THE OXFORD HANDBOOK OF

THE AMERICAN
PRESIDENCY

THE
OXFORD
HANDBOOKS
OF
AMERICAN
POLITICS

GENERAL EDITOR: GEORGE C. EDWARDS III

The Oxford Handbooks of American Politics is a set of reference books offering authoritative and engaging critical overviews of the state of scholarship on American politics.

Each volume focuses on a particular aspect of the field. The project is under the General Editorship of George C. Edwards III, and distinguished specialists in their respective fields edit each volume. The *Handbooks* aim not just to report on the discipline, but also to shape it as scholars critically assess the current state of scholarship on a topic and propose directions in which it needs to move. The series is an indispensable reference for anyone working in American politics.

THE OXFORD HANDBOOK OF

THE AMERICAN PRESIDENCY

Edited by

GEORGE C. EDWARDS III

and

WILLIAM G. HOWELL

OXFORD

UNIVERSITY PRESS

OXFORD
UNIVERSITY PRESS

Great Clarendon Street, Oxford OX2 6DP

Oxford University Press is a department of the University of Oxford.
It furthers the University's objective of excellence in research, scholarship,
and education by publishing worldwide in

Oxford New York

Auckland Cape Town Dar es Salaam Hong Kong Karachi
Kuala Lumpur Madrid Melbourne Mexico City Nairobi
New Delhi Shanghai Taipei Toronto

With offices in

Argentina Austria Brazil Chile Czech Republic France Greece
Guatemala Hungary Italy Japan Poland Portugal Singapore
South Korea Switzerland Thailand Turkey Ukraine Vietnam

Oxford is a registered trade mark of Oxford University Press
in the UK and in certain other countries

Published in the United States
by Oxford University Press Inc., New York

British Library Cataloguing in Publication Data
Data available

Library of Congress Cataloguing in Publication Data
Data available

Typeset by SPI Publisher Services, Pondicherry, India
Printed in Great Britain
on acid-free paper by
Ashford Colour Press Ltd., Gosport, Hants.

ISBN 978-0-19-923885-9 (hbk); 978-0-19-960441-8 (pbk)

1 3 5 7 9 10 8 6 4 2

Contents

PART I INTRODUCTION

PART II APPROACHES TO STUDYING THE PRESIDENCY

PART III PRECURSORS TO GOVERNANCE

PART IV   THE PUBLIC PRESIDENCY

PART V   THE LEGISLATIVE PRESIDENCY

PART VI   UNILATERAL ACTION

PART VII   DECISION MAKING

PART VIII   IMPLEMENTING POLICY

PART IX   JUDICIAL RELATIONS

PART X   INTERNATIONAL POLITICS

PART XI   REFLECTIONS

LIST OF FIGURES AND TABLE

FIGURES

TABLE

Abbreviations

AJPS	*American Journal of Political Science*
ALD	American Law Division
APD	American political development
APSR	*American Political Science Review*
AUMF	Authorization to Use Military Force
BOB	Bureau of the Budget
BRAC	Base Realignment and Closure
COS	chief of staff
CSRA	Civil Service Reform Act
DHS	Department of Homeland Security
DOJ	Dept of Justice
EOP	Executive Office of the President
EPA	Environmental Protection Agency
FEC	Federal Election Commission
FEMA	Federal Emergency Management Agency
FISA	Foreign Intelligence Surveillance Act
FISC	Foreign Intelligence Surveillance Court
GAO	Government Accountability Office
GOP	Grand Old Party
IO	international organization
JOP	*Journal of Politics*
MMA	Medicare Modernization Act
NAFTA	North American Free Trade Agreement
NIRA	National Industrial Recovery Act
NRC	Nuclear Regulatory Commission
NSA	national security assistant
NSD	National Security Directive
NSDM	National Security Decision Memorandum

NSPD	National Security Presidential Directive
OFBCI	Office of Faith-Based and Community Initiatives
OIA	Office of Intergovernmental Affairs
OIRA	Office of Information and Regulatory Affairs
OLA	Office of Legislative Affairs
OLC	Office of Legal Counsel
OLS	ordinary least squares
OMB	Office of Management and Budget
OPA	Office of Political Affairs
OPL	Office of Public Liaison
OSHA	Occupational Safety and Health Administration
PAP	Policy Agendas Project
PART	Program Assessment Rating Tool
PRA	Paperwork Reduction Act
PSQ	*Presidential Studies Quarterly*
SAP	Statement of Administration Policy
SDI	Strategic Defense Initiative
SES	Senior Executive Service
SUA	State of the Union address
TILI	take-it-or-leave-it
TSP	Terrorist Surveillance Program
UAP	unilateral action propensity
WHO	White House Office
WMD	weapon of mass destruction

About the Contributors

Meredith Barthelemy, Graduate Student in the Political Science Department, Duke University.

Terri Bimes, Lecturer at UC Berkeley and also research affiliate at the Institute of Governmental Studies.

John P. Burke, Professor of Political Science, University of Vermont.

Charles M. Cameron, Professor of Politics and Public Affairs, Princeton University.

Brandice Canes-Wrone, Professor of Politics and Public Affairs, Princeton University.

Jeffrey E. Cohen, Professor of Political Science, Fordham University.

John J. Coleman, Professor of Political Science, University of Wisconsin-Madison.

Robert F. Durant, Professor of Public Administration and Policy at American University in Washington, DC.

James N. Druckman, Associate Professor of Political Science, Northwestern University.

George C. Edwards III, Distinguished Professor of Political Science and George and Julia Blucher Jordan Chair in Presidential Studies at Texas A&M University.

Lee Epstein, Henry Wade Rogers Professor, Northwestern University School of Law.

Louis Fisher, specialist in constitutional studies for the Law Library of Congress.

Paul Gronke, Professor of Political Science, Reed College.

Hugh Heclo, Robinson Professor of Public Affairs, George Mason University.

William G. Howell, Associate Professor, Harris School of Public Policy, University of Chicago.

Karen M. Hult, Professor of Political Science, Virginia Polytechnic Institute and State University.

Lawrence R. Jacobs, Walter F. and Joan Mondale Chair for Political Studies, University of Minnesota.

Scott C. James, Associate Professor of Political Science, University of California, Los Angeles.

Tana Johnson received her Ph.D. in 2009 from the Harris School of Public Policy at the University of Chicago. She is currently completing a post-doctoral fellowship in the political science department at Vanderbilt University.

Anne M. Khademian, Professor, Center for Public Administration and Policy, Alexandria Virginia Tech.

Douglas L. Kriner, Assistant Professor of Political Science at Boston University.

Burdett A. Loomis, Professor of Political Science, University of Kansas.

Kenneth R. Mayer, Professor of Political Science, and Affiliated Faculty, Lafollette School of Public Affairs, University of Wisconsin-Madison.

Brian Newman, Assistant Professor of Political Science, Pepperdine University.

David C. W. Parker, Assistant Professor of Political Science, Montana State University.

James P. Pfiffner, University Professor in the School of Public Policy at George Mason University.

Jon C. Pevehouse, Professor of Political Science, University of Wisconsin.

Richard M. Pious, Adolph and Effie Ochs Professor, Barnard College, Graduate School of Arts and Sciences, Columbia University.

William G. Resh, Ph.D. student in the Department of Public Administration and Policy in the School of Public Affairs at American University.

David W. Rohde, Ernestine Friedl Professor of Political Science and Director of the Political Institutions and Public Choice Program, Duke University.

Jeffrey A. Segal, SUNY Distinguished Professor and Chair Department of Political Science, Stony Brook University.

Dennis M. Simon, Altshuler Distinguished Teaching Professor, Department of Political Science, Southern Methodist University.

Stephen Skowronek, Pelatiah Perit Professor of Political and Social Science, Yale University.

Charles E. Walcott, Professor of Political Science, Virginia Polytechnic Institute and State University.

Stephen G. Walker, Professor Emeritus, Department of Political Science, School of Government, Politics, and Global Studies, Arizona State University.

Richard W. Waterman, Professor of Political Science, University of Kentucky.

Stephen J. Wayne, Professor of Government, Georgetown University.

Keith E. Whittington, William Nelson Cromwell Professor of Politics in the Department of Politics, Princeton University.

B. Dan Wood, Professor and Cornerstone Fellow, Texas A&M University.

PART I

INTRODUCTION

CHAPTER 1

....

INTRODUCTION

....

GEORGE C. EDWARDS III
WILLIAM G. HOWELL

THE quantity and intensity of attention to the American presidency exceeds that devoted to any other political institution. And well it should. As the central feature on the American political landscape, it is only natural that scholars and commentators focus on the presidency. So much is written about the subject, in fact, that it is often difficult to know where we stand in our understanding of it.

We have designed this volume to help scholars assess where we are and the directions in which we need to move in presidency research. Never before has the academic literature on the American presidency received such an extended, and seemingly exhaustive, treatment. We have commissioned nearly three dozen essays that critically engage the scholarship on different dimensions of the American presidency. These chapters trace out common themes, debates, and controversies that define different areas of study; and, in one way or another, identify how recent research extends, corrects, or fine-tunes arguments and evidence offered by older works.

Each of these essays will quickly bring readers up to speed on scholarship on the American presidency during recent decades. The chapters in this volume, however, do not provide encyclopedic summaries of the literature. Rather, the essays *critically* assess both the major contributions to a literature and the ways in which the literature has developed. What are the major questions in a line of research? How satisfied should we be with the answers scholars have provided to these questions? To what significant questions have scholars devoted too little attention?

As this last query implies, we hope that this volume helps set the agenda for research on the presidency for the next decade. The authors of each chapter seek to identify weaknesses in the existing literature—be they logical flaws, methodological errors, oversights, or some combination therein—and to offer their views about especially productive lines of future inquiry. Equally important, perhaps, the authors also identify areas of research that are unlikely to bear additional fruits. These chapters offer a distinctive point of view, an argument about the successes and failures of past scholarship, and a set of recommendations about how future work ought to develop.

ORGANIZATION

Although this volume is large, it does not cover every aspect of the American presidency. Nor does it allot space to those topics it does cover in equal proportion to existing scholarship. Most obviously, we do not focus on presidential elections, for the simple reason that other volumes in the *Oxford Handbook of American Politics* series cover them in considerable detail. The preponderance of this volume is devoted to issues of governance, beginning at the moment a newly elected president forms a transition team, develops a policy agenda, and prepares to take office.

Our essays do not necessarily reflect the balance of current scholarship on the presidency. We made difficult but important decisions regarding the importance of the questions that various streams of research address and their contributions to our understanding of the presidency. Other subjects, which we think offer particularly promising avenues of research, receive considerably more attention than they currently do in the existing presidency subfield.

The first three chapters of this volume focus on approaches to studying the presidency—in particular, those that utilize the methods of quantitative analysis, game theory, and American political development. These essays delineate the distinctive characteristics of these approaches, their strengths and weaknesses, and, crucially, the substantive insights they have generated into the presidency itself. We do not argue that these are the only ways of studying the presidency, of course. Over the years, important research on the American presidency has employed sociological, psychological, and legal modes of inquiry. Several of the substantive essays that appear later in the volume reflect the contributions of these approaches to understanding specific areas of the presidency.

As we mentioned earlier, our focus is on governing. We include chapters on presidential transitions and agenda setting, critical precursors to governing. These also are areas representing emerging literatures where scholars can, and need to, make important strides in understanding these critically important topics.

Modern presidents have frequently adopted governing strategies based on obtaining public support. We explore thoroughly the president's key relationship with the public, including the public's expectations of the president, the president's responsiveness to the public, the president's ability to lead the public, and the related topics of presidential rhetoric and the public's evaluations of the president. We also include a chapter on the mass media, the key intermediary between the White House and the citizens.

Central to every president's job description, and most presidents' legacies, is working with Congress. One of the most established areas of presidential research focuses on the White House's attempts to influence the legislature. We have included chapters on the president as party leader, the impact of presidential legislative skills and public approval on congressional support, the consequences of divided government, and the role of interest groups in presidential politics.

We have also commissioned three essays on the politics of unilateral action. In the last decade, the study of presidential power has undergone an important reorientation, as scholars have cast their attention on the politics of direct presidential action. We no longer strictly equate power with persuasion, with an ability to convince others to do the president's bidding. Rather, scholars have recognized, presidents use executive orders, executive agreements, National Security Directives, proclamations, memoranda, and any number of other tools to act, to remake the policy landscape, and to place upon others the onus of coordinating a response. Since 2000 alone, dozens of journal articles, multiple books, and a special edition of *Presidential Studies Quarterly* have set their sights on these politics. We think their efforts warrant careful consideration.

One could argue that the essence of the president's job is making decisions—about foreign affairs, economic policy, and literally hundreds of other important matters. We devote three essays to examining various influences on decision making. It is easy to describe presidential decisions but much more challenging to explain them. We know a great deal more about how presidents have organized their White House staff, for example, than about how these arrangements have affected the kinds of advice they have received. These essays should be helpful to scholars wishing to pursue research focused on the very heart of the presidency.

Similarly, every president implements policy. Scholars devote relatively less attention to this topic than to many others in the presidency field, but the White House's performance in both the recovery from the destruction of Hurricane Katrina and the occupation of Iraq remind us again just how important it is for us to increase our understanding of implementation. Thus, we are pleased to have two chapters devoted to this topic.

An increasingly critical relationship for presidents is with the courts. In the ongoing war on terror, for example, the courts have asserted themselves, placing new checks on the exercise of presidential power, and new obligations on Congress to either authorize or revamp unilateral actions taken by the president. Twenty years hence, we hope that scholars will have a great deal more to say about president–judicial relations than they currently do. Thus, we include chapters focusing on the president's influence on the composition of the courts and the courts' checks on the president.

Distinctively, this book also considers how presidents operate in the international arena and how the international arena, in turn, affects the presidency, areas of research that remain in their infancy, at least among presidency scholars. Certainly these topics have received extensive treatment in international relations, public law, and history. Until recently, however, presidency scholars have largely ceded topics that relate to international affairs to other disciplines and subfields within political science. Although they have assembled extraordinary datasets on legislative success rates, public appeals, and appointments, presidency scholars have paid considerably less attention to the many things that presidents do on the international stage: negotiating bi- and multilateral agreements, building international coalitions, waging war, imposing economic sanctions, and interacting with international organizations. Although such topics stood at the very center of presidency research in the 1940s and 1950s, with scholars like Edwin S. Corwin and Clinton Rossiter offering extended treatments of presidential war powers, they no longer do. This volume's section on international politics, therefore, recognizes the extraordinary range of actions presidents take in the international arena, an emergent interest among international relations scholars in domestic politics, and the possibilities this presents for presidency scholars to recommit themselves to studying topics of monumental importance to both the presidency and nation.

In the final section, four senior distinguished presidency scholars step back and take a broad view to reflect on key themes on the presidency, the efforts of different scholars to understand it, and directions for future research.

A FINAL WORD

Over the past quarter century, the community of presidential scholars has functioned as just that—a group dedicated to the joint enterprise of increasing our collective understanding of the single most important public office in the world. It is our hope that the essays in this volume will help these and future scholars clarify the issues in existing research—its strengths, weaknesses, and tensions—and identify promising areas for new research. We are excited by the prospects for future scholarship and hope we have provided some of the tools to do the job.

PART II

APPROACHES TO STUDYING THE PRESIDENCY

CHAPTER 2

QUANTITATIVE APPROACHES TO STUDYING THE PRESIDENCY

WILLIAM G. HOWELL

IN the early 1980s, George Edwards took the presidency subfield to task for its failure to adopt basic norms of social science. While scholars who contributed to the various other subfields of American politics constructed hard theory that furnished clear predictions that, in turn, were tested using original datasets and the latest econometric techniques, too many presidency scholars, it seemed to Edwards, insisted on wading through a bog of anecdotes and poorly justified prescriptions. Unlike their would-be closest kin, congressional scholars, presidency scholars tended to prefer complexity to simplicity, nuance to generality, stories to data. Consequentially, Edwards noted, "Research on the presidency too often fails to meet the standards of contemporary political science, including the careful definition and measurement of concepts, the rigorous specification and testing of propositions, the employment of appropriate quantitative methods, and the use of empirical theory to develop hypotheses and explain findings" (Edwards 1983, 100). If the subfield hoped to rejoin the rest of the discipline and enter the modern era of political science, it would need to nurture and reward scholars conducting quantitative research.

Edwards did not sit alone with such sentiments. In a damning report to the Ford Foundation, Hugh Heclo summarized the state of the presidency literature circa 1977 as follows: "Political observers have written excellent interpretations of the presidency. Important questions about presidential power have been raised. But considering the amount of such writing in relation to the base of original empirical research behind it, the field is as shallow as it is luxuriant. To a great extent, presidential studies have coasted on the reputations of a few rightfully respected classics on the presidency and on secondary literature and anecdotes produced by former participants" (Heclo 1977, 30). By recycling over and over again a handful of old chestnuts and witticisms, Heclo observed, scholars had failed to establish even the most basic empirical facts about the presidency.

In the years that followed, others delivered similar lamentations. According to Stephen Wayne, the presidency field languished for lack of clearly defined concepts and standards of measurement. As he put it, "By concentrating on personalities, on dramatic situations, and on controversial decisions and extraordinary events, students of the presidency have reduced the applicability of social science techniques" (Wayne 1983, 6). A decade later, Gary King bemoaned the fact that "Presidency research is one of the last bastions of historical, non-quantitative research in American politics" (King 1993, 388). And jumping yet another decade in time, Matthew Dickinson observed that "American presidency research is often described as the political science discipline's poor stepchild. Compared, for example, to election or congressional studies, presidency research is frequently deemed less clearly conceptualized, more qualitative and descriptive, overly focused on the personal at the expense of the institution, and too prone to prescribing reforms based on uncertain inferences" (Dickinson 2004, 99).

Of course, not everyone agreed that more, and better, quantitative research constituted the solution to this dispiriting state of affairs. A variety of scholars made powerful cases for the value of legal analysis (Fisher 2002), carefully constructed case studies (Thomas 1983), and theoretically informed historical research (Skowronek 2002). And they plainly had cause to do so. Some of the best insights and most theoretically informed treatises on the American presidency come through biographical, historical, and case study research;[1] and there are many questions about the presidency that simply are not amenable to quantitative research. Hence, no one now, or then, could plausibly argue that quantitative research should wholly supplant any of the more qualitative modes of research.

Still, Edwards spoke for many when he recommended that presidency scholars direct greater investments towards more systematic data collection efforts and the development of statistical skills needed to conduct quantitative research. For the presidency subfield to recover its rightful stature in the discipline, a genuine science of politics would need to take hold among presidency scholars; and to do so, clear, falsifiable theory and systematic data collection efforts would need to replace the

---

[1] Many of the most influential books ever written on the American presidency do not contain any quantitative analysis of any sort. Prominent examples include: Corwin (1948); Rossiter (1956); Barber (1972); Schlesinger (1973); Greenstein (1982); Neustadt (1990); and Skowronek (1993).

subfield's preoccupation with personalities, story telling, reflective essays, and biographical accounts. Hence, by the early 1980s, "observation, data collection, quantification, verification, conceptual clarification, hypothesis testing, and theory building [became] the order of the day" (Hart 1998, 383).

This chapter surveys the state of quantitative research on the presidency a quarter century after Edwards issued his original entreaty. After briefly documenting publication trends on quantitative research on the presidency in a variety of professional journals, it reviews the substantive contributions of selected quantitative studies to long-standing debates about the centralization and politicization of presidential authority, public appeals, and presidential policy making. Though hardly an exhaustive account of all the quantitative work being conducted, this chapter pays particular attention to the ways in which recent scholarship addresses methodological issues that regularly plague studies of the organization of political institutions, their interactions with the public, and their influence in systems of separated powers.

PUBLICATION TRENDS ON THE AMERICAN PRESIDENCY

Though numerous scholars have complained about the arrested state of quantitative research on the American presidency, none, somewhat ironically, has actually assembled the data needed to answer some basic empirical questions: What proportion of articles in the field journal for presidency scholars is quantitative in nature? Has this proportion increased or decreased over the past several decades? Are articles published in this journal more or less likely to contain a quantitative component than are articles on the presidency that are published in the top professional journals? And how does the literature on the presidency compare to that on other political institutions, notably Congress? This section provides answers to these questions.

In a survey of publication trends between 1980 and 2004, I identified almost 500 articles on the American presidency published in prominent, mainstream American politics journals, as well as another 800 articles published in the flagship subfield journal for presidency scholars.[2] Among articles on the American presidency, I then

[2] I counted all articles with the words "presidency," "presidential," or "president" in the title or abstract and discussing the US president somewhere in their text; articles had to be published between 1980 and 2004 in the Weld journal for presidency scholars, *Presidential Studies Quarterly* (*PSQ*), or one of the top three professional journals in American politics more generally: *American Political Science Review* (*APSR*), *American Journal of Political Science* (*AJPS*), and *Journal of Politics* (*JOP*). Excluded were: articles written by undergraduates, articles that were fewer than five manuscript pages (not including references) or that were submitted to symposia, transcripts of speeches, rejoinders, responses, research notes, comments, editorials, updates, corrections, and book reviews. In total, 799 articles meeting these criteria were published in *PSQ*, 155 in *APSR*, 165 in *AJPS*, and 160 in *JOP*. I gratefully acknowledge the research assistance of Ben Sedrish, Charlie Griffin, and Tana Johnson.

identified those that were quantitative in nature.[3] The differences could not be more striking. Whereas the top journals in American politics published almost exclusively quantitative articles on the American presidency, the field journal for presidency scholars published them only sporadically. In a typical year, the proportion of quantitative presidency articles published in mainstream outlets was nine times as high as the proportion of quantitative presidency articles published in the subfield journal. And though some over-time trends are observed in these publication rates, in every year the differences across these various journals are both substantively and statistically significant. Nor are such differences simply a function of typical differences in publication trends between mainstream and subfield journals. When writing for their respective subfield journals, congressional scholars were seven times more likely to write articles with a quantitative component than were presidency scholars.

Who wrote the presidency articles that appeared in these various journals? For the most part, contributors came from very different circles. A very small percentage of scholars who contributed presidency articles to the top, mainstream journals also wrote for the subfield journal; and an even smaller percentage of scholars who contributed to the subfield journal also wrote for the mainstream journals. The following, however, may be the most disturbing fact about recent publication trends: of the 1,155 scholars who contributed research on the presidency to one of these journals between 1980 and 2004, only 51 published articles on the presidency in both the subfield journal and the mainstream American politics journals.

Unavoidably, such comparisons raise all kinds of questions about the appropriate standards of academic excellence, the biases of review processes, and the value of methodological pluralism. For the moment, though, let us put aside the larger epistemological issues of whether the top journals in political science are right to primarily accept quantitative articles on the presidency; whether the subfield journal for presidency scholars is right to provide a venue for research that does not follow these methodological orientations; or whether congressional scholars are right to incorporate these basic norms into the research that fills their own subfield's journal. I cannot possibly settle such issues here. From the vantage point of a graduate student or young professor intent on assembling a record that will secure employment and tenure at a major research university, the more practical conclusions to draw from these data could not be clearer: if you intend to publish research on the American presidency in one of the field's top journals, you would do well to assemble and analyze data. Though purely theoretical essays and case study research may gain entrée into the presidency subfield's premier journal—though, as we'll soon see, this

[3] To count, an article had to subject actual data to some kind of statistical analysis, however rudimentary. Articles were identified as quantitative if they reported the results of any kind of regression, Bayesian inference, data reduction technique, natural or laboratory experiment, or even a simple statistical test of difference of means. Hence, an article that reported an occasional public opinion rating, or even one that tracked trends in public opinion in a figure or table, was excluded; however, an article that analyzed the determinants of public opinion, that tested for structural shifts in public opinion, or that decomposed measures of public opinion was appropriately counted as quantitative. Case studies, first-person narratives, and biographies, though certainly drawing upon empirical evidence, were not counted as quantitative; and neither were game theoretic models or simulations.

too is changing—they appear to offer substantially fewer rewards in the discipline more generally.

If a subfield's alienation from the broader discipline is appropriately measured by the regularity with which its scholars publish in both top mainstream journals and their chosen subfield journal, then we have obvious cause for concern. For most of this period, few bridges could be found between the main publication outlet designated expressly for presidency scholars and the best journals in American politics. Indeed, if contributing to a subfield's journal constitutes a prerequisite for membership, then the vast majority of scholars assembling the literature on the presidency in the top journals cannot, themselves, be considered presidency scholars. With some notable exceptions, meanwhile, those who can lay claim to the title of presidency scholar, at least by this criterion, do not appear to be contributing very much to the most influential journals in American politics.

A LITERATURE'S MATURATION

Not all the news is bad. For starters, a modest shift in the methodological underpinnings of presidency research can be observed. The proportion of quantitative work on the American presidency in all journals has increased rather notably of late.[4] And the period between 2005 and 2007, when 34 percent of research articles published in the presidency subfield's flagship journal had a quantitative component, represents the high watermark in quantitative studies on the presidency. Moreover, an increasingly wide spectrum of scholars is now contributing to the presidency subfield's journal.[5] In both the mainstream and subfield journals, there exists a considerably richer body of quantitative research on the American presidency than was available as little as a decade ago.

Obviously, disciplinary progress should not be measured only by reference to the number of articles amassed, no matter what their methodological tendencies might be. The mere addition of quantitative articles on the American presidency does not ensure that students today know anything more about the office than did their immediate or more distant predecessors. Fortunately, though, recent developments in the presidency literature provide further cause for optimism. By attending to a host of standard problems of research design and causal inference, problems endemic to quantitative research throughout the social sciences, scholars have materially

[4] Between 1980 and 1984, 30% of articles on the presidency published in the four journals examined in this chapter had a quantitative component; between 2000 and 2004, 46% did so. The percentage of quantitative articles published in PSQ alone since 2000, the first full year that George Edwards served as the journal's editor, nearly tripled.

[5] Over two-thirds of those scholars who wrote on the presidency in both mainstream and subfield journals between 1980 and 2004 contributed an article to PSQ during Edwards's editorship.

enhanced the quality of research conducted on the American presidency, just as they have gained fresh insights into the institution itself. This section reviews some of the ways in which scholars have grappled with a host of methodological challenges in order to make fresh contributions to ongoing debates about the political control over the bureaucracy, public appeals, and presidential power.

Political Control of the Bureaucracy

In a series of highly influential articles in the 1980s and early 1990s, Terry Moe spelled out a political rationale for presidents to politicize the appointment process and centralize authority within the Executive Office of the President (EOP) (Moe 1985, 1987, 1990; Moe and Wilson 1994). Moe observed that in an increasingly volatile political world, one wherein opportunities to effect change are fleeting, power is always contested, and opposing factions stand mobilized at every turn, presidents and their immediate advisers have a strong incentive to hunker down, formulate policy themselves, and fill administrative agencies with people who can be counted on to do their bidding. Neutral competence and bureaucratic independence, Moe observed, do not always suit the president's political needs. Rather than rely upon the expertise of a distant cadre of civil servants, presidents, for reasons built into the design of a political system of separated powers, have considerable cause to surround themselves with individuals who are responsive, loyal, and like-minded.

By focusing explicitly on institutional incentives and resources, and by dispensing with the normative considerations that then pervaded much of the public administration work on bureaucratic design and oversight, Moe's research had a huge impact on the ways in which scholars thought about presidential power. The theory that Moe postulated, however, lacked the dynamic components needed to identify when, precisely, presidents would centralize or politicize authority and when they would not—that is, Moe's work did not generate any clear comparative statics. Moe's work, for the most part, did not examine the trade-offs involved in using appointments to control the bureaucracy for either agency performance or the need to pay back campaign debts through plush appointments in the executive branch. And crucially, for our purposes, Moe's empirical analysis resembled the existing literature's at the time. Evidence of centralization and politicization consisted of selected case studies of individual agencies and a handful of policies they helped write.

Fortunately, subsequent scholars picked up where Moe left off. Consider, for instance, Andrew Rudalevige's book *Managing the President's Program* (2002).[6] Using the Public Papers of the President, Rudalevige tabulated some 2,796 messages from the president to Congress on 6,926 proposals. He then drew a random sample of 400 proposals and examined their legislative "pre-histories." Specifically, Rudalevige

---

[6] For other recent quantitative works that examine presidential control over the bureaucracy, see Wood and Waterman (1991); Wood (1994); Waterman and Rouse (1999); Dickinson (2003); Lewis (2003); Krause and Meier (2003); Krause, Lewis, and Douglas (2006); Gailmard and Patty (2007).

identified whether each presidential proposal was the product of cabinet departments and/or executive agencies; of mixed White House/departmental origin, with department taking the lead role; of mixed White House/departmental origin, with White House taking the lead role; of centralized staff outside the White House Office, such as the Office of Management and Budget (OMB) or Council of Economic Advisors; or of staffers within the White House itself. So doing, Rudalevige constructed a unique dataset that allowed him systematically to investigate the regularity with which presidents centralized the policy-making process within the EOP.

Notably, Rudalevige discovered that many of the proposals that presidents submit to Congress are formulated outside of the confines of their immediate control. Only 13 percent of the proposals Rudalevige examined originated in the White House itself; and just 11 percent more originated in the EOP. Cabinet departments and executive agencies drafted almost half of all the president's legislative proposals. Moreover, Rudalevige found, the occurrence of "centralization" did not appear to be increasing over time. Though the proportion of proposals that originated within the EOP fluctuated rather dramatically from year to year, the overall trend line remained basically flat for most of the post-war period. Rudalevige did not find any evidence that presidents were centralizing authority with rising frequency.

The real contribution of Rudalevige's book, however, lay in its exploration of the political forces that encouraged presidents to centralize. Positing a "contingent theory of centralization," Rudalevige identified the basic trade-off that all presidents face when constructing a legislative agenda: by relying upon their closest advisers and staff, they can be sure that policy will reflect their most important goals and principles; but when policy is especially complex, the costs of assembling the needed information to formulate policy can be astronomical. Though Moe correctly claimed that centralization can aid the president, Rudalevige cautioned that the strategy will only be employed for certain kinds of policies aimed at certain kinds of reforms.

To demonstrate as much, Rudalevige estimated a series of statistical models that predicted where within the executive branch presidents turned to formulate different policies. His findings are fascinating. Policies that involved multiple issues, that presented new policy innovations, and that required the reorganization of existing bureaucratic structures were more likely to be centralized; those that involved complex issues were less likely to be. For the most part, the partisan leanings of an agency, divided government, and temporal indicators appeared unrelated to the location of policy formation. Whether presidents centralized, it would seem, varied from issue to issue, justifying Rudalevige's emphasis on "contingency."

Clearly, Rudalevige's work is not the final word on the issue of centralization. The micro foundations of his theory need further refinement. And the statistical tests might better account for the fact that presidents decide where to formulate policy with a mind to whether the policy will actually be enacted. We have here, though, a basis upon which to extend the norms of social scientific inquiry into studies of presidential control over the federal bureaucracy.

And this foundation is only strengthened with David Lewis's recent book *The Politics of Presidential Appointments: Political Control and Bureaucratic Performance* (2008).

Shifting our attention to trends in the politicization of the American presidency, Lewis's book systematically evaluates the ways in which presidents use appointments to advance their policy and patronage interests.[7] Whereas Rudalevige built an entirely new dataset to track trends in centralization, Lewis exploited existing datasets that, until now, had been ignored by political scientists—in particular, the Policy and Supporting Positions volumes (aka the "Plum Book") and the Office of Personnel Management's Central Personnel Data File. Both datasets allow Lewis to distinguish civil servants from political appointees throughout the federal government, and thereby assemble the most comprehensive inventory of presidential appointees ever conducted.

The first contribution of Lewis's research is to document some basic, though heretofore unknown, trends in politicization. He shows, for instance, that presidents do politicize today more than they did half a century ago. The upward trend, however, has hardly been monotonic. While it increased dramatically between 1960 and 1980, it actually declined under Clinton's watch, only to experience a resurgence under Bush. Trends in politicization, what is more, vary dramatically across different departments and agencies. Proportional to their size, the Office of Science and Technology Policy, Federal Housing Finance Board, and US Commission on Civil Rights experienced the largest increases in political appointments; the Council on Environmental Quality, Federal Mine Safety and Health Review Commission, and Trade and Development Agency, by contrast, all noted substantial reductions.

The core of Lewis's book, however, is devoted to examining the particular conditions under which politicization increases and decreases in different agencies, and the consequences this has for their performance. Lewis shows that the number of political appointees reliably increases when the presidency switches parties; and that certain kinds of political appointees tend to rise as the preferences of members of Congress and the president converge. Additionally, Lewis demonstrates that agencies with higher numbers of political appointees consistently receive lower Program Assessment Rating Tool (PART) grades, a finding that would appear to confirm the long-standing concerns raised by public administration scholars about the rise in politicization.

Together, Lewis and Rudalevige make at least two important contributions to the empirical study of the presidency. First, and most obviously, their research extends theoretical claims advanced by Moe and others about the organizational structure of the executive branch. Rudalevige and Lewis do not simply recognize that presidents have cause to centralize authority and politicize appointments. They explore the precise conditions under which presidents are most likely to pursue either strategy. So doing, Rudalevige and Lewis deftly shift the debate onto even more productive ground from where prior research on the topic had left it.

Second, Rudalevige and Lewis demonstrate how one might go about testing, using quantitative data, theory that previously had strictly been the province of archival research. Before these two books, no one had figured out how one might actually measure centralization or politicization. And as a consequence, different studies applied

---

[7] For other empirical work on political appointments, see Cameron, Cover, and Segal (1990); McCarty and Razaghian (1999); Binder and Maltzman (2002).

different definitions to suit the particular challenges of explaining political struggles over individual agencies and policy domains. It was often unclear, then, whether scholars offering contrasting observations genuinely disagreed with one another, or whether they simply were looking at different things. Plainly, future research on centralization and politicization will (and should) continue to rely upon case studies—there is much about both theoretical propositions that Rudalevige's and Lewis's data cannot address. But residing in the background of their work is gentle encouragement to expand not only the number of datasets assembled on the US presidency, but also the kind.

One can, of course, quibble with the particular measures of centralization and politicization that Rudalevige and Lewis introduce. Rudalevige, for instance, focuses on the initiation of new legislation, not on decision making more generally. Hence, his measure of centralization says very little about the tasks of executing existing policies and unilaterally issuing new ones. By focusing on political appointees, Lewis also leaves for future scholars the job of constructing other measures of politicization based on loyalty or partisan identification. Such scholarship might also consider alternatives to the overall proportion of employees of one type or another. After all, it is quite possible that presidents can gain control over some agencies or departments with just a few key political appointments, while others of equal size require a much more aggressive strategy. And nothing in Lewis's data distinguishes the particular responsibilities (and therefore influence) of political appointees and civil servants within different organizational structures.

Like all pathbreaking works, Rudalevige's and Lewis's books also leave certain questions unanswered. It is unclear, for instance, whether centralization and politicization are complementary strategies, or whether one is employed to the exclusion of the other. It is quite possible that presidents turn to associates within the White House for advice about policy issues that departments with a high proportion of civil servants typically oversee; and that presidents encourage policy development in those departments that are saturated with political appointees. Future scholarship therefore would do well to not only expand the kinds of data that Rudalevige and Lewis assemble, but also to link their analyses in a single analytic framework.

Public Appeals

In another influential book, *Going Public: New Strategies of Presidential Leadership*, Samuel Kernell (1997) recognized the rising propensity of presidents to bypass Congress and issue public appeals on behalf of their legislative agendas. To explain why presidents often abandon the softer, subtler tactics of negotiation and bargaining, the supposed mainstays of presidential influence during the modern era (Neustadt 1990),[8] Kernell emphasized the transformation of the nation's polity, beginning in

---

[8] With over a million copies sold, Neustadt's book remains far and away the most influential treatise on presidential power. And as does any classic, Neustadt's book has attracted a fair measure of controversy. For selected critiques, see Sperlich (1969); Moe (1993); Howell (2005).

the early 1970s, from a system of "institutionalized" to "individualized" pluralism. Under institutional pluralism, Kernell explained, "political elites, and for the most part only elites, matter[ed]" (Kernell 1997, 12). Insulated from public opinion, presidents had only to negotiate with a handful of "protocoalition" leaders in Congress. But under the new individualized pluralist system, opportunities for bargaining dwindled. The devolution of power to subcommittees, the weakening of parties, and the profusion of interest groups greatly expanded the number of political actors with whom presidents would have to negotiate; and compounded with the rise of divided government, such developments made compromise virtually impossible. Facing an increasingly volatile and divisive political terrain, Kernell argued, presidents have clear incentives to circumvent formal political channels and speak directly to the people.

But just as Moe did not posit a theory that specified when presidents would (and would not) centralize authority, Kernell did not identify the precise conditions under which presidents would issue public appeals. Kernell offered powerful reasons why presidents in the 1980s and 1990s went public more often than their predecessors in the 1950s or 1960s. But his book did not generate especially strong expectations about whether presidents holding office during either of these periods would be more or less likely to issue public appeals on one issue versus another. Additionally, Kernell did not identify the precise conditions under which such appeals augment presidential influence, and when they do not.

During the last decade a number of scholars, very much including Kernell himself, have extended the analyses and insights found in *Going Public*. Two areas of research have been especially prodigious. The first examines how changes in the media environment, especially the rise of cable television, have complicated the president's efforts to reach his constituents (Groeling and Kernell 1998; Baum and Kernell 1999; Cohen 2008). Whereas presidents once could count on the few existing television networks to broadcast their public appeals to a broad cross-section of the American public, now they must navigate a highly competitive and diffuse media environment, one that caters to the individual interests of an increasingly fickle citizenry. Hence, while structural changes to the American polity in the 1970s may have encouraged presidents to go public with greater frequency, more recent changes to the media environment have limited the president's ability to rally the public behind a chosen cause.

It should not come as much of a surprise, then, that public appeals do not always change the content of public opinion, which constitutes the second body of quantitative research spawned by Kernell's work (Cohen 1998; Edwards 2003; Barrett 2004). Though they may raise the salience of particular issues, presidential speeches typically do not materially alter citizens' views about particular policies, especially those that involve domestic issues. Either because an increasingly narrow portion of the American public actually receives presidential appeals, or because these appeals are transmitted by an increasingly critical and politicized media, or both, presidential endorsements of specific policies fail to resonate broadly.

Brandice Canes-Wrone has also examined the conditions under which presidents will issue public appeals; and given its methodological innovations, her research warrants discussing at some length (Canes-Wrone 2001, 2006; Canes-Wrone and Shotts 2004). By increasing the salience of policies that already enjoy broad-based support, Canes-Wrone argues, plebiscitary presidents can pressure members of Congress to respond to the (otherwise latent) preferences of their constituents. Further recognizing the limited attention spans of average citizens and the diminishing returns of public appeals, Canes-Wrone argues that presidents will only go public when there are clear policy rewards associated with doing so. Then, by building a unique database that links presidential appeals to budgetary outlays over the past several decades, Canes-Wrone shows how such appeals, under well-specified conditions, augment presidential influence over public policy.

Two methodological features of Canes-Wrone's work address fundamental problems that scholars regularly confront when conducting quantitative research on the presidency. First, by comparing presidential budget proposals with final appropriations, Canes-Wrone introduces a novel metric that defines the proximity of final legislation with presidential preferences. This is no small feat. When conducting quantitative research, scholars often have a difficult time discerning presidential preferences, and an even more difficult time figuring out the extent to which different laws reflect these preferences. The challenge, though, does not negate the need. If scholars are to gauge presidential influence over the legislative process, they need some way of identifying just how well presidents have fared in a public policy debate. Prior solutions to the problem—focusing on presidential proposals or accounting for what presidents say or do at the end of the legislative process—have clear limitations. Just because Congress enacts a presidential initiative does not mean that the final law looks anything like the original proposal made; and just because another law is enacted over a presidential veto does not mean that every provision of the bill represents an obvious defeat for the president. Moreover, even when such ambiguities can be resolved, it often remains unclear how observers would compare the "success" observed on one policy with the "success" claimed on another.

By measuring the differences between proposed and final appropriations, Canes-Wrone secures a readily interpreted basis for comparing relative presidential successes and failures across different policy domains. Now of course, the proposals that presidents themselves issue may be endogenous—that is, they may be constructed with some mind to how Congress is likely to respond—and hence not perfectly indicative of their sincere preferences. But for Canes-Wrone's analyses to yield biased results, presidents must adjust their proposals in anticipation of Congress's responses in different ways depending upon whether or not they issue public appeals. This is possible, perhaps, but the most likely scenario under which it is to occur would actually depress the probability that Canes-Wrone would find significant effects. If presidents systematically propose more extreme budgetary allotments when they plan to go public, anticipating a boost in public support from doing so, then Canes-Wrone may actually underestimate the influence garnered from public appeals. (But see Jordan and Primo 2008 for a slightly different critique.)

Budgetary appropriations provide a second benefit as well. Because presidents must issue budget proposals every year, Canes-Wrone sidesteps many of the selection biases that often arise in quantitative studies of the legislative process. The problem is this: the sample of bills that presidents introduce and Congress subsequently votes on, which then become the focus of scholarly inquiry, are a subset of all bills that presidents might actually like to see enacted. And because presidents are unlikely to introduce bills that they know Congress will subsequently reject, the sample of roll calls that scholars analyze invariably constitutes a non-random draw from the president's legislative agenda.

Without accounting for those bills that presidents choose not to introduce, two kinds of biases emerge. First, when tracking congressional votes on presidential initiatives, scholars tend to overstate presidential success. Hence, because Congress never voted on the policy centerpiece of Bush's second term, social security reform, the president's failure to rally sufficient support to warrant formal consideration of the initiative did not count against him in the various success scores that *Congressional Quarterly* and other outlets assembled. And second, analyses of how public opinion, the state of the economy, the partisan composition of Congress, or any other factor influences presidential success may themselves be biased. Without explicitly modeling the selection process itself, estimates from regressions that posit presidential success, however measured, against a set of covariates are likely to be misleading.

Unfortunately, no formal record exists of all the policies that presidents might like to enact, making it virtually impossible to diagnose, much less fix, the selection biases that emerge from most analyses of roll-call votes. But because presidents must propose, and Congress must pass, a budget every year, Canes-Wrone avoids these sample selection problems. In her statistical analyses, Canes-Wrone does not need to model a selection stage because neither the president nor Congress has the option of tabling appropriations. Every year, the two branches square off against one another to settle the terms of a federal budget; without the option to retreat, we, as observers, have a unique opportunity to call winners and losers fairly in the exchange.

B. Dan Wood's recent work (2007) offers other innovations to the quantitative study of presidential appeals on public opinion. Focusing on issues of economic leadership, Wood examines how presidential optimism and confidence about the economy affect economic actors' attitudes toward taking risks. He shows that presidents, through economic rhetoric, can produce tangible effects on consumer spending, business investment, and interest rates. Presidents can also strengthen their own public approval ratings by projecting strong images of economic leadership.

Wood's first methodological advancement to contemporary scholarship on presidential appeals concerns issues of measurement. Much of the existing scholarship examines the content of major speeches offered by the president. Wood, though, reminds us that presidents appeal to the public not only through major addresses like the State of the Union, but also through a continuous stream of news conferences, briefings, news releases, minor speeches, signing and veto statements, executive orders, and other ceremonial activities. Wood uses text-search technologies in order to parse the Public Papers of the President for every mention—tens of thousands in total—of the economy during the last half century. So doing, he compiles the single most comprehensive dataset of presidential appeals about the economy ever constructed.

The second methodological innovation concerns issues of modeling. Most previous research tracks public opinion just before and just after presidential appeals. Evidence of presidential influence, then, hinges upon the observation of differences between these two moments in time. The pre-/post-tests that predominate in the existing literature on public appeals, however, ignore the profoundly dynamic nature of elite–mass relations. In discussions over the economy, the public updates its views in light of presidential appeals, just as the president adjusts his rhetoric in light of his assessments of latent public opinion. Moreover, the impact of one upon the other is not instantaneous. It may take repeated addresses and significant time before the public updates its views about either the economy or the president. Recognizing these basic facts, Wood rightly abandons the static models that characterize prior research on the topic. In their place, Wood uses vector autoregression methods to address the endogenous relationship between elite appeals and public opinion and to account for the inertial tendencies of both. By carefully parsing these dynamic relationships, Wood raises both the methodological and analytical standards for conducting research on public appeals.

Policy Influence Beyond Legislation

Outside of elections and public opinion, the most common type of quantitative research conducted on the presidency has concerned the legislative process. Scholars have examined how different political alignments contributed to (or detracted from) the enactment of presidential initiatives (Wayne 1978; Edwards 1989; Bond and Fleisher 1990; Peterson 1990; Mayhew 1991; Edwards, Barrett, and Peake 1997; Coleman 1999; Bond and Fleisher 2000; Howell et al. 2000; Peake 2002). Following on from Aaron Wildavsky's famous claim that there exist two presidencies—one foreign, the other domestic—scholars have assembled a wide range of measures on presidential success in different policy domains (Wildavsky 1966; LeLoup and Shull 1979; Sigelman 1979; Edwards 1986; Fleisher and Bond 1988; Wildavsky 1989). Scholars have critically examined the president's capacity to set Congress's legislative agenda (Edwards and Wood 1999; Edwards and Barrett 2000). And a number of scholars have paid renewed attention to presidential vetoes (Cameron 1999; Gilmour 2002; Conley 2003; Cameron and McCarty 2004). Given the sheer amount of attention paid to the legislative process, one might justifiably conclude that policy influence depends almost entirely upon the president's capacity to influence affairs occurring within Congress, either by convincing members to vote on his behalf or by establishing roadblocks that halt the enactment of objectionable bills.

Recently, however, scholars have begun to take systematic account of the powers that presidents wield outside of the legislative arena. Building on the insights of legal scholars and political scientists who first recognized and wrote about the president's "unilateral" or "prerogative" powers (Cash 1963; Morgan 1970; Hebe 1972; Schlesinger 1973; Fleishman and Aufses 1976; Pious 1991), scholars recently have built well-defined theories of unilateral action and then assembled original datasets of executive orders, executive agreements, proclamations, and other sorts of directives to test them. In the past several years, fully six books have focused exclusively on the president's unilateral powers (Mayer 2001; Cooper 2002; Howell 2003; Warber 2006; Shull 2006; Krutz and Peake forthcoming), complemented by a bevy of quantitative articles (Krause and Cohen 1997; Deering and Maltzman 1999; Mayer 1999; Krause and Cohen 2000; Howell and Lewis 2002; Mayer and Price 2002; Howell 2005; Lewis 2005; Martin 2005; Marshall and Pacelle 2005).

Collectively, the emerging quantitative literature on unilateral powers makes two main contributions to our substantive understanding of presidential power. First, and most obviously, it expands the scope of scholarly inquiry to account for the broader array of mechanisms that presidents utilize to influence the content of public policy. Rather than struggling to convince individual members of Congress to endorse a bill and then cast sympathetic votes, presidents often can seize the initiative, issue new policies by fiat, and leave it to others to revise the new political landscape. Rather than dally at the margins of the policy-making process, presidents regularly issue directives that Congress, left to its own devices, would not enact. So doing, they manage to leave a plain imprint on the corpus of law.

Second, the literature highlights the ways in which adjoining branches of government effectively check presidential power. After all, should the president proceed without statutory or constitutional authority, the courts stand to overturn his actions, just as Congress can amend them, cut funding for their operations, or eliminate them outright. And in this regard, the president's relationship with Congress and the courts is very different from the one described in the existing quantitative literature on the legislative process. When unilateral powers are exercised, legislators, judges, and the president do not work cooperatively to effect meaningful policy change. Opportunities for change, in this instance, do not depend upon the willingness and capacity of different branches of government to coordinate with one another, as traditional models of bargaining would indicate. Instead, when presidents issue unilateral directives, they struggle to protect the integrity of orders given and to undermine the efforts of adjoining branches of government to amend or overturn actions already taken. Rather than being a potential boon to presidential success, Congress and the courts represent genuine threats. For presidents, the trick is to figure out when legislators and judges are likely to dismantle a unilateral action taken, when they are not, and then to seize upon those latter occasions to issue public policies that look quite different from those that would emerge in a purely legislative setting.

Some of the more innovative quantitative work conducted on unilateral powers highlights the differences between policies issued as laws versus executive orders. In his study of administrative design, for instance, David Lewis shows that modern agencies created through legislation tend to live longer than those created by executive decree (Lewis 2003). But what presidents lose in terms of longevity they tend to gain back in terms of control. By Lewis's calculations, between 1946 and 1997, fully 67 percent of administrative agencies created by executive order and 84 percent created by departmental order were placed either within the Executive Office of the President or the cabinet, as compared to only 57 percent of agencies created legislatively. Independent boards and commissions, which further dilute presidential control, governed only 13 percent of agencies created unilaterally, as compared to 44 percent of those created through legislation. And 40 percent of agencies created through legislation had some form of restrictions on the kinds of appointees presidents can make, as compared to only 8 percent of agencies created unilaterally.

In another study of the trade-offs between legislative and unilateral strategies, I show that the institutional configurations that promote the enactment of laws impede the production of executive orders, and vice versa (Howell 2003). Just as large and cohesive legislative majorities within Congress facilitate the enactment of legislation, they create disincentives for presidents to issue executive orders. Meanwhile, when gridlock prevails in Congress, presidents have strong incentives to deploy their unilateral powers, not least because their chance of building the coalitions needed to pass laws is relatively small. The trade-offs observed between unilateral and legislative policy making are hardly coincidental, for ultimately, it is the checks that Congress and the courts place on the president that define his (someday her) capacity to change public policy by fiat.

Quantitative work on the president's unilateral powers is beginning to take systematic account of unilateral directives other than executive orders and departmental reorganizations—most importantly, perhaps, those regarding military operations conducted abroad. Presidency scholars have already poured considerable ink on matters involving war. Until recently, however, quantitative work on the subject resided exclusively in other fields within the discipline. Encouragingly, a number of presidency scholars have begun to test theories of unilateral powers and interbranch relations that have been developed within American politics using datasets that were assembled within international relations (Howell and Pevehouse 2005, 2007; Kriner 2006; Shull 2006). Just as previous scholarship examined how different institutional configurations (divided government, the partisan composition of Congress) affected the number of executive orders issued in any given quarter or year, this research examines how such factors influence the number of military deployments that presidents initiate, the timing of these deployments, and their duration. Though still in its infancy, this research challenges presidency scholars to take an even more expansive view of presidential power, while also bridging long-needed connections with scholars in other fields who have much to say about how, and when, heads of state wield authority.

CONCLUDING THOUGHTS

This very brief survey offers mixed assessments of the quantitative literature on the US presidency. On the one hand, the publication rates of quantitative presidency research have been rather dismal. In the last twenty-five years, only one in ten research articles published in the subfield's premier journal had a quantitative component. By contrast, in the top American politics journals, almost nine in ten articles on the presidency did so. Additionally, the scholars who wrote about the presidency in top mainstream journals almost never contributed to the presidency subfield's premier journal, while those who contributed to the subfield's journal almost never wrote about the presidency in the top mainstream journals. Of the 1,000-plus authors who wrote about the American presidency in the four journals surveyed in this chapter, a minuscule 4 percent contributed to both the mainstream and the subfield outlets.

Signs, however, suggest that change is afoot. In the last several years, the presidency subfield's journal has published a greater proportion of quantitative studies, written by a wider assortment of scholars. And the more recent quantitative work being conducted on the presidency makes a variety of substantive and methodological contributions to the subfield. The literatures on bureaucratic control, public appeals, and unilateral policy making have made considerable advances in the past several years in large part because of the efforts of scholars to assemble original datasets and to test a variety of competing claims. On each of the topics considered here, quantitative analyses did considerably more than merely dress up the extant presidency literature—indeed, they stood at the core of the enterprise and constituted the key reason that learning occurred.

Moving forward, quantitative research on the US presidency confronts a number of challenges. Three, in my mind, stand out. First, much quantitative research on the presidency, as with quantitative research on political institutions generally, lacks strong theoretical footings. When conducting such research, scholars all too often proceed through the following three steps: (a) collect data on some outcome of interest, such as whether a proposal succeeds, a war is waged, an order is issued, or a public appeal is delivered; (b) haul out the standard list of covariates (public opinion, divided government, the state of the economy, etc.) that are used to predict the things that presidents say and do; and (c) estimate a statistical model that shows how well each covariate influences the outcome of interest, offering a paragraph or two on why each of the observed relationships does or does not conform to expectations. Though occasionally a useful exercise, this formulaic approach to quantitative analysis ultimately is unsustainable. Without theory, we cannot ascertain the covariates' appropriate functional forms; whether other important covariates have been omitted; whether some of the explanatory variables ought to be interacted with others; and whether endogeneity is a concern, and how it might be addressed. And without theory to furnish answers to such issues, the reader has little grounds for assessing whether or not the results can actually be believed. Rote empiricism, moreover, is no substitute for theory. For when different results emerge from equally defensible statistical models, theory is ultimately needed to adjudicate the dispute.

Second, greater attention needs to be paid to the ways in which adjoining branches of government (Congress and the courts), international actors (foreign states and international governing agencies), and the public shape presidential calculations, and hence presidential actions. At one level, this claim seems obvious. Ours, after all, is hardly a system of governance that permits presidents to impose their will whenever, and however, they choose (Jones 1994). The trouble, though, lies in the difficulty of discerning institutional constraints—and here, I suggest, there is room for continued improvement. Too often, when trying to assess the extent to which Congress constrains the president, scholars take an inventory of the number of times that vetoes are overridden, investigations are mounted, hearings are held, or bills are killed, either in committee or on the floor. Such lists are helpful, if only because they convey some sense of the variety of ways in which Congress checks presidential power. The deeper constraints on presidential power, however, remain hidden, as presidents anticipate the political responses that different actions are likely to evoke and adjust accordingly.[9] To assess congressional checks on presidential war powers, for instance, it will not do to simply count the number of times that Congress has invoked the War Powers Resolution or has demanded the cessation of an ongoing military venture. One must, instead, develop a theory that identifies when Congress is especially likely to limit the presidential use of force, and then assemble data that identify when presidents delay some actions and forgo others in anticipation of congressional opposition—opposition, it is worth noting, that we may never observe. The best quantitative research on the presidency recognizes the logic of anticipated response and formulates statistical tests that account for it.

Finally, scholars too often rely exclusively on those data that are most easily acquired, which typically involves samplings of presidential orders, speeches, and proposals issued during the modern era. But as Stephen Skowronek (1993) rightly insists, much is to be learned from presidents who held office before 1945, the usual starting point for presidential time series. Early changes in political parties, the organizational structure of Congress and the courts, media coverage of the federal government, and public opinion have long contributed to the development of the presidency. And, as Skowronek demonstrates, the similarities between modern and pre-modern presidents can be just as striking as the differences between presidents holding office since Roosevelt. When searching around for one's keys, it makes perfect sense to begin where the proverbial street lamp shines brightest. Eventually, though, scholars will need to hone their sights on darker spaces; and, in this instance, commit the resources required to build additional datasets of presidential activities during the nineteenth and early twentieth centuries.

It remains to be seen whether scholars can build a vibrant and robust body of quantitative scholarship on the presidency. To be sure, some trends are encouraging. Important advances have been made. But until the literature is better integrated into the discipline, and until quantitative research addresses some of the problems outlined above, there will be continued cause to revisit and reiterate the simple pleas that George Edwards issued more than a quarter century ago.

---

[9] For a survey of the recent game theoretic research that accounts for these interbranch dynamics, see Defigueiredo, Jacobi, and Weingast (2006).

REFERENCES

BARBER, J. 1972. *The Presidential Character: Predicting Performance in the White House.* Englewood Cliffs, NJ: Prentice Hall.

BARRETT, A. 2004. Gone Public: The Impact of Going Public on Presidential Legislative Success. *American Politics Review,* 32: 332–70.

BAUM, M., and KERNELL, S. 1999. Has Cable Ended the Golden Age of Presidential Television? *American Political Science Review,* 93/1: 99–114.

BINDER, S., and MALTZMAN, F. 2002. Senatorial Delay in Confirming Federal Judges, 1947–1998. *American Journal of Political Science,* 46/1: 190–9.

BOND, J., and FLEISHER, R. 1990. *The President in the Legislative Arena.* Chicago: University of Chicago Press.

—— —— 2000. *Polarized Politics: Congress and the President in a Partisan Era.* Washington, DC: Congressional Quarterly Press.

CAMERON, C. 1999. *Veto Bargaining: Presidents and the Politics of Negative Power.* New York: Cambridge University Press.

——and MCCARTY, N. 2004. Models of Vetoes and Veto Bargaining. *Annual Review of Political Science,* 7: 409–35.

——Cover, A., and SEGAL, J. 1990. Senate Voting on Supreme Court Nominees: A Neoinstitutional Model. *American Political Science Review,* 84: 525–34.

CANES-Wrone, B. 2001. The President's Legislative Influence from Public Appeals. *American Journal of Political Science,* 45/2: 313–29.

—— 2006. *Who's Leading Whom?* Chicago: University of Chicago Press.

——and SHOTTS, K. 2004. The Conditional Nature of Presidential Responsiveness to Public Opinion. *American Journal of Political Science,* 48/4: 690–706.

CASH, R. 1963. Presidential Power: Use and Enforcement of Executive Orders. *Notre Dame Lawyer,* 39/1: 44–55.

COHEN, J. 1998. *Presidential Responsiveness and Public Policy-Making: The Public and the Policies that Presidents Choose.* Ann Arbor: University of Michigan Press.

—— 2008. *The Presidency in the Era of 24-Hour News.* Princeton, NJ: Princeton University Press.

COLEMAN, J. 1999. Unified Government, Divided Government and Party Responsiveness. *American Political Science Review,* 93: 821–36.

CONLEY, R. 2003. George Bush and the 102nd Congress: The Impact of Public and Private Veto Threats on Policy Outcomes. *Presidential Studies Quarterly,* 33/4: 730–50.

COOPER, P. 2002. *By Order of the President: The Use and Abuse of Executive Direct Action.* Lawrence: University Press of Kansas.

CORWIN, E. 1948. *The President, Office and Powers, 1787–1948: History and Analysis of Practice and Opinion.* New York: New York University Press.

DEFIGUEIREDO, R., JACOBI, T., and WEINGAST, B. 2006. The Separation of Powers Approach to American Politics. In *The Oxford Handbook of Political Economy,* ed. B. Weingast and D. Wittman. New York: Oxford University Press.

DEERING, C., and MALTZMAN, F. 1999. The Politics of Executive Orders: Legislative Constraints on Presidential Power. *Political Research Quarterly,* 52/4: 767–83.

DICKINSON, M. 2003. Explaining the Growth of the Presidential Branch, 1940–2000. In *Uncertainty in American Politics,* ed. B. Burden. New York: Cambridge University Press.

—— 2004. Agendas, Agencies and Unilateral Action: New Insights on Presidential Power? *Congress & the Presidency,* 31/1: 99–109.

EDWARDS, G. 1983. Quantitative Analysis. In *Studying the Presidency*, ed. G. Edwards and S. Wayne. Knoxville: University of Tennessee Press.

—— 1986. The Two Presidencies: A Reevaluation. *American Politics Quarterly*, 14/3: 247–63.

—— 1989. *At the Margins: Presidential Leadership of Congress*. New Haven, CT: Yale University Press.

—— 2003. *On Deaf Ears: The Limits of the Bully Pulpit*. New Haven, CT: Yale University Press.

—— and BARRETT, A. 2000. Presidential Agenda Setting in Congress. In *Polarized Politics: Congress and the President in a Partisan Era*, ed. J. Bond and R. Fleisher. Washington, DC: Congressional Quarterly.

—— —— and PEAKE, J. 1997. The Legislative Impact of Divided Government. *American Journal of Political Science*, 41/2: 545–63.

—— and WOOD, B. D. 1999. Who Influences Whom? The President, Congress, and the Media. *American Political Science Review*, 93/2: 327–44.

FISHER, L. 2002. A Dose of Law and Realism for Presidential Studies. *Presidential Studies Quarterly*, 32/4: 672–92.

FLEISHER, R., and BOND, J. 1988. Are There Two Presidencies? Yes, but Only for Republicans. *Journal of Politics*, 50/3: 747–67.

FLEISHMAN, J., and AUFSES, A. 1976. Law and Orders: The Problem of Presidential Legislation. *Law and Contemporary Problems*, 40: 1–45.

GAILMARD, S., and PATTY, J. 2007. Slackers and Zealots: Civil Service, Policy Discretion, and Bureaucratic Expertise. *American Journal of Political Science*, 51/4: 873–89.

GILMOUR, J. 2002. Institutional and Individual Influences of the President's Veto. *Journal of Politics*, 64/1: 198–218.

GREENSTEIN, F. 1982. *The Hidden-Hand Presidency: Eisenhower as Leader*. New York: Basic Books.

GROELING, T., and KERNELL, S. 1998. Is Network News Coverage of the President Biased? *Journal of Politics*, 60/4: 1063–87.

HART, J. 1998. Neglected Aspects of the Study of the Presidency. *Annual Review of Political Science*, 1: 379–99.

HEBE, W. 1972. Executive Orders and the Development of Presidential Powers. *Villanova Law Review*, 17: 688–712.

HECLO, H. 1977. *Studying the Presidency: A Report to the Ford Foundation*. New York: Ford Foundation.

HOWELL, W. 2003. *Power without Persuasion: The Politics of Direct Presidential Action*. Princeton, NJ: Princeton University Press.

—— 2005. Power without Persuasion: Rethinking Foundations of Executive Influence. In *Presidential Politics*, ed. G. Edwards. Belmont, CA: Wadsworth.

—— and LEWIS, D. 2002. Agencies by Presidential Design. *Journal of Politics*, 64/4: 1095–114.

—— and PEVEHOUSE, J. 2005. Presidents, Congress, and the Use of Force. *International Organization*, 59/1: 209–32.

—— —— 2007. *While Dangers Gather: Congressional Checks on Presidential War Powers*. Princeton, NJ: Princeton University Press.

—— ADLER, S., CAMERON, C., and RIEMANN, C. 2000. Divided Government and the Legislative Productivity of Congress, 1945–1994. *Legislative Studies Quarterly*, 25: 285–312.

JONES, C. 1994. *The Presidency in a Separated System*. Washington, DC: Brookings Institution.

JORDAN, S., and PRIMO, D. 2008. *The Bad News About "Going Public."* University of Rochester, typescript.

KERNELL, S. 1997. *Going Public: New Strategies of Presidential Leadership*. Washington, DC: Congressional Quarterly Press.

KING, G. 1993. The Methodology of Presidential Research. In *Researching the Presidency: Vital Questions, New Approaches*, ed. G. Edwards, J. Kessel, and B. Rockman. Pittsburgh: University of Pittsburgh Press.

KRAUSE, G., and COHEN, D. 1997. Presidential Use of Executive Orders, 1953–1994. *American Politics Quarterly*, 25: 458–81.

—— and COHEN, J. 2000. Opportunity, Constraints, and the Development of the Institutional Presidency: The Case of Executive Order Issuance, 1939–1996. *Journal of Politics*, 62: 88–114.

—— LEWIS, D., and DOUGLAS, J. 2006. Political Appointments, Civil Service Systems, and Bureaucratic Competence: Organizational Balancing and Executive Branch Revenue Forecasts in the American States. *American Journal of Political Science*, 50: 770–87.

—— and MEIER, K. 2003. *Politics, Policy, and Organizations: Frontiers in the Scientific Study of Bureaucracy*. Ann Arbor: University of Michigan Press.

KRINER, D. 2006. Taming the Imperial Presidency: Congress, Presidents, and the Conduct of Military Action. Ph.D. dissertation, Harvard University.

KRUTZ, G., and PEAKE, J. Forthcoming. *Treaty Politics and the Rise of Executive Agreements: International Commitments in a System of Shared Powers*. Ann Arbor: University of Michigan Press.

LELOUP, L., and SHULL, S. 1979. Congress versus the Executive: the "Two Presidencies" Reconsidered. *Social Science Quarterly*, 59 /4: 704–19.

LEWIS, D. 2003. *Presidents and the Politics of Agency Design*. Stanford, CA: Stanford University Press.

—— 2005. Staffing Alone: Unilateral Action and the Politicization of the Executive Office of the President, 1988–2004. *Presidential Studies Quarterly*, 35/3: 496–514.

—— 2008. *The Politics of Presidential Appointments: Political Control and Bureaucratic Performance*. Princeton, NJ: Princeton University Press.

McCARTY, N., and RAZAGHIAN, R. 1999. Advice and Consent: Senate Response to Executive Branch Nominations 1885–1996. *American Journal of Political Science*, 43/3: 1122–43.

MARSHALL, B., and PACELLE, R. 2005. Revisiting the Two Presidencies: The Strategic Use of Executive Orders. *American Politics Quarterly*, 33/1: 81-105.

MARTIN, L. 2005. The President and International Commitments: Treaties as Signalling Devices. *Presidential Studies Quarterly*, 35/3: 440–65.

MAYER, K. 1999. Executive Orders and Presidential Power. *Journal of Politics*, 61/2: 445–66.

—— 2001. *With the Stroke of a Pen: Executive Orders and Presidential Power*. Princeton, NJ: Princeton University Press.

—— and PRICE, K. 2002. Unilateral Presidential Powers: Significant Executive Orders, 1949–99. *Presidential Studies Quarterly*, 32/2: 367–86.

MAYHEW, D. 1991. *Divided We Govern: Party Control, Lawmaking, and Investigations, 1946–1990*. New Haven, CT: Yale University Press.

MOE, T. 1985. The Politicized Presidency. In *The New Direction in American Politics*, ed. J. Chubb and P. Peterson. Washington, DC: Brookings Institution.

—— 1987. An Assessment of the Positive Theory of "Congressional Dominance." *Legislative Studies Quarterly*, 12/4: 475–520.

—— 1990. The Politics of Structural Choice: Toward a Theory of Public Bureaucracy. In *Organization Theory: From Chester Barnard to the Present and Beyond*, ed. O. Williamson. New York: Oxford University Press.

—— 1993. Presidents, Institutions, and Theory. In *Researching the Presidency: Vital Questions, New Approaches*, ed. G. Edwards, J. Kessel, and B. Rockman. Pittsburgh: University of Pittsburgh Press.

—— and WILSON, S. 1994. Presidents and the Politics of Structure. *Law and Contemporary Problems*, 57/2: 1–44.

MORGAN, R. 1970. *The President and Civil Rights: Policy Making by Executive Order*. New York: St Martin's Press.

NEUSTADT, R. 1990. *Presidential Power and the Modern Presidents*. New York: Free Press.

PEAKE, J. 2002. Coalition Building and Overcoming Gridlock in Foreign Policy, 1947–1998. *Presidential Studies Quarterly*, 32/1: 67–83.

PETERSON, M. 1990. *Legislating Together: The White House and Capitol Hill from Eisenhower to Reagan*. Cambridge, MA: Harvard University Press.

PIOUS, R. 1991. Prerogative Power and the Reagan Presidency. *Political Science Quarterly*, 106: 499–510.

ROSSITER, C. 1956. *The American Presidency*. New York: Harcourt, Brace & World.

RUDALEVIGE, A. 2002. *Managing the President's Program: Presidential Leadership and Legislative Policy Formation*. Princeton, NJ: Princeton University Press.

SCHLESINGER, A. 1973. *The Imperial Presidency*. Boston: Houghton Mifflin.

SHULL, S. 2006. *Policy by Other Means: Alternative Adoption by Presidents*. College Station: Texas A&M University Press.

SIGELMAN, L. 1979. A Reassessment of the Two Presidencies Thesis. *Journal of Politics*, 41/4: 1195–205.

SKOWRONEK, S. 1993. *The Politics Presidents Make*. Cambridge, MA: Harvard University Press.

—— 2002. Presidency and American Political Development: A Third Look. *Presidential Studies Quarterly*, 32 /4: 743–52.

SPERLICH, P. 1969. Bargaining and Overload: An Essay on Presidential Power. In *The Presidency*, ed. A. Wildavsky. Boston: Little, Brown.

THOMAS, N. 1983. Case Studies. In *Studying the Presidency*, ed. G. Edwards and S. Wayne. Knoxville: University of Tennessee Press.

WARBER, A. 2006. *Executive Orders and the Modern Presidency: Legislating from the Oval Office*. New York: Lynne Rienner.

WATERMAN, R., and ROUSE, A. 1999. The Determinants of the Perceptions of Political Control of the Bureaucracy and the Venues of Influence. *Journal of Public Administration Research and Theory*, 9: 527–69.

WAYNE, S. 1978. *The Legislative Presidency*. New York: Harper & Row.

—— 1983. An Introduction to Research on the Presidency. In *Studying the Presidency*, ed. G. Edwards and S. Wayne. Knoxville: University of Tennessee Press.

WILDAVSKY, A. 1966. The Two Presidencies. *Trans-Action*, 4: 7–14.

—— 1989. The Two Presidencies Thesis Revisited at a Time of Political Dissensus. *Society*, 26/5: 53–9.

WOOD, B. D. 1994. *Bureaucratic Dynamics: The Role of Bureaucracy in a Democracy, Transforming American Politics*. Boulder, CO: Westview.

—— 2007. *The Politics of Economic Leadership: The Causes and Consequences of Presidential Rhetoric*. Princeton, NJ: Princeton University Press.

—— and WATERMAN, R. 1991. The Dynamics of Political Control of the Bureaucracy. *American Political Science Review*, 85/3: 801–28.

CHAPTER 3

GAME THEORY AND THE STUDY OF THE AMERICAN PRESIDENCY

BRANDICE CANES-WRONE

THREE decades ago, a number of influential scholars criticized the study of the presidency for lacking theory and generalizable observations. Anthony King (1975, 173) pointed out that "general hypotheses are almost never advanced." Likewise, in a monograph of advice to the Ford Foundation, Hugh Heclo (1977, 38) observed that the field was focused on "history for its own sake" rather than developing an "understanding of how central government performs and how it might perform better." Echoing these sentiments, Joseph Pika (1982, 18) argued that scholarship in this area had earned a reputation for being "empirically and theoretically impoverished."[1]

These and other scholars have accurately noted that the deficiency is at least partially endemic to the subject itself; the study of the presidency is fraught with obstacles for producing general knowledge. There is no analog to the *Congressional Quarterly Almanac*, which provides congressional scholars with a wealth of data about legislative activity. To the contrary, data are often restricted or classified, and

I thank Chuck Cameron, William Howell, David Lewis, Nolan McCarty, and Jee-Kwang Park for helpful comments and conversations.

[1] Lengthier quotations from King (1975) and Pika (1982) are in Kessel (1984), which focuses on the lack of systematic empirical analysis. See Edwards (1980) and Edwards and Wayne (1983) for similar arguments regarding the lack of systematic empirical analysis.

a good deal of unrestricted information is scattered about the various presidential libraries (e.g., Heclo 1977). Scholars also face the challenge of distinguishing presidents' personal proclivities from institutional or structural phenomena in a world with only forty-three observations of presidents (e.g., King and Ragsdale 1988).

Undoubtedly, students of the presidency face more daunting challenges for empirical analysis than students of Congress, mass behavior, or even the courts. Yet, it is hard to argue that the presidency is less amenable to theory. Indeed, given the difficulties associated with empirical work, theory arguably plays an at least as useful, if not a more useful, role. It can guide scholars as to what sorts of data they should be collecting from government documents, presidential libraries, and other sources. It can identify institutional incentives, thereby enabling a researcher to distinguish these incentives from the personal tendencies of a particular president. And when data are classified or otherwise unavailable, theory can still provide insight.

Over the past thirty years, the critique that "general hypotheses [about the presidency] are almost never advanced" has become a less accurate description of the field. Some scholars have developed generalizations from comparative case studies (e.g., Skowronek 1993) or the quantitative analysis of large datasets (e.g., Edwards 1983; Bond and Fleisher 1990). Others have developed hypotheses deductively, i.e., deriving them from explicit axioms of human behavior and assumptions (e.g., Moe 1985). Within this class of work, perhaps the most radical break from traditional presidency scholarship has been the use of game theory.

In game theory, scholars utilize mathematics to analyze the strategic behavior of actors. By definition, the method assumes an actor's optimal decision depends on the behavior of other actors. For instance, a president's decision over whether to veto a bill depends on his (or her) expectations about congressional behavior. The mathematical exercise itself bears some similarity to the study of logic. In the "game" or context being studied, assumptions are formalized. The assumptions and hypotheses are then linked explicitly through the use of mathematical proofs.

The use of game theory to study the presidency has evolved from a scattering of papers by economists around twenty-five years ago to a literature that is dominated by political scientists and, correspondingly, investigates a range of topics that scholars of the presidency have long deemed important. Presidential appointments, executive orders, speech making, vetoes, agenda formation, and reputation have all been examined with game theoretic models. The purpose of this essay is to review a few of these topics in detail, pointing to how game theory has contributed to our understanding of these subjects, as well as how future research could use this technique to advance our understanding even further.

The three topics include presidential vetoes, public opinion, and Supreme Court nominations. This choice obviously excludes important work, ranging from Terry Sullivan's early (by standards of this literature) game theoretic models of bargaining (1990) to Chuck Cameron and Jee-Kwang Park's (2007) recent theory of agenda setting. What is lost in breadth, however, is hopefully compensated by depth that will encourage careful consideration of other topics. At the end of the essay, I identify several additional areas that seem especially suitable for new game theoretic analysis.

Also at the end of the essay, I devote special attention to concerns about the limitations of game theory. To what extent can it handle complex interactions? What about personal differences across presidents? What if a president is not a rational actor? The purpose of this section is not to suggest that game theory has no limitations; indeed, the purpose is to be up front about them. At the same time, we will reflect upon the severity of these limitations within the context of considering what game theory can do, both in isolation and in combination with other approaches.

PRESIDENTIAL VETOES

Prior to game theoretic analysis of the veto, scholarship tended to focus on the exercise of this policy tool rather than the influence generated by it. Examinations of individual presidents sought to explain personal differences in chief executives, with the veto being one aspect of this behavior. For instance, Neustadt (1990, 137–8) sheds light on how Eisenhower's lack of a political background made a "blunt" tool like the veto attractive. Similarly, Greenstein (2001, 120–4) discusses how Ford's lack of rhetorical skills, combined with his legislative experience, encouraged him to make use of the veto.

Complementing these accounts of individual differences were econometric/ statistical studies that elucidated patterns of vetoes across presidencies. In particular, these studies identified structural conditions associated with vetoes. For example, research demonstrated that vetoes are more likely the lower the percentage of seats held by the president's party, the lower the president's approval, the worse the state of the economy, the larger the number of bills passed by Congress, and in election years (e.g., Lee 1975; Copeland 1983; Rohde and Simon 1985; Woolley 1991). This scholarship also established that vetoes became more likely after the 1840s (Copeland 1983).

Against this background, game theoretic analysis has offered several contributions. Most significantly, it has redirected attention from observations of vetoes to how the policy tool affects presidential-congressional relations more generally. At the same time, game theory has provided insight into the factors that determine the exercise of vetoes. The models have subsequently improved empirical analysis by identifying appropriate econometric tests as well as by distinguishing the extent to which veto behavior is due to institutional pressures or, instead, a function of personal style.

The topics of the game theoretic models have been quite varied. Some of the earliest work focused on the policy influence generated by veto threats (e.g., Matthews 1989; Ingberman and Yao 1991a, 1991b). The most recurrent subject, perhaps not surprisingly, has been the effect of the veto on presidents' legislative influence (e.g., Hammond and Miller 1987; Brady and Volden 1998; Krehbiel 1998; Cameron 2000). Other scholarship has analyzed the impact of the veto on presidents' reputations with Congress (e.g., McCarty 1997) and budget politics (Kiewiet and McCubbins 1988).

Cameron and McCarty (2004) provide a list of eighteen theoretical contributions from this literature; there is no need to repeat or try to add to that list. Instead, it is worth linking some of these contributions to empirical work that preceded and, in some cases, resulted from the theoretical contributions. By doing so, we can see how game theory not only provides insight in isolation, but also, and arguably more importantly, shapes the sort of data gathered, the empirical specification employed, and the interpretation given to results.

Blame Game Politics

From a substantive perspective, perhaps the most unorthodox game theoretic analysis is Groseclose and McCarty's (2001) "blame game" model. Unlike most research on vetoes, Groseclose and McCarty focus on electoral causes, not merely policy-related ones.[2] Accordingly, the analysis is not simply about congressional–presidential interaction, but also the relationship between the general public and these elected officials. In the theory, the electorate does not know with certainty the president's policy preferences. Voters only have prior beliefs about these preferences, and these beliefs are updated after observing whether the president vetoes or signs a bill. The veto decision, of course, does not reveal the president's exact preferences but only sends the cruder signal of whether the president prefers the bill to the status quo. Consequently, depending on the content (or in the theory, the spatial location) of the bill that a president vetoes, the public may come to believe that he is more ideologically extreme than he really is.

In the blame game model, the president and Congress care about policy, but also about the president's approval ratings. The closer the public believes their preferences are to those of the president, the higher the president's approval. The most interesting case is when Congress hopes the president's approval ratings will decline. In that circumstance, Congress will attempt to make the president appear ideologically extreme by sending popular legislation the president does not prefer to current policy (and will therefore veto).

The predictions of this model improve our understanding of veto politics in numerous ways: they help explain well-established empirical regularities, suggest new ones, and identify conditions under which presidential veto usage would not necessarily be a function of personal style. For instance, the theory suggests that vetoes should be more likely in presidential election years, and this result comports with the aforementioned empirical evidence that vetoes are more likely in election years. Notably, the blame game model implies that this increase in election-year vetoes should be most prominent when Congress desires lower presidential approval ratings. Accordingly, and as the authors point out, we would expect this pattern to be greater under divided government.

[2] An important exception is Gilmour (1995), who argues that Congress and the president can have incentives for "strategic disagreement" even when policy incentives alone would induce compromise.

Data that I collected on presidential vetoes provide support for this prediction. These data involve the total number of annual vetoes from Eisenhower through George W. Bush, and are from the following sources: through 1984, King and Ragsdale (1988); 1984–8, Stewart and Harness (1992); 1989–2000, Thomson and Davis (2001); and 2001–7, "Vetoes by President George W. Bush" (2008). I exclude 1974 because the presidency shifts from Nixon to Ford in the middle of the legislative session.

Comparing the annual number of vetoes in presidential election years versus other years, these data suggest this difference is statistically significant and driven by the observations in which divided government occurred. In particular, for all years combined, the average number of vetoes in presidential election years is fourteen compared to an average of eight vetoes in other years ($p = 0.06$, two-tailed t-test). For observations of divided government, the analogous comparison is seventeen to ten ($p = 0.05$, two-tailed). By contrast, for observations in which the president's party has a majority in at least one of the chambers, the number of vetoes is nearly identical across presidential election years and other years; specifically, the average is eight for the former and seven for the latter ($p = 0.77$, two-tailed). Obviously, these comparisons are not meant to be any sort of definitive test. Rather, by providing preliminary support, they suggest that the blame game model may not only explain an often-noticed empirical pattern, but also predict circumstances under which this pattern of behavior should not be expected.

The blame game theory additionally offers new predictions about political phenomena that are rarely linked. For instance, it implies that vetoes should cause a decline in presidential popularity. Interestingly, the reason for the decline is not that the public is inherently opposed to vetoes; rather, blame game vetoes reveal that the president's preferences are out of step with those of the electorate. Groseclose and McCarty provide empirical support for this prediction.

Finally, the blame game predictions can help separate the extent to which veto behavior is due to structural conditions or instead a function of a president's personal style. Indeed, simple regressions of the total number of vetoes suggest that some of the conventional wisdom about individual style may be explained by institutional factors identified in the theory. For instance, in George W. Bush's first term, many commentators argued that his lack of vetoes indicated he was "veto averse," earning him the label "the man who won't veto" (York 2002). Yet Bush does not stand out as uniquely veto averse if compared to contexts in which a president's party held a majority in at least one of the chambers. More specifically, using the observations of the veto data for years of unified government, I ran a simple regression of the number of annual vetoes, which included an indicator for presidential election years, plus a set of indicators for the individual presidents. The model was estimated using ordinary least squares.

These results indicate that George W. Bush's behavior under unified government is similar to that of Johnson and Clinton (and cannot be compared to that of Nixon, Ford, and George H. W. Bush since these presidents always faced divided government). More specifically, with George W. Bush as the omitted dummy variable, the coefficient and standard error for the Clinton indicator are 0.343 (5.553) and for the Johnson indicator are 4.720 (4.178). In other words, neither the Clinton indicator nor the Johnson indicator is significantly different from the omitted indicator, which is for George W. Bush. Full results are available upon request.

As with the earlier tests, this empirical analysis is far from definitive; one could control for a host of other factors and/or account for differences between major versus minor legislation. However, the results demonstrate how the blame game theory can help distinguish personal versus institutional determinants of veto usage.

Vetoes and Legislative Influence

A major contribution of game theoretic models has been to delineate conditions under which vetoes should grant presidents policy influence, not only when we observe vetoes but—and at least as importantly—when we do not observe them. Of course, non-game theoretic work has long recognized that a veto threat, whether implicit or explicit, can benefit a president. However, game theoretic models, by delineating the conditions under which this influence exists, have contributed to empirical work in at least two ways. First, these models have suggested that standard econometric specifications for analyzing presidential influence may, under certain circumstances, be inappropriate. Second, this work has encouraged scholars to reconsider conventional wisdom about presidential veto power over the course of American history.

With respect to the first contribution, the theories of Kiewiet and McCubbins (1988) and McCarty and Poole (1995) recommend econometric specifications that estimate different effects of presidential veto power based upon the configuration of the status quo policy, presidential preferences, and congressional preferences. In particular, these models point to a "switching regime" specification in which the regimes depend upon whether the configuration of preferences is such that the veto should afford influence; more technically, the empirical model is an endogenous switching regime specification in which the regimes are estimated as a part of the econometric system. The theoretical work identifies the configuration of preferences associated with the various regimes, and, critically, reveals that one can mis-estimate veto influence if it is constrained to be constant across all configurations of preferences. For instance, one could fail to find any effect simply because most observations concerned configurations in which the veto should not generate any bargaining leverage.

It is worth pointing out that Krehbiel (1998, 204) takes issue with a specific assumption of Kiewiet and McCubbins (1988), as do I in Canes-Wrone (2001b, 200). In particular, both Krehbiel and I argue that the status quo for discretionary budgetary appropriations is zero (while Kiewiet and McCubbins argue it is based on the previous year's spending, the House proposal if it has passed a bill, and the Senate proposal if it has passed a bill). Independent of the substance of the disagreement, it points to an often-overlooked advantage of game theory. Because formalization requires scholars to be explicit about assumptions, readers know what the assumptions are and can easily build upon and critique the theory.

Game theoretic models of vetoes have not only aided econometric analysis, but also qualitative empirical work. For instance, Cameron (2000, 203–46) utilizes his models of veto bargaining to reinterpret, through narrative analysis, significant legislative battles between the president and Congress. Among other findings, Cameron provides evidence that the veto afforded Truman more influence over the Taft–Hartley bill than many previous accounts have presumed. McCarty (2007) goes back further in time to challenge the conventional wisdom that the veto afforded pre-Jacksonian (i.e., pre-1829) presidents only limited influence. As McCarty points out, this conventional wisdom is typically linked to the observation that vetoes were rare in the early republic. Utilizing recent game theoretic work, McCarty argues that a lack of vetoes does not imply a lack of veto power. He proceeds to provide evidence for this argument with a case study of negotiations over the Missouri Compromise (as well as from econometric analysis that compares presidents' legislative influence pre- and post-1829).

Among all subjects in presidential studies, the veto has arguably received the most attention from game theorists. This may be because the topic is central to legislative politics, and legislative scholars have been more apt to utilize game theory. Indeed, some of the most prominent game theoretic models have been developed by scholars who write prominently on legislatures (e.g., Kiewiet and McCubbins 1988; Brady and Volden 1998; Krehbiel 1998). Perhaps because so much of the work has not come from scholars who write primarily on the presidency, or perhaps for other reasons, many topics relating to vetoes remain low-hanging fruit for game theoretic analysis.

For instance, take the subject of signing statements. In these statements, which have existed since the nineteenth century, a president states his interpretation of a bill, commonly declaring he will not enforce certain provisions because he believes them to be unconstitutional. As Cooper (2005) points out in a recent *Presidential Studies Quarterly* piece, these statements arguably amount to a line-item veto. Yet, despite the fact that they have become much more common since the 1980s, we have little theory about their effects on veto politics. Do the statements have policy effects, and if so, under what conditions? Are these statements signaling presidential preferences, and if so, to whom?

PUBLIC OPINION AND POLICY

Scholars have long recognized that public opinion affects the president's actions and policy influence (e.g., Neustadt 1990; Edwards 1983). Yet despite the general sense that public opinion "matters," too little attention has generally been paid to *why* it matters and, correspondingly, why it seems to matter only some of the time. For example, many works document that presidents have expended increasingly large quantities of effort and time addressing the public or "going public," to use Kernell's language (2006; see also, e.g., Tulis 1987; Hager and Sullivan 1994). Yet as important as this contribution is unto itself, the literature as a whole initially paid insufficient attention to presidents' optimal employment of this strategy, leading to faulty conclusions about the causes and effects of the action. Likewise, a good deal of interesting work has been done on presidential popularity (e.g., Rivers and Rose 1985; Ostrom and Simon 1985; Cohen et al. 2000). Yet the lack of a deductive theory has led to a series of contradictory empirical findings, with an insufficient ability of the literature to reconcile or even explain them.

There are obviously other important topics concerning public opinion, too. However, as with the discussion of presidential vetoes, I will favor a more detailed description of how game theory has altered our substantive understanding of a subject—in this case, going public—over a broader survey. At the conclusion of the section I offer some suggestions for future research on other topics that concern public opinion.

Going Public

A variety of research testifies to the importance of presidential speeches and other rhetorical activities. Scholarship on American political development traces the increased significance presidents have attached to these activities over time (e.g., Tulis 1987; Skowronek 1993; Gamm and Smith 1998). Other research demonstrates that speeches tend to boost a president's popularity (e.g., Ragsdale 1984) and can increase the salience of issues (e.g., Cohen 1995, 1997; Hill 1998). Yet in contrast to this evidence that the activity is a central part of the modern presidency, empirical work originally suggested it did not afford any policy influence. Case studies documented prominent failed efforts of presidents to mobilize public opinion (see, for instance, Jacobs and Shapiro, 2000, on Clinton's efforts for nationalized health care or Tulis, 1987, on Wilson's appeal for a League of Nations). Moreover, case studies of successful appeals numbered "a very few," to use the words of Tulis (1987, 45).

Game theoretic analysis helped reconcile these seemingly contradictory findings by identifying why and when going public should encourage policy success. Miller (1993), for instance, focuses on the role of congressional committees. In the model, going public alters the center of congressional power from committees to the floor, which is assumed to have similar preferences to those of the president. Miller does not test the theory, but several empirical studies provide indirect support. For instance, Maltzman (1999) finds that the floor has more influence, relative to committees, when an issue is salient to the public. Also, Mouw and MacKuen (1992) demonstrate that when Reagan and Eisenhower went public, congressional agenda setters adopted more moderate positions. What Miller, Maltzman, and Mouw and MacKuen fail to establish is that congressional moderation or deference to the floor generally corresponds to presidential success; it may be, for instance, that the president has quite different policy preferences than the floor of the House or Senate has.

A simple game theoretic model that I developed (Canes-Wrone 2001b) took up this issue. In particular, the model examines how the relationship between the president's policy preferences and public opinion affects the extent to which major public appeals aid (or harm) the president's policy efforts. The theory predicts that presidents should only achieve success from these efforts when mass opinion supports the president's proposal over the status quo. Thus, presidents should not expect to generate influence from publicizing unpopular policies. Separately, the theory predicts that presidents will not go public about proposals on which they could reasonably expect a good deal of success without adopting this strategy; to the contrary, the strategy will be adopted only when Congress is otherwise unlikely to accede to the president's wishes.

Canes-Wrone (2001b) assumed that public appeals could alter the salience of issues, but not voters' positions about these issues. A good deal of empirical research supports these assumptions (see, for examples, Edwards, 2003, with regards to the difficulty presidents have in moving voters' positions, and Cohen, 1997, for evidence presidents can alter the salience of issues). However, some research suggests that when voters are uninformed about an issue, such as for many issues of foreign policy, presidents have a limited ability to move voters' positions. Accordingly, Canes-Wrone (2006, 30–4) describes a signaling model that grants presidents this ability.

Canes-Wrone (2001b, 2006) tests these models, and the empirical tests support the game theoretic predictions. Presidents obtain influence from public appeals, but this influence depends on presidents' strategic behavior in choosing the issues to promote to voters. In particular, the ex ante likelihood of policy success is inversely related to the likelihood of a public appeal. Additionally, the popularity of domestic initiatives is positively correlated with the likelihood of a president publicizing the initiative. This correlation does not exist for foreign policy initiatives, which is consistent with the claim that presidents have a greater ability to change public opinion about foreign affairs as well as with other arguments about differences between foreign and domestic policy (e.g., Canes-Wrone, Howell, and Lewis 2008).

Building off this theoretical work, Clinton et al. (1999) compared three game theoretic models of going public: a model based on Canes-Wrone (2001b), a model of public veto threats based on Ingberman and Yao (1991a, 1991b), and a new model of presidential credit claiming. In the Ingberman and Yao theories, as well as the version presented by Clinton et al., a president loses utility if he backs down from a public promise to veto a piece of legislation. Accordingly, even if a president prefers the legislation to the status quo, he can "credibly commit" to vetoing it by making public statements to this effect. By contrast, in the credit-claiming model, Clinton et al. highlight that presidents may go public to claim credit for policies that Congress would have enacted regardless. The credit-claiming model thus under-scores the difficulty of measuring a president's "true" preference, a topic to which many empirical analyses have given a great deal of attention (e.g., Kiewiet and McCubbins 1988; Cohen 1997; Canes-Wrone 2006).

Despite all of the recent theoretical work on going public, a large number of questions remain unexplored. For instance, to the best of my knowledge, no one has developed a theory of how targeted addresses—whereby presidents speak to a particular audience without national coverage—affect public opinion and presidential influence. A number of studies provide evidence that presidents have given more targeted addresses over time (e.g., Kernell 2006; Hager and Sullivan 1994). Correspondingly, Barrett (2004) analyzes all public statements—including major addresses, minor addresses, and written statements—as one group, and finds that they are associated with presidential success. Barrett does not analyze, however, whether this effect was driven by the targeted addresses or other parts of the data. More generally, we have little theory about whether targeted speeches should generate policy influence, or the circumstances under which we would expect them to do so. Separately, game theory could provide guidance on the ways in which a president's popularity affects his or her influence from going public. Kernell (2006) suggests that popularity should be an important factor, while the empirical tests of Canes-Wrone (2001a) do not support this prediction. I would be the first to argue that the issue is far from resolved, and that better theory could help guide new and valuable empirical analysis.

Other Research Frontiers Regarding Public Opinion

More generally, a number of topics regarding presidents and public opinion remain under-theorized. Most glaringly, the topic of presidential popularity cries out for more theory. Various empirical studies have been conducted, and many of these studies posit thoughtful hypotheses. At the same time, and my work on presidential approval is no exception (Canes-Wrone and de Marchi 2002), this literature has left open basic questions. What are the strategic interactions among the president, Congress, and the public with respect to the president's approval ratings? More generally, what are the micro-level foundations for any effects of presidential popularity, and what are the implications of these foundations for empirical testing? Game theoretic analysis, particularly if based on assumptions consistent with what we know about mass behavior, could help with these questions.

Another subject that could use more theorizing is presidential responsiveness to public opinion. Oftentimes, observers view a president's responsiveness to be purely a function of character. The president is labeled a "panderer" or, on the opposite end, someone unwilling to heed public opinion.[3] Political scientists are left with the job of identifying whether these evaluations hold up under closer scrutiny of these presidents' structural incentives.

Several recent pieces have taken up this challenge. Geer (1996), using Downsian-like formal modeling, suggests that the advent of opinion polls have increased presidents' incentives to follow rather than attempt to lead public opinion. By contrast, Jacobs and Shapiro (2000) develop case studies that indicate presidents have increasingly become less responsive because they have used polling to try to "craft" public opinion. As a part of this analysis, Jacobs and Shapiro contend that presidents are most likely to be responsive when there is insufficient time to shape voters' beliefs before the next

[3] President Bill Clinton is cited as an archetype of "politicians who will recast their positions at the drop of a hat—or, more to the point, the drop of a poll" (Berke 1995). Likewise, Douglas Brinkley argues: "Franklin D. Roosevelt, for example, was deemed a 'chameleon on plaid,' changing colors regularly to control the zeitgeist of the moment. Other presidents are submariners, refusing to zigzag in rough waters, preferring to go from Point A to Point B with directional certitude. Harry S. Truman and Reagan are exemplars of this modus operandi, and they are the two presidents [George W.] Bush has tried to emulate" (Brinkley 2006).

election. Canes-Wrone, Herron, and Shotts (2001) offer a game theoretic analysis that also suggests presidents will be more responsive as an election nears, but their theory does not focus on presidents' efforts to craft voters' positions. Instead, it analyzes a president's incentives to *pander* to public opinion by taking a popular position that he believes is not in voters' long-term interests. The Canes-Wrone, Herron, and Shotts model further suggests that unpopular as well as popular presidents will be less likely to pander to public opinion than presidents with average approval ratings. Canes-Wrone and Shotts (2004) and Canes-Wrone (2006) provide evidence for the theory.

It is not a criticism of these perspectives to point out that they leave many questions about presidential responsiveness unanswered. For instance, none focuses on how information dispersed by others—whether these others be candidates, parties, or interest groups—affects public opinion and hence presidents' incentives. Moreover, these theories treat each issue independently, yet clearly presidents develop a portfolio of policies. How important is the assumption of independence, and what are the implications for empirical analysis? Game theoretic analysis that builds off existing theories (or critiques them) could help deepen our understanding of these issues.

Supreme Court Nominations

In the words of President George W. Bush, the choice of whom to nominate for the Supreme Court constitutes "one of the most consequential decisions a president makes" (Hanson and Benforado 2006). The president, of course, does not have dictatorial control over this decision; the Senate must confirm judicial nominees. Yet, basic stylized facts present a murky picture of the extent to which the Senate influences the president's nominations. In particular, the Senate has rarely turned down the president's nominations and, even more puzzling, the nominees it has turned down are less ideologically extreme than ones who have sailed through confirmation. A series of recent game theoretic works, in combination with empirical analysis motivated by these theories, relate the stylized facts to a general understanding of the politics of Supreme Court nominations.

About a decade ago Moraski and Shipan (1999) developed a spatial model that identifies how the preferences of the president, Senate, and Supreme Court affect the president's optimal behavior with respect to nominations. These authors point out that earlier spatial modeling examined a senator's decision over whether to confirm a nominee, but these theories take the nominee as given rather than examining the president's choice of nominee (e.g., Segal, Cameron, and Cover 1992). The Moraski and Shipan theory, which is based on the setter model of Romer and Rosenthal (1978), shows how these incentives depend critically on the preferences of the justices continuing to serve on the Court. In particular, Moaraski and Shipan assume that senators care about how the new appointment will shift the Court's median. If the nomination is not accepted then policy reverts to the midpoint between the two most moderate justices (out of the remaining eight). A nominee is only turned down if a majority of senators prefer this reversion policy to the "new median" that would come about if the president's nominee were confirmed. Because few appointments— even ones that are ideologically extreme—shift the median of the Court dramatically, the president can often secure the confirmation of appointees who are ideologically extreme in relation to the Senate. And when the president cannot expect to do so, he simply nominates a more moderate or acceptable justice.

Moraski and Shipan (1999) provide support for the theory with data on presidents' Supreme Court nominations between 1949 and 1994. Several papers have questioned the verisimilitude of the theory, however, by critiquing central assumptions. These papers argue, among other things, that the Senate can filibuster nominations absent at least sixty votes in favor of closing debate. Johnson and Roberts (2005) show that with this assumption, the president's nominees should be turned down more often than they are. The authors proceed to explore (outside the context of a formal model) other factors, such as presidential popularity, which might explain presidents' success in securing confirmations. Rohde and Shepsle (2007) likewise develop a spatial model that assumes the Senate can filibuster nominees. They find that gridlock—i.e., the lack of any agreement between the president and Senate over an acceptable nominee—is quite plausible given partisan polarization. Factors that decrease the likelihood of gridlock include uncertainty about the revision policy and an ideologically moderate president.

Finally, Krehbiel (2007) develops a filibuster-based model with a different assumption about the reversion policy. Instead of basing it on the eight-member Court that exists without the president's nominee, the reversion policy remains at the earlier median; in other words, a senator's choice is between the old median that depends on the retiring justice and what would occur with the confirmation of the nominee. Thus, depending on the preferences of the justice that retires, Krehbiel's theory can explain why gridlock is less common than other filibuster-based models would suggest.

Overall, the game theoretic analysis of Supreme Court nominations has helped explain several empirical puzzles, such as why some nominees who are ideologically out of step with the Senate do not face much scrutiny, while other more moderate nominees fail to secure confirmation. Moreover, the models show how seemingly small differences in institutions—such as the reversion policy or the existence of a filibuster—can have dramatic implications for the politics of Supreme Court nominations. These are no small achievements. Still, the models leave unanswered some critical questions about this process.

For instance, existing models of Supreme Court appointments cannot explain Johnson and Robert's (2005) finding that presidential popularity affects the likelihood of confirmation. Nor do the theories shed light on the politics of scandal that have played so prominently in many recent battles over Supreme Court nominations. Finally, game theory could help delineate how the appointments process is affected by interest groups, which empirical analysis establishes are heavily involved in battles over the nominations (e.g., Caldeira and Wright 1998). Along these lines, Console-Battilana and Shepsle (2007) have recently developed a model in which the president and interest groups can offer inducements to senators in exchange for their votes on Supreme Court nominations.

ADDITIONAL SUGGESTIONS FOR FUTURE RESEARCH

New game theoretic research would not only advance our understanding of the politics surrounding presidential vetoes, public relations, and Supreme Court nominations, but many other topics as well. For instance, Howell's (2003) model of unilateral action answers many questions, but like most important work, raises new ones, too. How does the electorate's information about presidential and congressional preferences affect the desirability of unilateral action? Is it related to blame game politics? Separately, to what extent does uncertainty about the future affect presidents' incentives for unilateral versus legislative action? Take, for instance, a president's choice between achieving a trade agreement that is ratified through legislation versus enacting one through unilateral action. To what extent do the president's beliefs about future chief executives' preferences affect the desirability of each route, and how do the trade partners' beliefs influence these incentives? Theories that build off Howell's set-up could provide insight into these issues.

A second topic that has not received much recent attention from presidency scholars, let alone those who utilize game theory, is the relationship between the president and his party. Legislators and presidents often have starkly different incentives, yet we know little about the extent to which these actors accommodate each other when pursuing policy objectives. Over the past few years some conservatives have criticized the 107th–109th Congresses for being too accommodating of the president. For instance, the Honorable Mickey Edwards, a former representative from Oklahoma and long-time Republican, claims these congresses excessively catered to George W. Bush (Edwards 2008). Yet we have few expectations from the literature as to the sort of accommodation that is "normal," or what sort of behind-the-scenes bargaining we might expect under unified government. How powerful will congressional leaders be in this circumstance? What factors determine the degree to which Congress and the president acquiesce to each other's policy goals? Game theory could help delineate these factors.

A separate area that is ripe for more theory is presidents' efforts to *politicize* the bureaucracy, i.e., to make it more responsive to the president through modifications in structure and personnel. While works such as Moe's (1985) seminal article on the subject are theoretical—in the sense of stating assumptions and discussing their implications—explicitly game theoretic work has been scarce. An important exception is Lewis (2008), which examines the trade-off a president faces between control of bureaucratic agents and bureaucratic competence. Lewis shows, among other things, that presidents are more likely to politicize ideologically unsympathetic agencies and ones in which this change is less likely to affect competence. The model offers a valuable foundation, but leaves unexplored many questions for which game theory would be well suited. For instance, in the Lewis theory, as with standard principal–agent theory, agencies cannot attempt to insulate themselves from politicization. Yet some bureaucracy scholars have argued that bureaucrats can develop autonomy by building independent reputations (e.g., Carpenter 2001). An extension of Lewis that examined the way in which politicization might (or might not be) limited by bureaucrats' efforts for autonomy would help bridge these important literatures. Moreover, beyond the subjects of politicization and autonomy, there are many topics of presidential–bureaucratic relations, such as patronage, which are lacking in explicit game theoretic analysis.

LIMITATIONS AND MISCONCEPTIONS OF GAME THEORY

As an analytical tool, game theory can often improve upon our understanding of the world. We—in this essay and as a field—have witnessed this capacity with respect to a variety of topics. However, certain types of questions pose particular challenges for this methodological approach. Having spent most of the essay extolling the virtues and contributions of game theory, some acknowledgement of its limitations is in order. At the same time, I will seek to invalidate several commonly perceived limitations that are erroneous.

(Real) Limitation No. 1 and Techniques for Dealing with the Limitation: Technical Feasibility in Complex Environments

When the number of actors and actions are sufficiently large, and the informational assumptions sufficiently complex, game theoretic models can quickly become technically unfeasible. It is one thing to analyze bargaining among a small set of actors who share the same information; it is another to analyze a game with twenty actors, all of whom have private information, and all of whom are bargaining with each other over an extended period of time. Theorists have developed various lines of attack for dealing with such complexity, but all of these techniques have admitted drawbacks. For instance, sometimes a group of individuals—such as members of Congress or voters—are represented by a unitary actor (or smaller set of actors), who is assumed to be pivotal. This is a common tactic in work on congressional–presidential bargaining (e.g., McCarty 1997; Cameron 2000). Another approach, adopted by Baron and Ferejohn (1987) in their work on legislative bargaining, is to assume that actions at a particular point in time are not affected by previous actions; thus, an actor A would make the same bargaining offer to actor B regardless of what actor B had proffered in the earlier part of the game.[4]

In contrast to these tactics, which produce analytically general solutions, some game theorists have utilized computational methods to solve a complex game for particular parameter values. For instance, Bendor and Moe (1985) adopt this approach to develop a model of bureaucratic politics. Krehbiel, Meirowitz, and Romer (2005) recently developed a theory of partisan bias with this technique. To the best of my knowledge, no one has yet applied computational methods to the study of the presidency, but utilizing them may be fruitful for the study of certain types of complex interactions.

Misconception No. 1: Rationality

A standard critique of game theory is that it assumes rationality on the part of all actors. This critique is incorrect. Game theory can incorporate alternative assumptions of human behavior. The critical feature of a game theoretic model is that it involves strategic interaction; rationality is simply the most common assumption of human behavior, not an inherent requirement. Thus, the assumptions underlying Kahneman and Tversky's prospect theory (1979) or Simon's (1957) concept of bounded rationality can readily be incorporated. Such models tend to be more technically complex, but a number of scholars have risen to this challenge (e.g., see Butler 2007 for a game theoretic model that incorporates assumptions of prospect theory, and Bendor and Swistak 2001 for a model that incorporates bounded rationality).

Limitation No. 2: Game Theory Cannot Explain Everything in the World

A common pot-shot is that game theory does not explain some of the important things that presidents do and/or have done. This critique is obviously correct. First, there will be times that presidents are acting without thinking about strategic interactions. Of course, for these contexts, formal, non-game theoretic models of individual decision making (i.e., decision theoretic models) can be developed. Moreover, such models—like game theoretic ones—can be based on the assumptions of rational choice or on alternative assumptions. See, for instance, Patty (2006), which explains the phenomenon of midterm loss through a formal model of individual decision making under assumptions of prospect theory.

Yet even if we consider all types of formal models, I readily acknowledge that they will not explain every decision that a president has ever made. It goes without saying

---

[4] More technically, Baron and Ferejohn (1987, 306) assume stationary strategies, so that players' actions are not affected by the history of play within the game. McCarty (2000) uses this approach to analyze the impact of the presidential veto on particularistic/pork barrel spending.

that some interesting cases of history will be "off the equilibrium path" of any reasonable game or decision theoretic model—whether it assumes rationality or not. What formal theory can do is to help identify which behaviors are actually consistent with a theory based on reasonable assumptions about political actors' incentives and capacities, and which presidential actions, upon closer inspection, are not. The argument for utilizing game theory is not an argument that presidential scholars should abandon more traditional forms of research. Of course we want scholars delving into the archives, interviewing White House officials, and conducting surveys of mass opinion. And of course these methods will sometimes produce knowledge that game theory cannot. The argument for utilizing game theory is that it will sometimes produce knowledge that these other methods can or will not.

Misconception No. 2: Game Theory Merely Restates Things that We Already Know

Sometimes a game theoretic model will make a prediction that is entirely new to the literature. Immodestly, I will argue that the Canes-Wrone, Herron, and Shotts (2001) prediction about the relationship between presidential popularity and policy congruence/responsiveness is one such prediction; in particular, the theory suggests that the relationship is non-monotonic so that highly unpopular and highly popular presidents are less likely than presidents with average popularity to cater to public opinion. Other, entirely new predictions arguably come out of the theory of Groseclose and McCarty (2001) and the models of Supreme Court nominations, as described above. However, even when a prediction is not "entirely new," it often has value in eliminating other, equally appealing hypotheses. Thus, often a game theory model will produce intuitive predictions while simultaneously establishing that other, equally intuitive predictions are inconsistent with standard assumptions of presidential politics. In this case, a major contribution of the model will be the refutation of commonly held perspectives that do not hold up when subjected to rigorous logical consistency.

Limitation No. 3 and Misconception No. 3: Game Theoretic Models Often do not Produce a Unique Solution and these Sorts of Models have No Substantive Value

Another limitation, if one can call it such, is that game theoretic models often produce multiple solutions or equilibria. In other words, the models do not always make unique predictions about the actors' behavior. For example, a theory might have one equilibrium solution in which the president and Congress "always cooperate" as well as one in which they "always do not cooperate." The model may therefore provide less predictive power than empirical researchers would desire. Even in this case, however, it is worth remembering that the purpose of game theory is not to make unique predictions, but rather to explain the set of behavior predicted by a certain set of assumptions. By this criterion, if a game produces multiple equilibria, then that is something worth knowing unto itself. More generally, from a purely substantive perspective, the value of a theory depends on whether it offers a better understanding of the world, not whether it offers a unique prediction.

CONCLUDING THOUGHTS

Since the 1970s, when numerous scholars rightly attacked scholarship on the presidency for lacking general hypotheses, the field has come a long way. Much of this development has involved less formal theorizing and/or empirical analysis. A smaller but growing portion has involved game theoretic models. These models have shed light on questions ranging from why vetoes systematically lead to lower presidential popularity to why Senators often vote for Supreme Court nominees that hold ideologically extreme preferences (relative to the Senators).

Much of the game theory has been produced by scholars whose research is not heavily focused on the presidency. This situation is hopefully not a long-term equilibrium. Naturally we, as a field, welcome the insight of scholars who often research other subjects. Moreover, and equally obviously, we would not want all presidency scholars to devote themselves exclusively to producing game theoretic models. Visits to presidential libraries, interviews of White House officials, and the gathering of large datasets on presidential policy making will rightly remain central components of our field. Still, it would be unfortunate if most game theoretic models of presidential politics were produced by scholars who did not extensively study these politics. As this chapter has demonstrated, simple differences in the assumptions of the models can produce vastly different predictions; thus it would be a shame if the theories were only produced by "outsiders" to the field. Likewise, this chapter has highlighted the ability of game theory to develop hypotheses that can provide novel understandings of important phenomena. Accordingly, the ability and willingness of presidency scholars to read, critique, and, most importantly, to integrate this work into our field is important for its development.

REFERENCES

BARON, D. P., and FEREJOHN, J. 1987. Bargaining and Agenda Formation in Legislatures. *American Economic Review*, Papers and Proceedings of the Ninety-Ninth Annual Meeting of the American Economic Association, 77: 303–9.

BARRETT, A. W. 2004. Gone Public: The Impact of Going Public on Presidential Legislative Success. *American Politics Research*, 32: 338–70.

BENDOR, J., and MOE, T. M. 1985. An Adaptive Model of Bureaucratic Politics. *American Political Science Review*, 79: 755–74.

——and Swistak, P. 2001. The Evolution of Norms. *American Journal of Sociology*, 106: 1493–545.

BERKE, R. L. 1995. Stand Fast or Pander: What's a Candidate to Do? *New York Times*, Sept. 1: section 4, p. 1.

BOND, J. R., and FLEISHER, R. 1990. *The President in the Legislative Arena*. Chicago: University of Chicago Press.

BRADY, D. W., and VOLDEN, C. 1998. *Revolving Gridlock*. Boulder, CO: Westview Press.

BRINKLEY, D. 2006. Move Over, Hoover. *Washington Post*, Dec. 3: section B, p. 1.

BUTLER, C. K. 2007. Prospect Theory and Coercive Bargaining. *Journal of Conflict Resolution*, 51: 227–50.

CALDEIRA, G. A., and WRIGHT, J. R. 1998. Lobbying for Justice: Organized Interests, Supreme Court Nominations, and the United States Senate. *American Journal of Political Science*, 42: 499–523.

CAMERON, C. M. 2000. *Veto Bargaining: President and the Politics of Negative Power*. Cambridge: Cambridge University Press.

——and McCARTY, N. 2004. Models of Vetoes and Veto Bargaining. *Annual Review of Political Science*, 7: 409–35.

——and PARK, J.-K. 2007. A Primer on the President's Legislative Program. In *Presidential Leadership: The Vortex of Power*, ed. B. Rockman and R. Waterman. Oxford: Oxford University Press.

CANES-WRONE, B. 2001a. The President's Legislative Influence from Public Appeals. *American Journal of Political Science*, 45: 313–29.

——2001b. A Theory of Presidents' Public Agenda-Setting. *Journal of Theoretical Politics*, 13: 183–208.

——2006. *Who Leads Whom? Presidents, Policy, and the Public*. Chicago: University of Chicago Press.

——and DE MARCHI, S. 2002. Presidential Approval and Legislative Success. *Journal of Politics*, 64: 491–509.

——HERRON, M. C., and SHOTTS, K. W. 2001. Leadership and Pandering: A Theory of Executive Policy Making. *American Journal of Political Science*, 45: 532–50.

——HOWELL, W. G., and LEWIS, D. E. 2008. Executive Influence in Foreign versus Domestic Policy Making: Toward a Broader Understanding of Presidential Power. *Journal of Politics*, 70: 1–16.

——and SHOTTS, K. W. 2004. The Conditional Nature of Presidential Responsiveness to Public Opinion. *American Journal of Political Science*, 48: 690–706.

CARPENTER, D. P. 2001. *The Forging of Bureaucratic Autonomy: Networks, Reputations and Policy Innovation in Executive Agencies, 1862–1928*. Princeton, NJ: Princeton University Press.

CLINTON, J. D., Lewis, D. E., Riegg, S. K., and WEINGAST, B. R. 1999. Strategically Speaking: The Three Strategies of Going Public. Presented at the Annual Meeting of the American Political Science Association, Atlanta, GA.

COHEN, J. E. 1995. Presidential Rhetoric and the Public Agenda. *American Journal of Political Science*, 39: 87–107.

——1997. *Presidential Responsiveness and Public Policy-Making: The Public and the Policies that Presidents Choose*. Ann Arbor: University of Michigan Press.

COHEN, J. E., BOND, J. R., FLEISHER, R., and HAMMAN, J. 2000. State Level Presidential Approval and Senatorial Support. *Legislative Studies Quarterly*, 15: 577–90.

COOPER, P. J. 2005. George W. Bush, Edgar Allan Poe, and the Use and Abuse of Presidential Signing Statements. *Presidential Studies Quarterly*, 35: 515–32.

CONSOLE-BATTILANA, S., and SHEPSLE, K. A. 2007. Nominations for Sale. Harvard typescript.

COPELAND, G. W. 1983. When Congress and the President Collide: Why Presidents Veto Legislation. *Journal of Politics*, 45: 696–710.

EDWARDS, G. C., III. 1980. *Presidential Influence in Congress*. San Francisco: W. H. Freeman & Co.

—— 1983. *The Public Presidency: The Pursuit of Popular Support*. New York: St Martin's Press.

—— 2003. *On Deaf Ears: The Limits of the Bully Pulpit*. New Haven, CT: Yale University Press.

—— and WAYNE, S. J. (eds.) 1983. *Studying the Presidency*. Knoxville: University of Tennessee Press.

EDWARDS, M. 2008. *Reclaiming Conservatism: How a Great American Political Movement Got Lost: And How it Can Find its Way Back*. New York: Oxford University Press.

GAMM, G., and SMITH, R. M. 1998. Presidents, Parties, and the Public: Evolving Patterns of Interaction, 1977–1929. In *Speaking to the People: The Rhetorical Presidency in Historical Perspective*, ed. R. Ellis. Amherst: University of Massachusetts Press.

GEER, J. G. 1996. *From Tea Leaves to Opinion Polls*. New York: Columbia University Press.

GILMOUR, J. B. 1995. *Strategic Disagreement: Stalemate in American Politics*. Pittsburgh: University of Pittsburgh Press.

GREENSTEIN, F. I. 2001. *The Presidential Difference: Leadership Style from FDR to Clinton*. Princeton, NJ: Princeton University Press. First published 2000.

GROSECLOSE, T., and MCCARTY, N. 2001. The Politics of Blame: Bargaining before an Audience. *American Journal of Political Science*, 45: 100–19.

HAGER, G. L., and SULLIVAN, T. 1994. President-Centered and Presidency-Centered Explanations of Presidential Public Activity. *American Journal of Political Science*, 38: 1079–103.

HAMMOND, T. H., and MILLER, G. J. 1987. The Core of the Constitution. *American Political Science Review*, 81: 1155–74.

HANSON, J. D., and BENFORADO, A. 2006. The Drifters: Why the Supreme Court Makes Justices More Liberal. *Boston Review*, Jan./Feb.

HECLO, H. 1977. *Studying the Presidency*. New York: Ford Foundation.

HILL, K. Q. 1998. The Policy Agendas of the President and the Mass Public: A Research Validation and Extension. *American Journal of Political Science*, 42: 1328–34.

HOWELL, W. G. 2003. *Power without Persuasion: The Politics of Direct Presidential Action*. Princeton, NJ: Princeton University Press.

INGBERMAN, D., and YAO, D. 1991a. Circumventing Formal Structure through Commitment: Presidential Influence and Agenda Control. *Public Choice*, 70: 151–79.

—— —— 1991b. Presidential Commitment and the Veto. *American Journal of Political Science*, 35: 351–89.

JACOBS, L. R., and SHAPIRO, R. Y. 2000. *Politicians Don't Pander: Political Manipulation and the Loss of Democratic Responsiveness*. Chicago: University of Chicago Press.

JOHNSON, T. R., and ROBERTS, J. M. 2005. Pivotal Politics, Presidential Capital, and Supreme Court Nominations. *Congress & the Presidency*, 32: 21–48.

KAHNEMAN, D., and TVERSKY, A. 1979. Prospect Theory: An Analysis of Decision under Risk. *Econometrica*, 47: 263–91.

KERNELL, S. 2006. *Going Public: New Strategies of Presidential Leadership*, 4th edn. Washington, DC: Congressional Quarterly Press. First published 1987.

KESSEL, J. H. 1984. The Structures of the Reagan White House. *American Journal of Political Science*, 28: 231–58.

KIEWIET, D. R., and McCUBBINS, M. D. 1988. Presidential Influence on Congressional Appropriations Decisions. *American Journal of Political Science*, 32: 713–36.

KING, A. 1975. Executives. Pp. 173–256 in *Handbook of Political Science*, Volume 5, ed. F. I. Greenstein and N. W. Polsby. Reading, MA: Addison-Wesley.

KING, G., and RAGSDALE, L. 1988. *The Elusive Executive: Discovering Statistical Patterns in the Presidency.* Washington, DC: CQ Press.

KREHBIEL, K. 1998. *Pivotal Politics.* Chicago: University of Chicago Press.

—— 2007. Supreme Court Appointments as a Move-the-Median Game. *American Journal of Political Science*, 51: 231–40.

—— MEIROWITZ, A., and ROMER, T. 2005. Parties in Elections, Parties in Government, and Partisan Bias. *Political Analysis*, 13: 113–38.

LEE, J. R. 1975. Presidential Vetoes from Washington to Nixon. *Journal of Politics*, 37: 522–46.

LEWIS, D. 2008. *The Politics of Presidential Appointments: Political Control and Bureaucratic Performance.* Princeton, NJ: Princeton University Press.

McCARTY, N. 1997. Presidential Reputation and the Veto. *Economics and Politics*, 9: 1–27.

—— 2000. Presidential Pork: Executive Veto Power and Distributive Politics. *American Political Science Review*, 94: 117–29.

—— 2007. Vetoes in the Early Republic. Working paper, Woodrow Wilson School. Princeton University.

—— and POOLE, K. T. 1995. Veto Power and Legislation: An Empirical Analysis of Executive–Legislative Bargaining from 1961–1986. *Journal of Law, Economics, and Organization*, 11: 282–312.

MALTZMAN, F. 1999. *Competing Principals: Committees, Parties and the Organization of Congress.* Ann Arbor: University of Michigan Press.

MATTHEWS, S. A. 1989. Veto Threats: Rhetoric in a Bargaining Game. *Quarterly Journal of Economics*, 104: 347–69.

MILLER, G. J. 1993. Formal Theory and the Presidency. In *Researching the Presidency: Vital Questions, New Approaches*, ed. G. C. Edwards III, J. H. Kessel, and B. A. Rockman. Pittsburgh: University of Pittsburgh Press.

MOE, T. 1985. The Politicized Presidency. In *The New Direction in American Politics*, ed. J. E. Chubb and P. E. Peterson. Washington, DC: Brookings.

MORASKI, B. J., and SHIPAN, C. R. 1999. The Politics of Supreme Court Nominations: A Theory of Institutional Constraints and Choices. *American Journal of Political Science*, 43: 1069–95.

MOUW, C. J., and MacKUEN, M. B. 1992. The Strategic Agenda in Legislative Politics. *American Political Science Review*, 86: 87–105.

NEUSTADT, R. E. 1990. *Presidential Power and the Modern Presidents: The Politics of Leadership from Roosevelt to Reagan.* New York: The Free Press. First published 1960.

OSTROM, C. W., JR., and SIMON, D. M. 1985. Promise and Performance: A Dynamic Model of Presidential Popularity. *American Political Science Review*, 79: 334–58.

PATTY, J. W. 2006. Loss Aversion, Presidential Responsibility, and Midterm Congressional Elections. *Electoral Studies*, 25: 227–47.

PIKA, J. A. 1982. Moving beyond the Oval Office: Problems in Studying the Presidency. *Congress and the Presidency*, 9: 17–36.

RAGSDALE, L. 1984. The Politics of Presidential Speechmaking, 1949–1980. *American Political Science Review*, 78: 971–84.

RIVERS, D., and ROSE, N. L. 1985. Passing the President's Program: Public Opinion and Presidential Influence in Congress. *American Journal of Political Science*, 29: 183–96.

ROHDE, D. W., and SHEPSLE, K. A. 2007. Advising and Consenting in the 60-Vote Senate: Strategic Appointments to the Supreme Court. *Journal of Politics*, 69: 664–77.

——and SIMON, D. M. 1985. Presidential Vetoes and Congressional Response: A Study of Institutional Conflict. *American Journal of Political Science*, 29/3: 397–427.

ROMER, T., and ROSENTHAL, H. 1978. Political Resource Allocation, Controlled Agendas, and the Status Quo. *Public Choice*, 33: 27–43.

SEGAL, J. A., CAMERON, C. M., and COVER, A. D. 1992. A Spatial Model of Roll Call Voting: Senators, Constituents, Presidents, and Interest Groups in Supreme Court Confirmations. *American Journal of Political Science*, 36: 96–121.

SIMON, H. A. 1957. *Models of Man: Social and Rational.* New York: John Wiley & Sons.

SKOWRONEK, S. 1993. *The Politics Presidents Make: Leadership from John Adams to George Bush.* Cambridge, MA: Harvard University Press.

STEWART, W. J., and HARNESS, G. 1992. Presidential Vetoes, 1789–1988. Senate Publication 102–12.

SULLIVAN, T. 1990. Bargaining with the President: A Simple Game and New Evidence. *American Political Science Review*, 84: 1167–96.

THOMSON, J., and DAVIS, Z. 2001. Presidential Vetoes, 1989–2000. Senate Publication 107–10.

TULIS, J. K. 1987. *The Rhetorical Presidency.* Princeton, NJ: Princeton University Press.

Vetoes by President George W. Bush. 2008. Official U.S. Senate Reference at <http://www.senate.gov/reference/Legislation/Vetoes/BushGW.htm>. Accessed April 2008.

WOOLLEY, J. T. 1991. Institutions, the Election Cycle, and the Presidential Veto. *American Journal of Political Science*, 35: 279–304.

YORK, B. 2002. The Man Who Won't Veto: One Power that George W. Bush Eschews. *National Review*, June 17.

CHAPTER 4

HISTORICAL INSTITUTIONALISM, POLITICAL DEVELOPMENT, AND THE PRESIDENCY

SCOTT C. JAMES

SERIOUS students of the modern presidency warn against a tendency to exaggerate the importance of presidents in American politics. Congress is the Article I branch and it remains the dominant player in routine matters of policy making. The president's role is by no means inconsequential—the Constitution's deliberate inter-mingling of governing authority across separated branches assures this—but his influence is said typically to be felt only "at the margins" of the legislative process (Edwards 1990; Peterson 1990; Jones 1994. For a critical view, see Whittington and Carpenter 2003). This line of argument is widely influential. It serves as a useful caution to those of us who, in our capacity as citizens, find ourselves otherwise awash in the ubiquity of presidential action and imagery, and where casual observation would seem to argue on behalf of that institution's political preeminence.

On the other hand, this discrepancy between casual perception and rigorous finding is sufficiently jarring to warrant asking whether we miss something deeper about the significance of the presidency in American politics if we confine our attention too narrowly to routine policy processes or if we limit our measures of presidential importance to statistical scorecards of legislative victory. Informal indicators of that institution's significance abound in our politics and culture. Scholars regularly periodize American political history around the names and programmatic namesakes of *presidents* ("the Jeffersonian Era;" "the Age of Jackson;" "the New Deal Era;" "the Reagan Revolution"). *Presidential* elections most often set the basic terms of national political debate and define the issues on the public agenda. During moments of national crisis, distraught citizens who seek reassurance wait anxiously for *presidents* to speak. Scholars and pundits endlessly draw up lists of great *presidents* and debate their respective merits. It is the iconic representation of *presidents* that we carve into mountainsides and that populate our national currency.

The list goes on—from the profound to the pedestrian. My only point here is to suggest the possibility that we elide the most distinctive properties of the presidency and its enduring role in American politics by confining our attention to legislative policy outputs. As one scholar has recently argued, the significance of the American presidency may lie less in the *policies presidents pass* than in the *politics presidents make* (Skowronek 1996). This essay will argue that historical institutionalism and American political development (APD), as distinctive approaches to the study of politics, offer one particular avenue for those interested to explore the broader significance of the presidency in American politics. Every approach has its limits, but the advantage of these complementary approaches lies in their capacity to throw into relief that institution's distinguishing features, as well as its unique contribution both to the dynamics of American politics and to the processes of political change. Much has been gained by disciplinary efforts to devise a general theory of institutions—one shorn of the specifics of time and space—and by efforts to subsume the presidency and presidential behavior under its universal rules of action (Moe 1993). However, by their nature, theoretical truths are at best partial, and to the historical institutionalist and the student of APD, absorbing the presidency into a general theory of institutions runs the risk of suppressing its unique and most consequential attributes.

This chapter is organized into several parts. First, I introduce historical institutionalism and APD as analytic approaches to the study of politics. Following this, I introduce the presidency as an object of study and assess the institution's relevant features in light of the precepts identified. Next, I turn to several streams of research in which students of the presidency with an APD bent have made significant contributions. The first research stream examines more closely the presidency's unique status among American political institutions, a status based on its intimate relationship to "the People." A second examines the presidency's distinctive contribution to the politics of regime change. A third stream investigates the historically changing modalities of governance, isolating developmentally significant moments in the evolution of presidential politics. Here we will examine separately the evolution of "plebiscitary politics" and the rise of an "administrative presidency," two emblematic features of contemporary American politics. Nowhere in what follows do I present full-blown literature reviews, though additional citations for further reading are included in the bibliography to this chapter. Rather, I will concentrate on a smaller set of publications that have made a lasting impact on the literature—mostly works within the mainstream of APD, but, where productive, I also include non-APD work with important developmental claims. At each stage, we will consider APD's analytic take on questions of interest to students of the presidency and American politics, and the fruitful points of dispute that arise as competing interpretative claims impinge upon one another, pointing the way for fresh new lines of inquiry. By emphasizing seminal nodes in a literature, we will sharpen our understanding of the key lines of debate, as well as the central points of contention that drive research in the APD community.

Finally, for reasons I will discuss in detail, my interest in this chapter lies not in understanding the political development of the American presidency. Indeed, I will argue that a phrase like "the political development of the American presidency"—or any single institution for that matter—is conceptually misguided. Rather, it is more appropriate to speak of the presidency's contribution *to* American political development or American political development's impact *on* the presidency. In order to understand why this is a significant difference, we need to understand both what historical institutionalism and political development are, and what they are not. Only at that point can we fruitfully fold the presidency into our discussion and explore what it is that APD and historical institutionalism can contribute to its study and vice versa.

Historical Institutionalism

What is historical institutionalism? What does it share with the other institutional approaches to politics? Where does it part company with those alternatives? In the discussion that follows, I draw extensively from the work of Karen Orren and Stephen Skowronek (1994, 1996, 1998, and 2006), whose writings on historical institutionalism and political development represent major contributions to the subjects and to the advancement of APD as a subfield.[1]

Like other institutional approaches, historical institutionalism gives explanatory pride of place to the rules, routines, standard operating procedures, and norms of legitimate action that both enable and constrain political action. Institutions channel political behavior, imparting to individuals in a common organizational setting a shared identity, purpose, and direction. By their operation, institutions make particular actions either more probable or less; in the process, they render political behavior more predictable. Institutional approaches thus emphasize regularities in political action, especially as they arise from the organizational setting of politics. Institutions impart a degree of pattern and orderliness to the tumultuous world of

[1] For a significant alternative formulation to Orren and Skowronek, see Pierson and Skocpol (2002) and Pierson (2004). For additional reading, see also Steinmo, Thelen, and Longstreth (1992) and Hall and Taylor (1996).

political conflict and, as a result, make an essential contribution to theory-building endeavors at the heart of contemporary social science (March and Olsen 1989; Carpenter 2000, 2001).

What, then, makes *historical* institutionalism distinctive? First, as the name implies, historical institutionalism is significant because it takes seriously the temporal origins of political institutions. Attention to history contextualizes the process of institution building; it infuses local specificity into the organizational design of politics. By this understanding, institutions are created at precise moments in time, within a delineated political context, and they house embedded sets of cultural assumptions. That context durably defines the purposes to which new institutions are put: the goals they pursue; the values they embody; the norms of appropriate behavior they both adhere to and expect from others. Moreover, *because they are institutionalized,* these purposes carry forward in time, where they engage with other purpose-driven institutions over the division of legitimate political authority. In essence, historical institutionalism holds that the act of institutionalizing a grant of new authority "freezes" the politics of a given historical moment and, through the formulation of rules, routines, and norms, carries the politics and culture of that historical moment forward in time. Put simply, an institution is a congealed historical remnant; current politics is the dynamic expression of multiple interactions among institutionalized vestiges of a country's political past. In Orren and Skowronek's theoretical formulation, the political present is an amalgam of "multiple orders" rooted in a nation's political history. Developmentally significant politics implicate ongoing relations between institutions; "intercurrence"—political conflict arising from the discordant historical premises that underlie interaction in a multi-institutional setting—is the stimulant to new distributions of governing authority (an excellent recent application is Frymer 2007).

Second, as a corollary, historical institutionalists argue that institutional reform is always partial or incomplete (Tulis 1987; Schickler 2001). Rarely does reform—or even revolution—result in a complete uprooting or transformation of an organization's initial premises (de Tocqueville 1969). There are no full reversions to square one; rather, reforms layer new politics and new assumptions upon old politics and old assumptions. The partial character of reform creates new points of tension and conflict within institutional settings. It also complicates the constituent bases of institutional support and the coherent articulation of organizational purposes in the external environment of politics.

Finally, historical institutionalism recognizes that any institution—be it new or newly reformed—is thrust immediately into an ongoing political universe replete with other institutional actors, each engaged in a fierce combat for jurisdictional authority and political autonomy. It is this ongoing contestation among institutions over the scope of their political authority—and the political conflict that inevitably ensues—that is the central facet of political life and the dynamic element that drives political change. Relations between institutions are prone to conflict, as it is intrinsic to the nature of political institutions to reach beyond their existing sphere of authority in an effort to regulate the behavior of others, and to do so in a manner consistent with their own purposes and interests. By way of analogy, consider the manner in which, to advance their interests in an anarchical international system, nation-states with distinctive interests, practices, habits, and histories seek stable and predictable relations with other states, even as those relations remain fraught with tension and conflict and are periodically subject to renegotiation over the allocation of authority and control. So too, of necessity, domestic political institutions with historically distinctive ordering principles engage in their own form of "foreign relations" with other institutions, relations continuously rubbed raw by the friction arising from the regular and inevitable exercise of political interest. Because of this, within historical-institutional approaches to politics, concepts like "institutional fit," "equilibrium institutions," and "political order" are each subject to criticism for muting the tension and conflict characteristic of institutional relations and the dynamic force that drives political change.

Political Development

How does this discussion of historical institutionalism advance an understanding of American political development? What precisely is political development? As an initial statement, I will observe simply that students of political development seek to understand political change, its processes and dynamics as well as its consequences. By *processes* of political change, I mean the operations of mechanisms inherent in the design features of a given political system. Political processes provide channels for political action, enabling and constraining political forces and providing both a strategic and a tactical context for political leadership. By *dynamics* of political change, I refer to the distinctive interaction effects that arise from a historically given configuration of events or sequence of actions. These dynamics may strengthen or weaken established political authorities; they create openings that enhance or diminish political opportunities for political change; and, they may assist or hinder efforts to institutionalize a new status quo in the aftermath of political change.

   This initial formulation is a useful starting point. However, absent further elaboration, the "development = change" equivalence quickly runs into problems. Perhaps the most important of these is the overly broad reach of the "change" concept. While all instances of political development are rightly understood as instances of political change, not all instances of political change constitute instances of political development. Political change is a broader and more inclusive term than political development; the latter is at best a subset of the former. Political change takes a variety of shapes and forms: from the small, the incremental, and the incidental to the large-scale, the discontinuous, and the transformative. Political change, for example, can be observed in the massive growth over time in annual expenditures by the US government, the temporal swelling in the volume of legislative bills introduced and processed by a single session of Congress, or the tremendous secular expansion in federal programs like social security. On the other hand, political change is also observed at critical junctures in American political history, like the New Deal, when new national electoral alignments upend long-standing ruling coalitions, uproot standing policy commitments and their institutional supports, and inaugurate full-scale and durable regime change. Each of the first three illustrations of political change cited above might plausibly be characterized as an institutional trend, an institutional advancement, or even an instance of institutional evolution. They might even be entry points in a search for political development. However, only the final example, or so I will argue, is fairly characterized as an instance of political development.

To proceed further, then, we need to refine our initial formulation. If political development is a specific kind of political change, what kind exactly is it? Following Orren and Skowronek (2006), I will define political development as political change that results in *a durable shift in governing authority*. Political development occurs when political change reconfigures or reconstitutes the locus of legitimate government action. Durability is achieved when competing sources of authority, power, and influence acquiesce to these changes, adjust their expectations accordingly, and new modes of political interaction—new modalities of governance—arise and stabilize. Political development recasts the formal authority to regulate the actions and affairs of others, altering in its wake the underlying structure of access, influence, and prestige. Political development is *systemic*: individual institutions do not develop; polities do. Political development is also *structural* or *relational*: it is the fruit of conflict over existing lines of political authority that fundamentally recasts governing relations between two or more institutions.

APD AND THE PRESIDENCY

These last two points are critical, as they shape the APD approach to the presidency. It follows from the preceding that it is conceptually wide of the mark to speak of "the development of the American presidency" (or any other institution considered in isolation). Rather, it is better to speak of the ways in which the presidency has been implicated in the broader process of APD, both as a participant in the politics of systemic change and as one of many inheritors of reconstituted governing relations. None of this is meant to suggest that individual institutions themselves remain static over time and that, as such, they offer little of interest to students of APD. Needless to say, institutions may experience change of significant and even historic proportions: they may grow larger or smaller; they may become more experienced or less; they may exhibit improved or diminished capabilities; they may become infused with new leadership or resist such infusions; they may shed old constituencies and commitments or acquire new ones. However, these facets of institutional change only become implicated in political development when, by their actions, they are complicit in the reorganization of governing relations among competing institutions. Of course, where change in the structure and function of the presidency (or, again, any other political institution) has implications for change in broader modes of governance and their relations of authority, it becomes critical to understand the causal character of those changes: from where they originated; how they came to grow or diminish in size and influence; their contribution to destabilizing the political status quo; and their contribution to the character of reconstructed governance.

It will be important then to keep in mind the distinction I am making between institutional change or evolution, on the one hand, and political development on the other. The goal of this chapter is to identify productive lines of research for scholars interested in exploring the developmental implications of historical struggles over the relative distribution of governmental authority involving the presidency. As we will see, the study of the presidency is a particularly fruitful vehicle for exploring America's political development, just as the study of APD is an excellent vehicle for exploring institutional change in the presidency. The reason is precisely APD's systemic vantage point, which focuses attention on relations or modes of governance, the institutionalized authority relations that underpin and legitimize them, and the sources of tension that destabilize them over time and contribute to fundamental political change.

Governance Versus Leadership

Issues of governance have long interested students of the presidency. Yet, more often than not, this broad interest in governance has veered toward more practical questions of presidential leadership. From an APD perspective, the problem with the leadership focus is that it draws us toward the strategic and the tactical within a particular mode of governance. As Jeffrey Tulis (1987) has written, the leadership vantage point invites scholars to become institutional partisans. It asks us to look out from over the shoulder of presidents, to see the political world through their eyes. In classic Neustadtian terms, we find ourselves attempting to solve the perennial presidential leadership dilemma: "How can I make the office of the presidency work for me?" A stock of immediately recognizable questions follows: what does the president wish to accomplish? What are the power resources at the president's disposal to accomplish personal and political goals? What are the stock of arguments, ideas, and imagery that a president can draw upon to persuade interested publics to follow the president's lead? What types of individual psychology, personal traits, and professional skills do successful presidential leaders tend to possess in abundance?

I have no wish to disparage the leadership focus in presidency studies. Given the presidency-centered character of modern American democracy, questions regarding presidential leadership will and should loom large in the research agenda of presidency scholars. It has been responsible for many important works in the subfield and continues to offer promising lines of inquiry. Nor should I be read to suggest either that leadership is not important to governance or that the governance frame sheds no light on the challenges of leadership (see, for example, Skowronek 1996). The claim I wish to advance here is that "governance" offers a more productive framework for presidency scholars with an APD bent than does the "leadership" frame. A focus on governance immediately embeds presidential action in a thick network of overlapping institutional relationships, each implicated in relations of functional interdependence, with each nonetheless seeking to subordinate other sources of political authority in order to broaden its own field of autonomous action. In sum, the governance frame draws attention to the allocation of authority within a given political regime and the modalities of regular intercourse that arise within it. It does not *ignore* matters of leadership. More to the point, it recognizes that institutional leadership is lodged at numerous points in the political system—in Congress and among ally and opposition political parties; with department secretaries and at critical nodes inside the career bureaucracy; and among pressure groups, economic institutions, and other interest-bearing organizations. A governance vantage point recognizes that it is the conduct of normalized relations among competing institutional leaders and the adherence to accepted procedures for resolving disputes among them that diffuse conflict, impart stability and predictability to politics, and allow the political system to function and reproduce itself over time.

Little in the preceding paragraph clearly differentiates APD from non-APD scholarship. It is here, or so I will argue, that APD strikes out on its own. In the main, non-APD scholarship on the presidency focuses its attention on the strategic dealings of presidents within a stable institutional context, one in which presidents seek to maximize their returns to purposive action by deploying available resources rationally, subject to the constraints of information, time, and tactical ability. APD scholarship on the presidency, on the other hand, seeks to understand how and why the once-stable modes of governing relations within which presidents are embedded become disturbed and break down. It aims to identify the ways in which presidential action facilitates or impedes that breakdown, and to document the signature elements of new governing configurations, the factors behind their coalescence, and the location of the presidency within them. Often, purposive presidential action will be front and center as the explanation for systemic change. However, in some instances, that institution may simply be implicated in the reconstitution, as changing relations initiated elsewhere in the system reverberate throughout that system. For instance, Stewart (1989) argues that the electoral connection in combination with the parochial character of congressional representation impeded efforts to create a centralized budget authority in the nineteenth-century House of Representatives. The result was a developmentally significant transfer of budgeting authority from that institution to the presidency, formalized in the Budget and Accounting Act of 1920.

Patterned Development

A final aspect of APD worth noting is the special place it accords to instances of political development that exhibit overarching temporal patterns, be they particular historical trajectories or directionalities (Galambos 1970; Orren 1991), or patterns of a cyclical or recurrent character (Burnham 1970; Skowronek 1996; Smith 1997). Patterned development suggests the presence of deeper truths regarding the meaning and character of America's political-historical experience. It directs us toward the conditions and conjunctures that both occasion and bound systemic change, and invites us to reflect upon the implications of both the patterns of change and their limits for the future course of American democracy. Consider, for example, that during much of American political history, the presidency has exhibited a tremendous growth in stature, in responsibilities, and in power, often at the expense of competing political institutional authorities. Its scope of legitimate action has expanded significantly. We might call this the *presidentialization* of American politics. Indeed, it is difficult to recognize the contemporary presidency in the modest constitutional grants contained in Article II (for a contrary view, see Nichols 1994). While scholars and public commentators might reach different conclusions as to whether the presidentialization of American politics has on balance advanced or retarded the development of liberal democracy, there is little gainsaying the fact that citizens have come to expect presidents to supply the primary direction and motive force to American politics in a way that most of the Framers of the Constitution never envisioned—indeed, in a manner most of the Framers explicitly sought to proscribe.

For students of APD the crucial question is to understand why successive episodes of political development have, on balance, tended to reinforce and deepen the relative authority of presidents. Can we ascertain whether historical happenstance or deep structural dynamics has exerted the greater causal weight on the presidency's institutional evolution? Can we assess the implications for the quality of American democracy of a continuing presidentialization of its politics?

PRESIDENTS AND THE SOVEREIGN AUTHORITY: THE PRIMACY OF "WE THE PEOPLE"

"We are *one people* in the choice of President and Vice-President.".... This assertion culminated [Andrew] Jackson's efforts to redefine the presidency and the relation of the American people to their government. It was another appeal for recognition that it was the presidential office—not the legislature...—that embodies all the people. The president is the representative of the American electorate and directly responsible to them. By his actions and words he articulates and executes their will. (Remini 1984, 20–1)

One of the more arresting explanations for the rise of the presidency in American politics directs us to the historical construction of the office itself. Both American constitutional theory and its practice suggest that those political institutions that can most credibly claim to speak on behalf of the sovereign authority—"We the People"—will find its authority relative to rival institutions enhanced. For that reason, the intimate, long-standing, and unmatched relationship between the presidency and the broad American political community has been at the heart of its significance to students of APD. It goes a long way toward clarifying the rhetorical tendencies that emanate from the office—the constant impulse manifested by presidents both to speak *to* the American people and to speak *for* them (Ellis 1998). Unitary in structure and possessing a constituency coterminous with the Union's geographical boundaries, the presidency, it is argued, is the only political institution structurally capable of representing the nation as a whole, speaking coherently on its behalf, and directly shaping its shared identity, sense of political purpose, and historical mission (e.g., Bellah 1967; Roelofs 1992; Abbott 1990, 1996).

The constitutional design of the presidency was motivated in equal parts by a promise and a fear (James 2005). The *promise* was of a virtuous executive motivated by national service and insulated from direct constituency pressures and interest-based politics, one free to defend constitutional principle and the permanent national interest against the passions and interests stirring normal politics. The *fear* was of a people's presidency, one that would attract ambitious demagogues, harness plebiscitary authority to amass personal power, and subvert the delicate institutional balance and limits on government woven into the fabric of the Constitution. Both the promise and the fear required the Framers to proscribe a direct and unmediated relationship between presidents and the public. The political science of the Founding generation focused intently on the latent political power of the presidential office: presidents were the only elected officeholders with a national constituency, while the quadrennial presidential election was the only institutional setting in which "the People" might regularly congregate as a single community to agitate on behalf of great national questions. Because of this, presidents were uniquely situated to claim both a direct knowledge of and an intimate relationship with the sovereign authority. In the end, by constitutional design, the Founders famously sought to deflate presidential pretensions to speak on behalf of "We the People," most notably through the erection of an intermediary institution—the Electoral College.

Against this backdrop, arguably the single most important political development in the organization of American governance since the Founding is the forging of an increasingly *personal* relationship between presidents and the popular will. All manner of presidential scholarship refers to or taps into some aspect of this singular relationship (e.g., Ceaser 1979; Ketcham 1984; Tulis 1987; Skowronek 1996; Bimes and Skrowonek 1996; Bimes and Mulroy 2004). To students of American political development in particular, that relationship has been implicated causally both in processes of regime change and in transformations in the basic modalities of governance, as they operate across both the various branches and levels of government. At times it seems as if almost anything important we might wish to say about presidents and their involvement in America's political development flows directly from this relationship and its peculiar intimacy. Much of the presidency's own institutional history tracks successive episodes in the dismantling of barriers impeding direct and unmediated popular leadership: some conceptual (assertions of a special presidential mandate, emergency powers, a unitary executive); others institutional (the displacement of mediating institutions such as the congressional caucus, the political party, the cabinet, and the addition of the permanent bureaucracy); and still others technological (innovations in the speed and scope of presidential travel and communications). In all, episodes fostering ever more intimate linkages between presidents and the people have been critical to the historical reconstitution of American governance, fundamentally altering authority relations between the presidency, Congress, political parties, the courts, the bureaucracy, state governments, and other political institutions.

Much more remains to be explored. APD scholarship on the presidency needs to clarify further the origin and development of that unique relationship and probe its fundamental nature. The presidency has seemingly always been a magnet for public attention. From the Framers on, political elites have worried about its potentialities even as some have sought to unleash them. All of these things are more easily observed than explained. What are the unique properties of the presidency that compel public and elite attention over its alternatives? To some, the presidency derives its salient characteristics from its unitary structure, while for others, its relation to the coercive powers of the state plays the primary role. Some attribute its uniqueness to the institution's dual nature (the president as both head of government and head of state), while still others point to its prophetic character (presidents as "high priests" of the American civil religion). If it is true that this relationship to "the People" is fundamental—i.e., that it is a principal source of dynamism that drives political development—then it is imperative that we understand this seemingly enduring relationship. Is this relationship a structurally inevitable outgrowth of the Framers' constitutional design? Is its potency constant or variable—and, if the latter, with what kind of pattern or regularity? Are its effects on American politics truly consequential, and if so, how? Is its institutional growth and prominence irreversible absent fundamental political change?

Empirically, it is also necessary to unpack more fully the politics of the Founding generation and the presidency's place within its constitutional practice. Political scientists know much more about the Founders' theoretical vision for American government than its regular day-to-day operations (Ceaser 1979; Tulis 1987). Theories of American political development stand on the shoulders of close historical work covering and detailing the daily routines and practices of governance. No discipline is as well equipped as political science to do the necessary spade work to acquire and analyze the information on governing practices needed for the theoretical advancement of APD. While important early work has been done in this area (e.g., Young 1969; Cunningham 1978), conceptual and methodological advances in the discipline of political science since this time make it an area ripe for productive scholarly engagement. Such findings will provide a crucial empirical baseline against which to gauge the degree, the character, and the direction of subsequent change in the structures of governance, and thus for evaluating its developmental significance.

Precisely how was American governance configured in the years immediately following constitutional ratification? What, *in practice*, were the appropriate relations of authority among governing institutions that arose under that document? What did presidential practice look like within that setting? What were the typical sources of tension and conflict that arose? What were the mechanisms for resolving those disputes? What types of conflict could not be contained by the regular mechanisms of dispute resolution, and what developmental effects did they have over time? The more precisely we are able to specify the character and practice of governance in the early Republic, the more exact our theories of subsequent change will be.

PRESIDENTS AND THE POLITICS OF REGIME CHANGE

If questions of origin are a constant preoccupation of APD, so too are questions of fundamental change. In this section, we will observe the tenets of historical institutionalism and APD applied in ways that offer insight both into the presidency as an institution and into that institution's causal role in the dynamics of developmentally significant politics. Stephen Skowronek (1996) and Bruce Ackerman (1991, 1998) have made major contributions to the study of regime change, both partisan-programmatic and constitutional (also see Whittington 2007). Squarely situating both the governance frame and the presidency–public nexus at the center of their analyses, their research significantly advances our understanding of presidents as transformative agents in American political development. Skowronek's analysis highlights the presidency's discordant presence within the routine operations of American governance. An inherently disruptive office, when situated within the right historical conjuncture, this institutional dissonance opens the door for fundamental political change. Ackerman links presidential action to "constitutional moments." Locked in battles with institutional rivals over the allocation of governmental authority, Ackerman shows how, by reaching out to "We the People" in critical national elections, presidents have ratified new substantive readings of the Constitution and pressed their adoption upon reluctant courts by dint of these election-centered ratification processes.

The Presidency and Partisan-Programmatic Regime Change

For better or worse, then, the American presidency has proven itself more effective politically as an instrument of negation. Too blunt in its disruptive effects to build securely on what has come before, it has functioned best when it has been directed toward dislodging established elites, destroying the institutional arrangements that support them, and clearing the way for something entirely new.... The presidency is a battering ram, and the presidents who have succeeded most magnificently in political leadership are those who have been best situated to use it forthrightly as such.   (Skowronek 1996, 27–8)

In *The Politics Presidents Make* (1996), Stephen Skowronek elaborates a theory of regime change in which presidential action is the decisive catalyst. Regimes in Skowronek's analysis are constellations of policies, governmental machinery, and patterns of authority that define a historical era and give direction and purpose to political action. Regimes are fortified by explicit ideologies and sustained by electorally dominant coalitions; they are purposive, programmatic, and partisan in nature. Regimes are also historical constructions of finite duration. They are founded, elaborated, and ultimately prone to political exhaustion, as a changing public agenda increasingly calls into question a regime's basic commitments and justifications, and as vested partisan interests splinter over questions regarding the necessity or scope of reform. Finally, regimes are sequential: the construction of one follows upon the prior collapse of another. Skowronek identifies six regimes in American history: a brief Federalist regime (1789–1800); the Jeffersonian regime (1801–28); the Jacksonian regime (1829–60); a long Republican regime (1861–1932); the New Deal regime (1933–80); and a current Republican regime starting with Ronald Reagan (1981–present).

Presidents are the dynamic element that advances regime politics forward; by their actions and mobilization efforts they continually alter the basic terms on which politics is contested. For this reason, Skowronek characterizes the presidency as an intrinsically disruptive institution; the very nature of presidential action makes it hostile to the status quo. The presidency, in his conception, is a battering ram—a bull in a china shop; it is a more effective engine for upending the old than for nurturing the new. During moments of pronounced regime decay, an opposition president (one tied neither to the regime party nor to its programmatic commitments) can provide the necessary energy to displace ideological critics and dismantle their institutional supports. They can articulate new governing visions and assemble new partisan majorities dedicated to their realization. However, even during periods of national peace and prosperity, the disruptive impulse of the presidency is hard at work, challenging orthodox regime commitments, disturbing institutionalized policy settlements, and otherwise undermining the sources of party unity. Firmly ensconced in the routine processes of governance, each successive president challenges anew the terms of American politics, rendering a given regime less resilient over time and more vulnerable to challenge by opposition partisans, until once again the restless and disruptive energies of the presidency can be trained on an exhausted partisan regime to transform the direction of American politics.

The disruptive nature of presidential action derives in large part from its historical-institutional origins. The office's independent seat of action is written into the text of the Constitution, as is its mandate to employ that independence in defense of higher-law principles and the general welfare. Such constitutional obligations encourage incumbents to stand outside the normal currents of politics; each new president is invited to emulate the determined insistence of James K. Polk "to be *myself* president of the U.S." (Skowronek 1996, 12). As Alexander Hamilton famously observed in Federalist No. 72, owing to its design, the presidency would be a magnet for the nation's most politically ambitious, those individuals seeking to procure fame and cement for themselves a place in the nation's unfolding historical narrative (Madison, Hamilton, and Jay 1987, 412–16). As a consequence, each successive president takes office seeking to place his own unique stamp on the direction of American government. This persistent impulse to start anew rubs hard against the demand that presidents faithfully embrace the orthodox paths of their party and leads to presidential actions that challenge the status quo as a matter of course.

Skowronek's great achievement is to explain why, if all presidents desire to remake politics to their liking, i.e., to be regime founders, only a handful have been able to do so without undercutting the bases of their own partisan and public support—in Skowronek's terms, without losing control over the meaning of their own actions. In Skowronek's most important formulation, only those presidents most fortuitously situated in "political time"—those who are historically positioned to practice "the politics of reconstruction"—possess the structural preconditions necessary to recast national governing commitments without ceding control over the meaning of political change to their partisan and ideological opponents. Skowronek also posits a "waning of political time," an important component of which is the attenuating impact of the reconstructive energy. It is a legitimate question therefore to ask whether this additional move renders Skowronek's theory of political time largely retrodictive. Although subsequent writings appear to vindicate the theory's continuing predictive power (Skowronek 2008), no reconstructive presidency has been observed since 1981. If this phenomenon is largely a thing of the past, it begs the fundamental question: if not the presidency, from what institutional location is the energy for fundamental political change likely to come? Or does the possibility of fundamental political change still remain within the confines of America's traditional constitutional order?

The Presidency and American Constitutional Regimes

[T]he Presidency and the system of national elections had begun to interact together to generate a powerful legitimating dynamic.... [T]he president's unconventional [emancipation] proclamation had catalyzed a broad-ranging national debate that had already shaped the meaning of two general elections. When sustained leadership finally met with decisive voter response in 1864, the Republicans could claim that there was something more than a normal political victory involved.   (Ackerman 1998, 134–5)

It is a staple of American political thought that ordinary citizens, when speaking in their collective voice as "We the People," are the authoritative source for constitutional change. Article V of the Constitution lays out one particular method by which that sovereign voice may be actuated to legitimize authoritative alterations to that document. However, as Bruce Ackerman (1991, 1998) demonstrates, some of the most important changes to the Constitution have taken place extra-constitutionally—that is, by the political efforts of institutional actors working outside of Article V's formal stipulations. Indeed, the actions of presidents and the conduct of presidential elections have been central to the politics of constitutional change.

Ackerman sorts American politics into two distinctive species. The first, "normal politics," is the more typical. It is characterized by a host of infirmities that empirical political scientists take for granted, infirmities that limit the signaling potential of most American elections: issueless campaigning, voter inattention, depressed levels of voter turnout, the prevalence of insider and pressure group politics, and assorted collective action problems. The other species, "extraordinary politics," is, as the name implies, a rare occurrence. It is characterized by the presence of salient issues of high public import, citizen attention riveted to national politics and elite partisan debate, and high degrees of voter mobilization. Elections of this sort are analogous to ratification events, citizen judgments rendered in the solemn sovereign voice of "We the People," deliberative judgments with the authority to recast fundamental constitutional understandings.

Ackerman characterizes these moments of extraordinary politics as "constitutional moments," authoritative acts of higher law making transacted through the medium of presidential elections. Constitutional moments and the extraordinary politics they spawn pit the nation's governing institutions—Congress, the presidency, the Court, political parties, state governments, organized pressure groups, and ordinary voters (acting collectively through the institution of national elections)—in sustained public dialogue and fierce political struggle over the fundamental lines of legitimate political authority and the relative status of institutional rivals within those lines of authority. Judicial authority ultimately acquiesces to these reconstituted understandings—though not without considerable resistance—codifying them as part of the Constitution's formal commitments.

Like Skowronek, Ackerman adopts a governance framework. A constitutional regime is a stable governing arrangement with roles assigned to each institution. Ackerman also relies heavily on the presidency–public nexus, identifying presidents as critical players in "extraordinary politics" because of their intimate relationship to the national body politic. It is most often a president's challenge of the status quo and the ensuing pushback by challenged institutional rivals that drives political conflict, frames national questions, and fuels public debate over alternative constitutional futures. One example will suffice to illustrate Ackerman's broader argument regarding the potency of the presidency as an engine of political development. It involves the constitutional transformations of the 1930s, fundamental changes that legitimized Franklin Roosevelt's New Deal.

"Constitutional moments" are multi-election events. It is the sustained character of public deliberation over several years that makes "extraordinary politics" distinctive. Thus to understand the presidency's place in the development of New Deal constitutionalism, we begin with Franklin Roosevelt's election in 1932. A classic change election, that contest sent a clear signal that the nation demanded aggressive action to confront the effects of the Great Depression. However, even as Roosevelt took office in March 1933, the contours of that change remained ill defined. The 1932 election was, in the language of modern political science, more retrospective than prospective in character—more a repudiation of the past than the affirmation of a particular course of future action. As it subsequently evolved, the New Deal vision of activist federal government would pose a fundamental challenge to long-standing constitutional orthodoxies—a set of jurisprudential principles predicated on laissez-faire and a delimited sphere of action for the central government, especially in the areas of economic regulation and social welfare provision. By May 1935, Roosevelt had on several occasions stood by as the Supreme Court struck down New Deal policies as unconstitutional. Finally, on May 27, 1935, in *ALA Schechter* v. *US*, the Court struck at the National Industrial Recovery Act, the corporatist-inspired cen-terpiece of Roosevelt's "First New Deal."[2] In light of the *Schechter* decision, core elements of Roosevelt's "Second New Deal"—most notably the Wagner Labor Relations Act and the Social Security Act—also seemed ripe for Court attack.

Roosevelt threw himself into a vigorous electoral defense of his "Second New Deal," seeking a popular mandate for his constitutional vision of regulatory capital-ism in his reelection bid of 1936. A key bone of contention was the meaning of the Commerce Clause. A narrow reading limited the regulatory authority of the national government to not much more than the conveyance of goods and services across interstate lines. Roosevelt sought a more expansive interpretation, one that would read a de facto national police power into the Constitution and, with it, greatly expand the scope and reach of federal regulatory power. As Ackerman recounts it, Roosevelt declared the Court's *Schechter* ruling to be "more important 'than any decision of my lifetime ... more important than any decision probably since *Dred Scott*' " (Ackerman 1998, 297).

[A]re the people of the United States going to decide that their Federal Government shall in the future have no right under any implied power or any court-approved power to enter a national economic problem, but that that economic problem must be decided only by the states? ... The other part of it is this: Shall we view our social problems ... from the same point of view or not, that the Federal Government has no right under this or following opinions to take any part in trying to better national social conditions? Now that is flat and that is simple!

(Ackerman 1998, 297–8)

In Ackerman's analysis, political success required both that Roosevelt mount a public defense of his constitutional course of action and that he mobilize broad public support for its continuation, even "in the face of a withering constitutional critique led by the Court" and a Republican presidential candidate who "energetically called the People to rise up in defense of their traditional Constitution." "While Republicans might con-scientiously believe that their fellow citizens had made a tragic mistake," Ackerman writes, "they could hardly deny that the People had given decisive support to the Democrats with their eyes wide open. By raising the question of constitutional principle so eloquently during Roosevelt's first term of experimentation, the Supreme Court had

---

[2] The NIRA had sought to break the downward spiral of wage and price deflation and reinflate the economy by suspending the antitrust laws and cartelizing American industry.

played a key role in establishing, even to New Deal opponents, that the People were indeed supporting a change in their governing philosophy" (Ackerman 1998, 311).

Sustained presidential action and broad electoral mobilization had engendered a revolution in American constitutionalism. In the wake of Roosevelt's 1936 landslide reelection victory, as well as his determined, if misguided, efforts to pack the high tribunal with several new justices committed to the president's programmatic vision, the Court retreated, upholding the important elements of the Second New Deal. A reconstitution of governing authority had been ratified, along with a new and enhanced role for the presidency.

Changing Modalities of Governance and the Emergence of a Plebiscitary Presidency

In assessing the work of Skowronek and Ackerman on regime change, one is struck by the largely non-problematic status of what I have referred to as the presidency–public nexus. In their work that relationship is taken largely for granted, operating as an independent variable, especially in Ackerman's account. It provides the motive force; in conjunction with presidential action, it makes fundamental change both possible and seemingly irresistible. In light of the historical sweep of their research, one might reasonably infer that the relationship between presidents and the public has been, in the main, mostly a constant. In saying this, I do not mean to suggest that these authors identify no prerequisites or antecedent conditions necessary to activate this latent popular authority; they do. Nevertheless, the essential relationship seems to be assumed. The relationship between presidents and the people simply lies dormant, awaiting ignition.

That inference, however, is at odds with a second body of scholarship that treats the presidency–public nexus as a dependent variable—something with a discernible point of origin; something with a history of its own; something, in itself, that needs to be accounted for. Instead of positing a constant, these scholars observe a change of significant proportions, directing their research energies toward uncovering its origins and assessing its developmental consequences. Many labels have been attached to the phenomenon in question: "the people's presidency," "the public presidency," "the *going* public' presidency," "the plebiscitary presidency," "the personal presidency," "the rhetorical presidency," and "the mandated presidency" (Peirce and Longley 1981; Edwards 1983; Lowi 1985; Kernell 1986; Tulis 1987; Ellis and Kirk 1998; italics added). Each of these attests to the popular (as opposed to the constitutional) roots of modern presidential authority. However, as we will see shortly, these works diverge in their specific theoretical and historical claims, and they do so in ways productive for students of APD. Several questions still seek consensual answers: when and why did such a relationship first emerge? How has the character of that relationship evolved over time? What impediments to its full realization had to be (or perhaps still need to be) marginalized or dismantled? What has been the developmental impact of these changes upon the central modalities of American governance?[3]

It is worth noting that most of the works we will consider in this section were published late in the presidency of Ronald Reagan and, it would at least seem, written in reaction to it. In light of the widely perceived failures of the Johnson, Nixon, and Carter presidencies, many academics and public commentators had concluded that the modern presidency was incapable of supplying the effective leadership to national government that its supporters had initially promised (the promise of presidential government is well expressed in Burns 1965; its disillusionment is exemplified by Schlesinger 1973 and Heclo 1981). The Reagan presidency suggested that the critics and pundits might be wrong, especially in light of Reagan's victories against a Democratic House of Representatives in the budget battles of 1981. Many observers noticed the effective manner in which Reagan systematically cultivated public support for his policies. The president was widely touted as a "great communicator." David Gergen, Reagan's first communications director, would later observe, "For the first time in any presidency, we molded a communications policy around our legislative strategy" (Maltese 1992, 193).

APD scholars have grappled with how best to understand both the origins and the ramifications of Reagan's popular leadership. Does it represent a recent and qualitative break with past governing practice, or is it the culmination of a sequence of changes with deep historical roots? In what follows, I will arrange a small sampling of seminal works on this question. Each author locates the origin of contemporary presidential practice differently. By arranging them in reverse historical chronology we can observe the outlines of a patterned developmental sequence, with contemporary popular leadership arising out of both a series of contingent institutional changes and a prior set of conceptual innovations and normative adjustments.

In *Going Public* (1986), Samuel Kernell argues that contemporary popular leadership constitutes a clear break with past practice, the displacement of one mode of governance by another in the last quarter of the twentieth century. Of particular interest here, Kernell argues that these changes prompted profound adjustments in the routine ways in which presidents interact with other governing institutions. Systemic changes to the organization of the polity forced the demotion of an older set of practices—summed up in the concept of "the bargaining presidency"—with those better suited to the emergent modalities of contemporary American politics— the " 'going public' presidency."

The significance of Kernell's analysis for us lies in its governance focus. Kernell details the central institutional characteristics of the bargaining era: its committee

---

[3] By "modalities of governance" I mean simply the modal or the typical interactions arising in the course of routine intercourse between rival governing institutions.

system, with influence concentrated in powerful committee chairs; its insulated deliberation process, in which a small number of powerful individuals could strike deals and mobilize the support required to sustain them; its smaller and more homogeneous pressure group system; and its palpably less polarized partisan context. The cumulative effect of this institutional environment was to facilitate quiet backdoor deal making among elites, consensus building, mutual accommodation, and incrementalism. Richard Neustadt is perhaps the most important presidential scholar of the bargaining era. His seminal book *Presidential Power* (1960) details the strategic necessity of effective bargaining to successful presidential leadership.

Kernell details a confluence of institutional changes in the 1970s, the aggregate effect of which was to ignite a revolution in governance and erode the utility of bargaining tactics: the subcommittee revolution and rapid growth in congressional staff, which together expanded policy influence to many more legislators; the explosion in the number and diversity of organized interests in the pressure group system, which made congressional policy making more conflictual and pluralist deals harder both to strike and to enforce. Add to this the increasing prevalence of divided government and passage of congressional "sunshine" laws, which pried open quiet backroom deliberations to scrutiny by powerful interests, and the traditional practices of the bargaining era became increasingly ineffectual, with diminishing returns to presidents who employed them.

Presidents responded to the new rules of governance by trading the quiet negotiations of the bargaining regime for the more public and confrontational tactics of "going public"—going directly to the constituents of opinion-sensitive Congressmen and Senators, mobilizing their support, and pressuring legislators to embrace presidential positions or risk electoral punishment. Changes in the mode of governance resulted in changes to its character and temperament. The techniques of governing and electioneering grew increasingly indistinct; compromise and mutual adjustment between co-equal branches of government gave way increasingly to institutional confrontation and zero-sum struggle.

Kernell dates the emergence of popular leadership to the last quarter of the twentieth century. Theodore Lowi (1985), by contrast, pushes the timeline for the rise of "the plebiscitary presidency" further back, to the 1930s, and the "second constitutional regime" inaugurated by Franklin Roosevelt's New Deal. Lowi argues that the constitutional and governmental revolution wrought by the New Deal required a corresponding political revolution to sustain it. Prior to the New Deal, American government was, as it had historically been, Congress-centered government. Congress, in turn, was organized and operated by decentralized and heterogeneous patronage parties oriented toward patronage and distributive policy. The new programmatic government introduced by the New Deal required a degree of ideological homogeneity and partisan discipline that congressional patronage parties were structurally incapable of providing. Consolidating and sustaining the New Deal therefore necessitated that Roosevelt break free of congressional dominance and reliance upon patronage parties as intermediaries for mobilizing political support.

Roosevelt's political revolution was at its core a communications revolution, end-running traditional intermediaries like political parties and the institutional press. It embraced the new mass communications technologies, like polling, which allowed Roosevelt to probe more fully the opinion structures of his national constituency, and radio, which for the first time allowed presidents to reach into the living rooms of average citizens and forge a direct and unmediated relationship—a *personal* relationship—with the American people. In the end, Lowi sees the rise of plebiscitary governance as flowing seamlessly from the decision by Roosevelt to cultivate an intimate relationship between him and the mass public, a relationship institutional-ized and subsequently developed by successive presidents.

Jeffrey Tulis (1987) locates the origins of plebiscitary governance—"the rhetorical presidency," in his terms—back further still in the American historical past. One of Tulis's many insights is the observation that antecedent conceptual and normative revolutions were required before presidents could publicly embrace the new oppor-tunities and technologies that figure so prominently in Lowi and Kernell. To para-phrase Tulis, before presidents could act anew, they first required a new cognitive road map to tell them how to proceed. Additionally, any new plan of action also had to be judged legitimate by others—it had to be seen as appropriate in light of settled practice and norms of acceptable presidential behavior. Tulis identifies the ferment of the Progressive Era as the locus for this ideational revolution in the norms of appropriate action between presidents, Congress and the public, and he sees in the writings of Woodrow Wilson that revolution's most coherent theorist. Wilson would provide the most detailed blueprint for fundamental change in the relations of American governance, change that would relocate the presidency to center stage in national politics.

Woodrow Wilson indicted the Framers' "Newtonian" constitutional design, its reliance on the mechanical operation of oppositional forces—checks and balances—and its failure to provide the requisite energy and purpose required by modern democracies. "You cannot compound a successful government out of antagonisms," Wilson wrote in *Constitutional Government in the United States.* "Leadership and control must be lodged somewhere" (1908, 60, 54). Years earlier, Wilson had similarly taken Congress to task for its parochialism and domination by special interests, conditions that systematically undercut its ability to provide coherent direction on national issues (Wilson 1973). Wilson identified the presidency as the only institution capable of infusing American government with both programmatic direction and political discipline on matters of national policy. The presidency is the one truly *national* institution in American politics. Presidential elections are the only occasions in which the nation congregates to reflect on the state of the union; presidential candidates are the only aspirants to national office with an incentive to engage this national audience, to deliberate openly on national problems, and to put forward a vision of national policy direction and the public interest; only presidents, so elected, can claim an issue-based mandate to lead the country in new directions; and only a mandate-born presidency can engage Congress as first-among-equals and prod the legislative branch to embrace executive leadership and national goals.

Ellis and Kirk (1995, 1998) agree with Tulis to this extent: the rise of the presidential mandate, and the conceptual shift it represents, was a critical developmental moment in American politics. However, they take issue with Tulis's account of its historical origin, pushing its emergence much deeper into the nineteenth century. The invention of the mandate is a significant event in American political development because, prior to this moment, informed opinion held Congress, not the presidency, to be the people's branch. Against this, mandate theory posits an immediate and rivaled relationship between presidents and the public. For the first time, public opinion would be explicitly harnessed to executive action through the institution of presidential elections. Once accepted as legitimate—and this becomes critical—claims by rival institutions to a privileged understanding of the public interest were necessarily subordinate to presidential claims. Through the mandate, the nation at large provided explicit direction to presidents regarding their official course of action, a charge presidents were obligated to take up, directing their institutional energies against any and all obstructions that may be thrown up by Congress, the bureaucracy, the courts, and any other institutional source of opposition.

Kirk and Ellis locate the origins of the presidential mandate in the 1830s and Andrew Jackson's war against the second Bank of the United States. Jackson and the Congress were locked in a confrontation over the issue of the Bank's rechartering. The Whigs supported recharter and Jackson opposed it. With the 1836 presidential election fast approaching, Whig leaders struck on a plan to force early passage of congressional reauthorization. They would force a presidential veto, stir public indignation against the popular Jackson for his willful disregard of the People's Branch, and thus improve Whig chances for electoral victory. Instead, to the chagrin of Whig leaders, the electoral outcome vindicated the president's position and, as confrontation deepened over Jackson's decision to remove federal deposits from the national Bank, Jackson made explicit use of the mandate claim, using it to justify executive actions that explicitly defied the will of Congress, the official discretion of cabinet secretaries, and even settled constitutional understanding. Pressed to justify his course of action, Jackson turned to the recently concluded elections, the pattern of clear partisan contestation on the Bank issue, the personal mandate given Jackson's position by his reelection victory, and the duty he possessed in its wake to continue fearlessly his previous course of action.

While each of these scholars offers a competing interpretation for the origins of plebiscitary governance, none views positively its developmental consequences. Ellis and Kirk view "the mandated presidency" as having promoted the displacement of traditional political party organizations and the rise of plebiscitary mass politics. Tulis criticizes executive rhetorical leadership for subverting the deliberative processes of Congress, and advocates a "middle way" between modern rhetorical leadership and the pre-Wilsonian model. Kernell argues that "going public" has stoked the fires of a new politics of confrontation and interinstitutional political polarization. Lowi concludes that "the plebiscitary presidency" has nurtured presidential arrogance and encouraged the abuse of power.

CHANGING MODALITIES OF GOVERNANCE AND THE EMERGENCE OF AN ADMINISTRATIVE PRESIDENCY

The governance focus of APD and historical institutionalism also lends itself to a topic of considerable recent scholarship: the actions by recent presidents to assert greater institutional control over the policy actions of the federal bureaucracy, actions that have challenged traditional relations of authority among presidents, Congress, assorted clientele groups, and career administrators themselves. This struggle over bureaucratic control has been accompanied by a much-noted temporal dynamic: (1) an increasing centralization of bureaucratic oversight inside the White House itself, and (2) an increasing politicization of bureaucratic rule-making and enforcement processes by government officials acting at the behest of presidents. Strategic presidential appointments, executive orders, and signing statements are some of the modern-day instruments of so-called "direct" or "unilateral" executive action (Howell 2003; Cooper 2002; Mayer 2001; Moe 1985; Tiefer 1994; Weko 1995). In Nathan's (1975, 1983) classic formulation, they are emblematic of the modern "administrative presidency."

As I have noted throughout this chapter, APD seeks to understand historical origins of contemporary political patterns. In the case of the administrative presidency, the current institutional confrontation over bureaucratic authority might fairly be traced back to the Founding itself. The constitutional text seems virtually to mandate periodic showdowns between presidents and other institutional actors over the legitimate control of bureaucratic authority. To borrow Edwin S. Corwin's (1941, 200) apt phrase, it is "an invitation to struggle."

Article II of the Constitution vests "the executive power" in a president of the United States. It also obligates presidents to "take Care that the Laws be faithfully executed, "to "faithfully execute the Office of the President," and to "preserve, protect, and defend the Constitution of the United States." Institutional struggle over the meaning of these provisions and their relative pecking order was inevitable. Does a proper reading of the vesting clause grant plenary authority to presidents over the actions of the executive branch? Are cabinet secretaries discretionary officers in the performance of their jobs? Do presidents act legitimately when they imprint their own policy objective on the rule-making and enforcement functions of expert career bureaucrats? Alternatively, what precisely does it mean to execute "faithfully" the laws of the United States? What is the appropriate yardstick by which to measure the faithfulness of presidential actions? Faithfulness to *what*: the statutory letter of the law, the best interests of the nation, or the higher law obligations enshrined in the Constitution? Faithfulness to *whom*: the intent of the originating Congress, the political sentiment of the current Congress, the judgment of experienced bureaucratic experts, the current climate of public opinion, or the mandate of the last presidential election? And what about the president's own conscience and discretionary judgment as an elected leader responsible to the nation at large?

As this suggests, the APD impulse is to locate the deep structural tensions that propel forward the institutional struggle over bureaucratic authority and its resulting path of development. This impulse, however, is usefully leavened with respect for political contingency. It is the contingent character of politics that makes political development a fundamentally *historical* process. Underlying constitutional tensions may be ever present, but like plate tectonics, only periodically do they erupt into large seismic events. Under what political conditions have such conflicts exploded into the open? What confluence of explanatory factors is observable at these moments? Which factors are patterned (i.e., which recur over time), and which are historically delimited? What are the developmental consequences for relations of governmental authority?

In what follows below, I once again present a small handful of seminal writings on the historical origins of "the administrative presidency." Utilizing both APD and non-APD scholarship, we will identify some of the critical issues and themes, as well as important interpretative disagreements over how best to account for contemporary patterns. I have again chosen to arrange the materials in a manner that emphasizes the historical chronology. This will allow us better to observe how working backwards temporally helps to bring into view deeper issues regarding the historical construction of American politics, implicating the separation of powers, federalism, political parties, and the substantive and ideological content of reform movements in the enduring struggle to define the legitimate organization of governing authority.

Richard Nathan coined the term "the administrative presidency." In *The Plot that Failed* (1975) and later in *The Administrative Presidency* (1983), Nathan identified Richard Nixon and Ronald Reagan as the originating forces behind contemporary presidential efforts to wrest greater control from the federal bureaucracy. In Nathan's analysis, the administrative presidency was a bureaucratic strategy for reforming or turning back New Deal and Great Society programs with strong support in Congress. Nixon focused his animus on the social welfare bureaucracy, while Reagan targeted key institutions of business regulation, most prominently EPA and OSHA. An administrative approach was required because divided government and partisan polarization made congressional reform of these programs beyond presidential reach. Unilateral bureaucratic action was the most feasible strategy for moving the policy status quo in the face of legislative stalemate. Nixon's "administrative presidency" was ultimately cut short by Watergate. Reagan's efforts, however, proceeded apace. As one of his first official acts, Reagan issued Executive Order 12991, which transformed the newly created Office of Information and Regulatory Affairs into a White House clearinghouse for proposed regulatory rules. Henceforth, all new environmental and workplace regulations would have to pass presidential scrutiny before they could have the force of law. In addition, Reagan utilized his appointment power to apply strict political and ideological tests to applicants for cabinet, sub-cabinet, and agency administrator positions. Once installed, these presidential agents used the bureaucratic tools at their disposal—budget and staffing authority, personnel policy, and enforcement policy—to bring bureaucratic output closer into line with White House policy objectives.

Nathan's explanation emphasizes the structure of American politics since the 1960s. Terry Moe (1985), by contrast, pushes the origins of the administrative presidency deeper into America's historical past, to the era of the Great Depression and Franklin Roosevelt's New Deal. In Moe's account, a deeper structural transformation lies behind the presidential impulse to centralize administrative oversight and colonize bureaucratic processes. To paraphrase him, the most important facet of "the Roosevelt Revolution" may well have been a revolution in public expectations. Prior to FDR, the federal government did not play a central role in the daily lives of citizens. Moreover, when federal action was required, Congress was expected to play the leadership role. Roosevelt's New Deal and the consolidation of a modern activist state redrew the lines of public expectations. From that point forward, voters would expect the federal government to be on the front line, managing the nation's social welfare and economic prosperity. Moreover, within this enlarged sphere of federal responsibility, presidents would assume the predominant leadership role. Henceforth, citizens would hold presidents accountable for the performance of government. Recognizing their limited ability to affect governmental performance, Roosevelt and his successors would respond by devising new strategies to imprint their objectives on bureaucratic operations. The effect was a historically distinctive pattern of presidential behavior, one that led to centralized bureaucratic oversight in the White House and to politicized governmental operations through the use of presidential appointments (see also Weko 1995).

Sidney Milkis (1993) also locates the origin of "the administrative presidency" in Franklin Roosevelt's New Deal. However, where Moe identifies the electoral connection as his explanatory variable, Milkis stresses long-standing institutional impediments to national programmatic leadership and, consequently, the need for presidents to embrace new forms of administrative action. A primary interest is the creation of the Executive Office of the President—the "institutional presidency"—the existence of which is widely said to herald the emergence of "the modern presidency" (Greenstein 1978). Milkis maintains that a presidency with enhanced institutional capabilities was rendered necessary by deep incompatibilities between Roosevelt's brand of programmatic liberalism and the configuration of traditional political party structures. The strong national and ideological thrust of the New Deal ran headlong into the decentralized organization of the Democratic Party and its substantively heterogeneous coalition. Indeed, enactment of the New Deal had been possible in the first instance because of the emergency conditions of the Depression and Roosevelt's charismatic leadership. The president's programmatic gains were therefore vulnerable to reversal with a return to normalcy. Roosevelt's first solution to this problem was to try to impress a more national and ideologically liberal direction upon his party. Rather than work through traditional party channels like the congressional caucus to formulate policy and build political support, Roosevelt forged links to the public, using press conferences and the radio to press the Democratic Congress into action. Roosevelt also intervened in Democratic primaries in twelve states in an ill-fated attempt to defeat conservative Democrats and make the party more ideologically liberal. More successfully, Roosevelt also led the fight to end the two-thirds vote requirement for selecting Democratic presidential nominees, weakening Southern control over candidate selection.

The two-thirds rule notwithstanding, Roosevelt's efforts to remake the Democratic Party were unsuccessful. Frustrated, he turned instead to a build-up of institutional capabilities inside the presidency itself. The Executive Reorganization Act of 1939 created the Executive Office of the President and, within it, a staff of loyal advisers dedicated to presidential political and policy success. It also moved the powerful Bureau of the Budget from the Treasury Department and into the new EOP, strengthening its budgeting and programmatic capabilities as well. Additionally, Roosevelt broke with traditional party rules governing administrative appointments, relying instead on tests of personal and programmatic loyalty in staffing his New Deal.[4] In Milkis's account, the passage of the Executive Reorganization Act ushers in the era of the modern presidency by giving birth to an institutional presidency, one with enhanced capabilities both for overseeing executive administration and for providing it with ideological direction. Of equal developmental significance, as the Executive Office of the President grew in both complexity and resources, it increasingly came to duplicate a number of the functions traditionally performed by the party system, including communications and mobilization functions, electoral management, legislative liaison, and policy development. In sum, the institutional presidency would give ideologically sympathetic presidents the capacity to protect and expand on Roosevelt's programmatic legacy with less reliance upon traditional party organization, to the latter's long-term institutional detriment.

Stephen Skowronek (1982) and Peri Arnold (1986) press their analyses even further into America's past, locating the historical origin of modern bureaucratic politicization in the early twentieth century and the politics of the Progressive Era. Each observes in this period an incomplete wresting of administrative control away from a localist and patronage-seeking Congress by administrative reformers intent upon building a new American state. These reformers aspired to dismantle a traditional executive branch organized on patronage principles and to replace it with a modern Weberian state—centralized, hierarchical, expert, and professional—under the direct managerial control of the president. In keeping with the principles of the new science of public administration, these reformers would institutionalize a formal separation of politics and administration, with the latter organized along rationalist principles, insulated from legislative and partisan manipulation.

The road to a "managerial presidency" was first realized with the passage of the Budget and Accounting Act of 1920, the high point of Progressive Era administrative reform. That act created the Bureau of the Budget, the forerunner of today's Office of Management and Budget and the cornerstone of the modern Executive Office of the President. In passing the Budget and Accounting Act, Congress gave the president

---

[4] Roosevelt also extended merit service protection to first-term appointees in the several newly created New Deal agencies.

both the responsibility and the resources to intervene directly in the day-to-day operations of executive bureaux and agencies. However, of equal political signifi-cance, Congress would cede neither its own traditional authorization and oversight responsibilities, nor its prerogative to kill executive reorganization plans that ran counter to the political needs of legislators. The result was institutional stalemate. The structural preconditions for contemporary "centralization and politicization" were sewn into the basic fabric of this Progressive Era settlement, with presidents and Congress locked in permanent conflict over the authority to define the budgetary, staffing, and policy goals of bureaucratic programs, along with the basic lines of authority governing executive branch organization.

Nathan, Moe, Milkis, Skowronek, Arnold—for students of APD, the hard work lies not simply in choosing from among these competing interpretations, but in the exercise of historical judgment that brings order to the succession of explanatory forces that move the historical construction of American politics forward. The achievement exists not merely in the isolation of a critical moment, but in making cumulative sense of a sequence of patterned and contingent causal factors, the sum of which is important not merely because it recounts something significant about our political past, but because it provides fresh insight into our current political condi-tion. Historical institutionalism is a critical component of the APD approach. As we have seen, it instructs its practitioners to privilege the institutional arrangements of governance in a given period setting, to understand both the regular operations that reproduce period status quo and the sources of conflict made manifest by their routine interactions. APD itself calls on us further to probe the sources of instability inherent in these institutional arrangements, as well as the processes and dynamics that push American politics beyond tension-filled governing order and toward full-fledged political disorder and reconstitution. By applying these methodological strictures with discipline we not only acquire insight into the historical origins of contemporary politics, we also advance further the cause of a political science of American political development.

Conclusion: Beyond "Nameless" and "Faceless" Institutionalism

Writing in 1993, Terry M. Moe issued the call to serious students of the presidency "to stop thinking about presidents as people and to start thinking of them generically: as faceless, nameless institutional actors whose behavior is an institutional product" (Moe 1993, 379). This chapter has in part agreed with Moe's recommendation and in part disagreed. Like Moe, I would renew the call to researchers to embed presidential action in an institutional context, one that situates the presidency in an unending struggle with other institutions over the control of legitimate governing authority. The presidency is a formal constitutional role; attached to it are responsibilities and expectations, and a grant of powers to meet them. It interacts in a regularized fashion with a multitude of other institutional actors similarly understood. Both the responsibilities of the president and his powers have expanded dramatically since the Founding. But the former has greatly outpaced the latter, with predictable consequences for the contest to control the actions of others. We advance our theoretical understanding of the presidency where we build upon this basic insight.

On the other hand, I have strongly argued against viewing the presidency in strictly generic fashion—as a nameless, faceless institution possessing only those properties it shares in common with all complex organizations. Such an approach runs the risk of stripping individual institutions of their most defining attributes. It boils them down to their shared residue of sameness. A *historical* institutionalism does not invite us to return to a political science of idiosyncratic individuals. It does, however, open the door to the possibility that the specificities that distinguish individual institutions have explanatory significance. The presidency, I have maintained, is an institution with *particular* properties and a *particular* history, and it is only by understanding its unique attributes that we can assess its *particular* contributions to the unfolding politics of change in the United States and the development of its modalities of governance.

The study of the presidency is a gateway to some of the most significant aspects of our politics. Not only has that institution always been a focal point for political actors seeking purposeful political change, but presidential action has time and time again also made an indelible impact upon the direction, the character, and the temper of American politics. Historical institutionalists and students of APD have an opportunity to reach beyond the confines of the policy process and its estimations of presidential "agenda success" and to delve more deeply into the historical construction of American politics. The presidency is an obvious entry point for such questions. By understanding more fully its unique properties and political standing, and by examining its changing interface with other rivals for political authority, we will better position ourselves to theorize its manifold contributions to political change. And by better understanding the hows and whys of political change, we better position ourselves to understand, not only where as a country we have been, but also "where we are, and wither we are tending" (Lincoln 1992).

REFERENCES

Abbott, P. 1990. *The Exemplary Presidency: Franklin D. Roosevelt and the American Political Tradition.* Amherst: University of Massachusetts Press.
—— 1996. *Strong Presidents: A Theory of Leadership.* Knoxville: University of Tennessee Press.
Ackerman, B. 1991. *We the People: Foundations.* Cambridge, MA: The Belknap Press of Harvard University Press.

ACKERMAN, B. 1998. *We the People: Transformations.* Cambridge, MA: The Belknap Press of Harvard University Press.

—— 2005. *The Failure of the Founding Fathers: Jefferson, Marshall, and the Rise of Presidential Democracy.* Cambridge, MA: The Belknap Press of Harvard University Press.

A.L.A. Schechter Poultry Corp. v. United States, 295 US 495 (1935).

ARNOLD, P. E. 1986. *Making the Managerial Presidency: Comprehensive Reorganization Planning, 1905–1996.* Princeton, NJ: Princeton University Press.

BAILEY, J. D. 2007. *Thomas Jefferson and Executive Power.* New York: Cambridge University Press.

BELLAH, R. N. 1967. Civil Religion in America. *Daedalus,* 96: 1–26.

BENNETT, J. 1998. True to Form, Clinton Shifts Energies Back to U.S. Focus. *New York Times,* July 5: 10.

BESSETTE, J. M., and TULIS, J. (eds.) 1981. *The Presidency in the Constitutional Order.* Baton Rogue: Louisiana State University Press.

BIMES, T., and MULROY, Q. 2004. The Rise and Decline of Presidential Populism. *Studies in American Political Development,* 18/2: 136–59.

—— and SKOWRONEK, S. 1996. Woodrow Wilson's Critique of Popular Leadership: Reassessing the Modern–Traditional Divide. *Polity,* 29: 27–64.

BURNHAM, W. D. 1970. *Critical Elections and the Mainsprings of American Politics.* New York: W. W. Norton & Company.

BURNS, J. M. 1965. *Presidential Government: The Crucible of Leadership.* New York: Avon Books.

CARPENTER, D. P. 2000. State-Building through Reputation Building: Policy Innovation and Cohorts of Esteem at the Post Office, 1883–1912. *Studies in American Political Development,* 14/2: 121–55.

—— 2001. *The Forging of Bureaucratic Autonomy: Reputations, Networks, and Policy Innovation in Executive Agencies, 1862–1928.* Princeton, NJ: Princeton University Press.

CEASER, J. 1979. *Presidential Selection: Theory and Development.* Princeton, NJ: Princeton University Press.

COOPER, P. J. 2002. *By Order of the President: The Use and Abuse of Executive Direct Action.* Lawrence: University Press of Kansas.

CORWIN, E. S. 1941. *The President: Office and Powers,* 2nd edn. New York: New York University Press.

CUNNINGHAM, N. E., Jr. 1978. *The Process of Government under Jefferson.* Princeton, NJ: Princeton University Press.

DE TOCQUEVILLE, A. 1969. *The Ancien Regime and the French Revolution.* New York: Collins. First published 1856.

EDWARDS, G. C., III. 1983. *The Public Presidency: The Pursuit of Public Support.* New York: St Martin's Press.

—— 1990. *At the Margins: Presidential Leadership of Congress.* New Haven, CT: Yale University Press.

ELLIS, R. J. (ed.) 1998. *Speaking to the People: The Rhetorical Presidency in Historical Perspective.* Amherst: University of Massachusetts Press.

—— and KIRK, S. 1995. Presidential Mandates in the Nineteenth Century: Conceptual Change and Institutional Development. *Studies in American Political Development,* 9: 117–86.

—— —— 1998. Jefferson, Jackson, and the Origins of the Presidential Mandate. In *Speaking to the People: The Rhetorical Presidency in Historical Perspective,* ed. R. J. Ellis. Amherst: University of Massachusetts Press.

FAIRBANKS, J. 1981. The Priestly Functions of the Presidency. *Presidential Studies Quarterly,* 11: 214–32.

FRYMER, P. 2007. *Black and Blue: African Americans, the Labor Movement, and the Decline of the Democratic Party.* Princeton, NJ: Princeton University Press.

GALAMBOS, L. 1970. The Emerging Organizational Synthesis in Modern American History. *Business History Review,* 44/3: 279–90.

GREENSTEIN, F. I. 1978. Change and Continuity in the Modern Presidency. In *The New American Political System,* ed. A. King. Washington, DC: American Enterprise Institute.

HALL, P. A., and TAYLOR, R. C. R. 1996. Political Science and the Three Institutionalisms. *Political Studies,* 44/5: 936–57.

HECLO, H. 1981. The Presidential Illusion. In *The Illusion of Presidential Government,* ed. H. Heclo and L. M. Salamon. Boulder, CO: Westview Press.

HINCKLEY, B. 1990. *The Symbolic Presidency: How Presidents Portray Themselves.* New York: Routledge.

HOWELL, W. G. 2003. *Power without Persuasion: The Politics of Direct Presidential Action.* Princeton, NJ: Princeton University Press.

JAMES, S. C. 2000. *Presidents, Parties, and the State.* New York: Cambridge University Press.

—— 2005. Between the Promise and the Fear: The Evolution of the Presidency. In *The Institutions of Democracy: The Executive Branch.,* ed. J. Aberbach and M. A. Peterson. New York: Oxford University Press.

JONES, C. O. 1994. *The Presidency in a Separated System.* Washington, DC: Brookings Institution.

KERNELL, S. 1986. *Going Public: New Strategies of Presidential Leadership.* Washington, DC: Congressional Quarterly Press.

KETCHAM, R. 1984. *Presidents above Parties: The First American Presidency, 1789–1829.* Chapel Hill: University of North Carolina Press.

LINCOLN, A. 1992. "House Divided" Speech at Springfield, Illinois. In *Selected Speeches and Writings.* New York: Vintage Books. First published 1858

LOWI, T. J. 1985. *The Personal President: Power Invested, Promise Unfulfilled.* Ithaca, NY: Cornell University Press.

MADISON, J., HAMILTON, A. and JAY, J. 1987. *The Federalist Papers,* ed. I. Kramnick. New York: Penguin Books.

MALTESE, J. A. 1992. *Spin Control: The White House Office of Communications and the Management of Presidential News.* Chapel Hill: University of North Carolina Press.

MARCH, J. G., and OLSEN, J. P. 1989. *Rediscovering Institutions: The Organizational Basis of Politics.* New York: Free Press.

MAYER, K. R. 2001. *With the Stroke of a Pen: Executive Orders and Presidential Power.* Princeton, NJ: Princeton University Press.

MILKIS, S. M. 1993. *The President and the Parties: The Transformation of the American Party System since the New Deal.* New York: Oxford University Press.

MOE, T. M. 1985. The Politicized Presidency. In *New Directions in American Politics,* ed. J. Chubb and P. E. Peterson. Washington, DC: Brookings.

—— 1993. Presidents, Institutions, and Theory. In *Researching the Presidency: Vital Questions, New Approaches.,* ed. G. C. Edwards III, J. H. Kessel, and B. Rockman. Pittsburgh: University of Pittsburgh Press.

NATHAN, R. P. 1975. *The Plot that Failed: Nixon and the Administrative Presidency.* New York: John Wiley & Sons.

—— 1983. *The Administrative Presidency.* New York: John Wiley & Sons.

NEUSTADT, R. 1960. *Presidential Power: The Politics of Leadership.* New York: Wiley & Sons.

NICHOLS, D. K. 1994. *The Myth of the Modern Presidency.* University Park: Pennsylvania State University Press.

ORREN, K. 1991. *Belated Feudalism: Labor, the Law, and Liberal Development.* New York: Cambridge University Press.

——and SKOWRONEK, S. 1994. Beyond the Iconography of Order: Notes for a "New" Institutionalism. In *The Dynamics of American Politics,* ed. L. C. Dodd and C. Jillson. Boulder, CO: Westview Press.

————1996. Institutions and Intercurrence: Theory Building in the Fullness of Time. *Nomos,* 38: 111–46.

————1998. Regimes and Regime Building in American Government: A Review of Literature on the 1940s. *Political Science Quarterly,* 113/4: 689–702.

————2006. *The Search for American Political Development.* New York: Cambridge University Press.

NICOLS, D. K. 1994. *The Myth of the Modern Presidency.* University Park: Pennsylvania State University Press.

PEIRCE, N. R., and LONGLEY, L. D. 1981. *The People's President: The Electoral College in American History and the Direct Vote Alternative.* New Haven, CT: Yale University Press.

PETERSON, M. A. 1990. *Legislating Together: The White House and Capitol Hill from Eisenhower to Reagan.* Cambridge, MA: Harvard University Press.

PIERSON, P. 2004. *Politics in Time: History, Institutions, and Social Analysis.* Princeton, NJ: Princeton University Press.

——and SKOCPOL, T. 2002. Historical Institutionalism in Contemporary Political Science. In *Political Science: State of the Discipline,* ed. I. Katznelson and H. V. Milner. New York: W. W. Norton & Company.

REMINI, R. V. 1984. *Andrew Jackson: The Course of American Democracy, 1833–1845.* Baltimore: Johns Hopkins University Press.

ROELOFS, H. M. 1992. The Prophetic President: Charisma in the American Political Tradition. *Polity,* 25/1: 1–20.

SCHICKLER, E. 2001. *Disjointed Pluralism: Institutional Innovation and the Development of the U.S. Congress.* Princeton, NJ: Princeton University Press.

SCHLESINGER, A. M., Jr. 1973. *The Imperial Presidency.* Boston, MA: Houghton Mifflin.

SKOWRONEK, S. 1982. *Building a New American State: The Expansion of National Administrative Capacities, 1877–1920.* New York: Cambridge University Press.

——1996. *The Politics Presidents Make: Leadership from John Adams to Bill Clinton.* Cambridge, MA: The Belknap Press of Harvard University Press.

——2008. *Presidential Leadership in Political Time: Reprise and Reappraisal.* Lawrence: University Press of Kansas.

SMITH, R. M. 1997. *Civic Ideals: Conflicting Visions of Citizenship in U.S. History.* New Haven, CT: Yale University Press.

STEINMO, S., THELEN, K., and LONGSTRETH, F. (eds.) 1992. *Structuring Politics: Historical Institutionalism in Comparative Politics.* New York: Cambridge University Press.

STEWART, C., III. 1989. *Budget Reform Politics: The Design of the Appropriations Process in the House of Representatives, 1865–1921.* Cambridge: Cambridge University Press.

TIEFER, C. 1994. *The Semi-Sovereign Presidency: The Bush Administration's Strategy for Governing without Congress.* Boulder, CO: Westview Press.

TULIS, J. K. 1987. *The Rhetorical Presidency.* Princeton, NJ: Princeton University Press.

WEKO, T. 1995. *The Politicizing Presidency: The White House Personnel Office, 1948–1994.* Lawrence: University Press of Kansas.

WHITTINGTON, K. E. 2007. *Political Foundations of Judicial Supremacy: The Presidency, the Supreme Court, and Constitutional Leadership in U.S. History.* Princeton, NJ: Princeton University Press.

—— and CARPENTER, D. P. 2003. Executive Power in American Institutional Development. *Perspectives on Politics*, 1/3: 495–513.

WILSON, W. 1908. *Constitutional Government in the United States.* New York: Columbia University Press.

—— 1973. *Congressional Government: A Study in American Politics.* Gloucester, MA: Peter Smith. First published 1885.

YOUNG, J. S. 1969. *The Washington Community, 1800–1828.* New York: Columbia University Press.

PART III

PRECURSORS TO GOVERNANCE

CHAPTER 5

PRESIDENTIAL TRANSITIONS

JAMES P. PFIFFNER

TRANSITIONS of the presidency in the United States involve the legitimacy of the change in leadership as well as effectiveness of the government, particularly when one political party takes control from the opposing party. Thus, most scholarship on presidential transitions focuses on the test of democratic succession during party turnover transitions. This essay first examines the development and increasing complexity of the transition of the presidency in the second half of the twentieth century. The following section analyzes the key elements of a successful transition and suggests questions that future scholars might address. The final section offers possible directions for future scholars.

In order to study presidential transitions, one must first define them, and different scholars have used different criteria. In the narrowest sense, President Eisenhower held that there was really not a transition between administrations, but merely a transfer of power at noon on inauguration day (Henry 1961, 213). The more conventional narrow definition holds that a transition begins when the outcome of the election is determined and ends at noon on January 20, when the new president takes the oath of office. Charles O. Jones takes perhaps the most expansive approach, arguing that "the transition begins when a person decides to seek the presidency" (Jones 1998, 5). Although the conduct of a transition depends importantly, as Jones maintains, upon the candidate, transitions are also affected by the anticipation of a possible change of administration by both political appointees and members of the career services.

The author would like to thank John Burke, George Edwards and Jon Herbert for helpful comments on earlier versions of this essay.

Most scholars adopt the widely accepted bounds of transition as extending from about six months before the election to six months after inauguration. The governmental dynamics of a possible change in government begin well before election day. In the last few months before an election, new policy initiatives in the federal bureaucracy begin to decrease, as political appointees start to think about their careers after government, should the incumbent not be returned to office, and high-level career public servants calculate how their potential new masters will perceive them. Harrison Wellford, who worked on President Carter's transitions in 1976–7 and 1980–1, characterized the political power of a lame-duck president "as if it were a large balloon with a slow leak ... the leak will initially be small. . . . By the end of the year, he will have lost the attention of the permanent government and can accomplish very little" (Brauer 1986, xiv; Henry 1960, 708; Pfiffner 1996, 5). This diminution of power does not mean that a lame-duck president is without the means to exercise executive authority, but the lame-duck president's power tends to be limited to unilateral executive tools of power (e.g. presidential pardons and executive orders) rather than policy initiatives that involve Congress or broad public support (Cooper 2002; Howell 2003; Mayer 2001). Howell and Mayer (2005) have found that the use of unilateral tools peaks during the last days of an administration. This governmental dynamic, along with the preelection preparations of presidential candidates, extends the study of transitions to several months before the election itself.

The inauguration of a newly elected president does not guarantee full control of the government or policy success. Authority is transferred; power must be seized. So the study of transitions must also extend several months into the new administration. In order to gain control and put their own stamps on the government, new presidents must designate a White House staff, form a cabinet, nominate political appointees, get control of the bureaucracies in the executive branch, publicly announce a policy agenda, establish relations with Congress, worry about the budget—and throughout all of this maintain an effective public outreach/media capacity. A new administration will not have effective control of the government until all of these functions have been accomplished. The challenge confronting a new president is that all of this must be done simultaneously, making the conduct of transitions so difficult for presidents-elect and fascinating to scholars.

Although scholars have explained much about transitions that we did not know several decades ago, future scholars can make further progress in several directions. Conceptually, scholars still need to address more fully the crucial linkages between transitions and governance. Some work has been done here in terms of management (Burke 2000, 2004) and the policy agenda (Edwards 2003a; Mosher, Clinton, and Lang 1987; Pfiffner 1996), but more needs to be done. Empirically, although we know a lot about recruitment of political appointees (Mackenzie 1981, 1987, 2001, 2002, 2003; Patterson and Pfiffner 2001; Weko 1995), much more can be learned about the backgrounds of nominees and how they perform once in office.

THE INCREASING COMPLEXITY OF PRESIDENTIAL TRANSITIONS

The study of presidential transitions as such has come relatively recently in political science scholarship. Certainly transitions have always been important and sometimes crucial to presidencies, but scholars did not analyze them as a distinct issue until the second half of the twentieth century. This lacuna in presidential scholarship occurred largely because the presidency itself did not become large and bureaucratized until the mid-twentieth century. When the US government was smaller, transitions were simpler, but as the functions and structures of government have grown more complex over the second half of the twentieth century, transferring governmental authority has become more elaborate. Thus, the interaction between incoming and outgoing administrations has become more important to the smooth function of the United States government. In addition, the Twentieth Amendment, which moved inauguration from March 4 up to January 20, has compressed the time frame within which transitions must take place. With more to do and less time within which to do it, transitions have become more challenging.

Part of the reason that scholarship had not focused on transitions was that presidents-elect themselves did not organize their coming to office in any elaborate way. Often they took vacations to rest from the rigors of campaigning. For instance, shortly after the election of 1912, President Elect Woodrow Wilson left for the island of Bermuda for a rest. Before leaving, he announced that he would stay on as New Jersey's governor in January to try to finish his reform agenda. When in Bermuda, he wrote an introduction to his new book, and when the communications cable with the mainland went out for five days, he was pleased for the respite it provided (Henry 1960, 29–31). Presidents Wilson and Harding each took a month off after their election victories before preparing in earnest for taking office.

By the 1950s, the government had grown considerably, and Dwight Eisenhower took only two weeks as a working vacation in Georgia before returning to work full time on his transition. The Twentieth Amendment drastically reduced the time for transition preparation, and Eisenhower's inauguration would be the first to take place on January 20 rather than on March 4, as it had occurred since the time of George Washington. Eisenhower ran his transition from the Commodore Hotel in New York City and had the largest staff operation of any president-elect before him (Henry 1960, 488–9).

In the late summer of 1960, John Kennedy asked Richard Neustadt and Clark Clifford to prepare for him memoranda on a possible transition because, "If I am elected, I do not want to wake up on the morning of November 9 and have to ask myself, 'What in the world do I do now?'" (Neustadt 2000a, 4). During the 1960–1 transition, Kennedy spent more than $300,000 of his personal resources in addition to funds from the Democratic National Committee on transition operations. As a result, he established a commission on transitions that recommended that they be publicly financed so that a president elect could support staffers to work on preparations for taking office. In response to the recommendations, Congress passed the Presidential Transition Act of 1963. In 1968, Richard Nixon used the publicly provided funds and raised another million privately to fund his transition, although Nixon needed less preparation than most newly elected presidents because he had been vice president for eight years in the 1950s.

Jimmy Carter, who had little experience in Washington or the national government, was the first president to invest significant resources before the election to begin preparations for a possible transition. In the summer of 1976, he set aside $150,000 from his campaign to prepare for a possible transition, including a "Talent Inventory Program" to review possible nominations for offices, should he win the election. Frictions in the Carter transition organization between the campaign director (Hamilton Jordan) and transition director (Jack Watson) hindered Carter's initial months in office.

For the next party-turnover transition four years later, transition planning began even earlier, when in April 1980 Edwin Meese asked Pendleton James to quietly begin a personnel recruitment operation in Alexandria, Virginia, in preparation for a possible Reagan election victory. After Reagan won the election, his transition operation was the most elaborate in history, with 588 listings in the transition telephone directory and multiple task forces preparing policy recommendations. Transition teams spread throughout the government to prepare departmental and agency transitions. The earliest preparations began when Governor George W. Bush asked Clay Johnson to begin transition planning in the spring of 1999 (Johnson 2002). The Obama transition in 2008–9 was clearly well organized and quickly got its White House staff into place. Getting cabinet secretaries into office was marred by vetting problems in early 2009.

The Clinton and George W. Bush transitions into office were similarly elaborate, though not equally successful. President Elect Clinton ran his transition from Little Rock, Arkansas, complicating coordination with his transition team in Washington. He personally conducted a review of economic policy alternatives that brought various economists who presented their judgments on the best direction for economic policy, and he interviewed potential nominees for cabinet positions. The lack of firm control of the transition operation presaged the lack of discipline in the early months of the Clinton administration. George W. Bush, because of the uncertain outcome of the 2000 election, had less time to work with, but the previous governmental experience of his transition team, particularly Vice President-Elect Cheney, gave him an advantage. The decision to act as if they had won the election and conduct their transition operations accordingly made a big difference, and the decision to designate a chief of staff before the election helped provide discipline and control for the transition.

Thus, presidential transitions grew into elaborate operations and now play a significant role in the beginning of a new presidency. In the past, when the government was smaller and affected a smaller portion of the economy and society, less preparation for gaining control of the government was necessary. But with the scope and reach of the federal government so much greater since the mid-twentieth century, the coordination of the transfer of power across a much larger and more complex government makes transitions more important to the continuity and smooth functioning of the government.

The continuity of government, its effectiveness, and the success of a new president will all be affected by the new president's transition into office. Good planning during the transition can greatly improve the efficiency of the recruitment of political appointees and the likelihood of success with the president's policy agenda. Experience has shown that mistakes during transition will hurt a new administration and that tensions in the transition will carry over into the White House. The next section will take up the factors that affect the relative success of transitions.

ELEMENTS OF SUCCESSFUL TRANSITIONS

Most transition scholarship addresses the key factors that affect the success of transitions into office. This section examines what scholars have found to be the most important dimensions of presidential transitions, and it will address how performance during transitions affects the ability of a new president to get off to a successful start in governing. The keys to a successful transition entail mastering the following elements: early planning, White House staff, cabinet, presidential personnel, media relations, the policy agenda, and finally the overall shift from campaigning to governing. Some of these elements of success have been effectively addressed by scholars, but I note gaps in scholarship and point out potential new directions for research.

Planning Affects Success

Scholars of transitions and practitioners alike urge that planning for a possible transition begin early, that is, well before the election (e.g., Burke 2000, 377; Brauer 1986, xiv; Kumar and Sullivan 2003, xi; Pfiffner 1996, 6–15). A newly elected president needs to make a good first impression, and an effective transition can set a positive tone for a new administration. The candidate should undertake this planning with some care, however. If it is visible to the public, it will attract press attention, and opponents will charge that the candidate is measuring White House drapes before winning the election. Those in the presidential campaign will resent the planners and will see them as dividing the spoils of victory before the battle has been won. Thus, candidates must do this crucial planning discreetly.

Certain precautions can preclude unnecessary conflict. Someone with authority in the campaign as well as transition planning must clearly be in charge. This will help keep transition planners from exceeding their warrants, and it will reassure the campaigners that they will not be bypassed after the election. The Carter transition and early personnel recruitment suffered because of conflict between the staff of transition chief Jack Watson and that of campaign chief Hamilton Jordan (Burke 2000, 20–40, 398–400; Pfiffner 1996, 60–1). The leadership of transition planning should include some people with governmental experience, preferably those who have participated in previous transitions. Transition planners should initiate liaison with the General Services Administration, scout out office space, and establish mechanisms for receiving funds provided by the Presidential Transitions Act. Once the election has been won, the transition operation must ramp up quickly in order to manage the tasks that need to be completed before inauguration. The most important tasks that must be undertaken correspond to the major functions and offices of the presidency: White House staff, cabinet, personnel, media relations, Congress, and policy agenda.

The need for advanced planning stems from our electoral system. In a parliamentary democracy such as Britain's, a shadow government of ministers in the opposition party in Parliament is experienced in national policy and ready to take over the government, should they become the majority party. Permanent career civil servants extending to the top levels of government in parliamentary systems can facilitate a change in party control of the government. In the United States, however, the layering of politically appointed positions extends much further down into the bureaucracy and entails the replacement of thousands of appointees by a new administration in order to gain control of the government (Light 1995; Richardson and Pfiffner 1999). Recruitment, screening, and nomination of these appointees take considerable time, and involve extensive planning.

One of the consequences of this deep penetration of political appointees is the relative dearth of institutional memory in the White House. Although the executive clerk to the president and several military aides usually remain from one administration to the next, each new administration replaces virtually all White House staffers (often including secretaries and clerical assistants). According to Kumar and Sullivan, a new administration on inauguration day is faced with "no institutional memory, no predetermined organizational structure, no adopted policies, no outline of their responsibilities, and no manual to show how the palace works. In short, they arrive to an empty shell" (2003, xi). This exaggerates the situation somewhat, but not too much.

Some continuity resides in the departments and agencies, Congress, and the memories of those in the new administration who have served in previous White Houses, but the fundamental point is important. Richard Neustadt, in bemoaning the lack of institutional memory in the White House, advises newcomers to listen to their predecessors: "I [want to] make the point . . . as forcefully as possible, the sheer dependence of incomers on what outgoers can tell them" (Neustadt 2000a, 167). That is, much institutional memory is passed on by the outgoing administration rather than in permanent personnel (of which there are few) or White House files, most of which depart with the exiting president and remain under proprietary control for some time.

Neustadt illustrates the consequences of this lacuna of memory by recalling the Carter administration's "discovery" of a Soviet brigade in Cuba. Secretary of State Cyrus Vance reacted to this news with public statements about the secrecy with which the Soviets had acted and the dire implications of the new development. The problem (for the Carter administration) was that the Soviet brigade had been there since before the Cuban missile crisis of 1962; Kennedy had tried to convince the Soviets to remove the soldiers, but they had refused, and the United States had accepted their presence. This discovery embarrassed the administration and caused the Soviets to suspect the United States of artificially trumping up a crisis; the Soviets could not believe that President Carter was not aware of this very basic fact. Although this mini-crisis did not occur during the transition, it well illustrates the lack of institutional memory in the White House that Neustadt termed "typical" (Neustadt 2000a, 163–4; Neustadt and May 1986, 92–6).

The George W. Bush transition seems to have confirmed most of the conventional scholarly wisdom about the importance of planning. It was carried out quite successfully, despite the narrow time frame resulting from the litigation that eventually made Bush the president-elect (Burke 2004). The dispute over the election outcome did not stop transition operations and planning from continuing unabated. The Bush transition was effective in part because the candidate had asked his friend and personnel chief from his governorship, Clay Johnson, to begin planning a transition in the spring of 1999. Johnson did not raise any jealousy from the campaign, because everyone knew that he was a close friend of Governor Bush (Burke 2004, 23). After consulting with Republicans with previous transition experience and examining the scholarly literature, Johnson drew up a list of transition priorities that echoed many of the scholarly prescriptions for successful transitions (Johnson 2002; Burke 2004, 16–17). Overall, the Bush transition preparation and success in establishing a disciplined and organized White House was impressive, proving that preparation and experience can make an important difference in a new administration.

Future scholarship might address the need for planning and what type of planning is most effective. How do presidents-elect with little Washington experience operate differently than "insiders?" Are there systematic differences in the types of personnel recruited by the two different types of presidents elect? What is the best mix of governmental experience and personal loyalty for the transition team?

Transitions Shape the White House Staff

Once the election is over, factions within the winning campaign, centered around personalities, policy, or ideology, inevitably arise. Thus, the president-elect needs to designate a single person who can manage the transition with the authority of the president-elect (Burke 2000, 286–8). Edwin Meese performed this function for President-Elect Reagan in 1980–1 (Burke 2000, 97–100; Pfiffner 1996, 25). Preferably, this person will move into the White House as chief of staff on January 20. He or she, in consultation with the president-elect, should designate people to take charge of different policy and administrative areas, and these people will need to put together their own staff (Burke 2000, 381–9; Kumar et al. 2000).

If the White House is to be functioning on inauguration day, the top layers of the White House staff must be preparing their areas of responsibility well before January 20. The chief of staff position, now essential to each White House, needs to be one of the first offices the new president fills, since he or she will be central to organizing the White House and selecting staffers (Burke 2000, 116–27; Walcott, Warshaw, and Wayne 2001; Pfiffner 1993). The Reagan administration benefited from settling on the chief of staff issue early during the transition, and the Clinton transition suffered because the president did not designate the White House staff until the weeks immediately preceding the inauguration. President George W. Bush's transition staff convinced the president to designate a chief of staff (Andrew Card) even before the election.

In addition to choosing the top staff, the chief of staff must organize the White House and adapt it to the new president's preferences. The current scholarly consensus holds that the collegial and spokes-of-the-wheel models of White House organization, which had been successful earlier in the twentieth century, are no longer feasible. Consensus has settled on a modified chief of staff system. Although a chief of staff is necessary, some of the "strong" chiefs of staff have caused problems for their presidents: Adams (Eisenhower), Haldeman (Nixon), Regan (Reagan), and Sununu (Bush Sr.). Nevertheless, there must be a hierarchy of responsibility in the White House (Hult and Walcot 2004; Walcott and Hult 1995; Pfiffner 1993). Before inauguration, the chief of staff, in consultation with the president-elect, must establish the paper flow and decide how to control access to the president (Hult and Tenpas 2001; Arnold, Patterson, and Walcott 2001; Burke 2000, 381–9).

Future scholarship on transitions might look for patterns in the ways that transition personnel and organization affect the organization of the White House. How are rivalries within transitions settled, and do the winners include or exclude the losers once an administration is under way? Does planning for how the White House should be organized take place? What is the role of those with previous White House experience in transitions? Do presidents take the advice of their advisers on White House organization? How do the talents of individuals affect the formal organization of a new White House? Do those prominent in the campaign make good White House staffers?

Transitions Establish the Role of Cabinet

The most visible public decisions a president-elect must make include selecting his or her cabinet secretaries. These choices send out strong signals about the direction and composition of the new administration and may unite a divided party. President-Elect Clinton spent much time on the selection of his cabinet, but in doing so he set aside making decisions about his White House staff, a mistake that marred the effectiveness of his first weeks in office. Instead of immediately taking on the policy, personnel, and administrative tasks of the new administration, new White House staffers were jockeying for position, and lines of authority had to be established. With earlier decisions about who would play what role in the White House, the administration could have focused more quickly on its initial policy agenda (Burke 2000, 290–5). Delays in coming to final decisions on the White House staff can lead to unfavorable press attention as well as delays in pursuing policy initiatives. Drawing up lists of potential cabinet nominees before the election can help a new president-elect, but if some of the names leak, it will distract from the effectiveness of the campaign. Preferably, the president can nominate cabinet secretaries and send them to the Senate for confirmation during the first week of the new administration.

In order to reduce conflict and debilitating fights over turf and access, the president or chief of staff must establish clear "ground rules" for the role of cabinet secretaries and their relation to the White House staff. Conflict between staffers and secretaries is natural, because staffers are usually younger, have worked in the campaign, and have regular access to the president. Cabinet secretaries are usually older, have some independent political stature, and have large departments to run and turf to protect. Pressures from Congress, interest groups, and their own civil servants often pull cabinet secretaries in different directions than White House staffers, with their single constituent, would choose. As Presidents Nixon and Carter found out to their dismay, once authority is delegated to cabinet secretaries, for instance, in choosing their immediate subordinates, pulling it back into the White House is (in John Ehrlichman's simile) like trying to put toothpaste back into the tube. Attempts to establish "cabinet government," with significant delegation of policy initiative and personnel selection to cabinet secretaries, are no longer viable (Pfiffner 1996, 34–55).

We do not know enough about how the role of the cabinet has changed in the presidency and how that has affected the recruitment of cabinet secretaries. At what point in the transition should presidents-elect focus on cabinet choices? Is it important to choose the top levels of the White House staff before cabinet recruitment, as the Clinton transition experience seemed to indicate? When presidents recruit potential cabinet nominees, how do they explain the role of cabinet secretaries and how they interact with the White House staff? Are cabinet members disappointed in their new roles as were some of President Nixon's cabinet appointees? How do White House staffers learn how to relate to members of the cabinet, and how does that affect the smoothness with which a White House operates?

Presidential Personnel are Key to Policy

Cabinet secretaries comprise a subset of a much larger group of leaders of the new administration, and a secretary alone cannot effectively manage a cabinet department. Selecting the people who receive the political "plums" of presidential appointments to the new administration would seem to be an attractive job. However, the reality is that personnel recruitment is one of the most vexing jobs of a transition, in part because of the sheer volume of the job seekers and in part because of the political sensitivity of the choices the president makes. The skeleton of the personnel oper- ation must be set up before the election in order to organize the flood of applicants and to focus energy on those policy areas that the new president will want to emphasize. Pendleton James, who ran political recruitment for President Reagan, said that "Presidential Personnel has to be functional on the first day, the first minute of the first hour" (Kumar and Sullivan 2003, 8; Burke 2000, 129; Patterson and Pfiffner 2001; Weko 1995). Presidents-elect want to place their personal loyalists in executive branch positions, and presidents planning significant policy change will want to appoint ideological allies. "People are policy" was the mantra of the Reagan transition teams.

The president should designate the person heading the personnel operation to be the Director of Presidential Personnel in the new administration. When President Clinton designated Richard Riley, who had been in charge of personnel recruitment, as his nominee to be Secretary of Education, it significantly set back the transition personnel operation (Burke 2000, 295; Pfiffner 1996, 164). Transition leaders should take care that those who worked in the candidate's campaign do not feel that they have been given short shrift in consideration for positions in the administration, as happened with the Carter transition. At the same time, the new administration needs the most competent people for the job (Burke 2000, 406; Edwards 2001; Pfiffner 1996, 164–72). As with cabinet nominees, the dilemma facing the personnel operation is preparing lists of possible nominees for higher-level positions (assistant secretaries and above) and the danger of those lists leaking to the press or the campaign. The personnel operation must quickly establish a process for clearing and vetting potential nominees with those whom they must consult and for narrowing the number of possibilities to a manageable number for final decision.

Only top presidential appointees can make authoritative decisions for the new administration, and vacancies at the sub-cabinet level can impede the policy agenda. Thus the president and the personnel operation must settle disputes with dispatch and act quickly to make the top appointments. But the huge volume of applications for positions can drown the personnel operation in paper (or electrons), and FBI background checks and Senate confirmation hearings can cause considerable delays. Chase Untermeyer estimated that when he headed personnel recruitment for Presi- dent George H. W. Bush's transition, the personnel operation received more than 70,000 résumés and applications (Pfiffner 1996, 138). The Obama transition received more than 300,000 applications in the first month after the election.

As a result, the appointment process gets slower each year. Calvin Mackenzie calculated that it took President Kennedy an average of 2.4 months (from inaugur- ation to confirmation) to get an appointee into a position; by the Clinton adminis- tration it took an average of 8.5 months. Mackenzie judged that the Bush 2000–1 transition was the slowest yet in getting its political appointees on board (2003). Despite efforts to streamline the personnel process, future administrations cannot expect much improvement in the time it takes to place their appointees. Mackenzie summed up the challenges: "Staffing the highest levels of government has become a nightmare for contemporary presidents" (2003, 332).

A number of dimensions of personnel recruitment could be better understood with further research. Does previous White House or transition experience help create a more effective transition operation? Are private sector professional recruiters effective in the political context of a transition? Does more sophisticated electronic capacity affect the type of people who apply for jobs in the new administration? Where do most appointees come from: inside the beltway or further out in the country? How does this vary with the level of positions? Are there systematic differences in the types of nominees recruited by different parties? How can the quality of appointees be measured? Do the types of personnel recruited differ with whether presidents elect have had previous Washington experience? How are personnel winnowed from campaign to transition and from transition to White House staff and presidential appointment? How important is early liaison with the Senate in confirmation hearings? How can appointees' relations with career civil servants be smoothed (Maranto 2005)?

The Media can Make or Break a Transition

The nation will perceive the competence of the president-elect and the new administration primarily from what the press says about them. Therefore, the transition team must organize an effective press operation in order to set the tone for the new administration. During the transition, the press swarms over the whole transition operation, so it is crucial that one authoritative source of substantive information speaks for the transition. Because the press follows the transition with such intense interest, the transition headquarters must manage the news so that reporters have something of substance about which to write. If significant lulls occur without newsworthy stories from the transition, the press will ferret out their own stories, which may not portray the transition operation in a kind light, as happened with the Clinton transition in Little Rock in 1992.

In contrast to some of the other major areas of the campaign, media and press relations will benefit from continuity in personnel. Presumably campaign spokespersons will step into the top jobs in the press and communications offices after the president's inauguration. The press must perceive that the spokesperson for the president-elect, and later the president, actually speaks for the president, or they will develop back channels that will distort the new administration's message (Kumar 2001a, 2003).

Kumar's work has brought a new appreciation of the need for professional communications and press strategies for transitions. She maintains that the public perception of a new administration is crucial to its success, and consequently to its success with Congress (2001a, 2001b, 2001c, 2003). She argues that the press secretary provides most of the official information about the transition and that concern for how events will play in the press pervades every transition and White House. Her "lessons learned" (2001a) summarize the hard-won experience of the many communications aides that she interviewed. As the Clinton transition demonstrated, if the transition does not provide the press with substantive issues about which to write, reporters will focus on personalities and internal transitions tensions; this will not help the president-elect. Jones's scholarship argues that in representing the president the media relations personnel also represent the United States (Jones 1998, 133–73). Thus an effective press operation must exude competence and authority.

Future scholarship might explore how the organization and function of communications operations change from campaigns to transitions to the White House. What is the best type of experience for those working in the Office of the Press Secretary and Office of Communications? Do some communication strategies work better than others? How are the new media affecting the types of communications personnel that will be important to transitions and White Houses of the future?

The Initial Policy Agenda can Set the Tone

A quick start on a policy agenda can help a new president because the beginning of an administration provides the greatest opportunity to get important policy proposals through Congress (aside from national emergencies, such as 9/11). Executive orders and other unilateral actions by a new president can change policies and attract press coverage, and so some of these should be ready for the president's signature shortly after inauguration (Cooper 2002; Howell 2003; Mayer 2001). The broader policy agenda, however, usually involves Congress, and that is where the real policy challenges lie. A new Congress often seeks an accommodation with a new president, though it will not give him or her a free ride (Neustadt and May 1986, 72).

As new presidents move into their terms, they will have made choices that will inevitably alienate some members of Congress. Thus, in order to take maximum advantage of this narrow window of opportunity, presidents must get policy proposals to Congress quickly (Edwards 2003a; Light 1999). Early legislative victories can set the tone for a new administration, and so early action is necessary, but congressional capacity to handle a wide range of issues is limited. FDR's famous 100 days cannot easily be duplicated, except in extraordinary circumstances (Neustadt 1990, 230; 2000a, 21; 2000b).

Public opinion polls indicate that voters want presidents to keep their campaign promises, and most recent presidents have a reasonably good record of promise-keeping (Fishel 1985; Pfiffner 2004, 99–116). But a narrow focus on promise-keeping can hurt a new president. President Carter had his White House staff make a list of his campaign promises, and he tried to keep many of them. The result, however, was a long list of policy initiatives that diluted his early agenda. He fell foul of Congress early in his administration by refusing to limit his efforts to a narrow set of priorities that he would pursue in Congress. In contrast, Ronald Reagan, who had articulated a wide range of policy preferences during his campaign, was much more successful with the narrowly focused set of priorities that he pursued vigorously in the first months of his presidency (Pfiffner 1996, 122–7).

The new president's legislative liaison staff will be most intimately involved in pushing the policy agenda on the Hill. Thus, it is important to designate the head of the Office of Legislative Liaison as early in the transition as possible. This person will ideally have had extensive experience with both houses of Congress and will have friendly relationships with both sides of the aisle (Bowles 1987). President Carter's relationships with Congress suffered from the lack of Hill experience of his first legislative liaison chief, and President Reagan benefited from the experience and reputation of Max Friedersdorf, his head of congressional relations (Jones 1983; Pfiffner 1996, 111–27). President George W. Bush concentrated his energies on his tax cut priority and a few other initiatives, and despite the Republicans' narrow margins in Congress, he achieved several early victories, though not the broad success of Reagan's first months in office (Edwards 2003a; Ornstein and Fortier 2003).

What is the relationship between the policy priorities presidents emphasize in their campaigns and the policies they pursue as presidents? What is the role of the transition in translating campaign promises into early administration policy initiatives? Can the perception of a policy mandate be created? Does the perception of a mandate make any difference in what a new president can accomplish? Do the margins in Congress affect the type of policy agenda that can be effectively pursued? Does the presence or absence of divided government make any difference? Does the polarization of Congress affect the policy agenda of a new president? How much liaison with members of Congress do presidents-elect attempt? Does it make any difference in relations with Congress?

Shifting from Campaigning to Governing

The broadest and most important challenges that new presidents face entail the shift from campaigning to governing. Campaigns demand that you distinguish yourself from your opponent and draw sharp differences (or wedges) between you and the opposition. In contrast, governing calls for uniting the country and being president of "all the people." The time frame shifts from a short-term focus culminating in the election to longer-term concerns about implementing policies and developing institutions.

Effective campaigners do not necessarily possess the skills or talents that are essential to governing. Some people can do both well, but many cannot. William Galston, who worked in the Clinton campaign and White House, recalled the difficulty of telling some campaigners that in a campaign "your youthful zeal, your take-no-prisoners political skills, were just what we needed then, but this is something different. That's enormously difficult to do" (Kumar 2003, xiii). One of the emotionally most difficult jobs of a winning presidential campaign is telling many loyal campaigners that, despite their very hard work throughout the campaign and demonstrated loyalty to the candidate, they will not be moving with the new president into the government. Some campaigners understand this, but others see no reason why, as they helped the candidate get elected, they are not also qualified to help implement the campaign promises.

Some scholars argue that recent presidents have begun to erode the traditional normative distinction between campaigning and governing and that the two functions have increasingly overlapped. Hugh Heclo points out how governing now more closely resembles campaigning. Presidents and their staff tend to make public appeals for their policy initiatives (even if these tactics are not effective; Edwards 2003b), and they pay less attention to deliberation and close cooperation with Congress. Interest groups are highly skilled and continually attempt to affect policy, and presidents respond to and use these external actors to attempt to influence congressional behavior. But, Heclo argues, this tendency ignores important differences between the functions of campaigning and governing: (1) campaigning is about the clear end point of election, whereas governing must concern itself with the ongoing nature of the government; (2) campaigning is a zero-sum game, and thus adversarial, whereas governing must be inclusive if it is to be successful; and (3) campaigning is about persuasion, whereas governing should be about deliberation for a shared future (Heclo 2000, 11–12). He warns that "the permanent campaign" has superseded these important normative distinctions. As a result, "our politics will become more hostile than needed, more foolhardy in disregarding the long-term, and more benighted in mistaking persuasions for realities" (Heclo 2000, 33).

Charles O. Jones also argues that the distinction between campaigning and governing has become increasingly blurred. Technicians skilled in the use of campaign techniques for polling, fund raising, focus groups, and communications have come to dominate campaigns (Jones 1998, 52–82). After the election, the winning technicians often shift their skills to the effective pursuit of presidential policy agendas. Thus, argues Jones, "campaigning for elections" shifts to "campaigning for policy" (1998, 3). The link between campaigning and governing has not been fully explored, yet it is central to the significance of transitions. Future scholars might analyze more systematically the way that campaigns are conducted and how this affects the behavior and success of presidents when they come into office. Are transitions of the future more likely to resemble extensions of campaigns rather than preparation for governing?

SCHOLARLY ADMONITIONS

The elements of successful transitions just noted reflect scholars' interviews with participants in transitions, archival research, and close observation. Most participants in transitions would agree on the lessons reflected above. But scholars of transitions have also come to some conclusions that the staff of new presidents-elect will not necessarily heed. Scholars have made a number of "good government" types of recommendations, which they judge will improve governance, but which presidents-elect are not likely to follow.

Hubris

Richard Neustadt has pointed out the dangers of hubris for a new administration: "the transition hazards that afflict a President-to-be and his immediate associates are born of haste, hubris, and the unfamiliarity native to newness" (Neustadt 2000a, 157). Often those who have served in transitions will later admit that hubris is a danger. It is a danger that is easily understood—the winning campaigners have just defeated the "enemy;" they may have thrown "the bums" out of office; they have beaten the odds and won the most powerful prize in the world; they are thus competent and very smart—how could they not be tempted to believe in their own infallibility? The dangers of this hubris are: they may try to do too much; they may fail to listen to the outgoing administration; they may reject the good as well as the bad policies of the preceding administration; and they may needlessly alienate members of Congress or the career services in the executive branch with their arrogance (Neustadt 2000a, 161–3).

Hasty Decisions and Overreactions

Incoming administrations often go overboard in rejecting any policy connected with the previous administration of the other party and make early policy mistakes in doing so. Kennedy, overreacting against Eisenhower's seemingly cumbersome national security policy process, abolished much of Ike's apparatus, assuming it would be replaced. He did not establish a new systematic policy process, however, and arguably might have avoided his failure with the Bay of Pigs invasion of Cuba if he had had a more systematic national security policy process (Neustadt 2000a, 152–3). More broadly, Kennedy rejected Eisenhower's cabinet system in part just to distinguish himself from his predecessor (Neustadt 2000a, 83). President Carter, reacting against Nixon's White House-centered administration, began with hopes of establishing "cabinet government," but he soon changed his mind after cabinet secretaries did not seem to embrace presidential priorities. President George W. Bush rejected the Clinton administration's policy toward North Korea early in his term, but was not more successful and eventually had to return to similar policies.

Neustadt cautions new administrations to undertake new policies deliberately so as not to make mistakes born of haste. Jimmy Carter's broad policy agenda overestimated what was possible and consequently undermined how successful he would be with Congress. Presidents Ford and Carter, wanting to distinguish themselves from the Nixon administration and its notorious chief of staff, H. R. Haldeman, initially refused to designate a chief of staff. But acting as their own chiefs of staff, they became overwhelmed, and each designated a chief of staff for the remainder of their terms (Pfiffner 1993). In the spring of 1981, Ronald Reagan had to quickly reverse his proposal to reduce social security spending by shaving some benefits. Bill Clinton's "gays in the military" proposals slowed his transition into office, and his initial designees for Attorney General diverted the administration from its policy agenda. All of these incidents hurt the new administrations; they may have been inevitable, but taking Neustadt's advice might have helped them avoid the negative fallout from them.

Listening to Predecessors

The outgoing administration is likely to want to be helpful to a new administration, even of the opposite party. The White House staff is experienced and wants the United States government to be run effectively, even if they disagree with the policies of the incoming administration. Of course, the new administration does not need to take the advice, but listening to or soliciting suggestions from those who have occupied the positions into which new staffers will step can elicit valuable insights about the beginnings of a presidency. James A. Baker demonstrated his wisdom when, after Ronald Reagan designated him as his chief of staff, he went to visit and ask the advice of every living previous incumbent of the office.

The tendency of a new administration is to demand that all previous political appointees submit their resignations by January 20. Scholars, however, are likely to advise the transition teams to hold over some members of the previous administration in key positions for which continuity is important. The administration's appointees cannot make authoritative decisions or sign documents before the Senate confirms them, so it may be necessary to keep a high-level appointee from the previous administration on board until the new team gets confirmed.

Similarly, some administrations come to government believing that the career services will try to undermine new policies by dragging their feet or sabotaging them. Top-level career civil servants (and military leaders) are more likely to want to serve the new administration (and their own careers) by being as helpful as they can be. Ignoring or shutting out career civil servants can lead to early mistakes, redundant studies and delay of the new administration's policy agenda.

What civil servants *do* need is respect and clear policy direction from the new administration. Career civil servants possess much of the institutional memory that can save wheel spinning and facilitate the new administration's priorities. Political appointees are often competent and experienced; but several levels down from the top, it is possible that a new administration may try to reward its campaign supporters with important positions in the executive branch. Consequently, some important positions will likely be filled with less-than-competent appointees. Thus, scholars often recommend an overall reduction of the number of political appointees (Edwards 2001; Mackenzie 1987; Richardson 1987; Richardson and Pfiffner 1999).

In summary, scholars treat transitions as an essential part of the conduct of the presidency, and thus their approaches and analyses blend into the broader concerns of presidential scholarship. This survey of the most important scholarship on presidential transitions reveals a scholarly consensus on several points:

1. Transitions since the second half of the twentieth century have become more elaborate.
2. As the presidency and the government have become larger and more institution-alized, transitions have become more important to the success of a presidency.
3. It is thus important for candidates for the presidency to devote time and resources to transition planning, even before the campaign has been won.
4. The effectiveness of the government and the new presidency depend in important ways on the smooth transfer of authority from one administration to the next, whether the transition emphasizes change or continuity.

DIFFERENT APPROACHES TO TRANSITION SCHOLARSHIP

The first few scholars to study transitions approached them from a historical perspective. The "grandfather" of the scholarly analysis of presidential transitions was Lauren Henry, a scholar at the Brookings Institution who wrote the definitive (and only) study of party-turnover transitions from Taft–Wilson through Truman–Eisenhower, *Presidential Transitions* (1960). Henry's approach was explicitly histor-ical and his scope extensive. Historian Carl Brauer followed Henry's historical/chronological approach in his book *Presidential Transitions: Eisenhower through Reagan*, published in 1986. Brauer examined the presidential campaigns and placed the transitions into the context of the political history of the elections and the early months of the presidencies that he examined.

In contrast to the historical approach, most political scientists have chosen to examine transitions analytically, that is, by taking up the different challenges faced by each new president and analyzing them separately. Pfiffner, in *The Strategic Presidency: Hitting the Ground Running* (1988, 1996) devoted chapters to key factors essential to gaining control of the government: White House staff, cabinet, political appointments, the bureaucracy, the budget, and relations with Congress. John P. Burke examined transitions from Carter through Clinton in *Presidential Transitions: From Politics to Practice* (2000). In each of these cases he separated five key tasks for analysis: the pre-election effort, the post-election effort, filling the cabinet, crafting a policy agenda, and shaping the White House staff.

Other political scientists have approached transitions by examining the generic challenges that each new administration must face and presenting lessons learned that would be relevant to a new administration. Charles O. Jones, in *Passages to the Presidency* (1998), interviewed many transition veterans, and his book reflects their advice. Burke followed his book on the Carter through Clinton transitions with *Becoming President: The Bush Transition, 2000–2003* (2004) that drew lessons from the shortened Bush transition.

Since the incumbent could not run for the presidency in 2000, a group of political scientists, led by Martha Kumar, undertook the largest and most organized, non-partisan effort to prepare the next administration (Republican or Democratic) for transition into office. Kumar and Terry Sullivan published the results of the project in *The White House World: Transitions, Organization, and Office Operation* (2003). This work included sections on transitions themselves, the White House environment and operations, seven White House offices that are key to successful transitions, and analyses of the Bush 2000–1 transition. Their book summarized much of the research that they undertook in the White House 2001 Project, which was comprised of systematic, in-depth interviews with seventy-five former incumbents of key White House staff offices. The project made the interviews and briefing books for each of the key White House offices available to the transition teams of the two candidates, Vice President Gore and George W. Bush.

DIRECTIONS FOR FUTURE SCHOLARSHIP

Within several decades, the professional scholarship on presidential transitions has contributed significant insights into the operation of the presidency as well as to the practice of organizing transitions and the White House. What began as academic exercises (in the best sense of the term) has developed into sources of sound advice to new administrations coming into office. Transition teams, at least from the 1988–9 transition on, have consulted transitions scholars as well as their books and articles for guidance on how to make their own transitions more effective. In turn, transition participants have contributed their own time to provide interviews with scholars, both for the historical record and as advice for future transitions.

Transition research suffers from some inherent drawbacks. Scholars can measure some data objectively, such as the number of days to get cabinet secretaries confirmed, the number of days to make presidential appointments, the number of people in transition teams, and the amount of public and private money a transition spends. Nevertheless, these useful indicators do not capture what is most important about transitions, which is how effectively the incoming administration manages the shift from campaigning to governing.

The best scholarship on presidential transitions has exploited primary sources in some depth. The major works have made use of extensive interviewing of those who have personally participated in transitions (e.g., Burke 2000, 2003; Jones 1998; Kumar 2003; Pfiffner 1996). These same scholars have also done archival research in presidential libraries and in the private papers of former transition participants. More of these unpublished plans, memoranda, and reports undoubtedly exist, and ferreting them out presents challenges to scholars of future transitions.

Kumar's recorded and transcribed interviews constitute a rich vein of primary source recollections of transitions veterans that have not yet been fully mined. They will be available to scholars through the National Archives and Records Administration. Richard Neustadt worked in the Truman administration and advised every subsequent Democratic (and one Republican) administration as it came into office. Fortunately, scholars do not have to dig these memoranda out of archives, because Charles O. Jones has collected Neustadt's transition memoranda into one volume, *Preparing to be President: The Memos of Richard Neustadt* (2000). His memos to Kennedy exemplify Neustadt's concern with seeing the challenges of transitions from the perspective of the president. Jones places the memos in context with an introduction and a very useful, annotated essay on the scholarship of presidential transitions (2000a, 173–80). Jones also mentions in his bibliography a number of memoranda not publicly available but of potential use to scholars.

Most transition scholarship has focused on the incoming administration and what the president-elect must do to get control of the government. Much less attention has been paid to lame-duck administrations and what they do before leaving office. Presidential pardons have received some attention, and some high-visibility cases have called end-of-presidency pardons to public attention. Howell and Mayer (2005), however, have explored the use of unilateral powers at the end of administrations and found that they differ from periods earlier in presidential terms. In addition, the number of pages in the *Federal Register* increases in the last months of an administration facing a party-turnover transition. Future scholars might replicate these suggestive findings and pay more attention to the final months of administrations. Lame-duck presidents may try to accomplish unfinished business or limit the flexibility of their successor administrations. Similarly, career civil servants may alter their behavior in anticipation of a new set of political appointees.

Although some scholars have examined within-party transitions (Burke 2003; Pfiffner 1990), they remain under-studied. Ironically, transitions to a president of the same party may entail more bitterness than party-turnover transitions. The challenge of a new president of the same party is to differentiate himself from the previous president and put a unique stamp on the office. Bad feelings may arise when the newly elected president encourages contrasts with the previous leader, and loyal presidential appointees may resent being replaced with the new president's personal loyalists.

The conventional wisdom of transition scholars holds that there is insufficient time and resources to accomplish well all that must be done in the eleven weeks between election and inauguration. The Bush 2000–1 transition accomplished much in a shorter period of time. Future scholars might explore whether successful transitions can be accomplished in a shorter period of time and with fewer resources.

One major challenge that has not been fully met is scholarship connecting campaigns, elections, transitions, and the performance of presidents. John Burke has addressed the effect of transitions on the early performance of presidents, but more needs to be done in order to more fully understand this key linkage. What process and preparation will best prepare the candidate to become president? Are there systematic differences between Democratic and Republican transitions? How can we assess the effectiveness of governance in a new presidency? Can an effective transition lead to poor performance once a president is in office? Do those nominees who conduct the most effective campaigns and transitions make the best presidents? Is the "permanent campaign" inevitable, or can a president govern effectively without treating each important issue as a new campaign. How do divided government and the polarization of Congress affect transitions and presidencies?

Continuity of governance is crucial to the security of the United States, particularly during time of war. The war on terror will probably be with us for the foreseeable future, so continuity will be especially important. Examining previous incoming transitions during wartime (e.g., Truman, Eisenhower, Nixon) may shed light on how future transitions might minimize the danger during these perilous transitions.

Personnel recruitment presents a major organizational challenge in every transition. Research on different approaches to organization for personnel operations, the type of backgrounds of nominees and appointees, and evaluating the quality of appointees would fill important gaps in our understanding of transitions. In short, the fundamentals of presidential transitions have been analyzed in a rich, scholarly literature. Perhaps the broadest and most important questions that future scholars can address concern how transitions affect governance.

REFERENCES

ABSHIRE, D. (ed.) 2000. *Report to the President Elect 2000: Triumphs and Tragedies of the Modern Presidency.* Washington, DC: Center for the Study of the Presidency.

ADAMS, B., and KAVANAGH-BARAN, K. 1979. *Promise and Performance: Carter Builds a New Administration.* Lexington, MA: Lexington Books.

ARNOLD, P., PATERSON, B. H., and WALCOTT, C. E. 2001. The Office of Management and Administration. *Presidential Studies Quarterly,* 31: 190–220.

BOWLES, N. 1987. *The White House and Capitol Hill.* Oxford: Clarendon Press.

BRAUER, C. M. 1986. *Presidential Transitions: Eisenhower through Reagan.* New York: Oxford University Press.

BURKE, J. P. 2000. *Presidential Transitions: From Politics to Practice.* Boulder, CO: Lynne Rienner.

——2001a. A Tale of Two Transitions: 1980 and 1988. *Congress and the Presidency,* 28: 1–18.

——2001b. Lessons from Past Presidential Transitions: Organization, Management, and Decision Making. *Presidential Studies Quarterly,* 31: 5–24.

——2002. The Bush Transition in Historical Context. *PS: Political Science and Politics,* 31: 23–6.

——2003. A Tale of Two Presidential Transitions, 1980 and 1988. In Kumar and Sullivan 2003.

——2004. *Becoming President: The Bush Transition, 2000–2003.* Boulder, CO: Lynne Rienner.

CLINTON, W. D., and LANG, D. G. 1993. *What Makes a Successful Transition?* Lanham, MD: University Press of America.

COOPER, P. 2002. *By Order of the President.* Lawrence: University Press of Kansas.

DAVID, P. T. (ed.) 1961. *Presidential Election and Transition 1960–61*. Washington, DC: Brookings.

—— and EVERSON, D. (eds.) 1983. *The Presidential Election and Transition, 1980–81*. Carbondale: Southern Illinois University Press.

EDWARDS, G. C., III. 1989. *At the Margins*. New Haven, CT: Yale University Press.

—— 2001. Why Not the Best. In *Innocent until Nominated: The Breakdown of the Presidential Appointments Process*, ed. G. C. Mackenzie. Washington, DC: Brookings.

—— 2002. Strategic Choices in the Early Bush Legislative Agenda. *PS: Political Science and Politics*, 31: 41–5.

—— 2003a. Strategic Choices and the Early Bush Legislative Agenda. In Kumar and Sullivan 2003.

—— 2003b. *On Deaf Ears*. New Haven, CT: Yale University Press.

FELZENBERG, A. (ed.) 2000. *The Keys to a Successful Presidency*. Washington, DC: Heritage Foundation.

FISHEL, J. 1985. *Presidents and Promises*. Washington, DC: CQ Press.

HECLO, H. 1977. *A Government of Strangers: Executive Politics in Washington*. Washington, DC: Brookings.

—— 2000. Campaigning and Governing: A Conspectus. In *The Permanent Campaign and its Future*, ed. N. Ornstein and T. Mann. Washington, DC: AEI and Brookings.

HENRY, L. L. 1960. *Presidential Transitions*. Washington, DC: Brookings.

—— 1961. The Transition: Transfer of Presidential Responsibility. In *Presidential Election and Transition 1960–61*, ed. P. T. David. Washington, DC: Brookings.

Heritage Foundation. 1980. *Mandate for Leadership*. Washington, DC: Heritage Foundation.

HESS, S., with PFIFFNER, J. P. 2002. *Organizing the Presidency*, 3rd edn. Washington, DC: Brookings.

HOWELL, W. G. 2003. *Power without Persuasion*. Princeton, NJ: Princeton University Press.

—— and Mayer, K. 2005. The Last One Hundred Days. *Presidential Studies Quarterly*, 35: 533–53.

HULT, K., and WALCOTT, C. 2004. *Empowering the White House*. Lawrence: University Press of Kansas.

—— and TENPAS, K. D. 2001. The Office of Staff Secretary. *Presidential Studies Quarterly*, 31: 262–80.

JOHNSON, C. 2002. The 2001–2002 Presidential Transition: Planning, Goals, and Reality. *PS: Political Science and Politics*, 31: 51–3.

JONES, C. O. 1983. Presidential Negotiations with Congress. In *Both Ends of the Avenue*, ed. A. King. Washington, DC: AEI.

—— 1998. *Passages to the Presidency: From Campaigning to Governing*. Washington, DC: Brookings.

KUMAR, M. J. 2001a. The White House as City Hall: A Tough Place to Organize. *Presidential Studies Quarterly*, 31: 44–55.

—— 2001b. The Office of Press Secretary. *Presidential Studies Quarterly*, 31: 296–322.

—— 2001c. The Pressures of White House Work Life: Naked in a Glass House. *Presidential Studies Quarterly*, 31: 708–19.

—— 2003. The Office of Communication. In Kumar and Sullivan 2003.

—— and SULLIVAN, T. 2003. *The White House World: Transitions, Organization, and Office Operations*. College Station: Texas A&M University Press.

—— EDWARDS, G. C., III, PFIFFNER, J. P., and SULLIVAN, T. 2000. Meeting the Freight Train Head On: Planning for the Transition to Power. *Presidential Studies Quarterly*, 30: 754–69.

LEWIS, D. Forthcoming. *Politicizing Administration: Policy and Patronage in Presidential Appointments*. Princeton, NJ: Princeton University Press.

LIGHT, P. 1995. *Thickening Government*. Washington, DC: Brookings.

—— 1999. *The President's Agenda: Domestic Policy Choice from Kennedy to Clinton*. Baltimore: Johns Hopkins University Press.

MACKENZIE, G. C. 1981. *The Politics of Presidential Appointments*. New York: Free Press.

—— (ed.) 1987. *The In-and-Outers: Presidential Appointees and Transient Government in Washington*. Baltimore: Johns Hopkins University Press.

—— (ed.) 2001. *Innocent until Nominated: The Breakdown of the Presidential Appointments Process*. Washington, DC: Brookings.

—— 2002. The Real Invisible Hand: Presidential Appointees in the Administration of George W. Bush. *PS: Political Science and Politics*, 31: 27–30.

—— 2003. The Real Invisible Hand: Presidential Appointees in the Administration of George W. Bush. In Kumar and Sullivan 2003.

—— and SHOGAN, R. (eds.) 1996. *Obstacle Course*. New York: Twentieth Century Fund.

MARANTO, R. 2005. *Beyond a Government of Strangers*. Lanham, MD: Lexington.

MAYER, K. 2001. *With the Stroke of a Pen*. Princeton, NJ: Princeton University Press.

MOSHER, F. C., CLINTON, W. D., and LANG, D. G. 1987. *Presidential Transitions and Foreign Affairs*. Baton Rouge: Louisiana State University Press.

National Academy of Public Administration. 1983. *America's Unelected Government*. Cambridge, MA: Ballinger.

NEUSTADT, R. E. 1990. Hazards of Transition. Pp. 230–68 in *Presidential Power and the Modern Presidents*. New York: Free Press.

—— 2000a. *Preparing to Be President: The Memos of Richard E. Neustadt*, ed. C. O. Jones. Washington, DC: American Enterprise Institute Press.

—— 2000b. The Presidential ONE HUNDRED DAYS: An Overview. In Abshire 2000.

—— and MAY, E. 1986. *Thinking in Time*. New York: Free Press.

ORNSTEIN, N., and FORTIER, J. 2003. Relations with Congress. In Kumar and Sullivan 2003.

—— and MANN, T. 2000. *The Permanent Campaign and its Future*. Washington, DC: AEI and Brookings.

PATTERSON, B. 2000. *The White House Staff: Inside the West Wing and Beyond*. Washington, DC: Brookings.

—— and PFIFFNER, J. P. 2001. The White House Office of Presidential Personnel. *Presidential Studies Quarterly*, 31: 415–38.

PFIFFNER, J. 1990. Establishing the Bush Presidency. *Public Administration Review*, Jan./Feb.: 64–72.

—— 1993. The President's Chief of Staff: Lessons Learned. *Presidential Studies Quarterly*, 23: 77–102.

—— 1996. *The Strategic Presidency: Hitting the Ground Running*, 2nd edn. Lawrence: University Press of Kansas.

—— ed. 1999. *The Managerial Presidency*, 2nd edn. College Station: Texas A&M University Press.

—— 2001. Presidential Appointments: Recruiting Executive Branch Leaders. In Mackenzie 2001.

—— 2004. *The Character Factor: How We Judge America's Presidents*. College Station: Texas A&M University Press.

—— and HOXIE, R. G. (eds.) 1989. *The Presidency in Transition*. New York: Center for the Study of the Presidency.

RICHARDSON, E. L. 1987. Testimony. United States. Congress. Senate. Governmental Affairs Committee. 1988. Hearings on the Presidential Transition Effectiveness Act.

—— 1996. *Reflections of a Radical Moderate.* New York: Pantheon Books.

—— and PFIFFNER, J. 1999. Politics and Performance: Strengthening the Executive Leadership System. In Pfiffner 1999.

SHOGAN, R. 1977. *Promises to Keep: Carter's First Hundred Days.* New York: Thomas Y. Crowell.

STANLEY, D. T. 1965. *Changing Administrations: The 1961 and 1964 Transitions in Six Departments.* Washington, DC: Brookings.

SULLIVAN, T. 2002. Already Buried and Sinking Fast: Presidential Nominees and Inquiry. *PS: Political Science and Politics*, 31: 31–3.

THOMPSON, K. W. (ed.) 1986–7. Papers on Presidential Transitions and Foreign Policy Series. White Burkett Miller Center of Public Affairs and Lanham, MD: University Press of America.

Vol. 1, *History and Current Issues.*

Vol. 2, *Problems and Prospects.*

Vol. 3, *Political Transitions and Foreign Affairs in Britain and France.*

Vol. 4, *Some Views from the Campus.*

Vol. 5, *Reflections of Five Public Officials.*

Vol. 6, *Perceptions of Policy Makers.*

—— (ed.) 1993. *Presidential Transitions: The Reagan to Bush Experience.* Lanham, MD: University Press of America.

WALCOTT, C. E., and HULT, K. 1995. *Governing the White House.* Lawrence: University Press of Kansas.

—— WARSHAW, S. A., and WAYNE, S. 2001. The Office of Chief of Staff. *Presidential Studies Quarterly*, 31: 464–89.

WALKER, W. E., and REOPEL, M. R. 1986. Strategies for Governance: Transition and Domestic Policymaking in the Reagan Administration. *Presidential Studies Quarterly*, Fall: 734–60.

WARSHAW, S. A. 1996. *Powersharing: White House–Cabinet Relations in the Modern Presidency.* Albany: State University of New York Press.

WEKO, T. J. 1995. *The Politicizing Presidency: The White House Personnel Office, 1948–1994.* Lawrence: University Press of Kansas.

CHAPTER 6

PRESIDENTS AND THE POLITICAL AGENDA

B. DAN WOOD

AGENDA setting is the process whereby matters of concern for the political system become defined as policy problems for consideration on political agendas. Cobb and Elder (1972) define two different types of political agendas; a systemic agenda and an institutional agenda. The systemic agenda is broader in scope and more abstract than any given institutional agenda. The systemic agenda refers to the entire set of concerns recognized as politically relevant by the nation or its subunits at any point in time. The institutional agenda refers to those matters of concern that political institutions seriously consider at a given point in time. There may or may not be a hierarchical relationship between the systemic and institutional agendas. Issues may first be on the systemic agenda and then move to an institutional agenda. Alternatively, institutions such as the presidency can produce elevated attention to issues across the system.

Presidents should be important actors for determining what is on both the systemic and institutional agendas. As symbolic representatives of the nation-at-large, presidents are expected to be problem identifiers, policy purveyors, managers of the public good, international leaders, and unifying representatives of all the people. They are the most visible and important political actors in the US system and are assumed to have more information about most policy issues than other actors because of their role and supporting expertise. The media broadly publicize presidential issue stances and related information flowing from the presidency. Most Americans get most of their information about policy issues from the media.

Therefore, presidents should figure prominently in determining which matters of concern are on the systemic agenda.

Presidents should also figure prominently in determining which matters are on institutional agendas. In our system there are multiple institutional venues for addressing matters of concern. For executive venues, the president's capacity as an agenda setter should be obvious. Presidents are the chief executives in charge of policy administration. They propose budgets, issue executive orders, nominate top executives, and have substantial control over the activities of the federal bureaucracy. For judicial venues, presidents appoint justices to the federal bench, which can alter the types of issues they are likely to consider. Presidents also appoint attorneys in the Justice Department who can potentially pursue the administration's issue priorities across a wide range of cases and controversies. For the legislative venue, the presidency has specific legal powers through which it can affect Congress's agenda. Indeed, presidents can press the legislative branch on important issues at any time.

Additionally, expectations on the presidency have evolved over time. Beginning with Theodore Roosevelt, presidents proposed legislative programs. Since 1921, presidents have been initiators of the federal budget. The growing expectation of presidential leadership was greatly magnified by the Great Depression. Presidents since Franklin Roosevelt have been expected to issue an annual program to address the nation's most pressing needs. Moreover, citizens and other institutions now look to the presidency for policy leadership. Therefore, presidents should be important agenda setters both for the system and its various institutions.

Consistent with these assertions, various scholars conducting broad analyses of agenda setting in the US have claimed that presidents are important actors. Cobb and Elder (1972, 182) note, "By virtue of the offices they hold, Presidents... tend to enjoy a presumptive right to play a leading role in identifying and defining the problems that will command governmental attention." Kingdon (1995, 23) observes, "No other single actor in the political system has quite the capability of the president to set agendas in given policy areas for all who deal with those policies." Similarly, Baumgartner and Jones (1993, 241) claim that "No other single actor can focus attention as clearly, or change the motivations of such a great number of other actors, as the president."

Although it seems evident that presidents *should* be influential agenda setters at both the systemic and institutional levels, hard scientific evidence showing that presidents *are* influential agenda setters is limited. Assertions and qualitative evidence make for interesting prose, but science requires evaluating the extent to which presidents actually do affect political agendas, and the factors that condition these effects.

How dominant, if at all, are presidents in affecting what people think are the important issues facing the nation? Do presidents drive media attention to various issues? Or, do public and media attention generally precede presidential attention to particular issues? Do the media moderate relationships between presidential efforts at agenda setting and attention to issues across the system and various institutions? In which issue domains have presidents been most successful as agenda setters, and why? Does agenda setting typically work in a bottom-up fashion with systemic attention typically preceding presidential attention? Or, do institutions such as the presidency tend to drive systemic attention? Do presidents strongly affect Congress's agenda, or those of the courts and federal bureaucracy? Do presidents sometimes follow Congress, the courts, and the bureaucracy in attending to particular issues? Do institutional agendas interact horizontally? If so, then what is the nature of these interactions?

As the preceding set of research questions suggests, there are many facets to potential relationships between the president and political agendas. This list of questions is not exhaustive, but does represent some of the paths for extending social science knowledge. Few, if any, of these questions have achieved definitive answers, and research in this area is still in its infancy. Accordingly, this essay describes the current state of scientific research on the president and the political agenda. It also points toward gaps and limitations in the literature and areas for future research.

PRESIDENTS AND GENERAL THEORIES OF AGENDA SETTING

Understanding how and why issues become defined as policy problems is key to understanding agenda setting (Jones 1994, 23–7; Kingdon 1995, 109–10; Stone 1997, 137–232; Anderson 2006, 82–9). Issues abound in the American system. The number of issues that could potentially be on the systemic agenda at any point in time is extremely large. These include such matters as aging, death, disease, health care, crime, terrorism, war, violence, the economy, poverty, inequity, substance abuse, smoking, global warming, poor education, child abuse, etc. The list is endless. Policy problems arise from the long list of issues that continuously impinge on the system, but few issues become policy problems for potential consideration on the political agenda.

Although the number of potential issues to be considered is always large, there are limits on the system's ability to consider more than a few issues at a time. Issue space is scarce. People and institutions are limited in their cognitive abilities and typically attend to matters in a serial, rather than parallel fashion (Simon 1947, 1983; Jones 1994; Jones and Baumgartner 2005). As a result, new issues must compete with other issues already under consideration, as well as those that could potentially be considered.

Presidents are only one force impinging on the processes whereby issues become defined as policy problems. If presidents want to place their particular issues into consideration, then they must compete for scarce issue space with a variety of other influences. Other issues may be deemed more pressing due to their persistence or perceptions that they are more serious. Other political actors, including the Congress, courts, and media, can also be influential in determining what is under consideration. Focusing events, crises, or indicators may move competing issues higher on the list of priorities. Given that the mass media are quite important in determining systemic attention, presidents must also compete with or co-opt the media into promoting their issues. Thus, there is no certainty of success for presidents seeking to affect priorities on the systemic agenda.

The underlying conditions associated with issues are obviously important. As conditions become more severe or more global, there is a greater potential for bottom-up political mobilization. As these processes occur, perception can be as important as fact in determining how individuals and the system respond to particular issues (e.g., see Rochefort and Cobb 1994, ch. 1). Cascades of attention can develop that are beyond the ability of any individual to control (Kuran 1989, 1991, 1995; Lohman 1994; Mutz 1998; Wood and Doan 2003). As a result, presidents may sometimes be cast as responders to broader systemic influences that are inertial and ongoing, rather than as independent agenda setters. Alternatively, they might serve as facilitators of processes already in progress.

In a related vein, Downs (1972) argues that issues have a life of their own, passing through a cycle from pre-problem stage through alarmed discovery and euphoric enthusiasm to a gradual decline of public attention. Kingdon (1995, 90–115) also takes the perspective that problems are themselves independently important, but claims that issue definition is stochastic rather than cyclical. Focusing events, crises, symbols, indicators, and policy entrepreneurs can reinforce preconceptions of a problem and propel it to the forefront of the public's agenda. In this case the process is again subject to external forces that are beyond presidential control.

Similarly, Baumgartner and Jones (1993; see also Jones and Baumgartner 2005) note that positive feedback due to policy punctuations of various sorts can accelerate movement of issues to the political agenda. This view depicts agenda setting as a process in which issue attention has no permanent equilibrium. Most issues are characterized by negative feedback, which holds systemic or institutional attention in temporary stability. Negative feedback can be due to social norms, a sense that an issue lacks importance, or attitudes that the issue has been adequately addressed. Occasionally, however, events occur that can accelerate systemic or institutional attention to an issue. Altered perceptions due to events can produce positive feedback, or bandwagon effects of increasing attention. The resulting sharp changes are what Baumgartner and Jones call policy punctuations. This theory is intended to explain how issue attention across the system can be mostly stable, but occasionally dramatic changes will occur for some issues.

Baumgartner and Jones's studies span a range of issues and explore changing issue dynamics over long time spans by the media, Congress, and other actors. Consistently, scholars have also employed formal and statistical models of positive feedback in issue definition and report evidence supporting the policy punctuation perspective (Jones, Baumgartner, and True 1998; Jones, Sulkin, and Larsen 2003; Wood and Doan 2003).

Presidents also compete with other political actors when attempting to focus attention on their issue priorities. These actors include members of Congress, the courts, interest groups, policy entrepreneurs, and the mass media. Walker (1977) describes how members of Congress sometimes adopt issues as their own to act as policy entrepreneurs. Flemming, Wood, and Bohte (1997) demonstrate that the Supreme Court can sometimes be a powerful agenda setter for the system. More relevant to the presidency, Flemming, Wood, and Bohte (1999) explore relations between the president, Congress, the courts, and the media in their attention to three issues. They find that the courts most affect media attention to civil rights and civil liberties issues, while Congress most affects media attention to the environment. For all three issues, presidential influence is minimal, while the media tends to drive presidential attention to civil rights and the environment.

Presidents and the Systemic Agenda

Presidents must compete with a variety of influences if they want to focus systemic attention on their issue priorities. Their main paths for focusing systemic attention are through the mass media and making direct appeals to the public.

Presidents and the Media

Presidential relations with the media are symbiotic. Presidents need the mass media to communicate their policy agendas to the public. The mass media also need the presidency for information about an institution their audience cares about. This relationship is partially one of mutual self-interest since the two actors need one another. As a result, there will be a degree of cooperation between the White House and the media in coverage of the president's issues.

However, the degree of cooperation is limited by the diversity of interests represented by the media. Most news outlets are independent actors that care about their appearance of neutrality and perceptions of what appeals to their audience. The media does not, therefore, cater limply to every presidential need. Media independence means that presidents must be strategic when pursuing their policy agendas. They are in fact highly dependent on the mass media for transmitting their messages to the public.

Political science and the field of communications have a long tradition of examining how well the mass media transmit messages to the public. The seminal empirical work in this area is McCombs and Shaw (1972), who find a strong correlation between media coverage and citizen attention to particular issues. Many others (Erbring, Goldberg, and Miller 1980; Winter and Eyal 1981; Iyengar, Peters, and Kinder 1982; Behr and Iyengar 1985; Hill 1985) have documented a relation between media and citizen attention to policy issues. As expressed by Cohen (1963, 13), the press "may not be successful much of the time in telling people what to think, but it is stunningly successful in telling its readers what to think *about*." Given that the mass media is an important and independent actor, it follows that the president must either compete with or co-opt the mass media when attempting to focus systemic attention on presidential issue priorities.

Presidents depend on the mass media to transmit their messages. Indeed, the media constitute their primary voice to the outside world. Without the press or television, presidents would have little or no ability to communicate. As a result, presidential relations with the media are extremely important for understanding presidential influence in agenda setting.

Presidents recognize the importance of the press, and the White House devotes substantial effort toward cultivating good relations. As observed by Edwards and Wayne (2006, ch. 5), the presidential press operation provides a range of services, including briefings, background reports, press releases, interviews, and press conferences with high-level officials. Through these efforts the president attempts to focus the president's message for the media and the public, as well as control the content of the news stream (e.g., see Grossman and Kumar 1981; Maltese 1992; Rozell 2003).

Much research in this area finds that presidents are not completely successful in affecting the news stream. Gilberg et al. (1980) examined the president's 1978 State of the Union message and concluded that the president was not able to influence media content in the month following the president's message. Moreover, they found just the opposite: that the media had influenced the content of the president's speech. Wanta et al. (1989) reviewed four studies of how the president's State of the Union message influenced media content following the messages and found that the president affected the media's content only about half the time.

These early works focused on single presidential speeches and their effect on media attention to particular issues. However, modern presidents engage in a continuous effort to shape public perceptions. In this effort, they use a variety of tools including speeches, interviews, reports, press conferences, press releases, town meetings, and other forms of communication. Information from all of these sources flows into the news stream. As a result, a single speech such as the State of the Union may have little or no impact since it is just one of many cues directed at citizens. However, a sustained public relations campaign may well have a stronger impact that spreads more slowly and evolves more dynamically over time.

In accordance with these ideas, Wood and Peake (1998) expanded the presidential stimulus set to include broader and more dynamic measures of presidential communication. They employed a weekly time series measure encompassing all presidential rhetoric associated with three major foreign policy issues: the US–Soviet, Arab–Israeli, and Bosnian conflicts. Major foreign policy constitutes a domain in which presidents are widely perceived to be more influential than other political actors. However, Wood and Peake found that presidents are not very successful in driving media attention to these issue areas. Rather, international events and inertia drive most presidential attention to foreign policy issues. Thus, this work casts the president more as a passive responder to external influences than a driver of systemic attention to major foreign policy issues.

Edwards and Wood (1999) expanded this research by also considering domestic policy issues. They evaluated the interaction between presidential, media, and congressional attention for issues involving crime, education, and health care, as well as the Arab–Israeli and US–Soviet conflicts. For foreign policy their findings mirrored those of Wood and Peake (1998). However, for domestic policies they found a more interactive relation between the president and the media. Their statistical results showed that presidents affect media attention for education and health care, but not for crime. In the opposite direction, the media affected presidential attention to all three issues. This interactive relationship suggests that presidents are occasional leaders of the systemic agenda for domestic policies, as well as followers.

Peake (2001) replicated these studies for foreign policy using a set of lower-salience issues: the Caribbean, Central America, foreign aid, and foreign trade. He found that presidents are more influential of the media when issues are low in public salience. This finding suggests that when there is less preexisting overall systemic attention to an issue, the president may have a better chance of moving systemic attention toward presidential issue priorities.

Eshbaugh-Soha and Peake (2005) continued work in this tradition by evaluating the president's ability to influence media attention to economic issues. They analyzed presidential, media, and congressional attention to the general economy, spending, inflation/unemployment, and international economic matters. Their statistical analyses again showed an interactive relationship between the president and the media in all four issue domains, with little or no influence by Congress. Their statistical simulations revealed that presidential attention to economic matters influences media attention for all four measures. In the reverse direction, media attention to these same issues influenced presidential attention for three of the four issues.

Presidents and the Public

Research on the president's ability to influence the mass media is ongoing, but does not enable strong conclusions that presidents can consistently direct media attention toward their issue priorities. Since the mass media is the president's primary voice to the public, this leads toward skepticism about the president's ability to consistently focus public attention on their chosen issues.

Several studies have evaluated the direct relationship between presidential speeches and subsequent public concern about the issues addressed in those speeches. Cohen (1995) examined presidents' annual State of the Union messages and their potential impact on what people think are the most important problems facing the nation. Since 1946, the Gallup Poll has asked "What do you think is the most important problem in this country today?" In general, foreign policy and economic problems have dominated people's responses, with other issues occupying relatively minor parts of the issue space. Cohen's statistical analysis found that increased presidential attention to foreign, economic, and civil rights policy in the State of the Union message leads to increased public attention to these same issues in the first Gallup Poll after the speech.

However, these effects appear to be short lived. Cohen looked at the poll immediately preceding the next year's State of the Union message and observed that the elevated attention to the economy and civil rights had disappeared. However, he did not track the dynamics of changing public issue concern through time. Therefore, it is uncertain from this study whether presidents can produce elevated issue concern for more than a brief period after presidential speeches.

Cohen (1995) also did not consider the possibility that presidential issue priorities in the State of the Union message may actually be a response to, rather than a cause of, public issue concerns. Hill (1998) replicated Cohen's work to consider the possibility of reverse causality. He found such reverse causality for two of the three issues. Specifically, he found that presidential issue priorities for the economy and foreign policy are a function of preexisting public issue concerns for economic and foreign policy issues, but not for civil rights. In other words, presidential issue priorities are often a response to the public, so the president cannot be viewed as setting the public's agenda.

Edwards (2003, ch. 8) provided further evidence that should make us wary of the president's ability to consistently focus the public's attention. The most potent presidential tool for focusing public attention is the televised address. However, Edwards showed that broadcast viewership of major presidential addresses has declined significantly since the 1960s (see also Baum and Kernell 1999). By the late 1990s, only about 30 percent of American homes were watching the president's annual State of the Union message. For other presidential addresses the number was even smaller, and only about 7 percent of Americans were watching televised presidential news conferences. Additionally, people who are exposed to major presidential addresses generally could not recall the major points of those addresses. In other words, people are increasingly less attentive through time to presidential words, and those people who are attentive do not generally understand them. Both results paint a dim picture of the president's ability to focus public attention on presidential issue priorities.

Future Research

Research on the systemic agenda leads toward skepticism about the president's ability to consistently focus media and public attention toward the president's issue priorities. However, research in this area is limited, and we should not consider knowledge of presidential effects on media and public attention complete.

One limitation of past work dealing with the president's ability to affect the systemic agenda is its extensive focus on the concept of issue attention. Many scholars have been concerned with the question of whether presidential issue attention generally leads media and public attention, or vice versa. Issue attention is clearly important, because focusing issue attention is a prerequisite to agenda setting. However, *the issue attention concept should not be confused with agenda setting.*

Most past research has focused on issue attention over long time spans. However, presidents seeking to place their issue priorities under consideration by the system need to focus attention during relevant policy-making time spans. The window for policy action tends to be narrow and open for only a brief time (Kingdon 1995, 165–95). To set the political agenda, presidents need to focus attention during these critical periods, not over the long time spans considered by past research.

Similarly, timing should also be an important consideration to future research. For example, Wood (2007, ch. 4) notes that President Clinton successfully focused public attention on the growing federal deficit and debt between the time of his election and the passage of deficit reduction legislation in August 1993. As with the Clinton case, presidents should recognize that issues have a brief window of opportunity to be translated into policy. Therefore, future studies of presidential agenda setting should focus more closely on the time frames during which presidents actually intend to influence the media and public.

Additionally, issue selection should take on more importance for future agenda-setting research. Past research has paid little attention to issue selection, simply choosing what appear to be the most important issues over long time spans. However, presidents may not care uniformly about these issues and may even prefer that some issues be deemphasized. For example, Presidents Kennedy and Johnson should have cared far more about focusing attention on civil rights than, say, Eisenhower, Nixon, or Reagan. Yet, past studies of long-term issue attention have treated these administrations equally. To understand presidential agenda setting, researchers need to select issues that presidents are known to care about, and which they have made a concerted effort to bring to systemic attention.

Other concepts that might be considered in future research involve the interplay of the president, the media, and the public. Past research has considered the president and the media, and the president and the public. However, there has been no research that considers the president, the media, and the public simultaneously. Do presidents sequentially drive media and public attention to issues? Do public and media attention sequentially drive presidential attention? Do the media moderate relations between the president and the public? There is a potential for these relations to be quite complex, and future research should sort out the possibilities.

Future research might also explore variations in the president's agenda-setting ability as a function of presidential approval and the electoral cycle. Do popular presidents have more ability to capture public and media attention than those who are less popular? Does the phase of the electoral cycle bear on the president's ability to focus systemic attention? These are all ripe areas for future research on the president and the systemic agenda.

Future research should also establish stronger ties to the broader agenda-setting literature. For example, general agenda-setting theory suggests that the process occurs in an environment characterized by scarcity. Issue space is scarce and few issues can capture systemic or institutional attention simultaneously. As observed by

Jones and Baumgartner (2005), the system often processes issues in serial, rather than parallel, fashion. If this is true, then presidents must crowd out other issues if their own issues are to become prominent. In what manner and to what extent does this crowding-out effect actually occur? Future work should examine this question in more depth, as well as other questions implied by the broader agenda-setting literature.

Finally, past work on the president's ability to focus systemic attention has also been restricted to time series research designs. Although agenda setting is a process that occurs through time, these research designs are only one way to study the president's ability to influence systemic attention to issues. Experimental designs are one possible alternative. Early experimental research showed that if the president's name is attached to specific policy proposals, then some members of the public are more likely to support that proposal (Sigelman 1980; Conover and Sigelman 1982; Thomas and Sigelman 1985). Subsequent experimental research, however, suggested that identification of the president as supporting particular policies can fail to increase support, and may even diminish public support (Sigelman and Sigelman 1981; Glaros and Miroff 1983). These contradictory findings have sometimes been construed to mean that support for the president on particular policies depends on presidential popularity or credibility (Mondak 1993). Future researchers might also consider using survey experiments to study the president's ability to affect public attitudes about what issues are important (e.g., see Wood and Vedlitz 2007). Regardless, further experimental work should be done to explore the president's ability to affect systemic agendas.

PRESIDENTS AND INSTITUTIONAL AGENDAS

The American legal framework situates the president as a potentially important actor for influencing the agendas of political institutions. To be sure, the president is not a prime minister who leads the majority party and therefore by design dominates the agenda of the sitting government. However, the president does have both formal and informal power that should enhance the White House's potential for affecting the agendas of all three major institutions of American government.

Presidents and Executive Venues

The most obvious institutional agenda-setting power of the president relates to the role as chief executive. By design, presidents are largely responsible for the operation of the White House and much of the federal bureaucracy. Accordingly, they should have extensive ability to affect executive agendas.

However, a larger question should precede any analysis of presidential effects on executive agendas. Do presidents act independently, or are their own agendas affected externally? Concerning the president's internal agenda, Light (1991) argues that presidents develop issue priorities with an emphasis on reelection, establishing a historical legacy, and making good policy. They often face a cycle of declining influence through time so that it is also important to focus issue attention early in their administrations. Given constrained White House resources and bounded issue space for other institutions and the system, presidents must also limit the size of their agendas to a manageable issue set.

Past research is very limited on how much of the president's issue agenda is driven internally versus being a result of external forces. At the heart of this question is the so-called endogeneity problem. Presidential decisions to pursue a particular issue may depend, in part, on what presidents believe can be accomplished. Recognizing potential failure, to what extent do presidents moderate their agendas when they perceive that there might be strong opposition due to an unfriendly political environment?

Some past research has attempted to avoid the endogeneity problem using time series designs that explicitly model two-way relations. This work generally suggests that presidential issue attention depends on various external factors such as events, conditions, and incentives flowing from Congress, the courts, the bureaucracy, the media, and the public (Wood and Peake 1998; Edwards and Wood 1999). Various other studies mirror these findings, but also suggest an interactive relationship between the president's agenda and the agendas of Congress, the courts, and media (Edwards and Wood 1999; Flemming, Wood, and Bohte 1999; Peake 2001; Eshbaugh-Soha and Peake 2005).

Wood (2007, ch. 3) shows that presidents differ along partisan lines in their relative emphasis on particular economic issues. Democrats tend to emphasize unemployment and poor labor conditions more than Republicans. However, presidents of both political parties who serve during poor economic times place greater emphasis on economic conditions. For example, presidential emphasis on inflation for both Democrats and Republicans was much greater during the stagflation era of the 1970s, and presidential emphasis on the federal deficit varied with the relative severity of deficits and debt through time.

Wood (2007, ch. 3) also finds that presidential issue attention depends on various democratic influences. Presidents are more attentive to economic issues during election years. As presidential approval declines they emphasize the economy more. As citizens become more concerned about specific economic problems, presidents mirror citizens' concerns with increased issue attention.

Although these studies are a beginning, much more is required to fully understand the internal and external determinants of the president's issue agenda. For example, presidents may formulate their agendas with a strategic eye on the alignment of economic and political forces in the system. Do presidential issue priorities change with the incentives and constraints flowing from the macroeconomy? Do they change with changing public approval? Do presidential issue priorities change with drifting public liberalism? Do presidential issue priorities depend on the alignment of institutional forces in the federal system?

Regardless of whether presidential issue priorities are determined internally or externally, they can often use their prerogatives as chief executive unilaterally. One form of unilateral presidential action flows from executive power over the bureaucracy. Bureaucracies make major contributions to the ongoing policy-making processes of the United States. Congress delegates much policy-making authority to the bureaucracy through discretionary policy implementation and rule making. Presidents are the chief executives responsible for administering these activities and policies.

By now it is well understood that presidents have various tools for controlling bureaucratic processes (see for example Moe 1982, 1985; Scholz and Wei 1986; Wood 1988, 1990; Wood and Waterman 1991, 1993, 1994; Wood and Anderson 1993; Scholz and Wood 1998, 1999; Wood and Bohte 2004). Presidential tools of administrative control include political appointments, budgetary authority, executive orders, directives, and potential sanctions for non-compliant bureaucrats and bureaucracies.

Presidents are very powerful with respect to bureaucracies. Yet, there is little or no research exploring how presidents affect bureaucratic agendas. Do presidents differentially affect issue priorities being considered by bureaucracies? Do they differentially affect the probability of rule making in certain policy areas? Do they differentially affect bureaucratic issue priorities for research and development? More generally, do presidents systematically set the political agendas for public bureaucracies?

Cooper (2002) describes various other tools of unilateral presidential action. In particular, he details how presidents have used executive orders, proclamations, memoranda, directives, and presidential signing statements through time to circumvent or augment normal legislative processes. These mechanisms obviously expand the possibilities for presidential agenda setting.

There is a growing literature on the importance of unilateral presidential action to presidential policy making (Krause and Cohen 1997; Mayer 1999; Krause and Cohen 2000; Mayer 2001; Cooper 2002; Howell 2003). Many of these studies examine significant executive orders issued by presidents from Franklin Roosevelt through Clinton. They generally find that the number of executive orders issued by presidents depends on their political environment. They issue more executive orders near the end of their terms when there is less time for legislative action. Presidents issue fewer executive orders when they are popular and more during periods of unified government.

An unresolved question in the literature on unilateral action concerns the potential for interaction between the president's legislative choices and taking unilateral action (but see Marchbanks 2005). Presidents may choose either path in pursuing some issue priorities. However, these two venues are not substitutes for one another. Legislation is more permanent, but has higher political transaction costs. Presidents may need to bargain and compromise to achieve legislative success. On the other hand, unilateral action is easier to achieve, but can be overturned by the next president. Congress and the courts may also overturn unilateral action, but seldom do so (Howell 2003, 113–20). When do presidents choose legislation, versus taking unilateral action?

Unilateral action offers the president an important strategic advantage as an agenda setter. Howell (2003, 14) argues that unilateral action enables the president to act as an agenda setter not only for the executive branch, but for other institutions. "[T]he president moves policy first and thereby places upon Congress and the courts the burden of revising the new political landscape. Rather than waiting at the end of an extended legislative process to sign or veto a bill, the president simply sets new policy and leaves it up to Congress and the courts to respond." This ability to take unilateral action puts the president in the position of making the first move in the policy-making game, providing the president with an important institutional advantage. Under our system of separated and countervailing powers, the majorities necessary to reverse unilateral actions can be difficult to achieve, and presidents can usually veto efforts to overturn their actions.

Presidents and Judicial Venues

By design, presidents should be important agenda setters for the executive branch and through unilateral executive action for other institutions. However, the direct means whereby presidents should affect judicial venues are less obvious.

Judicial venues at the federal level consist of the dockets of the district courts, appellate courts, and Supreme Court. The dockets of the first two entities are subject to the normal flow of litigation and appeals throughout the US system. The president may affect the content of decisions by these courts through appointments and other means. However, these courts have no control over their own dockets, so presidents have only limited ability to affect their agendas.

Working through the Department of Justice, presidents can change policy emphases for cases filed by the government before the district and appellate courts. For example, during the 1960s Justice Department attorneys increased their emphasis on voting rights and racial discrimination cases. Later, Attorney General Ashcroft increased the number of cases filed by the US dealing with death penalty issues. More recently, there has been greater emphasis by the Justice Department on issues involving immigration. Thus, staffing the Justice Department is an indirect means whereby presidents can affect lower court agendas (e.g., see Savage 2006). However, presidents have no direct influence over the dockets of lower federal courts.

In contrast, justices fully determine the docket for the Supreme Court. At their discretion, the Court has the power to review cases and controversies involving federal law, presidential administrative actions, state law, and the rulings of lower courts at both the federal and state levels. The Supreme Court decides which cases to hear and when. At the case selection stage, the justices must filter through roughly 8,000 petitions for potential review (Pacelle 2006, 318). However, they only choose to hear oral arguments in fewer than 100 cases annually. With so many cases to consider and such a restricted agenda space, empirical research has shown that the justices use cues and signals that a case is worthy of consideration (Perry 1991).

Presidents have two means through which they can affect Supreme Court case selection. First, they may affect the manner in which the Court processes cues and signals through the appointment process. Presidential appointments to the Court can shape the present and future ideology of the Court. For example, Flemming and Wood (1997) show that the entry of new justices onto the Court systematically alters its relative liberalism. Other empirical research also suggests that presidents are fairly successful in appointing justices who mirror their own policy preferences (Segal 1990; Segal, Timpone, and Howard 2000; Kuersten and Songer 2003). However, through time presidential appointees to the Court can drift away from presidential preferences (Segal, Timpone, and Howard 2000). Such changes may affect the particular issues that the Court considers and the manner in which it decides those issues.

The retirement decisions of the justices also limit the president's influence on the Court's agenda through appointments. If no justices retire during a president's term, then the president can have no impact on the Court's future agenda or decisions. Additionally, the president shares influence through appointments with the Senate. Roughly 20 percent of all Supreme Court nominations fail. The potential for failure means that presidents tend to avoid extreme nominations. These limitations mean that appointment power can be a fairly blunt instrument for presidents wanting to shape the Supreme Court's agenda. Presidents may be successful using this approach, but such success may not be quick and there is little guarantee of the ultimate outcome. These reservations aside, there is little research addressing the question of how presidential appointments affect case selection by the Supreme Court (but for some related research see Segal 1990; Segal, Timpone, and Howard 2000).

A second mechanism for presidents affecting the Supreme Court's agenda is through the Office of the Solicitor General. The Office conducts all litigation on behalf of the United States before the Supreme Court and supervises the handling of litigation in the federal appellate courts. The Solicitor General decides which cases the government lost in lower courts should be appealed to the Supreme Court and also decides which cases the government should enter through amicus curiae briefs in lower courts. Before the Supreme Court, the Solicitor General is the government's attorney for all direct appeals of federal lower court decisions, and may also partici-pate through amicus briefs on behalf of the US government. As former Solicitor General Wade McCree stated, "It is the duty of the solicitor general to serve as a first-line gatekeeper for the Supreme Court and to say 'no' to many government officials who present plausible claims of legal errors in the lower courts" (quoted in Pacelle 2006, 317).

An important function of the Solicitor General is offering signals and cues on which cases are important. Oral arguments and written briefs of the Solicitor General are major sources of information for the Court in deciding which cases should be on the current year's docket (Bailey, Karnoie, and Maltzman 2005). Virtually every study of these relations suggests that the presence of the Solicitor General in a case is the most important cue determining Supreme Court case selection (e.g., see Caldeira and Wright 1988).

The Solicitor General is the most frequent litigant before the Supreme Court, and the most important external influence on case selection. Salokar (1992, 25) notes that the Court granted 69.8 percent of the Solicitor General's requests for certiorari (i.e., discretionary review) between 1960 and 1989. When the Solicitor General files an amicus petition to enter cases by private petitioners the Court is similarly inclined to grant review. Salokar attributes this success in getting cases on the Supreme Court's docket to being a "repeat player" who possesses advance intelligence, access to specialists, resources, expertise, and a high degree of credibility (see also Pacelle 2006, 317).

Salokar (1992, 68, 175) argues that the Solicitor General deploys power first and foremost for the administration. Although limited by staff attorneys and bureaucratic norms, the Solicitor General is sympathetic to, if not totally supportive of, the president's policy agenda. Given the importance of the Solicitor General to judicial decision making, it is unlikely that a president would appoint a Solicitor General whose preferences did not match his own. As noted by Segal (1990, 142) "evidence does exist that the president does intervene in important cases, and even when he does not the briefs filed by the solicitor general tend to match the ideological predispositions of the incumbent administration."

Although past research shows that the president, through the Solicitor General, can be fairly successful in placing issue priorities on the judicial venue, the Court is itself ultimately in control of its own agenda. This means that the president must depend on the goodwill of others in getting the administration's issue priorities before the Court. The president must appoint a responsive Solicitor General who will push the priorities of the administration. Further, a friendly Court is required that will agree to hear cases important to the administration. Thus, presidential agenda setting with the Supreme Court should depend on bureaucratic responsiveness and the changing composition of the Supreme Court through time (e.g., see Segal, Timpone, and Howard 2000).

Presidents and the Legislative Venue

There are now widespread expectations that the president will set at least part of the legislative agenda. The Constitution requires the president to present an annual State of the Union message. Through time, this message has evolved into a presidential opportunity to propose policy measures for legislative consideration. In this regard the Constitution also grants the president authority to recommend "such Measures as he shall judge necessary and expedient." These formal powers can potentially exert a strong influence on the congressional agenda.

Modern presidents take full advantage of these formal powers. However, they have not always done so. President Washington delivered his annual State of the Union messages to Congress in person. The focus was literally on the condition of the union and the challenges of building a new nation. President Jefferson used the State of the Union message to outline his administration's priorities and also sent written copies of the message to both chambers. However, over the next 112 years presidents issued their annual State of the Union messages in writing and did not lay out a formal legislative agenda.

President Theodore Roosevelt was an activist president who proposed numerous measures for congressional consideration. His belief was that "it was not only his right but his duty to do anything that the needs of the nation demanded unless such action was forbidden by the Constitution or by the laws" (Roosevelt 1913, 197). Accordingly, he worked closely with legislative leaders and sent several messages to Congress that defined a legislative program.

In 1913 President Wilson revived the tradition of delivering the State of the Union message in person when he sent Congress a complete set of legislative priorities labeled the New Freedom. As a political science professor, Wilson believed that strong presidential leadership of Congress was necessary if the nation was to cope with growing problems associated with industrialization and developing technology.

The Great Depression altered expectations of the presidency. Prior to the Great Depression, many viewed presidents as chief executives, but subservient to the policy-making powers of Congress. After the Great Depression, most viewed presidents as responsible for proposing and promoting an agenda that would secure the nation's well-being. Franklin Roosevelt's New Deal was an agenda of legislative proposals intended to lift the nation out of the economic crisis. The president also issued a plethora of other legislative proposals intended to address various social problems, from old age assistance to welfare, labor relations, banking, and industrial regulation.

Every president since Franklin Roosevelt has been expected to issue what has become known as the president's annual legislative program. Congress expects the president to issue an annual program to provide direction to the legislative agenda. By the 1950s, the president's program had become so ingrained that when President Eisenhower failed to issue one during his first year, he was soundly criticized by Congress, the media, and the public. The result of these changes is that the president is now expected to be a major agenda setter for Congress.

Beyond these constitutionally derived presidential prerogatives, Congress has also added to the president's agenda-setting authority through time. In 1921, Congress passed the Budget and Accounting Act to increase the fiscal responsibility and efficiency of government. This legislation required the president to propose a fiscal policy for the entire government and programs for every federal department and bureau. To support the president in this new agenda-setting power, the legislation created the Bureau of the Budget within the Treasury Department to assist the president with expert advice and administrative support. Since 1921, all presidents have been initiators of the annual federal budget and set forth fiscal programs encompassing the entire federal government.

The first three presidents affected by the Budget and Accounting Act—Warren Harding, Calvin Coolidge, and Herbert Hoover—complied with the requirements, but did not exert strong leadership to secure enactment of the budget (Sundquist 1981). However, presidents after the crisis of the Great Depression were more likely to take the initiative in budgeting.

The evolution of the presidency through time has also resulted in greater agenda-setting authority in certain issue areas. Early on, the president was deemed the primary national agenda setter in issues involving foreign and national security policy. Beginning with Washington, the chief executive became primarily responsible for conducting relations with other nations, negotiating treaties and agreements, managing national defense, and securing the nation. The Departments of State and Defense developed to assist the president in performing these tasks.

In 1947, Congress passed the National Security Act which enhanced the president's ability to gather foreign intelligence and provided an advisory staff for presidential initiatives relating to foreign and security policy. As a result of these institutional arrangements, the president is widely recognized as the entity which initiates matters relating to foreign and national security policy.

Congress has also added to presidential agenda-setting ability for economic matters. The Employment Act of 1946 (PL 79-304) and the Humphrey–Hawkins Act of 1978 (PL 95-523) require the president to maintain continuous surveillance of the economy, issue an annual economic report, and if there are signs of economic weakness to propose measures that would promote "maximum employment, pro-duction, and purchasing power." As a result, the president is now the most important institutional agenda setter for matters dealing with the nation's economy.

These institutional arrangements seemingly place presidents in a strong position to affect legislative agendas across a range of policy areas. Yet, much of the general agenda-setting work has emphasized Congress as the main agenda setter for the American system (Baumgartner and Jones 1993; Kingdon 1995; Jones and Baumgart-ner 2005). If this perspective is valid, then we should expect presidents to have limited impact on congressional agendas. We should also expect presidents to be responsive to, rather than determine, legislative agendas.

As noted earlier, Flemming, Wood, and Bohte (1999) examined relations between presidential, congressional, judicial, and media attention to three policy issues: civil rights, civil liberties, and the environment. Edwards and Wood (1999) look at relations between presidential, congressional, and media attention for health care, education, and crime. Eshbaugh-Soha and Peake (2005) examine presidential, con-gressional, and media attention to four economic issues: the general economy, spending, unemployment/inflation, and international economic matters. None of these studies found that presidents consistently affect congressional attention to these issues. Indeed, just the opposite seems to occur for some issues. Congress affects presidential attention to civil liberties, environmental, education, and some economic issues.

However, these studies are limited in that they do not consider presidential issue priorities and what is actually on Congress's "law-making" agenda. Instead, they look at how changing presidential attention through time, gauged through presidential remarks reported in *Public Papers of the Presidents*, is related to various measures of congressional hearing activity. Although presidential remarks and congressional hearing activity might be indicative of the respective presidential and legislative agendas, they are too indirect to reach strong conclusions about the president's ability to affect legislative agendas.

Fishel (1985) offers more direct evidence of presidential influence on legislative agendas. His work does not specifically reference theories of agenda setting. Instead, he is concerned with whether the promises presidents make during election campaigns result in subsequent legislative activity. He begins with the common public perception that presidents often renege on campaign promises and sets about to empirically test this hypothesis. His descriptive results (Fishel 1985, 42) show that presidential issue priorities during election campaigns usually translate into subsequent legislative activity. Kennedy submitted legislation to Congress on 61 percent of his campaign promises, Johnson on 70 percent, Nixon on 56 percent, Carter on 56 percent, and Reagan on 64 percent. Of these legislative proposals by the president, Congress passed 81 percent of Kennedy's proposals, 89 percent of Johnson's, 61 percent of Nixon's, 71 percent of Carter's, and 68 percent of Reagan's. Fishel's results suggest that presidents are very important legislative agenda setters, especially when they have made promises to the electorate.

More recently, Taylor (1998) quantifies who sets the congressional agenda by coding legislation before Congress that is classified as "major actions" and those listed among *Congressional Quarterly Almanac*'s Key Votes. Taylor's coding scheme identifies those bills initiated by the president, congressional leadership, presidential–congressional agreement, presidential–congressional disagreement, and other. He finds that presidents are relatively successful at setting the legislative agenda, but their influence is conditioned by various contextual factors such as the composition of Congress.

Edwards and Barrett (2000) offer the most comprehensive analysis of presidential agenda setting in Congress by examining all significant legislation initiated by the president that both passed and failed from 1953 through 1996. Their descriptive results show that presidents can almost always place significant legislation on the agenda of Congress. From 1953 through 1996 the president obtained agenda status for 98 percent of his legislative initiatives. On average about 35 percent of all significant legislation pending before Congress since 1953 was the result of a presidential initiative. This number varied from a high of 69 percent during the first year of the Kennedy administration to a low of zero in 1995–6 when President Clinton faced strong partisan opposition.

Edwards and Barrett (2000) also examine some of the conditions under which presidents are more or less successful in placing issues on the legislative agenda. They show that presidents are more successful at affecting the legislative agenda early in their terms. During their first two years presidents achieve on average about 41 percent of the House and Senate legislative agendas. During the third and fourth years this percentage drops to around 30 percent for the respective agendas. These numbers are also dependent on the presence or absence of divided government.

Edwards and Barrett (2000) show that during periods of divided government presidents initiate an average of 24 percent of all significant legislation before the House and Senate. In contrast, during periods of unified government they initiate about 57 percent of the House agenda and 47 percent of the Senate agenda. Thus, presidential success at achieving scarce agenda space depends strongly on the partisan composition of Congress.

Future Directions for Research

Concerning institutional agendas, past research strongly implies that institutional arrangements matter with respect to *how many* of the president's initiatives make it onto institutional agendas. They engage in more unilateral action during periods of unified government when there is little possibility of being overturned. They are more successful with the courts when the courts are friendly. Presidents are more successful with Congress during periods of unified government.

However, there is little past work that captures the strategic nature of the agenda-setting game between presidents and other political institutions and its potential importance for the *substantive make-up* of institutional agendas (but see Peterson 1990). For example, with respect to Congress presidents may decline to initiate legislation for certain issues under periods of divided government because there is little probability of achieving success. Similarly, members of Congress may decline to initiate legislation for certain issues under periods of divided government because of the perceived probability of a presidential veto.

These strategic calculations point to what may be another potential dimension of agenda-setting power—the ability to keep things off institutional agendas (e.g., see Bachrach and Baratz 1970; Crenson 1971). If there is little probability of presidents allowing legislation to become law, then there may be little reason for members of Congress to initiate legislation in the first place. Presidents often have incentives to keep things off political agendas, either for ideological reasons or due to self-interest. For example, President Reagan would never have been favorable toward more stringent environmental laws due to his strong pro-market convictions. As a result no new environmental legislation passed Congress during his presidency. Similarly, President Clinton would never have allowed Republicans to pursue large tax cuts for the wealthy after Republicans took control of Congress in 1995. It required the election of a Republican president in 2000 for this change to occur.

In the other direction, if there is little probability that Congress will take a presidential proposal seriously, then there is little reason for presidents to attend to an issue. For example, President Kennedy might have preferred to deal with the issue of civil rights early in his administration. After all, he had made promises to civil rights leaders during the 1960 presidential campaign. However, according to Beschloss (2007, 235–79), the president recognized that civil rights legislation would be impossible in the existing political environment. Therefore, he held off pushing civil rights legislation until 1963 when the political environment was more favorable.

Related to these arguments, Cameron (2000) explores the dynamic of veto bargaining by the president and Congress, and rational anticipation as it pertains to the substantive content of legislation. However, there has been no analogous work as it pertains to presidential and congressional agenda setting. To what extent do presidents and/or Congress fail to initiate policy making for certain issues because of a high perceived probability of failure? Which particular issues are more likely to be ignored by the president when facing a hostile Congress? Which particular issues will Congress fail to consider due to the high probability of a presidential veto? If we are to fully understand the relationship between the president and institutional agendas, then future research should move toward understanding how strategic interactions between the president, Congress, and courts affect what is proposed by the president and presidential effects on the composition of other institutional agendas.

Exploring these questions empirically will be difficult. It is difficult to measure non-agenda items and the reasons for their non-inclusion. However, game theoretic and experimental designs are well suited to exploring strategic interactions between institutional actors. Therefore, future research on the president's role in setting institutional agendas might move in this direction.

CONCLUSIONS

The idealized version of the policy process model (Jones 1975; Anderson 1977) depicts agenda setting as the first stage of a multistage progression. Although scholars may not consistently agree that policy making is as orderly as the idealized model, all policy making involves agenda setting prior to policy action. Thus, presidents wanting to affect policy must somehow affect policy agendas.

More generally, agenda setting is what presidents must do first if they are to pursue their own priorities on political agendas. Agenda setting is a critical element of presidential leadership. In order to be successful, they must first define issues in a manner that is conducive to action. They must persuade others to agree with their issue definitions. They must mobilize attention toward their issue priorities, and ultimately obtain support for their preferred solution. If presidents are unable to direct the system or other institutions in these processes, then it will be difficult for them to successfully exert policy leadership.

Public and scholarly expectations often leave the impression that presidents are powerful actors in this process. Popular media and textbook treatments of agenda setting and the presidency bolster this impression. To be sure, people look to the president for policy leadership, especially during times of crisis or after elections. Presidents are the symbolic representatives of the nation and during such times there are uncommon opportunities for pushing what might appear to be democratically authorized priorities.

However, thinking more critically about the president's role in setting political agendas leads toward the conclusion that during normal times presidents are not dominant of the system or its institutions. Presidential influence on political agendas depends strongly on the alignment of political forces within the system and across institutions. They must compete with a plethora of other forces when attempting to push their policy priorities. Alternatively, presidential issue priorities may not be ripe for consideration due to constraints on the agenda space or the dominance of more pressing matters. As with presidential power generally, the president's ability to set political agendas is limited by the American system of fragmented interests, separate but shared institutional authority, and competing power centers.

Presidents are also subject to forces beyond their control. Ongoing processes may at times make it seem mandatory that the president get on board to press issues that are already important within the system. Events can thrust matters onto political agendas, placing the president in the position of simply having to follow a course already in progress. Attention to issues often exhibits inertial or cyclical characteristics. Thus, there are many instances where the president is simply one of the players in a policy-making process that is already ongoing.

These constraints do not to diminish the importance of the president's role in setting political agendas. Presidents can be major impediments for issues that might otherwise move forward. If addressing an issue runs counter to presidential preferences or those of political supporters, then there is little possibility of the issue moving forward in the policy-making process. In the other direction, if an issue is consistent with presidential preferences or that of political supporters, then presidents can be important facilitators of the policy-making process. Without presidential participation there may be insufficient political force to achieve action. In either case, the American president is an important actor in setting political agendas; just not the hegemonic force depicted by the popular media or introductory textbooks.

References

ANDERSON, J. E. 1977. *Public Policy-Making*. New York: Holt, Rhinehart, & Winston.
—— 2006. *Public Policymaking*, 6th edn. New York: Houghton Mifflin.
BACHRACH, P., and BARAT, M. S. 1970. *Power and Poverty: Theory and Practice*. New York: Oxford University Press.
BAILEY, M., KARNOIE, B., and MALTZMAN, F. 2005. Signals from the Tenth Justice: The Political Role of the Solicitor General in Supreme Court Decision Making. *American Journal of Political Science*, 49: 72–85.
BAUM, M. A., and KERNELL, S. 1999. Has Cable Ended the Golden Age of Presidential Television? *American Political Science Review*, 93: 99–114.
BAUMGARTNER, F. R., and JONES, B. D. 1993. *Agendas and Instability in American Politics*. Chicago: University of Chicago Press.
BEHR, R. L., and IYENGAR, S. 1985. Television News, Real-World Cues, and Changes in the Public Agenda. *Public Opinion Quarterly*, 49: 38–57.

BESCHLOSS, M. 2007. *Presidential Courage: Brave Leaders and How They Change America 1789–1989*. New York: Simon & Schuster.

CALDEIRA, G., and WRIGHT, J. 1988. Organized Interests and Agenda Setting in the U.S. Supreme Court. *American Political Science Review*, 82: 1109–27.

CAMERON, C. M. 2000. *Veto Bargaining: Presidents and the Politics of Negative Power*. New York: Cambridge University Press.

COBB, R. W., and ELDER, C. D. 1972. *Participation in American Politics: The Dynamics of Agenda Building*. Baltimore: Johns Hopkins University Press.

COHEN, B. C. 1963. *The Press and Foreign Policy*. Princeton, NJ: Princeton University Press.

COHEN, J. E. 1995. Presidential Rhetoric and the Public Agenda. *American Journal of Political Science*, 1: 87–107.

CONOVER, P. J., and SIGELMAN, L. 1982. Presidential Influence and Public Opinion: The Case of the Iranian Hostage Crisis. *Social Science Quarterly*, 63: 249–64.

COOPER, P. J. 2002. *By Order of the President: The Use and Abuse of Executive Direct Action*. Lawrence: University of Kansas Press.

CRENSON, M. A. 1971. *The Un-Politics of Air Pollution: A Study of Non-Decisionmaking in Cities*. Baltimore: Johns Hopkins University Press.

DOWNS, A. 1972. Up and Down with Ecology: The Issue Attention Cycle. *Public Interest*, 28: 38–50.

EDWARDS, G. C., III. 2003. *On Deaf Ears: The Limits of the Bully Pulpit*. New Haven, CT: Yale University Press.

—— and BARRETT, A. 2000. Presidential Agenda Setting in Congress. In *Polarized Politics: Congress and the President in a Partisan Era*, ed. J. R. Bond and R. Fleisher. Washington, DC: Congressional Quarterly Press.

—— and WAYNE, S. J. 2006. *Presidential Leadership: Politics and Policy Making*, 7th edn. Belmont, CA: Thompson/Wadsworth.

—— and WOOD, B. D. 1999. Who Influences Whom? The President and the Public Agenda. *American Political Science Review*, 93: 327–44.

ERBRING, L., GOLDBERG, E. N., and MILLER, A. H. 1980. Front-Page News and Real World Cues: A New Look at Agenda-Setting by the Media. *American Journal of Political Science*, 24/1: 16–49.

ESHBAUGH-SOHA, M., and PEAKE, J. S. 2005. Presidents and the Economic Agenda. *Political Research Quarterly*, 58: 127–38.

FISHEL, J. 1985. *Presidents and Promises*. Washington, DC: Congressional Quarterly Press.

FLEMMING, R. B., and WOOD, B. D. 1997. The Public and the Supreme Court: A Pooled Time Series Analysis of Individual Justice Responsiveness to American Policy Moods. *American Journal of Political Science*, 41: 468–98.

—— —— and BOHTE, J. 1997. One Voice among Many: The Supreme Court's Influence on Attentiveness to Issues in the United States, 1947–1990. *American Journal of Political Science*, 41: 1224–50.

—— —— —— 1999. Attention to Issues in a System of Separated Powers: The Dynamics of American Policy Agendas. *Journal of Politics*, 61: 76–108.

GILBERG, S., EYAL, C., McCOMBS, M., and NICHOLAS, D. 1980. The State of the Union Address and the Press Agenda. *Journalism Quarterly*, 57: 584–8.

GLAROS, R., and MIROFF, B. 1983. Watching Ronald Reagan: Viewers' Reaction to the President on Television. *Congress and the Presidency*, 10: 25–46.

GROSSMAN, M. B., and KUMAR, M. J. 1981. *Portraying the President*. Baltimore: Johns Hopkins University Press.

HILL, D. B. 1985. Viewer Characteristics and Agenda Setting by Television News. *Public Opinion Quarterly*, 49: 340–50.

HILL, K. Q. 1998. The Policy Agendas of the President and the Mass Public: A Research Validation and Extension. *American Journal of Political Science*, 42: 1328–34.

HOWELL, W. G. 2003. *Power without Persuasion: The Politics of Direct Presidential Action.* Princeton, NJ: Princeton University Press.

IYENGAR, S., Peters, M. D., and Kinder, D. R. 1982. Experimental Demonstrations of the "Not-So-Minimal" Consequences of Television News. *American Political Science Review*, 76: 848–58.

JONES, B. D. 1994. *Reconceiving Decision-Making in Democratic Politics.* Chicago: University of Chicago Press.

—— and BAUMGARTNER, F. R. 2005. *The Politics of Attention: How Government Prioritizes Problems.* Chicago: University of Chicago Press.

—— —— and TRUE, J. L. 1998. Policy Punctuations: U.S. Budget Authority, 1947–1995. *Journal of Politics*, 60: 1–33.

—— SULKIN, T., and LARSEN, H. A. 2003. Policy Punctuations in American Political Institutions. *American Political Science Review*, 97: 151–69.

JONES, C. O. 1975. *Clean Air.* Pittsburgh: University of Pittsburgh Press.

KINGDON, J. W. 1995. *Agendas, Alternatives, and Public Policies.* New York: Harper Collins.

KRAUSE, G., and COHEN, D. 1997. Presidential Use of Executive Orders, 1953–1994. *American Politics Quarterly*, 25: 458–81.

—— —— 2000. Opportunity, Constraints, and the Development of the Institutional Presidency: The Case of Executive Order Issuance, 1939–1996. *Journal of Politics*, 62: 88–114.

KUERSTEN, A., and SONGER, D. 2003. Presidential Success through Appointments to the United States Courts of Appeals. *American Politics Research*, 31: 107–37.

KURAN, T. 1989. Sparks and Prairie Fires: A Theory of Unanticipated Political Revolution. *Public Choice*, 61/1: 41–74.

—— 1991. Now Out of Never: The Element of Surprise in the East European Revolution. *World Politics*, 44: 7–48.

—— 1995. *Private Truths, Public Lies: The Social Consequences of Preference Falsification.* Cambridge, MA: Harvard University Press.

LIGHT, P. C. 1991. *The President's Agenda: Domestic Policy Choice from Kennedy to Reagan.* Baltimore: Johns Hopkins University Press.

LOHMAN, S. 1994. The Dynamics of Informational Cascades: The Monday Demonstrations in Leipzig, East Germany, 1989–91. *World Politics*, 47: 42–101.

McCOMBS, M. E., and SHAW, D. L. 1972. The Agenda-Setting Function of Mass Media. *Public Opinion Quarterly*, 2: 176–87.

MALTESE, J. A. 1992. *Spin Control: The White House Office of Communications and the Management of Presidential News.* Chapel Hill: University of North Carolina Press.

MARCHBANKS, M. P., III. 2005. A Transaction Cost Approach to Unilateral Presidential Action. Ph.D. dissertation, Texas A&M University, College Station, TX.

MAYER, K. R. 1999. Executive Orders and Presidential Power. *Journal of Politics*, 61: 445–66.

—— 2001. *With the Stroke of a Pen: Executive Orders and Presidential Power.* Princeton, NJ: Princeton University Press.

MOE, T. M. 1982. Regulatory Performance and Presidential Administration. *American Journal of Political Science*, 26: 197–224.

—— 1985. Control and Feedback in Economic Regulation. *American Political Science Review*, 79: 1094–116.

MONDAK, J. 1993. Source Cues and Policy Approval: The Cognitive Dynamics of Public Support for the Reagan Agenda. *American Journal of Political Science*, 37: 186–212.

MUTZ, D. C. 1998. *Impersonal Influence: How Perceptions of Mass Collectives Affect Political Attitudes.* New York: Cambridge University Press.

PACELLE, R. L., Jr. 2006. Amicus Curiae or Amicus Praesidentis? Reexamining the Role of the Solicitor General in Filing Amici. *Judicature*, 89/6: 317–28.

PEAKE, J. S. 2001. Presidential Agenda Setting in Foreign Policy. *Political Research Quarterly*, 54: 69–86.

PERRY, H. W. 1991. *Deciding to Decide: Agenda Setting in the U.S. Supreme Court*. Cambridge, MA: Harvard University Press.

PETERSON, M. A. 1990. *Legislating Together: The White House and Capitol Hill from Eisenhower to Reagan*. Cambridge, MA: Harvard University Press.

ROCHEFORT, D. A., and COBB, R. W. 1994. Problem Definition: An Emerging Perspective. In *The Politics of Problem Definition: Shaping the Policy Agenda*, ed. D. A. Rochefort and R. W. Cobb. Lawrence: University Press of Kansas.

ROOSEVELT, T. 1913. *The Autobiography of Theodore Roosevelt*, Centennial Edition. New York: Charles Scribner's Sons.

ROZELL, M. J. 2003. Presidential Image-Makers on the Limits of Spin Control. In *The Presidency: Classic and Contemporary Readings*, ed. J. E. Cohen and D. Nice. Boston: McGraw-Hill.

SALOKAR, R. M. 1992. *The Solicitor General: The Politics of Law*. Philadelphia: Temple University Press.

SAVAGE, C. 2006. Civil Rights Hiring Shifted in Bush Era. *Boston Globe*, July 23.

SCHOLZ, J. T., and WEI, F. H. 1986. Regulatory Enforcement in a Federalist System. *American Political Science Review*, 80: 1249–70.

——and WOOD, B. D. 1998. Controlling the IRS: Principals, Principles, and Public Administration. *American Journal of Political Science*, 42: 141–62.

————1999. Efficiency, Equity, and Politics: Democratic Controls over the Tax Collector. *American Journal of Political Science*, 43/3: 1166–88.

SEGAL, J. A. 1990. Supreme Court Support for the Solicitor General: The Effect of Presidential Appointments. *Western Political Quarterly*, 43: 137–52.

——TIMPONE, R. J., and HOWARD, R. M. 2000. Buyer Beware? Presidential Success through Supreme Court Appointments. *Political Research Quarterly*, 53: 557–74.

SIGELMAN, L. 1980. Gauging the Public Response to Presidential Leadership. *Presidential Studies Quarterly*, 10/3: 427–33.

——and SIGELMAN, C. K. 1981. Presidential Leadership of Public Opinion: From "Benevolent Leader" to "Kiss of Death." *Experimental Study of Politics*, 7/1: 1–22.

SIMON, H. A. 1947. *Administrative Behavior*. New York: Free Press.

——1983. *Reason in Human Affairs*. Stanford, CA: Stanford University Press.

STONE, D. 1997. *Policy Paradox: The Art of Political Decisionmaking*. New York: W. W. Norton.

SUNDQUIST, J. L. 1981. *The Decline and Resurgence of Congress*. Washington, DC: Brookings Institution Press.

TAYLOR, A. J. 1998. Domestic Agenda Setting, 1947–1994. *Legislative Studies Quarterly*, 23: 373–97.

THOMAS, D. B., and SIGELMAN, L. 1985. Presidential Identification and Policy Leadership: Experimental Evidence in the Reagan Case. In *The Presidency and Public Policy Making*, ed. I. G. C. Edwards, S. A. Shull, and N. C. Thomas. Pittsburgh: University of Pittsburgh Press.

WALKER, J. L. 1977. Setting the Agenda in the United States Senate: A Theory of Problem Selection. *British Journal of Political Science*, 7: 423–46.

WANTA, W., STEPHENSON, M. A., Van SLYKE TURK, J., and McCOMBS, M. E. 1989. How the Presidents' State of the Union Talk Influenced News Media Agendas. *Journalism Quarterly*, 66: 537–41.

WINTER, J. P., and EYAL, C. H. 1981. Agenda Setting for the Civil Right Issue. *Public Opinion Quarterly*, 45: 376–83.

WOOD, B. D. 1988. Principals, Bureaucrats, and Responsiveness in Clean Air Enforcements. *American Political Science Review*, 82/1: 215–34.

——1990. Does Politics Make a Difference at the EEOC? *American Journal of Political Science*, 34/2: 503–30.

——2007. *The Politics of Economic Leadership*. Princeton, NJ: Princeton University Press.

——and ANDERSON, J. E. 1993. The Politics of U.S. Antitrust Regulation. *American Journal of Political Science*, 37: 1–39.

——and BOHTE, J. 2004. Political Transaction Costs and the Politics of Administrative Design. *Journal of Politics*, 66: 176–202.

——and DOAN, A. 2003. The Politics of Problem Definition: A Theory and Application to Sexual Harassment. *American Journal of Political Science*, 47: 640–53.

——and PEAKE, J. S. 1998. The Dynamics of Foreign Policy Agenda Setting. *American Political Science Review*, 92: 173–84.

——and VEDLITZ, A. 2007. Issue Definition, Information Processing, and the Politics of Global Warming. *American Journal of Political Science*, 51: 552–68.

——and WATERMAN, R. W. 1991. The Dynamics of Political Control of the Bureaucracy. *American Political Science Review*, 85: 801–28.

—— ——1993. The Dynamics of Political-Bureaucratic Adaptation. *American Journal of Political Science*, 37: 497–528.

—— ——1994. *Bureaucratic Dynamics: The Role of Bureaucracy in a Democracy*. Boulder, CO: Westview Press.

PART IV

THE PUBLIC PRESIDENCY

CHAPTER 7

PUBLIC EXPECTATIONS OF THE PRESIDENT

DENNIS M. SIMON

BASED upon decades of research and writing, there is a general recognition in our journals, textbooks, and readers that modern presidents face a wide variety of public expectations. These expectations are part of the historical inheritance that awaits every new president. They are, in a sense, imposed on every incumbent, regardless of party or ideology. These expectations shape how presidents are covered by the press as well as how they are perceived and evaluated by elites and the mass public.

Unlike the research on topics such as presidential approval (Gronke and Newman 2003), there is no corpus of work that constitutes the normal science on public expectations. Rather, the research is eclectic and touches upon numerous traditions in political science and other disciplines—the Founding era, political theory, institutional history, American political culture, political socialization, public opinion, elections, legislative relations, and media studies. There are both advantages and disadvantages to this state of affairs. The advantage lies in the richness of perspectives that is characteristic of an interdisciplinary study. At the same time, there are no long-standing and well-agreed-upon measures of public expectations; there are no field essays demonstrating both the continuity and innovations in the study of expectations; there is no identifiable research agenda for the future.

Broadly speaking, this disparate research identifies two sets of public expectations about the president. The first can be termed image-based expectations and refers to both the desirable personal traits of presidents and how presidents should conduct themselves in office. These flow from the very nature of the office created by the

Framers. The second consists of performance-based expectations that focus upon what presidents should accomplish in office. These expectations are grounded in the roles of the modern president and highlight the events and conditions for which the public holds the president responsible.

This essay uses a diverse body of research to examine the origin and development, the content, and the consequences of these expectations. The first section focuses on image-based expectations and the idealization of the presidency. The discussion then turns to performance-based expectations and the responsibilities imposed on occupants of the modern presidency. The concluding section offers an assessment of existing research and identifies the questions most likely to animate future research on what the American public expects of its presidents.

IMAGE-BASED EXPECTATIONS: HOW PRESIDENTS SHOULD BEHAVE

Image-based expectations refer to both the personal traits of presidents and how presidents should conduct themselves in office. The list of desirable qualities and behaviors is seemingly endless. For example, in his defense of presidential exceptionalism, Denton (2005, 32–3) summarizes the earlier writings of Rossiter (1956) and Hughes (1974) to include the following: bounce, affability, political skill, cunning, the newspaper habit, and senses of history, confidence, proportion, drama, timing, constancy, humanity, and perspective. Collectively, image-based expectations are a "collage of images, hopes, habits, and intentions" shared by the American people (Denton 2005, 37) and writers often encapsulate these expectations, at times derisively, using such labels as the "heroic presidency" (Miroff 1995, 1025), "cult of the presidency" (Cronin 1975, 23–30), and the "celebrity and Sun King" (Pious 1979, 3).

The Origins of Image-Based Expectations

The origins of image-based expectations can be found in the creation of the presidency at the Philadelphia Convention of 1787 and the subsequent efforts to win ratification of the Constitution. These origins flow from three developments. First is the adoption of a unitary executive. The proposal to house administrative authority in a single executive initially unsettled the delegates. Bowen (1966, 55) describes the response following James Wilson's motion that the executive consist of a single person:

A sudden silence followed. "A considerable pause," Madison wrote....*A single executive!* There was menace in the words, some saw monarchy in them. True enough, nine states had each its single executive—a governor or president—but everywhere the local legislature was supreme, looked on as the voice of the people which could control a governor any day. But a single executive for the national government conjured up visions from the past—royal governors who could not be restrained, a crown, ermine, a scepter!

The ensuing debate, in fact, focused upon whether a unitary executive office would be a danger to republican principles of government. Edmund Randolph characterized the proposed office as the "foetus of monarchy" (Farrand 1911, Vol. 1, 66) while, later in the proceedings, Hugh Williamson of North Carolina argued that the president "will be an elective King and will feel the spirit of one" (Farrand 1911, Vol. 2, 101). The debate, however, did not address the consequences of merging the symbolic and ceremonial roles of a head of state with the operational and practical responsibilities of a chief administrative officer. This blending of roles guaranteed that the president would be both politically and culturally salient. It is from this merger that image-based expectations would grow.

Second, recognizing that the most immediate purpose of the *Federalist Papers* was to sell the Constitution, Hamilton essentially forecast, with his usual certainty and tinge of arrogance, the kinds of individuals that would be chosen to serve as chief magistrate. In defending the "Rube Goldberg mechanism" (Roche 1961, 811) called the Electoral College, Hamilton argued in *Federalist* No. 68 that "talents for low intrigue, and the little arts of popularity" would not be sufficient to gain the office; rather, "there will be a constant probability of seeing the station filled by characters preeminent for ability and virtue" (Kramnick 1987, 395; see also Edwards 2004, 82–3). Such men of virtue, Hamilton noted in *Federalist* No. 71, would not succumb to "every sudden breeze of passion or to every transient impulse which the people may receive from the arts of men, who flatter their prejudices to betray their interests" (Kramnick 1987, 410). In effect, the *Federalist Papers* offered a promissory note about the character and abilities of those who would rise to the presidency.

Third, the credibility of this promise was bolstered by the widespread presumption that George Washington would be the first president (Riker 1984; Roche 1961). Washington was respected as a man of virtue and accomplishment. He was admired for his "dignity," "judiciousness," and "dedication to duty" (Barber 1992, 10). The delegates trusted Washington, as Barber (1992, 2) notes, "to invent a tradition as he went along." Most importantly, his character was admirable. According to McDonald (1994, 217), character in the eighteenth century

meant, in polite society, a persona that one deliberately selected and always wore; it was conventional practice to pick a role, like a part in a play, and attempt to act it consistently, always "to be in character." If one chose a character that one could play comfortably and play it long enough, by degrees it became a "second nature" that superseded one's primary nature, which was generally thought to be base.

Given this understanding, McDonald (1994, 217) concludes that "Washington differed from other mortals by picking a progression of characters during his lifetime, each nobler and grander than the last, and by playing each so well that he ultimately transformed himself into a man of extrahuman virtue." The prestige enjoyed by Washington among his contemporaries is difficult to overstate. He was the object of a "cult of veneration" in a "culture that was explicitly disdainful of the glorification of personality, a culture in which complete deference to higher authority was ridiculed and every form of power deliberately and systematically scrutinized" (Schwartz 1983, 20). The selection of Washington as president thus closed an implicit deal. Essentially, the Framers promised, via *The Federalist Papers*, an extraordinary individual as president, and their method—the system of electors—delivered on that promise by selecting George Washington to serve as the first.

As president, Washington did not betray the trust of his contemporaries. He established the ceremonial importance of the office with a "simplicity of tastes and manners" (McDonald 1974, 217). The ceremonies included his inauguration and Annual Messages to Congress along with receiving members of Congress and communicating with governors of the states (McDonald 1994, 215–16; Tulis 1987, 45–9). In addition, Washington developed protocols for hosting weekly dinners, greeting ordinary citizens at his residence, and for "seeing and being seen" during travel outside of the nation's capital (Tulis 1987, 69; McDonald 1994, 214). By definition, these activities set precedents and, symbolically, demonstrated that the office was "public property" (Denton 2005, 38).

In sum, the origin of image-based expectations is a product of both institutional design and Washington's service as the first president. The Framers created an office that was both ceremonial and ministerial. The prestige earned by Washington during the years of revolution was "an interest-gathering deposit later drawn upon to sanctify the presidency" (Schwartz 1983, 24). That the presidency would become a repository of high expectations, myth, legend, and hagiography is an unintended consequence of the Philadelphia Convention and the administration of Washington.

This process, in fact, is evident with the passing of Washington, who was memorialized as a virtuous and heroic leader as well as the symbol of the young Republic. Washington "personified the heroic archetype of the Anglo-American Whig tradition" (Schwartz 1983, 18; also see Schwartz 1987). Many deemed it fitting that Washington's successors, John Adams and Thomas Jefferson, were "the voice" and "the pen" in the drive for independence (McCullough 2001, 643). Most noteworthy were their near simultaneous deaths on July 4, 1826, the fiftieth anniversary of the Declaration of Independence. The response to their passing created a legend that included substantial religious overtones (Hay 1969). Against the backdrop of reports stating that mathematicians calculated the odds of this event as infinitesimal, speakers offering memorials described their deaths as a "fiat of the Almighty" and the "design of Providence" (Hay 1969, 545, 553). It was evidence, as Daniel Webster eulogized, that "our country and its benefactors, are objects of His care" (quoted in McCullough 2001, 648).

Associating the death of a president with religious themes was even more pronounced following the assassination of Abraham Lincoln. Lincoln was mortally wounded on the evening of Good Friday, April 14, 1865. His death on the following morning prompted Secretary of War Edwin Stanton to declare that "[N]ow he belongs to the ages" (Steers 2001, 134). The first wave of the eulogies, delivered primarily in churches on the morning of Easter Sunday, was awash with religious allusion. Lincoln was commonly compared to Moses (Steers 2001, 14). His assassination was described as the "final blood sacrifice by which the nation was purified" (Cheseborough 1994, 106). The mixing of political and religious symbolism would not subside with the passage of time. Just over ninety years later, the symbolism of this Good Friday assassination would prompt Clinton Rossiter (1956, 102) to call Lincoln "the martyred Christ of democracy's passion play."

This apotheosis of presidents is not limited to the biblical. Fueling the creation of legend and the expectation of presidential exceptionalism includes over a century and a half of monument building and public dedication ceremonies. Completing the presidential memorials in the capital city—for Washington, Lincoln, Jefferson, and Franklin Roosevelt—spanned the period from 1848, when the initial construction work on the Washington Monument began, to the dedication of the Franklin Roosevelt Memorial in 1997. There is also Mount Rushmore, "America's Shrine of Democracy" (Glass 1994, 266). The creation of this monument featured separate dedication ceremonies for Washington, Jefferson, Lincoln, and Theodore Roosevelt. Its completion ultimately allowed "Americans to connect with the sacred qualities carved into the mountain" (Glass 1994, 271) and, according to President George H. W. Bush, to have a "moment of communion with the very soul of America" (quoted in Glass 1994, 271). Finally, there are the presidential libraries and museums. As Hufbauer (2005) notes, these libraries are largely funded by supporters of former presidents who act as legend makers. The objective is to make these libraries "part of the civil religion of the United States" which is designed to elevate political "saints," "sacred places," and inspire "ritual practices" and "pilgrimages" (Hufbauer 2005, 7).

This history of elevating presidents and cultivating legends of presidential greatness is, in part, a *top-down process*. Congress appropriated the monies used to construct the memorials in the capital city. Their dedications, as with those associated with Mount Rushmore, were led by sitting presidents. Research also informs us, however, that the diffusion and perpetuation of beliefs about presidential exceptionalism is also a *bottom-up process*. This is certainly the lesson taught by numerous studies of political socialization. Children and adolescents hold a "highly idealized view" of presidents (Greenstein 1975, 1378). Presidents are regarded as individuals of "benevolence, protectiveness, and exceptional sagacity" (Greenstein 1960, 941). The president is an "ideal authority figure" (Hess and Easton 1960, 642) who exercises a "high degree of control over his political system" (Greenstein 1975, 1378; see also Sigel 1966, 1968). In his 1985 critique of this research, Cook (1985, 1087) notes that despite the methodological flaws, findings that children and adolescents are socialized to hold an idealized view of presidents are not subject to dispute.

The growth in the civics and government curriculum in high schools (Niemi and Smith 2001) as well as the content of textbooks and other standard readings on the presidency serve to reinforce this early socialization. The textbooks of the 1950s and 1960s exaggerated not only the power of the office but also the virtue of its occupants (Cronin 1975, 26–33; 1980, 75–118). Subsequent studies of the *textbook presidency* emphasize that this idealized portrayal of the office and its powers has not diminished over time (Hoekstra 1982; Sanchez 1996). The most recent review of textbooks by Adler "largely confirms Professor Cronin's observations and findings" (2005, 378). Research also shows that this idealization of the president persists into adulthood in the form of prototypes that encapsulate the qualities that "citizens believe best define an exemplary president" (Kinder et al. 1980, 316). These qualities include honesty, knowledge, and open mindedness along with not being power hungry, unstable, or weak (Kinder et al. 1980, 319). Other traits include sound judgment in a crisis, competence, taking firm stands on issues, and placing the country's interest ahead of politics (Edwards 1983, 190–196).

The Consequences of Image-Based Expectations

There are three consequences created by the idealization of the president in American politics and culture. First, expectations of how presidents should behave are both high and exaggerated. For example, Edwards (1983, 187–209) presents data illustrating that these expectations include the personal characteristics (e.g., intelligence), the private behavior (e.g., church membership), and the leadership style (e.g., compassion) of the president (see also Wayne 1982). The analysis presented by Greenstein (2000, 5–6) highlights expectations that include public communication, vision, and emotional intelligence. In the more symbolic sense, the public expects presidents to be sources of reassurance, progress, and legitimacy (Barber 1992, 6). The public will judge incumbents according to standards that fallible officeholders could not hope to satisfy completely. Another tendency is that news coverage often stereotypes presidents and tags them with liabilities that focus on their persona— Lyndon Johnson as "bombastic and long-winded," Gerald Ford as a "dullard," and George H. W. Bush as having problems with the "vision thing" (Greenstein 2000, 87, 123, 170). Importantly, these perceived discrepancies from an idealized president can also influence assessments of an incumbent's substantive performance in office (Waterman, Jenkins-Smith, and Silva 1999, 944–66; Jenkins-Smith, Silva, and Waterman 2005, 690–715).

Second, image-based expectations are potentially contradictory. This flows from a characteristic tendency in American political culture to hold contradictory ideas simultaneously (McCloskey 1963, 14). The heroic presidency coexists, for example, with skepticism toward political authority as well as a populist, egalitarian impulse in American political culture. The story associated with this cultural tendency is well illustrated in the work of Cronin (1975, 1980; Cronin and Genovese, 2004). Cronin presents these potential contractions as paradoxes grounded not in survey data but in this cultural ambivalence toward power and authority. Thus, the public expects the president to be decent but ruthless, a unifier and a divider, a statesman and a politician, programmatic and pragmatic, and a common person who achieves the uncommon in office (Cronin 1980, 3–22). Maintaining an appropriate presidential image requires influencing public perceptions and navigating these potential contradictions. A president must, in effect, be all things to all people (Hodgson 1980).

The third consequence of the image-based expectations of the president is the response of the White House to these expectations. The rise and diffusion of television in the 1950s enhanced the prominence of image-based expectations. The proportion of US households with a television set increased from 9 percent in 1950 to 87 percent in 1960 (US Bureau of the Census 1989, 523). This growth, in effect, nationalized popular culture by exposing viewers to the same commercials, programming, and political leaders. As a result, presidents have been increasingly obligated to play to these expectations before a mass audience. The televised debates during the presidential campaign of 1960 and President Kennedy's live press conferences produced two marriages—politician with celebrity and politics with entertainment. In addition to the standard established by Kennedy, there have been technological changes that allow news and entertainment to be delivered more rapidly as well as a shift in journalistic norms making reporters more adversarial and more attentive to the personal lives of politicians (Sabato 1991). In response, the White House has developed and refined a sophisticated Office of Communications that operates, in effect, as an in-house public relations firm (Kurtz 1998; Maltese 1994). The result is leadership as spectacle—a near-continuous "projection of images whose purpose is to shape public understanding and gain public support" (Miroff 2006, 256). Spectacle has become a "structural feature" of modern presidential politics, a "harmful" and "disturbing development" since it emphasizes "gesture over accomplishment and appearance over fact" (Miroff 2006, 280). It also stands in stark contrast to the eighteenth-century ideas of virtue and character, ideas that animated the creation of the office.

PERFORMANCE-BASED EXPECTATIONS: WHAT PRESIDENTS SHOULD ACCOMPLISH

Performance-based expectations represent public beliefs that the office of the president is equipped to influence conditions and events in the real world. The public expects the modern president to maintain peace, national security, prosperity, and domestic stability along with integrity or probity. The public also expects presidents to be innovative and successful policy leaders and, with respect to unanticipated events in the domestic and international arenas, to be a *responder-in-chief* who effectively resolves crises and influences the course of events. Unlike the image-based expectations of the president which were, in a sense, present at the creation, performance-based expectations are products of evolutionary change in the institution of the presidency and political thought about the nature of executive authority. It is an evolution that turns the Framers' understanding of the office on its head.

The Origins of Performance-Based Expectations

The office that emerged from the Philadelphia Convention was not energized for policy leadership. In addition to the qualified veto given the president in Article I of the Constitution, Article II assigns the president the authority to convene the Congress on "extraordinary occasions," the responsibility to "give Congress Information on the State of the Union," and the discretion to "recommend to their Consideration such Measures as he shall judge necessary and expedient." Although these provisions would allow the president to prod and, if necessary, block the actions of the legislative branch, the affirmative authority here is quite meager and does not "substitute in the long run and on a regular basis for congressional hegemony" over policy making (Wayne 1978, 7).

Moreover, as part of a general fear and distrust of popular politics, the Founders insulated the president from public opinion. First, the Electoral College, as it operated in the early Republic, left the president two layers removed from the voting public. The electorate, itself circumscribed at the time, voted for state legislators who, in turn, chose the electors. Second, as part of a general fear and distrust of popular politics, the Constitution built a wall of separation between the president and the public. Reflecting the prevailing distrust of public opinion, there was a strong norm against popular leadership (Tulis 1987, 25–60). Popular leadership refers to direct appeals to the public by candidates and officeholders in an effort to build support or gain advantage in a political dispute. The Founders regarded such appeals as a wholly inappropriate behavior for refined and educated gentlemen. They considered popular leadership to be demagoguery and regarded it as unwholesome and dangerous (Tulis 1995, 59–60). Filtering public sentiment and proscribing appeals to the public thus insulated the office, protecting it from popular politics. This insulation would make it difficult for any president to overcome his subordinate status in the policy-making process.

Although Andrew Jackson and Abraham Lincoln provided brief glimpses of assertive policy leadership (Ellis and Kirk 1998; Laracey 1998), such presidential activism was not the norm until the twentieth century. These early assertions triggered a significant backlash. In the 1830s, a coalition of Whigs in Congress challenged Jackson's unilateral actions, including his removal of deposits from the national bank. As a national party, the Whigs were vocal advocates of "legislative supremacy" (*Congressional Quarterly* 2000, 99) and opponents of "executive usurpations" (*Congressional Quarterly* 1975, 25) The Civil War also brought challenges to executive authority by a "whiggish" Congress. In 1863, Congress challenged President Abraham Lincoln for control of reconstruction policy in the Wade–Davis Manifesto which asserted that the "authority of Congress is paramount" and that if the president desired their support, "he must confine himself to his executive duties— to obey and execute, not to make the laws" (*Congressional Quarterly* 2000, 101). Such assertions of legislative authority reached their crescendo with the impeachment of Andrew Johnson in the Republican-led 40th Congress. As Pious (1979, 62) notes, it is "only a slight exaggeration to suggest that government-by-corpse was the logical extension of such Whig principles."

Following the Civil War, expectations of the president were minimal. The most cited study of this period was done by James Bryce, whose account of his travels in *The American Commonwealth* included a chapter entitled "Why Great Men Are Not Chosen President" (1891, 73–80). Bryce observed that such men are not chosen because "great men are rare in politics," "the method of choice does not bring them to the top," and "they are not, in quiet times, absolutely needed" (1891, 80). Citing the party-driven nomination system, Bryce concludes that "when the choice lies between a brilliant man and a safe man, the safe man is preferred" (1891, 74). The historical analysis of Lowi (1985, 22–44) attributes this lack of exceptionalism to the features of the traditional political system or the patronage state. As Lowi observes, the "presidents produced by the party-dominated selection process were very ordinary people with very ordinary reputations in the job precisely because they presided . . . over a patronage party in a patronage state dominated by a legislature" (1985, 40).

How and under what circumstances did this patronage state change? During the past two decades, there has been a marked and resurgent interest in both the political and institutional evolution of the presidency in an effort to answer this question. One of the central concerns of this scholarship is dating—fixing the time—when presidents first began to act as policy initiators and strategically engage in popular leadership to create the political leverage necessary to sell their programs. This effort has produced a spirited and engaging debate in which a number of scholars attempt to identify the moment in time that corresponds to a "big-bang transformation of the presidency" (Skowronek 2003, 748).

For Jeffrey Tulis (1987), the period of transformation—characterized as the rise of the rhetorical presidency—is the second decade of the twentieth century and the administration of Woodrow Wilson. He casts Wilson not only as the landmark practitioner of popular leadership but as the theorist of the modern presidency, articulating both a critique of the Madisonian system and a remedy that emphasizes the role of the president as a popular leader (Tulis 1987, 118–36). The political thought of Wilson and his subsequent reliance on popular leadership, Tulis argues, formed "the core of dominant interpretations of our whole political order" (1987, 4). Accordingly, Tulis concludes that Wilson engineered a "profound development in American politics" and a "true transformation of the presidency" (1987, 4; 7). In fact, Wilson introduced a "Second Constitutional Presidency" (Tulis 1995, 91–123).

Gamm and Smith (1998) challenge both the dating and the rationale for the rise of the rhetorical presidency. Their research leads them to conclude that the practice of going public began with the administration of Theodore Roosevelt. More importantly, they argue that the rhetorical presidency was pre-dated by the rise of candidate-centered campaigning. The watershed year was 1896, an election year in which the national candidates—especially Theodore Roosevelt, the Republican vice presidential nominee—assumed a direct and active role in electioneering and directed overt policy appeals to the public. This break with tradition was stimulated by the adoption of the Australian ballot, the growing independence of the press, and a shift in vote-getting strategies from entertainment to education and propaganda (Gamm and Smith 1998, 90–2). The authors then connect the innovations in this campaign with the rise of the rhetorical presidency and advance the general proposition that changes in campaign styles and strategies ultimately stimulated changes in strategies of presidential governance. "The changes wrought during his presidency," they argue, "proved permanent" (1998, 90). Gamm and Smith thus conclude that in his governing style, Theodore Roosevelt "became the architect of the modern presidency" (1987, 110).

Other studies credit Franklin Roosevelt with the rise of popular leadership and the emergence of the modern presidency. Fred Greenstein, for example, characterizes the FDR administration "not as a shift but rather a metamorphosis" (1978, 45; also see Skowronek 1993, 287–323). Lowi (1985) offers the most emphatic case. The era of Franklin Roosevelt was, according to Lowi, a revolution in four parts that included marginalizing the political party and establishing "a direct and unmediated relationship between the president and the people" (1985, 59). Thus arose a personal and plebiscitary presidency characterized by a reliance on the infant communication and polling industries (Lowi 1985, 62). The governing strategy fashioned by Roosevelt was transformative, for it provided the president with the political capital required to fund the other components of the Roosevelt revolution and to establish what Lowi, in *The End of Liberalism* (1979), calls the Second American Republic.

The reverberations of this change were felt in the intellectual community as well, for the Roosevelt example would alter how the discipline of political science would define and study the concept of presidential power. The centrality of policy initiation and popular leadership in Roosevelt's strategy of governance prompted a shift in presidential scholarship from a historical and constitutional approach (e.g., Corwin 1957) to a behavioral perspective in which power is characterized as an inherently unstable product of mass and elite evaluations (Neustadt 1960).

What distinguishes the era of Franklin Roosevelt from prior administrations known for political and policy innovations is the response of Congress and other elites. In the wake of FDR, there was no significant assertion of Whig principles as witnessed during and after the administrations of Andrew Jackson and Abraham Lincoln. Instead, Congress acted to institutionalize the Roosevelt example. The Employment Act of 1946 required the president to assume the role of economic manager while the National Security Act of 1947 unambiguously made the president the foreign policy leader (Sundquist 1981, 61–126). Further, Congress "by statute directed or invited the president to be chief legislator" in "seven broad policy fields—the budget, the economy, national security, manpower, the environment, housing, and urban growth" (Sundquist 1981, 147). The precedent of FDR's 100 Days would require future presidents to formulate an agenda complete with specific policy proposals. Mandating presidential activism triggered a generation of growth in the personnel employed by the Executive Office of the President (Stanley and Niemi 2003, 254–5). These policy-making responsibilities gave rise to the use of "central clearance" in evaluating legislative proposals from the departments of the executive branch (Neustadt 1954) and the necessity of a centralized process for "planning the president's program" (Neustadt 1955). Modern administrations now engineer what advertisers call an *annual rollout* of their agenda. This spectacle, in

Miroff's (2006) parlance, is highlighted by a nationally televised State of the Union address, the annual report of the Council of Economic Advisors, and the submission of the president's budget.

From the outset of the Republic through the era of Franklin Roosevelt, the decision to pursue a legislative agenda was essentially a matter of presidential temperament and discretion. There were no institutional requirements that a successor behave like his predecessor in office. Thus, William Howard Taft (2002) could articulate a "strict constructionist" view of the office that was at odds with the "stewardship theory" of Theodore Roosevelt (2002). The "understanding of executive power" exhibited by the three Republican successors of Woodrow Wilson "owed more to William Howard Taft than to Theodore Roosevelt", with President Coolidge, in particular, raising "inactivity to an art" (Milkis and Nelson 2003, 250, 258). After the era of FDR, however, the option of a limitationist approach—what Burns (1973, 108–12) calls the Madisonian model—was "off the table." The presentation of an agenda is not only mandated by law and political custom but also reinforced by the perception, among both elites and the mass public, that the White House is the focus of national policy leadership.

In this manner, the performance-based expectations of the public derive from the evolution of these modern roles and their institutionalization following the Franklin Roosevelt administration. Note, too, that as with their image-based counterparts, the performance-based expectations are reinforced by the *bottom-up process* of political socialization as well as the *textbook presidency.* Whereas image-based expectations focus upon exceptionalism in conduct, performance-based expectations are grounded on the assumption that any president is supplied with the requisite authority and power to excel in the modern roles of the office.

The historical significance of this development is substantial. As policy leadership became a mandatory part of the presidential job description, so too did the instrumental need to engage in popular leadership. Presidents—Democrat or Republican, liberal or conservative—would be expected to pursue a legislative agenda, and political necessity would demand that the president engage in what Hamilton termed the "little arts of popularity" (Kramnick 1987, 395). Because of these developments, the presidency evolved from an institution insulated from public opinion into one in which the fears of the Framers, as expressed in their understanding of popular politics, are now identical to the objectives of the modern president.

The Consequences of Performance-Based Expectations

Broadly speaking, there are three types of consequences associated with performance-based expectations. First, these expectations help us understand fluctuations in public support for presidents, both within and across administrations. Essentially, the public holds presidents accountable for a broad range of events and conditions in the real world (Gronke and Newman 2003). As economic managers, we expect presidents to ensure prosperity and hold them accountable for the state of the economy; as foreign policy leaders, we expect presidents to maintain peace and national security; as domestic policy initiators, we expect them to be innovators who formulate an agenda and effectively act to secure its passage and implementation (Ostrom and Simon 1985; Edwards 1983). In addition to the image-based expectation of honesty, we also expect presidents to maintain integrity or probity within their administrations (Newman 2003, 2002).

The modern roles of the president also create an expectation that the president will operate as a *responder-in-chief*. From the Cold War to the war on terror, we expect presidents to respond to events and crises in the international arena. We also expect them to manage events and developments that threaten domestic stability, be they labor disputes during the Truman administration or the threats of violence that prompted President Kennedy to act during the integration of the Universities of Mississippi and Alabama.

In effect, performance-based expectations establish a basic rule of the game— presidents are blamed for *bad* outcomes. Recessions, prolonged military conflict, scandals, and other adverse events exact a toll on the president's approval ratings, his future effectiveness, and the electoral fortunes of his party (e.g., Jacobson 2004, 151–206; Simon, Ostrom, and Marra 1991). Herein lays the trap of the textbook presidency. In the face of adverse outcomes and events in the real world, these expectations lead to a conclusion that a president did not exercise his authority and power in a competent manner (Peffley 1989). Seldom do political participants and commentators raise the question of whether presidents have, in fact, sufficient power and authority to meet these expectations. One prominent example is the expectation of prosperity that flows from the president's role of economic manager. A realistic view of the office would emphasize that presidential influence over fiscal policy is restricted by the power of the purse granted to Congress and that, on matters of monetary policy, the Federal Reserve Board is a regulatory agency independent of the executive branch. In fact, recent case studies demonstrate that the Federal Reserve Board is more likely to influence presidential economic policy than vice versa (Woodward 2000, 1994).

Second, the political value of public support, as measured by approval ratings, has altered the character of presidential politics. It has created a politics of prestige (Simon and Ostrom 1988) and a perpetual election or continuous referendum (Marra, Ostrom, and Simon 1990; Brace and Hinckley 1992) in which presidents, subject to continuous scrutiny in the polls, attempt to influence public opinion in order to sell their agenda and maintain the necessary levels of public support. As Kernell (1997) notes, the strategy of going public has become more commonplace since the 1960s. The growth of the welfare state spawned by Lyndon Johnson's Great Society, the demise of political parties as the primary mediators between presidents and the public, and technological advances in communications and travel spawned a new form of politics which disrupted the institutionalized pluralism of Washington and ushered in an era of individualized pluralism (Kernell 1997, 27–33).

It was in this milieu that popular leadership ceased to be a sporadic and extraordinary event and became a routine and essential component in the president's strategy of governance. The politics of prestige also acknowledges a growing capability of the White House to survey and analyze public opinion through standard polling techniques as well as qualitative research based upon such vehicles as focus groups. The work of Jacobs and Shapiro (2000) shows that in these endeavors, presidential operatives are less concerned with reading and responding to public opinion and more oriented to developing priming strategies and crafted talk to build support for an already established agenda and set of policy proposals.

The incentive to manipulate is all the greater given recent research on presidential approval. Gronke and Newman (2003, 504–7) identify a shift in the empirical research from using hard indicators of economic conditions (e.g., unemployment and inflation rates) to public perceptions of the economy (e.g., index of consumer sentiment) along with variables that measure media coverage of the economy. Because citizens evaluate the president according to their perceptions of economy, the new wave of research shows that the politics of prestige requires that presidents compete with other political actors and an adversarial media in attempting to influence these perceptions.

The role of perceptions is equally important in the case of war. The performance-based expectation is peace. What happens, then, in the case of protracted military conflict? One conclusion drawn from the empirical results reported in the literature is that the fundamental expectations are to make progress and to win, most preferably in a timely manner (Ostrom and Simon 1985; Kernell 1978; Mueller 1973). In the Second World War, progress was an easy concept to demonstrate. It was fundamentally geographic; the objective was to capture territory held by enemy, make the enemy armies retreat, and move toward the capital cities of Rome, Berlin, and Tokyo. Winning meant the surrender of the enemy. This was not the case with the war in Vietnam or the current war in Iraq. These wars were not territorial, the idea of progress was not geographic, and winning was not associated with the traditional concept of an enemy surrender. Thus, to maintain public support for themselves and for the military effort, politics of prestige requires presidents to develop public relations campaigns that would lead the public to perceive that progress was being made and that America was winning (for Vietnam, see Berman 1989; Gelb and Betts 1979; for Iraq, see Woodward 2006; Gelpi, Feaver, and Reifler 2005).

The third consequence pertains to the expectation of domestic policy innovation. Here, occupants of the White House face what Paul Light (1999) calls a "no-win presidency" (also see Edwards 2003). Research shows that despite the increased expenditures of effort and political capital, presidents typically fail in their efforts to produce major policy innovations. This is certainly the lesson to be drawn from Jimmy Carter and energy policy (Kellerman 1984, 185–219), Bill Clinton and health care policy (Jacobs and Shapiro 2000), and George W. Bush and social security (Edwards 2007). More generally, Light's (1999) analysis reveals that the necessary conditions for effective policy innovation are seldom met. Despite presidential aspirations and efforts, history promises few instances that are comparable to the gold standard of innovation established during Franklin Roosevelt's 100 Days.

PRESIDENTIAL EXPECTATIONS: TAKING STOCK AND LOOKING TO THE FUTURE

In addition to the disparate nature of the research pertaining to public expectations, there is no landmark or seminal work whose impact on subsequent research can be traced over time. However, it is possible to identify two distinct contributions within this body of research. The first is that this research provides us with a "dominant narrative" about the origin and development of public expectations. One part of the narrative explains how the idealization of the presidency and image-based expectations grew from an office occupied by a single individual whose duties were both ministerial and ceremonial. This narrative suggests that the growth of image-based expectations is monotonic over time, punctuated by elite-driven activity associated with the deaths of presidents and former presidents. It is sustained by political parties regularly lionizing their successful presidents and a widespread cultural belief in great persons and heroic leaders.

The narrative also addresses performance-based expectations. Our understanding here owes much to the "rediscovery of history" by scholars in political science (e.g., Skowronek 1993; Tulis 1987). This portion of the narrative tells us that there was no "big bang." The narrative suggests that prior to the administration of Franklin Roosevelt, the growth of performance-based expectations was neither linear nor monotonic. Rather, the growth was the product of an irregular development featuring extended periods in which the Whig concept of a limited presidency was dominant. Although debate over the utility of such constructs as the modern, pre-modern, and post-modern presidency will continue to refine the narrative (Skowronek 2003), it is also clear that since Franklin Roosevelt, there has been a distinct tendency to "look to the White House" (Jenkins-Smith, Silva, and Waterman 2005, 693) for solutions to emerging problems. This, in turn, suggests a monotonic growth in performance-based exceptions for those presidents who governed in the "shadow of FDR" (Leuchtenburg 1983). Unlike prior eras, sitting presidents and aspiring candidates implicitly but repeatedly claim that the office is well equipped to solve problems. Examples range from President Johnson's "War on Poverty" to President Carter's "moral equivalent of war" in attempting to fashion a national energy policy to President George W. Bush's education initiative designed to leave "no child behind."

This fundamental narrative also provides the context and rationale for the study of expectations using the methods of survey research. This is the second and empirical contribution of this research on public expectations. Recent progress here has been encouraging. By linking the idealization of the president to the psychological concept of a prototype, Kinder and his colleagues identify a set of personal and behavioral traits and construct a profile of the public's ideal president (1980, 319). They also demonstrate that the prototypes held by the individuals influenced their voting preferences for President Carter, the incumbent at the time of their study (1980, 321).

Building upon this study as well as the work of Edwards (1983) and Wayne (1982), Waterman, Jenkins-Smith, and Silva (1999) introduce further refinements in measuring expectations. Two surveys administered in 1996 asked respondents to rate an ideal president on four qualities and then to evaluate President Clinton on the same qualities (1999, 947–51). Their analysis provides direct evidence that public expectations of the ideal president are exaggerated, that there exists an expectations gap between this ideal and President Clinton, and that the magnitude of this gap influences approval of President Clinton and the likelihood of voting for Clinton or his 1996 opponent, Robert Dole (1999, 952–60; also see Jenkins-Smith, Silva, and Waterman 2005).

In sum, building an explanatory and historical narrative along with introducing precision in measuring expectations are what we, as a subfield, have done well with the work on prototypes constituting the "empirical core" of this research. In addition, based upon the early socialization studies, there is some evidence about the individual-level or micro process that leads to the idealization of the president. Clearly, elites drive the apotheosis and create shining and heroic images of presidents. These images, in turn, become the substantive content in the early phases of socialization. Thus, it is known that young children hold a rudimentary but idealized view of the president and that the initial years of education reinforce this view. However, little is known about how expectations vary over the remaining phases of the life cycle or how historical events change or reinforce the expectations of individuals. At the individual level, there is little work on the relationship between expectations and the demographic profile of citizens. Aggregate work on presidential approval offers little help in filling this void. As Gronke and Newman (2003, 508) observe, "the bases of expectations about presidential performance remain surprisingly unexplored."

It is important to note that this situation is not a "sin of omission" among members of the subfield. Rather, the situation is due primarily to the lack of data and thus an absence of opportunity. The data analyzed by Kinder and his colleagues (1980), Wayne (1982), and Edwards (1983) were not gathered as part of a regularized and repeated survey process. More recent work in studying prototypes is primarily based upon the yeoman efforts of scholars to obtain the funding necessary to conduct and analyze their own surveys (e.g., Waterman, Jenkins-Smith, and Silva 1999). Unlike scholars focusing on the study of partisan identification, political trust, and other attitudes, those interested in public expectations of the president are not blessed with a set of surveys asking the same questions over a long period of time. Questions about prototypes and beliefs about presidential power are not part of the regular battery of questions in national surveys.

Despite this state of affairs, it is possible to identify some interesting questions related to public expectations and to suggest some approaches that may prove useful for addressing them. The discussion assumes that, in principle, it is possible to replicate and refine the measures of prototypes that capture the idealization of the presidency inherent in image-based expectations (e.g., Kinder et al. 1980). The same holds true for measures that tap beliefs about the president's power and authority to satisfy the performance-based expectations (such as those reported in Edwards 1983, 194). An added variable of interest in this regard represents the "flip side of the expectations coin"—the tendency of the public to attribute exclusive responsibility for conditions and events to the president (Gomez and Wilson 2003, 2001). The underlying rationale of these suggestions is that there is a need to study how expectations vary across individuals in a given era and whether these expectations respond to the sources of change (e.g., aging, historical events) identified in the literature on political socialization.

Expectations, Political Socialization, and Zeitgeist

The bear market described by Cook in 1985 persists. There are few recent studies that focus upon the presidential images held by children, young adolescents, and high school students. As a result, there is little information for assessing the key question of whether the formation of image-based and performance-based expectations varies according to landmark events and, more generally, the temper of the times. Evidence from the Watergate era suggests that the formation of expectations may be subject to generational effects (Meadow 1982; Hershey and Hill 1975; Arterton 1975). These studies demonstrate that during the Watergate era, the image of the president among children and adolescents was decidedly less benevolent than in the Eisenhower–Kennedy era. However, there has been little study of subsequent periods. Did images of the president rebound during the Reagan administration? Was there a *Clinton effect* in the late 1990s? How did the tragedy of 9/11 and the subsequent war on terror influence the images and expectations of children and adolescents?

Absent such studies of children, research could target the eras in which different citizens came of age politically. An interesting research design would rely upon age cohorts to identify different political generations. It would then be possible to examine whether presidential prototypes and beliefs about the power and authority of the office vary by political generation. A related question pertains to the persistence of expectations formed during the process of political socialization. Although the presidency is not the focus of the research, there is evidence that "core political predispositions tend to be highly stable through the life span" (Griffin 2004; Jennings 2002; Sears and Funk 1999). The stability in attitudes may include expectations of the president, given the longevity of the *textbook presidency* noted earlier. Thus, a "persistence hypothesis" could be tested against an alternative proposition that ageing effects, representing the accumulation of life experiences, produce more realistic expectations of the president among older cohorts.

Expectations, Presidential Success, and the Political Calendar

It is also possible to hypothesize about period effects and the factors that may lead to adjustments of expectations. For example, an administration that is perceived as politically unsuccessful (e.g., Jimmy Carter) may lead to downward adjustments while administrations seen as successful (e.g., Ronald Reagan) may produce heightened expectations. Although political socialization and generational differences are long-term effects, these readjustments are akin to period effects—responses to the performance of specific administrations.

Another related line of inquiry pertains to the political calendar, which can be likened to a period effect. Presidential politics in America operates on a four-year cycle with an increasingly lengthy campaign that now begins just after the midterm election (Mayer 2008). The question arises as to whether expectations of the president vary according to this calendar. Campaigns are the nemesis of realistic expectations. The discourse focuses not on the limitations of presidential power but on the competence of the incumbent in using or misusing power that candidates assume exists. Although unrelated to presidential expectations, there is research that demonstrates the effects of campaigns on other attitudes (Valentino and Sears 1998). In this vein, an interesting study would examine measures of presidential expectations at inauguration, the end of year one in the cycle, during the midterm campaign, at the first official event of the primary season, and during the general election campaign. At a minimum, then, such a design would shed light on the manner in which campaigns themselves reinforce exaggerated expectations and account for their persistence over time. It also has the potential to uncover a four-year cycle of recalibration in public expectations.

Relationship between Image-Based and Performance-Based Expectations

The distinction between image-based and performance-based expectations is a useful heuristic in that it recognizes two distinct tracks in the history of the idealized presidency. It also acknowledges the simultaneous importance of personal qualities and performance. Another line of inquiry pertains to the relationship between these kinds of expectations. There are a few instances where scholars have explored the relationship (Jenkins-Smith, Silva, and Waterman 2005; Waterman, Jenkins-Smith, and Silva 1999; Peffley 1989; Waterman 1993). Questions remain about whether personal and performance evaluations of the president are independent or whether there is some form, under certain conditions, of a causal relationship between them.

Recent presidential history provides an interesting mix of cases. Consider the comparison of Presidents Carter and Clinton. The public evaluated Carter favorably on the personal dimension and unfavorably on the performance dimension whereas the public assessed Clinton most favorably on the performance but unfavorably on the personal (Fiorina, Abrams, and Pope 2003). Other off-diagonal presidents— evaluated favorably on the personal and unfavorably on the performance—include Gerald Ford and George H. W. Bush. A potentially fruitful avenue of research, then, would be to examine fluctuations in personal and performance evaluations over the course of an administration or several administrations. Such a design could provide the time series analyst with a veritable feast day of results.

Expectations and the Classroom

In surveying the relevant literature, perhaps the greatest curiosity is the persistence of the *textbook presidency*. From the initial analysis of textbooks by Cronin (1975) to the most recent replication of this exercise by Adler (2005), authors continue to exaggerate the power and authority of the president. As Adler (2005, 379) notes, students have the intellectual "problem of confused and misleading claims and characterizations of presidential power derived from the Constitution." This exaggeration is all the more perplexing given that those who instruct classes at the college level are far removed from the Roosevelt era as well as the textbooks of the 1950s and 1960s that exaggerated the authority of the office. Many tenured professors were either in graduate school during the Vietnam and Watergate eras or became the graduate students of those who were. Few instructors have not been schooled in Neustadt, who, in the last edition of his work, noted that "presidential weakness was the underlying theme of *Presidential Power*" (1990, ix). Many have read *The Imperial Presidency* (Schlesinger 1973), *All Things to All Men* (Hodgson 1980), *The Impossible Presidency* (Barger 1984), or similar works.

This curiosity leads to a number of questions. To what extent do courses that examine the presidency emphasize realism about and skepticism toward presidential power? Do students who enroll in courses that focus upon the presidency have more realistic expectation than students who do not enroll? Among those who enroll, are variations in the presidential expectations related to the readings assigned by the instructor or the instructor's approach to the topic? Relevant courses include both regular and Advanced Placement high school courses on American government, introductory college courses on American government, and more advanced university courses on the presidency. Addressing these questions requires using the classroom as a laboratory where such courses serve as the treatments in experimental or quasi-experimental designs. The pre-test and post-test would include measuring prototypes, understanding of the president's constitutional authority, and expectations about presidential performance. Such studies could also draw distinctions among the courses according to the textbook, the type of school, or the pedagogical methods of the instructor. In addition, control groups comprised of students who have not taken such courses would allow us to asses the impact of teaching the presidency.

Expectations and Public Discourse

There is no doubt that the celebration of strong presidents and forceful leadership is a prominent element of American political culture. In addition to believing that the office is endowed with substantial authority, Cronin demonstrates that the textbook presidency and the *cult of the presidency* which it feeds includes a normative component (1980, 76). This is a value-based belief that presidents *should* be powerful and that the effective exercise of this power is desirable (1980, 76–99).

Interestingly, in public discourse advocating presidential power, the partisanship and ideology of the advocates and opponents vary over time. Although Neustadt (1990) expresses concern with the weakness of the office, there is much in his analysis that celebrates the success enjoyed by Franklin Roosevelt in acquiring and using presidential power. Because of Neustadt's strategic perspective toward power, William Bluhm compares Neustadt to Machiavelli in *Theories of the Political System* (1965, 224–59). Other advocates of a strong presidency during the 1950s and 1960s include Arthur Schlesinger Jr. who wrote celebratory biographies of both Franklin Roosevelt (1960, 1959) and John Kennedy (1965), as well as James MacGregor Burns (1973, 1970, 1963, 1956). The authors of these and other works lauded a strong presidency as a vehicle for liberal and progressive causes (Cronin 1980, 88–90).

In the wake of the Vietnam War and the numerous scandals of the Nixon administration, there arose a concern with such issues as the scope of the president's authority to use military force, secrecy in government, and domestic surveillance of dissidents. Writers began to challenge the normative premise that the president *should* be powerful. Ironically, it was Arthur Schlesinger, Jr., a one-time celebrant of presidential power, who led the charge with publication of *The Imperial Presidency* (1973). Other works, such as *The Decline and Rise of Congress* (Sundquist 1981), essentially lauded what was called the reassertion of congressional authority.

This respite was short lived, however. By the late 1980s, a new school of advocates for a strong presidency emerged, arguing for eliminating the so-called reforms of the 1970s (e.g., War Powers Resolution). Unlike the earlier celebrants of presidential power, these advocates were conservative and Republican and "came to see a strong presidency as the only way to protect conservative ideals from the encroachments of a Democratic Congress, liberal courts, and obstreperous bureaucrats" (Rosen 2006, 1). One initial work was *The Fettered Presidency* (1989), an edited volume by L. Gordon Crovitz and Jeremy A. Rabkin. The foreword to this work was written by Robert Bork, who argued that "the president of the United States has been significantly weakened in recent years and that Congress is largely, but not entirely, responsible" (Crovitz and Rabkin 1989, ix). The volume includes contributions by Alan Keyes, Elliott Abrams, Jeane Kirkpatrick, Caspar Weinberger, C. Boyden Gray, and Theodore Olson. All share in the prescription of Robert Bork that the "president must make a public issue of congressional attempts to control his legitimate powers" (Crovitz and Rabkin 1989, xiv). A similar theme lies at the heart of *Energy in the Executive* by Terry Eastland (1992) which Rosen (2006, 3) judges as the "best intellectual history of the conservative embrace of executive power." Rosen (2006) goes on to note that the advocates of the *unitary executive* also include the Federalist Society and numerous individuals employed by the Office of Legal Counsel in the Department of Justice during the Reagan era and the most recent Bush administration.

This brief overview of the normative claim that presidents *should* be powerful and the theories justifying that claim identifies another path for inquiry. It appears that the advocacy of presidential power has a distinct partisan and ideological dimension. Just as importantly, it appears that the beliefs of liberals and conservatives about whether this power is beneficial or dangerous change over time. Future studies that focus on the intellectual history of this debate promise to be a fruitful line of inquiry for two reasons. First, they will shed light on how philosophical positions are contingent upon the political realities of a given era. Second, they will help the research community understand more thoroughly how public discourse itself serves to perpetuate the symbolic and substantive expectations of presidential exceptionalism in our politics and culture.

CONCLUSION

In a fundamental sense, the study of what the public expects of its presidents consists of two conversations. The first is academic and involves a conversation among ourselves, members of the academy who study the relationship between the president and the mass public. Of the future lines of research discussed, those pertaining to examining variations in expectations over time and space are central. They require doing "political science" in the sense of systematic design of studies, measurement, and testing. Addressing the questions associated with variations in expectations promises to advance the conversation within the academy.

The second conversation about expectations occurs in the "public square"—in classrooms, in the media, and in the political arena. More often than not, this conversation assumes that the authority of the office is substantial; it is grounded in the idealized view of the office. The conversation then focuses on the normative question of whether the president should be powerful, as well as speculative questions about the competence of incumbents and the projected competence of presidential aspirants. My suggestions pertaining to expectations in the "public square" are designed to study this second conversation in a more systematic fashion. This promises to inform the design and execution of our ongoing academic studies of public expectations and to help us understand why conversations about the presidency in the "public square" have not grown more realistic over time.

REFERENCES

ADLER, D. G. 2005. Textbooks and the President's Constitutional Powers. *Presidential Studies Quarterly*, 35: 376–88.

ARTERTON, F. C. 1975. Watergate and Children's Attitudes toward Political Authority Revisited. *Political Science Quarterly*, 90: 477–96.

BARBER, J. D. 1992. The *Presidential Character*, 4th edn. Englewood Cliffs, NJ: Prentice-Hall.

BARGER, H. M. 1984. *The Impossible Presidency: Illusions and Realities of Executive Power*. Glenview, IL: Scott, Foresman.

BERMAN, L. 1989. *Lyndon Johnson's War: The Road to Stalemate in Vietnam*. New York: W. W. Norton.

BLUHM, W. T. 1965. *Theories of the Political System*. Englewood Cliffs, NJ: Prentice-Hall.

BOWEN, C. D. 1966. *Miracle at Philadelphia*. Boston: Little, Brown.

BRACE, P., and HINCKLEY, B. 1992. *Follow the Leader: Opinion Polls and the Modern Presidency*. New York: Basic Books.

BRYCE, J. 1891. *The American Commonwealth*, 2nd edn. New York: Macmillan.

BURNS, J. M. 1956. *Roosevelt: The Lion and the Fox*. New York: Harcourt Brace Jovanovich.

—— 1963. *The Deadlock of Democracy: Four Party Politics in America*. Englewood Cliffs, NJ: Prentice-Hall.

—— 1970. *Roosevelt: The Soldier of Freedom*. New York: Harcourt Brace Jovanovich.

—— 1973. *Presidential Government: The Crucible of Leadership*. Boston: Houghton Mifflin.

CHESEBOROUGH, D. B. 1994. *"No Sorrow Like our Sorrow:" Northern Protestant Ministers and the Assassination of Abraham Lincoln*. Kent, OH: Kent State University Press.

Congressional Quarterly. 2000. *Congressional Quarterly's Guide to Congress*. 5th edn. Washington, DC: Congressional Quarterly.

—— 1975. Congressional Quarterly's Guide to U.S. Elections. Washington, DC: Congressional Quarterly.

COOK, T. E. 1985. The Bear Market in Political Socialization and the Costs of Misunderstood Psychological Theories. *American Political Science Review*, 68: 1079–93.

CORWIN, E. S. 1957. *The President, Office and Powers, 1787–1957*. New York: New York University Press.

CRONIN, T. E. 1975. *The State of the Presidency*. Boston: Little, Brown & Company.

—— 1980. *The State of the Presidency*, 2nd edn. Boston: Little, Brown & Company.

—— and GENOVESE, M. 2004. *The Paradoxes of the American Presidency*, 2nd edn. New York: Oxford University Press.

CROVITZ, L. G., and RABKIN, J. A. (eds.) 1989. *The Fettered Presidency: Legal Constraints on the Executive Branch*. Washington, DC: American Enterprise Institute.

DENTON, R. E., Jr. 2005. *Moral Leadership and the American Presidency*. Lanham, MD: Rowman & Littlefield.

EASTLAND, T. 1992. *Energy in the Executive: The Case for the Strong Presidency*. New York: Free Press.

EDWARDS, G. C., III. 1983. *The Public Presidency*. New York: St Martin's Press.

—— 2003. *On Deaf Ears: The Limits of the Bully Pulpit*. New Haven, CT: Yale University Press.

—— 2004. *Why the Electoral College is Bad for America*. New Haven, CT: Yale University Press.

—— 2007. *Governing by Campaigning: The Politics of the Bush Presidency*. New York: Pearson Longman.

ELLIS, R. J., and KIRK, S. 1998. Jefferson, Jackson, and the Origin of the Presidential Mandate. In *Speaking to the People: The Rhetorical Presidency in Historical Perspective*, ed. R. J. Ellis. Amherst: University of Massachusetts Press.

FARRAND, M. (ed.) 1911. *The Records of the Federal Convention of 1787*, 3 vols. New Haven, CT: Yale University Press.

FIORINA, M., ABRAMS, S., and POPE, J. 2003. The 2000 US Presidential Election: Can Retrospective Voting Be Saved? *British Journal of Political Science*, 33: 162–87.

GAMM, G., and SMITH, R. M. 1998. Presidents, Parties, and the Public: Evolving Patterns of Interaction, 1877–1929. In *Speaking to the People: The Rhetorical Presidency in Historical Perspective*, ed. R. J. Ellis. Amherst: University of Massachusetts Press.

GELB, L. H., and BETTS, R. K. 1979. *The Irony of Vietnam: The System Worked*. Washington, DC: Brookings Institution.

GELPI, C., FEAVER, P. D., and REIFLER, J. 2005/6. Success Matters: Casualty Sensitivity and the War in Iraq. *International Security*, 30: 7–46.

GILLON, S. M. 2000. *That's Not What We Meant to Do: Reform and its Unintended Consequences in Twentieth-Century America*. New York: W. W. Norton.

GLASS, M. 1994. Producing Patriotic Inspiration at Mount Rushmore. *Journal of the American Academy of Religion*, 62: 265–83.

GOMEZ, B. T., and WILSON, J. M. 2001. Political Sophistication and Economic Voting in the American Electorate: A Theory of Heterogeneous Attribution. *American Journal of Political Science*, 45: 899–914.

—— 2003. Causal Attribution and Economic Voting in American Congressional Elections. *Political Research Quarterly*, 56: 271–82.

GREENSTEIN, F. I. 1960. The Benevolent Leader: Children's Images of Political Authority. *American Political Science Review*, 54: 934–43.

—— 1975. The Benevolent Leader Revisited: Children's Images of Political Leaders in Three Democracies. *American Political Science Review*, 69: 1371–98.

—— 1978. Change and Continuity in the Modem Presidency. In *The New American Political System*, ed. A. King. Washington, DC: American Enterprise Institute.

—— 2000. *The Presidential Difference: Leadership Style from FDR to Clinton*. New York: Free Press.

GRIFFIN, L. J. 2004. "Generations and Collective Memory" Revisited: Race, Region, and Memory of Civil Rights. *American Sociological Review*, 69: 544–57.

GRONKE, P., and NEWMAN, B. 2003. FDR to Clinton, Mueller to ?: A Field Essay on Presidential Approval. *Political Research Quarterly*, 56: 501–12.

HAY, R. P. 1969. The Glorious Departure of the American Patriarchs: Contemporary Reactions to the Deaths of Jefferson and Adam. *Journal of Southern History*, 35: 543–55.

HERSHEY, M. R., and HILL, D. B. 1975. Watergate and Preadults' Attitudes toward the President. *American Journal of Political Science*, 19: 703–26.

HESS, R. D., and EASTON, D. 1960. The Child's Changing Image of the President. *Public Opinion Quarterly*, 24: 632–44.

HODGSON, G. 1980. *All Things to All Men: The False Promise of the Modern American Presidency from Franklin D. Roosevelt to Ronald Reagan*. New York: Simon & Schuster.

HOEKSTRA, D. J. 1982. The "Textbook Presidency" Revisited. *Presidential Studies Quarterly*, 12: 159–65.

HUFBAUER, B. 2005. *Presidential Temples: How Memorials and Libraries Shape Public Memory*. Lawrence: University Press of Kansas.

HUGHES, E. 1974. *The Living Presidency*. New York: Penguin Books.

JACOBS, L. R., and SHAPIRO, R. Y. 2000. *Politicians Don't Pander: Political Manipulation and the Loss of Democratic Responsiveness*. Chicago: University of Chicago Press.

JACOBSON, G. 2004. *The Politics of Congressional Elections*. 6th edn. New York: Pearson Longman.

JENKINS-SMITH, H. C., SILVA, C. L., and WATERMAN, R. W. 2005. Micro- and Macro-Level Models of the Presidential Expectations Gap. *Journal of Politics*, 67: 690–715.

JENNINGS, M. K. 2002. Generation Units and the Student Protest Movement in the United States: An Intra- and Intergenerational Analysis. *Political Psychology*, 23: 303–24.

KELLERMAN, B. 1984. *The Political Presidency: Practice of Leadership from Kennedy through Reagan*. New York: Oxford University Press.

KERNELL, S. 1978. Explaining Presidential Popularity. *American Political Science Review*, 72: 506–22.

——1997. *Going Public: New Strategies of Presidential Leadership*. Washington, DC: CQ Press.

KINDER, D. R., PETERS, M. D., ABELSON, R. P., and FISKE, S. T. 1980. Presidential Prototypes. *Political Behavior*, 4: 315–37.

KRAMNICK, I. (ed.) 1987. *The Federalist Papers*. New York: Penguin Books.

KURTZ, H. 1998. *Spin Cycle: Inside the Clinton Propaganda Machine*. New York: Free Press.

LARACEY, M. 1998. The Presidential Newspaper: The Forgotten Way of Going Public. In *Speaking to the People: The Rhetorical Presidency in Historical Perspective*, ed. R. J. Ellis. Amherst: University of Massachusetts Press.

LEUCHTENBURG, W. E. 1983. *In the Shadow of FDR*. Ithaca, NY: Cornell University Press.

LIGHT, P. C. 1999. *The President's Agenda: Domestic Policy Choice from Kennedy to Clinton*, 3rd edn. Baltimore: Johns Hopkins University Press.

LOWI, T. 1979. *The End of Liberalism: The Second Republic of the United States*, 2nd edn. New York: W. W. Norton.

——1985. *The Personal President*. Ithaca, NY: Cornell University Press.

McCLOSKEY, R. G. 1963. The American Ideology. In *Continuing Crisis in American Politics*, ed. M. D. Irish. Englewood Cliffs, NJ: Prentice-Hall.

McCULLOUGH, D. 2001. *John Adams*. New York: Simon & Schuster.

McDONALD, F. 1994. *The American Presidency: An Intellectual History*. Lawrence: University of Kansas Press.

MALTESE, J. A. 1994. *Spin Control: The White House Office of Communications and the Management of Presidential News*, 2nd edn. Chapel Hill: University of North Carolina Press.

MARRA, R. F., OSTROM, C. W., JR., and SIMON, D. M. 1990. Foreign Policy and Presidential Popularity: Creating Windows of Opportunity in the Perpetual Election. *Journal of Conflict Resolution*, 34: 588–623.

MAYER, W. G. (ed.) 2008. *The Making of Presidential Candidates*. Lanham, MD: Rowman and Littlefield.

MEADOW, R. G. 1982. Information and Maturation in Children's Evaluation of Government Leadership during Watergate. *Western Political Quarterly*, 35: 539–53.

MILKIS, S., and NELSON, M. 2003. *The American Presidency: Origins and Development, 1776–2002*, 4th edn. Washington, DC: Congressional Quarterly.

MIROFF, B. 1995. Review of Thomas Langston's *With Reverence and Contempt*. *American Political Science Review*, 89: 1025–6.

——2006. The Presidential Spectacle. In *The Presidency and the Political System*, 8th edn., ed. M. NELSON. Washington, DC: CQ Press.

MUELLER, J. 1973. *War, Presidents, and Public Opinion*. New York: Wiley.

NEUSTADT, R. E. 1954. Presidency and Legislation: The Growth of Central Clearance. *American Political Science Review*, 48: 641–71.

——1955. Presidency and Legislation: Planning the President's Program. *American Political Science Review*, 49: 980–1021.

——1960. *Presidential Power*. New York: John Wiley.

——1990. *Presidential Power and the Modern Presidents*. New York: Free Press.

NEWMAN, B. 2002. Bill Clinton's Approval Ratings: The More Things Change, The More They Stay the Same. *Political Research Quarterly*, 55: 781–804.

——2003. Integrity and Presidential Approval. *Public Opinion Quarterly*, 67: 335–67.

NIEMI, R. G., and SMITH, J. 2001. Enrollments in High School Government Classes: Are We Short-Changing Both Citizenship and Political Science Training? *PS: Political Science and Politics,* 34: 281–7.

OSTROM, C. W., JR. and SIMON, D. M. 1985. Promise and Performance: A Dynamic Model of Presidential Popularity. *American Political Science Review,* 79: 334–58.

PEFFLEY, M. 1989. Presidential Image and Economic Performance: A Dynamic Analysis. *Political Behavior,* 11: 309–33.

PIOUS, R. 1979. *The American Presidency.* New York: Basic Books.

RIKER, W. H. 1984. The Heresthetics of Constitution-Making: The Presidency in 1787, with Comments on Determinism and Rational Choice. *American Political Science Review,* 78: 1–16.

ROCHE, J. P. 1961. The Founding Fathers: A Reform Caucus in Action. *American Political Science Review,* 55: 799–816.

ROOSEVELT, T. 2002. The Stewardship Presidency. In *Understanding the Presidency,* ed. J. Pfiffner and R. Davidson, 3rd edn. New York: Longman. Originally published 1913.

ROSEN, J. 2006. Bush's Leviathan State. *New Republic,* July 18 (online version).

ROSSITER, C. 1956. *The American Presidency.* New York: Harcourt, Brace, & World.

SABATO, L. J. 1991. *Feeding Frenzy: How Attack Journalism Has Transformed American Politics.* New York: Free Press.

SANCHEZ, J. M. 1996. Old Habits Die Hard: The Textbook Presidency is Alive and Well. *PS: Political Science and Politics,* 29: 63–6.

SCHLESINGER, A. M., JR. 1959. *The Coming of the New Deal.* Boston: Houghton Mifflin.

—— 1960. *The Politics of Upheaval.* Boston: Houghton Mifflin.

—— 1965. *A Thousand Days: John F. Kennedy in the White House.* Boston: Houghton Mifflin.

—— 1973. *The Imperial Presidency.* Boston: Houghton Mifflin.

SCHWARTZ, B. 1983. George Washington and the Whig Conception of Heroic Leadership. *American Sociological Review,* 48: 18–33.

—— 1987. *George Washington: The Making of an American Symbol.* New York: Free Press.

SEARS, D. O., and FUNK, C. L. 1999. Evidence of the Long-Term Persistence of Adults' Political Predispositions. *Journal of Politics,* 61: 1–28.

SIGEL, R. S. 1966. Image of the American Presidency: Part II of an Exploration into Popular Views of Presidential Power. *Midwest Journal of Political Science,* 10: 123–37.

—— 1968. Image of a President: Some Insights into the Political Views of Children. *American Political Science Review,* 62: 216–26.

SIMON, D. M., and OSTROM, C. W., JR. 1988. The Politics of Prestige: Popular Support and the Modern Presidency. *Presidential Studies Quarterly,* 18: 741–59.

—— —— and MARRA, R. F. 1991. The President, Referendum Voting, and Subnational Elections in the United States. *American Political Science Review,* 85: 1177–92.

SKOWRONEK, S. 1993. *The Politics Presidents Make: Leadership from John Adams to George Bush.* Cambridge, MA: Harvard University Press.

—— 2003. Presidency and American Political Development: A Third Look. *Presidential Studies Quarterly,* 32: 743–52.

STANLEY, H. W., and NIEMI, R. G. 2003. *Vital Statistics on American Politics, 2003–2004.* Washington, DC: CQ Press.

STEERS, E., JR. 2001. *Blood on the Moon: The Assassination of Abraham Lincoln.* Lexington: University Press of Kentucky.

SUNDQUIST, J. L. 1981. *The Decline and Resurgence of Congress.* Washington, DC: Brookings Institution.

TAFT, W. H. 2002. The Strict Constructionist Presidency. In *Understanding the Presidency,* ed. J. Pfiffner and R. Davidson, 3rd edn. New York: Longman. Originally published 1916.

TULIS, J. K. 1987. *The Rhetorical Presidency*. Princeton, NJ: Princeton University Press.

—— 1995. The Two Constitutional Presidencies. In *The Presidency and the Political System*, ed. M. Nelson. Washington, DC: CQ Press.

TYLER, T. R. 1982. Personalization in Attributing Responsibility for National Problems to the President. *Political Behavior*, 4: 379–99.

US Bureau of the Census. 1989. *Statistical Abstract of the United States, 1988*. Washington, DC: Government Printing Office.

VALENTINO, N. C., and SEARS, D. O. 1998. Event-Driven Political Communication and the Preadult Socialization of Partisanship. *Political Behavior*, 20: 127–54.

WATERMAN, R. W. (ed.) 1993. *The Presidency Reconsidered*. Itasca, IL: F. E. Peacock Publishers.

—— Jenkins-Smith, H. C., and Silva, C. L. 1999. The Expectations Gap Thesis: Public Attitudes toward an Incumbent President. *Journal of Politics*, 61: 944–66.

WAYNE, S. 1978. *The Legislative Presidency*. New York: Harper & Row.

—— 1982. Great Expectations: What People Want from Presidents. In *Rethinking the Presidency*, ed. T. E. Cronin. Boston: Little Brown.

WOODWARD, B. 1994. *The Agenda: Inside the Clinton White House*. New York: Simon & Schuster.

—— 2000. *Maestro: Greenspan's Fed and the American Boom*. New York: Simon & Schuster.

—— 2006. *State of Denial*. New York: Simon & Schuster.

CHAPTER 8

....

PRESIDENTIAL RESPONSIVENESS TO PUBLIC OPINION

....

JAMES N. DRUCKMAN
LAWRENCE R. JACOBS

ONE of the defining features of the "modern" presidency is its pervasive public presence. It is unusual to turn on the television or open a newspaper without seeing the president. No other individual receives as much sustained and intense news coverage and public attention as the president.

The emergence of a public presidency is relatively recent. Before modern transportation and communications, the president's ability to reach Americans was restricted. White House use of these new opportunities included Herbert Hoover's appointment of the first press secretary; Franklin Roosevelt's decisions in the 1930s to use a new media form (radio) and strengthen existing ties with newspapers and film; and John Kennedy's introduction of television coverage of press conferences.

The new technological capacity became attractive to presidents when it served their political interests. Norms of governance that focused them on avoiding public promotion in favor of private negotiations with legislators and key interest groups generally constrained presidents early in the twentieth century. Presidents after Franklin Roosevelt, however, increasingly relied on their ability to appeal over the heads of Congress as a rare opportunity to augment their political capital and to unify divided elites. Kernell (1997) argues that changing institutional incentives in a more atomized environment, where power is dispersed, motivated presidents to widen their public presence. By so doing, presidents could pressure other elites in Washington to coalesce around their leadership and policy proposals.

The broader political system encourages and sustains the public presidency. Indeed, the media have developed a "beat" to cover the president's every word and action, and Americans have become accustomed to looking to the president as the principal policy maker and representative of the country.

Most research on the public presidency focuses on the direct and often unmediated appeals that modern presidents make to the general public. For example, these analyses track the frequency and type of presidential speeches and travel (e.g., Simon and Ostrom 1989). What makes the "public presidency" public, though, is not only its outward-oriented activities but also its emergence as the representative of the country. Citizens look to the president as a symbol of America, and his actions serve as a general expression of citizens' preferences. A favorite pastime of the media involves comparing the president's policies with public support. Whether the president's policies respond to public opinion is now a routine question.

Although the press now routinely covers and discusses presidential responsiveness to public opinion, the Framers of the US Constitution explicitly positioned the president to be independent of public opinion. The president was to be politically free to pursue what policies and administrative decisions he believed best furthered the country's overall interests. Most notably, the Electoral College made the selection of the president dependent on the independent judgment of the electors rather than on the popular vote. The president also received separate constitutional authority to free him from the risk in a parliamentary system of having the legislative branch bring him down through a vote of "no confidence." The Framers held a particular definition of "representation" in mind when they designed the president's role—he would represent the country through his independent decisions and as a symbol of the country who would, for example, welcome visiting heads of state.

This chapter examines the president's emergence as a "representative." It reviews different definitions of representation and examines research into the modern definition of presidential representativeness—the president's responsiveness to public opinion. We also highlight a number of complications that studies of responsiveness face, including the questions of whether citizens even possess "real preferences," what specific aspects of preferences leaders respond to, whose preferences they consider, and whether citizens' preferences merely reflect those of elites.

DEMOCRATIC REPRESENTATION
AND RESPONSIVENESS

The term democracy comes from two Greek words: "demos," meaning people, and "kratos," meaning rule. Hence, democracy is rule by the people. In its purest Athenian form, democratic government ensures citizens equal opportunities to directly participate in proposing and deciding on all laws. Modern democracies rely, instead, on a system of representation. In formal terms, the electoral system constitutes an institutional mechanism for millions of American citizens to select representatives who go to Washington, DC, on their behalf (see Urbinati 2006, 3).

The significance of electoral representation is open to divergent interpretations. The populist interpretation expects elections to foster government responsiveness to the citizens' preferences. Dahl (1971), for instance, insists that "a key characteristic of a democracy is the continuing responsiveness of the government to the preferences of its citizens." Elections create a concrete institutional mechanism for inducing responsive representatives through two linked processes: elected officials who are unresponsive to their constituents can be removed, and those who are intent on retaining their seats are motivated to respond to citizens' preferences so that they will not be removed (Dahl 1989).

The populist definition of representation—where the representative serves as a delegate for his or her constituents—faces, however, several sharply different alternative interpretations. The "trustee" view insists that representatives are elected to be responsible for (rather than to) citizens. Their job is to advance citizens' interests rather than respond to their often ill-informed wishes. As Burke (1949) explains in an often-cited speech to the electors of Bristol during the 1774 election to the British Parliament, "Your representative owes you, not his industry only, but his judgment; and he betrays, instead of serving you, if he sacrifices it to your opinion." Elections, in this trustee view, are a "method" for leadership selection: voters choose among competing candidates and then retreat to allow the deciders to make policy (Schumpeter 1947).

Pitkin (1967) reminds us that there are several other conceptions of "representation" that are not directly tied to elections. Representation can also occur, for example, through objects (e.g., flags or crowns) or people (e.g., heads of state) that "stand for" a body of people. People often salute flags or give them respect, for instance, because of what they symbolize. Leaders can create new forms of symbolic representation; "ground zero" in New York City, for instance, has been defined as standing for American resolve to fight terrorism. Individual leaders like modern presidents often attempt to construct an image of themselves as standing for the country's deepest shared commitments.

Indeed, the tendency to equate representation with democracy is relatively recent. For much of recorded history, a king or other ruler was authorized by heredity, by a divinity, or by some other higher power to serve as a representative. There was no expectation that rulers would respond to the wishes or wants of those who lived within their territory.

There are, then, competing conceptions of representation. A key feature differentiating these contending interpretations is whether and to what extent representatives *respond* to the expressed opinions of citizens. According to the populist definitions of representation, evidence that the decisions of elected officials correspond to their constituents' preferences indicates responsiveness which is required for adequate representation. By contrast, others have conceptualized representation in terms of symbols or independent judgment, assuming little or even no correspondence between the substantive policy decisions of government officials and the preferences of citizens.

Much recent work investigates whether and to what extent presidents respond to national public opinion—that is, whether their policies correspond with the policies or general ideology favored by most Americans. At its core, this growing body of research focuses on defining the *nature* of the public presidency: genuinely populist, as presidents often claim, or symbolic leaders and independent trustees that are unresponsive to Americans.

THE PRESIDENT AND PUBLIC OPINION

Scholars employ two general approaches to empirically studying opinion representation or responsiveness (Wlezien and Soroka 2007). One perspective focuses on the relationship between the public's policy preferences and system-level (collective) policy outcomes (rather than the individual actions of representatives). The other (dyadic) approach looks at the relationship between an individual representative, such as a member of Congress or the president, and his or her constituents' attitudes.

These studies, of course, vary in their focus and include explorations into the responsiveness of general public policy, of specific legislators, and of the chief executive. The extent to which the chief executive—in the US context, the president—responds to the public's preferences is of particular interest when it comes to questions of how democracies function.

As the most public and influential government official, the president's connection to public opinion is particularly important in sorting out normative debates about representation and empirically examining whether he is a leader or a follower of public opinion (Rottinghaus 2006, 720). The answer has significance for assessments of the policy-making process. As Canes-Wrone (2006, 192) observes, "The relationship between a chief executive and his or her public can significantly affect the ways in which formal institutions operate in practice."

Research on presidential representation tends to focus on national public opinion because of the national basis of his constituency. Wlezien and Soroka (2007, 12) explain that "U.S. Presidential responsiveness to public preferences is conceptually quite simple: The president represents a national constituency and is expected to follow national preferences." Analyses often explore the association between national opinion on various policies and presidential policy proposals or policy statements in his public speeches.

Presidential Understanding of Public Opinion

For a president to respond to the public's preferences, he must possess some knowledge about those preferences. Although various methods are available—including assessing constituent letters and interest group activities (Herbst 1994; Lee 2003; Rottinghaus 2007)—public opinion surveys from representative samples of voters constitute the most straightforward method for measuring citizens' preferences. Manza and Cook (2002a) explain, "Prior to the 1930s and the development of modern survey research, there were few direct ways to discern public attitudes on specific policy questions (Converse 1986). Since the mid-1930s, however, and especially in recent decades, the volume and sophistication of polling data and survey research has increased dramatically."

The increase in information about citizens' preferences affects the incentives and expectations of the president (e.g., Jacobs and Shapiro 1994, 2000). Specifically, since most presidents presumably hope to be reelected (when eligible), secure a place in history, and/or affect policy, it behooves them to be informed about citizens' opinions (since citizens vote and evaluate, and their evaluations affect the president's policy power; e.g., Kernell 1997). The assumption of journalists and researchers is that "greater information [about public opinion] facilitates responsiveness by giving political leaders the capacity to make reasoned judgments about where the public stands" (Manza and Cook 2002a; also see Geer 1996; Wlezien and Soroka 2007).

The political incentives to track public opinion create significant motivations for representatives—particularly presidents who have a massive constituency and relatively abundant resources—to develop private polling operations that give them control over the survey's content and access to information that may not be widely accessible (Jacobs and Shapiro 1995; Eisinger 2003; Heith 2004).

The Rise of Presidential Polling

Private presidential polling as a routine part of White House operations started in earnest with John Kennedy and then sharply increased in its amount and quality in the 1960s. The expansion of the White House's public opinion apparatus is most plainly evident in the number of its polls. Louis Harris supplied fifteen private polling reports to the Kennedy White House, often by relying upon ad hoc arrangements such as "piggy-backing" questions on surveys sponsored by other clients. Oliver Quayle, whom Harris had recommended to replace him when he became a pollster for major media organizations, provided most of the 110 surveys that Lyndon Johnson received. Nixon escalated the number of private surveys to 173, relying on a stable of trustworthy pollsters who had Republican "bona fides" to conduct his research, including established firms like Opinion Research Corporation and new upstarts—Robert Teeter (who later co-directed a polling firm that worked for the *Wall Street Journal* and directed George H. W. Bush's 1992 campaign) and Richard Wirthlin (who polled for President Reagan). Wirthlin conducted at least 204 private surveys for Reagan, although more probably remain to be publicly released by the Reagan Presidential Library.

We do not have archival records of subsequent presidential polling. Partial archival records, interviews, and journalistic accounts suggest, however, that private polling remains a substantial operation and that it continues to be closely integrated into the White House's decision making during the presidencies of George H. W. Bush, Bill Clinton, and George W. Bush.

There have been two changes in the extent and purpose of presidential polling since Kennedy. First, there has been an expansion of presidential polling not only in terms of the number of polls but also in terms of the amount of information collected and the sophistication of the instrument design (Jacobs and Shapiro 1995). Second, there has been a shift from polling on the public's policy preferences to polling also on its non-policy evaluations related to personal image and appeal (Jacobs and Burns 2004)—a potentially potent basis for appealing to voters that connects with more symbolic forms of representation that Pitkin (1967) examined.

Are Citizens' Preferences Real?

The focus on public preferences for more or less of something is sensible insofar as it echoes both theories of political strategy and assumptions of democratic theorists of representation. Numerous empirical studies of responsiveness point to Downs's (1957) median voter theorem as a starting point. The studies seek to explore the extent to which representatives adopt issue positions that correspond with those of the typical (e.g., median) voter (e.g., Page and Shapiro 1983, 175; Riker 1996, 5; Jacobs and Shapiro 2000, 13; Manza and Cook 2002a, 2002b). In this sense, candidates act responsively for strategic reasons; they try to adopt favorable positions on particular policies. They are political marketers who are highly attuned to consumer demands and intent on pinpointing and then emulating (i.e., moving in a congruent direction) the policy preferences of voters.

That citizens have well-defined directional preferences on various issues also is a standard starting point for democratic theorists. Bartels (2003, 50) explains that "most liberal democratic theorists... assume as a matter of course that citizens do, in fact, have definite preferences and that the primary problem of democracy is to assure that a government will respond appropriately to those preferences." Bartels points to Miller's (1992, 55) statement as an example: "democracy is predominantly understood as involving the aggregation of independently formed preferences."[1]

Yet, certain research on public opinion formation calls this basic assumption into question. Citizens may lack the information and motivation to form even basic

---

[1] For example, Canes-Wrone (2006, 23) begins her work on the relationship among presidents, policy, and citizens with the premise that "the electorate... [is] assumed to have these types of well-ordered preferences."

preferences in the first place. Bartels (2003, 48–9) nicely summarizes this perspective: "many citizens 'do not have meaningful beliefs, even on issues that formed the basis for intense political controversy among elites for substantial periods of time' (Converse 1964: 245) ... [even if] citizens have 'meaningful beliefs' ... those beliefs are not sufficiently complete and coherent to serve as a satisfactory starting point for democratic theory." If this is the case, "public opinion ... cannot constitute an independent causal factor" (Manza and Cook 2002a).

We see four possible reactions to these questions about whether there is a tangible, sensible, and relatively autonomous set of public preferences for policy makers to follow. First, the challenge to citizen competence might lead to the conclusion that presidential responsiveness to public opinion is unrealistic and, indeed, not possible because of the absence of "meaningful beliefs." The correlations of public opinion and policy that do occur might well be spurious. Wlezien and Soroka (2007, 11) explain that correlations do "not mean that politicians actually respond to changing public preferences, for it may be they and the public both respond to something else ... All we can say for sure is that the research captures policy responsiveness in a statistical sense." Instead of responsiveness, observed relationships could stem from the reverse—where it is the representatives shaping or manipulating their constituents' preferences—or from another exogenous factor, such as outside interest groups or world events (e.g., Jacobs and Shapiro 2000; Bartels 2003, 9; Jacobs and Page 2005).

A second, contrary, reaction is to lower the stringent standards for independent, well-defined policy preferences. Given the everyday demands on citizens and the unevenness of citizen cognitive capacity, individuals can use shortcuts to form preferences. For instance, the latest news reports on rising unemployment might provide a cue for voters that leads them to be supportive of government programs to retrain laid-off workers (Sniderman, Brody, and Fetlock 1991; Popkin 1994; Lupia and McCubbins 1998). In other words, citizens may harbor reasoned preferences even if they are not based on an intense scrutiny of facts and logic.

Third, one could argue that although most individuals lack coherent preferences on specific policies, they do have a general sense of whether they want "more" or "less" government (i.e., general ideology). This is the track taken by Erikson, MacKuen, and Stimson (2002, xxi, 289–91), who explain that "political leaders regularly ignore expressed public preferences on [specific policies] ... knowing that the preferences arise from a weak grasp of the central facts." Instead, "it is the general public disposition, the mood, which policy makers must monitor" (also see Kingdon 1984, 69, 89–91; Zaller 1992, 1998).

The fourth approach, and the one we endorse, opts for a middle road, or what Manza and Cook (2002a) call a "contingent view" (also see Hill and Hurley 1999). On some specific issues—particularly salient ones—the public is likely to possess reasoned and consistent opinions to which representatives have an incentive to respond. On other issues, the public's views may be more diffuse, in which case their specific policy opinions will be less meaningful. However, even in these latter domains, constituents' preferences are best construed not as the direct product of elite manipulation, but rather as reflecting numerous influences including their values, background, and interpersonal associations, as well as elite influence (and, under some conditions, manipulation). This view comports with recent research on public opinion that identifies clear limits to elite influence and portrays citizens as systematic (but not infallible) in the ways they process information and construct preferences, even though they may not regularly hold definitive, independent preferences (Page and Shapiro 1992; Chong 1996; Price and Tewksbury 1997; Brewer 2001; Druckman 2001; Edwards 2003; Chong and Druckman 2007a, 2007b, forthcoming; Druckman and Nelson 2003; Althaus and Kim 2006).

The notion of public opinion as contingent and variable in its degree of consistency and rationality revises much of the theoretical and empirical debate about representation. The tendency to define representation as a binary choice between elected officials who respond or do not respond to public preferences faces two challenges. First, as Pitkin (1967) suggests, representation has long existed without reference to public preferences or the expectation of popular sovereignty. Second, and more directly connected with the nature of public opinion, the formation of citizen policy preferences is not monolithic as a process or in terms of its outcomes. On salient issues on which the collective public has reached reasoned preferences and maintains them consistently, the potential for responsiveness is real. Without these conditions, responsiveness will be more difficult.

PRESIDENTIAL RESPONSIVENESS

We now turn to a review of five major and exemplary bodies of research that examine the *extent* and *nature* of presidential representation (also see, e.g., Jacobs 1992; Jacobs and Shapiro 1995, 2000; Cohen 1997; Burstein 2003). These works show how the president responds to what he knows about citizens' preferences.

First, Erikson, MacKuen, and Stimson (2002, i) offer a comprehensive model of American politics, exploring "interactions between citizen evaluations and preferences, government activity and policy, and how the combined acts of citizens and governments influence one another over time." Part of their model involves an investigation into presidential responsiveness to public opinion (from 1956 to 1996). To measure public opinion, they rely on an aggregated, global measure of policy liberalism that combines more than 1,500 survey questions; the measure captures the public's domestic policy leanings. Erickson et al. measure presidential policy activity or output by using the policy positions (as measured by interest group ratings) of legislators from the president's party who also tend to support presidential proposals (297). They report a strong relationship between presidential behavior and aggregated public opinion, suggesting a high level of responsiveness, both across presidents and within presidential terms. The authors conclude that "for the presidency... a shift in *Mood* yields an almost immediate shift in *Policy Activity*... Like antelope in an open field, [presidents] cock their ears and focus their full attention on the slightest sign of danger" (emphasis in original) (2002, 319–20).

Second, Canes-Wrone (2006) offers a more nuanced depiction of presidential responsiveness (also see Canes-Wrone and Shotts 2004). She constructs a formal theory to derive hypotheses about the conditions under which presidents will respond to the public. This leads to the prediction that "policy congruence between a president's positions and public opinion should be more likely the sooner the president faces a context for reelection" (2006, 159). She also expects increased congruency by unpopular presidents if the president's popularity rises as an election approaches (i.e., the relatively unpopular president's popularity is trending upward); in contrast, popular presidents follow the public when their popularity drops (i.e., is trending downward, in the face of a pending election) (2006, 159). To test these predictions, Canes-Wrone uses annual observations on numerous budgetary issues from the Nixon to the Clinton presidency. She measures public preferences with survey questions that asked citizens whether spending should be increased, decreased, or not changed on a given issue, and presidential activity with the president's proposed budgetary change on the issue. When a majority of the public agrees with the president's preference (e.g., both want increased spending on the issue), there is congruence (i.e., responsiveness); otherwise there is incongruence.

Canes-Wrone's research strongly supports her predictions—the president's congruence with national public opinion is much more likely as an election approaches, particularly among popular presidents when their popularity is decreasing, or, alternatively, with unpopular presidents when their popularity happens to be on the rise. She also finds that responsiveness in the second term, where reelection is not possible, declines (e.g., there is not an election proximity effect): without the prospect of facing an upcoming election, the fear of being punished by voters disappears as does the motivation to maintain favorable public approval. Canes-Wrone's findings usefully shift research from whether or not the president is responsive to investigations of the conditions under which the president responds. Moreover, her finding that responsiveness depends on the interaction between electoral cycle *and* presidential popularity suggests some revision to other responsiveness studies (e.g., Geer 1996; Cohen 1997; Manza and Cook 2002a, 2002b; Jacobs and Shapiro 2000).

Hers of course is not the final word, as suggested by a third body of recent research. Rottinghaus (2006) uses a distinct dataset and finds slightly different dynamics than Canes-Wrone. Whereas Canes-Wrone uses budget proposals to measure presidential action, Rottinghaus looks at presidential rhetoric. He performed a content analysis on a sample of public statements by presidents from Eisenhower through Clinton. For each statement, he recorded the policy discussed and the position taken. He links these data to issue-specific public opinion survey questions from at least one year prior to the president's statement. He investigates how often and when the president takes a congruent (i.e., responsive) position to a majority of the public (also see, e.g., Page and Shapiro 1983, 1992; Jacobs and Shapiro 1995). Rottinghaus (2006, 724–5) emphasizes that, unlike policy proposals made to Congress (which may reflect political compromises in anticipation of congressional response), politics is less likely to intercede on presidential positions as expressed in rhetoric (i.e., stated positions may more accurately reflect the president's true preference since political compromises may be less relevant). Also, the public's opinions are more likely to be meaningful on various issues rather than "arcane and not well understood" spending questions (also see Wlezien and Soroka 2007). Rhetoric also has the advantage of capturing the public persona of the president (Rottinghaus 2006, 720).

Consistent with others (e.g., Cohen 1997, 1999; Erikson, McKuen, and Stimson 2002; Canes-Wrone 2006), Rottinghaus (2006, 725) reports a high degree of responsiveness with 70 percent of the cases displaying a match between the president's positions and the prior opinion of the majority of the public. He also reports that the level of congruency has remained fairly constant over time and does not vary based on the importance of an issue. In contrast to Canes-Wrone, Rottinghaus reports marginal differences between first- and second-term presidents—"second-term presidents are as affected by public trends as first-term presidents" (2006, 727).[2] Thus, despite the impossibility of being reelected, second-term presidents respond as if they were running; this presumably stems from concern about "their historical legacy [and] helping to elect their successor" (Rottinghaus 2006, 729). The different findings by Canes-Wrone and Rottinghaus regarding second-term responsiveness are intriguing, suggesting possible differences across types of presidential behavior (e.g., budget proposals versus rhetorical position taking). Each study offers a substantial advance to our understanding of the conditions that promote or prohibit responsiveness (e.g., it depends on the type of responsiveness, venue of responsiveness, election cycle, popularity, etc.).

A fourth body of research extends a long-standing social science exploration of the role of information in decision making by investigating the *type* of information on public opinion that presidents decide to collect and use. Instead of exploring the conditions of responsiveness, Druckman and Jacobs (2006) investigate the type of public opinion to which presidents respond (also see Stevens 2002). Specifically, they ask: when do presidents rely on the public's opinion about specific policies (e.g., increase or decrease welfare spending) as opposed to the public's general support for more or less government (i.e., general ideological predilection)? (Rottinghaus and Canes-Wrone use the former type of data while Erickson et al. use the latter.)

Druckman and Jacobs argue that prior work that fails to consider multiple types of opinion may lead to misleading conclusions; for example, if a president tracks issue-specific opinions, then an empirical analysis looking only at aggregate trends may lead to faulty conclusions about responsiveness. Of even more importance is that the alternative measures of opinion carry distinct normative implications, with the issue-specific measures corresponding "with a populist version of democracy where policymakers exhibit respect for citizen competence" and the aggregate measure

---

[2] He also finds that presidents "with above average popularity in the first half of their second terms are significantly *more likely* to make congruent statements than when their popularity is below average" (2006, 728). This is the opposite of what Cane-Wrone finds. Rottinghaus also reports some intriguing variations in responsiveness based on communication media (e.g., television statements in the first term are less likely to be congruent).

treating citizens as if they are "relatively limited in their capacity to understand particular issues" (Druckman and Jacobs 2006, 454).

Druckman and Jacobs focus on Nixon's presidency and use a presidential action variable analogous to the one employed by Rottinghaus—that is, issue positions as expressed in public statements (also see Hobolt and Klemmensen 2006). On the public opinion side, Druckman and Jacobs turn to Nixon's own private opinion polls that they collected from presidential archives. These data have numerous advantages. For example, prior to deciding whether to respond to public opinion, presidents decide whether to monitor opinion in the first place. They make decisions about which data to collect, which itself provides an indication of responsiveness (also see Burstein 2003).[3] These data also reveal the specific types of data presidents collect, which, as we will discuss, suggest that presidents respond to multiple dimensions of opinions and not just directional issue preferences (e.g., they also respond to image perceptions). Finally, private polls offer unparalleled access into the inner workings of the president's decisions; these are the data that the president actually receives when deciding whether or not to respond (rather than publicly available data that may not match what the president sees).

Druckman and Jacobs find that when opinion data on specific policies were collected and thus available, the president relied on them and not on the general ideology data. On less important issues, however, the president often chose not to collect policy-specific data and instead relied on general ideology data. In short, presidents respond to different types of public opinion data on salient and less salient issues (also see Wlezien 2004).

The four bodies of recent research that we have reviewed all examine one interpretation of representation—whether elected officials respond to the policy preferences of citizens. The findings suggest that under varying political and institutional conditions presidents behave or give the appearance of serving as the public's delegate, responding to their wishes: their level and type of responsiveness vary depending on the electoral cycle, popularity, issue salience, and venue. These results appear to contradict the hopes of the Constitution's Framers and a range of political thinkers (from Burke to Schumpeter) that presidents (and perhaps other elected officials) would pursue their own judgment independent of public opinion.

The fifth body of research widens the conception of representation to examine the efforts of presidents to "stand for" citizens through static symbols and through their efforts to fashion particular impressions of themselves as embodying attractive values and traits. Recognizing that citizens' evaluations of presidential performance depend in substantial ways on what citizens think about the president's image—including performance traits such as strength and competence (e.g., Funk 1999)—Druckman, Jacobs, and Ostermeier (2004) explore how presidents work to improve image perceptions.

---

[3] For example, Rottinghaus's analyses are limited to the issues on which public survey organizations collected data, which presumably include only salient issues. Thus, his finding that salience does not moderate responsiveness may be a function of his focus on issues already salient enough to warrant data collection.

Using data from the Nixon administration, the authors show that the president significantly responded to the public's image perceptions. For example, Nixon increased his public comments on foreign affairs (i.e., he emphasized foreign affairs) when polls revealed the public's decreasing ratings of his performance traits. He specifically increased his comments on dovish diplomatic policy to counter the slide in the public's evaluations of his competence, while he emphasized both diplomatic and hawkish military policy to bolster the public's perceptions of him as strong. That Nixon used this approach to boost perceptions of his performance attributes was echoed in his own campaign's internal deliberation. For example, Nixon instructed his team to use his "major accomplishments: Cambodia, the Middle East, and the Vietnam Speech... [to] get across the courage, the independence, the boldness... of the President [and allow them] to come through" (excerpt from Haldeman 1994, Dec. 3, 1970). (Druckman and Holmes 2004 show that such foreign policy emphasis does in fact enhance impressions of the president's strength.)

This finding accentuates the importance of considering broad conceptions of representation. Presidents not only respond to the public's directional issue preferences, but they also react to changes in the public's perceptions of the president's persona. This is akin to a form of symbolic representation with responsiveness to preferences about image and not substantive policy. Interestingly, it also reveals the inherent link between image and issues insofar as presidents use issues (e.g., foreign policy efforts) to build image (Jacobs and Shapiro 1994). They do this via issue emphasis and not taking a policy position *per se*, with the goal of influencing (or manipulating) citizens' perceptions. In short, they respond to public opinion about their image by emphasizing specific issues in an attempt to shape subsequent public perceptions.

The vibrant and wide-ranging research on the president's different forms of responsiveness has made important contributions to the study of political representation in general and the investigation of the public presidency. It also raises significant questions for future research. The different data used in these studies in terms of the independent variable (i.e. the types of public opinion information) and the dependent variable (e.g., budgetary proposals and presidential rhetoric) accentuate the importance of attending to possible variations across types of presidential behaviors.

Future work can also contribute by examining whether citizens actually possess preferences in the first place. Indeed, nearly all studies of responsiveness, including the ones discussed here, largely conceive of preferences as the individuals' *directional* predilection, such as their support or opposition for a specific policy, or their liberal or conservative leanings. For instance, individuals have a preference to either increase or decrease taxes, extend or limit abortion rights, or for more or less government in general (in the case of Erikson et al.'s aggregated approach). Researchers then gather available survey data on the public's policy preferences and explore the degree to which outcomes reflect the direction of their preferences, implicitly assuming the preferences exist and are coherent.[4]

---

[4] Erikson, MacKuen, and Stimson (2002, 13–14) list policy agreement, along with competence and control, as three attributes citizens want from government.

CITIZENS' PREFERENCES AND DIMENSIONS
OF RESPONSIVENESS

One of the most daunting challenges for research on presidents as political representatives is accounting for the multiple dimensions of representation and of public evaluations. From the perspectives of citizens, an individual's evaluation of the president might consist of a combination of negative and positive evaluations of the president on different dimensions. An individual, for instance, may believe that the president holds the correct position on reducing welfare spending but lacks strength as a leader. If this individual supports both the welfare position and leadership skills, his or her attitude toward the president will depend on the relative magnitudes of that support for each, discounted by the relative salience or weights assigned respectively to the welfare position and the policy attribute of leadership strength (Enelow and Hinich 1984; Nelson and Oxley 1999; Druckman and Lupia 2006; Chong and Druckman 2007a). Even this illustration is relatively simple; the public often holds views about more than one policy or individual personality trait (i.e. they are also concerned about taxes and a foreign war as well as perceived honesty and empathy). A key element in this complex and multidimensional evaluation by citizens is the relative weight they assign to particular policies and personality traits; this helps to simplify their evaluation and make it more manageable.

The nature of citizen evaluations of presidents has an important implication for presidential representation. There are multiple dimensions of public opinions and evaluations to which the president can respond. Conventional studies—including all of those discussed above—look only at one of these elements: directional issue positions. Yet, there are others, including image and salience.

As we have mentioned, voters, and consequentially politicians, including the president, care about more than issues (e.g., Page 1978; Popkin 1994). They also expect officeholders to hold certain personal qualities including leadership skills, competence, trust, and empathy (Funk 1999). Voters prefer officeholders who possess each of these traits, and thus, responsiveness on image may be more salience based. For example, if citizens highly value competence, the president might work to develop expertise in certain areas (e.g., Druckman, Jacobs, and Ostermeier 2004). Failure to consider image responsiveness could lead one to conclude that a corrupt politician is "responsive" if he or she takes congruent issue positions.

Officeholders also may vary their responsiveness to issues or images that voters find more or less salient. For example, imagine that citizens care overwhelmingly about tax cuts—all other issues are far less important. Then, if the president takes a position that differs from citizens' preferences on tax cuts but that matches citizens' opinions on dozens of other low-salience issues, the conclusion might be that the president is generally responsive, even if he completely ignores taxes as an issue (e.g., failure to take action on an issue may mean the issue is not included in the data analyzed for responsiveness). Yet, on the tax issue that really matters, he is not responsive. Although analyses of representation often do not consider the interaction of responsiveness and salience, the little research that has been done reports that presidents are more directionally responsive on salient issues. This research does not, however, explicitly take account of whether the president focuses on the key issues in the first place (although see Hobolt and Klemmensen 2006)—that is, presidents may be initially unresponsive, perhaps as they attempt to reframe issues before moving into line with intense public concerns. A full account of responsiveness and representation requires attention to the multiple dimensions that make up citizens' opinions. The idea that citizens' preferences consist of multiple elements also is consistent with the public opinion data presidents tend to collect in their private polling operations. They do not only track directional issue positions, but they also carefully follow salience and image (e.g., Jacobs and Burns 2004).

Whose Preferences?

The president represents a "national constituency" and thus might be expected to "follow national preferences" (Wlezien and Soroka 2007, 12). Empirical studies, including those discussed above, operationalize public opinion by taking the majority view on an issue (e.g., Rottinghaus 2006) or the average percentage of the public supporting a policy (e.g., Druckman and Jacobs 2006). Although this approach is of obvious normative importance, it may neglect how responsiveness works in practice.

Ample evidence shows that distinct subgroups of citizens, particularly the wealthy and educated, participate in elections and a range of other political activities at far higher rates than others (Verba, Schlozman, and Brady 1995). Moreover, a growing body of research supplies systematic evidence of the influence of the economically advantaged on government actions. One study of income-weighted preferences and roll-call votes cast by US Senators in the late 1980s and early 1990s finds that Senators are consistently much more responsive to the views of affluent constituents than to the views of the poor (Bartels 2005). Another study reports that the American political system is a great deal more responsive to the preferences of the rich than to the preferences of the poor (Gilens 2005). A third study suggests that the policy stands of foreign policy decision makers are most influenced by business leaders, with the general public exerting no consistent significant effect and policy experts largely serving as conduits for the views of other elites, including business (Jacobs and Page 2005).

Although presidents present themselves as the symbol of the nation, the reality is that they are prone to privilege discrete segments of the country—especially those who are already advantaged. In one recent paper, Druckman and Jacobs (2007) investigate this type of segmented representation by pinpointing the groups to which Reagan responded during his presidency. Reagan's goal was to construct a new conservative coalition—one that would expand Barry Goldwater's economic libertarianism to include social conservatives (especially born-again Protestants and

Baptist fundamentalists), "supply-siders" who favored sharply lower taxes (even at the risk of higher budget deficits), and more general philosophical conservatives. Druckman and Jacobs examine the relationship between Reagan's publicly stated positions and the issue positions of these groups as revealed in Reagan's private polls. The authors find that Reagan responded to certain subgroups on issues of particular appeal to these groups. For example, on issues involving family values and crime, Reagan took policy positions that correlated only with those taken by fundamentalist Baptists and Christians (and not the general public). Similarly, on defense spending, Reagan responded particularly to the opinions of conservative Republicans, and on economic issues, he staked out positions consonant with those of high-income groups (e.g., more likely to be supply-siders).

These results suggest that presidents respond differentially to specific subgroups, based on strategic considerations. Moreover, these subgroups vary across not only economic but also political dimensions (also see Cohen 2006; Rottinghaus n.d.). Along these lines, Edwards (2004) shows how the very institutions of electing the president (i.e., the Electoral College) further contribute to politicians ignoring numerous groups; for example, despite its intent, the Electoral College fails to protect the interests of small states or racial minorities (in terms of ensuring presidential attention).

Future work needs to further identify which subgroups (e.g., different income groups, particular states, or ideological conservatives or liberals) matter most to a particular president and then isolate the distinct opinions of those groups. Identifying influential subgroups has normative implications in terms of who is and who is not being represented. The reality of representation is that all preferences are not treated equally.

Who Responds to Whom?

A good deal of democratic theory and research on political representation starts with the premise that the public possesses "independently formed preferences" (Bartels 2003, 50; also see Miller 1992, 55). This flies in the face of a massive amount of research showing that the preferences of citizens depend in part on elite action and rhetoric (e.g., Druckman and Lupia 2000). And, of course, presidents have incentives to shape public opinion given the purported relationship between opinion and policy outcomes (e.g., Erikson, MacKuen, and Stimson 2002; Manza and Cook 2002a, 2002b), the possible electoral consequences of public opinion, as well as the potential importance of the public's approval of the president for the president's power and policy-making success (e.g., Neustadt 1960; Edwards 1976).

While some suggest that "presidential drama," such as the occurrence of a major speech, can impact public opinion (e.g., Brace and Hinckley 1993), more recent evidence suggests this may not be the case (e.g., Edwards 2003). Presidential initiatives—such as pushing for a war—also can affect public opinion, although the president himself is limited in this sphere as well (e.g., Howell and Pevehouse 2007). It may be that modern presidents' most potent tool for shaping public opinion is their own rhetoric (e.g., Tulis 1987).

There are several ways in which presidential rhetoric might influence public opinion. Most straightforwardly, the president may impact the public's basic policy preferences. For example, a president may use his speeches to persuade Americans to change their attitudes toward immigrants. The president also might influence the public's agenda by pushing them to believe certain issues are more important than others. Cohen (1995, 1997) shows that from 1953 to 1989, the issues which the president discusses most in his State of the Union addresses are subsequently the issues that the public views as the most important to the nation (also see Lawrence 2004). Canes-Wrone (2006) argues (although does not explicitly show) that presidents can and do influence the salience the public assigns to each issue even though they do not shape directional issue opinions.[5] This type of presidential agenda influence differs from elite responsiveness to issues salient to the public (i.e., presidential responsiveness on salience, as discussed). Rather than addressing issues seen as important, the president seeks to strategically push citizens to prioritize some issues over others in ways that benefit the president.

Priming constitutes a related type of influence. In this case, presidential emphasis on a given issue (e.g., health care) or image (e.g., trust) leads citizens to then privilege that issue or image in their evaluations of the president (e.g., Iyengar and Kinder 1987; Druckman 2004; Druckman and Holmes 2004). For example, when the president emphasizes health care, citizens subsequently evaluate the president based on his health care position. Another example is when President Bush's speeches highlighted the threat of terrorist attacks. If Americans focus on the threat of terrorist attacks, they support aggressive policies (including restrictions on civil liberties) and offer more positive evaluations of the president.

Druckman, Jacobs, and Ostermeier (2004) offer evidence that presidents work to strategically prime advantageous issues and images by emphasizing domestic issues on which the citizens share their preferences. For instance, if the public generally agrees with the president's position on welfare spending, the president will focus his remarks on welfare so that citizens subsequently also focus on welfare when evaluating the president (and give him high ratings since they agree with his welfare position). Interestingly, in finding that the president focuses on issues where the public agrees with his position, Druckman, Jacobs, and Ostermeier also report that the president pays little or no attention to the actual salience (e.g., national importance) of the issue. In other words, the president emphasizes issues that work to his advantage—issues on which the public agrees with his positions—rather than issues that the public necessarily sees as inherently important.[6]

The possibility of the president shaping public opinion raises important questions about representation and how it should be studied. The normative implications of presidential influence depend on the nature of that influence. As Page and Shapiro

[5] Canes-Wrone (2006, 30–2) incorporates the possibility of very limited presidential influence on citizens' preferences (e.g., the president exerts influence only when he shares the public's policy preferences).

[6] Another means of presidential influence is framing (e.g., Edwards 2003; Entman 2004), which, as Chong and Druckman (2007b) explain, is closely linked or perhaps even synonymous with priming.

(1992, 356) explain, "To the extent the public receives useful interpretations, and correct and helpful information . . . the policy preferences it expresses can be considered more 'authentic,' or 'enlightened'. . . to the extent that the public is given erroneous interpretation or false, misleading, or biased information, people may make mistaken evaluations . . . and may express support for policies harmful to their own interests or values." Presidents who enlighten or educate public opinion enhance the likelihood of substantive representation working insofar as it facilitates responsiveness to "authentic" preferences. But presidents who successfully mislead— or consciously manipulate—undermine representation by debasing the foundation of responsiveness (i.e., public opinion).

This accentuates the importance of continued research into the conditions under which presidents can influence public opinion. Recent research suggests that presidents—particularly in recent years—face various hurdles to exerting an impact. In his exhaustive study of the impact of presidential rhetoric on public opinion, Edwards (2003, 241) concludes that "presidents typically do not succeed in their efforts to change public opinion." Edwards points to a number of factors that limit even charismatic presidents, including: citizens' predispositions, competition from many other actors (including the Congress, interest groups, and outside events), a dependence on the media to echo their messages, and the need to get citizens' attention in the first place. This insight is consistent with work on opinion formation that highlights various moderating variables that constrain elite influence (e.g., Chong and Druckman 2007b).

The evolution of the media also presents new challenges to presidents who hope to influence public opinion. Not only is it more difficult for presidents to gain access to national audiences via the media, but even when they do address the country at large, fewer and fewer citizens pay attention, given all the alternatives available in a new media age (e.g., Baum and Kernell 1999). The result is a decreased ability of the president to influence and/or lead the public. Cohen (2008, 187–8) explains that "the new media age has also affected the style of presidential leadership . . . they look more and more to narrower groups, such as special interests and their partisan bases" since these are the only groups they can reach. Cohen (2008, 289) continues, "Presidents might be responsive to the policy preferences of the target group, as presidents adjust their public stance to more closely match the group that they are trying to mobilize."

These changes obviously have implications for whose preferences the president responds to (as previously discussed). It also complicates the relative impact of the president, the Congress, and the media in responding to and influencing citizens' preferences. As Edwards and Wood (1999) demonstrate, it is often the president who is reacting to the media and world events, rather than vice versa (also see Hill 1998; Howell and Kriner 2007). Whether and how this relationship has changed in recent years remains an open question.

Two pressing topics in need of more study, then, include identification of the specific conditions under which presidents influence citizens' preferences and the concomitant normative implications of this influence, and a more thorough understanding of how changes in the media affects the public's relationship with presidents.

CONCLUSION

Presidential representation varies across dimensions and levels of salience. In addition to responding to the public's *policy preferences*, presidents make choices about their degree of attention to certain issues—potentially depending on the *salience* of these issues to the public. Representation may extend beyond policy issues to symbols and the president's *perceived personality*. Moreover, representation may be selective rather than responsive to the entire constituency. *Differential representation* may lead to particular presidential attentiveness to certain segments of the country (e.g., high-income earners and social conservatives). Finally, presidents may exercise influence on the policy preferences of citizens and, especially, the salience that is attached to particular issues or personality traits.

Presidential representation is much more complicated, multidimensional, and dynamic than investigations of whether the public's policy preferences align with the president's policies capture. One potential implication is that presidents enjoy significant leeway in shifting the nature of their representative relationship with Americans from policy to non-policy. The result, if this occurred, would be to expand the president's discretion and reduce policy responsiveness, at a substantial cost to popular sovereignty.

REFERENCES

ALTHAUS, S. L., and KIM, Y. M. 2006. Priming Effects in Complex Environments. *Journal of Politics*, 68: 960–76.

BARTELS, L. M. 2003. Democracy with Attitudes. In *Electoral Democracy*, ed. M. B. MacKuen and G. Rabinowitz. Ann Arbor: University of Michigan Press.

——— 2005. Economic Inequality and Political Representation. Revised paper presented at the Annual Meeting of the American Political Science Association, Boston, Aug. 2002.

BAUM, M. A., and KERNELL, S. 1999. Has Cable Ended the Golden Age of Presidential Television? *American Political Science Review*, 93: 99–114.

BRACE, P., and HINCKLEY, B. 1993. Presidential Activities from Truman through Reagan: Timing and Impact. *Journal of Politics*, 5/2: 382–98.

BREWER, P. R. 2001. Value Words and Lizard Brains. *Political Psychology*, 22: 45–64.

BURKE, E. 1949. Speech to the Electors of Bristol. In *Burke's Politics: Selected Writings and Speeches*, ed. R. Hoffmann and P. Levack. New York: Alfred Knopf.

BURSTEIN, P. 2003. The Impact of Public Opinion on Public Policy: A Review and an Agenda. *Political Research Quarterly*, 56: 29–40.

CANES-WRONE, B. 2006. *Who Leads Whom? Presidents, Policy, and the Public.* Chicago: University of Chicago Press.

——— and SHOTTS, K. W. 2004. The Conditional Nature of Presidential Responsiveness to Public Opinion. *American Journal of Political Science*, 45: 532–50.

CHONG, D. 1996. Creating Common Frames of Reference on Political Issues. In *Political Persuasion and Attitude Change*, ed. D. C. Mutz, P. M. Sniderman, and R. A. Brody. Ann Arbor: University of Michigan Press.

CHONG, D., and DRUCKMAN, J. N. 2007a. A Theory of Framing and Opinion Formation in Competitive Elite Environments. *Journal of Communication*, 57: 99–118.

————2007b. Framing Theory. *Annual Review of Political Science*, 10: 103–26.

————Forthcoming. Framing Public Opinion in Competitive Democracies. *American Political Science Review.*

COHEN, J. E. 1995. Presidential Rhetoric and the Public Agenda. *American Journal of Political Science*, 39/1: 87–107.

————1997. *Presidential Responsiveness and Public Policy Making*. Ann Arbor: University of Michigan Press.

————1999. The Polls: The Dynamics of Presidential Favorability, 1991–1998. *Presidential Studies Quarterly*, 29: 896–902.

————2006. The Polls: The Coalitional President from a Public Opinion Perspective. *Presidential Studies Quarterly*, 36/3: 541–50.

————2008. *The Presidency in the Era of 24-Hour News*. Princeton, NJ: Princeton University Press.

CONVERSE, J. 1986. *Survey Research in the United* States. Berkeley and Los Angeles: University of California Press.

CONVERSE, P. E. 1964. The Nature of Belief Systems in Mass Publics. In *Ideology and Discontent*, ed. D. E. Apter. New York: Free Press.

DAHL, R. A. 1971. *Polyarchy: Participation and Opposition*. New Haven, CT: Yale University Press.

————1989. *Democracy and its Critics*. New Haven, CT: Yale University Press.

DOWNS, A. 1957. *An Economic Theory of Democracy.* New York: HarperCollins Publishers.

DRUCKMAN, J. N. 2001. On the Limits of Framing Effects: Who Can Frame? *Journal of Politics*, 63: 1041–66.

————2004. Political Preference Formation. *American Political Science Review*, 98: 671–86.

————and HOLMES, J. W. 2004. Does Presidential Rhetoric Matter? Priming and Presidential Approval. *Presidential Studies Quarterly*, 34: 755–78.

————and JACOBS, L. R. 2006. Lumpers and Splitters: The Public Opinion Information That Politicians Collect and Use. *Public Opinion Quarterly*, 70: 453–76.

————————2007. Segmented Representation: The Reagan White House and Disproportionate Responsiveness. Unpublished manuscript, Northwestern University.

————————and Ostermeier, E. 2004. Candidate Strategies to Prime Issues and Image. *Journal of Politics*, 66: 1205–27.

————and LUPIA, A. 2000. Preference Formation. *Annual Review of Political Science*, 3: 1–24.

————————2006. Mind, Will, and Choice. In *The Oxford Handbook on Contextual Political Analysis*, ed. C. Tilly and R. E. Goodin. Oxford: Oxford University Press.

————and NELSON, K. R. 2003. Framing and Deliberation. *American Journal of Political Science*, 47: 728–44.

EDWARDS, G. C., III. 1976. Presidential Influence in the House: Presidential Prestige as a Source of Presidential Power. *American Political Science Review*, 70/1: 101–13.

————2003. *On Deaf Ears: The Limits of the Bully Pulpit*. New Haven, CT: Yale University Press.

————2004. *Why the Electoral College Is Bad for America*. New Haven, CT: Yale University Press.

————and WOOD, B. D. 1999. Who Influences Whom? The President, Congress, and the Media. *American Political Science Review*, 93/2: 327–44.

EISINGER, R. M. 2003. *The Evolution of Presidential Polling*. New York: Cambridge University Press.

ENELOW, J., and HINICH, M. 1984. *The Spatial Theory of Voting*. Boston: Cambridge University Press.

ENTMAN, R. M. 2004. *Projects of Power: Framing News, Public Opinion, and U.S. Foreign Policy.* Chicago: University of Chicago Press.

ERIKSON, R. S., MacKUEN, M. B., and STIMSON, J. A. 2002. *The Macro Polity.* New York: Cambridge University Press.

FUNK, C. 1999. Bringing the Candidate into Models of Candidate Evaluation. *Journal of Politics*, 61/3: 700–20.

GEER, J. G. 1996. *From Tea Leaves to Opinion Polls*. New York: Columbia University Press.

GILENS, M. 2005. Inequality and Democratic Responsiveness. *Public Opinion Quarterly*, 69/5: 778–96.

HALDEMAN, H. R. 1994. *The Haldeman Diaries: Inside the Nixon White House*. New York: G. P. Putnam's Sons.

HEITH, D. 2004. *Polling to Govern: Public Opinion and Presidential Leadership*. Palo Alto, CA: Stanford University Press.

HERBST, S. 1994. *Politics at the Margin: Historical Studies of Public Expression outside the Mainstream*. New York: Cambridge University Press.

HILL, K. Q. 1998. The Policy Agenda of the President and the Mass Public: A Research Validation and Extension. *American Journal of Political Science*, 42/4: 1328–34.

——and HURLEY, P. A. 1999. Dyadic Representation Reappraised. *American Journal of Political Science*, 43: 109–37.

HOBOLT, S. B., and KLEMMENSEN, R. 2006. Government Responsiveness in Words and Action: Policy Promises and Public Expenditure in a Comparative Perspective. Paper prepared for presentation at the Annual Meeting of the American Political Science Association, Aug. 31– Sept. 3.

HOWELL, W. G., and KRINER, D. 2007. Political Elites and Public Support for War. Unpublished manuscript, University of Chicago.

——and PEVEHOUSE, J. C. 2007. *While Dangers Gather: Congressional Checks on Presidential War Powers*. Princeton, NJ: Princeton University Press.

IYENGAR, S., and KINDER, D. R. 1987. *News That Matters: Television and American Opinion.* Chicago: University of Chicago Press.

JACOBS, L. R. 1992. The Recoil Effect. *Comparative Politics*, 24/2: 199–217.

——and BURNS, M. 2004. The Second Face of the Public Presidency: Presidential Polling and the Shift from Policy to Personality Polling. *Presidential Studies Quarterly*, 34/3: 536–56.

——and PAGE, B. I. 2005. Who Influences U.S. Foreign Policy? *American Political Science Review*, 99: 107–24.

——and SHAPIRO, R. Y. 1994. Issues, Candidate Image and Priming. *American Political Science Review*, 88/3: 527–40.

——————1995. The Rise of Presidential Polling. *Public Opinion Quarterly*, 59/2: 163–95.

——————2000. *Politicians Don't Pander*. Chicago: University of Chicago Press.

KERNELL, S. 1997. *Going Public*, 3rd edn. Washington, DC: CQ Press.

KINGDON, J. W. 1984. *Agendas, Alternatives, and Public Policies*. Boston: Little, Brown & Company.

LAWRENCE, A. B. 2004. Does It Matter What the Presidents Say? The Influence of Presidential Rhetoric on the Public Agenda, 1946–2003. Ph.D. dissertation, University of Pittsburgh.

LEE, T. 2003. *Mobilizing Public Opinion: Black Insurgency and Racial Attitudes in the Civil Rights Era*. Chicago: University of Chicago Press.

LUPIA, A., and McCUBBINS, M. D. 1998. *The Democratic Dilemma: Can Citizens Learn What They Need to Know?* New York: Cambridge University Press.

MANZA, J., and COOK, F. L. 2002a. A Democratic Polity? Three Views of Policy Responsiveness to Public Opinion in the United States. *American Politics Research*, 30: 630–67.

———— 2002b. The Impact of Public Opinion on Public Policy: The State of the Debate. In *Navigating Public Opinion: Polls, Policy, and the Future of American Democracy*, ed. J. Manza, F. L. Cook, and B. I. Page. New York: Oxford University Press.

MILLER, D. 1992. Social Choice and Deliberative Democracy. *Political Studies*, 40: 54–68.

NELSON, T. E., and OXLEY, Z. M. 1999. Issue Framing Effects and Belief Importance and Opinion. *Journal of Politics*, 61: 1040–67.

NEUSTADT, R. E. 1960. *Presidential Power and the Modern Presidents: The Politics of Leadership from Roosevelt to Reagan*. New York: Free Press.

PAGE, B. I. 1978. *Choice and Echoes in Presidential Elections*. Chicago: University of Chicago Press.

———— and SHAPIRO, R. Y. 1983. Effects of Public Opinion on Policy. *American Political Science Review*, 77: 175–90.

———— 1992. *The Rational Public: Fifty Years of Trends in Americans' Policy Preferences*. Chicago: University of Chicago Press.

PITKIN, H. 1967. *The Concept of Representation*. Berkeley and Los Angeles: University of California Press.

POPKIN, S. L. 1994. *The Reasoning Voter*, 2nd edn. Chicago: University of Chicago Press.

PRICE, V., and TEWKSBURY, D. 1997. News Values and Public Opinion. In *Progress in Communication Sciences*, Vol. 13, ed. G. A. Barnett, and F. J. Boster. Greenwich, CT: Ablex Publishing Corporation.

RIKER, W. H. 1996. *The Strategy of Rhetoric*, ed. R. Calvert, J. Mueller, and R. Wilson. New Haven, CT: Yale University Press.

ROTTINGHAUS, B. 2006. Rethinking Presidential Responsiveness: The Public Presidency and Rhetorical Congruency, 1953–2001. *Journal of Politics*, 68/3: 720–32.

———— 2007. Following the "Mail Hawks:" Alternative Measures of Public Opinion on Vietnam in the Johnson White House. *Public Opinion Quarterly*, 71/3: 367–91.

———— N.d. The Provisional Pulpit: Modern Conditional Presidential Leadership of Public Opinion. Unpublished manuscript, University of Houston.

SCHUMPETER, J. 1947. *Capitalism, Socialism, and Democracy*, 2nd edn. New York: Harper & Brothers Publishers.

SIMON, D. M., and OSTROM, C. W., JR. 1989. The Impact of Televised Speeches and Foreign Travel on Presidential Approval. *Public Opinion Quarterly*, 53/19: 58–82.

SNIDERMAN, P. M., BRODY, R. A., and FETLOCK, P. E. 1991. *Reasoning and Choice: Explorations in Political Psychology*. Cambridge: Cambridge University Press.

STEVENS, D. 2002. Public Opinion and Public Policy: The Case of Kennedy and Civil Rights. *Presidential Studies Quarterly*, 32/1: 111–36.

TULIS, J. 1987. *The Rhetorical Presidency*. Princeton, NJ: Princeton.

URBINATI, N. 2006. *Representative Democracy: Principles & Genealogy*. Chicago: University of Chicago Press.

VERBA, S., SCHLOZMAN, K. L., and BRADY, H. E. 1995. *Voice and Equality: Civic Voluntarism in American Politics*. Cambridge, MA: Harvard University Press.

WLEZIEN, C. 2004. Patterns of Representation: Dynamics of Public Preferences and Policy. *Journal of Politics*, 66: 1–24.

—— and SOROKA, S. 2007. Public Opinion and Public Policy. In *Oxford Handbook of Canadian Politics*, ed. J. C. Courtney and D. E. Smith. Oxford: Oxford University Press.

ZALLER, J. 1992. *The Nature and Origins of Mass Opinion*. New York: Cambridge University Press.

—— 1998. Monica Lewinsky's Contribution to Political Science. *PS: Political Science & Politics*, 31: 182–9.

CHAPTER 9

LEADING THE PUBLIC

GEORGE C. EDWARDS III

LEADING the public is at the core of the modern presidency. Gaining and maintaining office, obtaining support from an independently elected legislature, and increasing the party's representation in Congress depend on public opinion. As a result, the White House invests a substantial amount of staff, time, and energy into focusing the public's attention on the issues it wishes to promote and encouraging the public to see its proposals for dealing with those issues in a positive light (Kernell 2007). Most of the White House staff have at least some public relations responsibilities (Kumar 2007, 4–5).

Commentators on the presidency in both the press and the academy often assume that the White House can move public opinion if the president has the skill and will to effectively exploit the "bully pulpit." As Sidney Blumenthal has put it (1982, 24; also see 297–8), "the citizenry is viewed as a mass of fluid voters who can be appeased by appearances, occasional drama, and clever rhetoric." Books that purport to tell politicians just the right words to use in order to persuade the public receive substantial attention (see, for example, Lakoff 2004; Feldman 2007; Luntz 2007). Even those who lament the "plebiscitary presidency" may base their analyses on the premise of the president having established a direct and persuasive relationship with the public (see, for example, Lowi 1985).

Equally important, those in the White House share the premise of the potential of presidential leadership of the public. David Gergen (2000, 210), an experienced White House communications adviser, favorably cites Churchill's assertion that "Of all the talents bestowed upon men, none is so precious as the gift of oratory. He who enjoys it wields a power more durable than that of a great king. He is an independent force in the world." He goes on to add that Ronald Reagan turned television "into a powerful weapon to achieve his legislative goals" (2000, 210, 348). Blumenthal agrees, declaring that Reagan had "stunning success in shaping public opinion," which in turn was central to transforming his ideas into law (1982, 284; see also Baker 2006, 174).

In interviews in the 1990s, Jacobs and Shapiro (2000, 45, 106, 136) found among both White House and congressional staff widespread confidence in the president's ability to lead the public. Evidently President Clinton shared this view, as people close to him reported that he exhibited an "unbelievable arrogance" regarding his ability to change public opinion and felt he could "create new political capital all the time" through going public—a hubris echoed by his aides.

The administration's assumption of the potential for public leadership led it repeatedly to interpret its setbacks, whether in elections or on policies such as health care reform, in terms of its failure to communicate rather than in terms of the quality of its initiatives or its strategy for governing (Woodward 1996, 54, 126; Drew 1996, 19, 34–5). Each downturn in the president's health care reform bill's progress prompted new schemes for going public rather than a reconsideration of the fundamental framework of the bill or the basic strategy for obtaining its passage (Jacobs and Shapiro 2000, 115, 149). Ultimately, the president concluded that health care reform failed because he "totally neglected how to get the public informed... I have to get more involved in crafting my message—in getting across my core concerns" (quoted in Drew 1996, 66). In other words, his strategy was not inappropriate, only his implementation of it. The premise of the potential of presidential public leadership seems to be non-falsifiable.

Similarly, Clinton concluded that the principal cause of the Democrats' stunning defeat in 1994 was neither his presidency nor his policies. Instead, the main problem was communication. He had failed to communicate his accomplishments, and "the role of the President of the United States is message" (quoted in Drew 1996, 19). "I got caught up in the parliamentary aspect of the presidency and missed the leadership, bully pulpit function which is so critical" (quoted in Woodward 1996, 22).

One of Ronald Reagan's highest priorities was obtaining congressional support for the Contras in Nicaragua. The White House left no stone unturned in its efforts to make its case. The public was not persuaded, however (Edwards 2003, 51–5). Nevertheless, one White House official concluded that the problem was not in the potential of presidential leadership of the public but rather in "packaging of the activity, in terms of policy and presentation to the public. It wasn't well staged or sequenced" (quoted in Blumenthal 1982, 293).

The assurance with which presidents, scholars, and journalists accept the assumption of the potential of presidential public leadership belies our lack of understanding of that leadership. Until recently, we knew very little about the impact of the president's persuasive efforts because we had focused on the stimulus rather than the response in examining presidential public leadership. For example, the substantial and rapidly growing literature on presidential rhetoric (see Medhurst 2008; Bimes in this volume) focuses on analyzing *what* the president said rather than the impact of the president's rhetoric on public opinion (Edwards 1996). Other research examines the president's direct efforts to obtain public support (Edwards 1983; Kernell 2007) or to manage the news (Grossman and Kumar 1981; Maltese 1992; Kumar 2007) to encourage public views favorable to the White House rather than the impact of this activity on public opinion.

Yet one of the crowning ironies of the contemporary presidency is that at the same time that presidents increasingly attempt to govern by "going public," public support is elusive. In his memoirs, Ronald Reagan—the "Great Communicator"—reflected on his efforts to ignite concern among the American people regarding the threat of Communism in Central America and mobilize them behind his program of support for the Contras (1990, 471).

For eight years the press called me the "Great Communicator." Well, one of my greatest frustrations during those eight years was my inability to communicate to the American people and to Congress the seriousness of the threat we faced in Central America.

John F. Kennedy once suggested an exchange from *King Henry IV, Part I* as an epigraph for Clinton Rossiter"s classic work *The American Presidency* (Sorensen 1965, 392):

GLENDOWER: I can call spirits from the vasty deep.
HOTSPUR: Why, so can I, or so can any man.
        But will they come when you do call them?

Kennedy's sardonic proposal reflected both his own frustrations in leading the public and his skepticism about the potential of public leadership.

The premise that the president has considerable potential to move the public is so widespread and so central to our understanding of politics that we rarely focus on it explicitly. At the very least, we should not *assume* that presidents, even skilled presidents, succeed in leading the public.

INVESTIGATING PRESIDENTIAL
PUBLIC LEADERSHIP

A few studies have examined aggregate responses to the president's communications. Lyn Ragsdale (1984; see also 1987) found a short-term increase of about 3 percentage points in presidential approval following a televised presidential address, and Paul Brace and Barbara Hinckley (1992, 56) concluded that a major presidential address added 6 percentage points to the president's approval ratings. Yet we know that statistically significant increases in approval rarely occur following these speeches (Edwards 2003, 28–34; 2007, 82–6). Dennis Simon and Charles Ostrom (1989) concluded that presidential televised speeches typically had no impact at all on the president's approval.

Additional work concluded that presidents could influence public opinion a small amount on issues, but only when they themselves have high approval ratings (Page and Shapiro 1985; Page, Shapiro, and Dempsey 1987). Cohen (1997), however, found little impact of approval on public leadership. Other research has concluded, unsurprisingly, that people who approve of the president's performance are more supportive of policy stances of the president than those who disapproved (Sigelman 1980b; Kernell 1984).

Some essentially descriptive findings show public opinion changing over extended periods in line with presidents' views, including the testing of nuclear weapons (Rossi 1965), isolationism (Page and Shapiro 1992, 182), and both the escalation and the de-escalation of the Vietnam War (Mueller 1970, 69–74). These results suggest a public deference to the president on foreign policy issues.

Conversely, Benjamin Page and Robert Shapiro (1992, 242, 250) concluded opinion on relations with the People's Republic of China was not presidency driven, and Edwards (2009, 26–34) showed how Franklin D. Roosevelt was frustrated in his attempts to obtain public support for supporting America's allies and preparing for the Second World War.

Many of the studies indicating successful opinion leadership of issues do not focus on the presidency and often extend over several presidencies. Because their core concerns are not with presidential leadership, they do not make a systematic effort to correlate opinion with White House behavior or the context of public discourse over the relevant issues.

George Edwards (2003) has made the most extensive effort to gauge the impact of presidential efforts to lead the public. Selecting best-test cases, he focused on the opinion leadership of Bill Clinton and Ronald Reagan on a wide range of policies and efforts to defend themselves against scandal. He found that public opinion rarely moved in the president's direction. On most of Clinton and Reagan's policy initiatives, pluralities, and often majorities, of the public *opposed* the president. Moreover, movement in public opinion was typically *against* the president.

George W. Bush also invested heavily in governing by campaigning, and Edwards (2007) also studied the public's response to several of his principal initiatives, including social security reform and the war with Iraq. Once again, the public did not move in the president's direction. For example, even in the favorable context of the national trauma resulting from the 9/11 terrorist attacks, the long-term disdain of the public for Saddam Hussein, and the lack of organized opposition, the White House still made little headway in moving public to support the war, and once the war was over, the rally resulting from the quick US victory quickly dissipated.

Disaggregating Opinion

A pertinent question is whether aggregate national data mask movement that occurs among subgroups of the population. Perhaps the president's leadership changes a small but important segment of public opinion, perhaps those predisposed to support him. Or perhaps predispositions polarize responses to the president, with the opinions of some moving markedly toward the president while the opinions of others are moving in the opposite direction.

In their extensive treatment of trends in public opinion, Benjamin Page and Robert Shapiro (1992, ch. 7) and Robert Erikson, Michael MacKuen, and James Stimson (2002, 219, 369) found that there is a uniformity of preference change, with movement in public opinion coming from all strata. Edwards (2003, ch. 9) examined changes in opinion during the tenures of Presidents Reagan and Clinton across four issues and significant subgroups in the population. He did not find opinion change below the surface of the national totals.

Nevertheless, investigating opinion change among segments of the population, perhaps those that might be especially responsive to presidential appeals on certain issues or that were the target of special efforts by the White House, remains an important avenue of future research. Similarly, we should devise tests for determining whether presidential appeals at least contribute to maintaining the status quo in public opinion.

A Framework for Research

As a framework for his research on presidential leadership of the public, Edwards employed a simple model (Figure 9.1) that identified the critical elements in presidential public leadership and specified the relationships between these elements. The major elements of the model are the messenger (the president), the president's message, the audience (the public), and the public's response.

The specific questions we are likely to ask about the relationships in the model will differ, depending on whether the president is able to move public opinion with some regularity. If at least some chief executives are successful much of the time, we should begin at the left side of the model (the stimulus) and investigate each relationship as we moved to the right (the response). We would focus on explaining why some presidents are more successful than others in leading the public and ask about the nature of presidential appeals, their presentations of themselves, the public's perceptions of them, and the conditions under which the public pays attention, understands, and responds positively to them.

Conversely, if presidents—all presidents—are rarely able to move the public, our questions need to focus on explaining why presidential leadership of the public is not more effective. If even the most rhetorically skilled presidents find it difficult to move

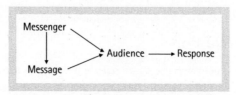

Figure 9.1 A simple model of presidential public leadership

the public, then studying variations in those skills among presidents will not reveal explanations for the president's difficulties. If all kinds of messages fail to resonate with the people, then the question is broader than the nature of the messages themselves. Our questions should center instead on investigating and explaining the *absence* of relationships in the model. For example, why do the messenger's characteristics not matter, why does the president not focus his messages more tightly, and why does the public not hear the president's messages?

Constraints on Opinion Change

Edwards (2003) devoted considerable attention to answering such questions. Space constraints prohibit a detailed review of his conclusions. In brief, he found that there is no magic associated with certain leaders and that the "charisma" and personality of leaders are not the keys to successfully leading the public. Even George Washington, who was better positioned than any of his successors to dominate American politics because of the widespread view of his possessing exceptional personal qualities, did not find the public particularly deferential.

The first step in the president's efforts to lead the public is focusing its attention. Despite an enormous total volume of presidential public statements, they are dispersed over a broad range of policies and wide audiences hear only a small portion of the president's remarks. The president rarely focuses a televised address on an issue before Congress and actually makes few statements on even significant legislation. In addition, the president faces strong competition for the public's attention from previous commitments of government, congressional initiatives, opposing elites, and the mass media. Even more importantly, the president often provides competition for himself as he addresses other issues, some on his own agenda and others that are forced upon him.

Presidents make a substantial effort to frame issues in ways that will favor their preferred policy options and to place their own performance in a favorable light. As I discuss below, however, there are many limitations on successful framing.

If the president is going to lead the public successfully, it must *receive* and *understand* his messages. Yet the White House finds it increasingly difficult to obtain an audience for its views (see also Baum and Kernell 1999)—or even airtime on television to express them (see also Cohen 2008). Those who are unaware of a message are unlikely to be know the president's positions. Moreover, many people who do pay attention miss the president's points. Because the president rarely speaks directly to the American people as a whole, the White House is dependent on the press to transmit its messages. The media are unlikely to adopt consistently either the White House's priorities or its framing of issues.

Perhaps most significantly, the president must overcome the predispositions of his audience if he is to change their minds about his policies or his performance (for an early study on predispositions see Glaros and Miroff 1983). Yet, most people ignore or reject arguments contrary to their predispositions. Those who pay close attention to politics and policy are likely to have well-developed views and thus be less susceptible to persuasion. Better-informed citizens possess the information necessary to identify and thus reject communications inconsistent with their values. They are also more sensitive to the implications of messages. In the typical situation of competing frames offered by elites, reinforcement and polarization of views are more likely than conversion among attentive citizens (Zaller 1992, 102–13).

It may seem that those with less interest and knowledge present the most potential for presidential persuasion. Such people cannot resist arguments if they do not possess information about the implications of those arguments for their values, interests, and other predispositions. However, these people are also less likely to be aware of the president's messages, limiting the president's influence. To the extent that they do receive the messages, they will also hear from the opposition how the president's views are inconsistent with their predispositions. In addition, even if their predispositions make them sympathetic to the president's arguments, they may lack the understanding to make the connection between the president's arguments and their own underlying values. Moreover, the more abstract the link between message and value, the fewer the people who will make the connection (Converse 1964; Jacoby 1988; Luskin 1987; Neuman 1986; Carmines and Stimson 1980; Zaller 1992, 48).

In addition, Kuklinski and his colleagues (2000) found that people are frequently *misinformed* (as opposed to uninformed) about policy, and the less they know, the more confidence they have in their beliefs. Thus, they resist correct factual information. Even when presented with factual information, they resist changing their opinions.

Zaller (1992, 1994) argues that those in the public most susceptible to presidential influence are those attentive to public affairs (and thus who receive messages) but who lack strong views (and thus who are less likely to resist messages). At best, such persons are a small portion of the population. In addition, these persons receive competing messages. There is no basis for inferring that they will be most likely to find the president's messages persuasive. Such a conclusion is especially suspect when we recognize that most attentive people have explicit or latent partisan preferences. The president is leader of one of the parties, and those affiliated with the opposition party must overcome an inherent skepticism about him before they can be converted to support his position.

Adjusting toward Equilibrium

We can also see the impact of predispositions by taking a very broad view of public opinion about public policy. In their sweeping "macro" view of public opinion, Erikson, MacKuen, and Stimson (2002, ch. 9) show that opinion always moves contrary to the president's position for the entire span of their analysis 1952–96. They argue that a moderate public always gets too much liberalism from Democrats and too much conservatism from Republicans. Because public officials have policy beliefs as well as an interest in reelection, they are not likely to calibrate their policy stances exactly to match those of the public. Therefore, opinion movement is typically contrary to the ideological persuasion of presidents. Liberal presidents produce movement in the conservative direction and conservatives generate public support for more liberal policies.

The public continuously adjusts its views of current policy in the direction of a long-run equilibrium path as it compares its preferences for ideal policy with its views of current policy to produce a policy mood (Erikson, MacKuen, and Stimson 2002, 344, 374). Thus, the conservative policy period of the 1950s produced a liberal mood that resulted in the liberal policy changes of the mid-1960s. These policies, in turn, helped elect conservative Richard Nixon. In the late 1970s, Jimmy Carter's liberal policies paved the way for Ronald Reagan's conservative tenure, which in turn laid the foundation for Bill Clinton's more liberal stances (see also Wlezien 1995, 1996).

Loss Aversion

Research in psychology has found that people have a broad predisposition to avoid loss (Kahneman and Tversky 1979, 1984) and place more emphasis on avoiding potential losses than on obtaining potential gains. In their decision making they place more weight on information that has negative, as opposed to positive, implications for their interests. Similarly, when individuals form impressions of situations or other people, they weigh negative information more heavily than positive. Impressions formed on the basis of negative information, moreover, tend to be more lasting and more resistant to change (Hamilton and Zanna 1972; Fiske 1980).

Risk and loss aversion and distrust of government make people wary of policy initiatives, especially when they are complex and their consequences are uncertain. Since uncertainty accompanies virtually every proposal for a major shift in public policy, it is not surprising that people are naturally inclined against change (Lau 1985). Further encouraging this predisposition is the media's focus on political conflict and strategy, which elevates the prominence of political wheeling-dealing in individuals' evaluations of political leaders and policy proposals. The resulting increase in public cynicism highlights the risk of altering the status quo.

The predisposition for loss aversion is an obstacle for presidential leadership of the public. Most presidents want to leave some substantial change at the core of their legacies. Yet those proposing new directions in policy encounter a more formidable task than advocates of the status quo. Those opposing change have a more modest task of emphasizing the negative to increase the public's uncertainty and anxiety to avoid risk. Michael Cobb and James Kuklinski (1997) found in an experimental study of opinion change on NAFTA and health care that arguments *against* both worked especially well. They found people to be both risk and loss averse, and arguments against change, which accentuate the unpleasant consequences of a proposed policy, easily resonated with the average person. In addition, they suggest that fear and anger, which negative arguments presumably evoke, are among the strongest emotions and serve as readily available shortcuts for decision making when people evaluate an impending policy initiative (on the role of emotion in political decision making, see Marcus, Neuman, and MacKuen, 2000; Miller 2007).

Exploiting Existing Opinion

Even if presidents are unlikely to *change* public opinion, there may be an important role for leadership of the public. Perhaps the White House can exploit *existing* public opinion as a resource for changing the direction of public policy. At the core of such a strategy is choosing the issues they emphasize and the manner in which they present their policy initiatives.

From the perspective of the White House, "the key to successful advocacy is controlling the public agenda" (Kumar 2007, 9). Although previous commitments, current crises, and unresolved problems left from their predecessors foist much of their agenda upon them, presidents still have substantial discretion to choose their own initiatives and the manner in which they present them to the public.

In the remainder of this section, I illustrate different aspects of potentially leading the public through exploiting existing opinion. There is very little literature that focuses on such leadership efforts. Thus, each of the facets of public leadership I discuss represents rich possibilities for our research agenda.

Framing Issues

The president is interested in not only what the public thinks about a policy but also *how* they are thinking about it. Structuring choices about policy issues in ways that favor the president's programs may set the terms of debate on his proposals and thus the premises on which the public evaluates them. As one leading adviser to President Reagan put it, "I've always believed that 80 percent of any legislative or political matter is how you frame the debate" (quoted in Boyd 1986, 22). Similarly, Stephen Skowronek (2005, 818) argues that setting the terms of discourse and thus structuring the choices of citizens "is the primal act of leadership."

Attempts to frame issues are as old as the Republic (see, for example, Riker 1984, 1986, 1996) and begin with campaigns for office. Each side of a political contest usually attempts to frame the debate to its own advantage. Byron Shafer and William Claggett (1995; see also Druckman, Jacobs, and Ostermeier 2004) argue that public opinion is organized around two clusters of issues, both of which are favored by a majority of voters: social welfare, social insurance, and civil rights (associated with Democrats) and cultural values, civil liberties, and foreign relations (associated with Republicans). Each party's best strategy is to frame the choice for voters by focusing attention on the party's most successful cluster of issues. John Petrocik (1991, 1996) has found that candidates tend to campaign on issues that favor them in order to prime the salience of these issues in voters' decision making (see also Hillygus and Shields 2008). Similarly, an important aspect of campaigning is activating the latent predispositions of partisans by priming party identification as a crucial consideration in deciding for whom to vote (Gelman and King 1993).

Framing and Priming

A *frame* is a central organizing idea for making sense of an issue or conflict and suggests what the controversy is about and what is at stake. Thus, a leader might frame welfare as an appropriate program necessary to compensate for the difficult circumstances in which the less fortunate find themselves, or as a giveaway to undeserving slackers committed to living on the dole.

Individuals typically have multiple values that are relevant for evaluating issue positions and are unlikely to canvass all their values in their evaluations. Thus, presidents cannot leave to chance the identification of which values are most relevant to the issues they raise. Because people use cues from elites as to the ideological or partisan implications of messages (Converse 1964)—the source of a message is itself an important cue (Zaller 1992, 42–8; Kuklinski and Hurley 1994; Mondak 1993)—the White House seeks to influence the values citizens employ in their evaluations (see Edwards 2003, ch. 7).

In framing, the president does not try to influence the public's values. Instead, the White House encourages the public to view issues, events, or the president's performance in terms of certain values the public already holds, hoping to increase the salience (and thus the accessibility) of those values in the public's appraisals of the president and his positions.

It is not clear whether an issue frame interacts with an individual's memory so as to *prime* certain considerations, making some more accessible than others and therefore more likely to be used in formulating a political preference, or whether framing works by encouraging individuals to deliberately think about the importance of considerations suggested by a frame. In either case, the frame raises the priority and weight that individuals assign to particular attitudes already stored in their memories.

Framing and priming have a number of advantages for the president, not the least of which is that they demand less of the public than directly persuading citizens on the merits of a policy proposal. The president does not have to persuade people to change their basic values and preferences. He does not have to convince citizens to develop expertise and acquire and process extensive information about the details of a policy proposal. In addition, framing and priming—because they are relatively simple—are less susceptible to distortion by journalists and opponents than direct persuasion on the merits of a policy proposal (see Jacobs and Shapiro 2000, 49–52).

Studying Presidential Framing

Despite the substantial efforts presidents make to frame issues, we know almost nothing about their success. The biggest obstacle to understanding the consequences of framing is that we know very little about the terms in which the public thinks about and discusses issues. Indeed, there is not a single study that has measured the terms of public discourse. We need to measure both changes in public discourse over time and White House efforts to frame debates. Such efforts should play a prominent role in the research agenda of scholarship on the presidency.

Scholars also need to be attentive to the limits on framing. Perhaps the most important is the presence of competing frames. Stephen Skowronek (2005, 818, 821, 826–7) makes it clear that "the political world seldom conforms to definitions and formulas; no matter how tight, skilled, or hands-on the controls exerted, events can be orchestrated to set terms only for so long." The president's opponents are unlikely to accept his terms of debate and "relentlessly and ruthlessly" provide an alternative view.

Studies that have found powerful framing effects have typically carefully sequestered citizens and restricted them to hearing only one frame, usually in the context of a controlled experiment. These frames tend to be confined to brief fragments of arguments, pale imitations of frames that often occur in the real world. The early work on presidential leadership of the public employed experimental designs. In effect, the authors framed choices as supporting or opposing the president. Lee Sigelman (1980a; see also Conover and Sigelman 1982) ascertained public opinion on six potential responses to the 1979–80 hostage crisis in Iran. He then asked those who opposed each option whether they would change their view "if President Carter considered this action necessary." In each case, a substantial percentage of respondents changed their opinions in deference to the supposed opinion of the president. In another experiment during the Reagan presidency, Dan Thomas and Lee Sigelman (1985) posed policy proposals to sample subjects. When informed that the president was the source of the proposals, enthusiastic supporters of Reagan evaluated them in favorable terms, but when the source was withheld, Reagan supporters evaluated these same proposals unfavorably.

Not all results were as positive, however. In another study, Lee and Carol Sigelman (1981) asked sample groups whether they supported two proposals, a domestic policy proposal dealing with welfare and a proposal dealing with foreign aid. Researchers told one of the groups that President Carter supported the proposals, while they did not mention the president to the other group. The authors found that attaching the president's name to either proposal not only failed to increase support for it, but also actually had a negative effect because those who disapproved of Carter reacted very strongly against proposals they thought were his. More than a decade later, Jeffrey Mondak (1993) found that reference to the president in issue surveys affected results only when other information was scarce. Moreover, the president needed a high level of approval before his policy endorsement constituted a supportive frame.

The environment in which the president usually operates is fundamentally different from that in an experiment or poll. The president's world is inhabited by committed, well-organized, and well-funded opponents. Intense disagreement among elites generates conflicting messages. John Zaller (1992, 99, ch. 9) argues that attitudes on major issues change in response to changes in relation to the intensity of competing streams of political communication. When there is elite consensus, and thus only one set of cues offered to the public, opinion change may be substantial. However, when elite discourse is divided, people respond to the issue according to their predispositions, especially their core partisan and ideological views (see also Berinsky 2007). Thus, when Paul Sniderman and Sean Theriault (2004; see also Sniderman 2000; Druckman 2004) offered people competing frames, as in the real world, they adopted positions consistent with their preexisting values (but see Chong and Druckman 2007).

Occasions in which elite commentary is one-sided are rare. Most issues that generate consensual elite discourse arise from external events, i.e. surprise attacks on the US, such as the terrorist assaults on September 11, 2001, or its allies, such as the invasion of Kuwait in 1990. Consensual issues also tend to be new, with few people having committed themselves to a view about them. In his examination of public opinion regarding the Gulf War, Zaller (1994) argues that the president's greatest chance of influencing public opinion is in a crisis (which attracts the public's attention) in which elites articulate a unified message.

Studies have also found that conversations that include conflicting perspectives (Druckman and Nelson 2003), credible advice from other sources (Druckman 2001a), pertinent predispositions (Haider-Markel and Joslyn 2001), differing levels of education (Huber and Lapinski 2006), and relevant expertise (Druckman and Nelson 2003) condition the impact of framing efforts. The strength of a frame also seems to be important in determining how much influence it may have (Chong and Druckman 2007).

In addition, for the president to frame issues for the public, people must perceive accurately the frame offered by the White House. We know very little about how people perceive messages from the president or other elites. Nor do we know much about how citizens come to understand public issues or develop their values and other predispositions that the president seeks to prime. (We also do not know whether the potential impact of frames is restricted to priming existing values or whether they may also affect understanding, which may in turn alter opinion.) There is reason to believe, however, that different people perceive the same message differently (see, for example, Kuklinski and Hurley 1994). With all his personal, ideological, and partisan baggage, no president can assume that all citizens hear the same thing when he speaks. Partisanship is especially likely to bias processing perceptions, interpretations, and responses to the political world (see Bartels 2002; Edwards 2003, ch. 9; Gaines et al. 2007).

A related matter of perception is the credibility of the source. Experimental evidence supports the view that perceived source credibility is a prerequisite for successful framing (Druckman 2001b; see also Druckman 2001a; Miller and Krosnick 2000). The president is likely to be more credible to some people (those predisposed to support him) than to others. Many people are unlikely to find him a credible source on most issues, especially those on which opinion is divided and on which he is the leader of one side of the debate.

Increasing the Salience of Popular Issues

Even if the president cannot change the public's views on issues, he may be able to influence *what* it is thinking about. Instead of seeking to change public opinion regarding an issue, the president may make appeals on policies that already have public support. The goal in such efforts is to make popular issues more salient to the public and thus encourage members of Congress to support White House initiatives that please the public.

In a context of polarized politics, persuasion may be particularly problematic, and thus the president may focus primarily on maintaining and mobilizing his electoral coalition. As Clinton press secretary Mike McCurry put it, "the truth is, most presidential communications are not aimed at the entire country; they're aimed at different segments of the total population" (quoted in Kumar 2007, 40). George W. Bush, for example, often sought to govern with a 50 percent plus 1 majority rather than seek to compromise with his opponents and create a more inclusive coalition (see, for example, Brownstein 2007). Similarly, in the 2004 presidential election the core Republican political strategy was to motivate the base rather than persuade the undecided (Draper 2007, 230). Mobilizing the president's core supporters usually involves making more salient to them issues about which they care and share a consensus.

A more complicated means of making issues salient to a wider segment of the public and thus adding to a supportive coalition is expanding the scope of conflict (Schattschneider 1960) by applying new attributes to them (see Jones and Baumgartner 2005, ch. 3; Jones 1994, ch. 4). In 1998, Bill Clinton wanted to use the new budget surplus to pay down the national debt rather than to cut taxes, as Republicans favored. He articulated the rationale for his position with an appeal in his State of the Union address that year to "save Social Security first." As one of his speechwriters put it, "The presidential pulpit had never been put to more effective use" (Waldman 2000, 216).

Stopping Republican proposals for tax cuts was not at the core of social security policy, and social security was not a matter of great public concern at that time. However, the president framed the issue of using the budget surplus to pay down the national debt as support for the popular policy of social security. Thus, Clinton increased the salience of the paying down the national debt by demonstrating its relevance to social security and thus its pertinence to the interests of millions of Americans. Republicans had to applaud the president's protection of this widely supported policy, giving him the upper hand in the battle over using the budget surplus. We should remember, however, that presidents are rarely in a position to frame a policy as central to the success of another, popular, policy.

More generally, there is no assurance that the president can exploit existing support for an issue by making it more salient to the public. First, the president's initiative must be popular. There is no point in making policy positions that lack public support more prominent in the public's thinking. Some presidential initiatives do have public support, but many do not. Ronald Reagan's efforts to decrease government spending on domestic policy and increase it on defense policy, win support for the Contras, and reduce regulation all typically lacked majority support. Bill Clinton's proposals for stimulating the economy, reforming health care reform, intervening in Haiti, and enacting NAFTA faced at least plurality opposition once his critics responded to them. George W. Bush's most ambitious proposals in his second term, reforming social security and immigration policy and maintaining his policy in Iraq, confronted a similar lack of popular support. Holmes (2007) found that presidents have become more likely to go public on behalf of nominees to the US courts of appeals who face opposition (and nominees were less likely to be confirmed when the president went public on their behalf).

Brandice Canes-Wrone has led the way on investigating the types of issues on which presidents go public (2006, 80, chs. 3–4). She found that presidents are "more likely to publicize a domestic initiative the more popular it is and almost never appeal to the public about an initiative likely to mobilize popular opposition." Although presidents often speak about foreign policy issues that lack popular support, she found that presidents are also more likely to publicize foreign policy initiatives if a majority of the public favors them and will generally avoid going public on initiatives that face mass opposition.

This research is an important first step. Yet Canes-Wrone only studied the small percentage of presidential statements made in nationally televised addresses, and, on domestic policy, only for spending on a few issues. In most instances, the president did not mention at all the policies she studied, and when he did, only for a sentence for two. We know that public statements cascade from the White House (Edwards 2003, ch. 6), and we need to examine the full range of presidential messages, especially when many of them are aimed at only segments of the public.

The second requirement for exploiting existing support for an issue by making it more salient to the public is that the president actually be able to increase the salience of the issue among the public. We know little about the president's success in increasing the salience of issues, but there is reason to be cautious about attributing influence to the White House. Bill Clinton sought to start national discussions on affirmative action and social security, trying to develop a consensus on how to reform them. He even participated on round tables with citizens to discuss the policies. The president's goal was laudable, but there is no evidence that he succeeded in stimulating national discussions, much less forging agreement on solutions.

Patrick Fett (1994) and Brandice Canes-Wrone (2006) contend that by publicizing an issue, the president increases the chances that it will become more salient to the public and thus increase the likelihood that members of Congress will support the president's proposal. Yet neither author actually examined the president's influence on issue salience, and it is highly questionable whether a few sentences—or even less—spoken by the president can influence the salience of issues months after they were spoken.

The agenda-setting literature provides mixed results about the ability of the president to influence the public agenda (see Wood in this volume). Behr and Iyengar (1985) found that presidential televised addresses devoted to a policy problem influence the public agenda, but such addresses are rare (Edwards 2003, ch. 6) and do not necessarily lead to support for the president's program. Indeed, Miller found that news that arouses *negative* emotions is what affects the public's judgments of what issues are important (Miller 2007).

Jeffrey Cohen (1997) found that presidents can influence the public's agenda through symbolic speech in State of the Union messages, at least in the short run. He also found, however, that presidents are only able to affect the public's agenda over time on foreign policy and that substantive policy rhetoric has no impact on the public's policy agenda. In general, Cohen found the president to have only a very modest impact on public opinion.

This influence may be even less than Cohen suggests, because presidential issue priorities in the State of the Union message may actually be a response to rather than a cause of public issue concerns. Kim Hill (1998) replicated Cohen's work to consider the possibility of reverse causality and found it operating for public concern with the economy and foreign policy, although not for civil rights. B. Dan Wood (2007, ch. 3) found that the intensity of presidential rhetoric on the economy responds to public concerns about economy. In other words, presidential issue priorities are often a response to the public rather than a cause of the public's agenda.

Increasing our understanding of presidents leading the public through increasing the salience of policies requires progress on several fronts. First, we need to develop better measures of the salience of issues over time. The "most important problem" question has many limitations for scholars, not the least of which is its narrow focus, asking respondents about *the* most important problem. An issue could become more salient without diminishing the significance of issues of war, the economy, and other matters.

We also need to disaggregate salience so we can identify the importance of issues among segments of the public, particularly within the president's electoral constituency. If this group is the focus of the White House's leadership efforts, we need to be able to isolate the salience of issues among its members. Polls taken by the Pew Research Center over several years, for example, have shown that Republican and Democratic voters frequently differ on the issues on which they evaluate candidates.

Naturally, we want to investigate the connection between presidential discourse and the public's response. To do so, we will need to measure various dimensions of the president's communications and include much more than televised addresses. Now that we have electronic access to all the president's public statements, this should not be a difficult task. Developing a theory for explaining how the salience of issues increases will require more effort but is central to our scholarly enterprise.

The ultimate goal of some scholars will be uncovering the relationship between presidentially driven changes in the salience of issues and congressional response to that change. Succeeding in this effort will require sensitivity to appropriate controls. For example, it is very likely that presidents will make extra efforts to pass legislation to which they devote significant attention in public. We will have to develop new measures to capture those efforts so we do not inappropriately attribute influence to the president's rhetoric. We also need to examine a range of issues, especially those that play a more prominent role in the public domain than appropriations bills.

Clarifying Opinion

Public opinion about matters of politics and policy is often amorphous. It lacks articulation and structure. Woodrow Wilson urged leaders to interpret public opinion and identify issues that "reflected majority will even if the majority was not yet fully aware of it. The leader's rhetoric could translate the people's felt desires into public policy." As Jeffrey Tulis (1984, 78–9) points out, success at interpretation requires understanding majority sentiment underlying the contradictions of factions and discordant views; and explaining people's true desires to them in an easily comprehended and convincing fashion.

Understanding Opinion

All presidents since John F. Kennedy have retained private polling firms to provide them with soundings of American public opinion, and in the last five administrations, pollsters have also played a significant role as high-level political advisers (Tenpas and McCann 2007; Heith 2004; Jacobs and Shapiro 1994, 1995; Eisinger 2003; Murray and Howard 2002). Technology is not a cure-all, however. Opinions are often rife with contradictions because the public often fails to give its views much thought or consider the implications of its policy stands for other issues (Feldman and Zaller 1992). Policy making is a complex enterprise, and most voters do not have the time, expertise, or inclination to think extensively about most issues, especially those distant from their everyday experiences.

The public may get its basic facts wrong. Before the war with Iraq in 2003, two-thirds of the public expressed the belief that Iraq played an important role in the 9/11 terrorist attacks. After the war, substantial percentages of the public believed that the United States had found clear evidence that Saddam Hussein was working closely with al-Qaeda, that the United States had found weapons of mass destruction in Iraq, and that world opinion favored the United States going to war in Iraq (Kull, Ramsay, and Lewis 2003–4). All of these beliefs were inaccurate, as even the White House admitted.

On the other hand, collective public opinion has properties quite different from those of individual citizens. There is evidence that the general public holds real, stable, and sensible opinions about public policy, which develop and change in a reasonable fashion in response to changing circumstances and new information. Changes that occur are usually at the margins and represent different trade-offs among constant values (Page and Shapiro 1992; Stimson 1991).

Understanding public opinion, then, is difficult, especially on new issues on which opinion is fluid. Yet on many issues, opinion is long established and stable. It is to the White House's advantage to articulate such opinion as consistent with its initiatives.

Articulating Opinion

In his study of agenda setting in the national government, John Kingdon (1995, 146–50) found that people in and around government believed strongly that there was such a thing as a "national mood," that they could measure it, and that it had consequences for policy. Baumgartner and Jones (1993, 236–7) argue that it is important for leaders to discern whether the flow of events favors their proposals, and to skillfully exploit the opportunity when it does.

To exploit amorphous or latent opinion effectively, the president must not only recognize it but also articulate that opinion in a clear and compelling manner. Michael Nelson (1988, 272) concludes that, above all, successful presidents require not only a strategic sense of the grain of history but also an ability to sense, define, and articulate the public mood to fulfill the historical possibilities of the time. Doing so may require waiting for opinion to mature to the point that it supports White House initiatives. The most effective means of articulating newly clarified opinion may be in the form of policy proposals that encapsulate the public's views.

Franklin D. Roosevelt was well aware that Americans were ambivalent about involvement in the Second World War. He carefully gauged public opinion and typically relied on events to change opinion about issues such as the nature of the threat posed by the Nazis and the Japanese and the appropriate national response to it. When opinion moved in the direction he wished to go, he quickly clarified and solidified this change by announcing policies consistent with it, such as aiding the Allies in June 1940 by asking Congress for the Lend-Lease bill (Edwards 2009, 27, 33). As Richard Hofstadter (1954, 316) put it, FDR was not able to move the public, but "he was able to give it that necessary additional impetus of leadership which can translate desires into policies."

Investigating strategies for articulating opinion will be difficult. We are just beginning to learn about the White House's understanding of public opinion, and there is much more to discover. Even more demanding will be measuring amorphous opinion and then determining whether the president's rhetoric resonated with the public.

Channeling the Public

Framing and clarifying issues or increasing their salience to take advantage of existing public opinion are short-term strategies that may prove useful to the White House. Channeling the public to support a broader party program is a longer process but one that may have significant consequences for politics and public policy. Channeling involves parties and leaders signaling to voters a commonality of interests and increasing the salience of these shared interests in voting decisions.

The rise of new issues has the potential to destabilize or even destroy party coalitions, and effective leaders will recognize and channel this potential to help build a new governing coalition. Following the passage of the 1964 Civil Rights Act, Republicans, led by Richard Nixon, saw that the alienation of many Southerners from their former home in the Democratic Party provided them the opportunity to engage in a "Southern strategy" to win converts among conservative white Southerners.

Edward Carmines and James Stimson (1989) have shown how the emergence of race as a new issue cleavage in the 1960s caused many Americans to change their party allegiances. However, Republican leaders also attracted support by stressing patriotism, religious values, and traditional (and thus conservative) positions on social issues to attract voters alienated by the Democrats' anti-war stances and apparent sympathy for views ranging from support for greater protections for alleged criminals to a wide separation between church and state. Republicans also began stressing economic issues (Smith 2007), which the emerging white middle class in the South found especially attractive (Shafer and Johnston 2006). When the Supreme Court made abortion a constitutional right in *Roe* v. *Wade* in 1973, opposition to abortion fit seamlessly with the Republicans' emphasis and further defined the parties, attracting additional adherents and mobilizing new legions of activists.

The result was Republican domination of presidential elections for two generations after 1964. Only two Democrats won in the four decades following that election, and only one, Jimmy Carter, running on the heels of Watergate in 1976, received a majority of the vote. The political landscape did not change because leaders persuaded people to alter their views about race, abortion, or other issues. Republican leaders attracted new voters to their party by reacting to events that were not of their making, such as the war in Vietnam, urban riots, and Supreme Court decisions. They responded by articulating views with which the voters agreed and making these views more salient in voting decisions (Hillygus and Shields 2008, ch. 5).

We know a fair amount about changes in party identification among the public, but scholars rarely focus on the role of leaders in influencing these changes. Although we have plenty of data on the dependent variable, party identification, examining the president's impact requires measuring the White House's efforts and effective controls for alternative explanations of party identification. Ideally, we would have individual-level data with which we could identify those who *changed* their party allegiance and the reasons for their change, including attentiveness to signals from the president.

Exploiting Fluid Opinion or Public Indifference

Although events, predecessors, and pressing needs of the time determine much of the White House's agenda, the government's attention to an issue is not solely a function of the severity of a problem (Jones and Baumgartner 2005, 241). Sometimes, the president may choose to advocate a policy to which the public has not been attentive. This inattention could be the result of the newness of an issue or a general lack of concern for a matter. In either case, the public is not clamoring for action and contending sides have not mobilized for action. Public indifference may signal a tolerance for a presidential initiative, providing an opportunity for the White House, which generally prefers to form opinion rather than change it after it has developed (Kumar 2007, 7).

Immediately after taking office in 1963, Lyndon Johnson began his War on Poverty. Poverty was not a pressing issue in the US at the time (Zarefsky 1986, 24), but such an effort animated liberals, and giving people a hand up is consistent with broad currents of American ideology. Thus, the White House launched what Jeffrey Tulis termed a "massive rhetorical campaign" to develop a sense of urgency about poverty, and the president made it the most visible theme of his first State of the Union message (1987, 161–172; see also Zarefsky 1986).

Opinion is especially likely to be open to supporting the White House on new issues, because people are less likely to have predispositions on them. Thus, the president has an opportunity to develop support among the public before an organized opposition develops. Ronald Reagan's advocacy of the Strategic Defense Initiative (SDI) may be an example of leading the public on a new issue (Edwards 2003, 57–9).

Opinion changes may well be temporary, however. Even under unusual circumstances when people have participated in intense deliberations with fellow citizens and listened to the testimony of politicians and policy experts, research finds changes of opinion to be largely temporary (Kuklinski et al. 2000; Luskin, Fishkin, and Jowell 2002). Members of the public who are the easiest to sway in the short run are those without crystallized opinions. However, opinions that people altered in response to presidential leadership may quickly be forgotten as issues fade into the background, the realities of daily life confront issue positions, or a better understanding of the implications of support for the president for basic values clarifies policy options. This slippage is especially likely to occur in foreign policy, the area where the president's influence on public opinion may be greatest.

The president is not always advantaged on new issues, however. Stem cell research was not on the minds of most voters until George W. Bush announced in a nationally televised address that he would allow the federal government to fund research using stem cells that had been created in the past in a process that destroyed human embryos, but he would not allow funding for stem cell research that would destroy additional embryos in the future. Although a majority of the public initially approved of the president's decision, Bush's advantage soon faded. By the following May, a majority of the public felt medical research using stem cells obtained from human embryos was morally acceptable and the percentage increased to nearly two-thirds by 2007. At that point, 60 percent of the public also wanted fewer or no restrictions on federal funding for stem cell research (Edwards 2009, 93–4).

Opinion may be fluid even on elements of highly salient ongoing policies. In September 2007, the Gallup Poll asked whether respondents favored the plan of General David Petraeus and President Bush to withdraw about 40,000 troops from Iraq by the summer of 2008, but not to make a commitment to further withdrawals until that time. Gallup also asked whether respondents supported a plan introduced by Democratic senators that called for the withdrawal of most US troops within nine months. The muddled results revealed that similar and large percentages of Americans favored each plan—and 45 percent of the public favored both plans. Although the president was not able to obtain the public's support solely for his preferred option, he was able to buy himself time to pursue his policy (Edwards 2009, 94–5).

On rare occasions, a crisis may hit the US, creating new issues overnight. The onset of the Great Depression in 1929, the taking of US hostages in Iran in 1975, and the terrorist attacks of September 11, 2001, are examples. In such cases, most in the public look to the White House to respond to the new problem rapidly. In most instances, this deference provides the president an opportunity to build support for his policies by demonstrating competence and resolution. Franklin D. Roosevelt exploited the crisis atmosphere to obtain passage of his New Deal legislation. George W. Bush won most of what he sought for fighting the war on terrorism abroad, investigating and prosecuting terrorism at home, and reorganizing the government to enhance domestic security.

Policies not directly relevant to the crisis are not likely to receive public support, however. Bipartisanship in one arena does not necessarily carry over in another. The public did not defer to Roosevelt's efforts to prepare the country for entry into the Second World War until events made their impressions (Edwards 2009). Similarly, the politics of the war on terrorism did not fundamentally alter the consideration of domestic policy issues in 2001–2. Those issues continued to divide the public and their representatives in Congress as they had before the September 11 attacks, as the differences between the parties emerged (Edwards 2007, ch. 5). Moreover, the public found Herbert Hoover and Jimmy Carter wanting in their response to crises and elected their opponents in the next elections.

There is no literature that focuses systematically on leading the public under conditions of fluidity or indifference. To do so requires first identifying issues on which opinion is fluid or indifferent. Then we must measure change in opinion, a challenge because there may be no measures of opinion prior to the president's raising an issue. Easier to deal with will be measuring opinion over time, a concern because any opinion change may be fragile. Naturally, we will have to control for other explanations for opinion change.

CONCLUSION

We have only just begun to study presidential leadership of the public systematically. Developing measures of presidential effort, public response, and appropriate controls should be high on our research agenda. So should a focus on explaining the frequent failure of the White House to move the public to support the president and his proposals.

There are several means by which presidents might increase their chances of success in leading the public by exploiting *existing* public opinion. At this point, we know little about them and need systematic studies of efforts to frame policy proposals and their consequences; the ability of the White House to increase the salience of its initiatives, clarify the public's wishes and show how they are consistent with its policies; define themselves and their parties in ways that channel existing opinion on the issues into support for a party program over the longer term; and exploit the public's opinion fluidity or indifference regarding an issue.

We also should consider the consequences of limits on the president's ability to lead the public. The adoption of a core governing strategy of changing public opinion based on a belief in the potential of persuasive leadership may encourage presidents to underestimate their opponents and eschew necessary compromises in the mistaken belief that they can move the public. In the process, the White House may suffer significant opportunity costs as it overlooks less dramatic, but more realistic, chances for success.

If presidents cannot persuade (and if, in polarized times, there is not a middle of the electorate that is persuadable), should presidents abandon attempts to govern from the center or to adopt an inclusive orientation to policy making? Do the limitations on presidential persuasion inevitably create incentives for polarizing politics in order to mobilize a president's base, which already agrees with his policies? Is one consequence of such a strategy that the president will rarely enjoy substantial public support and it is likely to fall to very low approval ratings in tough times?

The rudimentary state of our understanding of public leadership may be an advantage to scholars of the presidency. Answering these questions about leading the public, strategies for exploiting existing opinion, and the consequences of public leadership for governing provides bright opportunities for research on the presidency.

REFERENCES

BAKER, J. A., III. 2006. "Work Hard, Study... and Keep Out of Politics!" New York: G. P. Putnam's Sons.

BARTELS, L. 2002. Beyond the Running Tally: Partisan Bias in Political Perceptions. *Political Behavior*, 24: 117–50.

BAUM, M. A., and KERNELL, S. 1999. Has Cable Ended the Golden Age of Presidential Television? *American Political Science Review*, 93: 99–114.

BAUMGARTNER, F., and JONES, B. D. 1993. *Agendas and Instability in American Politics*. Chicago: University of Chicago Press.

BEHR, R. L., and IYENGAR, S. 1985. Television News, Real-World Cues, and Changes in the Public Agenda. *Public Opinion Quarterly*, 49: 38–57.

BERINSKY, A. J. 2007. Assuming the Costs of War: Events, Elites, and American Public Support for Military Conflict. *Journal of Politics*, 69: 975–97.

BLUMENTHAL, S. 1982. *The Permanent Campaign*. New York: Simon & Schuster.

BOYD, G. M. 1986. General Contractor of the White House Staff. *New York Times*, March 4: section A, p. 22.

BRACE, P., and HINCKLEY, B. 1992. *Follow the Leader*. New York: Basic Books.

BROWNSTEIN, R. 2007. *The Second Civil War: How Extreme Partisanship Has Paralyzed Washington and Polarized America*. New York: Penguin Press.

CANES-WRONE, B. 2006. *Who Leads Whom? Presidents, Policy, and the Public*. Princeton, NJ: Princeton University Press.

CAPPELLA, J. N., and JAMIESON, K. H. 1997. *Spiral of Cynicism: The Press and the Public Good*. New York: Oxford University Press.

CARMINES, E. G., and STIMSON, J. A. 1980. The Two Faces of Issue Voting. *American Political Science Review*, 74: 78–91.

———— 1989. *Issue Evolution: Race and the Transformation of American Politics.* Princeton, NJ: Princeton University Press.

CHONG, D., and DRUCKMAN, J. N. 2007. Framing Public Opinion in Competitive Democracies. *American Political Science Review,* 101: 637–55.

COBB, M. D., and KUKLINSKI, J. H. 1997. Changing Minds: Political Arguments and Political Persuasion. *American Journal of Political Science,* 41: 88–121.

COHEN, J. E. 1997. *Presidential Responsiveness and Public Policy-Making.* Ann Arbor: University of Michigan Press.

COHEN, J. E. 2008. *The Presidency in the Ear of 24-Hour News.* Princeton, NJ: Princeton University Press.

CONOVER, P. J., and SIGELMAN, L. 1982. Presidential Influence and Public Opinion: The Case of the Iranian Hostage Crisis. *Social Science Quarterly,* 63: 249–64.

CONVERSE, P. E. 1964. The Nature of Belief Systems in Mass Publics. In *Ideology and Discontent,* ed. D. E. Apter. New York: Free Press.

DRAPER, R. 2007. *Dead Certain: The Presidency of George W. Bush.* New York: Free Press.

DREW, E. 1996. *Showdown: The Struggle between the Gingrich Congress and the Clinton White House.* New York: Simon & Schuster.

DRUCKMAN, J. N. 2001a. Using Credible Advice to Overcome Framing Effects. *Journal of Law, Economics, and Organization,* 17/1: 62–82.

———— 2001b. On the Limits of Framing Effects: Who Can Frame? *Journal of Politics,* 63: 1041–66.

———— 2004. Political Preference Formation: Competition, Deliberation, and the (Ir)relevance of Framing Effects. *American Political Science Review,* 98: 671–86.

———— and HOLMES, J. W. 2004. Does Presidential Rhetoric Matter? Priming and Presidential Approval. *Presidential Studies Quarterly,* 34: 755–78.

———— JACOBS, L. R., and OSTERMEIER, E. 2004. Candidate Strategies to Prime Issues and Image. *Journal of Politics,* 66: 1180–202.

———— and NELSON, K. R. 2003. Framing and Deliberation: How Citizens' Conversations Limit Elite Influence. *American Journal of Political Science,* 47: 729–45.

EDWARDS, G. C., III. 1983. *The Public Presidency.* New York: St Martin's.

———— 1996. Presidential Rhetoric: What Difference Does It Make? In *The Future of the Rhetorical Presidency,* ed. M. J. Medhurst. College Station: Texas A&M University Press.

———— 2003. *On Deaf Ears.* New Haven, CT: Yale University Press.

———— 2007. *Governing by Campaigning: The Politics of the Bush Presidency,* 2nd edn. New York: Longman.

———— 2009. *The Strategic President: Persuasion and Opportunity in Presidential Leadership.* Princeton, NJ: Princeton University Press.

EISINGER, R. M. 2003. *The Evolution of Presidential Polling.* Cambridge: Cambridge University Press.

ERIKSON, R. S., MACKUEN, M. B., and STIMSON, J. A. 2002. *The Macro Polity.* New York: Cambridge University Press.

FELDMAN, J. 2007. *Framing the Debate: Famous Presidential Speeches and How Progressives Can Use Them to Change the Conversation (and Win Elections).* New York: Ig Publishing.

FELDMAN, S., and ZALLER, J. 1992. The Political Culture of Ambivalence: Ideological Responses to the Welfare State. *American Journal of Political Science,* 36: 268–307.

FETT, P. J. 1994. Presidential Legislative Priorities and Legislators' Voting Decisions: An Exploratory Analysis. *Journal of Politics,* 56: 502–12.

FISKE, S. T. 1980. Attention and Weight in Person Perception: The Impact of Negative and Extreme Behavior. *Journal of Personality and Social Psychology,* 38/6: 889–906.

GAINES, B. J., KUKLINSKI, J. H., QUIRK, P. J., PEYTON, B., and VERKUILEN, J. 2007. Same Facts, Different Interpretations: Partisan Motivation and Opinion on Iraq. *Journal of Politics*, 69: 957–74.

GELMAN, A., and KING, G. 1993. Why Are American Presidential Elections Campaign Polls So Variable When Votes Are So Predictable? *British Journal of Political Science*, 23: 409–51.

GERGEN, D. 2000. *Eyewitness to Power: The Essence of Leadership*. New York: Simon & Schuster.

GLAROS, R., and MIROFF, B. 1983. Watching Ronald Reagan: Viewers' Reaction to the President on Television. *Congress and the Presidency*, 10: 25–46.

GOLD, V. 1994. George Bush Speaks Out. *The Washingtonian*, Feb.

GROSSMAN, M. B., and KUMAR, M. J. 1981. *Portraying the President*. Baltimore: Johns Hopkins University Press.

HAIDER-MARKEL, D. P., and JOSLYN, M. R. 2001. Gun Policy, Opinion, Tragedy, and Blame Attribution: The Conditional Influence of Issue Frames. *Journal of Politics*, 63: 520–43.

HAMILTON, D. L., and ZANNA, M. P. 1972. Differential Weighting of Favorable and Unfavorable Attributes in Impressions of Personality. *Journal of Experimental Research in Personality*, 6/2–3: 204–12.

HART, R. P. 1987. *The Sound of Leadership: Presidential Communication in the Modern Age*. Chicago: University of Chicago Press.

HEITH, D. J. 2004. *Polling to Govern: Public Opinion and Presidential Leadership*. Palo Alto, CA: Stanford University Press.

HILL, K. Q. 1998. The Policy Agendas of the President and the Mass Public: A Research Validation and Extension. *American Journal of Political Science*, 42: 1328–34.

HILLYGUS, D. S., and SHIELDS, T. G. 2008. *The Persuadable Voter: Wedge Issues in Presidential Campaigns*. Princeton, NJ: Princeton University Press.

HOFSTADTER, R. 1954. *The American Political Tradition*. New York: Vintage.

HOLMES, L. M. 2007. Presidential Strategy in the Judicial Appointments Press. *American Politics Research*, 35: 567–94.

HUBER, G. A., and LAPINSKI, J. S. 2006. The Race Card Revisited: Assessing Racial Priming in Policy Contests. *American Journal of Political Science*, 50: 421–40.

JACOBS, L. R., and SHAPIRO, R. Y. 1994. Issues, Candidate Image, and Priming: The Use of Private Polls in Kennedy's 1960 Presidential Campaign. *American Political Science Review*, 88: 527–40.

——— 1995. The Rise of Presidential Polling: The Nixon White House in Historical Perspective. *Public Opinion Quarterly*, 5: 163–95.

——— 2000. *Politicians Don't Pander*. Chicago: University of Chicago Press.

JACOBY, W. G. 1988. The Sources of Liberal-Conservative Thinking: Education and Conceptualization. *Political Behavior*, 10: 316–32.

JONES, B. D. 1994. *Reconceiving Decision-Making in Democratic Politics*. Chicago: University of Chicago Press.

—— and BAUMGARTNER, F. R. 2005. *The Politics of Attention: How Government Prioritizes Problems*. Chicago: University of Chicago Press.

KAHNEMAN, D., and TVERSKY, A. 1979. Prospect Theory: An Analysis of Decision under Risk. *Econometrica*, 47: 263–92.

——— 1984. Choices, Values, and Frames. *American Psychologist*, 39: 341–50.

KERNELL, S. 1984. The Presidency and the People: The Modern Paradox. In *The Presidency and the Political System*, ed. M. Nelson. Washington, DC: Congressional Quarterly Press, 1984.

—— 2007. *Going Public*, 4th edn. Washington, DC: CQ Press.

KINGDON, J. W. 1995. *Agendas, Alternatives, and Public Policies*, 2nd edn. Boston: Little, Brown.

KUKLINSKI, J. H., and HURLEY, N. 1994. On Hearing and Interpreting Messages: A Cautionary Tale of Citizen Cue-Taking. *Journal of Politics*, 56: 729–51.

——— QUIRK, P. J., JERIT, J., SCHWIEDER, D., and RICH, R. F. 2000. Misinformation and the Currency of Democratic Citizenship. *Journal of Politics*, 62: 790–816.

KULL, S., RAMSAY, C., and LEWIS, E. 2003–4. Misperceptions, the Media, and the Iraq War. *Political Science Quarterly*, 118: 569–98.

KUMAR, M. J. 2007. *Managing the Presidents Message: The White House Communications Operation*. Baltimore: Johns Hopkins University Press.

LAKOFF, G. 2004. *Don't Think of an Elephant*. White River, VT: Chelsea Green Publishing Company.

LAU, R. 1985. Two Explanations for Negativity Effects in Political Behavior. *American Journal of Political Science*, 29: 119–38.

LOWI, T. J. 1985. *The Personal President*. Ithaca, NY: Cornell University Press.

LUNTZ, F. 2007. *Words that Work*. New York: Hyperion.

LUSKIN, R. C. 1987. Measuring Political Sophistication. *American Journal of Political Science*, 31: 856–99.

——— FISHKIN, J. S., and JOWELL, R. 2002. Considered Opinions: Deliberative Polling in Britain. *British Journal of Political Science*, 32: 455–87.

MALTESE, J. A. 1992. *Spin Control: The White House Office of Communications and the Management of Presidential News*. Chapel Hill: University of North Carolina Press.

MARCUS, G. E., NEUMAN, W. R., and MACUEN, M. 2000. *Affective Intelligence and Political Judgment*. Chicago: University of Chicago Press.

MEDHURST, M. J. 2008. From Retrospect to Prospect: The Study of Presidential Rhetoric, 1915–2005. In *The Prospect of Presidential Rhetoric*, ed. J. A. Aune and M. J. Medhurst. College Station: Texas A&M University Press.

MILLER, J. M. 2007. Examining the Mediators of Agenda Setting: A New Experimental Paradigm Reveals the Role of Emotions. *Political Psychology*, 28: 689–717.

——— and KROSNICK, J. A. 2000. News Media Impact on the Ingredients of Presidential Evaluations: Politically Knowledgeable Citizens Are Guided by a Trusted Source. *American Journal of Political Science*, 44: 301–15.

MONDAK, J. J. 1993. Source Cues and Public Approval: The Cognitive Dynamics of Public Support for the Reagan Administration. *American Journal of Political Science*, 37: 186–212.

MUELLER, J. E. 1970. *War, Presidents, and Public Opinion*. New York: Wiley.

MURRAY, S. K., and HOWARD, P. 2002. Variations in White House Polling Operations. *Public Opinion Quarterly*, 66: 527–58.

NELSON, M. 1988. The President and the Court: Reinterpreting the Court-Packing Episode of 1937. *Political Science Quarterly*, 103: 267–93.

NEUMAN, W. R. 1986. *The Paradox of Mass Politics; Knowledge and Opinion in the American Electorate*. Cambridge, MA: Harvard University Press.

PAGE, B. I., and SHAPIRO, R. Y. 1985. Presidential Leadership through Public Opinion. In *The Presidency and Public Policy Making*, ed. G. C. Edwards III, S. Y. Shull, and N. C. Thomas. Pittsburgh: University of Pittsburgh Press.

——— ——— 1992. *The Rational Public*. Chicago: University of Chicago Press.

——— ——— and DEMPSEY, G. R. 1987. What Moves Public Opinion? *American Political Science Review*, 81: 23–44.

PETROCIK, J. R. 1991. Divided Government: Is It All in the Campaigns? In *The Politics of Divided Government*, ed. G. W. Cox and S. Kernell. Boulder, CO: Westview Press.

——— 1996. Issue Ownership in Presidential Elections, with a 1980 Case Study. *American Journal of Political Science*, 40: 825–50.

RAGSDALE, L. 1984. The Politics of Presidential Speechmaking, 1949–1980. *American Political Science Review*, 78: 971–84.

——1987. Presidential Speechmaking and the Public Audience: Individual Presidents and Group Attitudes. *Journal of Politics*, 49: 704–36.

REAGAN, R. 1990. *An American Life*. New York: Simon & Schuster.

RIKER, W. B. 1984. The Heresthetics of Constitution Making: The Presidency in 1787, with Comments on Determinism and Rational Choice. *American Political Science Review*, 78: 1–16.

——1986. *The Art of Political Manipulation*. New Haven, CT: Yale University Press.

——1996. *The Strategy of Rhetoric: Campaigning for the American Constitution*. New Haven, CT: Yale University Press.

ROSSI, E. J. 1965. Mass and Attentive Opinion on Nuclear Weapons Test and Fallout, 1954–1963. *Public Opinion Quarterly*, 29: 280–97.

SCHATTSCHNEIDER, E. E. 1960. *The Semisovereign People: A Realist's View of Democracy in America*. New York: Holt, Rinehart & Winston.

SHAFER, B. E., and CLAGGETT, W. J. M. 1995. *The Two Majorities: The Issue Context of Modern American Politics*. Baltimore: Johns Hopkins University Press.

——and JOHNSTON, R. 2006. *The End of Southern Exceptionalism*. Cambridge, MA: Harvard University Press.

SIGELMAN, L. 1980a. Gauging the Public Response to Presidential Leadership. *Presidential Studies Quarterly*, 10: 427–33.

——1980b. The Commander in Chief and the Public: Mass Response to Johnson's March 31, 1968 Bombing Halt Speech. *Journal of Political and Military Sociology*, 8: 1–14.

——and SIGELMAN, C. K. 1981. Presidential Leadership of Public Opinion: From Benevolent Leader to Kiss of Death? *Experimental Study of Politics*, 7/3: 1–22.

SIMON, D. M., and OSTROM, C. W., JR. 1989. The Impact of Televised Speeches and Foreign Travel on Presidential Approval. *Public Opinion Quarterly*, 53: 58–82.

SKOWRONEK, S. 1993. *The Politics Presidents Make*. Cambridge, MA: Harvard University Press.

——2005. Leadership by Definition: First Term Reflections on George W. Bush's Political Stance. *Perspectives on Politics*, 3: 817–31.

SMITH, M. 2007. *The Right Talk: How Conservatives Transformed the Great Society into the Economic Society*. Princeton, NJ: Princeton University Press.

SNIDERMAN, P. M. 2000. Taking Sides: A Fixed Choice Theory of Political Reasoning. In *Elements of Reason: Understanding and Expanding the Limits of Political Rationality*, ed. A. Lupia, M. D. McCubbins, and S. L. Popkin. New York: Cambridge University Press.

——and THERIAULT, S. M. 2004. The Structure of Political Argument and the Logic of Issue Framing. In *Studies in Public Opinion: Attitudes, Nonattitudes, Measurement Error and Change*, ed. W. E. Saris and P. M. Sniderman. Princeton, NJ: Princeton University Press.

SORENSEN, T. C. 1965. *Kennedy*. London: Hodder & Stoughton.

STIMSON, J. A. 1991. *Public Opinion in America: Moods, Cycles, and Swings*. Boulder, CO: Westview.

TENPAS, K. D., and McCANN, J. A. 2007. Testing the Permanence of the Permanent Campaign: An Analysis of Presidential Polling Expenditures, 1977–2002. *Public Opinion Quarterly*, 71: 349–66.

THOMAS, D., and SIGELMAN, L. 1985. Presidential Identification and Policy Leadership: Experimental Evidence on the Reagan Case. In *The Presidency and Public Policy Making*, ed. G. C. Edwards III, S. A. Shull, and N. C. Thomas. Pittsburgh: University of Pittsburgh Press.

TULIS, J. K. 1984. The Two Constitutional Presidencies. In *The Presidency and the Political System*, ed. M. Nelson. Washington, DC: CQ Press.

—— 1987. *The Rhetorical Presidency*. Princeton, NJ: Princeton University Press.

WALDMAN, M. 2000. *POTUS Speaks*. New York: Simon & Schuster.

WLEZIEN, C. 1995. The Public as a Thermostat: Dynamics of Preferences for Spending. *American Journal of Political Science*, 39: 981–1000.

—— 1996. Dynamics of Representation: The Case of U.S. Spending on Defense. *British Journal of Political Science*, 26: 81–103.

WOOD, B. D. 2007. *The Politics of Economic Leadership*. Princeton, NJ: Princeton University Press.

WOODWARD, B. 1996. *The Choice*. New York: Simon & Schuster.

—— 1999. *Shadow*. New York: Simon & Schuster.

ZALLER, J. R. 1992. *The Nature and Origins of Mass Opinion*. New York: Cambridge University Press.

—— 1994. Elite Leadership of Mass Opinion: New Evidence from the Gulf War. In *Taken by Storm: The Media, Public Opinion, and U.S. Foreign Policy in the Gulf War*, ed. W. L. Bennett and D. L. Paletz. Chicago: University of Chicago Press.

ZAREFSKY, D. 1986. *President Johnson's War on Poverty: Rhetoric and History*. University: University of Alabama Press.

—— 1990. *Lincoln, Douglas, and Slavery: In the Crucible of Public Debate*. Chicago: University of Chicago Press.

CHAPTER 10

....

UNDERSTANDING THE RHETORICAL PRESIDENCY

....

TERRI BIMES

THE political science literature often gives the study of rhetoric short shrift. At a 1995 conference on "The Future of the Rhetorical Presidency," George Edwards (1996) struck a nerve in the field of presidential rhetoric when he equated the study of presidential rhetoric to literary criticism. After a review of several of the major works in the field of presidential rhetoric, Edwards concluded that most research on presidential rhetoric lacks clear hypotheses and systematic evidence. Moreover his subsequent finding in *On Deaf Ears* (2003) that going public rarely moves a national audience begs the question of why study rhetoric at all.

Is this assessment of the field of presidential rhetoric correct? The task of reviewing research on presidential rhetoric is complicated because it is a topic that bridges two disciplines—political communications and political science (Medhurst 1996; Stuckey and Antczak 1998; Windt 1986; Zarefsky 2004). The standards and assumptions of political communication scholars are typically much different from those of political scientists. While political scientists tend to focus on identifying and testing causal explanations, political communication scholars who study presidential rhetoric tend to be critical of using the scientific method. Martin Medhurst (1996, xv–xvi), Professor of Rhetoric and Communication at Baylor University and the former head of the Program in Presidential Rhetoric at Texas A&M University, understands presidential rhetoric as art, not science. He argues that "to reduce rhetoric to a linear, one-to-one, cause–effect relation between the message (cause) and audience reaction (effect) is to fundamentally misunderstand the nature of the art." It is not about "outcomes but rather judgment and power of interpretation that the speaker displays in assessing the situation, the appropriate language, arguments, timing, occasion and audience." Although there are some scholars who engage both fields (Roderick Hart, Kathleen Hall Jamieson, and Mary Stuckey to name a few), scholars working on presidential rhetoric within the political science field (Tulis 1987; Ellis and Kirk 1995; Wood 2007a) tend not to build on the work of political communication scholars. In addition, political scientists, such as Edwards, who approach the study of politics quantitatively are largely dismissive of political scientists who study presidential rhetoric in an interpretive, qualitative way.

For presidential rhetoric to become a more central subfield in political science, scholars operating in the political communications field as well as those in the political science need to find more rigorous ways to test their theories. Although much of the field is guilty of Edwards's charges, there are several recent exemplars in the presidential rhetoric field that run contrary to his assessment. New data sources, the deployment of sophisticated content analysis techniques, and systematic historical research (using both quantitative and qualitative methods) have generated noteworthy progress in recent years. Using these methods, scholars have made several advances in helping to explain historical patterns of presidential rhetoric (Ellis 2008) and the effects of political rhetoric on the public's attitudes and on elite opinion (Wood 2007a).

This chapter begins by considering the historical development of presidential rhetoric, with a particular focus on Jeffrey Tulis's agenda-setting study of the rhetorical presidency. Although a series of subsequent studies have challenged Tulis's specific claims, his analysis had a substantial influence on both political science and political communications scholarship on presidential rhetoric and thus is a useful lens for considering what we have learned about the development of presidential rhetoric. The chapter then turns to a consideration of the impact of presidential rhetoric on American politics, reviewing both quantitative political science studies and more interpretative works by political communications scholars. I conclude by considering directions for further work that will capitalize on the promise of new data sources to address substantively important questions.

HISTORICAL PATTERNS OF PRESIDENTIAL RHETORIC

How have presidents' conceptions of their role vis-à-vis the public changed over time? How have their rhetorical practices changed to reflect these transitions, and what impact have these changes had on our polity? What factors drive changes in the president's relationship with the public and in presidential rhetorical practices? These are the core questions that the literature on the rhetorical presidency has attempted to answer. The first major effort to provide answers emerged with the publication of the article "The Rise of the Rhetorical Presidency" (Ceaser et al.) in 1981 and Jeffrey Tulis's book *The Rhetorical Presidency* in 1987 (see also Thurow and Wallin 1984). These landmark works argue that the presidency underwent a major transformation with the administration of Woodrow Wilson. Tulis (1987, 132) asserts that Wilson's doctrine of popular leadership represented nothing less than "a major shift, indeed a reversal, of the founding perspective." After Wilson, presidents shifted from constitutional rhetoric and embraced a more popular, "inspirational" rhetoric, one that sought to "'interpret' the wishes of the people" and to use these public appeals to influence Congress through mass pressure. Terms such as "voice of the nation," the "permanent campaign," and the "nation's trumpet" capture this modern conception of popular leadership (Ceaser et al. 1981, 240).

The strength of Tulis's book is that he attempts to show empirically how these doctrines shape rhetorical practice. He makes two core claims about the development of the rhetorical presidency. First, the Framers sought to proscribe presidential popular leadership. These ideas, as explicated in the *Federalist Papers*, then shaped eighteenth- and nineteenth-century presidential rhetorical practice. Examining "approximately one thousand" unofficial speeches as well as official rhetoric, Tulis finds that although presidents went out on tours of the country in the nineteenth century, they confined themselves to ceremonial and non-policy-specific speech. These presidents may have been "public" figures in the sense of making ceremonial addresses, but they were not "popular" leaders. When presidents broke the norms governing popular leadership, the consequences were severe—most notably Andrew Johnson's impeachment following his 1866 "swing around the circle," an attempt to rally the public to support his lenient policy toward former Confederates.

Second, the writings of Woodrow Wilson dramatically transformed the norms governing presidential practice. Wilson's exposition of the doctrine of popular leadership constituted an informal second constitution legitimizing—and even requiring—popular presidential leadership. In Tulis's view, the key factor driving the emergence of the rhetorical presidency is doctrine. Without a change in doctrine, rhetorical leadership practices could not have changed so dramatically. Technological changes, the rise of the mass media, and the modern campaign have exercised only a secondary influence on the transformation of presidential rhetoric. They facilitate change rather than create it. The rise of television and radio did not change norms of presidential behavior but just permitted presidents to speak more often to more people.

Starting with Wilson, presidents began to pitch the delivery and the content of their official addresses for public consumption. Most telling, Tulis finds that the quality of speeches and messages has declined as presidents adopted this new mode of rhetoric, with bulleted policy lists and inspirational rhetoric replacing reasoned argument based on constitutional principles. Tulis (1987, 181) credits Wilson's doctrine with creating the energy necessary to justify policies, but argues that the rise of the rhetorical presidency is "more deleterious than beneficial"—a claim backed up by the work of his co-authors (Ceaser et al. 1981; Thurow 1996). The problem for modern leaders is that Wilson's second constitution mandating popular leadership did not simply replace the first Constitution but was layered on top of it. Modern presidents must navigate their way through these two conflicting constitutions and the result is that presidents lack a precise compass on how to lead. Presidents are simultaneously expected to be the head of state representing a stable constitutional order and a popular politician swaying the public to support new initiatives; the tensions between these divergent sets of expectations make the contemporary presidency a dysfunctional office.

The major drawback of Tulis's framework is that his evidence that written doctrines were the main cause of changes in rhetorical practices was indirect and far from conclusive. Drawing upon new evidence and a reexamination of historical materials, scholars have undermined many of the basic claims regarding the importance of doctrinal changes in driving changes in the president's relationship to the public and in rhetorical practices. These critiques provide a more accurate depiction of presidential rhetoric over time. Yet, it is to Tulis's credit that *The Rhetorical Presidency* generated such a lively research agenda. Indeed, a special issue of *Critical Review* published in 2008 was entirely devoted to assessing the lasting impact of Tulis's study.

CRITIQUES OF THE RHETORICAL PRESIDENCY

Critiques of the rhetorical presidency thesis fall into four areas: first, challenges to the claim that constitutional doctrine prohibited popular leadership; second, critiques focusing on nineteenth-century practice, noting repeated outbursts of popular presidential leadership that conflict with Tulis's account; third, critiques of Tulis's treatment of Wilson's doctrine of popular leadership, arguing that Wilson wanted to constrain not unleash presidential popular leadership; and fourth, political communications scholars have claimed that Tulis's understanding of rhetoric is too limited. In the end, although Tulis's specific hypotheses about the rise of the rhetorical presidency have been weakened, our understanding of the development of presidential popular leadership has advanced considerably as a result of the research inspired by his theory.

Constitutional Presidency

At the base of the rhetorical presidency thesis is the doctrine that the Constitution prohibited popular leadership. David Nichols (1994, 10) offers the most radical critique of Tulis's interpretation of constitutional doctrine, arguing that the president's role as popular leader is "a logical outgrowth of the decisions made at the Constitutional Convention and embodied in the Constitution." According to Nichols, the adoption of the Electoral College and the provision that the president report on the state of the union are evidence that the Founders viewed popular leadership as a source of authority for the president. Nichols makes the case that the Electoral College was *not* adopted primarily out of a concern to restrain popular leadership, as Tulis argues, but as a way to assuage those delegates who were concerned about the balance of representation between large states and small states as well as slave states and free states (for an alternative view see Edwards 2004). Nichols also points out that by requiring that the president report on the state of the union, the Founders institutionalized the president's agenda-setting role.

Laracey (2002) and Bimes (2008), in turn, argue that the Constitution was ambiguous at best on the propriety of presidential popular leadership. There was no explicit support or opposition for popular leadership written into the Constitution. Laracey argues that there were two "constitutional orthodoxies:" the Federalist view that opposed public leadership and the Anti-Federalist view that supported it. Bimes, in contrast, argues that the Framers' debates about the design of the presidency paid remarkably little attention to the question of how the president was to relate to the general public. Although it is unlikely that the Framers expected the president to be an active popular leader, they made little effort to specify constraints on how the president would relate to the public. For example, it was unclear what kind of people would be chosen as electors or even how they would be chosen (Storing 1981, 168).[1] Rather than specifying that electors would be selected by the state legislatures, the Constitution allowed the legislatures to determine how the electors would be chosen. This resulted in a mixed system in which roughly half of the states initially used some version of popular election.

The Constitution's ambiguity left it to the first several presidents, particularly George Washington, to work out the president's relationship to the public through their practice in office. Thus, even if one rejects Nichols's argument that the Framers were the authors of the rhetorical presidency, the Founding emerges from this literature as more vague and ambivalent about the president's role vis-à-vis the public than one would expect from Tulis's account.

Early Rhetorical Practice

Given this constitutional ambiguity, it is not surprising to find much more variation in nineteenth-century presidential practice than Tulis presents in his book. From the start, presidents claimed an allegiance to patrician norms of restraint, yet also repeatedly used their unique institutional position as the sole representative of the

---

[1] The Framers specified that the electors were not to be members of Congress or "holding an office of trust or profit under the United States" and that electors needed to meet the same eligibility requirements as members of the House of Representatives.

entire country as a tool in political battles with their opponents. Laracey argues that one of the chief ways presidents attempted to publicize their policy positions to a broader audience in the nineteenth century was by planting anonymous editorials in the presidential newspaper (Laracey 2002). Presidential newspapers, or so-called "presidential organs," provided a useful mechanism for presidents to get their opinions heard. In return for a lucrative contract to print all government documents, the editor of the administration newspaper acted as an informal presidential mouth-piece. Jackson explained his removal of deposits with an "unofficial" statement placed in the *Globe,* the presidential organ of his administration, claiming that a statement had to be made to "counteract the gross misrepresentations that were circulated, and that the full view of the case should be made to the people and representatives before the meeting of Congress" (as cited in Laracey 1998, 73). President Zachary Taylor ordered the editor of the presidential newspaper to attack members of Congress who voiced opinions that were inconsistent with his own on more than one occasion. When he clashed with Henry Clay over the issue of slavery in the western states, Taylor instructed his editor to publish an editorial critical of Clay's argument (Laracey 1998, 79).[2]

Tulis (1996) is skeptical that such anonymous editorials constitute a challenge to his theory. For Laracey to directly challenge his theory, Tulis suggests that Laracey needs to "show that the public 'blamed' presidents for controversial positions taken by their partisan organ in the same way the public blames misstatements or controversy on the president today." But a more specific test would be to examine what the public knew about the president's relationship to the newspaper. That is, the hurdle should be to show that it was widely known that the president was placing editorials in the newspaper and nevertheless there was no public outcry against the presidents' actions.

Regardless of the degree to which the public understood the president's relation-ship to the newspapers, the use of anonymous editorials in the presidential news-paper helps us understand the tensions surrounding popular leadership in the nineteenth century. Presidents were attempting simultaneously to appear to adhere to patrician leadership norms (in that they did not reveal their identity) while at the same time pushing against the boundaries of these norms (trying to exercise leader-ship through the editorials in the first place and evidently allowing their efforts to be discovered).[3]

---

[2] On a few notable occasions, nineteenth-century presidents used public letters as part of an effort to rally public support for their position or to pressure Congress or other adversaries. Most notably, John Adams drafted a series of 71 public letters in response to petitions critical of France's actions in the XYZ affair. Adams used the replies, which were reprinted in newspapers, to make explicit policy claims, attack his political foes, and build public support for the Federalists and for a military build-up against France (see Hoffman 1997 and Bimes 2008).

[3] It is also worth noting that presidential control of newspapers diminished over the first half of the nineteenth century due to increasing congressional control over printing contracts that had often been the lifeline for the survival of administration newspapers. With the creation of the Government Printing Office in 1860, presidents could no longer as easily exchange lucrative printing contracts for positive coverage. Presidents now had to use more direct means of getting coverage in the newspapers, such as public letters.

More directly, several presidents in the nineteenth century (including James Monroe, Andrew Jackson, Martin Van Buren, Zachary Taylor, and Andrew Johnson) attempted to use tours of the nation to establish and publicize their positions on issues, reaching beyond the goodwill tours of Washington. Ellis and Walker (2007) focus on Taylor's 1849 tour of Pennsylvania to assess the content of speeches and the public's reaction to them as gauged by partisan newspaper coverage. Whereas Tulis finds that Taylor's speeches consisted of platitudes, Ellis and Walker show that Taylor in several speeches explicitly took positions on the issues of his day, stating his support for the protective tariff, internal improvements, and his opposition to the extension of slavery. There was no backlash against Taylor's tour; instead local newspapers reported that the public was pleased to hear the president's policy positions. Ellis (2008) expands the scope of study to encompass tours from George Washington to George W. Bush. He finds that Jacksonian era presidents sought to use tours to satisfy democratic demands for accessibility, yet also confronted pressure to conform to patrician norms of proper decorum. It was acceptable for the president to put forward policy positions while on tour, but not to be overtly partisan.

Beyond simply using their speeches to discuss policy, several nineteenth-century presidents departed from the supposed strictures of patrician leadership by identifying themselves as direct representatives of the public and using this popular authority as a political weapon. Interestingly, it turns out that many of the most ambitious examples of popular leadership claims by nineteenth-century presidents came in their official rhetoric, such as their Annual Messages to Congress, rather than in speeches delivered while out on tour. Tulis's search for examples of popular leadership in the nineteenth century, however, is confined mainly to presidents' unofficial rhetoric. The rationale for this focus is Tulis's assumption that the form of official communication—the method of delivery (written) and the intended audience (Congress)—constrained the content of presidential messages. According to Tulis, presidents used official communications in the nineteenth century to reinforce the image of the presidency as the protector of the nation's principles, and not as a tool of public persuasion. Yet recent scholarship has shown recurrent examples of popular leadership in nineteenth-century presidents' official messages.

One way in which presidents exercised their role as popular leaders was by claiming an electoral mandate. From Tulis's theory, mandate claims should emerge around the turn of the century with Wilson's new doctrine of popular leadership that legitimizes public opinion as a basis for presidential authority. Tulis is not alone in thinking that the mandate is a modern twentieth-century practice. Dahl (1990, 359) credits Wilson with developing the theory of the mandate into its "canonical form."[4] Although twentieth-century presidents are more likely to make mandate claims than their nineteenth-century counterparts (Heidotting-Conley 2001, 56), Ellis and Kirk (1995), in their history of the mandate concept, find that by 1860, both Democratic

---

[4] Although Dahl (1990, 358) notes Jackson's and Polk's use of the mandate, he views these examples as more of an aberration in the nineteenth century. According to him, presidents between Polk and Wilson "seemed to have laid no claim to a popular mandate for their policies—when they had any."

and Republican presidents had endorsed the concept of a mandate. Similarly, Michael Korzi (2004, 95) deems the mandate claims of Andrew Jackson a "watershed event" in the way that presidents spoke about their relationship to the people. Presidents now interpreted their elections through the prism of a party mandate (for an alternative view, see Bimes and Mulroy 2004).

These mandate claims paralleled changes on the campaign trail as presidential discourse became more issue oriented, diluting patrician era norms that barred presidents from campaigning and expressing their views about the issues (Ellis and Dedrick 2000; Heale 1982; Korzi 2004). Several nineteenth-century presidential candidates ventured out on the campaign trail to make their issue positions heard (Harrison in 1840, Douglas in 1860, Seymour in 1868, Greeley in 1872, Blaine in 1884, Bryan in 1896).[5] Others spoke about politics from their front porch—but in front of large crowds brought in by their campaign (Harrison in 1888). Still other presidential candidates turned their acceptance addresses into major policy position papers (Tilden and Hayes in 1876).

The norms against popular campaigning did not disappear entirely. Instead, they coexisted uneasily with the expectation that presidential campaigns would be highly public contests fought out before a mass audience. Richard Ellis and Marc Dedrick (2000, 188) note that nineteenth-century presidential candidates, starting in the 1840s, found themselves "whipsawed between contradictory expectations. On one hand, they were not supposed to seek the presidential office; on the other, they were supposed to engage in a direct and honest dialogue with the people about the issues."

Once in office, several Democratic presidents went beyond the assertion that their policy views had been endorsed at the polls and staked out an independent power base as a populist leader. Bimes and Mulroy (2004) show that nineteenth-century Democratic presidents regularly used populist appeals that framed the president as the unique representative of the people in a battle against specific special interests. Andrew Jackson launched this populist script in the late 1820s, but it became a recurrent theme in Democratic presidential rhetoric. In his veto of the renewal of the Bank in 1832, Jackson charged the Bank with making the "rich richer and the potent more powerful." Sounding the same themes as Jackson, Polk, known as "Young Hickory," declared that the consequence of Clay's American System was to "[enrich] the favored few... at the expense of the many;" its effect was to "make the rich richer and the poor poorer;" and its tendency was to "create distinctions in society based on wealth and to give to the favored classes undue control and sway in Government" (Polk 1848, 2511). This rhetoric is significant in that it shows that nineteenth-century presidents not only claimed an electoral mandate from the people, but also used popular leadership to incite divisions within society. If aggressive popular appeals were a regular part of nineteenth-century presidential rhetoric, then Woodrow Wilson's doctrine of popular leadership, the linchpin in Tulis's study, loses its distinctiveness.

---

[5] Scott in the 1852 presidential election went on an electioneering tour but avoided talking about issues. Cleveland gave two substantive policy speeches, but he did not officially take the stump.

Wilson's Doctrine of Popular Leadership

A third challenge to Tulis's account is that it misconstrues the nature of Wilson's project as president. An examination of Wilson's telling of nineteenth-century presidential history reveals his own deep-seated reservations about popular leadership. In his two historical surveys of the United States, Wilson took to task the leadership of Thomas Jefferson, Andrew Jackson, Andrew Johnson, and William Jennings Bryan for not meeting his own ideals of statesmanship (Bimes and Skowronek 1996; see also Stid 1998). These leaders were "apostles of passion" who did not respect the important values of order and traditional practices. Unlike these leaders (at least in his characterization), Wilson believed that the "government ought to be guarded against the heats and the hastes, the passions and the thoughtless impulses of the people" (Link 1972, Vol. 7, 350). The job of the president was not to act on immediate popular opinion but to respond to a more refined sense of the public will (see Hogan 2006). Thus, it is hard to place Wilson as the central protagonist in legitimizing popular leadership when he believed that such leadership needed to be more constrained than that exhibited by several other nineteenth-century presidents.

The Rhetorical Presidency from a Communications Perspective

The last criticism of Tulis's rhetorical presidency thesis comes primarily from political communication scholars. Several of them have critiqued Tulis's account, with the main objection concerning Tulis's conceptualization of rhetoric. Martin Medhurst (1996) takes issue with Tulis's definition of rhetoric as being too "narrowly drawn," a claim echoed by Stuckey and Antczak (1998), Zarefsky (2002), Smith and Smith (1994), Ivie (1996), and Olson (2001). From the perspective of political communication scholars, the "rhetorical presidency" is not a contemporary problem to lament (or celebrate), but rather is an inherent feature of politics. For these scholars, rhetoric is not simply a popular appeal to a mass audience; nor is it a substitute for or false form of political action. It is itself a symbolic form of action that is endemic to political and social life. To Medhurst, contexts (persons, medium, message, events, and audiences) shape rhetorical practices, but these contexts are complex and indeterminate, making generalizations difficult. Consequently, political communications scholars who study presidential rhetoric have largely been unconcerned with how presidential rhetoric has developed over time (exceptions include Fields 1996; Jamieson 1990; Stuckey 2004; Beasley 2004) and instead have focused on the rhetoric of an individual president or a single speech or contend that the analysis of rhetoric transcends time. Hence, Zarefsky (2002, 24), in a chapter entitled "The Presidency Has Always Been a Place for Rhetorical Leadership," claims that presidents' rhetorical "goals and strategies have been remarkably stable even while the technology for pursuing them has changed with the culture." Notwithstanding these criticisms, it is striking that many authors working in the political communications field use

The Rhetorical Presidency as a backdrop for their more individualized case studies of presidential rhetoric (Ryan 1988; Stuckey 1991).

What is Left of the Rhetorical Presidency Thesis?

Although scholars have critiqued several key aspects of Tulis's rhetorical presidency thesis, his claim that the structure and tone of presidential rhetoric changed in the modern era finds some support in subsequent empirical studies. Lim (2002) and Teten (2003) undertake systematic analyses of presidential State of the Union addresses that provide cautious support for Tulis's claim that the tenor of presidential rhetoric changed significantly with Wilson's presidency. Lim (2002, 331) finds that the word "democracy" shows up only twice in annual messages prior to 1901, whereas the word appears 189 times between 1901 and 2000. Lim also finds that the words "constitution" and "constitutional" have declined as a percentage of inaugural and Annual Messages in the twentieth century, as the percentage use of the word "people" has increased over time. Teten, in turn, assesses whether presidents now use their rhetoric to identify themselves more closely with their audience than in the past. Specifically, he tracks the usage of the words "we" and "our" as a percentage of all words in each State of the Union address. Teten finds that these words constitute just 0.5 percent of the words in the Annual Messages before Wilson's administration. Wilson's 1914 State of the Union address makes much greater use of these words—they constitute 2.5 percent of the words in the speech. After that, Wilson's use of "our" and "we" drops back down for the rest of his term, but there is a gradual upwards trend overall starting with Wilson, so that by the 1950s–1990s, "we" and "our" constitute about 2 percent of the words in State of the Union addresses.

Most of Lim's and Teten's findings, which are calculated as the percentage of words in each speech, need to be placed in perspective of the decreasing length of annual State of the Union messages.[6] The number of words per State of the Union message had been growing rapidly in the late nineteenth century, from an average of about 10,000 words in the 1830s–1870s, to about 20,000 words at the turn of the century (Teten 2003). With Wilson's move to deliver the speech in person, the length of the speech plummeted to about 5,000 words, where it has hovered ever since. This is not surprising, given that a speech of 20,000 words would likely take more than four hours to deliver, but it does suggest that the form of delivery can have a systematic impact on how much is said. Interestingly, the increased percentage in use of the words conveying popular leadership coincides with the shortened length of the speech (see also Murphy 2008). Teten found that the sheer frequency of occurrence of the words "we" and "our" is roughly the same as before Wilson, even as they now constitute a greater percentage of the words used in the message.

---

[6] In this essay, I refer to State of the Union messages but include Annual Messages (a term that was historically used to refer to the State of the Union message) under this term.

At a more general level, Tulis is clearly correct that Wilson's successors give more speeches in person than did his predecessors in office, and that speeches delivered in person will have different characteristics from written messages. Twentieth-century presidents speak more frequently to the public than their nineteenth-century counterparts (Kernell 2006; Hart 1987). Faced with declining audience for their major messages (Baum and Kernell 1999; Kumar 2000; Cohen 2004; Wattenberg 2004), presidents and their surrogates seek out local venues and television talk shows to spread their message (Kernell 2006; Mutz 2001).

However, it is unclear what is driving the change in modern practice. If it is norms that are changing the shape of presidential rhetoric, then all post-Wilson presidents should follow the newly established norm. But the first few Republican presidents who served after Wilson proved reluctant to deliver their State of the Union messages in front of Congress and made only sparing use of public speeches. According to Kolakowski and Neal (2006), Wilson delivered six of his annual messages in person (1913–18); President Warren Harding, two (1921 and 1922); and President Calvin Coolidge, one (1923). Gamm and Smith (1998) mark Theodore Roosevelt as the key turning point in norms governing going public. They argue that the shift from party-dominated campaigns to candidate-centered campaigns helped usher in popular leadership among candidates (see also Ceaser 1979). Yet, their argument is stymied by the same timing difficulties as is Tulis's account. Roosevelt's immediate successor, William Howard Taft, was not an aggressive popular leader, nor were the Republican presidents of the 1920s.

The practice of "going public" only became a common presidential strategy decades later in the 1960s–1970s (Kernell 2006; Lewis 1997). Scholars seeking to explain variation in modern presidents' public activities have pointed to several variables other than norms. Lyn Ragsdale (1984) finds that presidents are more likely to make speeches in response to fluctuations in their popular approval ratings and policy events. Hager and Sullivan (1994) in turn find that technology (an index measure composed of lighted runways, speed of Air Force One, and television outlets) had a significant positive impact on the increase in presidential public activity for the 1949–84 period (although note the exception of press conferences which have actually declined over time. See Eshbaugh-Soha 2003). Lastly, divided party control (Powell 1999) may also increase the frequency of presidential speech making. These empirical studies are useful for showing change within the contours of the modern presidency, but are less useful for explaining longer-term historical change.

In sum, although scholars have challenged several of Tulis's specific empirical claims, his focus on presidential rhetoric as a lens to understand the development of the president's relationship to the mass public (and, through the mass public, with other institutional actors) constitutes a substantial contribution. The underlying problem, however, is that by focusing so much attention on two key moments—the Founding and Wilson's doctrinal innovations—Tulis neglects the many important changes in presidential rhetorical practices in the nineteenth century and in the decades following Wilson. The onset of presidential mandate claims in the Jacksonian era, the use of tours to advocate for policy positions, and the rise of Democratic presidential populism are important innovations that are elided in Tulis's account. Similarly, the routinization of going public in the late twentieth century does not follow closely from Wilson's presidency and instead is likely connected to changes in technology and in the Washington political community that took place in the 1960s–1970s (see Kernell 2006).

DOES PRESIDENTIAL RHETORIC MATTER?

The debate about the sources and timing of the rise of the rhetorical presidency presupposes that presidential popular leadership has a meaningful impact on American politics. In Tulis's account, along with that of Kernell and other scholars, presidents' reliance on public rhetoric persuades the public at times but at the cost of short-circuiting bargaining and deliberation. Critics of Tulis from the political communication perspective suggest that rhetoric moves the president's audience while also having broader symbolic impacts on the political system (e.g., in defining the presidency as an office; see discussion below).

Yet George Edwards's (2003) research on going public indicates that presidents are rarely successful in swaying public opinion. Edwards examines public attitudes on domestic and foreign policy priorities of Ronald Reagan and Bill Clinton and finds that neither was generally successful in swaying the public. Since Reagan and Clinton are widely credited as the most talented rhetorical leaders in recent decades, this finding makes it unlikely that one would find greater effects if one examined other presidents (see also Edwards 2007). Similarly, Edwards shows that presidential approval ratings do not increase following major speeches. If in the end rhetoric has no impact, it may make little sense to study the development of the rhetorical presidency.

Within the political science field, however, several recent studies have shown that rhetoric has an impact on agenda setting, spending priorities, and, at times, on the public's perception of economic conditions. Although presidents may not be able to use their rhetoric to increase their popular approval ratings or support for their policies, they may be able to draw the public's attention to certain issues (Cohen 1995; Hill 1998). Similarly, James Druckman and Justin Holmes (2004) show that respondents who watched President George W. Bush's January 2002 State of the Union address placed more weight on issues emphasized in the address in determining whether they approved of Bush's job performance. Druckman and Holmes employed a clever research design that includes an experimental component that allows them to control what the subjects watched and to measure their reactions shortly after the speech. They also incorporated a nationally representative sample from a panel survey in order to address concerns about the external validity of the experimental study. The panel survey shows that respondents who watched the speech based their evaluation of Bush more on his handling of terrorism than they had prior to the speech; by contrast, the terrorism issue did not have a heightened impact for non-watchers.

There is reason to be skeptical that particular speeches will have lasting effects priming the public because other studies have shown that presidential rhetoric often follows, rather than leads, media attention to issues (see Wood and Peake 1998; Edwards and Wood 1999). Thus, a single major speech may not generate sustained media (and thus public) attention to an issue. Nevertheless, the study provides a promising design for further research.

Brandice Canes-Wrone (2006) finds that presidents are generally successful in increasing spending on the issues that they target in their major speeches. Although there are difficult endogeneity issues involved in identifying the impact of presidential speeches (since presidents do not target a random sample of programs and instead may focus on areas in which support for change is already building), Canes-Wrone's statistical model attempts to account for this endogeneity and thus offers important evidence for the impact of presidential rhetoric on policy.

Most recently, B. Dan Wood (2007a) shows that presidential rhetoric about economic policy has a strong influence on the public's perceptions about the economy and can also influence presidential approval (see also Cohen and Hamman 2003). A key innovation is that Wood does not focus on a single major speech and instead develops a monthly measure of the intensity and tone of presidential remarks on the economy and on specific economic topics. As Wood notes, it is plausible that presidential rhetoric has greater impact when it is part of a sustained public relations campaign rather than an isolated high-profile speech. Furthermore, the public is likely to be particularly attentive to economic rhetoric given the importance of economic conditions for their everyday life. Thus, Wood's analysis may be a most-likely case for finding an impact for presidential rhetoric, and is thus compatible with Edwards's findings of the lack of impact of presidential rhetoric on support for their policies.

Using a sophisticated time series statistical modeling approach that accounts for potential reverse causality among his key variables, Wood shows that optimistic economic rhetoric does not have a substantial direct impact on presidential approval, but does have a significant indirect impact through its influence on media coverage of the economy and public perceptions of economic conditions. Wood's analysis also shows that optimistic economic rhetoric leads to changes in economic behavior; a sustained, optimistic presidential message leads to a more optimistic public assessment of economic news and conditions, which in turn leads to increased consumption and investment. The effects of "going public" are more fully covered in another chapter in this volume, but while the sweeping characterizations of major presidential influence implicit in much work on presidential rhetoric have not been sustained, there is good reason to believe that presidential rhetoric does, at times, influence public perceptions.

The Symbolic Presidency and the Impact of Rhetoric

Political communication scholars, along with some political scientists writing about presidential rhetoric, take the argument one step further and argue that rhetoric is important for what it can tell us about the symbolic dimensions of politics.

For example, Stuckey and Antczak (1998) argue that "presidential rhetoric has constitutive as well as instrumental consequences." In other words, presidential rhetoric can make certain identities and self-conceptions of citizens more prominent and can shape how citizens understand the issues facing the country and the role of the presidency in the political system.

These constitutive effects are highlighted by Zarefsky (2004), who argues presidential rhetoric is important because it attempts to define political reality for the public. These definitions can be politically consequential even if their effects are not at all what the president intended. Thus, Zarefsky (1986) argues that Lyndon Johnson's use of the rhetoric of war helped ensure the swift passage of his landmark anti-poverty program in 1964. But the "War on Poverty" language then undermined the successful implementation of the program by generating excessive expectations, which then encouraged the Johnson administration to exaggerate progress, ultimately sacrificing its credibility.

One might well challenge the causal force of rhetorical choices in generating the failure of the War on Poverty: after all, the power battles between big-city mayors and community organizers likely would have happened regardless of how Johnson's rhetoric framed the program, and the white backlash of the mid-1960s suggests broader forces at work in undermining the cause of Great Society liberalism (see Miroff 1986). Still, it seems likely that presidents are particularly well situated to frame public debate and understanding, and the choices they make—whether in describing a "war on poverty," "crisis of confidence," "war on terror," or "axis of evil"—can have a consequential impact on political debate. As of now, however, there is insufficient evidence to either prove or disprove that linkage.[7]

A major limitation of the political communication literature thus far has been that it has been short on systematic evidence that traces the conditions under which presidents' rhetorical choices have shaped the terms of political debate and the subsequent choices (rhetorical and otherwise) by members of Congress, the media, and mass public. Although there have been numerous examples in which individual presidents seem to have had an impact (Zarefsky 1986 on LBJ's rhetoric, Ryan 1988 on FDR's rhetoric, Medhurst 1993 on Eisenhower's rhetoric), it is not clear how pervasive this impact is or the conditions under which it is more likely to be manifested.

Kohrs Campbell and Jamieson (1990) elaborate on the potential political significance of presidential rhetoric beyond the question of direct persuasion of a mass audience (see also Jamieson 1990). In *Deeds Done in Words*, Kohrs Campbell and Jamieson provide a careful exploration of different categories of presidential speeches, and show that presidents adopt different rhetorical approaches that are specific to each genre. For example, the Inaugural Address requires a formal, ceremonial tone that seeks to symbolically unify the audience by reconstituting its members as "the people." The State of the Union address, by contrast, combines an assessment of the current situation (rooted in the specific constitutional requirement that the president "from time to time give to the Congress Information of the State of

---

[7] I take up the question of how one might establish that linkage below.

the Union") with concrete policy recommendations. Their core claim is that these genres help define the different roles of the presidency and its interactions with the other branches. Thus, "veto messages constitute the president in a legislative role; war rhetoric seeks to legitimize assumption of the role of commander-in-chief; the very act of speaking presidentially in self-defense against impeachment reminds the audience that the presumption of office resides in the speaking president" (see also Whittington 2000). In Kohrs Campbell and Jamieson's account (1990, 214), "these words are deeds; in their speaking, the 'presidency is constituted and reconstituted.' "

The difficulty with this account is that it is not entirely clear what impact these words have on the public's perceptions of the president or on other political actors' choices (see Edwards 1996 on this point). What would the impact be if a president used the Inaugural Address to attack his opponents—thus violating the understanding that the formal occasion is to be used to unify the nation symbolically? What would the impact be if a president did not use the State of the Union address to put forward concrete legislative proposals? Eisenhower was criticized in 1953 for failing to present an ambitious program to Congress, and he responded the following year with a formal program. However, it is not clear that the problem was the failure to abide by rhetorical expectations as opposed to the judgment that Eisenhower's concrete policy agenda fell short of contemporary expectations. Again, although intuitively it makes sense to argue that rhetorical choices have an impact on public understandings of the presidency as an office, pinning down the effects of these choices in relation to other factors has proven elusive.

Similarly, Hinckley's (1990) landmark study. The Symbolic Presidency emphasizes how presidents use their rhetoric to define the place of their office in the political system. Hinckley draws upon a content analysis of the Public Papers of the Presidents to examine how post-Second World War presidents have framed themselves and the government to the public. She argues that modern presidents consistently portray themselves as the symbolic representative of the Nation and the "People," while denigrating the role of Congress. Modern presidential rhetoric frames the president as doing the work of government, while other institutional actors are mere roadblocks. Hinckley suggests that the news media and many academics have largely embraced this characterization, and thus reinforce the symbolic redefinition of the office put forward by modern presidents. These rhetorical choices matter because they reinforce the rise of the president as the chief agenda setter and legislator in our political system. Implicit in Hinckley's argument is the claim that if the public—and the media—view the president as the person responsible for the work of government, this perception will encourage a long-term shift in power towards the White House and away from the "obstructionist" legislative branch. But once again, the evidence that presidents frame themselves in these terms is much stronger than is the evidence that these rhetorical strategies affect the public's understanding of the president's appropriate role.

Indeed, critics, such as Edwards (1996, 208), note that such claims about "constituting" the office leave unaddressed the question of how we can determine in practice whether presidential rhetoric "serves the institutional ends of the presidency." Indeed, one might argue that the real problem is the subtle shift from arguing that rhetoric can offer a lens to understand institutional relationships to the stronger claim—implicit in much of Kohrs Campbell and Jamieson's argument, in particular—that rhetorical choices have a direct, clear impact on public opinion, policy outcomes, and institutional power. Sustaining the latter claim requires systematic analysis of how the "audience" responds to presidential rhetoric, along the lines of Edwards (2003), Wood (2007a), Canes-Wrone (2006), Cohen (1995), and Rottinghaus (2006).

However, the former claim—understanding presidential popular leadership as one of several indicators of how the president relates to key constituencies in American politics and how this relationship has changed over time—is where communication scholars and political scientists have made the most progress thus far. Thus, we have considerable evidence that presidents seek to use their speeches to frame themselves as the unique representative of the American people, and that this rhetorical strategy began with nineteenth-century Democratic presidents and became routinized in the twentieth century. Similarly, studies such as Kohrs Campbell and Jamieson suggest that presidents continue to play multiple and distinct roles in our political system and that their rhetorical approaches are adapted to these different roles. The president's symbolic role of a chief of state is highlighted in the Inaugural Address, while the legislative role is more relevant to the State of the Union address.

From this vantage point, the core concerns of political communications scholars are not as distant from those of political scientists as it might seem at first glance. Presidential rhetorical practices may be important in ways that are more subtle than through their direct impact on public opinion and political outcomes. The types of appeals used by presidents can tell us about how they perceive their relationship to other institutional actors and also can help us understand what the public expects of the president.

If everyone goes public—the president, Congress, interest groups—it is quite plausible that the public will tune out the messages and not respond. Indeed, Kernell (2006) hypothesizes that going public may have lost its effectiveness precisely because of the plethora of voices and hyperpluralism. Yet a political system in which political actors compete through rhetorical appeals—even if these appeals ultimately largely neutralize one another and do not systematically favor one branch or party over the other—is still a much different political system than one characterized primarily by closed-door bargaining among elite representatives.

Understanding the rise of the rhetorical presidency—particularly in terms of what has and has not changed over time—is critical because the public, Congress, and the press expect the president to be a rhetorical leader and judge his performance accordingly. Even if they only rarely move the public, presidential rhetorical practices illuminate core institutional relationships in the American political system.

The key problem with much of the political communications literature has been the seamless move from arguing that rhetoric tells us about the president's symbolic relationship to the people to the more difficult claim that rhetoric has a substantial impact on concrete political outcomes. The latter claim requires the sort of research design which, with a few notable exceptions, has generally been in short supply.

NEW DATA SOURCES AND FUTURE RESEARCH DIRECTIONS

With the emergence of digitized speeches and messages and content analysis software tools, the subfield of presidential rhetoric is in the midst of an overhaul that promises to make it more systematic and rigorous. The new data sources can be directed towards addressing two key categories of substantive questions. The first category deals with questions about the causes of presidential rhetoric. What is the impact of such factors as party, technology, and changing norms on presidents' rhetorical strategies? Some of these questions have been examined in prior work, but the newly available data will allow future studies to be more systematic and refined than in the past. Rather than relying upon subjective coding of a potentially non-representative sample of presidential speeches, it is now feasible to develop time series measures of presidential rhetorical practices that can be modeled as a function of changes in technology, party alignments, and of the president's substantive agenda. The second category of research questions involves examining the impact of presidential rhetoric on public attitudes, elite opinion, and political outcomes. As noted above, Edwards, Wood, Canes-Wrone, and Druckman and Holmes have undertaken important recent studies in this area, which also hold considerable promise for further development.

Two new resources for scholarly research on presidential rhetoric bear emphasis. The Annenberg/Pew Archive of Presidential Campaign Discourse contains the transcripts of campaign speeches, television ads, and debates from 1952 to 1996.[8] On the governance side, John Woolley and Gerhard Peters of the American Presidency Project at the University of California, Santa Barbara, have created a searchable database of almost 80,000 documents from US presidents from 1789 to the present. The overriding suggestion for future research on presidential rhetoric is to draw upon recently developed content analyses to capitalize upon these rich new data sources, and to integrate these data with systematic analyses of public opinion, media coverage, and congressional debate. A few examples of the research being done using sophisticated new content analysis methods provides a hint of the important contributions that this approach promises to make in the near future.[9]

Roderick Hart (1984, 1987; Hart et al. 2005) has been a pioneer in the development of content analysis tools and their application to presidential rhetoric. Hart developed his DICTION program in the 1980s and has applied it to the examination of presidential campaign and governing addresses, while also revising the program over the years. In *Verbal Style and the Presidency: A Computer-Based Analysis* (1984), Hart

[8] This CD-ROM (The Annenberg/Pew Archive of Presidential Campaign Discourse) is available from The Annenberg School for Communication at the University of Pennsylvania. Note that the Goldwater campaign is not included on the CD-ROM.

[9] Another recent work that uses content analysis software to examine presidential rhetoric is Cheryl Schonhardt-Bailey (2005), who examines the different themes in John Kerry's and George W. Bush's national security speeches using the computer software Alceste. See also Yager and Schonhardt-Bailey (2007).

uses DICTION to assess presidential speech in terms of a series of attributes, such as Activity, Certainty, Realism, Familiarity, and Symbolism. He applies the program to speeches from Harry Truman to Ronald Reagan, finding that presidents varied considerably in their rhetorical style. Hart's next book, *The Sound of Leadership* (1987), analyzes nearly 10,000 public presidential speeches since the Second World War and documents how presidents speak more often and on a greater array of topics than in the past. As such, Hart's findings reinforce the argument made by other scholars, such as Kernell, that "going public" has become a routine strategy. More controversially, Hart argues that the act of speaking has taken the place of concrete action on policy—that is, presidents increasingly substitute rhetoric for governance. Much like the work in political communication reviewed above, this begs the question of how one can determine when rhetoric is a substitute for rather than a complement to policy actions. Designing a study that examines whether presidential messages have become more or less connected to their legislative lobbying efforts over time would be one possible way to systematically test this hypothesis. If one found that presidents now engage in sustained rhetorical campaigns for issues that are not connected to a major legislative (or administrative) drive, Hart's contention would be validated. However, it is also plausible that one would find that presidential rhetoric continues to work in tandem with legislative policy drives. In either case, the results would improve our understanding of the significance of presidential rhetoric.

By relying solely upon the computer to categorize words, these early works often confused the tone of statements. For example, Javkin (1985) pointed out that Franklin Roosevelt's famous declaration "we have nothing to fear but fear itself," would be classified as a pessimistic statement because "nothing" and "fear" are each considered pessimistic words. He suggests that Hart's software classifies John Kennedy as a less optimistic president largely because it misses how Kennedy often discussed problems facing the country (i.e., pessimism) as exciting challenges. In his recent book *Political Keywords* (2005), Hart and his co-authors move away from a straight application of DICTION to using the computer to provide all instances of the use of a word and then coding the context in which it was used.

Similarly, Dan Wood (2007a) uses a combination of machine and human coding in his study of presidential economic rhetoric from April 1945 to January 2005. He draws upon two new data sources to achieve this. First, Western Standard Publishing Company's puts out a CD-Rom that covers presidential messages and speeches from presidents Washington to Taft and from Hoover to the third year of Clinton's administration. To bring the analysis up to 2005, he downloaded the Weekly Compilation of Presidential Documents from Encyclopedia Britannica's OriginalSources. com.[10] Using PERL (Practical Extraction and Report Language) to extract every presidential remark on the economy from these sources, Wood (2007a, 20–6) then enlisted the help of coders to determine that the remark is indeed about the economy as well as to develop a dictionary of optimistic and pessimistic terms and then verify

[10] OriginalSources has an updated website that allows users to search presidential speeches and messages through the end of Clinton's administration.

the validity of the dictionary. By tracking presidential remarks on the economy in such a systematic way, Wood is able to go further than most researchers in assessing patterns of presidential usage as well as the impact of rhetoric. By developing more nuanced and valid measures of presidential rhetoric concerning the economy, Wood provides systematic evidence for the significant impact that the president can have on economic perceptions and expectations.

Wood's study highlights the importance of examining sustained presidential messages, rather than focusing simply on a single speech. That is, presidential rhetoric may have a cumulative impact on popular perceptions even if isolating the effect of a particular speech proves elusive. Again, the development of these new data sources will allow researchers to code sustained presidential messages regarding a range of topics in addition to the economy. The substantively important questions that could be addressed with this approach include: does a sustained presidential message impact the salience of domestic or foreign policy issues, and when can it move public opinion on such issues? How much do the president's individual style and personal issue priorities affect the emphasis and tone of his rhetoric regarding different issues? Under what conditions can a sustained presidential message influence media coverage of an issue? How do competing elites' responses challenge the ability of the president to sway the public? For the latter question, it might be useful to examine the interplay between presidential message campaigns and those of the opposing party's leadership. In each case, however, the key is to develop valid, systematic measures of the content, intensity, and tone of presidential messages that are comparable over time.

Conclusion

In the end, although earlier critiques of the field of presidential rhetoric for the absence of systematic evidence gathering and hypothesis testing were largely on target, the study of presidential rhetoric has made substantial progress in recent years. Tulis's landmark book, followed by the many critical studies it inspired, have together provided a more refined understanding of the development of the rhetorical presidency. Rather than a story marked by one or two key moments—such as the Founding and Wilson's presidency—the rhetorical presidency developed in fits and starts. Nineteenth-century presidents grappled with balancing the competing imperatives of satisfying patrician norms and capitalizing upon their growing popular authority to push their programs. Over time, an expansive model of popular leadership took hold in the nineteenth century, even as it coexisted with competing understandings. The tensions that Tulis associates with the post-Wilson presidency have characterized the office since the Founding. The manner in which presidents have negotiated these tensions has changed considerably—both in the nineteenth century and with the routinization of going public in the late twentieth century. The upshot is a richer sense of development than Tulis's initial conception provided.

An important question for the future is whether presidential rhetoric, coded in a fashion that combines systematic keyword searches and coding sensitive to context, as in Wood's study of speeches relating to the economy, has similar effects across issue areas. The president's ability to shape public perceptions could possibly be greater in the foreign policy arena, in which there are fewer competing information sources. Similarly, the study of presidential rhetoric can be integrated with the political behavior literature, which suggests hypotheses concerning which citizens will be most receptive to particular types of presidential appeals. For example, it may be that citizens who are at least moderately attentive to political news are the most likely to be responsive to presidential messages (see Druckman and Holmes 2004). The new data sources and content analysis tools should allow scholars of presidential rhetoric to move beyond debates concerning the normative properties of the "rhetorical presidency," and toward a systematic understanding of how presidents use popular appeals as one of several strategies in their competition with other institutional actors to influence political outcomes.

REFERENCES

ABBOTT, P. 1988. Do Presidents Talk Too Much? The Rhetorical Presidency and its Alternatives. *Presidential Studies Quarterly*, 18: 347–62.

BAUM, M., and KERNELL, S. 1999. Has Cable Ended the Golden Age of Presidential Television? *American Political Science Review*, 93: 99–114.

BEASLEY, V. B. 2004. *You, the People: American National Identity in Presidential Rhetoric.* College Station: Texas A&M University Press.

BENSON, T. W. 1996. Desktop Demos: New Communication Technologies and the Future of the Rhetorical Presidency. Pp. 50–74 in *Beyond the Rhetorical Presidency*, ed. M. J. Medhurst. College Station: Texas A&M University Press.

BIMES, T. 2008. The Practical Origins of the Rhetorical Presidency. *Critical Review*, 19: 241–56.

——— and MULROY, Q. 2004. The Rise and Decline of Presidential Populism. *Studies in American Political Development*, 8: 136–59.

——— and SKOWRONEK, S. 1996. Woodrow Wilson's Critique of Popular Leadership: Reassessing the Modern–Traditional Divide. *Polity*, 29: 27–64.

BOSE, M. 1998. Words as Signals: Drafting Cold War Rhetoric in the Eisenhower and Kennedy Administrations. *Congress and the Presidency*, 25: 23–41.

BURDEN, B., and SANBERG, J. N. R. 2003. Budget Rhetoric in Presidential Campaigns from 1952 to 2000. *Political Behavior*, 25: 97–118.

CANES-WRONE, B. 2006. *Who Leads Whom? Presidents, Policy, and the Public.* Chicago: University of Chicago Press.

——— and SHOTTS, K.W. 2004. The Conditional Nature of Presidential Responsiveness to Public Opinion. *American Journal of Political Science*, 48: 690–706.

CEASER, J. W. 1979. *Presidential Selection: Theory and Development.* Princeton, NJ: Princeton University Press.

CEASER, J. W., THUROW, G. E., TULIS, J., and BESSETTE, J. M. 1981. The Rise of the Rhetorical Presidency. Pp. 233–52 in *Rethinking the Presidency*, ed. T. E. Cronin. Boston: Little, Brown & Company.

CMIEL, K. 1990. *Democratic Eloquence: The Fight over Popular Speech in Nineteenth-Century America*. New York: William Morrow & Company.

COHEN, J. E. 1995. Presidential Rhetoric and the Public Agenda. *American Journal of Political Science*, 39: 87–107.

——2004. If the News Is So Bad, Why Are Presidential Polls So High? Presidents, the News Media, and the Mass Public in an Era of New Media. *Presidential Studies Quarterly*, 34: 493–515.

——and HAMMAN, J. A. 2003. The Polls: Can Presidential Rhetoric Affect the Public's Economic Perceptions? *Presidential Studies Quarterly*, 33: 408–22.

COLEMAN, J., and MANNA, P. 2007. Above the Fray? The Use of Party System References in Presidential Rhetoric. *Presidential Studies Quarterly*, 37: 399–426.

DAHL, R. A. 1990. Myth of the Presidential Mandate. *Political Science Quarterly*, 105: 335–72.

DRUCKMAN, J. N., and HOLMES, J. W. 2004. Does Presidential Rhetoric Matter? Priming and Presidential Approval. *Presidential Studies Quarterly*, 34: 755–78.

EDELMAN, M. 1988. *Constructing the Political Spectacle*. Chicago: University of Chicago Press.

EDWARDS, G. C., III. 1996. Presidential Rhetoric: What Difference Does it Make? Pp. 199–217 in *Beyond the Rhetorical Presidency*, ed. M. J. Medhurst. College Station: Texas A&M University Press.

——1999. Campaigning Is Not Governing: Bill Clinton's Rhetorical Presidency. Pp. 33–47 in *The Clinton Legacy*, ed. C. Campbell and B. Rockman. Chatham, NJ: Chatham House.

——2003. *On Deaf Ears: The Limits of the Bully Pulpit*. New Haven, CT: Yale University Press.

——2004. *Why the Electoral College is Bad for America*. New Haven, CT: Yale University Press.

——2007. *Governing by Campaigning*, 2nd edn. New York: Longman.

——and ESHBAUGH-SOHA, M. 2001. Presidential Persuasion: Does the Public Respond? Paper presented at the Annual Meeting of the Southern Political Science Association, Atlanta, GA.

——and WOOD, B. D. 1999. Who Influences Whom? The President, Congress, and the Media. *American Political Science Review*, 93: 327–44.

ELLIS, R. J. 1998. Accepting the Nomination: From Martin Van Buren to Franklin Delano Roosevelt. Pp. 112–33 in *Speaking to the People: The Rhetorical Presidency in Historical Perspective*, ed. R. J. Ellis. Amherst: University of Massachusetts Press.

——2008. *Presidential Travel: The Journey from George Washington to George W. Bush*. Lawrence: University Press of Kansas.

——and DEDRICK, M. 2000. The Rise of the Rhetorical Candidate. Pp. 85–200 in *The Presidency Then and Now*, ed. P. G. Henderson. New York: Rowman & Littlefield Publishers.

——and Kirk, S. 1995. Presidential Mandates in the Nineteenth Century. *Studies in American Political Development*, 9: 117–86.

——and WALKER, A. 2007. Policy Speech in the Nineteenth Century Rhetorical Presidency: The Case of Zachary Taylor's 1849 Tour. *Presidential Studies Quarterly*, 37: 248–69.

ESHBAUGH-SOHA, M. 2003. Presidential Press Conferences over Time. *American Journal of Political Science*, 47: 348–53.

FIELDS, W. 1996. *Union of Words: A History of Presidential Eloquence*. New York: Free Press.

FRIEDMAN, J. 2007. A "Weapon in the Hands of the People:" The Rhetorical Presidency in Historical and Conceptual Context. *Critical Review*, 19: 197–240.

GAMM, G., and SMITH, R. 1998. Presidents, Parties and the Public: Evolving Patterns of Interaction, 1877–1929. In *Speaking to the People: The Rhetorical Presidency in Historical Perspective*, ed. R. J. Ellis. Amherst: University of Massachusetts Press.

GERRING, J. 2001. *Party Ideologies in America, 1818–1996.* New York: Cambridge University Press.

GREENSTEIN, F. 2006. Presidential Difference in the Early Republic: The Highly Disparate Leadership Styles of Washington, Adams, and Jefferson. *Presidential Studies Quarterly,* 36: 373–30.

GRONBECK, B. E. 1996. The Presidency in the Age of Secondary Orality. Pp. 30–49 in *Beyond the Rhetorical Presidency,* ed. M. J. Medhurst. College Station: Texas A&M University Press.

HAGER, G. L., and SULLIVAN, T. 1994. President-Centered and Presidency-Centered Explanations of Presidential Public Activity. *American Journal of Political Science,* 38: 1079–103.

HAN, L. C. 2001. *Governing from Center Stage: White House Communication Strategies during the Television Age of Politics.* Cresskill, NJ: Hampton Press.

HART, R. P. 1984. *Verbal Style and the Presidency: A Computer-Based Analysis.* Orlando, FL: Academic Press.

—— 1987. *The Sound of Leadership: Presidential Communication in the Modern Age.* Chicago: University of Chicago Press.

—— 2000. *Campaign Talk: Why Elections are Good for Us.* Princeton, NJ: Princeton University Press.

—— 2002. Why Do They Talk That Way? A Research Agenda for the Presidency. *Presidential Studies Quarterly,* 32: 693–709.

—— JARVIS, S. E., JENNINGS, W. P., and SMITH-HOWELL, D. 2005. *Political Keywords: Using Language that Uses Us.* New York: Oxford University Press.

HEALE, M. J. 1982. *The Presidential Quest: Candidates and Images in American Political Culture, 1787–1852.* New York: Longman.

HEIDOTTING-CONLEY, P. 2001. *Presidential Mandates: How Elections Shape the National Agenda.* Chicago: University of Chicago Press.

HEITH, D. 2000. Presidential Polling and the Potential for Leadership. Pp. 381–407 in *Presidential Power: Forging the Presidency for the Twenty-First Century,* ed. R. Y. Shapiro, M. J. Kumar, and L. R. Jacobs. New York: Columbia University Press.

HILL, K. Q. 1998. The Policy Agendas of the President and the Mass Public: A Research Validation and Extension. *American Journal of Political Science,* 42: 1328–34.

HINCKLEY, B. 1990. *The Symbolic Presidency: How Presidents Portray Themselves.* New York: Routledge.

HOFFMAN, K. S. 1997. The Institutional Origins of the Popular Presidency. Ph.D. dissertation, University of Chicago.

—— 2002. "Going Public" in the Nineteenth Century: Grover Cleveland's Repeal of the Sherman Silver Purchase Act. *Rhetoric & Public Affairs,* 5/1: 57–77.

HOGAN, J. M. 2006. *Woodrow Wilson's Western Tour: Rhetoric, Public Opinion, and the League of Nations.* College Station: Texas A&M University Press.

IVIE, R. L. 1996. Tragic Fear and the Rhetorical Presidency: Combating Evil in the Persian Gulf. Pp. 153–78 in *Beyond the Rhetorical Presidency,* ed. M. J. Medhurst. College Station: Texas A&M University Press.

JAMIESON, K. H. 1990. *Eloquence in an Electronic Age: The Transformation of Political Speech-making.* New York: Oxford University Press.

JAVKIN, H. R. 1985. Review of *Verbal Style and the Presidency: A Computer-Based Analysis.* *Language,* 61: 735.

KERNELL, S. 2006. *Going Public: New Strategies of Presidential Leadership,* 4th edn. Washington, DC: CQ Press.

KIEWE, A., and HOUCK, D. 1991. *A Shining City on a Hill: Reagan's Economic Rhetoric, 1951–1989.* Westport, CT: Praeger.

KOHRS CAMPBELL, K., and JAMIESON, K. H. 1990. *Deeds Done in Words: Presidential Rhetoric and the Genres of Governance*. Chicago: University of Chicago Press.

KOLAKOWSKI, M., and NEAL, T. H. 2006. *The President's State of the Union Message: Frequently Asked Questions*. Congressional Research Service Report for Congress <http://crapo.senate.gov/monthly_feature/crs_state_union.pdf>. Accessed May 16, 2008.

KORZI, M. 2004. *A Seat of Popular Leadership: The Presidency, Political Parties, and Democratic Government*. Amherst: University of Massachusetts Press.

KUMAR, M. J. 2000. The President as Message and Messenger: Personal Style and Presidential Communications. Pp. 408–34 in *Presidential Power: Forging the Presidency for the Twenty-First Century*, ed. R. Y. Shapiro, M. J. Kumar, and L. R. Jacobs. New York: Columbia University Press.

LARACEY, M. 1998. The Presidential Newspaper: The Forgotten Way of Going Public. In *Speaking to the People*, ed. R. Ellis. Amherst: University of Massachusetts Press.

—— 2002. *Presidents and the People: The Partisan Story of Going Public*. College Station: Texas A&M University Press.

LEWIS, D. 1997. The Two Rhetorical Presidencies: An Analysis of Televised Presidential Speeches 1947–1991. *American Politics Research*, 25: 380–95.

LIM, E. T. 2002. Five Trends in Presidential Rhetoric: An Analysis of Rhetoric from George Washington to Bill Clinton. *Presidential Studies Quarterly*, 32: 328–48.

LINK, A. S. (ed.) 1972. *The Papers of Woodrow Wilson*, 7 vols. Princeton, NJ: Princeton University Press.

MEDHURST, M. J. 1993. *Dwight D. Eisenhower: Strategic Communicator*. Westport, CT: Greenwood Press.

—— 1996. A Tale of Two Constructs: The Rhetorical Presidency Versus Presidential Rhetoric. In *Beyond the Rhetorical Presidency*, ed. M. J. Medhurst. College Station: Texas A&M University Press.

MIROFF, B. 1986. Review of David Zarefsky, *President Johnson's War on Poverty: Rhetoric and History*. *American Historical Review*, 91: 1294.

MURPHY, C. 2008. The Evolution of the Modern Rhetorical Presidency: A Critical Response. *Presidential Studies Quarterly*, 38: 300–7.

MUTZ, D. C. 2001. The Future of Political Communication Research: Reflections on the Occasion of Steve Chaffee's Retirement from Stanford University. *Political Communication*, 18: 231–6.

NICHOLS, D. 1994. *The Myth of the Modern Presidency*. University Park, PA: Penn State Press.

OLSON, K. M. 2001. Rhetoric and the American President. *Review of Communication*, 1: 247–53.

OSTROM, C. W., JR., and SIMON, D. M. 1988. The President's Public. *American Journal of Political Science*, 32: 1096–119.

POLK, J. K. 1848. Fourth Annual Message. P. 2511 in *A Compilation of the Messages and Papers of the Presidents*, compiled by J. D. Richardson. New York: Bureau of National Literature, 1902.

POWELL, R. J. 1999. Going Public Revisited: Presidential Speechmaking and the Bargaining Setting in Congress. *Congress and the Presidency*, 26: 153–70.

RAGSDALE, L. 1984. The Politics of Presidential Speechmaking. *American Political Science Review*, 78: 971–84.

—— 1987. Presidential Speechmaking and the Public Audience: Individual Presidents and Group Attitudes. *Journal of Politics*, 49/3: 704–36.

—— 1993. *Presidential Politics*. New York: Houghton Mifflin.

ROTTINGHAUS, B. 2006. Rethinking Presidential Responsiveness: The Public Presidency and Rhetorical Congruency, 1953–2001. *Journal of Politics*, 68: 720–32.

RYAN, H. R. 1988. *Franklin D. Roosevelt's Rhetorical Presidency*. New York: Greenwood Press.

SCHONHARDT-BAILEY, C. 2005. Measuring Ideas More Effectively: An Analysis of Bush and Kerry's National Security Speeches. *PS: Political Science and Politics*, 38: 701–11.

SHOGAN, C. J. 1986. *The Moral Rhetoric of American Presidents*. College Station: Texas A&M University Press.

SMITH, C. A., and SMITH, K. B. 1994. *The White House Speaks: Presidential Leadership as Persuasion*. Westport, CT: Praeger.

STID, D. 1998. *The President as Statesman: Woodrow Wilson and the Constitution*. Lawrence: University Press of Kansas.

STORING, H. J. 1981. *The Complete Anti-Federalist*. Chicago: University of Chicago Press.

STUCKEY, M. E. 1991. *The President as Interpreter-in-Chief*. Chatham, NJ: Chatham House Publishers.

——2004. *Defining Americans: The Presidency and National Identity*. Lawrence: University Press of Kansas.

——and ANTCZAK, F. J. 1998. The Rhetorical Presidency: Deepening Vision, Widening Change. *Communication Yearbook*, 21: 405–41.

TETEN, R. L. 2003. Evolution of the Modern Rhetorical Presidency: Presidential Presentation and Development of the State of the Union Address. *Presidential Studies Quarterly*, 33: 333–47.

THUROW, G. E. 1996. Dimensions of Presidential Character. Pp. 15–29 in *Beyond the Rhetorical Presidency*, ed. M. J. Medhurst. College Station: Texas A&M University Press.

——and WALLIN, J. (eds.) 1984. *Rhetoric and American Statesmanship*. Durham, NC: Carolina Academic Press.

TULIS, J. K. 1987. *The Rhetorical Presidency*. Princeton, NJ: Princeton University Press.

——1996. Revising the Rhetorical Presidency. Pp. 3–14 in *Beyond the Rhetorical Presidency*, ed. M. J. Medhurst. College Station: Texas A&M University Press.

VAN BUREN, M. 1839. Third Annual Message. P. 1771 in *A Compilation of the Messages and Papers of the Presidents*, compiled by D. Richardson. New York: Bureau of National Literature, 1902.

WATTENBERG, M. 2004. The Changing Presidential Media Environment. *Presidential Studies Quarterly*, 34: 557–72.

WHITTINGTON, K. E. 2090. The Rhetorical Presidency, Presidential Authority, and Bill Clinton. In *The Presidency Then and Now*, ed. P. G. Henderson. Rowman & Littlefield Publishers.

WINDT, T. O., JR. 1986. Presidential Rhetoric: Definition of a Field of Study. *Presidential Studies Quarterly*, 16: 102–16.

——1990. *Presidents and Protesters: Political Rhetoric in the 1960s*. Tuscaloosa: University of Alabama Press.

WOOD, B. D. 2007a. *The Politics of Economic Leadership: The Causes and Consequences of Presidential Rhetoric*. Princeton, NJ: Princeton University Press.

——2007b. Presidential Saber Rattling and the Economy. Paper presented at the annual meeting of the American Political Science Association, Chicago, IL.

——and PEAKE, J. S. 1998. The Dynamics of Foreign Policy Agenda Setting. *American Political Science Review*, 92: 173–84.

YAGER, E., and SCHONHARDT-BAILEY, C. 2007. Measuring Rhetorical Leadership: A Textual Analysis of Margaret Thatcher's and Ronald Reagan's Speeches. Paper presented at the Annual Meeting of the American Political Science Association, Chicago, IL.

ZAREFSKY, D. 1986. *President Johnson's War on Poverty: Rhetoric and History*. Tuscaloosa: University of Alabama Press.

——2002. The Presidency Has Always Been a Place for Rhetorical Leadership. Pp. 20–41 in *The Presidency and Rhetorical Leadership*, ed. L. Dorsey. College Station: Texas A&M University Press.

——2004. Presidential Rhetoric and the Power of Definition. *Presidential Studies Quarterly*, 34: 607–19.

CHAPTER 11

....

PUBLIC
EVALUATIONS OF
PRESIDENTS

....

PAUL GRONKE

BRIAN NEWMAN

SINCE the 1930s, the Gallup organization has asked Americans "do you approve or disapprove of the way [the incumbent] is handling his job as president?" This is a fundamental question for democratic politics, tapping the public's evaluation of the nation's most powerful government official. Public support for the president shapes the give and take of politics in Washington, DC. High approval ratings can be a powerful resource for presidents as they work to achieve their policy goals while low or eroding ratings can make it harder to move the president's agenda (see Edwards in this volume for an extended discussion).

Reflective of its normative and political significance, survey measures of presidential approval have become ubiquitous; one website regularly updates an estimate of presidential approval based on results from seventeen polling organizations.[1] At the time of this essay, the Gallup organization alone has asked the approval question 262 times during George W. Bush's presidency.[2] Presidential approval is widely reported in news media, routinely discussed among the chattering classes, and has been analyzed at length by social scientists since John Mueller's (1970) seminal study. Almost four decades of research has taught us much about public evaluations of the president, but the march of history—new political and historical conditions—and

---

[1] Charles Franklin at <http://www.pollster.com>.
[2] Referenced from <http://pollingreport.com>, May 14, 2008.

the march of political science—theoretical and methodological advances—continue to raise novel questions that animate the study of presidential approval.

Three developments have significantly altered the political landscape of the United States and will stimulate new research on presidential approval. First, party polarization has become a central element of American national politics (e.g., McCarty, Poole, and Rosenthal 2006, but see Fiorina, Abrams, and Pope 2006). Second, outlets for news and public affairs have proliferated at a mind-numbing rate with the growth of cable television, talk radio, web-based news sources, and the blogosphere. As a consequence, the news audience has fragmented. Coupled with party polarization, a highly decentralized media market creates ever more possibilities and incentives for individuals to distrust media outlets they deem biased and rely on sources that reflect their own political predispositions, ultimately reducing the president's ability to marshal public opinion and counter party polarization (Cohen 2008). Third, the terrorist attacks of 9/11 and the subsequent war on terror have dramatically affected American politics during the George W. Bush administration, elevating the importance of threat and anxiety in the public's assessments of presidential power and leadership.

In the midst of these changes, theoretical and methodological advances in political science have altered the focus of presidential approval studies. While the first wave of presidential approval studies following Mueller sought to identify the major factors driving aggregate approval ratings, more recent work has placed the impact of these factors in a richer theoretical and empirical context (see Gronke and Newman 2003 for a description of the field's historical development).

In many instances, studies have taken these factors, which early research largely took as exogenously determined, and endogenized them, seeking to understand what causes them. These correlates of approval do not exist outside of the realm of approval but coexist with it, part of a constellation of attitudes that are shaped by things such as partisan predispositions, media coverage, presidential rhetoric, and other elite discourse as much as they are by objective real world conditions. For example, earlier work considered the direct impact of economic indicators such as inflation and unemployment on approval, while more recent work examines how perceptions of economic conditions, although certainly affected by real world conditions, can also be shaped by the president and other political actors (Wood 2007). Much of this research shifted from time series studies of aggregate approval to a new focus on the micro foundations of approval. This shift coincided with a move toward using individual-level survey data because the standard aggregate-level time series studies could not do much to explain how individuals evaluate the president, simply because these studies could only test the implications of underlying models (Edwards, Mitchell, and Welch 1995).

This work of endogenizing and contextualizing the foundations of presidential approval has opened broad new avenues of research. At the same time, new data sources have helped the discipline advance the research frontier. As noted above, it is now possible to construct estimates of aggregate approval based on a dozen or more public opinion polls, conducted on a daily (sometimes more often) basis, creating an almost instantaneous (and less error-prone) barometer of public approval. Some have used Stimson's (1999) algorithm to generate time series measures of concepts that previously could not be included in time series models simply for lack of data (e.g., Kelleher and Wolak 2006; McAvoy 2006, 2008). New survey designs, such as rolling cross-sections, more frequent use of panels, and experimental survey studies, may also open up new possibilities for examining the underpinnings of presidential approval.

Our purpose here is to review recent research that endogenizes and contextualizes the aspects of the political and economic environment that drive presidential approval and to identify important questions that should motivate future research. We proceed by describing the forces that shape approval and ways in which polarization, changes in the media market, and the post-9/11 context may alter their impact. We then explore the roots of these forces themselves, explaining how these forces depend on competition among political actors, including the president, and the media environment in which this competition occurs.

Our discussion then turns to the question of how the relative influence of these forces changes over time, sometimes with important consequences for the strength of public support. Research in this area points to a critical theoretical and normative question: who or what can determine the weight or relative influence of these factors? Can the president shape media coverage and public concern for various issues such that he can alter the criteria by which he is evaluated, thereby enhancing his public standing? We know that presidents attempt and sometimes succeed in doing this (e.g., Cohen 1995; Edwards and Wood 1999; Druckman, Jacobs, and Ostermeier 2004). To what extent is the public a victim of such presidential efforts and to what extent can the public resist them bringing to bear its own views of how the president should be evaluated? This is a question with deep implications for democratic accountability and one that recent work has only begun to examine.

The challenges presidents face in communicating with the public in the context of a fragmented media market give rise to new communication strategies that may heighten heterogeneity in the public's evaluations. Facing considerable difficulty communicating with the entire nation at any given time (e.g., Baum and Kernell 1999), presidents have shifted toward more narrowly defined audiences as these groups can be reached more easily (Cohen 2008). This strategy may have consequences for presidential approval as different parts of the public are exposed to different information, may understand the world in different ways, hold different political priorities, and encounter different cues about appropriate evaluative criteria. Rather than examining the public as a monolithic whole, some research has begun to explicitly consider heterogeneity, primarily focusing on partisanship and political sophistication. We review this research and highlight opportunities for advancing it. After encouraging further exploration of the contingencies of various influences on approval, we close with a call for connecting findings to broader statements about what shapes presidential approval and larger implications for fundamental issues of presidential politics.

THE FACTORS SHAPING PRESIDENTIAL APPROVAL

Evaluations of the president reflect a combination of relatively durable partisan predispositions that largely account for *levels* of public approval and more variable views of events and conditions that lead to *changes* in approval. We begin with partisanship, a predisposition that affects approval both directly and indirectly, as we discuss below. Most directly, partisanship shapes the level of approval, as Republicans in the public are far more likely than Democrats to approve of a Republican president, and vice versa. This is hardly surprising, but vitally important, especially in an era of party polarization. In the 1950s through the 1970s, approval ratings among Democrats and Republicans in the public differed on average by about 30 points. In the 1980s and 1990s, the partisan gap in approval often exceeded 50 points (Bond and Fleisher 2001), an increase of more than two-thirds.

During the George W. Bush administration, party polarization in approval increased even more, exceeding 70 points during much of the Bush presidency, more than doubling the partisan gap of the 1950s to 1970s (Jacobson 2007). Although individuals who identify with the president's party (in-partisans) have historically provided the president with a remarkably stable base of approval, even in the face of unfavorable conditions (Lebo and Cassino 2007), Republican approval of George W. Bush reached record levels of depth and stability when compared to his predecessors. Through 2005, on average, 91 percent of Republicans approved of Bush. Moreover, two-thirds of Republicans said they *strongly* approved of Bush (Jacobson 2007, 8). In contrast, especially as the Iraq War dragged on, Democrats' approval declined to record lows, reaching a mere 7 points in one November, 2005 Gallup poll. Democrats' disapproval ran deep as well, as just under two-thirds strongly disapproved of Bush in 2004–5 (Jacobson 2007, 8). These are not just gaps in approval, but opinion canyons. The impact of such enormous levels of polarization on presidential governance is beyond the scope of this essay but will surely animate retrospectives on the Bush White House.

Despite the relatively stable force of partisanship, public approval varies considerably over the course of a president's tenure in response to changing conditions, events, and actions. However, only some aspects of the political environment will affect approval. As a group, Americans are notoriously inattentive to politics. Few monitor every new political or economic development. Therefore, only those features of the political and social environment that are salient enough that individuals pay some attention to them and consider the president's responsibility for them will affect approval (Ostrom and Simon 1988; Edwards 1990).

It may seem obvious that a condition must be salient to influence evaluations of the president, but much remains to be discovered about the connections between salience and approval. Presidential approval studies that pay careful attention to salience almost uniformly rely on the "most important problem" question as a measure of salience (e.g., Ostrom and Simon 1985, 1988; McAvoy 2006). However, this question is not an ideal measure of salience. For example, after Iraq's military had been ousted from Kuwait in the Gulf War, the situation in the Persian Gulf remained salient to many, even though they may no longer have considered it a "problem" (Edwards, Mitchell, and Welch 1995). Developing valid and reliable measures of salience to incorporate into research on presidential approval remains an important task for future research.

Even if a particular aspect of the political environment is salient to the public, the public must consider the president responsible for it in order for that aspect to affect views of the president (Huwitz and Peffley 1987; Althaus and Kim 2006). If an individual is concerned about a particular problem such as unemployment because he has lost a job, he may not hold the president responsible for his lost job. In this case, the respondent's opinion about his own unemployment will not affect his opinion of the president. Similarly, the public may not hold a newly inaugurated president responsible for poor economic conditions inherited from the previous administration. A line of new research has just begun to study the ways the public forms attributions of presidential responsibility (e.g., Rudolph 2003a, 2003b; Arceneaux 2006; Malhotra and Kuo 2008) and promises to spark new insights into presidential approval.

Decades of approval studies have identified four features of the political environment that the public tends to find salient and assign as a responsibility of the president. First, every study of presidential approval finds that economic conditions affect presidential approval. Early research focused on the impact of objective economic indicators on approval (e.g., Mueller 1970; Kernell 1978; Ostrom and Simon 1985). Recent economic changes suggest that new aspects of the economy may be more germane now. In particular, economic globalization and increasing interdependence among national economies may make international economic conditions more relevant to economics and politics in the US. In this environment, the president has less power over domestic economic conditions. Will the public punish the president for economic conditions deeply affected by trade disputes, regional recessions, or a foreign stock market crash? One study found trade conditions with Japan had a significant relationship with Bill Clinton's approval ratings (Burden and Mughan 2003), but this study represents only the first effort to incorporate global economic realities into approval models.

Recently, scholars have examined the impact of public *perceptions* of economic conditions rather than objective economic indicators. This shift sparked a debate over whether prospective or retrospective views of economic conditions are most relevant to presidential approval (see especially MacKuen, Erikson, and Stimson 1992; Clarke and Stewart 1994; Norpoth 1996). Although this debate was one of the major substantive questions driving research in the 1990s, it has not been at the core of most recent studies.

Second, since Mueller (1970) first noted the importance of the "rally-round-the-flag" effect on presidential approval, scholars have agreed that major political events drive aggregate approval and shape individuals' evaluations of the president (see especially MacKuen 1983). However, beyond general agreement that events matter, there is precious little commonality in the ways events are treated. Studies vary widely in the ways they determine which events should be included and how they should be coded. As we noted elsewhere, "a unified event series would save significant labor, ease the temptation to use events to boost model fit, and limit suspicions that others have done so" (Gronke and Newman 2003, 509).

Third, war can have a dramatic effect on presidential approval. It has become standard to tap war's impact by including the log of the number of American troop deaths (e.g., Kernell 1978; Ostrom and Simon 1985; Hibbs 1987; Erikson, MacKuen, and Stimson 2002; Newman 2002; see also Gartner and Segura 1998). Recent research on support for war and the impact of casualty numbers on such support calls this approach into question as we describe below.

Fourth, perceptions of the president's personal character inform evaluations of the president. Mueller (1970, 27) argued *"an analysis of presidential popularity cannot rely entirely on the variables* [he included—a time counter, rally events, economic conditions, and war], *but must also incorporate parameters designed to allow for the special character of each administration"* (emphasis in original). However, most studies of presidential approval over the two decades following Mueller's writing did not pay great attention to these unique aspects, often simply adding a dummy variable for each presidential administration to capture individual idiosyncrasies. More recently, studies have explicitly examined the link between public views of the president's character and their evaluations of presidential performance, finding that public assessments of the president's competence, integrity, and favorability are significantly related to presidential approval (Kinder 1986; Greene 2001; Newman 2003, 2004; Kelleher and Wolak 2006; McAvoy 2008).

Some research has pointed to other influences on approval. Policy attitudes or global ideological identification can shape approval ratings at the individual level (e.g., Nicholson, Segura, and Woods 2002; Newman 2003), while aggregate approval tracks the public's aggregate policy mood (Erikson, MacKuen, and Stimson 2002). We encourage further development of the links between issue positions and presidential approval. We do not discuss approval's tendency to decline over time or the tendency for presidents to enjoy a honeymoon period of relatively high approval. Elite discourse and media coverage largely explain these trends (see Brody 1991; Edwards 1990, 123–5). To the extent that they are included in future research, we encourage the development of explanations of these tendencies rather than simply including these relatively atheoretical measures in models as controls.

THE FACTORS' ROOTS

As scholars turned from trying to isolate the correlates of aggregate approval to attempting to explain "the individual-level processes that lead to aggregate results" (Bond and Fleisher 2001, 530), they began to explore ways the factors shaping approval are themselves shaped by, or are endogenous to, the political environment.

Perceptions of political conditions and who is responsible for them are shaped by partisanship, personal experiences, and messages from the president, the president's political opponents, news media, pundits, friends, family, and co-workers, among other things. These complex interrelationships raise substantive and methodological questions that will drive research in the coming years. In this section, we discuss the ways research has shown these factors to be endogenous to the political environment and the puzzles that should drive future research.

Party Identification

Political scientists have long examined the underpinnings of party identification. Most relevant to presidential approval, MacKuen, Erikson, and Stimson (1989) found that the proportion of the public identifying with the two major parties responds to perceptions of the economy and aggregate presidential approval ratings (see also Green, Palmquist, and Schickler 1998; Erikson, MacKuen, and Stimson 1998). This finding demonstrates two challenges as we endogenize the attitudes that influence presidential approval. First, these attitudes and approval may influence each other. Just as party identification shapes evaluations of the president, those evaluations in turn may shape partisanship.

Second, the factors affecting approval often shape each other. In particular, an individual's reaction to conditions and events is colored by partisanship, which acts as a "filter through which changes in the environment are evaluated" (Ostrom and Simon 1988, 1101). Partisans often engage in motivated reasoning, a process of collecting and evaluating information with the goal of reaching conclusions that are consistent with their party predispositions (Taber and Lodge 2006). In-partisans discount new developments that cast the president in a negative light and emphasize more positive conditions, while out-partisans do the opposite. Thus, out-partisans might consider a sluggish economy a problem of the president's making, while in-partisans might consider economic conditions not all that poor, not all that important, or not the result of the president's actions (see Bartels 2002; Bond and Fleisher 2001; Rudolph 2003a, 2003b; Malhotra and Kuo 2008).

Economic Conditions

The task of endogenizing the factors shaping presidential approval has advanced furthest in the realm of economic perceptions. Where approval studies once considered economic conditions as essentially fixed and exogenous, now presidential approval models treat them as potentially malleable, conditioned on other aspects of the political environment and on an individual's prior political predispositions. Besides objective economic indicators, public perceptions of economic conditions and whether the president is responsible for them are conditioned by partisanship, media coverage, and elite discourse—*including presidential rhetoric* (e.g., Hetherington 1996; Nadeau et al. 1999; Nadeau and Lewis-Beck 2001; Rudolph 2003a, 2003b; Evans and Andersen 2006; Lewis-Beck 2006). As Wood (2007, 119) puts it, "when evaluating the economy, citizens take cues and receive information from a variety of sources ... [p]residential rhetoric, manifest through a stream of speeches and other public comments that are widely reported in the news, is one of those sources of cues and information." Thus, presidents are able to enhance their standing in the polls via an adroit use of communications, a finding with potentially negative implications. Although it may not be easy to shape perceptions of the economy, doing so may be far easier than improving the economy itself. Consequently, presidents have incentives to focus their administration's resources on strategic communication rather than solving real-life problems (Waterman, Wright, and St Clair 1999).

Wood's (2007) book presents the strongest evidence to date that the sustained communication efforts of presidential administrations do in fact alter public views of economic conditions. Wood's book is exemplary in dealing with the challenge of estimating how perceptions of the economy shape evaluations of the president and vice versa. Using time series data, he conducts Granger causality tests that uncover the direction of causality, demonstrating the continuing utility of aggregate time series methods even as scholars increasingly probe individual-level data to develop ever more elaborate models of approval.

Major Events

Efforts to explain the rally phenomenon (boosts in aggregate approval after a major event) raise two important questions. First, when do rallies occur? Early studies argued that rallies were the result of a reflexive surge of patriotic support for the president in a time of crisis. However, we now know that rallies are not automatic; they depend in part upon the political and media environment. After a major event, elite discourse about the president's handling of the event, media coverage of the event, and individuals' predispositions to approve of the president shape the size of any potential rally (see especially Brody 1991). For example, Peffley, Langley, and Goidel's (1995) study of the 1986 air strike against Libya found that those who watched Reagan's televised speech announcing the strike were more likely to rally than those who did not watch the speech. Similarly, Edwards and Swenson (1997) found that among those most predisposed to rally, individuals who paid attention to foreign policy news were the most likely to rally after Clinton's 1993 missile strike on Baghdad. Most recently, Baum and Groeling (2008) demonstrate that reactions to military use of force, one of the most important types of rally events, depend on media coverage of elite messages.

Thinking of rallies as contingent on the environment raises a second question: do party polarization and the proliferation of news outlets affect the size of rallies? Party polarization may influence who rallies and therefore the size of the rally. Presumably, individuals who were generally favorable toward the president but disapproved prior to the event are most likely to rally (Kernell and Hibbs 1981). For example, after Clinton's missile strike on Baghdad, in-partisans and independents who held generally favorable views of the president were most likely to rally (Edwards and Swenson 1997). Gronke and Brehm (2002) found that the impact of events differed according to the underlying "volatility" of public opinion, which was determined in part by the strength of partisan sentiments.

In a polarized world where in-partisans almost uniformly strongly approve of the president and out-partisans are cohesive in their strong disapproval, rally effects may be minimal simply because there is little room for movement. Out-partisans are especially unlikely to rally in a media context that is increasingly prone to broadcast critical commentary during a potential rally event. Although politicians may be hesitant to criticize the president during a crisis, talking heads and bloggers are always ready to do so. In addition, such criticism may make its way into mainstream news because of journalistic preferences for drama and presenting two sides to stories (Baum and Groeling 2008). Thus, although criticism of the president during a rally event was at one time relatively muted (Brody 1991), now those who wish can easily find criticism of the president. In the end, then, rallies in the midst of partisan polarization depend almost entirely on unaffiliated citizens. If presidents adopt a general strategy of mobilizing, catering to, and depending on, their base support as George W. Bush has, they may find few independents willing to rally. On the other hand, a media strategy targeted at unaffiliated, and often disinterested, citizens seems highly problematic. Future research should continue to think through the complex interactions of the political and media environment, partisan predispositions, and the shape, size, and frequency of future rallies.

War

As we noted earlier, recent research on support for war has raised problems with the standard inclusion of troop deaths as a measure of war's impact on presidential approval. Although most of this work takes some measure of support for a particular war as its dependent variable, Gelpi, Feaver, and Reifler (2005/6) briefly explored the impact of war casualties on approval for George W. Bush. Rather than leading inexorably to declines in approval, the impact of casualties depended on the military and political context. Over the whole period studied (January of 2003 to November of 2004), the log of American deaths in Iraq was unrelated to aggregate approval. However, casualty counts did negatively affect approval over some time periods. Despite the increase in deaths, presidential approval actually increased with the onset of military action and the fall of Baghdad. In contrast, after Bush declared an end to major combat, his approval dropped as troop deaths rose. Then, after the transfer of sovereignty to the Iraqi government, deaths once again showed no relationship with Bush's approval ratings.

Furthermore, Gelpi, Feaver, and Reifler found that the effect of casualties on support for the war depends on expectations of success and views of whether it was right to go to war with Iraq. Those who considered the war the right course of action and especially those who thought the US would ultimately succeed were casualty tolerant (see Berinsky and Druckman 2007 and Gartner 2008 for critiques of this work). In addition, the impact of casualties was muted for those who viewed the objective as the defense of the US and its allies, those who perceived elite consensus supporting the war, and those who were not concerned about multinational support for the conflict. Each of these factors conditioning the impact of casualties is, of course, shaped by elite debate, media coverage, and individuals' partisan predispositions. Elites hotly contested the justification for the war (especially as no weapons of mass destruction were found), the wisdom of building a broader coalition, and the likelihood of success; while most Republicans viewed the war's aims as right and were optimistic about success, most Democrats were at odds on both counts. Consequently, casualties may have had a larger effect on Bush's approval rating among Democrats than among Republicans. Although most studies on support for war do not examine the effect of casualties on presidential approval directly, their findings open avenues for future scholarship on approval during foreign conflicts.

This research questions the standard practice of simply including the log of the number of casualties as a control for the effect of war. Such a variable is too crude to capture the complex and contingent effects of casualties. Since at the time of this essay we remain in the war on terror, American troops will remain in Iraq for at least the near future, and Americans face the possibility of future military intervention across the globe, it is important to incorporate the nuances and contingencies uncovered in research on presidential approval, military conflict, and war casualties.

Perceptions of Presidents' Personal Character

Our understanding of views of presidential character remains in its infancy. While we are well aware that character matters, we know little about the source of these perceptions. Some evidence suggests that media coverage of presidential character shapes the public's perceptions (Shah et al. 2002), but this is an area ripe for further development. Presidents try to shape views of their character (e.g., Druckman, Jacobs, and Ostermeier 2004), but are they successful? To date, scholars have not adequately dealt with this question. The studies of character perceptions assume, but do not show definitively, that perceptions of the president's character affect evaluations of his performance, rather than the reverse. Although some experimental evidence shows indirectly that perceptions of character really do have some causal effect (Funk 1996), this is a vital direction for future research.

In addition, we know little about how the context in which character perceptions are shaped will alter those perceptions, even though new scholarship indicates that context is crucial. For example, Merolla, Ramos, and Zechmeister (2007) found that in a context of crisis—like a heightened threat of terrorist attack—the public views the president as more charismatic than when under less threatening conditions. This highlights both the importance of considering context and the potential that alternative dimensions of the broad construct "character" (like charisma) are relevant. Considering the context in which perceptions of character are formed may be especially critical since 9/11, and the ongoing war on terror may induce a sense of crisis in the public.

THE FACTORS' VARIABLE INFLUENCE

The first generation of approval research implicitly assumed that the impact of various factors on approval was constant over time (Edwards, Mitchell, and Welch 1995; Wood 2000). However, the issues, events, and conditions the public cares most about and the extent to which the president is held responsible for them change over time. Much of the theoretically and methodologically novel presidential approval research over the past two decades has found that the criteria used to evaluate the president varies depending on the context in which the evaluation occurs. At least four contextual factors can alter the evaluation calculus: divided versus unified government, individuals' level of anxiety, the longer presidential campaign, and messages from political actors reported in news media.

Divided government alters the degree to which the president is held responsible for negative economic conditions, ultimately decreasing the impact of such conditions on approval (Nicholson, Segura, and Woods 2002). Under divided government, it is more difficult for the public to award credit or assign blame for economic conditions to the president or to Congress, so presidential approval is decoupled from economic conditions. Under unified government, information and elite cues about economic conditions squarely implicate the president, whose approval ratings are therefore more sensitive to economic changes.

A growing body of research on emotion highlights the ways anxiety shapes political decisions (e.g., Marcus, Neuman, and MacKuen 2000; Brader 2006; Ladd and Lenz 2008). Much of this research argues that anxious individuals rely less on partisan cues and other cognitive short cuts, and instead seek more information and process it more rigorously. This process may make new features of the political environment salient to the public and ultimately relevant for evaluations of the president. As yet, scholars have not studied the role of anxiety or other emotions in presidential approval, but future research should do so, particularly since the potential of future terrorist attacks may have increased the public's anxiety levels.

The presidential campaign season may also prove a unique context for evaluating presidents. As two candidates, one of whom may be the sitting president, compete for votes, they inevitably try to make some conditions more salient than others and make arguments about who is responsible for current conditions. Do such campaigns alter the criteria of evaluating the president's current performance? This is an important question for substantive reasons since presidential campaigns are now over a year long, meaning that sitting presidents may have just over two years to govern in non-election mode. Methodologically, many of the surveys that enable individual-level studies of presidential approval are in the field during presidential campaigns (e.g., the National Election Studies and the National Annenberg Election Studies). If the criteria of evaluating presidents are unique during the period in which these surveys are conducted, conclusions drawn from them will be limited to this particular context.

The vast majority of studies examining the varying influences on presidential approval involve media coverage and elite discourse, particularly as they relate to the psychological phenomenon of priming. Miller and Krosnick (2000, 301) explain that "priming occurs when media attention to an issue causes people to place special weight on it when constructing evaluations of overall presidential job performance." For example, individuals who view news stories about US defense preparedness tend to place more weight on their views of the president's handling of national defense when evaluating the president's overall performance than individuals who have not seen these stories (Iyengar and Kinder 1987). Studies of priming have found time and again that exposure to stimuli (e.g., media coverage, elite messages, or real world events) emphasizing a particular consideration increases that consideration's influence on presidential approval evaluations (e.g., Iyengar and Kinder 1987; Krosnick and Kinder 1990; Krosnick and Brannon 1993; Miller and Krosnick 2000). In addition, Edwards, Mitchell, and Welch (1995) found that the impact of economic or foreign policy considerations depends on the salience of each at a given time, as measured by the amount of media coverage of each. Studies demonstrate varying impacts for several aspects of the political and economic environment, including perceptions of economic conditions (e.g., Iyengar and Kinder 1987; Kelleher and Wolak 2006), views of the Gulf War (Krosnick and Brannon 1993) and the Iraq War (Ladd 2007), and character perceptions (Kelleher and Wolak 2006). Major events can also prime specific considerations, which can account for part of the rally phenomenon (e.g., Krosnick and Kinder 1990; Krosnick and Brannon 1993; Ladd 2007).

WHO OR WHAT CAN DETERMINE THE FACTORS' INFLUENCE?

Research has convincingly demonstrated that the criteria of evaluation change in different contexts and in response to new information. We know less about the extent to which specific political actors, media content, or real world events alter the influence of particular factors on approval. In their initial priming study, Iyengar and Kinder (1987) concluded that "priming is greatest when the news frames a particular problem as if it were the president's business, when viewers are prepared to regard the problem as important, and when they see the problem as entangled in the duties and obligations of the presidency," once again highlighting the importance of salience and attribution of responsibility to the president. Since then, studies have begun to explore which political actors, news sources, or events can alter the impact of the main factors on approval, what types of considerations can be amplified or depressed in evaluations, and which individuals in the public are open or resistant to these effects. These efforts to define the extent to which the evaluative criteria are open to change should continue to be at the forefront of the next wave of research. They are important to our theoretical understanding of priming, an important concept in the study of public opinion, and they relate to a fundamental question for scholars of presidential approval: how much can presidents control their own public support?

In thinking about who or what can shape evaluative criteria, Chong and Druckman's (2007) recent work on framing is instructive. Their definition of framing makes their theory directly applicable to efforts to change evaluative criteria. As they put it, (2007, 637) "a speaker 'frames' an issue by encouraging readers or listeners to emphasize certain considerations above others when evaluating that issue." This is precisely what scholars refer to when describing the ways some stimulus increases the influence of the particular consideration in evaluations of the president. Recent priming and framing research finds that not everyone can alter the public's evaluative criteria. Trusted and credible sources are especially effective at priming and framing (e.g., Miller and Krosnick 2000; Chong and Druckman 2007). Can presidents alter the criteria by which they are evaluated? They certainly have incentives to convince the public to weigh favorable considerations more and unfavorable considerations less. Several studies demonstrate that presidential candidates attempt to prime considerations that generally favor them over their opponents in the hope that voters will make decisions based on those favorable considerations (e.g., Jacobs and Shapiro 1994; Druckman, Jacobs, and Ostermeier 2004). Experimental evidence indicates that presidents can alter the public's evaluative criteria, at least under some conditions. Watching the president's 2002 State of the Union address primed perceptions of Bush's leadership and handling of terrorism among some viewers (Druckman and Holmes 2004). However, presidents often compete with opposition political actors who have incentives to emphasize considerations unfavorable to the president and downplay considerations favorable to the president (Althaus and Kim 2006; Chong and Druckman 2007). Thus, presidents and their surrogates, opposition leaders, and news coverage may all be sending different messages that could potentially shift the standards of evaluation. Much more research is required to demonstrate presidents' power to influence the criteria by which they are evaluated and to delineate the limits of that power in the real world.

As presidents, other political actors, and news media compete to define evaluations, some messages may be more effective in altering evaluative criteria. Iyengar and Kinder (1987, ch. 9) found that news stories that highlighted the president's responsibility for a particular problem produced greater priming effects than stories about the same problem that did not draw such a link. Recent studies have expanded on this finding, showing that, at least under some conditions, individuals must view considerations as salient and applicable to evaluations of the president in order to change individuals' evaluative criteria (Edwards, Mitchell, and Welch 1995; Miller and Krosnick 2000; Althaus and Kim 2006).

In addition, Chong and Druckman (2007) argue that effective framing requires that the audience can understand both the consideration presented in the frame and its potential link to the president. Along these lines, Kelleher and Wolak (2006) found that from 1981 to 2000, familiar and easily understood considerations like economic perceptions were more open to priming by news coverage than less familiar and more complex issues like foreign policy. An important implication of message limits is that even if presidents are viewed as a credible source, they may not be able to prime any consideration they like, especially when other actors and conditions offer alternative evaluative criteria.

When presented with information that might alter their evaluative calculus, some individuals may reject these framing messages and retain their own calculus. For example, Democrats in Congress may argue that George W. Bush should be held responsible for soaring gas prices, while Republicans may argue that presidents have little influence over gas prices. Individual citizens consider these claims in light of their own political leanings and past information they have about gas prices, sometimes rejecting them, again limiting the power of the president and other actors to shape the criteria of evaluation (Zaller 1992).

Thus far, most research on resisting priming has focused on individuals' level of sophistication. Unfortunately, the research has not yet reached a consensus about the relationship between sophistication and susceptibility to priming. The early presidential approval studies of priming found that the least sophisticated were the most affected by priming (Krosnick and Kinder 1990), yet later work has found the opposite, that more sophisticated individuals are more open to priming (Krosnick and Brannon 1993; Miller and Krosnick 2000). This recent work contends that it requires significant sophistication to "interpret, store, and later retrieve and make inferences from news stories" and other potential primes (Miller and Krosnick 2000, 312). A potential path to resolution between these two positions is work that shows that sophistication interacts with message content such that individuals with lower sophistication levels are open to some primes while individuals with higher sophistication levels are open to different primes. For instance, among individuals with limited political knowledge, watching the 2002 State of the Union address increased the impact of Bush's leadership qualities on overall evaluations of his performance, while among individuals with higher knowledge levels, watching the speech increased the influence of views of the president's performance on terrorism (Druckman and Holmes 2004, see also Ladd 2007).

Beyond political sophistication, we would expect that partisanship would moderate the power of priming. Iyengar and Kinder (1987) found that Republicans were more open to priming on the traditionally Republican issues of inflation, defense, and arms control, while Democrats were more open to priming on traditionally Democratic issues of the environment, unemployment, and civil rights. Thus, "television news primes most effectively those viewers who are predisposed to accept the message in the first place" (1987, 93). Presumably, today's greater party polarization would continue to make partisanship an important force in resisting or amplifying the power of potential primes. We encourage future study of the impact of partisanship and party divisions on the power of priming.

Most of the work on priming has occurred in the experimental context. Many of the avenues we suggest for future research will require experimental studies as well. However, as scholars continue to study varying effects on approval, we encourage them to do the challenging work of applying new theoretical insights to the aggregate time series context. Althaus and Kim (2006) argue that experimental studies of priming ignore the influence of cumulative exposure to messages and urge examination of priming in the complex information environment of the real world. Some work has tested for priming effects in time series models, allowing the impact of several factors to vary over time (see Wood 2000; Holian 2006; Kelleher and Wolak 2006; McAvoy 2006). These studies demonstrate that aggregate analysis can be sensitive to changes in the public's evaluative calculus. Such studies increase our confidence in the experimental research by demonstrating that the significance of priming extends beyond the laboratory and into aggregate approval.

As we close our discussion of altering standards of evaluation, we note that the new media environment may be another element that alters presidents' power to prime the public. The proliferation of media outlets poses significant challenges to the executive branch's ability to set the news agenda. Presidents reach fewer people via a prime-time nationally televised speech because viewers uninterested in politics have many alternative entertainment outlets (Baum and Kernell 1999). In addition, critics of the president have many more venues through which to voice their criticism. They can convince smaller media outlets with more narrowly defined markets to carry their message or simply post their views online. Furthermore, any statement from the administration can and will be scrutinized, challenged, and critiqued in the blogosphere or on talk radio. The new media environment makes it much more difficult for any political leader to shape the information individuals are receiving.

Cohen (2008) argues that in this context presidents have an incentive to communicate with smaller, more defined groups. Thus, the president's partisans and those groups that share the president's policy views are likely to receive greater attention while the president will spend less time communicating with opposition groups. This communications strategy will advance polarization since the president's messages are crafted for his party's base, while critics of the president are not exposed to the president's communications and instead turn to sources critical of the president. This move toward segmented communication highlights the importance of examining heterogeneity in the ways the public learns about and evaluates the president.

HETEROGENEITY IN
PRESIDENTIAL APPROVAL

Although most studies, especially in the early decades of presidential approval research, examined the public as a relatively undifferentiated whole, we would not expect everyone in the public to care about the same issues or conditions, so we might expect various groups in the public to differ in their evaluations of the president. Heterogeneity across groups can affect approval in two ways, via different perceptions of political and economic conditions (e.g., Democrats may view the economy more favorably than Republicans or vice versa) and via different impacts of those conditions (Republicans may weigh their views of the economy more heavily than do Democrats). For example, Gilens (1988) found that differences in women's and men's attitudes on various issues explained much of the gender gap in approval of Ronald Reagan. However, women also put greater weight on their more liberal views of defense spending than did men when evaluating Reagan. Along the same lines, from 1978 to 1997, women's views of economic conditions were generally less positive than men's and they weighed their economic perceptions differently than men when evaluating presidents (Clarke et al. 2005).

From the beginning of presidential approval research, scholars have examined partisan differences in evaluative criteria (Mueller 1973, ch. 10). Most notably, several studies have found that Democrats' approval is most sensitive to unemployment and Republicans' approval tends to respond to inflation (Hibbs, Rivers, and Vasilatos 1982; Ostrom and Simon 1988; Lebo and Cassino 2007), while partisan groups often respond to major events in different ways (Baum 2002; Baum and Groeling 2008). In addition, partisans appear to use motivated reasoning to incorporate new information into evaluations of the president in ways that reinforce their partisan predispositions. In-partisans generally approve of the president even in the face of negative perceptions of the president's character or economic downturns, while out-partisans typically weigh negative perceptions of character traits and economic woes more heavily (Goren 2002; Lebo and Cassino 2007). Although research on heterogeneity has focused on partisanship, a few studies have examined differences related to gender (e.g., Gilens 1988; Clarke et al. 2005), race (Dawson 1994), and occupation (Hibbs, Rivers, and Vasilatos 1982), while many of the priming studies we cited above have explored heterogeneity across levels of sophistication.

We have much to learn about differences in the foundations of approval across the major groups in the American public. Some dimensions of American society have largely been ignored in this literature, such as income and religion. It may be worth exploring whether lower-income earners base their views of the president on different aspects of the economy than do higher-income earners. As we learn more about which groups weigh factors differently, larger questions of why heterogeneity exists in some instances, but not others, may arise. Here again we see a plethora of research questions drawing scholars ever deeper into the nuances of what drives presidential approval.

PULLING IT ALL TOGETHER

After spending several pages pointing to ways to explore ever more nuanced details of what was once a relatively basic model, we want to highlight the importance of pulling these details together to tell us something general about presidential approval. As we move toward understanding the micro foundations of approval by delving deeper into particular aspects of the model, contextualizing each factor, demonstrating how the levels and impact of various forces differ across the public and depend on elite discourse, news coverage, and other aspects of the political environment, we must continue to ask how these nuances affect our larger understanding of presidential approval. If men and women or Republicans and Democrats weigh their views of war differently, for example, what does this mean for the president's overall standing in the public? If in-partisans are more open to the president's attempts to prime them, what do we learn about aggregate approval ratings? How do the micro foundations we uncover translate into the macro-level trends that can affect the president's leverage in Washington?

The best work has effectively drawn connections between detailed individual-level analyses and aggregate approval ratings. For example, Ostrom and Simon (1988) worked through a series of simulations to illustrate how the individual-level effects their analyses identified would alter aggregate approval levels, while Krosnick and Kinder (1990, 510) note important consequences of their finding that the least knowledgeable are most susceptible to priming. In their words, "our findings suggest that change over time in popular approval—and thus the waxing and waning of presidential power—may depend the most on the citizens who know the least." Although their conclusions about who is most open to priming have since been challenged, we applaud their application of detailed findings to broader questions of the ways aggregate approval moves. In addition, some recent time series studies have enriched their models by explicitly including insights from individual-level studies, especially as they note the varying impact of particular factors over time (e.g., Kelleher and Wolak 2006; McAvoy 2006; Wood 2007). As we continue to develop more nuanced models, we must also continue the challenging work of integrating these advances into our comprehensive understanding of presidential approval.

Beyond linking findings to our general understanding of presidential approval, scholars must continue to connect their findings to the central questions of democratic politics that motivate the study of approval ratings. Many of the questions we identify ultimately relate to the fundamental issue of the public's competence in playing its democratic role. If citizens are susceptible to presidential priming strategies, they may overlook areas in which the president has failed and not hold him accountable for that failure. However, if citizens are capable and willing to reject such strategic messages and base their evaluations in part on more negative considerations presidents do not prime, perhaps the public may be checking its representatives effectively (see Zaller 1998).

In a related way, many of the questions we raise here relate to the degree to which presidents can shape opinion about themselves. Edwards (in this volume) discusses the president's ability to shape opinion more broadly, but we briefly highlight the issue here as well. As views of character, the economy, events, and war are shaped in part by elite debate, the president remains a central voice in this discourse and may therefore indirectly shape approval ratings. Moreover, if presidents can influence the criteria by which they are evaluated, they may have subtle tools to boost their public standing.

These questions relate not only to the public's ability to resist elite manipulation and hold the president accountable to what it sees as the president's chief duties, but also to the ability of other political actors to check presidents. If Congress, the press, or other political actors can work successfully against presidents' efforts to shape the criteria of presidential evaluation, if these other actors can convince the public to hold presidents accountable for failure in fundamental aspects of presidential performance, the system will provide a check on the executive. However, if presidents win the competition over framing the relevant criteria for evaluating themselves, they may avoid punishment for poor performance on particular dimensions.

Therefore, as Chong and Druckman (2007) emphasize, it is vital to study the president's power to set the public's evaluative criteria in a competitive context. They note that not all political actors have the same ability to frame an evaluation; some will be advantaged because they have the resources "to develop and disseminate their messages" (2007, 639). The president generally has ample resources to do so. Thus, presidents may be advantaged in competitions over the criteria by which they are evaluated. However, these other political actors, who often have incentives and capacity to frame evaluations of the president in different ways, may still limit presidents.

In the end, then, we see research exploring the extent to which the president, other political actors, and individuals in the public shape presidential approval as theoretically, empirically, and normatively important. Presidential approval research has always touched close to the heart of democratic politics. We are optimistic that future research will continue to do so.

References

ALTHAUS, S. L., and KIM, Y. M. 2006. Priming Effects in Complex Environments. *Journal of Politics*, 68: 960–76.

ARCENEAUX, K. 2006. The Federal Face of Voting: Are Elected Officials Held Accountable for the Functions Relevant to their Office? *Political Psychology*, 27: 731–54.

BARTELS, L. M. 2002. Beyond the Running Tally: Partisan Bias in Political Perceptions. *Political Behavior*, 24: 117–50.

BAUM, M. A. 2002. The Constituent Foundations of the Rally-Round-the-Flag Phenomenon. *International Studies Quarterly*, 46: 263–98.

—— and GROELING, T. 2008. Crossing the Water's Edge: Elite Rhetoric, Media Coverage and the Rally-Round-the-Flag Phenomenon, 1979–2003. *Journal of Politics*, forthcoming.

BAUM, M. A., and KERNELL, S. 1999. Has Cable Ended the Golden Age of Presidential Television? *American Political Science Review*, 93: 99–114.

BERINSKY, A. J., and DRUCKMAN, J. N. 2007. Public Opinion Research and Support for the Iraq War. *Public Opinion Quarterly*, 71: 126–41.

BOND, J. R., and FLEISHER, R. 1999. *Polarized Politics: Congress and the President in a Partisan Era*. Washington, DC: CQ Press.

———— 2001. Partisanship and Presidential Performance Evaluations. *Presidential Studies Quarterly*, 31: 529–40.

BRADER, T. 2006. *Campaigning for Hearts and Minds: How Emotional Appeals in Political Ads Work*. Chicago: University of Chicago Press.

BRODY, R. A. 1991. *Assessing the President: The Media, Elite Opinion, and Public Support*. Stanford, CA: Stanford University Press.

BURDEN, B. C., and MUGHAN, A. 2003. The International Economy and Presidential Approval. *Public Opinion Quarterly*, 67: 555–78.

CHONG, D., and DRUCKMAN, J. N. 2007. Framing Public Opinion in Competitive Democracies. *American Political Science Review*, 101: 637–55.

CLARKE, H. D., and STEWART. M. 1994. Prospections, Retrospections, and Rationality: The "Bankers" Model of Presidential Approval Reconsidered. *American Journal of Political Science*, 38: 1104–23.

———— AULT, M., and ELLIOTT, E. 2005. Men, Women and the Dynamics of Presidential Approval. *British Journal of Political Science*, 35: 31–51.

COHEN, J. E. 1995. Presidential Rhetoric and the Public Agenda. *American Journal of Political Science*, 39: 87–107.

——2008. *The Presidency in the Era of 24-Hour News*. Princeton, NJ: Princeton University Press.

DAWSON, M. C. 1994. *Behind the Mule: Race and Class in African-American Politics*. Princeton, NJ: Princeton University Press.

DRUCKMAN, J. N., and HOLMES, J. W. 2004. Does Presidential Rhetoric Matter? Priming and Presidential Approval. *Presidential Studies Quarterly*, 34: 755–78.

——JACOBS, L. R., and OSTERMEIER, E. 2004. Candidate Strategies to Prime Issues and Image. *Journal of Politics*, 66: 1205–27.

EDWARDS, G. C., III. 1990. *Presidential Approval*. Baltimore: Johns Hopkins University Press.

——MITCHELL, W., and WELCH, R. 1995. Explaining Presidential Approval: The Significance of Issue Salience. *American Journal of Political Science*, 39: 108–34.

——and SWENSON, T. 1997. Who Rallies? The Anatomy of a Rally Event. *Journal of Politics*, 59: 200–12.

——and WOOD, B. D. 1999. Who Influences Whom? The President and the Public Agenda. *American Political Science Review*, 93: 327–44.

ERIKSON, R. S., MACKUEN, M. B., and STIMSON, J. A. 1998. What Moves Macropartisanship: A Response to Green, Palmquist, and Schickler. *American Political Science Review*, 92: 901–12.

———— 2002. *The Macro Polity*. New York: Cambridge University Press.

EVANS, G., and ANDERSEN, R. 2006. The Political Conditioning of Economic Perceptions. *Journal of Politics*, 68: 194–207.

FIORINA, M. P., ABRAMS, S., and POPE, J. C. 2006. *Culture War? The Myth of a Polarized America*, 2nd edn. New York: Pearson Longman.

FUNK, C. L. 1996. The Impact of Scandal on Candidate Evaluations: An Experimental Test of the Role of Candidate Traits. *Political Behavior*, 18: 1–24.

GARTNER, S. S. 2008. The Multiple Effects of Casualties on Public Support for War: An Experimental Approach. *American Political Science Review*, 102: 95–105.

—— and SEGURA, G. M. 1998. War, Casualties, and Public Opinion. *Journal of Conflict Resolution*, 42: 278–300.

—— —— 2000. Race, Casualties, and Opinion in the Vietnam War. *Journal of Politics*, 62: 115–46.

GELPI, C., FEAVER, P. D., and REIFLER, J. 2005/6. Success Matters: Casualty Sensitivity and the War in Iraq. *International Security*, 30: 7–46.

GILENS, M, 1988. Gender and Support for Reagan: A Comprehensive Model of Presidential Approval. *American Journal of Political Science*, 32: 19–49.

GOREN, P. 2002. Character Weakness, Partisan Bias, and Presidential Evaluation. *American Journal of Political Science*, 46: 627–41.

GREEN, D., PALMQUIST, B., and SCHICKLER, E. 1998. Macropartisanship: A Replication and Critique. *American Political Science Review*, 93: 883–99.

GREENE, S. 2001. The Role of Character Assessments in Presidential Approval. *American Politics Research*, 29: 196–210.

GRONKE, P., and BREHM, J. 2002. History, Heterogeneity, and Presidential Approval. *Electoral Studies*, 21: 425–52.

—— and NEWMAN, B. 2003. FDR to Clinton, Mueller to ?? A Field Essay on Presidential Approval. *Political Research Quarterly*, 56: 501–12.

HETHERINGTON, M. J. 1996. The Media's Role in Forming Voters' National Economic Evaluations in 1992. *American Journal of Political Science*, 40: 372–95.

HIBBS, D. A., Jr. 1987. *The American Political Economy*. Cambridge, MA: Harvard University Press.

—— RIVERS, R. D., and VASILATOS, N. 1982. The Dynamics of Political Support for American Presidents among Occupational and Partisan Groups. *American Journal of Political Science*, 26: 312–32.

HOLIAN, D. B. 2006. Trust the Party Line: Issue Ownership and Presidential Approval from Reagan to Clinton. *American Politics Research*, 34: 777–802.

HUWITZ, J., and PEFFLEY, M. 1987. The Means and Ends of Foreign Policy as Determinants of Public Support. *American Journal of Political Science*, 31: 236–58.

IYENGAR, S., and KINDER, D. R. 1987. *News that Matters*. Chicago: University of Chicago Press.

JACOBS, L. R., and SHAPIRO, R. Y. 1994. Issues, Candidate Image, and Priming: The Use of Private Polls in Kennedy's 1960 Presidential Campaign. *American Political Science Review*, 88: 527–40.

JACOBSON, G. C. 2007. *A Divider not a Uniter: George W. Bush and the American People*. New York: Pearson Longman.

KELLEHER, C. A., and WOLAK, J. 2006. Priming Presidential Approval: The Conditionality of Issue Effects. *Political Behavior*, 28: 193–210.

KERNELL, S. 1978. Explaining Presidential Popularity. *American Political Science Review*, 72: 506–22.

—— and HIBBS, D. A., JR. 1981. A Critical Threshold Model of Presidential Popularity. Pp. 49–71 in *Contemporary Political Economy: Studies on the Interdependence of Politics and Economics*, ed. D. A. Hibbs, Jr., and H. Fassbender. New York: North-Holland Publishing Company.

KINDER, D. R. 1986. Presidential Character Revisited. In *Political Cognition*, ed. R. R. Lau and D. O. Sears. Hillsdale, NJ: L. Erlbaum Associates.

KROSNICK, J. A., and BRANNON, L. A. 1993. The Impact of the Gulf War on the Ingredients of Presidential Evaluations: Multidimensional Effects of Political Involvement. *American Political Science Review*, 87: 963–75.

KROSNICK, J. A., BRANNON, L. A., and KINDER, D. 1990. Altering the Foundations of Support for the President through Priming. *American Political Science Review*, 84: 497–512.

LADD, J. M. 2007. Predispositions and Public Support for the President during the War on Terrorism. *Public Opinion Quarterly*, 71: 511–38.

——and LENZ, G. S. 2008. Reassessing the Role of Anxiety in Vote Choice. *Political Psychology*, 29: 275–96.

LEBO, M. J., and CASSINO, D. 2007. The Aggregated Consequences of Motivated Reasoning and the Dynamics of Partisan Presidential Approval. *Political Psychology*, 28: 719–46.

LEWIS-BECK, M. S. 2006. Does Economics Still Matter? Econometrics and the Vote. *Journal of Politics*, 68: 208–12.

McAVOY, G. E. 2006. Stability and Change: The Time Varying Impact of Economic and Foreign Policy Evaluations on Presidential Approval. *Political Research Quarterly*, 59: 71–83.

——2008. Substance versus Style: Distinguishing Presidential Job Performance from Favorability. *Presidential Studies Quarterly*, 38: 284–99.

McCARTY, N., Poole, K. T., and ROSENTHAL, H. 2006. *Polarized America: The Dance of Ideology and Unequal Riches*. Boston: MIT Press.

MacKUEN, M. 1983. Political Drama, Economic Conditions, and the Dynamics of Presidential Popularity. *American Journal of Political Science*, 27: 165–92.

——ERIKSON, R. S., and STIMSON, J. A. 1989. Macropartisanship. *American Political Science Review*, 83: 1125–42.

——————1992. Peasants or Bankers? The American Electorate and the U.S. Economy. *American Political Science Review*, 86: 596–611.

MALHOTRA, N., and KUO, A. G. 2008. Attributing Blame: The Public's Response to Hurricane Katrina. *Journal of Politics*, 70: 120–35.

MARCUS, G. E., NEUMAN, W. R., and MacKUEN, M. 2000. *Affective Intelligence and Political Judgment*. Chicago: University of Chicago Press.

MEROLLA, J. L., RAMOS, J. M., and ZECHMEISTER, E. J. 2007. Crisis, Charisma, and Consequences: Evidence from the 2004 U.S. Presidential Election. *Journal of Politics*, 69: 30–42.

MILLER, J. M., and KROSNICK, J. A. 2000. News Media Impact on the Ingredients of Presidential Evaluation: Politically Knowledgeable Citizens are Guided by a Trusted Source. *American Journal of Political Science*, 44: 295–309.

MUELLER, J. E. 1970. Presidential Popularity from Truman to Johnson. *American Political Science Review*, 64: 18–34.

——1973. *War, Presidents, and Public Opinion*. Lanham, MD: University Press of America.

NADEAU, R., and LEWIS-BECK, M. S. 2001. National Economic Voting in U.S. Presidential Elections. *Journal of Politics*, 63: 159–81.

——NIEMI, R. G., FAN, D. P., and AMATO, T. 1999. Elite Economic Forecasts, Economic News, Mass Economic Judgments, and Presidential Approval. *Journal of Politics*, 61/1: 109–35.

NEWMAN, B. 2002. Bill Clinton's Approval Ratings: The More Things Change, the More They Stay the Same. *Political Research Quarterly*, 55: 781–804.

——2003. Personal Integrity and Presidential Approval: The Effects of Integrity Assessments, 1980–2000. *Public Opinion Quarterly*, 67: 335–67.

——2004. Presidential Traits and Job Approval: Some Aggregate-Level Evidence. *Presidential Studies Quarterly*, 34: 437–48.

NICHOLSON, S. P., SEGURA, G. M., and WOODS, N. D. 2002. Presidential Approval and the Mixed Blessing of Divided Government. *Journal of Politics*, 64: 701–20.

NORPOTH, H. 1996. Presidents and the Prospective Voter. *Journal of Politics*, 58: 776–92.

OSTROM, C. W, JR., and SIMON, D. M. 1985. Promise and Performance: A Dynamic Model of Presidential Popularity. *American Political Science Review*, 79: 334–58.

——1988. The President's Public. *American Journal of Political Science*, 32: 1096–119.

PEFFLEY, M., LANGLEY, R. E., and GOIDEL, R. K. 1995. Public Responses to the Presidential Use of Military Force: A Panel Analysis. *Political Behavior*, 17: 307–37.

RUDOLPH, T. J. 2003a. Who's Responsible for the Economy? The Formation and Consequences of Responsibility Attributions. *American Journal of Political Science*, 47: 698–713.

—— 2003b. Institutional Context and the Assignment of Political Responsibility. *Journal of Politics*, 65: 190–215.

—— 2006. Triangulating Political Responsibility: The Motivated Formation of Responsibility Judgments. *Political Psychology*, 27: 99–122.

SHAH, D. V., WATTS, M. D., DOMKE, D., and FAN, D. E. 2002. News Framing and Cueing of Issue Regimes: Explaining Clinton's Public Approval in Spite of Scandal. *Public Opinion Quarterly*, 66: 339–70.

STIMSON, J. A. 1999. *Public Opinion in America: Moods, Cycles, and Swings*. Boulder, CO: Westview.

TABER, C. S., and LODGE, M. 2006. Motivated Skepticism in the Evaluation of Political Beliefs. *American Journal of Political Science*, 50: 755–69.

WATERMAN, R., WRIGHT, W. R., and ST CLAIR, G. 1999. *The Image-Is-Everything Presidency*. Boulder, CO: Westview.

WOOD, B. D. 2000. Weak Theories and Parameter Instability: Using Flexible Least Squares to Take Time Varying Relationships Seriously. *American Journal of Political Science*, 44: 603–18.

—— 2007. *The Politics of Economic Leadership: The Causes and Consequences of Presidential Rhetoric*. Princeton, NJ: Princeton University Press.

ZALLER, J. R. 1992. *The Nature and Origins of Mass Opinion*. Cambridge: Cambridge University Press.

—— 1998. Monica Lewinsky's Contribution to Political Science. *PS: Political Science and Politics*, 33: 182–9.

CHAPTER 12

THE PRESIDENCY AND THE MASS MEDIA

JEFFREY E. COHEN

NEWS is the primary source of information for the overwhelming number of people in modern mass democracies. Citizens use information from the news to hold government leaders accountable for their actions in office, the policies they pursue, and the impacts of those policies. News is also important to officeholders, like the president. Through news coverage, political leaders gain access to the public, providing opportunities to lead the public and set its policy agenda.

ACCOUNTING FOR THE QUANTITY, CONTENT, AND TONE OF PRESIDENTIAL NEWS

The quality of news coverage affects the president's ability to lead the mass public. If the president receives little or no news coverage, he cannot lead the public through the news. If the news does not emphasize the issues the president wants highlighted, he cannot lead on that issue. Even if presidents receive plentiful news coverage on

I would like to thank Matthew Baum and George Edwards for their comments on an earlier version of this chapter.

issues they deem important, news critical of the president may undermine his ability to lead. Thus, the quantity, content, and tone of presidential news coverage affect the prospects for presidential leadership.

Before proceeding, what do we mean by presidential news? Presidential news can be thought of as all stories that mention the president or only those in which the president is an important subject or actor. The second definition is generally preferable. Most readers probably identify the second type as presidential news but probably do not consider stories that mention the president in passing as presidential news.

Quantity

As Cornwell (1959) noted fifty years ago, the quantity of presidential news indicates not only the importance of the president to the public, but also the importance of the public to the president. As the quantity of news about the president grew, the president became increasingly important to the public. As presidential importance grew, public support, in turn, became ever more vital to the president.

Presidents also value a high volume of presidential news, because due to the finite size of the new hole, as the president receives more news, competitors to the president, such as congressional leaders, will receive less news. The ideal situation for the president occurs when he is the sole voice in the news, when he "monopolizes" this public space, to use Miroff's (1982) useful terminology. When presidents appear to dominate the news, the citizenry may surmise that other political leaders tacitly approve of or support the president or at least there is no overt opposition to the president. Such one-message environments (Zaller 1992) may enhance presidential leadership of public opinion.

The Growth (and Decline) of Presidential News

Few studies have tried to assess the amount of presidential news historically (Cornwell 1959; Balutis 1977; Kernell and Jacobson 1987). These studies use human coders, which limits the amount of data that could be collected and coded, usually resulting in wide time gaps between data points. Moreover, the sampling frames are based more on convenience than properties of the population of news, which are unknown. From this tiny literature, we learn that the amount of presidential news has grown over the course of the nineteenth and twentieth centuries. But the paucity of data points limits our ability to describe the trend in detail or to test hypotheses about the sources of trends in presidential news. The massive cost of collecting and coding news about the president over time and across the large number of news outlets has been a major hurdle, limiting past data collection efforts.

Recently, machine readable databases of newspapers have opened up the opportunity to collect larger, more comprehensive, and denser presidential news data. Improved data may lead to finer-grained understandings of presidential news production processes. For instance, the ProQuest service has scanned the entire publication history of the *New York Times* (1857–present) into a machine readable format, and has more recently added the *Wall Street Journal, Chicago Tribune,* and *Los Angeles Times,* with more newspapers promised in the future.

Cohen (2008) exploited the *New York Times* database. Using a simple search request that asks for the word "president" and the president's name, he retrieved over 116,000 articles from the front page of the *New York Times* from 1857 through 1998. Note that this search retrieved all stories that mention the president and thus does not employ my preferred definition of presidential news offered above. We can compare presidential and congressional news using this methodology by searching for the terms "Congress" or "House of Representatives" or "Senate" but excluding "state senate" or "state house," which retrieves over 138,000 articles on Congress. Figure 12.1 plots the two series as percentages of front-page stories per year, to take account of the changing architecture of front pages (Barnhurst and Mutz 1997). Figure 12.2 plots the percentage of congressional news stories that also mention the president.

These figures provide a much more refined and detailed portrait of presidential and congressional news than earlier research. Like that research, these data show growth in both types of news. In the twentieth century, they track each other, but in the nineteenth century, congressional news clearly overshadowed presidential news coverage. Figure 12.2 provides another interpretative twist—as the twentieth century progressed, the president appears in congressional news stories in greater frequency. By the 1930s, over half of all front-page Congress stories also mention the president. By the 1970s, that figure often topped 70 percent. In the nineteenth century, the two institutions appear in the pages of the *Times* independently. In the twentieth century

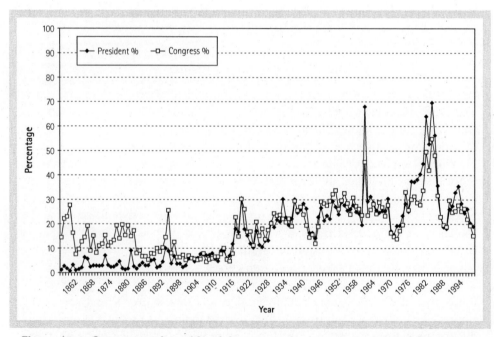

Figure 12.1 Congress and presidential news stories as a percentage of front-page news, *New York Times,* 1857–1998

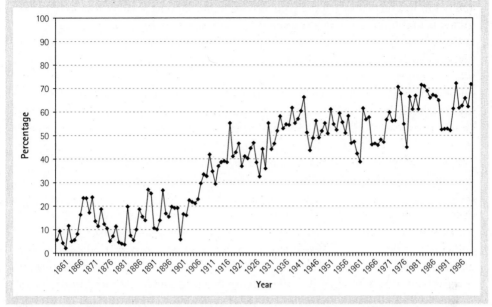

Figure 12.2 Percentage of Congress stories that mention the president on the front page of the *New York Times*, 1857–1998

they appear jointly. One can conjecture that when they jointly appear, it is likely that Congress is mentioned as a player in a presidential news story. Figure 12.1 also reveals declining amounts of news for both institutions beginning in the late 1970s (Farnsworth and Lichter 2006; Patterson 2000).

Cohen (2008) is particularly concerned with understanding the trends in presidential news. His theoretical model argues that the amount of news space is finite, forcing presidential news to compete with other events for front-page placement. From this idea, derived from theories of news production, Cohen suggests a number of hypotheses about both the long-term trend and short-term dynamics of presidential news coverage: presidents receive more news in their first year in office; news totals rise when the president visits foreign nations; increased federal spending will dampen presidential news totals; and the rise of the new media, like cable television, will depress presidential news totals. Yet Cohen analyzes only the *Times*. Of interest would be to see if other papers follow the same trends, and for the same reasons, as Cohen detects for the *Times*.

Comparing Presidential News Coverage across Media

The discussion thus far has focused on newspaper coverage. Television may be a more important source of presidential news because it is the primary source of news for the largest fraction of the US public, despite a shrinking audience. There are several reasons to compare the amount of news across news media forms. First, as new forms of media have come on line, people's news acquisition habits change. If the new form contains more or less news, and people switch from the old form to the new, then the amount of news that they could receive might change. For example, in the 1950s, television replaced newspapers as the most used news form; many newspaper readers stopped reading the newspaper, switching to television. In the current era, many newspaper and television news consumers are dropping those forms for internet-delivered news. What are the implications of these changes on the public's information level? Second, changes in the major news form may affect the president's ability to generate the amount, type, and tone of news coverage about him. Inasmuch as the president's ability to manage the news varies across news media types, his prospects for public and policy leadership might rise or fall.

Comparing newspaper and television coverage poses important challenges. The thirty-minute nightly broadcast tightly constrains television in both quantity and depth of coverage. Moreover, newspaper stories can be read at the reader's pace and reread, which may aid comprehension. These format differences make it difficult to compare the quantity of presidential news on television and in newspapers. For instance, should we compare the number of stories on both media? Or should we compare story length? Linguists offer methods for counting the number of words spoken per minute, for example, and archives of news broadcasts allow one to count story length in words. If we proceed with word counts, does a spoken word count equally with a written word count? When watching a television news broadcast, do facial expressions of the speaker add to the informational power of spoken words?

One recent study illustrates these issues. Farnsworth and Lichter (2006) content analyzed presidential news the during the first year of the Reagan (1981), Clinton (1993), and George W. Bush (2001) administrations for the three broadcast networks, the *New York Times, Washington Post,* and four regional newspapers. With the statement or soundbite as their unit of analysis, they collected approximately 16,000 television stories and 13,000 front-page newspaper stories on the president. How comparable are these totals? And what are we to make of the different metrics for story length? How do we compare an average broadcast story that lasts about 1 minute and 40 seconds with a story in a major national newspaper that runs 32.1 column inches or a story in a regional newspaper, which runs about 22 column inches (2006, 147, table 6.3)?

From linguistics we can estimate the number of words spoken per minute and we can also count the number of words per column inch. Thus we can convert broadcast time and column inches into the same units, words. For example, at an average speaking rate of 120 to 150 words per minute, there will be about 200–50 words spoken in an average network news story. The average column inch contains approximately 30 words. Thus the average newspaper story in national and regional papers will contain about 950 and 650 words respectively. Based on these metrics, one network will broadcast in the range of 330,000 to 415,000 words on the president per year. In comparison, a national newspaper will print about 970,000 words and a regional paper about 300,000 words per year on the president. With these rough calculations, a national newspaper will report several times as much presidential news as one of the big three networks, but regional newspapers appear to offer no more "information" in terms of quantity of words than the networks. But do these comparisons make sense? Are spoken and written words equivalent? Do the visuals of film provide viewers with other information, perhaps information that is not so easily conveyed through words?

The aim of these word-length calculations is not to present a precise metric for comparing the quantity of news coverage across media, but to raise the point that to make such comparisons we need some way of gauging news quantity and information impact across different media forms. This issue becomes even more daunting when we recognize that the internet is fast becoming a major source of news, draining off readers of newspapers and viewers of television, and that we also need to contend with the 24/7 cable news networks, which, over the past fifteen years or so, have become major news sources also. Few comparative analyses of cable versus other news forms now exist (Wicks and Walker 1993; Bae 2000). They suggest differences both across cable networks and between cable and the broadcast networks, but none directly pertains to the presidency and none compares cable to newspapers. There now exist a diversity of news forms and the audience for news is shrinking and splintering. In this context, how much presidential news is reaching citizens who use one form as opposed to another?

Content

If we can say little about the quantity of presidential news, we can say even less about its content. Few studies have tried to gauge the content or subject matter of presidential news. Two aspects of story content stand out as possible research topics. First, how symbolic versus substantive is presidential news? And second, which policies or issues are mentioned in presidential news?

Presidents often assume a symbolic role and play a leading role in many ceremonies and rituals. This symbolic-ceremonial aspect of presidential public activity is often thought an important resource for building public support (Waterman, St Clair, and Wright 1999). For instance, some observers contend that President George W. Bush's speech at the Washington National Cathedral shortly after the September 11 terrorist bombings altered his public image and rallied public support behind his leadership. How often and in what manner do news outlets report these symbolic-ceremonial activities? Do they more often portray the president as a symbolic-ceremonial leader or as a policy leader? We simply have no systematic data on these questions, nor do we have studies on the impact of ceremonial versus policy news on public opinion.

Similarly, we know little about news portrayal of the president as a policy leader or even which policy areas receive the most coverage in presidential news. Shields and Goidel (1996) is an exception with their comparison of presidential and congressional coverage on the national debt issue over a four-year period. They find considerably more presidential than congressional news, but we should be cautious in generalizing this finding to other policy areas.

The *New York Times* database of the Policy Agendas Project (PAP) provides us with one way to get a sense of the policy topics that figure in presidential news. The PAP coded over 40,000 randomly selected stories from 1946 through 2003, using the *Times* index as the database. The *Times* index poses some problems in coding a story as presidential. Only if the president was mentioned explicitly in the very brief index description did the data collectors code a story as presidential. By this standard, about 8 percent of stories were presidential. The use of the index probably undercounts the amount of time that the president appears in a story on a policy area as a major actor due to the limited amount of information in the index. Still, we may view the policy stories picked up by this method as ones that the *Times*, and perhaps the president, view as decidedly and unambiguously presidential.

Table 12.1 presents the breakdown for presidential news by the PAP policy categorization scheme. The first column presents the policy area percentage for all presidential stories. Four of the twenty-one policy areas account for slightly over

Table 12.1 Presidential news coverage by policy area, *New York Times*, 1946–2003

Policy area	Percentage of presidential news	Presidential percentage of all policy news	Percentage of sentences in the State of the Union address
Government operations	35.71	54.16	6.67
International affairs	15.09	9.48	19.03
Defense	13.13	17.10	15.46
Macroeconomics	6.75	38.55	15.85
Foreign trade	3.46	12.35	2.41
Law, crime, and family issues	3.25	4.31	4.23
Energy	2.56	11.23	2.26
Labor, immigration, and employment	2.41	7.74	5.25
Civil rights	2.29	9.91	2.98
Health	1.81	4.57	4.86
Education	1.75	3.64	4.36
Banking, finance, and domestic commerce	1.54	0.75	1.53
Social welfare	1.39	18.85	4.43
Environment	1.29	7.33	1.82
Transportation	1.23	2.95	1.29
Space, science, technology, and communications	1.17	3.74	1.61
Community development and housing	0.99	4.30	1.89
Agriculture	0.84	6.78	2.62
Public lands and water management	0.42	4.91	1.45

Source: Policy Agendas Project <www.policyagendas.com>.

70 percent of all presidential policy area stories—government operations (35.7 percent), international affairs (15.1 percent), defense (13.1 percent), and macroeconomics (6.8 percent). To a degree, the "two presidencies" emerge in news coverage of the president, which may reflect presidential policy priorities as well as news definitions for presidential policy leadership. What might account for this concentration of presidential news into four policy areas? It could be the actions and priorities of the president, a supply function, or it could be the way that journalists and perhaps the public define presidential news, a demand function, or some combination of the two.

There is some suggestion of presidential supply dynamics here. We can compare, from the PAP, presidential policy emphasis in his State of the Union address (SUA), one way of ranking presidential policy priorities. In their SUAs, presidents focus heavily on international affairs, defense, and macroeconomics, which together constitute about 50 percent of mentions, but presidents do not spend much time on government management, the other area that figured prominently in presidential news. Presidents also spread their attention more evenly across the remaining policy areas than we see in presidential news. Presidential policy attention seems more concentrated in news than it does in the president's own policy agenda, as reflected in the SUA.

Turning to the amount of presidential news within policy areas, these data suggest that presidents figure in over one-half of a policy area's mentions for only one policy area, government management (54.2 percent). Macroeconomics follows some distance behind at nearly 39 percent, and four other policy areas show presidential mentions ranging between 10 and 20 percent. But the bulk of policy areas fall below 10 percent. By these figures, the president does not appear to be the dominant policy actor in any policy area except government management. Given our conventional wisdom on presidential policy leadership, especially for the macroeconomy and international affairs, why don't we find the president in a greater percentage of stories on those policies? Perhaps the *Times* index does not record presidential activity very well, given the brevity of the index entries. Or it may be that presidents are not as active or do not take a policy leadership role as much as our conventional wisdom suggests. Clearly, more work needs to be done on the content of presidential news.

Tone and Bias

Another important topic relates to the direction of presidential news, referred to as tone, valence, or slant. Closely related is the topic of bias, as some observers use the direction of news as an indicator of bias. The ideas of tone and bias raise thorny conceptual issues. Bias in particular is used inconsistently, with various meanings or definitions.

Bias and Presidential News

Scholars conceptualize bias at least three ways (Entman 2007). First, bias may refer to news that distorts or falsifies reality, *distortion bias*. A second use of bias focuses on the equivalent treatment of both (or more) sides to an argument, *content bias*. Third, bias may refer to the motivations and mindsets of journalists, *decision-making bias*, which may affect how they write news stories.

Distortion bias claims are found most often among those who lament that the media are not treating their side fairly or accurately, such as conservatives arguing that the press is liberal, with liberals arguing the reverse. We are not going to resolve the distortion bias debates (D'Alessio and Allen 2000; Druckman and Parkin 2005; Gilens and Hertzman 2000; Groeling and Kernell 1998; Kahn and Kenney 2002). First, "no 'objective' standard of unbiased coverage exists against which actual coverage can be compared" (Gilens and Hertzman 2000, 371). Second, news, by definition, distorts reality. Reality is just too complex and voluminous to be reported in its entirety. News condenses reality, reporting some facts, while filtering out others. Reasonable people may disagree about which facts should be included and the emphasis that they should receive, disagreements that arise because people's values differ. Inasmuch as people hold different values, there will be disagreement over whether the news "got it right."

The hostile media hypothesis is related to the distortion bias issue, but instead of resolving distortion bias claims, the hypothesis aims to understand why some people see the media as hostile to their viewpoints (Comstock and Scharrer 2005, 91–3). In recent years Republicans and conservatives have been likely to view the media as hostile, that is, as congenial to Democrats and liberals (Eveland and Shah 2003). The effects of news will likely weaken if people view the media as hostile. When people see the media as hostile, they may disregard, discount, or misperceive news that is contrary to their predispositions (Comstock and Scharrer 2005, 93). An important question that has not received much scholarly attention asks if political leaders can influence whether the public views the media as hostile. Circumstantial evidence suggests that Republican and conservative leaders' complaint of a liberal bias in the media may have influenced the opinion of many Republicans and conservatives. How receptive would the public be to presidents who also complain about the treatment that they receive in the news media?

Tone and Presidential News

If we cannot resolve the distortion bias debates, we can more systematically deal with content bias. Entman's (2007) definitions of slant and content bias provide useful starting points. Slant "characterizes individual news reports and editorials in which the framing favors one side over the other in a current or potential dispute" (2007, 165). Content bias consists of "consistent patterns in the framing of mediated communication that promote the influence of one side in conflicts over the use of government power" (2007, 166). Although any story may be slanted, slant only becomes bias when it recurs systematically across stories and affects the distribution of power.

Presidential news may be slanted in many ways, for instance, to the Democrats or Republicans, a *partisan slant*, or in a liberal or conservative direction, an *ideological slant*. Most research on slant focuses on presidential elections, asking primarily whether the presidential candidates of the two major parties receive equal amounts of news coverage. D'Alessio and Allen's (2000) meta-analysis of the literature finds little indication of either partisan or ideological slant, and thus, they conclude there is not much bias in news coverage of presidential elections (Niven 2002).

Although there may be little partisan or ideological bias when we aggregate across news media, particular news organizations may be slanted in a partisan or ideological direction. For instance, Fox Cable News may be slanted toward Republicans and conservatives, with the *New York Times* slanted in the opposite directions (Gentzkow and Shapiro 2006; Groseclose and Milyo 2005). Assume a news system with two news organizations that are identical except one displays a Republican slant and the other a Democratic slant. At the level of the news system, bias in the news is the average of the slant of the two news outlets. Our hypothetical news system looks balanced, not biased. In a sense, this is D'Alessio and Allen's (2000) perspective in their meta-analysis.

But individual voters rarely expose themselves to a wide variety of news outlets. Depending on the news outlet that the voter relies upon most heavily, that voter's news diet may be filled with partisan or ideologically slanted news, and a slanted news diet may affect voting decisions (Della Vigna and Kaplan 2007; Druckman and Parkin 2005; Kahn and Kenney 2002). If Republican (or Democratic) slanted news outlets have in the aggregate larger audiences and/or those audiences are more likely to turn out, then partisan slant may affect election outcomes and evaluations of political leaders. In estimating the degree of bias, we need to do more than aggregate across news outlets; we need to also look at the size and political participation of their readers and/or viewers.

When studying presidents in office, as opposed to election settings, research more often focuses on whether presidential news is positive or negative, good or bad, for the president, that is, tone or valence. In a sense, tone is one type of news slant. Tone is important because presidents, politicians, commentators, and some scholars believe that positive news enhances presidential leadership, while negative news undercuts it. Moreover, presidents often believe that the media are biased against them by being more likely to run a negative than a positive news story. A key task of White House media operations is to ensure positive news coverage and to mitigate the harm of negative news through what is generally referred to as "spin control" (Kumar 2007; Kurtz 1998; Maltese 1992; Rozell 1993, 1995). This leads to two critical questions: what is the tone of presidential news and what determines that tonality?

We can define positive news as stories that present the president as a strong, successful, prudent leader, backed by the public and other political leaders, and define negative news as stories that portray the president as weak, indecisive, unsuccessful, beset by opponents, and lacking high levels of public support. Coding news according to such a definition is admittedly difficult, but possible (Brody 1991; Farnsworth and Lichter 2006; Grossman and Kumar 1981; Erikson, MacKuen, and Stimson 2001).

Often overlooked in the measurement of story tone is whether good or bad news reflects the events being reported on or the interpretation of journalists. Those who subscribe to the first model, that news tone reflects an event accurately, assume, often without stating overtly, the "mirror" model of journalism. The second model, that a story's tone is a function of journalistic interpretation of the event, raises the issue of decision-making bias. Decision-making bias suggests that reporters and editors interpose their own interpretations of an event into the news, for instance by selectively excluding or including information in stories. In other words, news is a social or journalistic construction. Presidents naturally tend to subscribe to this second way of viewing story tone. The White House expends a massive amount of resources on "news management" or "spin control" because they believe that they can alter the tone of a story. It is not clear how successful presidents are in affecting the tone of their news. An important research question asks how successful presidents are in managing their news and the tactics and factors that affect such success.

Whether a story deserves to be reported from a positive or negative angle is a question that we cannot answer definitively. Although we can assess the tone of a news story within tolerable limits of measurement error, it is difficult, expensive, and time consuming to collect large datasets, which are necessary to test rival hypotheses about the factors that affect tone in presidential news. Consequently, only a small number of large data collections exist (Grossman and Kumar 1981; Farnsworth and Lichter 2006). These studies are primarily descriptive and spend little time testing hypotheses about the factors that affect the tone of presidential news, but two recent studies that employ large datasets are more theoretical and analytical (Groeling forthcoming; and Cohen 2008).

Groeling (forthcoming), like Farnsworth and Lichter, utilizes Center for Media and Public Affairs data, sometimes exactly the same data as Farnsworth and Lichter use. Groeling's study is theoretically motivated, tests hypotheses derived from theory, and looks at the impact of news tone on public opinion, a necessary linkage. Groeling's theory begins with journalists' definition of newsworthiness. To journalists, a newsworthy story will contain one or more of these four characteristics: novel events, conflict, authority figures, and balance. Balance refers to the journalist presenting both sides of the story, which they sometimes also refer to as "objectivity" in reporting. Groeling's second theoretical element relates to political parties. Political parties are important to their members, such as members in Congress, by aiding in their re-election and other efforts. By combining these two theoretical assumptions, journalist news definitions and the importance of parties, Groeling derives some novel hypotheses. Two stand out: Attacks from the president's party will be especially newsworthy, as will support from the opposition. He finds that such public statements are highly likely to become news, and that attacks from presidential co-partisans are remarkably newsworthy.

Groeling also detects an unexpected result when looking at the moderating effects of divided government. When the president's party controls Congress, we see the natural alignment of co-partisan support and opposition criticism. Co-partisan support rarely makes the news, but opposition criticism does because it reflects conflict, and journalists can present it in a balanced way, offset against the president's point of view.

When the opposition controls Congress, matters change. The party controlling Congress is more newsworthy, having greater authority than the minority party. Divided government creates incentives for the president's party to support him and disincentives to oppose him. Support from the presidential (minority) party is not very newsworthy, according to Groeling's theory. But divided government creates incentives for the majority opposition party to mute its criticism of the president: to forge policy compromises, to take credit for policy accomplishments, and to appear as a responsible, governing party. The implication is clear—presidents receive less criticism in the news during divided than united government, an intriguing and seemingly counter-intuitive finding. Nicholson, Segura, and Woods's (2002) analysis finds marginally higher approval during divided than united government after controlling for the usual factors. Groeling's theory may provide one mechanism to understand the Nicholson et al. result.

Cohen (2008) analyzes two large datasets on the tone of presidential news, a time series of presidential news from the *New York Times* from 1946 through 1992 and a random sample of 5,000 news stories in the Lexis-Nexis database from 1980 through 1998, with nearly 1,000 stories about the president (Patterson 2000). Cohen derives several hypotheses based upon the assumption that presidential news must compete with other events for news space. Like Groeling, he begins with the proposition that the president's authoritative position makes him newsworthy. The president is also newsworthy because he is often embroiled in policy and political conflict. Moreover, as traditional news outlets have lost audience and readers to the new media, like cable and the internet, news organizations have an incentive to be more responsive to viewer tastes, to find stories and formats that appeal to readers and viewers. Thus, not only has soft news replaced hard news, but hard news has become increasingly negative and conflictual in an attempt to retain and attract viewers and readers.

Cohen's time series analysis of the *New York Times* finds an up tick in negative news associated with the era of new media. War, scandal, and a president with an active and large legislative policy agenda also display higher rates of negative news, while new presidents seem to enjoy a honeymoon, with lower levels of negative news. Groeling and Cohen provide us with the beginnings of an understanding of the factors that affect the tone of presidential news.

Content and Tone: The Indexing Hypothesis and the Information Environment

News concerning foreign policy and national security generally provides presidents with more positive news coverage than stories concerning domestic policy issues. There are several possible reasons for this. One, the potential threat to the nation that such issues raise may dampen partisanship and other political divisions. Two, presidents possess important information advantages, especially in the early stages of foreign policy issues and events. There are two aspects to this presidential informational advantage. First, he possesses more information and detail than almost anyone, including Congress. Second, the president can regulate the release of information to his advantage. All of this makes the news media highly dependent upon the presidency, unlike domestic policy, where journalists can turn to other sources who possess information independent of the president. Thus, for many foreign policy events, presidents are likely to receive positive news, especially in comparison to news about domestic policy. This is the indexing hypothesis, first articulated by Bennett. To quote Bennett: "mass media news professionals, from the boardroom to the beat, tend to 'index' the range of voices and viewpoints in both news and editorials according to the range of views expressed in mainstream government debate about a given topic" (1990, 106).

Numerous studies provide evidence supportive of the indexing hypothesis (Bennett 1990; Entman and Page 1994; Hallin 1986; Hallin and Gitlin 1994; Mermin 1999; Zaller and Chiu 2000), although some important questions remain. For instance, in some cases Congress publicly challenges the president and the news media reports on the ensuing interbranch debate between them. Why does Congress voice concern or opposition to the president's course of action on some foreign policy events but not others? Does the news media always report on these congressional differences with the president or only under some circumstances? If the latter, what are those circumstances? Entman's (2007) cascading model has been an attempt to address these questions, while also noting that the president begins with informational advantages and the news media remains dependent on the president, until Congress and other authoritative elites begin to voice opposition to the president. Still, Entman's model does not tell us what triggers congressional opposition, although he richly describes the process of news production once congressional opposition becomes public.

Although the indexing hypothesis was developed to account for the dominance and positive tone of the president in foreign policy news, Brody's (1991) and Zaller's (1992) informational environment models are closely related. These information environment ideas begin with the alignment of the political leadership, especially the president and Congress. The leadership can either line up on the same side of an issue or the leadership can disagree, which Zaller calls one-sided versus two-sided message flows. Generally, a one-sided message flow means that Congress supports the president, while congressional opposition indicates a two-sided message flow. The news media reflects the degree of support or opposition to the president in its reporting; in other words, it indexes Washington debate. Thus, media indexing may be applicable across all types of policies. If so, then factors other than presidential informational advantages may determine whether a one-sided or two-sided information flow develops. It is possible, however, that presidential information advantages activate one-sided message flows in foreign policy, while some other causal mechanism determines whether one- or two-sided information flows emerge in other policy areas.

COMPARING LOCAL AND NATIONAL MEDIA COVERAGE

Most research on presidential news focuses on the national news media but good reasons exist to also study coverage in the local media. First, presidents have increasingly steered their media efforts to the local media since Richard Nixon established the Office of Communication in the White House in 1969 (Maltese 1992). Presidential perceptions that the Washington press corps had become increasingly hostile and that presidents would be more able to influence local than national news coverage provided motivation to increase attention to the local media. Second, compared to the national media, the public holds the local media in relatively high regard and the local news commands a relatively large audience, even though, like most media, the audience has shrunk, especially for newspapers. In 2005, the public graded local newspapers and television with 72 percent and 73 percent favorability ratings, higher than any other type of news media (Pew Research Center for the People and the Press 2005).

Only recently have studies turned their attention to local coverage of the president, focusing on the impact of presidential trips to localities on the quantity and tone of newspapers serving the visited regions. Barrett and Peake (2007) look at coverage of presidential travel to localities, finding extensive coverage by the local press when the president visits the region, although the tone of that coverage varies often with the political characteristics of the region and newspaper. Eshbaugh-Soha and Peake (2006) focus on local coverage of George W. Bush's extensive, locally based campaign for his social security reforms, replicating many of Barrett and Peake's findings. Thus, presidential trips to localities may result in higher rates of presidential news coverage, but do not necessarily produce the positive news that presidents seek. The lack of tonality effect from local trips may in part derive from the controversy surrounding the topic or rationale for the trip, like Bush's social security reform efforts.

But presidents are concerned with news coverage beyond their local visits. Traveling around the nation involves high costs in terms of presidential time. Despite the increasing volume of presidential travel, the bulk of important presidential public activities occur in Washington on national matters, such as interactions with Congress. How often do Washington-based activities get covered in the local press and what is the tonality of such reports? Peake's (2007) and Eshbaugh-Soha's (2008) studies suggest that presidents receive measurable amounts of local coverage. Peake (2007) too shows that local coverage is not uniformly positive but follows local political alignments and newspaper endorsement patterns.

We are just beginning to understand the contours of local presidential news, but important questions remain. First, does the local press report on the same events as the national media? Shaw and Sparrow (1999) suggest some borrowing by the local from the national press in covering presidential election campaigns, but the local press also emphasizes events with local interest. Does the same hold for presidential news? Second, can presidents affect the amount, content, and tone of local news coverage? Which presidential activities and local media are most susceptible to successful presidential news management efforts? Third, what does local television coverage of the president look like?

NOTES TOWARD A THEORY OF
PRESIDENTIAL NEWS PRODUCTION

This review reveals the limited amount of data on presidential news. Obviously, we need more and better data, across time, across media outlets, and data that code news for a variety of characteristics. Other than saying that presidential news has increased in volume and frequency over the long haul, that it seems to be dropping in the age of new media, and that in this modern era negativity in presidential news appears to be climbing, we cannot say much else. We know very little descriptively about presidential news.

Theory about presidential news production is also underdeveloped. A theory of presidential news must be rooted in theories of news production. News production is a complex process (Shoemaker and Reese 1996). Characteristics of news organizations and their context, and the political leanings and professionalism of reporters, editors, and owners, affect the production of presidential news. Theories of news production tend to come from other disciplines, journalism and communications in particular. Presidency scholars and political scientists are more familiar with political institutions, and here they have the opportunity to add to our understanding of presidential news.

Commonly studies assume that the interactions between the president and journalists affect the amount and qualities of presidential news. Grossman and Kumar's (1981) exchange theory and Cook's "negotiating the news" model (1998; also Cook and Ragsdale 1998) are among the best and most insightful examples. For an exchange to exist, each party must have something that the other party wants. Presidents control information on their activities. Journalists control one access route to the public, the news. Presidents and journalists, however, do not always agree on how news about the president should be reported. Presidents in particular want good news; journalist prefer that news attract readers. This divergence builds tension into the relationship between presidents and journalists, which sometimes leads to conflict between them.

To a degree, the exchange metaphor mischaracterizes the presidential–journalist relationship. The notion of exchange comes from models of market-based relationships, between consumers and producers, who do not have the mismatch of incentives that characterizes the relationship between presidents and journalists. The major point of contention between consumers and producers is the price for the exchanged good. If they cannot agree on the price, the transaction will not go through. Exchanges between consumers and producers are voluntary, which is not the case between presidents and journalists, who need to interact no matter their degree of animosity, because presidents must reach the public, at least sometimes through the news, and journalists need content about the president to report on.

The relationship between presidents and reporters is better characterized with game theory. Students of the presidency and presidential–media relations have been slow to utilize and are often resistant to game theoretic approaches. Only recently have game theory approaches appeared in studies of the presidency, many of which have proved valuable in generating new approaches to understand presidential behavior. Krehbiel's (1998) pivotal politics model has helped us understand the dynamics of gridlock and the difficulty for presidents in realizing their legislative policy goals. The pivotal politics model has been extended and expanded to the veto (Cameron 2000) and executive orders (Howell 2003). Other game theoretic models have been developed for presidential going public behavior and the relationship between the presidency and the mass public (Canes-Wrone 2005). Canes-Wrone's (2001) game theory model helps explain why presidents sometime go public and at other times stay private. Lewis (2003) has offered a related model to explain the creation and form of executive agencies.

Game theory is certainly no panacea in understanding the relationship between the president and the news media, yet it has much to offer. For instance, Zaller's (1998) product substitution model, a non-technical "soft rational choice" game between presidential candidates and reporters during election campaigns, provides the only example that I know of that uses a game theoretic framework to understand presidential–reporter interactions. It provides some valuable insights and empirical tests: for instance, the more presidential candidates try to control the news, the more negative the news becomes. This model has direct implications for presidential–journalist relations outside of the electoral campaign context.

Game theory may also help us understand the dynamics of a seeming paradox. The modern White House has invested massive institutional resources into presidential image management (Waterman, St Clair, and Wright 1999), but in recent years there does not seem to be much pay-off—presidents are receiving less news and the news is increasingly negative. Why would "rational" actors invest so heavily and keep investing so heavily, with such bad outcomes? Game theory may open our eyes to trade-offs that presidents make so that they will accept what looks like a bad outcome, such as avoiding a worse outcome or to derive a better outcome on some other dimension.

A related theoretical tack recognizes that journalists and presidents have goals that they aim to realize. Oversimplifying reality, let us assume that presidents primarily use news to lead the public. That implies that presidents want a relatively high quantity of positive news. Again oversimplifying, let us assume that news organizations are primarily profit-maximizing institutions. They sell their product, the news, to consumers. Everything else being equal, they want to increase sales to as many readers as possible to maximize profits. Thus, news organizations will be highly sensitive to the public's taste or preference in news. Can we take these simple assumptions and offer any hypotheses about the characteristics of presidential news reviewed above?

First, let's assume that the public desires a certain amount of presidential news, an amount that has grown since the late nineteenth century. Both presidents and journalists thus have incentives to provide the public with news about the president and to feed this growing appetite for presidential news. The increase in presidential news buoys presidential leadership, making him appear more important to the public, while also restricting the news space that others, like congressional leaders, can occupy. As a result, those leaders may decline in importance to the public relative to the president.

In supplying newsworthy activities, presidents have a choice between symbolic-ceremonial ones and policy relevant ones. At the margins, symbolic-ceremonial activities may hold advantages over policy relevant activities because they are not likely to produce negative news. Early modern presidents, like Theodore Roosevelt, seemed to understand that symbolic-ceremonial activities resulted in positive news, and fed journalists hungry for presidential news with such activities (Ponder 1998).

Still, the public demands some news about presidents and public policies. Policy activities also enhance the importance of the president to the public. But many policies are controversial and divisive and at times political leaders will voice their disagreements with the president, a type of news story that presidents obviously dislike. Journalists, however, like to report on policy disagreements between presidents and other leaders, thinking that conflict-based stories will be interesting to readers. Given the possibility for negativity in policy-based news, and the need for there to be some policy news on the president, presidents will try to steer news to policy areas where policy conflict is either minimal or where the initial public reaction is to side with the president. In many instances, foreign policy and national security topics fit this bill.

This discussion ties together the three aspects of presidential news reviewed here: quantity, content, and tone. We know that over time the amount of presidential news has increased. This simple model also hypothesizes that much of the increase in presidential news will be ceremonial-symbolic or about foreign policy, both types of news that will tend to be more positive in tone than other types of presidential news. Many more hypotheses can be developed from the basic model presented here. The larger theoretical point is that it may be useful for theories of presidential news production to look at the incentives of presidents and journalists and how those incentives interact.

THE IMPACT OF PRESIDENTIAL NEWS ON PUBLIC OPINION

The ultimate rationale for studying the presidential news production process is to understand the impact of presidential news on the public, and thus learn something about presidential leadership. Like studies of presidential news, we know little empirically about the impact of presidential news on the public. And like studies of presidential news, theories of the impact of presidential news on the public must look outside of the presidency subfield for guidance, especially to political psychology. Finally, presidency scholars have been slow to use experimental designs, which may help unravel causal chains. Experiments, coupled with field studies, like surveys and content analyses, have something to offer in studying the impact of presidential news on public opinion.

I focus on the impact of presidential news on presidential approval, although there are other attributes of public opinion, such as the public agenda and opinion on issues, that also deserve attention. The approval question has received the most attention, not only by those who study the impact of news on public opinion, but also as a more general property of public opinion with regard to the presidency (Gronke and Newman 2003), and it provides a model for studying the effects of presidential news on other aspects of public opinion. A theory of news impact requires an understanding of the recipient, the communicator or message source, the relationship between the communicator and the recipient, as well as the message itself (Page, Shapiro, and Dempsey 1987).

News Reporting v. Events

Numerous studies have found that news affects public evaluations of the president. When the news is good or favorable to the president, public approval rises; when the news is bad, approval drops (Iyengar and Kinder 1987; Brody 1991; West 1991; Mutz 1992, 1994; Blood and Phillips 1995; Pan and Kosicki 1997; Nadeau et al. 1999; Shah and Watts 1999; Erikson, MacKuen, and Stimson 2001, ch. 2; Shah et al. 2002; Burden and Mughan 2003; Gronke and Newman 2003; Althaus and Kim 2006; Wolf and Holian 2006; but see Cohen 2008). The primary linkage between news and approval is that the public holds the president responsible for the state of the nation, i.e. the economy and foreign affairs.

In an important critique of the presidential approval literature, Brody (1991) argues that people experience politics and government vicariously, that is, through the news. When employing a news tone variable in several of his analyses, objective indicators such as the economy drop out of the estimated equations (also Erikson, MacKuen, and Stimson 2001). In effect, news imparts information about, for instance, the nation's economy to voters, who then use that news to evaluate the president. But it is not clear what it is about the news that affects presidential evaluations. Is it the events that the news reports on or is it the way that journalists report on those events that affects public opinion toward the president?

Few subscribe to the idea that the news media merely passively convey information to the mass public (Shoemaker and Reese 1996; see the discussion of the indexing hypothesis and the information environment above). News organization routines, the economics of news production, definitions of newsworthiness, among other factors, may affect how an event is reported. Inasmuch as these factors vary across news organizations, we may observe differences across news organizations in their coverage of events.

Yet even if such news reporting differences exist, they might not always have much impact on public attitudes regarding the president. People may utilize a particular frame of reference about an event no matter how it is reported. For example, voters may view a story that unemployment has risen as bad news, even if one news outlet emphasizes that a drop in employment will ease inflationary pressures, putting on positive note, while another emphasizes the impact of job losses on those affected, a negative perspective. For some events, the way a news organization reports on the event may not affect how people interpret or understand the event. If this is true, then there may be limits to politicians' and candidates' ability to "spin" the interpretations of events. In other words, counter-framing may not always be possible.

To settle this question requires that we distinguish the impact of events from reporting on those events. Past research has had difficulty making this distinction. Dalton, Beck, and Huckfeldt (1998, 124) conclude in their study of mass media effects on presidential voting, "[W]e find evidence of information effects, but it is not clear whether this is the media's independent influence or the effect of the campaign as transmitted by the press." The same can be said for approval or any other attribute of public opinion.

It matters whether events or news reports on those events affect public attitudes. If it is events, and not how events are reported, then not only will the president's attempt to manage the news have limited impact, but the news media will also only have limited impact on public opinion. To pursue this line of inquiry, we need to classify types of news and learn just how malleable or ingrained public frames are for each type of news, a difficult task. Experimental designs that vary how the same event is reported may help test this notion. Large-scale surveys that ask people which news outlets they use, coupled with content analyses of the news from those news organizations, may also provide a way to distinguish events from news, and their relative impact on public opinion.

Different Types of News may have Different Effects

Groeling (forthcoming) argues that not all "bad" news will sting the president equally. Criticism from members of the president's party, especially when his party controls Congress, seems to have stronger effects on approval than other types of negative news. In contrast, criticism from opposition party members is often "cheap talk," which the public takes less seriously.

Following this line of reasoning, presidential and party reputations may produce asymmetric effects on public opinion. For example, Democrats have a reputation for lowering unemployment, with greater tolerance for inflation, with the Republican reputation being the reverse. News that unemployment is rising might thus hurt Democratic presidents more than news of rising inflation, because the public expects Democrats to push unemployment down not up, but expect inflation to rise under Democrats. Democrats might not realize any public opinion benefit from news of easing unemployment because this is what the public expects.

There are other ways of differentiating news, with possible implications for news effects on public opinion. For instance, consider the distinction between soft and hard news (Baum 2002, 2003a, 2003b; Patterson 2000; Prior 2003, 2005). Causing some ambiguity, studies use the terms in two ways. One refers to types of news programs, with hard news being more traditional news platforms, such as evening news broadcasts, and soft news being non-news programs that might contain news content, such as *Oprah*. Second, soft news may refer to the content of the news story. Patterson (2000) defines hard news as stories about government, its leaders, public issues, and significant disruptions in daily life, such as weather and other disasters. In contrast, soft news concerns celebrities, sports, entertainment, fashion, lifestyle (Patterson 2000, 3). What are the implications of hard versus soft news on public opinion?

Baum (2003b) and Prior (2003) debate how much the public learns from hard versus soft news programs. Baum's by-product theory suggests that content on soft news programs will especially affect the attitudes of its audience, which tends to be less interested and informed than average hard news consumers. Moreover, content on soft news programs tends to be more personality focused than that found on hard news programs. One implication is that soft news programs may enhance the trend toward personality politics. Prior (2003) is less sanguine about soft news effects. We know little about how people process soft versus hard news, much less the implications for public evaluations of the president.

Furthermore, issues tend to become more salient to the public the more news coverage it receives. Issue salience may have important moderating effects on approval, with salient issues carrying more weight than less salient issues. If news coverage affects issue salience, then indirectly news may affect presidential approval through the mix of issues that new organizations report. Kelleher and Wolak (2006) argue that news primes people to use certain considerations in evaluating the president. Thus, when the amount of economic news increases, economic considerations become more important in evaluating the president. Similarly, news about personal attributes prime character assessments of the president (also Edwards, Mitchell, and Welch 1995). However, Wolf and Holian (2006) demonstrate in an experiment that issue salience may also erect a barrier to news effects on approval. Using two issues, social security and the Iraq War, they randomly exposed respondents to a simulated opinion piece that either supported or opposed George W. Bush's position on those issues. They found stronger treatment effects on social security than the Iraq War, arguing that the latter was more salient, that people had their minds made up about the war, and thus were resistant to change.

Issue salience may thus have a complex relationship to approval. News coverage may increase the salience of an issue, and thus prime the public to employ that issue in evaluating the president. But by heightening salience, news may immunize opinion on that newly salient issue to further news (and possibly presidential leadership) effects. However, how easily can news reporting affect the public salience of issues? The agenda-setting hypothesis assumes that almost any issue that receives heightened news coverage will result in increased public salience. News personnel may anticipate this public reaction and thus report on issues about which the public is predisposed to care.

The larger point is that much research on news effects on presidential approval tends to treat all news similarly, only distinguishing between "good" or "bad" news.

We need to make other distinctions. Differentiating among types of news, and their hypothesized effects, may be a profitable track to take in understanding the impact of news on presidential approval.

Recipient–Messenger Relationship: Credibility of News Organizations

We also need to take into account the reputation of news organizations. Research on communications effects finds that credible sources are more persuasive than less credible sources (Miller and Krosnick 2000). Over time the "credibility" of the news media has fallen (Robinson and Kohut 1988; Gillespie 2004; Pew Research Center for People and the Press 2007), which might account for why several recent studies fail to find a relationship between the tone of news and approval (Cohen 2004, 2008; Gaines and Roberts 2005). As news media credibility has fallen, people may rely less on news in evaluating the president. Credibility may also vary across news outlets. Currently local news organizations tend to receive higher marks from the public than national news organizations. If local news also tends to produce more positive news about the president than the national media, then the increasing attention that presidents give to localities and local news organizations makes sense. The credibility of news organizations may be an important intervening variable in assessing news effects on public opinion. Rarely has research incorporated this trait into studies of news effects.

Messenger: Types of News Organizations and Varieties of News Systems

Recent years have seen the emergence of new forms of news delivery, from talk radio and cable television to the internet, with a decline in audience for traditional news formats. Not only may each media form utilize a different news production process, leading to variability in presidential news across them, but the public may use each news form differently. And different types of people may use different news media forms.

Here it may be useful to distinguish between *news media forms* and *news media systems.* News media forms differentiate the ways that news is communicated, such as newspapers, broadcast television, cable television, the internet, etc. News media systems operate at a higher level of aggregation, and compare the mix of news media forms at any point in time. Over time the news media system has evolved from one dominated by broadcast television to what some have called the "new media age" (Baum and Kernell 1999; Prior 2007; Cohen 2008). The broadcasting age of roughly 1950–80 and the new media age (1980–present) differ (Cohen 2008; Prior 2007). There is a greater variety of news forms, greater economic competition, and variation in news content across outlets in the new media age. It is a much more decentralized system than the broadcasting age. This shift may have important implications for public attitudes towards the president.

First, the great variety of news outlets offering different news products allows people to gravitate to a news provider that reinforces their preexisting political orientations. Studies indicate that audience political characteristics vary across news outlets. For example, Fox Cable News watchers are more likely to be Republican and conservative than CNN viewers. These differences appear more a function of self-selection than media effects, e.g., Republicans and conservatives gravitate to Fox (Morris 2005; but see Prior 2007, 156–9).

Several studies indicate that exposure to media affects attitudes and perceptions. For instance, Barker (1999, 2002) finds that Rush Limbaugh's conservative talk radio program influences Democrats and liberals who listen to it. Kull, Ramsey, and Lewis (2003–4) find that those who watch Fox Cable News were more likely to misperceive important facts regarding the Iraq War, such as whether clear evidence was found linking Saddam Hussein to al Qaeda, whether weapons of mass destruction (WMDs) were found in Iraq, and whether world public opinion supported the US war, than those who tuned in to other networks or read newspapers. Kull, Ramsey, and Lewis speculate that differences in reporting about the war across news media may be one source of these misperceptions. They do not claim that Fox, for instance, falsified information, but by being less critical of the administration, which at various times argued the Saddam Hussein–al Qaeda link and the existence of WMDs, viewers might have developed these misperceptions. Importantly, these misperceptions statistically held even with controls for political attitudes, such as support for George W. Bush, which minimizes that these misperceptions were due solely to self-selection effects. Still, self-selection effects appear stronger and more widespread than these influence effects.

It is difficult to detect at the individual level media influence among those who self-select news because of consistency with their preexisting political views. Attitudes are not changed, but reinforced. Does lack of change indicate that news exposure reinforced preexisting attitudes or that it failed to affect the individual? Reinforcement is a type of effect even if it is difficult to detect empirically. We may be able to detect reinforcement effects at the aggregate level, however. When large numbers of the public self-select a news outlet, we should find a public that is increasingly polarized and somewhat immune (not even exposed) to contrary information. This may account for why Republicans appear supportive of George W. Bush and the Iraq War in the face of its long duration and mounting casualties, while Democrats seem unresponsive to the upturn in the economy under Bush's watch (Gaines and Roberts 2005). In such a news system, not only may presidential leadership efforts be blunted, but so may news effects.

Recipients: Differential Responses to News across Individuals

News may affect some people more than others. Zaller's (1992) response-acceptance theory provides a foundation. News cannot directly affect those who are not exposed to it, although they may be affected indirectly by conversations with others who are directly exposed. And those with well-developed attitudes about politics are unlikely to have their minds changed when exposed to news that runs contrary to their beliefs, although encountering congruent news may reinforce one's already hardened attitudes. Changes in recent decades may have reduced the size of the group susceptible to news effects—those who pay some attention to the news but who do not have strongly held political views. The audience for news has declined, reducing the number of directly exposed individuals. Since people often travel in relatively homogeneous social circles, it is likely that the non-exposed socially interact mostly with other non-exposed people, limiting the indirect effects of news conveyed through personal interactions.

In addition, the size of the group with hardened political attitudes has grown. Party identification is perhaps the most important general political predisposition. Through the lens of party identification, people interpret and understand the political world around them; the stronger one's sense of party identification, the greater resistance to the reception of contrary news. After years of decline, party identification rates have been growing. This means that the number of people who are both exposed to the news but may be resistant to its message has grown. Adding to this the growth in the number of non-exposed people, the number of people who can be moved by a news story has dwindled. This in part may account for the lack of impact of news tone on public opinion in the George W. Bush years (Gaines and Roberts 2005).

News Media Influence on the Public Agenda

Many of the above points apply to other aspects of public opinion, such as the public agenda and attitudes on policies and issues, both of which have important implications for presidential leadership. It appears that presidents may have greater ability to affect the public agenda than preferences on issues (Edwards 2003), although presidents have to compete with the news media for influencing the public agenda.

Presidential and media influence on the public agenda grows out of the large literature on agenda setting. Reacting to the minimal effects paradigm, the agenda-setting model suggests that the emphasis of issues in the news will affect the importance the mass public attributes to issues; issues that receive high volumes of news media attention will rank higher in importance to the mass public. Agenda-setting effects operate primarily through exposure, with numerous studies finding empirical support for this proposition that exposure to news affects the public's agenda at the aggregate as well as the individual level (Scheufele and Tewksbury 2007). These agenda-setting effects spill over to affect presidential approval and other evaluations through a priming effect. "Priming is the activation of knowledge stored in long-term memory following exposure to a stimulus" (Althaus and Kim 2006, 961). Thus, "the standards that people use to make political evaluations" are changed (Iyengar and Kinder 1987, 63). For instance, if economics rises on a person's agenda because of an increase in the amount of news about economic matters, the economic issue should weigh more heavily in evaluations of the president, as Iyengar and Kinder's (1987) classic experiments demonstrate.

Presidents and the news media may compete to affect the public agenda and, by implication, affect public evaluations of the president. Few studies compare the relative effects of the president and the news media on the public agenda, although several studies are relevant to addressing that issue. Presidential effects on the public agenda may be felt directly, as people watch presidential addresses, or indirectly, through news coverage of presidential activities. Cohen (1995), Hill (1998), and Druckman and Holmes (2004) find that major presidential speeches affect the public agenda, while Druckman and Holmes (2004) also show priming effects from presidential speeches on presidential approval. Plus, Young and Perkins (2005) demonstrate with aggregate data that the larger the audience for the presidential speech, the greater the affect on the public agenda.

Presidents may also influence the public agenda indirectly through news coverage of their activities and public statements on issues, but doing so requires that the president be able to affect the news. As noted in the first half of this chapter, presidents possess limited ability to affect news coverage, and some research contends that the news coverage of issues may affect presidential public activities, at least for some issues. Edwards and Wood's (1999) seminal study indicates that presidents tend to react to the news on foreign policy, but may lead the news for some domestic policy issues. Extending this line of inquiry, Peake (2001) finds that presidents seem to lead media attention on less salient foreign policy issues, while Eshbaugh-Soha and Peake (2005) find that the president and the media affect each others' economic policy attention.

This agenda-setting research holds great promise for advancing our understanding of media effects on public opinion with regard to the presidency, and should be a top research priority. The agenda-setting paradigm allows us to integrate questions from the news production research outlined above with media impacts on public opinion.

For example, the agenda-setting perspective assumes that mere exposure, a simple stimulus-response model, accounts for changes in the public's agenda. However, we need to entertain the prospect that agenda-setting effects will vary in strength across characteristics of the news production process and attributes of individuals and mass publics. The news production literature suggests that news personnel have strong incentives to anticipate (correctly) the public reaction to reported news, which may account for the strength of agenda-setting effects noted in the empirical literature. News organizations may vary in their ability or desire to correctly predict the public reaction to the news, that is, to incorporate anticipations of public reactions into their news production decisions. News organizations that invest more in market research should be better at predicting the public reaction than news organizations that rely on the hunches or gut feelings of news personnel, like editors and reporters, for example. Similarly, news outlets with a definite (political) agenda may be more resistant to public reactions, instead trying to lead the public in a particular direction. We can measure such attributes of news organizations and incorporate them as mediating variables.

The variety of news sources in the post-broadcast age (Prior 2007) creates opportunities to test the hypothesis that agenda-setting effects will vary across news organization characteristics. For instance, the hostile media phenomenon suggests that people who view a news source as "hostile" may be less inclined to follow that news source's agenda than those who do not see the news source as hostile. One may test this hypothesis, for example, by exposing experimental subjects to identical news stories from identified sources, which some respondents might view with hostility.

We also need to compare the impact of the president and the news media on the public agenda, as noted above. Baumgartner and Jones's Policy Agendas Project now has data that may enable a first stab at such a study, albeit with some limitations. Using a refined, comprehensive, and consistent policy coding scheme, they have collected data from 1946 to the early 2000s on the public agenda (the public's most important problem), the news agenda (from the *New York Times*), and presidential policy attention in the State of the Union address, three types of data necessary to assess the relative impact of the media and the president on the public agenda. Still, there are several limitations in using these data to test this hypothesis. First, the public agenda data are annually aggregated, which limit our ability to assess short-term changes in the public agenda, as in the work of Edwards and Wood (1999), Peake (2001), and Eshbaugh-Soha and Peake (2005), by using more refined temporal units. Second, although the *New York Times* may help set the national news agenda, it is but one news outlet, and despite the huge number of items from the *Times* included in their data collection, these data may not be dense enough to pick up the types of media effects that we are looking for. Still, the Policy Agendas Project data represent one of the best yet relatively untapped data sources to test some of the most important hypotheses and conjectures from the agenda-setting research program.

Studying News Effects on Public Opinion about the President

Future research on news effects needs to find a way to distinguish the effects of news from the events being reported. Future research also needs to distinguish among types of news, and also needs to take into account variability in the credibility of news organizations, the changing structure of the news media system, differences across forms of news media, and relevant differences across individuals. Political psychology may help deal with this long list of issues by offering two aids to improved understanding of the effect of news on opinion: a theoretical approach and a methodology. Political psychology theory provides useful concepts such as priming and framing and information processing. As noted above, presidency scholars are well trained in the intricacies of the institution. That training needs to be broadened to include other theoretical approaches and orientations. An institutional focus only takes us so far in understanding the kinds of questions raised in this essay, questions that are fundamentally about the relationship between the presidency and other components of the political system, in this case the news media and the mass public.

Experimentation is a methodology that political psychologists rely on heavily and have found useful; experiments have become increasingly popular across political science subfields as well (Druckman et al. 2006). Experimentation allows one to hold all variables constant, while manipulating the one of interest. Before we jump on the experimental bandwagon, we need to understand several of its limitations and pitfalls. (A thorough review of the issues in experimentation as it applies to political science can be found in Gaines, Kuklinski, and Quirk 2007.) Most experiments, even of the political psychology sort, take place in laboratories and among samples that are not representative of the population, such as college students. This raises important issues of generalization to the real world. Political psychologists are often interested in highly general processes, such as how individuals process information. Thus, it might not make much difference for those purposes whether a representative sample is used or not—the underlying theoretical proposition is that all people process information similarly.

But those who study the presidency want to know what impact news will have on presidential approval in the real world. How great an impact will news stories have on public evaluations of the president? How many and what types of people will change their attitude about the president after exposure to a type of story? How long lasting are those effects? We want to know something about real world implications. To make the leap from laboratory to real world, studies need to better mimic real world conditions.

The survey experiment is one way to ensure a representative population, but survey experiments are conducted in a real world context, for instance, when a president is popular or not, is a Democrat or a Republican, is first elected or nearing the end of his term, in an era or polarization or bipartisanship, during an election season or not, etc. The impact of an experimental manipulation might vary as the real world context varies. Researchers will thus need to repeat the same experiment during differing times to determine the stability or generality of its effects.

Moreover, the real world bombards people with political information from various sources. Experimental designs rarely take this into account. This point is important because if individuals' opinions and attitudes can be easily affected by exposure to an experimental manipulation, then the effects of exposure to one message may be readily undone by exposure to another message. In a sense, this is the message of Converse's (1964) non-attitudes thesis. Most people's opinions do not hold for long. Druckman (2004; Druckman and Nelson 2003) incorporates the rich information environment in which people live into his experimental design on counter-arguing.

Further, collection of data on characteristics of news, as proposed above, can be especially useful in identifying aspects of news that we want to experimentally manipulate. Knowing how often or under what conditions or for which media certain attributes of news stories appear will give us an idea of which types of experimental manipulations to undertake, which may provide another dimension of realism to experimental designs. Experimental designs to study the impact of news on public opinion should incorporate as much as possible what we know about the real world, which will facilitate generalizing experimental results to real world settings.

Turning to experimental designs does not mean that we should jettison traditional surveys for studying the impact of news on public opinion. Also useful would be to ask more detailed questions about the media outlets that people use and couple that information with content analyses of those media outlets. The major surveys, like the American National Election Study, ask only general questions about which media type a person uses (e.g., newspapers, television, etc.) and how frequently they use those media.

Such data, although useful, provide only the most general information on media use. They cannot account for the variation in news content across media types, such as newspapers or the different cable news channels. In an age with a greater variety of news outlets to choose from, and with those news outlets offering differing news content, we need more detailed information on media exposure. The National Annenberg Election Studies of 2000 and 2004 contain information on the specific newspaper that a person reads. Although it would surely be daunting, content analysis of those media, attached to these surveys could provide a nuanced sense of the impact of differing news media on public attitudes. The great limitation of the NAES surveys for our purposes is their focus on presidential election campaigns. They provide few questions on the president. Pew News Interest and Media Use surveys provide another valuable source of information with detailed questions on media use, but again these surveys lack a range of items on the president, although they usually ask a presidential approval question.

CONCLUSION

Data and theory interact in the pursuit of scientific understanding. Quality data allow one to test theories and their hypotheses. Theory tells us what types of data to collect. The topic of the presidency and the mass media lacks quality data and well-developed theory. At this point, the lack of quality data presents the major barrier to progress. We cannot describe the basic characteristics of presidential news very well. Without much sense of the characteristics of presidential news, it makes little sense to try to theorize about the presidential news production process. Without being able to describe presidential news very well, we cannot say much about the impact of such news on the public. We need better data on the quantity, content, and tone of presidential news, across time and news organizations. Electronic news archives and computer-generated data from them offer the hope of collecting such data relatively efficiently.

But more theoretical work also needs to be done. Presidency scholars have traditionally been trained to understand and study the institution. Institutional theories, although not irrelevant to the understanding of presidential news and its impact on the public, can only take us so far. Theories of news production from communications and journalism, rational choice theory, and political psychology also have much to offer. The topic of the presidency and the news media is an interdisciplinary one. Presidency scholars, to make progress on the questions raised in this chapter, need to better understand, utilize, and contribute to these other theoretical perspectives.

REFERENCES

ALTHAUS, S. L., and KIM, Y. M. 2006. Priming Effects in Complex Information Environments: Reassessing the Impact of News Discourse on Presidential Approval. *Journal of Politics*, 68: 960–76.

BAE, H.-S. 2000. Product Differentiation in National TV Newscasts: A Comparison of the Cable All-News Networks. *Journal of Broadcasting & Electronic Media*, 44: 62–77.

BALUTIS, A. P. 1977. The Presidency and the Press: The Expanding Public Image. *Presidential Studies Quarterly*, 7: 244–51.

BARKER, D. C. 1999. Rushed Decisions: Political Talk Radio and Vote Choice, 1994–1996. *Journal of Politics*, 61: 527–39.

—— 2002. *Rushed to Judgment: Talk Radio, Persuasion, and American Political Behavior.* New York: Columbia University Press.

BARNHURST, K. G., and MUTZ, D. 1997. American Journalism and the Decline in Event-Centered Reporting. *Journal of Communication*, 47: 27–53.

BARRETT, A. W., and PEAKE, J. S. 2007. When the President Comes to Town: Examining Local Newspaper Coverage of Domestic Presidential Travel. *American Politics Research*, 35: 3–31.

BAUM, M. A. 2002. Sex, Lies, and War: How Soft News Brings Foreign Policy to the Attentive Public. *American Political Science Review*, 96: 91–110.

—— 2003a. *Soft News Goes to War: Public Opinion and American Foreign Policy in the New Media Age.* Princeton, NJ: Princeton University Press.

—— 2003b. Soft News and Political Knowledge: Evidence of Absence or Absence of Evidence? *Political Communication*, 20: 173–90.

—— and KERNELL, S. 1999. Has Cable Ended the Golden Age of Television? *American Political Science Review*, 93: 99–114.

BENNETT, W. L. 1990. Toward a Theory of Press–State Relations in the United States. *Journal of Communications*, 40/2: 103–27.

BLOOD, D. J., and PHILLIPS, P. C. B. 1995. Recession Headline News, Consumer Sentiment, the State of the Economy and Presidential Popularity: A Time Series Analysis 1989–1993. *International Journal of Public Opinion Research*, 7: 2–22.

BRODY, R. 1991. *Assessing the President: The Media, Elite Opinion, and Public Support.* Stanford, CA: Stanford University Press.

BURDEN, B. C., and MUGHAN, A. 2003. The International Economy and Presidential Approval. *Public Opinion Quarterly*, 67: 555–78.

CAMERON, C. M. 2000. *Veto Bargaining: Presidents and the Politics of Negative Power.* New York: Cambridge University Press.

CANES-WRONE, B. 2001. A Theory of Presidents' Public Agenda Setting. *Journal of Theoretical Politics*, 132: 183–208.

—— 2005. *Who Leads Whom? Presidents, Policy Making and the Mass Public.* Chicago: University of Chicago Press.

COHEN, J. E. 1995. Presidential Rhetoric and the Public Agenda. *American Journal of Political Science*, 39: 87–107.

COHEN, J. E. 2004. If the News is so Bad, Why Are Presidential Polls so High? Presidents, the News Media, and the Mass Public in an Era of New Media. *Presidential Studies Quarterly,* 34: 493–515.

——2008. *The Presidency in an Era of Twenty-Four Hour News.* Princeton, NJ: Princeton University Press.

COMSTOCK, G., and SCHARRER, E. 2005. *The Psychology of Media and Politics.* Burlington, MA: Elsevier.

CONVERSE, P. E. 1964. The Nature of Belief Systems in Mass Publics. In *Ideology and Discontent,* ed. D. E. Apter. New York: Free Press.

COOK, T. E. 1998. *Governing with the News: The News Media as a Political Institution.* Chicago: University of Chicago Press.

——and RAGSDALE, L. 1998. The President and the Press: Negotiating Newsworthiness in the White House. Pp. 323–57 in *The Presidency and the Political System,* ed. M. Nelson, 5th edn. Washington, DC: CQ Press,.

CORNWELL, E. E., JR. 1959. Presidential News: The Expanding Public Image. *Journalism Quarterly,* 36: 275–83.

D'ALESSIO, D., and ALLEN, M. 2000. Media Bias in Presidential Elections. *Journal of Communication,* 50/4: 133–56.

DALTON, R. J., BECK, P. A., and HUCKFELDT, R.1998. Partisan Cues and the Media. *American Political Science Review,* 92/1: 111–26.

DELLA VIGNA, S., and KAPLAN, E. 2007. The Fox News Effect: Media Bias and Voting. *Quarterly Journal of Economics,* 122: 1187–234.

DRUCKMAN, J. N. 2004. Political Preference Formation: Competition, Deliberation, and the (Ir)relevance of Framing Effects. *American Political Science Review,* 98: 671–86.

——and HOLMES, J. W. 2004. Does Presidential Rhetoric Matter? Priming and Presidential Approval. *Presidential Studies Quarterly,* 34: 755–78.

——and NELSON, K. R. 2003. Framing and Deliberation: How Citizens' Conversations Limit Elite Influence. *American Journal of Political Science,* 47: 729–45.

——and PARKIN, M. 2005. How Editorial Slant Affects Voters. *Journal of Politics,* 67: 1030–49.

——GREEN, D. P., KUKLINSKI, J. H., and LUPIA, A. 2006. The Growth and Development of Experimental Research in Political Science. *American Political Science Review,* 100: 627–35.

EDWARDS, G. C., III. 2003. *On Deaf Ears: The Limits of the Bully Pulpit.* New Haven, CT: Yale University Press.

——2008. *Governing by Campaigning: The Politics of the Bush Presidency.* New York: Pearson.

——MITCHELL, W., and WELCH, R. 1995. Explaining Presidential Approval: The Significance of Issue Salience. *American Journal of Political Science,* 39: 108–34.

——and Wood, B. D. 1999. Who Influences Whom? The President, Congress, and the Media. *American Political Science Review,* 93: 327–44.

ENTMAN, R. M. 2007. Framing Bias: Media in the Distribution of Power. *Journal of Communication,* 57: 163–73.

——and PAGE, B. 1994. The Iraq War Debate and the Limits to Media Independence. In *Taken by Storm: Media, Public Opinion, and U.S. Foreign Policy in the Gulf War,* ed. W. L. Bennett. Chicago: University of Chicago Press.

ERIKSON, R. S., MACKUEN, M., and STIMSON, J. A. 2001. *The Macro Polity.* New York: Cambridge University Press.

ESHBAUGH-SOHA, M. 2008. Local News Coverage of the Presidency. *Harvard International Journal of Press/Politics,* 13: 103–19.

——and PEAKE, J. S. 2005. Presidents and the Economic Agenda. *Political Research Quarterly,* 58/1: 127–38.

————— 2006. The Contemporary Presidency: "Going Local" to Reform Social Security. *Presidential Studies Quarterly*, 36: 689–704.

EVELAND, W. P., JR., and SHAH, D. V. 2003. The Impact of Individual and Interpersonal Factors on Perceived News Media Bias. *Political Psychology*, 24: 101–17.

FARNSWORTH, S. J., and LICHTER, S. R. 2006. *The Mediated Presidency: Television News and Presidential Government*. Lanham, MD: Rowman & Littlefield.

FOOTE, J. S. 1990. *Television Access and Presidential Power: The Networks, the Presidency, and the Loyal Opposition*. New York: Praeger.

GAINES, B. J., KUKLINSKI, J. H., and QUIRK, P. J. 2007. The Logic of the Survey Experiment Reexamined. *Political Analysis*, 15: 1–20.

————— and ROBERTS, B. D. 2005. Hawks, Bears, and Pundits: Explaining Presidential Approval Rally Effects. Paper presented at the Midwest Political Science Association, Chicago, IL, Apr. 7–10.

GENTZKOW, M., and SHAPIRO, J. M. 2006. Media Bias and Reputation. *Journal of Political Economy*, 114: 280–316.

GILENS, M., and Hertzman, C. 2000. Corporate Ownership and News Bias. *Journal of Politics*, 62/2: 369–86.

GILLESPIE, M. 2004. Media Credibility Reaches Lowest Point in Three Decades. *Gallup Tuesday Press Briefing*, Sept. 23: 12.

GROELING, T. Forthcoming. *Singing from the Same Hymnbook: Party Cohesion in the Media*. New York: Cambridge University Press.

————— and KERNELL, S. 1998. Is Network News Coverage of the President Biased? *Journal of Politics*, 60/4: 1063–87.

GRONKE, P., and NEWMAN, B. 2003. FDR to Clinton, Mueller to ?? A Field Essay on Presidential Approval. *Political Research Quarterly*, 56: 501–12.

GROSECLOSE, T., and MILYO, J. 2005. A Measure of Media Bias. *Quarterly Journal of Economics*, 120: 1191–237.

GROSSMAN, M. B., and KUMAR, M. J. 1981. *Portraying the President: The White House and the News Media*. Baltimore: Johns Hopkins University Press.

HALLIN, D. 1986. *The Uncensored War*. Berkeley and Los Angeles: University of California Press.

————— and GITLIN, T. 1994. The Gulf War as Popular Culture and Television Drama. In *Taken by Storm: Media, Public Opinion, and U.S. Foreign Policy in the Gulf War*, ed. W..L. Bennett. Chicago: University of Chicago Press.

HOWELL, W. G. 2003. *Power without Persuasion: The Politics of Direct Presidential Action*. Princeton, NJ: Princeton University Press.

HILL, K. Q. 1998. The Policy Agendas of the President and the Mass Public: A Research Validation and Extension. *American Journal of Political Science*, 42: 1328–34.

IYENGAR, S., and KINDER, D. 1987. *News That Matters*. Chicago: University of Chicago Press.

KAHN, K. F., and KENNEY, P. J. 2002. The Slant of the News. *American Political Science Review*, 96/2: 381–94.

KELLEHER, C. A., and WOLAK, J. 2006. Priming Presidential Approval: The Conditionality of Issue Effects. *Political Behavior*, 28: 193–210.

KERNELL, S., and JACOBSON, G. C. 1987. Congress and the President as News in the Nineteenth Century. *Journal of Politics*, 49: 1016–35.

KREHBIEL, K. 1998. *Pivotal Politics: A Theory of U.S. Lawmaking*. Chicago: University of Chicago Press.

KULL, S., RAMSEY, C., and LEWIS, E. 2003–4. Misperceptions, the Media, and the Iraq War. *Political Science Quarterly*, 116/4: 569–98.

KUMAR, M. J. 2007. *Managing the President's Message: The White House Communications Operation.* Baltimore: Johns Hopkins University Press.

KURTZ, H. 1998. *Spin Cycle: Inside the Clinton Propaganda Machine.* New York: Free Press.

LEWIS, D. E. 2003. *Presidents and the Politics of Agency Design.* Stanford, CA: Stanford University Press.

MALTESE, J. A. 1992. *Spin Control: The White House Office of Communications and the Management of Presidential News.* Chapel Hill: University of North Carolina Press.

MERMIN, J. 1999. *Debating War and Peace: Media Coverage of U.S. Intervention in the Post-Vietnam Era.* Princeton, NJ: Princeton University Press.

MILLER, J. M., and KROSNICK, J. A. 2000. News Media Impact on the Ingredients of Presidential Evaluation: Politically Knowledgeable Citizens are Guided by a Trusted Source. *American Journal of Political Science,* 44: 295–309.

MIROFF, B. 1982. Monopolizing the Public Space: The President as a Problem for Democratic Politics. Pp. 218–32 in *Rethinking the Presidency,* ed. T. Cronin. Boston: Little, Brown.

MORRIS, J. S. 2005. The Fox News Factor. *Harvard International Journal of Press/Politics,* 10: 56–79.

MUTZ, D. C. 1992. Mass Media and the Depoliticization of Personal Experiences. *American Journal of Political Science,* 36: 483–508.

——1994. Contextualizing Personal Experience: The Role of the Mass Media. *Journal of Politics,* 56: 689–714.

NADEAU, R., NIEMI, R. G., FAN, D. P., and AMATO, T. 1999. Elite Economic Forecasts, Economic News, Mass Economic Judgments, and Presidential Approval. *Journal of Politics,* 61: 109–35.

NEUMAN, W. R. 1990. The Threshold of Public Attention. *Public Opinion Quarterly,* 54/2: 159–76.

NICHOLSON, S. P., SEGURA, G. M., and WOODS, N. D. 2002. Presidential Approval and the Mixed Blessing of Divided Government. *Journal of Politics,* 64: 701–20.

NIVEN, D. 2002. *Tilt? The Search for Media Bias.* New York: Praeger.

PAGE, B. I., SHAPIRO, R. Y., and DEMPSEY, G. R. 1987. What Moves Public Opinion? *American Political Science Review,* 81: 23–44.

PAN, Z., and KOSICKI, G. M. 1997. Priming and Media Impact on the Evaluations of the President's Performance. *Communication Research,* 24: 3–30.

PATTERSON, T. E. 2000. *Doing Well and Doing Good: How Soft News and Critical Journalism are Shrinking the News Audience and Weakening Democracy—And What News Outlets Can Do About It.* Joan Shorenstein Center for Press, Politics, and Public Policy, John F. Kennedy School of Government, Harvard University.

PEAKE, J. S. 2001. Presidential Agenda Setting in Foreign Policy. *Political Research Quarterly,* 54/1: 69–86.

——2007. Presidents and Front-Page News: How America's Newspapers Cover the Bush Administration. *Harvard International Journal of Press/Politics,* 12: 52–70.

Pew Research Center for the People and the Press. 2005. Public More Critical of Press, But Goodwill Persists: Online Newspaper Readership Countering Print Losses. June 26. <http://people-press.org/reports/display.php3?ReportID=248>.

——2007. Internet News Audience Highly Critical of News Organizations: Views of Press Values and Performance: 1985–2007. Aug. 9. <http://people-press.org/reports/display.php3?ReportID=348>.

PONDER, S. 1998. *Managing the Press: Origins of the Media Presidency, 1897–1933.* New York: St Martin's.

PRIOR, M. 2003. Any Good News in Soft News? The Impact of Soft News Preference on Political Knowledge. *Political Communication*, 20: 173–90.

—— 2005. News vs. Entertainment: How Increasing Media Choice Widens Gaps in Political Knowledge and Turnout. *American Journal of Political Science*, 49: 577–92.

—— 2007. *Post-Broadcast Democracy: How Media Choice Increases Inequality in Political Involvement and Polarizes Elections.* New York: Cambridge University Press.

ROBINSON, M. J., and KOHUT, A. 1988. Believability and the Press. *Public Opinion Quarterly*, 52: 174–89.

ROZELL, M. J. 1993. The Limits of White House Image Control. *Political Science Quarterly*, 108: 453–80.

—— 1995. Presidential Image-Makers on the Limits of Spin Control. *Presidential Studies Quarterly*, 25: 67–90.

SCHEUFELE, D. A., and TEWKSBURY, D. 2007. Framing, Agenda Setting, and Priming: The Evolution of Three Media Effects Models. *Journal of Communication*, 57: 9–20.

SHAH, D. V., and WATTS, M. D. 1999. News Coverage, Economic Cues, and the Public's Presidential Preferences, 1984–1996. *Journal of Politics*, 61: 914–43.

—— —— DOMKE, D., and FAN, D. P. 2002. News Framing and the Cueing of Issue Regimes: Explaining Clinton's Public Approval in Spite of Scandal. *Public Opinion Quarterly*, 66: 339–70.

SHAW, D. R, and SPARROW, B. H. 1999. From the Inner Ring Out: News Congruence, Cue-Taking, and Campaign Coverage. *Political Research Quarterly*, 52: 323–51.

SHOEMAKER, P. J., and REESE, S. D. 1996. *Mediating the Message: Theories of Influences on Mass Media Content.* White Plains, NY: Longman.

SHIELDS, T., and GOIDEL, R. K. 1996. The President and Congress as Sources in Television News Coverage of the National Debt. *Polity*, 28: 401–10.

WATERMAN, R. W., ST. CLAIR, G., and WRIGHT, R. 1999. *The Image-Is-Everything Presidency: Dilemmas in American Leadership.* Boulder, CO: Westview Press.

WEST, D. M. 1991. Television and Presidential Popularity in America. *British Journal of Political Science*, 21: 199–214.

WICKS, R. H., and WALKER, D. C. 1993. Differences between CNN and the Broadcast Networks in Live War Coverage. Pp. 99–112 in *Desert Storm and the Mass Media*, ed. B. S. Greenberg and W. Gantz. Cresskill, NJ: Hampton Press,.

WOLF, M. R., and HOLIAN, D. B. 2006. Polls, Elite Opinion, and the President: How Information and Issue Saliency Affect Approval. *Presidential Studies Quarterly*, 36: 584–605.

YOUNG, G., and PERKINS, W. B. 2005. Presidential Rhetoric, the Public Agenda, and the End of Presidential Television's "Golden Age." *Journal of Politics*, 67: 1190–205.

ZALLER, J. R. 1992. *The Nature and Origins of Mass Opinion.* Cambridge, MA: Cambridge University Press.

—— 1998. The Rule of Product Substitution in Presidential Campaign News. *Annals of the American Academy of Political and Social Science*, 560: 111–28.

—— and CHIU, D. 2000. Government's Little Helper: U.S. Press Coverage of Foreign Policy Crises, 1946–1999. Pp. 61–84 in *Decisionmaking in a Glass House: Mass Media, Public Opinion, and American and European Foreign Policy in the 21st Century*, ed. B. L. Nacos, R. Y. Shapiro, and P. Isernia. New York: Rowman & Littlefield.

PART V

THE LEGISLATIVE PRESIDENCY

CHAPTER 13

....

THE PRESIDENT AND CONGRESSIONAL PARTIES IN AN ERA OF POLARIZATION

....

DAVID W. ROHDE

MEREDITH BARTHELEMY

DURING the first six years of George W. Bush's presidency, his party controlled both chambers of Congress for all but a little over a year. In that period, Bush vetoed only a single bill. After the GOP lost control of the House and Senate in the 2006 midterms, the situation changed. Before Labor Day of 2007, the president had vetoed two more bills. As the Congress worked on the twelve regular appropriations bills in the summer of 2007, Bush had issued threats to veto at least nine of them. Moreover, his administration had threatened or advised a veto of about half of the major pieces of regular legislation then working their way through Congress (*CQ Weekly* 2007). These data would seem to suggest that whether the president and congressional majorities were of the same or different parties mattered a great deal in determining whether legislation was produced that reflected the president's views.

In this chapter we will discuss a portion of the research on Congress and the president produced over the last two decades that relates to presidential party leadership. Our main focus will be on whether the theoretical arguments and empirical findings of that research apply to the polarized partisan era of the "Republican Revolution" and the Bush presidency. The space available for this discussion in this multifaceted volume precludes an analysis of all works that bear on the matter, so we will focus on only a few aspects of the literature, particularly presidential success in the legislative process, the tendency to "go public," and the consequences of divided government.

PARTISAN POLARIZATION AND LAW MAKING

Until fairly recently, the view gleaned from the literature on presidential–congressional relations was that the role of political parties in both the Congress and the presidency was modest, and it followed from this that the president's role as party leader was of limited consequence. Shortly after the end of the Reagan presidency, George Edwards (1989) offered an extended analysis of presidential leadership of Congress. In the chapter that dealt directly with the president as party leader, Edwards (1989, 99) emphasized that "there are severe limitations to the responsiveness of members to appeals to party loyalty, the influence and reliability of party leaders, and the utility of favors and sanctions, and there are substantial obstacles to party unity." This viewpoint was not only representative of research on presidential–congressional relations, but also reflected more generally the work on congressional parties (see Rohde 1991, ch. 1). Moreover, Edwards (1989, 100) argued that changing congressional rules that would strengthen party discipline would "depend on the acquiescence of persons who have a stake in the status quo." He contended that "[t]he probability of such reforms occurring is very low, and once reforms are made, they require the active support of these same people to ensure that the power they allocate is used on behalf of the president. But there is little incentive for this to happen."

Yet despite the fact that this perspective was widely shared, we know that there was a sea change in the role of parties in Congress beginning with the Reagan administration, and with its roots even earlier. The independence of committees and the powers of their leaders were undermined, and the powers of party leaders were enhanced (Rohde 1991; Cox and McCubbins 1993; Sinclair 1995). This trend was amplified after the Republican congressional victories of 1994 (Aldrich and Rohde 1997–8, 2000a, 2005). These institutional changes, and the changes in the legislative process they induced, were widely seen to be linked to increasing partisan polarization in the US.

Aspects of Polarization

Political polarization by party is not an undifferentiated phenomenon; it has a number of aspects that can each affect the political process in different ways.

With no claim to be exhaustive, we will note briefly three important aspects here: polarization among elites, among activists, and among voters.

Elite Polarization

Elite polarization is the aspect that has been most apparent to analysts and about which there is little disagreement. Beginning in the late 1970s or early 1980s, ideological stratification among members of Congress along party lines began to intensify, reversing a pattern that had existed for decades (Rohde 1991; Poole and Rosenthal 2007; Jacobson 2007). For example, Jacobson (2007, 23) shows that average DW-Nominate scores of Democrats and Republicans in both the House and Senate have been moving further apart since the late 1960s, and now stand at levels of polarization not seen since the early twentieth century. (DW-Nominate scores are the result of a scaling technique for roll-call votes developed by Keith Poole and Howard Rosenthal. They indicate where members stand on a left–right spectrum. See Poole and Rosenthal 2007.) Jacobson notes that the same pattern is apparent in other roll-call measures such as ADA scores and party unity scores.

Aldrich and Rohde (2001, 281) offer another perspective on congressional polarization. They arrange the DW-Nominate scores of House members for the 91st and 105th congresses (1969–71 and 1997–9 respectively) into deciles, from the most liberal 10 percent of the House to the most conservative 10 percent. These data show that in the earlier Congress there were Democrats in every decile, and Republicans in every one but the most liberal. In the 105th Congress, on the other hand, there were only Republicans in the five most conservative deciles and only Democrats in the four most liberal deciles. Only one decile contained members of both parties. These data vividly portray the change in the pattern of ideological alignments in Congress. In the late 1960s, regardless of where a member of either party stood on the political spectrum, there were members of the other party with similar views. In the 1990s, however, only the Democrats were on the liberal side and only Republicans on the conservative side. The only place where members of both parties held similar positions was in a small range near the middle of the spectrum.

Since presidents do not participate in congressional roll calls, one cannot compute scores for them that are precisely comparable to the DW-Nominate scores of members. It is possible, however, to derive an analogous score for presidents by estimating the score of a hypothetical member who supported the president's view on all of the roll calls on which he took a position. Based on this measure, the estimated positions for the presidents from Truman through Clinton were always closer to the median score for their party than the median score for the House, and this remained true as the congressional scores polarized (Aldrich and Rohde 2000a, 68–9).

Activist Polarization

Standing between the officeholding elites we have just considered and the ordinary voters we examine next are partisan activists. As we will discuss further below, these actors have a disproportionate impact on various aspects of the political process, including what kinds of candidates each party nominates for office and the policy positions those candidates adopt. Democratic and Republican activists have always held contrasting positions to a degree, but evidence indicates that, like elites, the degree of ideological differentiation between the groups of activists has grown larger in the last three decades and is much greater than the differences between party identifiers.

For example, in 1996 a *New York Times* survey of major-party convention delegates and of the general public showed that the opinions of the delegates were extremely divergent on a range of issues (Aldrich and Rohde 2001, 278). The opinions of rank-and-file party identifiers were less in conflict than those of the activists, but the opinions of Democrats tilted toward the liberal side of the spectrum while those of Republicans tilted to the conservative side across all issues. Similar data for 2004 show even greater differences (Fiorina, Abrams, and Pope 2006, 17). Abramowitz (2006, 76) presents data on the standard deviations of scores on seven-point issue scales from the National Election Studies 1984–2004. This measure of polarization increased 23 percent among "active citizens" (those who engaged in at least one election activity in addition to voting) over the two decades. Abramowitz (2006, 83) also portrays the ideological distributions of both parties' active citizens in 2004. The two distributions are almost as disjoint as those of the representatives in the 105th Congress discussed above.

Polarization among Voters

The scholarly discussion of polarization among ordinary voters exhibits less consensus than that about elites and activists. The principal dissenters to the view that voter polarization is similar to the others are Fiorina and his co-authors (2006). They contend that the claim that the nation is in the midst of a "culture war" is vastly overdrawn and that the views of voters tend to be generally centrist on most issues. Over time, they contend, the increase in polarization on issues among the electorate as a whole has been modest. On the other hand, they say, voters have increasingly "sorted" themselves between the parties based on issues, creating what they (and we) have referred to as greater partisan polarization.

To some degree, the differences between Fiorina et al. and other analysts tend to be matters of emphasis and degree, but data provided by other researchers do indicate a substantial growth in polarization even among voters. Abramowitz (2006, 76), for example, shows that the standard deviation of issue scale scores increased 25 percent during 1984–2004, slightly *greater* than the increase among active citizens. Jacobson (2006) argues that partisan voters have perceived increasing divergence between their own policy positions and those of the opposition party and its candidates, while voters have perceived no increase in divergence between their positions and those of their own party and candidates. This asymmetry occurred despite the acknowledged increase in elite divergence noted above (see also Jacobson 2000). Brewer and Stonecash (2007) present evidence of increased partisan polarization based on cultural issues and see an important relationship between such polarization and class divisions. Finally, even Fiorina perceives important changes in the electorate related to polarization. He and a co-author note that the proportion of strong partisans in the electorate has increased over time, while the proportion of weak partisans and independents has decreased. "The result is an actual electorate (as opposed to an eligible electorate) that is considerably more ideological than the electorate of a generation ago" (Fiorina and Levendusky 2006, 108).

So What? The Possible Consequences of Polarization for Law Making

Having outlined some dimensions of polarization in American politics, we now consider the theoretical relevance of these developments with regard to presidential party leadership in Congress. Before we discuss this matter in relation to specific aspects of the literature, we want to deal briefly with the question in general: in what ways might polarization affect the law-making process, beyond merely leading to different values for certain parameters previous theory considers relevant? We argue that it is possible—even likely in some cases—that the various aspects of polarization could alter previous theoretical relationships and make new ones relevant in the law-making process.

John Aldrich (1994, 209) contended, in a discussion of the application of rational choice theory to the study of institutions, that the "fundamental equation" of rational choice theory in political science is: "Political outcomes are the product of goal-seeking behavior by actors, choosing within both a set of institutional arrangements and a particular historical context." Regardless of whether one considers rational choice to be the best avenue for research, we think that most analysts would agree that these elements—actors' goals, institutional rules, and political-historical context—are important for explaining patterns of political outcomes. We argue that the development of the various aspects of polarization we have discussed could affect each of these elements and the ways they interact with each other to shape outcomes.

Let us illustrate with some examples. Partisan polarization is an element of the political context. We have seen that there is evidence that the amount of polarization in each of its aspects has changed substantially over time. But polarization is also, in turn, related to other changes in the political context. One salient change is in the competitive situation regarding party control of Congress. During most of the post-war period, the Democrats seemed to have unshakeable control of the House and (for most of that time) the Senate. House control did, in fact, last for forty years, ending with the election of 1994. Before 1994, virtually no observer had serious doubt on a given election day which party would control the House after the next election, two years hence. That subjective certainty, we believe, conditioned all legislative relationships, both within the Congress and between the Congress and the White House. Republican presidents like Nixon and even Reagan knew it was highly probable that they would be dealing with opposite party control throughout their presidency.

Since 1994, however, things are radically different. On every election day, leaders and members of both parties know that majority control of both chambers is likely to be in doubt in the next election, and that their strategic choices during those two years could well determine the outcome. Every legislative choice is made with one eye (or all eyes) on the next election. Such a strategic context encourages constant electioneering, great emphasis on fund raising and providing benefits to contributors, and the incessant search for lines of attack that can undermine any positive public perceptions of the opposite party and of an opposition president. The situation encourages what has been called "the politics of blame" (Groseclose and McCarty 2001).

To be sure, all of these developments would likely have occurred to some degree as a result of greater competition even without polarization. But just as polarization played a role in increasing the competition for party control, it also raised the stakes for the actors of the outcome of the competition, and personalized the political conflicts among elites and activists. Is it plausible that these major changes would not affect the legislative interactions of the president and the congressional parties?

Furthermore, polarization has produced significant institutional changes in both the Congress and the White House. The congressional literature contains many discussions of the procedural changes that gave additional powers to the majority party in both chambers.[1] Of particular relevance here are those that undermined the independence and influence of committee chairs, those that enhanced majority party control of the floor agenda (especially leadership control of the House Rules Committee), and those that increased leaders' control of incentives that could influence members' legislative decisions (e.g., committee assignments). These tools in the hands of the president's party could guarantee a place on the agenda for his proposals (except in the decreasingly likely event that the congressional majority's preferences conflicted with the president's). They could also block the minority from offering their own proposals or from seeking changes in the president's bills. On the other hand, if controlled by the opposition party, such powers could potentially block access to the agenda for the president's initiatives and limit the ability of his allies to alter the other party's bills.

Polarization could also have affected the kinds of people who seek public office and how they behave if they are winners. That is, polarization could have produced different kinds of goals, or at least a different mix of goals, among the actors. A central part of the argument of Fiorina, Abrams, and Pope (2006) is that political elites have changed and that their preferences have become increasingly different from those of voters. Observers of the political scene frequently remark that American politics has become coarser, meaner, and more conflictual. Many analysts contend that the increased polarization of activists and their domination of congressional and presidential nominations have led to more officeholders with intense personal policy commitments, and to greater unwillingness to compromise among those without such commitments due to fear of activist retribution.

---

[1] See, for example, Rohde (1991); Aldrich and Rohde (1997–8, 2000a, 2000b, 2005); Sinclair (1995, 2006). Not all analysts, however, are convinced that these institutional changes have consequences over and above the effects of the distribution of preferences. See Krehbiel (1993, 1998) and Brady and Volden (2006).

Although we do not yet have a lot of systematic evidence that polarization produces differences in the types of candidates that seek office and are chosen as nominees (indeed the need for such research is part of our point here), there are some indications to that effect. For example, Brady, Han, and Pope (2007) analyze House primaries between 1956 and 1998. They show that candidates are cross-pressured by primary and general electorates, and that members who do well in general elections often do poorly in primaries. Primary losses are most likely to happen among ideologically moderate incumbents. They infer from over-time trends in primary losses that members responded to the large number of primary losses around 1970 by moving closer to the party extremes. This resulted in fewer primary losses after the early 1970s. These results are consistent with the idea that changes in primary competition led to more extreme and more ideological candidates being selected. Assuming these descriptions of changes among members of Congress are accurate, would we not expect such people to approach legislative interactions differently than those of an earlier era?

If this analysis is correct, then we must reconsider (although not necessarily change our view of) the theoretical arguments and empirical analyses regarding the president in the legislative process that have been viewed as persuasive regarding the past. It is quite possible that relationships that accurately described the earlier era may no longer obtain given the increased polarization. We now turn to an application of these ideas to the three aspects of presidential–congressional interaction.

AGENDA SETTING AND PRESIDENTIAL SUCCESS

Edwards and Barrett (2000) argue that setting the congressional agenda is important because items not under consideration have no chance of passing. For the president, then, getting his proposals on the agenda is a necessary condition for success in the legislative arena. Edwards and Barrett find that during the period of their analysis (1953–96) the president virtually always got his items on the agenda. The data for this study, however, include only two years after the GOP took control of Congress and polarization increased substantially. Did the same pattern obtain in later years? Moreover, even if the pattern persists, if the president refrains from making proposals because he perceives they have no chance, that is the functional equivalent of failing to get proposals considered. We will further consider this aspect of the endogeneity of the agenda at the end of this section. Another important consideration that we will discuss in connection with divided government is the significant impact polarization has had on the president's success in getting his proposals on the agenda.

Agenda-Setting Strategies

Edwards (2002) argues that especially in a more polarized era, as the complexity of a bill and the amount of proposed change from the status quo increases, opposition to the bill also increases. There are several strategies, then, that a president may utilize in setting his agenda. First, he may decrease the complexity of the bill or not stray too far from the status quo. Second, he may try to pass legislation through quiet negotiations with congressional leaders. Third, he may go public and take the case to the people, counting on their support for the president translating into a favorable vote for the president from their representative.

The relationship between the president and his party leaders in Congress also is important in the president's attempt to pass his legislation. Covington, Wrighton, and Kinney (1995) argue that the president may be able to affect legislative outcomes through his congressional party leaders' influence on the rank-and-file members. Edwards (1989, 34) asserts that, "if the party leadership [in Congress] is less dependable, if his fellow partisans in Congress are less amenable to his leadership, then the chief executive is more likely to be restricted to the more modest role of facilitator." Edwards argues that the president's leadership of his party must be a priority in his overall strategy. He must establish himself quickly and firmly as party leader in order for his party members to be counted upon for support (see also Bond and Fleisher 1990; Fleisher and Bond 2000).

Agenda Setting and Presidential Success in a More Polarized Era

It is difficult to imagine that the increase in polarization has not affected presidential agenda setting and legislative success, as intra- and interparty dynamics are significant determinants of both. The most relevant effect can be seen in the party elite, where the amount of diversity within and overlap between the two parties has significantly decreased. Although loyalty to the president of their own party is never a given, members consistently voting with their party is much more commonplace and expected than in previous eras. Barefoot Sanders (1967, 1), the director of legislative liaisons in the House from 1967 to 1968, notes that "These [northern Democrats] are usually solid Administration votes ... the principal need is for increased personal attention to their individual problems and frequent massage-type visits to let them know of our continuing appreciation for their support."

Thus, although the president must maintain responsiveness to his core partisans, maintaining such relationships is much easier than both trying to establish new ones with cross-pressured members or the opposition and expending the resources to gain their support. That is, starting out with a substantial level of solid loyalty and shared preferences with his base in Congress is a much easier way for the president to begin a vote than by facing a sizeable opposition or large groups of undecided members with which he must negotiate to change preferences. Recognizing this will, in turn, influence the president's decisions on the content of his agenda. The larger and more dependable the group of core supporters in Congress is, the more ambitious a president can be in fashioning proposals with a realistic chance of success. On the other hand, with fewer core supporters we would expect a more modest and limited agenda.

Considering the increase in member loyalty and decrease in intraparty diversity, is it easier for presidents in the polarized era to gain support for their legislation? On the one hand, current presidents have a more solid partisan base from which they can build their legislative coalition. With decreased interparty overlap, however, presidents are less able to appeal to members of both parties. The core legislative coalitions, in addition, are more stable than in previous eras; because fewer members find themselves cross-pressured, fewer members oscillate between sides on issues. Thus, presidents in a more polarized era find it more difficult to craft bipartisan coalitions on matters that are salient to the parties. Although presidents' party bases are more secure from issue to issue, if their base does not constitute both a numerical and legislative majority, then they have a much more difficult time in appealing to members of the opposing party than earlier presidents. Covington (1988) argues that a president's successful coalition-building efforts often depend not on his base, but rather on the marginal sources of support: cross-pressured members of Congress. If this is the case, then current presidents should have a more difficult time in building legislative majorities, all else equal, because there are fewer marginal sources of support to approach than there were for past presidents.

The consequences of changes in the nature of majority legislative coalitions through polarization—from broad and diverse to narrow and comparatively cohesive—is one important focus for future research on agenda setting and success. Although under unified government the president would have more party members as potential allies in the former case (e.g., Carter), partisan theories of legislative organization contend that the enhanced powers granted the majority party's leaders in the latter case may more than compensate in the struggle over policy outcomes.

Thus, it is not necessarily the case that all the implications of polarization are to undermine presidents' ability to achieve their legislative goals. Another feature of legislative interaction that may be affected in the opposite direction is the veto. Charles Cameron (1999) led the way in applying formal theory and systematic quantitative analysis to the study of vetoes and renewed scholarly interest in this presidential power (see also Krehbiel 1998; Gilmour 2002; Conley 2003; Cameron and McCarty 2004). Space limits preclude extended discussion of this literature, but we must note that Sinclair (2006, 247) shows that as polarization has increased, use of veto threats on major bills has also grown, although the increase is confined to divided government situations.

Of course the veto is an effective blocking tool for a president as long as he can maintain the support of a third of one chamber, but it can also be used as leverage to extract concessions toward the president's preferred position when the Congress's desire to pass a bill is sufficiently strong (see Sinclair 2006, 248). (Cameron 1999 termed this process "veto bargaining.") Polarized parties in Congress have thus strengthened the president's hand in this regard and increased the attractiveness of veto threats as a strategy because it is more likely that the president can hold the support of a sufficiently large portion of his party to make the veto a credible threat. Moreover, as Evans and Ng (2006) show, the interaction involving veto bargaining is not only related to the desire to affect the content of bills, but is also related to each party's message strategies to influence public opinion and, in turn, future elections.

Ornstein and Fortier (2002) direct attention to another feature of this more polarized era: September 11, 2001. They (2002, 50) argue that in terms of agenda setting and presidential success rates, "September 11 changed everything." They assert that Bush's education reform might have passed by a slim margin but that the rest of his agenda would have been in trouble. Once the war on terrorism became the focus of Bush's agenda, "the nation united, and bipartisanship became the watchword in Congress" (Ornstein and Fortier 2002, 50). Bush's approval ratings soared as the partisan interests in Congress decreased significantly and both Congress and the public rallied around the flag. As subsequent developments in the 2002 midterm elections and later revealed, however, the bipartisanship was generally short lived. Conflict over domestic matters quickly returned and intensified, and then extended to national security issues as public support for the war in Iraq waned. These later developments suggest the events of 9/11 had not given the president new leverage with the opposition party in the legislative arena on national security matters, but future research will have to assess the relationship across the full range of issues.

Measurements of Presidential Success

The increase in polarization has added another complication to the measurement of presidential success. If, as we have contended, politics is different in the more polarized era, how does this affect the comparisons across presidents in different eras of polarization? Does the fact that presidents in the polarized era face different challenges in coalition building than earlier presidents, for example, create problems in making comparisons across time? If the difference in politics between the two eras has contributed to differences in the ability to form successful coalitions, then comparing the influence of presidents across time on this issue may be complicated. Sullivan (1988), in seeking to accurately measure presidential influence within Congress, argues that a key factor in such an analysis is to distinguish the position changes of members that are due to the members' personal decision making from changes that are due to actual presidential influence. He finds that President Johnson built bipartisan coalitions by converting the positions of members from his opposition's base. Was part of Johnson's success due to the fact that the opposition party's base in the pre-reform era was closer to the center of the ideological spectrum than the parties' bases are now?

Edwards (1989) argues that in analyzing questions of this nature, policy agreement must be the main research focus. Members of the same party typically share many policy preferences and this has only been magnified in the polarized era. If the president simply has taken stands that are congruent with the normal policy positions of his party members in Congress, then is the president truly needed as the party leader? Is the president's role as party leader diminished when he does not have to mobilize his party members but rather only propose the issues with which they all agree?

Krehbiel (1993) seeks to assess more accurately the primary legislative function of parties: whether they can pass legislation that is different from laws that would be passed in the absence of parties. Krehbiel (1993, 238) asks that when casting party-line votes, "do individual legislators vote with fellow party members *in spite of their disagreement* about the policy in question, or do they vote with fellow party members *because of their agreement* about the policy in question?" He concludes that although parties are important contributors to the legislative process, partisanship does not explain much variation in outcomes at different stages of the construction of legislative policy.

Writing in the middle of the increase in polarization, Krehbiel (1993, 261) argues that "as party ties weaken among voters, congressional candidates are less conspicuously party-affiliated during an ever-present electoral cycle ... Eventually, electorally grounded non-partisanship invades the legislature." If, as we have contended, however, the increase in polarization has affected both party elites and the mass public, then the non-partisanship Krehbiel spoke of rests on a shaky foundation. Indeed, Bartels (2000) shows that the relationship between party affiliation and voting behavior has grown stronger in more recent presidential elections.

One challenge that faced presidential researchers prior to the polarized era is the significant amount of individuality unique to each president. These individual personality traits, leadership styles, and overall characteristics specific to each president can make comparisons between the leaders challenging. When applied to presidential–congressional relations, for example, was President Johnson more successful than Carter in getting his legislation passed because of factors such as the ideological composition of Congress and public sentiment toward Congress and the president, or because Johnson had a more persuasive leadership style unique to him? Similarly, one important question that the full consideration of George W. Bush's administration will have to address is the degree to which his decision to focus on a highly partisan strategy in dealing with Congress was strategic and, if so, whether it undermined or enhanced the enactment of his priorities.

The political environment also plays a part in this question because we often are forced to use controls for outlying events such as foreign conflicts and assassinations. For instance, can we rightfully compare George W. Bush's legislative record in the period directly after September 11 to another president's during a period of international stability? The combination of the reformed presidential nomination system of the 1970s and subsequent increased polarization may have led to presidential nominees that, while still representing the center of their parties, represent more extreme points on the ideological spectrum. Note that George W. Bush is the only president initially selected since 1994 and the increase in polarization that followed from the partisan shift that year. Clinton (and his running mate) had sought support on the grounds that they were different from and more moderate than previous nominees. That has not been a successful theme in either party since Clinton's nomination.

These developments offer reasons to question the current applicability of findings regarding presidential–congressional relations and presidential party leadership that were derived from analyses before polarization. They suggest the need to consider the impact of additional variables that are unique to presidents and presidencies in the more polarized era. These include, among others, a conflictual and divergent political context, leadership and governing styles that are rooted in ideology, and elite policy preferences that are closer to the extremes of the spectrum.

In addition to this type of reconsideration, however, we think that the adequate assessment of the relationship between agenda setting and partisan success requires some new approaches. Specifically, we believe that not enough attention has been paid to what is the central object of the legislative process: the substance of legislation. To be sure, there have been case studies of a number of bills that have produced useful details. There has not, however, been the same kind of systematic attention to legislative content as there has been to bill adoption or roll-call success.

Presidents and members of Congress seek to pass bills that contain particular policies and programs. Disagreements over the particulars of these features are often the focus of political conflict between the parties (or potentially between the president and his party's leadership). Who is successful and who is not, and to what degree, depends on the details of legislation Congress adopts. For example, when Bill Clinton and the 104th Congress battled over the passage of welfare reform, three successive bills were concerned involving two vetoes. Each of these bills was a Republican proposal, and in the end the president signed a bill he did not like very much. However, the final proposal that became law had moved closer to Clinton's preferences in many respects. He was more successful than he would have been had the first bill become law, but we can only judge these matters of relative success by focusing on the bills' specifics. Knowing who made an initial proposal that passed is useful information, but it often will not tell us what is most relevant because the content of the final bill may differ greatly from the original proposal. For example, in Nixon's first Congress (1969–70), he threatened to veto three of his own proposals because congressional Democrats had altered them substantially (Conley 2006, 171). We suggest that future work should seek to expand on the insights of the agenda-setting research discussed above by focusing on the sources of specific legislative proposals and on which of them were actually included in the bills that were adopted. Such analyses would provide a firmer assessment of the relative influence of the president and congressional party leaders over what ideas were under active consideration for final policy. While the work of Edwards and Barrett discussed above provided much new information, the criterion of a proposal having received legislative hearings sets a low bar for inclusion as an agenda item. Indeed, a congressional majority from the opposite party may have only held a hearing to berate the administration about its proposal.

In addition, developing a list of specific policy proposals would facilitate attention to another feature of the legislative agenda that has received relatively little attention: matters of priority and saliency. The quantitative research on agenda setting and success, whether concentrating on bills proposed or individual roll calls, has generally treated each item as equally important to the actors. Yet we know that presidents and congressional leaders regard various items differently. Indeed, variations in priority are often a basis for bargains across pieces of legislation. Various sources, such as public speeches and Statements of Administration Policy (SAPs), can offer indications of which proposals have the highest import for presidents and party leaders. Thus a focus on specifics would offer a variety of ways to assess better the legislative consequences of the strategic choices of the president and the party leaderships with regard to proposing and adopting policy options, and thereby the impact of presidential leadership on congressional parties.

One significant effort to consider legislative details is the work of Brandice Canes-Wrone (2001, 2005). In her analyses, Canes-Wrone compares presidential budget proposals to final appropriations to measure the degree to which final legislation reflects the president's preferences. This work has been justly praised (see Howell 2006, 312–13; Howell also notes the general difficulties of measuring the match between policy and presidential preferences). It is important to note, however, that spending measurements capture only one aspect of policy, even in spending bills. For example, in the struggle over the budget in 1995–6 that led to the government shutdowns, the tax and appropriations bills that were at the center of the fight involved both amounts of money and substantive policy, mostly due to legislative riders in the appropriations bills (see Aldrich and Rohde 2000b). If the final results of this battle had been legislation in which every appropriation amount matched exactly Clinton's proposals, but all of the legislative changes proposed by the GOP had been included, the administration would probably not have seen it as a presidential victory. It would be highly desirable if the substantial insights offered by Canes-Wrone's budgetary analysis could be built on by studies that tried to measure the qualitative aspects of final legislation and to employ those measurements in systematic analysis.

Going Public

As noted above, Edwards (2002) indicates that one strategy of presidential influence in Congress is going public. Kernell (2007, 2) defines going public as "a strategy whereby a president promotes himself and his policies in Washington by appealing directly to the American public for support." Tulis (1987, 4), in introducing the rhetorical presidency, similarly states that "since the presidencies of Theodore Roosevelt and Woodrow Wilson, popular or mass rhetoric has become a principal tool of presidential governance. Presidents regularly 'go over the heads' of Congress to the people."

Fett (1994) contends that if a president reveals his preferences and makes an issue well known to the public, then legislators may be forced into a constituency-oriented voting pattern on the issue. By publicizing an issue, the president increases the chances that his issue will become more salient to members' constituencies. Because the member does not want to hurt his reelection chances, he most likely will vote with his constituency on the issue. For the president, this strategy is successful if his issue preferences coincide with a majority of constituency preferences. Accordingly, this scenario most likely arises on party-line votes. The president mobilizes his core partisan supporters while ostracizing his core opponents, as they most likely represent constituencies whose preferences are not aligned with the president's.

Ornstein and Fortier (2002) examine how going public focuses on the costs of non-compliance rather than the benefits of compliance. They note that in 2001, George W. Bush traveled to states in which he had received strong electoral support but whose members were wavering in their presidential support. Although this strategy backfired in some cases—the visits induced some constituency voting patterns that were unfavorable to the president—Bush did pick up several Democratic votes in future legislation. In contrast to Ornstein and Fortier's focus on campaigning, however, Edwards (2003) concentrates on presidents' speeches and concludes that instances of those speeches moving public opinion substantially, either on evaluations of the president or support for specific policies, are rare if not non-existent.

The juxtaposition of these two analyses suggests future lines for additional research. Edwards convincingly demonstrates that presidents' opportunities for making gains in public support via speech making are limited. However, that is not the only avenue for going public. There can be alternative strategies or purposes that reflect broader interests, some of which are connected to rallying or maintaining party support in Congress. For example, the president's purpose may be to shift public attention away from a politically disadvantageous issue not discussed to the subject of a speech. Or the president may be trying to stave off a decline in support from his base, rather than the more ambitious goal of increasing support. Strategically, the president may focus on campaigning rather than speeches, as Bush did in 2002 when he used the campaign trail to force the Democrats to capitulate to his proposals for structuring the Department of Homeland Security. There are other possibilities, but assessing the success of such efforts requires more information about the particulars of each situation.

Once the president has gone public, he has publicly stated his issue position and has little room to compromise with Congress members without being accused of waffling. In this situation, the president reduces his ability to compromise; the members are the only ones left with this option. Reflecting one of the downsides of more homogeneous party coalitions, the president may risk his reputation, especially with his core supporters, by publicly contradicting his original issue position. "Staying private" (Covington 1987), then, by negotiating with members out of the public eye may help to avoid the appearance of contradictions. The need to stay private rather than go public thus may be greatest when, in order to compromise for support on final passage, the president must contradict positions taken earlier in the bargaining process.

Going Public in a More Polarized Era

The possibility of staying private on an issue in order to keep necessary issue contradictions equally private also raises questions. In this polarized era with a ubiquitous media presence, it is unlikely that these presidential position contradictions would not be made public at some point. In the 2004 election especially, the effort to exploit "flip-floppers" was quite visible. In order to gain electoral and party image advantages, the opposition may jump on the opportunity to reveal a presidential contradiction made obvious during the bargaining process. In this era, then, the negative consequences may be growing quite similar for going public or staying private when the president contradicts himself.

In addition, the increasingly conflictual political environment, largely a result of greater polarization, has decreased the president's ease in crafting bipartisan coalitions. Although staying private may be a plausible strategy for the president when crafting a bipartisan coalition, he must take into consideration one of the most significant elements in the polarized era, the motivated opposition. The president is not the sole determinant of whether an issue becomes salient. The opposition may want to increase the saliency of an issue that is disadvantageous to the president. To be sure, the president can do his part in not acting on an issue and trying to keep the issue from becoming publicized, but just because the president does not want an issue to become salient does not mean that it will not. In fact, the president's reluctance to publicize an issue may signal political weakness to the opposition and serve as motivation for them to go public.

So what is it precisely about modern politics that encourages presidents to go public? Kernell (2007, 71) argues that going public is a more fitting strategy for modern presidents for three main reasons: the current political relations discourage quiet and considerate bargaining; presidential nomination reforms have led to presidents who are more inclined toward and skilled at public relations; and the increased regularity of divided government has introduced a "zero-sum game that shrinks the availability of mutually acceptable policies and otherwise makes bargaining risky by rewarding reneging."

The regularity of divided government in light of greater polarization may have increased the appeal of going public rather than bargaining, as the odds of the president succeeding by going over the heads of his political opponents, though limited, may appear greater than by bargaining with them. It seems that the reformed presidential nomination system made it easier for extreme candidates to be sent to the presidency than in the pre-reform era. In the wake of subsequent polarization, presidential nominees still may represent the ideological center of their party, but the parties themselves have tilted toward the extremes of the ideological spectrum. Thus, what qualifies as the center of the parties in the polarized era may have been the extremes in the pre-reform era. The combination of increasingly ideologically divergent parties with increasingly common divided government has lessened the appeal of bargaining in favor of going public.

Under unified government, the president and congressional leaders have incentives to appear cooperative by settling disagreements harmoniously and in private. Party differences are resolved knowing that the higher collective good of the party image is the most important priority at stake. In this situation, then, going public can be costly to the party's reelection chances (as, for example, in Bush's efforts to pass immigration reform in 2006); staying private is the preferred strategy. Under divided government, however, a different dynamic arises. Negotiations move from the private to the public arena and politics becomes a more zero-sum game. The main priority often changes from policy to electoral advantage, significantly changing the political incentives. Kernell argues that presidents use going public for the same positive reasons that they bargain: to pass a bill, ratify a treaty, etc. Under divided government in this partisan era, the chances of cooperation so that the president can achieve these goals are very slim on a range of major issues. Constituent pressure may be one of the only ways in which opposing members will support the president.

Kernell hints at the effects that the increased polarization may have on the strategy of going public. In order to go public successfully, two key components must exist: the president must first mobilize public opinion and the public in turn must influence their representatives. With the increase in partisanship, however, members have become less susceptible to "political breezes the president can stir up in their constituencies" (Kernell 2007, 216). In addition, presidents in the more polarized era may need to adopt a counter-intuitive strategy when going public. With the increase in polarization, the president's support from his base is nearly a given as is the opposition from the other party's base. Given these two probable conditions, the independent voters are the ones left for the president to target. A highly partisan targeting strategy is unlikely to sway independent voters and, in fact, may undermine the president's ability in the long term to influence this group's vote. (Research on Bush's governing strategy, and on those of Obama, will help to shed light on the probabilities of success these strategic options offer.) With greater polarization, then, one going public strategy the president might consider turning to more often is that of playing down exactly what helped him get to the White House in the first place: his partisanship. Yet the types of people selected as presidential nominees, coupled with the need to avoid alienating the partisan base, may undermine the feasibility of such a strategy.

DIVIDED GOVERNMENT

A segment of the literature that is particularly relevant to this discussion involves the consequences of divided government. Since David Mayhew's pathbreaking book was published in 1991, researchers have focused a great deal of attention on the matter. (He updated his analysis with a second edition in 2005.) Mayhew was interested in divided government both because of its increased frequency and because many observers regarded it as consequential for the operation of government. He (1991, 1–3) noted that analysts from Woodrow Wilson to contemporary political actors shared the expectation that divided government would reduce the likelihood that important legislation would be enacted, while unified government (either because of the acceptance of presidential party leadership or due to shared preferences) would increase the likelihood. On the other hand, these analysts expected that divided government would increase the incidence of congressional investigations, as the opposition party sought political advantage.

Based on his analysis, Mayhew concluded that divided government neither significantly decreased the likelihood of passing major laws, nor increased the incidence of high-publicity congressional investigations. While subsequent research did not challenge Mayhew's most basic conclusion that important legislation can pass under both divided and unified government, the evidence from many varied perspectives indicates that divided government is less likely to be legislatively productive (Edwards, Barrett, and Peake 1997; Binder 1999, 2003; Howell et al. 2000). Moreover, the recent research reveals a variety of ways in which this tendency is likely to be reinforced in the context of high partisan polarization.

Divided Government and Polarization

Work by Conley (2002, 2006) offers some of the most current evidence on these issues. Building on previous analyses, Conley (2006, 152) focuses on "the ways in which unified or divided government *does matter* for presidential leadership." He argues that the impact of divided control is more varied than that of unified government, particularly over time. He (2006, 164–7) shows, for example, that while there is relatively little temporal variation in presidential success on roll calls under unified government during the post-war era, success has declined substantially in the "postreform/party unity era" (1981 on) compared to earlier periods. Furthermore, regarding this later period, he (2006, 172) concludes that "few landmark bills [using Mayhew's classification] are consistently connected with the president's stated policy objectives."

These results illustrate the consequences of the transformation of majority party power in Congress that has both resulted from and reinforced polarization. Given these institutional changes, the president is less able to focus the Congress's attention on his priorities when government control is divided. For example, Edwards and Barrett (2000, 122) show that in the 100th and 104th congresses almost none of the potentially significant bills on the congressional agenda were presidential initiatives. On the other hand, these same majority powers can guarantee serious consideration for virtually all presidential initiatives under unified government.

Furthermore, the decline of the proportion of moderate members in both chambers that has accompanied polarization makes it more difficult to secure the legislative compromises that are likely to be necessary under divided control to secure passage of important bills. Binder's (2003, 68) analysis shows that a one standard deviation increase in the proportion of moderates decreases the probability of gridlock by 9 percent, nearly the same as a shift from divided to unified government. Moreover, this consideration is closely tied to the kinds of candidates that are chosen by the parties to run for office and the kinds of strategic choices they make once elected. George Bush deliberately chose a highly partisan governing strategy (Sinclair 2008, 168) for his presidency. It is certainly true, as Fiorina (2008) argues, that this was not an inevitable consequence of polarization. We would argue, however, that current conditions make it more likely that someone like Bush (or a Democratic counterpart) would be nominated, and more likely that a strategy like Bush's would be chosen. Similarly, polarized politics would seem to increase the probability that the congressional nominating process will result in the choice of candidates who manifest the intense personal dislike for members of the opposition party that has characterized the Congress over the last two decades. This in turn makes legislative agreement more difficult under divided government, over and above the effects of policy disagreements and conflicting electoral interests.

Comparisons of the varying strategic contexts during the Clinton and George W. Bush administrations will help to discern better the consequences of divided versus unified government, especially if part of the focus is on legislative specifics as suggested above. The key issue here is not whether there are major bills adopted under each regime as Mayhew asserts. That is too minimalist a criterion. Rather we want to know whether there is systematic variation in the frequency of major policy initiatives being adopted and in the content of those initiatives, and whether those patterns have been altered by polarization.

Bush, in the wake of his reelection, claimed that he had political capital and intended to use it. Yet his waning approval appeared to have undermined his ability to rally his own party and to overcome Democratic resistance, leaving the administration with few significant victories in that Congress. After the 2006 elections, on the other hand, Bush was much more able to maintain his party's support in blocking Democratic initiatives, permitting the president to exploit fully his advantages in veto bargaining. This suggests that polarization may enhance the president's influence under divided government when the only goal that will often be feasible is to prevent the opposition from making significant departures from the status quo. Under unified government, on the other hand, where the president's ambition is to rally his co-partisans and induce Congress to adopt his new initiatives, the president's success will be dependent not only on his party's majority control, but also on maintaining significant public support. Without those conditions, especially with the current era's narrow majorities, his congressional partisans will likely be resistant to following his lead; they will think instead about maintaining their majority and their individual seats.

In addition to the consideration of passing legislation, research on divided government would profit by attention to Mayhew's other focus: investigations. There has not been much research on congressional oversight since the growth of polarization. Mayhew (1991) argues that the evidence shows that divided government does not lead to significantly more congressional investigations of the executive than unified government. Mayhew, however, focuses only on "high-publicity" investigations of topics that are already salient to the public. His results do not deal with the more routine and more numerous enquiries that are less visible to begin with, but could reveal politically damaging information. Public pressure will always compel Congress to investigate salient events like 9/11, but that does not mean they will investigate waste of aid to Iraq, formaldehyde in Federal Emergency Management Agency trailers, or the politicization of the executive branch (investigations of all of which were launched by rep. Henry Waxman (D-Calif.) in 2007). Moreover, some recent work on high-profile investigations indicates that even in that narrow category divided government yields more and longer hearings in both House and Senate (see Kriner and Schwartz 2008). More systematic attention to this subject, including comparisons of the 1980s and earlier to recent congresses, could give us a clearer picture of the consequences of partisanship and polarization for policy implementation and presidential unilateralism (Rudalevige 2006), and whether presidential party leadership in the current era may short-circuit the operation of this aspect of checks and balances.

CONCLUSION

In this chapter, we have sought to explore the potential effects of partisan polarization on presidential–congressional interactions within and between parties, and to reflect on the implications of those possible effects for previous theoretical arguments and empirical findings. In closing, we should offer some caveats about these arguments to avoid misunderstandings. First, we are not claiming that all legislative matters have become partisan. Despite increased polarization, much—indeed most—legislation involves little or no conflict (Aldrich and Rohde 2005, 263). However, most legislation that is highly salient to the president, the Congress, and the public is more likely to involve partisan conflict than was true twenty-five, or even fifteen, years ago. Furthermore, we do not imply that all legislative conflict has a partisan cast. It is still possible for parties to be internally divided on important issues, as recent battles over immigration reform and efforts to regulate greenhouse emissions demonstrate. But it is also true that such issues are fewer and less damaging to intraparty homogeneity than used to be the case. Thus, the implications of polarization we have considered are relevant to a large and important share of the political agenda. On those bills the president is likely to have naturally the vigorous support of his party's congressional leadership and the equally automatic opposition of the other party's leadership.

Obviously this is just a beginning of the discussion, and no firm conclusions can be offered. We have argued that both theory and preliminary evidence suggest that polarization among voters, activists, and elites has probably affected political interactions and policy by changing the political context, the preferences and goals of relevant political actors, and the institutional structure. Thus, we believe that students of presidential–congressional relations must think systematically about the relevance of polarization for existing theories. In addition, we must conduct new empirical analyses that parallel those that produced the most convincing patterns of evidence about the past to determine whether those relationships still hold in this arguably very different situation.

References

ABRAMOWITZ, A. 2006. Disconnected, or Joined at the Hip? Pp. 72–85 in *Red and Blue Nation*, Volume 1, ed. P. S. Nivola and D. W. Brady. Washington, DC: Brookings Institution.

ALDRICH, J. H. 1994. Rational Choice Theory and the Study of American Politics. Pp. 208–33 in *The Dynamics of American Politics: Approaches and Interpretations*, ed. L. C. Dodd and C. Jillson. Boulder, CO: Westview Press.

—— and ROHDE, D. W. 1997–8. The Transition to Republican Rule in the House: Implications for Theories of Congressional Politics, *Political Science Quarterly*, 112: 541–67.

———— 2000a. The Consequences of Party Organization in the House: The Role of Majority and Minority Parties in Conditional Party Government. Pp. 31–72 in *Polarized Politics*, ed. J. R. Bond and R. Fleisher. Washington, DC: CQ Press.

———— 2000b. The Republican Revolution and the House Appropriations Committee. *Journal of Politics*, 62/1: 1–33.

———— 2001. The Logic of Conditional Party Government: Revisiting the Electoral Connection. Pp. 249–70 in *Congress Reconsidered*, 7th edn., ed. L. C. Dodd and B. I. Oppenheimer. Washington, DC: CQ Press.

———— 2005. Congressional Committees in a Partisan Era. Pp. 249–70 in *Congress Reconsidered*, 8th edn., ed. L. C. Dodd and B. I. Oppenheimer. Washington, DC: CQ Press.

BARTELS, L. M. 2000. Partisanship and Voting Behavior, 1952–1996. *American Journal of Political Science*, 44/1: 33–50.

BINDER, S. A. 1999. The Dynamics of Legislative Gridlock, 1947–96. *American Political Science Review*, 93: 519–33.

—— 2003. *Stalemate*. Washington, DC: Brookings.

BOND, J. R., and FLEISHER, R. 1990. *The President in the Legislative Arena*. Chicago: University of Chicago Press.

BRADY, D. W., HAN, H., and POPE, J. C. 2007. Primary Elections and Candidate Ideology: Out of Step with the Primary Electorate. *Legislative Studies Quarterly*, 32/1: 79–105.

—— and Volden, C. 2006. *Revolving Gridlock*, 2nd edn. Boulder, CO: Westview Press.

BREWER, M. D., and STONECASH, J. M. 2007. *Split: Class and Cultural Divides in American Politics*. Washington, DC: CQ Press.

CAMERON, C. M. 1999. *Veto Bargaining: Presidents and the Politics of Negative Power*. New York: Cambridge University Press.

—— and McCARTY, N. M. 2004. Models of Vetoes and Veto Bargaining. *Annual Review of Political Science*, 7: 409–35.

CANES-WRONE, B. 2001. The President's Legislative Influence from Public Appeals. *American Journal of Political Science*, 45/2: 313–29.

—— 2005. *Who's Leading Whom?* Chicago: University of Chicago Press.

—— and SHOTTS, W. 2004. The Conditional Nature of Presidential Responsiveness to Public Opinion. *American Journal of Political Science*, 48/4: 690–706.

CONLEY, R. S. 2002. *The Presidency, Congress, and Divided Government: A Postwar Assessment.* College Station: Texas A&M University Press.

—— 2003. George Bush and the 102nd Congress: The Impact of Public and Private Veto Threats on Policy Outcomes. *Presidential Studies Quarterly,* 33/4: 730–50.

—— 2006. The Legislative Presidency in Political Time: Party Control and Presidential–Congressional Relations. Pp. 183–208 in *Rivals for Power,* 3rd edn., ed. J. A. Thurber. Lanham, MD: Rowman & Littlefield.

COVINGTON, C. R. 1987. "Staying Private:" Gaining Congressional Support for Unpublicized Presidential Preferences on Roll Call Votes. *Journal of Politics,* 49/3: 737–55.

—— 1988. Building Presidential Coalitions among Cross-Pressured Members of Congress. *Western Political Quarterly,* 41/1: 47–62.

—— WRIGHTON, J. M., and KINNEY, R. 1995. A "Presidency-Augmented" Model of Presidential Success on House Roll Call Votes. *American Journal of Political Science,* 39/4: 1001–24.

COX, G. W., and McCUBBINS, M. D. 1993. *Legislative Leviathan: Party Government in the House.* Berkeley and Los Angeles: University of California Press.

CQ Weekly. 2007. *Bills to Watch and Status of Appropriations,* Aug. 13: 2483–4.

EDWARDS, G. C., III. 1989. *At the Margins: Presidential Leadership of Congress.* New Haven, CT: Yale University Press.

—— 2002. Strategic Choices and the Early Bush Legislative Agenda. *PS: Political Science and Politics,* 35/1: 41–45.

—— 2003. *On Deaf Ears.* New Haven, CT: Yale University Press.

—— and BARRETT, A. 2000. Presidential Agenda Setting in Congress. In *Polarized Politics,* ed. J. R. BOND and R. FLEISHER. Washington, DC: CQ Press.

———— and PEAKE, J. 1997. The Legislative Impact of Divided Government. *American Journal of Political Science,* 41: 545–63.

EVANS, C. L., and NG, S. 2006. The Institutional Context of Veto Bargaining. Pp. 183–208 in *Rivals for Power,* ed. J. A. Thurber. Lanham, MD: Rowman & Littlefield.

FETT, P. J. 1994. Presidential Legislative Priorities and Legislators' Voting Decisions: An Exploratory Analysis. *Journal of Politics,* 56 /2: 502–12.

FIORINA, M. P. 2008. A Divider, Not a Uniter: Did It Have to Be? Pp. 92–111 in *The George W. Bush Legacy,* ed. C. Campbell, B. A. Rockman, and A. Rudalevige. Washington, DC: CQ Press.

—— with ABRAMS, S. J., and Pope, J. C. 2006. *Culture War? The Myth of a Polarized America,* 2nd edn. New York: Pearson, Longman.

—— and LEVENDUSKY, M. S. 2006. Rejoinder. Pp. 95–111 in *Red and Blue Nation,* Volume 1, ed. P. S. Nivola and D. W. Brady. Washington, DC: Brookings Institution.

FLEISHER, R., and BOND, J. R. 2000. Partisanship and the President's Quest for Votes on the Floor of Congress. Pp. 154–85 in *Polarized Politics,* ed. J. R. Bond and R. Fleisher. Washington, DC: CQ Press.

GILMOUR, J. B. 2002. Institutional and Individual Influences of the President's Veto. *Journal of Politics,* 64: 198–218.

GROSECLOSE, T., and McCARTY, N. 2001. The Politics of Blame: Bargaining before an Audience. *American Journal of Political Science,* 45: 100–19.

HOWELL, W. G. 2006. Executives: The American Presidency. Pp. 303–22 in *The Oxford Handbook of Political Institutions,* ed. R. A. W. Rhodes, S. A. Binder, and B. A. Rockman. Oxford: Oxford University Press.

—— ADLER, S., CAMERON, C., and RIEMANN, C. 2000. Divided Government and the Legislative Productivity of Congress. *Legislative Studies Quarterly,* 25: 285–311.

JACOBSON, G. C. 2000. Party Polarization in National Politics: The Electoral Connection. Pp. 9–30 in *Polarized Politics,* ed. J. R. Bond and R. Fleisher. Washington, DC: CQ Press.

JACOBSON, G. C. 2006. Comment. Pp. 85–95 in *Red and Blue Nation*, Volume 1, ed. P. S. Nivola and D. W. Brady. Washington, DC: Brookings Institution.

——2007. *A Divider, Not a Uniter: George W. Bush and the American People*. New York: Pearson, Longman.

KERNELL, S. 2007. *Going Public: New Strategies of Presidential Leadership*, 4th edn. Washington, DC: CQ Press.

KREHBIEL, K. 1993. Where's the Party? *British Journal of Political Science*, 23: 235–66.

——1998. *Pivotal Politics*. Chicago: University of Chicago Press.

KRINER, D., and SCHWARTZ, L. 2008. Divided Government and Congressional Investigations. *Legislative Studies Quarterly*, 33: forthcoming.

MAYHEW, D. R. 1991. *Divided We Govern*. New Haven, CT: Yale University Press.

——2005. *Divided We Govern*, 2nd edn. New Haven, CT: Yale University Press.

ORNSTEIN, N., and FORTIER, J. 2002. Relations with Congress. *PS: Political Science and Politics*, 35/1: 47–50.

POOLE, K. T., and ROSENTHAL, H. 2007. *Ideology and Congress*. New Brunswick, NJ: Transaction.

ROHDE, D. W. 1991. *Parties and Leaders in the Postreform House*. Chicago: University of Chicago Press.

RUDALEVIGE, A. 2006. *The New Imperial Presidency*. Ann Arbor: University of Michigan Press.

SANDERS, B. 1967. Memo, for the President, July 18, 1967, Congressional Liaison Aides, Box 19, Papers for Barefoot Sanders, LBJ Library.

SINCLAIR, B. 1995. *Legislators, Leaders, and Lawmaking*. Baltimore: Johns Hopkins University Press.

——2006. *Party Wars: Polarization and the Politics of National Policy Making*. Norman: University of Oklahoma Press.

——2008. Living (and Dying?) by the Sword: George W. Bush as Legislative Leader. Pp. 164–87 in *The George W. Bush Legacy*, ed. C. Campbell, A. Rockman, and A. Rudalevige. Washington, DC: CQ Press.

SULLIVAN, T. 1988. Headcounts, Expectations, and Presidential Coalitions in Congress. *American Journal of Political Science*, 32/3: 567–89.

TULIS, J. 1987. *The Rhetorical Presidency*. Princeton, NJ: Princeton University Press.

CHAPTER 14

....

LEGISLATIVE
SKILLS

....

STEPHEN J. WAYNE

LEGISLATIVE skills are the tactics presidents use to convince members of Congress to support their policy initiatives. They differ from legislative strategies in that they are the instruments utilized to achieve specific legislative objectives, whereas strategies are more generic in approach and more comprehensive in application. Legislative tactics tend to be action oriented and goal specific.

The need for legislative skills stems from the leadership expectations for contemporary presidents combined with the systemic constraints on them, constitutional, institutional, and political constraints that impede a president's ability to meet those expectations. The constitutional system fosters institutional rivalry; it creates "separate institutions sharing powers" (Neustadt 1960, 29), but requires joint institutional cooperation to transform presidential proposals into legislative enactments.

The political system also divides power more than it unifies it. Since the middle of the twentieth century, that system has produced extended periods of divided government (1946–8; 1954–60; 1968–76; 1980–92, 1994–2002,[1] 2006–8). It has also limited presidents' leverage over legislators of their own party by virtue of the decentralized nomination process, the absence of presidential coattails (since 1980), the reelection advantages of congressional incumbents, and the Twenty-Second Amendment to the Constitution which limits a president to two elective terms in office. These limits contribute to the president's leadership dilemma: how to achieve expected and

[1] The administration of George W. Bush began with a Republican House and an evenly divided Senate in which the vice president naturally voted with the Republicans. The defection of Republican James Jeffords (Vermont), and his decision to vote with the Democrats to reorganize the Senate, gave the Democrats control of that body until the midterm election in which Republicans gained a majority.

promised policy goals within a legislative body in which institutional independence is both a norm and ideal.

Part of the answer to that dilemma lies in the exercise of legislative skills by presidents, their staff, and subordinates in the executive branch. The conventional wisdom is that those contemporary presidents deemed to have had the greatest policy impact, Franklin Roosevelt, Lyndon Johnson, and Ronald Reagan, were successful in the congressional arena in large part because of their legislative skills (Edwards 1989, 168–9; Light 1982, 61–82). Although the generalizability of this skills proposition—the exercise of legislative skills by presidents is a principal factor contributing to their policy success in Congress—has been challenged (Edwards 1989, 211–12; Bond and Fleischer 1990, 41 and 52; and to some extent, Peterson 1990, 12, 266–7), practitioners and scholars still agree that skills matter at certain times, on certain votes, and with certain members. Scholars commonly assume that presidents can affect the outcome of their policy initiatives by what they propose, when they propose it, and how persuasive they are in convincing legislators to follow their lead (Peterson 1990, 218–67).

The persuasiveness thesis was famously articulated by Richard E. Neustadt in his classic study *Presidential Power*:

The essence of a President's persuasive task, with congressmen and everybody else, is to induce them to believe that what he wants of them is what their own appraisal of their own responsibilities requires them to do in their interest, not his. Because men may differ in their views on public policy, because differences in outlook stem from differences in duty— duty to one's office, one's constituents, oneself—that task is bound to be more like collective bargaining than like a reasoned argument among philosopher kings.   (Neustadt 1960, 40)

Neustadt's advice to presidents became the basis of a theoretical model that political scientists have used to justify the need for and utility of exercising presidential power. The perspective from which Neustadt saw the president's power dilemma, "from over the President's shoulder, looking out and down with the perspective of his place" (Neustadt 1960, xxi), was also adopted by students of the presidency, seeking to evaluate the effectiveness of individual presidents. It was a presidency-centered approach that focused on how presidents could overcome the hurdles they faced in an environment that was hostile to their exercise of leadership.

Scholars of presidential–congressional relations assumed that the president's legislative skills were a critical criterion in assessing their effectiveness in Congress. How to define these skills, much less measure their impact, has proven difficult, however. Initially, scholars used case studies to illustrate and support Neustadt's thesis (McConnell 1962; Paige 1968; Marcus 1977; Berman 1982; Kellerman 1984; Burke and Greenstein 1989), but extracting skills from other possible influences on behavior often turned on the subjective views of those involved in the process or who observed it up close.

There were other problems. There were too few cases from which to generalize. Idiosyncratic aspects of each case clouded underlying commonalities. Critics argued that the choice of a particular case because of its importance or the controversy it generated usually exaggerated presidential influence. Another approach and methodology, more consistent with the tenets of scientific research, was necessary, or so the critics argued (Wayne 1983, 45–6; Edwards 1983b, 99–124; Moe 1993, 337–85; King 1993, 387–412).

There were a few hypothesis-testing studies, using the Neustadt model as a frame of reference. Some of them focused on two variables that Neustadt believed to be central to the exercise of presidential power: reputation and prestige (Edwards 1983a; Kernell 1986; Gleiber, Shull, and Waligora 1998). Others looked at presidential activities directed at Congress, attempting to correlate those activities with legislative policy success (Covington 1988; Sullivan 1988; Lockerbie and Borrelli 1989; Covington, Wrighton, and Kinney 1995).

But this research also encountered problems. One involved circularity of reasoning. Assuming reputation and prestige to be key factors (independent variables) that contributed to the president's policy success does not take into account that these factors may themselves have been a consequence of policy successes. In other words, the relationship between reputation and prestige on one hand and legislative success on the other may be recursive. Under these circumstances, it is difficult to untangle cause and effect.

A second problem has to do with Neustadt's definition of influence, getting people to do something they might not otherwise do. Although we can surmise partisan, constituency, and ideological orientations as motives for behavior, they do not, in and of themselves, indicate the initial reactions to the legislation by members of Congress, much less their positions on it. Some legislators may not have given the matter much thought; others may have taken a certain stand for the purposes of increasing their political leverage with the president; some may be moved by personal experience that does not accord with their overall partisan or ideological beliefs. Yet unless their initial inclination or position is known, presidential influence on individual members cannot be systematically measured using Neustadt's definition.

For some, the presidency-centered approach itself presented the problem. The "n" was too small, the cases too detailed and too individualistic, the method of analysis too qualitative, and the conclusions too subjective. For others, the approach contained a normative bias, a preference for liberal, activist government and for the president to be its prime "mover and shaker." Conservatives disputed Neustadt's notion of "emergencies in policy" and the need for presidents to lead and Congress to follow. Some argued that the system has been capable of devising suitable policy solutions to the country's needs even when powers were divided (Mayhew 1991; Jones 1994) while others pointed to the dangers of a dominant president (Corwin 1984; Reedy 1970; Fisher 1985).

How then can legislative skills be identified? How can their impact on congressional policy output be determined? Some scholars turned to the congressional arena and social science methodology for the answers. They focused their attention on Congress because it is more open than the presidency, with more people making more decisions on the public record. Scholars can also analyze these decisions using statistical techniques and then infer presidential influence from the patterns of decision making.

Naturally, different approaches and methods can result in different findings. The congressionally centered, quantitative analyses have found much less evidence of presidential influence on congressional voting decisions than the more presidency-centered, qualitative studies have focused. Both types of studies, however, seemed to confirm the hostility of the environment in which presidents operate and the need for them to exercise influence to overcome the opposition to their proposals. But how influential can they be?

Which of these approaches and methodologies has the largest pay-offs for understanding presidential power? Which of them tells us the most about legislative skills, when they matter and what effect they have on congressional policy output? This essay explores these questions by first describing legislative skills in some detail, then summarizing the research on the impact of these skills on legislative policy output, and finally by posing some substantive and methodological issues that scholars and practitioners need to address.

THE NATURE OF
LEGISLATIVE SKILLS

Presidents use their legislative skills to affect congressional decision making. They do so by structuring the environment within Congress to maximize their chances for a successful policy outcome. They also try to affect individual voting decisions by members of Congress (Edwards 1980, 116–88; 1989, 186–212; Bond and Fleisher 1990, 29–33; Peterson 1990, 216–31). Structural instruments include setting the agenda, taking positions on issues that Congress is considering, and threatening to veto legislation that contains provisions to which presidents object. Interpersonal tactics comprise contact and consultation, bargaining and compromise, and rewards and sanctions.

Structural instruments that presidents use are coordinated and implemented by offices primarily within the Executive Office of the President. The Office of Management and Budget (OMB) and the White House policy offices oversee agenda preparation, position taking, and the coordination of veto threats; the outreach offices in the White House promote presidential policy initiatives within the public arena while the Office of Legislative Affairs, also White House-based, maintains ongoing relations with members of Congress, providing them with a conduit to and from the presidency.

In general, the internal executive policy-making and policy implementation processes drive the institutional components of the legislative presidency. They are directed toward the Congress as a whole or its committees while the interpersonal elements tend to be more ad hoc, dependent on the inclinations and involvement of the president and senior White House staff, and focus more on individual members of Congress, such as the leadership, committee chairs, and eventually the rank and file.

STRUCTURAL INSTRUMENTS OF PRESIDENTIAL INFLUENCE

Presidents try to affect congressional consideration of their policy proposals in strategic ways (Bond and Fleischer 1990, 18–21, 31; Peterson 1990, 218–31). They do so by proposing an agenda, prioritizing the items in it, packaging them in a manner that contributes to their enactment in the form and with the content that they desire, and then timing their introduction so as not to overload the congressional policy-making process.

Throughout Congress's consideration of legislation, presidents also take positions on how the legislation is being drafted, thereby signaling their approval, desire for modifications, or outright disapproval of the policy decisions that Congress is making. The signals may also contain a veto threat, a powerful negative weapon that a president can wield to prevent legislation to which the administration strongly objects from becoming law.

Agenda Setting

Presidents are expected to set the legislative agenda and have been doing so on a regular basis since the 1930s. The items in their agenda come from their electoral campaign, party platforms, and White House policy-making staff. The president presents his agenda to Congress in the State of the Union address, messages to the congressional leadership that accompany the administration's legislative proposals, and other communications, both public and private, that emanate from the White House.

Scholars who have examined the president's legislative agenda have found it large and diversified. Between 1949 and 2002, Andrew Rudalevige counted 7,800 legislative proposals that were initiated by presidents and 3,200 messages sent to Congress. "Of these, about two-thirds are largely domestic, one-fifth foreign, with the rest dealing with budget or reorganization issues cutting across both domains" (Rudalevige 2005, 426).

Mark Peterson tallied 5,069 domestic presidential policy initiatives from 1953 through 1984, with Democratic presidents having larger legislative agendas than Republicans. According to Peterson, most of the major proposals that came from the White House received some consideration by Congress; a little less than half of the minor ones did so as well (Peterson 1990, 95–6, 152–7).

George C. Edwards III and Andrew Barrett found that presidents proposed almost 34 percent of the 865 significant bills that Congress considered between 1953 and 1996. Not surprisingly, the White House introduced about twice as many significant bills during periods of unified government as during divided government (Edwards and Barrett 2000, 123–6). A study by congressional scholar Barbara Sinclair confirmed Edwards and Barrett's basic findings. Her examination of Congress between the years 1969 and 1998 found that presidents initiated 29 percent of the legislation. If the Republican Congress of 1995–6 is excluded, that percentage rises to 33 (Sinclair 2000, 142).

The large number of presidential policy initiatives indicates that presidential agenda setting became institutionalized in the second half of the twentieth century. Prior to this time, however, it was not. Lawrence H. Chamberlain's study of major legislation drafted between 1933 and 1940 found that most of it was formulated by Congress or by Congress and the president working together, not by the White House alone (Chamberlain 1946, 450–3).

Although agenda setting by presidents has become a contemporary expectation (Wayne 1978, 103–38), there has been considerable variation in the size, scope, and substance of the policy agendas presented to Congress. Franklin Roosevelt, Lyndon Johnson, Ronald Reagan, and Barack Obama proposed the most far-reaching and distinctive legislative agendas and were reputed to be the most successful in getting them enacted into law. In addition to their own legislative skills, their success was attributed to the size of their election victories, the partisan composition of the Congresses with which they dealt, and the nature of the times. The Great Depression of the 1930s, the Kennedy assassination and the civil rights revolution of the 1960s, and the stagnant, inflated economy and Iranian hostage crisis of the late 1970s, and the economic meltdown in 2008–9 all created environments which facilitated presidential leadership of Congress.

These four presidents were the exceptions, however. The norm has been more limited and less innovative agendas.

New presidents rarely begin with a clean policy slate, according to Charles O. Jones (Jones 1994, 164–7). Jones notes that ideas usually percolate for some time before they become major issues in political campaigns and acquire the public salience and support necessary to transform them into legislative initiatives and, eventually, policy outcomes.

Jones differentiates the agendas of contemporary presidents on the basis of their orientation (expansive, consolidation, maintenance, and contraction), ambitiousness (active, permissive, and reactive), consensus (low, moderate, and high), and their impact on future agenda building (limited, significant, and massive) (Jones 1994, 170). These categorizations are useful for making qualitative distinctions among the agendas of modern presidents but the categorization itself is of limited utility in generalizing about the scope and substance of presidential agenda setting.

Underlying Jones's typologies and his qualitative analysis is his normative judgment that the active, assertive presidential model, derived from Richard Neustadt's prescriptions for mid-twentieth-century presidents, is not consistent with the Framers' constitutional framework, may not be consistent with a particular president's ideological orientation, and may also be out of sync with the political climate at that time. For Jones, the hurdles that constrain presidential agenda-setting do and should outweigh the individualized impact presidents have most of the time (Jones 1994, 181).

Jones does concede, however, much like Neustadt, that presidents must assess the political environment, the policy needs of the country, and the institutional and partisan resources at their disposal when pointing Congress toward a particular course of action. That assessment is a critical component of leadership skills, one that affects a president's political capital down the road (Jones 1994, 181).

Prioritizing and Packaging

One component of a president's legislative skills is to identify agenda items. Another is to prioritize those items on the basis of their importance. A third is to package them in a way that enhances their chances for passage.

Congress needs to know how strongly presidents feel about their proposals and how much political capital they are willing to invest in them. There are many veto points at which legislation can be derailed or modified substantially. The White House must consider partisan, ideological, and regional perspectives, address constituency interests, and accommodate personal considerations of members of Congress.

Prioritizing enables presidents to take the policy initiative, frame the issue, shape press coverage, involve the public, and do so in a way that generates pressure on Congress. It also enables an administration to focus its energies on what presidents consider most important, resolve executive infighting, and direct White House re-sources to where they will do the most good (Light 1982, 158). Finally, setting priorities can facilitate coalition building, a process that is both time and labor intensive.

Presidential scholar Paul C. Light lauds the strategy that the Reagan administra-tion adopted of identifying a few priorities, focusing public attention on them, and cycling them over the course of the congressional calendar (Light 1982, 217–21). In contrast, he warns, waiting too long, inundating Congress with too many proposals at the same time, and not using the president's podium and perquisites to advance the administration's policy are mistakes that Jimmy Carter made that contributed to his poor relations with Congress and perceived lack of success in getting his policy proposals enacted (Jones 1988, 127–8; Light 1982, 44–9,157–8, 218–21).

There is a danger to priority setting, however. It raises the stakes for the president and inflates the consequences of failure. Clinton found this out when his health care reform package died in Congress. The priority he gave to that issue, the involvement of his wife in designing the proposal, and the time and energy his administration devoted to it magnified the political fallout from the failure of Congress to enact the president's plan and probably contributed to the Democrats' defeat in the 1994 midterm elections.

Related to prioritizing is packaging, the process by which proposals are framed to maximize presidential success. The key to packaging from the administration's perspective is getting the congressional leadership to "buy in" to the president's proposal and force centralized consideration of it in as few committees, with as few amendments, and on as few roll-call votes as possible. Offering constituency-oriented earmarks to members of Congress in exchange for their support often bloats the president's proposal, inflates its cost, and may delay its enactment.

The tactic of packaging works best for an administration at the beginning of its first term in office when presidents are most likely to receive the benefit of doubt from the public and members of Congress. Thus Reagan was able to keep his budget and tax proposals intact and get Congress to vote them up or down in the first years of his administration. When an administration is weak, however, it is Congress that creates the package, such as a continuing resolution to prevent the president from excising objectionable items. Presidents tend to face a congressional packaging problem more at the end of their term than at the start of it.

Prioritizing and packaging have lent themselves to qualitative analysis based largely on interview data (Wayne 1978, 128–33; Light 1982, 154–68), the accounts of participants observers (O'Brien 1974), and journalistic reports, but not to systematic quantitative analysis (see however, Felt 1992, 896–920). Although such strategic and tactical decisions are considered important to legislative success, their effect on congressional policy outcomes has been difficult to document, much less measure.

Timing

A fourth strategic decision that presidents must make is when to propose various parts of their agenda. Here they face a paradox. New presidents need time to increase their legislative effectiveness to acquire information, develop expertise, refine their proposals, and introduce them to Congress in a manner that increases their prospects for passage (Light 1982, 16–25). Yet a president's political capital in Congress declines over the course of an administration, especially in the second term. How to overcome the increasing effectiveness-decreasing political capital cycle is a agenda-setting paradox with which presidents must contend. Paul C. Light, who first presented this paradox in his book *The President's Agenda*, believes that presidents have little choice but to adopt a "move it or lose it" strategy (Light 1982, 33).

James P. Pfiffner also stresses the need to move quickly and "strike while the iron is hot" in his book *The Strategic Presidency*. Pfiffner argues that the early actions of a new administration are crucial (Pfiffner 1996, 112). Both Light and Pfiffner quote administration insiders as oracles of the 'hitting the ground running' philosophy. Their argument is based on the assumption that presidents are likely to encounter their most favorable political environment when they are first elected.

George C. Edwards III and Andrew Barrett confirm that presidents propose more policy initiatives to the first Congress they face than to the second (Edwards and Barrett 2000, 126). Barbara Sinclair also noted, "presidents have been highly prominent agenda setters in their first Congress and less so later in their terms" (Sinclair 2000, 142). Edwards and Barrett also found that control of government affects the scope of agenda setting. Presidential initiatives decline but congressional initiatives increase during a presidential term when partisan control of government is divided; when government is unified, the initiatives of both president and Congress decline in the second part of the president's term (Edwards and Barrett 2000, 126).

Presidents also move quickly to extend the political momentum generated by their election campaign into the governing arena. They wish to claim an electoral mandate, if possible, to add legitimacy and build support for their policy initiatives.

Although most presidential scholars do not give much credibility to the mandate claim (Dahl 1990, 355–72; Edwards 1980, 147–66; Rudalevidge 2005, 434–6), presidents still claim them. Examples include Johnson's pledge to pursue civil rights and social welfare programs and Reagan's to reduce the role of government in the domestic arena (Conley 2001, 86–115). On the other hand, George W. Bush's misreading of his 2004 win led him to pursue policies that had little public support, such as privatization of Social Security, immigration reform, and increasing troop levels in Iraq.[2]

To summarize, presidents try to influence Congress's agenda by establishing their policy priorities and introducing them at opportune points during the congressional law-making process. They try to take advantage of their election victories, and the most favorable partisan composition of Congress they are likely to encounter, by moving quickly on their most important initiatives, packaging them astutely, and cycling others over the course of the congressional calendar. The fewer the issues at any one time with which a president has to deal, the greater the attention and resources an administration can devote to them. Although such an effort enhances the chances for a successful policy outcome, it also raises the stakes for a president, making the final disposition of the issue a more important criterion for evaluating the president's legislative skills.

Evaluating Agenda Success

How successful have presidents been in getting their agenda adopted? They have been very successful in getting Congress to consider their agenda but less successful in getting it enacted into law. In their study of presidential agenda setting in Congress from 1953 to 1996, Edwards and Barrett report that presidents succeeded in actually achieving passage of only about half of the potentially significant items they propose during periods of unified government, but only a little more than one-fourth during periods of divided government (Edwards and Barrett 2000, 122–3). The authors calculate the overall success of presidents in getting their policy initiatives enacted into law as 42 percent; Congress's success rate for its own initiatives was less, only 25 percent (Edwards and Barrett 2000, 128). In situations of divided government, however, the records of the president and Congress are about the same. The authors conclude that presidents lead Congress under conditions of unified government but share power and policy outcomes more evenly during periods of divided government (Edwards and Barrett 2000, 131–3; Taylor 1988, 378–90; Sinclair 2004, 150–1).

Mark Peterson, using a different definition of significant legislation than Edwards and Barrett, found that Congress acted on 75 percent of the proposals presidents submitted to Congress between 1953 and 1984 (Peterson 1990, 96). Of these, Congress took serious action on 86 percent of the most important legislation presidents

---

[2] In a press conference held two days after the 2004 election, Bush said: "I've earned political capital in this election. And I am going to spend it for what I told the people I'd spend it on, which is, you've heard, the agenda: Social Security, tax reform, moving this economy forward, education, fighting and winning the war on terror" (George W. Bush, "Press Conference," Nov. 4, 2004).

introduced and 46 percent on less important presidential initiatives. Presidents were more successful on their major proposals, receiving all or part of what they requested 60 percent of the time, compared to 39 percent for their minor proposals (Peterson 1990, 157). Proposals entailing large policy changes were also more likely to receive congressional consideration than those proposing smaller changes, particularly if the matter had been considered by previous Congresses (Peterson 1990, 154). Peterson also states, however, that there was greater consensus on small proposals than larger ones (Peterson 1990, 154–5).

Andrew Rudalevige, who has also researched the impact of presidential proposals in Congress, had results that were similar to those of Peterson and Edwards and Barrett. During the second half of the twentieth century, he found that nine out of ten presidential proposals got at least a committee hearing and eight out of ten received serious consideration (Rudalevige 2005, 428). Of those that Congress considered, "presidents got basically what they wanted in a little less than 30 percent of cases, garnering substantial victories on another 20 percent" (Rudalevige 2005, 432). Rudalevige concluded that presidents may not be able to tell members of Congress what to think but they can tell them what to think about (Rudalevige 2005, 428).

In summary, presidents provide Congress with a legislative agenda, but only part of that agenda gets enacted into law, more when the government is unified than when it is divided (Steger 1997, 17–36), more in times of crises than during periods of politics as usual (Edwards and Wayne 2006, 507), more in foreign policy than in domestic affairs (Wildavsky 1966, 7–14; Shull 1991; Rudalevige 2005, 438), and more on relatively simple, smaller, less complicated, and less controversial bills than on the larger, more complex, innovative, and controversial measures (Peterson 1990, 154–7; Rudalevige 2005, 432).

What explains the varying levels of presidential agenda success? Is it skills alone or are these skills contingent on other factors such as the partisan composition and ideological orientation of Congress, public demands and pressures for specific policies, the popularity of the president or of the policy being proposed, and the services that presidents provide, or the size and proximity of the president's electoral victory?

Most political scientists believe that the political environment in which skills are excised has much to do with whether they are used successfully or not (Edwards 1989, 175–85; Bond and Fleisher 1990, 196–234). How skills and contingency factors interact to affect congressional voting behavior, however, has not received the same amount of attention by political scientists examining presidential influence in Congress. One reason, already noted, is that the exercise of legislative skills is not always observable, much less measurable (Fleisher, Bond, and Wood 2008, 192). Another is that the effect of the same skills differs from member to member and Congress to Congress. A third problem stems from the difficulty of systematically studying the impact of skills over time and across congresses. As a consequence, some political scientists have resorted to studying the impact of legislative skills indirectly, inferring skills from a president's general reputation and correlating that reputation, skilled or unskilled, with congressional voting patterns (Edwards 1989, 175–85; Bond and Fleisher 1990, 196–234).

Another tack has been to develop models that explain and predict when members are most likely to follow the president's lead and when they are not. In developing one such model, Charles Cameron and Jee-Kwang Park identify three causal mechanisms that create incentives for members of Congress to go along with presidential policy initiatives: burden sharing, executive coordination, and information superiority (Cameron and Park 2008, 56–9).

The authors contend presidents can do heavy lifting for members of Congress. By drafting legislation, incorporating executive branch expertise into it, and mounting a public campaign, presidents relieve members of Congress of some of their policy-making chores, giving them more time to address constituency issues which have bigger personal and political pay-offs for them. An administration can also better focus congressional and public attention on an issue and oversee and coordinate its consideration in two houses by multiple committees in a manner that helps to foster a desirable policy outcome. All of these presidential capacities benefit Congress collectively and some members individually. The services presidents provide reduce congressional input into legislative policy that the president desires, thereby producing a more favorable policy outcome from the president's perspective (Cameron and Park 2008, 59–76).

Position Taking

For presidents to influence Congress, legislators and their staff need to know the administration's positions on a wide range of issues. Where a president stands is critical information to legislators when they are considering legislation. The absence of a presidential position on pending bills or the failure to communicate one is normally interpreted as a sign of indifference by the administration and as a green light for Congress to work its will (Wayne 1978, 167).

The White House is not shy about making its opinions known, however. Since the Carter administration, the Office of Management and Budget (OMB), working closely with the executive departments and agencies and policy advisers in the White House, has issued Statements of Administration Policy (SAPs) on legislation as it moves from committee to the floors of both houses. Drafted by the relevant department, agency, or occasionally by the OMB, the SAP is coordinated and cleared within the executive branch and then communicated directly to Congress. It also appears on the OBM website.

Most statements indicate how strongly the administration feels about the decisions made on legislation. For example, the administration of George W. Bush strongly supported legislation drafted in the Republican-controlled House of Representatives that transformed his key first-term education, tax, and national security initiatives into law, but strongly opposed bills that would have curtailed or reversed the administration's policy on abortion, public–private competition (competitive sourcing), and sanctions imposed against Castro's Cuba (Wayne, unpublished research).

In addition to presenting general support or opposition of the legislative draft, the administration may also signal its concern about a constitutional issue, usually one in which the president believes that Congress has overstepped its authority, thereby restricting the executive's power to conduct foreign policy, manage the executive branch, or implement legislation. If Congress fails to modify or delete the objectionable item, the president may still approve the legislation but signal his displeasure in a signing statement that indicates how the administration intends to interpret and implement the law. Such statements reinforce the intent and effect of SAPs over the long haul. They indicate how far presidents are prepared to go to achieve their legislative objectives and prevent Congress from encroaching on executive authority. During his first six years in office, George W. Bush challenged over 800 provisions of legislative acts he signed into law, exercising in effect a line-item veto and generating considerable consternation in Congress (Savage 2006, A7).

Threatening Vetoes

Presidents have a more powerful tool than constitutional interpretations, however. They can threaten to veto legislation if it contains provisions to which they object. The threat of a veto is designed to give the president leverage in negotiations with Congress. The more Congress wants or needs to enact the legislation, the more influential a veto threat becomes.

President Clinton used the veto threat very effectively with the Republican-controlled Congress on appropriation bills after the closure of government in the winter of 1995–6. Similarly, President George W. Bush threatened to veto 145 bills during his first six years in office, bills that would have overturned agency rules, prevented public–private competition for federal contracts, and weakened, delayed, and repealed the military base closing bill known by its initials, BRAC. He actually vetoed twelve bills during his two terms in office (The American Presidency Project 2009).

Veto threats come in two forms: either the possibility of a veto is raised or one is promised if objectionable provisions remain in the legislation. In its first five years, the Bush administration promised to veto ten appropriation and four authorization bills that contained provisions or proposed amendments that would have reversed its policies on abortion, stem cell research, and sanctions against the government of Fidel Castro in Cuba.

For veto threats to work they have to be credible; in other words, presidents must follow through on them. Clinton's vetoes of a budget reconciliation bill in 2005, which closed the government, and his determination not to approve appropriations that short-changed his health, education, and environmental priorities as well as his two vetoes of what he considered draconian Republican welfare legislation, reinforced subsequent veto threats he made. In contrast, President George W. Bush's approval, over the objections of senior aides, of legislation that exceeded his budget requests undercut further the credibility of similar threats as long as the president's party controlled Congress.

Unified government creates far fewer incentives for presidents to veto legislation than does divided government. Charles Cameron estimated that presidents threatened vetoes on 14 percent of the legislation Congress considered between 1945 and 1996.

Of these, less than 4 percent occurred during periods of unified government; 23 percent occurred during divided government (Cameron 2000, 188).

With government mostly divided between 1968 and 2002, veto threats have become the rule and not the exception, according to Professor Barbara Sinclair (Sinclair 2000, 145). She notes that the George H. W. Bush administration threatened to veto over half the major legislative matters that the Democratically controlled Congress considered during that president's first two years in office, while Clinton threatened vetoes on 60 percent of the bills considered by the first two GOP-controlled congresses he faced from 1995 to 1998 (Sinclair 2000, 145).

Veto threats work, according to political scientists who have studied their impact. Charles Cameron concluded that they bring concessions, which, in turn, deter actual vetoes (Cameron 2000, 192). Barbara Sinclair found presidents to be more supportive of legislation at the end of the process than during the committee phase. She attributes this support to changes in the legislation that made it more palatable to the president. Bills that raised the possibility of a presidential veto had a greater likelihood of being changed in a manner that suited the president. Sinclair contends that the veto threat is effective because it moves legislation in the direction of the preferred position of the president (Sinclair 2000, 146–7). In the absence of such a threat, such movement will not usually occur (Sinclair 2004, 96).

Sometimes exercising a veto threat in private can be more effective than doing it in public because it facilitates behind-the-scenes bargaining and allows members of Congress to compromise with the president without looking weak in the process. Richard S. Conley found that President George H. W. Bush had more success with the 102nd Democratic Congress when the administration threatened quietly to veto relatively minor or ordinary legislation than when it went public with the threat. When the private negotiations stall or fail, however, the president has little choice but to go public to reinforce the seriousness of his position (Conley 2003, 736–50).

INTERPERSONAL TACTICS

Presidents and their aides also need to interact with members of Congress, particularly the leadership, if they are to be successful legislative presidents. They must make information available to Congress, attend to the needs and wishes of members with whom they must work, particularly committee chairs, and permit congressional input into executive policy making. Failure to reach out to Congress lessens the likelihood that their proposals will become public policy in the form and content they desire (Wayne 2006, 14–18). In the words of Lyndon Johnson: "There is only one way for a President to deal with Congress, and that is continuously, incessantly, and without interruption" (Kearns 1976, 226).

Contact and Consultation

Personal contact by a president and senior White House aides is a congressional expectation, one that tends to be highlighted in news media coverage (Edwards 1989, 117–18, 199–201; Christenson 1982, 255–6; Andres and Griffin 2006, 111–12). Keeping in close touch with the congressional leadership that directs, amplifies, and builds support for the president's initiatives is also expected (Wayne 1978, 149–50). Whether a president chooses to consult with the partisan or bipartisan leadership depends of the nature of the president's proposal and the strategic approach the White House has taken, the partisan composition of Congress, and the nature of the policy issue under consideration.

Contemporary vice presidents are also expected to play a key role in meeting with their party's congressional leadership, attending party caucuses, and applying muscle on the president's behalf. They convey their administration's perspective on legislation, assess the overall partisan support for presidential proposals and positions, and negotiate, especially if they came to the vice presidency with congressional experience. Vice President Richard Cheney was instrumental in working out a compromise on the legislation to establish a national intelligence director when House Republicans in 2004 threatened to gut a House–Senate compromise that President Bush publicly supported.

The White House office that orchestrates the administration's campaign on Capitol Hill as well as maintains ongoing contacts with rank-and-file members of Congress is the Office of Legislative Affairs. First established during the Eisenhower administration, the office's primary job is to improve the atmosphere for the president on Capitol Hill. Specific functions include identifying the positions of members on pending legislation, arranging for congressional input into White House decision making, and helping members of Congress with constituency-related problems (Wayne 1978, 139–68; Collier 1997, 16–18). The office also works with executive department and agency liaison agents to coordinate the legislative activities of the executive branch and to ensure that their policy initiatives and positions comply with the president's. "We didn't want secretaries to cut separate deals with Republican chairs who had oversight over them," said Pat Griffin, who headed the Clinton liaison operation during part of the president's first term (Griffin 2001).

A critical task for the president's legislative representatives is to keep tabs on congressional sentiment on key issues. They do so by working closely with their party's respective whips in the House and Senate, and occasionally with outside lobbyists representing groups that support the president's policy initiative. If congressional backing is uncertain, liaison aides may even generate a test vote by getting a "friendly" member to offer an amendment to indicate congressional sentiment on the issue.

With the exception of the congressional leadership, members of Congress must go through the White House Legislative Affairs Office to reach the president. Liaison aides arrange for telephone calls, group meetings, even informal occasions in which members communicate directly with the president. The office also disburses invitations to state dinners and other White House social events, seats in the president's box at the Kennedy Center, and even presidential souvenirs such as signing pens, cuff links, Christmas cards, and anniversary and birthday letters to constituents. For most members of Congress, such personal niceties mean a lot (Wayne 1978, 172; Collier 1997, 18; Andres and Griffin 2006, 111–12).

From an administration's perspective, members of Congress require constant "care and feeding." Anecdotal evidence suggests that the failure to reach out to members and address their personal and constituency needs can cost a president dearly. Nixon's increasing isolation from Congress and the low priority he placed on legislative interaction (Wayne 1978, 157, 160), Carter's refusal to engage in "politics as usual" with members of Congress (Wayne 1978, 212; Jones 1988, 104–5, 143–9), and the closed, secretive, non-consultative manner in which the White House of George W. Bush operated during his first term (Wayne 2006, 14–18) were resented by members of Congress and subsequently affected their cooperation with the White House.

Not only must presidents and their aides consult with members of Congress, but they must also consult widely within and outside the government. According to Andrew Rudalevige, how presidential initiatives are developed within the executive branch affects their legislative outcome. Looking at the impact of the growth and institutionalization of the presidency's internal policy-making structures and processes, Rudalevige found that the greater the centralization in the formulation of policy, the less likely the legislation Congress enacts would conform to the president's initial policy proposal (Rudalevige 2002, 134–51). Wide consultation inside and outside of the executive branch increases the chances for legislative enactment and minimizes the need to modify the proposal (Rudalevige 2002, 15, 113–23).

Rudalevige's conclusion is illustrated by the failure of the Clinton administration to consult with health care professions, the private health care industry, and Republican congressional staff during the period when the health care reform package was being developed. In the words of journalists Haynes Johnson and David Broder who evaluated the reasons that the legislation was unsuccessful in a Democratically controlled Congress:

The biggest mistake of all may have been the President's decision that the way to handle this issue was with a White House task force headed by his wife and his Oxford classmate ... Had Clinton ... instead awarded the job to the Health and Human Services Department ... the process would probably have followed traditional Washington patterns. Political appointees—many with extensive background in health policy—would have hooked up with the career officials in the department to assemble the options for review by the secretary. The "policy networks" would have spring to life. Think tank authors, academics, congressional staffers, and others would have put their ears to the meeting room walls and slipped their memos under the doors. So would staffs of the myriad interest groups with a stake in the policy.

(Johnson and Broder 1996, 112)

Bargaining and Compromising

Persuasion is still a principal way in which an administration tries to affect the voting decisions of individual members of Congress on issues of importance to the president.

Narrowing the playing field is essential. Presidents have neither the time, energy, nor need to persuade 535 members of Congress. On most issues they can depend on a core of partisan supporters and write off a core of opponents from the other party. The trick is to identify those who have not made up their mind and determine what it will take to get them on board. Frequently, members of Congress, especially from the president's own party, will feign neutrality, indecision, or even opposition in order to obtain something from the White House (Sullivan 1990, 1177, 1185).

It is the task of the White House Office of Legislative Affairs to identify these potentially "persuadable" members, their qualms about the proposal, and what they want in exchange for supporting the president's initiative. When Senators and Representatives go public with their views, positions harden and finding common ground becomes more difficult, especially within a highly polarized political environment.

Deal making can be a complex undertaking. Much depends on structuring the alternatives for members of Congress to make the proposal that the president supports the most acceptable one for most legislators intent on enacting legislation (Rudalevige 2005, 436).

Rewards and Sanctions

Presidents also have a variety of "goodies" to dispense. They can provide information, share the news media's spotlight, and acknowledge the contribution of certain members of Congress. Political favors include visiting constituencies, promising support for members' own pet projects, and aiding fellow partisans in reelection. Helping opposition party members is riskier, however, because it can strengthen the opposition and alienate the president's congressional supporters (Edwards 1989, 193).

Threatening or exercising sanctions is more problematic, in part because presidents lack such sanctions and in part because they do not usually work. The autonomy of congressional elections and the advantages of incumbents render most members of Congress invulnerable to the White House's political muscle. In fact, standing firm against the president on a policy that is not popular within a member's district or Senator's state is often regarded as a badge of courage, not a sign of betrayal, by those who count the most: constituents.

Personal attacks and slights emanating from the White House can also be dysfunctional. They are not taken lightly or easily forgotten by elected officials, who tend to be very sensitive to how they are perceived in public. Take the case of then Democratic senator Richard Shelby of Alabama, who criticized the components of Clinton's deficit reduction bill at a joint news conference with Vice President Al Gore standing at his side. The White House, furious with Shelby, had the OMB announce a transfer of 100 jobs from the NASA facility at Huntsville, Alabama, to the Johnson Space Center in Houston. Adding insult to injury, Senator Shelby was given only one ticket to a White House event honoring his alma mater's championship football team, the University of Alabama, while the state's other Senator was given eleven. The following year Shelby switched his allegiance to the Republican Party.

Although the circumstances were different, the end was the same for James Jeffords, Republican Senator from Vermont, whose attempts to amend the President Bush's "No Child Left Behind" proposal and extend the New England Compact on milk prices were rejected by the administration. Jeffords also was not invited to the Teacher of the Year ceremony at the White House honoring a Vermont educator. He subsequently defected from the Republican Party in June of 2001, voting to reorganize the Senate under Democratic control.

White House aides know their limits. In the words of Lawrence F. O'Brien who headed legislative affairs for John F. Kennedy and Lyndon B. Johnson, "I never expected any member to commit political suicide in order to help the President, no matter how noble our cause. I expected politicians to be concerned with their own interests: I only hoped to convince them our interests were often the same" (O'Brien 1974, 118).

Compromising on the scope and substance can be a more acceptable way for an administration to achieve legislative goals (Edwards 1989, 190–1). A problem with compromise is that it may dilute the president's initiative, anger his electoral supporters, even project an image of weakness which can damage a president's reputation and reduce his political capital later on. On the other hand, having a bully pulpit enables the president to present the compromise in favorable way to the public, take credit for the outcome, and improve relations with some members of Congress in the process.

EVALUATING THE IMPACT OF LEGISLATIVE SKILLS

Do the president's legislative skills really make a difference in what Congress does? Presidents and their White Houses obviously believe that they do since they devote considerable time, energy, and resources to the task of persuading Congress and the American people of the merits of their proposals. Nor would they need a White House legislative liaison office to lobby the Hill, a communications office to mount a public relations, issue-oriented campaign, or senior aides to organize a behind-the-scenes lobbying effort on their behalf.

Moreover, most members of Congress behave as if what the president says and does matters. They ritually complain when they perceive that the president neglects them or takes them for granted. Although they expect the president to propose policy initiatives, they also want to be consulted before that process reaches fruition. Moreover, they desire presidential support for their own legislative goals because such support improves the likelihood of success. Similarly, they want to avoid presidential opposition, particularly a veto on their pet constituency projects.

Although members of Congress are not likely to admit that presidential arm twisting was a principal factor in affecting their vote, they still assume that the president will be actively engaged in mobilizing support for his key policy proposals (Wayne 1978, 167).

There are numerous anecdotal examples to which lobbyists, executive branch officials, and, especially, liaison aides can point that illustrate the proposition that a president's legislative skills contribute to his administration's policy success (Andres and Griffin 2006, 761–70). Political scientists, however, are more skeptical about the extent of a president's personal influence and its impact on the overall support presidents receive in Congress.

Researchers who have applied quantitative methodologies to study congressional voting behavior have not discovered much evidence of a presidential imprint coming from the exercise of legislative skills. Aage R. Clausen found very little presidential influence on congressional voting decisions. In a study of roll-call votes in five major issue areas between 1953 and 1964, Clausen discovered presidential influence in only one of them, international intervention. In the other four issue areas he examined, civil liberties, agricultural assistance, social welfare, and government management, he noted that partisanship and constituency were the principal factors associated with congressional voting behavior (Clausen 1973, 222–30).

John W. Kingdon also studied congressional voting decisions. His data, however, came primarily from interviews with members of Congress and their staffs. Kingdon's respondents indicated relatively little presidential influence compared with the influence which they claimed fellow members and their own constituents exerted on them (Kingdon 1984, 20). Kingdon's study revealed that representatives of the same party as the president, particularly junior members, tended to pay more attention to the administration's arguments than do more senior members (Kingdon 1984, 190–1).

Similarly, presidential scholar George C. Edwards III's study of congressional roll calls on which presidents took positions concluded that presidents regarded as most skillful did not receive more support from members of Congress than those reputed to be less skillful. Edwards found the partisan identification of members and, to a lesser extent, the popularity of the president to have a greater effect on how members of Congress voted than did presidential position taking. On the basis of his analysis, Edwards concluded that presidents tend to be influential at the margins, not on most votes of most legislators on most issues (Edwards 1989, 212).

Jon Bond and Richard Fleisher also found little systemic evidence to support the legislative skills hypothesis. In their research Bond and Fleisher established a base line of support that presidents could expect to receive given the partisan composition of Congress, the popularity of the president, and the time frame within a term when the initiative was advanced (Bond and Fleisher 1990, 196–219). Analyzing important votes and close votes in which the margin of victory was 10 percent or less for each year from 1953 to 1984, Bond and Fleisher found no systematic effect of legislative skills on policy output (Bond and Fleisher 1990, 206–19). Although their analysis does not refute the thesis entirely, it does cast doubt on its validity (Bond and Fleisher 1990, 218–19).

Bond and Fleisher's analysis indicates that partisanship and ideology are more important influences and better explanations of presidential success or failure in

Congress (Bond and Fleisher 1990, 221–3). In fact, the authors go on to argue that the more polarized the political environment, the less the president's legislative skills should matter, given the importance of partisanship and the decline in the number of moderate, centrist legislators who presumably would have been more open than their more ideological colleagues to presidential persuasion (Bond and Fleisher 2000, 210). Unlike Edwards, however, Bond and Fleisher did not find presidential popularity to be a major contributor to favorable legislative outcomes for presidents.

STUDYING LEGISLATIVE SKILLS:
METHODOLOGICAL AND
SUBSTANTIVE ISSUES

Why the divergence of opinion on the importance of presidents' legislative skills on policy outcomes in Congress? Much has to do with the goals and perspective of the researchers and with their methods of analysis.

Case Studies: Strengths and Weaknesses

Practitioners that have participated in the policy processes, journalists covering day-to-day events, and scholars examining individual cases generally take a presidential-centered approach. They focus on presidential actions (cause) to explain congressional reactions (effect). These students of the presidency tend to examine a single or small set of policy proposals with which they are familiar. Those proposals tend to be the important presidential priorities, ones to which White Houses have devoted considerable time and resources, and often ones that have generated considerable controversy in Congress.

These authors frequently describe the cases in great detail. They note and evaluate deliberations in committees on the floors of the House and Senate; explain modifications to the president's proposals largely as a consequence of presidential interventions; and attribute presidential policy successes or failures to these interventions and to the legislative skills the president, top White House aides, and cabinet officials exert.

The advantage of the case study approach is that it presents an insider's perspective, describes the multiplicity of forces that affect legislative decision making, and suggests how these forces, singularly and together, contribute to the how and why of congressional policy judgments. Case studies try to mirror reality by showing its complexity. They have been used effectively to study presidential decision making on policy and organization (Allison 1971; Porter 1980; Burke and Greenstein 1989; Johnson and Broder 1996; Woodward 2004).

The principal disadvantage of case studies is the difficulty of generalizing from one case to another. Researchers choose cases to examine because of their importance, not because of their representative character. These cases usually involve major decisions, those in which the president is more likely to be actively involved. Moreover, the detail in which authors describe such cases usually emphasizes their distinctive features as opposed to their underlying commonalities. It becomes difficult to tell the forest from the trees.

Case studies do not facilitate theory building, although they may illustrate theories and may also be used to disconfirm them. Richard E. Neustadt used case studies to illustrate his insights about presidential power (Neustadt 1960), and Irving Janis detailed several case studies to support his conception of "groupthink" and its dangers (Janis 1982).

Another problem with reliance on cases is that the description and analysis often tend to be highly subjective. Inferences about casual behavior—the impact of a presidential conversation, promise, or deal—may be incorrect, can be self-serving, and naturally are limited by the perspective of the person making them.

Quantitative Studies: Strengths and Weaknesses

The goals of most political scientists are different from those of reporters and participant observers. Political scientists wish to generalize about behavior over time and among presidents and congresses. To do so, they need to examine hundreds, even thousands, of cases that reflect the same type of observable behavior, and then, using statistical methods, discern what those cases have in common. They have to simplify the cases they study to find commonalities, thereby eliminating much of the rich detail that accompanies the case study approach and situates those studies within a real world context.

The principal data on which political scientists rely when studying congressional voting decisions are recorded roll calls that occur in committees and on the floor. These votes are part of the public record, easily accessible to scholars, and amenable to statistical analysis. They also constitute an important set of legislative policy judgments, judgments on which the president's opinion is usually known.

Scholars aggregate roll-call votes by party, ideology, and region to discern patterns of decision making. In doing so, they provide a congressionally centered explanation of presidential effectiveness in contrast to the more issue-specific, presidential-centered approach that case studies adopt.

One issue that researchers must address is how to categorize and evaluate the individual roll calls and the members who voted on them. Vote categorization may be done on the basis of importance (key votes), closeness, subject matter (foreign or domestic), partisanship (party unity), and members can be categorized by party, ideology, region, years of service, electoral margin of victory, to name but a few of the more popular categories. Researchers usually evaluate the individual votes that comprise a set of roll calls equally, whether the set be key votes, close votes, partisan votes, or all votes (but see Edwards 1989; Bond and Fleischer 1990).

Methodological Problems

From the president's perspective, weighing all roll calls in a particular set as equal is problematic. With limited time, multiple responsibilities, many constituencies, and ever-changing issues that they must address, presidents do not have the time, energy, or even incentive to involve themselves continuously and deeply on all bills that come before Congress. Nor do they have the political capital to do so. As a consequence, the White House chooses its priorities carefully on the basis of its promises, political needs, and the partisan environment in which it finds itself. Once the priorities are determined, the White House usually orchestrates a campaign to get them adopted, using those legislative skills they think they will be most effective on members identified by their liaison aides as targets of opportunity.

Similarly, presidents act in discrete ways to affect specific bills at different stages of their consideration, not solely at the end when Congress votes on the legislation. They strike when the iron is hot or when they must do so to preempt or prevent Congress from enacting policies they oppose. Nor are the skills they use the same from administration to administration. Different presidents in different situations facing different political environments use different skills, sometimes in different ways. For these reasons, analyses of roll calls are not apt to highlight, much less find, a presidential needle in a haystack of congressional votes.

Scholars need to evaluate skills on the basis of their actual use, not simply the position taken by the president. Although position taking indicates an administration's policy preferences, it does not indicate the priorities the White Houses attaches to those preferences or the level of involvement of presidents and their top aides in getting congressional support.

Identifying an administration's priorities is not difficult. Most of them are part of the public record; they have been trumpeted in campaigns, press releases, presidential interviews, major addresses, and formal messages to Congress.

Ordering these priorities is another matter. Presidential candidates and even presidents themselves may be purposely ambiguous in establishing priority preferences so as not to alienate any of their electoral constituencies, give themselves more flexibility in dealing with Congress, and also to enlarge their discretion if public moods change and new issues arise.

Monitoring presidential interactions with Congress is another problem if those interactions are not made in the public arena. Telephone conversations, private correspondence, and impromptu meetings are difficult to identify, much less measure. Moreover, as noted previously, the initial inclinations of members toward the legislation before administrations try to exert influence may not be known.

Professor Terry Sullivan tried to tackle this latter problem by using White House whip counts, found in the Johnson Library, to discern the positions of members of Congress before the administration's congressional campaign got under way. But Sullivan found that the whip counts were not necessarily reliable. Members of Congress, particularly those of the president's party, often feigned positions to maximize their leverage in bargaining with the White House (Sullivan 1990, 1167–95).

Of course, there are also many sequential hurdles to overcome before a bill becomes a law in the committees and subcommittees, party caucuses, and with party leaders, in the decisions that affect floor consideration, the deliberations on the floor itself, and often, the House–Senate conferences that work out the differences in the bills that the two houses have passed. In addition, researchers need to consider substantive and stylistic changes in the legislation and the extent to which those changes contribute to or detract from the president's policy proposals as these proposals move through the legislative process.

The problems associated with ordering presidential priorities, identifying White House–congressional interactions, noting and evaluating the give and take that is part of the policy-making processes, and, especially, developing operational indicators of legislative skills and measures of their impact have led some researchers to use the legislative reputation of presidents as a basis for inferring their skills. They then test the validity of these inferences by examining patterns of congressional voting behavior to discern whether presidents deemed to be more skillful have had more legislative success, defined in terms of the level of support they receive on legislation on which they have taken a position. (Edwards 1989; Bond and Fleisher 1990). Although this research design does not directly test the skills hypothesis, it does indicate the limited systematic effect of the president's legislative skills on congressional voting behavior.

The skills research conundrum suggests that scholars will continue to debate the merits of the various approaches and methods by which legislative skills can be studied. This debate cannot help but affect the conception and practice of presidential leadership in Congress: the promises presidents make, the tactics they use, and the claims and blame they assert after the policy outcome is determined. The more frustrated or unsuccessful presidents are in their legislative leadership role, the more likely they will turn to the unilateral exercise of executive authority and to public relations campaigns to hype the issue on their own behalf.

IMPLICATIONS FOR PRESIDENTIAL LEADERSHIP

The limitations that the constitutional, institutional, and political systems impose on the exercise of presidential power in Congress create a variety of leadership problems for presidents. They widen the gap between promises and performance. The congressional hurdles that presidents must overcome increase the need for executive-initiated coalition building and for executive resources to be devoted to this task. They also increase the temptation for presidents to use unilateral instruments to achieve their policy goals and reinforce their leadership image. Finally, the ongoing problems of getting Congress to follow the president's lead provide incentives for suspending "politics as usual" and introducing crisis rhetoric as a means of enhancing presidential support. Crisis policy making undercuts the balance built into the constitutional system; it constrains and hurries the deliberations which the Framers believed would improve public policy outcomes; and it reduces the number of policy makers and the variety of interests and views that they represent.

Creating Unrealistic Expectations

If presidents' legislative skills have a marginal effect on legislative outcomes, then presidents and their aides should try to reduce public and congressional expectations. Such a reduction, however, would conflict with their political need to articulate a broad-based program that appeals to their electoral coalitions and project a strong leadership image. It might also conflict with the country's policy needs at any one point in time. The failure to address these needs promptly and effectively would probably contribute to greater public cynicism and more mistrust of government, particularly by those who are most directly and adversely affected by the issue. It might also run counter to the personal ambitions of presidents and their aides.

Increasing Organizational Demands

If policy and leadership expectations cannot be reduced, then presidents need to devote greater effort and more resources to their legislative activities. These efforts and resources would naturally take away from other presidential leadership roles and staffing needs, and, conceivably, from other internal and external institutional relationships.

Greater efforts at coalition building would probably involve the White House and executive departments in more extensive and constant campaigns and more interaction with organized interests, which in turn would undoubtedly fuel the public's perception of a government of, by, and for the special interests. The separation between the public and private might become less clear and, correspondingly, conflicts of interest more pronounced. Such conflicts could negatively impact on government recruitment and also on public trust of government.

The bottom line is that presidents would have to expand their efforts to extend their reach in the legislative arena. However, extending reach and gaining results may not go hand in hand because of the autonomy of institutional structures and incentives, the advantages of incumbency, and separate election cycles and political constituencies.

Encouraging Presidential Unilateralism

Scholars have pointed to increased presidential policy making that utilizes unilateral instruments of executive power (Mayer 2001; Howell 2003; Howell and Kriner 2008,

105–44). Lack of legislative influence is one incentive for using unilateral powers. The prospect of legislative gridlock is another. A third motivation would be to preempt congressional action (Howell and Kriner 2008, 112).

Increased reliance on unilateral executive authority, however, usually extends executive privilege, limits information available to Congress and the public, shortens the time frame for decisions, increases the partisan and ideological content of those decisions, and reduces the number of participants in the executive decision-making process—all undesirable consequences from the perspective of proponents of greater government visibility, more congressional involvement, less partisan and ideological policy judgments, and greater propensity for compromise and finding common ground among those with diverse views and interests. More presidential unilateralism would increase institutional rivalry between president and Congress, thereby making the president's job more difficult, reducing not increasing his political capital in Congress, and continuing the strident political rhetoric that has characterized Washington politics for the last three decades.

Elevating Problems to Crises

Suspending the normal give and take of everyday politics by describing policy issues as crises or declaring war on the problem has been another presidential tact that has followed from the executive's weakness in Congress. When the stakes are unusually high, the time is very short, and the need for action so acute that the legislative process needs to be short-circuited or circumvented, presidents have resorted to crisis rhetoric and unitary decision making as a means of blunting partisan opposition and building bipartisan support. Checks and balances are reduced or suspended, and Congress is expected to follow the leader, the president.

The danger here is obvious. Fewer minds, fewer interests, fewer thought-through consequences result in policy that has not been subjected to sufficient scrutiny nor received sufficient public support. Moreover, the go-along pressures of the moment may impede future criticism. Finally, policy solutions designed and imposed by presidents and their administrations have a greater likelihood of being personalized by those presidents, thereby making policy adjustments more difficult down the road, and if the policy is not viewed as successful, further reducing the president's political capital. Crying wolf too often makes it harder for presidents to deal with future crises when they occur because their credibility has been damaged.

In short, both president and Congress have a stake in making the system work by creating mechanisms for building policy consensus and for bridging the institutional and oftentimes political divide. Failure to do so reinforces the status quo orientation of the constitutional system, reduces trust in government, and encourages presidents to overreach and perhaps even circumvent Congress to redeem their campaign promises and resolve policy issues that become salient during their administrations.

REFERENCES

ALLISON, G. T. 1971. *Essence of Decision: Explaining the Cuban Missile Crisis.* Boston: Little Brown.

American Presidency Project. 2009. University of California, Santa Barbara. <http://www. presidency.ucsb.edu/data/vetoes.php>.

ANDRES, G., and GRIFFIN, P. J. 2006. Successful Influence: Managing Legislative Affairs in the Twenty-First Century. Pp. 141–62 in *Rivals for Power: Presidential–Congressional Relations,* ed. J. A. Thurber. Lanham, MD: Rowman & Littlefield.

BERMAN, L. 1982. *Planning a Tragedy: The Americanization of the War in Vietnam.* New York: Norton.

BOND, J. R., and FLEISHER, R. 1990. *The President in the Legislative Arena.* Chicago: University of Chicago Press.

——— (eds.) 2000. *Polarized Politics: Congress and the President in a Partisan Age.* Washington, DC: Congressional Quarterly.

BURKE, J. P., and GREENSTEIN, F. I. 1989. *How Presidents Test Reality: Decisions on Vietnam, 1954 and 1965.* New York: Russell Sage Foundation.

CAMERON, C. M. 2000. *Veto Bargaining: Presidents and the Politics of Negative Power.* New York: Cambridge University Press.

—— and PARK, J.-K. 2008. A Primer on the President's Legislative Program. Pp. 45–79 in *Presidential Leadership: The Vortex of Power,* ed. B. A. Rockman and R. W. Waterman. Oxford: Oxford University Press,

CHAMBERLAIN, L. H. 1946. *The President, Congress, and Legislation.* New York: Columbia University Press.

CHRISTENSON, R. M. 1982. Presidential Leadership of Congress. Pp. 255–70 in *Rethinking the Presidency,* ed. T. E. Cronin. Boston: Little, Brown,

CLAUSEN, A. R. 1973. *How Congressmen Decide.* New York: St Martin's Press.

COLLIER, K. E. 1997. *Between the Branches: The White House Office of Legislative Affairs.* Pittsburgh: University of Pittsburgh Press.

CONLEY, P. H. 2001. *Presidential Mandates: How Elections Shape the National Agenda.* Chicago: University of Chicago Press.

CONLEY, R. S. 2003. *The Presidency, Congress, and Divided Government: A Postwar Assessment.* College Station: Texas A&M University Press.

CORWIN, E. S. 1984. *The President: Office and Powers, 1987–1984,* 5th edn. New York: New York University Press.

COVINGTON, C. R. 1988. Guess Who's Coming to Dinner? The Distribution of White House Social Invitations and their Effects on Congressional Support. *American Politics Quarterly,* 16: 243–65.

—— WRIGHTON, J. M., and KINNEY, R. 1995. A Presidency-Augmented Model of Presidential Success on House Roll Call Votes. *American Journal of Political Science,* 39: 1001–24.

DAHL, R. A. 1990. Myth of the Presidential Mandate. *Political Science Quarterly,* 105: 355–72.

EDWARDS, G. C. III. 1980. *Presidential Influence in Congress.* San Francisco: W. H. Freeman.

—— 1983a. *The Public Presidency.* New York: St Martin's Press.

—— 1983b. Quantitative Analysis. Pp. 99–124 in *Studying the Presidency,* ed. G. C. Edwards III and S. J. Wayne. Knoxville: University of Tennessee Press.

—— 1989. *At the Margins.* New Haven, CT: Yale University Press.

—— and BARRETT, A. 2000. Presidential Agenda Setting in Congress. Pp. 109–33 in *Polarized Politics: Congress and the President in a Partisan Age,* ed. J. Bond and R. Fleisher. Washington, DC: Congressional Quarterly.

EDWARDS, G. C. III., and WAYNE, S. J. 2009. *Presidential Leadership: Politics and Policy Making*, 8th edn. Belmont, CA: Cengage/Wadsworth.

FELT, P. J. 1992. Truth in Advertising: The Revelation of Presidential Legislative Priorities. *Western Political Quarterly*, 45: 895–920.

FISHER, L. 1985. *Constitutional Conflicts between Congress and the President*. Princeton, NJ: Princeton University Press.

FLEISHER, R., BOND, J. R., and WOOD, B. D. 2008. Which Presidents Are Uncommonly Successful in Congress? Pp. 191–213 in *Presidential Leadership: The Vortex of Power*, ed. B. A. Rockman and R. W. Waterman. Oxford: Oxford University Press.

GLEIBER, D., SHULL, S. A., and WALIGORA, C. A. 1998. Measuring the President's Professional Reputation. *American Politics Quarterly*, 26: 366–85.

GRIFFIN, P. 2001. Conference on the White House Legislative Affairs Office. Miller Center at the University of Virginia.

HOWELL, W. G. 2003. *Power without Persuasion: The Politics of Direct Presidential Action*. Princeton, NJ: Princeton University Press.

—— and KRINER, D. 2008. Power without Persuasion: Identifying Executive Influence. Pp. 105–44 in *Presidential Leadership: The Vortex of Power*, ed. B. A. Rockman and R. W. Waterman. Oxford: Oxford University Press.

JANIS, I. L. 1982. *Groupthink: Psychological Studies of Policy Decisions and Fiascoes*. Boston: Houghton Mifflin.

JOHNSON, H., and BRODER, D. 1996. *The System: The American Way of Politics at the Breaking Point*. Boston: Little, Brown.

JONES, C. O. 1988. *The Trustee Presidency: Jimmy Carter and the United States Congress*. Baton Rouge: Louisiana State University Press.

—— 1994. *The Presidency in a Separated System*. Washington, DC: Brookings.

KEARNS, D. 1976. *Lyndon Johnson and the American Dream*. New York: Harper & Row.

KELLERMAN, B. 1984. *The Political Presidency: Practice of Leadership*. New York: Oxford University Press.

KERNELL, S. 1986. *Going Public: New Strategies of Presidential Leadership*. Washington, DC: CQ Press.

KING, G. 1993. The Methodology of Presidential Research. Pp. 387–412 in *Researching the Presidency*, ed. G. C. Edwards III, J. H. Kessel, and B. A. Rockman. Pittsburgh: Pittsburgh University Press.

KINGDON, J. W. 1984. *Agendas, Alternatives, and Public Policies*. Boston: Little, Brown.

LIGHT, P. C. 1982. *The President's Agenda: Domestic Policy Choice from Kennedy to Carter*. Baltimore: Johns Hopkins University Press.

LOCKERBIE, B., and BORELLI, S. A. 1989. Getting inside the Beltway: Presidential Skill and Success with Congress. *British Journal of Political Science*, 19: 97–106.

McCONNELL, G. 1962. *Steel and the Presidency*. New York: Norton.

MARCUS, M. 1977. *Truman and the Steel Seizure Case: The Limits of Presidential Power*. New York: Columbia University Press.

MAYER, K. 2001. *With the Stroke of a Pen: Executive Orders and Presidential Power*. Princeton, NJ: Princeton University Press.

MAYHEW, D. R. 1991. *Divided We Govern: Party Control, Lawmaking, and Investigations, 1946–1990*. New Haven, CT: Yale University Press.

MOE, T. 1993. Presidents, Institutions, and Theory. Pp. 337–85 in *Researching the Presidency*, ed. G. C. Edwards III, J. H. Kessel, and B. A. Rockman. Pittsburgh: Pittsburgh University Press.

NEUSTADT, R. E. 1960. *Presidential Power: The Politics of Leadership*. New York: John Wiley.

O'BRIEN, L. F. 1974. *No Final Victories*. Garden City, NY: Doubleday.

PAIGE, G. D. 1968. *The Korean Decision*. New York: Free Press.

PETERSON, M. A. 1990. *Legislating Together: The White House and Capitol Hill from Eisenhower to Reagan*. Cambridge, MA: Harvard University Press.

PFIFFNER, J. P. 1996. *The Strategic Presidency: Hitting the Ground Running*. Lawrence: University of Kansas Press.

PORTER, R. B. 1980. *Presidential Decision Making: The Economic Policy Board*. Cambridge: Cambridge University Press.

REEDY, G. 1970. *The Twilight of the Presidency*. New York: New American Books.

RUDALEVIGE, A. 2002. *Managing the President's Program: Presidential Leadership and Legislative Policy Formulation*. Princeton, NJ: Princeton University Press.

—— 2005. The Executive Branch and the Legislative Process. Pp. 419–51 in *The Executive Branch*, ed. J. Aberbach and M. Peterson. Oxford: Oxford University Press,

SAVAGE, C. 2006. Bush Challenges Hundreds of Laws. *Boston Globe*, A7. <www.boston.com/news/nation/articles/2006/04f/30/bush_challenges_hundreds_of_laws>.

SHULL, S. A. (ed.) 1991. *The Two Presidencies: A Quarter Century Assessment*. Chicago: Nelson Hall.

SINCLAIR, B. 2000. Hostile Partners: The President, Congress, and Lawmaking in the Partisan 1990s. Pp. 134–53 in *Polarized Politics: Congress and the President in a Partisan Age*, ed. J. Bond and R. Fleisher. Washington, DC: Congressional Quarterly.

—— 2004. Leading and Competing: The President and the Polarized Congress. Pp. 85–100 in *New Challenges for the American Presidency*, ed. G. C. Edwards and P. Davies. New York: Longman.

STEGER, W. 1997. Presidential Policy Initiation and the Politics of Agenda Control. *Congress and the Presidency*, 24: 17–36.

SULLIVAN, T. 1988. Headcounts, Expectations, and Presidential Coalitions in Congress. *American Journal of Political Science*, 32: 567–89.

—— 1990. Bargaining with the President: A Simple Game and New Evidence. *American Political Science Review*, 84: 1167–95.

TAYLOR, A. 1988. Domestic Agenda Setting, 1947–1994. *Legislative Studies Quarterly*, 23: 373–97.

WAYNE, S. J. 1978. *The Legislative Presidency*. New York: Harper & Row.

—— 1983. Approaches. Pp. 17–49 in *Studying the Presidency*, ed. G. C. Edwards III and S. J. Wayne. Knoxville: University of Tennessee Press.

—— 2006. Bush and Congress: Communication without Much Consultation. *Extensions*: 14–18.

WILDAVSKY, A. 1966. The Two Presidencies. *Transaction*: 7–14.

WOODWARD, B. 2004. *Plan of Attack*. New York: Simon & Schuster.

CHAPTER 15

PRESIDENTIAL APPROVAL AS A SOURCE OF INFLUENCE IN CONGRESS

GEORGE C. EDWARDS III

In the first edition of *Presidential Power*, Richard Neustadt (1960) articulated a relationship between "presidential prestige" and presidential influence in Congress. Nearly a generation later, Edwards (1976, 1977) provided an empirical structure for Neustadt's theorizing and used quantitative data and methods to perform the first test for his core proposition. Since that time, the question of the impact of the president's public approval on his success or support in Congress has been the subject of a substantial literature. This research has produced a wide range of findings: some scholars have found very strong relationships while others have concluded that the relationship between presidential approval and congressional support is weak or non-existent. Thus, although the White House invests enormous amounts of time and energy in its efforts to obtain public support for the president, it remains unclear (at least to political scientists) how—or if—this potential resource is translated into a tool of presidential leadership in Congress.

In this chapter, I focus on answering this perennial question. I argue that to determine the nature of the relationship between presidential approval and congressional support, we need to reason more carefully about the theoretical underpinnings of the relationship and employ more rigorous designs for tests that evaluate this theorizing.

VIEWS FROM THE WHITE HOUSE

One of the most puzzling aspects of the question of the impact of presidential approval is the contrast between recent findings of a lack of relationship between approval and presidential success in Congress and the virtually unanimous conclusion by participants in the legislative process on both ends of Pennsylvania Avenue and other close observers that public approval is an important source of presidential power. In this section, I devote detailed attention to the views of presidents, White House aides, and other Washington insiders because they represent the direct observations of politically savvy people who have a strong incentive to understand accurately the nature of legislative politics.

Ken Collier (1995, 1) found that among White House lobbyists, "many emphatically" asserted that a linkage exists between presidential approval and success in obtaining votes in Congress. This is a widely shared view among chief executives and their aides, who assert the importance of the president's public standing to an administration's legislative success.

Dwight Eisenhower, one of our most popular post-war presidents, went to considerable lengths to nurture his public support. According to Fred Greenstein, Ike "was fully aware that his popularity was essential to his ability to exercise influence over other leaders. As he once noted, 'one man can do a lot . . . at any particular given moment, if at that moment he happens to be ranking high in public estimation' " (1982, 99). Eisenhower's congressional liaison chief, Bryce Harlow, reports that Democrats in Congress saw that openly opposing Eisenhower was unpopular and thus became more cooperative (n.d., 53). Other observers have concluded that his popularity helped Eisenhower to preempt challenges from congressional Democrats (see, for example, Rovere 1956, 261–2; McPherson 1972, 105–6) and to bring around Republicans like Everett Dirksen (MacNeil 1970, 138, 142).

Lyndon Johnson understood well the advantage that public support afforded him. In his memoirs he declared, "Presidential popularity is a major source of strength in gaining cooperation from Congress" (1971, 443). Johnson aide Harry McPherson agrees, remembering that members of Congress "listened hard for evidence of how the President stood in their states in order that they might know how to treat him" (1972, 246–7).

Richard Nixon's chief of staff, H. R. Haldeman, wrote after the 1972 election that he felt things would be easier in Congress because of the Nixon landslide (1994, 532). On the evening of his second inauguration, Nixon recorded in his diary his concern over the drop he expected in his approval levels in response to the extensive Christmas bombing of North Vietnam. The polls could affect his ability to lead, "since politicians do pay attention to them" (1977, 753). Earlier, Nixon also expressed his concern at his dependence on his general support from the public when he wrote, "No leader survives simply by doing well. A leader survives when people have confidence in him when he's not doing well" (quoted in Safire 1975, 284).

In 1969, Nixon celebrated the landing on the moon by personally observing the splashdown of Apollo XI in the Pacific Ocean. When he returned home, he cashed in on the increased approval the publicity had brought him and had the Gallup Poll results sent to those members of Congress "who might have thought that it will now be sage to give in to their deepest desires and kick us in the teeth" (quoted in Ambrose 1989, 287). But, of course, this is just what would eventually happen. And his aides recognized that it was easier for members of Congress to vote against the president as his approval dropped (Collier 1995, 6). President Carter's aides were quite explicit about the importance of the president's public approval in their efforts to influence Congress. One stated, the "only way to keep those guys [Congress] honest is to keep our popularity high" (quoted in Goldman, Clift, and DeFrank 1977, 35. Also see the statement of Hamilton Jordan in the same article). One of the president's legislative liaison officials added, "When you go up to the Hill and the latest polls show Carter isn't doing well, there isn't much reason for a member to go along with him. There's little we can do if the member isn't persuaded on the issue" (quoted in Hager 1978). Another aide at the White House was even more explicit: "No president whose popularity is as low as this President's has much clout on the Hill" (quoted in Mathews et al. 1978).

President Reagan's administration was especially sensitive to the president's public approval levels. According to David Gergen, the head of the White House Office of Communication in Reagan's first term, "Everything here is built on the idea that the president's success depends on grassroots support" (quoted in Blumenthal 1981, 110).

During the presidency of George H. W. Bush, Newt Gingrich declared, "If the President's popularity is at 80 percent, I think the president can do whatever he wants" (quoted in Oreskes 1990). In a televised discussion in 1994, Fred McClure, the president's chief congressional liaison aide, and Tony Coelho, the former House Democratic whip, agreed that the higher the president was in the polls, the easier it was for him to obtain congressional support.

In early 1993, President Clinton's pollster, Stanley Greenberg, argued that at the beginning of Clinton's tenure "popular support is the key to congressional support" (quoted in Barnes 1993, 712). Similarly, Mandy Grunwald, another of Clinton's closest political advisers, maintained, "The President's popularity first had to be improved, then Congress could be moved by a popular president." "It's a bank shot, what you say to the American people bounces back to Congress" (quoted in Woodward 1994, 248, 141). George Stephanopoulos, at the core of the early Clinton presidency, found the president's low approval ratings were hurting his chances in Congress (1999, 294, 316).

Representative Lee Hamilton agreed: "when a President is riding high, his influence goes up, and when a President is in the dumps... his influence declines" (quoted in Apple 1994). Similarly, a senior legislative strategist on the staff of a senior

Democratic senator argued, "It's an absolute rule up here: popular Presidents get what they want; unpopular ones don't" (quoted in Rosenbaum 1993).

In the president's second term, a presidential aide found that "Clinton has come to believe that if he keeps his approval ratings up and sells his message as he did during the campaign, there will be greater acceptability for his program" (quoted in Mitchell 1997). Presidential strategist Dick Morris agreed. Noting that when Clinton was down in the polls, members of Congress began to desert him, Morris concluded, "A President doesn't just need a majority on Election Day. The President needs a majority every day of the week behind every bill that he has." Thus, it is not surprising that the president was convinced that he could not govern unless his poll numbers were high (Morris 1997, 33, 324; Mitchell 1997; Cannon 1998, 2934–5). White House officials also concluded that when the president's approval ratings were up, interest groups were afraid and wanted to cut a deal; when his ratings were down, groups were less willing to deal (Jacobs and Shapiro 2000, 104–5).

George W. Bush spent his second term mired low in the polls. One of the most visible results was the number of Republicans shedding their fear of publicly challenging the White House. "I think the biggest single challenge of putting votes together for our team, frankly, was the president's numbers," declared acting House majority leader Roy Blunt (quoted in Hulse 2005). The head of the White House's legislative liaison office in the president's first term, Nicholas Calio, agreed, observing that the lower Bush's approval sunk, the more Republicans in Congress opposed him (Brownstein 2007, 309). Political analyst Charlie Cook (2005) was blunter: "Bush's popularity or unpopularity has a tremendous impact on the behavior of members of Congress."

The fact that so many presidents, presidential aides, members of Congress, and other Washington insiders believe that presidential approval has an important influence on presidential support in Congress is not in itself conclusive evidence of such a relationship. They may simply be wrong. Nevertheless, we cannot ignore the widespread view of the significance of presidential approval by able people who have a substantial stake in correctly understanding the nature of presidential power. At the very least, the confidence of insiders should prompt us to take a careful look at the question.

THEORIZING ABOUT THE RELATIONSHIP

To reach meaningful conclusions about the impact of presidential approval on presidential success in Congress, it is essential that scholars test propositions that make theoretical sense. It is not difficult to place data in a regression equation, but the results will be useful only if they represent a theoretically meaningful relationship. We would not, for example, correlate the president's approval on his first day in office with his success in his fourth year. We would conclude that there would be no reason that the two would be related closely, and thus we would reject such a test as meaningless—no matter what the results showed.

Unfortunately, the authors of many of the studies that have examined the impact of presidential approval on congressional behavior have relied on little or no theorizing. As a result, theory has not guided the tests they employ and their findings cannot help us reach conclusions about the impact of presidential approval. This is equally true for studies that have found an impact and studies that have found no influence at all.

Before we discuss individual studies in more detail, it is useful to review the reasoning behind hypothesizing that presidential approval would influence votes in Congress. Why might senators and representatives respond to the public's evaluation of the president? To answer this question, we must reach out beyond the presidency literature to what we have learned about Congress and the public.

The Congressional Environment

Members of Congress live in a world characterized by uncertainty and insecurity. They depend on their constituents to retain their seats, which they usually wish to do. Yet the average representative's constituency includes nearly 700,000 individuals and the average senator's about six million. It is obviously not possible for any member of Congress to have direct knowledge of what more than a few of his or her constituents are thinking about politics and policy, and voters do little to help close this information gap. A relatively small and unrepresentative sample of citizens ever communicates with their representatives about policy issues (Dexter 1955–6, 1956; 1969, 330; Bauer, Pool, and Dexter 1963, 419–20; Tacheron and Udall 1966, 282–3; Rieselbach 1973, 216; Kingdon 1973, 56–7; Stolarek, Wood, and Taylor 1981; Times Mirror 1987, 57–78; West 1988). To compound their problems, members of Congress are unsure of other important matters directly relevant to their reelections, such as who voted for them in the last election, population shifts, the effects of redistricting, and the identity of their next challenger (Fenno 1977, 886–7; 1978).

With this lack of information comes a strong feeling of vulnerability. Members of Congress perceive themselves to be "unsafe at any margin" (Mann 1978) and "see electoral uncertainty where outsiders would fail to unearth a single objective indicator of it" (Fenno 1978, 10–11). The reforms of the early 1970s brought more open meetings and roll calls, making their actions more public than ever before, and the proliferation of politically active groups puts them under more scrutiny. Groups bring any deviation from their perspectives to the attention of relevant voters.

In addition, changes in the nature of campaigning have made it easier for challengers to mount effective campaigns in the right circumstances. Direct mail fund raising and campaigning, political action committees, polling firms, television advertising, and national party campaigns make it possible for challengers who can meet certain thresholds of name recognition, political skills, and resources to contest what might appear to be safe seats.

Over the years, scholars have focused much attention on the large margins by which most House members win reelection. Yet we must be careful about the inferences we draw from this fact. Gary Jacobson (1987) has shown that "[House] incumbents are not safer now than they were in the 1950s, the marginals, properly defined, have not vanished, the swing-ratio has diminished little, if at all; and so competition for House seats held by incumbents has not declined" (see also Erikson 1976; Collie 1981).

Despite appearances, House elections remain competitive, as the Framers intended them to be. The Senate, which the Founders designed to insulate members somewhat from the public, is even more subject to electoral competition. According to one senator, "The founding fathers gave senators six-year terms so they could be states-men for at least four years and not respond to every whim and caprice. Now a senator in his first year knows that any vote could beat him five years later—so senators may behave like House members. They are running constantly" (quoted in Ehrenhalt 1982).

A senator's constituency is usually larger and more diverse socially, economically, and politically than a House district. Moreover, because seats in the Senate are especially attractive to potential candidates, there are often effective, well-financed challenges to incumbent senators. Senators also receive more press coverage in office than representatives, and their constituents are more likely to hold them accountable on controversial issues. For this reason, senators do indeed run constantly for reelection (Cook 1986).

As one might expect, members of Congress are well aware of their electoral insecurity and have been raising and spending more campaign funds, sending more franked mail to their constituents, traveling more to their states and districts, and staffing more local offices than ever before (Johannes 1984; Parker 1986a, 1986b). They realize that with the decline of partisan loyalty in the electorate, they bear more of the burden of obtaining votes.

A primary task of members of Congress is to preempt an effective challenge to their reelection by demonstrating broad support and a lack of vulnerability in their constituencies. Thus, they are in most cases highly attentive to their constituents (Fenno 1978; Johannes 1984; Parker and Parker 1985; Parker 1986a, 1986b; Rivers and Fiorina 1991) and eager to avoid votes and stands on issues that might be a catalyst for strong opponents to emerge.

In such an environment, it should come as no surprise that senators and repre-sentatives are hypersensitive to the anticipated reaction of their constituents to their actions. They overestimate their visibility to their constituents and the extent to which the electorate is concerned about issues (Stokes and Miller 1962; Miller and Stokes 1963; Cnudde and McCrone 1966; Kingdon 1968; Davidson 1968; Mayhew 1974; Fenno 1978; Arnold 1990). Whether or not voters follow the issues of the day or know how members of Congress vote on them, the members certainly act as if their votes make a difference in their chances for reelection or elevation from the House to the Senate (Elling 1982; Fenno 1982; Hibbing 1984, 1986; Thomas 1985; Wright and Berkman 1986).

Such concerns make good sense, as recent research has found that the actual support of representatives of the president is the best predictor of the public's perception of their support. In addition, these perceptions interact powerfully with citizen's presidential approval to shape attitudes toward congressional incumbents (Gronke, Koch, and Wilson 2003).

Reinforcing this concern for public opinion are the role perceptions of members of Congress. Although good time series data on congressional role perceptions are lacking, and the way in which these perceptions affect behavior is unclear, there is some reason to believe that many senators and representatives feel they ought to reflect public opinion in their voting in Congress (Davidson 1968, 79–80, 117; Cavanaugh 1979). To the extent that this holds at any given time, it increases the sensitivity of members of Congress to the electorate.

The President

Members of Congress thus face an environment of uncertainty and vulnerability. They want to please their constituents, yet often do not know how the voters feel about matters of public policy or politics. Looming over this arena is the public official who is the most visible and whom senators and representatives must continuously take into account: the president.

The President as Surrogate

As the central figure in American politics, the president is the object of a constant stream of commentary and evaluation by all segments of society, including those that are unlikely to articulate specific policy preferences. Indeed, press coverage of the president and his policies exceeds that of all other political figures combined (Cornwell 1959; Balutis 1977; Gans 1979, 9; Grossman and Kumar 1981, 258–9, 265; Davis 1986; Ornstein and Robinson 1986). The president's standing in the public provides members of Congress with a guide to the public's views.

Because of the high visibility and frequency of presidential approval polls, it is safe to assume that members of Congress are aware of the president's standing with the public. In addition, senators and representatives learn of the public's opinion of the president from other political elites, political activists, leaders of interest groups, the press, attentive publics, and constituents. Some of what they hear may be echoes of their own actions in government.

Anticipated Reactions

The public's evaluations of the president are important not only as surrogates for broader opinions on politics and policy, but also as influences on congressional behavior. Members of Congress must anticipate the public's reaction to their decisions to support or oppose the president and his policies. Depending on the president's public standing, they may choose to be close to him or independent from him to increase their chances of reelection. As analyst William Schneider (1994) put it, "popularity is power. Members of Congress are all in business for themselves. If a President is popular, they'll support him because they want to be with a winner. If he starts losing popularity, they'll abandon him. Even members of his own party don't want to be associated with a loser."

A president with strong public support provides a cover for members of Congress to cast votes to which their constituents might otherwise object. They can defend their votes as supporting the president rather than on substantive policy grounds alone.

The context of high public approval allows the administration to seek congressional support with an implicit threat for failure to do so lurking in the background. Ultimately, the effectiveness of this strategy is tied to the potential for the White House to make the support of a senator or representative a campaign issue. Presidents high in the polls are in a position to make such threats. According to an aide to Ronald Reagan, for example, the president's contacts with members of Congress before the tax vote of 1981 were "merely a device to keep the congressmen thinking about what could happen next year. I'm sure Mr. Reagan is charming as hell, but that isn't what is important. It's his reminding these people that they could lose their jobs next year" (quoted in Light 1983, xiii). Similarly, White House political director Ed Rollins observed, "Time and again in 1981, members of Congress would tell me they opposed his [Reagan's] legislative agenda but couldn't risk voting against a president who was six to ten points more popular in their districts than they were" (1996, 106).

Members of Congress may also use the president's standing in the polls as an indicator of his ability to mobilize public opinion against his opponents. Senators and representatives are especially likely to be sensitive to this possibility after a successful demonstration of the president's ability to mobilize the public, as appears to have occurred in response to the efforts of Reagan's White House in 1981 (Kernell 1986, 115–23). As Richard Neustadt (1990, 264) put it, "Washingtonians ... are vulnerable to any breeze from home that presidential words and sighs can stir. If he is deemed effective on the tube, they will anticipate."

Richard Nixon agreed about the importance of the president's standing in the public, arguing that a strong incentive for members of Congress to support the president was "the fear that a popular president may oppose them in the next election" (1990, 282). As Vice President Walter Mondale (1993, 14) declared, "If the president has the American people on his side, Congress will take notice—because, like a hanging, the prospect of defeat in an election concentrates the mind."

Of course, a president without public support loses this advantage. One study found that members of Congress spent more time in their constituencies when the president's approval ratings were low, explaining how their views differed from his (Parker 1980, 547). Similarly, members of the president's party try to distance themselves from him if he is low in the polls. When Republican support for George W. Bush waned as the president sunk in the polls, Republican Senator John Thune of South Dakota maintained, "This is partly a function of approval ratings. People pay attention [to polls] and start saying, 'Let's take a more independent tack.' It is frankly self-interest, self-preservation" (quoted in VandeHei and Babington 2005, A5).

Moreover, members of Congress may avoid association with a president caught in the depths of the polls. Lyndon Johnson found fewer members of Congress eager to attend White House receptions or discuss matters of policy with him when his standing in the polls declined (Bowles 1987, 99, 102, 104). With approval ratings below 40 percent in 2006, George W. Bush did not make his first traditional campaign rally until the end of October. Few Republicans sought campaign appearances with him.

Low presidential approval ratings free members of Congress from supporting the president if they are otherwise inclined to oppose him. A senior political aide to President Carter noted:

When the President is low in public opinion polls, the Members of Congress see little hazard in bucking him... After all, very few Congressmen examine an issue solely on its merits; they are politicians and they think politically. I'm not saying they make only politically expedient choices. But they read the polls and from that they feel secure in turning their back on the President with political impunity. Unquestionably, the success of the President's policies bears a tremendous relationship to his popularity in the polls.   (Quoted in Bonafede 1979, 830)

In addition, low ratings in the polls may create incentives to attack the president, further eroding his already weakened position. Richard Nixon's legislative liaison chief William Timmons wrote to the president at the end of 1973 that when the chief executive's approval is low, "Its advantageous and even fun to kick him around" (1973, 3). After the arms sales to Iran and the diversion of funds to the Contras became a *cause célèbre* in late 1986, it became more acceptable in Congress and in the press to raise questions about Ronald Reagan's capacities as president. Disillusionment is a dangerous force for the White House.

It is prudent for members of Congress to anticipate voters' reactions to their support for the president. Their constituents hold them accountable for their legislative voting, especially on salient issues such as those on which the president has taken a stand (Canes-Wrone, Brady, and Cogan 2002). Strong supporters of unpopular presidents in competitive districts are particularly at risk, because senators and representatives who support the president more than constituents prefer are more likely to lose (Brady et al. 1996; Brady, Canes-Wrone, and Cogan 2000; Burden and Kimball 2002, 124–5; Gronke, Koch, and Wilson 2003). Regardless of party, the voters do not punish representatives who do not support the president's programs if they perceive his policies are to be unsuccessful, but strong supporters of the president are less fortunate (Alford and Hibbing 1984).

Midterm election results partly reflect a verdict on the president's performance (Campbell 1997). Polls have found that a significant percentage of voters see their votes for candidates for Congress as support for the president or opposition to him (see, for example, Pew Research Center for the People and the Press 2006). Republicans defeated in the election of 1974 had supported Richard Nixon more than had their colleagues who won reelection (Burnham 1975, 418; Congressional Quarterly 1975). In 1994, Democratic candidates were more likely to be defeated in districts where Bill Clinton was weak (Brady et al. 1996). Opinions about George W. Bush's job performance and his decision to invade Iraq were exceptionally strong predictors of

individual vote choices in the 2006 congressional elections (Jacobson 2007). Nearly 40 percent of voters cast ballots to oppose the president (Pew Research Center for the People and the Press 2006).

Abramowitz and Segal (1992, 121, 233, 238) found that the president's approval rating strongly influenced the vote in individual Senate races. Similarly, Atkeson and Partin (1985) found that in Senate races with an incumbent of either party, presidential approval had a strong and significant effect on voting. They concluded that voters in Senate races express their support for or dissatisfaction with the president by respectively rewarding or punishing candidates of his party—a national referendum effect.

Constraints on Influence

There are solid theoretical reasons for expecting members of Congress to be responsive to the president's standing in the public. Yet we should expect this responsiveness to be modest. We know that no matter how low a president's standing with the public or how small the margin of his election, he still receives support from a substantial number of senators and representatives. Similarly, no matter how high his approval levels climb or how large his winning percentage of the vote, a significant portion of the Congress still opposes his policies.

The president's public support must compete for influence with other, more stable factors that affect voting in Congress, including ideology, party, personal views and commitments on specific policies, and constituency interests. Although constituency interests may seem to overlap with voters' presidential approval, they are distinct. It is quite possible for constituents to approve of the president but oppose him on particular policies, and it is opinions on these policies that will ring most loudly in congressional ears. Members of Congress are unlikely to vote against the clear interests of their constituents or the firm tenets of their ideology solely in deference to a widely supported chief executive.

Both Neustadt and Edwards argue that we should view presidential approval (or "prestige") as a strategic influence, a factor that may affect the outcome in every case, but that will not necessarily determine the outcome in a specific case (Neustadt 1990, 78; Edwards 1989, 109–14). As Neustadt makes clear, public approval is a "factor operating mostly in the background as a conditioner, not the determinant, of what Washingtonians will do about a President's request." It "tends to set a tone and to define the limits of what Washingtonians do for him or do to him." However, "Rarely is there any one-to-one relationship between appraisals of his popularity in general and responses to his wishes in particular" (1990, 74).

Widespread support should give the president leeway and weaken resistance to his policies. Thus, public support gives a president, at best, leverage, but not control. On the other hand, when the president lacks popular support, this strengthens the resolve of those inclined to oppose him and narrows the range in which he receives the benefit of the doubt. The president's options are reduced, his opportunities diminished, and his room for maneuver checked; he loses crucial "leeway" (Neustadt 1990, 75, 77).

DESIGNING TESTS OF THE RELATIONSHIP

If we are to analyze the relationship between presidential approval in the public and presidential success in Congress properly, we must design tests that are theoretically meaningful. Otherwise, we are likely to obtain results that are theoretically irrelevant and, possibly, misleading.

There are two basic approaches to investigating the impact of presidential approval on congressional support for the White House. One is to approach the relationship with an implicit assumption that if approval has an influence, it is at the tactical level. Following this approach assumes, in effect, that if senators and representatives are attentive to the president's standing with the public, they include short-term changes in approval in their daily decision-making calculus and make rapid adjustments in their inclinations to support the president as the public changes its approval levels.

On the other hand, the theorizing in this chapter views presidential approval as a long-term, broad, strategic asset for presidential influence. Neustadt warned that we should ignore the month-by-month variations in presidential approval. They are unlikely to affect members of Congress, as "presidential influence is shielded from the vagaries of shifting sentiment." It is the large and stable shifts that are important (1990, 76, 81). Thus, we must fashion a test that is capable of capturing a broad influence rather than one that investigates a simple one-to-one impact.

The Independent Variable

There are several theoretically significant questions about measuring presidential approval, including the time period over which we measure approval, the segment of the public whose approval we measure, and the specific components of presidential approval on which we focus.

Shifts in Approval?

We have seen that if presidential approval has an impact on congressional support for the president, it will be a broad background influence rather than one that shifts rapidly and causes immediate change in congressional support. However, some authors, largely as a result of lack of explicit attention to theory, construct tests that do not evaluate theoretically meaningful relationships. For example, some scholars test for the impact of presidential approval by using the most recent poll taken before a vote as their indicator of presidential approval (see, for example, Bond and Fleischer 1990, ch. 7; Canes-Wrone and de Marchi 2002), exactly what Neustadt insisted we should ignore. There is no theoretical reason to expect such close associations between approval and congressional support, and findings of a lack of relationship between approval and presidential success in Congress reveal nothing about the type of relationship concerning which we have theorized. In addition, there is typically little variability in the dependent variable over short periods of time. Thus, the authors have stacked the deck both theoretically and methodologically against a positive finding.

The same problems arise when authors try to measure the "context" of presidential approval (whether at the time of a vote it had been increasing or decreasing or high or low compared to a previous period) (see Bond and Fleischer 1990; Mouw and MacKuen 1992; Collier and Sullivan 1995). This reduces the variability of the independent variable even further, since most of the time there will be "o" recorded for approval. Moreover, this approach also has the drawbacks of attempting to examine moment-to-moment influence. Finally, their equations do not contain a measure of the actual approval level of the president. Neither Neustadt nor his successors have theorized that members of Congress are sensitive to changes in presidential approval. On the contrary, Neustadt argued that short-term changes in approval are likely to be unimportant and that it is more significant whether approval is high or low. Thus, the authors, all skilled political scientists, make a good effort but ultimately miss the theoretical point that they are trying to test.

Ostrom and Simon (1985) measured presidential success in Congress as the cumulative percentage of winning votes on domestic policy for each Congress. However, they regress this cumulative dependent variable on the current month's presidential approval. This test lacks theoretical justification. There is simply no reason to think that such a measure of presidential success in Congress would be a function of the current month's approval. Although they find a strong impact of presidential approval on presidential success in Congress, we cannot be comfortable with their conclusion.

On the other hand, several studies (Edwards 1989, ch. 6; 1997; Rivers and Rose 1985; Brace and Hinckley 1992, ch. 4; Bond, Fleischer, and Wood 2003) use annual figures to measure presidential approval. Although they employ different measures of presidential success in Congress, each study finds positive and statistically significant relationships with presidential approval. Annual measures smooth out "the vagaries of shifting sentiment" and provide a better test of strategic influence.

Whose Approval?

In addition to the question of the time period over which we measure presidential approval is the issue of *whose* approval we measure. Most authors use the aggregate level for the entire nation to measure approval. Yet the theory underlying the influence of presidential approval on members of Congress is that they will be responsive to public opinion regarding the president out of concern for reelection or out of a desire to represent the views of their constituents.

If members of Congress respond to the president's standing in the public to increase the probability of their reelections, they should be most concerned with their reelection constituencies. There is substantial evidence that senators and representatives do not pay equal heed to all the voters they represent. They are likely to receive communications from their electoral supporters more frequently than from other constituents. In addition, whether their motivation is responsiveness or reelection, the constituents to whom members of Congress are most responsive are generally part of their electoral coalitions (MacRae 1958, 264; Miller and Stokes 1963; Dexter 1969; Oppenheimer 1971; Clausen 1973, 126–7, 182, 188; Kingdon 1973; Fiorina 1974; Markus 1974; Bullock and Brady 1977; Fenno 1978; Achen 1978; Stolarek, Wood, and Taylor 1981; Poole and Rosenthal 1984; Glazer and Robbins 1985; West 1988; Wright 1989; Roscoe 2003; Clinton 2006. See also Griffin and Newman 2005).

Fellow party identifiers form the core of incumbents' reelection constituencies. It follows that members of Congress should be more responsive to presidential approval among members of the electorate who share their party affiliation and compose the core of their electoral bases. Democratic members of Congress should be most responsive to Democratic party identifiers and Republican members to Republican party identifiers.

A failure to disaggregate presidential approval may lead to puzzling data and inappropriate inferences. For example, in 1984 President Reagan's approval rating averaged 55 percent for the year. This figure masked considerable variance, however: his approval rating among Republicans was 89 percent, but it was only 29 percent among Democrats. An analyst who compared the president's meager congressional support levels from Democrats that year to his overall approval ratings might erroneously conclude that there was no relationship at all, and the strong Republican support in Congress may seem equally baffling.

In addition, the correlation (r) between yearly averages of Democratic and Republican approval over the 34 years in which Republicans served as president from 1953 to 2006 is .47, The figure is .46 for the 20 years of Democratic presidents. These findings indicate that although the variables are related, they are conceptually distinct. Other sources explain about 80 percent of the variance in the two variables. The differences between Democratic and Republican approval are not surprising. In their survey of five decades of public opinion, Page and Shapiro (1992, 309–10) found that party groups display divergent movements in public opinion; that is, they change in different directions or by differing amounts (see also Lebo and Cassino 2007).

Bond and Fleisher (1990, 179, 187) argue that partisan opinion covaries with overall opinion, and conclude that they are safe with using only the latter. It is not appropriate to correlate partisan opinion with overall opinion, however, because the former is a large component of the latter. To do so is correlating opinion with itself. What matters is how Democratic and Republican opinion correlate, and, as we have seen, they are quite different.

They also claim that there is no difference between using partisan and overall approval (1990, 187), but they provide no results using partisan approval, and there clearly is a difference. The relationships between aggregate national presidential approval and presidential support among party groups in Congress are much weaker than the relationships between partisan approval and party groups in Congress (Edwards 1997).

The ideal measure of presidential approval would be approval among each incumbent's reelection constituency. By matching senators and representatives with their electoral constituencies, we would employ the most theoretically meaningful test of the relationship between public approval and congressional support.

Unfortunately, constituency-level data are rarely available. Nevertheless, scholars have made some progress in the effort to measure presidential approval among the constituents of members of Congress.

Cohen, Bond, and Fleischer (2000) exploited a set of polls taken in each state in September 1996. They found no relationship between state-level approval and support for the president's position on Senate votes in the third quarter of that year. The authors were not able to examine trends, of course, and they were not able to measure the reelection constituencies of senators because they lacked data on the approval of party identifiers, but the principle of attempting to measure constituency opinion was an important step forward.

In an explicitly exploratory analysis, Ponder and Moon (2005) pooled samples of data about members and their constituencies from the 1980–98 National Election Studies. When they regressed overall presidential support in the years of the study (even numbered years) on national, national party, and constituency approval, they found significant relationships. As the authors recognize, the study has many limitations, including a dependent variable incorporating potentially distorting one-sided votes in Congress, sometimes very small samples in a congressional district, and a lack of data on presidential approval among party groups in constituencies. Again, however, the authors are to be commended for trying to deal with theoretical issues that earlier studies did not address.

What Approval?

Borelli, Wrighton, and Bryan (1998) raise yet another element of any relationship between approval and congressional support. They advocate use of policy-specific approval ratings, such as those for the president's handling of the major policy dimensions of economic and foreign policy. When they regressed congressional support for presidential policy in these areas on approval ratings in the economic and foreign policy realms, respectively, they found a modest relationship.

This is another dimension of the relationship to which we might profitably devote more attention to theorizing. Do members of Congress make such fine distinctions among policy areas in responding to presidential approval? How should we specify equations focusing on the economy or foreign policy? How can we overcome the limitations on data and the inevitable small number of votes on most issue areas?

The Dependent Variable

The dependent variable, a measure of congressional support for the president, should also be appropriate for testing for strategic influence. As in the case of the independent variable, there are several theoretically significant decisions for scholars. First, we have already seen that it is necessary to disaggregate congressional behavior into party groups if we are to test the theoretical argument underlying the hypothesis of the impact of presidential approval on congressional behavior.

We have also seen that we should not seek to find influence on a vote-by-vote basis. Just as individual polls are not useful as indicators of presidential approval for testing the relationship between approval and congressional behavior, individual votes in Congress are not useful measures of presidential success in Congress. Broader measures that aggregate congressional votes provide better tests of strategic influence, the only impact with a foundation in theory.

Once the demands of theory are explicit, we are better positioned to make decisions regarding a measure of congressional support. Aggregate measures such as winning votes do not allow us to differentiate the votes of partisan groups. Without knowing who the president's supporters are, it is difficult to understand why they provide support. We cannot tell whether different members of Congress respond differently to various influences on their voting and thus lack a solid basis for inferences about the causes of congressional behavior.

In addition, such a measure will include many lopsided votes that are not useful tests of the president's influence. Because many of the issues on which the president takes a stand are not controversial and are decided by nearly unanimous votes, including them in a measure of support for the president can distort the results by inflating the measure. Furthermore, the number of these votes varies over time, and including them in a measure of presidential support can therefore frustrate attempts to correlate the measure with possible explanatory variables. Including these votes may also distort comparisons between the House and Senate because the upper chamber tends to have more unanimous votes, owing at least in part to its special responsibilities for confirming appointments and ratifying treaties, most of which are not controversial.

A yearly aggregate of presidential success in obtaining passage of legislation not only masks variability in support for the president among individual members of Congress or groups of members but also makes it impossible to compare the House with the Senate. It is also possible for the president to obtain substantial support on votes requiring extraordinary majorities, such as those for ratifying treaties, suspending the rules, or bringing cloture to debate, and still end up with a loss. Indeed, a "box score" of presidential success in Congress (Rivers and Rose 1985) has been so thoroughly discredited (see Edwards 1989, 17–19) that *Congressional Quarterly* stopped calculating it in 1975 and it requires little attention here.

Because of the limitations of aggregate measures, it is usually better to calculate presidential support for each member of Congress. This makes it possible to disaggregate the analysis as much as theory and independent variables will allow, and to compute aggregate figures for groups of representatives and senators when it is appropriate to do so. On the other hand, beginning with one aggregate figure to represent behavior makes it impossible to disaggregate the figure to the individual level.

Aside from the level of aggregation, we must decide which votes to include in a measure of presidential support. This decision is of critical importance, because we want to know whether variables that may explain behavior, such as public approval, operate uniformly across all issues and all votes, or influence some issues and votes more than others. Measures of presidential support that are very broad may mask important relationships that more exclusive measures reveal. Conversely, relationships that appear to hold across a wide range of issues and votes may actually be weak or non-existent on especially important matters or on specific issues.

I have discussed these issues in detail elsewhere (Edwards 1989, ch. 2) and space limitations prohibit an extensive discussion in this essay. Most scholars (see, for example, Edwards 1989; Bond and Fleischer 1990; Bond, Fleischer, and Wood 2003) have settled on including votes on which the winning side numbered less than 80 percent of those who voted. Although this figure is somewhat arbitrary, it is a reasonable cut-off, beyond which presidential influence appears to be largely irrelevant. Moreover, such a measure of support correlates highly with alternative measures. Edwards has also supplemented his measure of Nonunanimous Support with a measure based on *Congressional Quarterly's* Key Votes on which the president took a stand, but relying solely on such an indicator (Mouw and MacKuen 1992) risks distorting the measurement of presidential support because of the very small number and unrepresentative nature of key votes in any year.

There remains much work to be done on conceptualizing presidential support. Brandice Canes-Wrone and Scott de Marchi (2002) make a useful contribution to refining the dependent variable by hypothesizing that presidential approval affords the White House influence on bills that are salient to the public and complex enough so that public opinion is uncertain. It is on such cases, they argue, that members of Congress will turn to presidential approval as an indicator of public preferences or be responsive to the president out of concern that the president can influence public opinion on such issues. We now know that there is little basis for the latter concern, but, of course, members of Congress may not understand this.

They examined all House roll-call votes on passage on regulatory and social issues between 1989 and 2000, coding the former issues as those that are salient and complex. They found that presidential approval is significantly related to White House success on complex and salient issues. Moreover, they point out that such issues are common and the inclusion of foreign policy issues, which are often both complex and salient, likely would have bolstered the findings.

The authors do make the common errors of measuring only the end result of voting (winning or losing) rather than the actual votes of members of Congress and measuring approval immediately prior to each vote. Nevertheless, their study is an important milestone in efforts to theorize about the relationship between presidential approval and presidential success in Congress.

Any measures based solely on roll-call votes do not account for the many important decisions that members of Congress make in committees or other venues. Although there is evidence that roll-call votes reflect less visible decisions (Clausen 1973, 19–20; Unekis 1978), it is not certain that this is so, and Hall (1996) has shown that levels of participation are also important in the legislative process. As our theorizing suggests, members of Congress may be more willing to launch investigations and hold aggressive hearings when the president is low in the polls. Nevertheless, roll-call votes typically occur on a wide range of significant issues and are worthy of study in and of themselves, and roll-call votes are the only systematic data available on the decisions of the individual members of Congress.

Questions remain, however, about the points in the legislative process at which we should investigate the influence of presidential approval. Collier and Sullivan (1995) investigated whether members of Congress are more likely to change their stands following initial White House headcounts on issues before Congress when presidents enjoy high approval. They found no relationship between presidential approval and changes in voting stance. Yet, as we have seen, conversion is not at the core of theorizing about the impact of presidential approval. If public prestige is a source of presidential influence, it is likely to have its effect at the beginning of the process, when anticipated reactions have their effects, not at the end. The authors look only for evidence of change in the position of a member of Congress, however. Any measure of influence that requires change *following* an initial headcount risks missing much of the influence, and the change, that may have already occurred. In other words, the authors look for influence where they cannot find it—after it has taken place. The authors may be correct in their conclusion about changes in initial stances, but we cannot logically infer conclusions about the impact of presidential approval on presidential support in Congress from such a finding.

Other Key Questions

Questions about the principal components of tests of the impact of presidential approval on congressional support for the president do not exhaust the issues with which scholars must deal to make progress in understanding the relationship.

Direction of Influence

Investigating the impact of presidential approval on congressional support for the president assumes that members of Congress follow public opinion about the president rather than shape it. If the reverse were true, support for the president among members of Congress could not be a response to public approval of the president. That some members of Congress, particularly key members, do affect public opinion seems plausible, but the extent is unmeasured and perhaps unmeasurable. However, we know that citizens have a wide range of sources for information about the president in addition to their Representatives in Congress. Although we have seen that members of Congress are visible enough to their constituents that voters can form opinions about them and their broad levels of support for the president, we also know that representatives and senators are not visible enough throughout the year to influence greatly their constituents' approval of the president (Stokes and Miller 1962; Hinckley 1976, 1980; Mann 1978, 37, 39, 46; Hurley and Hill 1980; Songer 1981; Edwards 1983, 25).

A related issue is whether the public's approval of the president is as much consequence as cause of his success in Congress. There is no definitive answer to this question, partially because we lack information on the public's perception of the president's success in Congress, and the matter deserves attention. We do know that in the vast literature on presidential approval, no one has found that legislative success is an important explanation for the public's evaluation of the president. We also know that presidents can enjoy high approval after periods of relative failure with Congress or when they face a stalemate with the legislature. Ronald Reagan, for example, enjoyed his highest public approval years after his greatest success in Congress. Bill Clinton's approval began rising when he faced stalemate with an aggressive Republican Congress in 1995–6 and rose even higher when the House called for his impeachment in 1998.

Time-Varying Influence

Bond, Fleisher, and Wood (2003) introduced a new wrinkle into the study of the impact of presidential approval on congressional support when they theorized that the level of partisanship in a chamber conditions the relationship, so it varies over time and is strongest when there are more cross-pressured members in Congress and thus there is less partisanship. Employing new statistical techniques, they find support for their hypothesis. Although they use one annual measure of approval and success on roll-calls votes for each chamber each year, and thus have very small ns for any administration or time period, they raise an important issue that deserves further study.

Controls

We must always be alert to the possibility that a variable strongly influences both the president's public approval and congressional support, rendering any apparent relationship between them spurious. The president's party certainly has such an impact. However, we naturally control for this influence by examining the relationship *within* party groupings, as I have suggested. That is, if we look at the influence of presidential approval among, say, Republicans, on the presidential support of Republicans in Congress, we hold party constant.

Another possibility is that both the public and members of Congress may react to the president on the basis of his legislative proposals. In this case, presidential programs rather than approval would determine presidential support. This reasoning assumes, however, that the public and members of Congress respond to presidential programs similarly, which is unlikely given their differences in background, responsibilities, and access to information on presidential proposals. In addition, this line of reasoning assumes that both the public and members of Congress base their evaluations of the president solely on his legislative programs. Presidential approval and support would be little influenced by the president's failure to propose programs, policies not voted on by Congress (such as administrative decisions and most foreign policy), and his handling of other matters (scandals, State of the Union messages, and so on). These assumptions are difficult to accept.

It seems equally unlikely that both the public and members of Congress respond similarly to the president's general performance. The differences between the two groups preclude such an assumption. In addition, for such a relationship to hold, members of Congress would have to translate their general evaluations into specific votes on legislative proposals, which in turn would match changes in the public's general approval of the president. This is hardly likely.

Discriminating among Theories

In theorizing about the impact of presidential approval on congressional support, I have offered different explanations for why approval should matter. These theories concern issues of information, in which presidential approval serves as a proxy for voter preferences, and of anticipated reactions, in which members of Congress respond out of concern for voter punishment or reward for their support of the president. Although the explanations are related, it would increase our understanding of the relationship between approval and support if we could design a test that discriminated among these explanations.

We might compare the support of members of Congress most vulnerable to defeat with those in more secure electoral positions. If the former group was responsive to presidential approval and the latter group was not, for example, we might conclude that the punishment/reward motivation was the most important explanation. Under ideal conditions, such a test would involve disaggregating the support of members of Congress and correlating the support of various groups with opinion in their constituencies.

CONCLUSION

We in the presidency field have been somewhat cavalier about aligning our empirical tests with our theory in investigating presidential influence in Congress—and other subjects as well. In this chapter, I have emphasized the importance of theoretical thinking as a foundation for developing and testing hypotheses. When we develop tests based on a theoretical view of presidential approval as a broad, strategic influence on congressional voting, rather than a focused, tactical source of influence and as an influence based on responsiveness to electoral constituencies, we are more likely to ascertain the nature of the relationship between the public's approval of the president and congressional support for the White House.

I have also suggested a number of areas that deserve additional attention. Most important, however, is the principle of placing more emphasis on theorizing about the presidency and ensuring that we employ our rapidly developing methodological skills in the pursuit of answers to theoretically meaningful questions.

REFERENCES

ABRAMOWITZ, A. I., and SEGAL, J. A. 1992. *Senate Elections.* Ann Arbor: University of Michigan Press.

ACHEN, C. H. 1978. Measuring Representation. *American Journal of Political Science,* 22: 475–510.

ALFORD, J. R., and HIBBING, J. R. 1984. The Conditions Required for Economic Issue Voting: Actions Speak More Loudly than Partisan Affiliation. Paper presented at the Annual Meeting of the Midwest Political Science Association, Chicago, IL, April.

AMBROSE, S. E. 1989. *Nixon: The Triumph of a Politician, 1962–1972.* New York: Simon & Schuster.

APPLE, R. W., JR. 1994. Vote against Crime Bill is Lesson on Clout. *New York Times,* Aug. 17: A1 and B6.

ARNOLD, R. D. 1990. *The Logic of Congressional Action.* New Haven, CT: Yale University Press.

ATKESON, L. R., and PARTIN, R. W. 1985. Economic and Referendum Voting: A Comparison of Gubernatorial and Senatorial Elections. *American Political Science Review,* 89: 99–107.

BALUTIS, A. P. 1977. The Presidency and the Press: The Expanding Presidential Image. *Presidential Studies Quarterly,* 7: 244–51.

BARNES, J. A. 1993. White House Notebook: They Can Sell, but Can They Close? *National Journal,* Mar. 20: 712.

BAUER, R. A., POOL, I. DE S., and DEXTER, L. A. 1963. *American Business and Public Policy: The Politics of Foreign Trade.* New York: Atherton.

BLUMENTHAL, S. 1981. Marketing the President. *New York Times Magazine.* Sept. 13: 43, 110–18.

BONAFEDE, D. 1979. The Strained Relationship. *National Journal,* May 19: 830.

BOND, J. R., and FLEISHER, R. 1990. *The President in the Legislative Arena.* Chicago: University of Chicago Press.

——— and WOOD, B. D. 2003. The Marginal and Time-Varying Effect of Public Approval on Presidential Success in Congress. *Journal of Politic,* 65: 92–100.

BORELLI, S. A., WRIGHTON, J. M., and BRYAN, C. 1998. Policy-Specific Approval Ratings and Presidential Success on Roll Calls: An Exploration. *American Review of Politics,* 19: 267–82.

BOWLES, N. 1987. *The White House and Capitol Hill.* New York: Oxford University Press.

BRACE, P., and HINCKLEY, B. 1992. *Follow the Leader: Opinion Polls and the Modern Presidents.* New York: Basic Books.

BRADY, D. W., CANES-WRONE, B., and COGAN, J. F. 2000. Differences between Winning and Losing Incumbents. In *Change and Continuity in House Elections,* ed. D. W. Brady, J. F. Cogan, and M. P. Fiorina. Stanford, CA: Stanford University Press.

—— COGAN, J. F., GAINES, B., and RIVERS, R. D. 1996. The Perils of Presidential Support: How the Republicans Captured the House. *Political Behavior,* 18: 345–68.

BROWNSTEIN, R. 2007. *The Second Civil War.* New York: Penguin Press.

BULLOCK, C. S., III, and BRADY, D. W. 1977. Party, Constituency, and U.S. Senate Voting Behavior. Paper presented at the Annual Meeting of the Southern Political Science Association, New Orleans, LA, Nov.

BURDEN, B. C., and KIMBALL, D. C. 2002. *Why Americans Split their Tickets: Campaigns, Competition, and Divided Government.* Ann Arbor: University of Michigan Press.

BURNHAM, W. D. 1975. Insulation and Responsiveness in Congressional Elections. *Political Science Quarterly,* 90: 411–35.

CAMPBELL, J. E. 1997. The Presidential Pulse and the 1994 Midterm Congressional Election. *Journal of Politics,* 59: 830–57.

CANES-WRONE, B., BRADY, D. W., and COGAN, J. F. 2002. Out of Step, Out of Office: Electoral Accountability and House Members' Voting. *American Political Science Review,* 96: 127–40.

—— and DE MARCHI, S. 2002. Presidential Approval and Legislative Success. *Journal of Politics,* 64: 491–509.

CANNON, C. M. 1998. The Twilight Zone, Where Substance Reigns. *National Journal,* Dec. 12: 2934–5.

CAVANAUGH, T. E. 1979. Role Orientations of House Members: The Process of Representation. Paper delivered at the Annual Meeting of the American Political Science Association, Washington, DC, Aug.

CLAUSEN, A. R. 1973. *How Congressmen Decide: A Policy Focus*. New York: St Martin's.

CLINTON, J. D. 2006. Representation in Congress: Constituents and Roll Calls in the 106th House. *Journal of Politics*, 68: 397–409.

CNUDDE, C. F., and MCCRONE, D. J. 1966. Linkage between Constituency Attitudes and Congressional Voting Behavior: A Causal Model. *American Political Science Review*, 60: 66–72.

COHEN, J. E., BOND, J. R., and FLEISHER, R. 2000. State Level Presidential Support and Senatorial Support. *Legislative Studies Quarterly*, 15: 577–90.

COLLIE, M. 1981. Incumbency, Electoral Safety, and Turnover in the House of Representatives, 1952–1976. *American Political Science Review*, 75: 119–31.

COLLIER, K. 1995. The President, the Public and Congress. Paper delivered at the Annual Meeting of the Midwest Political Science Association, Chicago, IL, Apr. 6–8.

——1997. *Between the Branches: The White House Office of Legislative Affairs*. Pittsburgh: University of Pittsburgh Press.

——and SULLIVAN, T. 1995. New Evidence Undercutting the Linkage of Approval with Presidential Support and Influence. *Journal of Politics*, 57: 197–209.

Congressional Quarterly. 1975. 1974 Support in Congress: Ford Low, Nixon Up. *Congressional Quarterly Weekly Report*, Jan. 18: 148–57.

COOK, C. 2005. Expect Bush's Popularity to Track That of the Iraq War. *National Journal*. Feb. 12: 480.

COOK, T. E. 1986. The Electoral Connection in the 99th Congress. *PS*, 19: 16–19.

CORNWELL, E. E., JR. 1959. Presidential News: The Expanding Public Image. *Journalism Quarterly*, 36: 275–83.

DAVIDSON, R. H. 1968. *The Role of the Congressmen*. New York: Pegasus.

DAVIS, R. 1986. News Coverage of American Political Institutions. Paper presented at the Annual Meeting of the American Political Science Association, Washington, DC, Aug.

DEXTER, L. A. 1955-6. Candidates Make the Issues and Give Them Meaning. *Public Opinion Quarterly*, 19: 408–14.

——1956. What Do Congressmen Hear: The Mail. *Public Opinion Quarterly*, 20: 16–27.

——1969. The Representative and his District. In *New Perspectives on the House of Representatives*, 2nd edn., ed. R. L. Peabody and N. W. Polsby. Chicago: Rand McNally.

EDWARDS, G. C., III. 1976. Presidential Influence in the House: Presidential Prestige as a Source of Presidential Power. *American Political Science Review*, 70: 101–13.

——1977. Presidential Influence in the Senate: Presidential Prestige as a Source of Presidential Power. *American Politics Quarterly*: 481–500.

——1983. *The Public Presidency*. New York: St Martin's.

——1989. *At the Margins: Presidential Leadership of Congress*. New Haven, CT: Yale University Press.

——1997. Aligning Tests with Theory: Presidential Approval as a Source of Influence in Congress. *Congress and the Presidency*, 24: 113–30.

EHRENHALT, A. 1982. In the Senate of the '80s, Team Spirit Has Given Way to the Rule of Individuals. *Congressional Quarterly Weekly Report*, Sept. 4: 2175–82.

ELLING, R. C. 1982. Ideological Change in the United States Senate: Time and Electoral Responsiveness. *Legislative Studies Quarterly*, 7: 75–92.

ERIKSON, R. S. 1976. Is There Such a Thing as a Safe Seat? *Polity*, 8: 623–32.

FENNO, R. F., JR. 1977. U.S. House Members in their Constituencies: An Exploration. *American Political Science Review*, 71: 883–917.

—— 1978. *Home Style*. Boston: Little, Brown.

—— 1982. *The United States Senate: A Bicameral Perspective*. Washington, DC: American Enterprise Institute.

FIORINA, M. P. 1974. *Representatives, Roll Calls, and Constituencies*. Lexington, MA: Lexington Books.

GANS, H. J. 1979. *Deciding What's News*. New York: Vintage.

GLAZER, A., and ROBBINS, M. 1985. Congressional Responsiveness to Constituency Change. *American Journal of Political Science*, 29: 59–273.

GOLDMAN, P., with CLIFT, E., and DEFRANK, T. M. 1977. Carter Up Close. *Newsweek*, May 2: 32–50.

GREENSTEIN, F. I. 1982. *The Hidden-Hand Presidency*. New York: Basic Books.

GRIFFIN, J. D., and NEWMAN, B. 2005. Are Voters Better Represented? *Journal of Politics*, 67: 1206–27.

GRONKE, P., KOCH, J., and WILSON, J. M. 2003. Follow the Leader? Presidential Approval, Presidential Support, and Representatives' Electoral Fortunes. *Journal of Politics*, 65: 785–808.

GROSSMAN, M. B., and KUMAR, M. J. 1981. *Portraying the President*. Baltimore: Johns Hopkins University Press.

HAGER, B. M. 1978. Carter Seeks More Effective Use of Departmental Lobbyists' Skills, *Congressional Quarterly Weekly Report*, Mar. 4: 579–86.

HALDEMAN, H. R. 1994. *The Haldeman Diaries: Inside the Nixon White House*. New York: G. P. Putnam's Sons.

HALL, R. L. 1996. *Participation in Congress*. New Haven, CT: Yale University Press.

HARLOW, B. N.d. Oral History. Lyndon B. Johnson Library.

HIBBING, J. R. 1984. The Liberal Hour: Electoral Pressures and Transfer Payment Voting in the United States Congress. *Journal of Politics*, 46: 846–65.

—— 1986. Ambition in the House: Behavioral Consequences of Higher Office Goals among U.S. Representatives. *American Journal of Political Science*, 30: 651–65.

HINCKLEY, B. 1976. Issues, Information Costs, and Congressional Elections. *American Politics Quarterly*, 4: 131–52.

—— 1980. The American Voter in Congressional Elections. *American Political Science Review*, 74: 641–50.

HULSE, C. 2005. A Messy Congressional Finale. *New York Time*, Dec. 23.

HURLEY, P. A., and HILL, K. Q. 1980. The Prospects for Issue Voting in Contemporary Congressional Elections: An Assessment of Citizen Awareness and Representation. *American Politics Quarterly*, 8: 425–48.

JACOBS, L. R., and SHAPIRO, R. Y. 2000. *Politicians Don't Pander*. Chicago: University of Chicago Press.

JACOBSON, G. C. 1987. The Marginals Never Vanished: Incumbency and Competition in Elections to the U.S. House of Representatives, 1952–82. *American Journal of Political Science*, 31: 126–41.

—— 2007. The War, the President, and the 2006 Midterm Congressional Elections. Paper delivered at the Annual Meeting of the Midwest Political Science Association, Apr. 12–15.

JOHANNES, J. R. 1984. *To Serve the People*. Lincoln: University of Nebraska Press.

JOHNSON, L. B. 1971. *The Vantage Point: Perspectives of the Presidency, 1963–1969*. New York: Popular Library.

KERNELL, S. 1986. *Going Public*. Washington, DC: Congressional Quarterly Press.

KING, G. 1986. How Not to Lie with Statistics: Avoiding Common Mistakes in Quantitative Political Science. *American Journal of Political Science*, 30: 666–87.

KINGDON, J. W. 1968. *Candidates for Office.* New York: Random House.

—— 1973. *Congressmen's Voting Decisions.* New York: Harper & Row.

LEBO, M. J., and CASSINO, D. 2007. The Aggregated Consequences of Motivated Reasoning and the Dynamics of Partisan Presidential Approval. *Political Psychology,* 28: 719–46.

LIGHT, P. C. 1983. *The President's Agenda: Domestic Policy Choice from Kennedy to Carter (with Notes on Reagan).* Baltimore: Johns Hopkins University Press.

MacNeil, N. 1970. *Dirksen: Portrait of a Public Man.* New York: World.

McPherson, H. 1972. *A Political Education.* Boston: Little, Brown.

MacRae, D. 1958. *Dimensions of Congressional Voting.* Berkeley and Los Angeles: University of California Press.

MANN, T. 1978. *Unsafe at Any Margin.* Washington, DC: American Enterprise Institute.

MARKUS, G. 1974. Electoral Coalitions and Senate Roll-Call Behavior: An Ecological Analysis. *American Journal of Political Science,* 18: 595–608.

MATHEWS, T., with HUBBARD, H. W., THOMAS, R., CLIFT, E., and MARTIN, D. 1978. Slings and Arrows. *Newsweek,* July 31: 20.

MAYHEW, D. R. 1974. *Congress: The Electoral Connection.* New Haven, CT: Yale University Press.

MILLER, W. E., and STOKES, D. E. 1963. Constituency Influences on Congress. *American Political Science Review,* 57: 45–56.

MITCHELL, A. 1997. Clinton Seems to Keep Running Though the Race is Run and Won. *New York Times,* Feb. 12: A12.

MONDALE, W. 1993. Two Views from Pennsylvania Avenue. *American Prospect,* 14: 13–16.

MORRIS, D. 1997. *Behind the Oval Office.* New York: Random House.

MOUW, C., and MacKUEN, M. 1992. The Strategic Configuration, Personal Influence, and Presidential Power in Congress. *Western Political Quarterly,* 45: 579–608.

NEUSTADT, R. E. 1960. *Presidential Power: The Politics of Leadership.* New York: Wiley.

—— 1990. *Presidential Power and the Modern Presidents.* New York: Free Press.

NIXON, R. M. 1977. *RN: The Memoirs of Richard M. Nixon.* New York: Grosset & Dunlap.

—— 1990. *In the Arena: A Memoir of Victory, Defeat and Renewal.* New York: Simon & Schuster.

OPPENHEIMER, B. I. 1971. Senators' Constituencies: Suggestions for Redefinition. Paper presented at the Annual Meeting of the American Political Science Association, Chicago, IL, Sept.

ORESKES, M. 1990. Approval of Bush, Bolstered by Panama, Soars in Poll. *New York Times,* Jan. 19: A20.

ORNSTEIN, N. and ROBINSON, M. 1986. The Case of our Disappearing Congress. *TV Guide,* Jan. 11: 4–6, 8–10.

OSTROM, C. W., Jr., and SIMON, D. M. 1985. Promise and Performance: A Dynamic Model of Presidential Popularity. *American Political Science Review,* 79: 334–58.

PAGE, B. I., and SHAPIRO, R. Y. 1992. *The Rational Public.* Chicago: University of Chicago Press.

PARKER, G. R. 1980. Cycles in Congressional District Attention. *Journal of Politics,* 42: 540–8.

—— 1986a. *Homeward Bound.* Pittsburgh: University of Pittsburgh Press.

—— 1986b. Is There a Political Life Cycle in the House of Representatives? *Legislative Studies Quarterly,* 11: 375–92.

—— and Parker, S. L. 1985. Correlates and Effects of Attention to District by U.S. House Members. *Legislative Studies Quarterly,* 10: 223–42.

Pew Research Center for the People & the Press. 2006. October 2006 Survey on Electoral Competition: Final Topline Oct. 17–22.

PONDER, D. E., and MOON, C. D. 2005. A Tale of Three Variables: Exploring the Impact of Alternative Measures of Presidential Approval on Congressional Voting. *Congress & the Presidency,* 32: 157–69.

POOLE, K. T., and ROSENTHAL, H. 1984. The Polarization of American Politics. *Journal of Politics*, 46: 1061–74.

RIESELBACH, L. N. 1973. *Congressional Politics*. New York: McGraw-Hill.

RIVERS, D., and FIORINA, M. P. 1991. Constituency Service, Reputation, and the Incumbency Advantage. In *Home Style and Washington Work: Studies in Congressional Politics*, ed. M. P. Fiorina and D. Rohde. Ann Arbor: University of Michigan Press.

—— and ROSE, N. L. 1985. Passing the President's Program: Public Opinion and Presidential Influence in Congress. *American Journal of Political Science*, 29: 183–96.

ROLLINS, E. 1996. *Bare Knuckles and Back Rooms: My Life in American Politics*. New York: Broadway Books.

ROSCOE, D. D. 2003. Electoral Messages from the District: Explaining Presidential Support in the U.S. House of Representatives. *Congress & the Presidency*, 30: 37–54.

ROSENBAUM, D. E. 1993. Clinton's Plan for Economy May Hinge on his Popularity. *New York Times*, Apr. 29: A1.

ROVERE, R. 1956. *Affairs of State: The Eisenhower Years*. New York: Farrar, Strauss.

SAFIRE, W. 1975. *Before the Fall: An Inside View of the Pre-Watergate White House*. New York: Doubleday.

SCHNEIDER, W. 1994. It's Payback Time for GOP and Press. *National Journal*, Mar. 19: 696.

SONGER, D. R. 1981. Voter Knowledge of Congressional Issue Positions: A Reassessment. *Social Science Quarterly*, 62: 424–31.

STEPHANOPOULOS, G. 1999. *All Too Human: A Political Education*. Boston: Little, Brown.

STOKES, D. E., and MILLER, W. E. 1962. Party Government and the Saliency of Congress. *Public Opinion Quarterly*, 26: 531–46.

STOLAREK, J. S., WOOD, R. M., and TAYLOR, M. W. 1981. Measuring Constituency Opinion in the U.S. House: Mail Versus Random Surveys. *Legislative Studies Quarterly*, 6: 589–95.

TACHERON, D. G., and UDALL, M. K. 1966. *The Job of a Congressman*. Indianapolis: Bobbs Merrill.

THOMAS, M. 1985. Election Proximity and Senatorial Roll-Call Voting. *American Journal of Political Science*, 29: 96–111.

Times Mirror. 1987. *The People, Press, and Politics*. Los Angeles: Times Mirror.

TIMMONS, W. E. 1973. *Memorandum for the President*. Dec. 31. Folder: Executive–Legislative Relations—93rd Congress, 1st Session, William E. Timmons Files, Box 3, Gerald R. Ford Library, p. 3.

UNEKIS, J. K. 1978. From Committee to the Floor: Consistency in Congressional Voting. *Journal of Politics*, 40: 761–9.

VANDEHEI, J., and BABINGTON, C. 2005. Newly Emboldened Congress Has Dogged Bush This Year. *Washington Post*, Dec. 23: A5.

WEST, D. M. 1988. Activists and Economic Policymaking in Congress. *American Journal of Political Science*, 32: 662–80.

WOODWARD, B. 1994. *The Agenda: Inside the Clinton White House*. New York: Simon & Schuster.

WRIGHT, G. C., JR. 1989. Policy Voting in the U.S. Senate: Who Is Represented? *Legislative Studies Quarterly*, 14: 465–86.

—— and BERKMAN, M. B. 1986. Candidates and Policy in United States Senate Elections. *American Political Science Review*, 80: 567–90.

CHAPTER 16

....

THE
PRESIDENTIAL
VETO

....

CHARLES M. CAMERON

THE executive veto is one of the few puissant powers of the presidency embedded in
the Constitution (Article I, Section 7). America's constitutional design thus guaran-
tees the president a place at the legislative bargaining table even when a majority of
those around it are hostile to his aims. Using the veto or the threat of a veto, the
president can kill legislation he opposes or, more frequently, wrest policy concessions
from majorities loath to relinquish them. In fact, some of the most important
legislation of the past three-quarters of a century was killed, postponed, or substantially shaped through veto bargaining (Cameron 2000a, table 8.1). Perhaps of even
greater significance is the silent tempering of congressional legislation imposed by
the mere existence of the veto power. The executive veto should therefore be seen as a
foundation stone for America's distinctive system of interbranch bargaining. Even
after 200 years, that system remains a hallmark of American governance.

   This chapter reviews what political scientists have, and have not, learned about the
use of vetoes, the effects of vetoes, and the significance of the veto power. As is
often the case in institutional analysis, it is helpful to draw a distinction between
"micro-politics" and "macro-politics." The micro-politics of the veto concerns the
strategic logic of the veto as applied to individual pieces of legislation or bargaining
episodes between the president and Congress. I take the macro-politics of the veto to

   I thank Will Howell, Jeff Cohen, and Nolan McCarty for helpful comments on earlier versions of
this chapter.

concern: (1) the effect of structural features of the political environment (e.g., unified or divided party control of the government) on aggregate veto usage by the president; (2) the effect of veto usage on the popularity of the president; and (3) the overall effect of the president's veto power on bill content (including pork barrel legislation), the legislative productivity of Congress, and the stability of public policy.

Because vetoes are easy to count, modern political scientific studies of the veto focused first on the macro-politics of the veto, especially the covariates of aggregate veto use; Rohde and Simon 1985 stands out as perhaps the best of these studies. However, absent well-developed micro-theory or much of the needed data, examination of veto counts soon reached diminishing returns. In fact, most of the interesting macro-political questions remain open today. However, the main barrier to progress is no longer an absence of micro-theory; in addition, much new data is at hand, or soon will be. Rather, the main difficulty is a lack of institutional variation—we simply do not have any presidents without the veto power to study! I suggest below that progress in understanding the macro-politics of the veto may be possible but—somewhat paradoxically—probably awaits further theoretical development in areas *outside* the veto, especially theories of Congress and theories of the president's legislative program.

In contrast to the rather sparse achievements on the macro-political front, progress in understanding the micro-politics of the veto has been truly substantial. Indeed, it may not be too bold to claim this area as the most theoretically sophisticated and well developed in the entire field of presidential studies. Progress in understanding the micro-politics of the veto was so rapid because analysts were able to leverage off existing models of take-it-or-leave-it bargaining in political economy (Romer and Rosenthal 1978). However, a set of rather distinctively "presidential" variants was soon developed. In addition, because on-point data were readily available or at least obtainable with effort, the theoretical models quickly received extensive empirical testing, generally with substantial success. While incremental refinements would no doubt be valuable, at this point it is not glaringly obvious that the micro-political side of the veto literature contains gaping lacunae. What are perhaps more intriguing are entirely new points of departure.

The chapter is organized in the following way. The first section reviews the micro-politics of the veto. Here I am relatively terse despite the extensive literature, because of the availability of a recent, rather detailed survey of the theory and relevant empirics (Cameron and McCarty 2004). Instead I offer a non-technical overview, highlighting areas that an interested reader may wish to pursue further. The second section turns to the macro-politics of the veto. The section begins by pointing out the knotty problems that plague macro-political studies. I highlight three in particular: the "wheat from the chaff" problem, the "small-n" problem, and the "no institutional variation" problem. The latter is particularly difficult. Nonetheless, much has been learned and more could be. Finally, in a speculative vein, the third section suggests some new points of departure. I point to the possibility of theoretically modeling, and empirically studying, integrated presidential strategy, including the veto. This section elaborates on themes in Cameron 2006.

THE MICRO-POLITICS OF THE VETO

The presidential veto has been the subject of more intense theoretical scrutiny than any other tool of presidential governance. Much of the theory has received empirical testing, generally with success.

Basic Theory

Political scientists have developed two approaches to modeling the veto. The first, and most thoroughly studied, portrays the veto as part of a one-shot take-it-or-leave-it (TILI) bargaining game played by Congress and the president. That is, Congress presents the president with a bill; he may "take it" and sign it into law; or, he may "leave it" by using the veto, affording himself (and Congress) the reversion policy or status quo. If the reversion policy is unattractive to the president he is apt to take the bill; but if the reversion policy is more attractive than the bill, he would like to veto the bill. A constraint on the president, however, is the veto override: if both chambers of Congress vote by a two-thirds majority to overturn the veto, the bill becomes law despite the president's veto. The override provision means that, when the president tends to favor the reversion policy (as might happen under divided party government), Congress must make sufficient concessions to the president so he favors the bill, or it must make the bill so broadly appealing that two-thirds of Congressmen favor it over the reversion policy. In practice, this means that a president willing to use the veto can compel considerable concessions from Congress, so much so that a bill will appeal not only to members of one party but to many members of the other as well. Of course, if the president is a supporter of the bill rather than the reversion policy (as might occur under unified party government), the veto is irrelevant.

The TILI approach to the veto is derived from the celebrated "monopoly agenda setter" of Romer and Rosenthal (1978). This simple and powerful model affords a crisp, sharp interpretation of TILI bargaining in a one-dimensional spatial setting (for a simple explication see Cameron 2006). In turn, the TILI approach to the veto has been incorporated into standard accounts of law making under the separation of powers system (e.g., Krehbiel 1998; Brady and Volden 1998; Ferejohn and Shipan 1990).

The second approach, the distributive politics veto, is quite different. Developed in McCarty 2000a and 2000b, this approach significantly extends the standard model of pork barrel politics, the Baron–Ferejohn model (1989). In the basic Baron–Ferejohn model, a congressional entrepreneur distributes benefits over Congressmen so as to hold a majority coalition, given the likely counter-proposals that will follow a rejection of the entrepreneur's allocation. Typically, a minimum winning coalition receives benefits; those outside the coalition pay the bills. The distributive politics veto adds a presidential veto to the distributive politics framework. In the model, a veto leads to another attempt to build a coalition that will "stick." So the entrepreneur must assemble a coalition that will hold not only in the legislature; it must also pass muster with the president, given what is likely to ensue given a veto. Although McCarty 2000a considers universalistic presidents, he also considers—arguably more realistically—presidents with their own geographic constituency. Such presidents will use the veto as a shield differentially protecting their own constituents. In fact, McCarty's theoretical analysis shows the veto may decrease pork modestly but is even more likely to shift its allocation. However, as discussed in the subsection "Pork and Distributive Legislation," this prediction has yet to receive an empirical test.

Varieties of Veto Politics

The distinctions drawn in the theoretical literature are extremely useful in understanding actual veto politics. In particular, it is worth distinguishing simple vetoes and override politics; sequential veto bargaining; veto threats; blame game vetoes; and vetoes and agency policy making.

Simple Vetoes and Overrides

The theoretical literature draws a sharp distinction between the *veto power* and actual *vetoes*, a distinction with important empirical implications. The veto power arises from the president's constitutional ability to veto legislation. Because of the veto power, Congress may modify legislation to head off or avoid vetoes. So, the veto power may influence the content of legislation even absent any vetoes (I return to this point in the subsection on "Anticipation Effects"). Actual vetoes occur when Congress somewhat miscalculates what the president will accept, or both president and Congress play into a gamble over an override attempt. Thus, actual vetoes require both a policy disagreement between president and Congress, and some "incomplete information." Typically, the incomplete information concerns uncertainty by Congress about the preferences of the president, but it could involve uncertainty by both or either about the preferences or identity of the veto override player. In the case of the "blame game" model considered momentarily, the incomplete information concerns voters' knowledge about the preferences of the president. Because Congress's or the voter's beliefs about the president involve his policy "reputation," TILI models of vetoes explicitly address presidential reputation, including strategic reputation building and (in the case of the blame game) reputation breaking (Cameron 2000b).

Table 2.12 in Cameron 2000a summarizes empirical patterns in the 434 post-war vetoes from 1945 to 1992. Overall, vetoes were rare events—only about 2 percent of all enactments were vetoed. However, among very important enactments during divided party government, the veto rate was as high as 20 percent. Overall, Congress attempted to override about half of the post-war regular vetoes. (Recall that the Constitution allows the president to "pocket veto" legislation passed in the closing days of a Congress; pocket vetoes cannot be overridden. So-called "regular" vetoes (non-pocket vetoes) can be overridden by a two-thirds majority vote in both chambers of Congress.) Notably, Congress attempted to override about 80 percent of regular vetoes of consequential legislation during divided party government. The success rate on override attempts was about 45 percent.

Krehbiel (1998) presents an innovative analysis of how Congressmen's votes shift between the passage vote and the override attempt. He shows that "marginal" Congressmen are the most likely switchers—Congressmen near the veto pivot whose ideology makes them nearly indifferent between voting one way or the other (see also Wilkins and Young 2002). This is exactly the pattern predicted by models of "bribe" targeting (Groseclose and Snyder 1996). Such data, if combined with micro-level data on presidential lobbying, afford an opportunity to test and explore these models. Such a study would have larger implications about presidential–legislative interactions and lobbying strategies more generally.

Sequential Veto Bargaining

Law making does not always involve one-shot take-it-or-leave-it offers. If the president vetoes a bill, Congress can modify its content, re-pass it, and present it to him again. Cameron 2000a shows that this process of "sequential veto bargaining" has occurred many times, though it is generally restricted to the most consequential legislation. For less consequential legislation, a veto is generally a fatal event. Cameron suggests this fact reflects the steep opportunity costs involved in securing floor time (see Cox 2006 on "plenary time").

Sequential veto bargaining involves an active process of congressional learning about what the president is willing to accept (Cameron and Elmes 1994). Vetoes force Congress to revise its estimate and consequently offer concessions. Sequential veto bargaining can also involve a degree of bluffing by the president: he may veto a bill he would actually be willing to accept, in order to extract concessions in the successor bill. It is risky strategy, however, in that bargaining may break down and no bill be enacted.

Cameron 2000a presents data on sequential veto bargaining as well as case studies of prominent examples, including the passage of welfare reform in the Clinton administration.

Veto Threats

If Congress is somewhat unsure about what the president will actually accept, a veto threat—or conversely silence—can be somewhat informative about his preferences. In essence, silence implies consent. But a veto threat may well be a bluff, in that the president might actually be willing to accept a bill and uses the threat to angle for concessions. In fact, during divided party government, veto threats occur with extraordinary frequency and appear remarkably efficacious in extracting concessions (Cameron 2000a; Kernell 2006). For highly consequential legislation drafted during divided party government, it is hardly an exaggeration to say the president keeps up a veritable drum-beat of veto threats. Veto threats appear a powerful tool of presidential–legislative relations, one that is relatively under-studied given their frequent use and apparent effectiveness.

The theory of veto threats is laid out in Matthews (1989); a simple explication may be found in Cameron and McCarty (2004).

Blame Game Vetoes

On occasion, it will be more valuable for the party opposing the president to have a live issue rather than a done deal. In particular, by offering the president a piece of high-profile "veto bait," the opposition party can highlight for voters the president's stubborn insistence on an extreme and unpopular policy position. In this case, veto bargaining becomes a game played before spectators, with victory tied as much to their perceptions as to the enactment or failure of legislation. In the blame game, whatever action the president takes will be costly to him: either accept a bill with an unattractive policy, or veto it and pay a price in popularity. Blame game vetoes are characteristic of periods of high interparty ideological polarization, combined with divided party government.

Identifying blame game vetoes is somewhat tricky as ideally one would like to know the intention of Congress in proffering a bill to the president. However, likely signatures of the blame game include a high-profile bill offered immediately prior to a presidential election during divided party government; passed by a narrow majority along party lines so that a veto override is hopeless; and no veto override is attempted or an override fails by a wide margin. The Family Medical Leave Act vetoed by George H. W. Bush is usually taken as an archetypal blame game veto. More recently, President Bush's veto of a child health care bill in the 110th Congress may have been a blame game veto—upon passage in the House, the bill lacked some two dozen votes for a successful override. The second stem cell research bill vetoed by Bush (in 2007) also displays the signatures of a blame game veto. Cameron 2000b provides a list of some likely blame game vetoes in the post-war era.

A question that has received little attention is the interaction between the veto and the filibuster, especially in the context of the blame game. One usually thinks of the filibuster as a tool of the Senate minority, facing a majority party and its president (Wawro and Schickler 2006). But in the last George W. Bush Congress (the 110th), the Republican minority filibustered many bills that, presumably, President Bush would have vetoed. Why didn't the Republicans allow those bills to go forward and die from the veto? An interesting possibility is that the Republicans acted to protect their already damaged president from further blows to his popularity. But it may also have been true that very extreme Republicans were happy to bear the cost of filibustering (at present quite low, due to the use of "holds") in order to claim credit for defeating Democratic bills. For these Senators, filibustering brought more benefits than costs. And the extreme polarization of the Senate made the policy compromises necessary to beat the filibuster and veto very unattractive to Democrats, who saw the hope of imminently winning the White House anyway. Though a relatively small point, the filibuster–veto interaction in the 110th Congress illustrates the somewhat surprising turns veto politics can take.

The theory of blame game vetoes is due to Groseclose and McCarty (2001), though somewhat similar albeit informal arguments can be found in Gilmour (1995).

Cameron and McCarty (2004) provide a simple explication of the theory. I return to blame game vetoes in the subsection on "Presidential Popularity and the Electoral Cycle" where I discuss the effects of vetoes on presidential popularity.

Vetoes and Agency Policy Making

In an era of a vast administrative state, agencies can often undertake policy initiatives unilaterally, at the president's direction. Congress may attempt to reverse these actions, by passing legislation. However, the president can use the veto to protect the new "status quo" established at his direction. The combination of agency discretion and presidential veto implies a shift in power from Congress to the president, particularly if the courts (the other venue for reversing agency actions) are friendly to the president, perhaps because he has packed them with loyal co-partisans.

A recent dramatic example concerns "water boarding," a practice widely viewed as a form of torture, employed by the CIA against terrorism suspects at the direction of the president. In 2008, Congress enacted a bill prohibiting agencies from using the controversial practice and certain other extreme forms of interrogation. President Bush then vetoed the bill, which failed of an override. Consequently, extreme interrogation practices remained available to government agencies, who could continue under the effective protection of the presidential veto.

This example highlights uses of the veto that would never have occurred to the Founders, and points to the potential value of models of integrated presidential strategy. The theory of vetoes and agency policy making is elaborated in detail in Ferejohn and Shipan 1990; see also Howell 2003.

THE MACRO-POLITICS OF THE VETO

The macro-politics of political institutions concerns big-picture questions about institutional performance. Macro-political studies are particularly helpful in reaching empirically grounded, normative evaluations of political institutions. Unfortunately, from a normative point of view the literature on the macro-politics of the veto is weakest exactly where one would wish it strongest: the effects of the president's veto power on the overall content of legislation and the aggregate legislative performance of Congress. Does the president's veto power force ideologically extreme Congresses to moderate the content of legislation to avoid the veto, thereby benefiting moderate citizens? Does the president's veto power restrain Congress's frantic urge to pork-barrel? Or does it merely garner the president's co-partisans a bigger share of the spoils? Does the veto stabilize policy in specific domains? These remain open questions.

Before turning to these and related subjects, it is important to highlight three methodological problems that plague macro-political studies of the veto—or indeed macro-political studies of the other instruments of presidential power, such as public rhetoric, the legislative program, appointments, or executive orders.

Methodological Issues

Three methodological problems bedevil studies of the macro-politics of the veto. Analysts have found ways to address the first two; the third remains difficult.

The "Wheat-from-the-Chaff" Problem

One of the outstanding empirical realities of the veto is that not all vetoes are created alike. To illustrate, consider two pieces of legislation vetoed by President Harry Truman in the 80th Congress:

H.R. 723. For the relief of the legal guardian of Hunter A. Hoagland, a minor. Vetoed June 27, 1947. The veto message was laid before the House, referred to the Committee on Judiciary, and printed as H.R. Doc. No. 368. (93 Cong. Rec. 7822, 7823). Veto unchallenged.

   H.R. 3020 Labor–Management Relations Act, 1947 (Taft–Hartley). Vetoed June 20, 1947. The veto message was laid before the House and printed as H.R. Doc. No 334 (93 Cong. Rec. 7485–7488). The House overrode the veto on June 20, 1947 by a vote of 331 yeas to 83 nays (93 Cong. Rec. 7489). The Senate overrode the veto on June 23, 1947 by a vote of 68 yeas to 25 nays. (93 Cong. Rec. 7539). Veto overridden. (61 Stat. 136; Public Law 80–101). (Senate Library 1992 (Senate Publication 102–12))

The first concerns a bill of absolutely zero public policy importance, indeed of no interest to anyone other than Master Hoagland's guardian, the Congressman who served as his errand boy, and an anonymous drone in the executive branch who wished to protect the public fisc from a bad precedent. The second concerns one of the most important pieces of legislation of the twentieth century, one with substantial import for workplace relations in the United States and, arguably, for the political development of the country in the post-war years. The first veto is trivial to the point of inconsequentiality; the second of tremendous significance despite its failure (of course, Truman's veto of the Taft–Hartley Act played an important role in the presidential election of 1948).

   The vast majority of vetoes are of the first kind, not the second. For example, most of Grover Cleveland's 304 first-term vetoes struck down bills extending veterans benefits to individuals who did not qualify for them (Berdahl 1937). This form of "waste, fraud, and abuse" largely benefited Republicans and therefore presented an attractive target for the first (elected) Democratic president since the Civil War. Yet even taken as a whole and considering their value as symbolic politics, Cleveland's vetoes of private bills did not really amount to much. In modern times, most of President Truman's vetoes were also directed at private bills like the Hoagland give-away, inflating Truman's count to 180 regular vetoes and 70 pocket vetoes. A similar inflation occurred with President Eisenhower's vetoes. By Kennedy, however, passage of private bills had become less frequent; eventually, their enactment became rare.

A similar issue arises with pocket vetoes, which only rarely are of any policy significance. The relative inconsequentiality of most pocket-vetoed legislation reflects the legislative strategies of authors of more consequential legislation: the author of an even modestly consequential but clearly controversial bill typically schedules its floor passage earlier in the congressional session, so that a veto override attempt remains possible. Only relatively inconsequential bills are left at the end of the session to be pocket-vetoed (a few of President Gerald Ford's pocket vetoes offer a modest exception to this general rule).

The way in which trivial vetoes swamp important ones is a challenge for macro-political analyses of vetoes: how can one sort the wheat from the chaff? This problem is hardly unique to the study of the veto; rather, it is pervasive in the president's use of all his instruments of governance: public speeches, executive orders, legislative proposals, and so on.

At least in the case of vetoes, analysts have responded in two ways (aside from ignoring the problem). The first is to define the universe of vetoes as regular vetoes of non-private bills. This is a step in the right direction (which I pursue shortly), but it still mixes quite minor vetoes with extraordinary ones. A more ambitious effort, taking inspiration from Mayhew (1991), sorts vetoes into "significance categories" ranging from high to low. This effort was initiated by Wooley (1991) and Watson (1993), but pursued most aggressively in Cameron (2000a), which not only classified vetoed bills but also all enacted legislation from 1945 to 1994 into comparable importance categories. Consequently, this study could examine not only counts of vetoes but veto rates for enactments by importance category. This move turns out to be vital for understanding the macro-politics of the veto, because many minor pieces of legislation have been vetoed but the veto *rate* for such enactments is very low; conversely, far fewer pieces of important legislation have been vetoed but the veto *rate* for such legislation is amazingly high, at least under specific circumstances.

The sorting method employed in Cameron (2000a) combined newspaper coverage (as in Mayhew 1991) with coverage in *Congressional Quarterly Almanac*; consequently, the analysis was restricted to the post-war years. Recent advances in item-response scaling have allowed analysts much greater flexibility and power in using other sources with much longer data availability (see Clinton and Lapinski 2006). To a large degree, the item-response methods have solved the wheat-from-the-chaff problem. However, as noted in the following paragraphs, this methodological breakthrough has yet to be fully exploited in new studies of the veto.

The "Small-n" Problem

The second problem is intrinsic to macro-political analysis: the unit of analysis is typically a Congress or a president, and there have been relatively few of these. For example, at the time I write there have been only thirty-two post-war Congresses and eleven post-war presidents. Consequently, it is very difficult to discern reliable empirical patterns, except of the grossest variety (King 1993).

Analysts have responded to the small-n problem in two ways. The first is to abandon macro-politics in favor of micro-politics, where data can be abundant.

For example, rather than studying the number of vetoes per Congress (so one has thirty-two observations in the post-war era), one can study the probability of a veto per class of enactment or even individual enactment, so one has thousands of observations. Of course, this approach requires data on specific enactments beyond structural features per Congress; otherwise, the proliferation of observations is largely illusory. New data on legislation afford new opportunities in this area, for example, the Congressional Bills Project (see <www.congressionalbills.org>). The second approach to the small-n problem has been to acquire more macro-political data by extending modern datasets backward in time. Again, the outstanding example is Clinton and Lapinski (2006), which neatly extends the measurement of legislative significance backward to 1877. When these data are publicly released, it will be possible to calculate veto rates by legislative significance and reexamine the macro-politics of the veto over a much more extended time period. This is a potentially exciting development.

The "No Institutional Variation" Problem

The typical way to explore causal effects is through covariation: vary an exogenous variable and document the resulting response of the critical endogenous variable. This procedure works well for studying *vetoes*, but it faces a severe problem in studying the effects of the president's *veto power*: there have been no presidents without the veto power. The no-variation problem is, as scholars of Comparative Politics often point out, intrinsic to studying American national institutions non-comparatively (Huber and Gamm 2002).

One response to the no-variation problem is to be more comparative. Unfortunately, most cross-national comparisons seem too coarse or too distant to be apposite—one must compare not just apples and oranges but apples and elephants. Comparisons across the American states, however, can sometimes be illuminating, as shown perhaps most notably in Besley and Case (2003) and Huber and Shipan (2002). Although there are some notable exceptions—for example, Holtz-Eakin (1988) on the effects of the line-item veto—this is not a route that students of the veto have pursued with as much vigor as one might expect.

There is an alternative, however, that allows one to address American national institutions: use stronger theory to substitute for institutional variation. Sometimes this route allows one to interpret the behavioral variation one sees despite fixed American federal institutions, and at least place bounds on the size of possible effects. I return to this idea in the section on "Anticipation Effects."

When do Presidents Use the Veto? The "High Veto" Configuration

Little attention has been paid to the macro-politics of the veto of late, so let us quickly review the data. The top row in Figure 16.1 shows the number of regular vetoes of non-private bills per Congress from 1945 to 2008, the 79th to 110th

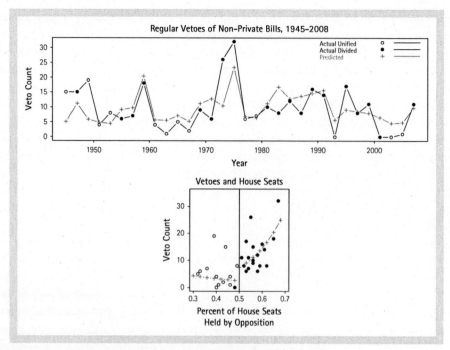

Figure 16.1. Regular vetoes of non-private bills since 1945

Congresses. As discussed above, excluding pocket vetoes and private bill vetoes enhances comparability over time and allows us to focus on vetoes with at least some policy consequence.

The number of vetoes per Congress ranged from zero to thirty-two. If these numbers seem relatively modest, it should be remembered that at any given time, most of the policy action in Congress revolves around a very small number of bills. If a Congress enacts as many a dozen important pieces of legislation, it is generally accounted extraordinarily productive (Mayhew 1991). Especially during divided party government, it is these consequential bills that disproportionately draw vetoes.

Several patterns immediately stand out. The first is *variation by presidency.* Here, the most notable pattern is Gerald Ford's heavy reliance on vetoes. Ford faced huge opposition majorities in Congress following the Democratic sweep in the 1974 election, a consequence of the Watergate scandal and the impeachment and resignation of President Nixon. In these incredibly inauspicious circumstances, Ford necessarily fell back on the veto as one of the few presidential governing tools expressly granted by the Constitution. Ford can be seen as the model of a president whose resources devolve down to the veto. Somewhat similar figures from earlier periods include Andrew Johnson and John Tyler.

Even in the relatively brief time span shown in the figure, one can discern other presidents who relied heavily on the veto. Eisenhower, for example, confronted a large activist Democratic opposition after the 1958 election. He too turned to the veto to force compromise. After the 1994 election, President Clinton faced a Congress controlled by the highly militant Gingrich Republicans. He wielded the veto skillfully to check their moves and compel them to moderate, however reluctantly.

President George W. Bush's first Congress or two (the 107th and 108th) also stand out as unusual. But they appear anomalous for their infrequent vetoes. No doubt the rarity of vetoes reflected the impact of the 9/11 terrorist attacks, which brought "wartime" legislation to the fore and made congressional Democrats quite deferential to the president. Arguably anomalous were the large number of unified party vetoes by President Truman in the 79th and 81st Congresses. However, most of the vetoed bills in those congresses were of relatively modest consequence so the apparent anomaly probably amounts to little.

The second notable pattern is *variation by unified and divided party control*. In the figure, unified party congresses are shown with open circles, divided party ones by black circles. Clearly, divided government typically brings forth vetoes; unified government does so to a much lesser degree. For instance, the mean number of regular, non-private bill vetoes per Congress since 1950 was about 3.5 during unified party government but somewhat over 12 during divided party government, about three and a half times greater. In fact, as shown in the figure, almost every divided party Congress had more than six vetoes; almost every unified party Congress had fewer than seven.

How can one explain the obvious variation in veto counts? Scholars who cut their teeth on spatial models of legislative politics (e.g., Krehbiel 1998; Brady and Volden 1998; Cox and McCubbins 2004) are likely to see the key explanatory variable as the spatial distance between the president and the median Congressman or, perhaps, that between the president and the median member of the opposition party. (One can easily calculate the relevant distances using Poole and Rosenthal's NOMINATE scores; but note the logical problems discussed in Clinton 2007.) The basic idea is: when this distance is small, the president is likely to view the proposed change in the status quo favorably. But when the distance is large, he is less likely to do so unless the bill is finely calibrated to his preferences or those of the veto pivot. So, a small error in placement will provoke a veto. Although the published empirical literature on the macro-politics of the veto does not contain models of this kind, in fact they perform very poorly in explaining veto counts (analysis not shown).

An earlier generation of political scientists would have taken the key explanatory variable to be the percentage of seats held by the president's opposition, especially in the House. And in fact, a simple three-variable model of this kind—where the variables are "divided party government," "percentage of House seats held by the opposition," and the interaction between the two—captures a considerable amount of the variation in veto counts. (Once one includes in the regression the percentage of opposition seats in the House, adding those in the Senate contributes nothing.) In the model, the interaction does most of the work.

The top panel in Figure 16.1 shows the fit from such a model. The fit is from a quasi-maximum likelihood Poisson regression which accounts for the over-dispersion in the data, but substantively almost identical results obtained in OLS, Poisson, or negative binominal models. It will be seen that the model tracks the modern experience rather well. The bottom panel in the figure examines the key relationship. Four patterns stand out. First, if the president's party controls the House, vetoes are relatively rare (about 5–6 per Congress). And, under those circumstances, vetoes are insensitive to the exact size of the president's majority. However, at about the 50 percent mark, there is a discontinuity, an apparent jump as party control changes. Then, after crossing the 50 percent mark, there is a regime change: as the percentage of House seats controlled by an opposition majority increases, the number of vetoes increases. As shown, the number of vetoes increases from a base of about 7.5 vetoes at 50 percent, at a rate of about one veto per percent point above 50 percent. The model thus appears to identify a "high veto configuration" in American politics: divided party government and a large opposition to the president in the House.

These patterns would probably have struck earlier generations of political scientists as "common sense." Nonetheless, they constitute something of a puzzle in light of contemporary, spatially oriented theories of Congress and the presidency. In those theories, there is no direct role for "percentage of seats held by the opposition." So how can we reconcile the macro-evidence and contemporary micro-theories? An obvious point is that the political process that generates veto counts involves more than an executive–legislative interaction over a given bill, as analyzed in veto micro-theory. Rather, the data-generating process involves all aspects of Congress including committee power, positive and negative agenda control, manipulation of floor rules, various possible party effects, and the preexisting distribution of status quo policies (Cox 2006; Krehbiel 2004). Together, these features determine which and how many preexisting or new policies receive attention and the content of the resulting legislation. Presumably, some of these features explain the close connection between veto counts and the percentage of House seats held by the opposition during divided party government. But what those features may be is unclear at present.

Whatever the causal mechanism underlying the "high veto configuration," it is worth examining the frequency with which the high veto configuration occurs. How frequently do presidents find themselves in a structural position that leads to many vetoes?

Figure 16.2 provides some insight. It displays the percentage of seats in the House held by the president's opposition, from 1850 to 2010. It also distinguishes unified party government (open circles) from divided part government (black circles). As shown, the "high veto configuration" was quite common in the latter half of the nineteenth century. It was relatively rare in the first half of the twentieth century, because of the infrequency of divided party government. But in the second half of the twentieth century, the high veto configuration became common again. In fact, the recent experience mirrors that of the late nineteenth century, though seat swings in the House are now more moderate (presumably due to better control of the macro-economy). Overall, the figure confirms Stokes and Iverson's famous conjecture that one party rarely dominates American politics for long (1962). Absent an extraordinary implosion by either the Republican or Democratic parties, the high veto configuration will reappear regularly. When it does, the stage is set for vetoes.

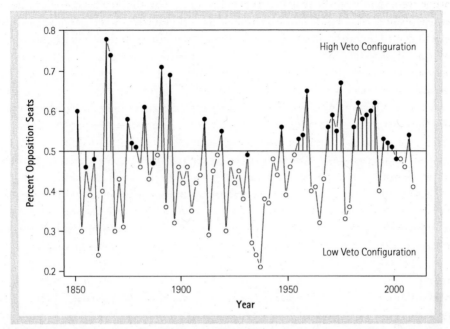

Figure 16.2. The frequency of the high veto and low veto configurations, 1851–2010

Presidential Popularity and the Electoral Cycle

The empirical literature on the macro-politics of the veto noted the possible impact of presidential popularity and the electoral cycle on veto frequency (Rohde and Simon 1985; Wooley 1991). Underlying this conjecture was a Neustadtian "bank balance" view of the presidency: popularity puts money in the president's bank account (as it were) so that popular presidents are "strong" presidents. And (in this view) Congress hesitates to "challenge" a strong president. Thus, the bank balance view suggests, a popular president vetoes little because Congress lies supine at his feet, while an unpopular lame-duck president vetoes more because Congress is resurgent and assertive.

Contemporary theories of Congress and the presidency have not adopted the bank balance view of the presidency. In fact, some contemporary theories turn the bank balance logic on its head.

Consider Groseclose and McCarty's model of blame game vetoes (see the subsection on "Blame Game Vetoes" above). In this model, president and Congress bargain before an audience of voters. And, Congress—especially a divided party Congress shortly before a presidential election—deliberately constructs its legislative offers to draw a veto and cast the president in as unfavorable a light as possible. When the "veto bait" provokes the intended presidential response, voters form an unfavorable impression of the president's policy views. As a result, his popularity declines. In other words, unpopularity does not cause vetoes; rather, vetoes cause unpopularity. Groseclose and McCarty test this prediction with data on presidential approval from

1956 to 1992. They find that major vetoes during divided party government indeed reduce presidential approval; minor vetoes and unified party vetoes do not.

In a rather different model, McCarty (1997) examines presidential incentives to build a policy reputation over the electoral cycle. Early in the cycle, the president has an incentive to veto bills in order to build a more extreme reputation and thereby extract concessions in subsequent, related legislation. Appreciating these incentives Congress, early in the presidential term, forbears from presenting the president with bills he will veto. Thus, a kind of early-term "veto honeymoon" emerges endogenously. The logic is not that Congress "challenges" a weak, lame-duck president; rather, Congress shrinks before an early-term, reputation-hungry president. McCarty examines data on the timing of vetoes and finds support for a veto honeymoon.

These studies, though employing essentially macro-political data, have strong roots in micro-theory. They offer a novel take on vetoes and presidential power. Somewhat strangely, their empirics have not been updated with longer time series or expanded with data from state governments. This is an obvious research opportunity.

Anticipation Effects: Bill Content, Legislative Productivity, and Policy Stability

The *possibility* of a veto is likely to insinuate itself into many calculations of Congressmen. For example: In light of the president's veto power, is it worth enacting this legislation? Or is it better to work on other matters? If we do go forward, how should we adjust the legislation's content to head off a veto? Call these "anticipation effects" of the veto power.

In gauging the size of anticipation effects, evidence from actual vetoes can be helpful. But anticipation effects may be considerable even absent any vetoes. Of course, if some presidents had the veto power and others did not, we might be able to estimate the size of anticipation effects directly. But since all presidents have the veto power, the "no-institutional variation" problem bites hard. One might despair, but sometimes it is possible to use well-elaborated theory to detect anticipation effects—at least in principle. Such efforts can be worthwhile, as they allow us to address silent but pervasive consequences of America's constitutional design.

Pork and Distributive Legislation

Will the president use the veto to restrain Congress's relentless urge to pork-barrel? This has been a recurrent hope of efficiency-minded students of the American political economy. The underlying logic is seemingly intuitive: Congressmen are loyal primarily to their small district and quite insensitive to the externalities their reelection efforts impose on the citizenry more broadly. But the chief executive (supposedly) has a more universal constituency and may interpose presidential power as a shield between citizens and Congress's worst urges.

In light of these expectations, it would be helpful to know the effect of actual vetoes on pork barrel legislation (e.g., spending on bridges, roads, dams or—seemingly—homeland security). How much pork have vetoes killed? During sequential veto bargaining over pork barrel legislation, do subsequent versions of vetoed bills contain changes in the allocation of benefits and costs? To the best of my knowledge, these questions have yet to receive systematic attention.

Again, however, the main effect of the veto is probably an anticipation effect: Congress is likely to shift or forgo pork in order to head off a veto.

The development of a carefully articulated theory of vetoes in distributive politics offers the hope of gauging the magnitude of these anticipation effects (McCarty 2000a; see the subsection on "Basic Theory" above). In particular, the key variable in McCarty's model of pork barrel vetoes is the size of the president's constituency (party) in Congress. Obviously, this variable changes dramatically over time (see Figure 16.2). In addition, there is considerable variation in the geographic distributions of support for Republican and Democratic presidents (Gelman 2008). By utilizing these two sources of variation and matching them with the geographic distribution of pork, it may well be possible to identify the magnitude of the anticipation effect in distributive politics. This appears to be a fruitful, and largely un-pursued, line of inquiry.

Ideological Legislation

Most legislation is not pork barrel legislation, at least not nominally. Rather, the legislation has an ideological tenor that translates into a left–right ideological position (Poole and Rosenthal 2007). How do vetoes affect the ideological positioning of enactments?

Cameron (2000a) presents evidence about bill positioning over sequences of vetoed and re-passed bills. Because the status quo policy remains fixed over such a sequence, one can compare the content of bills in a sequence by examining the movement in the cut-point between yeas and nays in an ideological space, like Poole and Rosenthal's first dimension NOMINATE space. That is, if the cut point on the roll call on the re-passed bill moves toward the president's ideal policy, the re-passed bill's content has presumably shifted toward the president. Cameron shows that this sort of repositioning in bill content is common and apparently substantial during sequential veto bargaining (which itself is rather common for highly consequential bills passed during divided party government). Somewhat similarly, Cameron presents evidence from content analysis of bills threatened with vetoes, and shows that congressional compromise is common after a veto threat (also see Kernell 2006).

This evidence indicates a powerful impact from actual vetoes. But one would like to go beyond these estimates to gauge the anticipation effect in bill positioning in non-vetoed enactments. Unfortunately, two problems present themselves. First, there is no generally accepted way to measure the ideological content of bills directly (if there were, it would be of immense value in testing theories of legislating).

Suppose, however, one *did* have a reasonable method for determining the ideological position of bills or groups of bills. It would be tempting to attribute the variation in bill positioning between unified and divided party government to the veto power, at least if one controlled for obvious attributes of Congress such as the preferences of the median voter or median majority member. But such an inference would be problematic because much else changes with the switch between unified and divided party government. In particular, the president's legislative program is apt to be very different and have different impacts on Congress (see, e. g., Larocca 2006). Suppose, for example, unified party presidents can shift bills toward their preferred position by drafting proposed legislation and presenting it to Congress, as suggested in Cameron and Park (2007). Then a Democratic president facing a Democratic Congress may be able to shift bills somewhat to the left. Conversely, bills from the same Congress facing a Republican president might shift to the right, due to the anticipation effect from the veto power. Attributing to the veto power all the measured change in bill locations between the first and second scenarios would overstate the impact of the veto power.

Can these problems be solved? Clearly, they are tough nuts to crack. But progress in measuring bill content and further progress in understanding the analytic foundations of the president's legislative program might open a new research frontier.

Congressional Productivity, Gridlock, and Policy Stability

Mayhew 1991 stimulated considerable interest in surges and slumps in congressional legislative productivity. Mayhew found little difference in the number of very important laws enacted by Congress between unified and divided party government. Some recent studies modify this conclusion to a degree; for example, Howell et al. find about a 28 percent reduction in the production of important legislation with the switch from unified to divided party government, and about a 39 percent increase with the converse switch (2000). These findings somewhat allay fears that the veto power allows the president to gridlock American politics across the board, when Congress and the executive have different policy preferences. Yet they still hint at a stabilizing impact from American constitutional design: policies are not likely to vary wildly with small shifts in majorities (Hammond and Miller 1987).

An obvious question is, what explains the differential productivity that seems to exist? How much is due to vetoes and the veto power when Congress and president are at loggerheads, and how much (if any) is attributable to presidential leadership when Congress and the executive have similar preferences? The analytical difficulties are the same as those discussed in the previous section: no institutional variation in the veto power and inadequately developed theories of the presidential legislative program. Here there is a major opportunity for theorists: better-developed theory might identify sources of variation that would allow a parsing of the different mechanisms.

A related area of inquiry concerns stability and change in policy domains. In other words, when are there surges in congressional production of, say, health policy legislation, energy legislation, environmental legislation, banking legislation, telecommunications legislation, and so on? What role does the veto play here (and, one might add, the presidential program)? Although there are many policy histories, relatively little systematic attention has been devoted to legislative change and stability in policy domains.

Toward Integrated
Presidential Strategy

Because the micro-politics of the presidential veto has been the subject of such extensive theoretical and empirical investigation, this area of presidential studies appears, if not "over-tilled" (to use Arnold's phrase), at least adequately tilled. If one expands one's definition of veto strategy, however, research opportunities abound.

Over the last decade presidential scholars have dramatically extended the theoretical and quantitative analysis of presidential governance tools. Perhaps most notably, Howell (2003) studies executive orders; Canes-Wrone (2006) studies "going public;" Edwards and Barrett (2000), Rudalevige (2002), Larocca (2006), Cameron and Park (2007), and Cohen (2008) study the president's legislative program; and Lewis (2008) studies presidential appointments. Cameron (2006) summarizes much of this work and notes that underlying all these tools of presidential power are three (and apparently only three) causal mechanisms: *veto power, proposal power,* and what he terms *"strategic pre-action."* In the latter, the president first changes a state variable affecting his or other's behavior, and then plays a game involving veto power or proposal power. The agency policy-making game discussed in the subsection on "Vetoes and Agency Policy Making" is an example of strategic pre-action, in that agency action creates a new status quo at the president's direction, then the president and Congress play a standard legislative game in which the veto power is critical.

If this claim is true, an opportunity arises to study *integrated presidential strategy.* By combining models of veto power, proposal power, and strategic pre-action, one might be able to consider simultaneously and interconnectedly how the president constructs a legislative program; mobilizes public attention through rhetoric; shapes congressional action with veto threats; forces concessions with vetoes; uses bribes to switch votes during overrides; employs executive orders to take unilateral action; pursues strategic appointments to effectuate agency policy making; oversees agency action; and protects it with the veto and judicial appointments.

Steps have already been made toward models of integrated presidential strategy. Examples include the models of executive orders and agency policy making, in which the president takes a direct step, then protects his initiative with the veto (Ferejohn and Shipan 1990; Howell 2003). But I am suggesting far more ambitious efforts, for example, by adding an appointment game onto the front of the agency policy-making game and including the trade-offs between responsiveness and competence studied in Lewis (2008), or incorporating a "going public" game (Canes-Wrone 2006) into models of the presidential legislative program (Larocca 2006; Cameron and Park 2007). Detailed empirical case studies of integrated strategy would be extremely helpful, particularly case studies informed by the theoretical advances of the last decade.

Models of integrated presidential strategy knitting together veto power, proposal power, and strategic pre-action would constitute a new vision of presidential governance, a vision reflecting the rise of the modern administrative state, polarized politics, the plebiscitary presidency, and the continuing reality of interbranch bargaining.

REFERENCES

ARNOLD, R. D. 1982. Over-tilled and Under-tilled Fields in Political Science. *Political Science Quarterly*, 97: 91–103.

BARON, D., and FEREJOHN, J. 1989. Bargaining in Legislatures. *American Political Science Review*, 83: 1181–206.

BERDAHL, C. 1937. The President's Veto of Private Bills. *Political Science Quarterly*, 52/4: 505–31.

BESLEY, T., and CASE, A. 2003. Political Institutions and Policy Choices: Evidence from the American States. *Journal of Economic Literature*, 41/1: 7–73.

BRADY, D. W., and VOLDEN, C. 1998. *Revolving Gridlock: Politics and Policy from Carter to Clinton*. Boulder, CO: Westview Press.

CAMERON, C. 2000a. *Veto Bargaining: Presidents and the Politics of Negative Power*. Cambridge: Cambridge University Press.

—— 2000b. Presidential Reputation and Bargaining. In *Presidential Power: Forging the Presidency for the 21st Century*, ed. R. Y. Shapiro, M. J. Kumar, and L. R. Jacobs. New York: Columbia University Press.

—— 2006. The Political Economy of the US Presidency. Pp. 241–55 in *The Oxford Handbook of Political Economy*, ed B. Weingast and D. Wittman. Oxford: Oxford University Press.

—— and ELMES, S. 1994. Sequential Veto Bargaining. Manuscript Columbia University. <http://www.princeton.edu/~ccameron/VetoBargain.pdf>.

—— and MCCARTY, N. 2004. Models of Vetoes and Veto Bargaining. *Annual Review of Political Science*, 7: 409–35.

—— and PARK, J.-K. 2007. A Primer on the President's Legislative Program. In *Presidential Leadership: The Vortex of Power*, ed. B. A. Rockman and R. W. Lightman. Cary, NC: Roxbury Press.

CANES-WRONE, B. 2006. *Who Leads Whom?* Princeton, NJ: Princeton University Press.

CLINTON, J. 2007. Law-Making and Roll Calls. *Journal of Politics*, 69/2: 455–67.

—— and LAPINSKI, J. 2006. Measuring Legislative Accomplishment 1877–1994. *American Journal of Political Science*, 50/1: 232–49.

COHEN, J. 2008. Recommend to their Consideration: The President's Legislative Policy Agenda, 1789–2002. Manuscript, Center for the Study of Democratic Politics, Princeton University.

COX, G. 2006. The Organization of Democratic Legislatures. Pp. 141–61 in *The Oxford Handbook of Political Economy*, ed. B. Weingast and D. Wittman. Oxford: Oxford University Press.

—— and MCCUBBINS, M. 2004. *Setting the Agenda*. Cambridge: Cambridge University Press.

EDWARDS, G. C., III, and BARRETT, A. 2000. Presidential Agenda Setting in Congress. Pp. 109–33 in *Polarized Politics: Congress and the President in a Partisan Era*, ed. J. R. Bond and R. Fleisher. Washington, DC: CQ Press.

FEREJOHN, J., and SHIPAN, C. 1990. Congressional Influence on the Bureaucracy. *Journal of Law, Economics, and Organization*, 6 (Special Issue): 1–20.

GELMAN, A. 2008. *Red State, Blue State, Rich State Poor State: Why Americans Vote the Way They Do*. Princeton, NJ: Princeton University Press.

GILMOUR, J. B. 1995. *Strategic Disagreement: Stalemate in American Politics*. Pittsburgh: University of Pittsburgh Press.

GROSECLOSE, T., and McCARTY, N. 2001. The Politics of Blame: Bargaining before an Audience. *American Journal of Political Science*, 45/1: 100–19.

—— and SNYDER, J. 1996. Buying Supermajorities. *American Political Science Review*, 90/2: 303–15.

HAMMOND, T., and MILLER, G. 1987. The Core of the Constitution, *American Political Science Review*, 81: 1155–74.

HOLTZ-EAKIN, D. 1988. The Line Item Veto and Public Budgets: Evidence from the States. *Journal of Public Economics*, 36: 269–92.

HOWELL, W. 2003. *Power without Persuasion: The Politics of Direct Presidential Action*. Princeton, NJ: Princeton University Press.

—— ADLER, S., CAMERON, C., and RIEMANN, C. 2000. Divided Government and the Legislative Productivity of Congress. *Legislative Studies Quarterly*, 25/2: 285–312.

HUBER, J., and GAMM, G. 2002. Legislatures and Political Institutions: Beyond the Contemporary Congress. In *Political Science: The State of the Discipline*, ed. I. Katznelson and H. Milner. New York: Norton.

—— and SHIPAN, C. 2002. *Deliberate Discretion: The Institutional Foundations of Bureaucratic Independence*. Cambridge: Cambridge University Press.

KERNELL, S. 2006. Presidential Veto Threat as a Negotiating Instrument with the Bicameral Congress. Working paper, Department of Political Science, University of California at San Diego. Available at SSRN: <http://ssrn.com/abstract=1154103>.

KING, G. 1993. The Methodology of Presidential Research. In *Researching the Presidency: Vital Questions, New Approaches*, ed. G. C. Edwards, J. H. Kessel, and B. A. Rockman. Pittsburgh: University of Pittsburgh Press.

KREHBIEL, K. 1998. *Pivotal Politics: A Theory of U.S. Lawmaking*. Chicago: University of Chicago Press.

—— 2004. Pivots. Pp. 223–40 in *The Oxford Handbook of Political Economy*, ed. B. Weingast and D. Wittman. Oxford: Oxford University Press.

LAROCCA, R. T. 2006. *The Presidential Agenda: Sources of Executive Influence in Congress*. Columbus: Ohio State University Press.

LEWIS, D. 2008. *The Politics of Presidential Appointments*. Princeton, NJ: Princeton University Press.

MATTHEWS, S. A. 1989. Veto Threats: Rhetoric in a Bargaining Game. *Quarterly Journal of Economics*, 103: 347–69.

MAYHEW, D. 1991. *Divided We Govern*. New Haven, CT: Yale University Press.

—— 2008. Presidential Elections and Policy Change: How Much of a Connection Is There? Pp. 153–79 in *Parties and Policies: How the American Government Works*, ed. D. Mayhew. New Haven, CT: Yale University Press.

McCARTY, N. 1997. Presidential Reputation and the Veto. *Economics and Politics*, 9: 1–26.

—— 2000a. Presidential Pork: Executive Veto Power and Distributive Politics. *American Political Science Review*, 94/1: 117–29.

—— 2000b. Proposal Rights, Veto Rights, and Political Bargaining. *American Journal of Political Science*, 44/3: 506–22.

POOLE, K., and ROSENTHAL, H. 2007. *Congress and Ideology*. Edison, NJ: Transaction Publishers.

ROHDE, D., and SIMON, D. 1985. Presidential Vetoes and Congressional Response: A Study of Institutional Conflict. *American Journal of Political Science*, 29/3: 397–427.

Romer, T., and Rosenthal, H. 1978. Political Resource Allocations, Controlled Agendas, and the Status Quo. *Public Choice*, 33/1: 27–44.

Rudalevige, A. 2002. *Managing the President's Program: Presidential Leadership and Legislative Policy Formulation.* Princeton, NJ: Princeton University Press.

Stokes, D. E., and Iverson, G. 1962. On the Existence of Forces Restoring Party Competition. *Public Opinion Quarterly*, 26/2: 159–71.

Watson, R. A. 1993. *Presidential Vetoes and Public Policy.* Lawrence: University of Kansas Press.

Wawro, G. J., and Shickler, E. 2006. *Filibuster: Obstruction and Lawmaking in the U.S. Senate.* Princeton, NJ: Princeton University Press.

Wilkins, V., and Young, G. 2002. The Influence of Governors on Veto Override Attempts: A Test of Pivotal Politics. *Legislative Studies Quarterly*, 27/4: 557–75.

Wooley, J. T. 1991. Institutions, the Election Cycle, and the Presidential Veto. *American Journal of Political Science*, 35/2: 279–304.

CHAPTER 17

....

THE CONSEQUENCES OF DIVIDED GOVERNMENT

....

JOHN J. COLEMAN

DAVID C. W. PARKER

PRESIDENT George W. Bush saw a new legislative environment in January 2007, and it could not have been an attractive sight. His party, "thumped" in the 2006 midterm election, as the president put it, had lost its Senate and House majorities. Divided government had returned.

And with the return of divided government, the president's legislative successes dipped markedly. Bush was unusually successful as a legislative leader during his first six years in office, scoring an average of 81 percent support from Congress on those votes on which he took a public position. And for a year and a half of those six, Bush faced divided government. But divided government in 2007 and 2008 proved not nearly as accommodating to the president's preferences as was divided government in the wake of 9/11 in 2001 and 2002. Presidential support fell to only 38 percent for 2007, as measured by *CQ Weekly*—one of the lowest presidential support scores recorded since it began keeping records. Only Bill Clinton fared worse, in 1995, when Republicans took control of both houses of Congress for the first time in forty years.

The loss of Capitol Hill to Democrats signaled a loss of the president's agenda control, and the president turned to a different toolset to implement his preferences. Prior to 2007, Bush had resorted to the veto only once. Over the next two years, Bush would use his veto pen more frequently. Unable to persuade Congress, President Bush relied on his formal constitutional powers in an attempt to blunt the Democratic legislative agenda.

For the new Democratic majorities in the House and the Senate in 2007, their elevation to majority status promised to expose the incumbent administration's mismanagement and to pass a wide array of popular proposals in short order. The early signs suggested great success in "draining the swamp" of executive branch malfeasance through aggressive use of congressional oversight hearings. Thomas Mann and his colleagues at Brookings tallied the number of oversight hearings during the first six months of the 109th Congress, a time of unified Republican government, and compared it to the number undertaken by Democrats over the same period in the 110th Congress, a time of divided government. The results are striking: over 600 oversight hearings were held in the latter Congress, an increase of more than 50 percent (Mann, Reynolds, and Hoey 2007). But the heavy production of significant legislation, as promised by the Democrats, did not fare as well.

The question of whether divided government affects government output and operation is part of a larger and older debate within political science. That debate concerns whether or not parties matter in a system of separated powers, and if they do, how? To ask about the state of scholarship on divided government is to ask whether scholars have developed any consensus on what place parties have in the American political system and what, if anything, parties do to alter political forces and outcomes. Therefore we begin by asking: what is the nature of political parties in a system of separated powers? We then jump ahead to discuss the most recent empirical manifestation of that debate: does party control of government matter? Lastly, we discuss what has yet to be learned about divided government and offer some thoughts about future research directions.

Parties, Responsible and Otherwise, in a Separated Powers System

Scholars have long been concerned with the adverse consequences of divided control of government (Wilson 1885; Key 1961; Sundquist 1983; Burns 1963; APSA 1950; Schattschneider 1942). Those studying political parties, in particular, have argued that parties serve to bring together what the Constitution puts apart. Woodrow Wilson criticized the constitutional architects for designing a "federal system that . . . parcels out power and confuses responsibility" (1885, 187). The answer, he contended, was responsible parties that brought "the legislature and executive side by side in intimate but open cooperation" (1885, 97–8). By implication, a government controlled by one party is more efficient, responsive, and productive. In particular, it will produce more legislation and generate less interbranch antagonism than one where party control is divided between the executive and legislative branches. E. E. Schattschneider wrote that "a major party mobilizes a majority in order to take control of government and accepts responsibility for the whole conduct of public policy" (1942, 63). Parties, in pursuit of the whole conduct of policy, seek ways to obtain control of both the executive and legislative branches; they are not content with controlling only one.

What do responsible parties do and why is unified government beneficial? Responsible parties (1) make policy commitments; (2) carry them out when in office; (3) develop policy alternatives when out of office; (4) differ sufficiently to offer voters a significant and substantive choice; and (5) run on their record in the next election (Ranney 1973, 43). Voters, in short, can hold the ruling party responsible for the conditions in the country for both failures and successes. Divided government, scholars argued, precluded this sort of responsibility.

To advocates of responsible parties, the president played a key role. The president was uniquely positioned to mobilize the public behind the party's program (Schattschneider 1942, 2), although the American political system—in particular the separation of powers and federalism—made presidential leadership of responsible parties difficult, even if desirable. Parties, Schattschneider emphasized, and especially the president's leadership, provided a welcome centralizing tendency to a system suffused with decentralization. In his critique of Congress and the federal constitutional system, Wilson laments that there is no one to be "*trusted* in order that when things go wrong it may be quite plain who should be punished" (1885, 187, emphasis in the original). The president should be the person to receive the blame for when things go wrong, but also be responsible for setting the nation's priorities and direction. Both Wilson and Schattschneider agree that the presidency is to provide the accountability in a system of responsible parties and that he should be judged on his ability to make good on his promises.

Wilson, once he became president, tried to put into practice what he preached. He proposed a wide array of legislative programs under the banner of the New Freedom and convinced the Democratic leadership within both houses to require members to pledge support for his legislative agenda. The Democratic congressional caucus became an arm of the presidency itself. Although much of Wilson's domestic agenda flew through Congress quickly during his first term, the limits of his ability to command Congress became all too clear at the close of the First World War with the return of divided government to Washington. Wilson's legislative successes declined. It was one thing to lead one's party, it was another to lead Congress. Unified government seemed to make both tasks easier, but by no means assured. Witness FDR's legislative successes between 1933 and 1935, in the depths of the Great Depression, and compare them to his inability over time, also during unified government, to build congressional southern Democratic support for a more expansive New Deal.

Critics of the responsible party vision argued that American parties served critical systemic needs for the American polity exactly because they were *not* responsible. Yes, parties did serve to put together what the Constitution set to put apart, as Wilson argued. Parties, however, are not responsible agents of the electorate, but merely tools through which officeholders win elections. American parties serve as a force for social cohesion and harmony in a tremendously heterogeneous society (Herring 1940; Pomper 1971, 918). American parties helped government govern—but not, however, because they highlighted difference and division and distinction. Parties were organizationally and regionally decentralized entities that had to tolerate a diversity of preferences among their ranks, build internal compromise at each level of government, and work with the leaders of the other major party due to the likelihood that fellow partisans would not all march in lockstep. There was no particular reason to assume unified government would be markedly different from divided government in the production of significant policy or other measures of output and performance.

Can presidents, according to the functionalist perspective, unite the party behind a common agenda? The answer is not only no, but presidents should not even try. "Localism and factionalism," according to Pendleton Herring, "are the twin demons the president must exorcise, and our presidents are reduced to using spells and incantations" (Herring 1940, 219). The president's place in the constitutional and party system is relatively weak. He does not, in Herring's view, have a party machine at his command like many legislators do. And members of Congress must satisfy constituents back in the district to win reelection, regardless of the president's particular policy priorities.

For the most part, the debate between the functionalists and the responsibilists remained at a theoretical and normative impasse (Coleman 2003). What, in fact, can American parties do, do they do it, and when do they do it? Up through the late 1980s, party scholars produced impressive studies on voting in Congress, on party identification in voting, and on party organization, including the provision of resources to candidates during campaigns, their recruitment activities, and the role of party activists. The solid empirical work vastly improved our understanding of how parties operated, but the old normative and theoretical debate between the responsibilists and the functionalists never quite went away.

After scholars in the 1980s and 1990s noted a heightened party polarization in evaluations of presidents' job performance, marked resurgence in party voting among the electorate, a surge in intraparty unity and interparty conflict in roll-call voting in Congress, and the increasing involvement of parties in electioneering, the question of whether parties were responsible or not reemerged with new vigor (e.g., Pomper 1998). Given that this resurgence was occurring largely during a time of divided government, when public trust in government was low and critics were lambasting the government's handling of key national problems, the responsibilist–functionalist dispute no longer made much sense. How could it be that responsibility and responsiveness were high during divided government, given the responsibilists' preference for unified government? How could it be that divided government was making it difficult to act, given functionalist promises that American parties were designed precisely to navigate between and provide a bridge over group differences? One thing was clear: the onset of divided government with these newly responsible and responsive parties created an empirical conundrum not easily explained by the field's dominant theoretical framework. It was to the apparent and possible negative consequences of divided government under this new party arrangement in the 1980s and early 1990s that party scholars now turned their attention.

DIVIDED WE GOVERN—OR NOT

E. E. Schattschneider long ago offered an explanation for why the volume of legislation produced by the president and Congress should not and does not vary between divided and unified governments: the nature of the American two-party system generated relatively moderate parties, creating an incentive to bargain and compromise (1942, 89–91). Nevertheless, the notion that unified control should yield greater legislative productivity did not disappear. The arrival of party polarization in the 1980s and especially 1990s seemed to undermine Schattschneider's notion that American parties were moderate and eager seekers of political compromise. Political observers bemoaned the arrival of gridlock and the apparent rise in incivility between the president and his opponents, and between partisans on Capitol Hill. Divided government, a relative rarity in the first half of the twentieth century, became commonplace and served as the latest explanation—joining the distinguished company of interest group dominance, iron triangles, the influence of the South in national politics, weak parties, political culture, and defective constitutional structure—for the seeming inability of government to act quickly and responsively.

To explain the inaction and political rancor, political scientists Benjamin Ginsberg and Martin Shefter (1990) posited that politicians in the post-war era, unable to establish decisive victories in the electoral arena with unified control of government, increasingly turned to other forms of "institutional combat." They argued that investigations, media revelations, and legal proceedings had become critical venues in the struggle for power during periods of divided government, with an eye to creating enough damage to the party in control that the electorate would have little choice but to establish unified control in order to clean up the mess.

The politics by other means thesis was met skeptically among many political scientists. David Mayhew's (1991) rejoinder to Ginsberg and Shefter made a convincing and seemingly sound empirical argument: divided government appeared to affect neither the ability of the president and Congress to enact significant legislation, nor the volume of congressional investigations of the executive branch. Using contemporary year-end summaries of significant legislation produced by the *Washington Post* and the *New York Times* and the policy evaluations of later scholarly experts, Mayhew found 12.8 significant acts signed into law on average in unified government and 11.7 in divided government (1991a, 76). The difference was not statistically significant. Using the front page of the *New York Times* as his guide, Mayhew identified 30 high-publicity investigations of the executive branch between 1946 and 1990. He identifies 15 during 18 years of unified party control, and 15 during 26 years of divided control, suggesting no discernible relationship between divided government and the frequency of congressional investigations.

Echoing past party literature, Mayhew argued that the American system of separated powers was the key. That system made it difficult for government to pass legislation regardless of party control of the presidency and Congress, while at the same time it "nudg[ed] officials toward deliberation, compromise, and supermajority outcomes." And the institutional jealousies woven into the Constitution, along with the responsibilities to different electorates, make it sensible for Representatives and Senators to seek out instances of waste, fraud, and abuse in the executive branch to advance their own political careers, even if the cost might be paid by a president of their own party.

Mayhew's *Divided We Govern* was a powerful empirical rejoinder to the normative pleas for responsible political parties. As Mayhew concludes, "political parties can be powerful instruments, but in the United States they seem to play more of a role as 'policy factions' than as, in the British case, governing instruments." American parties, no matter the wishes of Wilson or Schattschneider, should not and could not be responsible. Functionality, not responsibility, was the role of parties in the American system.

Keith Krehbiel's *Pivotal Politics* (1998) served to further advance the notion that divided party control means little in America's system of separated powers. Because successful navigation of America's legislative process requires supermajorities, gridlock will be a common feature of both divided and unified government. It should be equally difficult for the president and Congress to produce legislation in divided and unified government—proposed legislation requires majorities in both houses, the assent of sixty Senators in the Senate to foreclose a filibuster (and even more in previous decades), and the concurrence of two-thirds of the members in both houses to overturn a veto. These so-called "pivot" points in the system, Krehbiel argues, mean party majorities are equally thwarted in divided and unified government. Only radical change in the preferred policy by the electorate will unlock dramatic bursts of legislative activity.

Krehbiel's analysis is part of a deeper and broader critique of political parties. He argues in a series of articles that the alleged power of political parties—to induce individual legislators to vote against their preferences, to control the legislative agenda, and to stack congressional committees with party loyalists—does not match "what is [often] seen on the street" (Krehbiel 1999; also 1997, 2000; Krehbiel and Wiseman 2001). Standard measures of party strength, such as presidential support scores or party unity in roll-call votes, conflate the strength of parties with the individual preferences of legislators (1999, 2000). A truly strong president and party would be able to induce members to vote against their personal preferences (see Covington 1988).

Although precise and insightful, Krehbiel's approach is not without conceptual problems. Disentangling party effects from preference effects remains notoriously difficult, and some studies show that switching parties changes members' voting behavior, presumably in the absence of major shifts in preferences (McCarty, Poole, and Rosenthal 2001). Perhaps more important, Krehbiel relies on a thin conception of parties that separates congressional parties from the rest of the party universe. While one is reluctant to haul the shopworn "but what causes the preferences?" tool out of the analytical toolbox yet again, in this instance it is particularly pertinent. The preference cohesiveness found in Krehbiel's analysis did not "just happen," but was, at least arguably, the concerted result of the actions of party organizations, party activists, and, to some degree, party voters in the electorate. Parties, broadly construed, had a hand in creating the very preference unity that in Krehbiel's approach undercuts their ability to be considered significant and necessary parts of congressional analysis.

PARTY CONTROL MATTERS

Research since Mayhew's pathbreaking contribution has produced a range of results, including some that warn scholars about overemphasizing the importance of divided government. Jones (1994, 1997) finds that significant policy can be made in a variety of partisan arrangements. Skowronek (1993) reaches similar conclusions. The cycle of "political time" suggests that presidents can achieve spectacular short-term success by pursuing what amounts to a triangulation strategy between the two parties—a hallmark maneuver of the Eisenhower, Nixon, and Clinton presidencies—without having much long-term impact on their party's direction after they leave office. Examining the presidency of George H. W. Bush, Quirk and Nesmith (1994) suggest that factors other than divided government, such as budget deficits and confused signals from public opinion, predominantly account for policy deadlock.

Overall, however, the findings in recent research strongly support the premise that party control matters. Kelly (1993) argues that innovative legislation should be considered an important departure at its time of adoption and deemed significant years later by experts, rather than meet only one of these criteria. Using this definition, Kelly finds that the production of important legislation is significantly greater during periods of unified government. Howell et al. (2000) provide the most elaborate compilation of significant enactments, and find that while enactment of major legislation does not appear to vary significantly between unified and divided government, enactment of landmark statutes does so at a rate of about two or three statutes per congressional term.

Four studies merit extended discussion for their contribution to the debate. Edwards, Barrett, and Peake (1997) conclude that there is more potentially significant legislation that fails to pass during divided than unified government, especially when the president takes a clear stance against the legislation. Looking only at legislation that passes suffers from selection bias: successful legislation may be unusually likely to garner bipartisan support. Edwards, Barrett, and Peake conclude that divided government increases the chances of potentially significant legislation failing by 45 percent, and the president is crucial to this differential rate of failure.

Building on the concept of what failed to happen in the legislative arena, Binder (1999, 2003) argues that the number of bills passing is an incomplete measure of gridlock. The numerator is just as important as the denominator: any measurement of policy production must consider the size of the policy agenda facing Congress at any given moment. Like Mayhew, Binder uses the *New York Times* to develop a measure of the nation's policy agenda. Dividing the prospective policy agenda by items which the president and Congress actually enacted into law yields a gridlock score for each Congress (2003, 37–8). The policy production of the president and Congress—once the size of the prospective agenda is considered—is greater in periods of unified government.

Coleman (1999) advances a theoretical and empirical argument concerning party control. Employing a variety of legislative productivity measures yields the conclusion that Mayhew's findings are an outlier: other indicators of significant legislative output establish that unified government is more productive than divided. More importantly, Coleman theoretically accounts for the institutional features of policy making and party responsiveness to the public. Incorporating the public's policy mood and institutional features serving to block policy production—such as the filibuster pivot, transactions costs, and intraparty factionalism—Coleman finds that the unified government productivity premium is even more pronounced than in analyses not accounting for these features (1999, 830, table 3). Coleman emphasizes that not all divided government or unified government is of a piece: there is a range of contexts under which divided and unified government occur, and these contexts significantly differ in how they are likely to affect legislative productivity.

Epstein and O'Halloran (1996, 2001) focus on a different aspect of law making— delegation to the executive branch. They hypothesize that as the president and Congress diverge ideologically, congressional willingness to delegate discretion to the executive branch declines. Examining individual and party voting on delegating discretion, vetoes over discretion, the structure of delegation, and the strategic design of institutions, they find that in each instance, divided government negatively affects the decision to delegate additional power and responsibility to the executive branch (see also McCubbins, Noll, and Weingast 1989; Volden 2002; cf. Krause 2003).

These studies on the whole lend support to a conceptualization of political parties as cartels. Applied most notably to congressional parties by Cox and McCubbins (1993), this approach emphasizes how the shared fate of a brand name creates incentives for a majority party to organize and control policy making in a manner consistent with its policy preferences. If this is the president's party, a boost in productivity is a likely outcome. Aldrich (1995) notes that politicians create parties to overcome problems of collective action and to provide collective goods to their members. The electoral brand name, campaign finance, and public policy are among the goods or resources parties can provide (Sinclair 2006; Parker 2008). The cartel notion should, however, be extended with care when used to incorporate both the president and the congressional party. The diverging electoral bases of presidents and their partisan supporters in Congress, their varying and overlapping length of term, and the term limits facing presidents but not members of Congress, create ample opportunities to encourage defection from the cartel. Whether this encouragement for defection increases or not during divided government—and how much strain the president–congressional party cartel can withstand—are compelling questions for future research.

But if party does not matter, then why does the voting behavior of party switchers in Congress change dramatically—especially when the only thing that changed is how the member chose to label his aggregate preferences (McCarty, Poole, and Rosenthal 2001)?

LOOKING BEYOND LAWS

Much of the research on divided government has focused on legislative outputs. This is sensible, both practically and substantially. Although there can be and has been considerable debate about how one might measure significant legislation and whether a measure of productivity should also consider that which failed to pass, the enactment of laws as a practical matter is relatively easy to quantify. Substantially, the passage of laws is arguably the most important function of government and the place where one ought to search for the most sweeping consequences of divided control.

Since the early 1960s, the attention of presidential scholars has been heavily focused on the president's ability to persuade Congress on legislation, and this has contributed substantially to the study of party control of government. Recent research has, however, begun to draw scholarly attention back to presidents' unilateral use of power, including executive orders, executive agreements, proclamations, and signing statements (Cooper 2002; Howell 2003; Mayer 2001). Mayer and Price (2002) examine the president's issuing of significant executive orders and find no relationship between party control and the quantity of the orders. Employing a different measure of significant executive orders, Howell (2005) classifies 228 orders (from 1945 to 2001) as significant as opposed to 51 (from 1949 to 1999) in the Mayer and Price study. He finds strong evidence that divided government and large and cohesive congressional majorities dampen the president's issuance of significant executive orders. In tandem with the legislative productivity literature, this finding depicts presidents as seeking the arena that is most suited to advancing their agenda, whether that be during divided or unified government. With unified government, presidents can rely more on the legislative process, while with divided government, unilateral action becomes increasingly attractive.

The president's use of his commander in chief powers also varies systematically depending on party control. Howell and Pevehouse (2007) find that party control does not much affect the president's deployment of small numbers of troops abroad, or the president's actions in cases involving long-time American or Soviet Union allies. Significantly, however, they find that presidents facing opposite party control of Congress, especially if that party is large and cohesive, are generally less likely to exercise military force than presidents working with a Congress in which their party has a majority. They also find that presidents facing these conditions of a cohesive opposition majority party are less likely to respond militarily to specific conflicts and will take a longer time before deploying a military response to a foreign incident. Large, cohesive, opposite party majorities weaken the president's ability to raise public support for military action and weaken his ability to signal credible foreign policy commitments to foreign allies and adversaries.

Researchers have explored a number of other areas outside the confines of legislative production. Divided government is found to produce a variety of effects: rising deficits (McCubbins 1991), delayed executive appointments (McCarty and Razaghian 1999), and delayed judicial confirmations (Moraski and Shipan 1999; Binder and Maltzman 2002; Bell 2002). Cameron (2000) finds that various permutations of veto politics—veto use, threats, sequential veto bargaining, and "blame game" vetoes—increase in frequency and substantive significance during divided government, especially divided government with ideologically distinct parties. Nicholson, Segura, and Woods (2002), using National Election Study data from 1972 to 1994, find that divided government is related to higher presidential approval. Although divided government after 2006 did not rescue George W. Bush from his plummeting approval ratings, Bill Clinton emerged from the budget showdown with Congress in the winter of 1995–6 stronger and more popular than ever. If presidents win the competition for public approval in divided government, might that be one factor explaining how the presidency strengthened during the post-1945 era of divided government (cf. Bond, Fleisher, and Wood 2003)?

Mayhew (1991a) found in his initial analysis of high-publicity investigations of the executive branch that there was no difference in the number of probes undertaken in divided and unified government. But in a later account (Mayhew 2005), he identified a pattern of greater numbers of investigations during periods of divided party control. Any investigation of malfeasance contains within it the possibility of adverse consequences for the president. A committee-based charge of malfeasance is an inherently significant event that may or may not be made substantially more important by the media attention it receives. Are investigations of executive branch malfeasance rooted in the power of partisan majorities, and hence more likely to emerge in divided rather than unified government? Recent accounts suggest they are. Kriner and Schwartz (2008) and Dull and Parker (n.d.), using two different datasets of investigations, find more and longer congressional investigations of the president and executive branch during divided government.

DIRECTIONS FOR FUTURE RESEARCH

Our assessment of the research on party control of government is that this literature demonstrates broad and significant effects of divided government. This remains a fertile area for research. In this section, we identify several possible paths for future studies (see also Cameron 2002 for additional suggestions). We focus in particular on avenues that may benefit research into the presidency and largely set to the side other possible research directions regarding divided government.

Enlarging Datasets

Studies of divided government run into the classic problem of small-n. Most studies focus on the period after the Second World War and on congressional sessions, relying on a little over two dozen observations. Although it is possible to make statistical inferences from such a small sample, it is difficult to test many hypotheses without running into computational difficulties. There are two remedies for this. The first is to extend the time series. Scholars could push the time line back to the late nineteenth century, an era thought to feature greater party responsibility and a greater willingness on the part of the president to defer to Congress in law making, compared to the postwar era. Clinton and Lapinski's (2006) legislative importance estimates for all statutes passed by Congress between 1874 and 1994 provide one source of data. A second remedy is to make more refined measurements within a particular time series. Rather than measuring the consequences of divided government biennially, scholars could explore annual, quarterly, or monthly effects. Theory should drive which of these is employed. This remedy would allow for clearer tests of existing divided government hypotheses and the development of more sophisticated ones. For example, the simultaneous and perhaps interactive effects of presidential approval and party control on presidential persuasiveness are bluntly measured by congressional term and perhaps even by year. Generally, extending the time series this way will likely make it harder to find effects of party control, as this will typically be constant across months and quarters.

Resort to the Courts

Do the courts prove to be an especially attractive arena for the pursuit of political goals during divided government? Unable to get preferred legislation passed through Congress or signed by the president during divided government, are interest groups more likely to file suits or write amicus curiae briefs in the hope of pushing the courts to act where the president and Congress cannot? Or perhaps the exact opposite occurs. Those organizations and interest groups shut out of the legislative process during unified government, such as those of a liberal persuasion during the first six years of George W. Bush's administration, might turn more often to the courts as the place of last resort. The recent attention paid by interest groups to judicial nominations and their willingness to spend substantial sums on television, print, and internet advertising to either block or advance particular nominations underscores the relative lack of attention given by scholars to the third branch in considering the consequences of divided government. Interesting work has looked at factors explaining the Supreme Court's willingness to reargue cases (Hoekstra and Johnson 2003) and found that reargument is associated with increased levels of uncertainty on the Court, such as a minimum winning coalition or a large amount of ideological distance between the opinion writer and the Court median. Might external factors producing uncertainty, such as divided government and its possible impact on future judicial nominations by the president, also affect how the court approaches cases on its docket or its willingness to reargue a case?

Getting Comparative

Another approach to the limited-n problem is to expand our intellectual universe beyond national American government. This might prove salutary not only for the reason of enlarging datasets, but for theoretical reasons as well. To the extent that party theory is designed to explain outcomes at the American national level, it is not as general as it might be in the study of executive–legislative relations. Of course, context may be highly consequential for outcomes, but scholars can do a better job evaluating the significance of context by expanding the range of contexts they consider. Something that seems consequential to the president–Congress relationship at the American national level but nowhere else might well be reevaluated to determine if indeed it is as significant at the national level as first thought.

Three possibilities are worth pursuing. First, comparisons among the American states deserve more attention as an effort to understand executive–legislative relations under different forms of party control and independent executive action under those forms. Particularly at a time when state governments appear to be very active, they are an attractive arena in which to understand the significance of party control under varying circumstances.

Second, we would do well to look outward beyond the United States. Though divided government in the American form is relatively unusual, there might well be fruitful comparisons between divided and unified government in the United States and various forms of majority coalitions in other countries. Just as not all unified government or divided government is of a piece, neither are the governing coalitions in other systems.

Lastly, scholars could consider what amounts to comparative case studies of divided government across US history. The premise here is that an episode of divided government in the late nineteenth century might fundamentally differ from that in the 1950s, which might differ from the 1970s, which in turn might differ from the 1990s. Coleman (1999) advanced the idea that not all divided or unified government is equivalent; Conley (2002) finds support for this idea; and Mayhew (2005) touches on the possibility of enhancing analysis through comparisons across type of divided government. Classic case comparison methods would be fruitful here. Generally, in case comparisons, there are four categories: similar inputs, similar outcomes; similar inputs, different outcomes; different inputs, different outcomes; different inputs, similar outcomes. Episodes of divided government in American history might be compared to develop a sense of contextual richness—a sense of time and place, a sense of the experience of an episode of divided government by the actors on the ground—that is difficult to achieve in systematic quantitative analysis. At the least, this can enrich our understanding of how divided government plays out in practical terms. At the most, there is the promise of unearthing new, important explanatory factors about the consequences of divided government.

Thinking Across Time

The study of American political development emphasizes that sequence and timing matter in politics. Events early in a path take on disproportionate structural significance in determining or shaping later politics. The sequence in which subsequent events happen also heavily shapes future events. At a more general level, the same kind of analysis might be pursued through the application of game theory.

The logic of this research suggestion builds off our prior point about comparing episodes of divided government. How divided government plays out, and what consequences it has, may depend heavily on initial starting conditions, very early decisions, the sequence of later decisions, and the length of the entire episode of divided government. Did it matter for the way that divided government worked in the Bush years that 9/11 happened when it did and the Iraq War happened when it did? Most observers would certainly offer a casual "yes" in response to that question. The challenge for scholars is to determine whether that casual yes is correct, and if so, how.

The questions are multiple. Where in the sequence, for example, did a particular heated judicial confirmation case occur? What effects might that have had on later events, including presidential unilateral action, legislative productivity, oversight hearings, and investigations? How long did the episode of divided government last? Is there a theoretical reason to believe that the difficulties of governance and the difficulties of presidential leadership will grow or subside the longer divided government is in place? Is that true for both presidential persuasion and the use of unilateral action? What was the sequence of events that observers at the time attributed primarily to the existence of divided government and how might these have precluded future options by affecting interpretations of political actors at those times? Does it make any difference if the divided government starting point is a presidential rather than midterm election? Does the length of the gap between the current bout of divided government and its predecessor have any implications for how politics will proceed—i.e., how distant are the memories and how much turnover has there been? To what degree did previous periods of divided government produce institutional changes that a later period has to operate within? What kinds of events seem to have a particularly significant ability to increase or decrease the probability of certain other future events?

Politics happens in sequence and time. To be clear, we strongly advocate broadly systematic studies of the consequences of party control that do not delve into these details. We do, however, suggest that scholarly understanding of the consequences of divided government would grow even stronger by taking into account the kinds of questions posed in studies of American political development.

Evaluating Party Responsiveness

To date, little effort has been made to link the consequences of divided government to the theoretical questions that inspired the divided government research agenda: Do parties matter? And if so, how do they matter? How can research tie back to these founding questions?

Parties provide a linkage function between the people and their elected officials regardless of whether they are responsible or functionalist and regardless of whether they intend to do so or not. The crux of the debate between these two schools of thought is how parties serve to link the two. Responsible party theorists stress responsiveness and the implementation of policy. Functionalists stress the unifying function of parties and their ability to help elected officials win elections. Parties, of course, do both, and that is the point. Across history, they may be more or less responsible and more or less functional, but they are almost certainly some of both (Coleman 2003). Parties have to win elections and they have to implement policy; both imperatives require parties to be responsive to the electorate. The question should be: how does unified or divided government affect the responsiveness of parties?

As Coleman (1999) argues, responsiveness is the key to the party government model. That responsiveness, rather than raw numbers of enactments, should be most important to the party government school is unsurprising. Schattschneider was deeply interested in government responding to general and not just narrow interests. Responsiveness in that sense requires that government produce policy initiatives when the public demands them, but it also requires that government attend to maintaining the status quo when the public is content and uninterested in moving in new legislative directions. Skowronek suggests that the best way for the president of "articulation," also known as the "orthodox innovator," to find the most political trouble is by overreaching his public warrant for action. Generally, this means presidents like John Kennedy, Lyndon Johnson, and the two Bushes going beyond implementation of the dominant regime's policy prescriptions or straying away from its core premises.

Simply comparing the number of significant laws produced in a given congressional session is at the very least not the whole point of responsiveness. The important question is does government provide activism when the public demands it, and otherwise provide stability during periods of public satisfaction? In short, is unified government more responsive to the policy mood of the public than divided government? If so, is this due to changed presidential behavior? Our point here is not that scholars need to take a stance on whether such responsiveness is or is not desirable as a normative matter. The point is that to test and challenge theories empirically, scholars need to be sure they are truly testing the theory and not striking down straw men.

Consider, for example, the increased willingness to use legislative holds, cloture motions, and filibusters in the Senate and the rise of closed and modified rules in the House (Sinclair 2000, 2006). Certainly, the increased ideological distance between senators and representatives over the past three decades is partly responsible and a component of the larger pattern of increased party polarization, which makes it difficult to blame divided government alone for obstructionism. Consider this legislative obstructionism in the light of presidents' increasing reliance on unilateral action with executive orders, executive agreements, and so on (Cooper 2002; Howell 2003; Mayer 2001). With Congress pushing toward inaction, the president pushes toward action. This raises two questions. One is whether the president's increased use of unilateral action during divided government is caused by divided government, or is it more directly related to obstructionist tactics? This draws back to our earlier point that not all divided government is the same. If divided government has occurred more frequently while there has been a secular trend toward greater obstructionism, analysts need to be careful to disentangle cause and effect. A broader question is what impact do obstructionist and unilateral tactics have on the political system at large, and on political parties specifically, over the long term? What do they say about government responsiveness to the public?

We do not have a ready answer. Consider the initial "politics by other means" thesis. Frustration with the lack of electoral mandates and with divided control of government leads presidents and legislators to pursue their conflict in other venues. Unable to be responsive to the public, the president and legislators increasingly pull the courts and the bureaucracy into their conflicts, seeking an edge that they hope will yield electoral victories. The act of delay can serve to preserve and entrench past policy victories and rouse partisans to contribute funds and be energized, possibly increasing the likelihood of unified control in the future.

But here is another take on the same story. What if parties increased the use of obstructionist tactics exactly because they were being responsive and not because of any frustration with the inability to govern? The causal mechanism is not divided government at all, but rather the need to be responsive to an increasingly vocal party activist base. Parties would be responding responsibly, albeit yielding inaction by standard measures of government performance.

To date, responsiveness has been defined either explicitly or implicitly as an adequate response to public demands and to the alleviation of collective problems. Question marks might well be put around virtually every word in that depiction: "adequate" "response" to "public" "demands" and to the "alleviation" of "collective" "problems."

Studies of divided versus unified government have an action bias that arises from responsible party theory. There is an undercurrent that unified government can be more responsive, and responsive means action rather than inaction. Analysts, therefore, test whether the president was able to *do something* in unified government that he could not do in divided, or do something in divided that he need not do in unified. Research tests whether the president and Congress are more likely to *do more* in unified than divided government. These studies have created a rich base of knowledge about the consequences of party control. Indeed, the authors of this essay have contributed to that set of studies. It would be a worthy pursuit, however, for scholars to think more deeply about what responsiveness requires, what happens analytically if we do not assume that responsiveness requires the president and Congress to take action, how that intersects with the study of party control effects, and how that in turn affects our understanding and study of the presidency.

CONCLUSION

Digesting the excellent empirical work on divided government produced over the last two decades suggests that party control does indeed produce a range of consequences that vary across divided and unified control. No one suggests that important legislation is not signed into law by the president during divided government, that presidents do not issue important executive orders during unified government, or that presidents do not pursue military commitments and conflicts during divided government. The debate is about the quantitative differences on the margin between the two forms of party control, and in some studies the qualitative and substantive differences as well. The research shows consistently that divided government has specific, measurable, significant effects on public policy and government action.

In conclusion, we briefly revisit the theoretical questions that initially spawned the debate about the consequences of party control. What do parties do? Do they matter? What constitutes party responsiveness and responsibility? E. E. Schattschneider (1960) argued that parties are distinct from interest groups because they seek to expand the scope of conflict, suggesting that they are responsive to more than narrow interests.

But in practice, parties do not always seek to expand conflicts and at times can be subject to the concerns of narrow constituencies, maybe particularly so in times of extreme polarization when each small constituency can present itself as a vital part of the party coalition. Parties will expand the scope of conflict if they have the resource capability and if doing so is required to win elections. In a polarized political atmosphere, however, the cost of conflict expansion is great and generally unnecessary. Political parties might be just as apt to minimize the scope of conflicts if this leads to favorable electoral consequences. When asking whether parties are responsive or not it is worth asking to whom are parties responsive (Parker 2008). For researchers, it is also important to ask whether and how the tendencies toward conflict expansion and conflict contraction vary between the president and the rest of his party under conditions of divided and unified control. Several streams in the presidency literature, notably the various aspects of going public, suggest that modern presidents push toward conflict expansion. Studies of the political parties to which presidents belong, however, including the legislative parties and party organizations, suggest parties often have good reasons to narrow conflicts.

The irony is that parties, in seeking to be responsive to their supporters in the short run, may have made responsiveness less achievable in the long run by doing considerable damage to the system of separated powers. Responsibility, in that sense, might be shunting aside functionality. Pursuing responsiveness through obstruction and through politicization of the bureaucracy and the courts, parties over the last three decades may have made it more difficult for the president and Congress to govern—however scholars choose to measure governing.

REFERENCES

ALDRICH, J. H. 1995. *Why Parties? The Origin and Transformation of Political Parties in America.* Chicago: University of Chicago Press.

American Political Science Association. 1950. Toward a More Responsible Two-Party System: A Report of the Committee on Political Parties. *American Political Science Review,* 44: Part 2, Supplement.

BELL, L. C. 2002. Senatorial Discourtesy: The Senate's Use of Delay to Shape the Federal Judiciary. *Political Research Quarterly,* 55/3: 589–607.

BINDER, S. A. 1999. The Dynamics of Legislative Gridlock, 1947–96. *American Political Science Review,* 93/3: 519–33.

——2003. *Stalemate.* Washington, DC: Brookings Institute Press.

——and MALTZMAN, F. 2002. Senatorial Delay in Confirming Federal Judges, 1947–1998. *American Journal of Political Science,* 46/1: 190–200.

BOND, J. R., FLEISHER, R., and WOOD, B. D. 2003. The Marginal and Time-Varying Effect of Public Approval on Presidential Success in Congress. *Journal of Politics,* 65/1: 92–110.

BURNHAM, W. D. 1970. *Critical Elections and the Mainsprings of American Politics.* New York: Norton.

BURNS, J. M. 1963. *The Deadlock of Democracy.* Englewood Cliffs, NJ: Prentice-Hall.

CALVERT, R. L., MORAN, M. J., and WEINGAST, B. R. 1987. Congressional Influence over Policy Making: The Case of the FTC. In *Congress: Structure and Policy,* ed. M. D. McCubbins and T. Sullivan. New York: Cambridge University Press.

CAMERON, C. R. 2000. *Veto Bargaining: Presidents and the Politics of Negative Power.* New York: Cambridge University Press.

——2002. Studying the Polarized Presidency. *Presidential Studies Quarterly,* 32/4: 647–63.

CANES-WRONE, B., and DE MARCHI, S. 2002. Presidential Approval and Legislative Success. *Journal of Politics,* 64/2: 491–509.

CLARKE, H. D., ELLIOTT, E., and ROBACK, T. H. 1991. Domestic Issue Ideology and Activist Style: A Note on 1980 Republican Convention Delegates. *Journal of Politics,* 53/2: 519–34.

CLINTON, J. D., and LAPINSKI, J. S. 2006. Measuring Legislative Accomplishments, 1877–1994. *American Journal of Political Science*, 50/1: 232–9.

COLEMAN, J. J. 1999. Unified Government, Divided Government, and Party Responsiveness. *American Political Science Review*, 93/4: 821–35.

—— 2003. Responsible, Functional, or Both? American Political Parties and the APSA Report after Fifty Years. In *The State of the Parties: The Changing Role of Contemporary American Parties*, ed. J. C. Green and R. Farmer, 4th edn. Lanham, MD: Rowman & Littlefield.

CONLEY, R. S. 2002. *The Presidency, Congress, and Divided Government: A Postwar Assessment*. College Station: Texas A&M University Press.

COOPER, P. J. 2002. *By Order of the President: The Use and Abuse of Executive Direct Action*. Lawrence: University Press of Kansas.

COTTER, C. P., et al. 1984. *Party Organizations in American Politics*. New York: Praeger.

COVINGTON, C. R. 1988. Building Presidential Coalitions among Cross-Pressured Members of Congress. *Western Political Quarterly*, 41/1: 47–62.

COX, G. W., and MCCUBBINS, M. D. 1993. *Legislative Leviathan: Party Government in the House*. Berkeley and Los Angeles: University of California Press.

DOWNS, A. 1957. *An Economic Theory of Democracy*. New York: Harper Collins.

EDWARDS, G. C., III, BARRETT, A., and PEAKE, J. 1997. The Legislative Impact of Divided Government. *American Journal of Political Science*, 41/2: 545–63.

EPSTEIN, D. F., and O'HALLORAN, S. 1996. Divided Government and the Design of Administrative Procedures: A Formal Model and Empirical Test. *Journal of Politics*, 58/3: 393–417.

—— —— 2001. Legislative Organization under Separate Powers. *Journal of Law, Economics and Organization*, 17/2: 373–96.

FIORINA, M. P. 1992. *Divided Government*. New York: Macmillan Publishing.

FLEISHER, R., and BOND, J. R. 1988. Are There Two Presidencies? Yes, But Only for Republicans. *Journal of Politics*, 50/3: 747–67.

GINSBERG, B., and SHEFTER, M. 1990. *Politics by Other Means: The Declining Importance of Elections in America*. New York: W. W. Norton.

HERRING, E. P. 1940. *The Politics of Democracy*. New York: W. W. Norton & Company.

HERRNSON, P. S. 1988. *Party Campaigning in the 1980s*. Cambridge, MA: Harvard University Press.

HOEKSTRA, V., and JOHNSON, T. 2003. Delaying Justice: The Supreme Court's Decision to Hear Rearguments. *Political Research Quarterly*, 56/3: 351–60.

HOWELL, W. G. 2003. *Power without Persuasion: The Politics of Direct Presidential Action*. Princeton, NJ: Princeton University Press.

—— 2005. Unilateral Powers: A Brief Overview. *Presidential Studies Quarterly*, 35/3: 415–39.

—— ADLER, E. S., CAMERON, C., and RIEMANN, C. 2000. Divided Government and the Legislative Productivity of Congress, 1945–1994. *Legislative Studies Quarterly*, 25/2: 285–312.

—— and PEVEHOUSE, J. C. 2007. *While Dangers Gather: Congressional Checks on Presidential War Powers*. Princeton, NJ: Princeton University Press.

JONES, C. O. 1994. *The Presidency in a Separated System*. Washington, DC: Brookings Institute.

—— 1997. Separating to Govern: The American Way. In *Present Discontents: American Politics in the Very Late Twentieth Century*, ed. B. E. Shafer. Chatham, NJ: Chatham House.

KELLY, S. Q. 1993. Divided We Govern? A Reassessment. *Polity*, 25/3: 475–84.

KEY, V. O. 1955. A Theory of Critical Elections. *Journal of Politics*, 17/1: 3–18.

—— 1961. *Public Opinion and American Democracy*. New York: Alfred A. Knopf.

KIEWIET, D. R., and MCCUBBINS, M. 1991. *The Logic of Delegation: Congressional Parties and the Appropriations Process*. Chicago: University of Chicago Press.

King, G. 1993. The Methodology of Presidential Research. In *Researching the Presidency: Vital Questions, New Approaches*, ed. G. C. Edwards III, J. Kessel, and B. Rockman. Pittsburgh: University of Pittsburgh Press.

Krause, G. A. 2003. Coping with Uncertainty: Analyzing Risk Propensities of SEC Budgetary Decisions, 1949–97. *American Political Science Review*, 97/1: 171–88.

Krehbiel, K. 1997. Restrictive Rules Reconsidered. *American Journal of Political Science*, 41/3: 919–44.

—— 1998. *Pivotal Politics: A Theory of U.S. Lawmaking*. Chicago: University of Chicago Press.

—— 1999. Paradoxes of Parties in Congress. *Legislative Studies Quarterly*, 24/1: 31–64.

—— 2000. Party Discipline and Measures of Partisanship. *American Journal of Political Science*, 44/2: 212–27.

—— and Wiseman, A. 2001. Joseph G. Cannon: Majoritarian from Illinois. *Legislative Studies Quarterly*, 26/3: 357–89.

Kriner, D., and Schwartz, L. 2008. Divided Government and Congressional Investigations. *Legislative Studies Quarterly*, 33/2: 295–322.

McCarty, N., Poole, K. T., and Rosenthal, H. 2001. The Hunt for Party Discipline in Congress. *American Political Science Review*, 95/3: 673–87.

—— —— —— 2006. *Polarized America: The Dance of Ideology and Unequal Riches*. Boston: MIT Press.

—— and Razaghian, R. 1999. Advice and Consent: Senate Response to Executive Branch Nominations, 1885–1996. *American Journal of Political Science*, 43/4: 1122–43.

McCubbins, M. D. 1991. Party Politics, Divided Government, and Budget Deficits. In *The Politics of Economic Policy in the U.S. and Japan*, ed. S. Kernell. Washington, DC: Brookings Institution.

—— Noll, R. G., and Weingast, B. R. 1989. Structure and Process, Politics and Policy: Administrative Arrangements and the Political Control of Agencies. *Virginia Law Review*, 75/2: 431–82.

—— and Schwartz, T. 1987. Congressional Oversight Overlooked: Police Patrols versus Fire Alarms. In *Congress: Structure and Policy*, ed. M. D. McCubbins and T. Sullivan. New York: Cambridge University Press.

Mann, T. E., Reynolds, M., and Hoey, P. 2007. A New, Improved Congress? Op-ed chart. *New York Times*, Aug. 26.

Mayer, K. R. 2001. *With the Stroke of a Pen: Executive Orders and Presidential Power*. Princeton, NJ: Princeton University Press.

—— and Price, K. 2002. Unilateral Presidential Powers: Significant Executive Orders, 1949–99. *Presidential Studies Quarterly*, 32/2: 367–86.

Mayhew, D. R. 1974. *The Electoral Connection*. New Haven, CT: Yale University Press.

—— 1991. *Divided We Govern: Party Control, Lawmaking, and Investigations, 1946–1990*. New Haven, CT: Yale University Press.

—— 2004. *Electoral Realignments: The Collapse of an American Genre*. New Haven, CT: Yale University Press.

—— 2005. *Divided We Govern: Party Control, Lawmaking, and Investigations, 1946–1990*, 2nd edn. New Haven, CT: Yale University Press.

Moraski, B., and Shipan, C. R. 1999. The Politics of Supreme Court Nominations: A Theory of Institutional Constraints and Choices. *American Journal of Political Science*, 43/4: 1069–95.

Nicholson, S. P., Segura, G., and Woods, N. D. 2002. Presidential Approval and the Mixed Blessings of Divided Government. *American Journal of Political Science*, 50/1: 146–59.

PARKER, D. C. W. 2008. *The Power of Money in Congressional Campaigns, 1880–2006*. Norman: University of Oklahoma Press.

——and DULL, M. D. 2009. Divided We Quarrel: The Politics of Congressional Investigation, 1947–2004. *Legislative Studies Quarterly*, 34.

POMPER, G. 1971. Toward a More Responsible Two-Party System? What, Again? *Journal of Politics*, 33/4: 916–40.

——1998. The Alleged Decline of American Parties. In *Politicians and Party Politics*, ed. J. Geer. Baltimore: Johns Hopkins University Press.

QUIRK, P. J., and NESMITH, B. 1994. Explaining Deadlock: Domestic Policymaking in the Bush Presidency. In *New Perspectives on American Politics*, ed. L. C. Dodd and C. Jillson. Washington, DC: CQ Press.

RANNEY, A. 1973. *Curing the Mischiefs of Faction*. Berkeley and Los Angeles: University of California Press.

ROHDE, D. W. 1991. *Parties and Leaders in the Postreform House*. Chicago: University of Chicago Press.

SCHATTSCHNEIDER, E. E. 1942. *Party Government*. New York: Holt, Rinehart & Winston.

——1960. *The Semisovereign People*. New York: Holt, Rinehart & Winston.

SINCLAIR, B. 2000. *Unorthodox Lawmaking: New Legislative Processes in the U.S. Congress*, 2nd edn. Washington, DC: CQ Press.

——2006. *Party Wars: Polarization and the Politics of National Policy Making*. Norman: University of Oklahoma Press.

SKOWRONEK, S. 1993. *The Politics Presidents Make*. Cambridge, MA: Harvard University Press.

SORAUF, F. 1968. *Party Politics in America*. Boston: Little, Brown.

SUNDQUIST, J. L. 1983. *The Decline and Resurgence of Congress*. Washington, DC: Brookings Institute.

——1988–9. Needed: A Political Theory for the New Era of Coalition Government in the United States. *Political Science Quarterly*, 103/4: 613–35.

VOLDEN, C. 2002. A Formal Model of the Politics of Delegation in a Separation of Powers System. *American Journal of Political Science*, 46/1: 111–33.

WILSON, W. 1885. *Congressional Government*. Boston: Houghton Mifflin & Company.

CONNECTING INTEREST GROUPS TO THE PRESIDENCY

BURDETT A. LOOMIS

SINCE Franklin Roosevelt laid the foundations of the modern presidency, organized interests have paid increasing attention to that office and to the executive branch in general. Given the steady growth in the programmatic reach of the federal government, we can scarcely regard this as remarkable. What is noteworthy, and more than a bit disconcerting, is the relative lack of scholarly attention accorded the connections between organized interests and the executive branch in general, and the presidency in particular. Even as lobbying has increased and executive power has grown, scholars have largely concentrated on the myriad connections between legislators and interests, while paying far less attention to the presidency.

The Framers designed the Congress to encourage access from citizens and their organized groupings, and twentieth-century legislators have cultivated relationships with interest groups and many other organizations, such as corporations, universities, and various governmental units. More than 30,000 lobbyists have registered to represent interests on Capitol Hill; important hearings are filled to overflowing with these Washington representatives, who either press for or defend against change, or simply monitor the proceedings. All this makes sense, in that the stakes are high, and the wording of one sentence of a single bill can translate into millions of dollars in benefits or costs for a given group.

In a related vein, the American court system (both federal and state) encourages groups to pursue their interests within these highly accessible venues (O'Connor 2005). Organized interests of all stripes can use the courts both to win policy victories and to delay the imposition of change; for many interests, such as drug companies and many other large corporations, maintaining the status quo can be extremely profitable, even if just for a few months. Again, groups have powerful incentives to use the court system, either to delay change or to create it in a setting more positive than a bicameral legislature with a filibuster-prone Senate. Although scholarship on groups' use of the courts scarcely rivals that on Congress, it surpasses the work that emphasizes groups and the presidency, largely because data are more available.

Scholarly studies of the relations between the executive and groups must overcome serious obstacles, most notably that critical deliberations and decisions within the executive branch ordinarily cannot be scrutinized to the extent allowed by Congress or the courts. At the same time, formal relationships between the presidency and organized interests, through the Office of Public Liaison, for example, often focus scholars' attention on structural and personnel questions that prove far less significant than private communications between the president or his agents and an assortment of group representatives, many of whom, such as corporate leaders, never register as lobbyists. Indeed, in the wake of George W. Bush's election as president, Vice President Cheney would not even release the names of oil company executives who met with him to discuss energy initiatives for the new administration.

Nevertheless, the most powerful secular trend in American institutions since the 1930s has been the steady expansion of powers within the executive branch and especially the presidency. As presidents make increasing numbers of important decisions, interest groups must pay more attention to the White House. Likewise, the chief executive must find ways to bring organized interests into coalitions that will help advance administration policies. Just as members of Congress and groups travel back and forth along a two-way street of access, so too must presidents both respond to entreaties by organized interests and seek to enlist them as allies in pushing through their favored policy initiatives.

Contacts between organized interests and the executive branch range from private discussions with the president to various tactics designed to influence policies deep within the bowels of the executive branch—from seeking membership on advisory panels to providing background studies for budget personnel to participating in revolving door hiring that links bureaucrats to trade organizations. This chapter will not address the systematic relationships between groups and the overall executive branch, although that modest literature could use substantial strengthening (Piotrowski and Rosenbloom 2005; Furlong 2005). For example, in the comprehensive Aberbach–Peterson (2005) volume on the executive branch, there is no citation for lobbying and only a handful for interest groups.

How, then, do organized interests relate to the president and the institutional presidency? Scholars of both the presidency and interest groups have paid some attention to their mutual relations, but in general the relevant studies have been episodic and limited. There is, for example, no book-length study explicitly focused on the linkages between presidents and organized interests. Given the myriad contacts between all modern presidents and a range of organized interests, such a gap is remarkable—and especially so when the George W. Bush presidency *began* with various oil company executives meeting with Vice President Dick Cheney to develop the new administration's energy policy. To be sure, various scholars have examined presidency–group relations from the distinctive perspectives of the White House and of organized interests. The emerging trend in this work is to focus most attention on how the president enlists groups and coalitions to lobby for his own programs (Tenpas 2005; Peterson 2008). Still, organized interests participate in both policy making and electioneering (including fund raising) with the anticipation of pay-offs for cooperation. In fact, *being in a position to be used* by the president may stand as an effective lobbying technique for a group that depends on maintaining solid ties to the executive branch.

This chapter examines the core findings and trends within the patchy scholarship that links presidents, lobbying, and interest groups, and then suggests ways for scholars to construct a fuller understanding of the complex and often hidden relationships between the executive and organized interests.

INTEREST GROUPS, LOBBYING, AND THE PRESIDENCY: BASIC PATTERNS

Within the political science literature, at least three major perspectives shape analyses of linkages between the presidency and organized interests. First, over time the White House has put in place a well-articulated, though scarcely immutable, organizational structure that frames many of its relations with interest groups. This juncture of the institutionalized presidency and organized interests has been adequately documented— at least in terms of its growth and variations across administrations (Patterson 2000; Tenpas 2005).

Second, interest groups relate to the presidency differently than they do with Congress or the courts. Ordinarily, we think of groups approaching government with demands or requests for policy change or maintenance of the status quo. Although members of Congress do sometimes seek assistance from groups in mobilizing support, interest groups generally bring policy initiatives to the Congress, not the reverse. Given the reactive nature of the courts, groups almost always approach them. But organized interests, especially those that possess real clout, do not control the amount, direction, or tempo of contact with the White House. Instead, the presidency appears as likely to lobby, in Tenpas's (2005, 251 ff.) terms, from the "inside out" as groups are from the "outside in." That is, presidents seek to use their insider status and centralized communication capacities to build White House-based coalitions that will move their initiatives through the Congress

(Shaiko 1998; Peterson 2008). Such coalition building has historically stood at the heart of the American legislative process, in part because presidential coalitions, on civil rights legislation, for example, have required building support across the political parties (Jones 1994).

Since the 1980s, however, merely focusing on outside-in and inside-out lobbying would miss a key component of presidential relations with interest groups. A third major perspective on these linkages focuses on the growth of strong parties, increasingly supported by broad interest group coalitions. In many ways, heightened partisanship and polarization define the core of presidential–group relations from the Reagan presidency on (Peterson 1992a). For presidential scholars, this development is important in that congressional research provides both useful theory and robust empirical findings that should provide insights into group–presidency linkages in a political world dominated by strong parties and substantial polarization— trends largely encouraged during the eight years of the George W. Bush presidency (Aldrich and Rohde 2005; Sinclair 2006; Owens 2006).

The institutionalization of White House relations with organized interests, the coalition-based nature of these linkages, and the increasingly partisan and polarized context do offer solid foundations for understanding how the presidency interacts with groups, but some gaping holes remain in our knowledge. First, presidents and their top advisers regularly communicate with, seek to influence, and may be influenced by high-level representatives of organized interests. Top corporate executives and former political leaders (e.g., ex-Senate majority leaders Bob Dole and Tom Daschle, ex-Republican Party chair Haley Barbour, among others) can gain access to high-level White House staff, often without registering as lobbyists. We can discover many of these communications only long after they occur, and ascertaining their influence (either on or by groups) is exceptionally difficult.

Second, organized interests, often through broad industry (e.g., pharmaceuticals) or issue (e.g., environment) groupings, provide substantial funding to presidential candidates. Determining the influence of either firm- or industry- or issue-based contributions is difficult, but the aggregate figures from various industries and broad interests do affect the context of groups' interactions with presidents. Enhanced partisanship and polarization do nothing to make these potential linkages less significant. Groups invest hundreds of millions of dollars in presidential campaigns; understanding how groups calculate the return on these investments, if at all, would be well worth our efforts.

Third, congressional oversight of a unified party government (Congress and the presidency) has diminished considerably during most of the George W. Bush administration. With divided government, vigorous oversight can occur; unified governments in a partisan era may prove far less willing or capable of performing this critical task. Given the communication and information-gathering potential of the internet, it is at least possible that organized interests, such as MoveOn.com, using popular websites and blogs, could offer a surrogate for congressional oversight—as in the controversies over Attorney General Alberto Gonzales and the politicization of the Justice Department. This is virgin territory for organized interests, but the ability of the internet to allow for focused and often well-informed criticism of presidential policies and personnel could open up a new set of relationships between the White House and organized interests.

BUILDING A WHITE HOUSE STRUCTURE FOR INTEREST GROUP RELATIONS

Prior to the Ford administration (1974–7), there was no institutionalized White House structure to maintain regular contact with organized interests, but that does not mean that previous presidents failed to forge relationships with outside groups (Patterson 2000, 202–4). Instead, Democratic and Republican presidents in the modern (post-1933) era have all established linkages to certain groups. Given the coalitional nature of the Democratic Party, presidents from Roosevelt through Johnson kept in touch with an array of core groups, representing such interests as labor, racial and ethnic minorities, and urban populations (Pika 1987; Hart 1994). Likewise, Eisenhower maintained contact with Republican business constituencies through his cabinet members, such as Defense Secretary Charlie Wilson, the former CEO of General Motors, as well as Bryce Harlow, his key liaison to many lobbyists and groups (Burke and Thompson 2000). Even after President Ford began to institutionalize presidential linkages to groups, informal contacts have remained central to the relationships between the White House and interests, in large part because major policy decisions are ordinarily made outside the executive branch offices that attend to particular kinds of groups.

At the same time, as the clearinghouse for countless policies and initiatives that bubble up within the bureaucracy, the modern Executive Office of the President (EOP) must rely upon a well-developed structure in ordering its contacts with large numbers of organized interests. As one EOP scholar puts it, the president continually needs to address "an American society of organized disputers" (Patterson 2000, 201). The Office of Public Liaison (OPL), established by President Ford, provides a mechanism for the White House to keep in touch with groups, both to lobby to and to be lobbied by them, although presidential scholars have found more of the former than the latter (Tenpas 2005, 251). Peterson (1992a, 612) concludes this White House "approach was designed to fuse presidential and congressional perspectives by transforming the goals and resources of like-minded interest groups into the political assets of the White House." But, as Tenpas points out (2005, 252, emphasis added), "An *inadvertent* by-product of this formalized outreach [has been] the creation of a White House contact point for outside interests... [This] has the *unfortunate* consequence of creating a 'casework' office for organized interests."

Although the OPL, like all governmental units, is forbidden by the Anti-Lobbying Act to encourage citizens to pressure the Congress, it remains the purveyor of information to groups, often in the course of briefings within the White House (Peterson and Walker 1986; Peterson 1999). The line is fine between keeping groups informed and encouraging their active lobbying. On occasion, the OPL's entreaties can make or break a presidential initiative, as with Ronald Reagan's successful tax cuts in 1981 and tax increases in 1982 (Patterson 2000, 209–10). In the end, the OPL's dual roles as target for group entreaties and lobbyist for presidential initiatives encourage a regular and substantial two-way flow of information between the White House and a host of organized interests. The president's staff and the groups must listen to each other, if they hope to communicate their respective perspectives. This situation results in what Patterson labels "a bargain," between the White House and organized interests, which enhances linkages to many interests, even as presidential leadership has become increasingly partisan and programmatic.

Given the immense stakes that state and local governmental units have in federal policies and policy making, the Office of Intergovernmental Affairs (OIA) plays a parallel role to that of the OPL. States and localities continually lobby on an extensive range of federal issues (Cigler 1995), and the OIA serves both as target for these efforts and as the coordinator of executive coalition building, as presidents seek allies among state, cities, counties, and other governmental units. In contrast to the numerous organizations linked to the OPL, the OIA emphasizes the concerns of six major groups: The Council of State Governments, the National Association of Counties, the National Conference of State Legislatures, the National Governors Association, the National League of Cities, and the US Conference of Mayors (Tenpas 2005; Patterson 2000, 449). At the same time, it must respond to numerous issues raised by individual governors, big city mayors, and the elected officials from the most populous counties.

In addition, the Office of Legislative Affairs (OLA) and the Office of Political Affairs (OPA) both directly affect the web of relationships between groups and the White House, often in league with the OPL. The mobilization of organized interests within coalitions has become increasingly important to the success of presidential initiatives, especially within the context of a highly partisan, polarized Congress (Andres 1997). Although the respective missions of these two offices are distinct in theory, they often overlap, as Washington lobbying has grown in partisanship and become firmly intertwined with electoral politics.

Despite significant institutionalization of group-related offices within the EOP, all presidents shape how their administrations relate to groups. For example, Bill Clinton emphasized the Office of Environmental Initiatives, while George W. Bush established the Office of Faith-Based and Community Initiatives (OFBCI). These offices focused considerable attention on the presidents' respective constituencies and worked through relevant groups to forge and implement new policies. But as both insiders (DiIulio 2003) and outside scholars (Tenpas 2005, 254) note, simply establishing a White House office, as with Bush's OFBCI, does not mean that policies will emerge to satisfy either the administration or its constituencies.

Mark Peterson's (1992a; 1999, 177–8) typology of linkages between the presidency and interest groups offers a coherent perspective on the growth of the EOP structure, as well as the increasingly programmatic and partisan nature of this relationship. He

		Breadth of group interactions	
		Exclusive	Inclusive
	Programmatic	Liaison as governing party	Liaison as consensus building
Substantive focus of group interactions			
	Representational	Liaison as outreach	Liaison as legitimization

Figure 18.1 Typology of White House liaison with interest groups

Source: Peterson, 1992, 614.

juxtaposes the White House's *purpose* of group interactions with its *breadth* of these interactions (see Figure 18.1). Presidential interactions with groups through formal EOP offices most often occur as inclusive and symbolic "legitimization," although some focused outreach and generalized consensus building also takes place. But if the core of presidential relations with groups comes, as Peterson argues, in programmatic governing, the formal EOP offices are often out of the loop, as John DiIulio (2003) discovered during his short tenure as head of the Office of Faith-Based and Community Initiatives.

Still, the institutionalization of White House relations with organized interests continues to grow (Patterson 2000) and in some ways becomes more regularized, even as the overall presidential approach to groups has become increasingly partisan. This institutionalization means that groups may expect a relatively neutral treatment from EOP personnel, when in fact those very appointees have been selected on partisan political grounds and often act accordingly. To the extent that such underlying politicization dominates the actions of various EOP offices, the White House offers up the symbolism of broad representation and legitimacy in its contact with groups (Edelman 1964), even as recent presidents pursue much more narrow and politically directed policies that may reflect: (1) private contacts with interests; (2) the effects, direct or tangential, of campaign funding; and (3) the president's programmatic preferences—or some combination of these three elements of presidential–group relations.

LOBBYING AND THE PRESIDENCY: "OUTSIDE-IN" AND "INSIDE-OUT"

Students of lobbying rarely feel the need to assess who is lobbying whom. One central assumption of the interest group literature is that groups organize and petition the government for the redress of grievances or the enactment of preferred policies. The causal arrows move *from* organized interests *to* governmental institutions. By and large, this is an accurate assessment of most lobbying; Congress, state legislatures, courts, independent agencies, and most executive branch agencies are targets of lobbying efforts. And so is the presidency, especially for major interests that can obtain access. As Tenpas (2005) observes, however, the presidency is different, given its growing capacity to lobby from the "inside out," rather than merely reacting to "outside-in" attempts at influence. This means that the EOP–interest group linkage can take three distinct shapes. The president can act as lobbyist, he can be a target of lobbying, and he can be part of a continuing reciprocal relationship with numerous organized interests. To be sure, other institutional actors, such as congressional party leaders and top regulators, conduct business within a reciprocal framework. The two-way street of presidential lobbying, however, is singular in generating reciprocity when the initiation of action regularly comes from the governmental partner, not the outside petitioner.

Outside-in Lobbying and the White House

For all the incentives for groups to lobby the president and the EOP, there is little systematic knowledge about how such lobbying operates (for an exception, see Furlong 2005), at least beyond relationships established at the level of the OPL and other White House offices. Indeed, one major influence on outside-in lobbying is the manipulation of access within the EOP. For example, when Ronald Reagan replaced Jimmy Carter as president, many groups found their access to the White House either enhanced or severely restricted (Peterson 1992b); the same phenomenon occurred in the Clinton–Bush transition of 2001 (Peterson 2004). Still, for major industry and issues-based groups, the broad sweep of modern presidential powers requires that they pay close attention to the White House. In the end, despite real variations in the styles and extent of lobbying efforts directed at the White House, Pika (1991, 295) concluded, "1600 Pennsylvania Avenue is a 'must stop' for interest group representatives."

Although presidents can and do provide specific benefits to particular groups, such distributional policy making represents only one reason for organized interests to lobby the White House. Given the presidency's central position in American politics, groups often approach the EOP in search of assistance that only the president can provide. First, presidents can place items on the government's policy agenda, by including them in January's annual State of the Union address (Cohen 1995), by inserting them in the federal budget, and by using the "bully pulpit" to encourage attention from the media, the public at large, and various members of a given policy community. In this vein, George W. Bush signaled the importance of alternative energy sources with his allusions to switch grass as a source of ethanol in the 2006 State of the Union.

Second, through executive orders, presidents can have a direct impact on policy outcomes. Especially when legislative approval of a policy change appears unlikely, lobbying the EOP offers the best chance for achieving a favorable result on an important issue. Both Bill Clinton and George W. Bush addressed public land policies with executive orders, as they faced a Congress that would have slowed or stopped many of the proposed changes (Berry 2001).

Third, presidents can exercise the ultimate negative in American politics—the veto. When groups know that they will lose on Capitol Hill, they can turn to the White House to reject the legislation, thus requiring two-thirds majorities in each chamber to override this action. Moreover, even the threat of a veto can change the congressional context in terms of what will represent an acceptable compromise (Cameron 2000).

Fourth, organized interests understand the stakes inherent in presidential nominations to the cabinet, top regulatory jobs, and judicial positions; indeed, Supreme Court appointments have become highly contested since the mid-1980s, as presidents have made the justices' policy positions increasingly important as selection criteria. Although most lobbying over Robert Bork (1987) and Clarence Thomas (1991) focused on the Congress in bitter, high-profile struggles, key groups have directed more of their attention toward the president in recent years, as they have sought to ensure the selection of reliably liberal (Ruth Bader Ginsburg with Bill Clinton) or conservative (John Roberts and Samuel Alito with George W. Bush) justices. The significance of group efforts must be inferred from the selection of judges like Ginsburg, Roberts, and Alito, but their influence became manifest in at least one Bush nomination—that of White House counsel Harriet Meiers for the Supreme Court in 2005. Social conservative groups, representing the core of Bush's declining political support, reacted immediately and publicly to Meiers's nomination, arguing strenuously that she lacked adequate pro-life credentials, among other failings. Despite strong, long-time connections to Meiers, Bush quickly backtracked, accepting her withdrawal almost immediately (O'Connor, Yanus, and Patterson 2007).

Interest group lobbying on Supreme Court nominations has declined over the past twenty years, at least as reflected in appearances at congressional hearings (O'Connor, Yanus, and Patterson 2007). This trend may simply reflect a much better job of lobbying the president, if lobbying is defined as effectively communicating the kind of justice who will be acceptable. Even though Roberts and Alito attracted substantial opposition, their nominations played effectively to the Republican base, while Meiers proved just the opposite. In the end, the combination of party and related groups described by Mark Peterson (1992a) held sway for the Bush nominees' ultimate confirmations.

More generally, when contrasted with the highly permeable Congress, the limited number of access points in the EOP discourages groups from attempting to influence the president on all but the most important issues. On central societal issues such as trade, health care, and tax cuts, among others, many major groups will seek to weigh in, and presidents can often play one group off against another, again in contrast to the Congress, where the committee system allows some interests to systematically affect policy agendas across separate venues. Likewise, lobbying on policy details is best saved for the Congress, and in some instances the bureaucracy.

Obtaining access to the White House does not equate to achieving influence. Access can often be symbolic, even at the highest levels, largely because major domestic policy decisions and almost all foreign policy alternatives are driven by far more than group-based considerations. Furthermore, "The route to influence in the White House can start on Capitol Hill," in that groups can "amplify their influence" by building on the support of key members of Congress (Wilson 1997, 254). For this and many other reasons, Congress remains the preferred venue for most groups' attention. Lobbyists can often claim some partial success for their congressional efforts, while presidential lobbying—even if successful over time—may not provide for much credit claiming. In short, for most groups, lobbying the EOP is of questionable effectiveness, unlikely to lead to clear wins, and often blunted by various powerful internal administration forces. It is no wonder that lobbyists feel much more at home on Capitol Hill.

Even when lobbying the EOP does occur, scholars and journalists may find it difficult to pin down. In their interest group text, Lowery and Brasher note that executive secrecy hampers those who would study interest representation. They state (2004, 192), "[W]e have any number of stories about specific interactions between presidents and interest organizations. But they are probably atypical. Many became stories only when conflicts within and between interest organizations rose to public controversies." In the end, outside-in lobbying of the president is most influential when it can affect the choice and shaping of major agenda items, early in the policy process and often early in presidential tenures (Light 1999). Nevertheless, as the numbers of organized interests and lobbyists rise, and as the stakes of lobbying grow in importance, the ability to lobby the White House from the outside becomes all the more valuable. Thus, the access granted by the Bush administration to oil industry executives on energy policy or the pharmaceutical industry on Medicare D was worth a lot, in that it came at the agenda stage of policy development on issues that directly affected the groups' long-term financial health.

Inside-Out Lobbying I: The Presidential Advantage

Presidents lobby. They lobby the Congress. They "go public" (Kernell 1997) and lobby the people (or various segments of the population). And they often lobby organized interests, both as targets and intermediaries, as they go about building coalitions to support their policies. Given the variety of groups and issues, coalition building is at best problematic, especially on major policies. Still, the president has great built-in advantages in forming and employing group-based coalitions. It may well be that presidents need all the advantages they can muster, especially when they seek to enact initiatives that affect the society at large.

In theory, and generally in practice, presidents must represent general societal interests that transcend even large membership groups, such as labor unions, and broad interests, such as the manufacturing sector. Quirk and Nesmith (2005, 312) find that "the president is the main institutional advocate of general interests" in their study across five policy areas "notorious for interest group influence in federal policy-making." To be sure, emphasizing the general interest raises real difficulties for presidents, to the extent that they must move entrenched policies, supported by various interests, away from the status quo position.

Moreover, presidents and top EOP personnel, along with political appointees in cabinet departments, fall under the murky provisions of the Anti-Lobbying Act of 1919, which regulates their participation in "public engagement" strategies to encourage support for legislation (Shaiko 1998). In practice, the restrictions are real, but require *explicit* executive requests of groups or the public to take specific lobbying actions, such as sending emails to members of Congress (Lawson 2005). The president, his EOP staff, and his political appointees within the administration have great leeway in organizing coalitions and seeking the assistance of particular groups. Thus, the Clinton administration in 1993–4 developed campaign-style "war rooms" that reached out to a host of interests on major policy issues, most notably (and unsuccessfully) on health care reform and (successfully) on providing "100,000 Cops" to cities across the country (Shaiko 1998, 256–63). Although such actions appear, on the surface, to run counter to the Anti-Lobbying Act, the statute's interpretation allows for considerable latitude in EOP actions (Lawson 2005).

With their ability to set the policy agenda, their capacity to "go public," and their unique position in reaching out to a wide range of groups, both personally and through the EOP structure, presidents can take full advantage of their central position in American political life. Still, the obstacles to creating a series of successful ad hoc coalitions are great, in large part because these groupings must overcome a status quo that many organized interests, along with their congressional allies, are more than willing to defend. President Clinton, for example, discovered the profound nature of the difficulties of constructing a broad coalition of potentially conflicting interests when he sought systematic health care reform in the 1990s (Johnson and Broder 1996).

Ironically, a president's willingness to build group-based coalitions may flow in part from the grave limitations on his ability to move public opinion in a way that affects either support for his policies or the content of enacted policies (see, among others, Edwards 2003, 2007). If using the "bully pulpit" is largely ineffective in obtaining broad political support, the combination of directing communication to particular audiences and working directly with organized interests offers a different model for moving a policy agenda. Indeed, such a model appears to be the dominant approach to inside-out lobbying from the White House since the mid-1980s, characterized by a combination of ideology-tinged communications, appeals to groups, and multifaceted partisanship (Confessore 2003; Continetti 2006).

Inside-Out Lobbying II: Presidents and Group in a Partisan Era

Mark Peterson (1992a) has developed a useful framework for examining the interest group–presidency nexus from the White House vantage point. He categorizes the relations between groups and the White House along two dimensions:

(1) inclusive–exclusive and (2) representational–programmatic (see Figure 18.1). Thus, presidents will seek to represent interests or to back proposed policies that, taken together, make up a program. And they will either cast their nets widely or less so in soliciting interest group allies. Peterson argues that emphases on program and exclusivity have come to dominate the president's relations with organized interests. This is true largely because of the changing relationships between parties, the presidency, and organized interests since the early 1980s.

As Peterson (2008, 290) summarizes, in the 1960s and 1970s:

[T]he political parties became more fragmented, and the social movements... yielded an interest group system that at once challenged corporate political power and spawned a wide range of organizations.... As the century came to a close, the parties as represented in government regained strength, now with far greater internal ideological coherence and accentuated interparty polarization, while the interest group terrain included a vastly larger number of relevant organizations, more specialized policy niches, and arguably greater ideological and partisan division among interests than in the past.

Within this context, presidents have strong incentives to govern on programmatic grounds, rather than representational ones (see Sinclair 2006). Rather than seeking to reflect a broad consensus within the center of American politics, recent presidents have governed from their respective parties' programmatic perspectives. Sometimes, as with Ronald Reagan and George W. Bush, this choice comes from the president's governing philosophy; in other instances, as with George H. W. Bush and Bill Clinton, the rising partisanship either negated or penalized attempts to govern from the center.

Peterson proved prescient with his 1992 article, in that the 1994 Republican landslide would heighten partisan/programmatic tendencies within the GOP. George W. Bush's election as president would provide the final component for a full-blown experiment in parliamentary-style government (Owens 2006) in the United States. Congress scholars have clearly delineated the growth of partisanship and polarization (among others, Aldrich and Rohde 2005; Sinclair 2006), but they have provided little assessment of the Republicans' extensive efforts to extend their reach into the interest group community. Despite some journalistic attention (Continetti 2006; Confessore 2003), academics have largely ignored this phenomenon, widely labeled the "K Street Project" (Loomis 2007; Cigler and Loomis 2007).

Briefly put, the project began as a personnel screening and tracking project of the Republican leadership on Capitol Hill, working with key lobbyists, such as Grover Norquist, that sought to place Republicans in DC lobbying jobs for large corporations, trade associations, and major contract lobbying firms (including many law firms with lobbying wings). In practice, Norquist and Senator Rick Santorum (R-Pa.) met weekly to slot Republicans into the best lobbying jobs: "the lobbyists present pass around a list of jobs available and discuss whom to support.... 'The underlying theme was [to] place Republicans in key positions on K Street. Everybody taking part was a Republican and understood that that was the purpose of what we were doing' " (former Rep. Rod Chandler, quoted in Confessore 2003). Although the impetus for the K Street Project came from a combination of key lobbyists and top congressional leaders, the election of George W. Bush and his decision to govern in a highly partisan manner generated powerful and complex relationships between the Republican administration, the Republican Congress, and the increasingly Republican tilt of the Washington lobbying community. For example, in 2004, President Bush chose David Safavian, a close associate of the powerful lobbyist Jack Abramoff, to head the Office of Management and Budget's procurement office, with annual responsibilities of $300 billion in spending (Continetti 2006, 200 ff.).

With George W. Bush in the White House and given the federal government's reaction to the 9/11 attacks, conditions for growth were propitious on both the supply and demand sides of the lobbying business. The demand for Republican lobbyists rose with the onset of unified government and strengthened further after the 2002 and 2004 elections. As one lobbyist noted, "Having the White House [allowed Republican congressional leaders] to enforce the K Street Project." Post-9/11 spending meant that the federal pie grew much larger, very quickly, which opened the door to intense lobbying over new spoils, much of it controlled by the executive branch, with little congressional scrutiny. Moreover, by 2001, the Republican legislators had produced a large supply of relatively young, reasonably experienced, and generally ideological staffers, who were eager to make the traditional, and highly lucrative, move to the private sector. With their rise to majority status in 1995, congressional Republicans had filled hundreds of key jobs on committees and within the party leadership. Like their predecessors in such positions, these staff members became valuable candidates for top lobbyist openings, and the K Street project served as a ready vehicle to channel hundreds of loyal, well-connected Republicans into those jobs.

Holding the White House allowed Republicans to make a convincing argument that interests that hired Democratic lobbyists would be at a disadvantage. By 2003, for example, a GOP official could publicly boast in the *Washington Post* that 33 of 36 high-level lobbying positions had gone to Republicans, and by 2005 one Republican argued that Democrats were simply not a valuable commodity within the lobbying community (Continetti 2006, 46).

A real question remains, however, as to how much the president's "programmatic" inside-out lobbying of organized interests in support of his agenda has consistently supplemented the party-based congressional model. To be sure, during the 1995–2006 period, those Washington lobbyists who identified with the GOP and who often emigrated from Capitol Hill or the Bush administration were considered part of a team by both congressional leaders and, later, the White House. On a handful of major issues, such as instituting a Medicare drug benefit through the Medicare Modernization Act (MMA), the White House and congressional Republicans could put together a large coalition of more than 300 pharmaceutical interests (Peterson 2008, 308). The night-long congressional session in 2003 that enacted MMA has become legendary, with House Republican leaders holding open the vote on passage for more than three hours as they worked with the EOP to cobble together a majority through side payments and arm twisting that largely targeted GOP law makers (Sinclair 2006, 172–5).

If this was the best that presidential lobbying within a partisan context could do, however, the coalition-based reach of the White House through the K Street Project has proven less potent than many have claimed. Indeed, the EOP and the Republican leadership looked a lot like what George Edwards (1989) described in his Reagan-era analysis of presidential influence on congressional decisions; Bush's influence was marginal, but critical, as the EOP was part of the lobbying effort that swayed a handful of votes. Moreover, given the jury-rigged nature of the MMA, with its opponents on the right and left, the president and his coalition of groups lobbied for a highly compromised legislative package, not some clear programmatic result of a unified party government.

The most striking alternative to the programmatic explanation of presidential inside-out lobbying model also comes from Mark Peterson (2004, 2008), who labels Bush's relationship to organized interests a "government of chums." Peterson sees Bush's governing style as falling firmly within the "governing party" quadrant (2004, table 1), which emphasizes program and exclusive interest group coalitions. Yet, as Continetti (2006, 232, 234) argues, the party-based K Street Project produced more pork and earmarks—the measures of success for many lobbyists—than programmatic conservative victories that reflected core Republican values.

Bush did reward his "chums" from K Street and from corporate boardrooms, but not in any coherent, program-based way. Instead, he regularly signed appropriations bills and other legislation that included record numbers of earmarks; such rewards have been part and parcel of American presidential politics at least as far back as Andrew Jackson's reliance on spoils. Moreover, in the wake of the Democrats' 2006 capture of the Congress, increasing numbers of lobbying firms have returned to a bipartisan approach to hiring and to seeking influence (Birnbaum 2007). Presidents surely seek to build long-lasting coalitions with groups for partisan and programmatic reasons, but actively governing through interest groups with their diverse and often conflicting preferences, even within a single policy community, may prove easier for political scientists to model than for the EOP to implement. As long-time conservative activist and Washington lobbyist David Keene observed in the midst of the 2008 presidential campaign, "This is a town in which 90 percent of the people balance their access and income on the one hand with their principles on the other" (Kirkpatrick 2008).

RESEARCHING ORGANIZED INTERESTS
AND THE PRESIDENT

In assessing the state of scholarly knowledge on organized interests *and* the president, we simply do not know nearly as much as we should. Mark Peterson's four-celled schema does offer a useful framework for analyzing group–presidency relationships, especially in terms of how the president approaches organized interests. In addition, some scholars have offered valuable snapshots of the linkages between these major institutions in American politics (Furlong 2005; Tenpas 2005; Shaiko 1998, among others). In the end, however, as both organized interests and the presidency have grown in size and, arguably, influence, both subfields' scholarly communities have paid little explicit attention to the implications of the overlaps between them.

The problems are twofold. First, beyond Peterson's model, scholars have employed few useful ways of conceptualizing the group–president relationship, especially in terms of interests that seek to exert influence, although coalitional strategies that flow from the White House do offer a potentially fruitful approach for examining "inside-out" lobbying. Nevertheless, traditional lobbying—of decision makers by interests—has not whetted the imagination of researchers, despite the ever-expanding presidential reach over the past fifty years.

Second, potential scholarly projects immediately confront the difficulty in generating good data on meaningful White House activities that affect major policies. Although we know a fair amount about the OPL and other executive offices, including how they change between administrations, we have much less systematic information on how the president and top-level staff address policies of great significance to powerful organized interests. Thus, there is both a dearth of theory building on relationships between the presidency and organized interests, and a striking lack of information on these linkages, especially the traditional outside-in group activities.

Mapping the Mosaic of the Presidency and Organized Interests

Despite its unparalleled capacity to forge large coalitions of groups, the White House regularly places its inside-out lobbying within the broader context of multiple exchanges between large numbers of organized interests and both the president and the institutionalized presidency. Aside from the regular lobbying give-and-take between groups and the EOP, the most significant elements of these exchanges are: (1) the White House's control of the policy agenda and (2) the tremendous amount of "interested" money that flows into presidential campaigns.

The modern presidency dominates the setting of the national policy agenda. Not only do presidents ultimately control thousands of specific budget (and tax) decisions, with implications for thousands of organized interests, but they also dictate the amount and nature of attention directed at the dozens of issues that they could possibly emphasize before Congress, within the bureaucracy, and to the public. In the wake of 9/11 the presidency has taken on even greater powers, as it conducts a far-reaching, if ill-defined, war on terror (Fisher 2005; Howell and Pevehouse 2007). Putting aside the Bush administration's most extreme claims of executive power, presidential responsibilities have grown sharply, to the point that many policy and allocation decisions come from the executive, rather than from the

Congress. No matter how difficult the task, groups have great incentives to seek access to the EOP, given presidential responsibilities in the twenty-first century.

With the difficulties of obtaining access to the White House's decision-making process, the role of fund raising as a tool for gaining entrée has become all the more important. In 2004, for example, George W. Bush received almost $35 million from finance/insurance/real estate interests, and almost $5 million each from the agribusiness and energy sectors (Open Secrets 2008). Within the congressional lobbying literature, there is general acceptance that organized interests, through their contributions, can "buy the time" of legislators to work more diligently on their issues, to the exclusion of others (Hall and Wayman 1990). Both for specific interests, such as Halliburton, or industry segments, such as the oil and gas sector, this kind of a pattern might well exist within EOP.

Through Federal Election Commission data, scholars can determine a great deal about input side of the potential exchanges between interests and the president. We know relatively little about the output side, however, and even less about the decision-making process that could link contributions to executive choices on agendas, particular policies, or general approaches to issues. Still, the FEC contributions information does provide a window into one set of potential influences on presidential choices. At a minimum, scholars could track broad patterns of interests—by sector and industry—across time, as well as focus on specific groups, corporations, and other organizations that invest in presidential candidates, and especially incumbents.

Although the Center for Responsive Politics does much of this tracking, its overall perspective is to *assume* that following the trail of money will inevitably lead to the discovery of influence over agendas, policies, and spending. This is no more than a journalistic hunch, however, one not pursued rigorously by scholars in large part because good data on processes and outcomes are difficult to obtain. Indeed, the absence of good information on group-related decision processes, especially at the top levels of the EOP, stands as the greatest obstacle to generating definitive work on connections between the presidency and organized interests (Lowery and Brasher 2004). Gathering better data is a prerequisite for stronger analysis and theory testing. In particular, scholars should focus on (a) connections between EOP personnel and organized interests within the White House decision-making process and (b) improved data on White House decision outputs that could be linked to interest group politics.

Beyond the Organization Chart

If the White House's formal structure for dealing with groups has grown in a straightforward manner since the 1970s, the informal relations between modern presidents and organized interests remain underreported by journalists, understudied by political scientists, and underestimated by almost everyone, including presidents, who often have no stake in emphasizing their ties to particular groups or interests. Thus, if scholars have done a credible job in chronicling and assessing the growth of the formal group-related White House structure (e.g., Patterson 2000), they have failed to establish an understanding of the linkages between presidents and organized interests at the top levels of decision making.

There are several possible explanations for this failure. First, if most improbable, there may be few such top-level connections, leaving most linkages to either the institutional White House (OPL, for example) or the growing partisan/programmatic coalitions that include groups, congressional parties, and parts of the media (which I discuss below). Second, these connections may well exist, but have little systematic impact on policy. Again, this is possible, but less than likely, given the immense stakes that ride on so many presidential decisions. Third, organized interests consult widely with the executive branch, but largely below the presidential level. From this perspective, the president's major influence on policy derives from the increasingly politicized and partisan appointment of key bureaucrats, who interact extensively with group representatives over particular issues. (Mackenzie 2001). Finally, to the extent that high-level connections do exist, they are largely hidden behind a White House wall of secrecy, only occasionally coming to light, as in Cheney's 2001 summit with oil industry representatives.

The question is not so much *whether* we should examine such connections, but *how* we should do so. Perhaps scholars can only do such analysis in retrospect, as memoirs, documents, and the cumulative historical record provide the necessary information to allow for generalizations. For example, the various biographies, memoirs, and other historical treatments that address particular events could well offer enough data to allow for conclusions about patterns of influence (outside-in) and coalition building (inside-out). Thus, the Roosevelt, Truman, and Eisenhower administrations, given their relative longevity, might provide enough data about EOP dealings that we could arrive at some baseline understanding of how the modern presidency addressed group-based concerns at the very top levels of decision making. The key here is to cast a scholarly net widely enough to encompass a large number of decisions, as well as to obtain some rough consensus on the groups that did, or did not, gain access to the process. Within the Roosevelt administration, for instance, one could survey all biographies, along with the memoirs from and biographies about insiders such as Hopkins, Ickes, Corcoran, and Howe. Add to these a large number of policy-based books and articles on the Roosevelt presidency, and a substantial database would be developed.

A Presidential Policy/Organized Interest Database

Examining the relations between Congress and the executive, scholars such as David Mayhew (1990, 2005), Sarah Binder (2003), and Charles Jones (1994, 2005) have created databases that have allowed them to reach general conclusions about the nature of interbranch relations and the ability (or inability) of the president and Congress to address major policy issues. To the extent that organized interests influence presidential decisions, there should be an accounting of both group-related decisions and of executive actions that take group preferences into account. Given the current state of the literature, such goals might appear out of reach. For example, the extensive "Advocacy and Public Policymaking" project (Baumgartner et al. n.d.; see <http://lobby.la.psu.edu/>) has generated lots of outcomes data, but nothing that directly comments on internal EOP deliberations. Still, when one searches for particular policy histories with particular presidents, groups and lobbyists are frequently integral to the policy narratives that develop. Indeed, the idea of "interest group liberalism" (Lowi 1979) may well have been transformed into a nexus of "interest group conservatism" inside the George W. Bush administration (Weisberg 2005), with altogether different loose governing coalitions.

Moreover, presidents can frequently alter policies with executive actions. Given the amount of coverage on policies on lobbying and policy making in *National Journal, CQ Weekly, The Washington Post, The Hill, Roll Call,* and online in *Politico* and *Influence*, scholars might well track major legislation in terms of both participation by organized interests in the policy-making process and of estimates of winners and losers. If we could not do this with just the public record, we might well be able to do it through scoring by insider experts. In the end, the accounting of participation and "winners and losers" would be a rough estimate, but even substantial measurement error may well be acceptable, given the importance of assessing the impact of groups on presidential decisions, to say nothing of ascertaining the importance of group-based coalitions for assisting in presidential victories. If the post-1990 growth in the study of divided government in the wake of Mayhew's *Divided We Govern* is any indicator, the development of a roughly similar group participation/impact dataset could well encourage a similar accumulation of useful studies.

Interest Groups and Oversight in a Partisan Era

If the George W. Bush presidency has ushered in an era in which unified party control of government will again become relatively common, one further perspective on interest groups may prove useful. That is, if unified government leads to less oversight, it may increasingly fall to organized interests to generate much of the monitoring of government policies that congressional committees have traditionally provided. In practical terms, this may well result from a combination of both old (unions) and new (MoveOn.com) raising issues on the internet, which the traditional media then pick up. But even in a more conventional and theoretical formulation, interest groups may well shore up traditional congressional oversight (Epstein and O'Halloran 1995). Indeed, if we can consider lobbying by organized interests a subsidy to members of Congress, there is no reason to think that the subsidy would not cover assisting in oversight (Hall and Deardorff 2006). To the extent that presidential policy making has become programmatic in forming partisan coalitions, opposing coalitions will seek to work with congressional minorities to oversee the implementation of the enacted policies and raise issues for the next elections for subsequent presidential and congressional elections.

THE INCOMPLETE MOSAIC: ORGANIZED INTERESTS AND THE PRESIDENT

The White House has accumulated great power since the birth of the modern presidency during Franklin Roosevelt's administration, but we know precious little about how the EOP has interacted with interests, even as the number of groups, the amount of lobbying, and the campaign contributions by various interests have all grown steadily over the past fifty years (Polsby, Wildavsky, and Hopkins 2008). Students of the presidency, interest groups, and public policy should all place the exploration of relationships between organized interests and the presidency near the top of their research agendas.

Still, scholars have not focused on the relationships between organized interests and the president or the presidency, and perhaps for good reason. The pay-off is unclear, and the requisite data are difficult to amass. Groups do spend more time addressing the legislative branch, yet presidents often seek to speak over the heads of interests to the public at large. Nevertheless, the institutions of the presidency and of organized interests represent two elephants, in reasonably close proximity. They simply must take account of each other. The presidency has for thirty years formally, and at least thirty more informally, paid real attention to many subgroups and organized interests (Pika 1983). Contemporary reporting, especially since the mid-1990s, has increasingly tracked the politics of organized interests in Washington, DC, and some of this attention has focused on presidential politics, as well as the traditional legislative emphasis.

In addition, with campaign contribution data and dozens of policy case studies, both journalistic and scholarly, there are ample opportunities to gather enough information to begin to reach empirical conclusions, guided by theories of influence, exchange (Pika 1983), or partisan program (Peterson 1992b). To be sure, gathering data from current administrations may prove impossible, but there is no reason why reasonably complete pictures of group–presidency relations for past administrations cannot emerge, as the pieces of the mosaic become known and fitted together. Often, scholars congregate around data that are easy to obtain and easy to manipulate, such as surveys and congressional voting records. These data-driven fields generate lots of scholarship, much of it first rate, while other, arguably equally important fields, such as relationships between groups and the presidency, go largely unexplored. But the pieces of the mosaic are there—or can be found—and the rewards for putting them together should be great.

REFERENCES

ABERBACH, J. D., and PETERSON, M. A. (eds.) 2005. *The Executive Branch*. New York: Oxford University Press.

ALDRICH, J. H., and ROHDE, D. W. 2005. Congressional Committees in a Partisan Era. In *Congress Reconsidered*, 8th edn., ed. L. C. Dodd and B. I. Oppenheimer. Washington, DC: CQ Press.

ANDRES, G. 1997. Lobbying for the President Influencing Congress from the White House. In *The Interest Group Connection*, ed. P. S. Herrnson, R. G. Shaiko, and C. Wilcox. Chatham, NJ: Chatham House.

BAUMGARTNER, F. R., BERRY, J. M., HORNACKI, M., KIMBALL, D. C., and LEECH, B. L. Advocacy and Public Policymaking Project <http://lobby.la.psu.edu/>.

BERRY, J. B. 2001. <http://www.sierraclub.org/planet/200103/conservation.asp>.

BINDER, S. A. 2003. *Stalemate: Causes and Consequences of Legislative Gridlock*. Washington, DC: Brookings Institution.

BIRNBAUM, J. H. 2007. Lobbyists Profit from Power in Congress. *Washington Post*, Apr. 23: D1.

BURKE, B., and THOMPSON, R. G. 2000. *Bryce Harlow: Mr. Integrity*. Oklahoma City: Oklahoma Heritage Association.

CAMERON, C. M. 2000. *Veto Bargaining: Presidents and the Politics of Negative Power*. New York: Cambridge University Press.

CIGLER, A. J., and LOOMIS, B. A. 2007. Organized Interests, Political Parties, and Representation: James Madison, Tom DeLay and the Soul of American Politics. In *Interest Group Politics*, 7th edn., ed. A. J. Cigler and B. A. Loom. Washington, DC: CQ Press.

CIGLER, B. A. 1995. Not Just Another Special Interest: Intergovernmental Representation. In *Interest Group Politics*, 4th edn., ed. A. J. Cigler and B. A. Loomis. Washington, DC: CQ Press.

COHEN, J. E. 1995. Presidential Rhetoric and the Presidential Agenda. *American Journal of Political Science*, 39: 87–107.

CONFESSORE, N. 2003. Welcome to the Machine. *Washington Monthly*, July/Aug. Accessed at <www.Washingtonmonthly.com>.

CONTINETTI, M. 2006. *The K Street Gang: The Rise and Fall of the Republican Machine*. New York: Doubleday.

DILULIO, J. J. 2003. Inside the Bush Presidency: Reflections of an Academic Interloper. In *The George W. Bush Presidency: An Early Assessment*, ed. F. I. Greenstein. Baltimore: Johns Hopkins University Press.

EDELMAN, M. 1964. *Symbolic Uses of Politics*. Champaign-Urbana: University of Illinois Press.

EDWARDS, G. C., III. 1989. *At the Margins: Presidential Leadership of Congress*. New Haven, CT: Yale University Press.

—— 2003. *On Deaf Ears: The Limits of the Bully Pulpit*. New Haven, CT: Yale University Press.

—— 2007. *Governing by Campaigning: The Politics of the Bush Presidency*, 2nd edn. New York: Longman.

—— and KING, D. S. (eds.) 2007. *The Polarized Presidency of George W. Bush*. New York: Oxford University Press.

EPSTEIN, D. L., and O'HALLORAN, S. 1995. A Theory of Strategic Oversight: Congress, Lobbyists, and the Bureaucracy. *Journal of Law, Economics and Organization*, 11: 227–55.

FISHER, L. 2005. *Military Tribunals and Presidential Power: American Revolution to the War on Terrorism*. Lawrence: University Press of Kansas.

FURLONG, S. R. 2005. Exploring Interest Group Participation in Executive Policymaking. In *The Interest Group Connection*, 2nd edn., ed. P. S. Herrnson, R. Shaiko, and C. Wilcox. Washington, DC: CQ Press.

HALL, R. L., and DEARDORFF, A. V. 2006. Lobbying as Legislative Subsidy. *American Political Science Review*, 100: 69–84.

—— and WAYMAN, F. W. 1990. Buying Time: Moneyed Interests and the Mobilization of Bias in Congressional Committees. *American Political Science Review*, 84: 797–820.

HART, J. 1994. *The Presidential Branch: From Washington to Clinton*, 2nd edn. Chatham, NJ: Chatham House.

HOWELL, W. G., and PEVEHOUSE, J. C. 2007. *While Dangers Gather: Congressional Checks on Presidential War Powers*. Princeton, NJ: Princeton University Press.

JOHNSON, H., and BRODER, D. 1996. *The System: The American Way of Politics at the Breaking Point*. Boston: Little Brown.

JONES, O. C. 1994. *The Presidency in a Separated System*. Washington, DC: Brookings.

—— 2005. *The Presidency in a Separated System*, 2nd edn. Washington, DC: Brookings Institution.

KERNELL, S. 1997. *Going Public: New Strategies of Presidential Leadership*. Washington, DC: CQ Press.

KIRKPATRICK, D. 2008. As McCain Wins, Critics on Right Look Again. *New York Times*, Feb. 1: A1.

LAWSON, J. 2005. <www.fedlawyerguy.org/2005/01/antilobbying_act_changes.html>.

LIGHT, P. C. 1999. *The President's Agenda*, 3rd edn. Washington, DC: Brookings Institution.

LOOMIS, B. A. 2007. Does K Street Run through Capitol Hill? Lobbying Congress in a Republican Age. In *Interest Group Politics*, 7th edn., ed. A. J. Cigler and B. A. Loomis. Washington, DC: CQ Press.

LOWERY, D., and BRASHER, H. 2004. *Organized Interests and American Government*. Boston: McGraw Hill.

LOWI, T. J. 1979. *The End of Liberalism*, 2nd edn. New York: W.W. Norton.

MCKENZIE, G. C. (ed.) 2001. *Innocent until Nominated*. Washington, DC: Brookings Institution.

MAYHEW, D. J. 1990. *Divided We Govern*. New Haven, CT: Yale University Press.

—— 2005. *Divided We Govern*, 2nd edn. New Haven, CT: Yale University Press.

NOWNES, A. J. 2007. *Total Lobbying*. New York: Cambridge University Press.

O'CONNOR, K. 2005. Lobbying the Justices or Lobbying for Justice? The Role of Organized Interests in the Judicial Process. In *The Interest Group Connection*, 2nd edn., ed. P. S. Herrnson, R. G. Shaiko, and C. Wilcox. Washington, DC: CQ Press.

—— YANUS, A. B., and PATTERSON, L. M. 2007. Where Have All the Interest Groups Gone? In *Interest Group Politics*, 7th edn., ed. A. J. Cigler and B. A. Loomis. Washington, DC: CQ Press.

Open Secrets. 2008. At <http://www.opensecrets.org/bush/index.asp>. Accessed Sept. 7, 2008.

OWENS, J. E. 2006. American-Style Party Government: Delivering Bush's Agenda, Delivering the Congress' Agenda. In *Right On? Political Change and Continuity in George Bush's America*, ed. I. Morgan and P. J. Davies. London: Institute for the Americas/Brookings Institution Press.

PATTERSON, B. 2000. *The Ring of Power: The White House Staff and its Expanding Role in Government*. Washington, DC: Brookings.

PETERSON, M. 1992a. The Presidency and Organized Interests: White House Patterns of Interest Group Liaison. *American Political Science Review*, 86: 612–25.

PETERSON, M. 1992b. Interest Mobilization and the White House. In *The Politics of Interests*, ed. M. Petracca. Boulder, CO: Westview.

——1999. Clinton and Organized Interests: Splitting Friends, Uniting Enemies. In *The Clinton Legacy*, ed. C. Campbell and B. Rockman. Chappaqua, NY: Chatham House of Seven Bridges Press.

——2004. Bush and Interest Groups: A Government of Chums. In *The George W. Bush Presidency*, ed. C. Campbell and B. Rockman. Washington, DC: CQ Press.

——2008. Still a Government of Chums. In *The George W. Bush Legacy*, ed. C. Campbell, B. Rockman, and A. Rudalevige. Washington, DC: CQ Press.

——and WALKER, J. 1986. Interest Group Responses to Partisan Change: The Impact of the Reagan Administration upon the National Interest Group System. In *Interest Group Politics*, 2nd edn., ed. A. Cigler and B. Loomis. Washington, DC: CQ Press.

PIKA, J. A. 1983. Interest Groups and the Executive: Presidential Intervention. In *Interest Group Politics*, ed. A. J. Cigler and B. A. Loomis. Washington, DC: CQ Press.

——1987. Interest Groups and the White House under Roosevelt and Truman. *Political Science Quarterly*, 102: 647–88.

——1991. Opening Doors for Kindred Souls: The White House Office of Public Liaison. In *Interest Group Politics*, 3rd edn., ed. A. J. Cigler and B. A. Loomis. Washington, DC: CQ Press.

——1999. Interest Groups: A Doubly Dynamic Relationship. In *Presidential Policymaking: An End-Of-Century Assessment*, ed. S. A. Shull. Armonk, NY: M. E. Sharpe.

PIOTROWSKI, S. J., and ROSENBLOOM, D. H. 2005. The Legal-Institutional Framework for Interest Group Participation in Federal Administrative Policymaking. In *The Interest Group Connection*, 2nd edn., ed. P. S. Herrnson, R. G. Shaiko, and C. Wilcox. Washington, DC: CQ Press.

POLSBY, N. W., WILDAVSKY, A., with HOPKINS, D. A. 2008. *Presidential Elections*, 12th edn. Lanham, MD: Rowman & Littlefield.

QUIRK, P. J., and NESMITH, B. 2005. Who Serves Special Interests? The President, Congress, and Interest Groups. In *The Interest Group Connection*, 2nd edn., ed. P. Herrnson, R. Shaiko, and C. Wilcox. Washington, DC: CQ Press.

SHAIKO, R. G. 1998. Reverse Lobbying: Interest Group Mobilization from the White House and the Hill. In *Interest Group Politics*, 5th edn., ed. A. J. Cigler and B. A. Loomis. Washington, DC: CQ Press.

SINCLAIR, B. 2006. *Party Wars: Polarization and the Politics of National Policy Making*. Norman: University of Oklahoma Press.

TENPAS, K. D. 2005. Lobbying the Executive Branch. In *The Interest Group Connection*, 2nd edn., ed. P. S. Herrnson, R. G. Shaiko, and C. Wilcox. Washington, DC: CQ Press.

WEISBERG, J. 2005. Interest-Group Conservatism: George Bush's Philosophy of Government. <www.slate.com>, posted May 4.

WILSON, E. J., III. 1997. Interest Groups and Foreign Policymaking: A View from the White House. In *The Interest Group Connection*, ed. P. Herrnson, R. Shaiko, and C. Wilcox. Chatham, NJ: Chatham House.

PART VI

UNILATERAL ACTION

CHAPTER 19

GOING ALONE

THE PRESIDENTIAL POWER OF UNILATERAL ACTION

KENNETH R. MAYER

UNILATERAL action refers to the different types of administrative and policy changes that the president can initiate on his own without the cooperation, and sometimes over the objections, of Congress or the judiciary. The instruments of unilateral policy include executive orders, proclamations, administrative and National Security Directives, military orders, pardons, recess appointments, signing statements, and executive agreements.

Presidents have initiated unilateral actions from the beginning of the Republic. The list is long and includes: Washington's Neutrality Proclamation, Jefferson's Louisiana Purchase, Lincoln's Emancipation Proclamation, FDR's establishment of the Executive Office of the President and the internment of Japanese-Americans during the Second World War, Truman's desegregation of the military and US entry into the Korean War, Johnson's establishment of affirmative action requirements for federal contractors, Nixon's imposition of wage and price controls, Carter's implementation of the agreement to release American diplomats held by Iran, Reagan's cost–benefit analysis for federal regulations, and Clinton's creation of national monuments (Mayer 2001; Howell 2003; Cooper 2002). In the aftermath of 9/11, President George W. Bush authorized the air force to shoot down hijacked civilian aircraft, established military tribunals to try enemy combatants, authorized warrantless electronic surveillance of communications, and asserted that he was not bound by certain statutory provisions in legislation he was signing. Presidents have ordered the military into combat hundreds of times, mostly without explicit congressional authorization (Fisher 2004). There is no dispute that presidents have made substantial changes to policy and process relying on nothing but their own authority.

At first, research into unilateral powers was offered as an extension of the long-dominant "strategic presidency" approach, synonymous with Neustadt, which held that presidents had to negotiate the major elements of their agendas. In the strategic presidency model, presidents confront a purposely fragmented political system in which other major stakeholders have their own power bases and claims to legitimacy. In such a system, presidents find their formal authority insufficient to meet their obligations, and must therefore turn to other resources in order to leave their mark. As Neustadt put it, the keys to presidential success are the strategic resources that a president can bring to bear on the central task of persuasion: popularity, strategic acumen, political judgment, and presidential reputations as seen through the eyes of political elites. All of these factors condition the bargaining environment, especially as they affect the perceived costs and benefits of supporting or opposing the president. These contingent resources, wielded carefully, help a president convince others that they should see things as the president does, and do what the president asks because it is in their own interest.

The strategic model posits (or observes, it is not always clear which) that presidents use their formidable political powers as a bargaining tool, by persuading, cajoling, threatening, logrolling, and compromising with other political elites in order to get high-priority policies enacted. They must constantly engage other actors, especially members of Congress (Peterson 1990). The few advantages that the president has in this process come from what Neustadt calls the "President as Clerk," the fact that other political actors "have found it practically impossible to do their jobs without assurance of initiatives from him" (1990, 7).

A crucial element of the strategic presidency is that presidents rarely get their way by command. In Neustadt's view, commands are evidence less of presidential authority than "a painful last resort, a forced response to the exhaustion of all other remedies, suggestive less of mastery than failure—the failure of attempts to gain an end by softer means (1990, 24). Harry Truman noted what Eisenhower would discover moving from the military to the White House: "He'll sit here...and he'll say, 'Do this! Do that!' *And nothing will happen.* Poor Ike—it won't be a bit like the Army. He'll find it very frustrating" (cited in Neustadt 1990, 10).

Neustadt offered *Presidential Power* as both an empirical and normative work. The strategic model simply recognized the reality of how presidents actually behaved, and was a more accurate portrayal of the office than the more static public law approach as exemplified in Corwin (1957). Neustadt was also arguing that bargaining is the *preferred* mechanism of political change, both required by and appropriate to the constitutional separation of powers. "After all," notes Charles O. Jones in a retrospective tribute of Neustadt's contribution, "*Presidential Power* may have been written to correct what we were teaching about the presidency, but it was also written to serve the best interest of Presidents and other power holders" (2007, 42). Such was

Neustadt's influence on the field that it was nearly universal for presidency scholars to position their work in relation to *Presidential Power*, even when the intent was to travel in an entirely new direction.

The unilateral powers model has developed to the point where it constitutes a direct challenge to the strategic presidency, as well as a separate research paradigm in its own right, widely perceived as capturing a significant portion of what presidents actually do. And while it can be dangerous to characterize an entire literature, the logic of the unilateral powers model allows scholars to devise theoretically informed, data-driven, and methodologically rich studies that genuinely advance the state of knowledge. In fact, the president can often say "do this," and it happens, even if the formal authority is ambiguous (or even lacking). Neustadt cites Truman's seizure of the nation's steel mills in 1952 as a case of presidential failure that illustrates the president's weakness, a "painful last resort, a forced response to the exhaustion of other remedies" (1990, 24). Viewed another way, Truman's order becomes an astonishing example of unilateral presidential authority: in the face of a statute that provided a specific mechanism to resolve labor disputes, and having been denied legislative authority to seize private property for wartime use, Truman ordered Secretary of Labor Charles Sawyer to do it anyway. Sawyer complied. Thus, "a secretary of labor—illegally, as it turned out—seized billions of dollars of private property, and the steel mill owners both acquiesced to that seizure (initially, at least), on the basis of the president's word" (Mayer 2001, 18).

In a controversial challenge to the presidency subfield, Gary King critiqued the scholarly focus on individual presidents (and, implicitly, the strategic presidency model). King was blunt, arguing that the literature was theoretically underdeveloped and empirically thin. "Although probably more has been written about the presidency than all other areas of American politics combined, most work in the field is not yet to the point where concepts are to be measured and theories tested systematically" (1993, 387). King was not the first to lament the lack of theoretical progress in the subfield. In this volume, Howell notes that other scholars had been making similar arguments for at least a decade prior. In a similar vein, Terry Moe urged scholars to abandon efforts to construct ever more complex theories that attempted to chase down increasingly contingent relationships with more and more variables. Instead, he insisted, more progress would come from pursuing simple institutionally based theories (1993, 352–4). Studying unilateral action is ideally suited to this sort of work, focusing as it does on the multiple, specific, and easily identifiable instances in which presidents exercise their constitutional and statutory authority. The paradigm of unilateral action is built on a solid theoretical foundation, which generates a wide range of hypotheses that can be tested with a variety of methods.

In this chapter, I have two goals. The first is to set out the logic of the unilateral powers model, assess the state of empirical work on the model's predictions, and identify unresolved questions that can motivate future research. As a discipline, we have learned a great deal about how and why presidents use unilateral action to advance their policy goals. This work has been both descriptive and theoretical. Scholars have accurately accounted for the multitude of unilateral tools, and analyzed patterns of why and how presidents use them. This empirical work is informed by a deductive theory that generates hypotheses about what we expect to find. There are, as in any new theory, plenty of unanswered questions and phenomena that we cannot yet explain.

Beyond offering suggestions for future research, my second goal is to analyze a troubling implication of unilateral action theory: the prediction that, over time, presidents will use unilateral action to expand the reach of presidential authority and centralize power within the White House. This prediction is a straightforward application of the underlying theory. But if it is correct, it suggests that there may exist a point where presidential power becomes too concentrated, undermining checks and balances. Many observers claim that we had reached this point under George W. Bush, who used unilateral action aggressively especially after 9/11 and whose advisers hewed to a "unitary presidency" theory that takes a broad view of executive power. A final suggestion for future research, then, is whether the power of unilateral action is in fact characterized by a "ratchet effect." As a discipline, we need a better understanding of the countervailing forces that may constrain unilateral action—whether institutional, political, or electoral—and the conditions in which these pushbacks will occur.

The Theory and Logic of Unilateral Action

The theory of unilateral presidential action is based on two foundational assumptions. The first is that presidential behavior is determined by institutional structure and formal rules, not the president's psychological make-up, character, political skills, style, or specific policy preferences. This is alternatively referred to as a "structural theory" or "new institutionalism," following Moe and Wilson (1994) and Moe (1993). The theory's strongest form assumes that the scholars can ignore altogether the individual characteristics of a president, and focus their attention on institutional constraints and the power of established rules and processes.

Every introductory American government course observes that the president is the only elected official with a national constituency, a head of state as well as head of government, independent of the legislature. Neustadt noted the political consequences, although in the context of the argument that expectations exceed the realities of power: "no one else sits where he sits or sees quite as he sees; no one else feels the full weight of his obligations. Those obligations are a tribute to his unique place in our political system" (1990, 8). Presidents thereby confront a degree of accountability that no other political official faces, and a unique set of responsibilities. Presidents sit at the apex of the executive branch, and are held directly accountable for the success or failure of policy (whether or not they are actually responsible). Presidents are also situated in the midst of a complex institution, whether we think of this as the executive branch as a whole or the narrow presidential institution of the Executive Office of the President.

The political structure motivates presidents to seek control of policy; the institutional structure motivates presidents to seek control of process, "just as rational choice theories of Congress typically assume that legislators seek reelection" (Mayer 2001, 24). Moe and Wilson, in one of the early statements about unilateral powers, put it this way:

Presidents pursue interests that are often incompatible with, and indeed threatening to, the interests of most of the other major players. Their heterogeneous national constituency leads them to think in grander terms about social problems and the public interest, and to resist specialized appeals. Reelection, moreover, does not loom as large in their calculations (and in the second term, of course, it is not a factor at all.

Unlike legislators, presidents are held responsible by the public for virtually every aspect of national performance. When the economy declines, an agency falters, or a social problem goes unaddressed, it is the president who gets the blame, and whose popularity and historical legacy are on the line. All presidents are aware of this, and they respond by trying to build an institutional capacity for effective governance.   (Moe and Wilson 1994, 11)

Presidents thus have an especially powerful reason to align government policy with their own preferences. Skowronek (1993, 6) comes to the same conclusion (though via a very different route), arguing that "in the most precise signification, presidents disrupt systems, reshape political landscapes, and pass to successors leadership challenges far different from the ones just faced."

How presidents do this is a function of the second assumption: presidential action is prompted, recognized, and legitimized by constitutional vestments and statutory delegations, rather than purely strategic or political factors (or bargaining). This emphasis on formal authority as a foundation of presidential action is a significant departure from the strategic presidency paradigm. To Neustadt, presidential success or failure is almost entirely a function of individual skill, bargaining, persuasion, reputation, and prestige. The theory of unilateral action looks instead to specific legal authority, beginning with the Constitution, and extending to the many powers that Congress has delegated to the executive branch.

Those legal warrants provide substantial formal authority to presidents, not only because they are broad, but because they are often ambiguous. Scholars have long noted the relative brevity of Article II, especially when compared to the detailed legislative vestments in Article I. Many of the most important questions about the scope of the president's constitutional powers are irresolvable. Justice Robert Jackson's often-cited review of the legal questions is just as trenchant now as it was when he wrote it in his 1952 *Youngstown* concurrence: "A judge, like an executive advisor, may be surprised at the poverty of really useful and unambiguous authority applicable to concrete problems of executive power as they actually present themselves . . . A century and a half of partisan debate and scholarly speculation yields no net result but only supplies more or less apt quotations from respect sources on each side of any question. They largely cancel each other" (343 US 579, 634 (1951)). These constitutional grants provide a way for presidents to claim legitimacy, in ways unavailable to any other elected official.

Ambiguity begets discretion, as competing interpretations of constitutional and statutory language provide "residual decision rights" (Moe and Wilson 1994, 14). Presidents fill in the gaps in this language, competing with other institutions in setting the meaning of that language through precedent.

In filling the outlines of authority, presidents have crucial advantages over other institutions and actors. The key is the foundation of the president as chief executive, and as a unitary office (meaning, in this context, single, not in the "unitary executive" theory as articulated by Yoo 2005). Hamilton had already identified this presidential advantage in *Federalist* No. 70: "Decision, activity, secrecy, and despatch [*sic*], will generally characterize the proceedings of one man, in a much more eminent degree than the proceedings of any greater number." This gives the president substantial ability to act on his own; at a minimum, the president has important advantages over Congress, which as a majoritarian institution is far more inefficient.

Broad grants, ambiguity, and the potential for swift action are a compelling combination. Presidential authority is amplified by a unique institutional setting and powerful claims to legitimacy. In recognizing the potency of formal authority, unilateral theory presents a direct challenge to the Neustadtian conception of presidential weakness. Where he saw a clerk, the unilateral action theory sees authority. "The result is a governing structure that is conducive to growing presidential powers of unilateral action, and thus an expanding role for presidents in national policymaking" (Moe and Howell 1999, 176).

EMPIRICAL CLAIMS ABOUT UNILATERAL ACTION

These axioms are, of course, open to challenge (see Romano 1994 as an example). But as a starting point, they generate empirical predictions, and help identify the specific processes through which presidents exert their influence. The most obvious implication of the theory is that presidents will, in fact, rely on unilateral action to implement major policy changes and alter institutional arrangements. Given Neustadt's hold on the field, this may have once been a controversial claim, but a growing literature has validated it beyond any doubt. Recent explorations of the executive order, for example, have found one example after another of landmark policies. Both Howell (2003) and Mayer (2001), using very different methods and criteria, estimated that about 15 percent of executive orders issued since the 1930s have been significant.

Warber (2006, 39) found that about 38 percent of executive orders since FDR have had a policy component (as opposed to being symbolic or routine). Cooper (2002, 13) insists that counting the number of executive orders, significant or otherwise, is "an unhelpful exercise." Instead, he urges scholars to focus on the content of specific orders. In his view, the mere fact that a president can govern by decree is itself troubling enough, irrespective of how often that power is used.

Other instruments of unilateral policy include proclamations (Rottinghaus and Maier 2007); administrative directives (Cooper 2002), military orders (Fisher 2005), National Security Directives (Gordon 2007), signing statements (Bradly and Posner 2006; Cooper 2005), some appointments (Lewis 2005; Corley 2006), executive agreements (Martin 2007), pardons (Erler 2007; Whitford and Ochs 2006), and lame-duck policy making (Howell and Mayer 2005). These tools are linked by their reliance on direct, formal, presidential authority; the lack of direct influence from the other branches; and the endurance of the resulting policies, which often require substantial effort to reverse (if they can be undone at all). This literature is pluralistic in methodology, combining formal theory, quantitative analysis, thick description, and careful case studies.

Scholars have identified several characteristics that make unilateral action particularly attractive and effective. Chief among these is the president's crucial advantage of being able to make the first move. In doing so the president alters policy, and if either Congress or the judiciary objects, they must take affirmative action to undo what the president has just done (Moe and Howell 1999; Mayer 1999, 2001; Howell 2003). Even in cases where the president turns out *not* to have the necessary authority—as occurred with the steel seizures, for example—the ability to unilaterally alter policy necessarily puts other institutions and actors in a reactive posture.

The theory of unilateral action depicts an institutional struggle, in which presidents compete with Congress for policy control. In this competition, Congress has the advantage of superior formal power, but a relative institutional incapacity. Presidents have a narrower substantive range of powers, but they are more able to take decisive action and have the first-mover advantage.

The literature on unilateral action has also established that presidents will win most of these interbranch conflicts. Typically, neither Congress nor the judiciary is in a good position to respond. Congress is a notoriously inefficient institution, requiring a majority (at least) in order to do anything substantive. Legislators have minimal incentives to attend to Congress's institutional needs, and often act in ways that undercut Congress's collective authority (Mayer and Canon 1999). No single legislator, no matter how influential, is in a position to challenge the president's legitimacy or national constituency. Even when legislators can muster the necessary votes to enact legislation countermanding a presidential action, the prospect of a veto raises the vote threshold to a usually unobtainable two-thirds. Howell (2003, 114–16) found that from 1945 to 1998, Congress tried only forty-five times to formally overturn or amend an executive order or place general conditions on the use of executive orders. Only four of these legislative efforts succeeded, usually on minor matters. Other sources identify a higher rate of successful congressional responses. Olson and Woll (1999) identified 239 executive orders since the Cleveland administration that have been revoked or modified by statute; Warber (2006, 199) used these data to estimate that Congress responded to 3.8 percent of executive orders between 1945 and 1992. This discrepancy can, at least in part, be traced to differences in methods. Howell investigated cases where Congress explicitly tried to reverse or modify a specific executive order. Olson and Woll included in their count many instances in which Congress rescinded a delegated power that presidents had used to issue multiple executive orders.

The courts are in no better position. Judges must wait for an actual controversy, may seek to avoid involvement in interbranch disputes by denying standing or invoking the political questions doctrine, and often uphold presidential action in any event. Howell (2003) identified eighty-three federal court decisions since 1943 that addressed the legality or application of forty-five separate executive orders. Not only does this caseload cover a fraction of the total number of executive orders issued over the same period (1.1 percent of 4,086 executive orders), the judges sided against the president only 17 percent of the time.

The central tenet of unilateral action has been repeatedly confirmed:

If [the president] wants to develop his own institution, review or reverse agency decisions, coordinate agency actions, make changes in agency leadership, or otherwise impose his views on government, he can simply proceed—and it is up to Congress (and the courts) to react... Congress often finds this difficult or impossible to do. And the president wins by default. The ability to win by default is a cornerstone of the presidential advantage.

(Moe and Wilson 1994, 20)

UNILATERAL POWERS: THE CASE OF WARRANTLESS WIRETAPS

Few sequences in the past decade illustrate this pattern better than the dispute between Congress and the president over Bush's authorization of warrantless wiretapping, revealed by the *New York Times* in December 2005 (Risen and Lichtblau 2005). While the exact nature of the program remains secret, the contours are clear enough. In 1978, Congress enacted the Foreign Intelligence Surveillance Act (FISA, 50 USC § 1801 ff.), establishing a process to secure warrants for electronic surveillance of suspected foreign agents in the United States. FISA resolved an ambiguity in the existing legal framework. Abroad, presidents are generally free to conduct foreign intelligence surveillance without constraint, based on their foreign affairs and commander-in-chief powers. Although the Supreme Court has not specifically ruled on the question, in various cases justices have hinted strongly that such a power exists.[1]

Domestically, it is a different matter altogether: the government must obtain such a judicial warrant to conduct surveillance for intelligence, domestic security, or (especially) law enforcement purposes. *United States* v. *Katz*, 389 US 347 (1967), held that wiretaps and other electronic surveillance constituted a search under the Fourth Amendment and therefore required a warrant. *United States* v. *United States District Court* 407 US 297 (1972) held that the Fourth Amendment applied to electronic surveillance even for domestic intelligence or security purposes. The opinion takes pains to note that the case involves surveillance of a "domestic organization . . . composed of citizens of the United States and which has no significant connection with a foreign power, its agents, or agencies" (309 n. 8).

The distinction between domestic and foreign surveillance blurs when the target is a foreign power or agent operating inside the United States. In this circumstance, it is not immediately clear which set of rules applies: does the location of the surveillance—inside the USA—mean that a judicial warrant is required? Or does the intent and target of the surveillance—a suspected foreign agent wiretapped for the purpose of collecting foreign intelligence—mean that a warrant is not necessary? There has been no conclusive judicial ruling either way, and even Congress has taken notice of the constitutional uncertainties:

[The debate over surveillance] has centered around the power of the president to acquire information necessary for the national security and the constitutionality of warrantless electronic surveillance. This is not surprising since the United States Supreme Court has never expressly decided the issue of whether the president has constitutional authority to authorize electronic surveillance in cases concerning foreign intelligence. Whether the president has so-called "inherent power" to engage in warrantless electronic surveillance and, if such power exist, what limitations, if any, restrict the scope of that power, are issues which have troubled constitutional scholars for decades.   (US Congress 1977, 9)

As the unilateral theory predicts, presidents have exploited this ambiguity by setting their own rules for the collection of foreign intelligence and conduct of covert operations through executive orders and other directives establishing the permissible practices and review procedures (see Mayer 1991, esp. ch. 5).

FISA represented a congressional attempt to settle the issue through a statutory framework that specifically applied to the domestic/international question. The law required the executive branch to obtain a warrant from a special judicial panel, called the Foreign Intelligence Surveillance Court (FISC), before conducting electronic surveillance of suspected foreign agents inside the US. The intent was to "strike a

---

[1] Presidents have a constitutional power to use spies to track enemy movements during wartime, *Totten* v. *United States* 92 US 105 (1876); and to keep intelligence information secret, (*Chicago and Southern Air Lines* v. *Waterman S.S. Corp*, 333 US 103 (1948). In *United States* v. *United States District Court*, 407 US 297 (1972), the Court very carefully sidestepped the question of whether the Fourth Amendment applied when domestic surveillance involving a foreign agent or power. "[T]he instant case requires no judgment on the scope of the President's surveillance power with respect to the activities of foreign powers, within or without this country" (308).

balance between national security interests and civil liberties" by providing a degree of judicial oversight, even if the rules were looser than those for criminal courts (Bazan and Elsea 2006, 8).

Soon after 9/11—the precise date is not yet publicly known[2]—President Bush authorized the National Security Agency to conduct some domestic surveillance without obtaining these warrants. The key element was surveillance of international communications between a person in the US and another abroad, where there is "reasonable basis to conclude that one party to the communication is a member of al Qaeda, affiliated with al Qaeda, or a member of an organization affiliated with al Qaeda, or working in support of al Qaeda" (White House Press Briefing, Dec. 19, 2005). The administration's initial position was that this action was supported by both constitutional and statutory authorities. In a memo to Senate majority leader Bill Frist, Attorney General Alberto Gonzales claimed that "the NSA activities are supported by the President's well-recognized inherent authority as Commander-in-Chief and sole organ for the Nation in foreign affairs to conduct warrantless surveillance of enemy forces for intelligence purposes to detect and disrupt armed attacks on the United States" (US Department of Justice 2006, 1). No law could limit the president's constitutional powers.

The administration claimed a statutory grant as well, citing the September 18, 2001 Authorization to Use Military Force (AUMF). The AUMF permitted the president to

use all necessary and appropriate force against those nations, organizations, or persons he determines planned, authorized, committed, or aided the terrorist attacks that occurred on September 11, 2001, or harbored such organizations or persons, in order to prevent any future acts of international terrorism against the United States by such nations, organizations or persons.

President Bush asserted that the authorization to "use all necessary and appropriate force" includes the use of surveillance, thus carving out an exception under the provisions of FISA, which imposed criminal liabilities only when surveillance was "not authorized by statute" (50 US Code § 1806 (a)). The TSP, according to the administration, was authorized under both constitutional and statutory grants of power. Bush had set his own rules for authorizing the program, establishing it for only forty-five days at a time, with reviews by the Justice Department and the NSA (US Department of Justice 2006, 5).

This is the archetype of a unilateral action: a president implementing a major change in policy on his own, near an ambiguous constitutional bounder, and operating in secrecy.

Even inside the administration there was disagreement about the legal merits. At one point in 2004, with Attorney General John Ashcroft in hospital, Acting Attorney General James Comey refused to reauthorize the NSA program; this led to a dramatic

---

[2] Eric Lichtblau (2008, 257), one of the two *New York Times* reporters who broke the story, puts the date at October 4, 2001.

confrontation in Ashcroft's hospital room, as White House Counsel Alberto Gonzales and Chief of Staff Andrew Card unsuccessfully sought Ashcroft's approval of the document Comey refused to sign.

In the face of bipartisan criticism, coming even from Senate Judiciary Committee member Arlen Specter (R-PA), the administration backed away from its initial insistence that the TSP was authorized by both the Constitution and statute. Instead, the White House argued that FISA was cumbersome and ill suited to modern telecommunications which were far more sophisticated than the point-to-point telephone technology that existed when the statute was enacted. Attorney General Alberto Gonzales insisted that the process of seeking approval from the Foreign Intelligence Surveillance Court was too slow and burdensome, and that the "probable cause" threshold needed to obtain a FISC warrant was too high (see discussion in Banks 2007, 1254–60). TSP's defenders argued that the nature of modern communications rendered FISA's wiretapping provisions obsolete. Email, in particular, is usually broken up into many smaller "packets," which are then routed via servers located all over the world and reassembled at the destination (Kerr 2003, 613–15). It was possible that an email message might be routed through a node in the US, even if both the sender and recipient were located abroad. A strict reading of FISA might require a warrant to tap into this communication, even though the statute was not intended to apply abroad.

Critics insisted that, technological change notwithstanding, the TSP was patently illegal since FISA was the exclusive means of conducting any foreign intelligence surveillance inside the US. Congress had already amended FISA many times since 9/11, to update the original statute and provide for the same contingencies that the administration was citing (Fein 2007, 28). The FISC was extraordinarily deferential in any event, rejecting only five warrants in the history of the program, out of nearly 19,000 requested (Leonnig 2006). During congressional hearings on the nature of wartime executive power, Senator Patrick Leahy (D-VT) summarized the opposition view:

[FISA] expressly states it provides the exclusive source of authority for wiretapping for intelligence purposes. Wiretapping that is not authorized under this statute is a Federal crime. That is what the law says. It is also what the law means.   (US Congress 2006, 8)

Even so, the administration may have operated on the basis of a classified legal opinion that concluded that the word "exclusive" in the statute did not rule out alternative mechanisms for conducting domestic surveillance (Barnes 2008).

Many legal scholars rejected the administration defense, insisting that the AUMF could not be read as granting implied permission, because FISA itself had a provision that applied during a time of war; this specific statutory provision took precedence over any subsequent indirect language (Bradley et al. 2006). In any event, many legislators felt that the administration should have asked Congress for any needed changes, rather than simply ignore the statute altogether.

The administration had its defenders—Federal Appeals Court Judge Richard Posner argued that FISA imposed "crippling limitations" on the government's ability to conduct necessary surveillance (Posner 2006, 102)—and some legal scholars concluded that the legal question could reasonably go either way (Posner and Vermeule 2007, 80–2). But it seems fair to say that the balance of opinion in the legal and political science academic communities was solidly against the TSP (see, for example, Pfiffner 2008), as was the reaction among congressional Democrats. One critical account observed that "Democrats and even some Republicans denounced the NSA program as illegal and promised formal congressional investigations. A few congressmen called for an immediate end to the operation; others demanded Bush's censure, or even his impeachment" (Lichtblau 2008, 214).

From the standpoint of unilateral action, the salient point is that the president acted on his own authority to implement a major policy change, thereby dramatically altering the status quo and changing the terms of political debate. Congress, far from being able to stop the program, ultimately wound up *granting* the president the power necessary to continue the program (albeit with somewhat tighter congressional oversight). In August 2007, Congress passed the Protect America Act (PL 110–55), temporarily amending FISA to make it clear that warrants are not required when surveillance is "directed at a person reasonably believed to be located outside the United States" (50 USC 1805a). In July 2008, Congress made the change permanent, and, just as importantly, immunized telecom companies from lawsuits arising out of their participation in the surveillance program. Seven years after unilaterally changing the policy, Bush succeeded in permanently moving the policy to his preferred position.

Legal challenges to the TSP have fared no better. A federal district judge did declare the law unconstitutional. However, the 6th Circuit Court of Appeals overturned this decision, ruling that the plaintiffs failed to show standing (they could not show that they had, in fact, been subjected to surveillance, because the government refused to turn over any evidence, citing the state secrets doctrine), and the Supreme Court declined to hear the case (*American Civil Liberties Union et al. v. National Security Agency*, no. 06–2095–2140, July 6, 2007, 6th Cir.). The Obama administration is aggressively fighting several newer lawsuits, invoking the state secrets doctrine in order to block litigation.

Even though the president could not keep the program secret and had to settle for a degree of legislative oversight, in the end he still moved policy in his preferred direction.

EMPIRICAL PUZZLES AND A RESEARCH AGENDA

The substantial and growing literature on unilateral powers tells us a great deal about when presidents are likely to use their unilateral powers: reliance varies according to *issue area*, with more emphasis in foreign affairs; *timing*, with more emphasis at the beginning and end of a president's term; and with *popularity*, with presidents falling back on their formal authority when they lack public standing. These conclusions complement some elements of the strategic presidency model: presidents might prefer legislation to achieve their goals, as the strategic presidency model would predict, but opt for unilateral action as a second-best option when they face particularly strong congressional opposition or public dissatisfaction.

One seemingly obvious implication of the unilateral powers theory is, however, disputed: that presidents will use unilateral action when they do not have a congressional majority, or when their chances for legislative success are smallest. This has long been the conventional wisdom, as it seems only natural that presidents should take the path of least resistance. In an early study, Fleischman and Aufses (1976) predicted that executive orders should be more frequent under divided government because presidents have to act unilaterally when they cannot succeed in Congress. The argument has a great deal of intuitive appeal, and presidents themselves appear to subscribe to it: in 1995, Clinton adviser Paul Begala provoked the incoming GOP congressional majority with threats to end-run Congress by executive action. "Stroke of the pen, law of the land," he mused, "kind of cool" (Bennett 1995).

But the empirical evidence for what Lisa Martin calls the "evasion hypothesis" (2007, 444) is inconclusive. Some work confirms it: Corley (2006) finds that presidents make more recess appointments when they do not have enough votes in the Senate to confirm. Deering and Maltzman show that the number of executive orders is inversely related to the number of Senate seats held by the president's party, and that presidents issue more orders when their ideology becomes more distant from the median member of Congress (1999, 777). Case studies in civil rights emphasize the importance of presidential initiatives in the face of sustained congressional intransigence (Mayer 2001, ch. 6; Graham 1990). Last-minute pardons, executive orders, proclamations, and regulatory activity are common in the weeks before presidents leave office, when the normal accountability mechanisms are entirely absent (Howell and Mayer 2005). Presidents tend to issue more executive orders when their popularity declines, a finding consistent with a strategic process in which presidents compensate for political weakness (Mayer 1999; Mayer and Price 2002).

But other research contradicts these findings. Most studies of executive orders, for example, have found no evidence that unilateral action surges under divided government (Mayer 2001; Krause and Cohen 2000; Mayer and Price 2002). Typically, the number of executive orders goes *down* when the opposition controls Congress, or when presidents have low legislative success scores (Mayer 1999; Shull 1997) Marshall and Pacelle (2005) identify a split pattern in which presidents who are skilled at pushing their foreign policy initiatives in Congress issue more executive orders; in domestic policy the effect is reversed, with presidents relying more heavily on unilateral action when they encounter legislative roadblocks. Divided government, by itself, has no effect in either area.

The same holds for other kinds of unilateral action. Presidents have *unlimited* discretion in choosing between a treaty and an executive agreement when negotiating compacts with foreign governments. The choice of instrument, like the decision to issue a veto, is committed totally to presidential discretion. Presidents have long been suspected of using executive agreements to avoid the need for Senate ratification (Nathan and Oliver 1994), and it would be unsurprising to find the strongest effect when presidents are politically weak. But Martin finds that the conventional wisdom is as wrong here as it is for executive orders: presidents rely on executive agreements when they have congressional support, and on treaties when they have little political capital (2007).

These results, which can at best be described as "mixed," present an unresolved challenge to the unilateral powers model, since its underlying logic strongly suggests that the evasion hypothesis should be correct. What accounts for the conflicting outcomes?

One possibility is that presidents understand that pushing too hard might provoke a backlash, even if they do not know exactly where that point is. Deering and Maltzman (1999) suggest that presidents take the potential for congressional opposition into account, and will end-run Congress only when they are confident that the legislature will not overturn their executive orders. Martin concludes that reliance on an executive agreement can indicate that the president might not be able to enforce the resulting commitment, and that this signal is most powerful when a president faces strong internal dissent (2007, 461). Shull (1997) and Krause and Cohen (1997) hypothesize that presidents rely on unilateral action to supplement and cement congressional action, not as a circumvention device. Rottinghaus and Maier (2007) make a similar argument for proclamations, noting that most are based on congressionally delegated authority.

Howell's formal model of unilateral action (2003) offers a theoretical explanation for the observed effects. He incorporates an exogenous measure of presidential discretion that determines how far the president can move policy before either Congress or the judiciary reacts. In this model, the president moves first, choosing to alter existing policy or not. Congress and the judiciary then have an opportunity to restore the original policy; their choice of whether to respond or not is a function of how far the president moves policy, and the "amount of discretion this status quo accords the president (d)" (2003, 30). This parameter d is generally unspecified, varies from one policy area to the next, and is revealed only in the course of the game itself (2003, 30–1); we do not know in advance how far the president can move before triggering a pushback. It is certainly plausible to think that that presidential discretion is narrower under divided government (that is, d is smaller when the opposition has control of Congress).

Another possibility is that the pressure to act unilaterally stems from institutional practices that are not anchored to political or strategic factors. Studies of presidential pardons—another area, like the choice between executive agreements and treaties, where the president's authority is absolute and unreviewable—find that presidential action is shaped by institutional processes, which shape and refine the choices that make it to the Oval Office. "[I]n practice," writes Erler, "instead of being the exclusive wielder of the pardon power, the president is the last hurdle in a lengthy and convoluted process governed largely by executive branch officials" (2007, 428).

Yet, these explanations have the flavor of rationalization, in an effort to reconcile theory with a disconfirming empirical result. Other predictions of the unilateral action model are robust enough that the lack of a clear relationship here does not undermine the theoretical value of the approach itself. But the disparate and conflicting results strongly suggest that we do not have a complete understanding of the interbranch dynamics of unilateral action. We may be focusing on the most visible aspects of the presidential–congressional interaction, expecting to see an obvious sequence: presidential action leading to a court challenge or congressional effort to reverse. This will miss many instances when a president chooses not to act, or opts for moderation, because of an anticipated backlash. We will observe some instances of inaction—most noticeably Bill Clinton's reluctance to issue an executive order ending the military's policy of excluding homosexuals from the service. Clinton had the clear authority to take this step, and had promised to do so in the 1992 campaign. But he demurred because of intense congressional opposition, attempting to split the difference with his "don't ask-don't tell" policy in which gay soldiers could serve as long as they did not openly engage in homosexual activities. Congress then enacted this policy into law (10 USC 654), preventing future presidents from making unilateral changes. In other cases, though, Clinton was more than willing to act unilaterally in the face of congressional opposition, sometimes *intending* to provoke a reaction (Mayer and Price 2002).

Similarly, President George W. Bush backed away from an initial effort to rescind a last-minute Clinton regulation lowering the permissible levels of arsenic in drinking water. After initially suspending the regulation (which was finalized so late in the Clinton administration that it was actually published in the *Federal Register* two days after Bush took office, on January 22, 2001), President Bush backtracked in the face of a huge public outcry, implementing the Clinton-era rule in October. In this instance, not even a congressional majority could insulate the president from the consequences of his own attempt to act unilaterally (for an account of this regulation, see Howell and Mayer 2005, 543–6).

Are these two high-profile examples of pushbacks representative of a larger pattern? One way to find out would be a study of unilateral actions that a president considers, or which supporters urge, but which are ultimately not carried out: a political science equivalent of Sherlock Holmes's dog that did nothing in the nighttime. One clear consequence of the unilateral action model is that presidents retain substantial discretion in choosing whether to act alone or not, and what instrument to use. Obviously, not every contemplated action is carried out, and a careful study of what presidents choose *not* to do might shed light on what, precisely, prompts presidents to pull the plug on potential actions as they wend their way through the many layers of political and legal review, and what encourages presidents to press on.

Ultimately, we lack a reliable way of classifying these various actions, and as a field need a better sense of when presidents will push hard and when they will back down.

It may be that presidents are better off working closely with Congress, even when they could have adopted a unilateral approach. It may be that presidents take potential judicial reactions into account, or that different presidents show different levels of deference. So far, Howell (2005, 422) writes, "the deeper effects of judicial and congressional restraints remain hidden."

These puzzles offer at least five new questions that should inform the next generation of research on unilateral powers. I will describe the first three quickly; the last two require more extensive discussion.

The first question is accounting for the unexpected result that the number of executive orders and other unilateral actions tends to go *down* when presidents face congressional opposition, rather than up, as we would expect. There are already some explanations of why this occurs in trade policy, for example (Martin 2007), a promising theoretical model of executive orders (Howell 2003, esp. ch. 2), and an exploration of how Congress can check presidential unilateralism in the use of force (Howell and Pevehouse 2007).

A second research question is creating a fully articulated model of when the judiciary will become involved in disputes over presidential power, and the circumstances in which judges—and Supreme Court justices especially—will overturn a unilateral act. The literature has identified a clear empirical pattern of judicial caution in the face of unilateral action, and a basic theory explaining why judges show so much deference to the president. Howell (2003) constructed a model that accounts for some of the variance in judicial decision making on presidential orders. Given the many landmark decisions that have come down in the last few years on presidential war powers, surveillance, treatment of unlawful combatants, and military tribunals, this remains an important and fertile area for both theoretical and empirical work.

A third research path is a study of how, and how well, unilateral policies are implemented. Neustadt argued that presidential orders must be self-executing in that there must be no distance between the order itself and compliance (1990, 17). This is far too strict a condition: Neustadt meant it to apply only in the narrowest sense, based on his overall conclusion that presidents rarely get their way by command. The unilateral powers literature has, in contrast, established that presidents can rely on their authority over a broad range of policy, including issues that involve a complex implementation process. We also know that the presidents can make unilateral decisions where their authority is uncertain, or even lacking (Mayer 2001, 18). One area in which the existing literature on unilateral powers needs more depth is on the details of implementation. Although some case studies trace the particulars of how an order is given effect, the quantitative literature assumes that a unilateral order issued is a unilateral order carried out. It seems clear enough that on many issues a presidential assertion of unilateral power will be resisted (even if ineffectively) by legislators, interest groups, or the bureaucracy. Agencies may disagree on the merits of a particular action, or dispute the legal authorities on which a unilateral act relies. The Departments of State, Defense, and Justice disagreed sharply over the president's legal authority to authorize interrogation techniques or set the rules for the treatment of unlawful combatants (see Goldsmith 2007 for an account of these intramural fights). Regulatory agencies, as well as legislators, objected to President Reagan's executive order requiring cost–benefit analysis for major rules (Moe and Wilson 1994). How do these disagreements affect presidential decision making? Does the White House have to expend resources to ensure faithful agency execution of unilateral orders, or is compliance truly automatic? How do presidents monitor compliance?

Unilateralism and the Unitary Presidency

The fourth question is perhaps the most important: understanding the long-term consequences of the presidential advantages that stem from unilateral action. Theories of unilateral action predict that presidents will often succeed in their attempts to change policy or process, even over the objections of the other institutions of national government. This presents a troubling implication. If the ambiguities of presidential authority mean that the boundaries of presidential power are determined by precedent (Sunstein 1995, 15 calls this "common law constitutionalism"); if presidents have an incentive to act first, and generally succeed in changing policy; and if Congress and the courts face institutional hurdles in trying to counteract presidential initiatives, the long-term consequence should be a steady expansion of presidential power. Following this argument to its conclusion, at some point it must be that checks and balances become ineffective, as Congress and the judiciary are unable to protect their own institutional authority. Presidential power becomes uncontrollable and sinister.

The potential for imbalance is even greater if the first-mover advantage operates as a ratchet, in which powers once won are not given up. Presidents who stretch the limits of constitutional powers—Lincoln during the Civil War, Roosevelt in the Second World War—set precedents to which future presidents can point as justifying their own acts. The courts have implicitly accepted this argument through their "acquiescence doctrine," the principle that a "systematic, unbroken executive practice, long pursued to the knowledge of Congress but never before questioned, engaged in by Presidents who have also sworn to uphold the Constitution, making as it were such exercise of power part of the structure of our government, may be treated as a gloss on 'executive power' vested in the President by §1 or Art. II" (*Youngstown Sheet and Tube* v. *Sawyer* 343 US 579, 610–11, J. Frankfurter, concurring).

If this argument is correct, then presidential power can only grow, to the point where the Framers' fear of monarchism, or its modern-day equivalent, is realized.

Some scholars take the position that we have already reached this stage, in a contemporary literature that owes its roots to Arthur M. Schlesinger, Jr.'s 1973 *The Imperial Presidency*. In a chain of reasoning that would be familiar to any student of unilateral powers, Schlesinger argued that secrecy, presidential control of the military, and congressional passivity had resulted in an out-of-control presidency unbounded by constitutional limits. Koh, writing in 1990, argued that "congressional acquiescence and judicial tolerance in the post-Vietnam era have combined to elevate this pattern of executive dominance to quasi-constitutional status" (1990, 159). These pressures are especially acute during crises, as "the temptation for officials to expand their power and push beyond the boundaries of their constitutionally delegated authority increases proportionately to the level of the threat" (Kassop 2003, 510). The president, it appears, can use the commander-in-chief power to send the military anywhere, at any time, for any purpose, and there is nothing that Congress or the courts can do to stop him: Truman committed the US to the Korean War, George H. W. Bush sent US troops into Somalia; Bill Clinton deployed 20,000 soldiers to Bosnia, and repeatedly fired missiles into Iraq, all without any prior congressional authorization.

The danger, of course, is that the constitutional limits no longer suffice to check the use (or abuse) of power. In Koh's view, the only checks on executive unilateralism are foreign policy debacles like Bay of Pigs, Vietnam, or Iran-Contra, so unambiguous in their failures that Congress is compelled to respond.

Concerns about the unbalanced scope of executive power grew after 9/11, as President Bush made extensive use of unilateral powers: establishing a system of military tribunals to try enemy combatants, asserting the authority to declare US citizens as illegal combatants, engaging in extraordinary rendition, asserting the right to launch preventive wars, authorizing warrantless electronic surveillance outside the scope of the Foreign Intelligence Surveillance Act. David Gray Adler argued that these "sweeping assertions of authority as commander-in-chief have launched presidential power on a trajectory toward the realm of illimitable and unaccountable executive power, the nether world of American constitutionalism" (2006, 525). Louis Fisher cites the military tribunal order as a "stunning transformation from a republican form of government, characterized by legislative control and a vigorous system of checks and balances," to a process dominated by the president, with little oversight from the other branches (2005, 253). The president's power to order the troops around the globe was, in this view, morphing into a more general power to do just about anything in the name of national defense.

These concerns are entirely consistent with the overall theory of unilateral action, and follow the outlines of the argument about presidential initiative, congressional acquiescence, and a secular trend of increased presidential authority. What gave these assertions extra attention was the accompanying intellectual foundation for expanded unilateral presidential authority, in the form of the "unitary executive" thesis that takes a broad view of presidential power. Arguments about a unitary executive, in a sense, express a truism that the executive power is vested fully and exclusively in the president, and within these boundaries cannot be constrained by (in particular) legislative action. One form—I will call this the "weak" form—has as its primary prescription that the president is entirely responsible for the executive branch. One immediate consequence is that independent regulatory agencies, whose heads are insulated from presidential at-will dismissal, are unconstitutional (see, for example, Calabresi and Prakash 1994). Congress is not required to delegate authority to the executive branch, nor is Congress constitutionally required to establish any particular regulatory agency. But if Congress does delegate such authority or establish such an agency, legislators may not then limit the president's authority over agency officers. Just as no act of Congress could set limits on the president's discretion to veto a bill, no statute could set limits on the president's authority over the executive branch. Even in this weak form, the unitary presidency thesis is vigorously contested by, among others, Lessig and Sunstein (1994), and it is unlikely as a practical matter that federal judges will rely on the theory and declare wide swaths of the federal government regulatory structure unconstitutional.

In its "strong" form, the unitary executive theory defines the executive power and other enumerated presidential powers in broad, even sweeping terms, and further, claims that neither Congress or the judiciary may infringe on presidential discretion in these areas. The idea reached its apotheosis in a series of memos written within the Office of Legal Counsel (OLC) in the Department of Justice, the subunit that provides legal advice to the White House. After 9/11, OLC lawyers analyzed the questions surrounding the applicability of the Geneva Conventions to illegal combatants captured on the battlefield, the limits of interrogation techniques that could be applied, and how the military handled long-term detention of combatants.

These legal analyses took an extraordinarily broad view of presidential powers, using the ideas behind the unitary executive as their foundation. John C. Yoo, then Deputy Assistant Attorney General inside OLC, argued that the commander-in-chief power gives the president exclusive power over *all* decisions over the use of military force, even including the initiation of war, and further asserted that the president has unlimited capacity to take action to protect the national security of the United States. Not even Congress's Article I power to "declare war" serves as a limitation; Yoo argued that this power was merely hortatory, insisting that declarations of war have few substantive consequences and certainly are not required for the president to begin military action. "[I]t is clear," writes Yoo, "that Congress' power to declare war does not constrain the President's independent and plenary constitutional authority over the use of military force." (OLC memo, Sept. 25, 2001). Proponents of the unitary executive point to the well-known constitutional convention debate in which the legislative power to "make war" was changed to "declare war," in order to give the president the authority to repel sudden attacks (see Fisher 2004, 8–10). But Delahunty and Yoo (2002) elide this distinction, and assert that this change does not limit the president's authority to only sudden attacks, but applies broadly to any use of force. "The historical record," they write, "demonstrates that the power to initiate military hostilities, *particularly in response to the threat of an armed attack,* rests exclusively in the president" (Delahunty and Yoo 2002, 503; emphasis added). Moreover, the president's war-making power is unlimited, and subject to no congressional checks at all. Congress may not "place any limits on the President's determinations as to any terrorist threat, the amount of military force to be used in response, or the method, timing, and nature of this response. These decisions, under our Constitution, are for the President alone to make" (OLC memo, Sept. 25, 2001).

More controversially, Assistant Attorney General Jay Bybee concluded that the commander-in-chief power included the authority to capture and interrogate enemy combatants in any manner the president sees fit, and that not even statutes or international treaties could constrain the range of interrogation techniques that a president could authorize. In what became infamously known as the Torture Memos, Bybee wrote to White House Counsel Alberto R. Gonzales that "Congress can no more interfere with the President's conduct of the interrogation of enemy combatants than it can dictate strategic or tactical decisions on the battlefield. Just as statutes that order the President to conduct warfare in a certain manner or for certain goals would be unconstitutional, so too are laws that seek to prevent the President from gaining the intelligence he believes necessary to prevent an attack on the United States" (OLC memo, *Standards of Conduct for Interrogation under 18. U.S.S. §§ 2340–2340A*, Aug. 1, 2002).

Under these readings of the Constitution, the president's authority to use the military is unlimited. Presidents have the sole authority to command the military, to decide the circumstances in which military force will be used, to decide what constitutes a threat, to choose what tactics would be used, and to specify what surveillance techniques were allowable. No act of Congress, treaty obligation, or judicial order could limit this plenary authority. Yoo (2005, 154–6) argues that the only constitutional mechanism available to Congress is cutting off appropriations for the conduct of military action. This position is, in fact, consistent with the unilateral action model: the president unilaterally initiates a war, leaving it up to Congress to affirmatively restore the prior state of affairs by denying funding. The unitary executive has no room for checks and balances, stoking concerns about the reach of these powers and the potential for abuse.

Pious (2007, 67) has little patience for such a broad reading of the executive power, citing a broad literature that "makes it clear that presidents do not possess a monopoly of prerogative powers in war and foreign affairs, and in fact they cannot even claim all 'executive' powers." The foreign affairs and war powers vested in Congress, apart from the declare war clause, include the power to "define and punish piracies and felonies committed on the High Seas, and Offences against the Law of Nations," to "grant Letters of Marque and Reprisal, and make Rules concerning Captures on Land and Water," "To raise and support" armies and navies and "make rules for the government and regulation of the land and naval forces," to provide for the appointment of officers. It is simply untrue—indisputably so—that the commander-in-chief clause vests in the president sole and plenary authority over the military.

The unlimited reach of executive power described by Yoo and Bybee proved too much for the Bush administration: the president publicly repudiated the memos when their existence became public, sought legislative authorization for military tribunals and detention of combatants after being constrained by the Supreme Court, and asked Congress to provide for enhanced electronic surveillance. Bybee's successor at OLC, Jack Goldsmith, attacked the premise of unlimited presidential power: the argument that no statute could prohibit the president's authority to use any interrogation techniques, he wrote,

has no foundation in prior OLC opinions, or in judicial decisions, or in any other source of law...OLC's conclusion about presidential power was all the more inappropriate because it rested on cursory and one-sided legal arguments that failed to consider Congress's competing wartime constitutional authorities, or the many Supreme Court decisions potentially in tension with the conclusion.   (2007, 149)

Ramsey (2005) argues that the memos' broad statements about presidential power were the equivalent of dicta, in any event, since they were not germane to the underlying legal question about the applicability of treaties or statutes. The experience of the Bush administration suggests that at least some checks remain in place, though observers may differ in their assessment of how well those checks worked, or how long it took to reverse the initial policy.

To Posner and Vermeule, the post-9/11 controversies actually are a constitutional success, as an initial legislative and judicial deference to the executive in times of crisis rebalances after the immediate danger has passed. In particular, they dismiss concerns about the ratchet effect as overwrought, noting that in many prior emergencies the president clearly went far beyond the contemporary understanding of constitutional boundaries—Lincoln's suspension of habeas corpus or FDR's internment of Japanese-Americans—without permanent harm. After a time, a normal separation of balance was restored (2007, 4–5).

Where did the Bush administration fall in this spectrum—between an out-of-control executive acting with no constitutional constraints, and a predictable and reversible level of executive initiative that will eventually return to a pre-9/11 balance? What does the pattern of executive initiative and congressional and court response tell us about the unilateral action thesis that presidents will accrue power? I suggest that the answer lies in the same murky and unexplored territory as our lack of a complete understanding of the interinstitutional dynamics of executive action. Obviously, presidents push hard during emergencies and challenges to national security. President Bush was, at least initially, operating with an open-ended understanding of presidential powers. Many of his policies were clearly driven by that understanding, and were consistent with the "act first" character of the unilateral action model. At the same time, he eventually encountered a pushback, as both the legislature and (more importantly) the courts resisted these assertions of broad power. Perhaps the empirical findings on the drop in executive orders under divided government have identified a real phenomenon, with the institutional restraints on presidential power tightening when the opposition controls Congress.

UNILATERALISM AND SEPARATION
OF POWERS

These four suggested research questions have one element in common: when do the constraints on unilateral action come into play, and what triggers them? Can we make any statements about *when* the judiciary will turn back a presidential assertion of unilateral constitutional power? When Congress will respond with a legislative reaction? Here, I offer one final recommendation about a potential approach.

Much of the time, we look to what happens after a president issues an order: how legislators react and whether they attempt to enact counter-legislation; whether a court challenge emerges and what happens as it winds its way through the legal process (there is evidence that the judiciary is more likely to overturn a presidential action during divided government, though this may be because litigants are more likely to challenge orders during these periods; see Howell 2003, ch. 6). The presidency literature has established beyond much doubt that these responses are rare; the difficulty of restoring the *status quo ante* is a key element of the unilateral action model.

If we are concerned about the institutional capacity to respond to presidential initiative, though, perhaps we are looking in the wrong place. We might make more progress by looking at what happens *before* a president takes unilateral action, rather than after.

The ability to send troops into harm's way is the archetype of unilateral action: the president issues an order as commander-in-chief, and the troops are sent, aircraft launched, missiles fired. Congress, almost by definition, is unable to respond, as anything it does is necessarily after the fact, and in many cases the entire engagement will be over before members can vote on any legislation. As a practical matter, presidential discretion is unconstrained. And yet, Howell and Pevehouse find "evidence that Congress—imperfectly, intermittently, but remarkably predictably—continues to monitor the presidential use of force. More than occasionally, its members do things, or threaten to do things, that materially affect presidential decisions about war" (2007, 6). Most importantly, presidents evaluate the potential congressional reaction, and factor in, as well diplomatic relationships, the centrality of the strategic interests in play, and public opinion. Even when their discretion and authority is at its apex, presidents appear to consider the political costs of acting unilaterally and adjust their strategies accordingly.

These kinds of checks are far more difficult to see than the obvious and formal legislative or judicial sanction. When Congress enacts a statute that invalidates an executive order, or when the courts rebuff a military directive, we have an unambiguous record of what happened, and when. It is notoriously harder to identify subtler constraining forces: as I noted above, we need to know when a president chooses *not* to issue a proclamation, executive order, or directive, because of a fear of a congressional backlash. The findings about congressional influence over presidential uses of force suggest that we need to look beyond the obvious causal connections, and consider a broader range of possible influences on presidential unilateral action.

Where should we look for those effects? Since the main thread of the unilateral action theory is institutionally based, institutional processes are a good place to start. The same institutional structures that extend presidents' reach can moderate the scope of change, as institutional inertia pushes back against extravagant claims of power. Erler's (2007) work on presidential pardons, cited earlier, identifies some of these forces at work in the clemency process, as the established institutional mechanisms determine what the president sees and how choices are framed. Goldsmith's account of his time as head of the OLC notes that the office had a long-standing reputation as an independent source of legal advice, with "powerful cultural norms about the importance of providing the President with detached, apolitical legal advice" (2007, 33). Howell and Pevehouse sort through the complexity of even a purely presidential unilateral decision:

Though he sits alone atop his governing institution and retains considerable powers to ensure the compliance of those below him, when preparing for war, the president still must coordinate with all sorts of advisors within the Executive Office of the presidency; navigate tensions that often arise between the State and Defense departments; allay the concerns of current and past generals who, increasingly, have demonstrated a predilection for showing up on the evening news; and manage the production of often-conflicting intelligence reports that weigh on the president's case for war and the probable benefits of alternative courses of action.

(2007, 225)

The hard part is finding a way to characterize these institutional rules and processes in a way that is amenable to inferential tests, rather than simply piling on more and more thick description and complexity in a manner that inevitably leads us to conclude that "everything" matters.

A second dimension of these institutional checks is the political constraints that presidents face. Here, the most obvious are electoral effects: the impact of running for a second term, the effect of midterm elections, ineligibility for a third term. Public opposition to the continuing war in Iraq—certainly one of the most controversial policies of the Bush administration—undoubtedly played a role in the Democrats recapturing congressional majorities in the 2006 midterm elections. Midterm elections are often a referendum on the incumbent administration, especially when there is a national issue that can outweigh local considerations; the war was surely such an issue in 2006 (Mann 2006). In addition, the Twenty-Second Amendment imposes a stark limitation on what any single president can do, good or bad. Whatever one thinks of George W. Bush, it is a certainty that he will not be president after January 20, 2009.

The notion that informal or political checks on presidential power might prove effective is hardly new. In *Federalist* 72, Hamilton defended the Framers' decision to allow presidents to serve additional terms, as "necessary, to give the officer himself the inclination and the resolution to act his part well." Schlesinger, after considering what changes might solve the Imperial Presidency problem, concluded that no procedural rule could replace public vigilance as a check on presidential abuses of power: "As Madison said long ago, the country could not trust to 'parchment barriers' to halt the encroaching spirit of power" (1973, 418).

CONCLUSION

A decade or so after the subject first attracted sustained interest among presidency scholars, "unilateral powers" has become a major research agenda, with a consistent theoretical framework and a strong empirical tradition. In studying presidential attempts to use their legal and constitutional powers to effect policy change, scholars have established and defended the theoretical foundations of the approach, offered empirical tests of key hypotheses, and have continued to debate the normative dimensions of presidential action. This literature constitutes the most important theoretical development in the presidency literature since Neustadt's *Presidential Power*. There are, of course, many unanswered questions, offering opportunities to scholars pursuing the second generation of research.

Unilateral action raises important questions about the balance of power among the institutions of national government, and the effectiveness of congressional and judicial checks on executive energy. Whether or not these checks are effective, of course, is an empirical question, as is the separate question of whether the "ratchet effect" is real. And these empirical questions are themselves related to the normative issue of whether a particular presidential decision is correct, wrongheaded, or unconstitutional.

However, all of the questions about unilateral action have the same starting point, which is the formal constitutional or statutory basis of presidential action. The unilateral action theory presents a specific mechanism through which presidents shape policy, one very different in orientation than the strategic presidency that Neustadt made so famous.

REFERENCES

ADLER, D. G. 2006. The Law: George Bush as Commander-in-Chief: Toward the Nether World of Constitutionalism. *Presidential Studies Quarterly*, 36: 525–40.

BANKS, W. C. 2007. The Death of FISA. *Minnesota Law Review*, 9: 1209–301.

BARNES, R. 2008. Sentence in Memo Discounted FISA. *Washington Post*, May 23: A15.

BAZAN, E. B., and ELSEA, J. K. 2006. Presidential Authority to Conduct Warrantless Electronic Surveillance to Gather Foreign Intelligence Information. *Congressional Research Service Memorandum*, Jan. 5.

BENNETT, J. 1995. True to Form, Clinton Shifts Back to U.S. Focus. *New York Times*, July 5.

BRADLEY, C. A., and POSNER, E. A. 2006. Presidential Signing Statements and Executive Power. *Constitutional Commentary*, 23: 307–64.

——COLE, D., DELLINGER, W., DWORKIN, R., EPSTEIN, R., HEYMANN, P. B., et al. 2006. On NSA Spying: A Letter to Congress. *New York Review of Books*, 53/2. <http://www.nybooks.com/articles/18650>. Accessed Apr. 17, 2007.

CALABRESI, S., and PRAKASH, S. 1994. The President's Power to Execute the Laws. *Yale Law Journal*, 104: 541–666.

CANES-WRONE, B. 2006. *Who Leads Whom? Presidents, Policy, and the Public*. Chicago: University of Chicago Press.

CAREY, J. M., and SHUGART, M. S. 1998. Calling Out the Tanks or Filling Out the Forms? In *Executive Decree Authority*, ed. J. M. Carey and M. S. Shugart. New York: Cambridge University Press.

COOPER, P. J. 2002. *By Order of the President: The Use & Abuse of Executive Direct Action*. Lawrence: University Press of Kansas.

——2005. George W. Bush, Edgar Allan Poe, and the Use and Abuse of Presidential Signing Statements. *Presidential Studies Quarterly*, 35: 515–32.

CORLEY, P. C. 2006. Avoiding Advice and Consent: Recess Appointments and Presidential Power. *Presidential Studies Quarterly*, 36: 670–80.

CORWIN, E. S. 1957. *The President: Office and Powers 1787–1957*. New York: New York University Press.

CROVITZ, L. G., and RABKIN, J. A. 1989. *The Fettered Presidency: Legal Constraints on the Executive Branch*. Washington, DC: American Enterprise Institute.

DEERING, C. J., and MALTZMAN, F. 1999. The Politics of Executive Orders: Legislative Constraints on Presidential Power. *Political Research Quarterly*, 52: 767–83.

DELAHUNTY, R. J., and YOO, J. C. 2002. The President's Constitutional Authority to Conduct Military Operations against Terrorist Organizations and the Nations That Harbor or Support Them. *Harvard Journal of Law & Public Policy*, 25/2: 487–517.

EDWARDS, G. C., III. 2003. *On Deaf Ears: The Limits of the Bully Pulpit*. New Haven, CT: Yale University Press.

ERLER, H. A. 2007. Executive Clemency or Bureaucratic Discretion? Two Models of the Pardon Process. *Presidential Studies Quarterly*, 37: 427–88.

FEIN, B. 2007. Presidential Authority to Gather Foreign Intelligence. *Presidential Studies Quarterly*, 37: 23–36.

FISHER, L. 2002. A Dose of Law and Realism for Presidential Studies. *Presidential Studies Quarterly*, 32/4: 672–92.

——2004. *Presidential War Power*, 2nd edn. Lawrence: University Press of Kansas.

——2005. *Military Tribunals & Presidential Power: American Revolution to the War on Terrorism*. Lawrence: University Press of Kansas.

FLEISHMAN, J. L., and AUFSES, A. H. 1976. Law and Orders: The Problem of Presidential Legislation. *Law and Contemporary Problems*, 40: 1–45.

GAZIANO, T. F. 2000. The Use and Abuse of Executive Orders and Other Presidential Directives. *Texas Review of Law & Politics*, 5: 267–316.

GOLDSMITH, J. 2007. *The Terror Presidency: Law and Judgment inside the Bush Administration*. New York: W. W. Norton & Co.

GORDON, V. 2007. The Law: Unilaterally Shaping U.S. National Security Policy: The Role of National Security Directives. *Presidential Studies Quarterly*, 37: 349–67.

GRAHAM, H. D. 1990. *The Civil Rights Era*. New York: Oxford University Press.

HOWELL, W. G. 2003. *Power without Persuasion: The Politics of Direct Presidential Action*. Princeton, NJ: Princeton University Press.

HOWELL, W. G. 2005. Unilateral Powers: A Brief Overview. *Presidential Studies Quarterly,* 35: 417–39.

—— 2006. Executives: The American Presidency. In *The Oxford Handbook of Political Institutions,* ed. R. A. W. Rhodes, S. A. Binder, and B. A. Rockman. New York: Oxford University Press.

—— and MAYER, K. R. 2005. The Last 100 Days. *Presidential Studies Quarterly,* 35: 533 –53.

—— and PEVEHOUSE, J. C. 2007. *While Dangers Gather: Congressional Checks on Presidential War Powers.* Princeton, NJ: Princeton University Press.

ISSACHAROFF, S., and PILDES, R. H. 2005. Between Civil Libertarianism and Executive Unilateralism: An Institutional Process Approach to Rights during Wartime. In *The Constitution in Wartime: Beyond Alarmism and Complacency,* ed. M. Tushnet. Durham, NC: Duke University Press.

JONES, C. O. 2005. *The Presidency in a Separated System,* 2nd edn. Washington, DC: Brookings Institution Press.

—— 2007. Scholar-Activist as Guardian: Dick Neustadt's Presidency. In *Guardian of the Presidency: The Legacy of Richard E. Neustadt,* ed. M. J. Dickinson and E. A. Neustadt. Washington, DC: Brookings Institution Press.

KASSOP, N. 2003. The War Powers and its Limits. *Presidential Studies Quarterly,* 33: 509–29.

KERR, O. S. 2003. Internet Surveillance Law after the USA PATRIOT Act: The Big Brother That Isn't. *Northwestern University Law Review,* 97: 607–74.

KING, G. 1993. The Methodology of Presidential Research. In *Researching the Presidency: Vital Questions, New Approaches,* ed. G. C. Edwards, III, J. H. Kessel, and B. A. Rockman. Pittsburgh: University of Pittsburgh Press.

KOH, H. H. 1990. *The National Security Constitution: Sharing Power after the Iran-Contra Affair.* New Haven, CT: Yale University Press.

KRAUSE, G., and COHEN, D. 1997. Presidential Use of Executive Orders, 1953-1994. *American Politics Quarterly,* 25: 458–71.

—— —— 2000. Opportunity, Constraints, and the Development of the Institutional Presidency, 1939–1996. *Journal of Politics,* 62: 88–114.

LEONNIG, C. D. 2006. Secret Court's Judges Were Warned About NSA Spy Data. *Washington Post,* Feb. 9: A1.

LESSIG, L., and SUNSTEIN, C. R. 1994. The President and the Administration. *Columbia Law Review,* 94: 1–123.

LEWIS, D. E. 2005. Staffing Alone: Unilateral Action and the Politicization of the Executive Office of the President, 1988–2004. *Presidential Studies Quarterly,* 35: 496–514.

LICHTBLAU, E. 2008. *Bush's Law: The Remaking of American Justice.* New York: Pantheon Press.

MANN, T. E. 2006. How to Think about the November 2006 Congressional Elections. *Issues in Governance Studies,* 5.

MARSHALL, B. W., and PACELLE. R. L. 2005. Revisiting the Two Presidencies: The Strategic Use of Executive Orders. *American Politics Research,* 33/1: 81–105.

—— 2007. The President and International Commitments: Treaties as Signaling Devices. *Presidential Studies Quarterly,* 35/3: 440–65.

MAYER, K. R. 1999. Executive Orders and Presidential Power. *Journal of Politics,* 61: 445–66.

—— 2001. *With the Stroke of a Pen: Executive Orders and Presidential Power.* Princeton, NJ: Princeton University Press.

—— and CANON, D. T. 1999. *The Dysfunctional Congress: The Individual Roots of an Institutional Dilemma.* Boulder, CO: Westview Press.

—— and Price, K. 2002. Unilateral Presidential Powers: Significant Executive Orders, 1949–1999. *Presidential Studies Quarterly*, 32: 367–86.

Moe, T. M. 1985. The Politicized Presidency. In *The New Direction in American Politics*, ed. J. E. Chubb and P. E. Peterson. Washington, DC: Brookings Institution.

—— 1993. Presidents, Institutions, and Theory. In *Researching the Presidency: Vital Questions, New Approaches*, ed. G. C. Edwards III, J. H Kessell, and B. A. Rockman. Pittsburgh: University of Pittsburgh Press.

—— and Howell, W. G. 1999. The Presidential Power of Unilateral Action. *Journal of Law, Economics, and Organization*, 15: 132–79.

—— and Wilson, S. A. 1994. Presidents and the Politics of Structure. *Law and Contemporary Problems*, 57: 1–44.

Nathan, J. A., and Oliver, J. K. 1994. *Foreign Policy Making and the American Political System*, 3rd edn. Baltimore: Johns Hopkins University Press.

Neustadt, R. M. 1990. *Presidential Power and the Modern Presidents: The Politics of Leadership from Roosevelt to Reagan*. New York: Free Press.

Olson, W. J., and Woll, A. 1999. Executive Orders and National Emergencies: How Presidents Have Come to "Run the Country" by Usurping Legislative Power. CATO Institute Policy Analysis No. 358, Oct. 28.

Perine, K. 2007. Senate Democrats Split on Immunity Provisions in Foreign Surveillance Bill. *CQ Weekly Online*, Dec. 17: 3731. <http://library.cqpress.com/cqweekly/weeklyreport110–000002643983>. Accessed Apr. 22, 2008.

Peterson, M. A. 1990. *Legislating Together: The White House and Capitol Hill from Eisenhower to Reagan*. Cambridge, MA: Harvard University Press.

Pfiffner, J. P. 2008. Constraining Executive Power: George W. Bush and the Constitution. *Presidential Studies Quarterly*, 38: 123–43.

Pious, R. M. 2007. Inherent War and Executive Powers and Prerogative Politics. *Presidential Studies Quarterly*, 37: 66–84.

Posner, E. A., and Vermeule, A. 2007. *Terror in the Balance: Security, Liberty, and the Courts*. New York: Oxford University Press

Posner, R. A. 2006. *Not a Suicide Pact: The Constitution in a Time of National Emergency*. New York: Oxford University Press.

Ramsey, M. D. 2005. Torturing Executive Power. *Georgetown Law Journal*, 93: 1213–52.

Risen, J., and Lichtblau, E. 2005. Bush Lets U.S. Spy on Callers without Courts. *New York Times*, Dec. 16: A1.

Romano, R. 1994. Comment on "Presidents and the Politics of Structure." *Law and Contemporary Problems*, 7: 59–63.

Rottinghaus, B., and Maier, J. 2007. The Power of Decree: Presidential Use of Executive Proclamations, 1977–2005. *Political Research Quarterly*, 60: 338–43.

Rozell, M. J. 2002. *Executive Privilege: Presidential Power, Secrecy, and Accountability*, 2nd edn. Lawrence: University Press of Kansas

Sala, B. R. 1998. In Search of the Administrative President: Presidential "Decree" Powers and Policy Implementation in the United States. In *Executive Decree Authority*, ed. J. M. Carey and M. S. Shugart. New York: Cambridge University Press.

Schlesinger, A. 1973. *The Imperial Presidency*. Boston: Houghton Mifflin.

Shull, S. A. 1997. *Presidential–Congressional Relations: Policy and Time Approaches*. Ann Arbor: University of Michigan Press.

Skowronek, S. 1993. *The Politics Presidents Make: Leadership from John Adams to George Bush*. Cambridge, MA: Harvard University Press.

SMELTZER, J. D. 2004. Should Faith-Based Initiatives Be Implemented by Executive Order? *Administrative Law Review*, 56: 181–205.

STARKS, T. 2007. White House Scores on FISA Rewrite. *CQ Weekly Online*, Aug. 6: 2369. <http://library.cqpress.com/cqweekly/weeklyreport110–000002567012>. Accessed Apr. 22, 2008.

SUNSTEIN, C. R. 1995. An Eighteenth Century Presidency in a Twenty-First Century. *Arkansas Law Review*, 48/1: 1–22.

US Congress. 1977. *Foreign Intelligence Surveillance Act of 1977*. Senate. Committee on the Judiciary. S. Rept. 604. 95th Cong., 1st sess.

——1999. *Executive Orders: The Impact of Executive Orders on The Legislative Process: Executive Lawmaking?* House. Committee on Rules, Subcommittee on Legislative and Budget Process. 106th Cong., 1st sess. October 27.

——2006. *Wartime Executive Power and the National Security Agency's Surveillance Authority.* Senate. Committee on the Judiciary. 109th Cong., 2nd sess. Serial No. J-109–59. Feb. 6, Feb. 28, and Mar. 28.

——2007. *Presidential Signing Statements under the Bush Administration: A Threat to Checks and Balances and the Rule of Law?* House. Committee on the Judiciary. 110th Cong., 1st sess. Serial No. 110–6. Jan. 31.

US Department of Justice. 2001. *2000 Annual Foreign Intelligence Surveillance Act Report to Congress*. Apr. 27. <http://www.usdoj.gov/nsd/foia/reading_room/2000annualfisareportto-congress.htm>. Accessed Apr. 16, 2008.

——2006. *Legal Authorities Supporting the Activities of the National Security Agency Described by the President.* Memorandum to Senate Majority Leader from Attorney General Alberto Gonzales. Jan. 19.

WARBER, A. L. 2006. *Executive Orders and the Modern Presidency: Legislating from the Oval Office.* Boulder, CO: Lynne Rienner Publishers.

WEAVER, W. G., and PALLITTO, R. M. 2006. The Law: "Extraordinary Rendition" and Presidential Fiat. *Presidential Studies Quarterly*, 6: 102–16.

WHITFORD, A. B., and OCHS, H. L. 2006. The Political Roots of Executive Clemency. *American Politics Research*, 34: 825–46.

YOO, J. C. 1996. The Continuation of Politics by Other Means: The Original Understanding of War Powers. *California Law Review*, 84: 170–305.

——2002. War and the Constitutional Text. *University of Chicago Law Review*, 69: 1639–84.

——2005. *The Powers of War and Peace: The Constitution and Foreign Affairs after 9/11.* Chicago: University of Chicago Press.

CHAPTER 20

PREROGATIVE POWER AND PRESIDENTIAL POLITICS

RICHARD M. PIOUS

PREROGATIVE power involves unilateral actions taken within a governing institution. In presidential studies, it involves a decision taken by the president, based on his interpretation of his constitutional powers, by his own initiative and subject to constraints by other branches of government. The Madisonian doctrine of partial separation of powers, as embodied in the Constitution (Federalist Papers No. 47–51), provides each institution with partial agency in the workings of the other. Consequentially, presidential prerogatives involve presidential powers that are quasi-legislative (the veto power, the claim of power to dispense with execution of laws) and quasi-judicial (the pardon, commutation, and reprieve powers). In this chapter, the broadest possible definition of presidential prerogative is used, covering all powers a president may claim from the Constitution. The other chapters in this section, by contrast, assume a narrower definition of the term that focuses primarily on a set of mechanisms by which presidents make policies that are judicially enforceable, such as executive orders, executive agreements, National Security Directives, and proclamations.

Scholars of constitutional law for the past two centuries have asked doctrinal questions: of what does presidential prerogative consist? How far does executive power extend? Is the president's exercise of a prerogative constitutional and lawful? The important questions about prerogative power that political scientists have asked over the past several decades have dealt with the conditions under which a prerogative power is exercised, why it is substituted for a statutory authorization, and the politics created by that substitution. Their key questions have been the following: what is the relationship between prerogative governance and persuasive governance—the two main forms of presidential power? How do presidents attempt to legitimize their exercise of prerogative and under what circumstances do they succeed? The newest wave of political science research, relying on statistical correlations and formal models developed from political economy and rational choice, has asked the following questions: What is the logic of the politics involved in such substitutions? What patterns of presidential behavior (causal and associated relationships) and congressional and judicial responses can be specified from formal models?

CONSTITUTIONAL AMBIGUITIES

The Constitution does not specify with precision the constitutional powers of the three departments nor the boundaries that separate them (Cronin 1989). Article II sets out the powers of the executive. These may be characterized either as precise (e.g., the veto, the power to adjourn Congress if its houses do not agree, the power to call Congress into special session) or as imprecise because they involve ambiguities and limits that are not specified, or because they seem incomplete, or because the president claims the silences of the document (the removal power for example). In such cases, the president, in exercising prerogatives, may be charged by critics with infringing on the powers of other departments. Madison wanted checks and balances, and enumerated powers that would define and therefore confine executive power; Hamilton and others in the circle around Washington wanted vague general terms (executive power, commander-in-chief) that would permit vast expansions of executive power once the Constitution was ratified by state conventions suspicious of such power; and Hamilton's allies controlled the Committee on Style that drafted the final version. And so, Article II can be read through either a Madisonian or Hamiltonian interpretation (Bessette and Tulis 1981; Burns 1965; Eastland 1992).

Early constitutional commentators pointed out that Article II was defective because of its ambiguities. Abel Upshur observed in 1840, "The most defective part of the Federal Constitution, beyond all question, is that which relates to the executive department. It is impossible to read that instrument without being forcibly struck with the loose and unguarded terms in which the powers and duties of the president are pointed out ... the convention appears to have studiously selected such loose and general expressions as would enable the President, by implication and construction, either to neglect his duties or to enlarge his powers" (Upshur 1840, 116). Woodrow Wilson, writing as a political scientist in the 1880s, thought executive power involved merely the administration of government once Congress had enacted policy into law (Wilson 1885). Taft conceived of the office as "chief magistrate," seeing it in quasi-judicial terms (Taft 1916). Nothing in the debates at the constitutional convention or the state ratifying conventions settled the question of whether executive will is anterior and superior to the legislative's, or whether Congress makes policy and the president presides over its administration (in which case the executive is subsequent and subordinate), or whether the two institutions are concurrent and coordinate policy makers who may choose to act separately or may choose to abide by statutory frameworks that establish patterns of interbranch policy co-determination (Glennon 1990).

One aspect of separation of powers theory, as embodied in the constitutional text, provides the opportunity for presidents to assert prerogative power (Sorenson 1989), and ironically, it was Madison, the proponent of strict enumeration of executive powers, who opened the way for its expansion. Madison in *Federalist* No. 47 observed that the "accumulation of all powers legislative, executive and judiciary in the same hands, whether of one, a few or many, and whether hereditary, self-appointed, or elective, may justly be pronounced the very definition of tyranny" (Cooke 1961, 327). He pointed out, however, that if a *complete* separation of power were achieved (so that Congress exercised all legislative power and only legislative power, the president exercised all executive power and only executive power, and the Supreme Court and lower courts exercised all judicial powers and only judicial powers), the institution assigned all legislative power would be so powerful it would suck the other institutions into the "impetuous vortex" (Cooke 1961, 329). This is what the Framers believed had already happened in many of the states after constitutions were written incorporating complete separation clauses: legislatures were dominant and the post-colonial governors and courts were too weak to keep legislative power in check. What should be done to prevent the erosion of separation of powers? Madison's answer, developed in *Federalist* No. 47 and *Federalist* No. 51, involved three principles: first, provide the politicians in the three departments with the motivation to protect their prerogatives; second, provide "interior contrivances" such as a council of state for the executive (never adopted) and bicameralism in the Congress; and third, replace *complete* with *partial* separation of powers.

In a system of partial separation, some powers would overlap and some would blend, and, in some instances, one department could exercise powers considered to be a part of another department (Pyle and Pious 1984). And so, in spite of the fact that the Constitution assigned "the judicial power" to a Supreme Court, Congress has a power of subpoena, retains the power to hold witnesses at hearings in contempt, and conducts impeachments as a trial, and the president has a power to issue reprieves and pardons for offences against the United States. Similarly, Congress does not exercise all legislative powers: executive orders, executive agreements, military orders, and proclamations all can have the force of law. Partial separation works both ways: other departments may have a small share in administration, but for the most part, the doctrine allows the president to legitimize his claims of concurrent powers and helps him counter claims that he is confined to exercising solely executive powers and required to conform to the provisions of authorizing statutes. In practice, this means that in some of the most significant policy arenas, the president can cobble together a set of concurrent powers and institutional practices—first to set policy, then to implement it, and finally to pass judgment on it. Although Madison was a strong proponent of checks and balances and partial separation of powers, the president can fashion his own line of argument from partial separation to produce and legitimize just that outcome—creating a situation in which it is possible that significant war, diplomatic, and national security powers will fall into an "executive vortex" irrespective of whether or not there are provisions in the Constitution assigning them to Congress and the judiciary (Casper 1985; Kurland 1986).

Public law scholars, beginning in the early nineteenth century and continuing on today, have attempted to define the scope of executive prerogative and determine its limits (White 1948, 1951, 1954, 1958; Corwin 1957; Fausold and Shank 1991; Fisher 1995, 2000; Kelly 2006). Their work is usually set in the context of conflict between president and Congress over the question of separation of power boundaries (Henkin 1972; Koh 1990). Since the presidency of Franklin Roosevelt, they have focused on the vast expansion of executive power during the Depression, the Second World War, and the Cold War (Corwin 1941, 1949; Rossiter 1949; Patterson 1976; Bernstein 1976). They deal with silences: there is no removal power specified, for example, and neither is a treaty abrogation power. Does this mean Senate consent is required for removals and abrogations? Or, would this be merely "sterile symmetry?" They also deal with ambiguities: what does it mean to "take care that the laws be faithfully executed?" Is it a duty to follow congressional intent? Or, does it pose an opportunity to shape the meaning of law, through signing statements and instructions to departmental officers (Kelly 2006)? How does one construe general terms such as the executive power or the commander-in-chief title: as grants of power in and of themselves (Hamilton's view), or as placeholders for any subsequent specific enumerated powers (Webster's view)? The incomplete grants of power need to be completed. What relationship does a president have with department secretaries, when all the Constitution states is that he nominates them, may require their opinion in writing on departmental matters, and is to take care that laws be faithfully executed?

Public law scholars such as Edward Corwin were able to synthesize scholarship on various specific points in order to produce "institutional" studies of the powers of the office. These helped to clarify some issues and frame the debates over the limits of powers, though there is little evidence that presidents or their counsel made decisions about the use of prerogative powers based on what scholars believed to be their prerogatives. Presidents tended to act and scholars thereafter reacted, often with protestations at what they believed to be excesses of power (Schlesinger 1973). And doctrinal studies had serious limitations. They tended to be static statements of "the law" rather than descriptions of what presidents did and why. It was as if one could understand how a horse runs solely through a recitation of its anatomy. More was needed, and after the Second World War several schools of political science attempted to complement doctrinal studies with case studies of the different styles presidents use to legitimize their claims of prerogative.

PRESIDENTIAL CLAIMS: HARD AND SOFT PREROGATIVE

The outcome of 200-plus years of governance under the Constitution has *not* been to fill in the blanks. The constitutional architecture has not become more explicit, and presidential power has not been better enumerated, defined, or confined. Instead, presidents have been able to exploit the silences, ambiguities and incomplete constructions and have vastly expanded their prerogative powers, even at times developing novel interpretations of what seemed to be routine powers such as the pocket veto (Pious 1979; Hurtgen 1975; Hoekstra 1985, 1989; Mansfield 1987). These claims of prerogative may even involve extra-constitutional sources. The United States as a sovereign nation may do anything any other sovereign power may do, whether or not such a power (declaring neutrality) is explicitly stated in the Constitution (Adler and Genovese 2002; Adler and George 1998). Presidents claim that they, as agents of the American people, exercise these powers (known as concomitants of nationality) when the Constitution is silent. They claim on rare occasions a Lockean Prerogative—the responsibility in an emergency to act without prescription of the law, and sometimes against it (Arnhart 1979; Langston and Lind 1991). They note that the oath requires the president to "preserve, protect and defend" the Constitution, but that the oath does not mention faithful execution of the laws, which is left for a separate provision (Miller 1987). Therefore, under some circumstances, presidents may claim a "dispensing Power" that allows them to dispense with the execution of law (Burgess 1994) and issue "signing statements" to make such a case when they sign new bills into law.

While this dispensing power was initially claimed for emergencies, presidents since Jefferson have also claimed such a power might be exercised in a non-emergency situation for the greater good (Bailey 2004). Presidents rely on expansive interpretations of constitutional text, an effort in which "presidentialist" public law scholars and their own legal counsel and attorneys general have provided them with scholarly argumentation. In addition to explicit powers granted in Article II, they claim "inherent" and "implied" powers from the "Executive Power." They claim a "unitary executive" exists (Yoo 2006) armed with all executive functions. They use what seem to be potential checks (the impeachment clause) to argue that if a president might be impeached for high crimes and misdemeanors, he must have the power to ensure that such crimes do not occur in his administration—and the only way to ensure that is to have a power of removal, and a power to direct subordinates in their duties. They combine separate clauses to find "resulting" powers, such as the power to issue executive orders (Carey and Shugart 1998; Cooper 2002) and negotiate executive agreements.

Political scientists can distinguish between a claim of "hard" and "soft" prerogative (Pious 1996). It is not usually the case that a president has to choose between making a decision and basing it on a claim of prerogative or basing it on statutory authorization. Often there is no clear demarcation between prerogatives and statutes. Presidents rely on "soft" prerogative when they act unilaterally to resolve an issue, but later claim that they acted under color of statute law. They may use delegated powers in ways inconsistent with congressional intent (Bowman 1988). They claim that when they rely on prerogative and law, narrowly drawn delegations of power should be interpreted expansively. They argue that the courts should uphold delegations of power that might in domestic affairs be considered unconstitutionally broad when they also involve inherent presidential powers, especially in foreign affairs. They argue that a broad constitutional prerogative is permitted when it involves carrying out congressional intent, even where no specific statutory provision can be found. They claim that the president has the prerogative to enforce "the mass of legislation" in a particular area, exercising executive powers that are not specifically mentioned in the statute, such as impoundment (Fisher 2000).

A related argument is that there is a "peace of the United States" that the president is bound to enforce. Presidents combine commander-in-chief powers and statutes to claim that they possess quasi-judicial enforcement powers involving strikes (Roche 1952; Wilmerding 1952; Corwin 1953), civil insurrection (Kohn 1972; Dennison 1974; Belz 1988; Pollitt 1958), alleged subversive and fifth column activities (Fairman 1942; Rostow 1945), and terrorism (Cole and Dempsey 2002; Pious 2006). They are also able in national emergencies to exercise powers that go beyond or contravene statute law (Baldwin 1897; Robinson 1973; Miller 1980). Similarly, they combine their prerogatives with statutes such as the National Emergencies Act and the International Emergency Economic Powers Act to go beyond the authorizations of statute law (Sturm 1949; Relyea 1976; Klieman 1979; Fuller 1979; Genovese 1979).

And so, scholars examining presidential statements or those of their counsel (such as Opinions of the Attorney General) will almost always encounter justifications that cite statutes extensively, even though the interpretation of these statutes involves the "prerogative" to interpret their meanings that defy congressional intent.

PREROGATIVE GOVERNANCE

Politics involves the substitution of decisional rules in order to influence the "who gets what, when, and why" fundamentals. In the case of prerogative politics, it involves the substitution of presidential fiat and unilateral action for statutory authorization and collaborative decision making (Moe 1999; Moe and Howell 1999). The interesting question for political analysis occurs when such decision making is optional: should a president ask Congress for legislation or implement policy through executive order? Should he spend funds appropriated by Congress or unilaterally assert a power to impound or defer? Should he go to Congress for a declaration of war or authorization for hostilities, or should he assert a prerogative as commander-in-chief to engage in hostilities? Should the president follow a framework law that requires him to obtain a judicial warrant before authorizing electronic surveillance in intelligence matters, or should he assert the prerogative to do so without warrant?

Since the 1970s, political scientists have dealt with these questions, some through institutional studies of the presidency, others by using quantitative methods or the logic of game theory. Aside from methodological differences, another distinction may be drawn: some studies deal with the routine processes of governance (nominations, vetoes, executive orders, signing statements, primarily in domestic policy spheres), while others deal with war powers, foreign affairs, diplomacy, and national security matters, and are more likely to involve studies of discrete decisions. The former are open (documents published in series) and subject to congressional and public discussion before and after the prerogative is exercised. The latter decisions usually involve secrecy and presidential *faits accomplis*, followed by eventual disclosure. The open politics of routine domestic prerogative is fundamentally different from the closed politics of "high prerogative."

The "when" question has recently been subjected to rigorous quantification in order to develop associated and sometimes causal statements. The study of executive orders, for example, has indicated that presidents are more, not less, likely to issue them when they are popular and have partisan advantage in Congress. They are less likely to issue executive orders or use force in times of split government (Howell 2003; Howell and Pevehouse 2007). Similarly, presidents have been more likely to risk use of American forces in hostilities when their public approval ratings are high. On the other hand, various studies have indicated that presidents are more likely to exercise the veto in times of split government (Cameron 2000). If there is any generalization that does seem to hold, it is that prerogative power will be employed when the president believes that he must act (Carter in hostage crisis in Iran, Reagan in hostage crisis in Lebanon), but if the action became public (a requirement for obtaining congressional authorization) it would precipitate either a domestic or an international crisis (or both) for the president that would damage him politically. A president will act, if necessary without congressional or public support, when he believes he has no choice. He may event act against the prescription of law (Ford in the evacuation of Saigon).

We also know more about the "how" question. In emergency situations, presidents may well call Congress into special session and seek legislative authorization to act, but this is not always the case, even when presidents are popular. Bush, for example, issued a secret executive order to the NSA authorizing wiretapping and electronic surveillance without warrants. And while he acted publicly to authorize military tribunals based on his power as commander-in-chief, he acted secretly in authorizing treatment of detainees and questioning that went beyond common understandings of American obligations under international law (Pious 2007).

The assertion of prerogative leads to the institution of prerogative governance. This involves the unilateral assertion of a power to decide and act, an imposition of a chain of command from the White House through the Executive Office of the President and into the departments (in the case of the Pentagon, from the president directly to the Secretary of Defense), and the issuance of self-executing orders to officials in the departments, resulting in *faits accomplis* to deal with the issue. Control of information is a crucial component in prerogative governance, whether it involves secrecy, selective leaks, or framing and spin (Pallitto and Weaver 2007). Routine classification systems are not useful, but sensitive compartmentalized information (that is circulated among a handful of officials) is organized by top presidential staffers. Decision making is concentrated in a small group setting, itself subject to intensive analysis by political scientists (George 1980). Once decisions have been made and implemented, information is kept close. Members of Congress who are briefed with classified information may not share it with aides or colleagues. Attempts by congressional committees to investigate decisions may be met with claims of executive and departmental secrecy. In court cases, the doctrine of state secret may be employed for similar purposes (Fisher 2006).

Presidents and their staff believe that secrecy aids in subsequent legitimization efforts. Presidents will claim they acted for reasons of national security and in the national interest. They need not argue that their opponents do not have the national interest at heart. Rather, they claim they cannot reveal all that went into their decisions in order to protect their intelligence capabilities and sources, but indicate that if their opponents knew what they knew, they would have acted in the same way. In other words, since their opponents cannot know what they know, their opposition is misinformed. They continue by appealing to their own party to close ranks out of loyalty, and for the opposition to support the administration in a spirit of bipartisanship: politics should stop at the water's edge. But secrecy often backfires. Deceptions and distortions are eventually unearthed by the investigative media, or disclosed by adversaries. Presidential credibility becomes an important issue. In some cases, decisions to evade the law or act against its provisions require cover-ups, and when these unravel, officials may be prosecuted. That in turn can leave the president and other high officials vulnerable to legal sanctions or even impeachment.

Outcomes of Prerogative Governance

The outcomes of prerogative power have been the province of historians ever since the creation of the presidency, and more recently of political scientists who have developed case studies of particular presidential decisions and their legitimization (or delegitimization) by the courts (Marcus 1977). There have been several attempts to develop a systematic analysis of the outcomes (Rossiter 1948). These efforts were primarily descriptive, and involved classifying prerogative outcomes according to their policy impacts (Pious 1979).

Frontlash

If the policy worked (Washington's proclamation of Neutrality), there was a "frontlash" effect. Mastery in the situation would quiet the critics and enable the president to retain support of party and public. His own party would unite and not only praise the policy but also defend the prerogatives; the opposition would be split and disheartened, and no coherent critique of the prerogative would be sustained. Congress would pass laws "perfecting" the president's initiatives (such as broad delegations of power), pass supportive resolutions, or provide retrospective authority or funding. It would also provide subsequent authorizations, and might immunize or indemnify officials if the legality of their actions was in question. Often, in subsequent elections, the president would consolidate his party's political position. The institutional impact would be an expansion of presidential power (as influence) and also an expansion (through the precedent of the "living presidency") of the powers of the office. The institutional self-confidence of the executive branch would increase, while Congress would play a supportive role, as happened in the aftermath of the Second World War. Ever since Jefferson, presidents and their supporters have fused plebiscitary claims based on "the will of the people" with prerogative claims (Bailey 2004).

These claims could transmute into what critics referred to as an imperial presidency (Schlesinger 1973). Prerogative could be taken to extremes and justified through the election, and powers could be abused in the name of national security. Secrecy systems could enable the president and his officials to evade checks and balances, as well as democratic accountability. The president could concentrate power into an "Executive Vortex" by using quasi-legislative powers to bypass statute law, and quasi-judicial powers to bypass both constitutional and statutory civil and military courts established by Congress. In areas such as the war on terror, the executive could establish what in effect was a "state within a state" without reference to international commitments, domestic legislative standards, or judicial procedures such as warrants and the writ of habeas corpus. Rose points out, however, that one person's imperial president is another's leader, and that to some extent, disagreements over policy and the success or failure of decisions usually precede constitutional debates (Rose 2000). Had Johnson or Nixon won the war in Vietnam quickly, it is doubtful either would have been called an imperial president, or that debates over war powers would have become so significant.

Backlash

What then happens when a presidential initiative loses public and congressional support? What if the policy succeeds, but only at a high cost? What if it fails? It is likely that checks and balances will come into play *after the fact*. And, attacks on a presidential policy will lead critics to attack the prerogatives that put it into play (Schlesinger 1973). In Congress, the president's party will become dispirited and divided, while the opposition is emboldened. Even in periods of party government there may be investigations and oversight, while in periods of split government Congress may follow on with framework legislation that promotes interbranch policy collaboration (Sundquist 1981). Congress may pass obstructive or prohibitory legislation, impose funding cut-offs or conditions, or directly cut programs. It may pass resolutions condemning the presidential action, or it may require additional reporting and consultation for future decisions. It may take reprisals, such as holding up nominations, failing to pass unrelated legislation, or holding up reorganization plans until they are modified to suit congressional interests. Courts may resuscitate the doctrine of separation of powers and find that indeed boundaries existed and were transgressed (Verkuil 1989; Chemerinsky 1983). Members of Congress may bring court cases to challenge presidential prerogative. Private parties may sue for damages on the grounds that presidents and their subordinates did not act according to law. Prosecutions may result, involving the original offenses or subsequent attempts to cover them up. Congress may pass measures attempting to overturn the policy, and, in exceptional circumstances, the courts will check the president or his subordinates. When the policy proves to be an unmitigated disaster (e.g., Vietnam, Iraq), the public shifts support away from the president's party in subsequent elections.

We can distinguish this effect from policy disagreements expressed in the use of prerogative, such as Jackson's veto, use of a removal power, and subsequent censure—none of which prevented his chosen successor Van Buren from winning the next presidential election. The institutional effect of backlash is that the living presidency does not incorporate the precedent. The party system institutionalizes constraints on presidential power, as happened for both Democratic and Whig conceptions of the office after Jackson. Congress is likely to pass framework legislation to limit the president, such as the War Powers Act of 1973, the Budget and Impoundment Act of 1974, and the Foreign Intelligence Surveillance Act of 1978. And once the president's standing is weakened, Congress may take reprisals on other issues so that the president's failed exercise of prerogative affects his reputation in the Washington community and his public standing, consequently limiting his options and his possibility of mastery tomorrow by what he had done yesterday (Neustadt 1960).

Overshoot and Collapse

There are times when presidential assertions of prerogative so overstep the bounds of legality or the constitutional understandings of the day that a crisis of legitimacy ensues. The impeachment of Andrew Johnson over the removal power, the resignation of Richard Nixon over the Watergate cover-up, and the paralysis in the latter stages of the Reagan administration over the Iran-Contra affair are three examples of presidential assertions of prerogative that led to a crisis of legitimacy and subsequent collapse. The president loses the battle for public opinion and much of his party "runs for the tall grass" (in Pat Buchanan's comparison of legislators with panicked elephants). The congressional debate turns against his position. High-ranking officials are investigated by Congress and grand juries for criminal offenses. There is talk in Congress of censure or impeachment. The president and his top aides are distracted with investigations. Turnover occurs in the ranks, and eventually the president seeks resignations of top officials and replaces them with others who have the confidence of Congress. In both the Watergate and Iran-Contra affairs, those who held day-to-day governing power had the confidence of Congress (Kissinger as the "Super-K" of State and the NSC during Watergate, and Schultz at State and former Senator Howard Baker at the White House Office in the later stages of Iran-Contra)—in effect creating a quasi-parliamentary system. Such scandals precipitate sharp drops in presidential approval ratings, which are accompanied by similar drops in approval scores on administration-sponsored legislation.

The institutional effects of a collapse are to weaken the presidency as an institution. After the Johnson impeachment played out, a system of "Congressional Government" described by Woodrow Wilson placed most governing power in the hands of congressional committee leaders and department secretaries (Wilson 1885). After Nixon's resignation, a Democratic Congress passed framework legislation designed (somewhat unsuccessfully) to rein in presidential budgeting, war powers, and intelligence operations (Sundquist 1981). After the Nixon presidency, some commentators argued that the "imperial" presidency had become an "imperiled" presidency (Crovitz and Rabkin 1989; Eastland 1992; Silverstein 1997). President Ford, who was not elected, and President Carter, who narrowly eked out a victory, both lacked mandates and were subject to the strictures of congressional oversight and framework laws designed to limit their prerogatives. In fact, both presidents exercised war and national security prerogatives and bypassed the framework laws, especially the War Powers Act (Franck and Weisband 1979).

These accounts of prerogative governance did not go beyond description. They could not explain why some exercises of prerogative led to backlash or collapse while others did not. To move to causal explanations, one would have to move beyond the study of specific decisions into comparative case studies, as well as statistical correlations. The development of formal models would also be helpful in generating hypotheses that could be rigorously tested.

EXPLAINING PREROGATIVE POLITICS

Why do presidents substitute prerogative for statutory authority? Before discussing some of the newer methodological approaches, we can glean some insights from traditional political science literature. If we organize the study of presidential decision making in terms of concentric circles (Patterson 1988), we would begin at the center with presidential personality, character, and leadership traits. In one pioneering study of presidential failure in the use of war powers, a political scientist (Barber 1972) argued that the "active/negative" personality type (i.e., someone committed to using powers extensively, but who lacked enjoyment of politics and tended to view events negatively) was most likely to rigidify rather than demonstrate flexibility and resilience in the use of war powers. While the argument is not necessarily persuasive—e.g., Lincoln could be viewed as an active/negative but demonstrated great flexibility and never rigidified around successful or failed policies (Hoekstra 1989)—it nevertheless remains a pathbreaking approach to thinking about why a president might rely on prerogative. Future lines of development, building on more recent presidents, will have to contend with both the Reagan and Clinton personalities, along with FDR, which make it clear that decisions to rely on prerogative cannot be ascribed to whatever demons beset Johnson and Nixon. Yet it may be the case that some decisions are either triggered by personality traits or encouraged by them. But what traits? Do those of the fox matter, irrespective of whether they enjoyed politics? If so, we would still have to account for the Reagans and Wilsons.

The first ring around the president would be the advisory system. Small group research, primarily about significant foreign policy issues, makes it clear that there are many dysfunctions. But the literature does not usually deal with issues of prerogative, and so it would be necessary to tease out discussions that focused on these issues. There are, however, accounts by participants and historians of decisions such as the Iran-Contra affair (Bowman 1988) and the Destroyer Deal (Jackson 2003) which make it clear that presidents (a) use legal advice instrumentally rather than analytically, to justify decisions they have already made; (b) operate under situational constitutionalism, in which precedent means nothing, and neither do past positions taken by presidents of their party; and (c) seem to lack a learning curve on constitutional issues (with the exception of military tribunals under FDR). One of the contributions made by studies of the advisory system (and its dysfunctions) is the insight that the institutionalized presidency and the cabinet departments tend to funnel a category of "non-solvable" problems up the advisory system. Anything that is solvable tends to be diverted before it reaches the president's desk, though the White House may engage in credit taking. What are left are issues whose complexity, uncertainty, unpalatable trade-offs, and often non-linear effects make them unsuitable for resolution by Congress. It may be the case that certain categories of these issues also require that something needs to be done, and that presidents are then tempted to resolve them with their own powers. The part of the institutionalized presidency that deals with legal issues (the Office of Legal Counsel and Attorney General in the DOJ) now has sufficient legal briefs to provide an institutional memory that can be accessed with low transaction costs (Baker 2006; Clayton 1995). It may now be the case that positions defending executive prerogatives have been so routinized that they have become orthodox for the office, irrespective of the personality of the incumbent or the party affiliation. Carter, Clinton, and both Bushes, for example, tested the limits of existing understandings on war powers. The remaining issue would not involve the traditional dichotomy between "active" and "passive" presidents, but rather whether the president and legal counsel would be willing to take the final steps to illegality and abuse of power under cover of executive prerogative.

The outer ring of power that might influence the decision about prerogative would be the congressional party (and the opposition congressional party). Here the example of FDR in the Destroyer Deal proves instructive. Roosevelt consummated the deal through an executive agreement, but this was a late decision; for several months, he and other officials believed that a treaty might be needed, and that Congress would have to pass a statute implementing such a treaty. Yet when FDR enquired, it was clear that his own congressional party leaders were just as happy to have the president conclude the deal on his own constitutional authority (though thereafter they passed many implementing statutes). In another example, Truman refused to implement provisions of the Taft–Hartley Act during the steel strike. His decision to substitute the power of commander-in-chief (eventually overturned by the Supreme Court) involved political calculations. Truman expected to run for reelection and expected Taft to oppose him; he had vetoed the Taft–Hartley Act and Congress had passed it over his veto. Bypassing the provisions of the law would enable him to satisfy the steelworkers' union, buttressing his electoral coalition, and also would serve as revenge against his Republican foes in Congress who had defeated him in the veto contest.

To better understand the relationships between the party system and the use of prerogative, we could utilize the concept of regime: presidents who seem to push the envelope and take the most risks in instituting prerogative governance are those who stand against the dominant regime (Skowronek 1993). In electoral terms, it could be said that they win deviating elections (Nixon, Reagan) or that they attain office alienated from the dominant regime (Tyler, Andrew Johnson). A hypothesis worthy of further research might be to examine whether the positioning of the president "makes" a high-stakes variant of prerogative politics, or whether the prerogative politics that most presidents make becomes risky because of the positioning against the dominant regime.

THE RESEARCH AGENDA

Each method of advancing the study of presidential prerogative has made important contributions. Each, in the future, can exploit new opportunities, either through interdisciplinary borrowings from other approaches, or through analysis of new claims and new forms of behavior in the Clinton and Bush presidencies.

Doctrinal Studies

Doctrinal research will focus on four approaches to governance that have gained currency in the Bush presidency and are likely to be carried on by theorists of the national security state. The first development is the attempt to "restore" the powers of the presidency against what some theorists see as attempts at congressional encroachment. This involves the "unitary executive" theory, as developed by John Yoo and others (Yoo 2006). In this approach, the executive possesses certain "core functions" which may not be transgressed. These include extensive powers as commander-in-chief that cover national security and domestic security activities, as well as purely military activities. In addition, presidents are the "sole organ[s] of communication,"[1] which in this view goes far beyond the power to communicate to the governments of other nations, but instead covers complete control over foreign policy.

Second (and stemming from developments in the Nixon and Reagan years), the executive combines presidential prerogatives with legislation in order to develop a "soft" prerogative that intermingles constitutional and statutory authority. And since the Truman and Johnson presidencies, the doctrine of an international police power, first developed by Theodore Roosevelt, has been extended to include multilateral commitments, treaty commitments, UN and NATO resolutions, and other international actions that presidents claim authorize their actions. Clinton, for example, relied on a NATO authorization for the bombing of Serbia, even though Congress had deadlocked and been unable to pass a resolution authorizing his action. The use of such resolutions warrants further study—particularly the interpretations of United Nations resolutions on Iraq, and the interpretations of Geneva Conventions relating to treatment of detainees in the aftermath of invasions of Afghanistan and Iraq (Pious 2007).

Third, the Bush presidency has developed a "with or without" approach to statutory authorization. Eavesdropping, for example, may be conducted by administration officials with a warrant under the Foreign Intelligence Surveillance Act, or without a warrant according to an executive order. The antecedents extend back to Washington and Lincoln, but in those times, prerogative came first (i.e., the declaration of neutrality, the suspension of habeas corpus), followed by congressional perfecting of the initiative. In the current system there is a concurrent approach, first developed by Theodore Roosevelt, who announced when he put into effect an executive agreement on sugar imports with Santo Domingo that he would be happy to effect it as a treaty—whenever the Senate consented to it.

Finally, a system of parallel governance in some policy arenas has been created, in which the president exercises a combination of executive, legislative, and judicial powers. For example, courts martial and federal district courts try some terrorists, but so do military tribunals established by the president by military order; the FBI conducts eavesdropping under the Patriot Act, but the National Security Agency conducts it without warrants, under authority of an executive order; the FBI issues National Security Letters to telecommunications carriers, while the Pentagon (without legal authority) issues informal letters to the same effect based on directives from the Secretary of Defense (Pious 2007). Are there emergency situations in which parallel governance might be justified? And in some cases, such as the "ticking bomb" scenario, would it make sense to legalize what otherwise could never be legal (i.e., torture)? Or does it make more sense to follow Justice Jackson's dissenting opinion in *Korematsu*, in which he did not take issue with the internment of Japanese and Japanese-Americans

---

[1] Justice Sutherland's opinion in *US* v. *Curtiss-Wright Export Corp.*, 299 US 304 (1936) at 319.

during the Second World War, but argued that the courts should be the last, not the first, to give up on the limits of governmental power in emergencies.

Power Stakes, Reputation, and Prerogative

The principle of consilience may be utilized to open up a useful line of research that unites Neustadt's power stakes (the need to make decisions today with an eye on how they will affect options for the exercise of influence at a later date), with the presidential choice to rely on prerogative power. One example would be Franklin Roosevelt's decision to reach an agreement with the United Kingdom on the transfer of destroyers for bases in the Caribbean. At all stages, FDR thought about his power stakes: he held up the deal until Churchill agreed to promise publicly that in the event of British capitulation, the Royal Navy would scuttle the destroyers (a humiliation for Churchill who agreed most reluctantly); and he refused to approve the Navy's draft of the deal that transferred sovereignty to the US. Doing so would have required substitution of the British racial code on the island for the strict segregation of the US South, and would have put strains on FDR's congressional party. It also would have allowed imports from the islands to arrive without being subject to the tariff, further straining the Northern and Southern wings of the party. Thus, the final decision to make the deal an executive agreement rather than seek congressional approval was made in order to keep members of Congress from having to go on record with a controversial vote.

The case study approach lends itself to this kind of analysis, which could also be used to indicate when presidents back off on asserting their prerogative claims. FDR's willingness to accept a legislative veto in the Lend-Lease legislation, and Ford's acceptance of a legislative veto in legislation authorizing a Sinai observer force, would be two examples of how political calculations trump constitutional claims. Similarly, Carter's signaling to Congress that, although he believed the War Powers Act to be unconstitutional, as a matter of political expediency a Democratic president would not pursue military hostilities against the wishes of a Democratic Congress is an indication of a tactical decision to forgo a claim of hard prerogative and instead substitute a decisional rule involving coordinate decision making. Another useful line of inquiry involves the impact that exercise of prerogative may have on presidential reputation. Franklin Roosevelt is reputed to have asked his aides for "something I can veto" in order to enhance his reputation in Congress. Do calculations about reputation and influence affect the exercise of prerogative power, especially the power to veto? Some of the "veto bargaining" literature (discussed below) has begun to explore these issues (McCarty 2000).

Prerogatives and Behavioral Social Science

The case study approach can be utilized to determine whether prerogative power or the persuasive approach is better suited for crisis diplomacy (Holder 1986; Pious

2001). Small group decision-making studies can be linked to the decision to rely on prerogative power. Having to go to Congress may foster more collegial discussions, require the preparation of more thorough materials in order to "make the case," and foster a more collaborative and less arbitrary style of decision making, but as yet we do not have systematic studies that demonstrate that effect. Nor do we have more than speculative biographical assertions that the capacity to bypass Congress creates the arbitrary atmosphere of the Palace Guard (Rather 1974).

Since the 1990s, political scientists have used massive databases to quantify the use of prerogative power, especially recess appointments, vetoes and signing statements, and the issuing of executive orders and executive agreements (Cameron 2000; McCarty and Poole 1995; McCarty 1997, 2000; Howell 2003; Warber 2006). These involve time series and associations of factors such as split versus party governance, high versus low presidential approval ratings, length of time in office, routine versus crisis situations, domestic versus foreign policies, and Republican versus Democratic presidents. We are beginning to develop an understanding of what factors are causal and associated with changes in "normal" outputs based on prerogative. It is also possible to quantify the responses of courts to assertions of presidential prerogative (Ducat and Dudley 1989; Howell 2003), as well as congressional responses. Some studies confirm what political scientists and journalists already knew: bills are more likely to be vetoed in divided government, and Congress makes concessions when it re-passes measures after vetoes (Cameron 2000). Others are counter-intuitive, such as the finding that executive orders are more likely in periods of party government rather than split government (Howell 2003).

Unilateral Action and Game Theory

The most recent development in the study of prerogative involves efforts to model the logic of substitution of prerogative power for legislative authorization. One version provides a variant of political economy and rational choice spatial modeling to calculate policy pay-offs and determine whether the president obtains better spatial positioning through unilateral action or through passage of a statute (Howell 2003). The initial formal models are simple, but the authors admit they are deliberately "unrealistic" since they are simplified to illustrate the fundamental logic of the choice; this is followed by modeling that is more complex and realistic. Future work in the area of executive orders will want to distinguish among different types of orders: executive or military; secret or open; those implementing statute or treaty law or those based solely on constitutional clauses. It is likely that distinguishing between national security "one-off" singular issues (i.e. whether or not to authorize military tribunals), versus those that involve an ongoing and routine stream of policy (such as expanding the national park system), will give us a better sense of the use of prerogative power than lumping all categories together.

Similarly, the preliminary efforts to model veto games, especially those using spatial models to develop hypotheses about when presidents will veto, when Congress will respond and in what manner, and under what circumstances the game will end with a veto or will result in accommodation and legislation being passed, will require more complex approaches (Cameron 2000). The essence of all vetoes cannot be accurately described along a spatial continuum, since some bills involve valences and "value politics" without much room for compromising spatially, such as abortion and other "rights of the unborn" funding cut-offs, in which the issue is not "more or less" money but the morality of the activity. Other legislation involves the scope of governmental power, issues involving federalism, perhaps, or presidential war powers, or powers of the judiciary. Policy differences may be discontinuous and not subject to movement along a continuum. Not all pay-offs can be expressed in terms of spatial positioning even on issues where spatial positioning is important. In budget and tax issues that are spatially defined, for instance, other pay-offs involve media coverage and public opinion, which translates into public approval and prestige ratings. A great deal of veto politics concerns the calibration of spatial shifts involving the bill with the external pay-offs. This would affect the rational choice about when and how to communicate, to posture, to make offers of compromise, to walk away, or to negotiate again. Each of these factors should be built into future models, even though their complexity will increase.

The early formal "veto bargaining" models restricted themselves to a presidential choice to veto or not to veto. Yet public law and other scholars of presidential–congressional interactions have long been aware, and have long researched, other outcomes. These include a willingness: (a) to permit a bill to become law, followed by a decision to defer spending, or to ask for rescission of spending; (b) to adopt a "signing statement" interpreting law in ways inconsistent with legislative intent; (c) to hold off on spending because of technicalities; (d) to use provisions of statutory impoundment (i.e., failure to conform with statutory requirements); and (e) to use other techniques (e.g., quarterly allocations by OMB) to ensure that spending conforms to presidential priorities, even when the president signs a bill that purportedly allocates funds according to the dictates of a "winning" congressional coalition. The work of the "veto scholars" in the future needs to incorporate the ways in which presidents play spending games.

Veto bargaining literature may want to exploit some of the knowledge of political behavior gleaned at the state level. Consider the influence of the executive veto on pork barrel distributions by the legislature. The original veto bargaining models posited that there will be a lower level of distributive spending when the veto is brandished or applied. Yet empirical findings about a similar executive power at the state level—the item veto—indicate that the governor gains great influence over spending bills passed by the state legislature. But spending is not lowered, and instead is actually increased to conform to gubernatorial priorities. One might hypothesize that at the national level a presidential veto power in the appropriations process does not result in lowered expenditures, but rather, through the additional accretion of presidential influence in Congress, the level of expenditure *increases* to conform to presidential priorities (McCarty 2000). This in fact seemed to be the case during the brief use of the item veto in the Clinton presidency, when enhanced rescission reduced congressionally mandated expenditures by 1 percent, but allowed Clinton to amass political power sufficient to increase executive priorities by a far higher amount. This also would be the case in 2007 during the veto bargaining between president and Congress over the Iraq War, since any presidential victory would result in increasing the length of stay of US forces, and likely increase both the direct war expenditures as well as pork barrel funding in the defense budget that in the past has accompanied appropriations.

The study of presidential prerogative power is likely to advance on all three fronts: through doctrinal approaches, behavioral approaches, and the use of formal modeling. So long as the imprecision of the original constitutional language is compounded by "ambition countering ambition," the system of partial separation of powers and checks and balances will provide the temptation for presidents to act unilaterally, and the need for political scientists to observe, analyze, and evaluate the impact of their actions.

References

ADLER, D. G., and GEORGE, L. N. (eds.) 1998. *The Constitution and the Conduct of American Foreign Policy.* Lawrence: University of Kansas Press.
—— and GENOVESE, M. 2002. *The Presidency and the Law: The Clinton Legacy.* Lawrence: University Press of Kansas.
ARNHART, L. 1979. "The God-Like Prince:" John Locke, Executive Prerogative, and the American Presidency. *Presidential Studies Quarterly,* 9: 121–30.
BAILEY, J. D. 2004. Executive Prerogative and the "Good Officer" in Thomas Jefferson's Letter to John B. Colvin. *Presidential Studies Quarterly,* 34: 732–55.
BAKER, N. V. 2006. *General Ashcroft: Attorney at War.* Lawrence: University of Kansas Press.
BALDWIN, S. E. 1897. Absolute Power, An American Institution. *Yale Law Journal,* 7: 1–19.
BARBER, J. D. 1972. *The Presidential Character: Predicting Performance in the White House.* Englewood Cliffs, NJ: Prentice-Hall.
BELZ, H. 1988. Lincoln and the Constitution: The "Dictatorship Question" Reconsidered. *Congress and the Presidency,* 15: 147–64.
BERNSTEIN, B. J. 1976. The Road to Watergate and Beyond: The Growth and Abuse of Executive Authority since 1940. *Law and Contemporary Problems,* 40: 58–86.
BESSETTE, J. M., and TULIS, J. (eds.) 1981. *The Presidency in the Constitutional Order.* Baton Rouge: Louisiana State University Press.
BOWMAN, M. 1988. Presidential Emergency Powers Related to International Economic Transactions. *Vanderbilt Journal of Transnational Law,* 11: 515–34.
BURGESS, C. 1994. When May a President Refuse to Enforce the Law? *Texas Law Review,* 72: 631–67.
BURNS, J. M. 1965. *Presidential Government.* Boston: Houghton Mifflin.
CALABRESE, S. 1994. The Vesting Clauses as Power Grants. *Northwestern University Law Review,* 88: 1377–405.
CAMERON, C. M. 2000. *Veto Bargaining: President as the Politics of Negative Power.* New York: Cambridge University Press.
CAREY, J. M., and SHUGART, M. S. 1998. *Executive Decree Authority.* New York: Cambridge University Press.

CASPER, G. 1985. The Constitutional Organization of the Government. *William and Mary Law Review*, 26: 177–98.

CHEMERINSKY, E. 1983. Controlling Inherent Presidential Power: Providing a Framework for Judicial Review. *Southern California Law Review*, 56: 863–912.

CLAYTON, C. W. 1995. *Government Lawyers*. Lawrence: University of Kansas Press.

COLE, D., and DEMPSEY, J. X. 2002. *Terrorism and the Constitution*. New York: New Press.

COOKE, J. E. (ed.) 1961. *The Federalist Papers*. Middleton, CT: Wesleyan University Press.

COOPER, P. J. 2002. *By Order of the President: The Use and Abuse of Executive Direct Action.* Lawrence: University Press of Kansas.

CORWIN, E. S. 1941. Some Aspects of the Presidency. *Annals of the American Academy of Political and Social Science*, 21: 122–31.

——1949. The Presidency in Perspective. *Journal of Politics*, 11: 7–13.

——1953. The Steel Seizure Case: A Judicial Brick without Straw. *Columbia Law Review*, 53: 53–66.

——1957. *The President: Office and Powers, 1787–1948*. New York: New York University Press.

CRONIN, T. E. (ed.) 1989. *Inventing the American Presidency*. Lawrence: University Press of Kansas.

CROVITZ, L. G., and RABKIN, J. A. (eds.) 1989. *The Fettered Presidency: Legal Constraints on the Executive Branch.* Washington, DC: American Enterprise Institute for Public Policy Research.

DENNISON, G. M. 1974. Martial Law: The Development of a Theory of Emergency Powers, 1776–1861. *American Journal of Legal History*, 18: 52–79.

DUCAT, C. R., and DUDLEY, R. L. 1989. Federal District Judges and Presidential Power during the Postwar Era. *Journal of Politics*, 51: 98–118.

EASTLAND, T. 1992. *Energy in the Executive: The Case for the Strong Presidency*. New York: Free Press.

FAIRMAN, C. 1942. The Law of Martial Rule and the National Emergency. *Harvard Law Review*, 55: 1253–302.

FAUSOLD, M. L., and SHANK, A. (eds.) 1991. *The Constitution and the American Presidency*. Albany, NY: SUNY Press.

FISHER, L. 1995. *Presidential War Power*. Lawrence: University Press of Kansas.

——1997. *Constitutional Conflicts between Congress and the President*, 4th rev. edn. Lawrence: University Press of Kansas.

——2000. *Congressional Abdication on War and Spending*. College Station: Texas A&M University Press.

——2006. *In the Name of National Security*. Lawrence: University Press of Kansas.

FRANCK, T. M., and WEISBAND, E. 1979. *Foreign Policy by Congress*. New York: Oxford University Press.

FRANKLIN, D. P. 1991. *Extraordinary Measures*. Pittsburgh: University of Pittsburgh Press.

FULLER, G. 1979. Note: The National Emergency Dilemma: Balancing the Executive's Crisis Powers with the Need for Accountability. *Southern California Law Review*, 52: 1453–511.

GENOVESE, M. 1979. Democratic Theory and the Emergency Powers of the President. *Presidential Studies Quarterly*, 9: 283–9.

GEORGE, A. L. 1980. *Presidential Decisionmaking in Foreign Policy: The Effective Use of Information and Advice.* Boulder, CO: Westview Press.

GLENNON, M. J. 1984. The Use of Custom in Resolving Separation of Powers Disputes. *Boston University Law Review*, 64: 109–48.

——1990. *Constitutional Diplomacy*. Princeton, NJ: Princeton University Press.

HENKIN, L. 1972. *Foreign Affairs and the Constitution*. Mineola, NY: Foundation Press.

HOEKSTRA, D. J. 1985. Presidential Power and Presidential Purpose. *Review of Politics*, 47: 566–87.
——1989. Neustadt, Barber and Presidential Statesmanship: The Problem of Lincoln. *Presidential Studies Quarterly*, 19: 285–99.
HOLDER, J. S. 1986. The Sources of Presidential Power: John Adams and the Challenge to Executive Primacy. *Political Science Quarterly* 101: 601–16.
HOWELL, W. G. 2003. *Power without Persuasion: The Politics of Direct Presidential Action.* Princeton, NJ: Princeton University Press.
——and PEVEHOUSE, J. C. 2007. *While Dangers Gather: Congressional Checks on Presidential War Power.* Princeton, NJ: Princeton University Press.
HURTGEN, J. 1975. The Case for Presidential Prerogative. *Toledo Law Review*, 7: 59–87.
JACKSON, R. H. 2003. *That Man: An Insider's Portrait of Franklin D. Roosevelt.* New York: Oxford University Press.
KELLY, C. S. (ed.) 2006. *Executing the Constitution: Putting the President Back into the Constitution.* Albany, NY: SUNY Press.
KING, K. L., and MEERNIK, J. 1999. The Supreme Court and the Powers of the Executive: The Adjudication of Foreign Policy. *Political Research Quarterly*, 52: 801–24.
KLIEMAN, A. S. 1979. Preparing for the Hour of Need: The National Emergencies Act. *Presidential Studies Quarterly*, 9: 47–64.
KOH, H. H. 1990. *The National Security Constitution.* New Haven, CT: Yale University Press.
KOHN, R. H. 1972. The Washington Administration's Decision to Crush the Whiskey Rebellion. *Journal of American History*, 59: 567–84.
KURLAND, P. B. 1986. The Rise and Fall of the "Doctrine" of Separation of Powers. *Michigan Law Review*, 85: 592–613.
LANGSTON, T. S., and LIND, M. E. 1991. John Locke and the Limits of Presidential Prerogative. *Polity*, 24: 49–68.
LOBEL, J. 1989. Emergency Power and the Decline of Liberalism. *Yale Law Journal*, 98: 1384–433.
LOCKE, J. 1988. *John Locke: Two Treatises of Government*, ed. P. Laslett. New York: Cambridge University Press.
MCCARTY, N. M. 1997. Presidential Reputation and the Veto. *Economics and Politics*, 9/1: 1–26.
——2000. Presidential Pork: Executive Veto Power and Distributive Politics. *American Political Science Review*, 94: 117–30.
——and POOLE, K. T. 1995. Veto Power and Legislation: An Empirical Analysis of Executive and Legislative Bargaining from 1961–1986. *Journal of Law, Economics and Organization*, 11: 282–312.
MANSFIELD, H. C., JR. 1987. The Modern Doctrine of Executive Power. *Presidential Studies Quarterly*, 17: 237–52.
——1993. *Taming the Prince: The Ambivalence of Modern Executive Power.* Baltimore: Johns Hopkins University Press.
MARCUS, M. 1977. *Truman and the Steel Seizure Case.* New York: Columbia University Press.
MATTHEWS, S. A. 1989. Veto Threats: Rhetoric in a Bargaining Game. *Quarterly Journal of Economics*, 104: 347–69.
MAYER, K. R. 2001. *With the Stroke of a Pen: Executive Orders and Presidential Power.* Princeton, NJ: Princeton University Press.
MILLER, A. 1980. Reason of State and the Emergent Constitution of Control. *Minnesota Law Review*, 64: 585–633.
——1987. The President and the Faithful Execution of the Laws. *Vanderbilt Law Review*, 40/2: 389–406.
MOE, T. 1999. Unilateral Action and Presidential Power: A Theory. *Presidential Studies Quarterly*, 29: 850–72.

—— and HOWELL, W. G. 1999. The Presidential Power of Unilateral Action. *Journal of Law, Economics and Organization*, 15: 132–79.

MONAGHAN, H. P. 1993. The Protective Power of the Presidency. *Columbia Law Review*, 93: 1–74.

NEUSTADT, R. E. 1960. *Presidential Power*. New York: John Wiley & Sons.

PALLITTO, R. M., and WEAVER, W. G. 2007. *Presidential Secrecy and the Law*. Baltimore: Johns Hopkins University Press.

PATTERSON, B. H. 1988. *The Ring of Power*. New York: Basic Books.

PATTERSON, J. T. 1976. The Rise of Presidential Power before World War II. *Law and Contemporary Problems*, 40: 39–57.

PIOUS, R. M. 1979. *The American Presidency*. New York: Basic Books.

—— 1996. *The Presidency*. Boston: Allyn & Bacon.

—— 2001. The Cuban Missile Crisis and the Limits to Crisis Decisionmaking. *Political Science Quarterly*, 116: 81–105.

—— 2006. Public Law and the "Executive" Constitution. In *Executing the Constitution*, ed. C. Kelley. Albany, NY: SUNY Press.

—— 2007. Torture of Detainees and Presidential Prerogative Power. In *The Polarized Presidency of George W. Bush*, ed. G. C. Edwards III and D. S. King. New York: Oxford University Press.

—— Forthcoming. The President and Military Tribunals. In *The Constitutional Presidency*, ed. J. M. Bessette and J. Tulis. Baltimore: Johns Hopkins University Press.

POLLITT, D. H. 1958. Presidential Use of Troops to Execute the Laws: A Brief History. *North Carolina Law Review*, 36: 117–41.

PYLE, C. H. 1970. CONUS Intelligence: The Army Watches Civilian Politics. *Washington Monthly*, 1 : 4–16.

—— and PIOUS, R. 1984. *The President, Congress and the Constitution*. New York: Free Press.

RATHER, D. 1974. *The Palace Guard*. New York: Harper & Row.

RELYEA, H. 1976. Declaring and Terminating State of Emergency. *Presidential Studies Quarterly*, 6: 36–42.

ROBINSON, D. L. 1973. The Routinization of Crisis Government. *Yale Law Review*, 63: 161–74.

—— 1987. *To the Best of my Ability: The Presidency and the Constitution*. New York: Norton.

ROCHE, J. P. 1952. Executive Power and Domestic Emergency: The Quest for Prerogative. *Western Political Quarterly*, 5: 592–618.

ROSE, R. 2000. *The Postmodern President*, 2nd edn. New York: Chatham House.

ROSSITER, C. L. 1948. *Constitutional Dictatorship*. Princeton, NJ: Princeton University Press.

—— 1949. Constitutional Dictatorship in the Atomic Age. *Review of Politics*, 2: 395–418.

ROSTOW, E. V. 1945. The Japanese American Cases: A Disaster. *Yale Law Journal*, 54: 489–533.

SCHLESINGER, A. M., JR. 1973. *The Imperial Presidency*. Boston: Houghton Mifflin.

SCHUBERT, G. A. 1953. The Steel Case: Presidential Responsibility and Judicial Irresponsibility. *Western Political Quarterly*, 6: 61–77.

SCHWARZ, F. A. O., and HUQ, A. Z. 2007. *Unchecked and Unbalanced*. New York: New Press.

SILVERSTEIN, G. 1997. *Imbalance of Powers*. New York: Oxford University Press.

SKOWRONEK, S. 1993. *The Politics Presidents Make*. Cambridge, MA: Belknap Press of Harvard University Press.

SMITH, J. M. 1960. *Powers of the President during Crises*. Washington, DC: Public Affairs Press.

SORENSON, L. 1989. The Federalist Papers on the Constitutionality of Executive Prerogative. *Presidential Studies Quarterly*, 19/2: 267–83.

SPITZER, R. L. 1988. *The Presidential Veto*. Albany, NY: SUNY Press.

STURM, A. 1949. Emergencies and the Presidency. *Journal of Politics*, 11/1: 121–44.

SUNDQUIST, J. L. 1981. *The Decline and Resurgence of Congress*. Washington, DC: Brookings Institution.

TAFT, W. H. 1916. *Our Chief Magistrate and his Powers*. New York: Columbia University Press.

THOMAS, G. 2000. As Far as Republican Principles Will Admit: Presidential Prerogative and Constitutional Government. *Presidential Studies Quarterly*, 30: 534–53.

UPSHUR, A. P. 1840. *A Brief Inquiry into the Nature and Character of our Federal Government*. New York: Da Capo Press, 1971.

VERKUIL, P. R. 1989. Separation of Powers: The Rule of Law and the Idea of Independence. *William and Mary Law Review*, 30: 301–41.

WARBER, A. 2006. *Executive Orders and the Modern Presidency: Legislating from the Oval Office*. Boulder, CO: Lynne Rienner Publishers.

WHITE, L. 1948. *The Federalists*. New York: Free Press.

——1951. *The Jeffersonians*. New York: Free Press.

——1954. *The Jacksonians*. New York: Free Press.

——1958. *The Republican Era*. New York: Free Press.

WILMERDING, L. 1952. The President and the Law. *Political Science Quarterly*, 67: 321–38.

WILSON, W. 1885. *Congressional Government*. Boston: Houghton Mifflin.

WINTERTON, G. 1979. The Concept of Extra-Constitutional Executive Power in Domestic Affairs. *Hastings Constitutional Law Quarterly*, 7: 1–46.

YOO, J. 2006. *War by Other Means*. New York: Atlantic Monthly Press.

CHAPTER 21

ASSESSING THE UNILATERAL PRESIDENCY

RICHARD W. WATERMAN

NEUSTADT (1980, 27) famously reminds us "President's 'powers' may be inconclusive when a President commands, but always remain relevant as he persuades." Yet, as Congress becomes more ideologically polarized (Brady and Volden 2005; Krehbiel 1998), as there is a greater propensity for divided government (Cameron 2000), and as the Washington community becomes more politically hostile to the idea of a bargaining presidency (see Kernell 1997; though see Edwards 2003), can presidents lead by persuasion alone? If not, what else can presidents do to facilitate leadership?

One answer is that presidents can employ a variety of political resources to accomplish unilaterally what they can no longer do through traditional legislative means. According to Moe and Howell (1999a, 132), a president has the "formal capacity to act unilaterally and to make law on his own." Unilateral action consists of everything from issuing executive orders and proclamations, to making executive agreements with other nations, to initiating foreign policy through National Security Directives, to interpreting the law through presidential memoranda and signing statements. In each case, presidents govern directly through executive fiat. In this chapter, I survey the literature on the president's unilateral powers and examine the implications of the related unitary executive model. I begin by examining the relationship between unilateral power and Neustadt's bargaining model.

AN ALTERNATIVE TO NEUSTADT'S BARGAINING MODEL

Richard Neustadt articulated a model of presidential bargaining in 1960, periodically revising and updating it for the next four decades. The central tenet of the model is the idea that presidents do not have the power to command. Rather, they must secure influence through a process of bargaining and compromising with other Washington elites, but particularly with members of Congress. To build the congressional coalitions which are necessary to govern, presidents must rely on their political skill and personal reputations. Yet, if presidents only can influence Congress, as the title of Edward's (1989) book suggests, "at the margins," and if building coalitions is an increasingly difficult process, as Seligman and Covington (1989) argue, then is a bargaining strategy sufficient to promote presidential power and leadership?

To answer this question we must look at Neustadt's basic model. His argument is cogent and compelling. Neustadt argues that presidents must use their resources wisely if they are to have influence in Washington. Leadership does not derive from specific constitutional delegations of authority (the president's constitutional authority is vague), so presidents lack the ability to command. In fact, one of the case studies that Neustadt employs to demonstrate the ineffectiveness of the command strategy was initiated by unilateral action. Truman's executive order, which permitted the US government to seize the nation's steel mills, was subsequently rebuked by the Supreme Court (see Marcus 1994).

If presidents cannot command, then how precisely can they lead? Neustadt's answer is straightforward. They must lead by persuasion; that is, they must be able to bargain and compromise with other policy actors, but mostly with Congress, if they are to accomplish their main objectives. To help them in this process, presidents have certain resources at their disposal. For example, Dwight Eisenhower had a reputation for leadership which was based on his war and post-war experiences. He had the potential, then, to translate this reputation into real influence with members of the Washington establishment, particularly on matters of foreign policy. But political resources are finite. Those presidents who overused their political currency, such as Lyndon Johnson and Richard Nixon, eventually lost the ability to be effective leaders.

The political calculation for modern presidents, then, is difficult. They must build up and use their political resources wisely. If they hoard them, as Eisenhower did, then they are not effective leaders. Leadership requires vision and a willingness to act. On the other hand, a president with vision, such as Lyndon Johnson, used his resources unwisely, and while he left an amazing record of accomplishment in the end, he also lost the ability to govern. Successful presidents, then, are those like Franklin Roosevelt and Harry Truman, who were more effective at using the tools of bargaining and compromise to get what they wanted (e.g., Roosevelt with the New Deal, the Second New Deal, Lend-Lease, etc.; Truman and the Marshall Plan).

While Neustadt's basic insights are still relevant today and offer many useful guides for presidential leadership (e.g., by his seventh year in office, George W. Bush's governance approach left him with few political resources to build congressional coalitions, even with members of his own party), Neustadt's model was initially designed to describe the president's relationship in a political world that existed almost fifty years ago. Much has changed since that time. The relationship between presidents and such external political actors as Congress, the media, and interest groups is far more confrontational than it once was. As politics becomes more of a contact sport, and as gridlock permeates the relationship between the White House and Capitol Hill, presidents find that they have less room to negotiate, build coalitions, bargain, and compromise. For this reason, presidents in recent decades have employed, to a far greater extent than their predecessors, a variety of unilateral powers. For example, as Howell (2005, 417) notes, "During the first 150 years of the nation's history, treaties (which require Senate ratification) regularly outnumbered executive agreements (which do not); but during the last 50 years, presidents have signed roughly ten executive agreements for every treaty that was submitted to Congress." And while "the total number of executive orders has declined, presidents issued almost four times as many 'significant' orders in the second half of the twentieth century as they did in the first." Presidents also are making greater use of presidential signing statements and National Security Directives either to express their policy views or to design and initiate foreign policy. Since these techniques generally do not get the same level of media scrutiny as treaties, vetoes, or legislation, and since they rarely are challenged by Congress or the courts, they provide a potent source of presidential influence.

This greater use of unilateral power has important implications for Neustadt's bargaining model. As Howell (2005, 421) writes, "The ability to move first and act alone . . . distinguishes unilateral actions from other sources of influence. Indeed, the central precepts of Neustadt's argument are turned upside down, for unilateral action is the virtual antithesis of persuasion." A new theory, one that bridges the gap between negotiation and unilateral action, therefore is required. Thus far, Howell (2003) provides the most fully developed and cogently articulated alternative to Neustadt's traditional bargaining model, though for another critique see Mayer (2001, ch. 1). Howell (2003, 27) writes,

A theory of unilateral action should have two characteristics. First, it should account for the president's first-mover advantage . . . Second, whenever presidents contemplate a unilateral action, they anticipate how Congress and the judiciary will respond. The limits to unilateral powers are critically defined by the capacity, and willingness, of Congress and the judiciary to overturn the president. Rarely will presidents issue a unilateral directive when they know that other branches of government will subsequently reverse it.

This means that presidents cannot act unilaterally with impunity on any issue. They will not act unilaterally if there is a high probability that Congress or the courts will reverse their action. A study by Olson and Woll (1999) for the Cato Institute finds that 206 executive orders were terminated or changed by Congress between the beginning of Franklin Roosevelt's presidency and George H. W. Bush's presidency (see also Warber 2006, 111). On the other hand, Moe and Howell (1999a) identified thirty-six attempts by Congress to overturn executive orders and found only one was successful. Howell (2003) also finds limited evidence that Congress overturns executive orders. Presidents do not have an unfettered ability to issue executive orders without considering the will of Congress (see Howell and Kriner 2008). In addition to Congress, the courts also can invalidate executive orders, though as is the case with Congress, they rarely do so (see Howell 2003, 136–7).

Congress also may decide not to fund a program a president creates via executive order. In this case, presidents can transfer funds from other accounts to pay for programs that they create unilaterally (as Kennedy did when he created the Peace Corps), but in the long term, if an executive order requires funding, then a president must bring Congress on board. Hence, an executive order can be a tool that can position a president to be in a better bargaining position with Congress. Thus, as Howell (2003) reminds us, Neustadt's bargaining model and the use of unilateral power need not be mutually exclusive approaches to the development of presidential power. Rather, presidents can, at times, use their unilateral powers to develop a stronger bargaining relationship with Congress. Extrapolating from Neustadt, wise use of unilateral power (like other presidential resources) can advance presidential influence with Congress. This is important because for many issues, particularly for those that are highly salient, presidents generally still seek change through the traditional legislative route.

Still, even on some high-profile issues, presidents seek change through unilateral action, especially if the bargaining approach fails. For example, in 2007, after Congress failed to enact significant immigration reform legislation, President George W. Bush instituted many of the reforms he had proposed legislatively through unilateral action, particularly those related to making the borders more secure (e.g., ideas attractive to his conservative base).

Unilateral action therefore offers an alternative to the Neustadt bargaining model for presidents who seek to increase their political influence. But it does more than that. It also reverses the constitutionally prescribed role of the president and the Congress. In traditional bargaining models, Congress acts first. The president then can either sign the legislation or act as a veto player, blocking action that he does not like or using the veto to negotiate a more favorable outcome (Cameron 2000). With unilateral action, the president moves first with Congress playing the veto role. The president now not only takes on the role of policy initiator and adopter, but Congress is forced to muster a majority of votes in both houses to pass legislation invalidating the president's action. Even if Congress has a majority, sixty votes in the Senate are necessary to successfully adopt a cloture vote ending a filibuster, and if the bill is passed and the president vetoes it, a two-thirds vote in both congressional chambers is required to override the veto. As a result, overturning unilateral action is a formidable task, one that requires considerable and prolonged congressional action. As for the judiciary, it too may move to invalidate unilateral action. Since, however, the courts often cite executive orders, signing statements, and other unilateral actions to justify their decisions and have generally shown deference to these presidential actions, the likelihood of a judicial reversal is relatively small. Consequently, when presidents issue executive orders, or take other unilateral action, they know that the chance of reversal by Congress or the courts is minimal.

Howell's model is designed only to explain the issuing of executive orders, but the logic of presidents acting first with Congress or the courts essentially playing the veto role also applies to other unilateral powers, though thus far executive orders are more likely to secure congressional and media attention than are other types of unilateral powers. Congress may not even be provided with the details of a National Security Directive until years after it is issued. Likewise, until very recently, presidential signing statements have received relatively little media or scholarly attention. Therefore, unilateral action provides the promise of increased authority, without a palpable legislative or judicial check, often outside of the klieg lights of public and media attention. This makes them a highly attractive option for presidents who seek political influence.

If presidents are rational strategic actors, as Moe (1985) suggests, then unilateral power also provides another benefit. Presidents can use this authority to manipulate the policy agenda. They can do so by creating bureaucratic structures unilaterally (Moe and Wilson 1994). With regard to the legislative branch, if Congress is set to adopt a policy that a president does not like, the president can preempt action by issuing an executive order that will satisfy enough members of Congress to forestall legislative action. If policy is located within the "gridlock interval"—a region in policy space where the ideological alignments of members of Congress are not favorably predisposed to the enactment of legislation—policy action is therefore unlikely (Brady and Volden 2005). Under these circumstances, presidents can move an issue to a new position in policy space—that is, outside of the gridlock interval—where legislative action is more feasible. Likewise, if presidents want to block major change, they can issue executive orders that move an issue directly into the gridlock interval. A strategic president, then, can use unilateral powers to set the policy agenda, encourage congressional action, or, alternatively, discourage it (see Howell 2003, 35). On many issues, then, unilateral power provides presidents with a considerable ability to act.

UNDERSTANDING UNILATERAL POWER

While there are a number of unilateral powers, political scientists focus most of their attention on executive orders.

Executive Orders

As Mayer (2001, 65) writes, "Executive orders are a potent instrument of presidential authority." Still, presidents can use them to make all policy, so when are they most likely to issue them? This is an important question, for if presidents issue a greater number of executive orders when they are confronted with divided government or when congressional gridlock exists, then one can argue that presidents are rational and strategic actors who use directives to overcome the constraints presented by the separation of powers. Yet if they issue more executive orders during propitious legislative times, such as during periods of unified government, then it suggests that presidents issue more directives when there are few risks that Congress will overturn them. In this case, presidents either would be risk averse or merely issue orders perfunctorily as a means of implementing legislation. What, then, does the evidence from the literature tell us?

One early study by Morgan (1970) argues that presidents are more likely to issue executive orders when Congress is unwilling to pass legislation. Other scholars also adopted this strategic argument (see Cooper 1986; Wigton 1996). But the evidence from studies of divided government suggests otherwise. For instance, Shull (1997) finds that presidents issue more total executive orders during periods of unified rather than divided government (see also Gleiber and Shull 1992; Gomez and Shull 1995). Mayer (1999; 2001, 99–102) examines presidents who faced both unified and divided government during their terms in office and finds that both Clinton and Eisenhower issued more executive orders during periods of unified government. Krause and Cohen (1997) argue that the number of seats the president's party holds in the House is positively correlated with the number of executive orders presidents issue, while a negative correlation exists between the number of Senate seats and the number of directives issued. But, Cohen and Krause (2000) provide no empirical evidence that the number of executive orders is related to the number of seats held by the president's party in either the House or the Senate. In a more recent study, Warber (2006, 66) concludes that during periods of unified government, presidents issue more routine executive orders. As for policy-oriented executive orders, Democrats issue a greater number during periods of unified government, while Republicans issue more under divided government, though Warber admits to having only two years of unified Republican rule in his dataset (not enough to make a reliable generalization).

The literature on executive orders and divided government is nicely summed up by Howell (2003, 70), who writes,

Though presidents may want to exercise their unilateral powers more often during periods of divided government, they should have a harder time doing so. When Congress is controlled by the opposite party, legislative restrictions on presidential powers are greatest. Presidents, ironically, enjoy the broadest discretion to act unilaterally precisely when they have the weakest incentives to take advantage of it—during periods of unified government. It is possible then, that the heightened incentives to act unilaterally are cancelled out by the losses in discretion to do so, nullifying any effect divided government might have on presidential policy making.

If divided government is an impediment to presidential action, then is there any evidence that presidents act strategically? There is if we focus instead on ideological differences between Congress and the president. Adopting the rational choice modeling approach introduced by Krehbiel (1998) and Brady and Volden (2005),

Deering and Maltzman (1999), Moe and Howell (1999a, 1999b), and Howell (2003) reconceptualize and reexamine the issue. Their argument is more sophisticated than the divided government literature because it includes both incentives for presidents to issue more executive orders (e.g., when gridlock exists and traditional legislative action is not probable), as well as the risks of such actions (that is the possibility that Congress can overturn a presidential directive).

Presidents also act strategically to thwart congressional action, or to secure legislation that is more consistent with their preferences. These models are multidimensional, examining both the incentives and constraints a strategic president must consider. As Deering and Maltzman (1999, 770–1) write,

A President's willingness to issue an executive order depends upon both his positive power to get legislation enacted by Congress and his negative power to stop legislation overturning such an executive order. Viewed in this light, presidential decisions regarding executive orders reflect strategic calculation. A President may find it difficult or impossible to change the status quo via legislative action. But in these same circumstances he may be able to maintain an executive order against hostile legislative action with judicious use of the veto. Under such conditions, an executive order will be the preferred institutional device for pursuing presidential policy goals.

The primary focus in Deering and Maltzman's research compares a president's ideal point with the ideological location of the median member of Congress (on a liberal to conservative scale). If the ideology of the median member is in accord with the president, then legislation is the preferred political arena. But as Krehbiel (1998) and Brady and Volden (2005) demonstrate, this condition is often not met. Presidents increasingly confront a large and expanding gridlock interval. As a result, the likelihood that important legislation will be enacted is decreasing. Under these circumstances, depending on their policy preferences, presidents can either effectively enact legislation unilaterally by issuing an executive order that reflects their personal preferences, moderate hostile congressional action (by issuing an order that gives the president less than he prefers by appealing to congressional moderates, hence forestalling more radical congressional action), or block an issue permanently by moving it squarely into the gridlock region. Thus, presidents can use executive orders for a variety of strategic reasons. Which option a president adopts depends on a calculation involving the potential costs versus the expected benefits of executive action.

Using this approach, Deering and Maltzman (1999, 777) find that "both a President's level of congressional support and his likelihood of being overturned by a congressional veto override are inversely related to the number of executive orders issued." On the other hand, while they find a positive relationship between the number of Senate seats and executive orders, they find no evidence either that the number of House seats matters or that a dummy variable representing divided government affects the president's propensity to act unilaterally. These findings are consistent with the thesis that presidents issue a greater number of executive orders when ideological congruence between the president and Congress is low and when the risks of executive action also are low.

Howell (2005, 43) likewise argues that "unilateral activity peaks during periods of congressional gridlock, and declines when Congress is better equipped to legislate on a wide array of policy issues. Presidents on average issue 'more significant orders' when the majority in Congress is relatively small and internally divided, and fewer when the majority party is larger and more unified." Howell's research provides additional support for the idea that presidents act strategically when they issue executive orders. Accordingly, we would expect a traditional Neustadt bargaining strategy to work best when the president and the median legislative member are not divided ideologically, that is, when there is a larger potential for presidents to be able to bargain and compromise with legislators. Persuasion should work best when presidents and members of Congress are already in ideological accord. But when this groundwork for a bargaining president is not present, Howell argues that presidents have strong incentives to use their unilateral powers.

While Howell (2003) and Deering and Maltzman (1999) employ the preference-base theoretical model introduced by Krehbiel (1998), Chiou and Rothenberg's (2007) research is more in line with the party-based effects argument posited in the congressional literature by Cox and McCubbins (1993, 2005). They argue that Howell's model is based on a unicameral legislature. Furthermore, other than examining the potential effects of divided government, Howell does not include specific measures to control for party-based effects (see also Dickinson 2004; Marshall and Pacelle 2005), though Chiou and Rothenberg pay little attention to the role of the courts (which Howell does). Chiou and Rothernberg introduce and test four party-based models. They find that their measure of the *unilateral action propensity* (UAP) is only significantly related to the issuing of executive orders when a president can "sway his party's legislative contingent" (Chiou and Rothenberg 2007, 22). They therefore advocate a presidential influence model based on party effects. Theoretically and empirically speaking, the unilateral presidency literature is now following directly in the footsteps of the same preference-based and party-based models that are currently being debated in the congressional literature.

While the preference and party-based models examine how and why presidents employ their unilateral powers, Cohen and Krause (2000) raise another important issue: whether presidents faced the same constraints in issuing executive orders over time. They include *time* in the equation by comparing a period when the presidency was first becoming institutionalized (1939–68) with a period when institutionalization was fully completed (1969–96). They argue that presidents acted differently in each period. Presidents were more opportunistic before "the presidency developed as an institution" (2000, 90). Presidential issuing of executive orders in the institutionalizing period can best be characterized by a president-centered model in which presidents act rationally and opportunistically (see Moe 1985). Once institutionalization occurred, however, presidents were constrained by expectations related to such factors as the state of the economy and the growth of the federal bureaucracy, and their behavior was more consistent with a presidency-centered model. Thus, different leadership strategies involving differential use of unilateral power should be identifiable at different periods in American history. As the political environment changes, the nature of presidential leadership changes, which means presidents will use their unilateral powers in different ways at different times (see Waterman 2007).

Others look at time from a different perspective. They examine time within presidential administrations. That is, do presidents issue more executive orders during their first or last year in office? Cohen and Krause (2000) find that since the institutionalization of the presidency, which they demarcate at 1969, presidents have issued more executive orders after their first year in office. For other results, see Mayer (2001), Howell and Mayer (2005), and Warber (2006).

Additional research raises another important question: What effect do executive orders exert on the formulation of public policy? While many studies simply examine the circumstances under which presidents act unilaterally, it is important to determine whether executive orders have a substantive impact as well. In an early study, Morgan (1970) found that the impact of a president's executive orders on discrimination constrained his successors' behavior. In a more recent study, Howell and Lewis (2002) examine the effects of executive orders on agency structure. They examine 425 agencies created between 1946 and 1995 and find that agencies presidents create through executive orders are less insulated from direct presidential control than are agencies created by Congress. From a practical perspective, this means that presidents who seek to control the bureaucracy will secure greater influence if they create an agency by executive order than if they follow a traditional legislative approach (see also Lewis 2003; Dodds 2006).

As this summary suggests, while there is a copious and varied literature examining executive orders, one key methodological issue is in need of greater attention: how does one count executive orders? Is it appropriate to include a count of all executive orders or are some directives more important than others? If so, then how does one measure the concept of a "significant order?" Many scholars simply analyze the total number of all executive orders as if they have the same common characteristics. But other than being issued by a president, there are important differences in the content of executive orders. As Howell (2003, 78–9) notes:

This approach, unfortunately, fails to distinguish significant from insignificant orders. This is of crucial importance, for the vast majority of executive orders, like laws, concern rather mundane affairs: renaming agencies, amending the retirement status of personnel...To the extent that we are interested in explaining when presidents set policy, however...we must find some method of separating those orders that are significant from those that are not.

Howell's analysis primarily focuses on significant orders. He uses three separate sources to identify them: "mentions of orders in federal court cases and in Congress for the 1945–1983 period; and mentions in the *New York Times* for the 1969–98 period" (Howell 2005, 430). His later work then uses the electronic search engine of the *Times* to examine all front-page mentions from 1945 to 2001 (ibid.). Mayer (2001, 83–4) uses a somewhat different schematic, examining such factors as whether an order received press attention, whether Congress held hearings, whether it is discussed in the legal literature, whether presidents themselves publicized the order by publishing it in the *Public Papers of the President,* and whether it created new institutions with substantive power.

Warber (2006) further differentiates executive orders by type. Following King and Ragsdale (1988), he examines executive orders by policy categories. He also content-analyzes all executive orders issued since 1936, when the US Congress mandated their publication in the *Federal Register*. He identifies four categories: symbolic, routine, policy, and hybrid orders, with policy orders being the most substantive. Routine orders tend to merely specify the manner in which a law will be carried out and who is responsible for implementation. Contrarily, Warber (2006, 143) coded an executive order as a policy directive "if it is either departing from the status quo of a specific policy that has already been implemented, or interpreting and implementing legislation that diverts from the original intent of Congress. In essence, an order is a policy initiative when its main function is presidential lawmaking." It is therefore important that, according to Warber (2006, 39), presidents in recent years have made greater use of policy rather than routine orders: 61.6 percent of all orders issued by Carter were policy orders, while the percentages for Reagan, G. H. W. Bush, and Clinton were 62.5, 62.1, and 73.9 respectively. While the number of orders issued each year does not reflect a clear pattern, presidents are making greater use of policy-related executive orders in recent years.

In summary, presidents can use unilateral resources such as their executive orders in routine and non-controversial ways, or they can seek to control policy. It is the latter case that is of most concern to scholars who perceive a dangerous trend in the growth of unilateral power. A concern with presidential power also lies at the heart of the debate about other unilateral powers.

Other Unilateral Powers

While there is an expanding literature with regard to executive orders, other resources of the unilateral presidency have received far less scholarly attention, particularly from political scientists. While Howell (2005, 47) notes that presidents over the past fifty years are making much greater use of executive agreements than treaties, the literature in this area lacks the same theoretical and empirical rigor developed by scholars of executive orders.

The first major study of executive agreements was conducted by an unlikely source, a civil servant working for the US government. Wallace McClure's 1941 study criticizes the treaty process for being undemocratic (e.g., it requires more than a majority in each house of Congress to secure passage of a treaty) and argues that presidents should make greater use of their executive agreement power (McClure 1967; see also McDougal and Lans 1945a, 1945b). From an operational perspective, McClure (1967, xii) notes that "personal judgment" was required in compiling the list of executive agreements, because prior to 1929, when the State Department commenced the *Executive Agreement Series*, there was no single data source for this unilateral technique.

In a more skeptical rebuttal, Borchard (1944) is concerned that executive agreements are replacing treaties. Likewise, Spindler (1953) critically examines the arguments for changing the Constitution, in particular the Bricker amendment, which would have limited executive power in making both treaties and executive agreements (see also Bricker 1953). The same skepticism is displayed by Paige (1977). His work fits with a number of studies from the 1970s that were critical of the expansion of presidential power in foreign affairs (Fisher 1972; Berger 1972; Schlesinger 1973; Gilbert 1973).

Johnson and McCormick (1978, 469–70) attempt to empirically address the issues raised by both sides. They note that "critics have argued that the foreign policy powers of Congress have eroded drastically through unilateral action by the Executive Branch." They provide a systematic survey "of all non-classified US foreign policy commitments from 1946 to 1972." Specifically, they "determine the extent to which Congress and the Executive Branch have participated in the making of international agreements over the 27 year period." They find (1978, 473–4):

The overwhelming percentage—almost 87 percent—of all United States agreements between 1946 and 1972 have been statutory. By contrast, executive agreements and treaties account for only 7 percent and 6 percent, respectively, of all agreements in this same period. These aggregate figures strongly suggest that Congress has not been left out of the agreement process; indeed it has participated in the vast majority of them. At the same time, though, the data confirm the notion that the treaty process has been replaced as the official instrument of foreign policy commitment. But again, in contrast to the conventional wisdom, treaties have been replaced not by executive agreements; but rather, by statutory agreements—instruments involving both Houses of Congress as well as the Executive Branch.

Furthermore, Johnson and McCormick (1977, 119) find that "treaties in the post-World War II period have been used mainly for important military commitments, not for trivial matters."

While Johnson and McCormick provided empirical evidence, the normative debate over the appropriateness of using executive agreements continued. Bloom (1985, 155) argues that the "demands of the executive branch are enormous" and provides an ardent defense of expanded executive power, including the broader use of executive agreements. On the other hand, Paul (1998) argues that the expansion of presidential power inherent in the use of such techniques as executive agreements has undercut presidential accountability. Likewise, Margolis (1985) examines whether executive agreements exclude the Senate from its constitutional treaty ratification function on important foreign policy matters (see also Tribe 1995).

While the literature on executive agreements is not inconsiderable, political scientists have contributed relatively little attention to this issue (see Klarevas 2003, 394). Surprisingly, the same is true of other unilateral powers. For example, Cooper (2005, ch. 7) identifies presidential signing statements as a tool of the unilateral presidency. They are not the equivalent of an executive order or an executive agreement, in that a new policy is established. But they do allow presidents to directly interpret the law.

Like many aspects of the unilateral presidency, the technique did not foster controversy when it was first used by James Monroe. It was not until the Reagan administration that presidents made consistent use of signing statements. To emphasize their greater importance, Reagan's second Attorney General, Edwin Meese, even added signing statements to the *Legislative History of the US Code, Congressional and Administrative News* (published by West Publishing Company) so they "could be available to the court for future consideration of what that statute really means" (Kelley 2005, 27). The Supreme Court relied on presidential signing statements in deciding both the *Chadha* and *Bowsher* cases in the 1980s.

Two developments are noteworthy with regard to the use of signing statements. First, presidents have vastly expanded their use of signing statements compared to past presidents. As Kelley (2005, 30–1) writes,

From the Monroe administration to the Carter administration, the executive branch issued a total of 75 signing statements that protected the presidential prerogatives and a total of 34 statements instructing the executive branch agencies of the interpretation of sections of the bill. From the Reagan administration through the Clinton administration, the number of both categories jumped drastically. The number of statements protecting the executive branch prerogatives went from 75 for all presidents up to Carter to 322, and the number of instructions to executive branch agencies on the interpretations of provisions of the law went from a total of 34 to 74.

George W. Bush then issued "435 statements, mostly objecting to encroachments upon presidential prerogative" during his first term (Kelley 2005, 31).

The second development reflects the use of signing statements, not merely to interpret the law, but as a surrogate for a line-item veto. This innovation commenced with the presidency of George W. Bush. As Savage (2007, 231) writes,

For years, political observers had puzzled about why Bush, who was so aggressive about exerting his executive prerogatives in every other respect, was not vetoing bills. As the full scope of Bush's use of signing statements became clear, so did the answer to the mystery: Bush's legal team was using signing statements as something better than a veto—something close to a line item veto.

In a variety of signing statements, the Bush administration would identify parts or sections of laws that it intended to ignore—in essence announcing that it would not execute the law because it believed the section in question was unconstitutional. In a report on signing statements issued in July 2006, the American Bar Association warned, "A line-item veto is not a constitutionally permissible alternative, even when the president believes that some provisions of a bill are unconstitutional" (quoted in Savage 2007, 245).

Despite the greater use of signing statements by presidents since Reagan, few political scientists pay attention to this development. *Boston Globe* reporter Charlie Savage received a Pulitzer Prize for his extensive research on the executive torture signing statement (see Savage 2007, ch. 10), while the most comprehensive scholarly studies to date are by Kelley (2003, 2005, 2006), Rudalevige (2005), and Cooper (2002, 2005).

In fact, Cooper (2002) provides the most detailed examination to date of a wide range of unilateral powers. Cooper's masterful work examines various tools of the unilateral presidency, including executive orders, presidential memoranda, presidential proclamations, National Security Directives, and presidential signing statements. He demonstrates that presidents can use unilateral power not only for legitimate purposes, but also to hide their intentions from the public and other Washington elites. For example, while executive orders are widely read, presidents can bury detail in presidential memoranda, which receive far less media or scholarly attention. Likewise, presidents can issue National Security Directives implementing foreign policy without informing Congress until much later, if at all. Cooper's book raises serious questions about the accountability of unilateral power, particularly when it is designed to avoid the light of public scrutiny. Hence, as with so much of the literature on the president's unilateral powers, he examines how it can be both "used and abused" (Cooper 2002, x).

Of particular interest is his examination of National Security Directives (NSD). Presidents have referred to them under a variety of different names including NSDS, National Security Action Memoranda, National Security Decision Memoranda (NSDMs), Presidential Directives, and National Security Presidential Directives (NSPDs) (Cooper 2005, ch. 6). Cooper quotes Lyndon Johnson to define a National Security Directive: "A National Security Action Memorandum was a formal notification to the head of a department or other governmental agency informing him of a presidential decision in the field of national security affairs and generally requiring follow-up action by the department or the agency addressed" (Cooper 2005, 144). They originated during the Truman and Eisenhower administrations as "NSC Policy Papers." They "have many of the same effects as executive orders, but they are not defined as such and therefore are not covered by the Federal Register Act." Furthermore, the "vast majority of these directives are classified" (ibid.); some are not even shared with members of Congress. National Security Directives therefore have the potential to make foreign policy, outside the usual reporting arrangements set aside for executive orders, and sometimes without even the knowledge of Congress. They have been used to set and change US foreign policy and played a central role in such various issues as Iran-Contra during the Reagan years, "the US sponsored coup in 1953 that put the Shah back on the throne, the bloody US coup that ousted the Arbenz government in Guatemala, and the . . . prosecution of the Vietnam War" (ibid. 143). Furthermore, they "have become increasingly attractive tools" (Cooper 2005, 151).

What the literature on executive orders, executive agreements, presidential signing statements, and National Security Directives has in common is (1) that presidents can secure significant additional influence from various unilateral powers, and (2) that there is a greater tendency in recent decades for presidents to use these powers, particularly in important policy areas. It is becoming more understandable why presidents use their unilateral powers. What is less apparent is the theoretical rationale behind this greater use of unilateral power. Specifically, given the limited constitutional powers that presidents possess, what is the justification for using unilateral power? Signing statements issued by George W. Bush provide an answer. Savage (2007, 237) writes,

Among the laws Bush challenged (via signing statements) included requirements that the government provide information to Congress, minimum qualifications for important positions in the executive branch, rules and regulations for the military, restrictions affecting the nation's foreign policy, and affirmative action rules for hiring. In his signing statements, Bush instructed his subordinates that the laws were unconstitutional constraints on his own inherent power as commander-in-chief and as the head of the "unitary" executive branch and thus not need be obeyed as written.

What, then, is the unitary executive?

THE UNITARY EXECUTIVE

Another major development in the unilateral power literature, one that has all but been ignored by political scientists, is the ascendancy of the *unitary executive or unitary presidency* literature. As of the spring of 2005, George W. Bush referenced the unitary executive ninety-five times in various signing statements and executive orders (Kelley 2005, 1). For example, in his October 4, 2006 signing statement on the Department of Homeland Security Appropriations Act, the Bush White House states, "The executive branch shall construe such provisions in a manner consistent with the constitutional authority of the President to supervise the unitary executive branch" (The American Presidency Project, <americanpresidency.org>). While political scientists have largely ignored this debate (though see Kelley 2005; Fisher 2006) for more than a decade, legal scholars have provided a solid rationale for this expansive theory of executive power. What, then, is the unitary executive model and why does it warrant scholarly attention?

According to constitutional expert Richard Fallon (2004, 184), the unitary executive theory is based on the idea that "the Constitution establishes one president, vested with the whole executive power." This unitary executive "must therefore be able to supervise and control all who work for him." A central concept of the unitary executive is the idea of "departmentalism" or "coordinate construction." As Yoo, Calabresi, and Colangelo (2004, 6) write, "This approach holds that all three branches of the federal government have the power and duty to interpret the Constitution and that the meaning of the Constitution is determined through dynamic interaction of all three branches."

Kelley (2005, 5) notes, "The unitary executive rests upon the independent power of the president to resist encroachments upon the prerogatives of his office and to control the executive branch. The three integral components of the unitary executive are the president's power to remove subordinate policy-making officials at will, the president's power to direct the manner in which subordinate officials exercise discretionary executive power, and the president's power to veto or nullify such officials exercises of discretionary executive power." Kelley (2005, 6) also writes that the unitary executive "largely draws from two sources within the Constitution— the 'Oath' and 'Take Care' clauses of Article II." In addition, proponents of the unitary executive adopt an expansive interpretation of the executive vesting clause, and, as I will demonstrate below, tend to construe congressional authority over perceived executive functions (such as treaty making or the war power) rather narrowly (see Yoo 2005).

Because the unitary executive places considerable authority in the president's hands, one primary concern is that it may tilt power so far in the president's direction that it will permanently undermine the Founders' carefully devised system of separation of powers and checks and balances, thereby creating a permanent imperial presidency (Savage 2007). Yoo, Calabresi and Nee (2004, 109) draw a direct connection between the unitary executive (with its broader use of unilateral power) and the imperial presidency. In their analysis of the unitary executive they write, "the period between 1889 and 1945 saw a tremendous growth in presidential power, as strong Presidents like the two Roosevelts and Wilson . . . helped remake the institution of the presidency into the primary institution for mobilizing and implementing political will. Their administrations set the stage for the imperial presidency that would dominate modern times."

In contrast to the political science literature on unilateral power, which is both quantitative and qualitative, the literature on the unitary executive is normative, generally addressing issues about the *proper scope* of presidential power; that is, whether presidents *should or should not* exert vastly increased executive power (in defense see Calabresi and Yoo 1997; Calabresi and Rhodes 1992; for critical views see Fitts 1996; Percival 2001; Marshall 2006). As a result, the *motivations* behind scholarship in this area have come under direct attack.

For example, Fisher (2006) criticizes proponents of the unitary executive model for promoting an ideologically driven model of presidential leadership. The unitary executive model is subject to such criticism because it is often advocated by conservatives who otherwise adopt a strict constructionist view of the Constitution. When addressing the issue of executive power, however, they generally ignore the arguments contained in Madison's Notes from the Constitutional Convention. They also present a highly selective delineation of history. As Calabresi and Yoo (1997, 1463) write in one of their four monumental studies of the history of the American presidency (see also Yoo, Calabresi, and Colangelo 2004; Yoo, Calabresi, and Nee 2004; Calabresi and Yoo 2003), "we approach this historical research project as constitutional lawyers and not as legal historians. We are interested in history in this project, but only in the way that lawyers are interested in history." In other words, they cite history that supports their legal argument while ignoring or downplaying evidence that is not consistent with their case. It is this selective citation of history that opens the unitary model to the charge that it is merely promoting an ideology rather than making a cogent argument based on the complete historical record. If Fisher is correct, then what are the implications of an ideologically based unitary model?

One possibility can be found in the motives of those who expound the unitary executive model. Kelley (2005, 10–11) states that the "unitary executive has mostly been championed by the founding members of the 'Federalist Society,' a group of conservative lawyers who nearly all worked in the Nixon, Ford, and Reagan White Houses and who understood the type of political climate the president operated in and understood what it took in order to succeed. Thus, the individuals who have written the most prolifically towards the unitary executive theory were also former members of the Reagan legal team—Calabresi, Ed Meese, Michael Stokes Paulsen, Douglas Kmiec, and Johnathan Yoo to name a few." One of the most conservative members of the US Supreme Court, Justice Antonin Scalia, also is identified as a proponent of the unitary executive theory.

Is it therefore possible that the advocates of the unitary executive are writing, not simply to posit an intellectual point of view, but rather to provide a critical rationale for later judicial adoption of the unitary executive model? Since political scientists convincingly demonstrate that justices render decisions on the basis of their attitudes or ideology (Segal and Spaeth 2002), Fisher's point and the sudden rash of law review articles on this subject suggests that it may be an attempt to provide a legal rationale for pro-unitary executive judges. If so, then the proponents of the unitary executive would welcome future court decisions which would further expand the scope of presidential power.

To better understand the possible ideological emphasis in this literature, I briefly examine one important point in the debate over the unitary executive: What is Congress's role in declaring war? Obviously, if the Constitution is interpreted to mean that Congress must declare war first, then presidents would be on shaky legal ground when going to war unilaterally. To counter this argument, Yoo (2005, 9) argues, "The Constitution did not intend to institute a fixed, legalistic process for the making of war." Rather, "flexibility means that there is no one constitutionally correct method for waging war. The president need not receive a declaration of war before engaging the U.S. armed forces in hostilities. Rather, the Constitution provides Congress with enough tools through its control over funding to promote or block presidential war initiatives." In advancing this argument, Yoo reduces Congress's power to declare war to nothing more than an acknowledgement that a state of war actually exists, essentially informing citizens and other participants of the changed nature of their legal status versus another nation.

If we are to accept Yoo's legal reasoning, then the unitary executive is proactive, while Congress is placed in a highly defensive position; deciding whether or not to provide funding for troops that most likely are already in the field of battle. Congress also can impeach the president if it believes that the war was not in the nation's interests. But both courses of action follow the advent of military action.

The centerpiece of Yoo's argument is that the declaration of war is not necessary for a unitary executive to conduct military action. With regard to US colonial history, Yoo (2005, 61) notes, "The declaration of war's main purpose lay not in authorizing military operations, but in triggering the governor's exercise of his domestic powers, such as the authorization of martial law." Yet Yoo (2005, 77, emphasis added) suggests that the declaration may have a more important purpose when he later writes, "The declaration acted as a permission slip for the states to initiate hostile activities, but only against identified enemies. Without a declaration of war, international law would consider such naval attacks [by states acting against a warring nation] as piracy rather than as legitimate combat under the law of wars. In short, *the declaration of war clothed what would have been an illegal act by the states—sending warships against another nation—with a legal status in international law."*

By acknowledging that a declaration of war was necessary to make a war legal, it can be surmised that without a declaration no similar legal standing exists. If we follow this line of reasoning then a declaration of war indeed would have far more important implications than merely serving notice to citizens or state officials that a state of war exists. It would provide the necessary step to make that war legal with regard to international law. Does this mean then that presidents are above international law until a declaration of war is issued by Congress? Yoo does not address such issues.

Of course one can argue that Yoo's discussion of the declaration function is related to the states and not the presidency. If, as Yoo argues, the presidency has inherent power under the executive vesting clause, then could one argue that the president's actions are legal even if the actions of states and US citizens are not? But this inference sets the legal standing of the president aside from that of all other citizens. If such is the case, then Nixon's famous statement that whatever the president does is legal is operational and the only mechanisms of accountability would be political (e. g., cutting funding or impeaching the president), not legal.

While this line of reasoning raises controversial issues, American history is replete with examples of US presidents taking the nation into battle, whether it is limited actions against pirates or Native Americans, or whether it is a full-fledged war such as Korea, without a formal declaration. And there are reasons for placing greater energy in the executive. As Yoo (2005, 20) notes, "the demands of the international system promote vesting the management of foreign affairs in a unitary, rational actor. The rational actor can identify threats, develop responses, evaluate costs and benefits, and seek to achieve national strategic goals through value-maximizing policies and actions." In short, "a unitary rational actor remains an ideal to guide foreign policy. It seems that the presidency best meets the requirement for taking rational action on behalf of the nation in the modern world" (for an alternative view see Fisher 2004; Corwin 1984).

What is most surprising about this literature is that while the legal stakes are extraordinarily important, essentially defining the parameters of presidential power for years to come, political scientists until very recently have been essentially AWOL in this debate. There are few references to the unitary executive debate in the political scientist literature (Bumgarner 2007; Fisher 2006; Kelley 2005). Given the potential long-term repercussions, it is a debate that political scientists should join, with both qualitative and quantitative evidence. In this regard, the *Presidential Studies Quarterly* should be commended for its special issues, one on unilateral power in 2005 and another on inherent presidential power in 2006. Such issues of the *PSQ* serve to bring unilateral power and the unitary executive to the attention of a wider range of presidential scholars and political scientists.

CONCLUSIONS

Research on the president's unilateral powers is, for the most part, a fairly recent development. Only during the past decade or so have presidential scholars systematically paid attention to a wide range of unilateral powers and the implications of presidential unilateral action. This may be the result of the power of Neustadt's bargaining model, which essentially defined the presidential literature for the past half century. While Neustadt's insights are still prescient and deserve further quantitative analysis, it is fair to say that his approach is no longer the only model of presidential leadership in town. New unilateral models and theories of the presidency are quickly adding to our understanding of a strategic presidency, one that seeks to govern effectively in an increasingly hostile political world where public and elite expectations often outstrip a president's actual constitutional ability to govern. Rather than admit failure, presidents are seeking out new political techniques and employing long-established resources in new ways. While this development is rational from a presidential perspective, it does raise legitimate questions about the proper scope of presidential power. Thus, the issues raised by the unitary executive and the president's unilateral powers provide fodder for additional qualitative and quantitative studies of the presidency, as well as more developed theories that will better help us to understand the continuing evolution of the presidential office and presidential power.

REFERENCES

BERGER, R. 1974. *Executive Privilege: A Constitutional Myth*. Cambridge, MA: Harvard University Press.

———1972. The Presidential Monopoly of Foreign Relations. *Michigan Law Review*, 71: 1–58.

BLOOM, E. T. 1985. The Executive Claims Settlement Power: Constitutional Authority and Foreign Affairs Applications. *Columbia Law Journal*, 85/1: 155–89.

BORCHARD, E. 1944. Shall the Executive Agreement Replace the Treaty? *Yale Law Journal*, 53/4: 664–83.

BRADY, D., and VOLDEN, C. 2005. *Revolving Gridlock: Politics and Policy from Jimmy Carter to George W. Bush*. Boulder, CO: Westview Press.

BRICKER, J. W. 1953. Making Treaties and Other International Agreements. *Annals of the American Academy of Political and Social Science*, 289, Congress and Foreign Relations: 134–44.

BUMGARNER, J. 2007. The Administrative, Politicized, Unitary Presidency in the Neo-Administrative State: A Fish Out of Water? Paper presented at the Annual Meeting of the Midwest Political Science Association, Chicago, IL.

CALABRESI, S. G., and RHODES, K. H. 1992. The Structural Constitution: Unitary Executive, Plural Judiciary. *Harvard Law Review*, 105/6: 1153–216.

—— and Yoo, C. S. 1997. The Unitary Executive during the First Half-Century. *Case Western Reserve Law Review*, 47: 1451–561.

—— —— 2003. The Unitary Executive during the Second Half-Century. *Harvard Journal of Law and Public Policy*, 26: 668–801.

CAMERON, C. 2000. *Veto Bargaining: Presidents and the Politics of Negative Power*. New York: Cambridge University Press.

CHIOU, F.-Y., and ROTHENBERG, L. S. 2007. Presidential Unilateralism: Theory and Evidence. Paper presented at the Annual Meeting of the Midwest Political Science Association, Chicago, IL.

COHEN, J. E., and KRAUSE, G. A. 2000. Opportunity Constraints, and the Development of the Institutional Presidency: The Issuance of Executive Orders, 1939–1996. *Journal of Politics*, 62: 88–114.

COOPER, J., and WEST, W. F. 1988. Presidential Power and Republican Government: The Theory and Practice of OMB Review of Agency Rules. *Journal of Politics*, 50/4: 864–95.

COOPER, P. J. 1986. By Order of the President: Administration by Executive Order and Proclamation. *Administration & Society*, 18: 233–62.

—— 2002. *By Order of the President: The Use & Abuse of Executive Direct Action*. Lawrence: University Press of Kansas.

—— 2005. George W. Bush, Edgar Allen Poe and the Use and Abuse of Presidential Signing Statements. *Presidential Studies Quarterly*, 35/3: 517–32.

CORWIN, E. S. 1984. *The President: Office and Powers 1787–1984*, ed. R. W. Bland, T. T. Hindson, and J. W. Peltason. New York: New York University Press.

COX, G. W., and McCUBBINS, M. D. 1993. *Legislative Leviathan: Party Government in the House*. Berkeley and Los Angeles: University of California Press.

—— —— 2005. *Setting the Agenda: Responsible Party Government in the US House of Representatives*. Cambridge: Cambridge University Press.

DEERING, C. J., and MALTZMAN, F. 1999. The Politics of Executive Orders: Legislative Constraints on Presidential Power. *Political Research Quarterly*, 52: 767–84.

DICKINSON, M. J. 2004. Agendas, Agencies, and Unilateral Action: New Insights on Presidential Power. *Congress & the Presidency*, 31: 99–109.

DODDS, G. G. 2006. Executive Orders from Nixon to Now. Pp. 53–71 in *Executing the Constitution: Putting the President Back into the Constitution*, ed. C. S. Kelley. Albany: State University of New York Press.

EDWARDS, G. C. III. 1989. *At the Margins: Presidential Leadership of Congress*. New Haven, CT: Yale University Press.

—— 2003. *On Deaf Ears: The Limits of the Bully Pulpit*. New Haven, CT: Yale University Press.

FALLON, R. H. 2004. *The Dynamic Constitution: An Introduction to American Constitutional Law*. New York: Cambridge University Press.

FISHER, L. 1972. *The President and Congress: Power and Policy*. New York: Free Press.

—— 2004. *Presidential War Power*. Lawrence: University Press of Kansas.

—— 2006. The "Unitary Executive:" Ideology Versus the Constitution. Paper Presented at the Annual Meeting of the American Political Science Association.

FITTS, M. A. 1996. The Paradox of Power in the Modern State: Why a Unitary, Centralized Presidency May Not Exhibit Effective or Legitimate Leadership. *University of Pennsylvania Law Review*, 144/3: 827–902.

GILBERT, A. 1973. *Executive Agreements and Treaties, 1946–1973*. New York: Thomas-Newell.

GLEIBER, D. W., and SHUL, S. A. 1992. Presidential Influence in the Policy-Making Process. *Western Political Quarterly*, 45/2: 441–68.

Gomez, B. T., and Shull, S. A. 1995. Presidential Decision Making: Explaining the Use of Executive Orders. Paper presented at the Annual Meeting of the Southern Political Science Association, Tampa, FL.

Howell, W. G. 2003. *Power without Persuasion: The Politics of Direct Presidential Action.* Princeton, NJ: Princeton University Press.

—— 2005. Unilateral Powers: A Brief Overview. *Presidential Studies Quarterly,* 35: 417–39.

—— and Kriner, D. 2008. Power without Persuasion: Identifying Executive Influence. Pp. 105–44 in *Presidential Leadership: The Vortex of Power,* ed. B. A. Rockman and R. W. Waterman. New York: Oxford University Press.

—— and Lewis, D. E. 2002. Agencies by Presidential Design. *Journal of Politics,* 64: 1095–114.

—— and Mayer, K. R. 2005. The Last One Hundred Days. *Presidential Studies Quarterly,* 35/3: 533–53.

Johnson, L., and McCormick, J. M. 1977. Foreign Policy by Executive Fiat. *Foreign Affairs,* 28: 117–38.

——————1978. The Making of International Agreements: A Reappraisal of Congressional Involvement. *Journal of Politics,* 40/2: 468–78.

Kelley, C. S. 2003. The Unitary Executive and the Presidential Signing Statement. Dissertation completed at Miami University, Oxford, OH.

—— 2005. Rethinking Presidential Power: The Unitary Executive and the George W. Bush Presidency. Paper presented at the Annual Meeting of the Midwest Political Science Association, Chicago, IL.

—— 2006. The Significance of the Presidential Signing Statement. Pp. 73–89 in *Executing the Constitution: Putting the President Back into the Constitution,* ed. C. S. Kelley. Albany: State University of New York Press.

Kernell, S. 1997. *Going Public: New Strategies of Presidential Leadership.* Washington, DC: Congressional Quarterly Press.

King, G., and Ragsdale, L. 1988. *The Elusive Executive: Discovering Statistical Patterns in the Presidency.* Washington, DC: Congressional Quarterly Press.

Klarevas, L. 2003. The Law: The Constitutionality of Congressional–Executive Agreements. *Presidential Studies Quarterly,* 33/2: 394–408.

Krause, G. A., and Cohen, D. B. 1997. Presidential Use of Executive Orders, 1953–1994. *American Politics Quarterly,* 25: 458–81.

Krehbiel, K. 1998. *Pivotal Politics: A Theory of US Lawmaking.* Chicago: University of Chicago Press.

Lewis, D. E. 2003. *Presidents and the Politics of Agency Design: Political Insulation in the United States Government Bureaucracy, 1946–1997.* Stanford, CA: Stanford University Press.

Light, P. C. 1999. *The President's Agenda: Domestic Policy Choice from Kennedy to Carter.* Baltimore: Johns Hopkins University Press.

Lowi, T. J. 1985. *The Personal Presidency: Power Invested, Promise Unfulfilled.* Ithaca, NY: Cornell University Press.

McClure, W. 1967. *International Executive Agreements: Democratic Procedure under the Constitution of the United States.* New York: AMS Press.

McDougal, M. S., and Lans, A. 1945a. Treaties and Congressional–Executive or Presidential Agreements: Interchangeable Instruments of National Policy, Part 2. *Yale Law Journal,* 54: 181–351.

——————1945b. Treaties and Congressional–Executive or Presidential Agreements: Interchangeable Instruments of National Policy, Part 2. *Yale Law Journal,* 54: 534–615.

Marcus, M. 1994. *Truman and the Steel Seizure Case: The Limits of Presidential Power.* Durham, NC: Duke University Press.

MARGOLIS, L. 1985. *Executive Agreements and Presidential Power in Foreign Policy.* New York: Praeger Publishers.

MARSHALL, B. W, and PACELLE, R. L., JR. 2005. Revisiting the Two Presidencies: The Strategic Use of Executive Orders. *American Politics Research,* 33: 81–105.

MARSHALL, W. P. 2006. Break Up the Presidency? Governors, State Attorneys General, and Lessons from the Divided Executive. *Yale Law Journal,* 115: 2448–79.

MAYER, K. R. 1999. Executive Orders and Presidential Power. *Journal of Politics,* 61: 445–66.

—— 2001. *With the Stroke of a Pen: Executive Orders and Presidential Power.* Princeton, NJ: Princeton University Press.

MOE, T. M. 1985. The Politicized Presidency. Pp. 235–71 in *New Directions in American Politics,* ed. E. Chubb and P. E. Peterson. Washington, DC: Brookings Institution.

—— and HOWELL, W. G. 1999a. The Presidential Power of Unilateral Action. *Journal of Law, Economics and Organization,* 15: 132–79.

—— —— 1999b. Unilateral Action and Presidential Power: A Theory. *Presidential Studies Quarterly,* 29: 850–73.

—— and WILSON, S. A. 1994. Presidents and the Politics of Structure. *Law and Contemporary Problems,* 57/1: 1–44.

MORGAN, R. P. 1970. *The President and Civil Rights: Policy Making by Executive Order.* New York: St Martin's Press.

NEUSTADT, R. E. 1980. *Presidential Politics: The Politics of Leadership from FDR to Carter.* New York: John Wiley & Sons. First published 1960.

New York Times (editorial). 2006. Veto? Who Needs a Veto? *New York Times,* May 5: A24.

OLSON, W. J., and WOLL, A. 1999. Executive Orders and National Emergencies: How Presidents Have Come to "Run the Country" by Usurping Legislative Power. *Policy Analysis,* 358: 1–29.

PAIGE, J. 1977. *The Law Nobody Knows: Enlargement of the Constitution—Treaties and Executive Agreements.* New York: Vantage Press.

PAUL, J. R. 1998. The Geopolitical Constitution: Executive Expediency and Executive Agreements. *California Law Review,* 86/4: 671–773.

PERCIVAL, R. V. 2001. Presidential Management of the Administrative State: The Not-so-Unitary Executive. *Duke Law Journal,* 51/3: 963–1013.

ROCKMAN, B. A., and WATERMAN, R. W. 2008. Two Normative Models of Presidential Leadership. Pp. 331–47 in *Presidential Leadership: The Vortex of Power,* ed. B. A. Rockman and R. W. Waterman. New York: Oxford University Press.

RUDALEVIGE, A. 2005. *The New Imperial Presidency: Renewing Presidential Power after Watergate.* Ann Arbor: University of Michigan Press.

SAVAGE, C. 2007. *Takeover: The Return of the Imperial Presidency and the Subversion of American Democracy.* Boston: Little, Brown & Company.

SCHLESINGER, A., JR. 1973. *The Imperial Presidency.* Boston: Houghton Mifflin.

SEGAL, J. A., and SPAETH, H. J. 2002. *The Supreme Court and the Attitudinal Model, Revisited.* Cambridge: Cambridge University Press.

SELIGMAN, L. G., and BAER, M. A. 1969. Expectations of Presidential Leadership and Decision-Making. In *The Presidency,* ed. A. Wildavsky. Boston: Little, Brown & Co.

—— and COVINGTON, C. R. 1989. *The Coalitional Presidency.* Chicago: Dorsey Press.

SHULL, S. A. 1997. *Presidential–Congressional Relations: Policy and Time Approaches.* Ann Arbor: University of Michigan Press.

SPINDLER, J. F. 1953. Executive Agreements and the Proposed Constitutional Amendments to the Treaty Power. *Michigan Law Review,* 51/8: 1202–17.

TRIBE, L. H. 1995. Taking Text and Structure Seriously: Reflections on Free-Form Method in Constitutional Interpretation. *Harvard Law Review,* 108: 1221–303.

WARBER, A. L. 2006. *Executive Orders and the Modern Presidency: Legislating from the Oval Office.* Boulder, CO: Lynne Rienner Publishers.

WATERMAN, R. W. 2007. *The Changing American Presidency.* Cincinnati: Thomson Learning/ Atomic Dog.

WIGTON, R. C. 1996. Recent Presidential Experience with Executive Orders. *Presidential Studies Quarterly,* 26: 473–84.

YOO, J. 2005. *The Powers of War and Peace: The Constitution and Foreign Affairs after 9/11.* Chicago: University of Chicago Press.

——CALABRESI, S. G., and COLANGELO, A. J. 2004. The Unitary Executive in the Modern Era. *Iowa Law Review,* 90: 601–731.

————and NEE, L. D. 2004. The Unitary Executive during the Third Half-Century, 1889–1945. *Notre Dame Law Review,* 80: 1–109.

PART VII

DECISION MAKING

....

CHAPTER 22

ORGANIZATIONAL STRUCTURE AND PRESIDENTIAL DECISION MAKING

....

JOHN P. BURKE

HAD this handbook been published in the mid-twentieth century, an article on organizational structure and presidential decision making would undoubtedly have not been included, nor would the need for attention to it have been discernible by presidency scholars. Prior to the presidency of Franklin D. Roosevelt (and indeed almost to the end of his second term), little in the way of White House organization existed. Presidents relied on a small number of aides, countable on one hand (Burke 2000, 3–6). The cabinet rather than the White House staff was the primary source of policy advice. Change would come following the adoption of the recommendations of the Brownlow Committee in 1939, which led to the statutory creation of the Executive Office of the President (see Polenberg 1966; Arnold 1998, 81–117). Although the initial organizational efforts were modest, the groundwork was laid. Through the Truman and Eisenhower presidencies the organization of the White House staff increased in both size and complexity (see Henderson 1988, 13–32; Sloan 1990; Hart 1992).

By 1960, with the publication of the first edition of Richard Neustadt's *Presidential Power*, scholars began to take account of the organizational environment of the presidency. In a chapter titled "Men in Office," Neustadt detailed both the growing complexity of the staff resources at the president's disposal as well as the differing managerial styles of FDR, Truman, and Eisenhower in their respective attempts to marshal those resources in the exercise of presidential influence (Neustadt 1990, 128–51).

By the Nixon presidency, signs of a highly organized, "institutional presidency" were clear. Hult and Walcott note the emergence of a "standard model" of White House staff organization under Nixon, which would be largely adopted by his successors (Hult and Walcott, 2004, 166–7, 175–6; Walcott and Hult 2005). Others have also noted a hardening, by the 1970s, of the institutional characteristics of the presidency (Ragsdale and Theis 1997; Burke 2000, 24–52; Ponder 2000, 10–13; Dickinson and Lebo 2007).

Three important works at the time began to capture the impact of organization upon the presidency: Richard Tanner Johnson's *Managing the White House* (1974), Irving Janis's *Victims of Groupthink* (1972), and Graham Allison's *Essence of Decision* (1971). Although different in emphasis, each would frame important strands of research on the relationship of organization and decision making.

THE IMPACT OF FORMAL AND COLLEGIAL DECISION STRUCTURES

Stanford University business school professor Richard Tanner Johnson's *Managing the White House* proved influential on several counts. First, surveying presidencies from FDR to Nixon, Johnson discerned three patterns of deliberative organization: competitive, formalistic (often termed hierarchical in other studies), and collegial. The first, a *competitive* arrangement, is restricted to the Roosevelt presidency. It consists of a system at the center of which and as an ongoing directive force stands the president. A small number of advisers are directly on call for presidential assignments, their duties generally overlap, and the president fosters rivalries among them. In *formalistic* arrangements, such as those of Eisenhower and Nixon, there is much delegation of authority to top advisers and the presence of an orderly system in which the information and advice that reaches the president is funneled through a large hierarchical structure of clearly designated organizational channels and specified roles. The third pattern, a *collegial* system, involves a small group of decision makers like a competitive system. However, they operate in a group setting. Whereas the formalistic model might be likened to a hierarchical organizational pyramid, with the president at its apex, the collegial model resembles a wheel: the president at the hub with advisers at the end of the spokes, directly connected to the president, and, along the rim, to each other.

Johnson's second contribution was to recognize that each of the three systems has distinctive strengths and weaknesses. Competitive systems maximize presidential control and favor the politically feasible and bureaucratically doable, but they place enormous demands on the president's time, limit information through their attenu-ated channels, and create interpersonal tension. Formalistic systems gather informa-tion and advice more widely, but their organizational complexity may lead to distortion as they move up the system. Johnson also argues that formal arrangements undervalue political pressures, are prone to lengthy searches for optimal policy (rather than the satisficing doable), and tend to respond slowly in crisis situations. Collegial systems can achieve a degree of optimality and doability, are less demanding than competitive system on the president's time, and can "fuse the strongest elements of divergent points of view" (Johnson 1974, 7). But they also have a drawback: they require astute presidential management in maintaining a positive group dynamic.

Johnson's work would prove important both in recognizing these different *organ-izational* patterns—at least the vernacular of which other scholars would widely utilize—*and* in beginning to recognize the related dimension of *presidential* manage-ment of them. The latter, however, was not well articulated in his study, particularly in differentiating and explaining the different degrees of success in presidencies that use similar systems (e.g. Kennedy and Johnson as collegial decision makers; Eisenhower and Nixon as formalistic ones). The categories also seem to operate too rigidly: presidents *both* rely upon formal organizations *and* meet in group settings. Like many typologies, Johnson's has classificatory strength and elegance, but actual staff operations rarely match the ideal types and are usually more muddled and complex (Burke and Green-stein 1989, 21, 274–5; Ponder 2000, 9; but see Haney 1997, 8–9). To be fair: Johnson does acknowledge the presence of "mixed models," but they are ones in which one pattern is "dominant" (Johnson 1974, 233). However, significant differences do seem to exist in the deliberative arrangements of presidents who fall within the same category and in the extent to which they reap the benefits and bear the costs associated with it.

But that said, Johnson's typology may remain heuristically useful. Utilizing John-son's categories, Meena Bose's comparative analysis of Eisenhower's and Kennedy's national security decision making, for example, found both formal and informal channels of advising, as well as a more positive assessment of the Eisenhower process than Johnson's characterization of it as "organized absenteeism" (Johnson 1974, 74). As for Kennedy, " 'collegial' is an imperfect description." According to Bose (1998, 100), "in 1961, those processes were so fluid that Kennedy did not really represent the hub of an informally coordinated advisory network." Burke and Greenstein found similar complexity and higher quality in the Eisenhower system in their study of Vietnam decision making. They particularly note that more formal arrangements have under-appreciated strengths while collegial systems have under-appreciated weaknesses (Burke and Greenstein 1989, 276–81). Patrick Haney also makes product-ive use of Johnson's schema (Haney 1997). His research is particularly instructive in its focus on *crisis* decisions and for its careful selection of case studies from the Truman through the George H. W. Bush presidencies. He has matched pairs of cases for four presidencies: Truman (Berlin airlift and Korean War), Eisenhower (Dien Bien Phu and Suez), Johnson (Tonkin Gulf and Tet offensive), Nixon (Jordanian civil war and the October 1973 war), plus one case for the G. H. W. Bush presidency (Panama invasion).

Haney also detects—beyond Johnson's schema—the presence of informal, unofficial networks of decision makers and ad hoc groups of advisers (Haney 1997, 128; also see Ponder 2000, 9). The latter have been noted in various accounts of presidential "wise men" by journalists and historians (e.g. Isaacson and Thomas 1986), and in some of the revisionist accounts of Eisenhower's decision making (Sloan 1990, 302–4; Burke and Greenstein 1989, 56, 279–81). Informal channels may be beneficial in expanding available information, but the presence of "back channel" avenues may also bear costs. Both the effects of informal channels on decision making and their relations to more official structures merit further systematic analysis.

Comparison of Roger Porter's (1980) similarly tripartite typology to Johnson's is also revealing. Porter drops the FDR-limited competitive model, replacing it with a version of Alexander George's (1972) notion of "multiple advocacy." Porter's remaining categories, "centralized management" and "adhocracy," resemble Johnson's formal and collegial systems. Porter's analysis of each differs, however. He views centralized management more favorably. It leads to more careful review of policy options, although it can value policy formulation over implementation. Adhocracy generally produces low-quality, non-comprehensive reviews of policy and may be less politically responsive if the president fails to consult widely. By contrast, Johnson sees a collegial arrangement as more politically astute and, in general, as a sort of "happy medium" between the "extremes" of the competitive and the formal (Johnson 1974, 6–7). Differences in their typologies and in their predictive effects are indicative of the need for further research on the basic deliberative arrangements used in a variety of presidencies as well as what effects they might have on decision making.

Indeed, emphasis on formal versus collegial or centralized management versus adhocracy may not reveal the full organizational dynamic at work. David Mitchell has helpfully noted, for example, a conceptual muddle in how relationships between presidents and advisers are conceptualized that also invites further exploration. Rather than treating all as structural difference, he argues that this is only one dimension. The other dimension may be more usefully conceptualized as "operations:" "the nature of the interaction between advisers and leaders *during* the decision-making process *within* a given structure" (Mitchell 2005, 3; also see Haney 1997, 3).

THE IMPACT OF THE SMALL GROUP ON DECISION MAKING

In 1972, *Victims of Groupthink* by Yale University social psychologist Irving Janis appeared. Based on case studies focusing exclusively on presidential decision making in small group settings, Janis sought to demonstrate that poor policy choices were made by participants who were otherwise highly intelligent, substantively experienced, and politically sophisticated. Janis attributes this failure in decision outcome to a particular pathology of small groups: the emergence of "groupthink." The structure and dynamics of the small group, in his view, can without corrective lead to a largely unconscious "concurrence-seeking" tendency, which generates uncritical thinking, the stifling of dissent, and optimistic and premature closure in favor of flawed policy options. His case study of Kennedy's April 1961 Bay of Pigs invasion decision is the most notable in the book and perhaps the most persuasive: it represented groupthink at its worse and led to a "perfect failure." But Janis also explores the possibility of remedy. In his analysis of deliberations during the October 1962 Cuban missile crisis, he details corrective steps to avoid groupthink. Janis's second edition of the book is especially notable for its clarification of the causal logic surrounding the antecedents and consequences of groupthink (1982, 174–8, 243–5), which had been noted in critiques of the first edition (Longley and Pruitt 1980, 75–7). Janis (1989) subsequently incorporated his work on groupthink into a broader theory of leadership and decision making.

There has been some validation of Janis's theory and findings as well as extensive scholarly discussion (Hart 1991, 1994; George 1997) and a twenty-fifth anniversary symposium (Organizational Behavior and Human Decision Processes 1998). Some studies have sought to expand the application of Janis's theory to other cases—e.g., the Iran hostage rescue mission (Smith 1985), Iran-Contra (Hart 1994), university decision making (Hensley and Griffin 1986), and the *Challenger* space shuttle disaster (Esser and Lindoerfer 1989). Others have offered more comprehensive case analyses. Herek, Janis, and Huth's (1987) study of nineteen presidential decisions utilizes Janis and Mann's (1977) seven signs of defective decision making, which very closely track with the seven symptoms produced by groupthink that Janis lists (1982, 244). They conclude that defects in process correlate with decision failure.

Other research has detected potential flaws in Janis's argument (Whyte 1989; McCauley 1989; Haney 1994; George 1997, 39–42; Fuller and Aldag 1997). Alternative accounts have reached different conclusions regarding the presence or absence of groupthink, even in the cases Janis presents (on the Bay of Pigs invasion, see Stern 1997; on the Cuban missile crisis, see Welch 1989; Gaenslen 1992, 174–6; Purkitt 1992; on the Korean invasion, see Preston 1997; on Johnson's Vietnam decision making, see Burke and Greenstein 1989, 281–6; Mulcahy 1995). Another area of contention is whether concurrence seeking is, in fact, always an organizational pathology. Concurrence seeking, for example, may not always be counter-productive: groups need to reach consensus in the long run (Longley and Pruitt 1980, 77).

Analysts also need to factor in types of decision tasks: simple or routine decisions may call for early consensus, contrary to Janis (Longley and Pruitt 1980, 78). Likewise, based on Katz and Kahn's (1978) distinction of problems and dilemmas as two different decision tasks, early concurrence seeking may actually be beneficial for deliberations involving problems but detrimental to dilemma-based decisions (Longley and Pruitt 1980, 78).

Another issue is whether the eight "symptoms of groupthink" (Janis 1982, 244) are in fact the result of concurrence seeking. According to Longley and Pruitt, the illusions of invulnerability and unanimity "appear to be antecedents of premature concurrence rather than consequences," while the belief in the inherent morality of the group and the stereotyping of outgroups "seem unrelated to concurrence seeking." In fact, the eight symptoms of groupthink "appear to be a loose bag of partially related ideas" (Longley and Pruitt 1980, 79–80).

The "antecedent conditions" of concurrence seeking may especially mask some causal confusion in Janis's argument. These conditions foster concurrence seeking according to Janis. Yet some may be powerful independent variables in their own right, bypassing the intervening phenomenon of group dynamics-grounded concurrence seeking. Leaders may be directive and fail to instill impartial leadership (one of Janis's antecedent conditions), which may in turn lead to groupthink as Janis argues. But leaders may exert a powerful influence in their own right, one that may have only limited or indirect effects on *group* dynamics—hence "leaderthink" rather than groupthink. The organization of groups might likewise be more directly consequential. Members' backgrounds, ideology, and the absence of norms requiring methodical procedures (others of Janis's antecedent conditions) may point to organizational factors with more direct bearing on decision dynamics but less mediation through group concurrence seeking.

On another organizational front, the more attenuated continuity of staff and advisory resources in the US presidential system compared to parliamentary governments (plus the greater political heterogeneity and coalitional composition of the latter) may also be important antecedent—but not groupthink-related—factors (Hart, Stern, and Sundelius 1997, 11). Alexander George has also pointed to another set of neglected antecedents: the larger and necessary trade-offs that constrain group deliberations such as time management and the need for acceptability and support (George 1980, 1–3; 1997, 44–50).

Schafer and Crichlow's (1996) quantitative study is especially interesting in this regard, because they use Herek, Janis, and Huth's (1987) dataset but push the analysis back one step from analysis of the *signs* of defective decision making produced by groupthink to its *antecedents*. Schafer and Crichlow found that some of the antecedent conditions that Janis identified do not correlate with faulty decision making (i.e. time constraint, recent decision failure, and stress). More importantly, although some antecedents do correlate with information-processing errors (leadership, group procedures, and patterns of group behavior), an index of these antecedent conditions "has more explanatory power" in its own right—explaining twice as much variance—than an index based on groupthink-based information-processing errors. According to their research, groupthink may explain some defective decision making, but the "real problem lies in structural arrangements" that precede information processing in the group setting (Schafer and Crichlow 1996, 427).

Structural arrangements take us full circle back to the broader organizational arrangements that Richard Tanner Johnson and others have emphasized, especially the more potentially hypotheses-rich—but not exclusively groupthink-based—dynamics of collegial systems. Schafer and Crichlow also offer prescriptive optimism. As they note, situational factors that are less subject to human control are weak predictive antecedents, while leadership style, organizational norms, and internal procedures are highly consequential and malleable to leadership efforts (1996, 429). They present similar findings in their extended study of thirty-one decisions from 1975 through 1993 (Schafer and Crichlow 2002).

As Hart, Stern, and Sundelius (1997, 11) point out, "It seems eminently reasonable, therefore, to treat groupthink as a contingent phenomenon, rather than as a general property of foreign policy decision making in high-level groups." They argue, in turn, that research should move "beyond groupthink" and recognize two core ideas: (1) "Policy-making and advisory groups take a variety of shapes and forms, and they perform widely different functions in the foreign policy process;" and (2) "Policy-making and advisory groups are embedded in an institutional and political context that constrains and facilitates their performance" (Hart, Stern, and Sundelius 1997, 12).

THE IMPACT OF BUREAUCRATIC ROUTINES, POLITICS, AND INTERESTS

Graham T. Allison's *Essence of Decision* (1971) presents two additional ways in which organizations have impact on decision making. In both the original work and a second edition (Allison and Zelikow 1999), the aim is to explicate the deliberations of Kennedy and his advisers during the Cuban missile crisis through the framework of three different analytical models: the nation-state as rational actor (Model I), organizational process (Model II), and governmental politics (Model III). The work is important as an examination of Kennedy's decision making, but it has captured enduring scholarly attention for its three models and the different explanatory light each sheds. For our purposes the latter two models are of particular interest since they raise organizational concerns, but in very different ways.

Analysis under Model II focuses on "existing organizational components, their functions, and their standard operating procedures for acquiring information... defining feasible options...and implementation." What rational-actor Model I "characterizes as 'acts and choices' are thought of instead as *outputs* of large organizations functioning according to regular patterns of behavior" (Allison and Zelikow 1999, 5–6; emphasis in original).

Model III is only in part attentive to organizational impact. Its general emphasis is on the "politics of a government." Deliberations are understood neither as rational choices (Model I) nor as organizational outputs (Model II) but as "a resultant of bargaining games among players." Analysis under Model III focuses on "the players whose interests and actions impact the issue in question, the factors that shape player's perception and *stands*, the established procedure or '*action channel*' for aggregating competing preferences, and the *performance* of the players" (Allison and Zelikow 1999, 6; emphasis in original). Unfortunately, in some ways, Model III is a bit of an explanatory hodge podge. At times, it has a flavor of Neustadtian individualism writ large across an array of actors—not just the president—in its emphasis on the importance of power positions, power as persuasion, and persuasion as bargaining (Allison and Zelikow 1999, 258–60). At other points, the authors emphasize political gamesmanship, manipulation of decision rules, and agenda setting. The "pull and haul of politics" is also a factor, and even groupthink is included in the mix (278–87).

But what is notable from an organizational perspective is Model III's inclusion of Rufus E. Miles's "law of bureaucratic politics:" "Where you stand depends upon where you sit" (Allison and Zelikow 1999, 307; Miles 1978). Here organization has impact, but at one step removed. Bureaucratic position at the "home agency" can powerfully affect the interests expressed by participants in subsequent, collective decision settings. The law is not an iron one, but more probabilistic. As the authors note in the second edition, "No paragraph from the first edition of this book attracted more criticism." "Depends" does not mean, as some readers took it to mean, "always determined by." Rather "we mean that where you stand is 'substantially affected by' where you sit." Participants can resist their particular organizational interests, but that influence is a strong one: "Knowledge of the organizational seat at the table yields significant clues about a likely stand" (Allison and Zelikow 1999, 307).

Both Model II and Model III may be problematic conceptually. Model II, as Welch notes, "does not operate at the moment of decision," but rather takes into account organizational constraint on the "formation of options," and, later, their implementation. As a result, it "has nothing to say about the decisions themselves;" that falls by default to other models or explanations (Welch 1992, 117).

Model III has clearly received more attention than Model II. Works have appeared with titles and content emphasizing bureaucratic politics and governmental process (see, e.g., Destler 1974; Halperin 1974; Allison and Szanton 1976; Rourke 1978; Kozak and Keagle 1988) as well as a journal symposium (*Mershon International Studies Review* 1998). However, there has been "comparatively little attention to Model II" (Welch 1992, 120), which is an important omission from an organizational perspective.

There is some irony here. Bendor and Hammond find Model II "one of the strongest sections" of the work (1992, 309). According to Welch, "despite the considerably greater attention analysts have paid to Model III, the body of theory it has spawned is far less clear, far less plausible, and more difficult to test" (Welch 1992, 120; also see Bendor and Hammond 1992, 302; Hart and Rosenthal 1998). Ascertaining the impact of bureaucratic position on decision interests—Miles's law—has been especially difficult to deal with, as Allison and Zelikow themselves acknowledge in the second edition of the work. Hoyt and Garrison, for example, note that bureaucratic rivalry need not be directly related to the actor's bureaucratic position, but to their individual policy preferences. Furthermore, "individuals operating in a group context are often driven to alter the group's structure and processes in an effort to enhance the strength of a preferred policy option" (Hoyt and Garrison 1997, 249).

Nor is the impact of bureaucratic position easy to operationalize with the other elements of Model III such as political pull and haul and gamesmanship. The Model III grab-bag thus compromises theoretical parsimony. As Robert Art pointed out in an early critique: "One of the central difficulties with the bureaucratic politics paradigm [is that] we must qualify it with so many amendments before it begins to work that when it does, we may not be left with a bureaucratic paradigm, but may in reality be using another one quite different" (Art 1973, 473). And, as Bendor and Hammond note, "a well-crafted model must strike a balance between simplicity and complexity. Too simple a model misses key aspects of the problem one is trying to understand; too complex a model is analytically intractable and yields few testable hypotheses" (Bendor and Hammond 1992, 302).

The relation between the Models II and III is also confusing, and they may not be mutually exclusive. Welch notes that in a later article on bureaucratic politics (Allison and Halperin 1972), the two models seem "conflated...relegating organizational processes to the status of 'constraints' within the bureaucratic politics paradigm" (Welch 1992, 118). Aspects of one model also reappear in the other. Parochial priorities and the perceptions of organization-bound members are part of Model II (Allison 1971, 81), but they seem closer to the bureaucratic interests of Model III than the organizational routines of Model II (Welch 1992, 118). Rosati regards Models II and III *together* as a "bureaucratic politics model of decision making," noting the later Allison and Halperin article (Rosati 1981, 233–5). Also, where does Allison come out in the end? The three models do not appear to be analytically equal (Model I seems especially weaker in its explanatory power). One might read *Essence of Decision* in a kind of Goldilocks manner: in the end, the porridge of Model III is "just about right."

These conceptual difficulties aside, there has been considerable work that has sought to test Allison's models beyond the Cuban missile crisis. Some studies support the utility and explanatory value of Model III: ABM deployment (Halperin 1972), the impact of the State Department's country director system (Bacchus 1974), ICBM development (Beard 1976), the Skybolt decision (Ciboski 1977), the SALT I negotiations under Johnson and Nixon (Rosati 1981), the 1980 Iran hostage rescue (Smith 1984), and Vietnam decision making (in part, Preston and Hart 1999). Leon V. Sigal's (1978) study of the decision to drop the atomic bomb is of special interest, since he calls attention to the role of bureaucratic politics in committee deliberations *before* a decision reaches the principals, which is important and insightful given the structured hierarchy of national security decision making.

Others studies are more doubtful about the bureaucratic politics approach: 1976 Korean militarized zone crisis (Head 1988), and naval budgets and procurements (Rhodes 1994). Even in Allison's key case, the Cuban missile crisis, the causal strength of Model III is open to criticism. According to Krasner, members of ExCom "often do not stand where they sit. Sometimes they are not sitting anywhere" (Krasner 1972, 165). As for bargaining, Welch notes that ExCom members "engaged in no 'bargaining' of any kind; never did one player assent to X only on condition of receiving Y as a quid pro quo" (Welch 1992, 132–3). Barbara Kellerman (1983) takes the argument further by emphasizing that three additional models also help explain ExCom's deliberations: the (non-bureaucratic politics) dynamics of small groups, the role of the dominant leader, and the cognitive and other psychological processes of the various participants in decision making.

One particularly telling weakness in Allison's Model III—indeed, if not in all three—is the place of the president. As Rosati and others (Bendor and Hammond 1992, 315; Krasner 1972, 166–9) have noted, Allison underestimates the role and impact of the president; one among a number of other actors. Yet Rosati argues that this may obtain in only some decision situations where presidential interest is low, and it calls for a broader contextual understanding of the decision setting. Rosati offers a 2 × 2 typology, arraying levels of presidential involvement against those of bureaucratic agencies. High levels of presidential interest will likely trump bureaucratic forces, but the latter will emerge more markedly when presidential concern is low (Rosati 1981, 248–51). Process, moreover, "varies as differences exist in the context and the styles of the participants. It is through the interaction of context, structure, participants, and process that a decision outcome is produced" (Rosati 1981, 251; on organizational structures and bureaucratic politics, see Hammond 1986). More generally, according to Bendor and Hammond, "What is odd about the model—a model of politics in a hierarchy—is that it says almost nothing about how hierarchy affects the politics" (1992, 317).

Has the bureaucratic politics approach lead to a productive line of research? It has certainly spawned a cottage industry of critiques. There is some evidence that it has served as a useful "on-ramp" to the super-highway of rational choice theory (see Bendor and Moe 1985; Hammond 1986; Bendor and Hammond 1992). It has been tested in particular decision cases—with differing assessments—as noted above. In Welch's view, however, "it has not led to an accumulation of useful knowledge of the kind to which its pioneers aspired" (Welch 1998, 210).

Welch's assessment may or may not be correct, but he does pose some useful questions calling for further study and clarification: what is the relationship between individual preferences and power versus organizations' preferences and power? Do organizations have clear and immutable interests, or do these change over time (and why)? How does policy choice relate to bureaucratic games—Equilibrium? Vector sum? A function of institutional design or structure? (Welch 1998, 214). And, as noted in the discussion on groupthink (especially the research of Schafer and Crichlow 1996, 2002), are bureaucratic politics and interests more an intervening variable, masking more powerful forces at work at an institutional or individual level? As Welch (1998, 215) observes, "when we articulate a 'bureaucratic politics' theory, we must be careful to ensure that variables at these other levels of analysis are not doing all of the interesting work in explaining or predicting policy choice—one of the primary criticisms of Allison's formulation (see Krasner 1972, 171; Art 1973, 472–73)." Hart and Rosenthal note, however, that bureaucratic politics may be a useful "middle range" or mid-level hypothesis providing the right "kind of balance between explanatory scope and in-depth process knowledge required for policy-relevant insights into manipulable variables" (1998, 236).

Organizational culture—which potentially offers a broader and deeper under-standing of how institutions can affect members' values and preferences—has been relatively under-studied from the perspective of decision making. Allison and

Zelikow do note its presence as a factor in their discussion of Model II in the second edition of *Essence of Decision* (Allison and Zelikow 1999, 145, 157). David Drezner has noted that "idea-infused" or "missionary" organizations, due to their relative newness, often develop organizational cultures blocking the intrusion of competing ideas. But there is a price: "this insulation also lessens the missionary institution's influence over the crafting of foreign policy." Preexisting bureaucracies will thwart the participation and influence of new actors (Drezner 2000, 733). In general, "Organizational culture as a means of propagating ideas is crucial to determining outcomes" (Bendor, Taylor, and Van Galen 1987; Brehm and Gates 1997), and it "is consistent with recent rationalist work...emphasizing the role of organizational culture as an important factor in bureaucratic politics" (Drezner 2000, 734).

As for the models and their propositions as exemplars of "good" social science, some have been highly critical (see Bendor and Hammond 1992; Welch 1992, 1998). According to Welch, "None of Allison's three models is a fully-specified causal model relating dependent and independent variables; instead, each is meant to be pretheoretical, or, better, 'metatheoretical,' since it merely invites the reader to 'think about X as if it were Y'" (Welch 1992, 114–15). But why not embrace that (assuming it is true), given the research that followed? *Essence of Decision* may have been a bit ragged in spots as rigorous social science, but it contributed in incalculable ways to how we have subsequently thought about and undertaken research on decision making—and should continue to do so. Falsification and improvement is good science too.

FURTHER ISSUES

Analysis of the strengths and weaknesses of the literature in these three areas of research is important in its own right. However, there are a number of additional issues that merit further consideration concerning the relationship of organizational structure and presidential decision making.

Independent or Dependent Variable?

One of the interesting tensions in studies of presidential decision making is the issue of what causes what: what is the independent variable and what is dependent? For some, especially those who approach the issue from the perspective of presidential studies, organizational structure is a dependent variable to presidential organization and management of decision-making systems. Greenstein, for example, has noted the importance of "organizational capacity" as one of a number of factors in analyzing the effects of leadership on the presidency, in accounting for differences among presidents, and in determining success or failure. That capacity includes two managerial components: the ability to "forge a team" and "minimizing the tendency of subordinates to tell their boss what they sense he wants to hear." And it incorporates two, more institutional, factors: an "ability to avail themselves of a rich and varied fare of advice and information" and "proficiency at creating effective institutional arrangements" (Greenstein 2004, 218–19).

For others the causal relationship is more complex. For Margaret Hermann and Charles Hermann (1989; also see Hermann 2001; M. Hermann et al. 2001), the leader matters when the "decision unit" is the "predominant leader," but single groups and multiple autonomous actors can also form the decision units and they can be self-contained or subject to influence from external forces (thus allowing group and institutional structure to come into play). According to Mitchell, "differences among presidents' leadership styles result in the formation of different advisory systems." But in turn, those systems act as intervening variables, which have "important consequences" in their own right: "different advisory systems result in variations in the presidential decision-making process" (Mitchell 2005, 2).

What those differences are and how they affect decision making vary from study to study. For Mitchell, four types of processes likely result, based on a presidential preference for formal or collegial structures and on whether presidents pursue a high or low degree of policy-making centralization in the White House. Mitchell especially emphasizes that the "way in which presidents and advisers resolve disagreements has implications for the outcome of the process. Specifically, the choice of 'unstructured solution' or method for resolving disagreements results in variations in decision outcomes" (Mitchell 2005, 2–3). In his view, such an approach has merit because of the importance of centralization of policy making in the White House as a key variable and the fact that "previous studies have only dealt superficially with the connection between decision process and decision outcomes" (Mitchell 2005, 2; also 217). For his part, Mitchell analyzes five cases: the Nixon–Kissinger negotiations to end the Vietnam War, Carter's negotiations with the Soviet Union on SALT II, Reagan's strategic arms negotiations in START I, Clinton and Bosnia, and George W. Bush's pre- and post-9/11 foreign policy. He does not analyze any cases from the Ford, George H. W. Bush, or pre-Nixon presidencies.

Whether centralization can deliver on the promise of a better understanding of presidential decision making remains an open question. At a minimum, it may allow us to better understand differences in presidencies that choose similar structures but operate quite differently (e.g. both Carter and Clinton were collegial, but the former was more highly centralized than the latter). Yet as Rudalevige (2002) has cautioned, centralization of policy formulation in the White House staff occurs less frequently than is anecdotally assumed, nor is there evidence that it has been increasing over time.

Also, as Ponder has noted in his study of Carter's domestic policy decision making, centralization can vary from policy issue to issue across even one presidency. He terms this "policy shift," and it can lead to different levels and types of staff activity: staff as "directors," centralizing policy making; staff as "facilitators," widely brokering agreements; and staff as "monitors," delegating policy making to broader bureaucratic entities (Ponder 2000, 35–47). "Process and roles shift," Ponder explains, "as presidential incentives and staff resources expand or contract" (Ponder 2000, 17).

Thomas Preston, drawing on the work of Margaret Hermann and work he has co-authored with her (Hermann and Preston 1999; also see Preston and Hermann 2004), develops, like Mitchell, a more encompassing typology, one grounded in case studies. In his study, Preston analyzes five cases: Truman and the Korean War, Eisenhower and Dien Bien Phu, Kennedy and the Cuban missile crisis, Johnson and the 1967–8 bombing halt in North Vietnam, and George H. W. Bush and the Gulf War. He also offers a general analysis of several foreign policy episodes in the Clinton presidency but provides no analyses of the Nixon, Ford, Carter, or Reagan presidencies.

The two dimensions Preston uses differ from Mitchell's more organizational-level concerns: for Preston both dimensions are grounded in *leader-related* attributes (high versus low expertise and interest in policy, and high versus low need for power/control). Yet like Mitchell, each combination in the typology bears organizational implications. Presidents high on a need to control will favor hierarchical systems but they will differ in their deference to the views of their advisers depending on the degree of their substantive policy expertise and interest. Likewise, presidents with low control needs will favor more informal, less hierarchical structures, but with continued differences in deference based on policy expertise and interest. Preston offers a robust theory and analysis of organizational preference grounded in personality and leadership style (Preston 2001, 16–17). Moreover, it is one, based on his typology, that is generalizable, predictive, and subject to cross-presidential comparison—the veritable methodological "hat trick." Yet, it too may promise more than it can deliver: decision-making structure is a dependent variable, and at times its independent effects and/or mediating causal role seem underdetermined.

Should organizational factors serve as the primary independent variables, as in Mitchell? Or should leadership style predominate, as in Preston? Whatever the answer, however, both Mitchell and Preston are on target in noting questions that still need to be answered. For Mitchell: "Are some advisory systems more or less prone to engage in bureaucratic politics? ... Which advisory systems are more prone to lead to breakdowns or policy failures? In what ways do advisers go about influencing the decision-making processes given a type of presidential management?" (Mitchell 2005, 218). So too with Preston, who asks:

Is it possible to develop objective, scientific techniques for assessing presidential personality and leadership style at a distance? Can subjective, impressionistic accounts of presidential personality and style be replaced by approaches allowing for clear and consistent measurement and comparison across presidents? Can we build theoretical models that allow us to predict the general parameters of a future president's style and decision making behavior based upon measures of their personal characteristics?   (Preston 2001, 3)

Sometimes the questions are as instructive as the particular answers.

In my own work, presidential organization and management of decision making are key, as are the basic collegial and hierarchical (or some combination thereof) systems that are thereby established. At the same time, however, I also take into account the institutional development of the White House staff system—a process occurring across administrations. Centralization is one component of institutionalization, but so too are emergence of hierarchy within the various parts of the staff system and the development of staff bureaucratization, which may generate the bureaucratic politics and other bureaucracy-determined forces that a presidential staff system was initially designed to guard against (Burke 2000).

Organizational Structure, Role, and Multiple Advocacy

The linkage between organizational structure and the particular roles of participants in decision making is important in establishing the causal impact of organization. Findings are divided; some studies discern personalistic-based patterns, others detect institutional factors at work (Garrison 1999, xvi–xvii). Still others find a mix, depending on the composition of the group and its open or closed nature (Hermann, Hermann, and Hagan 1987; Hermann and Hermann 1989). In Ponder's theory of policy shift and his three different types of staff activity, there is a president-led dynamic at work, as well as one that may result from the presence of "organizational routines" (Ponder 2000, 17). This focus on *role* is important, and Ponder sees it not as random or individually determined but linked to a broader dynamic that is both presidential and organizational.

Jean A. Garrison's study of national security policy making in the Nixon and Carter presidencies is also instructive. She notes the presence of "three types of influence maneuvers or relationships: structural, procedural, and interpersonal," which form adviser "games" (Garrison 1999, xix, 20–8). These gaming roles are not, as might be expected, simply the result of individual calculation and motivation, but stem from a complex dynamic that reflects broader institutional development, the features of a particular structure of advisory arrangements, as well as the social-psychological context in which they operate.

Alexander George's proposal for a system of multiple advocacy—the exposure of the president to robust and diverse streams of policy information and advice—is both an empirically and normatively important argument about the relationship of role and structure (George 1972; 1980, 191–209). Structurally, for multiple advocacy to work, there must not only be alternative channels of advice but, within those channels, participants must have approximately equal intellectual and bureaucratic resources and there must be adequate time for verbal give and take. Multiple advocacy does not, however, simply involve free debate or adversarial proceedings, but is a structured, balanced process. Role expectations are also important, and they are linked to structure. Presidents must be willing and able to participate in and manage the process. Equally important, George posits that key members of a decision group— in foreign policy, the national security adviser most notably—must act as "managerial custodians" of the process. The role of the latter includes balancing the resources of participants, strengthening weaker advocates, bringing in new participants to argue for unpopular options, establishing alternative channels of advice, arranging independent evaluation of policy options, and identifying and correcting broader malfunctions in the decision-making process (George 1980, 195–6).

Normatively, the premise of multiple advocacy is that it improves the deliberative process and thereby contributes to better policy decisions. But it is also empirically grounded. George does document how some presidents have practiced it and that it has contributed to the quality of their decision making: Eisenhower's 1954 decision not to intervene in Indochina and Johnson's 1964 decision not to proceed with a multilateral force for NATO. Additional research has substantiated George's findings (on Eisenhower, see Burke and Greenstein 1989, 286–9; Bose 1998, 37–41, 90–107). Porter has tested the model with respect to Ford's economic decision making (Porter 1980, 26–9, 241–52). Moens's analysis of Carter's foreign policy decision making is also instructive. Not only does he note that multiple advocacy is directed at some of the pathologies of groupthink and bureaucratic politics (1990, 12–14), but the general argument of the book concerns Carter's initial efforts to embrace multiple advocacy and the travails of how he failed to achieve it.

Multiple advocacy is not without its critics (see Walcott and Hult 2005, 314–16). George's initial 1972 article produced a strong dissent by I. M. Destler (1972) and a rejoinder by George. It is time consuming and may not be a good fit for some presidents' deliberative style. Its role constraints may operate too strongly, especially the prohibition against the NSC adviser providing policy advice to the president and the potential it has for weakening the adviser's leverage over the process. As I have argued, however, there may be some possibilities to achieve a more limited role of "honest broker," close in many respects to what the job of managerial custodian entails but with a recognition that some expansion of that role may be both necessary and possible (Burke 2005a).

The Problem of Presidential Fit

One area where further research is needed concerns the degree to which decision-making arrangements fit or otherwise reflect the needs of the president. At a general level, decision structures do need to match presidential predilections; certain types of structures may not mesh well with how a president processes information or reflect the types of settings in which a president feels most comfortable. Nor is this just a matter relating to how a president "thinks." Alexander George has explicitly noted a range of personal needs beyond just the cognitive: emotional support in making weighty decisions, the need to gain understanding and support among policy advisers, and the benefit of obtaining political support and legitimacy for decisions from the wider audience of Congress and the public (George 1980, 81). George's expanded conception of presidential needs invites systematic investigation. Advisory arrangements and broader organizational structures clearly differ in their ability to satisfy these needs.

Also note how this broader conception of presidential needs may be problematic for George's own goal of multiple advocacy, which may not always be a good fit with a president's cognitive needs or interpersonal style. Paul Kowert's (2002) research is instructive here. Not only must leaders guard against too little advice, but some must guard against too much. Some presidents are "open leaders" who thrive on information and advice (e.g. Eisenhower in his analysis), others are "closed leaders" who are comfortable in a more restricted setting (e.g. Reagan in his analysis). Although open leaders "are generally more capable of learning and improving the quality of their decision making over time," each type can also suffer if placed in the wrong organizational setting (Kowert 2002, 24). Open leaders in a closed advisory structure experience information deficit and the emergence of pathologies such as groupthink. Closed leaders in a more open setting confront information overload and often face decision deadlock, as would be the case perhaps under conditions of multiple advocacy.

The oft-held notion that an advisory system must fit a president like a suit of clothes also invites questioning. Presidential needs and personal predilections may contribute both positively and negatively to decision making. Have advisory systems accentuated the positive but guarded against the negative? To what extent can they balance recognition of the president's personal needs against other needs of effective decision making? Are patterns discernible, both positive and negative, among presidents? To what degree does an effective process require more than simple, personal fit?

Dynamics of Time

Much of the analysis of decision making tends to be discrete: case studies focusing on a particular policy episode or comparative case studies focusing on similar episodes but in different administrations. There is little analysis of similar decisions within one administration for the purposes of understanding the impact of time, particularly organizational change or learning behavior. There may be good reasons for this. To take one example: Mitchell finds that "Presidents rarely change their advisory systems once they are established. Indeed, presidents become bound by their advisory systems and it is only after prolonged inability to formulate policy or policy failure that they will adjust the advisory system" (Mitchell 2005, 208).

Other research has noted organizational change over time. In his study of national security policy making, Newmann (2003) found that presidents begin with a standard interagency process, but then evolve toward a more tight-knit circle of advisers. Other evidence indicates change in both the role of advisers and the organization and processes even within a single administration. There was a marked change under President Ford when Brent Scowcroft replaced Henry Kissinger as NSC adviser, and NSC staff operations and the role of the NSC adviser changed markedly over the tenure of Reagan's six NSC advisers. The role of the White House chief of staff has also similarly changed over time: Sherman Adams to Wilton Persons under Eisenhower, James Baker to Donald Regan and then to Howard Baker under Reagan. These changes in organization and role within a particular presidency, in turn, suggest a more complex dynamic at work than a simple matter of presidential fit; the president remained a constant throughout.

It is not clear which argument is right. There may be similar patterns of staff arrangements that persist through a presidency. There may be similar evolutions in organizational arrangements across presidencies. There may be significant differences over time in the experiences of one president using basically the same staff system throughout an administration. There are also may be significant differences that occur as individual presidents alter their staff and deliberative arrangements over time. Each possibility suggests the need for further research and explanation. *Individual* roles can also change over time—witness the devolution in Condoleezza Rice's role as an honest broker during her tenure as national security adviser (Burke 2005b). Is this a result of personal preference or strategy? Presidential preference? Some organizational dynamic? The policy issue at stake? And with what consequences on decision making?

A related issue concerning time is organizational learning. Janis's (1972, 1982) analysis of changes made in the Kennedy presidency after the Bay of Pigs fiasco is often cited as the classic case, and there has been some attention to the issue of "institutional memory" (see Burke 2000, 61, 213–15; Feldman 1993, 274–6). Yet presidency scholars have not studied learning behavior extensively. As Martha Feldman (1993, 276–80) observes, there is a substantial discussion of the topic in the general literature on organizations, and it is "one of potentially great importance in the study of the presidency" (276).

Haney is one of the few analysts to directly address the issue of learning. He finds in his case studies from Truman to George H. W. Bush that "The clearest examples of on-the-job learning ... are from the Johnson and [George H. W.] Bush administrations, and each is related to a significant performance failure." Both experienced negative feedback, but absent that, "I would suggest that presidents generally think things that 'ain't broke' do not need fixing" (Haney 1997, 135). Ponder has also discussed the issue, particularly with reference to Carter's energy policy (Ponder 1999).

Elsewhere the pickings are slim. As Stern and Verbeek (1998, 208) observe, "much of the research on governmental politics is event-centric—focusing on one case at a time. Of interest is to what extent and why do certain areas of foreign policy display more or less stable procedural and substantive patterns over time (cf. C. Hermann 1990)." They note the need for more attention to organizational learning, but they do cite some research on how parochial interests block change by altering the composition of the decision units (Hoyt 1997), and how high levels of zero-sum conflict block change through stalemate or deadlock (Hermann, Hermann, and Hagan 1987; Hermann and Hermann 1989, 368–9, 373). These findings may be limited, however. As Hoyt and Garrison note (1997, 271), "where the foreign policy small group literature has been deficient has been in examining just how groups evolve in terms of their structure and composition"—the big picture question.

Organizational Structure and Decision Making in Context

Another area where the impact of organizational structure merits further research relates to the context in which that structure is situated. For those studies that treat organization as an independent variable affecting decision process and outcome, there may be factors that more broadly affect how effectively particular structures operate. Particular areas and types of policy may be one such factor—e.g., Theodore Lowi's (1964, 1968) typology of distributive, redistributive, regulatory, and constituent policy. A significant amount of the case studies of presidential decision making concern foreign and national security issues, perhaps stemming from the interest in decision making by scholars in the field of international relations not just in presidential studies. Domestic and economic policy case studies have surely not been neglected, but they do appear to be overshadowed. If the "two presidencies" thesis is right—to take but one example—do differences in policy domain have effect on the appropriateness and operations of particular organizational structures?

Of particular note with respect to broader context is the work of Karen Hult and Charles Walcott. In a 1987 article, they note a number of contextual factors that may foster the increasing differentiation and complexity of organizational structure:

- Increasing uncertainty
- Increasing value heterogeneity
- Passage of time through the presidential term
- Passage of time across different administrations (Walcott and Hult 1987, 115–17).

In *Governing Public Organizations* (1990), they argue that the political dimension of the policy process—which they term "governance"—must be factored in when determining the appropriateness of a particular organizational arrangement in a particular policy area. To simplify their argument a bit, staff arrangements become appropriate depending on the degree of certainty, uncertainty, and controversy along two dimensions: (1) preferences about outcomes or goals, and (2) beliefs about causation (i.e. the means used to produce policy goals). Their typology produces nine organization possibilities. But to take just a few by way of example: more collegial arrangements are appropriate where outcomes are certain but beliefs about causation are uncertain (and vice versa). Hierarchical staff systems work best when both outcomes and causation are certain. "Adversarial/multi-Party advocacy" is appropriate when outcomes are uncertain and beliefs about causation are controversial (see Hult and Walcott 1990, 72).

But there are also potential limitations to their theory (and to any where context weighs heavily) when it is applied more narrowly to presidential decision making. One is the degree to which controversy or disagreement about goals or causation is known beforehand or whether they emerge only *in situ*, that is, as particular decisions are made within a preexisting staff arrangement. The former raises the issue of how malleable existing structures are in order to make changes to accommodate differences in governance. Existing structures may be present, moreover, for good reasons of their own (e.g., presidential needs) that must then be balanced off against the organizational needs of governance. With respect to controversy or disagreement that emerges *in situ*, the issue of malleability is especially complicated: alteration of organization in midstream. Furthermore, even if the various facts about the political dimensions of governance are ascertainable beforehand, most decisions that reach the level of presidential choice are often precisely those marked by high levels of disagreement, where both goals and beliefs about causation are marked by controversy. Here Hult and Walcott call for a decision setting that is "indeterminate:" "Decision making becomes particularly difficult.... In general, no particular structure seems more appropriate than any other" (Hult and Walcott 1990, 77). Still, Hult and Walcott have a point about the effects of the broader political context on the appropriateness of effective deliberative structures.

Greater attention to the stages of the decision-making process also seems warranted. Most studies of decision making focus on the principals—the president and a circle of high-level advisers. Yet for many decisions, especially non-crisis ones, this is merely the final stage of a process in which the table has been set and the menu already planned. These early stages may also reflect organizational and institutional factors at work. In national security policy making in recent presidencies, for example, although the principals are important, so too are the dynamics and organization of the deputies' committee below them, and working groups below that. In other policy areas, the organization of domestic and economic advising units may be consequential, as well as those of congressional and other liaison works. Much descriptive research has been done on these various components of the White House staff, but much remains to be done in linking their organization to subsequent stages of decision making.

The relationship of the broader political environment to decision-making structures is another area where context might matter. The impact of Congress especially deserves more systematic investigation. The legislative debate on the National Security Act of 1947 had great impact, for example, on the organization of the National Security Council and its staff. In the late 1950s, the investigative subcommittee led by Senator Henry Jackson (D-WA) was highly influential in Kennedy's dismantling of much of the formal national security structure under Eisenhower. Presidential reorganization authority, which is often legislatively set, is another area where Congress has often had an organizational impact (see Arnold 1998; Rudalevige 2002, 42–62, 126–7). Rudalevige's (2002) analysis of the contingent nature of centralization also opens an interesting area for further research. Do decision-making structures differ in those policy-making areas where White House centralization is high compared to those where agencies and departments are more heavily involved? Whether a president centralizes or does not centralize policy development in the White House, does the presence of a favorable or a sympathetic Congress and its bearing on legislative success have effect on the organizational structures utilized?

A Normative Dilemma

In many studies of decision making, an implicit normative assessment complements the analysis of empirical differences. In Richard Tanner Johnson's case, for example, a collegial system is a *happy* medium, while for Alexander George multiple advocacy is best. Assessing the merits of a decision-making process and its organization, however, can be tricky since that assessment is often based on the perceived success or failure of a policy outcome. In some cases, but perhaps few, the linkage may be clear: an outcome (such as Kennedy's 1961 Bay of Pigs invasion) is a decided fiasco and it can be clearly linked to problematic deliberations beforehand.

Determining success is more difficult. Assessment here may require a normative judgment about the outcome itself, as well as counterfactual comparison to other outcomes that might have been selected but were not, plus convincing evidence and a strong empirical argument linking outcome back to process. A hard case: commentators on the Cuban missile crisis of 1962 often take it as a success, and perhaps for good reason; it did avoid a nuclear showdown. But could other courses of action, not taken, have been plausibly more successful? Was the outcome, even if deemed successful, a product of the process, its organization, and dynamics or was it largely determined by President Kennedy's caution and personal beliefs and preferences?

One approach to this dilemma is simply to be up front in making a normative assessment (e.g. on the Korean War see Paige 1968, 325–55). Another is to take the participants' normative frame of reference as definitive: did they achieve what they wanted to achieve? Subjective normative assessments have also been avoided by relying on the intersubjective judgments of scholars and other experts, with the hope that collective judgments will cancel out individual biases. Herek, Janis, and Huth (1987) are especially sophisticated in this regard: the outside experts enlisted for their study were unaware of the authors' hypotheses, selected the sample of cases, selected bibliographic sources on the cases, and then rated the decision outcomes (also see Schafer and Crichlow 1996, 426–7; 2002, 50–1).

Still another approach is to emphasize the instrumental—attention to decision-making means rather than direct assessment of ends or outcomes. That is, to focus on the *quality* of the process rather than the intrinsic merits of the decision taken. As Greenstein and I have noted, "Our comparative advantage as students of decision making is not in judging what policies are warranted. It is in establishing whether alternatives were systematically and rigorously addressed" (Burke and Greenstein 1989, 3). Among the more interesting and systematic attempts to evaluate the quality of decision processes are Haney's six-part analytic assessment (1997, 126) and Herek, Janis and Huth's (1987, 204–5) use of Janis and Mann's (1977) seven signs of defective decision making. In these studies, authors still make evaluative judgments, but they are about the process and its relation to effective decision making, not judgments about policy ends.

At the same time, there are two costs to an approach based on instrumental reasoning. The first is whether actual decision makers realistically approach the requisites of "rational" decision making. There is a long line of argument here, including, among others, Herbert Simon's (1946) notions of satisficing and bounded rationality, Charles Lindblom's (1959, 1965) concept of "muddling through," John Steinbruner's (1974) cybernetic theory, Amos Tversky and Daniel Kahneman's (1974) analyses of heuristic decision shortcuts under conditions of uncertainty, Robert Jervis (1976) on images, consistency, and prior expectations, and Robert Axelrod (1976) on prior beliefs structures, causal relationships, and cognitive maps. The second cost is the loss of normative linkage to policy ends: effective, well-organized decision processes cannot guarantee good or effective policy ends, indeed a high-quality process might lead to a policy choice that is normatively unacceptable or a decision fiasco.

WHAT DO WE WANT TO KNOW? AND WHY DO WE WANT TO KNOW IT?

Analysis of the impact of organization upon decision making is a rich and thriving vein of research. As Ponder observes, "The perception has been that knowledge about the presidency is noncumulative, ad hoc, and good only for understanding one or a few presidencies and/or the nature of the times in which they served" (Ponder 2000, 189). Analysis of the literature on presidential decision making, at a minimum, indicates that this perception is wrong. Much remains to be done, but much has been already done, even if the groundwork is a bit patchy and uneven.

Connections clearly need to be strengthened to other disciplines where parallel research, even of presidential decision making, has been undertaken. Much of the more recent work on groupthink, for example, is the product of social psychologists rather than political scientists, much less presidency scholars. I suspect that there is a robust literature in various disciplines concerned with organization and management, such as in business administration, that is well worth tapping for further insight.

As a discipline, we also need to think more deeply about what we want to know and why we want to know it. Various research projects approach the topic with different questions in mind. Some are narrowly empirical and ask what are the critical independent variables that explain some posited dependent variable. The goal here is to build a nomothetic—general law derived—understanding. That is a noble effort, yet given the complex interrelation between organization on the one hand, and presidential preference, management, and decision needs on the other, causality is complex if ever-changing.

Indeed, there is an interesting internal debate between Allison and Zelikow in one of the endnotes to *Essence of Decision*. Allison adheres to Carl Hempel's understanding of scientific explanation: events can be understood based on particular circumstances, general laws, and the possibility of prediction. For Zelikow, the scientific paradigm does not carry over to the philosophy of history: "history can usefully draw attention to plausible possibilities, suggesting scrutiny and questions, but cannot provide laws of government behavior" (Allison and Zelikow 1999, 12). Neither is right, yet neither is wrong.

Research must also recognize the contingent nature of the questions asked. Sometimes, the goal is to understand a particular decision, as in the case of the Cuban missile crisis. This is an effort that we should embrace, and not dismiss as descriptively limited, by the way. It is of vital importance that political scientists undertake case analysis, rather than, as Bendor and Hammond suggest, that it be "a task characteristic of historians" (Bendor and Hammond 1992, 318). Political scientists ask different questions and sift through the material in their own discipline-informed ways. Sometimes the goal is prescriptive: Neustadt's goal of effective presidential power. Sometimes the aim is more comparative in nature. Much can be gleaned from an analysis of one presidency. Much can also be gleaned from more comparative case studies that treat more than one presidency. Each holds constant certain variables that parsimoniously reveal effects on dependent variables. But in holding some variables constant, the development of general laws is made more difficult—the bane of mid-level theory—since it leaves unexamined factors that might well be of causal significance.

We must also factor in practical value. Groupthink, multiple advocacy, honest broker, collegial and formal systems, and bureaucratic politics—to list just a few— are not just topics of scholarly inquiry but concepts that have seeped into the general political vocabulary. Moreover, it is a vocabulary of those who put organizations into practice and participate in and utilize their results. It is an audience that we should not ignore.

On the first page of *Essence of Decision*, Allison quotes President Kennedy from his foreword to Theodore Sorensen's *Decision-Making in the White House* (1963, xi–xii):

The essence of ultimate decision remains impenetrable to the observer—often, indeed to the decider himself. . . . There will always be the dark and tangled stretches in the decision-making process—mysterious even to those who may be most intimately involved.

In some sense, Kennedy may be right. But as the work of Allison, Janis, Johnson, and scholars who have followed in their path indicates—even of Kennedy's own deliberations—there is considerable light to be shed through analysis of the impact of organization upon decision making.

References

Allison, G. T. 1971. *Essence of Decision: Explaining the Cuban Missile Crisis*. Boston: Little, Brown.
——and Halperin, M. H. 1972. Bureaucratic Politics: A Paradigm and Some Policy Implications. *World Politics*, 24 (Spring Special Supplement): 40–79.
——and Szanton, P. 1976. *Remaking Foreign Policy: The Organizational Connection*. New York: Basic Books.
——and Zelikow, P. 1999. *Essence of Decision: Explaining the Cuban Missile Crisis*, 2nd edn. New York: Longman.
Arnold, P. E. 1998. *Making the Managerial Presidency: Comprehensive Reorganization Planning, 1905–1996*. Lawrence: University Press of Kansas.
Art, R. J. 1973. Bureaucratic Politics and American Foreign Policy: A Critique. *Policy Sciences*, 4/4: 467–90.
Axelrod, R. (ed.) 1976. *Structure of Decision: The Cognitive Maps of Political Elites*. Princeton, NJ: Princeton University Press.
Bacchus, W. L. 1974. *Foreign Policy and the Bureaucratic Process: The State Department's Country Director System*. Princeton, NJ: Princeton University Press.
Beard, E. 1976. *Developing the ICBM: A Study in Bureaucratic Politics*. New York: Columbia University Press.
Bendor, J., and Hammond. T. H. 1992. Rethinking Allison's Models. *American Political Science Review*, 86: 301–22.

—— and MoE, T. 1985. An Adaptive Model of Bureaucratic Politics. *American Political Science Review*, 79: 755–74.

—— TAYLOR, S., and VAN GAALEN, R. 1987. Stacking the Deck: Bureaucratic Missions and Policy Design. *American Political Science Review*, 81: 873–96.

BOSE, M. 1998. *Shaping and Signaling Presidential Policy: The National Security Decision Making of Eisenhower and Kennedy*. College Station: Texas A&M University Press.

BREHM, J., and GATES, S. 1997. *Working, Shirking, and Sabotage: Bureaucratic Responses to a Democratic Public*. Ann Arbor: University of Michigan Press.

BURKE, J. P. 2000. *The Institutional Presidency: Organizing and Managing the White House from FDR to Clinton*. Baltimore: Johns Hopkins University Press.

—— 2005a. The Neutral/Honest Broker Role in Foreign Policy Decision Making: A Reassessment. *Presidential Studies Quarterly*, 35: 229–58.

—— 2005b. Condoleezza Rice as NSC Advisor: A Case Study of the Honest Broker Role. *Presidential Studies Quarterly*, 35: 554–75.

—— and GREENSTEIN, F. I. 1989. *How Presidents Test Reality: Decisions on Vietnam, 1954 and 1965*. New York: Russell Sage.

CIBOSKI, K. 1977. The Bureaucratic Connection: Explaining the Skybolt Decision. Pp. 374–88 in *American Defense Policy*, 4th edn., ed. J. E. Endicott and R. W. Stafford. Baltimore: Johns Hopkins University Press.

DESTLER, I. M. 1972. Comment: Multiple Advocacy, Some Limits and Costs. *American Political Science Review*, 66: 785–90.

—— 1974. *Presidents, Bureaucrats, and Foreign Policy: The Politics of Organization Reform*. Princeton, NJ: Princeton University Press.

DICKINSON, M. J., and LEBO, M. J. 2007. Reexamining the Growth of the Institutional Presidency, 1940–2000. *Journal of Politics*, 69: 206–19.

DREZNER, D. W. 2000. Ideas, Bureaucratic Politics, and the Crafting of Foreign Policy. *American Journal of Political Science*, 44: 733–49.

ESSER, J. K., and LINDOERFER, J. S. 1989. Groupthink and the Space Shuttle Challenger Accident: Toward a Quantitative Case Study. *Journal of Behavioral Decision Making*, 2/3: 167–77.

FELDMAN, M. S. 1993. Organization Theory and the Presidency. Pp. 267–88 in *Researching the Presidency: Vital Questions, New Approaches*, ed. G. C. Edwards III, J. H. Kessel, and B. A. Rockman. Pittsburgh: University of Pittsburgh Press.

FULLER, S. R., and ALDAG, R. J. 1997. Challenging the Mindguards: Moving Small Group Analysis beyond Groupthink. Pp. 55–93 in *Beyond Groupthink: Political Group Dynamics and Foreign Policy-Making*, ed. P. 't Hart, E. K. Stern, and B. Sundelius. Ann Arbor: University of Michigan Press,

GAENSLEN, F. 1992. Decision-Making Groups. Pp. 165–94 in *Political Psychology and Foreign Policy*, ed. E. Singer and V. Hudson. Boulder, CO: Westview.

GARRISON, J. A. 1999. *Games Advisors Play: Foreign Policy in the Nixon and Carter Administrations*. College Station; Texas A&M University Press.

GEORGE, A. L. 1972. The Case for Multiple Advocacy in Making Foreign Policy. *American Political Science Review*, 66: 751–85.

—— 1980. *Presidential Decision-making in Foreign Policy: The Effective Use of Information and Advice*. Boulder, CO: Westview.

—— 1997. From Groupthink to Contextual Analysis of Policy-Making Groups. Pp. 35–53 in *Beyond Groupthink: Political Group Dynamics and Foreign Policy-Making*, ed. P. 't Hart, E. K. Stern, and B. Sundelius. Ann Arbor: University of Michigan Press.

GREENSTEIN, F. I. 2004. *The Presidential Difference: Leadership Style from FDR to George W. Bush*. Princeton, NJ: Princeton University Press.

HALPERIN, M. H. 1972. The Decision to Deploy the ABM: Bureaucratic and Domestic Politics in the Johnson Administration. *World Politics*, 25: 62–95.

——1974. *Bureaucratic Politics and Foreign Policy*. Washington, DC: Brookings Institution.

HAMMOND, T. H. 1986. Agenda Control, Organizational Structure, and Bureaucratic Politics. *American Journal of Political Science*, 30: 379–420.

HANEY, P. J. 1994. Decision Making during International Crises: A Reexamination. *International Interactions*, 19: 177–91.

——1997. *Organizing for Foreign Policy Crises: Presidents, Advisers, and the Management of Decision Making*. Ann Arbor: University of Michigan Press.

HART, J. 1992. Eisenhower and the Swelling of the Presidency. *Polity*, 24: 673–91.

HART, P. 't. 1991. Irving L. Janis' *Victims of Groupthink*. *Political Psychology*, 12: 247–78.

——1994. *Groupthink in Government: A Study of Small Groups and Policy Failure*. Baltimore: Johns Hopkins University Press.

——and ROSENTHAL, U. 1998. Reappraising Bureaucratic Politics. *Mershon International Studies Review*, 42: 233–40.

——STERN, E. K., and SUNDELIUS, B. 1997. Foreign Policy-Making at the Top: Political Group Dynamics. Pp. 3–34 in *Beyond Groupthink: Political Group Dynamics and Foreign Policy-Making*, ed. P. 't Hart, E. K. Stern, and B. Sundelius. Ann Arbor: University of Michigan Press.

HEAD, R. 1988. Crisis Decision-making: Bureaucratic Politics and the Use of Force. Pp. 72–90 in *Bureaucratic Politics and National Security: Theory and Practice*, ed. D. C. Kozak and J. M. Keagle. Boulder, CO: Lynne Rienner.

HENDERSON, P. G. 1988. *Managing the Presidency: The Eisenhower Legacy: From Kennedy to Reagan*. Boulder, CO: Westview.

HENSLEY, T. R., and GRIFFIN, G. W. 1986. Victims of Groupthink: The Kent State University Board of Trustees and the 1977 Gymnasium Controversy. *Journal of Conflict Resolution*, 30: 497–531.

HEREK, G. M., JANIS, I. L., and HUTH, P. 1987. Decision Making during International Crisis: Is Quality of Process Related to Outcome? *Journal of Conflict Resolution*, 31: 203–26.

HERMANN, C. F. 1990. Changing Course: When Governments Choose to Redirect Foreign Policy. *International Studies Quarterly*, 34: 3–21.

——STEIN, J., SUNDELIUS, B., and WALKER, S. 2001. Resolve, Accept or Avoid: The Effects of Group Conflict on Foreign Policy Decisions. *International Studies Review*, 3: 133–68.

HERMANN, M. G. 2001. How Decision Units Shape Foreign Policy: A Theoretical Framework. *International Studies Review*, 3: 47–81.

——and HERMANN. C. F. 1989. Who Makes Foreign Policy Decisions and How: An Empirical Inquiry. *International Studies Quarterly*, 33: 361–87.

——————and HAGAN. J. D. 1987. How Decision Units Shape Foreign Policy Behavior. Pp. 309–36 in *New Directions in the Study of Foreign Policy*, ed. C. F. Hermann, C. W. Kegley, and J. N. Rosenau. Boston: Unwin Hyman.

——and PRESTON, T. 1999. Presidents, Leadership Style, and the Advisory Process. Pp. 351–681 in *The Domestic Sources of American Foreign Policy: Insights and Evidence*, 3rd edn., ed. E. R. Wittkopf and J. M. McCormick. Lanham, MD: Rowman & Littlefield.

——————KORNAY, B., and SHAW, T. M. 2001. Who Leads Matters: The Effects of Powerful Individuals. *International Studies Review*, 3: 83–131.

HOYT, P. D. 1997. The Political Manipulation of Group Composition: Engineering the Decision Context. *Political Psychology*, 18: 771–90.

——and GARRISON, J. A. 1997. Political Manipulation within the Small Group: Foreign Policy Advisers in the Carter Administration. Pp. 249–74 in *Beyond Groupthink: Political Group*

Dynamics and Foreign Policy-Making, ed. P. 't Hart, E. K. Stern, and B. Sundelius. Ann Arbor: University of Michigan Press.

HULT, K. M., and WALCOTT, C. E. 1990. *Governing Public Organizations: Politics, Structures, and Institutional Design*. Pacific Grove, CA: Brooks/Cole.

—————— 2004. *Empowering the White House: Governance under Nixon, Ford, and Carter*. Lawrence: University Press of Kansas.

HYBEL, A. R. 1999. A Fortuitous Victory: An Information Processing Approach to the Gulf War. Pp. 333–50 in *The Domestic Sources of American Foreign Policy: Insights and Evidence*, 3rd edn., ed. E. R. Wittkopf and J. M. McCormick. Lanham, MD: Rowman & Littlefield.

ISAACSON, W., and THOMAS, E. 1986. *The Wise Men*. New York: Simon & Schuster.

JANIS, I. L. 1972. *Victims of Groupthink: A Psychological Study of Foreign-Policy Decisions and Fiascoes*. Boston: Houghton Mifflin.

—— 1982. *Groupthink: Psychological Studies of Policy Decisions and Fiascoes*, 2nd. edn. Boston: Houghton Mifflin.

—— 1989. *Crucial Decisions: Leadership in Policymaking and Crisis Management*. New York: Free Press.

—— and MANN, L. 1977. *Decision Making: A Psychological Analysis of Conflict, Choice, and Commitment*. New York: Free Press.

JERVIS, R. 1976. *Perception and Misperception in International Politics*. Princeton, NJ: Princeton University Press.

JOHNSON, R. T. 1974. *Managing the White House: An Intimate Study of the Presidency*. New York: Harper & Row.

KATZ, D., and KAHN, R. L. 1978. *The Social Psychology of Organizations*. New York: Wiley.

KELLERMAN, B. 1983. Allison Redux: Three More Decision-Models. *Polity*, 15: 351–67.

KOWERT, P. A. 2002. *Groupthink or Deadlock: When do Leaders Learn from their Advisors?* Albany: State University of New York Press.

KOZAK, D. C., and KEAGLE, J. M. (eds.) 1988. *Bureaucratic Politics and National Security: Theory and Practice*. Boulder, CO: Lynne Rienner.

KRASNER, S. D. 1972. Are Bureaucracies Important? (Or Allison Wonderland). *Foreign Policy*, 7: 159–79.

LINDBLOM, C. E. 1959. The Science of "Muddling Through." *Public Administration Review*, 19: 79–88.

—— 1965. *The Intelligence of Democracy*. New York: Free Press.

LONGLEY, J., and PRUITT, D. G. 1980. Groupthink: A Critique of Janis's Theory. In *Review of Personality and Social Psychology*, ed. L. Wheeler. Beverly Hills, CA: Sage.

LOWI, T. J. 1964. American Business, Public Policy, Case-Studies, and Political Theory. *World Politics*, 16: 677–715.

—— 1968 Four Systems of Policy, Politics, and Choice. *Public Administration Review*, 32: 298–310.

McCAULEY, C. 1989. The Nature of Social Influence in Groupthink: Compliance and Internalization. *Journal of Personality and Social Psychology*, 57: 250–60.

Mershon International Studies Review. 1998. Whither the Study of Governmental Politics in Foreign Policymaking? A Symposium. *Mershon International Studies Review*, 42: 205–55.

MILES, R. E., JR. 1978. The Origin and Meaning of Miles' Law. *Public Administration Review*, 38: 399–403.

MITCHELL, D. 2005. *Making Foreign Policy: Presidential Management of the Decision-Making Process*. Burlington, VT: Ashgate.

MOENS, A. 1990. *Foreign Policy under Carter: Testing Multiple Advocacy Decision Making*. Boulder, CO: Westview.

MULCAHY, K. V. 1995. Rethinking Groupthink: Walt Rostow and the National Security Advisory Process in the Johnson Administration. *Presidential Studies Quarterly*, 25: 237–50.

NEUSTADT, R. E. 1990. *Presidential Power and the Modern Presidents: The Politics of Leadership from Roosevelt to Reagan*. New York: Macmillan.

NEWMANN, W. W. 2003. *Managing National Security Policy: The President and the Process*. Pittsburgh: University of Pittsburgh Press.

Organizational Behavior and Human Decision Processes. 1998. Symposium on Groupthink. *Organizational Behavior and Human Decision Processes*, 73: 103–374.

PAIGE, G. D. 1968. *The Korean Decision*. New York: Free Press.

POLENBERG, R. 1966. *Reorganizing Roosevelt's Government: The Controversy over Executive Reorganization, 1936–1939*. Cambridge, MA: Harvard University Press.

PONDER, D. E. 1999. The Presidency as a Learning Organization. *Presidential Studies Quarterly*, 29: 100–14.

——2000. *Good Advice: Information and Policy Making in the White House*. College Station: Texas A&M University Press.

PORTER, R. B. 1980. *Presidential Decision Making: The Economic Policy Board*. Cambridge: Cambridge University Press.

PRESTON, T. 1997. "Following the Leader:" The Impact of U.S. Presidential Style upon Advisory Group Dynamics, Structure, and Decision. Pp. 191–248 in *Beyond Groupthink: Political Group Dynamics and Foreign Policy-Making*, ed. P. 't Hart, E. K. Stern, and B. Sundelius. Ann Arbor: University of Michigan Press,

——2001. *The President and his Inner Circle: Leadership Style and the Advisory Process in Foreign Affairs*. New York: Columbia University Press.

——and HERMANN, M. G. 2004. Presidential Leadership Style and the Foreign Policy Advisory Process. Pp. 363–80 in *The Domestic Sources of American Foreign Policy: Insights and Evidence*, 4th edn., ed. E. R. Wittkopf and J. M. McCormick. Lanham, MD: Rowman & Littlefield,.

——and 't HART, P. 1999. Understanding and Evaluating Bureaucratic Politics: The Nexus between Political Leaders and Advisory Systems. *Political Psychology*, 20: 49–98.

PURKITT, H. E. 1992. Political Decision Making in Small Groups: The Cuban Missile Crisis Revisited—One More Time. Pp. 219–46 in *Political Psychology and Foreign Policy*, ed. E. Singer and V. Hudson. Boulder, CO: Westview.

RAGSDALE, L., and THEIS, J. J., III. 1997. The Institutionalization of the American Presidency, 1924–92. *American Journal of Political Science*, 41: 1280–318.

RHODES, E. 1994. Do Bureaucratic Politics Matter? Some Disconfirming Findings from the Case of the U.S. Navy. *World Politics*, 47: 1–41.

ROSATI, J. A. 1981. Developing a Systematic Decision-Making Framework: Bureaucratic Politics in Perspective. *World Politics*, 33/2: 234–52.

ROURKE, F. E. (ed.) 1978. *Bureaucratic Power in National Politics*. Boston: Little, Brown.

RUDALEVIGE, A. 2002. *Managing the President's Program: Presidential Leadership and Legislative Policy Formulation*. Princeton, NJ: Princeton University Press.

SCHAFER, M., and CRICHLOW, S. 1996. Antecedents of Groupthink: A Quantitative Study. *Journal of Conflict Resolution*, 40: 415–35.

——— 2002. The Process–Outcome Connection in Foreign Policy Decision Making: A Quantitative Study Building on Groupthink. *International Studies Quarterly*, 46: 45–68.

SIGAL, L. V. 1978. Bureaucratic Politics and the Tactical Use of Committees: The Interim Committee and the Decision to Drop the Atomic Bomb. *Polity*, 10: 326–64.

SIMON, H. A. 1946. *Administrative Behavior*. New York: Free Press.

SLOAN, J. W. 1990. The Management and Decision-Making Style of President Eisenhower. *Presidential Studies Quarterly*, 20: 295–314.

SMITH, S. 1984. Policy Preferences and Bureaucratic Position: The Case of the American Hostage Rescue Mission. *International Affairs*, 61: 9–25.

——1985. Groupthink and the Hostage Rescue Mission. *British Journal of Political Science*, 15: 117–23.

SORENSEN, T. 1963. *Decision-Making in the White House: The Olive Branch and the Arrows*. New York: Columbia University Press.

STEINBRUNER, J. D. 1974. *The Cybernetic Theory of Decision*. Princeton, NJ: Princeton University Press.

STERN, E. K. 1997. Probing the Plausibility of Newgroup Syndrome: Kennedy and the Bay of Pigs. Pp. 153–89 in *Beyond Groupthink: Political Group Dynamics and Foreign Policy-Making*, ed. P. 't Hart, E. K. Stern, and B. Sundelius. Ann Arbor: University of Michigan Press,.

——and VERBEEK, B. 1998. Introduction: Whither the Study of Governmental Politics in Foreign Policymaking? A Symposium. *Mershon International Studies Review*, 42: 205–55.

TVERSKY, A., and KAHNEMAN, D. 1974. Judgment under Uncertainty: Heuristics and Biases. *Science*, 185: 1124–31.

WALCOTT, C. E., and HULT, K. M. 1987. Organizing the White House: Structure, Environment, and Organizational Governance. *American Journal of Political Science*, 31: 109–25.

————1995. *Governing the White House: From Hoover through LBJ*. Lawrence: University Press of Kansas.

————2005. White House Structure and Decision Making: Elaborating the Standard Model. *Presidential Studies Quarterly*, 35: 303–18.

WELCH, D. A. 1989. Crisis Decision Making Reconsidered. *Journal of Conflict Resolution*, 33: 430–45.

——1992. The Organizational Process and Bureaucratic Politics Paradigms: Retrospect and Prospect. *International Security*, 17: 112–46.

——1998. A Positive Science of Bureaucratic Politics. *Mershon International Studies Review*, 42: 210–16.

WHYTE, G. 1989. Groupthink Reconsidered. *Academy of Management Review*, 14: 40–56.

CHAPTER 23

INFLUENCES ON PRESIDENTIAL DECISION MAKING

KAREN M. HULT

CHARLES E. WALCOTT

In April 2006, responding to repeated questions about his support for embattled Defense Secretary Donald Rumsfeld, President George W. Bush strongly stated: "I am the decider."[1] As with most US presidents, however, it was less clear how broadly that claim applied, who else participated in decision making, the sources of information and advice on which the president based his decisions, and what influences were paramount in making them.

The scholarly literature that explores such topics is broad and varied. It traverses disciplinary lines and ranges in emphasis from description to explanation to prescription. Differing theoretical orientations and diverse methodological techniques abound. Over the last two decades, this scholarship has exhibited increasing analytical and methodological self-consciousness and growing sophistication. Moreover, the research for the most part has remained solidly anchored in the political and policy challenges confronting presidencies and the broader political system. In the future, we argue that more attention should be paid to looking beyond crisis decision

---

[1] The full quote was: " 'I listen to all voices, but mine is the final decision,' he said. 'And Don Rumsfeld is doing a fine job. He's not only transforming the military, he's fighting a war on terror. He's helping us fight a war on terror. I have strong confidence in Don Rumsfeld. I hear the voices, and I read the front page, and I know the speculation. But I'm the decider, and I decide what is best. And what's best is for Don Rumsfeld to remain as the secretary of defense' " (Bush 2008).

making and to exploring possible generalizations across policy spheres, perhaps within the context of a contingency framework. We contend that empirical research and accompanying explanatory theory on presidential decisions and decision making should continue to be problem driven (Shapiro 2005). In the short to medium run, we believe scholars should place primary emphasis on probing for patterns in decision processes and in influences on substantive outcomes, not on searching for additional decision theories or elaborating on potential influences.

Whether the emphasis is substantive, analytical, or normative, most attention in focusing on presidential decision making revolves around the extent, the nature, and the impact of presidential agency. What are the influences on presidential decisions? To what extent are they actually *presidential* decisions? What are the effects (and on whom) of such decisions?

After a brief discussion of the perimeters of our discussion, we first explore the range of factors that scholars have identified as primary shapers of presidential decisions. Then, we turn our attention to presidential advisers who help shape the agenda, frame many of the problems, and filter much of the information presidents cope with in making decisions. Exploration of the analytical, methodological, and prescriptive dimensions of contemporary scholarship on presidential decisions and decision making occupy the following sections. We conclude with suggestions for future work.

Analytical Prelude

At the outset, it may be helpful to sketch the boundaries of our discussion. First, an analysis of scholarship on presidential decision making must begin with the challenge of defining the focal concept, "decision." The term can refer to anything from an individual's cognitive process to a small group interaction to a formal declaration to a long-term, iterative process. People make choices all the time, but "big" decisions can take years and involve scores of actors. Indeed, the concept "decision" encompasses so many diverse phenomena that one can question its utility. At the very least, any use of the term requires that its meaning in context be specified.

Here we address this issue provisionally by viewing decisions as "choice opportunities" (following Boin et al. 2005). Thus a decision is a point that analysts identify at which a decision maker selects or dismisses (at least temporarily) a particular action or position. Whether one views decisions as "choice based" or "rule based" is among the issues James G. March (1994) contends analysts should confront. Although we do not do so here, it appears that most presidency scholars take the former view, seeing decision makers as typically "making choices among alternatives by evaluating their consequences in terms of prior preferences" (March 1994, viii); only rarely, however, do scholars articulate or justify their analytical stances. To fully review the relevant literature on presidential decision making, we will look beyond choice opportunities to view decision making as a broader social process as well. In doing so, we will of necessity move across levels of analysis, among decisional contexts and into a thicket of alternative conceptions of what "decision making" is. The result will be to identify what Harold Guetzkow (1950) long ago characterized as "islands of theory"—separate but potentially related clusters of theory and data that he hoped ultimately would be linked. Unfortunately, in the area of decision making in the US presidency, such linkages are mostly lacking.

Second, we focus primarily on policy decisions and decision processes, probing varying influences and dynamics. At the same time, the emphasis on policy should not obscure the fact that political concerns (reflecting, for example, ideological or partisan purposes and objectives) and considerations of communications with various publics permeate most presidential choices and the associated decision-making processes. In the White House, distinctions between policy and politics tend to blur in practice.

Third, although relatively few works on US presidential decision making outside of foreign policy explicitly identify the focal "decision unit" (see, e.g., Hermann and Hermann 1989), it appears to be a useful concept in helping identify both the ultimate decision maker and patterns of decision making. An "authoritative decision unit" is "an individual or set of individuals with the ability to commit the resources of the society and, when faced with a problem, the authority to make a decision that cannot be readily reversed" (Hermann 2001, 48). Such units may "shape policy decision making across diverse situations and issues as well as different political settings" (Hermann 2001, 48). US presidential decisions and decision making probably are mostly best characterized as having a "predominant leader" as the decision unit (that is, an "individual with the power and authority to commit or withhold government resources in regard to the problem at hand"; Hermann 2001, 58). Yet viewing the decision unit as a "single group" may better capture the dynamics on other occasions (e.g., during a national security or domestic crisis). Not only does this suggest that the structuring of presidential decision making is an empirical question, but it also opens avenues for comparative analyses within and across presidential decisions and among national executives.

INFLUENCES ON PRESIDENTIAL DECISION MAKING

As the islands of theory metaphor suggests, scholarship on presidential decision making has explored multiple influences and relied on differing theoretical streams. One way to begin to make sense of these numerous factors and theories is to examine them by level of analysis. Doing so draws attention to the primary drivers of decision processes and highlights the complex dynamics scholars seek to untangle. It exposes as well the wide variety of dependent variables and seeming scholarly over-attentiveness to independent variables. Since few recent works stress single factor explanations, this section concludes by looking at dominant combinations and emphases.

The once common debate between "personal" and "institutional" influences on presidential decision making has mostly disappeared. Moreover, studies that employ the "predominant leader" as the decision unit examine numerous potential shapers of decisions and decision processes (such as chiefs of staff, vice presidents, national security assistants), including but hardly limited to presidents.

Individuals

Works on the presidency are not always as explicit as they might be about the extent to which "individual" influences such as "personality" or childhood illness are idiosyncratic to particular presidents or vary along identifiable dimensions such as "decisiveness" and "emotional intelligence" from which scholars can generalize. However, we can place most recent work in the latter category, even as the relevant dimensions and extent of observed variation differ.

Scholars have paid considerable attention to presidential leadership or management style. Like the concept "decision," however, scholars employ "style" in many different ways. Colin Campbell (1983, 1986, 1991), for example, argues that "executive leaders' management styles" shape both how they organize their advisory systems and how they seek out and process advice; his supporting evidence comes from case analyses. Like Campbell, Margaret Hermann and her colleagues focus on "authoritative leaders" in various national settings; they contend that three dimensions are especially important in tapping leadership style: "how leaders react to constraints, process information, and are motivated to deal with their political environments" (M. Hermann et al. 2001, 94. See also Hermann and Preston 1994 and Hermann 1995 for applications to US presidents). Although Hermann and Preston mostly have probed these ideas in studying foreign policy choices, they suggest that leadership styles also can be applied to domestic policy issues; the styles of individual leaders, however, may change depending on their expertise (M. Hermann et al. 2001, 100).

Working within the Hermann et al. decision unit framework, Jonathan Keller (2005a) similarly treats leadership style as a multidimensional concept; his work additionally employs comparative case analysis rather than looking at individual or large numbers of cases. He distinguishes between presidents who tend to be "constraint respecters" and those who are "constraint challengers." In classifying presidents, he examines several dimensions, including their openness to information and their sensitivity to political context; individuals' placement on these dimensions in turn is influenced by their task vs. interpersonal emphasis, their need for power, their distrust for others, and their nationalism (2005a, 840 ff.). Informally testing his predictions on Presidents Kennedy and Reagan making specific decisions during international crises, Keller concludes that high levels of task emphasis and need for power were associated with more centralized decision processes and a tendency to suppress dissent; he also finds that leadership style acted as a "moderating variable."

Other scholars explore the ties between presidential personality and decision making. Employing a "trait-based approach to presidential psychology," Fred Greenstein (2004) suggests that the "cognitive style with which [presidents] process the tidal wave of advice and information" that they confront and their "emotional intelligence" affect decision making. As Greenstein acknowledges, of course, it sometimes is difficult to identify and obtain valid indicators of such traits that might be applied to individuals before and during their presidencies; even more problematic is systematically linking presidential traits and decision outcomes.

In contrast, political scientist and psychiatrist Stanley Renshon (2003, 26 ff.) argues that "a leader's judgment is not primarily an act of cognition or general intelligence" (2003, 32). Renshon seeks to integrate "the quality of analysis, reflection, and ultimately insight that informs the making of consequential decisions" into what he calls "judgment." He probes the psychological characteristics of "good judgment," emphasizing, for example, reflective skills and "strategic empathy." Renshon also hypothesizes links between good judgment and decision consequences, most of which await systematic testing.

Many others, however, do focus on cognitive factors in decision making. Among the myriad such factors that might influence presidential decision making, perhaps most attention has concentrated on information processing (Schafer and Crichlow 2002). Scholars emphasize possible negative effects on decisions, including failures to see, seek out, use, and share information (e.g., Bazerman and Chugh 2006; Keller 2005a). Among the potential problems Alexander George (1980) warned against were over-reliance on single information channels and failure to probe the premises on which advice is based. More generally Boin et al. note that "heuristic shortcuts in processing information introduce biases" in assessing choice situations (2005, 31). At the same time, Paul Kowert (2002) cautions that presidents vary in the volume of information that they can usefully absorb without suffering cognitive overload, while Margaret Hermann (1995, 150) observes that presidents are likely to differ in the "degree of control they need over policymaking," including channels for managing information.

Despite the mounting and frequently impressive body of work on cognitive constraints on decision makers, until recently relatively little has been incorporated systematically in studies of presidential decision making. To this point, an emphasis on information processing seems most promising (cf. Rudalevige 2005a). Meanwhile, as in the social sciences more generally, scholars are devoting more attention to the emotional pressures and limits on decision makers (cf. Maitlis and Ozcelik 2004). Greenstein lists "emotional intelligence" as a key characteristic of presidential leadership, and offers useful examples. Much of the systematic work in this area, however, focuses on crises. Based on a meta-analysis of US presidential decision making during international crises, Boin et al. (2005) express concern about "the frequent occurrence of stress-induced breakdowns of prudent leadership" (45), while noting that "some do better than others at compartmentalizing stress" (26).

Small Group Dynamics

Whether the focal decision unit is a predominant leader or a single group, many presidential decisions involve the interactions of groups of advisers. As 't Hart, Stern, and Sundelius (1997, 12) observe, there are "many faces of small groups in the policy process." Varying groups and volatile interpersonal dynamics may be particularly prevalent during perceived crises: "As a rule crisis decision making takes place in some type of small group setting in which political and bureaucratic leaders interact and reach some sort of collective decision" (Boin et al. 2005, 45; cf. 't Hart Stern, and Sundelius 1997, 15).

Irving Janis (1982) has famously detailed the dangers of "groupthink." The findings of historical and laboratory studies suggest that the "main problem [is] that individuals in groups often do not share and use information effectively in advising leaders or reaching collective decisions" (Boin et al. 2005, 46). High conflict in groups may foster paralysis, while high pressure to conform may allow incompletely scrutinized actions. Movement toward these extremes may be amplified by the informality that frequently characterizes interactions in crisis groups: "procedural rules and institutional safeguards that stabilize regular modes of policymaking tend to disappear" (Boin et al. 2005, 46).

Structuring

A related influence on decisions and decision making may be how the information, advisory, and decision processes that presidents rely on are structured. Many scholars focus on the overall organization of presidential management and advisory systems, sometimes using Richard Tanner Johnson's (1974) over-broad distinctions among formalistic, collegial, and competitive arrangements. Others take a more disaggregated look at the structuring of the numerous offices that have emerged and evolved over the twentieth century in the Executive Office of the President (e.g., Dickinson 2003; Hult and Walcott 2004; Lewis 2008; Walcott and Hult 1995). Still other scholars examine the structuring and interaction of specific White House and EOP units such as the National Security Council staff (e.g., Inderfurth and Johnson 2004), the White House chief of staff's office (e.g., Cohen, Dolan, and Rosati 2002; Walcott, Warshaw, and Wayne 2003), the counsel's office (e.g., Borrelli, Hult, and Kassop 2003), and the communications operation (e.g., Kumar 2007).

Although some of the research on structuring is descriptive in orientation or explores structures as dependent variables in broader analyses of institutional evolution, a good deal of it points to the role of structures in shaping both decision processes and the quality of decisions. A careful comparison of Dwight Eisenhower's and Lyndon Johnson's decisions on US troop strength in Vietnam, for example, highlighted the value of the formal procedures of the Eisenhower national security decision system, supplemented by the president's informal contacts in and out of government and his own vigilant monitoring, compared with Johnson's more informal processes and LBJ's tendency to exclude those who disagreed (Burke et al. 1989; cf. Moens 1990 on Carter's foreign policy decision making). Alexander George and others have argued for the value of "multiple advocacy" in high-stakes decision settings, highlighting the importance of exposing presidents to varying points of view, strongly advocated. Even so, based on their own and others' research, Boin et al. conclude that it is often difficult for presidents to rely fully on multiple advocacy in crises due to severe time constraints; during most of the international crises examined, key decisions were made almost simultaneously in diverse decision forums (2005, 49–50; 't Hart 1997).

In more routine decision arenas, multiple advocacy also may help increase the range of information and argument to which decision makers are exposed, in turn raising the likelihood of "better" decisions (see, e.g., Bogenreider and Nooteboom 2004; Farnham 2004; Haas 2003). Hult and Walcott (2004) argue that the White House decision memo system has persisted because presidents have found it valuable as an instrument of multiple advocacy. Yet the utility of multiple advocacy likely varies with, *inter alia*, the type of decision being made, the availability of a skilled "custodian" of the process, and the degree of presidential time, commitment, energy, and attention. Moreover, there often will need to be ways to bring the advocacy process to at least temporary closure—in order that the president may both reach a decision and then turn attention to issues of implementation and communication. In dealing with the execution and explanation of decisions, the participation of others with expertise different than that of those involved in policy advocacy may well be necessary. Once more, the ambiguity of the concept "decision" is highlighted as is the difficulty of drawing boundaries around the focal phenomenon.

Environment

As much as some presidents try to include others in and out of the national executive branch in their decision processes, many by design, necessity, or happenstance will be excluded and not directly influence decisions. Yet, scholars typically view them and other more or less ill-defined "environmental" actors and factors as shaping how and what presidents decide.

Exactly what this "choice environment" (Redd 2002, 338) encompasses varies, but it frequently includes Congress, the federal courts, constituency groups, public opinion, and global leaders. Barbara Farnham, for example, emphasizes the importance of the "domestic political context" to foreign policy decisions, especially their "acceptability...to some minimum number of relevant groups and individuals" (2004, 443), suggesting that, consistent with poliheuristic decision theory (see below), advisers and presidents begin assessing possible responses by first screening them for their acceptability. At the same time, Newmann (2001) underscores the importance of the international environment in restricting decision possibilities.

George trains his attention on the institutional context in which top decision makers and their advisers are ensconced, stressing the relevance of the "diversity of types of relationships that may develop among executives, advisers, and other autonomous political actors" (1997, 50). It may be especially important to focus on this network of relationships when examining decision making in new presidencies that confront perceived crises. Potter contends, for example, that "breaks with consistency with past policy and the loss of personal relationships" with a changing administration help account for his finding that the probability of an international crisis involving the United States (between 1918 and 2001) declines the longer a president is in office (2007, 302).[2]

Others move beyond personal relationships to examine other possibly relevant features of the environment. The availability of necessary financial resources, presidential approval levels, and partisan support in Congress doubtless are elements of a president's decision calculus, as are media coverage and public interest. Scholars have greater difficulty firmly linking environmental factors to presidential decision making, confined for the most part to unearthing suggestive evidence in documents, interviews, and memoirs and comparing events and approval trends with presidential behavior without being able to firmly establish the processes linking them.

Interplay

Research has identified myriad factors as possible influences on presidential decisions. Typically, scholars conclude that multiple influences intertwine to shape presidential decision processes and decision outcomes. Just as frequently, however, they also give primacy to a small number of key factors.

Schafer and Crichlow (2002), for example, studied the links between the foreign policy decision process and the effects of thirty-one decisions on national interests and on levels of international conflict (as judged by twenty-one foreign policy experts).[3] They found that the "structure of the decision group and how it processes information" critically influenced the decision outcomes (Schafer and Crichlow 2002, 66). The "situational context" in which the decision was made—for instance, "the stress level, the concerns of [international organizations] and allies, and the level of interests at stake in the decision" (Schafer and Crichlow 2002, 51)—was not important.

Margaret Hermann's work suggests possible qualifications to such findings. She contends that a president's leadership style interacts with the problem context to shape how the president structures decision making, which in turn influences how problems are defined, information is processed, and alternatives produced (Hermann 1993, 1995). George H. W. Bush, for example, "wanted team players around

---

[2] In his analysis, Potter controlled for presidential age, vice presidential experience, and time to the next election. His findings are consistent with "newgroup syndrome" (e.g., Stern and Sundelius 1997, 127–8).

[3] The time frame of the analysis was 1975–93. It included thirteen decisions made during the Reagan presidency, six under Carter, and two each under Ford and Clinton. The other decisions examined were made in Israel and the UK, in the Begin, Rabin, and Thatcher governments (see Schafer and Crichlow 2002, 49).

him who would be loyal and interested in participating in 'bull sessions' and building consensus." Yet when he "felt himself backed into a corner" (e.g., before the invasion of Panama, during the Clarence Thomas selection to the US Supreme Court), the president appeared to shift from a "team building system [to] one characterized by formal control and a problem focus [and] became a director and an ideologue" (Hermann 1995, 155).

In other work, Schafer similarly highlights the interplay between individual leaders and decision context. Applying Alexander George's Verbs-in-Context system of operational code analysis, Schafer and Walker (2006) compare how Bill Clinton and Tony Blair behaved in international relations. Although the two had "remarkably similar cooperative belief systems toward democracies, Blair was less cooperative, both strategically and tactically, than Clinton" toward non-democracies (Schafer and Walker 2006, 575). This latter difference (also supported by event data on the two countries' actions) is inconsistent with the predicted effects of the cultural and institutional differences between the US and the UK. Schafer and Walker conclude by suggesting that the beliefs and values of individual leaders may be especially important "in a weakly structured environment with relatively high uncertainty, such as when a democracy confronts a non-democracy, [where] the absence of shared expectations and institutional norms" reduces constraints (Schafer and Walker 2006, 579).

Others caution against pushing such a leader-centered approach too far. Issues of institutional design as well as time, attention, and financial restraints also are important (see, e.g., Boin et al. 2005).

ENTER THE STAFF: INFLUENCES OF PRESIDENTIAL AIDES

At least since the presidency of Herbert Hoover, presidents have been assisted by multiple staff members who perform professional tasks such as working with the press, dealing with Congress, and advising on policy issues. Over time, the White House staff has increased in size (albeit sporadically and with few increases after the 1970s), specialization, and hierarchical structuring; it has been joined by aides elsewhere in the EOP as well as informal presidential advisers in and out of government. Senior staffers may be key participants in presidential decision making, offering substantive input, political advice, and emotional sustenance. Advisers can help link presidents to broader policy and political environments, and staffers' perceptions affect presidential views and understanding of the world. Meanwhile, relationships among presidential aides, although examined less frequently, may influence the decision context in which presidents operate or shift presidential attention to management tasks.

Not surprisingly, most of the research on advisers that is related to presidential decision making focuses on presidential–advisory interactions and arrangements. Fewer scholars examine the possible effects of staff relations with each other on the decision contexts in which presidents operate. Once more, substantive decision outputs or outcomes receive somewhat less attention than do decision process concerns.

Presidents and Advisers

Whether the decision unit is the president as predominant leader or as a member of a small group, advisers usually are involved in examinations of presidential decision making. Research has focused at varying levels of aggregation.

First, scholars have devoted considerable attention to presidential advisory systems. Within the decision units framework, some have explored the ways in which presidential leadership styles have shaped their advising arrangements (e.g., Hermann 1995; Mitchell 2005; Preston 2001). Others examine how staffers have assisted presidents in "counteracting their constitutional weaknesses" (Rudalevige 2005a, 285).

From a rational choice institutionalist perspective, advisers—in formal or informal positions—can be seen as key components of a president's "informational institutions" (Rudalevige 2005b, 339). Yet the very existence of staffers with varying kinds of expertise underscores the likely information asymmetries that exist between presidents and their advisers. These relationships are affected as well by the "power games" among advisers that help shape the procedural rules influencing the information presented (Garrison 1999). One possible mechanism to mitigate the negative effects of both information asymmetry and gaming has been what Moe (1985) labels centralization: the emergence and stabilization of a White House Office (WHO) staff whose primary loyalty is to the president. This is scarcely a guaranteed strategy, of course. Anecdotes abound suggesting how adverse selection, opportunism, and moral hazard might lead White House staffers to capitalize on information asymmetry or stress personal or other loyalties. Still needed is more careful empirical analysis of the effects of centralization on presidential decision making.

Staff structuring is another way that presidents seek to compensate for informational and advisory shortfalls. As noted earlier, multiple advocacy is among the structural attempts to provide top decision makers with diverse information and arguments. Similarly, the "staffing system" first introduced by Dwight Eisenhower and continued by presidents beginning with Richard Nixon seeks to ensure that information, analyses, and decision options are reviewed by relevant actors in the WHO and elsewhere; it has been called part of a "standard model" of White House governance that also includes monitoring by a chief of staff (Hult and Walcott 2004; Walcott and Hult 2005). Both Matthew Dickinson and Andrew Rudalevige contend that "redundant staff structures" (Dickinson 2005, 259; cf. Dickinson 1997) and "multiple sources of competing information (parallel processing)" (Rudalevige 2005b, 346) are especially useful in assisting presidential decision making. Although

a

these works differ in emphases and terminology, they share the proposition that a presidential decision process that relies on multiple sources of diverse information and permits critical scrutiny of analyses and advice will generate more useful information and advice as well as better-informed, if not necessarily always "effective" decisions.

Less common are systematic efforts to empirically probe this expectation, especially across a range of policy arenas or kinds of decisions. One exception is Patrick Haney's (1997) study of foreign policy crises. Reanalyzing Haney's data and using his decision criteria, Dickinson finds that "redundant staff structures and competitive staff practices perform more effectively" (2005, 259, 279). Rudalevige (2005b) makes an illustrative foray by examining three administrations and three decision areas.

Shifting to the interpersonal level of analysis, other work concentrates on the relationships of advisers with presidents. Research grounded in the poliheuristic perspective of decision making has examined "the effects of the presence of advisers on strategy selection and choice and the influence of strategy selection on choice," typically in foreign policy settings (Redd 2002, 335). Poliheuristic theory conceives of decision making as a two stage process: decision makers (1) screen alternatives based on cognitive heuristics, and then (2) assess the remaining options using a more analytic process (see, e.g., Mintz 2003a; Mintz et al., 1997). Among the experimental findings are the importance of the sequence of adviser involvement and the nature of the information and guidance they provide (Redd 2002). Political advisers "acted as sensitizing mechanism[s] for decision makers," influencing their foreign policy choices (Redd 2002, 356). Systematic empirical examination in real world settings remains to be done.

Finally, a good deal of the more adviser-specific research focuses on advisory tasks and associated roles (e.g., Garrison 1999; Ponder 2000). Among the advisory roles that have received attention is that of the "neutral/honest broker," a "particular variant" of George's (1980) notion of the "managerial-custodian" in national security decision processes (Burke 2005, 230). Roger Porter, who oversaw Gerald Ford's Economic Policy Board, noted that honest brokers "do more than simply insure due process [for those with differing views]. They promote a genuine competition of ideas, identifying viewpoints not adequately represented or that require qualification, determining when the process is not producing a significantly broad range of options, and augmenting the resources of one side or another so that a balanced presentation results" (1980, 26). Case study analyses have underscored the broker role's positive impact on decision making and the difficulties that arise when it is not exercised or when trust in the broker's neutrality is low (see, e.g., Bose 1998; Burke et al. 1989; Cohen 2002; Herek, Janis, and Huth 1987).

Scholars frequently have viewed the broker role as being among the tasks of two specific contemporary advisers, with its performance critically affecting decision making and decisions: the national security assistant (NSA) and the White House chief of staff. Since Congress created the NSA in 1947 (initially as the "executive secretary" of the National Security Council), the assistant's position and responsibilities have evolved with presidencies, occupants, and events. NSAs have varied in their policy advocacy and implementation responsibility (e.g., Burke 2005, 240). Nonetheless, Burke views "the broker role as a kind of foundational [*sic*] basic to the job of NSC advisor" (2005, 241). Performance of the role and its contributions to presidential decision making, however, may be both complemented and weakened as NSAs engage in policy advocacy, are publicly visible, serve as "political watchdogs," or become enmeshed in decision implementation (Burke 2005, 241–9; Daalder and Destler 1999; Lord 1988).

Likewise, studies of the office of the chief of staff (COS) typically focus on the importance of honest brokerage (cf. Walcott et al. 2003, 129–30). The COS's job includes supervision of the White House's formal staffing system as well as control of personal access to the president. Practice varies, but often the NSA shares these tasks where national security issues are involved. A perception of impartiality is essential to the effective working of the White House. This role coexists with that of adviser and advocate (Walcott, Warshaw, and Wayne 2003, 130 ff.), with the potential for tension as a result. Sullivan (2004, 7–8) examines this tension between "orchestration" and "initiative," noting that it affects not only the COS but also others in the White House for whom the chief is administratively responsible. For Sullivan, this tension between orchestration and initiative is an "operational dilemma" whose resolution follows no set script, but must be worked out in the context of the personalities and issues salient at any given time. In the case of the COS, the tension is heightened by the multiplicity of claims and criteria that typically must be attended to in an office that former incumbents characterize as the locus of the integration of policy and politics (cf. Walcott, Warshaw, and Wayne 2003, 130 ff.)

Sullivan (2004, 9–10) identifies a second "operational dilemma" that afflicts not only the COS but also other top advisers and, implicitly, the president: "reaction vs. projection." White House decision making is famously short-term oriented, usually described by such terms as "firefighting," if not "crisis management." The president's aides, and especially the COS, are responsible for trying to create resources within the administration for focusing on the longer-term objectives inherent in a president's agenda.

Research on the impact of COS roles, strategies, and styles has been sparse, limited mostly to interviews with former incumbents of the office and focused primarily on providing advice to future chiefs (e.g., Kernell and Popkin 1986; Walcott, Warshaw, and Wayne 2003; Sullivan, 2004). Cohen and Krause (2000), however, go beyond this in systematically looking at survey data from White House staffers in two administrations; based on this evidence, they report findings on the impact of the "management style" of varying COSs on perceived presidential accessibility and on assessment of White House operations. Although they find no direct link to decision outcomes, the study does include information related to when and how COSs channeled information and advice to the president. More recently, Cohen, Hult, and Walcott (2006) have broadened the analysis to three administrations and focused on the effects of differences in style (distinguishing among "stronger" and "weaker" COSs) across and within administrations, finding significant evidence of both. Once more, however, no links with substantive presidential decisions are studied.

Finally, of course, we should note that advisers are vulnerable to many of the same cognitive and emotional challenges and limitations that presidents confront.

Significantly less work has systematically explored these issues and their effects. Nor has the impact of differential adviser skill on presidential decisions been examined carefully. The influence of the experience of advisers, however, has received more attention. For the most part, scholars agree that past experience with foreign policy crises (e.g., Boin et al. 2005, 36) and length of tenure in the White House (Potter 2007) are associated with improved decision outcomes for both presidents and their advisers.

Relationships among Advisers

Much of what scholars know about the relationships of presidential advisers with each other is based on memoirs, biographies, journalists' reports, and occasional public showcasing. Rich and informative glimpses also emerge from studies relying on interviews and careful examination of public documents and presidential papers (e.g., Kumar 2007). Yet only rarely is the emphasis on finding patterns in or generalizing about the features and dynamics of advisory relations or on their possible influences on decision making.

Unfortunately, scholars have not replicated John Kessel's pathbreaking work (1983, 1984) on White House staff structures for information, communication, influence, and organization in presidencies following the Reagan administration. His findings, however, highlight the variation in reported respect, expertise, and influence of staffers both within and between administrations (cf. Cohen, Hult, and Walcott 2006 on COSs). They also point to the more stable organizational features of White House staffing. Even so, research has not addressed the effects of any of these dynamics on information flows or on presidential decision making and decisions.

ANALYTICAL ISSUES REDUX

Quite clearly, work on presidential decision making is rich and variegated. It is both difficult and arguably unwarranted, however, to distill this scholarship into a small handful of testable hypotheses or broadly applicable generalizations. This section highlights the common features and some of the disconnects and gaps in this work.

Conceptual Emphases

Analyses of presidential decision making, considered as a whole, share several characteristics. First, as we have seen, potentially relevant studies of decision making rely on a variety of decision theories. Considerable contemporary attention has focused on more cognitive approaches such as poliheuristic and information-processing theories. Others employ ideas drawn from rational choice institutionalism and bureaucratic politics. Numerous scholars also work within the decision unit framework. In examining this research, one is readily reminded of Guetzkow's comments about islands of theory. Only rarely have the analyses and expectations of decisional theories been pitted against each other, as Graham Allison did in his classic work on decision making during the Cuban missile crisis (Allison and Zelikow 1999). Moreover, presidency scholars are only beginning to apply some of the newer theoretical approaches (e.g., Rudalevige 2005b), and little interchange is apparent between foreign policy and presidency scholars. Meanwhile, with notable exceptions, relatively few presidency scholars appear to be very familiar with contemporary work in psychology. Meanwhile, numerous dependent variables surface in decision-making analyses.

Second, much research examines decision making under "crisis" conditions. Without doubt, such analyses are crucial both empirically and normatively, perhaps in particular when examining US presidents and senior advisers. For example, Boin et al. (2005, 45) note their "great concern" about the "frequent occurrence of stress-induced breakdowns" in the empirical research (e.g., Herek, Janis, and Huth's 1987 meta-analysis of US presidential decision making in international crises). Considerably less clear, however, is how much can be learned when comparing such crisis settings to other decision contexts. Moreover, without comparison to other kinds of decision outcomes, some critics of groupthink contend that a "focus on fiascoes makes it difficult to say anything about the determinants of fiascoes" (Fuller and Aldag 1997, 72). Of even greater concern may be whether the same theoretical dimensions, interrelationships, and primary factors are apt even to be relevant in non-crisis situations, rather than whether and how the findings about the nature of crisis decision processes and dynamics can be generalized. It may be, for instance, that the psychological characteristics of presidents and senior advisers recede in influence as individual capacity for rapid sense making or for impulse control become less important and factors like expertise, representative decision mechanisms, or presidential interest grow more significant.

Reflecting both the emphasis in the presidential decision literature on crisis and the position of the president as commander-in-chief, a third feature of presidential decision research is its emphasis on examining national security advice and decision making. Still, significant work has examined other policy arenas as well (e.g., Porter 1980; Ponder 2000). Looking within US "domestic" policy, for example, Ponder (2000) finds that presidential use of staff and the amount of centralization of advice varies by policy issue.

Finally, examinations generally are oriented toward either decision processes or decision outputs and outcomes. Somewhat less frequent is explicit acknowledgement of the distinctive analytical demands of variance and process analyses (see Hult, Walcott, and Weko 1999; Scott 2007). Appropriate levels and units of analysis also vary considerably. Seemingly the most promising but also the most difficult to bound and challenging to study is the decision (cf. Quirk 1989). Compelling as well given the multiple dimensions of analysis and the evident variation within and between presidencies and policy arenas is a "contingentist' perspective" (Durant 1998). A "problem-contingency view," for example, proposes that how decisions are made ("decision structuring") often will, and arguably should, fit the prevailing decision context (e.g., Hult and Walcott 2004; cf. Peters 2001, Rudalevige 2005b). Some research also suggests that decision outcomes would be expected to be more "successful" as the fit between decision context and decision structuring grows closer; such a proposition also awaits further testing.

Methodological Observations

Most presidential decision-making research is firmly anchored in what some have called scientific realism (e.g., Shapiro 2005). Yet its research designs and methods are diverse. Although not all of the work has emphasized *presidential* decision making, poliheuristic models have been tested and explored using case studies, time series analysis, process tracing, and experimentation (Mintz 2003b, 5; cf. Mintz et al. 1997; Redd 2002). Dickinson and Lebo (2007) apply fractional integration to the institutionalization process of the White House staff, key decision participants, and an arena in which presidents decide. Other scholars have relied on comparative case studies (e.g., Mitchell 2005; Newmann 2003), surveys (e.g., Cohen 2002), and document analyses (e.g., Hult and Walcott 2004).

In addition, a relatively wide range of data sources is available. Scholars have examined, *inter alia*, the papers, diaries, memoirs, and biographies of presidents and staffers; congressional and executive branch documents, reports of key decision participants (e.g., Pritchard 2007) and about them (e.g., Mann 2004); and interviews and surveys. Nonetheless, significant constraints are evident. First, available data are limited. The end of the National Archives and Records Administration's program of exit interviews with senior officials as they left government service has meant the loss of immediate familiarity with and observations about their work. Meanwhile, the 1988 Presidential Records Act and President George W. Bush's executive order expanding required approval for the release of documents have both slowed and possibly limited the documents available for scholarly inspection, a concern deepened by scarce financial resources and the flood of electronic communications. Probably even more limiting have been the effects of almost two decades of investigations into the communications of presidents and presidential staff (over, for example, Whitewater properties and the Clinton–Lewinsky scandal in the Clinton administration and the exposure of Valerie Plame under George W. Bush), which have led many communications not to be placed in written form of any kind for fear of litigation.

Second, of course, are the well-known limitations of much of the information that is available. Oral histories are of uneven quality and scope. Like those in oral histories, responses in interviews and surveys sometimes appear "scripted," producing reliable but scarcely valid data. All three are subject as well to problems with, for example, the sampling of respondents, non-respondent bias, and the choice and sequence of questions. Meanwhile, presidency scholars who rely on archival records wrestle with the possibility that documents were never sent or were written to conceal or reframe information, to mislead, or "for the record." Finally, as Ian Lustick (1996) cautions more generally, presidency scholars also must be cautious in selecting the historical materials they choose to inform their work lest other selection biases enter.

Over time, presidential decision-making research has grown in methodological diversity, self-consciousness, and sophistication. Even so, calls continue for more, and more systematic, empirical testing of decision making under varying conditions and greater comparison over kinds of decisions and through time (e.g., George 1997; Dickinson and Lebo 2007). Efforts focused on searching for possible patterns linking particular kinds of decision structuring and outcomes also remain needed (e.g., Mitchell 2005). Mintz is among those who call for greater use of "automated coding techniques to construct large-scale data sets" of decisions (2003b, 166).

Emphasis on Prescription

Perhaps not surprisingly, scholars of presidential decision making frequently join government officials, citizens, and pundits in offering advice for future decisions and for the design of appropriate decision processes (e.g., Boin et al. 2005, ch. 7; Moens 1990). Considerable progress has been made in assembling materials on ways that presidents and others might cope with varying decision tasks. Yet the prescriptive enterprise often is problematic.

Many areas await additional and more systematic empirical grounding before recommendations can be made with relatively high degrees of confidence. At the same time, an emphasis on prescription inevitably highlights some research questions while obscuring others. This in turn threatens to compromise scholarly capacity to understand presidential decision dynamics more fully, including the limitations of human agency and of structural design.

CONCLUSIONS: ACHIEVEMENTS, GAPS, AND NEXT STEPS

As this overview should suggest, the scholarly literature on presidential decision making is diverse and rich, yielding many insights. Even so, much work remains. Calls for what research on presidential decision making should focus upon abound. Some concentrate on critical independent variables. Schafer and Walker, for instance, call for an "agent-centered approach" that emphasizes leaders' beliefs, hypothesizing that beliefs are likely to "act as different types of causal mechanisms under different circumstances" (2006, 579, 580). Others highlight the role of information and information processing in presidential decisions. Rudalevige (2005b) suggests that the design and impact of the informational institutions that surround presidents deserve systematic attention, with the decision as the unit of analysis (cf. Dickinson 2005). Although most scholars treat the decision or "decision episode" as the primary unit of analysis, Paul 't Hart (1997) instead recommends focusing on "interaction patterns" between high-level officials and stakeholders. As we have noted throughout, the ambiguity of the notion of decision itself may well be part of the difficulty in settling on critical questions and speaking across theoretical and methodological divides.

In addition, a considerable amount is known about the evolution of informational and advisory structuring within and across presidencies. Still needed, however, are more sustained efforts to examine the existence and the nature of any relationships between these arrangements and decision outcomes (Dickinson 2005, 278).

It seems to us that the most promising research on presidential decision making is likely to be "problem-driven" (Shapiro, 2005), rather than designed *primarily* to refine theories or apply new methodological techniques. We have mentioned several areas that merit particular attention. Certainly, the processes by which presidents choose to take or not to take specific actions might be traced in efforts to identify whether and how certain mechanisms operated to enhance, impede, or block information and participation (e.g. Rudalevige 2005b). Examination of decision outputs (e.g., formulation of the No Child Left Behind legislation, the issuing of a signing statement on the use of torture) and selected outcomes (for example, legislative passage, changes in agency behavior) also deserve attention, especially comparison among policy arenas and over time. As in the study of governance more generally, we have a generally good sense of the range of influences that may shape decision making and specific decisions (such as staff structuring, the degree of advisory centralization, levels of uncertainty and controversy); we know considerably less, however, about how they operate and interact in differing contexts. Systematic, theoretically informed investigation of multiple decisions over both time and space appears to us to be the most appropriate and potentially fruitful avenue for future research. Explicit definition and examination of varying focal decision units also seems needed.

Few doubt that US presidents frequently confront decision settings that are complex, sometimes volatile, and often ambiguous. Yet, in many, if not most, cases they must choose, even if it is to postpone, avoid, or delegate choosing, all the while knowing that today's choice may well shape future events, opportunities, and constraints both the next day and possibly beyond. For their part, analysts of presidential decisions and decision making struggle with capturing the nuance, uncertainty, and idiosyncrasy while seeking to unearth patterns and test hypotheses. Although the challenges facing policy makers and scholars are scarcely orthogonal, they differ in purpose, immediacy, cost, and audience. We continue to grapple with what it means for a president to be "the decider."

References

ALLISON, G. T., and ZELIKOW, P. D. 1999. *The Essence of Decision: Explaining the Cuban Missile Crisis*, 2nd edn. New York: Addison Wesley Longman.

BAZERMAN, M. H., and CHUGH, D. 2006. Decisions without Blinders. *Harvard Business Review*, 8: 88–97.

BEACH, L. R., and CONNOLLY, T. 2005. *The Psychology of Decision Making: People in Organizations*, 2nd edn. Thousand Oaks, CA: Sage.

BOGENREIDER, I., and NOOTEBOOM, B. 2004. Learning Groups: What Types Are There? *Organization Studies*, 25/2: 287–313.

BOIN, A., 'T HART, P., STERN, E., and SUNDELIUS, B. 2005. *The Politics of Crisis Management: Public Leadership under Pressure*. New York: Cambridge University Press.

BORRELLI, M., HULT, K., and KASSOP, N. 2003. The White House Counsel. In *The White House World: Transitions, Organization, and Office Operations*, ed. M. J. Kumar and T. Sullivan. College Station: Texas A&M University Press.

BOSE, M. 1998. *Shaping and Signaling Presidential Policy: The National Security Decision-Making of Eisenhower and Kennedy*. College Station: Texas A&M University Press.

BURKE, J. P. 2005. The Neutral/Honest Broker Role in Foreign Policy Decision Making: A Reassessment. *Presidential Studies Quarterly*, 35: 229–58.

—— and GREENSTEIN, F. I., with BERMAN, L., and IMMERMA, R. 1989. *How Presidents Test Reality: Decisions on Vietnam, 1954 and 1965*. New York: Russell Sage.

BUSH, G. W. 2006. "I'm the Decider." At <http://www.cnn.com/2006/POLITICS/04/18/rumsfeld/>. Accessed 13 Jan. 2007.

CAMPBELL, C. 1983. *Governments under Stress: Political Executives and Key Bureaucrats in Washington, London, and Ottawa*. Toronto: University of Toronto Press.

—— 1986. *Managing the Presidency: Carter, Reagan, and the Search for Executive Harmony*. Pittsburgh: University of Pittsburgh Press.

—— 1991. The White House and Cabinet under the "Let's Deal" President. In *The Bush Presidency: First Appraisals*, ed. C. Campbell and B. A. Rockman. Chatham, NJ: Chatham House Publishers.

COHEN, D. 2002. From the Fabulous Baker Boys to the Master of Disaster: The White House Chief of Staff in the Reagan and G. H. W. Bush Administrations. *Presidential Studies Quarterly*, 32: 463–83.

—— DOLAN, C. J., and ROSATI, J. A. 2002. A Place at the Table: The Emerging Foreign Policy Roles of the White House Chief of Staff. *Congress & the Presidency*, 29: 119–49.

—— HULT, K. M., and WALCOTT, C. E. 2006. The Chief of Staff in the Modern White House: An Empirical Exploration. Paper presented at the Annual Meeting of the American Political Science Association, Philadelphia, PA, Aug. 31–Sept. 3.

—— and KRAUSE, G. A. 2000. Presidents, Chiefs of Staff, and the Structure of White House Organization: Survey Evidence from the Reagan and Bush Administrations. *Presidential Studies Quarterly*, 30: 421–42.

DAALDER, I. H., and DESTLER, I. M. 1999. Introduction; The Role of the National Security Adviser. Oral History Roundtable, the National Security Project. Washington, DC: Brookings Institution, Oct. 25. <http://www.brookings.edu/fp/research/projects/nsc/transcripts/19991025.htm>.

DICKINSON, M. J. 1997. *Bitter Harvest: FDR, Presidential Power, and the Growth of the Executive Branch*. New York: Cambridge University Press.

—— 2003. Bargaining, Uncertainty, and the Growth of the White House Staff, 1940–2000. In *Uncertainty in American Politics*, ed. B. C. Burden. New York: Cambridge University Press.

DICKINSON, M. J. 2005. Neustadt, New Institutionalism, and Presidential Decision Making: A Theory and Test. *Presidential Studies Quarterly*, 35: 259–88.

—— 2008. The Politics of Persuasion: A Bargaining Model of Presidential Power. In *Presidential Leadership: The Vortex of Power*, ed. B. A. Rockman and R. W. Waterman. New York: Oxford University Press.

—— and LEBO, M. J. 2007. Reexamining the Growth of the Institutional Presidency, 1940–2000. *Journal of Politics*, 69: 206–19.

DURANT, R. 1998. Agenda Setting, the "Third Wave," and the Administrative State. *Administration & Society*, 30: 211–47.

FARNHAM, B. 2004. Impact of the Political Context on Foreign Policy Decision Making. *Political Psychology*, 25/3: 442–63.

FULLER, S. R., and ALDAG, R. J. 1997. *Challenge the Mindguards: Moving Small Group Analysis beyond Groupthink.* Ann Arbor: University of Michigan Press.

GARRISON, J. A. 1999. *Games Advisers Play: Foreign Policy in the Nixon and Carter Administration.* College Station: Texas A&M University Press.

GEORGE, A. L. 1980. *Presidential Decisionmaking in Foreign Policy: The Effective Use of Information and Advice.* Boulder, CO: Westview.

—— 1997. From Groupthink to Contextual Analysis of Policy-Making Groups. In *Beyond Groupthink: Political Group Dynamics and Foreign Policy-Making*, ed. P. 'T Hart, E. K. Stern, and B. Sundelius. Ann Arbor: University of Michigan Press.

GREENSTEIN, F. I. 1982. *The Hidden Hand Presidency: Eisenhower as Leader.* New York: Basic Books.

—— 2004. *The Presidential Difference: Leadership Style from FDR to George W. Bush*, 2nd edn. Princeton, NJ: Princeton University Press.

GUETZKOW, H. 1950. Long Range Research in International Relations. *American Perspective*, 4/4: 421–40.

HAAS, M. L. 2003. Ideology and Alliances: British and French External Balancing Decisions in the 1930s. *Security Studies*, 12 /4: 34–79.

HAGAN, J. D. 2001. Does Decision Making Matter? Systemic Assumptions vs. Historical Reality in International Relations Theory. *International Studies Review*, 3: 5–46.

HANEY, P. J. 1997. *Organizing for Foreign Policy Crises: Presidents, Advisers, and the Management of Decision-Making.* Ann Arbor: University of Michigan Press.

HEREK, G. M., JANIS, I. L., and HUTH, P. 1987. Decision Making during International Crises: Is Quality of Process Related to Outcome? *Journal of Conflict Resolution*, 38: 203–26.

HERMANN, C. F., GROSS STEIN, J., SUNDELIUS, B., and WALKER, S. G. 2001. Resolve, Accept, or Avoid: Effect of Group Conflict on Foreign Policy Decisions. *International Studies Review*, 3: 133–68.

HERMANN, M. G. 1993. Leaders and Foreign Policy Decision Making. In *Diplomacy, Force, and Leadership*, ed. D. Caldwell and T. J. McKeown. Boulder, CO: Westview Press.

—— 1995. Advice and Advisers in the Clinton Presidency: The Impact of Leadership Style. In *The Clinton Presidency: Campaigning, Governing, and the Psychology of Leadership*, ed. S. A. Rensho. Boulder, CO: Westview Press.

—— 2001. How Decision Units Shape Foreign Policy: A Theoretical Framework. *International Studies Review*, 3: 47–81.

—— and HERMANN, C. F. 1989. Who Makes Foreign Policy Decisions and How: An Empirical Inquiry. *International Studies Quarterly*, 33: 361–87.

—— and PRESTON, T. 1994. Presidents, Advisers, and Foreign Policy: The Effect of Leadership Style on Executive Arrangements. *Political Psychology*, 15: 75–96.

—— —— Korany, B., and Shaw, T. M. 2001. Who Leads Matters: The Effects of Powerful Individuals. *International Studies Review,* 3: 83–131.

Hult, K. M., and Walcott, C. E. 2004. *Empowering the White House: Governance under Nixon, Ford, and Clinton.* Lawrence: University Press of Kansas.

—— and Weko, T. 1999. Qualitative Research and the Study of the Presidency. *Congress & the Presidency,* 26: 133–52.

Inderfurth, K. F., and Johnson, L. K. 2004. *Fateful Decisions: Inside the National Security Council.* New York: Oxford University Press.

Janis, I. 1982. *Groupthink: Psychological Studies of Policy Decisions and Fiascoes,* 2nd edn. Boston: Houghton Mifflin.

Johnson, R. T. 1974. *Managing the White House.* New York: Harper & Row.

Keller, J. W. 2005a. Constraint Respecters, Constraint Challengers, and Crisis Decision Making in Democracies: A Case Study Analysis of Kennedy versus Reagan. *Political Psychology,* 26: 835–67.

—— 2005b. Leadership Style, Regime Type, and Foreign Policy Crisis Behavior: A Contingent Monadic Peace? *International Studies Quarterly,* 49: 205–31.

Kernell, S., and Popkin, S. L. 1986. *Chief of Staff: Twenty-Five Years of Managing the Presidency.* Berkeley and Los Angeles: University of California Press.

Kessel, J. H. 1983. The Structures of the Carter White House. *American Journal of Political Science,* 27: 430–63.

—— 1984. The Structures of the Reagan White House. *American Journal of Political Science,* 28: 231–58.

Kowert, P. A. 2002. *Groupthink or Deadlock: When Do Leaders Learn from their Advisers?* Berkeley and Los Angeles: University of California Press.

Kramer, R. W., and Gavrieli, D. A. 2004. Power, Uncertainty, and the Amplification of Doubt: An Archival Study of Suspicion inside the Oval Office. In *Trust and Distrust in Organizations: Dilemmas and Approaches,* ed. R. M. Kramer and K. S. Cook. New York: Russell Sage.

Kumar, M. J. 2007. *Managing the President's Message: The White House Communications Operation.* Baltimore: Johns Hopkins University Press.

Lewis, D. E. 2008a. The Evolution of the Institutional Presidency: Presidential Choices, Institutional Change, and Staff Performance. In *Presidential Leadership: The Vortex of Power,* ed. B. A. Rockman and R. W. Waterman. New York: Oxford University Press.

—— 2008b. *The Politics of Presidential Appointments: Political Control and Bureaucratic Performance.* Princeton, NJ: Princeton University Press.

Lord, C. 1988. *The Presidency and the Management of National Security.* New York: Free Press.

Lustick, I. 1996. History, Historiography, and Political Science: Multiple Historical Records and the Problem of Selection Bias. *American Political Science Review,* 90: 605–18.

Lyons, M. 1997. Presidential Character Revisited. *Political Psychology,* 18: 791–811.

Maitlis, S., and Ozcelik, H. 2004. Toxic Decision Processes: A Study of Emotion and Organizational Decision Masking. *Organization Science,* 15: 375–93.

Mann, J. 2004. *Rise of the Vulcans: The History of Bush's War Cabinet.* New York: Viking.

March, J. G. 1994. *A Primer on Decision Making: How Decisions Happen.* New York: Free Press.

Mintz, A. 2003a. Integrating Cognitive and Rational Theories of Foreign Policy Decision Making: A Poliheuristic Perspective. In *Integrating Cognitive and Rational: Theories of Foreign Policy Decision Making,* ed. A. Mintz. New York: Palgrave Macmillan.

MINTZ, A. 2003b. Theory Development and Integration in Foreign Policy Analysis: Directions for Future Research. In *Integrating Cognitive and Rational: Theories of Foreign Policy Decision Making*, ed. A. Mintz. New York: Palgrave Macmillan.

——— GEVA, N., REDD, S. B., and CARNES, A. 1997. The Effect of Dynamic and Static Choice Sets on Political Decision Making: An Analysis Using the Decision Board Platform. *American Political Science Review*, 91: 553–66.

MITCHELL, D. 2005. Centralizing Advisory Systems: Presidential Influence and the U.S. Foreign Policy Decision-Making Process. *Foreign Policy Analysis*, 2: 181–206.

MOE, T. M. 1985. The Politicized Presidency. In *The New Direction in American Politics*, ed. J. E. Chubb and P. E. Peterson. Washington, DC: Brookings Institution.

MOENS, A. 1990. *Foreign Policy under Carter: Testing Multiple Advocacy Decision Making*. Boulder, CO: Westview Press.

NEWMANN, W. W. 2001. Causes of Change in National Security Processes: Carter, Reagan, and Bush Decision Making on Arms Control. *Presidential Studies Quarterly*, 31: 69–103.

——— 2003. *Managing National Security Policy: The President and the Process*. Pittsburgh: University of Pittsburgh Press.

PETERS, B. G. 2001. *The Future of Governing: Four Emerging Models*, 2nd edn., rev. Lawrence: University Press of Kansas.

PFIFFNER, J. P. 2007. The First MBA President: George W. Bush as Public Administrator. *Public Administration Review*, 67: 6–20.

PONDER, D. E. 2000. *Good Advice: Information and Policymaking in the White House*. College Station: Texas A&M University Press.

PORTER, R. B. 1980. *Presidential Decision Making: The Economic Policy Board*. New York: Cambridge University Press.

POTTER, P. B. K. 2007. Does Experience Matter? American Presidential Experience, Age, and International Conflict. *Journal of Conflict Resolution*, 51: 351–78.

PRESTON, T. 2001. *The President and his Inner Circle: Leadership Style and the Advisory Process in Foreign Affairs*. New York: Columbia University Press.

PRITCHARD, C. L. 2007. *Failed Diplomacy: The Tragic Story of How North Korea Got the Bomb*. Washington, DC: Brookings Institution Press.

QUIRK, P. 1989. What Do We Know and How Do We Know It? Research on the Presidency. *Presidency Research*, 12: 9–30.

REDD, S. B. 2002. The Influence of Advisers on Foreign Policy Decision-Masking. *Journal of Conflict Resolution*, 46: 335–64.

RENSHON, S. A. 2003. Psychological Sources of Good Judgment in Foreign Policy. In *Good Judgment in Foreign Policy: Theory and Application*, ed. S. Renshon and D. Larson. Lanham, MD: Rowman & Littlefield.

RUBENZER, S. J., and FASCHINGBAUER, T. R. 2004. *Personality, Character, and Leadership in the White House*. Washington, DC: Brassey's.

RUDALEVIGE, A. 2005a. *The New Imperial Presidency: Renewing Presidential Power after Watergate*. Ann Arbor: University of Michigan Press.

——— 2005b. The Structure of Leadership: Presidents, Hierarchies, and Information Flow. *Presidential Studies Quarterly*, 35: 333–60.

SCHAFER, M., and CRICHLOW, S. 2002. The *Process–Outcome* Connection in Foreign Policy Decision Making: A Quantitative Study Building on Groupthink. *International Studies Quarterly*, 46: 45–68.

SCOTT, W. R. 2007. *Institutions and Organizations: Ideas and Interests*, 3rd edn. Thousand Oaks, CA: Sage Publications.

SHAPIRO, I. 2005. *The Flight from Reality in the Human Sciences*. Princeton, NJ: Princeton University Press.

SCHAFER, M., and WALKER, S. G. 2006. Democratic Leaders and the Democratic Peace: The Operational Codes of Tony Blair and Bill Clinton. *International Studies Quarterly*, 50: 561–83.

SIMONTON, D. K. 2006. Presidential IQ, Openness, Intellectual Brilliance, and Leadership: Estimates and Correlations for 42 U.S. Chief Executives. *Political Psychology*, 27: 511–26.

STERN, E. K., and SUNDELIUS, B. 1997. Understanding Small Group Decisions in Foreign Policy: Process Diagnosis and Research Procedure. In *Beyond Groupthink: Political Group Dynamics and Foreign Policy-Making*, ed. P. 't Hart, E. K. Stern, and B. Sundelius. Ann Arbor: University of Michigan Press.

SULLIVAN, T. (ed.) 2004. *The Nerve Center: Lessons in Governing from the White House Chiefs of Staff*. College Station: Texas A&M University Press.

SYLVAN, D. A. 1998a. Introduction. In *Problem Representation in Foreign Policy Decision Making*, ed. D. Sylvan and J. F. Voss. New York: Cambridge University Press.

——1998b. Reflecting on the Study of Problem Representation: How Are We Studying It, and What Are We Learning? In *Problem Representation in Foreign Policy Decision Making*, ed. D. Sylvan and J. F. Voss. New York: Cambridge University Press.

'T HART, P. 1997. From Analysis to Reform of Policy-Making Groups. In *Beyond Groupthink: Political Group Dynamics and Foreign Policy-Making*, ed. P. 't Hart, E. K. Stern, and B. Sundelius. Ann Arbor: University of Michigan Press.

—— STERN, E. K., and SUNDELIUS, B. 1997. *Beyond Groupthink: Political Group Dynamics and Foreign Policy-Making*. Ann Arbor: University of Michigan Press.

WALCOTT, C. E., and HULT, K. M. 1995. *Governing the White House: From Hoover through LBJ*. Lawrence: University Press of Kansas.

—— —— 2005. White House Structure and Decision Making: Elaborating the Standard Model. *Presidential Studies Quarterly*, 35: 303–18.

—— WARSHAW, S. A., and WAYNE, S. 2003. The Office of Chief of Staff. In *The White House World: Transitions, Organization, and Office Operations*, ed. M. J. Kumar and T. Sullivan. College Station: Texas A&M University Press.

CHAPTER 24

....

THE PSYCHOLOGY
OF PRESIDENTIAL
DECISION MAKING

....

STEPHEN G. WALKER

PAST discussions of the research agenda for presidential decision making distinguish the "personal" and the "institutional" presidencies (Neustadt 1960; Burke
2000, 1–24; Cameron 2000, 106–10; Preston 2001, 253–4). This dichotomy reminds
us that the president does not make all the decisions attributed to the institution.
Greenstein's (1967, 1987) conceptualizations of action dispensability and actor
dispensability address the issues raised by this distinction by asking whether
decisions and actions emanating from the presidency should be attributed to the
individual or elsewhere within the institution and whether the identity of the
president influences the decisions and actions in question. Personal presidency
scholars tend to emphasize that the identity of the president is indispensable to
explain the characteristics of decisions and actions that fall under the general
category of leadership style (Neustadt 1960; Greenstein 2004). Institutional presidency scholars often substitute a general model of rational choice for the idiosyncratic traits of the president in their models of presidential decision making,
arguing that the context of the decision influences choices within the White
House especially in the domestic political arena (Cameron 2000; Defigueiredo,
Jacobi, and Weingast 2006).

 The author would like to thank George Edwards, Fred Greenstein, William Howell, Margaret
Hermann, Deborah Larson, Akan Malici, Tom Preston, Charles Taber, and David Winter for comments
on earlier versions of this chapter.

Most of the research in political psychology has focused on the person rather than the institution. How far have we come and how far do we have to go in understanding the psychology of presidential decision making? I shall argue in this chapter that there has been considerable progress in conceptualizing and measuring the psychological characteristics of US presidents. The analysis of their impact on presidential decision making lags behind, however, and largely ignored is the systematic analysis of linkages between individuals, decisions, and outcomes. I shall argue further that an alliance between psychological theories of the personal presidency and rational choice theories of the institutional presidency may have a multiplier effect on progress in analyzing presidential decision making in the domestic and foreign policy domains. Specifically, I suggest a future research agenda for studies of the personal presidency that focuses on decisions rather than individuals and on the psychological sources of risk orientation and strategic choice as features of presidential decision making. Such a perspective may be both fruitful and attractive to other research agendas on the presidency, especially rational choice research programs that focus on the institutional presidency.

The president of the United States is widely regarded as the most powerful leader in the world. Does it follow that who leads the United States matters? If so, then exactly *how* and *why* does it matter? Attempts by political psychologists to grapple with the question of the impact of individual differences hinge on Greenstein's important distinctions of action dispensability and actor dispensability. Unless there is a clear link between a leader's actions and a historical event, the leader's actions are dispensable in the explanation of the event. And unless it is clear that another leader would have acted differently, the leader's identity is dispensable in the explanation of the action. These distinctions address the task of establishing criteria for linking a leader's identity (personality) with actions (decisions) leading to events (outcomes). This task led Greenstein to "unpack" various dimensions embedded in the concepts of personality, decision making, and political outcomes. He recommended as well several research strategies to test for the presence or absence of connections among these three constructs.

Greenstein's efforts offer a useful template within which to organize an appraisal of the research by political psychologists who have studied US presidents over the past thirty years. He suggests a pattern of progress among single case studies, typological studies, and aggregative studies in which "one chooses (a) to diagnose a single actor, (b) to classify actors and explain the origin and behavior of the types in the classification, or (c) to make use of knowledge obtained from the study of individuals and types in order to explain aspects of the larger system of which they are a part" (Greenstein 1987, 16). This a, b, c sequence can also work in reverse by reasoning backward from knowledge of the psychological requirements of institutions and systems to the types of leaders that fit these requirements and a judgment about whether or not a leader or candidate has them (Greenstein 1987, 138–9). Other sequences are also possible.

CONCEPTUALIZING AND MEASURING PRESIDENTIAL PERSONALITY

Greenstein (1987, 2–5) cautions at the beginning of his inquiry into the relationship between the personalities and decisions of political leaders that psychologists and political scientists mean different things when they refer to a political leader's personality. Psychologists refer to personality as encompassing all of the psychological characteristics of a leader while political scientists exclude political attitudes and limit personality to the clinician's traditional concerns with a leader's ego defense and inner conflicts. As Greenstein (1987, 5–6) points out, this distinction between a leader's cognitive processes and beliefs versus extra-cognitive processes and desires does not hold up under scrutiny and is ultimately a source of confusion regarding personality's meaning as a concept. It is probably more useful to conceptualize these distinctions as different dimensions of an individual's personality, which invite separate examination in this chapter while allowing for them to be related as well in important ways. George (1969, 195) has also recommended this approach as a research strategy with the argument that the methods of a clinical psychologist and a political scientist are sufficiently different to justify a division of labor in studying relatively unconscious emotional and motivational processes versus relatively conscious cognitive processes.

A related issue is whether personality characteristics are best conceptualized as stable traits or transitory states. A closer examination of this question suggests that the answer depends partly on the design and purpose of the research. Individuals may have relatively stable traits that differentiate them from one another at least in degree when they are placed in similar situations; however, the same characteristic may vary for the same individual across situations, as different environmental conditions arouse it in different degrees. For example, two individuals in the same situation may exhibit different degrees of extroversion[1] and continue to differ to the same degree as the situation changes from an informal to a formal occasion for decision making; however, both individuals may also manifest greater extroversion in the informal setting than in the formal setting. Comparing the two individuals *within* the same situation indicates that the degree of extroversion is a stable trait while studying the same individual *across* situations reveals that the degree of extroversion is a transitory state. Some psychological characteristics may be relatively hard-wired by genetics, as studies of adult twins separated at birth and growing up in quite different environments have shown (Hibbing, Alford, and Funk 2005). Other characteristics are clearly learned and may vary widely over time and across situations for the same individual. In order for either kind of psychological characteristic to influence behavior, it needs to be aroused either

---

[1] This personality trait is a personality orientation in which the individual is oriented toward the external environment while introversion is an inward-looking orientation. Some one who is lower in extroversion is usually assumed to be higher in introversion (see Kowert 2002, 15–16).

unconsciously or consciously by stimuli from the individual's decision-making environment.[2]

As psychoanalytic theory has waned in popularity under the methodological influence of experimental behaviorism and the influence of a theoretical revolution in psychology, cognitive and neuroscientific theories have become more prominent analytical platforms for linking personality and politics (Tetlock and Levi 1982; Nisbett and Ross 1980; Fiske and Taylor 1991; Marcus, Neuman, and MacKuen 2000; Ledoux 2002). In this essay I shall focus on particular examples of important research into connections between personality and politics by political psychologists who span the older and the newer approaches. I examine the history of research in three different areas—personality, world view, and cognitive processes—with links to presidential decision making. The research projects that I select below for discussion show how each area of research developed along the lines suggested by Greenstein's single-case, typological, and systems template for studying personality and politics.

Personality Studies

Perhaps the most famous study of presidential personalities is *Woodrow Wilson and Colonel House* (1956), a psychobiography of Woodrow Wilson by Alexander and Juliette George. The Georges argue that the psychodynamics of his personality, acquired from childhood socialization experiences, decisively influenced Wilson's actions during the debate over US ratification of the Versailles Treaty. According to Greenstein, this argument and the accompanying evidence presented by the Georges meet the criteria of action and actor indispensability for claiming that individual differences made a difference in the outcome of the debate. Wilson fulfilled the condition of action indispensability by occupying a strategic position in the decision-making environment within which his actions doomed the treaty to failure. His confrontation with opposition leaders in the US Senate aroused inner conflicts within Wilson that required him to defend his ego by refusing to make compromises necessary to gain ratification. He thereby met the condition of actor indispensability, because another president without these psychodynamics in his personality would likely have made concessions that brought about ratification and did not gut the treaty (Greenstein 1987, 63–93). The Wilson study represents the psychoanalytical theoretical orientation of many early psychological studies of presidential decision making and illustrates as well some of the methodological problems of the single case study.

How does one move from a single case study to a typological theoretical analysis and a systematic empirical comparison with other presidents and their decisions? It is possible to stretch the single case study into a longitudinal analysis of the same leader for different decision-making episodes or collect additional data that may point to the "correct" clinical interpretation of the single case (Weinstein 1981; Post 1983, 2003;

---

[2] For discussions of the importance of this issue in studying leaders, see Hermann (1980), Kowert and Hermann (1997), and Kowert (2002, 11–15) who also cite relevant psychological studies regarding this debate.

Immelman 1993; Walker 1995; George and George 1998). Such early comparative efforts were valuable heuristically in comparing US presidents, but the authors' methods of classifying them into the typologies were not always developed sufficiently to avoid some methodological problems. The most prominent and influential example of this kind of research was the pathbreaking study by David Barber (1972) who developed a famous typology of US presidents that categorized their orientation toward the role of president as either active or passive and positive or negative. The intersection of these two sets of traits defined a president's leadership style, reflected aspects of the leader's character, and predicted performance of the presidential role. George (1974) identified several problems with this approach to the study of US presidents, which include theoretical vagueness (the types are too general and too simple), latent circularity (using the president's political behavior to identify personal traits and then explaining his behavior with these traits), and a lack of reproducibility (no coding rules to reproduce the author's judgments). Two important research programs by Winter and Hermann, respectively, addressed these pitfalls by applying reproducible content analysis methods to the public statements of US presidents in an effort to study more systematically their personalities and leadership styles "at a distance" (Schafer 2000).[3]

David Winter analyzes the motivational imagery in the inaugural addresses of US presidents. He asks which motivations, the needs for achievement, power, or affiliation, characterize each president's personality. He argues that the particular mix of motivations in each case supplies a leader with a direction and energy for action and influences his conception of the leader's role (Winter 2003, 153). There is also a large body of research in psychology that has provided Winter with hypotheses about the links between these motivations and the political behavior of leaders (Winter 1973). Since these measurements are taken at the start of the leader's term in office, they avoid circularity and meet the test of temporal precedence for establishing their causal influence on subsequent political behavior. The measurements are comparable for the entire group of presidents through George W. Bush, because the coding of their respective inaugural addresses is done with explicit, reproducible coding rules and the results are counted with a standardized metric (image frequencies per 1,000 words).

Although Winter identifies the dominant motivations of each US president compared to the others and correlates these differences with variations in their political behavior, including conflict management strategies and the selection of advisers, he stops short of explicitly developing a typology of motivational profiles that is logically exhaustive and mutually exclusive. Instead, he identifies links between the needs for power, affiliation, and achievement and various behavioral characteristics in laboratory experiments, such as differences in risk orientation, impulse control,

---

[3] Schafer (2000, 512) notes that studying the personal characteristics of leaders at a distance draws "on assumptions and methods found in three different academic fields—psychology, political science, and speech communications . . . The most important assumption made with at-a-distance techniques is that it is possible to assess psychological characteristics of a leader by systematically analyzing what leaders say and how they say it." A survey of at-a-distance methods with applications is Post (2003).

and bargaining styles under different conditions of threat. He and his associates then test the external validity of these outcomes in the experiments with correlational analyses linking individual motivations with several behaviors exhibited by US presidents, such as charismatic leadership and decisions for war by power-motivated executives or peace-seeking decisions and susceptibility to scandals by affiliation-motivated occupants of the White House (Winter 2003, 159).

Margaret Hermann (2003) has developed criteria for extracting indicators of a leader's personality traits from the texts of interviews rather than prepared speeches. She has constructed profiles of over 122 political leaders, including eighty-seven heads of state, that span all of the US presidents since the Second World War. She argues that these relatively spontaneous verbal comments by leaders reveal several personality traits that are relevant for explaining a leader's actions (see also Weintraub 2003). She measures these traits with explicit coding rules that have been automated so that a computer with the appropriate dictionary and software for parsing grammar can reliably retrieve, code, and calculate the indices. They include parts of speech and vocabulary (verbal behavior) that indicate: (1) belief in the ability to control events, (2) the need for power, (3) self confidence, (4) conceptual complexity, (5) task focus, (6) in-group bias, and (7) distrust of others, which she employs to predict and explain leadership style (actual behavior in office).

Hermann (2003) uses different traits to predict different aspects of leadership style: (a) belief in control over events and need for power influence a leader's reaction to constraints, (b) self-confidence and conceptual complexity influence a leader's openness to contextual information, (c) task focus influences a leader's motivation for seeking office, and (d) in-group bias and distrust of others influence a leader's motivation toward the world. The independent variables in each of these hypotheses except for hypothesis (c) are dichotomized and crossed to create several typologies of leadership style relating to the dependent variables in these hypotheses. She also combines several dichotomies of leadership style, including a leader's motivational focus (task vs. relationship), reaction to constraints (challenges vs. respects), and openness to information (open vs. closed), to generate a general typology of eight general leadership styles.

World Views and Cognitive Processes

The notion of "Weltanschauung" or world view is a multifaceted concept which, like personality, can have more than one meaning. As a philosophical term it refers to beliefs about how the world works, especially how historical events unfold and the role of individuals and institutions in society. When a society or group shares such a system of beliefs to guide the conduct of public affairs, it constitutes an ideology. It is possible to analyze the contents of a world view to see if it represents current realities or future aspirations and to argue over its merits as a philosophy of life. When political psychologists analyze a leader's world view, however, they also ask other questions: What are the properties of a leader's world view that relate to political behavior? How do these properties influence a leader's decisions? This focus on the functions of beliefs in decision making produces several insights into how leaders process information and make choices.

First, beliefs serve a diagnostic function by ordering incoming information into categories within the context of a belief system aroused by the stimulus, which allows the decision maker to make associations between the new information and past experiences that resemble the incoming stimulus (George 1979). Second, these past experiences stored in memory also serve as general principles or analogies that prescribe appropriate actions in response to the stimulus (George 1969; Khong 1992). The influence of such cognitive mechanisms on decision making is higher when the stimulus is ambiguous or information is relatively scarce (Holsti 1976). Under these circumstances they reduce cognitive uncertainty, allowing a leader to identify problems and make choices consistent with this cognitive architecture.

The quality of the ensuing decisions depends on how appropriate the leader's beliefs are as guides for making decisions and how open the leader is to considering incoming information that may be inconsistent with previously held beliefs. On the one hand, a leader may be relatively unreceptive to new information and pay attention primarily to information that is consistent with his or her predispositions (Jervis 1976). On the other hand, a leader may exhibit the capacity for learning, i.e., for altering beliefs in response to new information and changing his behavior (Levy 1994). In the former case beliefs have a biased steering effect on decisions, overriding the potential influence of new information on a leader's choices. In the latter case beliefs have a realistic mirroring effect, reflecting the influence of new information on a leader's subsequent decisions (Schafer and Walker 2006).

Operational code analysis focuses on a leader's beliefs about political strategy, the power relations between self and other, and the friendly or hostile nature of others in the political universe (George 1969, 1979, 1987; Walker 1990; Walker, Schafer, and Young 2003). The research program on operational codes has evolved from single case studies of particular leaders informed by a common set of research questions to a typology of operational code belief systems in which the image of others is a master philosophical belief influencing other beliefs about the political universe as well as instrumental beliefs about the most effective strategies and tactics for realizing fundamental political values (George 1969; Walker 1983). The refinement and application of this typology includes quantitative-statistical studies of the belief systems, learning, and decision making of Abraham Lincoln, Theodore Roosevelt, Woodrow Wilson, and every US president since the Second World War (Walker and Schafer 2008). The application of the typology to US presidents Theodore Roosevelt and Woodrow Wilson, for example, reveals that Roosevelt was a pragmatic idealist during both of his terms in office while Wilson shifted from a dogmatic idealist in his first term to a pragmatic realist during his second administration and then back to a dogmatic idealist at the end of the First World War (Walker and Schafer 2007).

The image of others as a master belief in a political leader's world view has a long and distinguished history in political psychology (Boulding 1956; Rosati 1987; White 1991). The framing effect of defining others as friends, collaborators, competitors, adversaries, or enemies, for example, assigns an identity that cues other beliefs about how to interact with them. Image theorists have worked out the defining properties of different images, such as friendly/hostile orientations, strong/weak capabilities, good/bad intentions, superior/ inferior cultures attributed to others (Cottam 1977; Herrmann 1985; Cottam 1986). Depending on the configuration of such properties attributed to a particular other, the self may be likely to categorize "other" as a threat of conflict or an opportunity for cooperation calling for different behavioral responses (Herrmann 1985; Cottam 1994; Herrmann and Fischerkeller 1995; Herrmann et al. 1997). For example, Cottam's (1994) analysis of the images of US presidents in dealing with Latin American countries shows support for image theory's predictions that, depending on whether the image of "other" is a Dependent (weak capability/inferior culture/hostile orientation), Enemy (equal capability/equal culture/hostile orientation), or Neutral (weak capability/ equal culture/friendly orientation), US presidents are more or less likely to use coercive instruments of foreign policy and escalate to military intervention.

Generally missing from these analyses are fully specified models of the cognitive and extra-cognitive processes *during* decision making, which act as causal mechanisms connecting the world views and political behavior of US presidents and other political leaders. Some significant exceptions to this generalization are applications of formal computational models and game theory to the study of leaders and their belief systems (Taber 1992, 1998; Herrmann and Fischerkeller 1995; Marfleet and Walker 2006). Rules for processing information or playing games are the basis for computer simulations of decision-making processes, which process beliefs and information about the environment and calculate a decision as a response. They address the problem of external validity by constructing a knowledge base extracted from real world sources to represent a belief system about a particular domain of action.

The computer simulations or rules of play, respectively, act as inference engines to interpret a particular historical event and generate the alternatives preferred as choices by policy makers who subscribe to the beliefs or images in these formal models. Taber identifies three paradigms of American foreign policy, militant anti-Communism, pragmatic anti-Communism, and isolationism, extracted from the public statements by several US policy makers in the *Congressional Record*, 1949–60. Marfleet and Walker's simulation model interfaces with automated content analysis software to retrieve a leader's operational code belief system and infer a subjective game from public statements (see Schafer and Walker 2006; Maoz and Mor 2002). Some image theorists have also inferred games from qualitative content analyses of images of others (Hermann and Fischerkeller 1995). This approach addresses directly and more formally the process validity issue, which correlational studies leapfrog, historical case studies handle less systematically, and experiments have to qualify on external validity grounds.

Cognitive and Extra-Cognitive Processes

Psychological models often do not include rich analyses of the political decision-making process because they assume that relevant contextual features, such as institutional rules and structural constraints imposed by the environment, are outside of their scope. It is convenient to recognize such limits in order to avoid a charge of reductionism by critics who would accuse psychological models of claiming too much explanatory power. I suggest here that the optimum solution to this conundrum is a theoretical alliance with rational choice models that explicitly supply what psychological models lack. Less optimum solutions would be simply to respect a division of labor between psychological analysis and the domains of other models or to pit psychological models against rational choice models as rival explanations for the same phenomena. The division of labor argument is that the analyst needs to choose between them, based on the scarcity or abundance of information and time for decision (Holsti 1976). The rivalry argument is that one set of conditions is endemic to politics, and therefore, one model is generally superior to the other (Green and Shapiro 1994; Geva and Mintz 1997).

Decisions in politics often are responses to what Voss (1998) terms "ill-structured" problems, which resemble the conditions of scarcity of information or time that render rational choice models implausible as descriptions of political decision making. In the foreign policy domain, occasions for decision are often "ill structured," and various cognitive biases are most likely to be influential causal mechanisms (Larson 1985; Khong 1992; Etheredge 1985). Such mechanisms offer explanations as middle range theories of particular phenomena without necessarily embedding them within a general theory of human behavior (Elster 1993; Hedstrom and Swedberg 1998). For example, Larson (1985, 342) concluded that "self-perception, schema, and attribution theories were most useful in explaining policymakers' interpretations of Soviet actions and salient cutting points in the evolution of the Cold War belief system." Cognitive dissonance theory and learning theory were less fruitful causal mechanisms, because their predictions were not supported by archival evidence. However, US leaders did have preexisting idiosyncratic or expert schemata that influenced their adoption of new beliefs.[4]

Recent research by neuroscientists with new instruments permitting a biological perspective on psychological processes have returned to prominence the presence and influence of extra-cognitive, emotional processes and systems. Brain scans are able to locate the parts of the brain that contain emotional and motivational systems as well as the parts of the brain that contain cognitive systems. This research shows that the former react to incoming stimuli faster than the latter, and the three kinds of systems interact to influence the behavioral response of the individual (Marcus, Neuman, and MacKuen 2000; LeDoux 2002). The implications of this research are to give new emphasis to the influence of extra-cognitive processes in human behavior. Humans can act first and rationalize their actions later, supporting Zajonc's

---

[4] Psychologists define a schema as "a cognitive structure that represents knowledge about a concept or type of stimulus, including its attributes and the relations among those attributes" (Fiske and Taylor 1991, 98). There are different kinds of schemata, including a person schema, an object schema, and an action schema. An action schema is also called a script, as it defines the actions called for in response to a particular stimulus whereas person or object schemata simply define the characteristics of the stimulus (see Fiske and Taylor 1991, 98 ff.).

(1980) claim that "preferences need no inferences." In his initial dealings with Stalin, for example, Truman employed a "code of the politician" action and person schema with a positive emotional valence learned in Missouri politics, which associated Stalin with the persona of Boss Pendergast and a script that politicians keep their word. When Stalin's subsequent actions violated this script, Truman searched for an appropriate behavioral response and formulated a new script to justify it (Larson 1985, 350–1). The new information that Stalin was not following the script associated with this schema aroused an emotion with a negative emotional valence and an alternative script as a "get tough" or "straight one-two-to-the-jaw" tactic instead of FDR's "kid glove" approach in dealing with Stalin and his emissaries (Larson 1985, 335; see also Fiske and Taylor 1991, 407–61).

Neuroscience research supports the inference that opportunities and threats are basic categories that leaders use to interpret and respond to the environment. These categories resonate with feelings of novelty and anxiety aroused by incoming stimuli that the emotional surveillance system of the human brain recognizes as outside the normal flow of information. In the absence of novelty and anxiety signals from the surveillance system, individuals make decisions based on previously learned habits and routines stored in the disposition system (Marcus, Neuman, and MacKuen 2000). New feelings of novelty and anxiety are immediate and unconscious until their intensity level reaches a threshold that engages conscious feeling and thought. By that time they may have already shaped a behavioral response unless there is sufficient time and awareness to reason to a choice of action.

Even if cognitive, motivational, and emotional biases structure the diagnostic stage of the decision-making process by specifying goals and eliminating some alternatives from the menu for choice, it is still likely that decision makers use rational choice procedures to make their choices. They do try to estimate the consequences of alternative choices and select the one that maximizes benefits and minimizes costs. Therefore, it is plausible to use such models to explain the prescriptive stage of the decision-making process while also recognizing that different individuals and groups are more likely to conform or deviate from this procedure because of differences in their personalities or particular features of the occasion for decision (Mintz 1997; Kowert and Hermann 1997; Greenstein 1987). These caveats make decision making a process of "bounded rationality" (Simon 1957, 1985; March and Simon 1958; Tetlock 1998). The popular emphasis among political psychologists on boundaries rather than rationality in this phrase needs to be revisited and rebalanced, however, so that both terms are recognized as capturing important features of the political decision-making process (Lupia, McCubbins, and Popkin 2000, 9–11).

It is only relatively recently that an alliance solution has become a popular topic for discussion (Lupia, McCubbins, and Popkin 2000; Mintz 2002; Bueno de Mesquita and McDermott 2004; Schafer and Walker 2006). The argument on behalf of the alliance solution is the same as the solution in the story of Goldilocks and the Three Bears for selecting baby bear's porridge over mama bear's or papa bear's porridge— it's just right (neither too hot nor too cold). Unlike the rivalry position that claims too much and the division of labor position that claims too little on behalf of psychological models, the alliance position strikes a balance in providing an explanation for political decision making. Theoretically, the strength of psychological models is their diagnostic powers while the strength of rational choice models is their prescriptive powers, which address different stages of the decision-making process. Psychological models explain which information is gathered (perceived) plus which goals are deemed relevant. Given this information, rational choice models represent how and why a decision maker decides to choose among alternative choices.

Conceptualizing and Measuring Presidential Decision Making

Can a decision-making process that emphasizes reflection and time for deliberation be rational and avoid or minimize a response based on unrecognized cognitive or motivated biases? The answer is "yes" if you do not ask too much of the rationality criterion. A minimalist model of rationality would specify that a decision-making unit be purposeful (goal oriented) in its deliberations, mindful (actively engaged in considering different alternatives), and calculating (identifying the positive and negative consequences of each alternative). To the extent that each of these characteristics is present, the procedural rationality of the decision-making process increases (Lake and Powell 1999; Langer 1989; Lau 2003). However, it is possible for one of these features to decrease as another one increases. As an individual or group becomes actively engaged in considering different alternatives, "bolstering" by an individual or "groupthink" by several individuals may portray the consequences of one of the alternatives as more attractive in order to distance it from another alternative (Tetlock 2000; George 1980, 38–9; Janis 1972).

The cognitive complexity of thought and communication processes measures the strength of procedural rationality. In order to meet the three criteria above to some degree, cognitive processes of differentiation and integration need to occur as exhibited in recorded statements about a situation or decision. The processes indicate the level of cognitive complexity associated with information processing. Differentiation refers to the recognition of at least two distinct dimensions of judgment in these statements while integration notes the existence of conceptual connections between differentiated dimensions. Studies of the integrative complexity exhibited by political decision makers indicates that under conditions of value conflict, moderate stress, and accountability to others, they are likely to exhibit more differentiation and at least some integration in the complexity of their thought processes (Suedfeld, Guttieri, and Tetlock 2003). Given the emotionally charged conditions and relative uncertainty about goals, alternatives, and outcomes in the political domain, it is not surprising that leaders do not exhibit higher levels of integrative complexity (Tetlock 2000; Braybrooke and Lindblom 1963).

Generally, decision makers try to be as rational as they can or as much as the situation demands. The cognitive shortcuts to choice in psychological models are not always employed by individuals. When it is necessary or desirable to be actively rather than habitually or mechanically engaged in making choices, they are capable and motivated as cognitive managers to be strategic thinkers and deciders (Langer 1989; Tetlock 2000; Suedfeld, Guttieri, and Tetlock 2003). Even if a decision maker's unconscious motivational and emotional biases initiate the processes of cognition and choice (Zajonc 1980; Marcus, Neuman, and MacKuen 2000), it is possible to correct for their influence with offsetting, conscious decision-making procedures (Janis and Mann 1977; George 1972, 1980). When the decision-making process breaks down or when there is no opportunity to introduce rational thought processes into the decision-making process, psychological models have the most relevance in both diagnosing the occasion for decision and prescribing the choice (Janis 1972; Burke and Greenstein 1989; 't Hart, Stern, and Sundelius 1997; Suskind 2004).

One way to buy time and gain insight is to make the decision-making process *social* rather than *individual* by designing an advisory system for a predominant leader or by altering the decision-making process so that a single group or a coalition of autonomous actors becomes the decision unit (Hermann 2001). This step is a controversial solution, however, that moves the debate between psychological and rational choice theorists into another venue. On the one hand, some economists argue that the impacts of idiosyncratic personality traits and affect are said to "cancel each other out" at the level of collective decision making and "are perhaps best ignored as behavioral noise" (Thaler 1991 and Arrow 1987, cited in Marcus, Neuman, and MacKuen 2000, 24). On the other hand, social psychologists argue that small groups and large organizations are not simply free markets of ideas but heavily regulated arenas in which variations in leadership and structural features create institutionalized biases in the decision-making processes that produce choices (Hermann and Preston 1994; Stern 1997; Schafer and Crichlow 2002).

The most notorious effect of such biases is "groupthink," the tendency toward concurrence seeking within groups, which leads to premature closure in the consideration of relevant information and the identification of different options for choice (Janis 1972). The sources of groupthink include the presence of stress resulting from a short time in which to make a decision involving high stakes, the influence of leaders and other senior members within a group whose biases can guide deliberations and stifle discussion of unpopular options, and the homogeneity of the group's composition. To the extent that the leader's personality and power influence group structure, rational decisions depend on the leader's commitment to a rational decision-making process (Suskind 2004). The most important structural variables related to outcomes are the presence of a methodical procedures norm, the absence of a gatekeeper who stifles dissent, and the presence of value disagreement among group members. These structural characteristics and their implementation in the form of surveying objectives and alternatives are significantly associated with successful achievement of national interests and lower levels of international conflict. They represent a collective calculus of optimizing benefits and minimizing costs. Experienced and knowledgeable group members and teamwork also enhance the likelihood of successful achievement of national interests, but they are not significantly related to avoiding international conflict (Schafer and Crichlow 2002, 56–60).

These results reinforce the argument in this essay that an alliance of psychological and rational choice models is likely to be a fruitful approach in studying the psychology of presidential decision making. In this argument a rational choice model is just one more psychological model, but one which avoids or minimizes information-processing errors. Human beings are willing and able to follow rational choice procedures to the extent that circumstances either permit or demand. It is important not to confuse routine decisions governed by habit and prior information with those decisions in which opportunities or threats are detected and the decision-making process follows the norms of rational choice. A leader such as the president of the United States has the power to organize the decision-making process so that such norms govern leader–adviser interactions leading to the point of decision.

Psychological studies of presidents and advisers reveal that the leader's personality has at least three kinds of effects on the rational quality of the decision-making process between the president and his advisers. They are (1) who serves as advisers (Winter 1973, 2003), (2) how the advisers are organized (George 1980; Kowert 2002), and (3) what options are identified and advocated as choices (Etheredge 1978). Hermann and Preston (1994) have developed typologies of leadership style and their impact on the advisory process. After a review of personality traits identified by previous authors, they suggest a leader's personal orientations (task vs. process focus and preference for formal or informal control) are influential in accounting for the selection and organization of advisers and the operating characteristics of the advisory system. They also suggest that context (such as domestic or foreign policy domain) and expertise (previous experience and interest) are important in how leaders engage in decision-making activity.

In a subsequent study of US presidents, Preston (2001, 14–31, 252–67) applied these insights in constructing typologies of leadership style in leader–adviser interactions for six US presidents (Truman, Eisenhower, Kennedy, Johnson, G. H. W. Bush, and Clinton) and testing the predictions for each leader with case studies of their decision making. He shows that these leaders varied in their leadership styles across the domestic and foreign policy domains, depending on their level of expertise in each domain and the personal characteristics of cognitive complexity and need for power. Truman and Johnson were cognitively less complex and tended to exhibit an erratic, Maverick style in processing information from advisers in the foreign policy domain, where they were less experienced, vs. a more vigilant, Sentinel style in the domestic policy domain where they were more experienced. Kennedy, Eisenhower, Clinton, and Bush were cognitively more complex. The first three leaders were also more experienced in foreign policy and tended to exhibit a highly sensitive, Navigator style in processing information in this domain while playing a less sensitive, Observer role in domestic policy issues. Clinton's higher expertise with domestic issues and lower expertise in foreign policy matters led to a reversal of the Observer and Navigator styles across domains in his case.

These variations in sensitivity to context were accompanied by variations in level of involvement in the decision-making process, depending on their respective expertise in each domain and their personal needs for power. A high need for power (Kennedy, Eisenhower, and Johnson) translated into more active involvement as Directors in their respective areas of expertise and somewhat less active involvement as Magistrates in the less familiar domain. This trend continued for those presidents (Clinton and Bush) who had a low need for power and displayed Administrator or Delegator styles, depending on whether the domain was one in which their previous expertise was higher or lower.

A Holistic View of Rational Decision Making

Decision-making models divide into different levels of rationality, united by a common concern with making goal-directed (purposeful) choices. Some models are less mediated by conscious thought processes than others, such as learned habits and skills that govern responses to familiar stimuli. Driving a car, playing tennis, and other complex behaviors are purposeful and even planned in advance, e.g., choosing a route to a destination or selecting a strategy against another player, even though these decisions appear reactive rather than proactive in their execution. Their rationality may also not be apparent, because the connection between intentions, actions, and consequences may be thwarted by the actions of others or segmented, interrupted by other activities between the decision and execution stages, even though they are united by a common goal or purpose that is successfully attained. Formal rational choice explanations focus most explicitly on the choice process between or among alternatives whereas cognitive explanations emphasize the judgment process that precedes the actual decision. Advocates of cognitive explanations criticize rational choice explanations as unrealistic descriptions of how leaders and groups actually make political choices while advocates of rational choice models argue that they make accurate predictions of political decisions (Lau 2003). It is likely that both positions are correct and also that each argument is flawed.

The cognitivist claim about descriptive inaccuracy rests on an excessively narrow definition of "rational choice" in which a decision maker makes elaborate calculations regarding the probability and utility of different outcomes associated with different alternatives before making a decision. Political choices are often responses to "ill-structured" problems that do not have available the information necessary to make such highly technical and complex calculations. At the same time, the context for political decisions does not require such information in order to make rational choices that are predictable. Instead, rational choices require information about the constraints of the political decision-making environment and information about the preferences of the decision maker for outcomes circumscribed by those constraints. In a democratic political system, for example, the main constraint may be the electoral imperative, the necessity to make decisions that will keep a leader in office (Mayhew 1974; Fenno 1978). Political survival in other kinds of political systems may not employ elections as the mechanism for staying in office, but the logic of the situation is the same: it is rational to make choices that ensure one's political survival (Bueno de Mesquita et al. 2003).

Cognitivists are correct that highly stylized and formal models of rational choice, which require precise numerical measurements of probabilities and utilities, do not describe most political decision making. Originally developed for calculating gambling strategies to win money in various games of risk, these models do not automatically describe the procedures for making choices among political alternatives (McDermott 2001; Boettcher 2005). However, it is appropriate to level a similar criticism at psychological models of decision making based on laboratory experiments with college sophomores as subjects. The descriptions of choices between alternatives made by laboratory subjects regarding surgery vs. radiation treatments for cancer or choosing between different disease inoculation strategies for at-risk populations do not necessarily translate accurately into generalizations about how political decisions are made (McDermott 2001; Boettcher 2005). The key issue is the external validity of the model and not whether humans are complex calculators or simple estimators of consequences. The point is that they can do both kinds of operations, depending on the available information and the context for decision.

The Goldilocks "just right" solution is to study real decisions in the real world with models of choice that reflect measurement and calculation procedures realistically used by decision makers. Lau (2003, 33–37) distinguishes between compensatory and non-compensatory models of choice that meet minimum conditions of rationality. Both models require some criteria for choosing among alternatives. The former identify each alternative's consequences and calculate the balance between them into an overall evaluation. The choice is the option with the highest overall evaluation. Compensatory strategies of rationality have to figure out how to weigh positive and negative consequences in a way consistent with these criteria and how to aggregate them into an overall evaluation with a commensurate mathematical metric. Non-compensatory models of choice do not trade off positive against negative consequences for an alternative. They do not need commensurable measures of the criteria and do not use a mathematical aggregation formula. Negative information is sufficient to eliminate an alternative. Alternatives are assessed according to (a) pre-existing minimum levels of each criterion, (b) the most important criterion, or (c) a combination of these two steps to identify the best alternative. A model that combines non-compensatory and compensatory features is the poliheuristic decision model (Mintz 1997). This model of decision making has two stages in processing alternatives: a non-compensatory stage narrows the alternatives according to a relevant heuristic (rule)[5] that eliminates those options that do not meet a particular criterion, e.g., the electoral imperative in democracies, and then the remaining alternatives are the subject of a compensatory analysis of the trade-offs between them.

---

[5] Whereas schemata are ideas about the environment, heuristics are the rules for testing these ideas. They can act as shortcuts to organize and interpret incoming information even in the absence of explicit object, person, or action schemata (see Fiske and Taylor 1991, 381–93).

Presidential Decision-Making Models

A non-compensatory rationality model of presidential decision making is Farnham's (1997) analysis of Franklin Roosevelt's decision making during the 1938 Munich crisis. She advances a political decision-making model that combines sensitivity to context with a non-compensatory decision rule to resolve value conflicts—the acceptability principle. It states that a leader will choose the option that meets a threshold of acceptability among all politically relevant groups in the decision-making environment. Groups are politically relevant if they have a veto power, at least in the leader's mental calculus of decision, along with more impersonal contextual features such as material constraints, institutional norms and precedents, and available information. She argues that this principle requires a leader to engage rather than avoid the task of making choices, forgo cognitive shortcuts in the search for information, and make more sophisticated judgments rather than trade off gains and losses mechanically when faced with a value conflict. The Munich crisis in Europe became the catalyst for FDR to resolve the value conflict between international and domestic imperatives by supporting the democracies in their rearmament efforts against the fascist dictatorships. Although this choice satisfied fully neither the isolationist nor the interventionist sectors of US public and elite opinion, it was acceptable to both and appeared to Roosevelt as a feasible response to the Axis threat.

A key task involved in making rational choices is estimating the consequences of different alternatives. Risk is generally defined by the probabilities of good and bad consequences associated with an alternative. These probabilities are difficult to calculate in practice except for games of chance such as dice or cards. There is a tendency for decision makers in calculating risk to look at the magnitudes (variance) between good and bad consequences associated with an alternative. This insight is the core of prospect theory, a non-compensatory rationality model developed by Kahneman and Tversky (1979) to represent how individuals actually make choices between alternatives. Depending on whether the decision maker "frames" the decision in the domain of losses or the domain of gains, she or he will weight the good or the bad consequences associated with an alternative differently in calculating whether to choose it versus another alternative. In the simplest case, if the status quo is framed as a bad situation (domain of losses) for the decision maker, she or he will be risk acceptant, i.e., more accepting of a chance of bad consequences in choosing a decision that offers a chance of good consequences. Conversely, if the status quo is framed as a good situation (domain of gains) for the decision maker, she or he will be risk averse, i.e., less accepting of bad consequences in choosing an alternative with a chance of good consequences.

A study of foreign policy decisions by US presidents Dwight Eisenhower and Jimmy Carter offers support for these predictions by prospect theory. McDermott (2001) analyzes President Eisenhower's decision making during the U-2 crisis with Russia and the crisis with Britain and France over the Suez war. She finds that in the first crisis Eisenhower was operating in the domain of losses and made the risky decision to deny that the American U-2 plane shot down over Soviet territory was engaged in espionage. In the second crisis the president was located in the domain of gains and chose the less risky decision to oppose rather than support the Anglo-French occupation of the Suez canal in Egypt. Similarly, President Jimmy Carter in the domain of gains initially chose a low-risk policy of granting the exiled Shah of Iran asylum for medical treatment until Iranian students retaliated by occupying the US embassy and seizing American personnel. This move shifted the president's location from the domain of gains to the domain of losses and led to his high-risk decision to launch a military rescue of the hostages. In both sets of case studies, the decisions to take high-risk decisions by the two presidents resulted in foreign policy failures while the decisions to choose low-risk decisions produced foreign policy successes.

The acceptability principle and prospect theory are models of bounded rationality mechanisms, because they do not meet the requirements of a compensatory model of rational choice, which employ quantitative measures and probabilities of the likelihood of good and bad consequences associated with different alternatives (Lau 2003, 33–4). They either ignore or do not have available some of this information and employ instead decision heuristics such as acceptability thresholds or reference points to choose an alternative. There is a somewhat parallel distinction between models of cardinal and ordinal games. Cardinal game models measure the outcomes (consequences) for each player with quantitative scores (utilities) while ordinal game models simply rank the outcomes, limiting the possible mathematical calculations to determine the optimal choice by each player in the game. The level of measurement in cardinal games is often difficult to employ in politics unless the metric is money or votes or some other conventional interval measure.

Two other features of classical game theory models also make their application to political decision-making problematic: (1) they assume that the players know the utilities for their own respective choices *and* for the other players; (2) they also assume that players make simultaneous choices in order to simplify the mathematical solutions for calculating the optimal choice for each player (Morrow 1994). These assumptions do not meet the conditions of external validity for political decision making. Each player often does not have accurate and complete information about all players' utilities. They also make choices sequentially, alternating over time rather than choosing simultaneously together. Game theory has developed models that relax these two assumptions, however, which political scientists have begun to apply to the study of decision making by US presidents toward the congressional and judicial branches and the bureaucracy in the executive branch (Defigueiredo, Jacobi, and Weingast 2006).

The two-sided information assumption, that each player knows the ranked preferences for all outcomes, is particularly problematic. Unless this assumption is met, the players may literally be playing different games. However, it is possible to reduce this difficulty and make the analysis feasible with the following adjustments in research design: (1) permit pre-play communication between players, which can clarify the preference rankings of both players; (2) allow alternating moves and repeated plays of the game, which has the effect of revealing the preferences of each player by the moves they make; (3) model the subjective game of each player and do a second-order analysis of the choices each player makes in the sequence of alternating moves to see if they act "rationally" within the boundaries of their own subjective games and learn from the exchange of moves between players. These three steps are also consistent with what decision makers appear to do in the political domain, which makes the external validity of these adjustments plausible (Brams 1994, 2002; Cameron 2000; Maoz and Mor 2002; Marfleet and Walker 2006).

In recent years "a new separation of powers approach" has appeared in institutional studies of the presidency, which exploits these methodological solutions in applying game theory to study strategic choices by presidents in dealing with the bureaucracy and the other two branches of the federal government (Defigueiredo, Jacobi, and Weingast 2006). A prominent example is Cameron's (2000) study of presidential decision making toward Congress, which is primarily institution oriented rather than person oriented regarding the exercise of the veto power. His model emphasizes that veto decisions are more likely under divided government than when both branches are controlled by the same political party. His explanation for this difference does not take individual presidential differences into account, arguing that the highly structured, institutional setting for executive–legislative relations provides a situation for rational choices to be made. Although past presidential scholars, e.g., Neustadt (1960), do refer to presidential will and skill as influential in the effective exercise of the veto power in bargaining with Congress, Cameron concludes (2000, 107) that, "No path could be seen for developing Neustadt's insights. And so they remained largely in the state he left them."

Nevertheless, Cameron does recognize that will and skill do matter even if he does not know how to measure them *ex ante*. He subsumes them instead under the concept of "reputation," defined as beliefs about the president inferred from a record of previous behavior by a given president. He argues that the use of dynamic game theory models of repeated play and incomplete information reveals and updates a player's reputation in successive plays of the game. Starting from an initial period in which a model simply assumes the president is one of three types of leaders—accommodating, compromising, or recalcitrant—the risk of a presidential veto is calculated with one of these reputations as a variable in the analysis. If a leader does not live up to this assumption either by threatening or implementing a veto as anticipated, then the reputation of the president is adjusted via Bayesian updating in successive periods until a better fit occurs between his reputation and his actual use of the veto power (Cameron 2000, 83–122).

This "revealed preferences/repeated play" solution for learning the president's reputation has two shortcomings. It does not explain *why* the president has a particular reputation nor does it measure reputation *ex ante*, which gives the ensuing analysis a certain tautological quality in spite of the random assignment of the type of reputation for the initial period of repeated plays of the veto bargaining game. A psychological analysis of the president's personality or an application of prospect theory's framing criteria to the situation initially facing the president may reinforce or offer a rival hypothesis about the assumption assigned to a particular president by the "Harsanyi maneuver"[6] of randomly assigning a reputation (Cameron 2000, 100). For example, the findings by political psychologists regarding leadership style and risk orientation offer hypotheses about particular presidents in Cameron's dataset of presidential vetoes (Preston 2001; Hermann 2003; Winter 2003; Greenstein 2004; Boettcher 2005). A comparison may validate both personal and institutional analyses of presidential decision making, or each one may explain deviant cases in the other's research program. This alliance across the research agendas of the personal and institutional presidencies could thereby have a multiplier effect on the understanding of presidential decision making with each explanation complementing and deepening the other.

Prospect theory is situation oriented rather than personality oriented in its identification of a reference point and risk orientation (McDermott 2001). Individual differences, however, qualify significantly the generalizations about risk orientation in prospect theory (Kowert and Hermann 1997). It appears that there are at least two types of US presidents that vary in their risk orientation, because they vary in conceptual complexity, needs for affiliation and power, and belief in the ability to control events. Boettcher (2005) argues that security-motivated leaders such as Kennedy (high need for affiliation and high conceptual complexity) are risk averse while potential-motivated leaders such as Truman (high task emphasis and high need for power and belief in control over events) are risk acceptant in their decision making. Other reference points are also possible, such as a leader's aspiration level for the magnitude of future success. Depending on whether the aspiration level is higher or lower than the success level of the status quo, the decision maker locates himself in the domain of gains or losses and is risk averse or risk acceptant (Boettcher 2005).

Finally, a cognitive psychological approach linking world views to strategic choices is the identification of ordinal *subjective games* for players in a strategic interaction episode (Maoz 1990; Maoz and Mor 2002; Schafer and Walker 2006). There are a few pilot studies applying sequential game theory to presidential decision making in subjective games in the foreign policy domain (Walker and Schafer 2009). This approach has not been applied to US presidents in the domestic policy domain and is perhaps more suited to the "ill-structured" problems of analyzing foreign policy decisions where two players may play different games due to cross-cultural differences and the absence of institutional rules.

Rational institutionalists theorize that two players are more likely to play the same game in a highly structured situation, such as the domestic policy arena existing between the presidency and the Congress (Cameron 2000, 71–7). If the dynamics of the President–Congress game were based solely on institutional constraints between the executive and legislative branches, there would be no need for doing a

---

    [6] Cameron (2000, 100) notes, "A feasible method for adding incomplete information to models of strategic interaction long eluded game theorists. In the late 1960s, however, the mathematician and philosopher John Harsanyi conquered the technical difficulties.... [S]ometimes called the 'Harsanyi maneuver' in his honor... [the] basic idea is to convert a game of radically incomplete information into a much more tractable game of imperfect information."

psychological analysis of each player's subjective game. However, there are too many examples of important legislation that becomes deadlocked even when the president and Congress are unified by party affiliation for this simple model to be valid. Therefore, it may be desirable at least in particular cases to construct the president's subjective game based on his beliefs, in order to explain his choices and the outcomes of strategic interactions between the executive and legislative branches (Marfleet and Walker 2006).

CONCLUSION

The review of empirical research that informs this essay suggests that (1) presidential personality traits, motivations, world view, and cognitive processes are most directly linked empirically to the pre-decision, diagnostic stage of the decision-making process; (2) the empirical link between these personal characteristics and the actual assessment of alternative decisions and outcomes in the choice stage of the decision-making process is neither as strong or direct; (3) so long as a president exhibits and promotes mindful (active) examination of the options and evidence for projecting the consequences of different alternatives, it is not necessary to meet the criteria of classical models of rationality—bounded rationality models are also models of rational choice; (4) the degree of rationality depends on the degree to which positive and negative consequences are identified and taken into account when making a choice; (5) the ability and the incentive to be rational varies by decision domain and level of decision; (6) strategic political decisions combine strong incentives to be rational with strong limits on the ability to identify consequences and calculate which alternative to choose; (7) measurements of motivations and world views (creating typologies), cognitive processes of judgment (scaling integrative complexity), risk orientation (ranking outcomes), and choice calculation (constructing subjective games) are consistent with the incentives and the limits for making rational strategic choices in the political domain.

How should a research agenda for studying presidential decision making be organized so as to exploit a potential alliance of psychological and rational choice models in particular instances of decision making by US presidents? First, it should focus most directly on decision making *per se*, which is conceptualized as choosing among alternatives. Second, it should explicitly recognize that decision making is not either/or regarding rationality—it is a matter of degree and also contingent. Decision making follows the dictates of rationality within the limits of the occasion for decision and corresponding conceptions of what rationality means. Third, it should adopt a Goldilocks solution to the measurement and calculation issues that accompany the study of rational decision making in the political domain. Fourth, a key feature of political decision making is that decisions in the real world are strategic in two senses: (a) they are *strategic choices* in the individual sense that they are directed toward a particular outcome or end state—often as part of a series of decisions with this outcome as their purpose; (b) they are *strategic interactions* in the social sense that the successful achievement of this outcome depends on the actions of others in response to a decision at one or more points in the series. The actions of others may be decisive in whether the initial outcome is supplanted by a final outcome that is better or worse (Lake and Powell 1999; Signorino 1999; Defigueiredo, Jacobi, and Weingast 2006). Fifth, unless a strategic perspective is adopted to analyze presidential decisions, the links among personalities, decisions, and outcomes will probably remain under-theorized in the study of presidential decision making.

Finally, an alliance of political psychologists and presidential studies scholars in pooling data collection efforts should enhance the multiplier effect of bridging conceptual gaps regarding what we know about the personal and institutional presidencies. Most of the past research reviewed in this chapter focuses on a few presidents and a couple of decisions by each one. Psychological studies of presidential decision making should consider shifting future research toward a larger number of cases and longitudinal studies from single-case and cross-sectional comparative studies. In order to measure change in the dependent variables representing presidential choices, it is desirable to have a lot of cases so that variation can be observed (Edwards 1983; Cameron 2000; Howell 2006). This empirical objective can be readily achieved in two steps: shift the primary definition of the "case" from the president to the decision and collect event chronologies of White House–Congress interactions in the domestic policy domain and between the US government and other states in the foreign policy domain. These datasets would likely fuel quantitative-statistical studies as well as computational modeling analyses of presidential decision making and complement the efforts of political psychologists to profile the personalities of US presidents from their public and private statements.

REFERENCES

ARROW, K. 1987. Rationality of Self and Others in an Economic System. Pp. 201–15 in *Rational Choice: The Contrast between Economics and Psychology*, ed. R. Hogarth and M. Reder. San Diego: Academic Press.

BARBER, D. 1972. *The Presidential Character: Predicting Performance in the White House.* Englewood Cliffs, NJ: Prentice-Hall.

BOETTCHER, W. 2005. *Presidential Risk Behavior in Foreign Policy.* New York: Palgrave.

BOULDING, K. 1956. *The Image.* Ann Arbor: University of Michigan Press.

BRAMS, S. 1994. *Theory of Moves.* Cambridge: Cambridge University Press.

——2002. Game Theory in Practice. Pp. 392–404 in *Millennial Reflections on International Studies*, ed. M. Brecher and F. Harvey. Ann Arbor: University of Michigan Press.

BRAYBROOKE, D., and LINDBLOM, C. 1963. *A Strategy of Decision.* New York: Free Press.

BUENO DE MESQUITA, B., and MCDERMOTT, R. 2004. Crossing No-Man's Land. *Political Psychology*, 25/2: 271–87.

—— SMITH, A., SIVERSON, R., and MORROW, J. 2003. *The Logic of Political Survival.* Cambridge, MA: MIT Press.

BURKE, J. 2000. *The Institutional Presidency,* 2nd edn. Baltimore: Johns Hopkins University Press.

—— and GREENSTEIN, F. 1989. *How Presidents Test Reality.* New York: Russell Sage Foundation.

CAMERON, C. 2000. *Veto Bargaining.* Cambridge: Cambridge University Press.

COTTAM, M. 1986. *Foreign Policy Decision Making.* Boulder, CO: Westview.

—— 1994. *Images and Intervention.* Pittsburgh: University of Pittsburgh Press.

COTTAM, R. 1977. *Foreign Policy Motivation.* Pittsburgh: University of Pittsburgh Press.

DEFIGUEIREDO, R., JACOBI, T., and WEINGAST, B. 2006. The New Separation of Powers Approach to American Politics. Pp. 199–222 in *The Oxford Handbook of Political Economy,* ed. B. Weingast and D. Wittman. New York: Oxford University Press.

EDWARDS, G. 1983. Quantitative Analysis. Pp. 99–124 in *Studying the Presidency,* ed. G. Edwards and S. Wayne. Knoxville: University of Tennessee Press.

ELSTER, J. 1993. *Political Psychology.* Cambridge: Cambridge University Press.

ETHEREDGE, L. 1978. *A World of Men.* Cambridge, MA: MIT Press.

—— 1985. *Can Governments Learn?* New York: Pergamon.

FARNHAM, B. 1997. *Roosevelt and the Munich Crisis.* Princeton, NJ: Princeton University Press.

FENNO, R. 1978. *Home Style.* Glenview, IL: Scott, Foresman & Company.

FISKE, S., and TAYLOR, S. 1991. *Social Cognition,* 2nd edn. New York: McGraw-Hill.

GEORGE, ALEXANDER. 1980. *Presidential Decisonmaking in Foreign Policy.* Boulder, CO: Westview.

GEORGE, A. 1969. The Operational Code. *International Studies Quarterly,* 13/2: 190–222.

—— 1972. The Case for Multiple Advocacy in Foreign Policymaking. *American Political Science Review,* 66/3: 751–85.

—— 1974. Assessing Presidential Character. *World Politics,* 26: 234–82.

—— 1979. The Causal Nexus between Cognitive Beliefs and Decision-Making Behavior. Pp. 95–124 in *Psychological Models of International Politics,* ed. L. Falkowski. Boulder, CO: Westview.

—— 1987. Ideology and International Relations. *Jerusalem Journal of International Relations,* 9/1: 1–21.

—— and GEORGE, J. 1956. *Woodrow Wilson and Colonel House.* New York: John Day.

GEORGE, J., and GEORGE, A. 1998. A Reply to Weinstein, Anderson, and Link. Pp. 77–144 in *Presidential Personality and Performance,* ed. A. George and J. George. Boulder, CO: Westview.

GEVA, N., and MINTZ. A. 1997. *Decisionmaking on War and Peace.* Boulder, CO: Westview.

GREEN, D., and SHAPIRO, I. 1994. *Pathologies of Rational Choice Theory.* New Haven, CT: Yale University Press.

GREENSTEIN, F. 1967. The Impact of Personality on Politics. *American Political Science Review,* 61: 629–41.

—— 1987. *Personality and Politics.* Princeton, NJ: Princeton University Press.

—— 2004. *The Presidential Difference,* 2nd edn. Princeton, NJ: Princeton University Press.

HEDSTROM, P., and SWEDBERG, R. 1998. *Social Mechanisms.* Cambridge: Cambridge University Press.

HERMANN, M. 1980. Explaining Foreign Policy Behavior Using the Personal Characteristics of Leaders. *International Studies Quarterly,* 24/1: 7–46.

—— 2001. How Decision Units Shape Foreign Policy. Pp. 47–82 in *Leaders, Groups and Coalitions,* ed. M. Hermann. Special Issue of *International Studies Review.* London: Blackwell.

HERMANN, M. 2003. Assessing Leadership Style. Pp. 178–214 in *The Psychological Assessment of Political Leaders*, ed. J. Post. Ann Arbor: University of Michigan Press.

—— and PRESTON, T. 1994. Presidents, Advisers, and Foreign Policy. *Political Psychology*, 15/1: 75–96.

HERRMANN, R. 1985. *Perceptions and Behavior in Soviet Foreign Policy*. Pittsburgh: University of Pittsburgh Press.

—— and FISCHERKELLER, M. 1995. Beyond the Enemy Image and Spiral Model. *International Organization*, 49/3: 415–50.

—— VOSS, J., SCHOOLER, T., and CIARROCCI, J. 1997. Images in International Relations. *International Studies Quarterly*, 41/3: 403–33.

HIBBING, J., ALFORD, J., and FUNK, C. 2005. Are Political Orientations Genetically Transmitted? *American Political Science Review*, 99: 153–69.

HOLSTI, O. 1976. Foreign Policy Viewed Cognitively. Pp. 18–54 in *The Structure of Decision*, ed. R. Axelrod. Princeton, NJ: Princeton University Press.

HOWELL, W. 2006. Executives: The American Presidency. Pp. 303–22 in *The Oxford Handbook of Political Institutions*, ed. R. Rhodes, S. Binder, and B. Rockman. New York: Oxford University Press.

IMMELMAN, A. 1993. The Assessment of Political Personality. *Political Psychology*, 14/4: 725–41.

JANIS, I. 1972. *Victims of Groupthink*. Boston: Houghton-Mifflin.

—— and MANN, L. 1977. *Decision Making*. New York: Free Press.

JERVIS, R. 1976. *Perception and Misperception in International Politics*. Princeton, NJ: Princeton University Press.

KAHNEMAN, D., and TVERSKY, A. 1979. Prospect Theory. *Econometrica*, 47/2: 263–91.

KHONG, Y. 1992. *Analogies at War*. Princeton, NJ: Princeton University Press.

KOWERT, P. 2002. *Groupthink or Deadlock*. Albany: State University of New York Press.

—— and HERMANN, M. 1997. Who Takes Risks? *Journal of Conflict Resolution*, 41/5: 611–37.

LAKE, D., and POWELL, R. 1999. *Strategic Choice and International Relations*. Princeton, NJ: Princeton University Press.

LANGER, E. 1989. *Mindfulness*. Reading, MA: Addison-Wesley.

LARSON, D. 1985. *Origins of Containment*. Princeton, NJ: Princeton University Press.

LAU, R. 2003. Models of Decision-Making. Pp. 19–59 in *The Oxford Handbook of Political Psychology*, ed. D. Sears, L. Huddy, and R. Jervis. New York: Oxford University Press.

LEDOUX, J. 2002. *Synaptic Self*. New York: Viking Penguin.

LEVY, J. 1994. Learning and Foreign policy. *International Organization*, 48/2: 279–312.

LUPIA, A., MCCUBBINS, M., and POPKIN, S. 2000. Beyond Rationality. Pp. 1–22 in *Elements of Reason*, ed. A. Lupia, M. McCubbins, and S. Popkin. Cambridge: Cambridge University Press.

MCDERMOTT, R. 2001. *Risk-Taking in International Politics*. Ann Arbor: University of Michigan Press.

MAOZ, Z. 1990. *National Choices and International Processes*. Cambridge: Cambridge University Press.

—— and MOR, B. 2002. *Bound by Struggle*. Ann Arbor: University of Michigan Press.

MARCH, J., and SIMON, H. 1958. *Organizations*. New York: John Wiley.

MARCUS, G., NEUMAN, W. R., and MACKUEN, M. 2000. *Affective Intelligence and Political Judgment*. Chicago: University of Chicago Press.

MARFLEET, G., and WALKER, S. 2006. A World of Beliefs. Pp. 53–72 in *Beliefs and Leadership in World Politics*, ed. M. Schafer and S. Walker. New York: Palgrave.

MAYHEW, D. 1974. *Congress: The Electoral Connection*. New Haven, CT: Yale University Press.

MINTZ, A. 1997. The Poliheuristic Theory of Decision Making. Pp. 81–102 in *Decision Making on War and Peace*. Boulder, CO: Westview.

—— 2002. *Integrating Cognitive and Rational Theories of Foreign Policy Decision Making*. New York: Palgrave.

MORROW, J. 1994. *Game Theory for Political Scientists*. Princeton, NJ: Princeton University Press.

NEUSTADT, R. 1960. *Presidential Power*. New York: Macmillan.

NISBETT, R., and ROSS, L. 1980. *Human Inference*. Englewood Cliffs, NJ: Prentice-Hall.

POST, J. 1983. Woodrow Wilson Re-examined. *Political Psychology*, 4/2: 289–306.

—— 2003. *The Psychological Assessment of Political Leaders*. Ann Arbor: University of Michigan Press.

PRESTON, T. 2001. *The President and his Inner Circle*. New York: Columbia University Press.

ROSATI, J. 1987. *The Carter Administration's Quest for Global Community*. Columbia: University of South Carolina Press.

SCHAFER, M. 2000. Issues in Assessing Psychological Characteristics at a Distance. *Political Psychology*, 21 /3: 511–28.

—— and CRICHLOW, S. 2002. The Process–Outcome Connection in Foreign Policy Decision Making. *International Studies Quarterly*, 46/1: 45–68.

—— and WALKER, S. 2006. *Beliefs and Leadership in World Politics*. New York: Palgrave.

SIGNORINO, C. 1999. Strategic Interaction and the Statistical Analysis of International Conflict. *American Political Science Review*, 93/2: 279–98.

SIMON, H. 1957. *Models of Man*. New York: John Wiley.

—— 1985. Human Nature in Politics. *American Political Science Review*, 79/2: 203–304.

STERN, E. 1997. Probing the Plausibility of Newgroup Syndrome. Pp. 153–90 in *Beyond Groupthink*, ed. P. 't Hart, E. Stern, and B. Sundelius. Ann Arbor: University of Michigan Press,.

SUEDFELD, P., GUTTIERI, K., and TETLOCK, P. 2003. Assessing Integrative Complexity at a Distance. Pp. 246–70 in *The Psychological Assessment of Political Leaders*, ed. J. Post. Ann Arbor: University of Michigan Press.

SUSKIND, R. 2004. *The Price of Loyalty*. New York: Simon & Schuster.

TABER, C. 1992. POLI: An Expert System Model of U.S. Foreign Policy Belief Systems. *American Political Science Review*, 86/4: 888–904.

—— 1998. The Interpretation of Foreign Policy Events. Pp. 29–52 in *Problem Representation in Foreign Policy*, ed. D. Sylvan and J. Voss. Cambridge: Cambridge University Press.

TETLOCK, P. 1998. Social Psychology and World Politics. Pp. 869–912 in *Handbook of Social Psychology*, ed. D. Gilbert, S. Fiske, and G. Lindzey. New York: McGraw-Hill.

—— 2000. Coping with Trade-Offs. Pp. 239–63 in *Elements of Reason*, ed. A. Lupia, M. McCubbins, and S. Popkin. Cambridge: Cambridge University Press,.

—— and LEVI, A. 1982. Attribution Bias. *Journal of Experimental Social Psychology*, 18/1: 68–88.

THALER, R. 1991. *Quasi-Rational Economics*. New York: Sage.

'T HART, P., STERN, E., and SUNDELIUS, B. (eds.) 1997. *Beyond Groupthink*. Ann Arbor: University of Michigan Press.

VERTZBERGER, Y. 1998. *Risk Taking and Decisionmaking*. Stanford, CA: Stanford University Press.

VOSS, J. 1998. On the Representation of Problems. Pp. 8–28 in *Problem Representation in Foreign Policy*, ed. D. Sylvan and J. Voss. Cambridge: Cambridge University Press.

WALKER, S. 1983. The Motivational Foundations of Political Belief Systems. *International Studies Quarterly*, 27/2: 179–201.

—— 1990. The Evolution of Operational Code Analysis. *Political Psychology*, 11/2: 403–18.

WALKER, S. 1995. Psychodynamic Processes and Framing Effects in Foreign Policy Decision-Making. *Political Psychology*, 16/4: 697–718.

—— and SCHAFER, M. 2007. Theodore Roosevelt and Woodrow Wilson as Cultural Icons of U.S. Foreign Policy. *Political Psychology*, 28/6: 747–76.

—— —— 2009. Operational Code Analysis and Foreign Policy Decision Making. In *Methods and Theories of Foreign Policy Analysis*, ed. A. Mintz and S. Redd. New York: Palgrave.

—— —— and YOUNG, M. 2003. Profiling the Operational Codes of Political Leaders. Pp. 215–45 in *The Psychological Assessment of Political Leaders*, ed. J. Post. Ann Arbor: University of Michigan Press.

WEINSTEIN, E. 1981. *Woodrow Wilson*. Princeton, NJ: Princeton University Press.

WEINTRAUB, W. 2003. Verbal Behavior and Personality Assessment. Pp. 137–52 in *The Psychological Assessment of Political Leaders*, ed. J. Post. Ann Arbor: University of Michigan Press.

WHITE, R. 1991. Empathizing with Saddam Hussein. *Political Psychology*, 12/2: 291–308.

WINTER, D. 1973. *The Power Motive*. New York: Free Press.

—— 2003. Measuring the Motives of Political Actors at a Distance. Pp. 153–77 in *The Psychological Assessment of Political Leaders*, ed. J. Post. Ann Arbor: University of Michigan Press.

ZAJONC, R. 1980. Feeling and Thinking: Preferences Need No Inferences. *American Psychologist*, 39/2: 151–75.

PART VIII

IMPLEMENTING POLICY

....

CHAPTER 25

....

PRESIDENTIAL AGENDAS, ADMINISTRATIVE STRATEGIES, AND THE BUREAUCRACY

....

ROBERT F. DURANT

WILLIAM G. RESH

In the aftermath of the Republicans seizing majorities in Congress for the first time in forty years after the 1994 midterm elections, Democratic President Bill Clinton opined: "I had overemphasized in my first two years... the importance of legislative battles as opposed to the other things that the president might be doing. And I think now we have a better balance of both using the Presidency as a bully pulpit and the President's power of the Presidency to do things, actually accomplish things, and... not permitting the Presidency to be defined only by relations with Congress" (Ginsberg 2007, 175). Likewise, with major initiatives stymied by Congress in 2007, advisers to President George W. Bush noted that "there are a lot of tools in the tool box for any president" besides legislation for attaining policy goals (Ruttenberg and Meyers 2007).

Dubbed the "administrative presidency" by Richard Nathan (1983) and referenced more recently as "presidential administration" by Elena Kagan (2001), what Clinton and Bush's advisers allude to is a toolbox full of administrative strategies that presidents of both parties in the modern era have used to advance their policy agendas. These strategies consist not only of loyal presidential appointees aligning agency budgets, structures, personnel, decision rules, and rule making with presidential policy preferences, but also of the use of such "unilateral" tools as executive orders, presidential proclamations, presidential bill signing statements, executive agreements (rather than treaties), and National Security Directives.

The persistent use of administrative strategies by presidents, including Barack Obama, to advance their policy agendas indicates that presidents either believe such strategies work or that they have no choice but to use them in an American political system of checks and balances, diffused responsibilities, competing legitimacies, and continuing congressional and bureaucratic agendas (Jones 2005). Citing Article 2, Section 3, of the US Constitution "to take care that the laws be faithfully executed," the unitary executive theory, and claims of executive privilege, presidents justify their actions in noble terms. They insist that they are duty bound to use administrative strategies to affect federal agencies' exercise of discretion (see, for example, Fisher 2004, 2007a, 2007b; Rozell 1994). These justifications notwithstanding, presidents' use of administrative strategies is inherently pragmatic: they understand that "administration is policy" (Nathan 1983), that decisions made within agencies can have political implications, and that these implications may affect their own and their party's reelection chances.

Several assumptions underlie this pragmatism. Presidents and leading scholars assume that administrative strategies will provoke fewer challenges from opponents because they are "low-visibility" and "below-the-radar-screen" initiatives that will be difficult to track and monitor, offer first-mover advantages to the White House, and take advantage of the collective action problems of the Congress in responding to them. But how effective are administrative strategies for advancing presidential agendas? With agencies routinely becoming battlegrounds for control among presidents, the Congress, and the judiciary because of the discretion they exercise when implementing often vague, contradictory, and ambiguous statutes, sorting out the answer to that question is challenging. In this chapter, we review how scholars have done so. In the process, we identify what we know, don't know, and need to study to inform better both practice and theoretical debates over the efficacy of five major administrative tools: centralizing policy making in the White House, establishing regulatory clearance and program evaluation in the Office of Management and Budget (OMB), reorganizing agencies, appointing loyalists to run them, and wielding unilateral tools.

Our argument is threefold. First, the verdict is still out on the efficacy of various administrative tools, primarily because our understanding is predicated on an otherwise excellent research base that is a mile wide, an inch deep, and stovepiped substantively and methodologically in ways that need integration. Consequently, we need to go beyond studies explicitly focused on administrative strategies to gain a fuller appreciation of the opportunities and constraints they afford presidents trying to advance their policy agendas administratively. If we do not, researchers will fail to benefit from a variety of theoretical insights, frameworks, and propositions for testing that can advance our understanding appreciably (see also Durant 2009; Rudalevidge 2009). Second, although it is intuitively pleasing to assume and even illustrate first-mover advantages to presidents because of immediate collective action problems in Congress and deference of the courts to presidential actions, nowhere near enough research exists on the subsequent *implementation* of these initiatives (individually and as they interact with each other) within the bureaucracy. Without this research, confident assessments and theories of the efficacy of these strategies will elude us. Needed especially are studies assessing the effect of such resource constraints as inadequate funding, inadequately trained personnel, lack of control over key elements of implementation structures, unavailability of needed infrastructure, misalignment of management systems, and lack of subsystem and issue network support. Finally, with the devolution of many federal responsibilities to networks of public–private–non-profit partners in the late twentieth and early twenty-first centuries, even our present understanding, research designs, and methodologies need adjusting if practice and theory building are to advance appreciably (Light 1999b; Milward and Provan 2000).

THE REALPOLITIK OF CENTRALIZING POLICY MAKING IN THE WHITE HOUSE

Leading presidential scholars have claimed that efforts to centralize policy-making control within the White House are inevitable and growing over time, regardless of presidential party. Proffered by Terry Moe (1985, 1993; Moe and Wilson 1994), part of this theory portrays presidents as having first-mover advantages over Congress; having fewer collective action problems within the White House and the Executive Office of the President (EOP) than Congress to make policy; and fearful of shirking, moral hazard, and adverse selection problems with the bureaucracy. Anticipating that their political futures and presidencies can ride on any of the bureaucracy's actions or inactions, the arc of history has seen presidents replicating agency policy-making capabilities within the White House. Examples of this tendency are abundant and include the exclusion of the State Department from planning on Nixon's trip to China; the exclusion of State and the Department of Defense from Ronald Reagan's planning on the Strategic Defense Initiative; the writing of rules in the Clinton White House for policy initiatives related to restricting cigarette marketing to children, for patients' rights, and for tobacco manufacturing and vending (Ginsberg 2007); and the second Bush administration reviewing "raw" intelligence data in the White House in the prelude to the Iraq War. Most recently, the Obama administration has created a number of policy "czars" in the White House.

Scholarship over the past two decades has leavened immensely our understanding of the opportunities and implementation challenges of centralization efforts through rigorous historical, interpretive, and data analysis of the growth of this "institutional presidency" (Arnold 1998; Burke 2000; Dickinson 1999; Hart 1995; Hult and Walcott 2004; Krause and Cohen 2000; Kumar and Sullivan 2003; Ragsdale and Theis 1997; Walcott and Hult 1995; Weko 1995). Some have identified a fundamental irony of the procedure: given its growth, the institutional presidency is now just as bureaucratized and riven with the same turf wars, information hoarding, and internecine conflicts as in the agencies that centralization of policy making was designed to counteract. Despite recent increases in party discipline in Congress (Thurber 2002), no one contends that these challenges have eroded presidents' abilities to exercise more hierarchical authority over minions working within the institutional presidency than party leaders in Congress exercise over rank-and-file members. Nevertheless, the tendency for these bureaucratic pathologies to emerge has disabused scholars of the image of a smoothly functioning, presidentially responsive, White House bureaucracy faithfully carrying out presidential as opposed to institutional, personal, and subunit policy preferences.

Researchers also have demonstrated how centralization can occasion conflict between the White House and Congress, as well as between the White House and cabinet members, federal agencies, and the career bureaucracy. Formulating policy in the White House rather than in the departments and agencies into which Congress members routinely have access, power, and influence can be viewed by solons as an attempt to circumvent their policy preferences. In eras of unified party government (like major portions of the first six years of the George W. Bush administration), irresponsible congressional oversight may pose little challenge to presidential agendas as long as veto threats do not threaten congressional funding and earmarks. In periods of divided government such as those most typical during the modern presidential era, however, "disempowered" Congress members may hold contentious oversight hearings, withhold appropriations to carry out presidential agendas, prohibit the use of existing funding for them in appropriations bills and legislative reports, and hold up confirmations of appointees.

Likewise, marginalized cabinet members, agency heads, and federal bureaucrats can gain back much of their potency during implementation of administrative initiatives. In effect, the president proposes but cannot implement these initiatives, and most are not self-executing. Thus, in yet another paradox of centralization, implementation success depends precisely on those actors the White House has tried to circumvent through centralization. The White House can certainly monitor, prod, and pressure these agents to carry out policy. However, information asymmetry now shifts in favor of the implementers and away from the White House, bringing with it the same possibilities for shirking, moral hazard, and adverse selection that complicate policy implementation at all levels of government. Moreover, as John Kingdon (2002) notes more generally, while agenda setting rests in the hands of elected officials, alternative specification rests in the hands of experts in the bureaucracy and the issue networks to which they belong. And in trying to circumvent that reservoir of knowledge, careerist networks, and subsystem allies, presidents risk policy and political missteps, frustrations, and ultimate failures (Heclo 1977). Lost are career bureaucrats' institutional memories about what works, what does not, and how to bring initiatives to fruition through coalition building (Heclo 1977).

Prior research by Rudalevige (2002) also identifies a third set of constraints on centralization strategies of which students of policy implementation (Hill and Hupe 2002; Pressman and Wildavsky 1973) are well aware: the complexity of the policy proposals and the bureaucratic structures necessary to implement them constrain the use of centralization strategies by presidents. Using *The Public Papers of the Presidents*, Andrew Rudalevige's statistical analysis of trends in the sources of policy proposals from 1949 to 1996 finds that the greater the number of issues involved, the more novel the policy, and the more necessary reorganizations of agencies to implement them, the less likely presidents find centralization of policy making in the White House attractive. Yet Rudalevige's analysis identifying these constraints raises additional questions that may be beyond the ken of statistical analysis to address, questions that only archival research can inform. These include questions about process; bargaining strategies among actors in the White House and between the White House and agencies; and how history, present context, and political and administrative contingencies affect these types of decisions.

A fourth set of constraints on the ability of White House policy centralization to advance presidential agendas comes from the agency design and evolution literature. Longitudinal work by scholars applying the principals of the new institutional economics and transaction cost analysis leads one to posit that centralization strategies may be constrained by the path dependency that agency design puts them on (Lewis 2003; Wood and Bohte 2004). Agencies designed by presidents are on average more susceptible to presidential influence than those created by Congress. The former are designed to insulate the agency from congressional influence, while those created by the latter tend to use commission formats that make it harder for presidents to influence their operations, limit the number and types of presidential political appointees allowed in agencies, and require party-balancing and staggered terms of appointees.

A fifth set of constraints identified in recent research on the implementation of centralization in the White House involves factors impinging on the choice of specific centralization strategies. Most notable in this regard is Karen Hult and Charles Walcott's (Hult and Walcott 2004; Walcott and Hult 1995) important two-volume study of the evolution of White House organizational structures (covering Presidents Herbert Hoover to Jimmy Carter). One of the few studies of administrative strategies informed by organizational theory/behavior research and that does not involve principal–agent models, Hult and Walcott's work portrays White House organization as the interaction of four factors: partisan learning (i.e., choosing the same kind of structures as presidents of the same party); environmental expectations; organizational dynamics related to size, complexity, and the need for structural differentiation; and presidential preferences, objectives, and strategies.

These factors do not preclude presidential success, but they do complicate it by raising questions about how well presidential predilections can be aligned with these needs. An important body of organizational research on leadership, for example, suggests that mismatches can arise between what complexity demands, what partisan emulation requires, and what presidents prefer (for a summary, see Rainey 2003). This research also renders dubious the malleability of presidential leadership styles to accommodate these various factors, as they may shift across different policy areas. Likewise, organizational behavior theorists have long recognized that combat within subunits of any organization results in decisions getting delayed and pushed upwards to the executive level (see Rainey 2003). If that tendency to push decisions upwards comports with presidential decision-making predispositions to "control" decisions, no problem. If it does not, however, this tendency can cause delays, drift, and ultimately diminish timely presidential control of policy agendas. Finally, and more directly related to the presidency literature, Martha Kumar's (2007) recent study of White House efforts during the second Bush administration to centralize communication messages across the government shows that it worked well in keeping the administration "on message." However, the price paid was a persistent failure to recognize and adjust to unexpected events.

Having noted these five sets of constraints on White House centralization strategies, there is still a great deal we do not know and that merits future research. Places to start include determining the relative importance of the factors that Hult and Walcott identify; the conditions under which they take on different relative importance; and how much history, context, and contingencies (unexpected events) affect these determinations over time. We also do not know what difference all this makes in terms of policy outcomes. Does centralization make implementation more or less difficult once policies are announced? Do certain structures produce better or worse policy outcomes (e.g., the separate White House intelligence operation that led to the Iraq War)? Nor do we know how all this affects relationships with agencies in the long run. In answering these questions, statistical analysis is possible for answering the "what happens?" aspects of these questions, while research designs predicated on "thick" contextual analysis are the only ways to address the "how and why" questions (see Goodin and Tilly 2006).

We also need contextual analyses to improve our understanding of how agencies react strategically to White House centralization efforts, not only on the particular issue involved, but also on other issues important to the White House. Consider, for example, recent Central Intelligence Agency efforts to leak information on White House interference in intelligence gathering. Does centralizing policy making in the White House push bureaucratic program managers more firmly into the arms of congressional allies, and thus constrain policy agendas during both policy formulation and implementation? Do activist Democratic presidents have an easier time centralizing policy making in the White House than Republicans because activist-minded program managers are less likely to protest to congressional allies? Do program bureaucrats withhold critical information from the White House in the hope of embarrassing the administration when centralization produces policies they do not like?

Finally, it is possible that yet another constraint on the implementation of centralization strategies is the ongoing change in governance structures in the United States. In many areas, and for a broad spectrum of policies and programs, authority has been diffused to other public, private, and non-profit actors to determine policies in which presidents have a stake (Agranoff 2007; Light 1999b; Lynn 2006). Yet the tools of the administrative presidency are focused largely on federal and state agencies acting as direct deliverers of goods, services, and opportunities (Durant and Warber 2001). There is much research ground to till in these areas before we can be certain whether networked governance arrangements constrain the implementation of traditional centralization tools, enhance them, require new tools, or prompt even more reliance on central clearance of regulatory, contract, or agency guidance efforts (the topic of the next section).

THE REALPOLITIK OF CENTRALIZING REGULATORY REVIEW AND PROGRAM EVALUATION IN OMB

As Jerry Mashaw writes, "much public law is legislative in origin but administrative in content" (1997, 106). That content is comprised of an average 4,000 rules promulgated and interpreted annually by the federal bureaucracy (Kerwin 2007). Not surprisingly, then, presidents since Richard Nixon have used the OMB for pre-clearance of rules and regulations issued by executive branch agencies. This review grew more intense, however, after the Paperwork Reduction Act (PRA) of 1980 created the Office of Information and Regulatory Analysis (OIRA) within OMB, and President Reagan issued Executive Order 12291 requiring formal cost–benefit analyses of major rules. Clinton then used his Executive Order 12866 to extend the regulatory review process to independent agencies by requiring them to submit their annual regulatory agendas to OIRA, and he issued prompt letters asking agencies to promulgate rules it desired (Kagan 2001). George W. Bush next tried to compound clearance requirements by extending OMB pre-clearance to the guidance documents that agencies issue for implementing policy (see below). Bush also added the Program Assessment Rating Tool (PART) evaluation of agency progress on strategic planning (among other things) and linked progress on those measures to Senior Executive Service (SES) performance ratings (Gilmour and Lewis 2005). Part of that review incorporated inherently political judgments regarding whether programs were needed, could be performed in the private sector, or constituted inherently government functions.

All this has led many political scientists to conclude that presidents use these administrative tools strategically to coordinate agency rule making. Yet prior research suggests otherwise. One practical constraint on these clearance and evaluative techniques is the serious mismatch existing between the OMB's staffing levels and the workload noted above. Quite ironically, staffing at OMB has actually declined in recent years (Rubin 2003), precisely at a time when workload has increased significantly. Nor, until recent efforts by OIRA director George Graham during the second Bush administration to close the gap, has the skill mix of OMB examiners kept up with the kind of scientific literacy informing many health, safety, and environmental regulations coming out of the federal bureaucracy. Relatedly, retaining OMB personnel has become a challenge in the face of difficult and long work hours (Rubin 2003).

Likewise, William West (2006) concludes that OIRA has neither the aim nor the capacity to ensure overall planning and coordination of rule making, and fails to give the implementation of its recommendations much thought. His findings corroborate what the Comptroller General found nearly two decades ago when OIRA had more staff and fewer responsibilities: "little if any effort is made in the review process to think about the implementation of different programs in a comprehensive and comparative way" (West 2006, 445) or "to reduce conflicts [and] to ensure consistent application of the regulatory analysis process" (Comptroller General 1981, 53). Such findings have been well documented by policy implementation scholars (Elmore 1979–80) who are never cited in the presidential literature: the tendency for those practicing "top-down" (centralized) rather than "bottom-up" (decentralized) planning to consider implementation at all, let alone in a comprehensive way (see also Durant 2009). Thus, evidence exists that central clearance of regulations can definitely be effective in delaying, stopping, modifying, or promoting particular regulations, but strategic coordination is nowhere near as sought nor as practical as many scholars assume.

Preliminary research examining the implementation of PART evaluations by the Bush administration also offers mixed evidence of implementation success (Gilmour and Lewis 2005). To the extent that targeting of Democratic Party-affiliated programs for lower levels of funding indicates success in furthering Republican Party objectives, implementation seems to be effective from President Bush's perspective. Research also indicates, however, that variation in PART ratings of departmental programs by different examiners may mean less control using this technique than presidents might seek, but still more than they might have without it.

All this again raises issues that prior research has not adequately addressed and that should be explored in the future using both quantitative and qualitative research designs. For example, does Congress get any more involved in trying to checkmate or influence rule-making or funding recommendations when presidents try to advance policies that agencies and their clients disagree with? Not necessarily, if one extrapolates from the Reagan and second Bush administrations. OIRA either resubmitted to agencies for reconsideration or killed an average of eighty-five rules per year during the Reagan presidency. Even then, Congress was unable to extract very few White House concessions (Ginsberg 2007). Nor were agency program bureaucrats willing to risk making trouble, with the administration controlling other incentives like budgets, performance reviews, and the potential to select only sympathetic careerists for SES positions (Golden 2000). Similarly, a 2003 Government Accountability Office (GAO) study showed that Bush's OIRA had significantly influenced twenty-five of the eighty-five major rules it studied, again with impunity (West 2006). One possibility, as yet unexplored by researchers, is that Congress pursues its own course below the radar screen; rather than take on presidents directly, they wait to undermine implementation of regulations by underfunding, staffing, or modifying their implementation through appropriations riders, during hearings, or in legislative reports.

West's findings also beg further study. Since presidents have different priorities and limited political capital, does implementation success have to mean strategic integration of presidential preferences across all policy arenas? And what does cohesiveness and coordination really mean? Does it mean resolving fights among agencies or does it mean setting a plan and holding agencies accountable for realizing it? The bottom line may be that presidents may only feel they need to act strategically on rules they and their electoral coalition (past and potential) care about, a much more efficient way to approach rule review.

Survey research and, particularly, interviews with key White House, agency, interest group, and OMB actors can help answer these questions. Other research questions amenable to these techniques follow logically. From a White House perspective, does it make a difference in terms of implementation success whether presidents are using this (or any other) administrative strategy to make things happen (affirming policy) or to stop things from happening (negating policy)? For example, delaying the issuing of agency rules stops things from happening and is much more difficult to challenge. Indeed, if challenged in court, this only imposes additional delay that works in the favor of a deregulatory president. Making things happen in promoting new regulations, however, can again be foiled during implementation by congressional opponents, the courts, and interest groups stymieing funding or imposing delays.

Also, does the success of centralization (and any other tool of presidential administration) depend on a coordination or alignment of *all* the tools of the administrative presidency, as a study of the Reagan administration's efforts to reorient natural resource policy has chronicled (Durant 1992; also see Durant 2009)? Perhaps cutbacks in OMB personnel, for example, have unintentionally undermined a more comprehensive strategic and coordinative approach for regulatory rule making. It is also possible that if delaying or stopping rules from being issued is a president's goal, fewer resources and greater responsibilities are guaranteed to delay rule making.

Research using contextual analysis and grounded theory also are needed to see whether the White House or the agencies take an anticipatory reaction perspective in selecting rules to centralize and prompt and, if they do, what constraints these considerations impose on presidential agendas. The Clinton strategy of writing rules from the White House suggests they do, but can we generalize that finding to all regulatory review situations? Indeed, the entire White House–OMB–agency relationship (or dyadic relationships among these actors) needs sorting out in future research. What strategies do agencies use during negotiations with an overworked OMB staff during either ex ante (rule clearance) or ex post reviews (like PART scores)? What is the impact of interest groups generally, and different types of groups, on rule-making processes? The few who have studied these relationships offer mixed evidence on the influence of interest groups (Golden 1998; West 2006; Yackee 2006). Moreover, faced by requirements for strategic planning and performance measurement exercises by Congress (namely, the Government Performance and Results Act of 1993), what constraints (if any) do these impose on advancing presidential agendas?

Finally, researchers again have to ask what contemporary shifts from the traditional administrative state to the networked state mean for policy centralization (Durant and Warber 2001). Is this development yet one more factor pushing presidents into centralizing policy making in the White House or regulatory clearance and program evaluation into OIRA, or will it have countervailing tendencies? On the one hand, these developments mean more power to the agencies that award contracts, thus making it attractive for presidents to control the largesse that is handed out. Consider how the second Bush White House tried systematically and persistently to affect the awarding of projects and contracts from agencies. On the other hand, with subnational actors making so many policy decisions, policy-making power may shift to loyal presidential political appointees in agency regional offices. The Bush administration's efforts to require OMB clearance of agency guidance documents suggest that centralization pressures may trump decentralization pressures. Greater empirical study of this question is important as networking trends are unlikely to abate soon.

THE REALPOLITIK OF APPOINTMENT POWERS

Contemporary presidents appoint nearly 3,000 political appointees to executive branch agencies. In doing so, they hope that appointees can alter the incentive structures within agencies to reward bureaucrats' compliance with presidential agendas (e.g., with promotions), to punish them for failure to do so (e.g., with poor performance reports and undesirable job transfers), and to reallocate funding to initiatives preferred by their presidents (Lewis 2008). Appointees also are expected to try to alter the skill mix within agencies to emphasize presidential priorities, to fast-track for promotions positions symbolizing those priorities, and to contract out positions to reduce or increase the capacity of any agency to perform presidentially preferred policies.

The most oft-heard battle cry for doing so has been for presidents and their appointees to "hit the ground running" with these initiatives in the early days of a new administration before their honeymoon with Congress wanes (Maranto 2005; Michaels 1997; Pfiffner 1996). Paradoxically, presidents are not only more likely to get their way in the early days of their administration, but they are also more likely to make big mistakes or make decisions that put their administration on a path-dependent track that ultimately undermines their policy agendas (Light 1999a). Even were this not the case in some situations, however, researchers have identified constraints on implementing appointee strategies. Here we examine three of these constraints, and what we know—and do not yet know—about their general application: (1) sufficient delegation of authority for appointees to affect does not always exist, (2) presidentializing the SES is more complex than previously assumed, and (3) carrot-and-stick "incentives" wielded by political appointees are not effective in all contexts.

Opportunities and Constraints on Discretion

While literature on the presidency as it relates to administrative strategies fails to address this issue, recent work on congressional discretion by rational choice theorists offers a parsimonious deductive theory of congressional delegation that shows how and why levels of discretion available for presidential appointees to work with will vary. For instance, David Epstein and Sharyn O'Halloran's (1999) analysis of policy initiatives undertaken between 1947 and 1992 shows how Congress members can either write detailed legislation limiting bureaucratic discretion, or they can write vague laws with wide discretion that presidential appointees can try to alter. In the case of the former, they impose constraints on presidential appointment powers, spending limits, staffing ceilings, reporting requirements on agency rule making, and hammer requirements. These constraints, in turn, can give appointees trying to advance presidential agendas administratively little room to maneuver.

Research by public policy scholars suggests that the amount of bureaucratic discretion available for appointees to manipulate for presidential goals can be further constrained by variations in discretion *within* a statute. In an important conceptual essay typically not cited in the presidency literature, Helen Ingram and Anne Schneider (1990) argue that discretion can vary across six different dimensions of a statute. These include discretion over the goals of the legislation; what objectives to shoot for; what agents to use in carrying out the law; what specific tools to use (regulations, subsidies, guaranteed loans); what rules to follow (e.g., consider risks to health but not costs); and what assumptions to work under (normative, behavioral, and instrumental). This research suggests that even when a statute gives generally broad grants of discretion, misalignments can arise between the discretionary factors that political appointees need to alter to advance presidential policies and how much discretion they actually have to do so. For instance, Congress stipulated in the 1970 Clean Air Act that the EPA could not consider costs when assessing the health hazards of the six criteria pollutants designated in the act. More recently, the No Child Left Behind Act precludes the federal government from setting national performance standards, while the Personal Responsibility and Work Opportunity Act sets limits on how long persons can receive welfare.

Absent systematic research, the impact on appointee strategies of variations in discretion across and within statutes remains conjecture. Thus, not only do propositions derived from this research need to be tested to assess their general validity as constraints or opportunities affecting appointee success, they suggest subtopics for exploration. For example, do amounts of flexibility associated with the various types of discretion identified by these scholars tend to affect the pursuit of presidential strategies differently? Also worthwhile is studying what effect insulation of these aspects of discretion from presidential control has on the *effectiveness* of policy implementation by agencies—the presumed goal of presidential administration tactics.

In pursuing this agenda, there is a growing literature in public administration that quantitatively assesses the effects of goal ambiguity (Chun and Rainey 2005) and red tape (Bozeman 1993) on bureaucratic effectiveness. Presidency scholars might derive propositions suitable for testing from this literature to help inform their research (e.g., the greater the number of procedures or amount of transaction costs involved in personnel decisions, the less the discretion, and the more unlikely appointees will be able to marshal appropriate numbers and skills needed to advance presidential agendas).

Finally, a robust and evolving literature on public budgeting and finance that is rarely cited in presidential studies suggests additional opportunities and constraints on political appointees seeking to make major policy redirections administratively. The good news for presidents and their appointees is that opportunities do exist for fundamental shifts in budget priorities (Jones and Baumgartner 2005). Likewise, while early research on budgeting found evidence of only incremental budget shifts at the macro-budgetary level, more recent research finds significant yearly shifts in budget allocations within departments and among programs (i.e., at the micro-budgeting level). The bad news for presidents seeking major policy redirection administratively, however, is that those opportunities do not come often (Kingdon 2002; Baumgartner and Jones 2005). What is more, while presidents have grown enamored of linking budgets to performance as an administrative tool for advancing their policy agendas, performance budgets have been difficult to implement (Joyce 2004; also see Gilmour and Lewis 2005; but see Moynihan 2008).

Opportunities and Constraints on Appointee Loyalty, Competence, and Opportunities

Even if sufficient levels and types of discretion are available for presidential appointees to use to advance presidential agendas, success assumes that appointees are loyal to those agendas, have the skills to advance them, and can acquire sufficient resources to carry them out (e.g., personnel with needed skill, budgets, and congressional support). Conventional wisdom asserts that the greater the number of appointees that presidents can appoint, and the deeper they can place them in the bureaucracy, the greater control presidents will have over the bureaucracy. But how valid are these assumptions? If inaccurate, they impose severe constraints on appointee strategies for advancing presidential agendas administratively.

The evidence regarding implementation success is again inconclusive, hobbled by gaps in research and failure to consult related literatures. Appointees are chosen for a variety of reasons other than loyalty, including rewarding campaign contributors, pacifying interest groups, and cultivating congressional favor (Pfiffner 1996). The idea that all these appointees are initially, let alone persistently, loyal to presidential agendas lacks face and empirical validity in all cases (Edwards 2001). Moreover, appointees may lack not just policy knowledge, but also the management skills needed to perform their jobs (Cohen 1998). This is especially a problem the deeper one places appointees in an agency because the talent pool of individuals shrinks appreciably due to relatively lower wages. These appointees also tend to have briefer tenures because they try to advance to positions of higher levels of responsibility and pay. Thus, paradoxically, less-than-competent and inexperienced appointees can become dependent on the career bureaucrats they are sent to control. Also, the tendency for even initially loyal and skilled appointees to be more responsive to agency interest groups, bureaucrats, and congressional oversight committees over time can compromise or derail appointees' implementation of presidential policy aims (Durant 1992; Maranto 2005; Nathan 1983; Weko 1995).

Yet another paradox of appointee strategies that can constrain success is that the greater the number of political appointees in an agency, the greater the number of layers of hierarchy between a president and the top levels of the career service and, hence, the less control presidents actually have over career bureaucrats (Light 1995). And even when political appointees are loyal, skilled, and close to decisions vital for advancing presidential agendas, practical realities constrain them. With the average number of appointees in departments and agencies totaling 15 to 20 persons, and in independent agencies approximately 11 appointees, the magnitude of the task is immense (Rosenbloom and Kravchuk 2005).

Certainly, one finds examples of successes and failures in the extent to which political appointees are able at least partially to advance presidential agendas administratively (Durant 1992, 2007; Lynn 1984; Rainey and Thompson 2006). Indeed, research on the implementation of the Civil Service Reform Act (CSRA) of 1978 shows that all is not lost when it comes to presidential appointee strategies. Enacted in 1978, the CSRA created, among other things, an SES, 10 percent of whom could be presidential appointees. It also made top-level careerists in the SES subject to performance bonuses and allowed them to apply performance management techniques to the work of their subordinates. Performance measurement was expected to give appointees a better means for gaining responsiveness to presidential policy agendas.

Survey research indicates that if changing the partisan composition of higher-level civil servants in the SES increases the likelihood of loyalty to Republican presidential agendas, then at least partial success of politicization strategies can work. For instance, Joel Aberbach and Bert Rockman (2000) show that the percentage of Republicans in the career SES has increased significantly from the Nixon years when Democrats prevailed by sizeable margins. At the same time, the percentage of respondents reporting left-of-center ideology fell significantly (from 52 to 35 percent). They attribute this shift partially to Democratic departures from the SES as Reagan appointees applied the full range of administrative strategies available to them; to Republican appointees using partisan criteria for appointing career bureaucrats to the SES; and to shifts in party identification by bureaucrats to advance their careers in a changed partisan climate. These findings, of course, rest on analyses from an era dominated by Republican presidents, and they need to be extended to the Clinton, George W. Bush, and Obama eras and tested.

The rub, of course, is not only that surveys involve self-reporting of partisan attitudes, but that partisan attitudes do not necessarily translate into behavioral outcomes conducive to advancing presidential agendas administratively (Wilson 1989). Career bureaucrats report to multiple principals, have typically self-selected into agencies that share their program goals, and may not support all the particulars of a president's agenda even if they share partisan identification. What is more, surveys to date have been too narrow in the sampling universe they tap. Hopefully, future survey research will tap the perceptions of congressional oversight committee members and staff, White House and OMB staff, and other network actors in assessing how well appointees have been able to advance presidential agendas.

Nor should survey research designs alone address the question of political appointee effectiveness in advancing presidential agendas. These might be supplemented by in-depth interviews that allow respondents to address issues and patterns identified in surveys. Useful, too, are the "soak-and-poke" techniques that so richly informed Herbert Kaufman's (1981) study of federal bureau chiefs, Richard Fenno's (2003) work on congressional home style, and, more recently, Martha Kumar's (2007) study of the White House communications office. Working individually or in teams, researchers might use these techniques to track the experiences of political appointees during various phases of a presidential administration or, alternatively, to track the experience of an agency as appointees come and go over a president's term(s) in office. Theoretically informed comparative case studies that examine the link between appointee loyalty, success or failure in implementing presidential agendas, and exogenous constraints on success would be valuable. Also, as with all the other strategies covered in this chapter, quantitative and qualitative studies are needed that look at the interaction of these politicization efforts with other tools of presidential administration. For example, does greater politicization result in greater or less use of unilateral strategies, or produce fewer rule deferrals or reversals by the OIRA?

Lastly, and again related to changes in governance patterns, future research should assess whether perennial pleas to limit the number of political appointees, and where they are placed, still make sense. It is possible that the rise of networked public–private–non-profit governance may propel presidents toward greater numbers of appointees, placed deeper than ever into the career bureaucracy, and with political rather than management backgrounds (Durant and Warber 2001). Presidents may see such appointees as having better negotiating, bargaining, and coalition maintenance skills than careerists. Alternatively, politicizing the SES may become less attractive, with presidents relying again on OMB or other unilateral tools to review rules and guidance documents. Only empirical research will tell.

(Mis)reading Bureaucrats' Motivations?

Any strategy for advancing presidential agendas that relies on altering the behavior of career bureaucrats depends on how well appointees understand what motivates careerists. It also depends on whether even the most savvy appointees have the opportunities and skills to alter incentives to take advantage of those motivations or realign them accordingly. In turn, even well-motivated bureaucrats cannot advance presidential agendas if they lack the financial, staffing, expertise, training, and subsystem backing to implement those goals effectively.

Having said this, however, prior research indicates that presidential appointees are often their own worst enemies when it comes to understanding careerist motivations by inadvertently self-imposing constraints on their ability to advance presidential agendas. At the extremes, they tend to overstate the tendency for bureaucrats to oppose or embrace presidential agendas, and they devise extreme motivational strategies accordingly (Durant 1992). "Bureauphobes" distrust careerists, worry about shirking and moral hazard problems because of the technical information asymmetry bureaucrats enjoy, and thus keep careerists at arm's length by adopting "jigsaw puzzle" or "mushroom house" management styles. In the former, appointees keep their overall goals to themselves, sharing disconnected bits of information with different careerists. In the latter, they reveal nothing to careerists, a tendency color- fully described as "keeping them in the dark and feeding them manure." "Bureau- philes" err by assuming that careerists will uncritically embrace presidential initiatives, by automatically using a participative management style, and by trusting careerists to do the right thing without recognizing perverse bureaucratic incentives.

Scholars representing a variety of research traditions have effectively challenged these motivational assumptions about careerists. Principal–agent and formal mod- eling theorists, for instance, have shown how information asymmetry favoring bureaucrats overstates the importance of technical expertise, undervalues the im- portance of political information which appointees have in abundance, and ignores interest groups and fire-alarm oversight as alternative information sources for political appointees (among others) (Epstein and O'Halloran 1994; Hammond and Miller 1985; Hopenhayn and Lohmann 1996; Lupia and McCubbins 1994). From a more qualitative research perspective, Hugh Heclo (1977) long ago demonstrated that appointees should not treat federal bureaucrats as a homogeneous lot favoring or opposing presidential agendas. He identified four types of bureaucrats (program, staff, reformers, and institutionalists) with different motivational bases, some of whom would be amenable to change by appointees. Moreover, if ignored, political appointees would suffer from not tapping into their expertise, passive bureaucratic resistance, or active resistance by those ignored. As such, Heclo urges a contingent cooperation strategy for appointees, a point refined by Durant (1992).

Important and statistically creative research by Wood and Waterman (1994) also has advanced our understanding of motivations. Their mix of qualitative case studies, interviews, archival research, and quasi-experimental, time series analyses of the outputs of eight federal regulatory agencies (e.g., numbers of EPA enforcement decisions) consistently finds bureaucrats responding to the use of a full range of administrative strategies, including changes in political appointees. More recently, Marissa Golden's (2000) comparative case analysis of four agencies (the National Highway Safety Administration, the Civil Rights Division of the Justice Department, the Food and Nutrition Service in the Agriculture Department, and the Environ- mental Protection Agency) reinforces these points, and how these strategies can become constraints on appointees if not used wisely to reshape incentives.

Applying A. O. Hirschman's "exit, voice, and loyalty" concepts as a theoretical framework, Golden finds some evidence during the Reagan era of all three behaviors, but support for following presidential agendas was the default option. However, the loyalty she identifies also confirms that bureaucrats are rational-utility maximizers who respond to savvy manipulations of incentives by appointees. These include how political appointees wield the tools of the administrative presidency (i.e., their style, seriousness, and consistency), make use or benefit from agency contextual factors (e.g., availability of employment for various professionals in agencies), and tap into professional norms of neutral competence.

Both Wood and Waterman's and Golden's findings, however, are suggestive only; they have yet to be tested more broadly in regulatory and non-regulatory settings. In pursuing that agenda, studies might try to sort out the relative importance of the factors Golden identifies as motivating bureaucrats to comply with presidential agendas. They can be aided in this task by a substantial amount of motivational theory in the organizational change and development literatures that might place these studies on alternative theoretical grounds and offer propositions suitable for testing in them (for summaries, see Fernandez and Rainey 2006; Perry, Mesch, and Paarlberg 2006). To date, students of presidential administration have not availed themselves of these theories (also see Durant 1992 for an exception). Until they do, however, it is clear from existing research that appointees who take one-size-fits-all motivational approaches to implementing presidential agendas are likely to be frustrated.

THE REALPOLITIK OF REORGANIZATION TOOLS

Another assumption underlying the successful implementation of presidential administration is that presidents and their political appointees can partially alter the context of agency decision making in favor of presidential agendas through agency reorganizations. But in these situations, substantial constraints on appointees advancing presidential agendas exist. First, presidents are decidedly less able to seize first-mover advantages or to take advantage of Congress's collective action problems. Members of Congress care deeply about programs that affect their reelection chances, as do interest groups. As public administrationist Harold Seidman (1998) long ago established, agency structure is less about management effectiveness and more about power, access, and influence.

Recent research from formal modelers, rational choice theorists, and new institutional economics perspectives extends these insights, in the process identifying formidable constraints on appointees using reorganization strategies. They show how battles between winning and losing coalitions (including presidents and Congress members) drive agency design and evolution. Each coalition tries to insulate policies from changes by the other and to make them more responsive to their own preferences in the future (e.g., Lupia and McCubbins 1994; Wood and Bohte 2004). Also relevant for anticipating implementation difficulties involving reorganizations is work by B. Dan Wood and John Bohte (2004). From their structured probit analysis testing a transaction cost theory for understanding variations in agency design of 141 organizations created between 1879 and 1988, one logically posits that implementation will be more difficult whenever agencies are created during times when presidential–legislative conflict, coalitional conflict, electoral turnover, and party hegemony are high.

Studies like these suggest that how an agency has been created will offer either opportunities or constraints on administrative reorganization strategies for advancing presidential agendas. These are hypotheses, however, until tested explicitly in research on the implementation of reorganization strategies. Research is also needed on *why* variations occur. Future research might start with the four conditions listed by Wood and Bohte and see if, how, and why presidential success regarding reorganization powers varies, both in terms of structural realignment and the policies presumed to follow. Also potentially profitable would be future research assessing whether all types of transaction costs are equal in the constraints they impose on presidential or appointee reorganization strategies for advancing policy agendas.

Nor does prior research suggest why and how reforms in structures in single agencies occur over time and what opportunities and constraints they pose for implementing presidential agendas through reorganization strategies. A model of this longitudinal approach is Amy Zegart's (1999) research on agency design and evolution in the national security policy arena. Taking a qualitative approach to testing propositions derived from new institutionalist theories, her study provides reasons to challenge the conventional wisdom (derived mostly from the study of domestic regulatory policy) that Congress and interest groups not only constrain but dominate presidents in these efforts (e.g., McCubbins 1985; Moe 1985, 1989, 1993). She finds that presidents and bureaucrats tend to prevail over Congress and interest groups in the national security domain when it comes to implementing agency structures that favor their interests. At a minimum, this suggests that presidential appointees may face fewer reorganization difficulties in national security than in domestic agencies, a hypothesis that is readily testable.

It is also again striking how a literature purporting to understand agency structures and processes is so typically uninformed by organization theory, behavior, and development research. The closest the majority of research on reorganization comes to doing so, as noted, is mentions of Weberian bureaucracy and the use of simplistic principal–agent theories in multiple principal and multiple agent situations that are the norm rather than the exception (Meier and O'Toole 2006). We hope that presidential scholars will apply well-established relationships between strategy and structure and the aligning of environments and organizational structures to studying the success or failure of reorganization strategies in advancing presidential agendas (see Hult and Walcott 2004; Walcott and Hult 1995). As organizational and behavioral theorists well know, reorganization is disruptive, and the power of informal group norms, mental schemata, and laws to circumvent formal structural arrangements is profound. This does not bode well for advancing presidential agendas through reorganization, especially in light of the other constraints on administrative strategies articulated in this essay. But theory building depends on exploring these issues further.

THE REALPOLITIK OF UNILATERAL TOOLS

What opportunities and constraints during implementation do presidents face when trying to advance their agendas using unilateral tools? Again, there is much we do not know at this point. This is largely because early research has quite naturally focused on why, when, for what purposes, and with what consequences for democratic constitutional values unilateral tools like executive orders, signing statements, proclamations, and National Security Directives are used (Cooper 1986, 2002, 2005; Fisher 2007a, 2007b; Howell 2003; Mayer 2001; Moe and Howell 1999; Pious 2007; Ragsdale and Theis 1997; Rozell 1994; Warber 2006). To give a flavor for the promise and constraints of these tools, we limit our coverage in this section to two of the most studied types of unilateral controls: executive orders and presidential signing statements.

Kenneth Mayer's (2001) research is illustrative of some of the finest work that has been done on when and why executive orders become attractive to presidents as vehicles for advancing their policy agendas. Most significantly for our discussion, he finds that their use can be constrained by political costs, they are sometimes attractive to presidents as other constraints on their options mount, and they can be designed to impose political constraints on others. Applying the logic of the new institutional economics, he finds that presidents issue executive orders to alter bureaucratic incentives, as bargaining chips with Congress, to curry electoral support, to symbolize their own or their parties' policy priorities, and to put successors in awkward political positions. Mayer's work also confirms suspicions that presidents use executive orders to compensate for the constraints imposed on them when declines in their popularity occur. However, he refines this argument by noting that increases in usage occur only when long-term declines in popularity occur (i.e., six months or more). Elaborating and extending Mayer's research, Adam Warber (2006) recently content analyzed 5,000-plus executive orders issued by presidents from 1936 to 2001. His work adds credence to prior findings that a focus on policy over purely administrative matters has occurred over the years. Importantly, his research also suggests that both Congress and the courts (also see Howell 2003; Pious 2007) have been passive in challenging the implementation of executive orders.

A similar tale applies to the implementation of presidential signing statements. Viewed largely as ceremonial documents, they have risen in media salience because of the way President George W. Bush has used them to assert prerogatives in fighting the war on terror. Bush is not the first president to use signing statements to advance policy goals. He *is* the first, however, to expand their use systematically beyond nullifying specific legislative provisions. He has used them instead to "reposition and strengthen the powers of the presidency relative to Congress" (Cooper 2005, 516). Long before Bush, however, public law scholar Phillip Cooper called attention to the strategic uses and policy impacts of these documents. Cooper shows their increasing use as *de facto* line-item vetoes. Presidents signal to the bureaucracy and the courts what they do not like about legislation they are signing, why (typically challenging them on constitutional grounds), and what should not be implemented (Cooper 2002, 2005).

These substantial contributions to our understanding of their importance and strategic use for advancing presidential agendas notwithstanding, more systematic studies of all types of unitary tools are critical for advancing theory building and resolving debates related to the efficacy of unilateral strategies. Most needed again are studies of what happens to these initiatives once they are issued. Some of this has been done for particular executive orders, and we have learned much from them (including the tendency for courts to assume congressional assent to them if they fail to overturn or continue to fund them) (Mayer 2001).

Still, more theoretically grounded studies must be pursued across a more robust range of unilateral tools before we can accept contemporary arguments that they give presidents policy advantages. Leading theorists, for example, argue that the magnitude of presidential initiatives and Congress's constraints on collective action give presidents a distinct first-mover advantage. But even if true, this advantage does not mean that unilateral tools are useful in all circumstances, implemented effectively, or result ultimately in outcomes consistent with presidential aims.

For example, using executive orders or presidential signing statements to stop things from happening may be relatively easier (but still vulnerable to challenge) than executive orders designed to make things happen. Funding to make things happen must come from Congress or by reallocating resources from other programs, an appropriation or reprogramming of funds that may be politically difficult. Congress also can legislate precise statutory instructions on the use of funds by, among other things, inserting spending limitation riders into appropriations or using authorization bills to limit how money can be used. Moreover, executive orders may come too late in the budget cycle to have any impact until funding requests are funded in later fiscal years, at which time a president's successors may unilaterally revoke the original executive order or events may overtake its priority or relevance. Likewise, agencies may lack the personnel skills, tools, or organizational culture conducive to carrying the order out (Durant 2007). And in an era of networked government where parts of various public, private, and non-profit organizations must work together to implement policy, unilateral tools affecting only parts of that assembly line of actors may lack sufficient traction to advance presidential agendas.

Granted, the same kind of constraints on implementation exist for legislative initiatives by presidents (Howell 2005). But unless we assume that symbolism is the primary aim of presidents in using unilateral tools, our understanding of them begs the same kind of systematic empirical research agenda that policy scholars have pursued in studying the implementation of statutes (e.g., Elmore 1979–80; Mazmanian and Sabatier 1989). While we know after nearly four decades of study the factors that make implementation of laws more or less difficult, we do not know if the same factors affect the implementation of unilateral tools in the same way, or if other factors are involved.

In pursuing such a research agenda, one underutilized approach might involve selecting a range of executive orders (or presidential signing statements, proclamations, or national security directives) on various substantive criteria (e.g., by policy type, policy arena, or policy domain) and studying their fate over time. From this research, scholars might begin understanding and building a theory of implementation for executive orders (and other unitary tools). In this regard, the work of implementation scholars again might be useful in deriving propositions suitable for testing (Elmore 1979–80; Mazmanian and Sabatier 1989). Here, such factors as the extent of behavioral change required by the unilateral tool, the complexity of the implementation structure involved in carrying it out, and the validity of the causal (i.e., cause–effect) theory underlying it might be predictors of success or failure. Moreover, the insights of network theorists might again be useful when studying the implementation of unitary tools that involve public–private–non-profit partnerships with state governments, private contractors, and/or non-governmental organizations (Agranoff 2007; Milward and Provan 2000).

CONCLUSION

This chapter has offered a broad overview of some of the most important and promising lines of inquiry for improving our understanding of the promise versus the performance of administrative strategies designed to advance presidential agendas. We also have tried to show the importance and promise of integrating insights from not only literature that directly addresses these issues, but also the largely untapped research literatures that have implications for the study of administrative strategies. Offered in the process has been a robust, theoretically driven, and methodologically diverse research agenda that promises to improve our understanding of an approach to presidential leadership that shows few signs of abating in the future.

REFERENCES

ABERBACH, J. D., and ROCKMAN, B. A. 2000. *In the Web of Politics: Three Decades of the U.S. Federal Executive.* Washington, DC: Brookings Institution Press.

AGRANOFF, R. 2007. *Managing within Networks: Adding Value to Public Organizations.* Washington, DC: Georgetown University Press.

ARNOLD, P. E. 1998. *Making the Managerial Presidency: Comprehensive Reorganization Planning, 1905–1996,* 2nd edn. Lawrence: University Press of Kansas.

BAUMGARTNER, F. R., and JONES, B. D. 1993. *Agendas and Instability in American Politics.* Chicago: University of Chicago Press.

BOZEMAN, B. 1993. A Theory of Government "Red Tape." *Journal of Public Administration Research and Theory,* 3: 273–304.

BURKE, J. P. 2000. *The Institutional Presidency: Organizing and Managing the White House from FDR to Clinton,* 2nd edn. Baltimore: Johns Hopkins University Press.

CHUN, Y. H., and RAINEY, H. G. 2005. Goal Ambiguity and Organizational Performance in U.S. Federal Agencies. *Journal of Public Administration Research and Theory*, 15: 529–57.

COHEN, D. M. 1998. Amateur Government. *Journal of Public Administration Research and Theory*, 8: 450–97.

Comptroller General. 1981. *Improved Quality, Adequate Resources, and Consistent Oversight Needed if Regulatory Analysis is to Help Control the Cost of Regulations*. Washington, DC: GAO Report to the Chairman, Committee on Governmental Affairs, US Senate, GAO/PAD-83-6.

COOPER, P. J. 1986. By Order of the President: Administration by Executive Order and Proclamation. *Administration & Society*, 18: 233–62.

—— 2002. *By Order of the President: The Use and Abuse of Executive Direct Action*. Lawrence: University Press of Kansas.

—— 2005. George W. Bush, Edgar Allan Poe, and the Use and Abuse of Presidential Signing Statements. *Presidential Studies Quarterly*, 5: 515–32.

DICKINSON, M. J. 1999. *Bitter Harvest: FDR, Presidential Power, and the Growth of the Presidential Branch*. Cambridge: Cambridge University Press.

DURANT, R. F. 1992. *The Administrative Presidency Revisited: Public Lands, the BLM, and the Reagan Revolution*. Albany: State University of New York Press.

—— 2007. *The Greening of the U.S. Military: Environmental Policy, National Security, and Organizational Change*. Washington, DC: Georgetown University Press.

—— 2009. Back to the Future: Toward Revitalizing the Study of the Administrative Presidency. *Presidential Studies Quarterly*, 39: 89–110.

—— and WARBER, A. L. 2001. Networking in the Shadow of Hierarchy: Public Policy, the Administrative Presidency, and the Neoadministrative State. *Presidential Studies Quarterly*, 31: 221–44.

EDWARDS, G. C., III. 2001. Why Not the Best? The Loyalty–Competence Trade-Off in Presidential Appointments. In *Innocent until Nominated*, ed. G. C. Mackenzie. Washington, DC: Brookings Institution Press.

ELMORE, R. F. 1979–1980. Backward Mapping: Implementation Research and Policy Decisions. *Political Science Quarterly*, 94: 601–16.

EPSTEIN, D., and O'HALLORAN, S. 1994. Administrative Procedures, Information, and Agency Discretion. *American Journal of Political Science*, 38: 697–723.

—— —— 1999. *Delegating Powers: A Transaction Cost Politics Approach to Policy Making under Separate Powers*. Cambridge: Cambridge University Press.

FENNO, R. F., JR. 2003. *Home Style: House Members in their Districts*. New York: Longman.

FERNANDEZ, S., and RAINEY, H. G. 2006. Managing Successful Organizational Change in the Public Sector. *Public Administration Review*, 66: 168–76.

FISHER, L. 2004. *The Politics of Executive Privilege*. Durham, NC: Carolina Academic Press.

—— 2007a. Invoking Inherent Powers: A Primer. *Presidential Studies Quarterly*, 37: 1–22.

—— 2007b. The Law: Presidential Inherent Power: The "Sole Organ" Doctrine. *Presidential Studies Quarterly*, 37: 139–52.

GILMOUR, J. B., and LEWIS, D. E. 2005. Does Performance Budgeting Work? An Examination of the Office of Management and Budget's PART Scores. *Public Administration Review*, 66: 742–52.

GINSBERG, B. 2007. *The American Lie: Government by the People and Other Political Fables*. Boulder, CO: Paradigm Publishers.

GOLDEN, M. M. 1998. Interest Groups in the Rule-Making Process: Who Participates? Whose Voices Get Heard? *Journal of Public Administration Research & Theory*, 8: 245–70.

GOLDEN, M. M. 2000. *What Motivates Bureaucrats? Politics and Administration during the Reagan Years*. New York: Columbia University Press.

GOODIN, R. E., and TILLY, C. 2006. *The Oxford Handbook of Contextual Political Analysis*. Oxford: Oxford University Press.

HAMMOND, T. H., and MILLER, G. J. 1985. A Social Choice Perspective on Expertise and Authority in Bureaucracy. *American Journal of Political Science*, 29: 1–28.

HART, J. 1995. *The Presidential Branch: From Washington to Clinton*. Chatham, NJ: Chatham House.

HECLO, H. 1977. *A Government of Strangers*. Washington, DC: Brookings Institution Press.

HILL, M., and HUPE, P. 2002. *Implementing Public Poilcy*. Thousand Oaks, CA: Sage Publications.

HOPENHAYN, H., and LOHMANN, S. 1996. Fire-Alarm Signals and the Political Oversight of Regulatory Agencies. *Journal of Law, Economics, and Organization*, 12: 196–213.

HOWELL, W. G. 2003. *Power without Persuasion: The Politics of Direct Presidential Action*. Princeton, NJ: Princeton University Press.

——— 2005. Unilateral Powers: A Brief Overview. *Presidential Studies Quarterly*, 35: 417–39.

HULT, K. M., and WALCOTT, C. E. 2004. *Empowering the White House: Governance under Nixon, Ford, and Carter*. Lawrence: University Press of Kansas.

INGRAM, H., and SCHNEIDER, A. L. 1990. Improving Implementation through Framing Smarter Statutes. *Journal of Public Policy*, 10: 67–88.

JONES, B. D., and BAUMGARTNER, F. R. 2005. *The Politics of Attention: How Government Prioritizes Problems*. Chicago: University of Chicago Press.

JONES, C. O. 2005. *The Presidency in a Separated System*, 2nd edn. Washington, DC: Brookings Institution Press.

JOYCE, P. G. 2004. *Linking Performance and Budgeting: Opportunities in the Federal Budget Process*. Washington, DC: IBM Center for the Business of Government.

KAGAN, E. 2001. Presidential Administration. *Harvard Law Review*, 114: 2245–385.

KAUFMAN, H. 1981. *The Administrative Behavior of Federal Bureau Chiefs*. Washington, DC: Brookings Institution.

KERWIN, C. M. 2007. *The Management of Regulation Development: Out of the Shadows*. Washington, DC: IBM Center for the Business of Government, 2008 Presidential Transition Series.

KINGDON, J. W. 2002. *Agendas, Alternatives, and Public Policies*, 2nd edn. New York: Longman.

KRAUSE, G. A., and COHEN, J. E. 2000. Opportunity, Constraints, and the Development of the Institutional Presidency: The Issuance of Executive Orders, 1939–1996. *Journal of Politics*, 62: 88–114.

KUMAR, M. J. 2007. *Managing the President's Message: The White House Communications Operation*. Baltimore: Johns Hopkins University Press.

——— and SULLIVAN, T. (eds.) 2003. *The White House World: Transitions, Organization, and Office Operations*. College Station: Texas A&M University Press.

LEWIS, D. E. 2003. *Presidents and the Politics of Agency Design: Political Insulation in the United States Government Bureaucracy, 1946–1997*. Stanford, CA: Stanford University Press.

——— 2008. *The Politics of Presidential Appointments: Political Control and Bureaucratic Performance*. Princeton, NJ: Princeton University Press.

LIGHT, P. C. 1995. *Thickening Government: Federal Hierarchy and the Diffusion of Accountability*. Washington, DC: Brookings Institution Press.

——— 1999a. *The President's Agenda: Domestic Policy Choice from Kennedy to Clinton*, 3rd edn. Baltimore: Johns Hopkins University Press.

——— 1999b. *The True Size of Government*. Washington, DC: Brookings Institution Press.

LUPIA, A., and McCUBBINS, M. D. 1994. Learning from Oversight: Fire Alarms and Policy Patrols Reconstructed. *Journal of Law, Economics, and Organization*, 10: 96–125.

LYNN, L. E., JR. 1984. The Reagan Administration and the Renitent Bureaucracy. In *The Reagan Presidency and the Governing of America*, ed. L. M. Salamon and M. S. Lund. Washington, DC: The Urban Institute.

——2006. *Public Management: Old and New*. New York: Routledge.

McCUBBINS, M. D. 1985. The Legislative Design of Regulatory Structure. *American Journal of Political Science*, 29: 721–48.

MARANTO, R. 2005. *Beyond a Government of Strangers: How Career Executives and Political Appointees Can Turn Conflict to Cooperation*. Lanham, MD: Lexington Books.

MASHAW, J. L. 1997. *Greed, Chaos, and Governance: Using Public Choice to Improve Public Law*. New Haven, CT: Yale University Press.

MAYER, K. R. 2001. *With the Stroke of a Pen: Executive Orders and Presidential Power*. Princeton, NJ: Princeton University Press.

MAZMANIAN, D. A., and SABATIER, P. A. 1989. *Implementation and Public Policy*. Lanham, MD: University Press of America.

MEIER, K. J., and O'TOOLE, L. J. JR. 2006. *Bureaucracy in a Democratic State: A Governance Perspective*. Baltimore: Johns Hopkins University Press.

MICHAELS, J. E. 1997. *The President's Call: Executive Leadership from FDR to George Bush*. Pittsburgh: University of Pittsburgh Press.

MILWARD, H. B., and PROVAN, K. G. 2000. Governing the Hollow State. *Journal of Public Administration Research and Theory*, 10: 359–79.

MOE, T. M. 1985. The Politicized Presidency. In *The New Directions in American Politics*, ed. J. E. Chubb and P. E. Peterson. Washington, DC: Brookings Institution Press.

——1989. The Politics of Bureaucratic Structure. In *Can the Government Govern?*, ed. J. E. Chubb and P. E. Peterson. Washington, DC: Brookings Institution Press.

——1993. Presidents, Institutions, and Theory. In *Researching the Presidency: Vital Questions, New Approaches*, ed. G. C. Edwards III, J. H. Kessel, and B. A. Rockman. Pittsburgh: University of Pittsburgh Press.

——and HOWELL, W. G. 1999. The Presidential Power of Unilateral Action. *Journal of Law, Economics, and Organization*, 15: 132–79.

——and WILSON, S. A. 1994. Presidents and the Politics of Structure. *Law and Contemporary Problems*, 57: 1–44.

MOYNIHAN, D. P. 2008. *The Dynamics of Performance Management: Constructing Information and Reform*. Washington, DC: Georgetown University Press.

NATHAN, R. P. 1983. *The Administrative Presidency*. New York: John Wiley & Sons.

O'TOOLE, L., MEIER, K. J., and NICHOLSON-CROTTY, S. 2005. Managing Upward, Downward, and Outward: Networks, Hierarchical Relationships, and Performance. *Public Management Review*, 7/1: 45–68.

PERRY, J. L., MESCH, D., and PAARLBERG, L. 2006. Motivating Employees in a New Governance Era: The Performance Paradigm Revisited. *Public Administration Review*, 66: 505–14.

PFIFFNER, J. P. 1996. *The Strategic Presidency: Hitting the Ground Running*, 2nd edn. Lawrence: University Press of Kansas.

PIOUS, R. M. 2007. Inherent War and Executive Powers and Prerogative Politics. *Presidential Studies Quarterly*, 37: 66–84.

PRESSMAN, J. L., and WILDAVSKY, A. 1973. *Implementation*, 3rd edn. Berkeley and Los Angeles: University of California Press.

RAGSDALE, L., and THEIS, J. J., III. 1997. The Institutionalization of the American Presidency, 1924–92. *American Journal of Political Science*, 41: 1280–318.

RAINEY, H. G. 2003. *Understanding and Managing Public Organizations*. San Francisco: Jossey-Bass Publishers.

—— and THOMPSON, J. 2006. Leadership and the Transformation of a Major Institution: Charles Rossotti and the Internal Revenue Service. *Public Administration Review*, 67: 596–604.

ROSENBLOOM, D. H., and KRAVCHUK, R. S. 2005. *Public Administration: Understanding Management, Politics, and Law in the Public Sector*, 6th edn. New York: McGraw-Hill.

ROZELL, M. J. 1994. *Executive Privilege: The Dilemma of Secrecy and Democratic Accountability*. Baltimore: Johns Hopkins University Press.

RUBIN, I. S. 2003. *Balancing the Federal Budget: Eating the Seed Corn or Trimming the Herds?* New York: Chatham House Publishers.

RUDALEVIGE, A. 2002. *Managing the President's Program: Presidential Leadership and Legislative Policy Formulation*. Princeton, NJ: Princeton University Press.

—— 2009. The Administrative Presidency and Bureaucratic Control: Implementing a Research Agenda. *Presidential Studies Quarterly*, 39: 10–24.

RUTTENBERG, J., and MEYERS, S. L. 2007. With Rove's Departure, a New Era. *New York Times*, Aug. 15.

SEIDMAN, H. 1998. *Politics, Position, and Power: The Dynamics of Federal Organization*, 5th edn. New York: Oxford University Press.

THURBER, J. A. (ed.) 2002. *Rivals for Power: Presidential–Congressional Relations*, 2nd edn. Lanham: Rowman & Littlefield.

WALCOTT, C. E., and HULT, K. M. 1995. *Governing the White House: From Hoover through LBJ*. Lawrence: University Press of Kansas.

WARBER, A. L. 2006. *Executive Orders and the Modern Presidency: Legislating from the Oval Office*. Boulder, CO: Lynne Rienner Publishers.

WEKO, T. J. 1995. *The Politicizing Presidency: The White House Personnel Office, 1948–1994*. Lawrence: University Press of Kansas.

WEST, W. F. 2006. Presidential Leadership and Administrative Coordination: Examining the Theory of a Unified Executive. *Presidential Studies Quarterly*, 36: 433–56.

WILSON, J. Q. 1989. *Bureaucracy: What Government Agencies Do and Why They Do It*. New York: Basic Books.

WOOD, B. D., and BOHTE, J. 2004. Political Transaction Costs and the Politics of Administrative Design. *Journal of Politics*, 66: 176–202.

—— and WATERMAN, R. W. 1994. *Bureaucratic Dynamics: The Role of Bureaucracy in a Democracy*. Boulder, CO: Westview Press.

YACKEE, S. W. 2006. Sweet-Talking the Fourth Branch: The Influence of Interest Group Comments on Federal Agency Rulemaking. *Journal of Public Administration Research and Theory*, 16: 103–24.

ZEGART, A. B. 1999. *Flawed by Design: The Evolution of the CIA, JCS, and NSC*. Stanford, CA: Stanford University Press.

CHAPTER 26

THE PRESIDENCY–BUREAUCRACY NEXUS

EXAMINING COMPETENCE AND RESPONSIVENESS

ANNE M. KHADEMIAN

In *A Government of Strangers,* I am at pains to point out the inevitable tension that exists between the political demand for change and institutional demand for continuity.

(Hugh Heclo, interviewed in Pfiffner 2007, 420)

SCHOLARSHIP concerned with presidential influence upon the structure and processes of the bureaucracy has long been framed by the twin priorities of governing from the White House: responsiveness and neutral competence (Finer 1941; Friedrich 1940; Kaufman 1956; Mosher 1968; Heclo 1975, 1977; Seidman 1986; Aberbach and Rockman 1988; Rourke 1992; West 2005; Dickinson and Rudalevige 2004/5, 2007). Presidents need a responsive and energetic bureaucracy able to embrace the agenda of a successful campaign, yet continuity and competence require stable and expert-based organizations to provide the infrastructure of democratic governance. At the height of this debate, these two governing objectives were viewed as competing priorities in a struggle that responsiveness was winning (Heclo 1975; Aberbach and Rockman 1988; Seidman 1986; Moe 1985). Over the past two decades, however, a predominantly institutional focus on the presidency has advanced this debate by reexamining and reincorporating neutral competence as a potent force in presidential governance (Cameron 1999; Dickinson and Rudalevige 2004/5, 2007; Dull 2006; Miller 2000; Knott and Miller 1987; Moe and Howell 1999b).[1]

This chapter first examines the ways in which the literature engages neutral competence and how neutral competence matters for presidential governance of the bureaucracy. It examines three areas of the literature: studies of the management and reorganization of the bureaucracy, studies that apply economic theory to questions of presidential influence, and studies of direct "unilateral" presidential action. As the competence–responsiveness debate has matured, so too has our understanding of the institutional presidency. Building on this point, the chapter then identifies two related research topics in the institutional presidency.

First, recent advances in our understanding of the competence–responsiveness debate present opportunities for combining theories of leadership with scholarship on the institutional presidency. As our understanding of the presidency as an institution has deepened (Arnold 1998; Moe 1985: Moe and Wilson 1994; Burke 2000; Lewis 2003; Walcott and Hult 2005; Weko 1995; Miller 2000; Rudalevige 2002; Hult and Walcott 2004; Bertelli and Feldmann 2007), so too might our understanding of leadership exercised within the institution. The chapter thus applies theories of leadership developed in the field of public administration to the study of the presidency. In particular, it considers the extent to which these leadership models shed light on questions of whether and how presidents utilize ambiguity as an institutional resource. Additionally, the chapter explores useful connections between the fields of political science and public administration. As others have recommended (Meier and O'Toole 2006), public administration would benefit from empirical investigations of its normative assertions, and political science would benefit from the recognition of bureaucratic complexity found in the public administration literature.

A PLACE FOR NEUTRAL COMPETENCE

In the waning years of the Reagan White House—an administration recognized for its effectiveness in commanding responsiveness to the presidential agenda—Joel Aberbach and Bert Rockman (1988) observed a trend toward increased centralization and deinstitutionalization of the bureaucracy:

[1] The term "new institutionalism" has been widely used to describe a variety of approaches representing a revived study of institutions, from sociological perspectives that emphasize the role of the environment in institutional evolution and behavior (DiMaggio and Powell 1983; Meyer and Rowan 1977),

Politics provides energy and revitalization while bureaucracy brings continuity, knowledge, and stability. One can exist without the other but only to the detriment of effective government. The problem for government and, in our view, the public interest is not to have one of these values completely dominate the other, but to provide a creative dialogue or synthesis between the two. In recent times, the dialogue has turned into monologue as deinstitutionalization and centrist command has grown apace. (608)

Harold Seidman similarly identified the importance of institutional competence in the bureaucracy—and noted the lack of presidential appreciation for its benefits. "What the White House identifies as bureaucracy's inherent deficiencies are often its strengths," he wrote. "Effective functioning of the governmental machine requires a high degree of stability, uniformity, and awareness of the impact of new policies, regulations and procedures on the affected public. The bureaucracy all too frequently is not asked for its advice on the 'how to,' for which it does have the knowledge and experience to make a contribution" (1998, 63).

Terry Moe (1985) explained the presidential impulse toward responsiveness as a governing strategy. Presidents, he argued, draw upon politicization and centralization to achieve responsiveness from the bureaucracy. Politicization, in Moe's usage, refers to the strategic reliance upon partisan and presidential loyalty in the appointment of executive branch personnel, while centralization specifically denotes the concentration of decision-making authority within the Executive Office of the President (EOP). It is inevitable, he argued, that presidents would continue to apply strategies of politicization and centralization to boost the bureaucracy's responsiveness to their agendas. This truth reflects a conjunction of several considerations important to presidents, including: their own political ambitions; the vast expectations placed upon them to govern with a clear and visible vision; the contending constraints on time, resources, and organizational knowledge that they must balance; and obstacles to change posed by bureaucratic inertia and policy sub-governments. Given all of this, presidents face strong incentives to establish an "administrative presidency," whereby they govern through the use of administrative techniques. As a result, we have witnessed the increasing use of strategic appointments throughout the bureaucracy based upon presidential loyalty, as well as the employment of the Office of Management and Budget (OMB) and the Office of Information and Regulatory Affairs to centralize and influence decision making across the federal bureaucracy (Nathan 1983; Durant 1991, 1992; Waterman 1989).

Left adrift in the wake of this argument was the notion that organizational requirements for neutral competence could play an important role in presidents' administrative decisions. Arguments citing the constitutional and legal dimensions of the presidency, as well as the responsibilities of the president to reorganize,

to economic perspectives, emphasizing the relationship between individual and organizational priorities and institutional design and evolution (North 1990; Ostrom 1990), understandings of institutions through the lenses of history, routines, and organizational learning (March and Olsen 1984). The term "new" is used here to capture a broad return to institutionalism that has, to varying degrees, integrated behavioral concerns with structural concerns to examine the implications for institutional development and government action.

manage, and sustain the capacity of the executive branch, fell out of favor with scholars attempting to explain the growth of the office and the behavior of the president (Cook 2007; Moe 1990). Some observers noted a shift away from presidential interest in the managerial aspects of the presidency, understood as conscious choices by presidents to abandon the organizational principles of presidential governance (Moe 2003). Others have focused on the ad hoc and impulsive nature of management reforms (Carroll, Fritschler, and Smith 1985). Still others have noted the inevitability of the trend away from purposeful reorganization and management and the incompatibility of objective non-partisanship with service to a president (Arnold 1998; West 2005). To accomplish a broad agenda, scholars have argued that presidents rally and sustain broad popular support for presidential policy initiatives, which elevates the strategies and practices of the campaign to daily presidential governance (Blumenthal 1980; Edwards 2000; Ornstein and Mann 2000; Klein 2005).

In this highly politicized context of the "permanent campaign," presidential appointments take on a heightened strategic relevance. Rather than serving as a means to bring specialized expertise and management competence to the operation of executive branch organizations, appointments become a way to ensure loyalty to the presidential policy agenda as part of a broader strategy of policy monitoring (Wood and Waterman 1991; Waterman 1989; Schmidt 1995). Two sets of findings seem to confirm the politicization and centralization trends identified by Terry Moe, as well as Ronald Moe's assertions that presidents have abandoned administrative principles as governing strategy. First, studies indicate that presidential attempts to harness the bureaucracy in service of White House ambitions through the initiation of new management programs, or the redesign of agencies within the EOP and the broader executive branch, have yielded few returns (Aberbach and Rockman 1976; Cronin 1975; Roberts 1997; Thompson 2000). Second, and by contrast, presidents have effectively pursued administrative control in the post-Second World War presidency through the use of strategic appointments (Weko 1995; Schmidt 1995; Rudalevige 2002).

The significance of neutral competence, however, is gradually being reasserted by scholars, and is taking on an increasingly important role in our understanding of the presidency and the bureaucracy (Campbell 1986; Cameron 1999; Dickinson and Rudalevige 2004/5; Dull 2006; Miller 2000; Moe and Howell 1999b). Rather than pitting it as a trade-off with responsiveness, scholars have developed a new understanding of competence as a component of broader strategies of responsiveness. Responsiveness, in other words, remains a dominant objective. But its effective pursuit may require neutral competence, depending on political circumstances. Neutral competence may also emerge as an unintended consequence of management efforts forged by centralization and politicization. We see these advances in our understanding of the competence and responsiveness debate in the literature on reorganization and management, the application of economic theory to presidential design and management of the bureaucracy, and the research in direct presidential action and the bureaucracy.

Competence as a Strategy in Reorganization and Management

A new trend in American politics scholarship reassesses presidential efforts to reorganize and manage the bureaucracy (Pfiffner 1991; Weko 1995). For example, in his study of the Office of Management and Budget's) implementation of the Bush Administration's Program Assessment and Rating Tool (PART), Matthew Dull poses the question: "Why commit scarce resources to an initiative like PART when previous efforts neither took hold nor delivered discernable political benefit?" (2006, 188). His argument helps move the debate over the utility of presidential management efforts away from a perspective of neutral competence versus responsiveness and integrates the two in a framework of institutional bargaining and learning. The study makes this contribution in two parts. First, it examines "policy competence" as a means for the OMB to credibly pursue its work in a complex setting of shared power. Importantly, in Dull's terminology, "policy competence" denotes an analytic concept distinct from "neutral competence," which he defines as a professional norm. Second, Dull's work also analyzes PART as a cognitive tool that facilitates learning or problem solving for participants in the OMB and across government.

First, a neutral and transparent implementation of PART, Dull argues, builds the policy competence of the OMB—i.e., "the knowledge and adaptive capacity of available policy staff and resources" (2006, 191). In contrast to an approach characterized by the strategies of centralization and politicization with an emphasis on control, policy competence as a strategy is essential for the OMB to convincingly engage powerful institutions long recognized as resistant to presidential oversight (Rourke 1984; Heclo 1977). A competent OMB, in short, is understood as vital for engaging and influencing the work of federal agencies.

Second, Dull argues that policy competence is accomplished, in part, through an understanding of PART as a means for learning or problem solving. Rather than view the PART process as a tool for control, Dull makes the case for PART as a cognitive framework that allows participants in the budget process to hone objectives, assign meaning to the findings, and negotiate priorities for the future. It is through this process that policy competence as a reputational characteristic of the OMB emerges. It is through an understanding of budget reform as a mechanism for framing and addressing problems, however, that competence takes on theoretical importance. Viewed as a cognitive device for participants, we can see the implementation of PART as a means to articulate relationships, share knowledge, and acknowledge program challenges. In his analysis of the perspectives of career executives on the influence of political appointees on agencies' work, Steven Stehr found that "top bureaucrats are already inclined to share influence." Hence, efforts to control or dominate the bureaucracy "lead to ignoring valuable input from career personnel" (1997, 81). Based on Dull's findings, the implementation of PART in a neutral and transparent manner serves as a means of tapping that "valuable" input. Conceiving of PART as a problem-solving device, on the other hand, explains why OMB personnel would take the time to gather that "valuable input" in the first place.

Matthew Dickinson and Andrew Rudalevige (2007) also illustrate the rise of neutral competence as a factor in explaining presidential management and reorganization efforts. The authors examine the institutional transformation of the Bureau of the Budget (BOB) in the hands of President Roosevelt, and eventually the renamed Office of Management and Budget (OMB) in the hands of President Nixon. The conventional wisdom depicts the agency under President Roosevelt as an example of institutionalized neutral competence. Nixon's OMB, by contrast, serves as a prime example of responsive competence. "Ideally," according to Dickinson and Rudalevige, "all presidents desire an OMB that is both politically responsive and administratively competent" (2007, 4). But unfortunately, the authors discover that "the overriding lesson of the post-Nixon era is that it is difficult, if not impossible, to combine political responsiveness and administrative competence within a single staff agency" (36). The similarities between Roosevelt and Nixon are more striking than the differences, in that both sought to ensure responsiveness through this important agency. Varied political circumstances, however, drove different strategies for reaching this responsiveness goal.

This analysis of the BOB/OMB under Roosevelt and Nixon provides two important insights for the competence and responsiveness literature. First, the push toward politicization is not without concern for neutral competence, even though neutral competence has seemed less relevant in the characterization of the presidency as permanent campaign, or in accounts of presidents' attempts to control the bureaucracy. As Rudalevige's (2002) earlier work shows, how and when presidents rely upon centralization and politicization as governing strategies is contingent upon the complexity of the issues at hand. Employment of the strategies is also contingent upon the interplay between presidential priorities and the skills, capacities, and professional competencies of the agencies supporting presidential efforts, as well as those on the receiving end of presidential management efforts (Eisner and Meier 1990; Martino-Golden 2001; Kettl 1986; Khademian 1992). Responsiveness, they argue, is the goal. Whether a president draws upon neutral competence or the strategies of centralization and politicization depends upon the political and temporal context. Bertelli and Feldmann's (2007) assessment of loyalty in presidential appointments presents a similar set of constraints on use of the "ally principle" or the politicization strategy as a means to accomplish broader presidential objectives.

Second, Dickinson and Rudalevige (2007) reengage the early twentieth-century dichotomy between politics and administration by bringing historical evidence to bear on the normative arguments for their separation. Like early observers of the dichotomy, the authors contextualize the governing demands for neutral competence, or administration, as well as responsiveness, or politics (Lynn 2001). The emphasis placed on one value over the other will vary depending upon political circumstances. And like the early proponents, Dickinson and Rudalevige demonstrate that "dichotomy" is too strong a characterization of the dynamic tension between competence and responsiveness that cannot be restrained by practices, boundaries, or mandates. Both priorities tend to spill into the other (Walker 1989; Lynn 2001). Unlike early and more recent critics of the dichotomy (Waldo 1984;

Sayre 1951, 1958; Moore 1995), Dickinson and Rudalevige draw a distinction between the application of neutral competence as a strategy versus a more politicized strategy. The strategic choice or blend of the two rests with the best means to achieve responsiveness given the politics and policies of the time.

A variety of research agendas attempt to map out the implications of centralization and politicization as management strategies in terms of effectiveness, while also detailing these strategies in practice (Weko 1995; Rudalevige 2002). The presidential motivation for centralizing regulatory processes (Shapiro 2007), appointing presidential allies (Bertelli and Feldmann 2007; Lewis forthcoming), or increasing the number of political appointments (Light 1995, 2004) is made evident by the institutionally driven strategies of centralization and politicization. Yet, scholars are still uncovering the nuance and complexity of these pursuits. For example, as a package, changes in the regulatory process throughout the Bush administration have increased presidential influence over the regulatory process and resulted in its subtle slowing. Shapiro finds, however, that the motivation behind distinct initiatives, such as the OMB-initiated Electronic Rulemaking project, complicates the picture. A long-term OMB interest in utilizing the internet to enhance public access and transparency in the development of regulations can also slow the regulatory process by increasing the information administrators must consider in rule making. This can be a desirable outcome for regulatory opponents. Similarly, changes in the Office of Information and Regulatory Affairs (OIRA) have brought more scientific expertise into the office, and hence increased its clout in deliberations with regulatory agencies. While strengthening the hand of the presidency in regulatory affairs, the effort to enhance the expertise or capacity of the OIRA—i.e., its neutral competence—again provides an interesting counter to the straightforward trends in politicization as a responsiveness strategy (Shapiro 2007).

Summary Observations

Perhaps most influential in the competence–responsiveness debate has been the detailed research that identifies the quest for competence in practice. Neutral competence, the authors discussed here find, has been pursued at different points in time as a defining feature in the work of the OMB. Responsiveness remains a central goal; however, executing a presidential agenda requires the selective use of centralization and politicization, on the one hand, balanced with the pursuit of neutral competence on the other. This empirical finding shifts the theoretical effort to explain the choice of strategies, as well as the ways in which different strategies might be integrated into the institutional presidency. Examples of the coexistence of neutral competence and responsiveness as governing priorities provide a more solid picture of the realities of controlling the bureaucracy from the White House. While the priorities of presidents change rapidly, policy is conducted within established and expert agencies. To accomplish presidential goals, the White House requires the competence to engage and learn with the expert agencies. In the next section, the application of economic theory to the presidency is examined for additional contributions to the competence–responsiveness debate.

Competence and Consequence: Economic Theory and the Presidency

Terry Moe (1985) has argued that the lack of knowledge available about the relationship between organizational design and performance in the public sector provides an incentive for presidents to centralize and politicize in their attempts to direct the executive branch. Building from applications of economic theory to the study of bureaucracy, however, recent scholarship further demonstrates the rise of neutral competence as a factor in (or consequence of) presidential influence upon the design and behavior of the bureaucracy (Miller 2000; Whitford 2002; Lewis 2003).

Gary Miller examines the presidential choice to build neutral competence into bureaucratic design by posing a broader question about bureaucratic efficiency in a democracy. "Trying to design a set of governmental institutions that will encourage the benign aspects of the state while limiting its capacity for exploitation," he argues, "has been a persistent puzzle throughout history" (2000, 289). Principal–agent theory, on the one hand, defines the challenge as the need to develop and implement incentives that constrain or motivate self-interested agents to act in accordance with the priorities of principals—making bureaucrats do what the public, as represented through elected officials, mandates. However, Miller argues, if this is the solution, we need to know "why modern states insulate bureaucrats in civil service protections? And why are bureaucrats able to use the cry of 'political interference' to their own political advantage?" (324).

The answer, Miller argues, rests with the fact that the control by a principal (in this case, by an elected official) over agent productivity (i.e., the implementation of government programs by civil servants) results in a moral hazard—it is not optimal because, of the potential for principal exploitation. Miller builds his argument from the work of Holmstrom (1982) and Eswaran and Kotwal (1984), who theorize about the moral hazard present in relationships between the efficiency of a company, its self-interested ownership, and the work of self-interested employees. In an effort to achieve efficient outcomes, a solution to the potential for shirking by employees may be addressed by one structure, yet the same approach can present opportunities for subversion by the owner. "The problem in any social organization," Miller argues, "is not that of finding an efficient incentive system; rather, the problem is finding an efficient incentive system that members believe will not be subverted by the owner of the residual" (2000, 297). Applied to a public organization in a democratic setting, this type of principal influence over a range of bureaucratic decisions can result in interventions by elected officials to favor parochial interests to the detriment of the broader public welfare (Olson 1965, 1982; Rauch 1994).

Miller argues that the solution is not more principal control, as principal–agent theory suggests, but *less*—a solution achievable by building neutral competence into the design of bureaucratic programs. Delegation to professional non-partisan managers represents a credible commitment to the public by principals to restrain their own political influence. In a conclusion that could serve as advice to presidents bent on politicization and centralization, Miller notes that governments "should and sometimes do" adopt constraints on control in order to be efficient (2000, 325). This splendid argument integrates a century of debate and research to make the case for neutral competence as an active and efficient means for governing the bureaucracy.

In a test of "canonical principal–agent theory," Andrew Whitford finds evidence of the emergence of neutral competence as a governing strategy when the decision-making structure of the Nuclear Regulatory Commission (NRC) was decentralized during the Reagan administration (2002, 168). Specifically, decentralization of policy formulation and implementation processes in the NRC resulted in greater autonomy of the regional offices from national political control. "After decentralization," writes Whitford, "finding themselves insulated from national control, bureaucrats became more task-oriented" (185). According to Whitford, the direct relationship between the rise of neutral competence, in the form of more autonomous professional judgment, and the shift in organizational design demonstrates the limitations of principal–agent theory for the study of bureaucracy. Structure, he found, mattered a great deal for the behavior of political agents in the NRC. This contradicts the expectations of principal–agent theory, which relies upon the establishment of incentive systems, supervision, and selection criteria for agents to ensure compliance with principals' priorities. Whitford's findings also bolster the point made by Moe (1985) regarding the lack of knowledge about organizational structure and perform-ance to guide presidential efforts to influence the bureaucracy. The Reagan admin-istration pursued decentralization as a means to "decrease governmental activism," yet "the increased responsiveness of bureaucrats to the task environment actually increased governmental activism by the NRC" (2002, 187). Neutral competence and attention to the task environment emerged from the autonomy intended to reduce regulatory activity.

David Lewis (2003), in contrast, draws upon the new economics of organization (Moe 1985, 1989) to explicitly frame questions of organizational design and structure as questions of political influence. Lewis (2003) argues that debates over agency structure provide a foundation for the exercise of presidential influence. The location of an agency, its governing structure, the procedures for decision making, the professionals that dominate agency decision making, and the conditions under which appointed officials serve together create the framework for oversight and influence in the future. Lewis builds his study from two basic premises. First, design politics are debates over who will get what, when, and how, and are rooted in the constitutional separation of powers over the development and execution of govern-ment policy. Second, distinct logics that reflect the varied bases of constitutional authority guide the debates over agency design. Whereas members of Congress have often preferred agencies to be insulated from political (i.e., presidential) influence, presidents have sought to reduce fragmentation and duplication for a more centrally coordinated bureaucracy.

Lewis (2003) develops testable hypotheses for the conditions under which presi-dents and members of Congress will seek to shape the bureaucracy in a rational, comprehensive, and presidentially accessible manner; when the politics of isolation and fragmentation are likely to take hold; and when presidents are likely to go it alone and create agencies by unilateral action (see also Howell and Lewis 2002). His findings provide empirical evidence of durability among agencies designed to be isolated. Agencies created outside of the purview of cabinet offices, and equipped with fixed-term leadership and party-balancing procedures for appointments, last longer and have a greater opportunity to develop neutral competence, as Whitford (2002) found. Lewis's study illustrates the nuts and bolts of agency design in the context of competing branches of government. His work establishes a more complex reality of presidential choices associated with the design of the bureaucracy, and explains the emergence of neutral competence as a consequence of political choices.

Summary Observations

In these applications of economic theory to bureaucratic design, neutral competence emerges from a variety of sources: as an efficient solution to the moral hazard of political interference, as an unintended consequence of decentralization, or as a product of political debate in which congressional interests that promote isolation from the president play a prominent role. In each case, the opportunity for neutral competence to emerge depends upon a structural arrangement rather than the pursuit of competence as a presidential goal. In each case, the admonitions of earlier advocates of neutral competence (Heclo 1975; Seidman 1986) confront the reality of political bargaining, the challenges of producing public goods and services, and limited knowledge about the relationship between structure and performance. This injects another possible understanding into the neutral competence-responsiveness debate—the idea that competence sometimes arises as an unintended consequence.

Direct Presidential Action: The Pursuit of Responsiveness

A third line of research stems from the claim that presidents often create and design agencies unilaterally, without the permission or cooperation of Congress (Howell and Lewis 2002; Lewis 2003). Presidents use executive orders, National Security Directives, signing statements, the creation of an agency or council, and so on, to accomplish responsiveness. Explaining when and why presidents act unilaterally and toward what end is the theoretical goal of this research (Moe and Howell 1999a; Howell and Lewis 2002). At a macro level, researchers seek to explain the gradual transformation of the federal government from a congressionally dominated system characterized by "isolated" and "durable" agencies to one dominated by the president and a professional executive branch and driven partly by the use of direct presidential action (Moe and Wilson 1994; Howell 2003; Moe and Howell 1999a, 1999b; Mayer 2001; Cooper 2005; Warber 2006).

This research builds from a familiar premise and challenges a common assumption about the power of the presidency. The premise is that the institutional capacity of the president is at odds with the expectations for presidential leadership. In order to govern, and to fulfill popular expectations of them, presidents follow the common strategies of politicization and centralization. Presidents can pursue these strategies in a number of ways, many of which involve unilateral actions. The effectiveness of unilateral actions therefore poses a challenge to long-standing arguments that the presidency is ultimately constrained in its influence by the need to negotiate action in a shared-power system (Neustadt 1990).

This challenge has been taken on both empirically and theoretically. In terms of empirics, scholars are documenting and examining the particular actions presidents have taken to expand the power of the executive relative to the other branches of government. Such attempts include the use of executive orders, signing statements, and other forms of direct action to influence policy. As Kenneth Mayer states, "Presidents have used executive orders to alter the institutional and political contexts in which they operate" (2001, 29), very much to the advantage of the presidency (Mayer 2001; Cooper 2002). The challenge has also been addressed theoretically by scholars examining the motivation behind presidential uses of unilateral action, as well as the conditions under which unilateral action is exercised in a system of shared powers (Howell 2003; Moe and Howell 1999b).

The evidence for unilateral action and the growth of presidential influence is indeed strong. But considerable progress has also been made in contextualizing presidential decisions regarding the bureaucracy across a variety of circumstances. This contextual grounding begins with the observation that "ambiguity" is a fundamental presidential resource (Moe and Howell 1999b). Fortunately for presidents, ambiguity abounds in the Constitution. Vague specifications of presidential authority pertain to matters as important as the president's role as commander-in-chief of the armed forces and his or her responsibility to "take care that the laws be faithfully executed." There is, in short, a great deal of room for presidential interpretation of these powers when applied to a wide range of circumstances (Moe and Howell 1999b).

Ambiguity also arises from other sources, such as legislative mandates that are open to broad interpretation, a lack of consensus within the congressional majority or minority party, and in the banter of day-to-day policy making. Presidents can exploit this ambiguity through unilateral action by incorporating significant information and transaction cost advantages (Howell 2003). Presidents have better information regarding the work of the executive branch, and members of Congress are often dependent on the president for access to this information. Presidents may also enjoy lower transaction costs for direct action than the legislature does, depending on the relative unity of Congress. Thus, the degree of consensus and cooperation in any given Congress will influence the strategic use of unilateral action by presidents. Presidents create more agencies unilaterally (Howell and Lewis 2002), issue more executive orders (Mayer 2001), and engage in direct and dramatic action in foreign and military affairs more aggressively (Howell 2003) when Congress is divided along partisan and ideological lines (Howell and Lewis 2002). "Presidential power expands," writes William Howell (2003, 101), "at exactly the same times when, and precisely the same places that, congressional power weakens . . . for it is the check each places on the other that defines the overall division of power." In sum, conditions of ambiguity create the context for unilateral action that facilitates this expansion of presidential power.

Consider this proposition in the wake of the 9/11 terrorist attacks on the World Trade Center in New York City and the Pentagon in Arlington, Virginia. President Bush's silence and apparent confusion in the immediate aftermath of the attacks was a metaphor for the shock and uncertainty felt by the government, and, indeed, the nation. When the president found his voice on a visit to ground zero in New York City, however, he began to provide certainty through a series of swift unilateral actions, as well as through negotiations with Congress in which he seemed to hold the upper hand. When Congress took the lead in proposing a department that the president did not want to create (Kettl 2007), Bush countered with a personnel system that would directly challenge public sector unions and bring performance assessment squarely under the authority of federal employees in the Department of Homeland Security (DHS) (Moynihan 2005). Whereas members of Congress fought to make FEMA and its all-hazards approach the organizing premise of the work of DHS, the administration initially wrenched control over hundreds of millions of dollars in grant money from FEMA and placed it with its Justice Department counterpart, the Office of Domestic Preparedness, which emphasized terrorism prevention and response training (Khademian 2004). In these debates, we see the explicit connections between bureaucratic structures and the priorities and institutional preferences of policy makers responding to 9/11. Presidential priorities to centralize homeland security management in an Office of Homeland Security located in the EOP were countered by congressional preferences for a more consolidated organizational response in the form of the DHS, whose leadership would be subjected to Senate approval and regularly required to testify before Congress. The clout of the participants in this structural debate was made evident by those agencies left out of the merger, such as the FBI and the CIA, thus allowing them to preserve significant autonomy from the president and Congress.

Summary Observations

The study of unilateral action contributes to the competence–responsiveness debate in several ways. First, along with the earlier literature discussed in this chapter, it contextualizes presidential efforts to accomplish responsiveness. Unilateral actions are conditioned by the degrees of consensus and organization in Congress. President Bush's direct action to establish an Office of Homeland Security in the wake of the 9/11 attacks was gradually undone by a Congress that established consensus around a new DHS. Unilateral actions, however, are also conditioned by presidential capacity to identify and exploit ambiguity and opportunity. When legislation for a new DHS was proposed in Congress over President Bush's objections, the administration utilized the opportunity to pursue significant personnel reform through the implementation of a performance-based system.

Second, this literature raises the question of whether an increasingly powerful presidency will have an interest in or need to utilize neutral competence as a strategy or goal in the design and oversight of the bureaucracy. The work of Miller (2000), Dull (2006), and Dickinson and Rudalevige (2004/5, 2007) suggests that competence continues to be a governing force, though not always a welcome or anticipated one. The work of Whitford (2002), in particular, suggests that unilateral action does not necessarily produce an administrative-enhancing result—bureaucracies can establish neutral competence in decentralized space. Moe's (1985) warning that our organizational knowledge is little help for presidents seeking to accomplish mandates and high performance resonates in this debate. The power to tap ambiguity through the unilateral creation of an agency or policy can result in unanticipated consequences that may or may not enhance responsiveness or further the presidential agenda.

LEADERSHIP AND THE INSTITUTIONAL PRESIDENCY: RECONNECTING POLITICAL SCIENCE AND PUBLIC ADMINISTRATION

Literature that advances the competence and responsiveness debate presumes an institutional focus on the presidency, rather than a focus on the individual characteristics of any given president. Here we have examined research that identifies the contextual and environmental constraints that frame presidential choices regarding agency creation and design; the unanticipated consequences of presidential strategies aimed at influencing bureaucratic decision making; and the strength of concerns over capacity that can temper the institutional progression toward governance of the bureaucracy through centralization and politicization. An institutional focus upon structure, incentives, norms, and the dynamics of interaction with other institutions allows us to see longer-term trends, recognize changes over time, and apply the findings from presidential oversight of the bureaucracy to other institutions.

But the debate between individual versus institutional analysis as a means to examine the presidency remains vibrant (Edwards, Kessel, and Rockman 1992). The terrorist attacks of 9/11, for example, laid bare the politics of structure and made prominent the role of individual leadership as long-established systems and processes gave way to ambiguity. Why the attacks occurred and what response the US would put forth were open questions waiting for presidential leadership to assign meaning to them and move forward. Scholars have long understood the importance of leadership in the assignment of meaning (Smircich and Morgan 1982), particularly in times of crisis. Prominent examples of this include Franklin Roosevelt's introduction of the New Deal to address the chaos and ambiguity of the Great Depression (McJimsey 2000), and Abraham Lincoln's framing of a national logic for making sense of and continuing to fight the Civil War (Paludan 1994). Yet, as Colin Campbell has noted, "no president or administration can be fully understood without linking character and performance to the task of governance" (1986, 5), or, we might add, the strengths and potential of government institutions.

Ambiguity as a resource for the institutional presidency rests within the grant of authority in the Constitution, as well as in the mandates, processes, and debates of the policy-making process. Utilization of that resource, however, rests with the initiative of the individual president and his or her ability to assign a meaning to circumstances, to offer a solution in a crisis that sticks, or to take action that is perceived as legitimate and essential. As Moe and Howell (1999b) point out, "Presidents are particularly well suited to be first-movers and to reap the agenda powers that go along with it" (1999b, 138). But how and when presidents become first-movers, and what they may or may not do with the consequent agenda powers, is perhaps a matter of individual leadership style.

In the wake of Hurricane Katrina, Don Kettl (forthcoming) argues that leaders across the federal government understood the disaster and hence the appropriate response in different ways. Katrina was not a typical hurricane. In any catastrophe of such a scale, as in the case of 9/11, citizens and government officials look to the president to give meaning to the catastrophe and to engage the capacity of government to focus and respond accordingly. A key challenge of leadership and good management is not only knowing what to do to address a problem, but knowing how to define or interpret the problem (Pondy, Bohland, and Thomas 1988). President Bush's initial response to Hurricane Katrina was to express confidence in the agencies, governments, and personnel responding to the catastrophe (Sylves 2006). Declared an "incident of national significance" under the terminology of the National Response Plan, following existing plans and procedures was the initial approach. But as the scale of the disaster became more evident, the response less adequate, and the confusion more rampant, the meaning assigned to the disaster shifted explicitly toward the restoration of law and order to prevent rising violence and "protect the people from the criminal element through the presence of military forces" (Tierney, Bevc, and Kuligowski 2006, 71). As many have observed, the poor response of the federal government in the initial days following the storm, and the competence demonstrated by the United States Coast Guard and the National Guard, has since fostered a militaristic understanding and approach to disaster management, or "faith in the ability of the military and armed force to solve problems in both the international and domestic spheres" (Tierney, Bevc, and Kuligowski 2006, 77). This stands in contrast to an understanding of disaster management built upon civilian and community-based capacities to respond.

Whether ambiguity exists in the wake of disasters, or in the vague text of a congressional mandate, what guides the assignment of meaning for potential unilateral action? As our understanding of the institutional presidency deepens (Arnold 1998; Moe 1985: Moe and Wilson 1994; Burke 2000; Lewis 2003; Walcott and Hult 1995; Weko 1995; Miller 2000; Rudalevige 2002; Hult and Walcott 2004; Bertelli and Feldmann 2007), does our understanding of presidential leadership need to adjust as well? Within the literature on the institutional presidency, we have come to understand presidential leadership as the purposeful pursuit of policy and personal goals through the use of bureaucratic oversight to ensure responsiveness to the presidential agenda. Yet, just as the literature on the competence and responsiveness debate has highlighted the role of context in promoting neutral competence in presidential governance, perhaps leadership efforts are more contingent on institutional context than our explanations currently allow.

One way to investigate this question is to tap into the literature on leadership in public organizations. Within public administration, a normative tradition has advocated different models of leadership for the public or common good. Arguments for leadership that is value driven (Cook 1998) or conservative in its orientation in order to protect the integrity and mandated purpose of public organizations (Terry 1995, 1998) contrast with arguments for leadership that is entrepreneurial in the effort to create public value (Moore 1995; Behn 2001). And efforts to understand public leadership in a shared-power world (Crosby and Bryson 2005), or in a manner that facilitates public responsibility for problem solving (Heifetz 1994), contrast with a more traditional focus on leadership within a single institution whereby the role of the leader is to promote and protect the distinctive competence of any given organization (Selznick 1957). A criticism of this literature, however, derives from the lack of empirical evidence demonstrating how public sector leadership is actually practiced, as well as a dearth of knowledge about the real perceptions of public sector employees about what constitutes good leadership (Trottier, Van Wart, and Wang 2008; Van Wart 2003). This is a more general criticism leveled against the public administration literature (Meier and O'Toole 2006). While this literature asserts the importance of values, and the role of public administration in implementing and preserving them, little empirical research exists to identify value-driven actions and the effectiveness of such actions in practice.

However, these models of leadership could be applied to the investigation of how presidents might utilize ambiguity or assign meaning to problems or policies. The potential here is twofold. First, these leadership models direct attention to specific aspects of presidential governance—such as shared powers, the value of distinctive competencies of executive branch agencies such as the OMB, broad governing norms and practices, and "windows" or opportunities for dramatic "entrepreneurial" policy change orchestrated by a president. As presidents face different circumstances and different opportunities, do the applicable models of leadership change as well? Are presidents more inclusive in their assignment of meaning under some circumstances, while behaving more unilaterally in others? Is an entrepreneurial approach to the use of ambiguity contingent on the competencies of executive branch agencies that a president might draw upon or create? A significant limitation for President Bush's efforts to establish the Office of Homeland Security as the primary coordinating authority for the government's response to 9/11 was the limited capacity of the office to manage the assigned responsibilities (Lawlor 2008).

Second, examinations of these leadership models would provide one way to link the concerns of public administration and political science. In their assessment of both fields and the study of the bureaucracy, Meier and O'Toole (2006) argue for more empirical investigations of normative arguments present in public administration. The relevance of normative arguments, they suggest, should be recognized and engaged in political science, while empirical assessment of public administration claims is also important. Such efforts might also shed light on management reforms in particular, which seem to reflect a current fad without much grounding in political reality. As one group of commentators examining the "supply side" management policies of the Reagan administration put it: "It is a tendency rather than a theory, a collection of precepts that fit together uneasily, and an operational code driven by a new mix of political necessity and ideological orthodoxy" (Carroll, Fritschler, and Smith 1985, 807). These tendencies and operational codes, however, might also reflect the normative and institutional parameters that presidents see in their respective leadership styles. Rather than existing merely as quickly constructed vehicles for pursuing an agenda, management reforms may be manifestations of various understandings of leadership in complex institutional settings.

Indeed, the research of Miller (2000), Dull (2006), and others investigated in this essay finds new relevance in neutral competence, traditionally considered to be a normative imposition on presidential governance rather than an operational reality. It may very well be the case that the ways in which presidents exercise unilateral action, manage the bureaucracy, or attempt to set policy are influenced by models of leadership that emerge from the complexities of the institutional presidency. These complexities might promote a drive toward centralization and politicization as leadership strategies, but might also increase our recognition of the importance of neutral competence, shared power, or the role of constituents in problem solving.

References

ABERBACH, J., and ROCKMAN. B. 1976. Clashing Beliefs in the Executive Branch: The Nixon Administrative Bureaucracy. *American Political Science Review*, 70/2: 456–88.
————1988. Mandates or Mandarins? Control and Discretion in the Modern Administrative State. *Public Administration Review*, 48/2: 606–12.
ARNOLD, P. E. 1998. *Making the Managerial Presidency: Comprehensive Reorganization Planning, 1905–1996*. 2nd rev. edn. Lawrence: University Press of Kansas.
BEHN, R. 2001. *Rethinking Democratic Accountability*. Washington, DC: Brookings Institution Press.
BERTELLI, A., and FELDMANN, S. 2007. Strategic Appointments. *Journal of Public Administration Research and Theory*, 17/1: 19–38.
BLUMENTHAL, S. 1980. *The Permanent Campaign: Inside the World of Elite Political Operatives*. Boston: Beacon Press.
BURGER, P., and LUCKMANN, T. 1967. *The Social Construction of Reality*. New York: Anchor.
BURKE, J. 2000. *The Institutional Presidency*. Baltimore: Johns Hopkins University Press.
BURNS, J. 1982. *Leadership*. New York: Harper Perennial.
CAMERON, C. M. 1999. *Veto Bargaining: Presidents and the Politics of Negative Power*. New York: Cambridge University Press.

CAMPBELL, C. 1986. *Managing the Presidency: Carter, Reagan and the Search for Executive Harmony*. Pittsburgh: University of Pittsburgh Press.

CARROLL, J., FRITSCHLER, A. L., and SMITH, B. 1985. Supply Side Management in the Reagan Administration. *Public Administration Review*, 45/6: 805–14.

CONLEY, R. 2006. Reform, Reorganization, and the Renaissance of the Managerial Presidency: The Impact of 9/11 on the Executive Establishment. *Politics & Policy*, 34/2: 304–42.

COOK, B. J. 1998. Politics, Political Leadership and Public Management. *Public Administration Review*, 58/3: 225–30.

—— 2007. *Democracy and Administration: Woodrow Wilson's Ideas and the Challenges of Public Management*. Baltimore: Johns Hopkins University Press.

COOPER, P. J. 2002. *By Order of the President: The Use and Abuse of Executive Direct Action*. Lawrence: University Press of Kansas.

—— 2005. George W. Bush, Edgar Allan Poe, and the Use and Abuse of Presidential Signing Statements. *Presidential Studies Quarterly*, 35/3: 515–32.

CRONIN, T. E. 1975. Everybody Believes in Democracy until He Gets to the White House: An Examination of White House–Departmental Relations. Pp. 362–93 in *Perspectives on the Presidency*, ed. A. Wildavsky. Boston: Little, Brown.

CROSBY, B., and BRYSON, J. 2005. *Leadership for the Common Good: Tackling Public Problems in a Shared Power World*. San Francisco: Jossey-Bass.

DICKINSON, M. J., and RUDALEVIGE, A. 2004/5. Presidents, Responsiveness, and Competence: Revisiting the "Golden Age" at the Bureau of the Budget. *Political Science Quarterly*, 119: 633–54.

—— —— 2007. Institutionalizing Responsiveness: Roosevelt, Nixon and the Evolution of the Office of Management and Budget. Paper prepared for presentation at the Annual Meeting of the American Political Science Association, Chicago, IL, Aug. 30–Sept. 1, 2007.

DIMAGGIO, P. J., and POWELL, W. 1983. The Iron Cage Revisited Institutional Isomorphism and Collective Rationality in Organizational Fields. *American Sociological Review*, 48: 147–60.

DULL, M. 2006. Why PART? The Institutional Politics of Presidential Budget Reform. *Journal of Public Administration Research and Theory*, 16/2: 187–215.

DURANT, R. 1991. Fire Alarms, Garbage Cans and the Administrative Presidency. *Administration and Society*, 23/1: 94–122.

—— 1992. *The Administrative Presidency Revisited: Public Lands, the BLM, and the Reagan Revolution*. Albany: State University of New York Press.

EDWARDS, G. 2000. Building Coalitions. *Presidential Studies Quarterly*, 30/1, 47–78.

—— KESSEL, J. H., and ROCKMAN, B. A. 1992. *Researching the Presidency: Vital Questions, New Approaches*. Pittsburgh: University of Pittsburgh Press.

EISNER, M. A., and MEIER, K. 1990. Presidential Control Versus Bureaucratic Power: Explaining the Regan Revolution in Antitrust. *American Journal of Political Science*, 34/1: 269–87.

ESWARAN, M., and KOTWAL, A. 1984. The Moral Hazard of Budget Breaking. *Rand Journal of Economics*, 15: 578–81.

FELDMAN, M. 1993. Organization Theory and the Presidency. In *Researching the Presidency: Vital Questions, New Approaches*, ed. G. Edwards, J. Kessel, and B. Rockman. Pittsburgh: University of Pittsburgh Press.

FINER, H. 1941 Administrative Responsibility in Democratic Government. *Public Administration Review*, 1: 335–50. Reprinted in *Bureaucratic Power in National Politics*, ed. F. Rourke, 3rd edn. Boston: Little, Brown, 1978.

FRIEDRICH, C. 1940. Public Policy and the Nature of Administrative Responsibility. *Public Policy*, 1: 3–24. Reprinted in *Bureaucratic Power in National Politics*, ed. F. Rourke, 3rd edn. Boston: Little, Brown, 1978.

GREENSTEIN, F. 2002. The Contemporary Presidency: The Changing Leadership of George W. Bush: A Pre- and Post-9/11 Comparison. *Presidential Studies Quarterly*, 32/2: 387–96.

HECLO, H. 1975. OMB and the Presidency: The Problem of Neutral Competence. *Public Interest*, 38: 80–98.

——1977. *A Government of Strangers*. Washington, DC: Brookings Institution Press.

HEIFETZ, R. 1994. *Leadership without Easy Answers*. Cambridge, MA: Harvard University Press.

HOLMSTROM, B. 1982. Moral Hazard in Teams. *Bell Journal of Economics*, 13: 32–40.

HOWELL, W. 2003. *Power without Persuasion: The Politics of Direct Presidential Action*. Princeton, NJ: Princeton University Press.

——and LEWIS, D. 2002. Agencies by Presidential Design. *Journal of Politics*, 64/4: 1095–114.

HULT, K. 2003. The Bush White House in Comparative Perspective. Pp. 51–77 in *The George W. Bush Presidency: An Early Assessment*, ed. F. I. Greenstein. Baltimore: Johns Hopkins University Press,.

——and WALCOTT, C. 2004. *Empowering the White House: Governing under Nixon, Ford and Carter*. Lawrence: University of Kansas Press.

KAUFMAN, H. 1956. Emerging Conflicts in the Doctrines of Public Administration. *American Political Science Review*, 50: 1057–73.

KETTL, D. 1986. *Leadership at the Fed*. New Haven, CT: Yale University Press.

——(ed.) 2004. *The Department of Homeland Security's First Year: A Report Card*. New York: The Century Foundation.

——2007. *System under Stress: Homeland Security and American Politics*. Washington, DC: CQ Press.

——Forthcoming. *The Next Government of the United States*. New York: W. W. Norton.

KHADEMIAN, A. 1992. *The SEC and Capital Market Regulation: The Politics of Expertise*. Pittsburgh: University of Pittsburgh Press.

——2004. Strengthening State and Local Terrorism Response. In *The Department of Homeland Security's First Year*, ed. D. Kettl. New York: Century Foundation.

KLEIN, J. 2005. The Perils of the Permanent Campaign: Can the Public Live with an Administration that is Cutting Corners and Ignoring the Details? *Time*, Oct. 30: <http://www.time.com/time/columnist/klein/article/0,9565,1124237,00.html>.

KNOTT, J., and MILLER, G. 1987. *Reforming Bureaucracy: The Politics of Institutional Choice*. Englewood Hills, NJ: Prentice Hall.

LAWLOR, B. 2008. Department of Homeland Security: Realizing the Vision. Center for Technology, Security and Policy, Virginia Tech. Occasional Paper Series.

LEWIS, D. 2003. *Presidents and the Politics of Agency Design: Political Insulation in the United States Government Bureaucracy, 1946–1997*. Stanford, CA: Stanford University Press.

——2005. The Presidency and the Bureaucracy: Management Imperatives in a Separation of Powers System, in *The Presidency and the Political System*, ed. M. Nelson, 8th edn. Washington, DC: Brookings.

——Forthcoming. *The Politics of Presidential Appointments: Political Control and Bureaucratic Performance*. Princeton, NJ: Princeton University Press.

LIGHT, P. 1995. *Thickening Government: Federal Hierarchy and the Diffusion of Accountability*. Washington, DC: Brookings Institution Press.

——2004. Fact Sheet on the Continued Thickening of Government. The Brookings Institution 23-Jul-04 <http://www.brookings.edu/papers/2004/0723governance_light.aspx>.

LYNN, L. 2001. The Myth of the Bureaucratic Paradigm: What Traditional Public Administration Really Stood For. *Public Administration Review*, 61/2: 144–60.

MCJIMSEY, G. 2000. *The Presidency of Franklin Delano Roosevelt*. Lawrence: University Press of Kansas.

MARCH, J., and OLSEN, J. 1984. The New Institutionalism: Organizational Factors in Political Life. *American Political Science Review*, 78: 734–49.

MARTINO-GOLDEN. M. 2001. *What Motivates Bureaucrats? Politics and Administration during the Reagan Years*. New York: Columbia University Press.

MAYER, K. 2001. *With the Stroke of a Pen*. Princeton, NJ: Princeton University Press.

MEIER, K., and O'TOOLE, L., JR. 2006. *Bureaucracy in a Democratic State: A Governance Perspective*. Baltimore: Johns Hopkins University Press.

MEYER, J. W., and ROWAN, B. 1977. Institutional Organizations: Formal Structure as Myth and Ceremony, *American Journal of Sociology*, 83: 340–63.

MILLER, G. 2000. Above Politics: Credible Commitment and Efficiency in the Design of Public Agencies. *JPART* 10/2: 280–328.

MOE, R. C. 1990. Traditional Organizational Principles and the Managerial Presidency: From Phoenix to Ashes. *Public Administration Review*, 50: 129–40.

—— 2003. *Administrative Renewal: Reorganization Commissions in the 20th Century*. Lanham, MD: University Press of America.

MOE, T. M. 1985. The Politicized Presidency. In *New Directions in American Politics*, ed. J. E. Chubb and P. E. Peterson. Washington, DC: Brookings.

—— 1989. The Politics of Bureaucratic Structure. In *Can the Government Govern?*, ed. J. E. Chubb and P. E. Peterson. Washington, DC: Brookings Institution Press.

—— 1995. The Politics of Structural Choice: Toward a Theory of Public Bureaucracy. In *Organization Theory: From Chester Barnard to the Present and Beyond*, ed. O. E. Williamson. Oxford: Oxford University Press.

—— and HOWELL, W. G. 1999a. Unilateral Action and Presidential Power: A Theory, *Presidential Studies Quarterly*, 29/4: 850–72.

—— —— 1999b. The Presidential Power of Unilateral Action. *Journal of Law, Economics, and Organization*, 15/1: 132.

—— and WILSON, S. A. 1994. Presidents and Political Structure. *Law and Contemporary Problems*, 57: 1–44.

MOORE, M. 1995. *Creating Public Value: Strategic Management in Government*. Cambridge, MA: Harvard University Press.

MOSHER, F. 1968. *Democracy and the Public Service*. Oxford: Oxford University Press.

MOYNIHAN, D. 2005. Homeland Security and the U.S. Public Management Policy Agenda. *Governance*, 18/2: 171–96.

NATHAN, R. 1975. *The Plot that Failed: Nixon and the Administrative Presidency*. New York: John Wiley.

—— 1983. *The Administrative Presidency*. New York: Prentice Hall.

NEUSTADT, R. 1990. *Presidential Power and the Modern Presidents*. New York: Free Press. First published 1960.

NORTH, D. C. 1990. *Institutions, Institutional Change, and Economic Performance*. New York: Cambridge University Press.

OLSON, M. 1965. *The Logic of Collective Action: Public Goods and the Theory of Groups*. Cambridge, MA: Harvard University Press.

—— 1982. *The Rise and Decline of Nations: Economic Growth, Stagflation, and Social Rigidities*. New Haven, CT: Yale University Press.

ORNSTEIN, N., and MANN, T. (eds.) 2000. *The Permanent Campaign and its Future*, Washington, DC: American Enterprise Institute.

OSTROM, E. 1990. *Governing the Commons: The Evolution of Institutions for Collective Action*. Cambridge: Cambridge University Press.

PALUDAN, P. S. 1994. *The Presidency of Abraham Lincoln*. Lawrence: University Press of Kansas.

PFIFFNER, J. (ed.) 1991. *The Managerial Presidency*. Pacific Grove, CA: Brooks/Cole Publishing Company.

—— (ed.) 2007. The Institutionalist: A Conversation with Hugh Heclo. *Public Administration Review*, 67/3: 418–23.

PONDY, L., BOHLAND, R., and THOMAS, H. 1988. *Managing Ambiguity and Change*. New York: Wiley.

RAUCH, J. 1994. *Demosclerosis: The Silent Killer of American Government*. New York: Time Books.

ROBERTS, A. 1997. Performance Based Organizations: Assessing the Gore Plan. *Public Administration Review*, 57/6: 465–78.

ROURKE, F. 1984. *Bureaucracy, Politics, and Public Policy*, 3rd edn. Boston: Little, Brown.

—— 1992. Responsiveness and Neutral Competence in American Bureaucracy, *Public Administration Review*, 52/6: 539–46.

RUDALEVIGE, A. 2002. *Managing the President's Program: Centralization and Legislative Policy Formulation, 1949–1996*. Princeton, NJ: Princeton University Press.

SAYRE, W. 1951. Trends of a Decade in Administrative Values. *Public Administration Review*, 11/1: 1–9.

—— 1958. Premises of Public Administration: Past and Emerging. *Public Administration Review*, 18/2: 102–5.

SCHMIDT, D. 1995. The Presidential Appointment Process, Task Environment Pressures, and Regional Office Case Processing. *Political Research Quarterly*, 48/2: 381–401.

SCHNEIDER, A., and INGRAM, H. 1993. Social Construction of Target Populations: Implications for Politics and Policy. *American Political Science Review*, 87/2: 334–47.

SEIDMAN, H. 1986. *Politics, Position and Power: The Dynamics of Federal Organization*, 4th edn. New York: Oxford University Press.

SELZNICK, P. 1957. *Leadership and Administration: A Sociological Interpretation*. Evanston, IL: Row, Peterson.

SHAPIRO, S. 2007. An Evaluation of the Bush Administration Reforms to the Regulatory Process. *Presidential Studies Quarterly*, 37/2: 270–90.

SMIRCICH, L., and MORGAN, G. 1982. Leadership: The Management of Meaning. *Journal of Applied Behavioral Science*, 18/3: 257–73.

STEHR, S. 1997. Top Bureaucrats and the Distribution of Influence in Reagan's Executive Branch. *Public Administration Review*, 57/1: 75–83.

SYLVES, R. 2006. President Bush and Hurricane Katrina: A Presidential Leadership Study. *Annals of the American Academy*, 604: 26–56.

TERRY, L. 1995. *Leadership of Public Bureaucracies: The Administrator as Conservator*. Thousand Oaks, CA: Sage.

—— 1998. Administrative Leadership, Neo-managerialism, and the Public Management Movement. *Public Administration Review*, 58/3: 194–200.

THOMPSON, J. 1967. *Organizations in Action*. New York: McGraw-Hill.

—— 2000. Reinvention as Reform: Assessing the National Performance Review. *Public Administration Review*, 60/6: 508–21.

TIERNEY, K., BEVC, C., and KULIGOWSKI, E. 2006. Metaphors Matter: Disaster Myths, Media Frames, and their Consequences in Hurricane Katrina. *Annals of the American Academy*, 604: 57–81.

TROTTIER, T., VAN WART, M., and WANG, X. 2008. Examining the Nature and Significance of Leadership in Government Organizations. *Public Administration Review*, 68/2: 320–33.

VAN WART, M. 2003. Public Sector Leadership Theory: An Assessment. *Public Administration Review*, 63/2: 214–28.

WALCOTT, C., and HULT, K. 2005. White House Structure and Decision Making: Elaborating the Standard Model. *Presidential Studies Quarterly*, 35/2: 303–18.

WALDO, D. 1984. *The Administrative State*, 2nd edn. New York: Holmes & Meier.

WALKER, L. 1989. Woodrow Wilson, Progressive Reform, and Public Administration. *Political Science Quarterly*, 104/3: 509–25.

WARBER, A. L. 2006. *Executive Orders and the Modern Presidency: Legislating from the Oval Office*. Boulder, CO: Lynne Rienner.

WATERMAN, R. 1989. *Presidential Influence and the Administrative State*. Knoxville: University of Tennessee Press.

WEKO, T. J. 1995. *The Politicizing Presidency: The White House Personnel Office*. Lawrence: University Press of Kansas.

WEST, W. 2005. Neutral Competence and Political Responsiveness: An Uneasy Relationship. *Policy Studies Journal*, 33/2: 131–48.

WHITFORD, A. 2002. Decentralization and Political Control of the Bureaucracy. *Journal of Theoretical Politics*, 14/2: 167–93.

WOOD, B. D., and WATERMAN, R. W. 1991. The Dynamics of Political Control of the Bureaucracy. *American Political Science Review*, 85/3: 801–28.

PART IX

JUDICIAL RELATIONS

CHAPTER 27

....

NOMINATING FEDERAL JUDGES AND JUSTICES

....

LEE EPSTEIN
JEFFREY A. SEGAL

WITHOUT a doubt, presidents have strong incentives to concern themselves with appointments to the federal bench. Some have used them to shore up electoral support for their party or themselves, such as Ronald Reagan's nomination of the first female justice, Sandra Day O'Connor. For other presidents—perhaps the majority—policy or ideological goals move to the fore. Abe Fortas, Lyndon Johnson's first appointment to the Court, may have been a long-time friend of the president's, but Fortas also was a New Deal liberal who shared Johnson's views on problems of race, poverty, and governmental actions to remedy them.

Equally without doubt is that in an unconstrained world, all the president's appointments to the federal courts would perfectly reflect his partisan or ideological (or even occasionally personal) goals. The president is not so unfettered, however (e.g., Moraski and Shipan 1999; Nemacheck 2007). While the Framers of the Constitution expected the new nation's chief executive to play a crucial role in naming federal judges—they did, after all, list the power of appointment in Article II, that is, among the president's powers—those same Framers gave the Senate an equally

We thank the National Science Foundation and the Northwestern University School of Law Beatrice Kuhn Research Fund for supporting our research on the federal courts. We adapt some of the material in this chapter from our book *Advice and Consent: The Politics of Judicial Appointments* (Oxford University Press, 2005).

crucial role: the power to "consent" to the president's choices. Because it is the Senate, not the president, which has the final say on nominees, that body can impose an effective restraint on presidents' choices even if it does not completely control the selection of those candidates (see, e.g. Epstein et al. 2006; Cameron, Cover, and Segal 1990; Segal, Cameron, and Cover 1992).

In short, the president surely has objectives he would like to accomplish via appointments to the bench. But to achieve them he must act strategically, attending to the preferences and likely actions of the Senate, as well as certain norms senators expect him to follow. If he does not, he runs the risk of seeing his candidates defeated, in which case he cannot accomplish his objectives, whatever they might be.

Both parts of this claim—the president's goals and the constraints he confronts in attempting to achieve them—deserve some consideration. In what follows, we make use of the large extant literature to explore what we know and, importantly, what we do not know about both. We also consider what scholars have said about whether presidents ultimately achieve their goals; that is, we consider the question of whether presidents get what they want in their judicial appointments.

PRESIDENTIAL GOALS

Well before the departures of Chief Justice Rehnquist and Sandra Day O'Connor from the US Supreme Court, the George W. Bush administration was hard at work compiling a list of replacements. Possible candidates were mostly sitting judges—including the two Bush eventually appointed, Roberts and Alito, and several he did not, such as Michael Luttig and Edith Clement (Toobin 2007; Greenburg 2007).

If Bush's predecessors are any indication, a range of actors contributed to his list. Certainly some, perhaps the vast majority, came from inside the executive branch—perhaps even from the president himself. Bill Clinton actively engaged in the process of generating candidates for the appointments that eventually went to Ginsburg and Breyer, as did Lyndon Johnson and Richard Nixon before him. By all indications, President G. W. Bush was no different (Goldman et al. 2007; Greenburg 2007).

Beyond the president and his advisers, trusted senators, party leaders, and organized interests too play a role in recommending candidates. During the second Bush presidency no group was more involved than the Federalist Society, an organization devoted to counterbalancing what it decries as the "orthodox liberal" ideology that "dominates" the legal community. Of the George W. Bush administration's first seventy nominees to the lower courts, twenty were "recommended directly" by this organization (Lewis, 2001). What is not clear, though, is whether the Society's recommendations had an independent impact on the president's selections, or whether it was was simply putting forward the same names that inevitably would have appeared on the president's list. More generally, the influence of organized interests at this stage in the process is a rather unexplored area, deserving of far more scholarly attention.

In addition to groups, advisers, and party leaders, perhaps sitting justices or judges lobbied (or consulted with) the Bush administration. If so, this would not be without precedent. In the 1850s, the entire Supreme Court asked President Franklin Pierce to appoint John Campbell to the bench (Abraham 1999, 84). Over a century later, as John Dean (2001) tells it, Chief Justice Warren Burger (1969–86) "constantly supplied [the administration] with names" for "his" court. When Richard Nixon attempted to fill two vacancies in 1971, Burger suggested Hershel Friday, an Arkansas attorney who had a connection to Justice Harry Blackmun, a childhood friend of Burger's. At the same time, Burger lobbied against the appointment of a woman—so much so that Nixon's Attorney General, John Mitchell, dreaded telling Burger that Mildred Lillie, a California state judge, was on the president's list. Though Nixon did not appoint Lillie, neither did he nominate Burger's candidate, Friday. In fact, according to Dean, only Nixon and Mitchell knew that William H. Rehnquist would get the nod. All other advisers were kept out of the loop until the last possible moment.

But why choose Rehnquist, and not Friday, Lillie, or any of the other dozen or more prospective nominees Nixon considered? More generally, why do certain names and not others make initial lists, why will some candidates advance in the process to an even shorter list, and why will one ultimately rise above the pack?

According to Nemacheck (2007), Goldman (1997), and others who have addressed this question, the answer lies at least in part with the administration's goals. Undoubtedly, judicial appointments can work to accomplish many aims, but, as we hinted at the outset, almost all fall under the rubric of politics. In some instances, politics has centered largely on partisan aims, with the idea being that the president attempts to exploit judicial appointments to advance his party's interests or his own; in other cases, politics has been primarily about policy, or the notion that the president seeks to nominate judges and justices who share his political or ideological preferences.

Partisan and Electoral Goals

It seems odd to think that judicial appointments could help advance the president's and his party's ambitions, electoral or otherwise. After all, most Americans lack even a passing familiarity with courts and judges; in 2007 they could not, for example, name the Chief Justice even though he was appointed just two years earlier. Even more to the point, when asked before the 2004 presidential election, "What issue or problem... is most important for the next president to address?" fewer than 0.5 percent said "The Supreme Court."[1] Of the lower courts, the North Carolina senator

[1] Health Care Agenda for the New Congress Survey, Nov. 2004, accessed via Roper Center for Public Opinion Research, University of Connecticut.

Jesse Helms said it best: "You go out on the street of Raleigh, N.C., and ask 100 people, 'Do you give a damn who is on the Fourth Circuit Court of Appeals?' They'll say, 'What's that?' " (Sontag 2003).

On the other hand, when judges or their decisions attract media attention, Americans are not only aware of the controversy but also may have strong opinions that they occasionally express in their ballots. The storm over George H. W. Bush's nomination of Clarence Thomas in 1991 provides a case in point. As Overby et al. (1992) demonstrate, after initial public opinion polls indicated that blacks over-whelmingly believed Thomas when he said he had not sexually harassed Anita Hill, several senators from states with large minority populations voted to confirm Thomas.

But some may have paid a price. Wyche Fowler of Georgia, for one, was defeated at least in part because pro-choice white women were unhappy with his support for the anti-*Roe* Thomas. Similarly, the Republican Arlen Specter (Pennsylvania) nearly lost his reelection bid, receiving only 49.1 percent of the vote in 1992, compared with 56.4 percent in his previous election in 1986. More generally, researchers tell us that across the United States, voters who disapproved of Thomas were 14 percent more likely to vote for the challenger than the incumbent. On the other hand, voters who disapproved of Thomas were 18.6 percent more likely to vote for their senator if she or he failed to back Thomas (see Overby et al. 1992; Wolpert and Gimpel 1997). Whether reelection bids are helped or hurt by less controversial votes, though, has not been well established, and so is yet another area that would benefit from greater attention.

The link between judicial nominations and the president's achievement of partisan goals also may be less direct and can play out in a multitude of ways. In making his appointments to the lower courts, Franklin D. Roosevelt often contemplated how they might help shore up approval for his policies among Democrats within the Senate (Goldman 1997, 41). The Eisenhower and Kennedy administrations used their appointment power somewhat differently. They tried to strengthen their respective parties, with both Ike and JFK occasionally supporting candidates proposed by competitors within their party.

Other presidents have placed a great deal of weight on geography at least in part to advance their or their party's electoral objectives. Richard Nixon was nearly obsessed with making appointments that would help his 1972 reelection bid, and in particular, with enhancing the Republican Party's appeal to Southerners by appointing a justice from that region. And Nixon was surely not the first, as Daniels (1978) and Freund (1988) have shown. Hoover's failed nomination of John Parker of North Carolina, for example, was also perceived by Progressives and liberal Democrats as a Republican Southern Strategy.

Religion too was once part of an electoral calculus—such as when Dwight Eisen-hower appointed the Catholic William J. Brennan Jr. (1946–90) to the Court to attract Catholic voters. That two Jewish and five Catholic (Alito, Kennedy, Roberts, Scalia, and Thomas) justices now sit on the Court, however, is telling. While the new Catholic majority on the Court has come under some scrutiny (see, e.g. Gerhardt

2006), as a general matter religion (and region) has taken a back seat to race, sex, and ethnicity as vehicles for furthering partisan goals. Though presidents serving in the 1950s and 1960s contemplated some of these factors, it was Jimmy Carter who emphasized them. When Carter took office, only eight women had ever served on a federal court. Owing almost exclusively to the 144 new judgeships created by the Democratic legislature during his tenure, Carter was able to appoint 40 women to the nation's trial (29) and appellate (11) courts. He also appointed 37 black judges—nearly double the number of all his predecessors combined. To some, Carter's commitment to diversifying the federal bench reflected a genuine concern on his part about human rights (Clark 2003). That may be true, but surely he believed that appointing women and blacks would do little to damage his standing with crucial Democratic constituencies.

In other cases, presidents have used the power of appointment to pay off prior political debts. In 1952 Earl Warren, then the governor of California, saw that his chances for obtaining the Republican presidential nomination were faltering, and so he threw his and his state's support to General Eisenhower rather than Eisenhower's rival, senator Robert Taft of Ohio. One year later, Eisenhower nominated Governor Warren to replace Chief Justice Fred Vinson.

This much we know from the many detailed accounts and case studies of particular nominations. What we lack is more systematically developed and more generalized knowledge. For example, we know that in specific cases—most notably, Thomas—the president or his party can lose support over judicial nominees. But how typical is this? This seems an especially important question to raise because, at least in the case of Thomas, the appointment was probably something of an anomaly. Owing primarily to charges of sexual harassment, it was a highly visible confirmation battle for a seat on the nation's most visible tribunal, the US Supreme Court.

Likewise, can the president or his party actually score points via appointments? Certainly, many presidents (and commentators) seem to believe they can. Nixon's emphasis on the South, Ronald Reagan's commitment to appoint a woman to the Supreme Court, and Carter's attempt to diversify the bench provide obvious examples. The question we raise, and that we hope future scholars will address, is whether this is a rational strategy. That is, if presidents pursue it, do they succeed in building capital with crucial constituencies? This seems an especially important question to raise at a moment when the next president likely will be tempted to appoint Hispanics to the bench, but especially to the Supreme Court, on which no Hispanic has ever served.

Ideological Goals

Despite our lack of general knowledge about the efficacy of attempts to advance electoral or partisan goals through appointments, we know it is fairly common. But it is not the only political force at work; actually, according to many scholars, candidates' ideologies or policy values may be even more important (e.g., Epstein and Segal 2005; Moraski and Shipan 1999; Nemacheck 2007).

If so, this is hardly a new motivation. Thomas Jefferson hoped to rid the judiciary of judges attached to a "Federalist" philosophy—in other words, virtually every jurist appointed by his predecessors, George Washington and John Adams. Richard Nixon may have talked about appointing strict constructionists to the bench, but what he meant were judges who would "not be favorably inclined toward claims of either criminal defendants or civil rights plaintiffs" (quoted in Dean 2001, 16). President George W. Bush was even more transparent, publicly equating ideology with particular approaches to constitutional interpretation. As he said at the first presidential debate in October 2000, "I don't believe in liberal, activist judges. I believe in strict constructionists. And those are the kind of judges I will appoint."

As many commentators have noted, the manifestations of this emphasis on ideology are easy enough to spot. At least since 1869, only 10 percent of all appointments to the federal bench have fallen outside the president's own political party (a rough indicator of ideology), and when cross-party appointments do occur they may well go to an ideological soul mate, such as when Nixon appointed the conservative Democrat Lewis Powell (see generally Barrow, Zuk, and Gryski, 1996). Bush II was no exception. Of his 252 appointments to the district and appellate courts (through 2006), 86 percent went to Republicans, and almost all of those proposed as possible contenders for a seat on the Supreme Court had a noticeable connection to the Republican Party (Goldman et al. 2007).

By the same token, the majority of appointments to the federal courts have engaged in what Goldman (1997) calls "past party activism"—in other words, activities designed to advance their party's interest, such as campaigning, organizing, or fund raising. Goldman's data run back to the Roosevelt years but equally high—or even higher—levels might have existed in earlier years as well. Ulysses S. Grant may himself have been "bored" by politics, but his advisers made clear to the president that he "needed to pack the [Supreme] Court with Republican loyalists." As a result, Grant "resolved at the outset that a safe Republican record would be a basic requirement for nomination, to which he added geographic suitability." "Other qualifications," Henry Abraham reports, "appeared not to matter" (Abraham 1999, 95).

Why does such a high fraction of judicial seats go to activists? One answer is that service to prominent party members may be precisely why the candidate came to the administration's attention. Perhaps more importantly, though, service may reveal something about the candidate's ideological commitments. This is obviously crucial to presidents hoping to advance their agendas through the courts. Only by "minimizing uncertainty" over a candidate's sincere policy preferences can the president hope to realize such goals (Nemacheck 2007).

Along these lines, service to the party may help. But because partisanship does not always neatly translate into ideological compatibility, presidents and their advisers resort to other methods to learn about and thus reduce uncertainty over a candidate's preferences. The "litmus tests" employed during the Reagan years are legendary. But ideological screening pre-dates that administration and, of course, has hardly been limited to conservatives. Skirmishes with anti-New Deal judges and justices prompted FDR to seek out nominees who shared his policy visions. Knowing that, those proposing names for FDR's consideration were unhesitant to stress their candidates' commitments to "liberalism" and "progressive" causes. "Active opponents of the New Deal," Goldman (1997, 33) writes, "were not seriously considered." And if a doubt existed, the Roosevelt administration scrutinized a candidate's background, in much the same way as successor administrations now do. Clearly, the goal here was precisely the same as it was during the Reagan years. FDR wanted to avoid "mistakes"—judges and justices who did not share his political vision.

The types of screening mechanisms used today—interviews, questionnaires, and analyses of the written record—are rather obvious manifestations of the president's interest in appointing judges and justices with the "right" values. But there are also the markers of age, race, and gender. Beginning with age, presidents dating back to the earliest days of the Republic have valued relative youth. John Jay was only 43 when George Washington nominated him to serve as the first Chief Justice of the United States. President John Adams's initial appointee, Bushrod Washington, was just 36. One hundred and fifty years later, Eisenhower named the 43-year-old Potter Stewart to the Supreme Court, and in 1962, Kennedy appointed Byron White, who at 44 was just a month younger than the president himself. Some commentators say the emphasis on youth reflects the president's interest in creating a legacy. That begs the question of what kind of legacy, however. In many instances the answer is an ideological one. When Franklin Roosevelt appointed his securities and exchange commissioner, the 40-year-old William O. Douglas, to the Supreme Court, the president knew precisely what he was doing. Roosevelt was attempting to establish allegiance to his economic policies for decades to come.

Race and gender too may be political markers. It seems unlikely that it was merely electoral concerns that drove Jimmy Carter (and Bill Clinton) to place emphasis on appointing blacks and women to the bench. Rather, they may have assumed that blacks and women would be liberal jurists.

Given the attention to learning about candidates' preferences through screening processes, how well does it work? Do some markers work better than others? Are race and gender as effective ideological screening? Overall, do presidents succeed in appointing judges and justices who share their ideological commitments and work to advance their policy goals? As we explain at the end of this chapter, scholars have generally answered both in the affirmative, though a few qualifications are in order. First, because most of the work along these lines has focused on the Supreme Court, we know far less about the lower courts. More research is needed before we can reach any firm conclusions. Second, even studies on the Supreme Court are now beginning to question the longevity of presidential legacies (see, e.g., Epstein et al. 2007). While it seems clear that presidents typically are successful in appointing justices who share their ideological commitments in the short term, by the end of their justices' first decades in service, the picture is far murkier.

CONSTRAINTS ON THE PRESIDENT

Based on our discussion of ideological goals, it would seem that presidents should simply locate the closest ideological surrogate and nominate him or her for a position on the bench. But even if they could do this with certainty, it is not always the most rational move. As we mentioned at the outset, the problem is that the president is hardly an unconstrained actor. Rather, in making nominations he must take into account the preferences and likely actions of senators, along with various rules that structure their interaction.

When it comes to the lower courts, the vast majority of nominees (about four out of every five) are rather handily confirmed by the Senate—at least in part because presidents have adhered to norms within the Senate (see generally Gerhardt 2001, 2003). Most of these are intended to ensure that senators from the state where the nominee will serve and who belong to the president's party (i.e., home-state senators) have some role in filling vacancies on the lower federal bench (but especially in the district courts, which do not cross state lines). We think here of the norm of senatorial courtesy. Operative since the days of the Washington administration, courtesy holds that home-state senators of the president's party can block a nomination without supplying a reason. Should a home-state senator invoke courtesy, the nomination is usually doomed. Typically, senators invoke courtesy through "blue slips," which are sheets of light blue paper that the Senate's Committee on the Judiciary sends to the home-state senators, regardless of their party affiliation. The home-state senators, in turn, decide whether to support the nomination. If one or both of the home-state senators withhold their blue slips or otherwise object to the nomination, it is up to the Judiciary Committee's chair to decide whether to go forward with the nomination.

The factors that lead to a chair's interpretation of senatorial courtesy are not well known, but that interpretation has great consequences for nominations to the lower federal courts. This is not true, though, for Supreme Court nominations. When region exerted a greater influence on the selection of justices, home-state senators did occasionally attempt to block such nominations, but these days courtesy and blue-slipping are not in much evidence over candidates to the Supreme Court. Unlike district court nominees, senators, though free to submit Supreme Court names to the administration, have little expectation of seeing their favored candidate get the nod.

On the other hand, presidents can hardly ignore the Senate when contemplating Supreme Court nominations. Because senators have shown their willingness to reject candidates for the high court, failure to attend to them at the nomination stage can be perilous. What this means in practice, as many scholars have outlined it, is that presidents must pay heed to the fact that electorally oriented senators vote on the basis of their constituents' "principle concerns in the nomination process" (Cameron, Cover, and Segal 1990, 528; see also Watson and Stookey 1995; Segal,

Cameron, and Cover 1992). Those concerns primarily (though not exclusively) center on whether a candidate for the Supreme Court is (1) qualified for office, and (2) sufficiently proximate to the senator (and his or her constituents) in ideological space. Because these are the concerns of senators who can stand in the way of a successful appointment, they too must become the concern of presidents.

Qualifications

Beginning with qualifications, it is certainly true that presidents have nominated unqualified, even unsavory people to serve as federal judges. We think here of G. Harrold Carswell, a little-known federal judge from Florida whom Richard Nixon (unsuccessfully) sought to place on the US Supreme Court. Carswell's record on the bench was so deficient—he was reversed far more frequently than any other judge in his circuit—that even his supporters had a hard time justifying confirmation. About the best they could muster was the infamous defense uttered by senator Roman Hruska (R-Neb.): "Even if [Carswell] is mediocre, there are a lot of mediocre judges and people and lawyers. They are entitled to a little representation, aren't they?" (quoted in Harris 1971, 110).

Yet, and despite the lack of formal criteria outlined in the US Constitution, most presidents have sought to appoint persons of professional merit to the bench. One reason is that they themselves may prefer highly qualified candidates. If the president is concerned with leaving a lasting legacy to the nation in the form of jurists who will continue to exert influence on the law well after he leaves office, then professional merit may come into play. While this entire subject deserves more systematic inquiry, it does seem that many judges universally acclaimed as great by contemporary legal scholars were also universally perceived as exceedingly well qualified at the time of their nomination. Falling into this category are Supreme Court Justices Oliver Wendell Holmes (1902–32), Benjamin Cardozo (1932–8), William J. Brennan (1956–90), and more recently Antonin Scalia (1986–), and the circuit court judge Richard Posner (1981–). In some instances, as we explain later, the appointing presidents would have been pleased with the legacy they left (for example, Ronald Reagan and Scalia). In others, their displeasure is a matter of public record (Dwight Eisenhower thought Brennan a "mistake"). Either way, though, it is hard to deny the effect that outstanding jurists have had on the course of American legal history, an effect that transcends their appointing president.

There is another reason—one that directly implicates the Senate. As we have noted throughout, the president cannot achieve any of his goals—whether focused on advancing his partisan or policy interests—unless the Senate confirms his candidates. And senators, as systematic research indicates, are more likely to support candidates they perceive as qualified for office (see, e.g. Epstein et al. 2006; Cameron, Cover, and Segal 1990; Segal, Cameron, and Cover 1992). This was true during the nation's earliest days and it remains so even today, an era in which many commentators claim that professional merit is immaterial to the Senate's deliberations and that only the candidate's ideology (relative to senators') matters (e.g., Choi and Gulati 2004).

Ideology

Still, we cannot ignore ideology. While there is no doubt that professional merit acts as a constraint on the president, it now takes a back seat to ideology (Epstein et al. 2006). Just as the president hopes to make appointments that reflect his ideology, so too do senators. And their votes reflect that objective. According to Epstein, Segal, and Westerland (2008), the predicted probability of a senator voting for a moderately qualified candidate is a highly unlikely 0.06 when the candidate and senator are ideological extremes; that figure increases to highly likely 0.91 when they are at the closest levels.

The suggestion here is obvious: When the president's and senators' political preferences overlap, the president is far freer to select a nominee of his own choosing (Nemacheck 2007; Moraski and Shipan 1999). In those circumstances, the administration's primary task becomes one of selecting the closest surrogate from among the pool of qualified nominees.

On the other hand, when the president and Senate are ideologically distant, the president is far more constrained. Moraski and Shipan (1999) argue that in order to see his candidates confirmed, he must modulate, moving to the right or left as necessary (also see Nemacheck 2007). Ford's nomination of the moderate John Paul Stevens rather than the conservative Robert Bork in light of an overwhelmingly Democratic Senate is a prime example of this kind of presidential pragmatism. The Senate responded in kind, voting 98–0 to confirm Stevens. Of course, not all "compromise" candidates receive unanimous votes, but the inclination of most (though certainly not all) presidents to move toward the Senate may well explain why the rejection rate of Supreme Court nominees is not higher than it is.

This much we know. But many questions about the role of ideology remain. First, while scholars have demonstrated that senators began to place more emphasis on ideology in the late 1950s and then even more (though no less on qualifications) during and after Robert Bork's nomination, we are not sure why. Bork (1990, 348) himself lays the blame—or credit, depending on one's perspective—on the Court and, in particular, its "increasingly political nature … which reached its zenith with the Warren Court." If Bork's explanation is right, it suggests that the emphasis placed by appointers on ideology is entirely rational—a point to which we return in the final section of the chapter.

A second set of questions centers on issues of measurement. Examining the effect of senators' ideologies on the president's decisions requires valid and reliable measures of the political preferences of the president, his nominee, and the senators—not to mention a method for comparing them. Commentators have developed many possible approaches (see, e.g., Epstein et al. 2006; Bailey 2007) but each has its own set of problems. To assess the ideological distance between the nominee and the senator, Epstein et al. (2006), for example, use as their "bridge" candidates nominated by presidents whose party held a majority in the Senate at the time of nomination. The assumption here is that presidents whose party controls the Senate face relatively fewer constraints in nominating a candidate who reflects their ideological preferences than do presidents whose party does not control the Senate. While this enjoys some support in the literature, it is obviously imperfect.

These measurement differences, not surprisingly, can influence substantive interpretations. Thus Bailey and Chang (2001), who more carefully measure interinstitutional preferences measures than Moraski and Shipan (1991), find far less robust results on the influence of congressional preferences on presidential nominations.

Overcoming the Constraints

Yet another set of questions are more general in nature: Short of appeasing senators—whether by taking into account their recommendation or their political preferences—what might a president do to work around the constraints he confronts? What strategies does he have at his disposal to see his nominees confirmed? While these questions deserve far more systematic attention from scholars, we can speculate on a few possible answers.

One, as Johnson and Roberts (2004) note, is to "go public," that is, to convince Americans that his candidate is very well suited for the position and that only the partisan, ideological Senate can stand in the way. Following in the footsteps of many of his predecessors, George W. Bush attempted a form of this strategy. Throughout 2004 and into 2005, he accused Senate Democrats of "using unprecedented obstructionists tactics" to block his nominees, while simultaneously attempting to appear "above politics": "Every judicial nominee should receive an up-or-down vote in the full Senate, no matter who is President or which party controls the Senate." "It is time," Bush says, "to move past the partisan politics of the past, and do what is right for the American legal system and the American people."[2]

Sticking by his nominees turned out to be a good strategy for Bush but it is an indirect approach at best. By playing to the public, Bush was lobbying citizens to contact their senators. Other presidents (and Bush as well) have attacked the problem more directly, by seeking to cut deals with legislators or, more dramatically, by maneuvering around the Senate altogether. Bill Clinton took the former route in his quest to appoint his (and Hillary Rodham Clinton's) former classmate at Yale Law School and co-chair of his California election committee, William Fletcher, to the Ninth Circuit. Hoping to change the ideological composition of the left-of-center Ninth, Senate Republicans balked at the appointment of the liberal Fletcher. They agreed to proceed only if Fletcher's mother, the also-liberal Judge Betty Fletcher, vacated her seat on the Ninth and if the president appointed a candidate

---

[2] Quote available at: <www.whitehouse.gov/infocus/judicial nominees>.

suggested by Republican senator Slade Gorton to replace her. The "throw Momma from the bench" strategy eventually worked. Clinton was able to appoint his friend William Fletcher, but only by appointing a Republican to fill the other seat (Wilson 2003).

This sort of bargaining seems to be a regular feature of the appointments game. More unusual, but hardly unknown, are attempts to work around the Senate entirely. Ulysses Grant's Attorney General, Ebenezer Hoar, in an effort to create a more professional judiciary, tried to evade senatorial courtesy by refusing to give home-state senators a say in nominations. Jimmy Carter, in his quest to diversify the bench, also tried to eliminate senatorial courtesy, this time by establishing merit commissions for the selection of appellate court judges. A decade or so later, George H. W. Bush, in retaliation for the Senate Judiciary Committee's leak to the press of Anita Hill's affidavit to the Justice Department accusing Clarence Thomas of sexual harassment, said he would restrict senators' access to FBI reports (Gerhardt 2003).

These efforts were not terribly successful: senators retaliated against Grant and refused to confirm Ebenezer Hoar for a position on the Supreme Court. Carter too generated his own share of problems. He may have succeeded in diversifying the bench, but his approach led to "embarrassment and splintering in his own party," and the merit commissions he established were eventually abolished. As for Bush, when the Judiciary Committee, no longer privy to the FBI reports, decided to delay Bush's appointments until it could conduct its own investigations, the administration changed its policy. But it was too late. As Gerhardt (2003) explains, "The delay was fatal to over two dozen subsequent judicial nominees, because the nominees' earliest opportunities for hearings would not have been until 1992 at which point the Senate slowed the process to a complete standstill pending the outcome of the presidential election." More generally, while it is true that presidents are free to nominate whomever they like to the federal courts in pursuit of whatever goals move them, the Senate can attempt to curtail that freedom—whether through senatorial courtesy, forced bargains, or nay votes.

Do Presidents Get What they Want?

Failure to pay heed to the Senate can, of course, result in the president's least favored alternative: the rejection of his nominee. But assuming confirmation in the Senate, to what extent can the president achieve success once his nominees take their seats on the federal bench? If we define success in terms of the typical goal of presidents—to appoint ideological surrogates to the bench, that is, judges who will etch into law their president's political values—then many presidents would complain. Actually, they are notorious whiners about their judicial appointees, especially to the US Supreme

Court. No discussion of presidential influence over federal justices is complete without Theodore Roosevelt's quip that he could "carve out of a banana a Judge with more backbone" than Oliver Wendell Holmes (1902–32), or Truman's claim that Justice Tom Clark (1949–67) was "my biggest mistake." Eisenhower too purportedly labeled his appointment of the liberal Earl Warren "the biggest damn fool mistake I ever made," and apparently thought much the same of the equally liberal William J. Brennan Jr. (1956–90). Likewise, we cannot imagine that Richard Nixon was pleased with the leftward turn of his once-conservative appointee Harry Blackmun (1970–94) any more than George H. W. Bush probably appreciates the liberal trend of David Souter's (1990–) decisions.

Thus, prominent political scientist Henry Abraham declares, "there is a considerable element of unpredictability in the judicial appointing process" (cited in Epstein and Segal 2005, 120). Constitutional scholar Laurence Tribe (1985, 60), on the other hand, refers to the "myth of the surprised president." By this he means, "in areas of particular and known concern to a President, Justices have been loyal to the ideals and perspectives of the men who have nominated them."

Who has the better case? As it turns out, generally, Tribe does. At least at the level of the Supreme Court and at least in the short term, systematic research demonstrates that presidents can influence the law via their appointments (e.g., Segal, Timpone, and Howard 2000; Epstein and Segal 2005). We should not be entirely surprised by this finding. If presidents were unable to entrench their political values on the Court through their justices, attention to the ideology of nominees would be entirely irrational—they would be better off using appointments to pursue partisan-electoral goals. But that is not the case. At least for their first decade or so in office, justices carry their president's ideological commitments into their decisions, and that trend may be on the rise, as Figure 27.1 shows. There we plot the results of regression analyses comparing the justices' ideology ("ideal points") based on their voting patterns in their first and tenth terms with the ideology (or "ideal point") of their appointing president.[3] The closer a justice is to the line, the better his president's ideology corresponds to the justice's first-term (top panel) or tenth-term (bottom panel) ideal point estimate. Justices above the line are more conservative than we would expect based on the ideology of their appointing president; justices below it are more liberal. For justices on the line, their president's most preferred position perfectly (or nearly so) predicts their own.

Assuming that most presidents hope to identify nominees as close as possible to their own ideology and make their ultimate selection "after a careful and highly ideological search" (Strauss 2007) we would expect them to succeed—and, as Figure 27.1 shows, they typically do. Of course, there are some deviations. Based on

---

[3] We measure the justices' ideology via Andrew D. Martin and Kevin Quinn's (2002) term-by-term ideal point estimates (updated scores are available at: <http://mqscores.wustl.edu/measures.php>). Martin and Quinn derive them by analyzing the votes cast by the justices via a Bayesian modeling strategy. To determine the president's ideology, we rely on Keith Poole's Common Space scores (available at: <http://voteview.org/dwnl.htm>), which in turn assess ideology by analyzing the president's positions over bills before Congress.

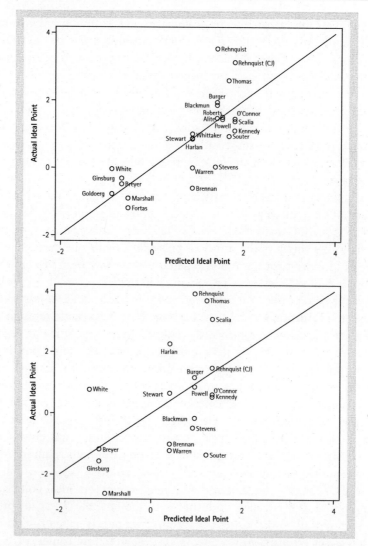

Figure 27.1 Actual ideology during a justice's first and tenth terms plotted against predicted ideology (based on the ideology of the appointing president)

Note: The superimposed lines are where X = Y. The closer a circle is to the line, the better the prediction.

these data, it is no wonder that President Eisenhower deemed Brennan a "mistake." Then again, if Eisenhower appointed Brennan for electoral, rather than ideological, reasons—to court the Catholic vote—perhaps we should not be surprised by the lack of concordance between Eisenhower's political views and Warren's votes.

On the other hand—and this is the key point—"mistakes," regardless of why they occur, are few and far between. By and large, presidents are successful with their appointees. Take George W. Bush's two nominees, Chief Justice Roberts and Justice Alito. If we were to use Bush's ideology to predict their voting patterns during their first terms on the Court, we would be nearly right on the money for both (for Alito, the prediction is 1.53; his actual ideal point estimate is 1.45. For Roberts, the prediction is 1.53; the actual value is 1.51). Also, note that even justices famous for eventually making significant moves to the right or left tended to reflect their president's ideology commitments in their first term. Justice Souter provides a case in point. Based on the ideology of Souter's appointing president, George H. W. Bush, we would have expected a moderately conservative justice, and that is what we observe in Souter's initial term.

Because many presidents have been sufficiently ideologically close to the confirming Senate to nominate nearly whomever they want, and many have actively sought to appoint justices who share their political outlook, Figure 27.1 is not particularly startling. But it is nonetheless suggestive. Politics in part pervades the appointments process because the outcomes of that process—justices on the Supreme Court—are themselves political, and predictably political. More often than not, they vote in ways that would very much please the presidents who appointed them.

But what about the circuit courts? When the president makes an appointment from a state in which one or both senators belong to the president's party—meaning that senatorial courtesy may be in effect—the relationship between presidential ideology and the judges' voting is not particularly strong. Actually, for these appointments, it is impossible to distinguish the Democrat Lyndon Johnson's judges from the Republican Richard Nixon's. Alternatively, when a president makes an appointment without the constraint of senatorial courtesy, the resulting nominee is far more likely to share the president's ideology. For these appointments, the association between the president's political preferences and his judges' voting is quite respectable and, actually, not altogether different than the one we found for Supreme Court justices.[4]

LASTING LEGACIES?

That justices and, under some circumstances, circuit court judges vote in ways that reflect the political values of their appointing presidents is welcome, though we doubt surprising, news for those presidents. Less welcome is that their influence may be more circumscribed than they may suspect or, of course, desire. Presidents may wish to sway individual jurists and the courts they serve, but to date the evidence that they do so is not as clear cut.

[4] Analyses supporting these claims appear in Epstein and Segal (2005, ch. 5). Suffice it to note here the correlation between presidential ideology and the votes of circuit court judges when senatorial courtesy was in effect is +.23; it jumps to +.49 when senatorial courtesy was not in effect. See also Giles, Hettinger, and Peppers (2001).

Justices?

While presidents often get what they want in the short term by appointing like-minded individuals to the bench, ten years after appointment, the picture clouds considerably. Underscoring this point is the bottom panel of Figure 27.1. Here, we see a substantial decrease in the association between the president's and his justices' ideologies—the correlation between the two drops from .70 to .51—suggesting a problem for administrations that seek to leave lasting imprints on the Court. Souter is the classic example—a justice who sharply departed from the values of his appointing president within a decade of service. But, as we can see, there are others, including Blackmun, Harlan, and White.

Why can time dampen any legacy presidents hope to leave to the nation? To our knowledge, scholars have yet to address this question systematically, but they have offered several testable hypotheses. For one, even if a president nominates an ideological ally, nothing prevents that ally from rethinking his or her jurisprudence over time (see generally Friedman 1986). Witness Harry Blackmun (1970–94), who early in his career on the Court joined the three other conservative Nixon appointees to uphold the death penalty. But just before he retired, Blackmun declared that "no sentence of death may be constitutionally imposed" and that "from this day forward" he "no longer shall tinker with the machinery of death" (*Callins* v. *Collins*, 510 US 1141 (1994)).

The passage of time also means that justices will be hearing issues to which their appointing president (and Senate) probably never gave much thought. While Abraham Lincoln's appointees supported him on cases related to the Civil War, they regularly rejected his views on crucial issues—military courts, legal tender, and the Fourteenth Amendment—that arose after the war ended (and after Lincoln was assassinated). Likewise, when Ronald Reagan appointed Anthony Kennedy, criminal law was a far more salient political matter to the president than, say, gay rights. Nonetheless, it was Kennedy who wrote the opinion disallowing states from prohibiting persons of the same sex from engaging in sodomy—an opinion that Reagan very likely would have condemned.

Finally consider the Court's swing justice during her last few terms, Sandra Day O'Connor. Over time, this Reagan appointee grew more liberal in her political preferences and with that movement came a change in her voting behavior. So, for example, based on the calculations of one team of scholars, the probability of the Court upholding an affirmative action program in 1992 was rather small (about .32); by the time the Court heard a challenge to the University of Michigan law school's affirmative action plan in its 2002 term, the odds had increased to over 50 percent—largely because of O'Connor's move to the left (Martin, Quinn, and Epstein 2005). At the end of the day, O'Connor did, in fact, provide the key vote to uphold the Michigan law program, surely a vote that her appointing president would have appreciated about as much as he would have liked Kennedy's opinion in the sodomy case.

Courts?

Long-lasting legacies in the form of individual justices willing to maintain their appointing presidents' ideological commitments are possible but far from certain. While further research is needed to understand why some justices drift and some do not, we can speculate that at least part of the explanation centers on the types of issues coming before the Court or on factors idiosyncratic to particular justices. Serendipity may play an even greater role in determining whether presidents can leave their imprint on the Supreme Court or entire circuits.

To illustrate the point, Segal, Timpone, and Howard (2000, 172–6) and Segal and Spaeth (2002, 217–22) compare the cases of Reagan and Nixon. Few presidents, as they note, had as much opportunity to influence the Supreme Court as Reagan did. The conservative Republican reached out again and again to social conservatives, calling for the return of school prayer, the reversal of *Roe* v. *Wade* (1973), and reductions in the rights accorded to the criminally accused. While campaigning for Republican Senate candidates in 1986, Reagan argued, "We don't need a bunch of sociology majors on the bench" (quoted in *New York Times* 1986, 32).

As luck would have it, Reagan made four appointees to the high court and had the opportunity to fill hundreds of vacancies on the lower federal courts. Yet the Supreme Court Reagan left was no more conservative than the one he inherited. Moreover, despite his appointees, the twentieth century ended with organized school prayer still unconstitutional and *Roe* v. *Wade* still the law of the land.

The more moderate Richard Nixon, in contrast, had a greater impact in pulling the Court to the right. The Warren Court, he declared in his 1968 campaign, had gone too far in protecting criminal forces in society. He wanted to replace liberals with justices who would not be, as we noted earlier, "favorably inclined toward claims of either criminal defendants or civil rights plaintiffs." Nixon won the election, earning the opportunity, like Reagan, to name four new members of the Supreme Court.

Though a variety of factors worked to constrain the conservative thrust of Nixon's Court—not the least of which was the president's own moderation on issues such as the Equal Rights Amendment and affirmative action—Nixon was successful in ways that Reagan was not. Under the leadership of his Chief Justice, Warren Burger (1969–86), the Court declined to declare capital punishment unconstitutional *per se*, and it limited the reach of the Warren Court's *Mapp* and *Miranda* decisions, which had restricted the use of evidence and confessions illegally obtained. The Burger Court increased the ability of states to ban obscene materials and refused to equalize state spending between school districts. It also turned down the opportunity to extend the right to privacy to homosexual conduct.

An overview of the percentage of liberal votes on the Supreme Court during ten presidential administrations shores up the basic point of this story: presidents have had varying degrees of success in transforming the Supreme Court (Segal and Spaeth 2002). After the Eisenhower administration, the Court grew increasingly liberal during the presidencies of the Democrats John Kennedy and Lyndon Johnson, and then increasingly conservative when the Republicans Richard Nixon and Gerald Ford were in office—just as we might expect and just as those presidents would have likely desired. As the only modern-day president without the opportunity to appoint any justices, Jimmy Carter obviously had no impact on the Court. Yet Reagan, perhaps the most conservative president of the twentieth century, oversaw a Court, as we suggest above, that was only marginally less liberal than it was during the Ford and Carter years—despite his four appointments to the bench.

Why some presidents seem to have more influence on the ideological direction of the Court than others has a good deal to do with the justices their appointees replace, and not simply with whom the president nominates. At the time Richard Nixon took office in 1969, the justices of the liberal Warren Court voted about seven times out of ten in favor of parties alleging a violation of their rights or liberties. The four justices that Nixon replaced (Warren, Black, Fortas, and Harlan) were even slightly more liberal than average. The four he appointed, in contrast, were quite conservative, voting in favor of liberal interests in about a third of all cases, lowering the Court's overall support for rights and liberties claims to about 50 percent (from about 70 percent during the tail end of the Warren Court). On the other hand, while Ronald Reagan did place the extremely conservative Antonin Scalia on the Court, Scalia took the seat of then-associate justice William H. Rehnquist, another strong conservative. As a result, Scalia's appointment did not have a discernible effect on the direction of Court decisions. Nor did Reagan's other appointments. While they were conservative, they too supplanted other (relatively) conservative justices, leaving the president's short-run impact on the high court fairly negligible.

We should note that similar problems afflict the president's ability to change the ideological direction of the courts of appeals. If, for reasons political or economic, few vacancies exist across or within the circuits, a president's influence will be negligible, obviously. But even when they are able to appoint many judges, moving the circuits is still no easy task.

PACKING THE COURTS

Given the discretion and power held by federal judges, especially Supreme Court justices, and the effect of their political outlooks in shaping how they use that discretion and power, Chief Justice Rehnquist (1987, 348) found it "normal and desirable for Presidents to attempt to pack" the judiciary.

Whether or not packing the courts is a laudable goal, a variety of factors can conspire against presidents seeking to achieve it. When it comes to the lower courts, judges are constrained by the Supreme Court, and presidents by the tradition of senatorial courtesy. Moreover, for judges and occasionally justices too, presidents may be more interested in pursuing electoral or partisan objectives rather than those centering on policy. Such was the case when Eisenhower selected the Catholic Democrat William Brennan or when Reagan redeemed his campaign promise by naming a woman, Sandra Day O'Connor, to the Court. So too, changing attitudes can rob a president of the long-lasting influence he may have wished from one of his justices.

But the public that elected Richard Nixon in 1968 desired and received a more conservative Supreme Court. Though the Reagan revolution did not make the courts substantially more conservative in their decision making, it did guarantee another generation of conservative domination, and provided four of the five votes (all but that of Clarence Thomas, a George H. W. Bush appointee) needed to select George W. Bush as the forty-third president.

It is thus no wonder why presidents have taken so seriously their constitutionally assigned task of appointing federal judges. They may whine about disappointing appointees; and they may fail to pack the courts. But they do seem rational in their anticipation that the federal judges and justices they name can help ensure their ideological legacy at least in the first few years after they depart from office.

REFERENCES

ABRAHAM, H. J. 1999. *Justices, Presidents, and Senators*. Lanham, MD: Rowman & Littlefield.

BAILEY, M. A. 2007. Comparable Preference Estimates across Time and Institutions for the Court, Congress and Presidency. *American Journal of Political Science*, 51: 433–48.

—— and CHANG, K. H. 2001. Comparing Presidents, Senators, and Justices: Interinstitutional Preference Estimation. *Journal of Law, Economics, and Organization*, 17: 477–506.

BARROW, D. J., ZUK, G., and GRYSKI, G. S. 1996. *The Federal Judiciary and Institutional Change*. Ann Arbor: University of Michigan Press.

BORK, R. 1990. *The Tempting of America*. New York: Simon & Schuster.

CAMERON, C. M., COVER, A. D., and SEGAL, J. A. 1990. Senate Voting on Supreme Court Nominees: A Neoinstitutional Model. *American Political Science Review*, 84: 525–34.

CARTER, S. L. 1994. *The Confirmation Mess: Cleaning up the Federal Appointment Process*. New York: Basic Books.

CHOI, S., and GULATI, M. 2004. A Tournament of Judges? *California Law Review*, 92: 299–322.

CLARK, M. L. 2003. Carter's Groundbreaking Appointment of Women to the Federal Bench: His Other "Human Rights" Record. *American University Journal of Gender, Social Policy and Law*, 11: 1131–63.

DANIELS, W. J. 1978. The Geographic Factor in Appointments to the United States Supreme Court: 1789–1976. *Western Political Quarterly*, 31: 226–37.

DEAN, J. W. 2001. *The Rehnquist Choice*. New York: Free Press.

EPSTEIN, L., and SEGAL, J. A. 2005. *Advice and Consent: The Politics of Judicial Appointments*. New York: Oxford University Press.

—— —— and WESTERLAND, C. 2008. The Increasing Importance of Ideology in the Nomination and Confirmation of Supreme Court Justices. *Drake Law Review/American Judicature Society*, 56: 101–27.

—— LINDSTADT, R., SEGAL, J. A., and WESTERLAND, C. 2006. The Changing Dynamics of Senate Voting on Supreme Court Nominees. *Journal of Politics*, 68: 296–307.

EPSTEIN, L., MARTIN, A. D., QUINN, K. M., and SEGAL, J. A. 2007. Ideological Drift on the U.S. Supreme Court. *Northwestern University Law Review,* 101: 1483–542.

FREUND, P. A. 1988. Appointment of Justices: Some Historical Perspectives. *Harvard Law Review,* 101: 1146–63.

FRIEDMAN, R. 1986. Tribal Myths: Ideology and the Confirmation of Supreme Court Nominations. *Yale Law Journal,* 95: 1283–320.

GERHARDT, M. J. 2001. Norm Theory and the Future of the Federal Appointments Process. *Duke Law Journal,* 50: 1687–715.

—— 2003. Federal Judicial Selection in the New Millennium: Judicial Selection as War. *UC Davis Law Review,* 36: 667–93.

—— 2006. Why the Catholic Majority on the Supreme Court May Be Unconstitutional. *University of St. Thomas Law Journal,* 4: 173–92.

GILES, M. W., HETTINGER, V. A., and PEPPERS, T. C. 2001. Picking Federal Judges. *Political Research Quarterly,* 54: 623–41.

GOLDMAN, S. 1997. *Picking Federal Judges.* New Haven, CT: Yale University Press.

—— SLOTNICK, E., GRYSKI, G., and SCHIAVONI, S. 2007. Picking Judges in a Time of Turmoil. *Judicature,* 90: 252–83.

GREENBURG, J. C. 2007. *Supreme Conflict: The Inside Story of the Struggle for Control of the United States Supreme Court.* New York: Penguin Press.

HARRIS, R. 1971. *Decision.* New York: Dutton.

JOHNSON, T. R., and ROBERTS, J. M. 2004. Presidential Capital and the Supreme Court Confirmation Process. *Journal of Politics,* 66: 663–83.

LEWIS, N. A. 2001. A Conservative Legal Group Thrives in Bush's Washington. *New York Times,* Apr. 18: A1.

MARTIN, A. D., and QUINN, K. M. 2002. Dynamic Ideal Point Estimation via Markov Chain Monte Carlo for the U.S. Supreme Court, 1953–1999. *Political Analysis,* 10: 134–53.

—— —— and EPSTEIN, L. 2005. The Median Justice on the U.S. Supreme Court. *North Carolina Law Review,* 83: 1275–322.

MORASKI, B. J., and SHIPAN, C. R. 1999. The Politics of Supreme Court Nominations: A Theory of Institutional Choice and Constraints. *American Journal of Political Science,* 43: 1069–95.

NEMACHECK, C. L. 2007. *Strategic Selection.* Charlottesville: University of Virginia Press.

New York Times. 1986. Reagan Aims Fire at Liberal Judges. Oct. 9: A32.

OVERBY, L. M., HENSCHEN, B. M., WALSH, M. H., and STRAUSS, J. 1992. Courting Constituents? An Analysis of the Senate Confirmation Vote on Justice Clarence Thomas. *American Political Science Review,* 86: 997–1003.

REHNQUIST, W. H. 1987. *The Supreme Court: How It Was, How It Is.* New York: Morrow.

ROSS, W. G. 2002. Attacks on the Warren Court by State Officials: A Case Study of Why Court-Curbing Movements Fail. *Buffalo Law Review,* 50: 483–612.

SEGAL, J. A., CAMERON, C. M., and COVER, A. D. 1992. A Spatial Model of Roll Call Voting: Senators, Constituents, Presidents, and Interest Groups in Supreme Court Confirmations. *American Journal of Political Science,* 36: 96–121.

—— and SPAETH, H. J. 2002. *The Supreme Court and the Attitudinal Model Revisited.* New York: Cambridge University Press.

—— TIMPONE, R. J., and HOWARD, R. M. 2000. Buyer Beware? Presidential Success through Supreme Court Appointments. *Political Research Quarterly,* 53: 557–95.

SILVERSTEIN, M. 1994. *Judicious Choices.* New York: Norton.

SONTAG, D. 2003. The Power of the Fourth. *New York Times,* Mar. 9, Section 6: 40.

STRAUSS, D. A. 2007. Memo to the President (and his Opponents): Ideology Still Counts. *Northwestern University Law Review Colloquy*, 102: 49–53. <http://www.law.northwestern.edu/lawreview/colloquy/2007/22/>.

TOOBIN, J. 2007. *The Nine: Inside the Secret World of the Supreme Court.* New York: Doubleday.

TRIBE, L. H. 1985. *God Save This Honorable Court.* New York: Random House.

WATSON, G. L., and STOOKEY, J. L. 1995. *Shaping America: The Politics of Supreme Court Appointments.* New York: Harper Collins.

WILSON, S. 2003. Appellate Judicial Appointments during the Clinton Presidency: An Inside Perspective. *Journal of Appellate Practice and Process*, 5: 29–47.

WOLPERT, R. M., and GIMPEL, J. G. 1997. Information, Recall, and Accountability: The Electorate's Response to the Clarence Thomas Nomination. *Legislative Studies Quarterly*, 22: 535–50.

YALOF, D. A. 1999. *Pursuit of Justices.* Chicago: University of Chicago Press.

CHAPTER 28

JUDICIAL CHECKS ON THE PRESIDENT

KEITH E. WHITTINGTON

IN a system of separated powers, the president faces several formal checks on his power as well as a variety of informal checks. The vertical check is perhaps the most important one: the power of the electorate to periodically review the president's performance and remove him or his party from office. But as theorists of "delegative democracy" have emphasized (O'Donnell 1994), well-functioning constitutional systems have horizontal as well as vertical checks on presidential power. As a formal matter, this means Congress and the courts. Relative to other countries, there are sharp limits to presidential power and the legislature is quite important in the United States. But on the margins, scholars actively debate over how effectively Congress operates as a constitutional check on the presidency (Levinson and Pildes 2006). Judicial checks on the presidency provide a supplementary tool for limiting executive power. The question is just how meaningful that tool has been.

The judicial check on the presidency is not as encompassing as the legislative check. Some policy domains fall largely outside of judicial purview, and the questions that can be addressed in the courts, as well as their possible remedies, are more limited than in the legislative arena. Nonetheless, a wide range of executive branch policy decisions can be challenged in the courts. As a consequence, the judiciary provides a potential avenue for checking claims of presidential and executive branch power as such and specific exercises of that power to make substantive policy.

Presidential power and the judicial check interact in several ways. Presidents gain legal authority to act primarily from the US Constitution and from federal statutes, and legal limits on presidential actions primarily derive from those two sources of law as well. The judiciary may review the constitutionality of presidential and executive actions, but it more commonly reviews whether the executive has adequate statutory authority for the actions that it wants to undertake. Although such statute-based decisions can be more easily overridden through legislative action than can constitutionally based decisions, they can provide an important vehicle for limiting the executive. Relatedly, judicial checks on the presidency are only a portion of the judicial checks on the executive branch as a whole. The courts can expand or limit the powers of the presidency not only through their review of the direct exertions of the asserted constitutional prerogatives of the office of the presidency, but also through its more routine review of policy making by the executive agencies that the president might influence.

As the reference to statutes already suggests, Congress matters when thinking about the judicial checks on the presidency. The judiciary is partly constituted by the legislature, and the legal web within which the courts and the executive operate is partly of the legislature's making. Moreover, when the courts square off against the executive it is of potential consequence whether the legislature is in the courts' corner, sitting on the sidelines, or likely to favor the executive. Judicial checks on the presidency are more likely to be effective when the president is ideologically and politically isolated.

This chapter reviews the judicial checks on the presidency from two perspectives. The first lays out the doctrinal framework within which the courts consider executive power. The second considers the theoretical and empirical research on how these judicial checks operate in practice.

THREE ASPECTS OF DOCTRINE

A variety of legal doctrines relevant to the judicial checks on the executive exist, but only three are considered in this chapter: political question doctrine, doctrinal frameworks for evaluating assertions of presidential power, and *Chevron* doctrine for judicial review of administrative action. Together they provide a fairly comprehensive portrait of the legal rules that the courts have established to guide how the judicial check should be applied against the executive.[1]

---

[1] The classic and still useful study of the constitutional and legal rules surrounding the presidency is Corwin (1984).

Political Questions

The key role of political question doctrine is to delineate certain questions as beyond the purview of the courts to address. The roots of the doctrine trace back to the beginning of the Supreme Court's history. The 1803 case of *Marbury* v. *Madison* (5 US 137) is primarily remembered today as the first invalidation of a federal law by the Supreme Court. But of greater note at the time was the fact that William Marbury was asking the Court to oversee how the Jefferson administration was fulfilling its constitutional duties and to issue a directive to Secretary of State James Madison to disobey the president and deliver up Marbury's commission to the office of justice of the peace. The administration did not recognize the Court's jurisdiction over the dispute, refusing to even argue the case, and it was widely expected that the executive branch would refuse to comply with any orders that the Marshall Court might issue in the matter. Holding the statutory provision that had brought Marbury to the Court unconstitutional allowed Chief Justice John Marshall to lecture the administration for its bad behavior without having to follow through with an order that could be ignored, saving the pretense of a judicial check if not the reality (Graber 1999). In the course of his lecture, Marshall argued that the courts could review and correct executive actions that were non-discretionary and affected vested legal rights. He thought that the mechanical task of delivering a judicial commission fell in that category. He admitted, however, that the "province of the courts is, solely, to decide on the rights of individuals, not to inquire how the executive, or executive officers, perform duties in which they have a discretion. Questions in their nature political, or which are, by the constitution and laws, submitted to the executive can never be made in this court" (170).

Marshall's suggestion that some actions by the executive (and legislature) were not reviewable by the courts was elaborated elsewhere. Most notably, the Court gave form to the political question doctrine in *Luther* v. *Borden* (48 US 1 [1840]), which resulted from the armed confrontation of two different groups claiming to be the legitimately constituted government of Rhode Island. "[F]ortunately for our freedom from political excitements in judicial duties, this court can never with propriety be called on officially to be the umpire in questions merely political. The adjustment of these questions belongs to the people and their political representatives ... These questions relate to matters not to be settled on strict legal principles. They are adjusted rather by inclination, or prejudice or compromise, often. Some of them succeed or are defeated even by public policy alone, or mere naked power, rather than intrinsic right" (51). Most notably for present purposes, Congress in exercising its own constitutional power to guarantee republican governments in the states and secure against insurrections had authorized the president to call out the militia when requested by the state government. It was within the sole discretion of the president to determine when the militia was needed and to whose aid it should be sent. Such discretionary power could be abused, but there were no "other hands in which this power would be more safe, and at the same time equally effectual" (44). For the early courts, they could exercise review over "ministerial" or non-discretionary acts, but political decisions ranging from the mustering of the militia to the calculation of pensions to the implementation of Reconstruction policy were beyond judicial review (Mashaw 2008).

The modern political question doctrine was summarized by Justice William Brennan in *Baker* v. *Carr* (369 US 186 [1962]), the legislative apportionment case. Political question cases involved issues that had been committed to another branch for resolution, lacked judicially manageable standards for resolution, were inextricably bound up in policy considerations, or required deference to other branches in order to avoid chaotic or embarrassing questioning of settled decisions (217). Ironically, beginning with *Baker*, the Court has been increasingly willing to find a wide array of cases to be justiciable, shrinking the practical significance of the doctrine (Barkow 2002).

Foreign policy, and especially presidential action in foreign policy, is one of the few areas in which political question doctrine is still routinely invoked. Even as the courts have invited litigation on questions such as legislative apportionment and the seating of legislators that they once regarded as beyond their purview, they continue to decline hearing challenges to the presidential commitment of military forces abroad or presidential termination of treaty obligations (Nzelibe 2004).

The Scope of Presidential Authority

A second doctrinal framework is intended to help guide the courts in providing substantive answers to questions involving assertions of presidential power. A historic divide for thinking about such issues falls between formalist and functionalist approaches. Formalist approaches to the separation of powers attempt to develop relatively clear rules from the available legal materials and broader principled considerations to distinguish the roles, powers, and duties of the various institutions of government. Functionalist approaches eschew rules in favor of broad standards and case-by-case pragmatism.

Both approaches were represented in the landmark Steel Seizure Case during the Korean War. In *Youngstown Sheet & Tube Co.* v. *Sawyer* (343 US 579 [1952]), a divided Court turned back President Harry Truman's use of federal troops to intervene in a labor strike in order to keep the steel mills operating during the war (Marcus 1977). Justice Hugo Black, a former New Deal Senator, emphasized his characteristic formalist approach in the majority opinion for the Court. The power to determine the conditions under which the government could seize property was a law-making power, and the president neither had the power to make such a law on his own nor had he been delegated the power to act under these circumstances by statute. Justice Robert Jackson, a former New Deal Attorney General, emphasized his characteristic functionalist approach in a concurring opinion. Jackson agreed that Truman's actions were unwarranted, but emphasized the need for integrating "dispersed powers into a workable government" and that "[p]residential powers are not fixed but fluctuate, depending on their disjunction or conjunction with those of Congress." He laid out three "practical situations" that the Court might confront: cases in which presidents acted in pursuance of a legislative delegation, when their authority would be at a "maximum;" cases in which presidents acted in the absence of legislation, when their authority would turn on the "imperative of events;" and cases in which presidents acted in conflict with the will of Congress, when their authority is at its "lowest ebb" (635–7).

Jackson's approach has proven to be far more influential than Black's. Although it rules little out (even at his "lowest ebb," the president still has an unspecified core of powers that Congress could not breach), Jackson's *Youngstown* concurrence directs future judges to evaluate the totality of the circumstances in which presidents might act and to consider the degree of support that they might have in Congress. *Youngstown* itself suggests that the Court might sometimes intervene to check the president, but Jackson's concurrence gave wide latitude to the Court and encouraged deference when the other two branches had found a "workable" solution to practical problems.

Since *Youngstown*, the Court has had occasion to review numerous separation-of-powers disputes, including assertions of presidential power. Administrations have sometimes relied on the constitutional authority of the presidency itself to support its claims in court, and they have met with some success, especially in the realm of foreign policy where the Court is inclined to view the president's own constitutional authority as relatively robust. In the midst of the New Deal, the Court influentially asserted in *United States v. Curtiss-Wright Export Corp.* (299 US 304 [1936]) that under the Constitution the president was the "sole organ of foreign affairs." Presidents have welcomed this bit of news. Moreover, the courts have frequently referred back to Justice Arthur Sutherland's opinion in that case to support the inherent and pre-dominant power of the president in the realm of foreign policy and to justify judicial deference to presidential actions in the international arena. This assumption of presidential predominance also tends to influence how the courts interpret statutes affecting presidential power relating to foreign affairs, such that the judiciary tends to give the benefit of the doubt to executive discretion whenever possible (Adler and George 1996). The Jackson concurrence in *Youngstown* has encouraged administra-tions to appeal to statutory support for their actions whenever possible to supplement pure constitutional claims (Quint 1989). When a majority of the Court decided to push back against the second Bush administration's terrorist detention policies, the strategy it chose borrowed from Jackson's playbook—telling the administration that it needed clearer statutory authorization for its policies but refraining from deciding whether such policies would be constitutionally out of bounds (Cleveland 2005).

The normative and legalist literature follows the same divisions that have appeared on the Court. Both formalism and functionalism have had advocates among jurists and scholars. Since the Reagan era, conservatives have made a particularly prominent bid to reemphasize the value of formalism in thinking about the constitutional separation of powers as well as other jurisprudential domains, though there is hardly ideological homogeneity on these points (Sunstein 1987). Functionalist accounts are often driven by the assumption that the constitutional text and original understand-ing provide few clues as to its meaning and implications regarding the conduct of foreign policy, and its structure may primarily suggest an "invitation to struggle" between the branches (Corwin 1984). If constitutional scholars and constitutional law are to have a role at all in regulating foreign affairs, then perhaps it must be built upon contemporary normative considerations and prudential judgments (Ramsey 2007). But formalists would argue that such judgments are readily contestable along familiar political lines and the formal features of the Constitution may offer more guidance to current actors than functionalists tend to assume. As a result, scholars contest both the terms of the debate and the merits of particular arguments within the debate.

A related cleavage in the normative and legalist literature relates to the proper scope of presidential power under the Constitution and the judicial role in checking that power. Put another way, was the "sole organ" language in *Curtiss-Wright* misguided and did *Youngstown* go far enough? It seems fair to say that most scholars writing in this area in the post-Vietnam era would prefer to see a more aggressive judiciary (as well as a more aggressive Congress) checking the foreign policy powers of the president. A predominant concern in the literature involves developing critiques of the *Curtiss-Wright* line of thinking on the Court and arguing that a combination of judicial deference to presidential exertions of power and judicial encouragement through things like the sole organ doctrine have helped to foster an "imbalance of powers" in the American constitutional system, especially in the realm of foreign policy. A central goal of this scholarship is to provide the intellectual tools to encourage a more active judicial check on presidential power and a more limited view of presidential prerogatives. There are advocates of presidential power and/or judicial deference, however, and they have raised a variety of challenges to the scholarly mainstream. Such scholars have argued that the courts have been generally right to recognize that the presidents have particular authority over foreign policy (Powell 2002; Yoo 2005), or that presidents have broad authority over the workings of the executive branch (Calabresi and Yoo 2008). Although sometimes giving way to broad polemics, such disagreements also create opportunities for creative and detailed examinations of the textual, historical, normative, and prudential arguments at play in this debate.

Judicial Deference to Administrative Agencies

A third stream of doctrine is intended to guide the courts in their evaluation of the interpretation of federal statutes offered by executive branch officials. Executive administrators are the first interpreters of federal law and routine policy makers under federal statutes. The interpretations of federal law and policies that they adopt in pursuance of those legal statutory grants of authority and statutory mandates are potentially subject to judicial review. The availability and scope of judicial review of administrative decision making are themselves matters of statutory design and the subject of negotiation for contending sides during the legislative process (Stephenson 2006).

In the late nineteenth and early twentieth centuries, the courts accommodated a massive shift of policy-making authority from both the legislature and the courts themselves to the executive branch. As courts became more skeptical of how executive branch officials were using that policy-making discretion in the 1960s and 1970s, they began to build a more elaborate edifice of administrative law to aggressively review executive decisions. Courts became more assertive in reviewing both the procedures used by agencies in making decisions and the substantive outcomes of agency decision making (Rodriguez 2008).

The Supreme Court significantly remade the doctrinal landscape of administrative law in *Chevron v. Natural Resource Defense Council* (467 US 837 [1984]). The Environmental Protection Agency under Ronald Reagan altered an interpretation of a provision of the Clean Air Act that had been adopted by the Carter administration. In a unanimous decision authored by Justice John Paul Stevens, the Court turned back a challenge to the policy change by an environmental interest group. Laying out a new standard of administrative deference, *Chevron* held that so long as the statute is ambiguous on the precise question at issue, the courts should defer to any reasonable interpretation made by the executive (843–4). Such statutory ambiguities, the Court assumed, were to be understood as congressional delegations of policy-making authority to the executive branch. Administrative policy making was to be checked by Congress, not the courts, except in the most egregious of cases (Vermeule 2006).

The normative and legal scholarship has been divided over the wisdom of "*Chevron* deference." Many administrative law scholars would prefer more rigorous judicial scrutiny of executive decisions, arguing that *Chevron* gives the executive branch a green light to ignore legislative purposes and make bad policy. Others are less sanguine about either the public-regarding qualities of the underlying statutes or the ability of judges to reach better policy outcomes than the executive branch. The question of whether the judiciary should defer to the executive in the interpretation of ambiguous statutes can be framed as a debate over whether judicial intervention will improve or worsen public welfare and whether judicial deference in cases of statutory ambiguity effectively frees the administration from the bounds of law (Rodriguez 2008; Garrett 2008). Many scholars were skeptical of deference, especially in the context of substantive executive decisions that they found misguided. Nevertheless, this normative debate rests on key empirical assumptions about the behavior of judges and consequences of judicial intervention in these contexts and about the process by which executive branch agencies interpret and apply the law. Relatively little work has been done investigating those assumptions, however, and this is a ripe area of research.

THE JUDICIAL CHECK IN PRACTICE

The established doctrinal frameworks relating to executive power encourage an assumption of legislative–executive cooperation and judicial deference to executive decision making. The executive enjoys many practical advantages in court as well. The judicial check on the executive is often limited, though certainly not toothless. A growing body of theoretical and empirical work on executive relations with the courts provides an improving picture of how the courts interact with the executive branch. This work cuts against the standard emphasis within the judicial politics literature that federal judges within the American political system are sufficiently insulated and motivated to be independent policy makers and will generally act to advance their own policy preferences. The two strands of work can be reconciled by considering the ways in which presidents help staff the courts and shape judicial views about policy. But, some immediate tensions remain over the extent to which judges are influenced by external factors like presidential popularity or preferences. And there are challenges in synthesizing studies that focus on the behavior of the judiciary as it is constituted and studies that attempt to place the judiciary within a broader, more dynamic context.

Constituting Courts

The president has some natural advantages in winning support for his actions in the courts. Foremost among those advantages is the federal judicial selection process. Robert Dahl (1957) influentially characterized the Supreme Court as part of a larger, national political coalition. Presidents routinely have the opportunity to place individuals who share their central commitments on the bench, and throughout American history successful political parties have been able to gain control over the Court in a relatively short period of time through the appointments process. Electoral instability, divided government, and the idiosyncrasies of individual vacancies and appointments can complicate that basic pattern. Nonetheless, a growing body of work in a Dahlian vein has emphasized the basic utility of this perspective on the judiciary (Graber 2005). The courts are constituted by those holding elective office, and they tend to act as governing partners with allies in the other branches.

The federal judiciary may not be as responsive to political trends as other institutions are, but the courts do not tend to be wildly out of step with public sentiment or dominant political coalitions. Within that context, the president has a particular opportunity to put his stamp on the judiciary. Presidents select judicial nominees, and that gives them a distinctive agenda-setting benefit. Judicial nominees, especially to the Supreme Court, routinely reflect presidential priorities, whether narrowly political or broadly ideological, within their particular coalitional contexts. Thus, Harry Truman selected personal confidants to the Court and Dwight Eisenhower and Richard Nixon looked for nominees who would win points with swing voters in the national electorate (Yalof 1999). Franklin Roosevelt, Harry Truman, and Dwight Eisenhower all placed individuals open to racial civil rights appeals on the Court, despite representing political coalitions that were much more divided on the issue (McMahon 2004). Theodore Roosevelt sought out potential justices who shared his own Hamiltonian vision of the Constitution. Similarly, it seems likely that potential candidates' views on presidential power were relevant considerations for the second Bush administration in choosing its Supreme Court nominees. Moreover, it has been common for presidents to look within the executive branch itself when searching for judicial nominees, whether selecting government lawyers such as Assistant Attorney General William Rehnquist, or those holding broader responsibilities such as Secretary of State John Marshall. Other Supreme Court nominees, from Roger Taney to Samuel Alito, had notable executive branch experience, even if they did not come directly from the executive branch at the time of their nomination to the high court. After the Jeffersonian backlash that included an impeachment, justices and presidents may have learned to keep more of a distance than they did at the start of the Republic, when justices were known to put off the Court's business so as to campaign for the president's reelection or help conduct foreign policy. Nonetheless, many justices have maintained some personal or political connections to like-minded presidents.

None of this suggests that judges are simply presidential pawns. Although presidents have a significant advantage in the judicial confirmation game, Senators do impose checks on the presidential selection of nominees. Presidents must anticipate senatorial preferences when choosing nominees, or risk delayed or contentious confirmations, or even failed nominations. The judiciary is a collective body, and its members represent the layered influences of multiple presidential administrations. Once placed on the bench, judges serve long terms of office and are not readily accountable to the president or party that appointed them. A potential judicial nominee represents a package of legal views, and the particular issue or set of issues that was salient to an individual's selection to the bench may not remain salient over time or predict how the judge might act on other issues. Individuals acting in the judicial role may well behave differently than they would have if they had been acting in a legislative or executive capacity, where the incentives, pressures, and perceived obligations are different. All of this complicates the path of presidential influence on the courts, and how the courts might, in turn, check the presidency. Even justices appointed by a single president do not necessarily vote as a cohesive bloc across a full range of issues over the length of their tenure on the Court (Lindquist, Yalof, and Clark 2000). Famously, Truman's own appointees to the Court split over the question of whether he had the power to seize the steel mills in the *Youngstown* case.

Substantial work still needs to be done at both the micro level of individual case studies and particular issues, as well as the macro level of systematic effects across wide swaths of cases to understand the relationship between judges, the changing environment, the commitments of the coalition that brought them to office, and the circumstances of their appointment. Dahl seems clearly correct that presidents are unlikely to appoint judges known to be actively hostile to the president's agenda, but we do not yet have an adequate theoretical or empirical appreciation of the presidential agenda in making appointments and how presidents might prioritize and balance conflicting considerations. "Mistaken" appointments may more often be an example of choice under constraints rather than genuine error. More work needs to be done about those choices and how they affect the ultimate operation of the judicial check on the presidency.

Litigation and Implementation

Presidents also possess significant advantages in the litigation process. The Solicitor General serves as the chief litigator before the Supreme Court for the federal government and is responsive to the presidential agenda. The Solicitor General has substantial discretion over which cases to advance through the judicial hierarchy, which cases to join with the weight of government support, how to frame issues, and what arguments to make. In advancing the president's case before the Court, the government lawyers bring significant resources, expertise, and experience to developing arguments to persuade the justices. Moreover, the Solicitor General signals to the justices the preferences of the president, which facilitates convergence by sympathetic justices to the president's position (Bailey, Kamoie, and Maltzman 2005). Indeed, the justices even request that the Solicitor General intervene in selected cases where knowing the administration's views on a politically salient issue appears useful to the Court (Johnson 2003). As a litigator, the Solicitor General is relatively successful, winning cases and shaping doctrines on behalf of the president.

Presidents can also attempt to limit the significance of the judicial check in other ways. At the extreme, presidents can influence the implementation of judicial decisions and can threaten the prestige and authority of the judiciary. Many of the most controversial policies of the second Bush administration's war on terror are covert and difficult for the courts to monitor. The prospect of easy presidential evasion of judicial decisions mitigates the judicial check and can lead judges to temper their own actions to avoid being exposed as impotent (Vanberg 2001). When the issue is important enough to presidents, and when they have the political support, they have even been willing to challenge the courts more openly. Presidents such as Thomas Jefferson, Abraham Lincoln, and Franklin Roosevelt have claimed an authority to interpret the law equal to or greater than that of the Court's. But presidents rarely find it in their interest to engage in such open confrontations, instead lending their support to the authority of the courts, precisely because the courts tend to serve presidential interests (Whittington 2007).

More prosaically, presidents can seek favorable legislative terms that can insulate their decisions from judicial review. Although the second Bush administration notoriously avoided seeking specific statutory backing for its foreign policy initiatives, the post-September 11 Authorization for the Use of Military Force was designed (at least to some of its White House proponents) to be both sweeping and vague so as to give the administration maximum flexibility in conducting the war on terror. Presidential administrations routinely emphasize to judges a variety of legislative policies that might provide legal support for the particular actions that they have taken, even if they also claim that the president could take such actions on their own constitutional prerogative. Truman sought to cloak his actions in the *Steel Seizure Case* with legislative support, as did the Bush administration in the terrorism detention cases. But the Court was ultimately unconvinced that the weight of congressional policy pronouncements cut in favor of those presidential actions, especially since the most specific statutes relating to the policies at issue seemed to cut against presidential decisions. The steel strike resolved itself in short order, but the Bush White House did return to the Republican Congress to get more specific statutory support for its detention policies in an attempt to deter judicial scrutiny.

Congressional Support

Congress thus has an important role to play in laying the groundwork for judicial review of executive policy making. The most basic question is whether to cover some policy ground with a statute at all. Once Congress is actively involved, the details of statutory design set the conditions for later executive discretion. To the extent that legislators trust the long-term policy preferences and value the administrative flexibility of the executive, statutory grants of authority may be relatively broad and the requirements for judicial review of administrative decisions may be relatively weak. Congress can encourage judicial oversight of the executive, however, by drafting tighter statutory language that hems in executive discretion and provides greater guidance to reviewing judges. Law makers can also provide explicit mechanisms for judicial review of administrative decision making, or shift some important policy decisions out of executive hands entirely (McCubbins, Noll, and Weingast 1987; Moe and Wilson 1994; Stephenson 2006). The judiciary can only check the executive in an effective fashion if the judges are provided with the opportunities to do so, which requires relatively sophisticated, well-organized, and persistent litigants. Congress may also facilitate judicial review of the executive by nurturing a broader litigation-rich environment in which organizations have both formal channels and practical incentives to pursue a variety of legal challenges to government policies (Frymer 2007; Farhang 2006).

The Court itself emphasizes the degree of congressional support as an important factor in its decision making. Congress had provided other mechanisms for resolving labor disputes in the steel industry and had not taken action to authorize Truman's intervention in the wartime strike. The administration was forced to rely directly on the Constitution and a more nebulous web of legislative policies to support the seizure of the steel mill, which the Court found inadequate. Whether the legal resources actually available to the executive branch to justify a particular policy action empirically matter to judicial outcomes remains untested. Assessing legal variables is difficult, but in this case they may be essential to understanding the ways in which congressional support for presidential action may influence the degree of judicial deference to the president.

Judicial Decision Making

A fundamental issue for presidents is how the courts treat their claims to presidential power. Ducat and Dudley (1989) developed the first broad empirical study of how judges responded to such cases. Their work focused on federal district court rulings since the Second World War, but the analysis has since been extended to the US Supreme Court (Yates and Whitford 1998). Judges are called upon to review a wide variety of substantive policy decisions made by the executive branch, but these studies are particularly interested in cases relating to the powers of the presidency and the executive office. As the pro-presidential flavor of established doctrine might suggest, presidents win more often than they lose such cases. But their win rate is not uniform.

In considering how the judiciary and the presidency interact in such cases, judicial scholars have focused on the tension between the intrinsic preferences of the judges and external factors that might push them away from acting on those inclinations. Of particular interest are those factors that might lead judges to be more deferential than might otherwise be expected. A ready starting point for analyzing judicial voting behavior is the recognition that judges have regular and politically salient proclivities, judicial philosophies, or ideologically meaningful "attitudes" regarding the substantive content of law. Presumably, federal judges are independent enough to be able to express these attitudes in the cases they decide. If judges are sufficiently independent and single-minded, they may only act on those preferences and be unresponsive to other considerations. Alternatively, judges might be sensitive to various "outside" pressures. Legal materials like statutory text and precedent may hem in judicial discretion. Popular opinion or the views of other government officials may affect judicial willingness to act on their own preferences. A great deal of the judicial politics literature emphasizes the extent to which judges act as independent policy makers. There are both theoretical and empirical challenges to that emphasis, and these studies of the judicial check on the presidency likewise highlight the potential importance of factors other than judicial ideology in determining judicial decisions.

Studies of the Supreme Court and the lower courts regarding presidential power bear out the predominant view that judicial ideology matters to judicial decision making. But, they also suggest that judicial ideology can be tempered (or exacerbated) by other factors. Judges tend to give favor to their own appointing president. Moreover, the degree of public support for the president at the time of the litigation appears to affect judges. Presidents who are riding high in the polls can anticipate better treatment in the courts than those who suffer from low public approval (Yates 2002). Determining whether judges are being influenced by the president's political standing or are reaching an independent but similar conclusion about the merits of the president's case as the general public may require more work to tease out.

The courts are particularly deferential to the president in foreign policy. Over much of the twentieth century, the Supreme Court had assumed that the president had enhanced constitutional authority in the realm of foreign policy (Silverstein 1996). There is certainly reason to doubt whether this view in its strongest form is fully consistent with understandings and practices in the early Republic, but there is little question that a "two presidencies" thesis has been influential in legal and political circles in the modern era (Barron and Lederman 2008; Lavinbuk 2005).

Both district court judges and Supreme Court justices in the post-war era have been more deferential to claims of presidential power in the foreign policy context than in the domestic context. Although legal scholars have in recent decades questioned the appropriateness of this deference, the president has substantial legal support to back his claims in this area. Judges are also likely to be hesitant to second-guess the president in an area in which the stakes are high but their own expertise is limited.

But presidents do not invariably win such contests. They lose support in the courts when they move out of their core area of competence and authority. Courts generally defer to presidents in cases involving issues such as the treaty-making or commander-in-chief powers. But presidential success is much less certain when the issues shift, even within the general domain of foreign affairs. Courts are willing to be more active when presidential powers touch on matters of traditional judicial concern, such as civil liberties and domestic security (King and Meernik 1998). Even in wartime and in evaluating war powers, the Court has often examined whether the president was acting alone, as Truman was in *Youngstown*, or whether he had the support of Congress. An isolated president is vulnerable to the judicial check in a way that a president fortified by legislative support is not (Issacharoff and Pildes 2004).

The Court has invited non-compliance and backlash when it obstructs measures that are viewed by the political branches as necessary to national security, whether in habeas cases in the Civil War, military commission cases in the Second World War, or anti-Communism cases in the Cold War. The Court must tread lightly in such cases, and often it reserves imposing serious checks on government power until after the crisis has passed. There are the tantalizing exceptions like *Youngstown*, in which the Court stepped in during the war itself to limit the president. But in such cases, the Court may well judge that either Congress is notably absent or the apparent crisis has passed and opened space for reexamination of presidential policies.

But most cases that the Court hears do not have that degree of political salience. In a large-scale study of civil rights and liberties cases since the Second World War, Epstein et al. (2005) find no evidence of special judicial deference to the government in war-related cases during wartime. Surprisingly, however, they do find that cases seemingly unrelated to the war are affected by the wartime environment, with the government becoming more successful in turning back individual rights claims in such cases. In a related analysis of criminal and non-criminal cases involving executive decision making heard in the federal court of appeals, Clark (2006) finds that circuit court judges become more deferential to prosecutors in criminal cases during wartime but less deferential to the executive in non-criminal cases in a wartime environment. Uncovering these patterns of behavior is an important first step in examining how the judicial check on the presidency is affected by war, and these results are all the more intriguing because they do not fit easily with any preexisting account of how the courts respond to war. More work clearly needs to be done to investigate and extend these results and to develop new theories of the judicial check in wartime.

The Supreme Court's change of approach to administrative law doctrine in the *Chevron* decision coincided with increasing attention to administrative law from scholars working in empirical and positive political theory traditions. In an influential analysis, Cohen and Spitzer (1994) argued that the more conservative Supreme Court adopted the deferential *Chevron* doctrine so as to rein in the more liberal lower courts from interfering with the policy decisions then being made by the Reagan administration. *Chevron*, by this reading, was a tool through which the Supreme Court hoped to control the judicial hierarchy so as to advance its policy objectives. *Chevron* was a landmark case, but it was not the only signal that the Supreme Court sent to the lower courts and the executive branch. The theory would predict that the Court would fine-tune its desired level of deference as the control of the composition of the lower courts and the executive agencies changed over time. Stephenson (2004) finds, however, that the Court did not adjust its signals as the theory would predict. Although some individual justices may have tailored their votes in such a direction, the Court as a whole sent deferential signals to a relatively convergent lower court at a time when the administration was moving away from its preferences. Cohen and Spitzer assumed that the Supreme Court was primarily concerned with sending doctrinal signals about deference with its cases, but the Court may have been more focused on the policy outcomes of the particular cases that it reviews. If so, immediate policy congruence between the Court and the agency decision under review should determine the level of deference that the Court deploys, not the prospective relationship between the courts and the administration in power or taking power. Smith (2007) tests this hypothesis, and finds substantial support for the traditional attitudinal explanation for the voting behavior of the justices. The justices reacted to the ideological distance between themselves and the president at the time the administrative policy was adopted, not to the distance between themselves and the sitting president at the time the Court heard the case.

Similar results have been found for the appellate courts. Humphries and Songer (1999) examine the effect of a party-based measure of judicial ideology while seeking to control for various legal factors that might influence judicial review of administrative decisions. They find that both the partisan character of the judge and legal features of the case affected how judges voted on the executive policies that came before them. Scholars have recently begun to investigate the "panel effects" on the behavior of circuit court judges, since those judges hear each case as a temporary member of a randomly selected panel. Anticipating the votes of their fellow panelists, and thinking ahead to other actors such as the Supreme Court who might choose to review their decisions, circuit court judges may well behave differently depending on the composition of the particular panel on which they happen to sit. Each panel offers a distinctive strategic context.

One application of panel effects comes in the context of administrative law. Examining circuit court cases reviewing EPA and NLRB decisions, Miles and Sunstein (2006) also find that judges appointed by different presidents of different parties have predictable tendencies in such cases. In keeping with recent work in other contexts, however, they also find that judges moderate their behavior when placed on mixed panels, in this case panels that included a member of the other party. Whether the cause of such moderation is primarily sociological, as Miles and Sunstein contend, or strategic, as others have suggested (Cross and Tiller 1998), remains ripe for further exploration (Kastellec 2009).

This leaves open the question of whether the political branches respond to such tendencies in judicial behavior. Executive actors might regard the prospect of judicial review of their actions as too remote to be worth anticipating, or find judicial preferences over the relevant policies to be too difficult to anticipate. Must the courts actively utilize the judicial check for it to be effective? Some emerging studies suggest that the political branches do anticipate judicial review of administrative decision making. Howard and Nixon (2002), for example, examine the auditing policies used by regional IRS offices as a function of circuit court ideology and find that local auditing practices do vary with the composition of the circuit court. Similarly, Canes-Wrone (2003) reports that the Army Corps of Engineers alters its behavior in granting permits for the development of wetlands depending on the composition of the lower courts. The effect of judicial composition on bureaucratic decision making in the issuing of wetland permits is comparable to the effect of the composition of Congress on such decisions.

The ways in which the White House might also adjust to the judicial check are still largely unexplored territory. In making law, Congress responds to the constitutional rules that the Supreme Court has laid down, but the legislative response is not always rapid or carefully calibrated to meet the Court's preferences (Pickerill 2004). The White House has the institutional tools to track the latest signals emerging from the judiciary and to analyze and disseminate the relevant pronouncements of the courts on any given policy. The legal opinions of the Office of Legal Counsel within the Department of Justice provide formal interpretations of the law for executive officials, coordinating the legal position and strategy of the executive branch (Kmiec 1993). In doing so, they can anticipate judicial review and extend the judicial influence into internal executive deliberations by embracing and replicating positions laid out by the courts. Instead, however, they could develop a counter-narrative that resists the legal frameworks and conclusions of the courts in order to justify policies that would likely be disfavored by the courts (Johnsen 2007). It is also possible for these opinions to leverage the authority of judicial decisions to push interpretations of the law that have not yet been clearly articulated by the courts, but that might be used to shape policy making internal to the executive branch or in negotiations between the executive and legislative branches. Through the internal adjustment of the procedures that agencies use to make decisions and adjudicate administrative cases, the executive can also potentially manipulate the effectiveness and availability of judicial review of administrative outcomes. The Justice Department's reform of the adjudication of cases in immigration courts after September 11, for example, had both the practical and formal effect of insulating such decisions from judicial review by Article III courts (Rana forthcoming).

MORE TO BE DONE

There is reason to be skeptical of the judicial check on the presidency as a heroic force in American politics. The judiciary is part of the broader political system, and the courts have particularly strong ties to the presidency. Presidents play an important role in shaping the judiciary, beginning with the Supreme Court. They have a strong voice in the litigation process, and they exercise an important measure of power in implementing judicial decisions and fostering support for or opposition to the courts. The Supreme Court has often been supportive of presidential power and the substantive policies of the executive branch over time. The Court has established doctrinal frameworks that are generally supportive of the presidency, though it has opened some important space for resisting executive action, especially when the executive is seen as operating against the will of Congress.

An emerging body of work examines the theoretical and empirical foundations of the judicial relationship to the executive. Most of this work has focused on judicial behavior and the most basic political correlates between the political orientation of the actors involved and judicial deference to administration policy. Recent work has begun to push further. Some studies have examined how presidents help shape the judicial agenda. Others have examined the conditions under which the courts might be more or less deferential to the executive. Still others have begun to examine how non-judicial institutions, most notably the executive, have responded to the judiciary and anticipated judicial review of their actions.

These new avenues of study are still in the early stages of development. There is a great deal of theoretical and empirical work left to be done. We will undoubtedly see in the future more sophisticated studies of judicial behavior and the conditions under which the courts impose checks on the executive, or fail to do so. Examining the influence of legal variables on judicial outcomes is difficult, but there are indications that such variables can matter for how successful presidents are in court. More work needs to be done to push these suggestions forward to bolster our confidence and understanding of the issues on which, or the legal conditions under which, courts might be more likely to defer to the executive. Theoretical and empirical investigation will be needed in turn to shed light on whether these variations are best understood as evidence of instances in which formal law matters to judicial decision making or as proxies for political and institutional circumstances in which presidents are more or less advantaged.

Even more intriguing, however, is the possibility of further work examining the executive and how it responds to the courts, or fails to do so. Executive reactions to the courts can be harder to observe than judicial voting behavior in cases, which can hamper empirical work, but understanding how both institutions think about and react to one another will ultimately be essential to understanding the operation of the judicial check. Relatively little is known about how judicial signals are processed within the executive branch and how legal interpretations are made, permeated, and

implemented through the executive branch. Not only might administration preferences and attitudes potentially deter the courts from utilizing their powers to check
the executive, but the efficacy and ultimate meaning of judicial decisions are affected
by subsequent interpretations and actions of executive branch officials. In short, the
judicial check will matter more if the executive branch anticipates it and adjusts its
behavior accordingly. Further theoretical and empirical investigation is needed to
flesh out whether and under what conditions the executive anticipates judicial
action.

REFERENCES

ADLER, D. G., and GEORGE, L. N. (eds.) 1996. *The Constitution and the Conduct of American Foreign Policy.* Lawrence: University Press of Kansas.

BAILEY, M. A., KAMOIE, B., and MALTZMAN, F. 2005. Signals from the Tenth Justice: The Political Role of the Solicitor General in Supreme Court Decision Making. *American Journal of Political Science,* 49: 72–85.

BARKOW, R. E. 2002. More Supreme Than Court? The Fall of Political Question Doctrine and the Rise of Judicial Supremacy. *Columbia Law Review,* 102: 237–336.

BARRON, D. J., and LEDERMAN, M. S. 2008. The Commander in Chief at the Lowest Ebb: A Constitutional History. *Harvard Law Review,* 121: 941–1111.

CALABRESI, S. G., and YOO, C. S. 2008. *The Unitary Executive: Presidential Power from Washington to Bush.* New Haven, CT: Yale University Press.

CANES-WRONE, B. 2003. Bureaucratic Decisions and the Composition of the Lower Courts. *American Journal of Political Science,* 47: 205–14.

CLARK, T. S. 2006. Judicial Decision Making during Wartime. *Journal of Empirical Legal Studies,* 3: 397–419.

CLEVELAND, S. H. 2005. *Hamdi* Meets *Youngstown:* Justice Jackson's Wartime Security Juris-prudence and the Detention of Enemy Combatants. *Albany Law Review,* 68: 1127–44.

COHEN, L. R., and SPITZER, M. L. 1994. Solving the *Chevron* Puzzle. *Law and Contemporary Problems,* 57: 67–110.

CORWIN, E. S. 1984. *The President: Office and Powers, 1787–1984, History and Analysis of Practice and Opinion,* 5th rev. edn., ed. R. W. Bland, T. T. Hindson, and J. W. Peltason. New York: New York University Press.

CROSS, F. B., and TILLER, E. H. 1998. Judicial Partisanship and Obedience to Legal Doctrine: Whistleblowing on the Federal Courts of Appeals. *Yale Law Journal,* 107: 2155–76.

DAHL, R. A. 1957. Decision Making in a Democracy: The Supreme Court as a National Policy-Maker. *Journal of Public Law,* 6: 279–95.

DUCAT, C. R., and DUDLEY, R. L. 1989. Federal District Judges and Presidential Power during the Postwar Era. *Journal of Politics,* 51: 98–118.

EPSTEIN, L., HO, D. E., KING, G., and SEGAL, J. A. 2005. The Supreme Court during Crisis: How War Affects Only Non-War Cases. *New York University Law Review,* 80: 1–116.

FARHANG, S. 2006. The Litigation State: Public Regulation and Private Lawsuits in the American Separation of Powers System. Ph.D. dissertation, Columbia University.

FRYMER, P. 2007. *Black and Blue: African Americans, the Labor Movement, and the Decline of the Democratic Party.* Princeton, NJ: Princeton University Press.

GARRETT, E. 2008. Legislation and Statutory Interpretation. In *The Oxford Handbook of Law and Politics*, ed. K. E. Whittington, R. D. Kelemen, and G. A. Caldeira. New York: Oxford University Press.

GRABER, M. A. 1999. The Problematic Establishment of Judicial Review. In *The Supreme Court in American Politics*, ed. H. Gillman and C. Clayton. Lawrence: University Press of Kansas.

——— 2005. Constructing Judicial Review. *Annual Review of Political Science*, 8: 425–51.

HOWARD, R. M., and NIXON, D. C. 2002. Regional Court Influence over Bureaucratic Policy-making: Courts, Ideological Preferences, and the Internal Revenue Service. *Political Research Quarterly*, 55: 907–22.

HUMPHRIES, M. A., and SONGER, D. R. 1999. Law and Politics in Judicial Oversight of Federal Administrative Agencies. *Journal of Politics*, 61: 207–20.

ISSACHAROFF, S., and PILDES, R. H. 2004. Between Civil Libertarianism and Executive Unilateralism: An Institutional Process Approach to Rights during Wartime. *Theoretical Inquiries in Law*, 5: 1–45.

JOHNSEN, D. E. 2007. Faithfully Executing the Laws: Internal Legal Constraints on Executive Power. *UCLA Law Review*, 54: 1559–612.

JOHNSON, T. R. 2003. The Supreme Court, the Solicitor General, and the Separation of Powers. *American Politics Research*, 31: 426–51.

KASTELLEC, J. P. 2009. Hierarchical and Collegial Politics on the US Court of Appeals. Unpublished working paper.

KING, K. L., and MEERNIK, J. 1998. The Sole Organ before the Court: Presidential Power in Foreign Policy Cases, 1790–1996. *Presidential Studies Quarterly*, 28: 666–86.

KMIEC, D. W. 1993. OLC's Opinion Writing Function: The Legal Adhesive for a Unitary Executive. *Cardozo Law Review*, 15: 337–74.

LAVINBUK, A. N. 2005. Rethinking Early Judicial Involvement in Foreign Affairs: An Empirical Study of the Supreme Court's Docket. *Yale Law Journal*, 114: 855–904.

LEVINSON, D. J., and PILDES, R. H. 2006. Separation of Parties, Not Powers. *Harvard Law Review*, 119: 2311–84.

LINDQUIST, S. A., YALOF, D. A., and CLARK, J. A. 2000. The Impact of Presidential Appointments to the U.S. Supreme Court: Cohesive and Divisive Voting within Presidential Blocs. *Political Research Quarterly*, 53: 795–814.

McCUBBINS, M. D., NOLL, R. G., and WEINGAST, B. R. 1987. Administrative Procedures as Instruments of Political Control. *Journal of Law, Economics and Organization*, 3: 243–77.

McMAHON, K. J. 2004. *Reconsidering Roosevelt on Race: How the Presidency Paved the Road to Brown*. Chicago: University of Chicago Press.

MARCUS, M. 1977. *Truman and the Steel Seizure Case: The Limits of Presidential Power*. New York: Columbia University Press.

MASHAW, J. L. 2008. Administration and the Democracy: Administrative Law from Jackson to Lincoln, 1829–1861. *Yale Law Journal*, 117: 1568–9.

MILES, T. J., and SUNSTEIN, C. R. 2006. Do Judges Make Regulatory Policy? An Empirical Investigation of Chevron. *University of Chicago Law Review*, 73: 823–81.

MOE, T. M., and WILSON, S. A. 1994. Presidents and the Politics of Structure. *Law and Contemporary Problems*, 57: 1–44.

NZELIBE, J. 2004. The Uniqueness of Foreign Affairs. *Iowa Law Review*, 89: 941–1010.

O'DONNELL, G. 1994. Delegative Democracy. *Journal of Democracy*, 5: 55–69.

PICKERILL, J. M. 2004. *Constitutional Deliberation in Congress: The Impact of Judicial Review in a Separated System*. Durham, NC: Duke University Press.

POWELL, H. J. 2002. *The President's Authority over Foreign Affairs: An Essay in Constitutional Interpretation*. Durham, NC: Carolina Academic Press.

QUINT, P. E. 1989. Reflections on the Separation of Powers and Judicial Review at the End of the Reagan Era. *George Washington Law Review*, 57: 427–58.

RAMSEY, M. D. 2007. *The Constitution's Text in Foreign Affairs*. Cambridge, MA: Harvard University Press.

RANA, S. Forthcoming. Streamlining the Rule of Law: How the Department of Justice is Undermining Judicial Review of Agency Action. *Illinois Law Review*.

RODRIGUEZ, D. B. 2008. Administrative Law. In *The Oxford Handbook of Law and Politics*, ed. K. E. Whittington, R. D. Kelemen, and G. A. Caldeira. New York: Oxford University Press.

SILVERSTEIN, G. 1996. *Imbalance of Powers: Constitutional Interpretation and the Making of American Foreign Policy*. New York: Oxford University Press.

SMITH, J. L. 2007. Presidents, Justices, and Deference to Administrative Action. *Journal of Law, Economics, and Organization*, 23: 346–64.

STEPHENSON, M. C. 2004. Mixed Signals: Reconsidering the Political Economy of Judicial Deference to Administrative Agencies. *Administrative Law Journal*, 56: 657–738.

——— 2006. Legislative Allocation of Delegated Power: Uncertainty, Risk, and the Choice between Agencies and Courts. *Harvard Law Review*, 119: 1036–70.

SUNSTEIN, C. R. 1987. Constitutionalism after the New Deal. *Harvard Law Review*, 101: 421–510.

VANBERG, G. 2001. Legislative–Judicial Relations: A Game-Theoretic Approach to Constitutional Review. *American Journal of Political Science*, 45: 346–31.

VERMEULE, A. 2006. *Judging under Uncertainty: An Institutional Theory of Legal Interpretation*. Cambridge, MA: Harvard University Press.

WHITTINGTON, K. E. 2007. *Political Foundations of Judicial Supremacy: The Presidency, the Supreme Court, and Constitutional Leadership in U.S. History*. Princeton, NJ: Princeton University Press.

YALOF, D. A. 1999. *Pursuit of Justices: Presidential Politics and the Selection of Supreme Court Nominees*. Chicago: University of Chicago Press.

YATES, J. 2002. *Popular Justice: Presidential Prestige and Executive Success in the Supreme Court*. Albany: State University of New York Press.

——— and WHITFORD, A. 1998. Presidential Power and the United States Supreme Court. *Political Research Quarterly*, 51: 539–50.

YOO, J. 2005. *The Powers of War and Peace: The Constitution and Foreign Affairs after 9/11*. Chicago: University of Chicago Press.

PART X

INTERNATIONAL POLITICS

CHAPTER 29

PRESIDENTS, DOMESTIC POLITICS, AND THE INTERNATIONAL ARENA

DOUGLAS L. KRINER

WHILE the twentieth century witnessed the dramatic expansion of presidential power across the gamut of national policy making, nowhere do presidents appear to be as firmly in command of the body politic as in their conduct of the nation's foreign relations. As America's chief diplomats, presidents have committed the United States to over 200 treaties and more than 14,000 executive agreements since the end of the Second World War. Through diverse measures such as mutual defense pacts, commitments to international conventions and institutions, and free trade protocols, presidents fundamentally shape the nation's posture in the world. International crises also have bolstered presidential power in the international arena; in the wake of natural disasters, economic panics, reports of human rights abuses, or outbursts of armed conflicts, other actors both at home and abroad look to the president to coordinate the American response. Finally, executive power is at its peak in the international realm when presidents deploy American military might around the globe, usually absent any prior congressional authorization (Schlesinger 1973; Fisher 1995, 2000; Rudalevige 2005). Whether by dispatching troops to restore democracy in

Haiti in 1994, combat genocide in the Balkans in the late 1990s, or preempt an alleged imminent threat to the United States from Iraq at the dawn of the twenty-first century, presidents have repeatedly cloaked themselves in the mantle of commander-in-chief to pursue a host of foreign policy objectives.

For almost half a century, presidency scholarship on foreign policy has systematically minimized the importance of other domestic political actors in constraining presidential discretion in the international arena. With perhaps the second most quoted aphorism in presidency studies ("the United States has one president, but has two presidencies") Aaron Wildavsky (1966, 7) firmly aligned presidential foreign policy scholarship with the realist paradigm then dominant in international relations (IR) (Morgentheau 1948, 1951). In contrast to domestic affairs, in foreign and defense policy Wildavsky argued, "it no longer makes sense for Presidents to 'play politics'" (1966, 14). Unfettered by the political constraints that hamper their freedom of action in the domestic arena, presidents in the nuclear age chart and implement a foreign policy course driven by their perceptions of the national interest, not crude political calculations.

Presidents are preeminent because of the institutional advantages they enjoy vis-à-vis other domestic political actors in the international realm. Lacking strong electoral incentives and independent resources with which to challenge the president for preeminence in foreign policy, Congress largely, and perhaps even logically, defers to the executive (Hinckley 1994; Fisher 1995, 2000; Deering 2005). If Congress is unwilling or unable to defend its institutional prerogatives in foreign affairs, the courts are equally reticent to intervene on its behalf (Silverstein 1997). And finally, in stark contrast to the rich array of organized interests demanding a seat at the table in the domestic arena, in foreign policy the interest group community is "weak, unstable and thin" (Wildavsky 1966, 10). Forced by bold strokes of presidential initiative into a reactive role, Congress and the courts all too often appear powerless to respond to what presidents have effected unilaterally (Howell 2003; Canes-Wrone, Howell, and Lewis 2008). As a result, for over four decades Edward Corwin's (1940, 200) famous declaration that the constitutional distribution of war powers across the branches created "an invitation to struggle" was replaced by a consensus view asserting presidential dominance.

Ironically, many of the most important challenges to this dominant realist paradigm have come from within international relations. In his seminal article, Robert Putnam (1988) argued that virtually all international disputes, from multinational wrangling over trade deals, to treaty negotiations, to interstate crisis bargaining and threats to use force, are best modeled as two-level games with simultaneous strategic interactions occurring at both the international and domestic levels. Moreover, domestic politics, according to Putnam, are of more than passing importance. In fact, because an executive "will normally give primacy to his domestic calculus" (457), the bargaining environment and distribution of preferences at the domestic level largely determine the available strategies, bargaining leverage, and ultimate prospects for success of a nation's leadership on the international stage (see also Schelling 1960; Allison 1971).

A decade later, Helen Milner (1998) emphasized the continued need for closer analysis of the linkages between domestic politics and IR by taking aim at a central tenet of realism: that states are unitary actors seeking to maximize a uniformly held, exogenous set of policy preferences comprising the "national interest." Rather, Milner emphasized that executives, legislatures, interest groups, and even the public at large all vie for influence over foreign policy decisions and that the "national interest" itself is the end product of their internal bargaining. "Actors domestically have distinct preferences, and fashioning some single national preference is dependent on the resources the actors possess and the institutions in which they operate." As a result, Milner warned, "the national interest cannot just be assumed; it must be explained" (772).

A growing number of IR scholars have embraced Putnam's and Milner's clarion calls and demonstrated the importance of domestic politics in shaping international relations, including the most critical policy decision at the heart of the realist paradigm, the use of force (*inter alia* Bueno de Mesquita et al. 1999, 2003; Maoz and Russett 1993; Lake 1992; Siverson 1995; Morgan and Campbell 1991; Fearon 1994, 1997). However, while these advances in IR offer both a strong theoretical framework and empirical evidence demonstrating that domestic political dynamics can have significant ramifications for interstate conflict behavior, most tell us very little about *which* domestic actors are most important in foreign policy decisions, through *what* mechanisms they affect presidential decision making, and *how* these actors' power and influence wax and wane across changing political and contextual environments. Lamenting what Bruce Bueno de Mesquita and David Lalman (1992) called "the black box of domestic politics" (8), Milner argues that a major objective for future theory building is "to develop a systematic way to explore which and how domestic factors affect international politics" (1998, 773). Presidency scholars possess a wealth of analytic tools to peer into that box and illuminate the processes at work affecting foreign policy outcomes.

For too long, presidency scholarship has remained mired in the two presidencies debate, focusing primarily on whether the president's institutional advantages when acting in the international arena manifest themselves in greater legislative success rates in foreign versus domestic policy (Wildavsky 1966; Wildavsky and Oldfield 1991; Sigelman 1979; Edwards 1986; Shull 1991; Rohde 1994; Fleisher and Bond 2000). However, the great strides presidency scholars have made in meticulously detailing how interbranch factors and other domestic political pressures affect virtually every aspect of presidential strategic behavior in the domestic realm suggest that they are uniquely positioned to describe how these same factors also drive presidential action in the international arena. In the domestic domain, presidency scholarship has demonstrated how domestic political pressures affect everything from where policy is made (Rudalevige 2002), to what strategies presidents employ to build support for their legislative agendas (Kernell 1997; Canes-Wrone 2005), to how they seek to influence the bureaucracy to implement enacted policies in accordance with their policy preferences (Lewis 2003; Moe 1998; Moe and Wilson 1994). By applying this analytic lens and theoretical advances in IR to the American case, future presidency research can both further American politics scholars' understanding of the continued importance of other domestic political actors and pressures in shaping foreign policy making, and also contribute to IR scholarship by illuminating in more detail the precise pathways through which various domestic factors combine to effect changes in policy.

RETHINKING THE TWO PRESIDENCIES

Although the president is undeniably the most prominent and influential actor guiding the American ship of state in international affairs, an emerging literature at the nexus of IR and American politics reexamines the conventional wisdom and asserts that in certain political and strategic environments other domestic political actors, particularly Congress, can influence presidents' decision calculus in the international arena. The logic driving most of these analyses is anticipatory. Presidents calculate that a Congress controlled by the opposition party is considerably more likely for a variety of ideological and partisan electoral reasons to challenge their conduct of foreign affairs than is a legislature controlled by the president's partisan allies. Thus, when choosing their foreign policy strategies, presidents look to the partisan balance of power on Capitol Hill, anticipate the amount of leeway Congress will grant them to pursue their policy preferences, and adjust their conduct of policy making accordingly.

Consequently, the evidence for these anticipatory mechanisms is usually indirect and primarily consists of covariance between executive behavior in foreign policy making and the strength of the president's party in Congress. For example, within international commerce, a number of scholars have argued that the presidential drive toward trade liberalization is retarded in periods of divided government versus unified government. The greater accommodation of protectionist positions held by many in the legislature is a result both of Congress crafting its delegation of trade authority to the president differently to maximize responsiveness to congressional pressures in divided government and of presidents anticipating congressional objections and moderating their policy initiatives accordingly (O'Halloran 1994; Lohmann and O'Halloran 1994; Milner 1997; though see Coleman 1996; Hiscox 1999). Furthermore, Helen Milner and Peter Rosendorf (1996, 1997) argue that presidential capacity to negotiate and implement new international trade agreements is also a function of divided versus unified government (though see Karol 2000).

Similarly, a diverse set of scholars have argued that the partisan composition of Congress is an important *ex ante* predictor of presidential conduct of military affairs. Using multiple datasets and operationalizations of interbranch partisanship,

David Clark (2000) and William Howell and Jon Pevehouse (2005) demonstrate strong correlations between rates of conflict initiation and the balance of party power across the branches: the stronger the president's party in Congress, the more frequently presidents are willing to exercise American military might abroad. In more recent work, Howell and Pevehouse (2007) go beyond simple event count models to examine the factors driving presidential responses to specific opportunities to use force abroad. Having identified more than 16,000 foreign crises to which the United States could have responded militarily since the end of the Second World War, their empirical analysis demonstrates that the partisan composition of Congress significantly affects a president's willingness to intervene in a given crisis, even after controlling for a host of international factors. These statistical results comport with earlier qualitative work by Lindsay (1992), Brands (1987), and others suggesting that presidents carefully assess the level of support for or opposition to military action within Congress when contemplating the use of force.

The partisan distribution of power on Capitol Hill also seems to affect the scale of a military venture. Kevin Wang (1996) explores the influence of congressional partisanship on the severity of presidential responses to thirty-two crises in the International Crisis Behavior Project from 1954 to 1986. Wang finds a strong, positive correlation between the size of the president's party in Congress and the scale and intensity of the American military action (see also Kriner 2007). Furthermore, the influence of Congress's partisan composition on military policy making does not end once American troops are deployed in the field. Rather, the partisan composition of Congress remains one of the most important predictors of the duration of a major military venture. Presidents confronted by a strong partisan opposition in Congress wage consistently shorter military actions than do their peers buoyed by large co-partisan majorities on Capitol Hill (Clark 2000; Kriner 2007).

Using multiple datasets and methodological approaches, this emerging literature collectively offers compelling indirect evidence that Congress, despite its institutional weaknesses, continues to exercise a check on presidential conduct of foreign policy, even in the military arena where presidential powers appear strongest. However, all of these studies share a common, implicit, and untested assumption: that Congress, the courts, and other domestic political actors possess the means to impose costs on the president should he or she pursue a foreign policy course that deviates too far from their preferences.

In some areas, such as trade, Congress has repeatedly used its formal legislative tools to real effect (O'Halloran 1994; Keech and Pak 1995; Shoch 2001). In treaty making more generally, David Auerswald and Forrest Maltzman (2003) argue that, even though the Senate rarely refuses to ratify presidential pacts, the upper house routinely employs the revision process to limit presidential autonomy and bring policy into greater alignment with congressional policy preferences. Even in the use of force, where presidents at first blush appear most preeminent, Congress has on occasion succeeded in using the formal legislative tools at its disposal to affect fundamentally the policies of the commander-in-chief, as it did in Cambodia, Somalia, and Rwanda.[1]

Yet, history is replete with examples of congressional failure when attempting to influence foreign policy through legislative means, and scholars offer no shortage of explanations for why failure is the most likely outcome. The legislative process itself is fraught with procedural hurdles and steep transaction costs, which make building coalitions for passage difficult even when both branches of government are working toward the same goal (Weingast and Marshall 1988; Epstein and O'Halloran 1999; Moe and Wilson 1994; Moe and Howell 1999; Howell 2003). Moreover, supermajoritarian requirements—specifically the need for sixty votes in the Senate to end a minority filibuster and for two-thirds majorities in both chambers to override a presidential veto—virtually preclude successful legislative challenges to a staunchly defiant president (Krehbiel 1996, 1998; Brady and Volden 1998; Cameron 2000; Deering 2005). Indeed, for many analysts, this repeated failure of Congress to check legislatively the expansion of presidential power in war making animates their arguments of congressional impotence in foreign affairs (Hinckley 1994; Meernik 1994; Gowa 1998, 1999; though see Grimmet 2001). Recent failures by the Democratic 110th Congress to legislate an end to the war in Iraq, despite considerable public support for an expeditious withdrawal, only further reinforce the conventional image of congressional weakness.

Given this track record of repeated legislative failure, why would presidents moderate or even abandon their preferred policies in anticipation of Congress's response? Recent research suggests one possible answer. Although Congress has demonstrated little capacity to write its preferred foreign and particularly military policies into law, it has historically exercised a number of formal tools at its disposal to influence presidential conduct of foreign affairs (Auerswald and Cowhey 1997; Auerswald 2000; Grimmet 2001). For example, Congress can propose and publicly debate varied legislative initiatives to constrain the commander-in-chief. Such actions can range from spending measures to cut off funds for policies of which it disapproves, to invoking the War Powers Resolution and its ninety-day withdrawal clock, to more creative measures, such as the Webb amendment under consideration in the

---

[1] In 1970, Congress enacted Public Law 91-652 cutting off funding for President Nixon's clandestine expansion of the ground war in Indochina into Cambodia. More than twenty years later, after the death of eighteen American servicemen in Mogadishu, Congress enacted PL 103-139 cutting off funding for military actions in Somalia after March 31, 1994. And finally, with the Somalia tragedy foremost in their collective conscious, members of Congress a year later passed PL 103-335 to insure that the Clinton administration's limited aid mission to Rwanda did not expand by cutting off funding for any humanitarian military presence within the genocide-ravaged country. It should be noted, however, that in the Vietnam case, Congress succeeded only after extensive negotiations with the Nixon administration and after the troops in Cambodia had already been withdrawn; nevertheless, it is not clear whether Nixon ever would have withdrawn the troops of his own accord absent the outcry and action in Congress. Similarly in the Somali context, President Clinton had announced his intentions to withdraw by that date prior to the legislation's passage. Efforts to cut off funding at an earlier date were defeated. For examples of congressional legislative challenges to presidential military policy from the pre-Second World War era, see Johnson (1995).

110th Congress, that hamstring presidential flexibility to conduct military policy making solely according to his or her preferences. Alternatively, congressional committees and the legislative entrepreneurs at their helms can also seek to influence foreign policy making through their capacity to superintend the executive via aggressive investigative oversight (Aberbach 1990; Fowler and Hill 2006; Kriner and Schwartz 2008). A quick perusal of Mayhew's (1991) list of high-profile congressional probes reveals a large number involving foreign policy—including inquests into who "lost" China, the conduct of major military operations in Korea, the Dominican Republic, and Vietnam, the Iran-Contra scandal, and the ongoing investigations into the Bush administration's missteps in Iraq. Even more mundane presidential actions in the international arena have not escaped the attention of Congress and its committees; for example, Jeffrey Peake, Glen Krutz, and Walt Jatkowski (2007) have identified over 850 House and Senate hearings devoted either to investigations or oversight of executive agreements and treaties between 1973 and 2004. Finally, individual members of Congress are also extraordinarily active in shaping the national debate over foreign policy issues through their informal maneuverings in the "public sphere." Through speeches on the floor, press conferences, media events, and tours in their states and districts, members of Congress can engage and shape the national debate over major issues on the political agenda. Indeed, in David Mayhew's (2000) extensive survey of over two hundred years of American history, almost a full quarter of all informal congressional "actions" in the public sphere involved major issues of foreign policy.

In his analysis of twenty major uses of force since 1945 that involved new deployments of ground troops or the sustained use of American firepower, Douglas Kriner (2007) employs hazard models with time-varying covariates to examine the influence of both these failed formal legislative initiatives and more informal congressional actions on the expected duration of a military venture. Even though none of these congressional actions legally compelled a president to alter or abandon his chosen military course, Kriner's hazard analyses demonstrate strong correlations between both categories of congressional engagement and changes in the predicted duration of an ongoing military action. After controlling for combat casualties, shifts in public opinion, the state of the economy, and other developments in the political and strategic environment, congressional actions to authorize the use of force correlated with increased expected durations for the use of force. Similarly, congressional investigative hearings and the introduction of legislative initiatives to curtail the use of force, regardless of whether or not they passed even a single chamber, yielded substantial decreases in a conflict's predicted duration. This echoes insights by David Auerswald and Peter Cowhey (1997) that even failed efforts to invoke the War Powers Resolution or other formal levers at Congress's disposal may have considerable indirect influence on presidential decision making. Moreover, even the informal maneuverings of individual members of Congress in the public sphere reported by the mass media had a significant impact on predicted changes in duration, particularly the "costly" signals generated by opposition party support for the president's handling of military affairs and calls for de-escalation or withdrawal from the president's partisan opponents (see also Baum and Groeling 2005; Howell and Kriner 2007b).

Yet, all of these studies challenging the conventional tenets of the two presidencies paradigm raise three important questions that future research must address. First, while it presents compelling empirical and historical evidence that Congress can influence presidential conduct of foreign and defense policy, existing research primarily demonstrates correlations between congressional partisanship or formal and informal actions and changes in patterns of policy making. Literatures within American politics and international relations suggest several possible mechanisms by which even failed legislative initiatives or other congressional actions that lack the force of law may influence presidents' decision calculus. However, in some cases the complete causal chains connecting specific actions to concrete changes in policy are ambiguous, and hard evidence that the proposed mechanism is indeed effecting observed policy changes is largely lacking.

Second, the bulk of prior research has focused exclusively on the capacity of Congress to affect presidential foreign policy making, particularly in the military arena. Yet, other domestic actors, particularly the courts and organized interest groups, frequently engage the policy-making process. Given the paucity of explicit grants of constitutional foreign policy and war powers to the executive branch, particularly in contrast to the extensive grants of military authority to Congress in Article I (Lofgren 1986; Koh 1990; Ely 1993; Glennon 1990; Adler and George 1996; though see Pious 2007), the judiciary possesses strong legal grounds on which to overturn presidential overreaches in the international arena. Moreover, the courts frequently have ample opportunities to do so as organized interests and even members of Congress have repeatedly petitioned the courts for redress against perceived usurpations of presidential war powers.[2] In most of these cases, the judiciary has ruled either that individual members of Congress lack standing to sue, that the issues are not yet ripe, or that the cases involve inherently "political questions" beyond the reach of the bench (Franck 1992; Sheffer 1999; see Fisher 2005 for a review).[3]

However, several recent decisions striking down elements of the Bush administration's conduct of the war on terror represent a departure from past precedent and may herald growing judicial influence in foreign policy matters.[4] Louis Fisher (2005)

---

[2] For example, during conflicts in Vietnam (*Mitchell* v. *Laird*), the Persian Gulf (*Dellums* v. *Bush*), Kosovo (*Campbell* v. *Clinton*), and Iraq (*Doe* v. *Bush*), individual members of Congress have filed suit asking federal courts to exercise their powers of judicial review and strike down unilateral presidential maneuverings in foreign policy as unconstitutional.

[3] In 1995, Congressman Vic DeFazio introduced amendments to the War Powers Resolution to codify the right of individual members of Congress to seek injunctive relief from federal courts if the president had failed to comply with any provision of the Resolution. However, the amendments failed to pass (Grimmett 2004). The courts have shown similar reluctance to adjudicate interbranch disputes in other aspects of foreign policy aside from war powers, including the Supreme Court's oft-cited dismissal of Senator Barry Goldwater's suit against the Carter administration for unilaterally withdrawing the United States from the Mutual Defense Treaty with Taiwan in order to open full diplomatic relations with the People's Republic of China.

[4] See *Hamdi* v. *Rumsfeld*, *Rumsfeld* v. *Padilla*, *Rasul* v. *Bush*, *Hamdan* v. *Rumsfeld*, and *Boumediene* v. *Bush*.

rightly notes that the substantive scope of these rulings pales in comparison to the dramatic assertions of unilateral presidential power over the conduct of the war on terror. Additionally, even these decisions challenging presidential power have left many issues to be resolved by the lower courts, mitigating their immediate impact and opening the door to policy drift. However, this recent judicial activism does challenge the conventional script stressing the judiciary's reticence to enter major foreign policy debates (Silverstein 1997; see also King and Meernik 1999 for a critique of judicial deference theories). Moreover, if even failed congressional actions may influence presidential decision making indirectly, future scholarship should explore whether court rulings, through the same mechanisms, have indirect effects beyond the immediate substance of the case in question on other aspects of presidential policy making.

Similarly, organized interests, particularly in specific areas of foreign policy, are increasingly active through both formal and informal channels (Hook 2005; Smith 2000; Grossman and Helpman 2002; Haney and Vanderbush 1999). As in domestic affairs, interest groups may play a catalytic role in spurring Congress or the courts to challenge presidential policies. Influential interest groups can provide officials with information about public opinion (Powlick 1995) and forge the "electoral connection" that raises the salience of foreign policy issues for key members of Congress and encourages them to act. They may also prime public awareness and even shift public opinion on an issue, compelling congressional action or encouraging the court that there is support for judicial restraints on presidential assertions of power in foreign policy. Future research would do well to explore how interest groups use the same mechanisms as other domestic actors to make their mark on foreign policy.

A third and final limitation of existing scholarship is that it only begins to explore the variance in when other political actors will possess the ability and political will to employ these mechanisms to affect the president's conduct of foreign policy. Prior studies emphasized the importance of Congress's partisan composition and argued that the strength of the legislative check on the president is directly proportional to the strength of the opposition party. Yet, even a strong opposition party will have few incentives to challenge the president's foreign policies, even when they diverge from its preferences, in certain conditions and circumstances. Future scholarship must explore in considerably greater detail how these baseline partisan incentives are conditioned by the overarching political and strategic environment in which the president and other domestic political actors must interact.

The next section draws on literatures from within American politics and international relations to identify three mechanisms through which other domestic political actors can retain some measure of influence over the president's conduct of the nation's IR, even when they are unable to legally compel him to change course. While the discussion frequently focuses on military policy making, the insights gained are applicable to other areas of foreign policy making. The final section examines the ways in which political and strategic considerations moderate the capacity and willingness of Congress, the courts, and organized interests to use these mechanisms to influence presidential decision making in the international arena.

THREE MECHANISMS OF DOMESTIC
POLITICAL INFLUENCE

Through a variety of channels, legislatures, courts, and other domestic political institutions can influence the foreign policies that presidents formulate and implement. This section focuses on three.

Mechanism 1: Raising or Lowering Domestic Political Costs

Congress and the courts have, in isolated cases, exercised their formal constitutional authority to coerce presidents to alter or abandon their foreign policy initiatives. Nevertheless, over 150 years of American history make clear that if enacting legislation forcing presidents to abandon their military ventures and comply with congressional mandates or issuing judicial rulings overturning executive actions were the only means through which other domestic actors could influence presidential foreign policy making, then presidents would, in all but the rarest of circumstances, exercise power virtually unchecked by the other branches. Indeed, the repeated failure of both branches to meet the expectations of the Founders and use the formal powers at their disposal to curb presidential usurpations of power has given rise to the dominant conventional wisdom of legislative and judicial impotence in international policy making.

Yet, Congress, the courts, and even interest groups need not legally compel the president to change course to influence his or her strategic decision making. Indeed, recent developments in IR suggest that even failed formal legislative challenges to the president and informal actions, such as investigative hearings and publicity campaigns, may have significant ramifications for the president by raising the political costs of a chosen policy course. Presidents, as rational actors, weigh the expected costs and benefits of all available policy alternatives and adopt the policy that maximizes their expected utility. Estimates of the domestic costs they stand to incur from a given policy option are critically important parts of that calculation. A number of leading IR theorists have argued that because of the capacity of other domestic political elites to exact costs on the executive for failed or unpopular policies, democratic leaders face higher levels of institutional constraints on their freedom of action in the international arena than do autocratic leaders (Morgan and Campbell 1991; Lake 1992; Prins and Sprecher 1993; Siverson 1995). This, in turn, they contend, explains many of the different patterns of conflict behavior observed across regime types.

While this IR literature is theoretically rich and offers the critically important insight that domestic politics may still influence executive behavior even in the absence of formal, legal challenges to its authority, the precise pathways through which other domestic actors impose these political costs are often unclear. For example, Zeev Maoz and Bruce Russett (1993, 626) speak in general terms of the "complexity of the democratic process" and the concomitant need for "securing a broad base of support for risky policies" to explain the critical importance of the domestic constraints on democratic executives when contemplating the use of force. Bruce Bueno de Mesquita and colleagues are more specific and argue that domestic political institutions critically affect states' conflict behavior primarily because they influence leaders' likelihood of retaining office given alternative policy outcomes (Buneo de Mesquita and Lalman 1992; Bueno de Mesquita and Siverson 1995; Bueno de Mesquita et al. 1999, 2003). Because democratic leaders face higher electoral costs if they fail militarily, democracies are more selective in the wars they initiate and more likely to win the conflicts they fight; moreover, the strength of this dampening effect only increases with the level of public electoral participation (Reiter and Tillman 2002).

Yet, even within this research tradition important questions remain. How do other domestic political actors, most importantly the legislature, affect the electoral costs democratic leaders risk when acting militarily? Does open legislative support for or opposition to the executive's policies moderate or exacerbate these likely costs and, in turn, indirectly influence his or her conflict behavior? If so, what types of legislative actions affect executive calculations of these potential electoral costs? Can other actors, such as the courts or interest groups, which enjoy popular legitimacy or engage the public directly, also influence the likely costs of a military course for the executive?

An extensive literature within American politics suggests at least one way in which the maneuverings of Congress and other domestic actors can affect presidential policy making in the international arena—through their influence on public opinion. Scholars have long analyzed presidents' use of the "bully pulpit" to court popular support for their policy proposals (Tulis 1987; Peterson 1990; Mouw and MacKuen 1992; Kernell 1997; Canes-Wrone 2001). However, such presidential efforts to sway the public and rally it behind administration policies frequently fail, even in foreign and defense policy (Edwards 2003). Indeed, recent scholarship emphasizes the growing importance of other political elites, particularly in Congress, who battle the president to manipulate public opinion in pursuit of their own policy and partisan electoral goals (Jacobs et al. 1998; Jacobs and Shapiro 2000; Caldwell 1991).

A growing literature has compiled considerable evidence that the public claims asserted by Congress and reported in the mass media do have significant influence over popular attitudes on major questions of foreign policy, including the use of force. Research by Richard Brody (1991, 1994), John Zaller (1992, 1994), and others finds that in the absence of open congressional criticism of the president's policies, many in the public rally around the flag and the commander-in-chief. However, when opponents of the president's policies in Congress renew their attacks on the administration and its policies, citizens react to familiar partisan or ideological cues and the rally effect attenuates. In a similar vein, in their study of variation in popular support for the invasion of Iraq, William Howell and Jon Pevehouse (2007) find that popular attitudes were heavily influenced by the balance of elite discourse individuals observed on local television news broadcasts. Survey respondents exposed to more reports of congressional opposition to the Bush administration's war plans were less likely to support a preemptive strike against Saddam Hussein than were their peers with similar demographic characteristics who hailed from regions that received more pro-war coverage in their local media outlets.

Alternatively, other scholars propose a more indirect means for elites to affect popular opinion through their capacity to shape the lens through which the public views major events and developments occurring abroad. For example, a growing literature on the mediated pathways through which conflict events, such as combat casualties, affect public opinion emphasizes how they are framed by elites (Boettcher and Cobb 2006). The sensitivity of the American public to casualties may vary considerably according to whether trusted political elites rally behind a military venture or criticize it (Berinsky 2007), and whether the response of these elites bolsters public confidence in the mission's ultimate success or spurs public doubt about the prospects for military victory (Feaver and Gelpi 2004; Gelpi, Feaver, and Reifler 2006).

However, existing studies attempting to demonstrate strong causal linkages between the actions of other domestic elites, changes in public opinion, and ultimately shifts in policy generally suffer from three primary limitations. The first, and perhaps most important, complicating factor is that the relationships between changing elite cues and shifts in public opinion are almost certainly endogenous. For example, members of Congress surely take the pulse of their district when deciding their public positions, just as these public positions and actions in turn influence and mold opinion in their states and districts. A number of opinion analysts have openly speculated that the causal arrow runs primarily from elites to the public and that this is particularly true in foreign affairs, the policy arena in which the public relies most heavily on elite cues for information (Zaller 1992; Zaller and Chiu 1996; Jordan and Page 1992; Berinsky 2007; Baum and Groeling 2005). However, armed only with traditional methodological approaches and standard observational data, demonstrating conclusively the independent capacity of Congress and other domestic political actors to shape and mold public opinion is difficult.

One way in which future research might overcome these difficulties is through adopting more advanced empirical methods, such as Bayesian vector autoregressive analyses, that are well suited to teasing out endogenous relationships (Freeman, Williams, and Lin 1989). Presidency scholars have already employed similar methods to untangle the complicated and highly endogenous relationships governing agenda setting with considerable success (Wood and Peake 1998; Edwards and Wood 1999; Peake 2001).

Alternatively, future scholars may make further use of experimental research to demonstrate the causal impact of congressional and other domestic actors' cues on the public's foreign policy attitudes. The ability to manipulate elite cues and randomly assign respondents to various treatment and control groups eliminates concerns about endogeneity. Moreover, it also avoids objections about identification that plague studies relying solely on observational data. For example, studies that seek to show correlations between rhetoric emanating from Congress (Howell and Kriner 2007a) or changing patterns of media coverage (Baum and Groeling 2004, 2005) and corresponding shifts in public opinion implicitly assume that the public is actually receiving the signals elite actors are sending. In a laboratory setting, we can be sure that respondents are receiving the elite cues under investigation and that observed differences in opinion across treatment and control groups are the result of these treatments. Recently, a number of scholars have employed survey-embedded experiments suggesting that, in a controlled environment, even nuanced congressional and interest group signals can have considerable influence on levels of popular support for both anticipated and ongoing military actions (Howell and Pevehouse 2007; Howell and Kriner 2007a, 2007b).

However, the same factors that improve the internal validity of experimental research also hinder its external validity. From survey experiments alone, it is next to impossible to assess the relative capacity of any one domestic political elite to influence public opinion in a competitive media environment against a backdrop of unfolding real world events. As a result, future presidency researchers should continue to push forward using both experimental methods and greater collection and analysis of observational data to tease out the intricate relationships between presidents, other domestic elites, and public opinion in foreign policy.

The second major limitation of existing research is its almost exclusive focus on Congress's ability to precipitate swings in popular support for the president. A notable exception is experimental work by William Howell and Douglas Kriner (2007b) suggesting that the public statements of trusted interest groups may also wield considerable influence over support for ongoing and proposed military actions. This experimental finding suggests that the courts, which scholars have long argued zealously guard their institutional legitimacy, may also have a considerable impact on foreign policy making when they rule against the president in foreign affairs that extends well beyond the limited scope of the ruling itself. As a result, even minor judicial defeats, such as those suffered by the Bush administration in *Hamdi*, *Hamdan*, and *Rasul*, may have important indirect consequences for the president through their ripple effects on public opinion. Scholars would do well to expand the scope of analysis and examine in much greater detail the capacity of other domestic political actors besides Congress to mold public opinion in the international arena.

Finally, further research is needed to complete the causal chain and demonstrate the impact of these changes in public opinion on policy decisions. A great deal of work has already begun to illustrate the policy consequences of public opinion in the international realm. New research has replaced the Almond–Lippman consensus with growing evidence that, through a variety of cognitive shortcuts, the mass public is able to form cohesive, consistent, even rational beliefs on major questions of foreign affairs (Page, Shapiro, and Dempsey 1987; Page and Shapiro 1992;

Holsti 1992, 2004; Peffley and Hurwitz 1992) and that the public uses this information when evaluating actors and policies in the political and electoral arenas (Aldrich, Sullivan, and Borgida 1989; Aldrich et al. 2006; Nincic and Hinckley 1991; Hurwitz and Peffley 1987). Moreover, a growing literature has taken the next step and documented the critical importance of changes in public opinion in shaping US foreign policy making in a number of important cases (Sobel 1993, 2001; Klarevas 2002, Larson and Savych 2005; Baum 2004b). These case studies are particularly useful in tracing the full causal processes through which changes in public opinion entered the decision calculus of foreign policy makers and in turn changed the course of policy. However, future scholars should endeavor to collect more systematic empirical evidence of the routine influence of shifts in public opinion, precipitated by support or opposition to the president's policies by other domestic political elites, on the conduct of American foreign policy.

Yet, manipulating public opinion and bringing popular pressures to bear on the president to change his or her policy course is but one way through which Congress, the courts, and organized interests can raise or lower the domestic political costs of a given foreign policy course. Indeed, the almost exclusive focus on the opinion dynamic has caused many scholars to overlook the much broader political consequences of domestic opposition to presidential foreign policies. At least since Richard Neustadt (1960), presidency scholars have warned that costly political battles in one policy arena frequently have significant ramifications for presidential power in other realms. Indeed, two of Neustadt's three "cases of command"— Truman's seizure of the steel mills and firing of General Douglas MacArthur— explicitly discussed the broader political consequences of stiff domestic resistance to presidential assertions of commander-in-chief powers. In both cases, Truman emerged victorious in the case at hand; yet, Neustadt argues, each victory cost him dearly.

By forcing the president to defend his or her international agenda, domestic criticisms may sap energy from other initiatives on the home front. Political capital spent shoring up support for a president's foreign policies is capital unavailable for his or her future policy agenda. Moreover, any weakening in the president's political clout may have immediate ramifications for his or her reelection prospects, as well as indirect consequences for congressional races (Jacobson 2004; Waterman, Oppenheimer, and Stimson 1991; Campbell and Sumners 1990; Campbell 1986). Indeed, Democratic efforts to tie Republican incumbents to President Bush and his war policies paid immediate political dividends in the 2006 midterms, particularly in states, districts, and counties that had suffered the highest casualty rates in the Iraq War (Kriner and Shen 2007; Grose and Oppenheimer 2007). In addition to boding ill for the president's perceived political capital and reputation, such partisan losses in Congress only further imperil his programmatic agenda, both international and domestic. Future research should explore in considerably greater detail these alternative pathways through which challenges to a president's foreign policies by other domestic actors may have significant political ramifications for his or her future power prospects.

Mechanism 2: Signaling to Foreign Actors

A growing game theoretic literature within IR suggests a second mechanism through which other domestic political actors may influence presidential strategic behavior without compelling him or her to change course—by sending signals of American resolve or disunity to foreign actors. Virtually all strategic interactions in the international system involve state leaders sending signals about their expectations of and intentions toward other state actors. When calculating the expected costs and benefits of a given policy response, national leaders must weigh the credibility of foreign states' promises or threats made during negotiations (Fearon 1994, 1997). Whether domestic political elites publicly support or oppose the executive's position greatly influences the credibility of the threats and commitments he or she can make to other states and in turn the probability with which democracies resort to military force (Schultz 1998, 1999, 2001; in the US case see Auerswald 2000; Baum 2004a).

Moreover, signaling dynamics may also critically affect presidential behavior in other areas of foreign affairs. For example, Lisa Martin (2000, 2005) emphasizes the importance of signaling to explain why presidents sometimes prefer to pursue their policy aims through formal treaties rather than executive agreements. The very existence of executive agreements, which free the president from the constitutional requirement of securing a two-thirds majority in the Senate for ratification, begs the question of why presidents would ever opt for the more cumbersome treaty process (Margolis 1986; Nathan and Oliver 1994; Moe and Howell 1999). Martin argues that, when presidents decide to negotiate a treaty, the requirement for Senate confirmation sends a strong signal to the president's negotiating partners that a broad-based domestic political consensus exists within the United States to comply with the terms of the agreement. By contrast, when presidents pursue an executive agreement instead of a treaty, their decision may belie potential domestic resistance to the administration's positions, which in turn diminishes the credibility of presidential pledges to abide by the terms of the agreement. As a result, concerns about signaling may encourage presidents to submit to the requirements and institutional constraints of the treaty-making process, even if executive agreements would afford them considerably more freedom of action and control over policy making.

In the treaty-making process and even in executive agreements, the vast majority of which require the assent of at least one chamber of Congress (Krutz and Peake 2006), supporters and opponents of the president's policies have a strong institutional position from which to send signals about the credibility of the president's negotiating positions. And in the context of military actions, other domestic actors, but most importantly Congress, appear well positioned to affect the signals sent from Washington to foreign governments. For example, public displays of legislative support for the president's conduct of military operations enhance the credibility of presidential threats to use force or commitments to stay the course of an ongoing engagement. Indeed, the desire for this strong signal of domestic support has motivated many presidents to ask Congress for its blessing to launch a military action, even as they claim independent constitutional authority as commander-in-chief to order the invasions unilaterally. Conversely, congressional investigations into alleged executive misconduct of foreign affairs, the informal maneuverings of influential Congressmen in the public sphere, and even failed formal legislative initiatives to constrain the president, may all undermine the credibility of the administration's signals to other nations.

The logic suggesting that Congress, the courts, and interest groups—even if they cannot legally compel the president to change course—can influence his or her decision making by affecting the signals sent to foreign actors is compelling. However, a significant limitation with the existing signaling literature is that the precise expectations for how signals of domestic disunity vs. resolve will affect presidential behavior in specific contexts are often indeterminate.

Consider, for example, the ramifications of various domestic signals for the use of force. Kenneth Schultz (2001) argues that public signals of support for the president's position from other domestic political actors strengthen the credibility of presidential threats to use force. On average, Schultz contends, such signals of resolve allow presidents to avoid engaging in military conflicts because the targets of American demands will be more likely to back down to the president's highly credible threats to use force. However, from another perhaps more Machiavellian perspective, vocal support from other domestic political actors may only bolster presidential ambitions to use American military might to pursue their policy objectives and secure the boost in popular support that regularly follows in the wake of a military action (Lee 1977; Kernell 1978; Sigelman and Johnston-Conover 1981; Brace and Hinckley 1992), particularly one supported by other domestic elites (Brody 1991; Lian and Oneal 1993).

There is similar ambiguity about the exact policy ramifications of domestic signaling after American troops are deployed in the field. Throughout American history, presidential administrations have warned that any public dissent from Congress or other actors undermines the soldiers in the field and hardens enemy resistance in the hopes of outlasting American political will to stay the course. However, even if correct, how presidents will react to these heightened strategic costs of staying the course may vary considerably from case to case. In some instances, presidents may judge that the costs of continuing a mission are no longer worth the expected benefit and therefore will withdraw American forces earlier than they otherwise would. Alternatively, presidents may remain undeterred in their decision to stay the course and the resulting heightened costs on the ground required to achieve American objectives only increase the eventual duration of the nation's military commitment.

Future research should recognize these alternative pathways through which signaling may influence presidential conduct of American military policy and explore in more detail how the case-specific political and strategic environments affect the probability of each type of presidential response. Furthermore, while previous studies have most thoroughly examined Congress's role in affecting the credibility of the signals the executive can send to foreign actors, the theoretical logic also suggests that both the courts and organized interests can have a similar impact. Particularly with the help of the mass media in amplifying critiques of administration policy from judicial sources or highly engaged interest groups, these other domestic political actors may have considerable influence on the scope and tone of the signals emanating from Washington. Future research should expand the scope of analysis to explore in more detail the influence of court decisions and the high-profile maneuverings of key interest groups on presidential policy making through the signals they send to foreign actors.

A final limitation of the signaling literature that future scholars should address is the limited direct evidence that signaling, as opposed to other mechanisms, such as increased domestic political costs, is a key force driving policy outcomes. Most of the empirical evidence collected to date in support of signaling hypotheses simply reports patterns of presidential behavior that are consistent with signaling expectations. However, there is little direct evidence that signaling is the precise mechanism causing the observed trends. Certainly presidents and other administration officials frequently allude to the importance of domestic signals in their public pronouncements. Furthermore, some recent archival research from the Reagan Presidential Library shows administration officials, even in classified memoranda, openly worrying about the response of foreign actors to congressional opposition and its adverse effects for the military situation on the ground in specific cases (Kriner 2007). Future research should examine whether similar calculations affected presidential conduct of other types of military deployments in other eras. Moreover, aside from military policy making, future scholars could also identify cases in which presidents quietly grappled with the decision of whether to pursue their diplomatic agenda through the treaty process or through an executive agreement and search for evidence that signaling dynamics entered their decision calculus. In so doing, presidency scholars can harness their traditional skills in archival and historical research to accumulate more extensive and varied evidence that signaling dynamics affect the conduct of presidential policy making across multiple areas of foreign policy.

Mechanism 3: Influencing the Foreign Policy Agenda

Much of the emerging literature challenging the traditional two presidencies framework has emphasized the indirect but still meaningful ways in which other domestic actors can check, restrain, and curtail presidential initiatives in the international arena. Yet, Congress and other actors can do more than take a merely reactive role in foreign affairs. Through oversight hearings, public debates, and publicity campaigns, members of Congress and interest groups can play a key role at the initial stage of the policy-making process by helping set the foreign policy agenda with which the president must grapple.

In the domestic realm, American politics scholars have long emphasized that the power to move policy items onto and off of the political agenda is a critically important source of influence over policy making (Cobb and Elder 1972; Light 1991; Baumgartner and Jones 1993). While many scholars have proclaimed the president's privileged position as an agenda setter (Huntington 1965; Edwards 1989; Bond and Fleisher 1990; Cohen 1997), others note the ongoing competition between the president, Congress, and other actors over which issues are prioritized atop the government's agenda (Walker 1977; Jones 1994). Moreover, this competition has surely only intensified with the proliferation of organized interest groups since the 1970s determined to push their programmatic agendas in Washington (Berry 1999).

Recently, George Edwards, B. Dan Wood, and Jeffrey Peake have sharpened the scope of analysis to assess the relative influence of various actors specifically on the foreign policy agenda. Surprisingly, Edwards and Wood (1999) fail to find much evidence of presidential influence over the agendas of the media and Congress in foreign affairs (though see Hill 1998). Rather, the political branches, particularly the president, appear to respond primarily to events unfolding abroad and changes in media attention to various foreign crises (see also Wood and Peake 1998). Peake's (2001) examination of agenda-setting dynamics underlying an additional set of less prominent foreign policy issues provides some important qualifiers; on issues of less critical importance and with less permanence on the policy agenda than US–Soviet relations and the Arab–Israeli conflict, Peake finds evidence of considerably more interaction. The media and events continue to have a strong effect on the political agenda, but presidential or congressional attention to an issue also appears to influence the priorities of the other branch.

Given Peake's results, future scholars should probe further the capacity of Congress to shape presidential conduct of international affairs in a proactive manner through their ability to move policy areas of interest to the legislature higher onto the president's agenda. Moreover, a robust literature within political communications suggests that the influence of the media on the president's foreign policy priorities— so strong in Edwards and Wood's analysis—may provide an additional vehicle for congressional influence over the presidential agenda.

In the early and mid-1990s, a number of political communications scholars proposed and discussed the implications of a "CNN effect" by which media attention to foreign crises largely overlooked by politicians in Washington, particularly humanitarian disasters, could catapult a given issue onto the political agenda. By raising public consciousness of an issue and increasing the political costs of inaction, media attention could provide the impetus for government engagement (McNulty 1993; Shaw 1996; Neuman 1996; Robinson 1999, 2002). Yet, others remain skeptical (see Gilboa 2005 for a review). For example, Jonathan Mermin (1999) notes that one of the supposed quintessential examples of the "CNN effect," the sustained media coverage of famine in Somalia which allegedly prompted the Bush administration to launch Operation Restore Hope, emerged only *after* other political elites, particularly members of Congress, had moved the issue onto the agenda through committee hearings and statements in the press (see also Livingston and Eachus 1995).

Indeed, a mounting body of empirical evidence suggests that the media amplifies official objections to the president's policies and priorities by "indexing" the scope and tone of their foreign policy coverage to the level of opposition voiced by Washington elites (Bennett 1990, 1996; Bennett, Lawrence, and Livingston 2006;

Mermin 1999; Entman and Page 1994; Zaller and Chiu 1996). Above all, political communications scholars emphasize the importance the media attributes to Congress, which in the words of Scott Althaus and colleagues is "the chief institutional locus of elite opposition" (1996, 409). In the absence of overt criticism from other domestic political elites, media scrutiny of the president's policies sharply declines. By contrast, as intragovernmental opposition arises, particularly in Congress, the media grows more assertive in questioning the administration's policies and openly discussing other foreign policy priorities.

From an indexing perspective, the media does not form its own agenda exogenously. Rather, it relies heavily on Congress and other government sources to guide its coverage. When these domestic actors disagree with the president's set of priorities, the media may be a powerful ally in amplifying domestic objections and springboarding their concerns onto the political agenda.[5] To be sure, the media certainly retains some independent capacity to affect the agenda and public opinion more broadly (see Baum and Potter 2008 for a review). Nevertheless, extensive media coverage of a foreign crisis, perhaps motivated by Congress or other organized interests, can move foreign emergencies onto the policy agenda in Washington and force presidents to grapple with issues they might otherwise prefer to avoid.

Undoubtedly, the president remains an important, and perhaps even the pivotal, agenda setter in Washington, particularly in foreign affairs. President Bush, more than any other actor on the domestic or international stage, brought Iraq's alleged development of weapons of mass destruction onto the government's agenda; through his control over the presentation and subsequent debate of the issue, Bush exercised almost unbridled control over the course of American foreign policy over the last five years of his presidency. Nevertheless, future research should probe in what set of political and strategic conditions other actors, primarily Congress but perhaps increasingly interest groups, bolstered by the media, can move a foreign policy issue onto the American policy agenda and compel presidential action.

Consider, for example, the domestic politics precipitating US military intervention in civil war-torn Liberia in the later summer of 2003. While President Bush may have wanted to dispatch American troops to Liberia to help implement the faltering ceasefire agreement and spur the self-imposed exile of Liberian leader and indicted war criminal Charles Taylor, staunch opposition from many in the Pentagon and from most leaders and rank and file in his own party in Congress made doing so a politically perilous proposition. With the early signs of an insurgency already beginning to surface in Iraq, an unpopular intervention in Liberia was a potential flashpoint with the military hierarchy and congressional Republicans that the president might logically have wished to avoid. However, through a series of public speeches and hearings congressional Democrats, led by the Congressional Black Caucus, championed the cause for American intervention and even introduced

---

[5] If operative, indexing not only helps Congress move its concerns onto the agenda, even when the president is resistant; rather, through indexing the media also amplifies congressional opposition to presidential foreign and military policies, which in turn may bolster Congress's capacity to influence public opinion.

legislation calling on the president to act. Moreover, the mass media only amplified congressional calls for action; more than 100 stories mentioning Liberia appeared on network and CNN news broadcasts during June and July alone. By raising the salience of Liberia, even at a time when the United States was already engaged in a full-scale war in Iraq, activists in Congress, aided by the media, forced the issue firmly onto the political agenda, eliminated any hopes that the issue would simply fade away, and compelled the administration to decide on a course of action that would displease either its partisan allies in Congress or a large segment of the concerned public.

Future scholars should explore the capacity of domestic elites to influence the foreign policy agenda in other political and strategic contexts; and equally important, additional research is needed to improve our understanding of how this agenda-setting mechanism interacts with the other signaling and political costs mechanisms to determine the ultimate impact of other domestic actors on foreign policy outcomes.

The Political and Strategic Determinants of Domestic Influence

Four decades have passed since Wildavsky proclaimed presidential ascendance in the international realm. While the "two presidencies" thesis continues to capture many of the institutional advantages presidents hold when forging the nation's foreign and defense policy, we must not allow these advantages to obscure the more subtle, yet still tangible ways in which other domestic political actors affect their conduct of international affairs. None of the literatures reviewed seeks to overturn the conventional wisdom that presidents have significant advantages vis-à-vis potential opponents in the international realm. The ebb and flow of over 150 years of American history testifies to the rapid expansion of presidential power in foreign policy making, particularly when directing the nation's armed forces abroad. However, breaking free from the confines of the two presidencies framework is critically important given recent developments within IR that have opened the door for a collaborative research agenda with implications across subfields toward which presidency scholars have much to contribute.

Drawing on new literatures at the nexus of American politics and international relations, this chapter has described three mechanisms through which Congress, the courts, and organized interests, through varied formal and informal actions, may affect presidential decision making in the international arena, and it has reviewed and critiqued the empirical evidence supporting the proposed pathways of influence. While this recent research has greatly sharpened our understanding of how domestic politics can affect presidential calculus in foreign affairs, much work remains to be done. The mechanisms themselves need to be refined further and each step along the causal chain connecting the actions of Congress, the courts, and interest groups to eventual policy outcomes laid bare.

Yet, equally importantly, future research must move beyond identifying the mechanisms through which other domestic actors can influence presidential foreign policy making to explore the considerable variance across cases and time in the willingness and capacity of other domestic political actors to use the means at their disposal to check presidential discretion in foreign policy making. For example, one of the most important predictors of Congress's ability to assert itself and defend its institutional prerogatives is the strength of the president's partisan opposition. However, even a Congress dominated by a strong opposition party will not always act to challenge the president's conduct of foreign affairs. Potential opponents of the president's policies do not operate in a political vacuum.

In his analysis of the frequency and timing of legislative challenges to the president's conduct of ongoing military operations, Douglas Kriner (2007) finds that the emergence of opportunities in both the political and strategic environment critically influences when and to what degree the president's opponents in Congress confront his policies both on the floor and in the hearing room. When popular support for the president and his military policies is strong, openly challenging the commander-in-chief is unlikely to afford any political advantage and may even backfire. However, as public support for a venture begins to wane and as developments on the ground, such as spikes in American casualties, create opportunities for congressional action in the strategic environment, the president's congressional opponents grow more willing to attack. Indeed, if conditions deteriorate enough, even the president's partisan allies may feel sufficiently compelled to abandon their leader. Additional work is needed to explore in more detail how changes both at home in Washington and abroad in the field affect the calculations of Congress, the courts, and organized interests of whether and how to challenge presidential decision making in the military arena and in the foreign policy realm more generally.

In a similar vein, James Lindsay (2003) emphasizes the importance of the overarching strategic environment in driving domestic institutional checks on presidential foreign policy powers. In times of crisis when security concerns are high, other actors logically defer to the president. As these tensions subside, other actors reengage in the policy-making process. In the current context of the war in Iraq, the gradual reduction of tensions following the September 11 attacks, in addition to the dramatic shift in partisan control of Congress, may explain the increased willingness of both the legislature and the judiciary to challenge President Bush's conduct of the multifaceted war on terror.

Finally, the capacity and willingness of Congress, the courts, and outside interest groups to influence presidential conduct of international relations may vary significantly across policy areas. For example, an important predictor of congressional involvement in foreign policy making is the salience of a given issue to its members' constituents. Policies with significant economic consequences, such as trade policy, which lies at the intersection of domestic and foreign policy, may thus attract considerably more congressional attention than policies with little immediate domestic impact. Similarly, William Howell and Jon Pevehouse (2005) find that the partisan composition of Congress only affects the frequency of major uses of force, which have the greatest potential to shape congressional electoral outcomes (Carson et al. 2001; Gartner, Segura, and Barratt 2004; Kriner and Shen 2007; Grose and Oppenheimer 2007). By contrast, Congress appears to have little interest in or influence over minor military maneuvers. Similarly, the capacity of organized interests to affect policy making through the mechanisms outlined above may also vary by issue area according to the size and scope of the interest group environment mobilized around that policy. Even the courts may be more reticent to strike down presidential assertions of power in some areas of foreign policy, such as the use of force, but more likely to do so in other policy areas, such as those involving civil liberties (King and Meernik 1999). Future scholarship should continue to probe this variance in domestic political actors' eagerness and ability to influence presidential conduct of foreign affairs across policy venues.

Moving forward along these and similar research trajectories will not only enrich the presidency subfield's already substantial contribution to the American politics literature on the role of interinstitutional dynamics in shaping policy making, which heretofore has focused primarily on the domestic realm. But it will also help illustrate the precise mechanisms through which domestic politics, in certain strategic and political environments, can generate the observed cross-state disparities in conflict and negotiating behavior observed in IR.

References

ABERBACH, J. 1990. *Keeping a Watchful Eye: The Politics of Congressional Oversight.* Washington, DC: Brookings Institution Press.

ADLER, D., and GEORGE, L. (ed.) 1996. *The Constitution and the Conduct of American Foreign Policy.* Lawrence: University of Kansas Press.

ALDRICH, J., SULLIVAN, J., and BORGIDA, E. 1989. Foreign Affairs and Issue Voting: Do Presidential Candidates "Waltz" before a Blind Audience? *American Political Science Review*, 83: 123–41.

——GELPI, C., FEAVER, P., REIFLER, J., and SHARP, K. T. 2006. Foreign Policy and the Electoral Connection. *Annual Review of Political Science*, 9: 477–502.

ALLISON, G. 1971. *Essence of Decision: Explaining the Cuban Missile Crisis.* Boston: Little, Brown.

ALMOND, G. 1960. *The American People and Foreign Policy.* New York: Praeger.

ALTHAUS, S., EDY, J., ENTMA, R., and PHALEN, P. 1996. Revising the Indexing Hypothesis: Officials, Media and the Libya Crisis. *Political Communication*, 13/4: 407–21.

AUERSWALD, D. 2000. *Disarmed Democracies: Domestic Institutions and the Use of Force.* Ann Arbor: University of Michigan Press.

——2006. Senate Reservations to Security Treaties. *Foreign Policy Analysis*, 2: 83–100.

—— and COWHEY, P. 1997. Ballotbox Diplomacy: The War Powers Resolution and the Use of Force. *International Studies Quarterly*, 41: 505–28.

—— and MALTZMAN, F. 2003. Policymaking through Advice and Consent: Treaty Consideration by the United States Senate. *Journal of Politics*, 65: 1097–110.

BACHRACH, P., and BARATZ, M. 1962. The Two Faces of Power. *American Political Science Review*, 56: 947–52.

BAUM, M. 2004a. Going Private: Public Opinion, Presidential Rhetoric, and the Domestic Politics of Audience Costs in U.S. Foreign Policy. *Journal of Conflict Resolution*, 48: 603–31.

—— 2004b. How Public Opinion Constrains the Use of Force: The Case of Operation Restore Hope. *Presidential Studies Quarterly*, 34: 187–226.

—— and GROELING, T. 2004. Crossing the Water's Edge: Elite Rhetoric, Media Coverage, and the Rally-Round-the-Flag Phenomenon, 1979–2003. Paper read at Annual Meeting of the American Political Science Association.

—— —— 2005. What Gets Covered?: How Media Coverage of Elite Debate Drives the Rally-Round-the-Flag Phenomenon, 1979–1998. In *In the Public Domain: Presidents and the Challenges of Public Leadership*, ed. L. C. Han and D. Heith, Albany: State University of New York Press.

—— and POTTER, P. 2008. The Relationship between Mass Media, Public Opinion and Foreign Policy: Toward a Theoretical Synthesis. *Annual Review of Political Science*, 11: 39–65.

BAUMGARTNER, F., and JONES, B. 1993. *Agendas and Instability in American Politics*. Chicago: University of Chicago Press.

BENNETT, W. L. 1990. Toward a Theory of Press–State Relations in the United States. *Journal of Communication*, 40: 103–25.

—— 1996. An Introduction to Journalism Norms and Representation of Politics. *Political Communication*, 13: 373–84.

—— LAWRENCE, R., and LIVINGSTON, S. 2006. None Dare Call it Torture: Indexing and the Limits of Press Independence in the Abu Ghraib Scandal. *Journal of Communication*, 56: 467–85.

BERINSKY, A. 2007. Assuming the Costs of War: Events, Elites, and American Public Support for Military Conflict. *Journal of Politics*, 69/4: 975–97.

BERRY, J. 1999. *The New Liberalism: The Rising Power of Citizen Groups*. Washington, DC: Brookings Institution Press.

BOETTCHER, W. A., III, and COBB, M. D. 2006. Echoes of Vietnam? Casualty Framing and Public Perceptions of Success and Failure in Iraq. *Journal of Conflict Resolution*, 50/6: 831–54.

BOND, J., and FLEISHER, R. 1990. *The President in the Legislative Arena*. Stanford, CA: Stanford University Press.

BRACE, P., and HINCKLEY, B. 1992. *Follow the Leader*. New York: Basic Books.

BRADY, D., and VOLDEN, C. 1998. *Revolving Gridlock: Politics and Policy from Carter to Clinton*. Boulder, CO: Westview Press.

BRANDS, H. W. 1987. Decisions on American Armed Intervention: Lebanon, Dominican Republic and Grenada. *Political Science Quarterly*, 102: 607–24.

BRODY, R. 1991. *Assessing the President: The Media, Elite Opinion, and Public Support*. Stanford, CA: Stanford University Press.

—— 1994. Crisis, War and Public Opinion. In *Taken by Storm: Media, Public Opinion, and U.S. Foreign Policy in the Gulf War*, ed. W. L. Bennett and D. L. Paletz, Chicago: University of Chicago Press.

BUENO DE MESQUITA, B., and LALMAN, D. 1992. *War and Reason: Domestic and International Imperatives*. New Haven, CT: Yale University Press.

BUENO DE MESQUITA, B., and SIVERSON, R. 1995. War and the Survival of Political Leaders: A Comparative Study of Regime Types and Political Accountability. *American Political Science Review*, 89: 841–55.

——MORROW, J., SIVERSON, R., and SMITH, A. 1999. An Institutional Explanation of the Democratic Peace. *American Political Science Review*, 93: 791–807.

————————2003. *The Logic of Political Survival*. Cambridge: Cambridge University Press.

CALDWELL, D. 1991. *The Dynamics of Domestic Politics and Arms Control*. Columbia: University of South Carolina Press.

CAMERON, C. 2000. *Veto Bargaining: Presidents and the Politics of Negative Power*. Cambridge: Cambridge University Press.

CAMPBELL, A., CONVERSE, P., MILLER, W., and STOKES, D. 1960. *The American Voter*. New York: Wiley.

CAMPBELL, J. 1986. Presidential Coattails and Midterm Losses in State Legislative Elections. *American Political Science Review*, 80: 45–63.

——and SUMNERS, J. 1990. Presidential Coattails in Senate Elections. *American Political Science Review*, 84: 513–24.

CANES-WRONE, B. 2001. The President's Legislative Influence from Public Appeals. *American Journal of Political Science*, 45/2: 313–19.

——2005. *Who Leads Whom?: Presidents, Policy and the Public*. Chicago: University of Chicago Press.

——HOWELL, W., and LEWIS, D. 2008. Toward a Broader Understanding of Presidential Power: A Re-evaluation of the Two Presidencies Thesis. *Journal of Politics*, 70: 1–16.

CARSON, J., JENKINS, J., ROHDE, D., and SOUVA, M. 2001. The Impact of National Tides on District-Level Effects on Electoral Outcomes: The U.S. Congressional Elections of 1862–1863. *American Political Science Review*, 45: 887–98.

CLARK, D. 2000. Agreeing to Disagree: Domestic Institutional Congruence and U.S. Dispute Behavior. *Political Research Quarterly*, 53: 375–401.

COBB, R., and ELDER, C. 1972. *Participation in American Politics: The Dynamics of Agenda Building*. Boston: Allyn & Bacon.

COHEN, J. 1997. *Presidential Responsiveness and Public Policymaking: The Public and the Policies that Presidents Choose*. Ann Arbor: University of Michigan Press.

COLEMAN, J. 1996. *Party Decline in America: Policy, Politics and the Fiscal State*. Princeton, NJ: Princeton University Press.

CONLEY, R. 1999. Derailing Presidential Fast-Track Authority: The Impact of Constituency Pressures and Political Ideology on Trade Policy in Congress. *Political Research Quarterly*, 52: 785–99.

CONVERSE, P. 1964. The Nature of Belief Systems in Mass Publics. In *Ideology and Discontent*, ed. D. Apter. New York: Free Press.

CORWIN, E. 1940. *The President, Office and Powers: History and Analysis of Practice and Opinion*. London: Oxford University Press.

DEERING, C. 2005. Foreign Affairs and War. In *The Legislative Branch*, ed. P. Quirk and S. Binder. New York: Oxford University Press.

DESTLER, I. M. 2005. *American Trade Politics*. Washington, DC: Institute for International Economics.

EDWARDS, G. 1986. The Two Presidencies: A Reevaluation. *American Politics Quarterly*, 14: 247–63.

——1989. *At the Margins: Presidential Leadership of Congress*. New Haven, CT: Yale University Press.

—— 2003. *On Deaf Ears: The Limits of the Bully Pulpit.* New Haven, CT: Yale University Press.

—— and WOOD, B. D. 1999. Who Influences Whom? The President, Congress and the Media. *American Political Science Review,* 93: 327–44.

ELY, J. (ed.) 1993. *War and Responsibility: Constitutional Lessons of Vietnam and its Aftermath.* Princeton, NJ: Princeton University Press.

ENTMAN, R., and PAGE, B. 1994. The Iraq War Debate and the Limits to Media Independence. Pp. 82–101 in *Taken by Storm: Media, Public Opinion, and U.S. Foreign Policy in the Gulf War,* ed. W. L. Bennett and D. L. Paletz. Chicago: University of Chicago Press.

EPSTEIN, D., and O'HALLORAN, S. 1999. *Delegating Powers: A Transaction Cost Politics Approach to Policy Making under Separate Powers.* New York: Cambridge University Press.

FEARON, J. 1994. Domestic Political Audiences and the Escalation of International Disputes. *American Political Science Review,* 88: 577–92.

—— 1997. Signaling Foreign Policy Interests: Tying Hands Versus Sinking Costs. *Journal of Conflict Resolution,* 41: 68–90.

FEAVER, P., and GELPI, C. 2004. *Choosing your Battles: American Civil–Military Relations and the Use of Force.* Princeton, NJ: Princeton University Press.

FISHER, L. 1995. *Presidential War Power.* Lawrence: University of Kansas Press.

—— 2000. *Congressional Abdication on War and Spending.* College Station: Texas A&M University Press.

—— 2005. Judicial Review of the War Power. *Presidential Studies Quarterly,* 35: 466–95.

FLEISHER, R., and BOND, J. 2000. *Polarized Politics: Congress and the President in a Partisan Era.* Washington, DC: Congressional Quarterly Press.

FOWLER, L., and HILL, S. 2006. Guarding the Guardians: U.S. Senate Oversight of Foreign and Defense Policy, 1947–2004. Paper presented at the Annual Meeting of the American Political Science Association, Philadelphia.

FRANCK, T. 1992. *Political Questions/Judicial Answers: Does the Rule of Law Apply to Foreign Affairs?* Princeton, NJ: Princeton University Press.

FREEMAN, J., WILLIAMS, J., and LIN, T. 1989. Vector Autoregression and the Study of Politics. *American Journal of Political Science,* 33: 842–77.

GARTNER, S., SEGURA, G., and BARRATT, B. 2004. War Casualties, Policy Positions, and the Fate of Legislators. *Political Research Quarterly,* 53: 467–77.

GELPI, C., FEAVER, P., and REIFLER, J. 2006. Casualty Sensitivity and the War in Iraq. *International Security,* 30: 7–46.

GILBOA, E. 2005. The CNN Effect: The Search for a Communication Theory of International Relations. *Political Communication,* 22: 27–44.

GLENNON, M. 1990. *Constitutional Diplomacy.* Princeton, NJ: Princeton University Press.

GOWA, J. 1998. Politics at the Water's Edge: Parties, Voters and the Use of Force Abroad. *International Organization,* 52: 307–24.

—— 1999. *Ballots and Bullets.* Princeton, NJ: Princeton University Press.

GRIMMETT, R. 2001. Congressional Uses of Funding Cutoffs since 1970 Involving U.S. Military Forces and Overseas Deployments. Congressional Research Service. Code RS20775.

—— 2004. The War Powers Resolution: After Thirty Years. Congressional Research Service. Code RL32267.

GROSE, C., and OPPENHEIMER, B. 2007. The Iraq War, Partisanship, and Candidate Attributes: Explaining Variation in Partisan Swing in the 2006 U.S. House Elections. *Legislative Studies Quarterly,* 32: 531–57.

GROSSMAN, G., and HELPMAN, E. 2002. *Interest Groups and Trade Policy.* Princeton, NJ: Princeton University Press.

GROSSMAN, M., and KUMAR, M. 1981. *Portraying the President: The White House and the News Media.* Baltimore: Johns Hopkins University Press.

HANEY, P., and VANDERBUSH, W. 1999. The Role of Ethnic Interest Groups in U.S. Foreign Policy: The Case of the Cuban American National Foundation. *International Studies Quarterly,* 43: 341–61.

HILL, K. 1998. The Policy Agendas of the President and the Mass Public: A Research Validation and Extension. *American Journal of Political Science,* 42: 1328–34.

HINCKLEY, B. 1994. *Less Than Meets the Eye: Foreign Policy Making and the Myth of the Assertive Congress.* Chicago: University of Chicago Press.

HISCOX, M. 1999. The Magic Bullet? RTAA, Institutional Reform, and Trade Liberalization. *International Organization,* 53: 669–98.

HOLSTI, O. 1992. Public Opinion and Foreign Policy: Challenges to the Almond–Lippman Consensus. *International Studies Quarterly,* 36: 439–66.

——— 2004. *Public Opinion and American Foreign Policy.* Ann Arbor: University of Michigan Press.

HOOK, S. 2005. *U.S. Foreign Policy: The Paradox of World Power.* Washington, DC: CQ Press.

HOWELL, W. 2003. *Power without Persuasion: The Politics of Direct Presidential Action.* Princeton, NJ: Princeton University Press.

——— and KRINER, D. 2007a. Bending so as Not to Break: What the Bush Presidency Reveals about Unilateral Action. In *The Polarized Presidency of George W. Bush,* ed. G. Edwards and D. King, Oxford: Oxford University Press.

——— ——— 2007b. Political Elites and Public Support for War. Typescript.

——— and PEVEHOUSE, J. 2005. Presidents, Congress and the Use of Force. *International Organization,* 59: 209–32.

——— ——— 2007. *While Dangers Gather: Congressional Checks on Presidential War Powers,* Princeton, NJ: Princeton University Press.

HUNTINGTON, S. 1965. Congressional Responses to the Twentieth Century. In *The Congress and America's Future,* ed. D. Truman, Englewood Cliffs, NJ: Prentice-Hall.

HURWITZ, J., and PEFFLEY, M. 1987. The Means and Ends of Foreign Policy as Determinants of Presidential Support. *American Journal of Political Science,* 2: 236–58.

JACOBS, L. 2007. The Promotional Presidency and the New Institutional Toryism: Public Mobilization, Legislative Dominance, and Squandered Opportunities. In *The Polarized Presidency of George W. Bush,* ed. G. Edwards and D. King, Oxford: Oxford University Press.

——— LAWRENCE, E., SHAPIRO, R., and SMITH, S. 1998. Congressional Leadership of Public Opinion. *Political Science Quarterly,* 113: 21–41.

——— and SHAPIRO, R. 2000. *Politicians Don't Pander: Political Manipulation and the Loss of Democratic Responsiveness.* Chicago: University of Chicago Press.

JACOBSON, G. 2004. *The Politics of Congressional Elections.* New York: Pearson Longman.

JOHNSON, R. D. 1995. *The Peace Progressives and American Foreign Relations.* Cambridge, MA: Harvard University Press.

JONES, C. 1994. *The Presidency in a Separated System.* Washington, DC: Brookings.

JORDAN, D., and PAGE, B. 1992. Shaping Foreign Policy Opinions: The Role of TV News. *Journal of Conflict Resolution,* 36: 227–41.

KAROL, D. 2000. Divided Government and U.S. Trade Policy: Much Ado About Nothing? *International Organization,* 54: 825–44.

KEECH, W., and PAK, K. 1995. Partisanship, Institutions and Change in American Trade Politics. *Journal of Politics,* 57: 1131–42.

KERNELL, S. 1978. Explaining Presidential Popularity. *American Political Science Review,* 71: 44–66.

——1997. *Going Public: New Strategies of Presidential Leadership*. Washington, DC: Congressional Quarterly Press.

KING, K. L., and MEERNIK, J. 1999. The Supreme Court and the Powers of the Executive: The Adjudication of Foreign Policy. *Political Research Quarterly*, 52: 801–24.

KLAREVAS, L. 2002. The Essential Domino of Military Operations: American Public Opinion and the Use of Force. *International Studies Perspectives*, 3: 417–37.

KOH, H. 1990. *The National Security Constitution: Sharing Power after the Iran-Contra Affair*. New Haven, CT: Yale University Press.

KREHBIEL, K. 1996. Institutional and Partisan Sources of Gridlock: A Theory of Divided and Unified Government. *Journal of Theoretical Politics*, 8: 7–40.

——1998. *Pivotal Politics: A Theory of U.S. Lawmaking*. Chicago: University of Chicago Press.

KRINER, D. 2007. After the Rubicon: Congressional Constraints on Presidential Warmaking. Boston University typescript.

——and SCHWARTZ, L. 2008. Divided Government and Congressional Investigations. *Legislative Studies Quarterly*, 33: 295–321.

——and SHEN, F. 2007. Iraq Casualties and the 2006 Senate Elections. *Legislative Studies Quarterly*, 32: 507–30.

KRUTZ, G., and PEAKE, J. 2006. The Changing Nature of Presidential Policy Making on International Agreements. *Presidential Studies Quarterly*, 36: 391–409.

LAKE, D. 1992. Powerful Pacifists: Democratic States and War. *American Political Science Review*, 86: 24–37.

LARSON, E., and SAVYCH, B. 2005. *American Public Support for U.S. Military Interventions from Mogadishu to Baghdad*. Santa Monica, CA: RAND.

LEE, J. 1977. Rally around the Flag: Foreign Policy Events and Presidential Popularity. *Presidential Studies Quarterly*, 7: 252–6.

LEWIS, D. 2003. *Presidents and the Politics of Agency Design: Political Insulation in the United States Government Bureaucracy, 1946–1997*. Stanford, CA: Stanford University Press.

LIAN, B., and ONEAL, J. 1993. Presidents, the Use of Military Force, and Public Opinion. *Journal of Conflict Resolution*, 37: 277–300.

LIGHT, P. 1991. *The President's Agenda: Domestic Policy Choice from Kennedy to Reagan*. Baltimore: Johns Hopkins University Press.

LINDSAY, J. 1992. Congress and Foreign Policy: Why the Hill Matters. *Political Science Quarterly*, 107: 607–28.

——2003. Deference and Defiance: The Shifting Rhythms of Executive–Legislative Relations in Foreign Policy. *Presidential Studies Quarterly*, 33: 535–46.

LIPPMANN, W. 1922. *Public Opinion*. New York: Macmillan.

LIVINGSTON, S., and EACHUS, T. 1995. Humanitarian Crises and U.S. Foreign Policy Reconsidered. *Political Communication*, 12: 413–29.

LOFGREN, C. 1986. Government from Reflection and Choice. In *Constitutional Essays on War, Foreign Relations, and Federalism*. New York: Oxford University Press.

LOHMANN, S., and O'HALLORAN, S. 1994. Divided Government and U.S. Trade Policy: Theory and Evidence. *International Organization*, 48: 595–632.

McNULTY, T. 1993. Television's Impact on Executive Decision-Making. *Fletcher Forum of World Affairs*, 17: 67–83.

MAOZ, Z., and RUSSETT, B. 1993. Normative and Structural Causes of the Democratic Peace. *American Political Science Review*, 87: 624–38.

MARGOLIS, L. 1986. *Executive Agreements and Presidential Power in Foreign Policy*. New York: Praeger.

MARTIN, L. 2000. *Democratic Commitments*. Princeton, NJ: Princeton University Press.

MARTIN, L. 2005. The President and International Commitments: Treaties as Signaling Devices. *Presidential Studies Quarterly*, 35: 444–65.

MAYHEW, D. 1991. *Divided We Govern: Party Control, Lawmaking, and Investigations 1946–1990*. New Haven, CT: Yale University Press.

——2000. *America's Congress: Actions in the Public Sphere, James Madison through Newt Gingrich*. New Haven, CT: Yale University Press.

MEERNIK, J. 1994. Presidential Decision-Making and the Political Use of Force. *International Studies Quarterly*, 38: 121–38.

MERMIN, J. 1999. *Debating War and Peace: Media Coverage of U.S. Intervention in the Post-Vietnam Era*. Princeton, NJ: Princeton University Press.

MILNER, H. 1997. *Interests, Institutions and Information: Domestic Politics and International Relations*. Princeton, NJ: Princeton University Press.

——1998. Rationalizing Politics: The Emerging Synthesis of International, American, and Comparative Politics. *International Organization*, 52/4: 759–86.

——and ROSENDORFF, B. P. 1996. Trade Negotiations, Information, and Domestic Politics: The Role of Domestic Groups. *Economics and Politics*, 8: 145–89.

————1997. Democratic Politics and International Trade Negotiations: Elections and Divided Government as Constraints on Trade Liberalization. *Journal of Conflict Resolution*, 41: 117–46.

MOE, T. 1998. The Presidency and the Bureaucracy: The Presidential Advantage. In *The Presidency and the Political System*, ed. M. Nelson, Washington, DC: CQ Press.

——and HOWELL, W. 1999. The Presidential Power of Unilateral Action. *Journal of Law, Economics and Organization*, 15: 132–79.

——and WILSON, S. 1994. Presidents and the Politics of Structure. *Law and Contemporary Problems*, 57: 1–44.

MORGAN, C., and CAMPBELL, S. 1991. Domestic Structures, Decisional Constraints, and War. *Journal of Conflict Resolution*, 35: 187–211.

MORGENTHAU, H. 1948. *Politics among Nations: The Struggle for Power and Peace*. New York: Knopf.

——1951. *In Defense of the National Interest: A Critical Examination of American Foreign Policy*. New York: Knopf.

MOUW, C., and MacKUEN, M. 1992. The Strategic Configuration, Personal Influence, and Presidential Power in Congress. *Western Political Quarterly*, 45: 579–608.

NAGEL, J. 1975. *The Descriptive Analysis of Power*. New Haven, CT: Yale University Press.

NATHAN, J., and OLIVER, J. 1994. *Foreign Policymaking and the American Political System*. Baltimore: Johns Hopkins University Press.

NEUMAN, J. 1996. *Lights, Camera War: Is Media Technology Driving International Politics?* New York: St Martin's Press.

NEUSTADT, R. 1960. *Presidential Power: The Politics of Leadership*. New York: Wiley.

NINCIC, M., and HINCKLEY, B. 1991. Foreign Policy and the Evaluation of Presidential Candidates. *Journal of Conflict Resolution*, 35: 333–55.

O'HALLORAN, S. 1994. *Politics, Process and American Trade Policy*. Ann Arbor: University of Michigan Press.

PAGE, B., and SHAPIRO, R. 1992. *The Rational Public: Fifty Years of Trends in Americans' Policy Preferences*. Chicago: University of Chicago Press.

————and DEMPSEY, G. 1987. What Moves Public Opinion? *American Political Science Review*, 81: 23–44.

PEAKE, J. 2001. Presidential Agenda Setting in Foreign Policy. *Political Research Quarterly*, 54: 69–86.

——KRUTZ, G., and JATKOWSKI, W. 2007. The Forgotten House? Treaties, Executive Agreements and the Role of the United States House of Representatives. Paper presented at the Annual Meeting of the American Political Science Association, Chicago, IL.

PEFFLEY, J., and HURWITZ, M. 1992. International Events and Foreign Policy Beliefs: Public Responses to Changing Soviet–American Relations. *American Journal of Political Science*, 36: 431–61.

PETERSON, M. 1990. *Legislating Together: The White House and Capitol Hill from Eisenhower to Reagan*. Cambridge, MA: Harvard University Press.

PIOUS, R. 2007. Inherent War and Executive Powers and Prerogative Politics. *Presidential Studies Quarterly*, 37: 66–84.

POWLICK, P. 1995. The Sources of Public Opinion for American Foreign Policy Officials. *International Studies Quarterly*, 39: 427–51.

PRINS, B., and SPRECHER, C. 1993. Institutional Constraints, Political Opposition, and Interstate Dispute Escalation: Evidence from Parliamentary Systems, 1946–89. *Journal of Peace Research*, 36: 271–87.

PUTNAM, R. 1988. Diplomacy and Domestic Politics: The Logic of Two-Level Games. *International Organization*, 42: 427–60.

REITER, D., and TILLMAN, E. 2002. Public, Legislative and Executive Constraints on the Democratic Initiation of Conflict. *Journal of Politics*, 64: 818–26.

ROBINSON, P. 1999. The CNN Effect: Can the News Media Drive Foreign Policy? *Review of International Studies*, 25: 301–9.

——2002. *The CNN Effect: The Myth of News, Foreign Policy and Intervention*. New York: Routledge.

ROHDE, D. 1994. Partisanship, Leadership, and Congressional Assertiveness in Foreign and Defense Policy. In *The New Politics of American Foreign Policy*, ed. D. Deese, New York: St Martin's Press.

ROSEN, J. 2007. DeMint Rips War "Wimps." *The State*, May 30.

RUDALEVIGE, A. 2002. *Managing the President's Program*. Princeton, NJ: Princeton University Press.

——2005. *The New Imperial Presidency: Renewing Presidential Power after Watergate*. Ann Arbor: University of Michigan Press.

SCHELLING, T. 1960. *The Strategy of Conflict*. Cambridge, MA: Harvard University Press.

SCHLESINGER, JR., A. 1973. *The Imperial Presidency*. Boston: Houghton Mifflin.

SCHULTZ, K. 1998. Domestic Opposition and Signaling in International Crises. *American Political Science Review*, 92: 829–44.

——1999. Do Democratic Institutions Constrain or Inform? Contrasting Two Institutional Perspectives on Democracy and War. *International Organization*, 53: 233–66.

——2001. *Democracy and Coercive Diplomacy*. New York: Cambridge University Press.

SHAW, M. 1996. *Civil Society and Media in Global Crises: Representing Distant Violence*. London: Pinter.

SHEFFER, M. 1999. *The Judicial Development of Presidential War Powers*. Westport, CT: Praeger.

SHOCH, J. 2001. *Trading Blows: Party Competition and U.S. Trade Policy in a Globalizing Era*. Chapel Hill: University of North Carolina Press.

SHULL, S. 1991. *The Two Presidencies: A Quarter Century Assessment*. Chicago: Nelson-Hall.

SIGELMAN, L. 1979. A Reassessment of the Two Presidencies Thesis. *Journal of Politics*, 41: 1195–295.

——and JOHNSTON-CONOVER, P. 1981. The Dynamics of Presidential Support during International Conflict Situations: The Iranian Hostage Crisis. *Political Behavior*, 3: 303–18.

SILVERSTEIN, G. 1997. *Imbalance of Powers: Constitutional Interpretation and the Making of American Foreign Policy.* New York: Oxford University Press.

SIVERSON, R. 1995. Democracies and War Participation: In Defense of the Institutional Constraints Argument. *European Journal of International Relations,* 4: 481–9.

SMITH, T. 2000. *Foreign Attachments: The Power of Ethnic Groups in the Making of American Foreign Policy.* Cambridge, MA: Harvard University Press.

SOBEL, R. 1993. *Public Opinion in U.S. Foreign Policy: The Controversy over Contra Aid.* Lanham, MD: Rowman & Littlefield.

——2001. *The Impact of Public Opinion on U.S. Foreign Policy since Vietnam: Constraining the Colossus.* New York: Oxford University Press.

STOLBERG, S. 2007. Opposition Undercuts Troops, Cheney Says of Spending Bill. *New York Times,* Mar. 13.

TULIS, J. 1987. *The Rhetorical Presidency.* Princeton, NJ: Princeton University Press.

WALKER, J. 1977. Setting the Agenda in the U.S. Senate: A Theory of Problem Selection. *British Journal of Political Science,* 7: 433–45.

WANG, K. 1996. Presidential Responses to Foreign Policy Crises: Rational Choice and Domestic Politics. *Journal of Conflict Resolution,* 40: 68–97.

WATERMAN, R., OPPENHEIMER, B., and STIMSON, J. 1991. Sequence and Equilibrium in Congressional Elections: An Integrated Approach. *Journal of Politics,* 53: 372–93.

WEINGAST, B., and MARSHALL, W. 1988. The Industrial Organization of Congress; Or, Why Legislatures, Like Firms, are not Organized as Markets. *Journal of Political Economy,* 96: 132–63.

WILDAVSKY, A. 1966. The Two Presidencies. *Trans-Action,* 4: 7–14.

——and OLDFIELD, D. 1991. The Two Presidencies Thesis Revisited at a Time of Political Dissensus. In *The Beleaguered Presidency,* ed. A. Wildavsky. New Brunswick, NJ: Transaction Publishers.

WOOD, B. D., and PEAKE, J. 1998. The Dynamics of Foreign Policy Agenda Setting. *American Political Science Review,* 92: 173–84.

YOO, J. 2005. *The Powers of War and Peace: The Constitution and Foreign Affairs after 9/11.* Chicago: University of Chicago Press.

ZALLER, J. 1992. *The Nature and Origins of Mass Opinion.* New York: Cambridge University Press.

——1994. Elite Leadership of Mass Opinion: New Evidence from the Gulf War. Pp. 186–209 in *Taken by Storm: Media, Public Opinion, and U.S. Foreign Policy in the Gulf War,* ed. W. L. Bennett and D.L. Paletz. Chicago: University of Chicago Press.

——and CHIU, D. 1996. Government's Little Helper: U.S. Press Coverage of Foreign Policy Crises, 1945–1991. *Political Communication,* 13: 385–405.

CHAPTER 30

....

PRESIDENTS AND INTERNATIONAL COOPERATION

....

JON C. PEVEHOUSE

RESEARCH examining the interactions between domestic politics and international relations has blossomed in recent years. Some of this work discusses how domestic political debates shape a country's incentives to engage in international cooperation. Other work examines how international factors influence decisions by key domestic actors. Most importantly, nearly all of this work implicates the American presidency in important ways.

As the rise of globalization has led to the blurring of lines between international and domestic issues, research in both American politics and international relations has begun to reflect these increasingly permeable borders. No longer can scholars of American politics hide behind the age-old dictum that "politics stops at the water's edge." Nor can international relations scholars claim that America, even with the world's largest military and largest economy, is immune to the ebbs and flows of the international system. All states are increasingly interdependent, forcing domestic institutions to confront issues emanating from the international system: economic recessions, environmental degradation, trade regulation, security issues, and human rights abuse. This interdependence often requires interstate cooperation to coordinate responses to international events. Cooperation often requires new policies at home, placing domestic politics front and center in the question of international policy coordination.

This chapter will discuss this fast-growing literature as well as promising areas for future research. It proceeds as follows. First, it briefly reviews the state of the field of international relations and domestic politics and examines how this literature has developed over the years. Second, it highlights some of the recent literature on two-level games—i.e., the idea that presidents simultaneously play a bargaining game at the domestic level (with Congress) and at the international level (with other states). Third, it examines new literature that links presidents to questions of international cooperation, in particular, cooperation that occurs within international organizations.[1] Some of this work suggests that presidents delegate to international organizations for domestic strategic reasons. Others argue that international organizations can help provide information to key constituencies regarding a president's behavior.

Before beginning, three general points are in order. First, the international relations literature on cooperation and domestic politics rarely focuses specifically on the American presidency, but attempts to generate broad cross-national predictions about how executives relate to international institutions. Yet, as we will see, the literature clearly implicates the American presidency in many ways. When turning from broad theoretical models to empirical testing, for instance, the vast majority of this work relies on examples or data from the United States.

In addition, this broad approach to executives should be seen as an opportunity for scholars of American politics. Theories of the American executive branch help refine predictions about national–international linkages. Key to this cross-subfield work is a serious engagement in each area. Future work would benefit from this opportunity to use extant theories and empirical work across subfields.

To take a simple example discussed below, some theories have assumed that Congress can help the president bargain more successfully in the international realm since an executive can always claim her hands are tied by domestic forces. Yet, studies of the presidency have shed important light on the conditions under which presidents have greater or lesser autonomy from congressional checks (e.g., Howell 2003). Presumably, any rational state negotiating with the president could see these conditions and adjust their bargaining strategy accordingly. This adjustment of bargaining strategy would likely influence the expected outcomes of international bargaining given domestic constraints. Better ideas concerning the interaction of international and domestic politics need strong cross-disciplinary research engaging both areas of inquiry. To this end, this review of the literature presents the broader theories of international cooperation with an eye towards the American presidency.

---

[1] I limit my focus to questions of cooperation through international organizations because much of the recent theoretical and empirical development in the field has occurred in this area. Throughout this chapter, I refer to international organizations and international institutions interchangeably. International organizations, which tend to have a physical presence (e.g., the United Nations), are usually conceived of as a subset of institutions, which can be legal entities only (e.g., an international treaty). In this review, I exclude a broader definition of international institutions that would include international norms.

Second, the chapter examines the question of international cooperation broadly defined. This serves as a way to limit the scope of inquiry, rather than a judgment on the quality of work relating presidents and other international behavior, such as conflict. In addition, within the realm of international cooperation, the chapter frequently focuses on international institutions. Although nation-states have various methods of engaging in cooperation, international relations scholars spend much of their time examining institutions as ways to instantiate cooperation (see Abbott and Snidal 1998). Special attention to these institutions, therefore, has some obvious advantages.

Third and finally, this review is not meant to be comprehensive. Some empirical and theoretical literature will inevitably be missed. Rather than cover all relevant ground, however, it focuses on the core theoretical and empirical debates in the literature surrounding the presidency and international cooperation.

THE STATE OF THE FIELD(S)

Why is the field of research regarding presidents and international cooperation growing so quickly? Put another way, what accounted for the previous dearth of research in this area? There are several related reasons for this state of affairs. For several decades, realist approaches held strong sway over the study of international relations. Many mainstream realist approaches, especially structural realism, assume a unitary actor at the domestic level (e.g., Morgenthau 1985; Waltz 1979). That is, many realists "black-box" the internal politics of states. State actions occur largely in response to the exigencies of the international system rather than due to behavior at the domestic level. In such a theoretical framework, there is no room for presidents (or any other domestic institution) to influence outcomes (for a recent example, see Gowa 1999).

Similarly, many realists are pessimistic about the potential for international cooperation and give little credence to the power of international institutions (e.g., Mearsheimer 1994/5). They hold that international organizations have little independent role in shaping outcomes, but merely reflect the interests of the strong states in the international system. For many realists, knowing the preferences of the strong states means knowing the preferences of international organizations. Thus, there is little reason to focus analytical attention on these international bodies. It is fair to say that throughout the Cold War, the predominance of realist thought meant that little serious attention was paid to either presidents or international institutions.

At this same time, a small but vibrant community of scholars investigated the determinants of American foreign policy behavior (e.g., Rosenau 1961; Hermann 1980). Yet this literature, which often focused on the individual attributes of presidents, paid almost no attention to how international institutions either constrained or empowered those presidents. These scholars were far more interested in how certain processes constrained presidents who, according to realist theories, should have been pursuing the national interest, yet often failed to do so. Unfortunately, many of these scholars focused more on the psychology of individuals and groups, rather than the domestic institutions in which the decision makers were embedded.

Finally, the field of American politics and its attendant studies of the presidency paid little heed to international factors and their role in shaping the behavior of the executive branch. This is in part because presidency scholars chose to focus on domestic policy issues over foreign policy. The lacuna also reflected the power of the two presidents thesis, which pervaded research for many years (Wildavsky 1966). Advocates of this position held that presidents were given a much freer hand in making foreign policy than in domestic policy. If one accepts the theory that Congress will demur more frequently on international issues, there will be, by definition, fewer interesting questions surrounding foreign policy issues like international cooperation.

Yet, in the past twenty years, there has been a marked increase in the number of studies examining domestic politics and international relations (IR), including many focusing on international institutions. What led to this increased attention? First, the end of the Cold War and the fall of realism as the dominant IR theory have been crucially important. Realism was criticized for its inability to predict the sea change in international politics brought about by the end of the Cold War. Similarly, it is hard to tell the story of the decline of the Soviet Union without reference to domestic politics. Thus, many in the IR community began to revisit the idea that domestic factors were important explanatory variables. Second, the increasing globalization of the world economy meant increasing interaction between domestic forces and their international counterparts. Third, there has been a notable rise in the number of international organizations (IO) since the 1970s (Pevehouse, Nordstrom, and Warnke 2004). If these organizations served little purpose, as realists maintained, why did states continue to form them at such a rapid pace? Many studies thus began to examine the domestic impetus for IO formation and membership. Finally, even if the two presidencies thesis is correct (Canes-Wrone, Howell, and Lewis 2008), meaningful debates persist over foreign policy issues; and other research suggests underlying similarities regarding domestic and international policy (Howell and Pevehouse 2005).

Of course, the literatures reviewed here are not without some weaknesses. Theories that have emphasized the politics surrounding the executive branch tend to black-box international interactions, whereas those studies that take politics at the international level seriously often have very thin conceptions of domestic politics and the American presidency. That is, the literature to date has chosen to emphasize the importance of presidents or the international cooperation, not both. In doing so, both sides have missed considerable opportunities to create a richer set of theories pertaining to executives and international institutions.

Two-Level Games

One of the most influential efforts to theorize the strategic interaction that characterizes politics in the domestic and international arena was Robert Putnam's work on two-level games. Putnam's (1988) basic insight was that state leaders were playing two simultaneous bargaining games in their attempts to achieve international cooperation: an international negotiation game against other states and a domestic negotiation game against a set of domestic interests (often, but not exclusively, a legislature). Putnam formalizes an earlier insight by Schelling (1960) that a president can invoke domestic constraints (e.g., existing laws or requirements for legislative ratification) to gain leverage in international negotiations—an idea that many since have labeled the "Schelling conjecture." By credibly claiming her winset is restricted at the domestic level, a president can gain a better bargain at the international level. According to Putnam (1988, 434): "At the national level, domestic groups pursue their interests by pressuring the government to adopt favorable policies, and politicians seek power by constructing coalitions among these groups. At the international level, national governments seek to maximize their own ability to satisfy domestic pressures, while minimizing the adverse consequences of foreign developments."

While Putnam's formulation of Schelling's insight has become a popular theory in international relations, empirical support for the idea of two-level games has been mixed. In a collection of case studies, Evans, Jacobson, and Putnam (1993) find little evidence that executives claim to be tied down domestically to gain international leverage. They also suggest that the framework itself was theoretically underspecified, making hypothesis testing difficult.

Information, Institutions, and Two-Level Games

Despite these weaknesses, Putnam's formulation has spawned a number of extensions (Milner 1997; Iida 1993; Mo 1994; and Tarar 2001). Central among these is the theoretical and empirical work by Milner (1997), who develops a formal model with three domestic actors—an executive, a legislature, and interest groups—which yields predictions that run counter to Schelling and Putnam's logic. Milner finds that under conditions where domestic ratification is less certain, presidents have a more difficult time negotiating internationally. Rather than maximize the "national interest" at the interstate level, leaders must prioritize negotiating a domestically acceptable agreement that may or may not be acceptable to international partners.

What variables predict conditions of uncertain domestic ratification? Milner focuses on three: the structure of domestic preferences, the nature of domestic institutions, and the internal distribution of information. Regarding domestic preferences, Milner shows that when the executive faces strong opposition in the legislature, the probability of international cooperation declines. In her words, "divisions at home seem to undermine a country's international bargaining strength" (236).[2] As for domestic institutions, Milner considers their degree of formality—specifically, whether legislatures have a formal ratification role (e.g., the US Senate) or an implicit one (e.g., most parliamentary systems). Finally, she examines how interest groups can facilitate the bargaining process domestically by serving as information providers. She concludes that the presence of at least one "endorser," an interest group favoring ratification of an agreement, is an important condition for legislative approval. These endorsers can provide information to legislators who are otherwise ignorant of international issues and are generally skeptical of international engagement. Even in the presence of two opposing interest groups, the probability of cooperation rises when compared to a situation where no endorser exists.

Ironically, Milner's overall predictions for international cooperation are more pessimistic than Schelling, Putnam, and even many realist scholars. The key mechanism driving Milner's conclusion is fear on the part of legislators and interest groups about the distributional consequences of international agreements. These actors fear the adjustment costs; in particular, that these costs of cooperation could fall disproportionately on their interests. Moreover, Milner argues that these actors have difficulty in dividing the spoils from international agreements. Thus, they push presidents to design agreements that maximize legislator preferences to secure ratification, making life more difficult for the executive at the international level.

Milner's careful analysis has brought important insights to the consideration of executives and international agreements. Her counter-intuitive predictions concerning domestic politics led to an important revision of the Schelling conjecture upon which scholars continue to build (see Butler 2004; Tarar 2005). She also provided a general model of domestic politics and international relations that tapped concepts familiar to students of domestic political institutions (e.g., divided government) yet moved beyond the substantive area of international trade, upon which most studies of presidential–congressional relations had focused (e.g., Lohman and O'Halloran 1994). Finally, her model also drew important links to well-known findings in American politics concerning the nature of interest groups as information providers (Epstein and O'Halloran 1993).

There are, however, reasons to push Milner's analysis forward. Empirically, Milner undertakes several case studies to provide illustrative support for her model; however, the large number of key variables in her model precludes her from finding cases where each important factor varies. Theoretically, Humphreys (2007) generates a similar model that adds the possibility of strategic behavior on the part of the legislature and introduces multidimensional preferences instead of single-dimensional winsets. According to Humphreys, these changes reverse Milner's prediction: the presence of a ratifier can assist presidents in achieving a better deal at the international level. Unfortunately, while Humphrey's model more closely mirrors the reality of domestic and international negotiations, he provides no empirical evidence to support

---

[2] Milner also emphasizes the importance of executive or presidential preferences, especially in contexts where leaders can initiate international bargaining.

his conclusions, nor does he confront the fact that extant empirical literature has found mixed evidence of the Schelling conjecture.

Finally, Milner's assumptions about international politics are quite sparse (by her own admission), in that she presumes an anarchic international environment free of institutions. While she speculates that relaxing the anarchy assumption and/or the introduction of international institutions could allow for a more propitious environment for international cooperation, these alternative assumptions are not incorporated into the model. While there are certainly limits to the number of variables that can be captured in any model, it is possible that the nature of the international game directly affects the nature of the gains and losses at the domestic level. If this is the case, it would be wise to more closely examine the international level to anticipate the circumstances under which legislators care enough about outcomes to threaten non-ratification. Put simply, if the anticipated benefits of an international agreement are low, or the expected compliance of other members is low, legislators may lack incentives to impinge on presidents at the international negotiation stage.

Congress, Delegation, and Two-Level Games

In another key work in the area of two-level games, Martin (2000) draws less-pessimistic conclusions about international cooperation and domestic politics while making a key contribution to theories of two-level games. Like Milner, she focuses on domestic political institutions, especially the president and Congress. Martin, however, moves beyond the idea of Congress as ratification body by noting several other mechanisms by which Congress can influence the negotiation process. In wielding the power of the purse, creating roadblocks to implementation, and threatening oversight, Congress "possess[es] numerous subtle and indirect mechanisms of influence" (51). Of course, presidents can anticipate these stumbling blocks and may attempt to negotiate around them at the international level. The important lesson to take from this possibility, Martin emphasizes, is that we may rarely witness direct congressional influence on the president concerning international cooperation. Rather, the anticipated effects will be subsumed into the president's negotiation strategy, making the detection of congressional influence more difficult.

Martin then investigates several hypotheses concerning the nature of legislative–executive politics regarding international cooperation. Two of these are particularly relevant to this discussion: the delegation hypothesis and the influence hypothesis. The delegation hypothesis, which builds upon models of executive oversight found in American politics, suggests the conditions under which Congress will delegate authority to the president to negotiate at the international level (e.g., Weingast and Moran 1983; McCubbins and Schwartz 1984; Lupia and McCubbins 1994).

Martin contends that legislators choose to delegate to the executive branch for a variety of reasons, including overcoming informational asymmetries in the area of foreign affairs. Due to their scant knowledge of foreign affairs and the lack of interest among constituents, legislators delegate foreign policy to the executive, while still keeping their oversight power.[3] Yet, as Martin recognizes, conditions may determine how comfortable legislators are with that delegation decision. Divided government, for instance, plays a key role: legislators of the president's party will be more likely to delegate to the executive due to the higher probability of preference homogeneity between them.

Through a quantitative examination of sanctions episodes and a qualitative examination of US food aid policy, Martin finds support for the delegation hypothesis. Congressionally imposed economic sanctions are more likely under divided government, since Congress cannot be assured the president will pursue sanctions on his own. Drawing on the history of American food aid, Martin finds evidence that behavior considered to be "abusive of executive authority" leads Congress to enact numerous reporting requirements, particularly under divided government.

The influence hypothesis, by contrast, questions whether executives can evade legislative "interference" in foreign affairs. After all, if a president anticipates congressional opposition to an international agreement, he or she could attempt to unilaterally create international cooperation through an executive agreement—skirting ratification requirements.[4] To test this hypothesis, Martin quantitatively examines the percentage of all international agreements concluded as executive agreements from 1953 to 1992 (where all international agreements are the sum of executive agreements and ratified international treaties). She initially finds little support for her influence hypothesis; contrary to expectations, as the number of the president's co-partisans in Congress increases, so does the percentage of international agreements concluded as executive agreements. Yet, the substantive effect of this finding is quite small—the predicted increase in the percentage of executive agreements as the total number of international agreements, when moving from very low congressional support to very high, hovers between 1 and 2 percent.

Using a disaggregated measure, however, Martin finds that the level of congressional support for the president has no influence on the number of executive agreements, although congressional support positively influences the number of international treaties signed. This result suggests that the president does need congressional support to conclude international agreements and, rather than attempting to evade ratification, concludes more treaties under times of unified government, knowing the path to ratification will be easier.

Martin's work, much like Milner's, provides a rich understanding of the constraints faced by the president. Her logic of delegation provides an alternative set of causal mechanisms to Milner's bargaining-based theory, while suggesting a larger set

---

[3] Canes-Wrone, Howell, and Lewis (2008) make a similar argument in the context of the two presidencies thesis: that Congress has delegated authority in some foreign policy issue areas. Thus, the presence of interbranch struggles over foreign policy will be over issues on which Congress has affirmatively chosen not to delegate, creating a bias towards rejecting the two presidencies thesis when examining behavioral measures such as roll-call votes.

[4] Martin limits her sample of executive agreements to internationally relevant ones. For a broader analysis of these agreements, which reaches a different conclusion than Martin, see Howell (2003).

of conditions that are more propitious for international cooperation. Moreover, Martin's recognition that executives may anticipate congressional opposition—thus allowing Congress influence over negotiations without direct, observable behavior—provides an important reminder to those undertaking empirical investigation of executive–legislative relations in foreign policy.

Like Milner, however, Martin pays scant attention to the nature of the international game being played by the executive, ignoring the question of whether the substance of the international agreement matters. Martin does investigate whether cooperation is more successful at the international level conditional on congressional involvement, but the international institutions and agreement themselves are rarely examined. This could be important if there are differences across different international agreements based on substantive issue area. And while Martin does vary the issue areas of her empirical investigation, there is little comparison between them.

Given Martin's theoretical mechanisms, in particular her emphasis on information, this gap could be problematic. For example, Congress is likely to be more informed concerning issues of trade or immigration, compared to other foreign policy issues such as the environment or foreign aid. Given that information dynamics play a key role in congressional decisions to delegate, one wonders if her findings are conditional on issue area. Perhaps even periods of unified government are not sufficient to spur delegation if Congress feels its competence in a particular area is high or the treaty poses clear and potentially large adjustment costs. The resounding bipartisan rejection of the Kyoto Protocol under the Clinton administration, for example, suggests that some of Martin's dynamics may depend on the nature of the international agreement. Further hypotheses could be developed to link the underlying causal mechanisms in Martin's work to the nature of the international cooperation.

Opening the International Black Box

In general, the move to unpack institutions at both the domestic and international level is afoot. In a recent example, Mansfield, Milner, and Pevehouse (2008) utilize the idea of veto players in the context of domestic ratification when examining state accession to preferential trade agreements. Specifically, they use cross-national time series data measuring the extent of preference divergence within domestic institutions across pairs of states (dyads) from 1950 to 2000. Their measure of preference divergence is taken from Henisz (2002), who uses three domestic factors: the presence of an effective legislative branch to check presidential power, the alignment of party power across the executive and the legislative branches (e.g., the presence of divided government), and the heterogeneity of preferences within the legislative branch (i.e., the probability that two representatives picked at random will hail from the same party).

For their dependent variable, the authors measure the depth of proposed integration in the trade agreement. That is, did the agreement call for a modest decline in tariffs, the wholesale adoption of free trade, the adoption of a common tariff structure across all members, the coordination of macroeconomic policies such as inflation control, the elimination of barriers to labor mobility, or the adoption of a common currency? They hypothesize that the presence of veto players in democracies will lessen the probability of deeper cooperation, since these more extensive arrangements raise the likelihood of more significant adjustment costs and/or material benefits. Adopting Milner's (1997) logic, they suggest the higher potential for costs will make the conclusion of a ratifiable agreement less likely.

Indeed, consistent with previous research (Mansfield, Milner, and Rosendorff 2002), they find that while democracies are more likely than non-democracies to join these international trade agreements, the relationship is conditional: as the number of veto players rises in democracies, the probability of entering into deep international cooperation declines. Their results are important since they suggest presidents will face more intense pressures if proposing deeper cooperation in international institutions. Thus, while the domestic story clearly remains important, delving deeper into the international side of the equation appears to yield important insights as well.

In sum, the literature on two-level games has grown substantially in IR. Two important themes of this work deserve consideration. First, only a small subset of the literature deals with the content of international institutions, although there are efforts under way to fill this gap. To date, the main thrust of the two-level games literature, from the IR perspective, has been pinpointing the factors that promote cooperation among states. That is, what domestic factors shape state incentives to cooperate with one another? Given the classic concern of IR with cooperation under conditions of anarchy, this emphasis was once warranted. Now that IR has moved past the first-order question of whether states cooperate, however, it has begun to think more systematically about the function, design, and success of that cooperation. The next step for the two-level games literature is to take these emerging insights concerning the design (Koremenos, Lipson, and Snidal 2000), the functionality (Goldstein et al. 2000; Rosendorff 2005), and the enforcement potential (Simmons 2000; von Stein 2005) of those international regimes, and tie them to our theories of two-level games.

Authors such as Milner and Martin have elucidated very specific causal mechanisms that shape the incentives of domestic political actors vis-à-vis international cooperation. Yet, domestic actors presumably have preferences concerning the design, functionality, and enforcement properties of international cooperation. That is, the next natural step in the research agenda is to flesh out the preferences of presidents and Congress over the form—rather than just the fact—of international cooperation. For example, might all members of Congress (regardless of partisanship) be willing to delegate to the president if the IO's rules guarantee American veto power over policy? Conversely, more egalitarian voting rules in the organization may sharpen political debates in the US, raising the prospect of a partisan showdown over whether to delegate in the first place. Congressional preferences over particular international issues, and how they play into two-level games, remain largely uninvestigated theoretically and empirically.

Indeed, perhaps the only study to pursue this research avenue, by Reinhardt (2003), reveals important constraints on the ability of presidents to leverage domestic opposition once the probability of enforcement by international institutions is considered. In short, Reinhardt argues that "the benefits of tying hands [in order to promote international cooperation] occur in proportion to the ex ante probability of enforcement" (99). Reinhardt bases his conclusion on a formal model of WTO institutional bargaining assuming the presence of divided government. His model takes an important step towards combining the insights of the two-level games literature using well-specified theories of international institutions, and accounts of domestic politics.

Second, as discussed in this section, the empirical evidence concerning two-level games is mixed. While some large-n studies have confirmed the importance of domestic factors in shaping incentives for cooperation, many qualitative studies have not. Yet, as Martin reminds us, the influence of legislatures may be both subtle and subject to anticipatory action by presidents. A lesson can be taken from the use of force literature: Congress has never activated the time limit provisions of the War Powers Act since its adoption. Yet, to say that this is evidence of congressional inactivity regarding war and military force is to overlook important congressional behavior (see Howell and Pevehouse 2007). Similarly, just because the list of non-ratified treaties for the US may be small, this does not suggest congressional indifference.

Here, future empirical work should examine insights from American politics to learn more about other mechanisms through which Congress can influence the president in addition to the threat of non-ratification of treaties. Vocalizing opposition to executive policy choices provides one possible route. This opposition may actually undermine a leader's international bargaining credibility in situations where perceptions of resolve are important (e.g., the use of force; see Schultz 1998). Vocal opposition can also turn public opinion against the president (Howell and Pevehouse 2007). Alternatively, Congress can tighten oversight of executive agencies, threaten public hearings, or use the power of the purse. Again, the key point is that presidents may anticipate this behavior and adjust their international bargaining strategies accordingly, or decline to participate in international negotiations if failure at home looms.

In the next section, we examine a burgeoning literature which largely takes cooperation as a given, but explores the ways in which extant international institutions can serve or frustrate the goals of presidents. This newer literature examines why presidents might surrender some policy autonomy to an IO. In other words, the key question is not how domestic politics constrains international cooperation, but rather how domestic politics might promote it. Moreover, for this body of literature, the focus at the international level becomes the interaction of presidents with international institutions rather than interaction with other nation-states.

DELEGATION FOR SELF-RESTRAINT

Two major strands of literature have blossomed in the past decade relating the president and the international system generally, and IOs in particular. We can divide these works into two broad camps: those emphasizing delegation (at the international level) and those emphasizing information. In this section, we review literature suggesting that presidents have incentives to limit their own policy autonomy in order to gain bargaining leverage domestically. While the two-level games conception of delegation occurs at the domestic level, these scholars have noted that presidents may delegate authority to international institutions, tying their own hands to boost their leverage domestically.

Delegation and American Trade Policy

Goldstein (1996) makes a delegation argument concerning the president and Congress in the area of trade policy; however, rather than Congress delegating to the president, the president delegates to an international institution. Goldstein examines the case of the 1988 Canadian–US free trade agreement, where binational panels were given the right to arbitrate disputes that arose between the two countries. Goldstein's puzzle emanates from the fact that these panels consistently ruled in favor of Canada, the weaker of the two parties to the agreement. Moreover, the US trade bureaucracy began to change its own behavior based on these panel rulings. Why, Goldstein asks, did the more powerful US actors not anticipate this outcome and design a system more favorable to their own interests? Why did the US not push for an *ex post* revision of the procedure or refuse to implement the judgments of the panels, since they did not automatically become US law?

Goldstein's answer arises from her model of executive–legislative bargaining and delegation. Goldstein adopts the widely held assumption that the president's preferences lean towards free trade (given its broad, welfare-maximizing benefits), while preferences of Congress lean towards protectionism (given each legislator's narrow, district-level interest in preventing the adjustment costs of free trade). Historically, however, Congress would be overwhelmed by demands from interest groups for protection. To remedy this problem, Congress delegated trade authority to the president to create a buffer between it and interest groups, creating so-called "fast-track" authority (today known as "Trade Promotion Authority").

Yet, over time, interest groups found other ways to promote protectionism through agencies such as the International Trade Commission, which could determine whether other states had adopted "unfair" trade policies. Through liberal interpretation of what constituted "unfair" policies, these agencies could erect "defensive" trade barriers. The creation of the binational panels under the Canadian–US trade agreement became a way for the president to delegate authority to determine "unfair" policies to an international body which was more likely to hold pro-free trade preferences. Thus, in cases where US agencies accused Canada of unfair practices, the final judgment on the issue would come from the binational panels, which consistently ruled against the US "defensive" measures.

According to Goldstein, the delegation of this authority to an international institution allowed the president to shift policies closer to his ideal point, away from Congress's as well as the domestic trade bureaucracy's ideal point.[5] Thus, having received the power to set unilateral tariff policy through fast track, the president then sought to curb attempts to erect barriers in response to complaints of "unfair" trade practices through federal agencies. By shifting authority to an international institution, the president effectively circumvented both Congress and the bureaucracy.

Obviously Goldstein only examines one case of this delegation story, but there are broader lessons to be learned from her study. Whereas Milner and Martin argue that factors like divided government will shape whether executives are able to commit to international agreements in the first place, Goldstein's study draws our attention to two additional issues. First, executives may find themselves in positions where their own ideal points on *particular issues* are far from the median member of Congress (which may or may not correlate with the presence of divided government), or even the ideal points of administrative agencies. Rather than serve as a constraint, this preference divergence provides an impetus to engage in international cooperation.

Second, Goldstein draws our attention to the *form* of international cooperation. Not just any trade agreement would accomplish the delegation goals of the president. The particulars of the Canada–US trade agreement mattered: the creation of binational panels that were relatively insulated from Congress was key to the delegation effort. This turn towards examining specific institutional functionalities is one that should continue in the literature since many of the causal theories put forth depend crucially on the international institution's ability to perform certain functions. After all, it is possible that preferences concerning delegation are conditional on the content of the international agreement—a possibility discussed below.

Delegation and Human Rights

In a very different empirical context, Moravcsik (2000) argues that executive incentives to delegate authority to international human rights institutions can be interpreted as attempts to create credible commitments to these policies. In his words: "Establishing an international human rights regime is an act of political delegation akin to establishing a domestic court or administrative agency" (220). In particular, he argues that newly democratic countries will join IOs that intrude on state sovereignty in order to commit current and future governments to protect human

---

[5] Normally, a president would have more control over an agency within the executive branch, but the ITC is unique in that it is designed to be independent. For example, the president is constrained by law to appoint a bipartisan commission, which places limits on her ability to manipulate the ideal point of the ITC.

rights. This "lock-in" is particularly effective since third parties (other members of the IO) will be committed to enforcing the conditions of the agreement and can be counted on to punish any reneging.

More relevant to our discussion here, however, is Moravcsik's assertion that well-established democracies, such as the US, will *not* pay the costs associated with joining human rights regimes. A key factor driving Moravcsik's idea of delegation is political uncertainty—because new democracies face high future uncertainties, an executive will lock in policies today, raising the costs of future defections tomorrow, even if he or she is not in power. Well-established democratic regimes, such as the US, do not face such political uncertainty, nor do they have difficulty making endogenous credible commitments to particular policies. Moreover, Moravcsik argues, older democracies are more likely to have established strong reputations promoting human rights, and thus do not gain any reputational benefit from joining human rights organizations.

Importantly, Moravcsik's study goes beyond Goldstein's argument that the distribution of domestic preferences drives presidents to commit to international institutions. Rather, Moravcsik highlights the incentives presidents have to lock in a new status quo in order to limit the autonomy of future presidents. Essential to his argument is the idea that international agreements increase the cost of defection over domestic policies. The study has important limits, however. Some of the assumptions Moravcsik adopts are specific to human rights issues, and he makes few attempts to generalize the theory outside this realm. And even within this area, he only examines one case: the formation of the European Court of Human Rights (ECHR) after the Second World War.

Does Moravcsik's theory tell us anything about presidential behavior in the American context? While the answer is likely no in the area of human rights, one can easily imagine other issue areas where it provides insight. In particular, the idea of locking in a particular set of policies through international organizations is a powerful one, even if states such as the US can make fairly credible commitments to future policy endogenously (e.g., by setting up a costly administrative agency). Environmental issues may provide one example. US policy in this area has varied widely by administration due to disparate preferences across political parties. The US has not committed to some key international environmental treaties—most notably, the Kyoto Protocol—yet future administrations will no doubt attempt to lock in particular environmental policies by acceding to these organizations. Magnifying this effect is the possibility that America's international partners could inflict higher costs on the US through mechanisms established in the agreement.

The presence of time-inconsistent preferences may provide another incentive for self-restraint. Aware that they will face temptation to renege on promises in the future, executives may view self-constraint as a logical policy response. Key to each of these logics, however, is that an international commitment raises the costs of backing out relative to a purely domestic commitment. Domestic laws may be easier to amend than international agreements are, and domestic administrative agencies can be captured, as in the Goldstein trade example. Of course, this begs an important question that Moravcsik skirts: why would a rational legislature allow their hands to be tied in the first place? This brings us back to the question of ratification in two-level games, to which we return below.

Other work in the area of human rights and international cooperation has made arguments similar to Moravcsik, but has reached different empirical conclusions concerning established democracies. Hafner-Burton, Mansfield, and Pevehouse (2008) conduct a cross-national time series statistical analysis to examine whether new democracies systematically join human rights organizations in comparison with other types of political regimes. They generalize Moravcsik's logic to suggest that a variety of human rights organizations besides the ECHR could create costly commitments to future human rights policies. Indeed, the authors find that newly democratized states are statistically more likely to accede to human rights organizations than other types of political regimes, although the effect does not hold for human rights treaties.[6] They also find, contra Moravcsik's predictions, that more democratic states are more likely to join human rights organizations, controlling for those that have democratized.

This finding suggests that Moravcsik's conclusions could be confined to his single case study. Indeed, the desire to tie hands in the face of future leadership turnover or time-inconsistent preference is one that arises in all democracies. The key challenge is determining under what conditions presidents will find the intrusion of an international commitment less costly compared to future policy uncertainty. Answering this question requires an understanding of how much presidents value future policy continuity, the level of uncertainty regarding future policy outcomes, and the costliness of the commitment internationally. Theories developed in American politics may offer more leverage on the first two questions, while international relations theories may contribute to our understanding of the third.

Of course, Hafner-Burton, Mansfield, and Pevehouse's empirical evidence is consistent with other theories that have little to do with delegation at the domestic level. For example, established democracies may join human rights institutions to signal a commitment to promoting human rights abroad or to pressure other members to improve their own human rights performance. Again, better theory is needed to elucidate the circumstances under which presidents will favor utilizing delegation to IOs rather than internal commitment devices. Such a theory would permit more refined empirical testing about the exact causal mechanisms at work.

Finally, as previously noted, a potential tension exists between the delegation literature and the literature on two-level games. That is, presidents may strongly prefer to delegate to an international institution, either due to a particular preference distribution (e.g., Goldstein) or to instantiate credible commitments (e.g., Moravscik). Congress, however, is not an ignorant bystander in this process. Any argument

---

[6] Mansfield and Pevehouse (2006) find that democratizing states join *all* types of international organizations more frequently than other regime types, but they also find that stable democracies join more than any non-democratic regime type.

contending that presidents can enhance their own power through delegation must confront the question of why Congress would acquiesce to such a maneuver. While several possible explanations exist, chances are that most accounts will need to apply extant theories of executive–legislative interactions developed in the context of American politics.

For example, Schultz (2003), drawing on the logic of self-restraint, makes a hand-tying argument in the security realm. He argues that "working through international organizations also creates a way for the president to commit himself to a [military] operation, by increasing the costs of turning back" (109). Because presidents generally possess better information and enjoy first-mover advantages in the field of security, Schultz contends they can often preempt congressional opposition and "induce legislators to shy away from efforts to deauthorize, defund, or otherwise limit the mission" (109). And while these various advantages certainly apply to the use of military force (Howell and Pevehouse 2007, 6–9), it remains unclear whether the president enjoys them in other issue areas as well.

INFORMATION AND APPROVAL SEEKING

In IR theory, the liberal challenge to realism largely derived from a set of claims advanced by Keohane (1984) and others, touting the ability of international institutions to help engender cooperation among rationally egoistic states in an anarchic system. According to proponents, international institutions, by providing information to interested parties about the state of the world and/or the behavior of others, could help quell states' fears of cheating, aid in punishing defectors, and assist policy coordination (Abbott and Snidal 1998).

Over the past decade, many scholars have recognized that the informational benefits of international institutions do not stop at the international level. In both the security and economic realms, scholars have increasingly argued that IOs provide information that is useful to other actors within states or useful to state leaders for domestic purposes.

Presidents, Public Opinion, and Approving the Use of Force

In the realm of security and foreign policy, Chapman and Reiter (2004) argue that international institutions, such as the UN Security Council, provide important signals to the American public about the potential costs and benefits of potential military action. They argue that presidents care deeply about public opinion regarding potential uses of military force, and thus are only likely to use force when the proposed venture is popular. The public, for its part, has little reason to trust the pronouncements of the president since they assume he will naturally favor the use of force, even when force may not be justified. In other words, the public presumes slack in the principal–agent framework. In equilibrium, then, the public may be unwilling to back the use of force.

As emphasized by the principal–agent literature, third parties can help ameliorate the slack problem by providing fire alarms. While opposition political parties could serve this role (see Schultz 2001), so could IOs. By consulting the UN Security Council, presidents can signal that they are responding to important threats rather than engaging in reckless behavior. When the Security Council votes to approve a use of force, this is a clear indication that neutral third parties support the mission, leading the public to look more favorably upon the military effort.[7] Of course, this assumes the public and the UN Security Council have similar preferences, a point to which we return momentarily.

Empirically, Chapman and Reiter find that the "rally round the flag" effect associated with American uses of force between 1945 and 2001 is higher when Security Council approval is received. Their empirical results are robust to the inclusion of a litany of control variables including the severity of the use of force, whether the US initiated the use of force, the presence of allies, and numerous economic variables. They conclude that their findings suggest an interesting substitution effect: executives can turn to international institutions to "constrain" their behavior in an attempt to lessen the constraint of domestic public opinion.

The Chapman and Reiter finding does beg the question of selection: why would a president propose a use of force to the Security Council if there was a high risk of rejection, a rejection which could turn public opinion strongly against using force? Might a president attempt to anticipate Security Council responses and only seek authorization in cases where approval was likely, and might those be the same cases where a rally effect would naturally take place? Chapman and Reiter do attempt to control for this possibility by introducing variables that represent the cases where this dynamic is most likely, i.e., a direct attack on the American homeland or on US troops. Still, a fuller attempt to deal with selection would give more confidence in the results.

A process related to these selection dynamics is addressed by Fang (2007), who contends that even leaders interested in private rents may seek approval from international institutions such as the Security Council. Fang creates a formal model where voters want to elect a leader who is concerned with choosing the "best" policy, rather than a "biased" leader who will pursue private benefits. Fang assumes that consultation with an IO will help a leader choose a better policy, and thus an "unbiased" leader will consult with the institution to maximize her reelection chances. Yet, upon seeing this behavior, Fang argues that a pooling equilibrium will result: biased leaders will also consult the institution to feign interest in the public good. Indeed, according to Fang, this is the power of institutions—by creating

---

[7] Voeten (2005) also argues that the UN Security Council can legitimize the use of force, but he has little discussion of the domestic implications of the process.

electoral incentives for good leaders to consult the institution, even leaders who may not want to consult the institution must, since they do not want to appear publicly biased.

Fang does not explore the mechanisms through which international institutions improve policy outcomes; however, one possibility is that institutions convey information. By publicly vetting a potential policy, a leader opens herself to criticism by the IO, removing doubts that she is acting only in her own best interests. Fang also notes that the power of the institution to constrain biased leaders grows as the public maintains favorable ratings of the institution itself. Yet, while some scholars contend that publics (even in the US) have a positive view of many IOs (see Kull 2002), their overall knowledge of international institutions may be low—a point to which we return below.

Information, Bias, and the Logic of Approval Seeking

The claim that international institutions can bolster cooperation by providing information to publics has also been extended in work by Thompson (2006) and Chapman (2007). Thompson (2006) uses insights from theories of Congress to examine the conditions under which information provided by international institutions can educate the public (Krehbiel 1992; Gilligan and Krehbiel 1989). According to these theories, the distribution of preferences within the institution matters; approval from an institution perceived to be biased in favor of a president is unlikely to affect public sentiment because observers expect this support. An institution with more heterogeneous preferences, however, can provide a more informative signal, since it is less clear *ex ante* that the president would receive strong support from that institution.

Thompson's information transmission theory suggests that the Security Council's preference structure may elevate its influence: because a wide variety of interests are represented on the Council, especially the presence of the permanent five veto players (Russia, China, France, Great Britain, and the US), any signal from that body will be informative to the American (or any other) public. Yet, the theory applies more generally to institutions that embody diverse preferences, because "formal IOs that are neutral, with heterogeneous and representative memberships are uniquely capable of providing credible information" (30). Interestingly, however, Thompson only identifies two audiences interested in this information: foreign publics and their leaders, who must take public support into consideration in making their own political decisions. Of course, this assumes that other states' regimes are democratic or at least representative, which may or may not be the case. But more importantly, Thompson ignores what may be the main target audience: the president's own public. And while it does not detract from the overall power of Thompson's theory, it would seem that a key impetus for seeking public support from a group of other states may be to inform one's own public and/or neutralize domestic opposition, per Schultz's argument.

This issue is taken up by Chapman (2007), who develops a formal model outlining the conditions under which presidents will seek authorization to use force from international institutions. Similar to Thompson, Chapman contends that institutions that are perceived as biased against an executive can provide more credible information.[8] For Chapman, the important audience is the president's constituents, who base their decision to support a policy goal on the feedback they receive from the international body. The audience cares about the feedback because they assume that opposition from a pivotal member in an IO will lead to higher costs of using force—or, more broadly, shifting the status quo. Public opposition to a policy makes an executive less likely to implement it, conditional on the perceived costs of going against the public's wishes and the cost of the use of force itself.

Chapman recognizes, moreover, that the public may discount support or opposition, depending on the perceived preferences of the pivotal member of the IO. Support for a policy from an IO that is biased against the state will provide credible information, but opposition from that organization does not guarantee more costs, since opposition was anticipated. Similarly, support from an institution biased in favor of the state is rarely beneficial, but opposition from such an institution could be quite costly. The hypothesis deduced from these comparative statics suggests that leaders who desire public support will choose to consult institutions that are perceived as "biased" against them, since the benefits are potentially large and the costs generally small.

Chapman's model nicely creates the possibility for variation regarding the question of when presidents will consult IOs. For Chapman, the pivotal member of an organization may differ based on the issue (e.g., environment versus security), the time frame (e.g., Cold War versus post-Cold War), and the institution (e.g., UN Security Council versus NATO). Thus, he escapes the need to argue that the bias within institutions is generally fixed over time—a critique that could be leveled at Thompson. This flexibility, however, entails costs. As discussed more fully below, Chapman's model demands that the public have knowledge of the pivotal player's preferences across these various issues, time frames, and institutions—an ironic assumption, given that a key principle of the model is the notion that the public observes the organization in the first place because it suffers from information shortages.

In addition, while Chapman's argument suggests intriguing hypotheses about the incentives of presidents to risk rejection by IOs, taken to its logical conclusion, the argument conjures potentially strange predictions. In the case of the 2003 Gulf War, for example, it suggests that George W. Bush should have attempted to garner approval for the conflict in the halls of the Arab League or the Organization of the Islamic Conference. Approval from such bodies would clearly convey valuable

---

[8] For Chapman, "bias" is defined as the location of the preference point of the pivotal member relative to the audience and the status quo. A bias against a state occurs when the pivotal member's ideal point is closer to the status quo than the audience, while a bias towards the state is the contrary.

information to domestic and international audiences; and although the probability of winning approval verges on zero, the costs of failing to secure approval may also be very small. Yet, we find few cases of presidents engaging in approval seeking from extremely biased institutions. If the costs of rejection are truly minimal and the benefits large, why would the president not make an attempt? This suggests other factors could be at play: the cost of approval seeking, for example, in terms of delay and reputational harm. That is, there seems to be an upper bound as to how biased the institution could be for presidents to even consider consulting them, and this is likely due to factors outside Chapman's model.

Elections, Presidents, and Trade Policy

The arguments linking international institutions, executives, and other domestic political actors are not confined to security affairs. Mansfield, Milner, and Rosendorff (2002) make an information provision argument with regard to economic organizations, specifically preferential trade agreements. They begin with the assumption that presidents value reelection. And while voter support is important for achieving this outcome, so might be the support of interest groups. To secure rents for these interest groups, an executive may increase tariffs higher than is preferred by the median voter. And while the public may have little knowledge of tariff levels, they do observe the price of goods (which rises with higher tariffs). If the price of goods grows too much, voters will attempt to remove the president from office.

Importantly, however, other macroeconomic factors may also increase the price of goods, resulting in a push to unseat an incumbent. Unfortunately, presidents cannot credibly inform the public that a rise in the price of goods was due to behavior other than rent seeking, since voters know that executives have incentives to raise tariffs to seek rents. International institutions can serve an important purpose for presidents in this regard. By signing a trade agreement committing a state to low tariffs, leaders can create a source of credible information regarding the underlying causes of poor economic outcomes. Much like the Security Council for Chapman and Reiter as well as Fang, trade agreements serve as the "alarm bell" for opportunistic behavior on the part of the executive. Since other members of the trade agreement face strong incentives to report unilateral increases in tariffs that violate the agreement, voters can monitor messages from the trade agreement concerning the origins of economic downturns. In the absence of a message from the international institution, voters assume the economic downturn was beyond the control of the president and she is reelected.

Mansfield, Milner, and Rosendorff empirically test the observable implication of their hypothesis: pairs of democratic states will be more likely to join preferential trade agreements than either pairs of autocratic states or mixed pairs (where only one state is a democracy). Examining all pairs of countries from 1951 to 1992, they find that pairs of democratic states are about twice as likely mixed pairs, and four times as likely as autocratic pairs, to form a preferential trade agreement. The Mansfield,

Milner, and Rosendorff work is valuable in extending the information-related bene-fits of IOs to the economic realm as well as providing an extensive theoretical framework for how presidents can benefit from the provision of information from international institutions.

A key question begged by Mansfield, Milner, and Rosendorff's work, which relies on the American public's knowledge of international events, is exactly how much the public knows about foreign affairs. Indeed, the papers linking IOs to public opinion contain a curious tension. On one hand, all suggest that, consistent with most empirical findings, the public is relatively ignorant about foreign affairs and suffers from large information asymmetries vis-à-vis the president. Otherwise, the pronouncements of the president would carry greater credibility. Yet, the arguments also demand the public to be attentive to signals from IOs regarding policy. In some issue areas, this may not be a stretch. Scholars such as Holsti (2004) have found that the mass public is relatively informed on issues of war and peace. But even though an average American could express knowledge of an incipient conflict involving the United States, it does not necessarily follow that they would be knowledgeable about an IOs position on that conflict. It is also unclear that international sources would be the first place voters would turn to for this information.

Of course, some of these arguments suggest that presidents have the power of the pulpit—they affirmatively choose to join an institution to convey information. Still, for some authors, the knowledge requirement for the public is sizeable. In particular, Chapman's model depends on the ability of voters to know the location of the ideal point of the pivotal member across time, issues, and institutions in order to give proper weight to the opinion of that institution. If they lack the knowledge of other states' preferences or the identity of the pivotal member, it is unclear how the public could evaluate information from the institution. One is tempted to suggest that the public discounts it or gives it little weight in their overall calculations of the desirability of a course of foreign policy action. When confronted with a situation of asymmetric information vis-à-vis both the president and the international insti-tution, the voter likely pays little attention to IO endorsements—even those that are difficult to achieve and thus the most informative.

Mansfield, Milner, and Rosendorff confront a potentially more daunting problem. While the public may be relatively more informed about matters of war and peace, it is unlikely that they closely monitor decisions of preferential trade arrangements (for example, Goldstein's binational panels in the US–Canada agreement). If true, this consideration undermines the ability of such agreements to serve as an effective fire alarm, giving a president less incentive to join the organization. One counter to this claim is that the alarm will not be pulled by the organization itself, but rather other member states who will loudly protest unilateral tariff increases. Indeed, this is an important mechanism since numerous preferential trade agree-ments lack formal institutional bodies to make such pronouncements (see Pevehouse 2008). In instances where other states must pull the fire alarm, however, the public must not perceive other states to be biased. Otherwise, any signal risks becoming uninformative, as in the Chapman and Thompson frameworks. Moreover, it begs the question of the value added of having an institution rather than relying on other states to identify one's own cheating behavior.

The final issue regarding these information-based theories of IOs concerns domestic alternatives. In the previous section, it was argued that international self-constraints were superior to domestic ones. Yet, in terms of information, it is less clear why executives do not rely on Congress and/or congressional opposition as a substitute for international sources of credible information. In the eyes of voters, Congress has less working knowledge of foreign affairs than the executive, who possesses large advantages in terms of information. Moreover, recent research has shown that the public closely follows debates over foreign affairs within Congress (Mermin 1999), and that detectable shifts in public opinion occur as Congress shifts its discussions of various policy options (Howell and Pevehouse 2007, ch. 7).

Given that large bodies of evidence indicate that the public follows Congress on foreign affairs, whereas little evidence suggests that voters shift in response to cues from international institutions, one wonders why Congress does not serve as a natural check against non-credible public pronouncements by the president. In other words, unless on a particular issue the incentives of Congress on the whole are perfectly aligned with the president, one can assume that any pronouncement about policy (e.g., tariff increases, the use of force, etc.) is credible given the constant presence of some domestic opposition. That is, why do executives face any problems of credibility vis-à-vis the public given congressional incentives to serve as a check on the president?

This is not to say that leaders will not seek endorsements and signals from IOs for other reasons, such as elite or public opinion in other countries, especially if doing so is relatively costless. But it is not clear that seeking approval from international sources helps the president to solve problems at home. Indeed, one area for future theorizing and empirical work would be to consider the relative costs and benefits of "staying domestic" versus "going international." This general question applies to the literature on self-restraint as well as approval seeking. Each option no doubt offers distinct costs and benefits at both the domestic and international level. Future scholarship would do well to explicitly compare the strategies from the perspective of the president.

Conclusions and Future Directions

This chapter began by noting the extensive growth in the literature linking domestic politics and international relations. Much of this literature bears directly on studies of the American president and her role in engaging in international cooperation. Of course, even though this fast-growing literature has pushed boundaries on the theoretical and empirical frontier, more work remains to be done.

There are several important questions in this area that remain underexplored. First, the work that has drawn significant insights from theories of American politics, especially in the field of two-level games, can do more to incorporate factors relating to the international realm. These theories often make restrictive assumptions about or pay little attention to the nature of international bargaining partners, the organization or agreement under consideration, or even the prospects that the organization will operate successfully. Theoretically, it is the same question asked by scholars of congressional models of delegation: to which agents are the principals comfortable delegating? As previously discussed, particular rules in an institution may be more attractive for presidents to solve credibility or time-inconsistency problems, but Congress may resist such attempts. By exploring how variation in the structure of international institutions (e.g., voting rules, enforcement mechanisms) influences domestic decision-making processes, future scholarship can move beyond the generality of the two-level games literature to emphasize particular conditions where domestic and international forces impinge on each other.

Second, the literature emphasizing the international side of the executive–IO linkage has often overlooked important domestic conditions that could make existing theories richer. For example, a key issue in the past decade in American presidency research has been the increasing use of unilateral executive instruments to achieve executives' policy goals (Howell 2003; Mayer 2001). As suggested in this essay, numerous IR scholars assume these mechanisms are inherently less credible than international commitments because they are easily altered or overturned domestically. Yet, as Howell (2005, 423) argues, "Congress has had a difficult time enacting laws that amend or overturn orders issued by presidents." This implies that IR scholars may overestimate the need for international solutions.

In addition, as a second-order question, how do other states perceive American commitments made via executive orders? Martin (2000) contends that congressional involvement in the policy process makes international cooperation more successful, but more systematic empirical work on the success of cooperation with respect to international versus domestic policy changes is in order. Moreover, does the fact that presidents "regularly invent new [policy mechanisms] or redefine old ones in order to suit their own strategic interests" undermine widely held assumptions in IR theory about the nature of democratic systems, such as their institutional constraints or promising advantages (Lipson 2003)? In other words, IR scholars often portray a far more idyllic and cooperative domestic scene in democracies than may actually exist.

Finally, much of the literature discussed here relies on public opinion as an important causal mechanism. Yet, as previously discussed, marked disagreement exists regarding how much the public knows about various issue areas. Future empirical research would do well to build on our scholarship of the public's knowledge of international affairs generally and international institutions more specifically. This has theoretical and empirical import: if the public knows more than theorists believe, the information asymmetries between the president and the public may be reduced, ameliorating her credibility problem in conveying her true intentions. Likewise, scholars would do well to square the increasingly common assumption that the president faces credibility problems resulting from informational asymmetries with the sizeable literature in American politics suggesting that presidents can shift public opinion under certain conditions (Kernell 1997). If presidents can lead, it suggests a public less wary of their pronouncements than is assumed by much of the IR literature.

Relatedly, scholars could do more do emphasize the role of the president in shaping the public opinion environment for Congress. Extant research in American politics suggests that presidents can play some role in legislative debates over policy through the mechanism of public opinion (Canes-Wrone 2005). As previously suggested, empirical work has also shown that Congress can play a key role in shaping opinion on foreign affairs, which in turns influences the president (Howell and Pevehouse 2007). While these arguments are not necessarily contradictory, they do suggest more work needs to be done to outline the precise conditions under which public opinion helps empower or constrain the president in international affairs. Specific to the previous discussion, one key question concerns the robustness of these theoretical models to a relaxation of the assumption that the public pays heed to the signals of IOs, as opposed to those of the president or Congress. Is Congress a key factor in the public's knowledge of international cooperation? Does the salience of a particular international issue increase or decrease the president's ability to engage in self-restraint or approval seeking?

The answers to these questions lie in wait for future scholars. Indeed, much of the exciting research in international relations lies at the border with American politics. Given the growing importance of global trade, international finance, globalization, and transnational security issues, both fields have much to learn from each other. The good news is that there is increasing interest in this work among each field. The Midwest Political Science Association has created an entire division in their annual program entitled "Domestic Politics and International Relations." Moreover, the University of Chicago Press has launched a book series engaging this exact topic. Outlets for work in this area are clearly expanding. As more work meaningfully engages both fields, including the theory and evidence within them, this area of research will no doubt continue to blossom.

References

ABBOTT, K., and SNIDAL, D. 1998. Why States Act through Formal International Organizations. *Journal of Conflict Resolution*, 42/1: 3–32.

BUTLER, C. 2004. Modeling Compromise at the International Table. *Conflict Management and Peace Science*, 21: 159–77.

CANES-WRONE, B. 2005. *Who's Leading Whom?* Chicago: University of Chicago Press.

—— HOWELL, W., and LEWIS, D. 2008. Toward a Broader Understanding of Presidential Power: A Reevaluation of the Two Presidencies Thesis. *Journal of Politics*, 70/1: 1–16.

CHAPMAN, T. 2007. International Security Institutions, Domestic Politics, and Institutional Legitimacy. *Journal of Conflict Resolution*, 51/1: 134–66.

—— and REITER, D. 2004. The United Nations Security Council and the Rally round the Flag Effect. *Journal of Conflict Resolution*, 48/6: 886–909.

EPSTEIN, D., and O'HALLORAN, S. 1993. Administrative Procedures, Information, and Agency Discretion. *American Journal of Political Science*, 38/3: 697–722.

EVANS, P., JACOBSON, H., and PUTNAM, R. (eds.) 1993. *Double-Edged Diplomacy: International Bargaining and Domestic Politics*. Berkeley and Los Angeles: University of California Press.

FANG, S. 2007. The Informational Role of International Institutions and Domestic Politics. *American Journal of Political Science*, 52/2: 304–21.

GILLIGAN, T., and KREHBIEL, K. 1989. Asymmetric Information and Legislative Rules with a Heterogeneous Committee. *American Journal of Political Science*, 33/2: 459–90.

GOLDSTEIN, J. 1996. International Law and Domestic Institutions: Reconciling North American "Unfair" Trade Laws. *International Organization*, 50/4: 541–64.

—— KAHLER, M., KEOHANE, R., and SLAUGHTER, A.-M. 2000. Introduction: Legalization and World Politics. *International Organization*, 54/3: 385–99.

GOWA, J. 1999. *Ballots and Bullets*. Princeton, NJ: Princeton University Press.

HAFNER-BURTON, E., MANSFIELD, E., and PEVEHOUSE, J. 2008. Democratization and Human Rights Regimes. Working paper: Harris School for Public Policy, University of Chicago.

HENISZ, W. J. 2002. The Institutional Environment for Infrastructure Investment. *Industrial and Corporate Change*, 11/2: 355–89.

HERMANN, M. 1980. Explaining Foreign Policy Behavior Using the Personal Characteristics of Political Leaders. *International Studies Quarterly*, 24/1: 7–46.

HOLSTI, O. 2004. *Public Opinion and American Foreign Policy*. Ann Arbor: University of Michigan Press.

HOWELL, W. 2003. *Power without Persuasion: The Politics of Direct Presidential Action*. Princeton, NJ: Princeton University Press.

—— 2005. Unilateral Powers: A Brief Overview. *Presidential Studies Quarterly*, 35/3: 417–39.

—— and PEVEHOUSE, J. 2005. Presidents, Congress, and the Use of Force. *International Organization*, 59/1: 209–32.

—— —— 2007. *While Dangers Gather: Congressional Checks on Presidential War Powers*. Princeton, NJ: Princeton University Press.

HUMPHREYS, M. 2007. Strategic Ratification. *Public Choice*, 132/1–2: 191–208.

IIDA, K. 1993. When and How Do Domestic Constraints Matter? Two Level Games with Uncertainty. *Journal of Conflict Resolution*, 34: 403–26.

KEOHANE, R. 1984. *After Hegemony: Cooperation and Discord in the World Political Economy*. Princeton, NJ: Princeton University Press.

KERNELL, S. 1997. *Going Public: New Strategies of Presidential Leadership*. Washington, DC: Congressional Quarterly Press.

KOREMENOS, B., LIPSON, C., and SNIDAL, D. 2000. The Rational Design of International Institutions. *International Organization*, 55/4: 761–99.

KREHBIEL, K. 1992. *Information and Legislative Organization*. Ann Arbor: University of Michigan Press.

KULL, S. 2002. Public Attitudes towards Multilateralism. Pp. 99–190 in *Multilateralism and U.S. Foreign Policy: Ambivalent Engagement*, ed. S. Patrick and S. Forman. Boulder, CO: Lynne Rienner.

LIPSON, C. 2003. *Reliable Partners: How Democracies Have Made a Separate Peace*. Princeton, NJ: Princeton University Press.

LOHMANN, S., and O'HALLORAN, S. 1994. Divided Government and U.S. Trade Policy. *International Organization*, 48: 595–632.

LUPIA, A., and McCUBBINS, M. 1994. Learning from Oversight: Fire Alarms and Police Patrols Reconstructed. *Journal of Law, Economics, and Organization*, 10/1: 96–125.

McCUBBINS, M., and SCHWARTZ, T. 1984. Congressional Oversight Overlooked: Police Patrols and Fire Alarms. *American Journal of Political Science*, 2: 165–79.

MANSFIELD, E., MILNER, H., and PEVEHOUSE, J. 2008. Democracy, Veto Players, and the Depth of Regional Integration. *World Economy*, 31/1: 67–96.

—— —— and ROSENDORFF, B. P. 2002. Why Democracies Cooperate More: Electoral Control and International Trade Agreements. *International Organization*, 56: 477–513.

—— and PEVEHOUSE, J. 2006. Democratization and International Organizations. *International Organization*, 60/1: 137–67.

MARTIN, L. 2000. *Democratic Commitments: Legislatures and International Cooperation*. Princeton, NJ: Princeton University Press.

MAYER, K. 2001. *With the Stroke of a Pen: Executive Orders and Presidential Power*. Princeton, NJ: Princeton University Press.

MEARSHEIMER, J. 1994/5. The False Promise of International Institutions. *International Security*, 19/3: 5–49.

MERMIN, J. 1999. *Debating War and Peace: Media Coverage of U.S. Intervention in the Post-Vietnam Era*. Princeton, NJ: Princeton University Press.

MILNER, H. 1997. *Interests, Institutions, and Information: Domestic Politics and International Relations*. Princeton, NJ: Princeton University Press.

MO, J. 1994. Two-Level Games with Endogenous Domestic Coalitions. *Journal of Conflict Resolution*, 38: 402–22.

MORAVCSIK, A. 2000. The Origins of Human Rights Regimes: Democratic Delegation in Postwar Europe. *International Organization*, 54/2: 217–52.

MORGENTHAU, H. J. 1985. *Politics among Nations*, 6th edn., rev. K. Thompson. New York: Alfred Knopf.

PEVEHOUSE, J. 2008. Regime Type and the Flexibility of International Cooperation. Working paper: Harris School for Public Policy, University of Chicago.

—— NORDSTROM, T., and WARNKE, K. 2004. The Correlates of War 2 International Governmental Organizations Data Version 2.0. *Conflict Management and Peace Science*, 212: 101–19.

PUTNAM, R. 1988. Diplomacy and Domestic Politics: The Logic of Two-Level Games. *International Organization*, 42: 427–60.

REINHARDT, E. 2003. Tying Hands without a Rope: Rational Domestic Response to International Institutional Constraints. Pp. 77–104 in *Locating the Proper Authorities*, ed. D. Drezner. Ann Arbor: University of Michigan Press.

ROSENAU, J. 1961. *International Politics and Foreign Policy: A Reader in Research and Theory*. Glencoe, IL: Free Press.

ROSENDORFF, B. P. 2005. Stability and Rigidity: Politics and Design of the WTO's Dispute Settlement Procedure. *American Political Science Review*, 99/3: 389–400.

SCHELLING, T. 1960. *The Strategy of Conflict*. Cambridge, MA: Harvard University Press.

SCHULTZ, K. 1998. Domestic Opposition and Signaling in International Crises. *American Political Science Review*, 94/4: 829–44.

—— 2001. *Democracy and Coercive Diplomacy*. New York: Cambridge University Press.

—— 2003. Tying Hands and Washing Hands: The U.S. Congress and Multilateral Humanitarian Intervention. Pp. 105–44 in *Locating the Proper Authorities*, ed. D. Drezner. Ann Arbor: University of Michigan Press.

SIMMONS, B. 2000. International Law and State Behavior: Commitment and Compliance in International Monetary Affairs. *American Political Science Review*, 96/4: 819–35.

TARAR, A. 2001. International Bargaining with Two-Sided Domestic Constraints. *Journal of Conflict Resolution*, 45/3: 320–40.

—— 2005. Constituencies and Preferences in International Bargaining. *Journal of Conflict Resolution*, 49/3: 383–407.

THOMPSON, A. 2006. Coercion through IOs: The Security Council and the Logic of Information Transmission. *International Organization*, 60: 1–34.

VOETEN, E. 2005. The Political Origins of the UN Security Council's Ability to Legitimize the Use of Force. *International Organization*, 59: 527–57.

VON STEIN, J. 2005. Do Treaties Constrain or Screen? Selection Bias and Treaty Compliance. *American Political Science Review*, 99/4: 611–22.

WALTZ, K. 1979. *Theory of International Politics*. New York: McGraw Hill.

WEINGAST, B., and MORAN, M. 1983. Bureaucratic Discretion or Congressional Control? Regulatory Policymaking by the Federal Trade Commission. *Journal of Political Economy*, 91/5: 765–800.

WILDAVSKY, A. 1966. The Two Presidencies. *Trans-Action*, 4: 7–14.

CHAPTER 31

WAR'S CONTRIBUTIONS TO PRESIDENTIAL POWER

WILLIAM G. HOWELL

TANA JOHNSON

THE original architects of our system of government and the scholars who subsequently studied it presumed that among stimulants to presidential power, war would know no equal. The Founders worried that through war a presidency might morph into a monarchy. At mid-twentieth century, political scientists credited wars with the emergence of a modern presidency, one wholly distinct from its predecessor. By Nixon's time, at least one historian argued (Schlesinger 1973), wars had catapulted the presidency out of the modern and into the imperial realm. And lest anyone doubt such claims—and few of prominence have—George Bush's stewardship through wars in Afghanistan and Iraq and a clandestine global war on terror would appear iron-clad proof that wars invariably lead to the aggrandizement of executive authority.

Viewed from another perspective, however, the last half century of US history has not treated the proposition kindly. Since the Second World War, major wars have proven disastrous for presidents. Public dissatisfaction with the Korean War drove Truman's approval ratings into the twenties; concerns about an escalating Vietnam War convinced Johnson not to seek reelection in 1968; and the current Iraq War put the Bush presidency clearly on the defensive. Minor wars, such as Lebanon and

Somalia, yielded costs of their own—diverting resources away from other policy initiatives, requiring justification at home and abroad, and causing substantial embarrassment to the president himself. Political scientists, meanwhile, have unearthed precious little quantitative evidence that presidential power—that is, the president's ability to influence the content and implementation of public policy—expands during times of war. Many analyses reveal no relationship between war and presidential power, and some actually uncover a negative one. Though adamantly argued, and almost universally presumed, the claim, at least in its current formulation, remains theoretically underdeveloped and empirically unsubstantiated.

This chapter traces the evolution of the argument, as well as its empirical record. It then offers critiques that are meant to guide future research on the topic. New scholarship may yet demonstrate that at least some wars positively influence some elements of some presidents' power. It is certainly possible that a robust relationship between war and presidential power may yet be documented. But having developed appropriate theoretical and empirical models, we anticipate, scholars will also gain a deeper appreciation for the toll that wars can take on presidential power.

An Idea's Articulation

People have written about a bond between war and presidential power for a very long time. For centuries, no less, statesmen and scholars have insisted that wars contribute mightily to presidential power. Some have gone so far as to argue that the relationship between the two warrants the status of "law" or "axiom." So convinced were they that wars, all wars, augment presidential power that almost none seriously contemplated the relationship's possible debasement.

The Founding Era

Shunning centuries of European precedent, the US's Founders opted to vest a legislature, rather than an executive, with the preponderance of war-making authority. Madison's core arguments in the *Federalist Papers* and the Pacificus–Helvidius debates, Hamilton's admissions of legislative dominance in war offered in the same outlets, a plain reading of Articles I and II of the Constitution, and early jurisprudence collectively demonstrate that the nation's Founders intended Congress to dictate whether, and when, the nation's military would be mobilized. To be sure, the precise division of war-making authority was (and continues to be) contested. Under certain circumstances—notably, when Congress was not in session or when military action was required to repel sudden attacks—the Founders allowed presidents to wage war independently. And consensus appeared more fleeting when the conversation turned to the appropriate division of other foreign policy powers. As a matter of both principle and standard practice, though, the Founders plainly intended Congress to bestride those national debates that specifically concerned war, whether large or small.

A handful of scholars dispute this characterization, insisting that the Founders intended to grant presidents ample discretion over decisions involving war (Yoo 2006a). Such views, though, are in a distinct minority, and other scholars have adequately addressed them (Adler 1988, 1998; Berger 1974; Fisher 2004). Rather than attend to matters of action, therefore, we wish to raise antecedent ones of motivation. Why did the Founders vest Congress, rather than the president, with primary authority over decisions involving war? And more specifically, what harms did the Founders intend to avert by granting Congress the most significant war powers?

Several considerations guided the Founders' decision, and each warrants brief mention. First, the Founders worried that American presidents would, as European monarchs had, use the military for their own private purposes. As John Jay recognized in *Federalist* No. 4, "absolute monarchs will often make war when their nations are to get nothing by it, but for purposes and objects merely personal, such as a thirst for military glory, revenge for personal affronts, ambition, or private compacts to aggrandize or support their particular families or partisans" (Rossiter 1999, 14). And it was for precisely this reason, Hamilton recognized in *Federalist* Nos. 69 and 70, that the Constitution entrusts these decisions to a legislative body of men rather than a single executive. While lauding the imperatives of "decision, activity, secrecy, and dispatch" (392)—all hallmarks of a unitary executive—Hamilton took pains to distinguish the president's military responsibilities from the vast war-making powers bestowed upon European monarchs. Hamilton famously admitted that the president's power "would be nominally the same with that of the king of Great Britain, but in substance much inferior to it" (385–6).

The Founders further hoped that by giving Congress the preponderance of war powers, war itself would become a rare event. Having just emerged from one military conflict, the Founders were hardly eager to begin another. And in the executive, Madison wrote to his friend Thomas Jefferson in 1798, there lies "the branch of power most interested in war, and most prone to it. [The Constitution] has accordingly with studied care, vested the question of war in the Legislature" (Hunt 1900–10, Vol. 6, 302). So doing, Madison and his compatriots hoped, the pace of war would predictably decelerate. "This system will not hurry us into war," James Wilson proclaimed during the state conventions to adopt the federal Constitution. Quite the opposite, "it is calculated to guard against it" (as quoted in Ely 1993, 3).

Some thirty years later, in his *Commentaries on the Constitution*, Joseph Story reiterated these themes. "Large bodies necessarily move slowly; and where the co-operation of different bodies is required, the retardation of any measure must be proportionally increased" (1833, 1166). Story recognized that foreign affairs occasionally required the "dispatch, secrecy, and vigour" of a unitary executive (60). The rapaciousness of war, though, convinced him, as it did the Founders, that it was best commenced only after the careful deliberations of a legislative body.

At one point in the constitutional convention, Pierce Butler of South Carolina offered an amendment to grant Congress the power to declare both war and peace. The amendment was roundly rejected on the grounds that the president, through his treaty-making authority, might negotiate a settled peace. And well and good this was, the Founders reasoned, for the process for declaring peace should be made eminently easier than that for ushering in a state of war. George Mason of Virginia registered his support "for clogging rather than facilitating war; but for facilitating peace" (Madison 2007, 419). Reflecting on this proposed amendment several decades later, Joseph Story noted: "The history of republics has but too fatally proved, that they are too ambitious of military fame and conquest, and too easily devoted to the views of demagogues, who flatter their pride, and betray their interests. It should therefore be difficult in a republic to declare war; but not to make peace" (1833, 1166).

A third motivation also reveals itself, and this last one is especially important for the purposes of this chapter. The Founders anticipated that through war presidents would find the means by which to exalt their power more generally. The problem with vesting war-making powers in a single individual was not merely that he (someday she) would use it inadvisably or frequently, but that by plunging the nation into a state of war he might disrupt the larger constitutional order. So doing, future presidents might undo what the Founders had worked so hard to create: a system of governance with three distinct branches of government, each with the incentives and resources to check the others, the result of which would be a robust, though admittedly dynamic, overall balance of power.

To be sure, additional threats to the balance of powers lay within Article II—in the pardon power, in the possibility of electing a president for multiple terms, and in the unitary nature of the office. The Founders, though, ultimately granted these powers and structural arrangements because they deemed them necessary to overcome some of the evident failings of the Articles of Confederation. The Founders expressly did not grant the president primary authority over decisions involving war, however, precisely because doing so presented too great a risk. To presidential power, wars were a stimulant *nonpareil*—more than any other, they promised to undermine the nation's fragile and altogether untested system of governance.

On this basic fact, there was virtual unanimity. In *Federalist* No. 8, Alexander Hamilton recognized that "it is the nature of war to increase the executive at the expense of the legislative authority" (Rossiter 1999, 36). Echoing these sentiments, Madison argued in *Helvidius* No. 4 that "war is in fact the true nurse of executive aggrandizement." To justify the conclusion, Madison noted that:

In war, a physical force is to be created; and it is the executive will, which is to direct it. In war, the public treasures are to be unlocked; and it is the executive hand that is to dispense them. In war, the honours and emoluments of office are to be multiplied; and it is the executive patronage under which they are to be enjoyed. It is in war, finally, that laurels are to be gathered; and it is the executive brow they are to encircle. The strongest passions and most dangerous weaknesses of the human breast; ambition, avarice, vanity, the honourable or venial love of fame, are all in conspiracy against the desire and duty of peace.

(Frisch 2007, 87)

Hamilton and Madison, of course, disagreed about the merits of a powerful presidency. But on their particular assessment of war's contribution to presidential power, the two adversaries stood together. And on the basis of such judgment, they opted to vest Congress with the authority to declare war.

Those who opposed the Constitution at the time, of course, took such arguments even further. For them, the assignment of almost any war powers to the presidency inexorably led not merely to the expansion of executive power, but the unraveling of a republic into tyranny. The *Anti-Federalist Papers* bristle with condemnation against an "elective king" whose war powers permit, even encourage, the concentration of virtually all government authority. Writing under the pseudonym Cato, George Clinton recognized the president as "the generalissimo of the nation, [who] of course has the command and control of the army, navy and militia; he is the general conservator of the peace of the union." By taking the nation to war, Clinton insisted, the president would brandish powers that no government of a free people should retain. "Will not the exercise of these powers therefore tend either to the establishment of a vile and arbitrary aristocracy or monarchy?" (Storing 1981, 116).

Primary among the Anti-Federalists' fears was the possibility that the president, as commander-in-chief, would use the army as an instrument of his own empowerment. Many of the controversies surrounding the existence of a standing army and the subservience of state militias to a federal militia stemmed from abiding concerns that presidents would employ the military as the arm of their dominion. Though Congress might ostensibly have the authority to declare war, who had the power to stop a president intent on using the military as he saw fit? Speaking before the Virginia ratifying convention, Patrick Henry intoned: "Away with your President, we shall have a King: the army will salute him Monarch; your militia will leave you and assist in making him King, and fight against you: and what have you to oppose this force? What will then become of you and your rights? Will not absolute despotism ensue?" (Ketcham 2003, 214). With the military and through war, Henry and his fellow Anti-Federalists warned, presidents would trample upon every individual right that the Constitution stood to protect.

Anti-Federalists and Federalists, of course, interpreted the Constitution very differently, and they held wildly divergent views about the consequences of ratification. Anti-Federalists expected that presidents would exploit their narrowly defined powers, and that the Constitution therefore was best rejected. Federalists pointed out that the Constitution granted all important decisions about war to Congress, and hence deserved to be ratified. The two sides, though, fundamentally agreed about the dangers of vesting excessive war powers in a single man, and were deeply preoccupied by the possibility that through war a president might eventually become, for all intents and purposes, a king.

Calamitous Wars and Vindication

The next 175 years would appear to provide ample justification for the Founders' fears. Lincoln's indomitable control over the federal government during the Civil War, Wilson's efforts to mobilize a country through the First World War, and Roosevelt's unprecedented involvement in the domestic economy during the Second World War reaffirmed the powerful relationship between war and presidential power. Each of these three wars ushered in massive changes to national policies concerning the tax code, wage and price controls, civil rights and civil liberties, and labor–management relations. The wars altered the design of the administrative state itself, yielding an extraordinary expansion of federal agencies—many of which were under the immediate control of presidents—that assumed primary responsibility for writing and implementing all sorts of public policy. And during each of these wars, virtually all actions taken by the federal government seemed to emanate first from the White House.

Consider what the two most famous mid-century presidency scholars—Edward Corwin and Clinton Rossiter—had to say about the matter. Corwin devoted an entire chapter of his masterwork, *The Presidency: Office and Powers*, to the issue of presidential power during times of war. Reflecting on the three largest wars, Corwin saw the president's constitutional powers at their apex. Lincoln, Wilson, and Roosevelt all flexed their Article II powers, and Congress and the courts promptly withdrew from a fight that they were well accustomed to having. Indeed, Corwin observed, Congress during these wars actively supplemented the president's constitutional powers with new statutory authority over all sorts of policy domains. As a result, presidents could be seen setting price controls, regulating speech, transforming the federal bureaucracy, issuing economic sanctions, assuming control over manufacturing plants, and constraining individual liberties like never before. And through it all, the courts refused to interfere—at least as long as troops remained in the field. Corwin concluded, "the principal canons of constitutional interpretation are in wartime set aside so far as concerns both the scope of national power and the capacity of the President to gather unto himself all constitutionally available powers in order the more effectively to focus them upon the task of the hour" (1957, 262).

At war's end, Corwin further observed, presidential power did not always revert to its pre-war status. Admittedly, some influence was ceded to the adjoining branches. Upon a war's termination, judges were more willing to rule against a president; and Congress simultaneously attempted to reclaim some of the authority it had previously delegated. These efforts, though, hardly negated the extraordinary expansion of presidential power witnessed during times of crisis, especially the two world wars.[1] Hence, when presidents confront altogether new crises, they benefit from the powers claimed during past ones. Says Corwin, "in each successive crisis the constitutional results of earlier crises reappear cumulatively and in magnified form" (1957, 262). Though wars may be needed to engender presidential power, they are not needed to sustain it.

---

[1] In this regard, Corwin distinguishes the Civil War from the First and Second World Wars. The former did not fundamentally alter the office of the presidency, says Corwin, while the latter two plainly did.

In even less qualified terms, Clinton Rossiter developed many of the same arguments. Rossiter raised the issue of war when trying to account for the astronomical rise of presidential power during the nation's first 200 years of history. He noted, "In such time, 'when the blast of war blows in our ears,' the President's power to command the forces swells out of all proportion to his other powers" (1956, 12). This influence, however, was hardly confined to the conduct of war. By Rossiter's account, it spilled over into all sorts of policy domains that may or may not relate to the war effort:

Another axiom of political science would seem to be this: great emergencies in the life of a constitutional state bring an increase in executive power and prestige, always at least temporarily, more often than not permanently. As proof of this point, we need only think of the sudden expansion in power that the Presidency experienced under Lincoln as he faced the rebellion, under Wilson as he led us into a world war, or under Franklin Roosevelt as he called upon Congress to extend him "broad Executive power to wage war" against depression. Each of these men left the Presidency a stronger instrument, an office with more customary and statutory powers, than it had been before the crisis.   (1956, 64–5)

This expansion, moreover, is not the result of great presidents in great wars. Rossiter admonishes:

Nor should we forget lesser Presidents in lesser crises, for these men, too, left their mark on the office. When Hayes dispatched troops to restore peace in the railroad strike of 1877, when McKinley sent 5,000 soldiers and marines to China during the Boxer uprising, and when Harry Truman acted on a dozen occasions to save entire states from the ravages of storm or fire or flood, the Presidency moved to a higher level of authority and prestige—principally because the people had now been taught to expect more of it.   (1956, 65)

According to Rossiter, presidents can claim new influence over the doings of government, even without launching a massive war or keeping troops in the field for excessive periods of time. The equivalent of a battalion or two will often suffice, and the effects may be felt almost immediately.

Vietnam and the Rise of an Imperial Presidency

If the Second World War produced a distinctively "modern" presidency, as many presidency scholars have suggested, future wars yielded still more opportunities for presidents to augment their power. With the Korean and Vietnam wars, in particular, members of Congress would appear to have abdicated what remained of their constitutional war powers. And in assuming primary control over the conduct of war, presidents managed to expand their influence more generally. By Nixon's second term, presidents had so distorted the constitutional order that the nation's very system of governance appeared to be in crisis. In 1973, Arthur Schlesinger Jr. summarized the views of many constitutional law scholars and historians by heralding the emergence of an "imperial presidency."

Schlesinger's core argument rests on the premise that presidential power ebbs and flows during times of peace and war. In *The Imperial Presidency*, Schlesinger regularly refers to war as the "health of the presidency" (2004a, 82). We have inherited a "war-magnified presidency" (127), he intones. For throughout American history, Schlesinger insists, wars have "nourished the presidency" (122).

For Schlesinger, presidential power was "resurgent" in the Second World War, "ascendant" in the Korean War, and "rampant" in the Vietnam War. In each of these wars, presidents further encroached on Congress's constitutional war powers—such that by the Vietnam War, the practice of war appeared altogether out of sync with the principles laid out in Articles I and II. These facts, though, had consequences that went well beyond decisions about military matters. Indeed, Schlesinger recognized, with war power firmly in their grasp, modern presidents could lay claim to all sorts of foreign and domestic policies. The translation of war power into general power appeared entirely self-evident. After all, Schlesinger asked, "If the President were conceded these life-and-death decisions abroad, how could he be restrained from gathering unto himself the less fateful powers of the national policy?" (2004a, xxvii).

In two ways, Schlesinger's argument differs from Corwin and Rossiter's. First, Schlesinger saw a direct connection between the size of a war and the amount of power accrued by the president. Whereas Rossiter suggested that almost any war will redound to the benefit of the presidency, Schlesinger primarily feared large-scale and long-standing military enterprises. "The more acute the crisis," he insisted, "the more power flows to the president" (2004b, 46). Second, whereas Corwin and Rossiter saw successive wars steadily contributing to presidential power, Schlesinger argued that periods of executive expansion and decline coincided with periods of war and peace. "While war increased presidential power," Schlesinger noted, "peace brought a reaction against executive excess" (2004a, xiv). Whether presidents were weak or strong, for Schlesinger, fundamentally depended on whether the nation was at war. It was precisely for this reason, then, that Schlesinger late in life saw an interminable and pervasive "war against terror" as such a threat to the nation's system of governance. Lacking temporal and physical boundaries, a war against terror might irreparably distort the balance of powers among the executive, legislative, and judicial branches of government.

Still, the Founders' basic concerns and Corwin and Rossiter's observations resonate with Schlesinger. Wars, these various men saw, catapulted the president to the top of the federal government. With the nation's troops engaged in battle, presidents wielded unprecedented influence over all sorts of domestic and policy initiatives. Relief from such a state of affairs, if relief was possible, ultimately depended upon the return of peace.

EMPIRICAL EVIDENCE ON WAR AND PRESIDENTIAL POWER

The close of the Vietnam War and the concurrent congressional resurgence did not silence discussions of an imperial presidency. They merely put them on hold. For many scholars, the subsequent thirty years of US history—with military deployments in the Middle East, Central America, Africa, and Eastern Europe—reaffirmed the ways in which wars propel executive efforts to claim (and reclaim) power (Fisher 2004; Rudalevige 2005). And twenty-first-century military operations in Iraq and Afghanistan, combined with a nebulous "war on terror," would seem to further confirm the linkages between war and presidential power (Irons 2005; Savage 2007; Schlesinger 2004; Schwarz and Huq 2007; Yoo 2006a). Ironically perhaps, John Yoo summarizes conventional wisdom on the topic: "the inescapable fact is that war shifts power to the branch most responsible for its waging: the executive" (Yoo 2006b).

Bush's recent actions have attracted considerable debate, much of it politically charged. Such normative considerations, however, warrant no further mention here. We are principally concerned with factual assessments about the relationship between war and presidential power. And on this topic, there is much more to say. During the last several decades, a reasonably large body of quantitative evidence has amassed on the ways in which wars contribute to presidential power in a wide variety of domains—in the types of laws that Congress enacts, the policies that presidents issue unilaterally, the decisions that judges render, the design of the bureaucracy, and the public's assessments of the president's performance in office. This section briefly summarizes the main findings in each of these domains.

Legislation

Though they have scrutinized almost every imaginable correlate of congressional voting behavior, scholars have paid less attention to the precise relationship between war and presidential influence. The findings that do exist, however, yield little support for theories of an imperial presidency. Andrew Rudalevige (2002), for instance, tracks the fate of presidential initiatives put before Congress during the post-Second World War era. He finds that "critical external events" prompt an 18-percentage point increase in the probability that Congress enacts a bill that is in line with presidential preferences. Unfortunately, the analysis does not test the effect of war *per se*, for war is merely one of several scenarios that are coded as critical external events. Other studies that do explicitly control for war, meanwhile, offer more tempered assessments of its influence on presidential power. Jeffrey Cohen (1982) investigates presidential legislative success during three time periods: 1861–96, 1897–1932, and 1933–72. In the quantitative analysis, war's effect is positive and statistically significant in the earliest era, but not in either of the two latter periods. Cohen concludes that "wars are less able now to build congressional support for the president" (528).

By expanding the definition of war to include not only "hot" wars like Korea and Vietnam but also the Cold War between the United States and the Soviet Union, and by further restricting the analysis to foreign policy initiatives, some scholars have unearthed evidence of a relationship between war and presidential influence in Congress. Examining roll-call votes taken between 1947 and 1988, Meernik (1993) finds that hot and cold wars encourage congressional support for the president's foreign policy and defense proposals. According to Meernik, presidents enjoyed greater levels of support in both the House and Senate during the first half of the Cold War; and greater levels of support in the Senate during the Korean War and Vietnam Wars.

Other scholars reach similar conclusions, but code for altogether different periods of the Cold War. Jeffrey Peake (2002) examines presidents' ability to convince members of Congress to vote for the executive's preferred foreign policy bills during 1947–98. Identifying the entire Cold War period between 1947 and 1990, he finds a positive and significant effect. Brandon Prins and Bryan Marshall (2001) examine foreign, defense, and domestic policies introduced between 1953 and 1998. Identifying the first half of the Cold War between 1953 and 1973, they find a significant positive effect for foreign and defense policies, but not for domestic policies. Eugene Wittkopf and James McCormick (1998) take a different approach, investigating whether the demise of the Cold War has eroded congressional support for presidents' foreign policy initiatives. Wittkopf and McCormick examine initiatives introduced between 1983 and 1996 and code for three stages during this time frame: Cold War (1983–8), transitional period (1989–90), and post-Cold War (1991–6). Wittkopf and McCormick conclude that conflict between Congress and the president has risen in the post-Cold War era. Given the authors' varying approaches to coding the Cold War years, it is difficult to know how to interpret these collective findings. It is worth noting, though, that whatever influence the Cold War bestowed upon the president, it did so only in foreign policy.

To be sure, ascertaining presidential power on the basis of roll-call votes on presidential initiatives is extraordinarily difficult. Presidents, after all, do not randomly select elements from their policy agenda to put before Congress. Rather, presidents select those policies that they think stand a decent chance of passage, and set aside the rest. If such selectivity is a function of war—and there are ample reasons to believe that it is—then systematic biases are introduced that, uncorrected, may obscure war's genuine effects on presidential power. Some of the best quantitative work on presidential power within Congress, therefore, considers budgets. For here, presidents do not have the luxury of selecting when to express a preference about an issue publicly, and when to stay silent. Each year presidents must submit to Congress a detailed budget proposal on every facet of the government's operations—a fact that alleviates, though certainly does not eliminate, concerns about selection bias.

If wars expand presidential influence over the appropriations process, we can expect to observe two kinds of evidence: first, that presidents during times of war request higher amounts of funding for their preferred programs; and second, that Congress appropriates amounts that better reflect presidential priorities. The existing literature, however, does not satisfy either expectation. Kiewiet and McCubbins (1985) speak to the first point. Though their data do not distinguish those programs that presidents support or oppose, Kiewiet and McCubbins are able to track all budget requests for domestic programs. Examining submitted budgets for thirty-seven federal agencies from fiscal years 1948 to 1979, Kiewiet and McCubbins uncover a statistically significant *and negative* relationship between war and presidential funding requests. A follow-up study of sixty-three non-defense agencies during fiscal years 1948 to 1985 further demonstrates that Truman cut his domestic appropriations proposals during the Korean War (1991). Kiewiet and McCubbins also find some evidence that Johnson and Nixon scaled back their budgetary requests during the Vietnam War, though the effect is much weaker.

Unfortunately, Kiewiet and McCubbins do not distinguish those programs that presidents support or oppose, making it difficult to conclusively determine whether presidential power actually weakens during times of war. It is possible that during periods of war presidents request cutbacks on domestic policies that they oppose, and peacetime equivalent funding for programs that they support. If true, then presidential power does not appear diminished. We can rule out the possibility, however, that presidents request peacetime equivalent funds for programs that they oppose and increases for programs that they support. And nowhere is there any evidence that wars systematically encourage presidents to solicit higher levels of spending for domestic programs as a whole.

Brandice Canes-Wrone, William Howell, and David Lewis (2008) investigate whether congressional appropriations better align with presidential priorities during times of war than during times of peace. Analyzing appropriations data from fiscal years 1969 to 2000, the authors show that foreign policy appropriations better reflect presidential requests than do domestic policy appropriations—a finding that is consistent with the two-presidencies hypothesis. The authors uncover very little evidence, however, that wars systematically augment presidential power. When isolating the Vietnam War, a slight positive effect between war and congressional appropriations is observed. When expanding the definition of war to include other military conflicts during the period, however, the observed relationship vanishes.

Unilateral Activity

If the president cannot count on congressional submissiveness during war, then perhaps he can bypass the legislature entirely. William Howell (2003) shows that the issuing of significant executive orders has peaked during the New Deal, the Second World War, the Korean War, the early stages of the Vietnam War, and the Iran hostage crisis. Regression analyses confirm that presidents issue greater numbers of important orders when the United States is at war, and the relationship is often—although not always—statistically significant. In a similar vein, Glen Krutz and Jeffrey Peake (2006) consider the circumstances under which presidents, between 1949 and 1998, forewent international treaties and instead utilized executive agreements with other countries. While treaties necessitate a supermajority in the Senate for ratification, executive agreements require only a simple majority in both houses. During the Cold War, Krutz and Peake find, presidents used a greater number of executive agreements vis-à-vis treaties than since the Cold War's end in 1989.

Do these findings definitively prove that presidential power increases during wartime? No. It is certainly true that presidents can employ unilateral directives to accomplish things that would not survive the legislative process. An increase in unilateral activity, however, does not necessarily indicate an expansion of presidential power, writ large. For starters, wars may introduce important substitution effects, as presidents issue more executive orders and agreements but fewer laws and treaties. Additionally, the observed increase in unilateral activity may have nothing to do with an expansion of presidential power, but rather it may simply reflect the greater foreign policy workload that wars present. Finally, these findings do not expressly compare the content of the orders that presidents issue to the policy preferences that they hold. If presidents are more inclined to compromise their policy preferences during times of war, an increase in unilateral activity does not necessarily indicate a concurrent expansion of executive power.

Bureaucratic Design

Other scholars have looked beyond unilateral activity, focusing instead on ties between the White House and other arms of the federal government. For example, presidents may wield their wartime power by fashioning bureaucratic organs that are especially and enduringly responsive to the executive branch. David Lewis (2003) points out that agencies created by unilateral directives are less likely to be insulated from presidential control, in part because they tend to lack governing boards, fixed terms for political appointees, or party-balancing limitations. Lewis further finds a positive and statistically significant correlation between war and the number of administrative agencies created through unilateral directives between 1946 and 1995. Canes-Wrone, Howell, and Lewis (2008), however, explicitly test whether administrative agencies exhibit more characteristics of presidential control during times of war. The relevant coefficient is not always of the expected sign and is never statistically significant. As with presidential power vis-à-vis the legislative branch, the evidence regarding the bureaucracy appears mixed.

Judicial Decision Making

The empirical record does not support the notion that Congress and administrative agencies consistently bow to presidential preferences during periods of war. Yet it is possible that the judiciary, lacking powers of either the purse or sword, may be especially prone to do so. Examining federal cases that challenge presidential power, some scholars find that judges indeed are more likely to side with the chief executive when foreign or military affairs are at stake (Ducat and Dudley 1989; Yates and Whitford 1998). These particular studies, however, only identify whether the substantive content of a case relates to international affairs. They do not consider whether judges rule differentially during periods of war and peace.

Those scholars who have examined judicial decision making when the nation is actually at war offer different conclusions about the correlates of presidential power. Clark (2006) provides the most direct test of the proposition. Examining appellate court rulings on non-criminal cases over a 100-year period, Clark does not find any evidence of heightened judicial deference to the executive during periods of war. In fact, Clark provides evidence that appellate judges are significantly more likely to rule against the president during wartime. He concludes that "constitutional checks and balances placed on executive power do not necessarily collapse during wartime" (416).

Howell (2003) also investigates every executive order that was challenged on constitutional or statutory grounds in a federal court between 1942 and 1998. He finds that courts affirm executive orders 83 percent of the time, and so doing, they occasionally provide justification for further expansions of presidential power. Howell unearths no evidence, however, that either the frequency of court challenges or the propensity of judges to side with the president systematically vary according to whether the country is at war.

Based on the current empirical record, presidents cannot count on judicial favoritism during times of war. But Clark and Howell's studies, of course, are hardly the last word on the judiciary's treatment of the presidency during periods of war. It is quite possible that judges hear very different types of cases during times of war than during times of peace, even if the size of their caseloads remains roughly constant. Moreover, on especially high-profile cases, judges may delay rendering a decision until after a military conflict has subsided. Recognizing such possibilities, Clark cautions that "much further analysis [is required] before a broad claim may be staked about the nature of non-criminal adjudication during wartime" (416).

Public Opinion

The notion that Congress, the bureaucracy, and the judiciary submit more readily to the chief executive in times of war is intuitively appealing. The existing empirical record, however, does not unambiguously corroborate the claim. Another possibility may resuscitate the conventional account of war and presidential power: military deployments may enhance the public's opinion of the president, affording him greater political capital and flexibility to pursue his policy agenda. We cannot possibly summarize the vast literatures on war and public opinion. We can, however, take inventory of those empirical findings that speak directly to the influence of war on the president's approval ratings. Depending upon their sampling frame and analytic focus, scholars have uncovered a variety of findings—some positive, some negative, many null—on how wars influence the president's public standing.

Some scholars have identified empirical evidence that wars tend to augment the president's public standing. Barbara Norrander and Clyde Wilcox (1993), for example, suggest that military deployments prompt members of the general public to identify more closely with the president's political party. They find that survey respondents who supported the 1991 deployment of troops to the Persian Gulf tended to view the Republican Party more warmly and to change their party self-identification accordingly. Suzanne Parker further suggests that the beneficial impact of the first Gulf War enhanced not only Bush's overall approval rating, but also the public's evaluations of his handling of economic affairs (1995).

It is not clear, however, that other wars had an equivalently positive effect on presidential approval ratings. Post-World War II surveys of public opinion trends do not yield much evidence of a consistent relationship between uses of force and evaluations of presidential performance. For instance, Patrick James and Jean Sebastien Rioux (1998) find that the use of force negatively affects presidential approving ratings. Marra, Ostrom, and Simon (1990), on the other hand, demonstrate that the use of force enhances presidential approval ratings, but only when the use is extensive and employed in a "major" region of the world. For minor uses and minor regions, the estimated effects fail to achieve statistical significance. Although other scholars have found some evidence that international crises and perceived threats boost evaluations of presidential performance, the observed increases tend to be short lived (Brace and Hinckley 1991; Huddy et al. 2005; Ostrom and Simon 1985).

A still larger body of research probes the "rally around the flag" phenomenon, defined as "the propensity of the American public to put aside political differences and support the president during international crises" (Baker and Oneal 2001, 661). Starting with John Mueller (1970, 1973), scholars have identified a wide range of international events, ranging from US–Soviet summits to the seizure of US hostages, that potentially induce rally effects. Much of this work, though, underscores the phenomenon's fragility, leading George Edwards to conclude that "[M]ost rally events do not produce rallies at all. Instead, the polls taken after most of them show a loss of support...Even the rallies that do occur may be short-lived" (1990, 146). Those analyses that focus on the subset of wars as potential triggering events tend to confirm Edwards's view. For example, analyses by Michael MacKuen (1983) and Helmut Norpoth (1984) indicate that the Vietnam War hurt President Johnson's approval ratings, but the authors disagree over the war's effect on his successor. Norpoth argues that the conflict in Vietnam enhanced President Nixon's standing, while MacKuen asserts that Nixon's reduction in troop deployments was not translated into approval. Other scholars find that ongoing major wars, such as Vietnam and Korea, effectively erase rally effects associated with new, unrelated crises (Lian and Oneal 1993; MacKuen 1983; Norpoth 1984; Oneal and Bryan 1995; Oneal, Lian, and Joyner 1996).

More recent work by William Baker and John Oneal (2001) extends the analysis back to the 1940s and through the 1990s, concluding that presidents cannot count on US troop deployment to elicit a politically significant rally in public opinion. Of the 167 events examined, only 65 resulted in increases in the executive's approval ratings. Baker and Oneal do find that rallies spike in particular circumstances, such as when the United States plays the role of both "originator" and "revisionist" in a conflict. Military ventures occurring while the United States is already involved in a war, however, actually diminish the size of a rally.

Most analyses of rally events focus on aggregate data. Foreign crises, however, need not evoke a common response from all members of the public. Wars may not convert opponents of the president into supporters. Rather, rallies may appear most pronounced—when they appear at all—among those individuals who already are predisposed to support the president. Examining a panel of survey respondents before and after a military strike against Iraq in 1993, George Edwards and Tami Swenson find that Democrats were significantly more likely to rally behind Bill Clinton than were either Independents or Republicans. They conclude: "Rather than being a distinctive phenomenon, a rally event seems to be an additional force that pushes potential supporters over the threshold of approval" (1997, 208).

Still other work finds that certain elements of war—namely, the occurrence of US casualties—actually dampen public support for the president. Jamie Carson and his colleagues (2001) investigate the influence of Civil War casualties on votes for incumbents in the Republican-controlled Congress in the 1862–3 midterm elections and unearth both positive and negative effects, depending on the variable employed. Doug Kriner and Frances Shen (2007) find similar evidence during the Vietnam War. And David Karol and Edward Miguel (2007) discover that Iraq War casualties substantially decreased George W. Bush's vote share in the 2004 elections (see also Gartner and Segura 1998; James and Rioux 1998; Marra, Ostrom, and Simon 1990; Ostrom and Simon 1985). Of course, debates persist about the functional form of the relationship between casualties and public opinion and the relevance of political elites in assigning meaning to war events (Berinsky 2007; Berinsky and Druckman 2007; Gelpi, Feaver, and Reifler 2006). None of these scholars, however, claims that casualties ever induce higher presidential approval ratings.

Scholars have devoted more attention to war's influence on presidential approval ratings than to any other correlate of presidential power. The collective evidence in support of a war-inspired imperial presidency is decidedly mixed. Some scholars do find that approval ratings surge during times of war; the findings, however, are neither robust nor indicative of a sea change in public sentiment. Ongoing wars often suffocate new rallies tied to unrelated foreign crises; existing supporters of the presidents tend to propel rallies when they do occur; and certain elements of war, notably US casualties, threaten reduced public support for the president.

RECONCILING EXPECTATIONS AND EVIDENCE

Evidence of executive largesse during periods of war hardly matches expectations. Many analyses of the impact of war on elements of presidential influence yield null findings. Those gains that are observed tend to be short lived. And when they explicitly model the direct and opportunity costs of war, scholars often observe evidence that military deployments actually hamper approval ratings and other vestiges of presidential power. On the whole, though, it is difficult to know what to make of these findings. Both empirical and theoretical limitations to this research make it extraordinarily difficult to determine whether claims about an imperial presidency are either wrong or simply in need of refinement.

Empirical Issues

From our vantage point, the existing quantitative literature on war and presidential power has three overriding limitations. The first concerns the literature's breadth of coverage. Simply put, the existing research is spotty. We have no systematic evidence about the influence of wars on the willingness of Congress to delegate authority to the president, to ratify treaties, or to grant fast-track authority. As previously indicated, our understanding of judicial decision-making on cases involving presidential power is especially thin. And we lack any empirical evidence about issues that traditionally have fallen within the purview of international relations—such as how wars influence the relationship between presidents and either foreign states or international organizations, or whether wars facilitate the signing of more advantageous bilateral and multilateral agreements. For all that the existing quantitative literature does address, ample lines of inquiry remain wholly unexplored.

Second, most of the existing empirical work on presidential power treats war as a control variable, rather than as the key explanatory variable of interest. As a result, scholars evaluate war's effect on presidential power, at best, only indirectly. Tellingly, few scholars provide a detailed theoretical rationale for including a control for war or even cite other researchers who have established the importance of this variable. Only the empirical work on public opinion treats war as a central focus of study. This literature, however, has the weakest relationship to presidential power. Whereas the work on Congress, the courts, and the bureaucracy specifically models how presidential policies are written or implemented, the literature on public opinion merely identifies one possible correlate of presidential influence.

The third limitation of the existing literature concerns the various definitions of war. Many studies identify only those periods in which the United States was involved in hot wars, such as Korea, Vietnam, and the two Persian Gulf Wars.[2] Other scholars opt to cast a wider net, recognizing such smaller deployments as those that occurred in the 1980s and 1990s in Panama, Somalia, Haiti, Bosnia, and Kosovo. And still other scholars focus on the Cold War between the United States and the Soviet Union, and

---

[2] Unfortunately—yet not surprisingly, due to the challenges of obtaining decades-old data—these analyses often exclude the two world wars, which had provided much of the initial inspiration for Corwin, Rossiter, and others who warned of imperial presidents.

various periods therein. Over time, defining wars in different ways may make a great deal of sense. It is quite possible—probable even—that different wars affect presidential power in different ways, and scholars would do well to account for their distinguishing characteristics. It seems perfectly reasonable to expect that a war's size, popularity, duration, and ultimate success may crucially define its contributions to presidential power. In the short run, however, the existence of multiple definitions of war makes it difficult to compare results across studies.

Without an agreed-upon definition of war, it is also difficult to ascertain the varying influences that long-standing military commitments in a single country or region can have on presidential power. During the course of one war, changes in the number of troops deployed, revelations about its costs and benefits, and evolving sentiments about whether the venture itself was justified may further condition the influence of war on presidential power. The Vietnam War, for instance, started out as a series of small deployments of military advisers, steadily escalated into a fully-fledged war under a Democratic president, and then morphed into a seemingly intractable campaign under a Republican president. There is no reason to expect that the nation's involvement in Vietnam in the mid-1960s had the same impact on presidential power as its involvement in the early 1970s. With the exception of the work on public opinion, however, the existing literature on war and presidential power aims to uncover the average effect of war and tends to ignore its considerable variance.

Theoretical Issues

Gallons of ink have been spilled on the proposition that wars augment presidential power. But most work on the subject has taken the form of a simple assertion made over and over again, rather than a well-developed theory whose micro foundations are specified with increasing clarity. As Stephen Skowronek points out, "the politics behind the imperial presidency thesis was never very fully articulated; what there is could be summarized in a single sentence: imperial ambitions breed imperial powers" (Skowronek 2008). Even if they satisfactorily resolve all of the empirical issues identified above, scholars still need theory in order to uncover evidence of a robust relationship between war and presidential power. For without theory, scholars cannot readily identify which elements of presidential power are likely to expand, and the precise conditions under which they will do so.

Periodically, one can detect the glimmers of a theory; in each instance, however, basic problems remain unresolved. Madison suggests that wars will unleash a president's passion for fame and glory. Presumably, though, in his own mind at least Madison and his compatriots designed a constitutional system that would constrain such tendencies. For Rossiter, wars led to the expansion of presidential power "principally because the people had now been taught to expect more of it" (1956, 65). There is something unsatisfying, though, about an argument taking the basic form: presidential power expands; witnessing such expansion, the public expects more of the president, and therefore presidential power expands even further. Schlesinger, meanwhile, offers a more conditional argument, admitting that different wars affect presidential power in different ways, and stipulating that while transitions from peace to war lead to expansions of presidential power, transitions from war to peace lead to contractions. The theoretical foundations to these claims, though, are altogether missing: with a compelling historical narrative about the ascendance of an imperial presidency as backdrop, Schlesinger advances these propositions not on the basis of well-defined first principles, but instead on their self-apparence.

Madison, Rossiter, and Schlesinger each offer the seeds of a theory, but no more. As a consequence, we lack answers to foundational questions. If wars constitute a boon to presidential power, for instance, what is the precise cause of the phenomenon? Does an expansion of presidential power result from the voting habits of a deferential Congress? Or, does it reflect the propensity of an impressionable public to rally behind its president? Could the rulings of a judiciary lacking the powers of either the purse or sword be to blame? Each of these possibilities teaches us very different lessons about the workings of our system of governance. And each rests upon very different assumptions about the behavior of political actors.

Take, for instance, the possibility that congressional checks on presidential power slacken during times of war. Scholars have shown that with regard to the war itself, Congress appears perfectly willing to defer to the president—especially when the war is popular and successful. It is less clear, though, why a popular, successful war ought to encourage individual members of Congress to side with the president on altogether separate issues. What theory of congressional behavior, for instance, predicts that a Democratic member of Congress would oppose a Republican president's tax cuts during times of peace, but support them during times of war? Similarly, why would a Republican member of Congress oppose a Democratic president's welfare initiative during times of peace, but support it during times of war? In either instance, the precise qualities of war and the foundations of congressional behavior that might evince such an about-face remain entirely mysterious.

If one is to advance an argument that the president's legislative initiatives will fail in peace but succeed in war, one must be able to identify whose behavior changes within Congress. Presumably, all peacetime opponents do not become wartime supporters. After all, only a handful of members need to reconsider their position for a policy initiative's fate to change. Unfortunately, though, the extant literature says little about the identity of these members. One wonders whether the president's newfound success—if such success genuinely exists—derives primarily from co-partisans rallying behind their leader, from moderate partisan opponents willing to grant the president some slack in a crisis, or from an altogether random assortment of members changing their positions for largely idiosyncratic reasons.

Lacking a theory, we also cannot know which elements of the president's agenda might revive when the nation turns to war. The right barometer may concern a policy initiative's proximity to the war effort: those policies that most immediately concern war (e.g. funding for defense systems) may be most affected, those that are tangentially related to war (e.g. civil liberty protections) may be partially affected, while those that are unrelated to war (e.g. social welfare policies) may be completely unaffected. Alternatively, the extent of peacetime opposition to a bill might be the critical indicator: those bills that require just a handful of new supporters may find their way into the law books during times of war, while those that require many more continue to languish in congressional committees. Alternatively, war may not have any impact on actual voting behavior, but instead modify the agenda that Congress considers. Wars, by this account, do not alter roll-call votes; rather, they change the types of bills that come before a legislative body.

Many of the same concerns apply to the courts, the public, or any other potential repository of presidential power set loose during times of war. The theory of judicial decision making that would explain why judges might uphold elements of the president's domestic policy program during times of war, but overturn them during times of peace, remains entirely elusive. Similarly, it is unclear why public opponents of the president would come around to his position when the nation stands on a war footing, only to reassert their opposition the moment that US troops come home. Judges or the public may in fact behave as described. We just do not have any theory that predicts such behavior.

To build such a theory, scholars must look beyond the office of the presidency and the individual who resides within it. Rather, we require accounts that specify how wars figure into congressional voting behavior, judicial decision making, and bureaucratic activity, because it is in these various locations that unilateral powers may be checked and legislative initiatives obstructed. As its foundations, a theory of war and presidential power requires theories of political institutions. Presidency scholars must resist the temptation to look inward. Only by engaging the broader discipline and building off of the insights of Congress, courts, and bureaucracy scholars will we fundamentally deepen our understanding of what happens at the nexus of war, presidential power, and public policy making.

THE WORK AHEAD

Recently, David Mayhew called upon scholars, when developing causal stories about institutional change, to pay more attention to events. And among all possible events, Mayhew highlighted the overriding importance of wars. "Wars," Mayhew wrote, "seem to be capable of generating whole new political universes." Unfortunately, the exact features of these universes, and the opportunities for different political actors to advance their policy agendas within them, remain unexplored. According to Mayhew, "political scientists who study American domestic politics have under-appreciated [war's] effects," preferring instead to read from a "peacetime script" (2005, 473).

Mayhew went on to document how five major US wars led to the enactment of sweeping policy changes, the emergence of new issue regimes, alterations in electoral coalitions, and redefinitions of the two major parties. It stands to reason, however, that wars also disrupt the fundamental balance of powers with the federal government. Indeed, we have inherited a long tradition of scholarship, tracing all the way back to the nation's founding, that argues precisely this point. If wars are to play a more central role in the work of political scientists generally, they certainly warrant greater attention from presidency scholars.

It will not do to continue reiterating again and again the basic assertion that war and presidential power go hand in hand. If theoretical progress is to be made, scholars must not presume such comity but instead initiate the harder work of scrutinizing it. And empirically, scholars must do more than include war as one among many background controls in standard regression models. Instead, they must design tests that directly evaluate war's variable contributions to presidential power.

Considerable work lies ahead. Future scholarship should evaluate the precise origins of the presumed relationship between war and presidential power, as well as the conditions under which it is more and less likely to hold. It should account for both war's benefits and costs to presidential power. It should allow for the possibility that different wars, and different stages of the same war, have different implications for presidential power. And it plainly must recognize that wars may influence different elements of presidential power in altogether different ways. The unqualified argument that all wars reflexively increase all dimensions of presidential power undoubtedly is wrong. But thankfully so, we think, for the questions raised by the topic are considerably more interesting, and more nuanced, than the standard formulation supposes.

In an era when war is common, and when the president stands at the center of national policy debates, these issues are ripe for exploration. And the last several years have only made them more so. Regional wars in Afghanistan and Iraq, and global wars against terrorism, have presented unique opportunities for the president to expand his power in a wide variety of policy domains, from civil liberties to domestic surveillance to the design of the judiciary. And as these wars have continued, and their costs have mounted, the president also has watched other policy reforms run aground. As scholars, we need to better understand war's impact on the domestic policy-making apparatus, and the president's ability to advance his agenda within it.

REFERENCES

ADLER, D. G. 1988. The Constitution and Presidential Warmaking: The Enduring Debate. *Political Science Quarterly*, 103: 1–36.

——1998. Court, Constitution, and Foreign Affairs. In *The Constitution and the Conduct of American Foreign Policy*, ed. D. Adler and L. George. Lawrence: University of Kansas Press.

BAKER, W., and ONEAL, J. 2001. Patriotism or Opinion Leadership? The Nature and Origins of the "Rally round the Flag Effect." *Journal of Conflict Resolution*, 45: 661–87.

BERGER, R. 1974. *Executive Privilege: A Constitutional Myth.* Cambridge, MA: Harvard University Press.

BERINSKY, A. 2007. Assuming the Costs of War: Events, Elites, and American Public Support for Military Conflict. *Journal of Politics,* 69/4: 975–97.

—— and DRUCKMAN, J. 2007. Public Opinion Research, Presidential Rhetoric, and Support for the Iraq War. *Public Opinion Quarterly,* 71/1: 126–41.

BRACE, P., and HINCKLEY, B. 1991. The Structure of Presidential Approval: Constraints within and across Presidencies. *Journal of Politics,* 53/4: 993–1017.

CANES-WRONE, B., HOWELL, W., and LEWIS, D. 2008. Executive Influence in Foreign versus Domestic Policy Making: Toward a Broader Understanding of Presidential Power. *Journal of Politics,* 70/1: 1–16.

CARSON, J., JENKINS, J., ROHDE, D., and SOUVA, M. 2001. The Impact of National Tides and District-Level Effects on Electoral Outcomes: The U.S. Congressional Elections of 1862–63. *American Journal of Political Science,* 45/4: 887–98.

CLARK, T. 2006. Judicial Decision Making during Wartime. *Journal of Empirical Legal Studies,* 3/3: 397–419.

COHEN, J. 1982. The Impact of the Modern Presidency on Presidential Success in the U.S. Congress. *Legislative Studies Quarterly,* 7/4: 515–32.

CORWIN, E. 1957. *The President, Office and Powers, 1787–1948: History and Analysis of Practice and Opinion.* New York: New York University Press. First published 1940.

DUCAT, C. R., and DUDLEY, R. L. 1989. Federal District Judges and Presidential Power. *Journal of Politics,* 51/1: 98–118.

EDWARDS, G. 1990. *Presidential Approval: A Sourcebook.* Baltimore: Johns Hopkins University Press.

—— and SWENSON, T. 1997. Who Rallies? The Anatomy of a Rally Event. *Journal of Politics,* 59: 200–12.

ELY, J. H. 1993. *War and Responsibility: Constitutional Lessons of Vietnam and its Aftermath.* Princeton, NJ: Princeton University Press.

FISHER, L. 2004. *Presidential War Power,* 2nd edn. Lawrence: University Press of Kansas.

FRISCH, M. (ed.) 2007. *The Pacificus–Helvidius Debates of 1793–1794: Toward the Completion of the American Founding.* Indianapolis: Liberty Fund.

GARTNER, S., and SEGURA, G. 1998. War, Casualties and Public Opinion. *Journal of Conflict Resolution,* 42/3: 278–300.

GELPI, C., FEAVER, P., and REIFLER, J. 2006. Success Matters: Casualty Sensitivity and the War in Iraq. *International Security,* 30/3:7–46.

HOWELL, W. G. 2003. *Power without Persuasion: The Politics of Direct Presidential Action.* Princeton, NJ: Princeton University Press.

HUDDY, L., FELDMAN, S., TABER, C., and LAHAV, G. 2005. Threat, Anxiety, and Support of Antiterrorism Policies. *American Journal of Political Science,* 49/3: 593–608.

HUNT, G. (ed.) 1900–10. *The Writings of James Madison.* New York: G. Putnam's Sons.

IRONS, P. 2005. *War Powers: How the Imperial Presidency Hijacked the Constitution.* New York: Metropolitan Books/Henry Holt & Co.

JAMES, P., and RIOUX, J. S. 1998. International Crises and Linkage Politics: The Experiences of the United States, 1953–1994. *Political Research Quarterly,* 51/3: 781–812.

KAROL, D., and MIGUEL, E. 2007. The Electoral Cost of War: Iraq Casualties and the 2004 U.S. Presidential Elections. *Journal of Politics,* 69/3: 633–48.

KETCHAM, R. (ed.) 2003. *The Anti-Federalist Papers and the Constitutional Convention Debates.* New York: Signet Classic.

KIEWIET, D. R., and McCUBBINS, M. 1985. Appropriations Decisions as a Bilateral Bargaining Game between President and Congress. *Legislative Studies Quarterly,* 10/2: 181–201.

——— 1991. *The Logic of Delegation.* Chicago: University of Chicago Press.

KRINER, D., and SHEN, F. 2007. The Casualty Gap: Death, Inequality and America's Wars. Typescript, Boston University.

KRUTZ, G., and PEAKE, J. 2006. The Changing Nature of Presidential Policymaking on International Agreements. *Presidential Studies Quarterly,* 36/3: 391–409.

LEWIS, D. E. 2003. *Presidents and the Politics of Agency Design.* Stanford, CA: Stanford University Press.

LIAN, B., and ONEAL, J. 1993. Presidents, the Use of Military Force and Public Opinion. *Journal of Conflict Resolution,* 37/2: 277–300.

MACKUEN, M. 1983. Political Drama, Economic Conditions, and the Dynamics of Presidential Popularity. *American Journal of Political Science,* 27: 165–92.

MADISON, J. 2007. *The Debates in the Federal Convention of 1787 which Framed the Constitution of the United States of America.* Amherst, NY: Prometheus Books. First published 1787.

MARRA, R., OSTROM, C., and SIMON, D. 1990. Foreign Policy and Presidential Popularity: Creating Windows of Opportunity in the Perpetual Election. *Journal of Conflict Resolution,* 34/4: 588–623.

MAYHEW, D. 2005. Wars and American Politics. *Perspectives on Politics,* 3/3: 473–93.

MEERNIK, J. 1993. Presidential Support in Congress: Conflict and Consensus on Foreign and Defense Policy. *Journal of Politics,* 55/3: 569–87.

MUELLER, J. 1970. Presidential Popularity from Truman to Johnson. *American Political Science Review,* 64/1: 18–34.

——— 1973. *War, Presidents and Public Opinion.* New York: Wiley.

NORPOTH, H. 1984. Economics, Politics, and the Cycle of Presidential Popularity. *Political Behavior,* 6/3: 253–74.

NORRANDER, B., and WILCOX, C. 1993. Rallying around the Flag and Partisan Change: The Case of the Persian Gulf War. *Political Research Quarterly,* 46/4: 759–70.

ONEAL, J., and BRYAN, A. L. 1995. The Rally round the Flag Effect in U.S. Foreign Policy Crises, 1950–1985. *Political Behavior,* 17: 379–401.

——— LIAN, B., and JOYNER, J. 1996. Are the American People "Pretty Prudent"? Public Responses to U.S. Uses of Force, 1950–1988. *International Studies Quarterly,* 40: 261–80.

OSTROM, C., and SIMON, D. 1985. Promise and Performance: A Dynamic Model of Presidential Popularity. *American Political Science Review,* 79: 334–58.

PARKER, S. 1995. Toward an Understanding of "Rally" Effects: Public Opinion in the Persian Gulf War. *Public Opinion Quarterly,* 59/4: 526–46.

PEAKE, J. 2002. Coalition Building and Overcoming Gridlock in Foreign Policy, 1947–1998. *Presidential Studies Quarterly,* 32/1: 67–83.

PRINS, B., and MARSHALL, B. 2001. Congress Support of the President: A Comparison of Foreign, Defense, and Domestic Policy Decision Making during and after the Cold War. *Presidential Studies Quarterly,* 31/4: 660–78.

ROSSITER, C. 1956. *The American Presidency: The Powers and Practices, the Personalities and Problems of the Most Important Office on Earth.* New York: Harcourt, Brace & World.

——— (ed.) 1999. *The Federalist Papers.* New York: Mentor Books. First published 1961.

RUDALEVIGE, A. 2002. *Managing the President's Program: Presidential Leadership and Legislative Policy Formation.* Princeton, NJ: Princeton University Press.

RUDALEVIGE, A. 2005. *The New Imperial Presidency: Renewing Presidential Power after Watergate*. Ann Arbor: University of Michigan Press.

SAVAGE, C. 2007. *Takeover: The Return of the Imperial Presidency and the Subversion of American Democracy*. Boston: Little, Brown & Company.

SCHLESINGER, A. 1973. *The Imperial Presidency*. Boston: Houghton Mifflin.

—— 2004. *War and the American Presidency*. New York: W. W. Norton & Company.

SCHWARZ, F., and HUQ, A. 2007. *Unchecked and Unbalanced: Presidential Power in a Time of Terror*. New York: New Press.

SKOWRONEK, S. 2008. The Imperial Presidency Thesis Revisited: George W. Bush at the Point of No Return. In *Presidential Leadership in Political Time: Reprise and Reappraisal*, ed. S. Skowronek. Lawrence: University of Kansas Press.

STORING, H. 1981. *The Complete Anti-Federalist*. Chicago: University of Chicago Press.

STORY, J. 1833. *Commentaries on the Constitution*, Volume 3. Boston.

WITTKOPF, E., and McCORMICK, J. 1998. Congress, the President, and the End of the Cold War. *Journal of Conflict Resolution*, 42/4: 440–66.

YATES, J., and WHITFORD, A. 1998. Presidential Power and the United States Supreme Court. *Political Research Quarterly*, 51: 39–50.

YOO, J. 2006a. *The Powers of War and Peace: The Constitution and Foreign Affairs after 9/11*. Chicago: University of Chicago Press.

—— 2006b. How the Presidency Regained its Balance. *New York Times*, Sept. 17: 15.

PART XI

REFLECTIONS

CHAPTER 32

THE PARADIGM OF DEVELOPMENT IN PRESIDENTIAL HISTORY

STEPHEN SKOWRONEK

ALTHOUGH scholars have accumulated a vast store of knowledge about the state of the presidency, findings about current operations do not speak for themselves. The meaning of the practices we observe today and of the effects they register hinge on our understanding of how the office was originally designed and subsequently reconfigured. Consider some well-known facts: presidents routinely appeal directly to the public for support of their policy preferences; presidents often choose to act unilaterally rather than work through Congress; presidents labor to gain control over the agencies of the executive branch; it is hard for presidents to alter public opinion. The large literatures devoted to each these observations indicate that they are laden with significance, but they are not transparently so. They claim our attention as they confirm or confound assumptions about the office, assumptions rooted in a construction of its history.

The dominant construction of presidential history—the one implicit in the bulk of the literature investigating how the office currently operates—highlights innovation and reinvention. Great transformative processes dominate the narrative: the "democratization" of the presidency, the "institutionalization" of the presidency, the "nationalization" and "internationalization" of the affairs of state. These themes bring into view an institution so altered by twentieth-century developments as to appear qualitatively different from its nineteenth-century predecessor. They hold in their sights a historic shift in governing arrangements, a systemic reorientation of political action around presidential initiative and national direction. It is this paradigm of development that anchors the research agenda of presidential studies today and lends significance to current findings about the operations of the office.

The paradigm of development keeps analytic attention riveted on conditions of office holding uniquely shared by contemporary incumbents. It sets apart "the modern presidency" as the object of our investigations and diminishes the contemporary significance of incumbents of earlier times (Greenstein 1978, 1983, 1988; James 2005). Historical study is thereby directed toward investigations of a characteristic sort. Researchers are prompted to fill in the back story, to describe the making of the modern presidency and the reconfiguration of American government and politics at large around a newly empowered executive.

This line of inquiry has, in fact, grown more productive as scholars have begun to challenge and replace shorthand assumptions about the natural evolution of government or the reflexive responsiveness of American institutions to changing circumstances. The "rise" of the modern presidency over the early decades of the twentieth century is now treated as a political problem in its own right, a problem of institution building where up-and-running arrangements of government, which had been geared to operate very differently over the course of the nineteenth century, had to be reorganized and accommodated to wholly new operating norms. Rather than simply point to precursors of the institutions and practices that now define the modern presidency, scholars are attending to the political processes by which new institutional resources were created, and they are delving into the subtle mechanisms by which new expectations about governmental operations as a whole took hold (Patterson 1976; Skowronek 1982; Arnold 1986; Gillman 1989; Milkis and Tichenor 1994; Arnold 1996, 2003; Whittington and Carpenter 2003; Farrar-Myers 2007).

Significantly, it is not just historical research that keeps the developmental paradigm vital. Research on the contemporary side of presidential politics also serves to sustain the narrative. Findings about current operations often take the form of updates in which scholars reassess the emergent configuration of power and adjust our expectations and understandings of the modern presidency accordingly. For example, when Terry Moe described "the politicized presidency" in the 1980s, he was calling into question the operational significance of the norm of neutral competence that had first inspired the expansion of executive offices; in practice, Moe observed, the ideal of neutrality gave way to presidential demands for "responsive competence" (Moe 1985). Similarly, when Samuel Kernell described the growing prominence of "going public" as a leadership strategy in the 1980s, he was pointing to institutional developments that were making interbranch bargaining more difficult while encouraging plebiscitary appeals (Kernell 1986). Likewise, when Lyn Ragsdale and John Theis moved the date of the "institutionalization" of the presidency from the traditional demarcation of the end at the New Deal into the 1970s, they were not only pointing to a far more extended interregnum of instability and transformation than previously acknowledged, but also recasting debate over the explanation for the presidency's "growth" (Ragsdale and Theis 1997; Krause 2002; Dickinson 2003; Dickinson and Lebo 2007). The common impulse in such work is to keep assumptions about the modern presidency abreast of current trends. The overall effect is to describe an office that is still very much in the making, to underscore its inherently dynamic qualities, and to sustain a forward-looking portrait of contemporary operations.

The attractions of thinking about presidential history in this way are obvious. Attention to the development of the office tracks very real changes in the institutional infrastructure of presidential power and keeps scholarship attuned to innovation in the practices of presidential leadership. There is nothing arcane about this history; it is unabashedly directed toward the illumination of contemporary political affairs. But although there is still much that sustains it, all is not well with the paradigm of development. In recent years, the assumptions of this history have been growing increasingly unsettled and controversial. Investigations on the contemporary side are raising questions about the back story, and investigations into past practices are contesting basic understandings of the current state of play. History is fast emerging as a battleground over the orientation of the entire field.

CRACKING OPEN THE OLD STORYLINE

The paradigm of development was stamped on contemporary understandings of the presidency very early on. Generations ago, when political science was in its infancy, progressive intellectuals began to look to the executive branch as a vital source of solutions to the new challenges of governing in modern America. These scholars issued a radical critique of the governing arrangements of the nineteenth century and pre-scribed an executive-centered overhaul to surmount their limitations. They justified various innovations—innovations meant to strengthen the national government, to activate the presidency through the mobilization of public opinion, to enhance insti-tutional capacities for central direction and coordination—as necessary and integral parts of a new order in government and politics. Many of them took an active role in government to help bring to fruition the changes they were prescribing. For the eighty years between 1885, when Woodrow Wilson's *Congressional Government* described the historical marginalization of the presidency in a political system that was deeply flawed, and 1965, when James MacGregor Burns's *Presidential Government* described a wholly new system and began to raise questions about the leadership qualities it was fostering, political science, progressive reform, and presidential prominence expanded in tandem. The progressives' juxtaposition of old and new, then and now, traditional and modern, set the analytic contours of presidential history and bequeathed to presidential studies its preoccupation with the novelty, the promise, and the capacity of emergent forms.

Among the factors now clouding the dominant storyline, none is more important than the realignment of intellectual support for presidential empowerment. No sooner had Burns identified a new order in government and politics then progressive scholars began to back away from it. Their sober second thoughts about "presidential government" threw into contention the political significance of its development, and this uncertainty opened the door to a more critical history in which the heroes of the progressive narrative—Woodrow Wilson first and foremost among them—were recast as the culprits in a new narrative of political degradation (Ceaser et al. 1982; Bimes and Skowronek 1998). Today that early revision is being superseded by another, even more destabilizing one. As the case for presidential empowerment was taken over in recent decades by a conservative insurgency in American politics, scholars with a very different political orientation began to rework the storyline. Not content simply to recast the familiar characters, these revisionists have now pushed an entirely different history into contention.

But it is not just that the politics of presidential advocacy has changed. The paradigm of development has come in for a number of empirical challenges as well. The time has passed when it is sufficient simply to describe the trappings of a new, presidency-centered government; scholars today are demanding a demonstration of categorically different political effects. Consider, for example, evidence presented by George Edwards showing that much of what presidents actually accomplish is still best explained with reference to the interaction of original constitutional constraints with contingencies, like the configuration of partisan support in Congress, that operate like a deal of the cards. When it comes to legislative outcomes in particular, the modern accouterments of presidential power and leadership appear, in Edwards's analyses, to make a difference only "at the margins" (Edwards 1989, 2003).

To the extent that certain essentials still hold sway, a history demarcating fundamental change will be seen as unduly preoccupied with mere window dressing. Recent work taking in the full sweep of the past experience echoes that point. For example, I have pointed to political contexts for leadership that have recurred since the beginning of our constitutional history and to corresponding leadership effects that persist across the traditional/modern divide (Skowronek 1993, 2008). More direct still is the challenge issued by David Nichols. He has declared that the "modern presidency" is a "myth" which fundamentally misconstrues the original constitutional design. As Nichols sees it, to the extent that presidential power has grown more imposing over the years, it has drawn directly from the initial endowments of the office, and to the extent that recent presidents are thought to embody something else or represent something more, they have largely disappointed: "they are modern presidents only to the extent that they fail to live up to expectations created by the 'modern Presidency' " (Nichols 1994, 5).

Studies like these leave the paradigm of development exposed, and notwithstanding the very real contributions of work ongoing within that frame, the questions now being raised about the assumptions and expectations behind it have begun to wedge the whole of presidential history open to reexamination. This essay pursues a few of these openings and examines the issues and controversies emerging within and among them. It would be premature to assert that that we are in the midst of a paradigmatic shift in our understanding of presidential history. In some ways, the challenges now on the table stand to strengthen the development thesis, for they will, if nothing else, force a clearer specification of the significance of the many obvious changes wrought by the innovations of the twentieth century. Nonetheless, it is fair to say that the paradigm of development no longer conveys the whole picture, that the picture it does convey is not quite as clear as it once was, and that alternative understandings of presidential history are beginning to bid for center stage. Although it is not at all certain how all this will shake out, a long-settled conception of the relationship between past and present in presidential politics is being contested today on a variety of fronts. In the balance is the significance of what we observe in presidential politics today.

Development as Institutional Derangement

The progressive scholars who championed a presidency-centered reconstruction of American government during the first half of the twentieth century placed their faith in the flexibility, adaptability, and responsiveness of America's basic governing arrangements. They were pragmatists who viewed the state as an instrument for solving problems and an arena for experimentation. They were part of an intellectual "revolt against formalism," which is to say they were inclined to discount structural impediments in new conceptions of the government's role and to view the formalities of American constitutional design as technical problems to be overcome in adapting American government to a new day (White 1947). Woodrow Wilson launched his academic career with a biting assault on the rigidity of the separation of powers (1885), and even when he came around to accepting the Constitution, he insisted that its interpretation be "sufficiently broad and elastic to allow for the play of life and circumstance" (1908). Henry Jones Ford, whose influential history of American politics traced the implications of democratization over the course of the nineteenth century, pointed to the presidency's potential for popular leadership as a home-grown mechanism for overcoming the conservative bias of the government's original design. Presidential leadership, in Ford's famous phrase, was "the work of the people *breaking through* the constitutional form" (1898, 293).

According to the progressives, modern democracy demanded modes of political thinking and governmental action. Eighteenth-century norms of constitutional government could not be allowed to stifle popular demands for more responsive institutions. These scholars had little patience with originalism, essentialism, or history itself insofar as they presented constraints on political possibility. By the time Charles Merriam joined Franklin Roosevelt's Committee on Administrative Management and began to oversee the work that would inspire the Executive Reorganization Act of 1939, it was a fixed assumption of progressive scholarship that the arrangements of government were a reflection of the social interests they served and that a robust democracy could change those arrangements as necessary to keep current with the evolving interests of the greater part (Merriam 1925).

The first wave of scholarship to reassess the paradigm of development was driven by a profound disillusionment with what progressive experimentation had wrought and by a corresponding skepticism about the flexibility and adaptability of American institutions. At the center of this work was a rediscovery of the significance of forms and a confrontation with the developmental dilemmas generated when tinkering with the basic arrangements of American government. Analysts pointed to inefficiencies in efforts to recast extant institutions, to structural limits in their redeployment for new ends, to the risks of a general derangement of the affairs of state in the politics of reform.

This pivotal shift in scholarly thinking about the presidency is marked rather clearly in Arthur Schlesinger Jr.'s posthumously published personal journal. In his entry for April 27, 1967, the great progressive historian wrote: "The irony is that all of us for years have been defending the presidential prerogative and regarding the Congress as a drag on policy. It is evident that this delight in a strong presidency was based on the fact that, up to now, strong presidents in American history have pursued policies of which one approved. We are now confronted by the anomaly of a strong presidency using these arguments to pursue a course which, so far as I can see, can lead only to disaster" (Schlesinger 2007, 260). A few years later, Schlesinger would publish *The Imperial Presidency,* a history of presidential power laying out dynamics of political aggrandizement and institutional overreach that had led the Republic, step by step, into a constitutional crisis (Schlesinger 1973).

Exposing the pride of twentieth-century institutional development as the source of a profound governing crisis cut hard against the progressive project. It is notable, however, that these post-progressive critics were not questioning the notion that American government had, in fact, been reconstituted over the course of the twentieth century. Indeed, in reflecting back on the long-term consequences of redesigning American government around a newly empowered presidency, they tended to present the case for development more starkly than ever before. Theodore Lowi, for example, characterized America's decades-long investment in presidential power as nothing less than the creation of a "Second Republic" (Lowi 1985). Nor did these critics doubt that some sort of transformation had been necessary, even inevitable. Lowi's assessment of the situation in the early twentieth century is virtually indistinguishable from that of the progressives whose handiwork he called into question: economic and social changes demanding a new response from government had reached "great and undeniable proportion" (Lowi 1985, 41).

The difference was that Lowi, Schlesinger, and others were looking backward and finding a flawed transformation, a reconstruction of American government and politics that was rife with unfortunate trade-offs, unintended effects, and high political costs. Moreover, by rendering development itself problematic, these critics were actively promoting a reevaluation of the older forms of government that had been displaced by it. The dilemmas they identified pointed back to certain verities that had been essential to the effective operation of American government in its early decades, and although their work implied that the practical effect of development had been to render those old practices inaccessible, it also cautioned against dismissing the early history of the presidency as an irrelevance. Looking to the past as a repository of values that had been lost or squandered, post-progressive scholarship redeployed it as a vital source of critical insight into contemporary operations.

Consider, for example, the developmental problem specified by Jeffrey Tulis in his examination of the emergence of the modern presidency's new rhetorical practices (Tulis 1987). Tulis's analysis reconstructs the rationale behind the Framers' original proscription of plebiscitary democracy. He not only recovers the values implicit in the precautions they took to avoid direct popular appeals, he also anchors the operations of their constitutional design in processes of interbranch deliberation that could not but be short-circuited by presidents having direct recourse to the people. At the same time, Tulis recognizes that the progressives' critique of the traditional practices anchored by the Constitution had merit, that the Framers' arrangements were wanting by the standards of modern democracy. His key point is not that progressive reformers were wrongheaded in their ambitions but that they vastly underestimated what was demanded institutionally by their desire for a more democratic system.

Whereas the reformers' principles anticipated a very different kind of constitution, their reforms did not, Tulis observes, replace the old structure. New practices were simply layered over the old forms, leaving modern presidents to "inhabit an office structured by two systemic theories" (Tulis 1987, 146). Because a sweeping change in the meaning and purposes of American government was enacted through adaptations and reconceptualizations rather than through outright reconstitution of the basic institutional framework, American government and politics were left to operate according to two different and incompatible standards of legitimacy, neither of which was likely to be realized in practice. Modern rhetorical practices would come to subvert the integrity of interbranch deliberations as they were constructed in the original frame, and the original forms dictating interbranch deliberation would come to frustrate modern expectations for programmatic action.

One might well wonder whether discarding old forms and building anew would be any less fraught with difficulties. Sidney Milkis's (1993) assessment of a twentieth-century shift in the institutional locus of presidential power from patronage parties to the programmatic bureaucracies suggests that it is not. The developmental process Milkis describes was less a matter of layering than of outright displacement, but, as with Tulis, his analysis turns on a dilemma. Milkis recaptures the logic and value of the old party structure as it connected the presidency to vibrant democratic institutions at the local level and provided a continuously operating mechanism for holding presidential power collectively accountable; at the same time, he recognizes an inherent incompatibility between the state-based parties of the nineteenth century, which used the federal bureaucracy as a repository of local patronage, and twentieth-century demands for more extensive and effective administrative capacities at the national level.

Milkis argues that the progressives, being creatures of their own time and history, tended to identify parties *per se* as antithetical to their cause and to look to an administratively empowered presidency as an alternative foundation of their new democracy. Because they did not build a new system of party accountability commensurate with their new system of administrative power but rather built the administrative presidency at the expense of traditional party ties, they created an executive that was dangerously out of balance. More imposing in the institutional resources at its command, it would also be further removed from local institutions of mass participation and thereby less easily held to account by a democratic collectivity (see also Milkis and Rhodes 2007).

The paradoxes of layering and displacement hardly exhaust the mechanisms of institutional derangement which critics of the modern presidency have identified in the processes of development. By far the most serious of all assessments of development gone awry concern the exercise of presidential war powers. Analyses of the dynamics of presidential overreach in this area from scholars such as Arthur Schlesinger (1973, 2005), Lewis Fisher (1995), and David Adler (1988, 2003, 2006; also Fisher and Adler 1998) draw characteristically on a resurrection of values embedded in the original design. They capture the logic of the whole host of war powers explicitly granted to Congress under Article I of the Constitution and offer a corresponding reassessment of the practice, increasingly commonplace after the Second World War, of presidents committing troops abroad unilaterally. They then document the ease with which arguments on behalf of pragmatism, adaptability, and flexibility undermined constitutional standards and limits.

It is notable that although these works focus their critical attention on how the war power developed after the Second World War, their most important analytic claim turns on an interpretation of how things developed in the wake of the American Revolution. Fisher and Adler, in particular, rely on a reading of the Constitution that treats its arrangement of war powers as a ratification of principles of 1776, most especially of the categorical rejection in the Declaration of Independence of monarchical practices in favor of the supremacy of representative assemblies. To the extent that this assessment of the Constitution is correct, presidential war powers will be narrowly construed and current practices will be seen to have little constitutional foundation. But, as we shall see later, an alternative reading of the sequence of development between the Declaration and the Constitution yields very different conclusions about current practices, and therein lies one of the most important scholarly controversies surrounding the development of the presidency today.

All told, these post-progressive explorations of developmental dilemmas and historical paradoxes forced some very basic questions to the fore—how much innovation can a given framework of government accommodate before it becomes hopelessly compromised? At what point does the insinuation of new ideals into old institutions begin to place the entire system at cross-purposes? The answers arrived at suggested that many of the most important effects of institution building were unforeseen by those advocating change, and that as adjustments to the new state of affairs were made throughout the system, the difficulties of dealing with the fallout were compounded.

Animated as it was by an acute sense that something had gone fundamentally wrong in the process of change, this first-wave of reassessments set a research agenda in which development would be scrutinized as a problem rather than celebrated as a solution, where the governing arrangements of the distant past would command equal attention, and where certain essential truths about American institutions could be discovered in the fallout from progressive tinkering with fundamentals.

By the same token, this first-wave critique set up a second, more thoroughgoing reassessment. Having discovered so much of value in nineteenth-century practice, and having relied for their critique of modern arrangements on strong assertions about how things had operated before, the critics opened the whole of presidential history to more intense scrutiny. Scholars were naturally directed by this critique to look more closely at these original conditions, to examine this time when institutional deliberation was held in such high regard, when political parties served as potent instruments of collective responsibility, and when checks and balances really held sway. Equally provocative were the critics' future premonitions. Their portraits of the derangement of contemporary institutions pointed to a simmering crisis of political legitimacy, a crisis that, if not belied by the ensuing decades of anticipation, has proven rather slow to come to a boil. On both counts, the post-progressive critique of the modern presidency spurred historical research in ways that would prove difficult to contain within the developmental frame and that would begin to blur the modern/traditional divide itself.

DEVELOPMENT OR MORE OF THE SAME?

Using the standard date of 1939 to demarcate presidential history, more than a quarter of all American presidents would now be categorized as "modern." Larger numbers should promote more robust analyses, and yet, adding presidents to this exclusive club has tended instead to bring the coherence of the analytic category itself into question. As indicated at the outset of this essay, some scholars have responded to this problem by updating the modern construct to take account of emerging trends and late-breaking developments. Others have gone further to propose a historical division within the modern period. They would separate out a "post-modern presidency" on one dimension of action or another so as to reduce variability and ensure comparability among the presidents brought under review (Barilleaux 1988; Rose 1991). Most interesting for our purposes are those who have grown impatient with the whole business of "drawing lines" in presidential history. These scholars have begun to question the underlying presumption of categorical differences distinguishing historically contiguous groups of incumbents.

As John Woolley summarizes this new disposition, the "modern presidency" construct is a methodological crutch at best; at worst, it is an impediment to candid evaluation of the current state of affairs. It insinuates into analysis sweeping empirical claims about the prior operations of the office and about the effects of institutional development for which there is at present scant evidence. "The bodies of research available," Woolley concludes, "suggest *none* of the following: a dramatic change at some specific point in time, dramatic reduction in the variability among modern presidents, or enduring enhancement—or decline—in the influence of modern presidents." Moreover, "past forecasts of a continuing trend in the relative power of the modern presidency have not been borne out" (Woolley 2005, 20).

Woolley is not saying that there are no patterns to be observed in presidential history, nor is he asserting categorically that the office has not developed in significant ways over time. What he is calling into question is the historical paradigm stamped on presidential studies by progressive scholarship, in particular the unexamined premise that the innovations of the twentieth century changed the government fundamentally. Whereas the first wave of scholars to challenge the progressives' storyline accepted their bifurcated historical frame and took aim at how development had actually occurred, Woolley captures the more open-ended and more strictly empirical voice of recent work that questions whether, to what extent, and exactly where significant development is to be discerned. His methodological prescription—stop "drawing lines" and start "defining variables"—is a call for empirical research that is more attentive to the variations among presidents *within* periods, more amenable to comparisons among presidents *across* periods, and more alert to institutional dynamics that move *through* the standard period divisions.

Although strains in the bifurcated frame of the dominant paradigm were first introduced by awareness of an increasingly diverse and unwieldy group of "modern" presidents, they have been deepened in recent years by scholars who, in looking backward, have found incumbents of earlier days thinking and acting in ways that call our sense of the "traditional" presidency into question. Students of the modern presidency have, of course, always been aware of precursors, they have always sought out "proto-moderns" that foreshadow current practices (Arnold 1996, 2003), and some have traced in detail the gradual emergence of new conceptions of the president's political position and governing role (Ellis and Kirk 1998; Farrar-Meyers 2007). But recent work has been far more aggressive in challenging received categories and rearranging the contours of presidential history as a whole.

New scholarship on the presidency of Thomas Jefferson illustrates this difference quite clearly. Jefferson has long been understood as an innovator in the presidency, but earlier studies tended to cast his efforts at party building and his invention of informal instruments of executive influence as reaffirmations of original norms of political consensus and legislative primacy. In contrast, current work finds President Jefferson enacting a wholly original conception of his office, a conception that rejected formalist reasoning, embraced plebiscitary notions of executive entitlement, and grounded expansive power claims directly in public opinion (Ackerman 2005; Bailey 2007). In other words, recent scholarship suggests that after Jefferson, the modern difference was less conceptual than technological. More generally, it suggests that historical period alone no longer provides an adequate explanation for whatever variation might be observed in the executive invocation of plebiscitary standards of legitimacy.

Although this newfound impulse to challenge assumptions about the distinctiveness of modern presidency and to test for a modern difference is still in the start-up phrase, it promises to be a growth stock in historical research in coming years. At present, the most pointed skepticism has been directed at the shorthand characterizations of nineteenth-century practice found in the work of leading theorists of the modern presidency. Consider for example an opening salvo by Daniel Galvin and Colleen Shogan (2004) which takes issue with Terry Moe's portrait of the presidency in the modern bureaucratic state. Moe asserts that the rise of the national government and the development of an activist state exposed a gaping incongruity between the president's constitutional powers and his newfound governing responsibilities, and that this, in turn, has prompted certain behaviors characteristic of the modern presidency. In particular, Moe suggests that the incentive structure of the modern American state is such that recent incumbents have been prompted to try to enhance their control over the administrative apparatus by politicizing executive branch operations and centralizing authority over it (Moe 1985). As noted earlier, Moe directed his thesis at the misplaced norms of "neutral competence" which had legitimized the early construction of overhead management tools in the Executive Office of the President.

Galvin and Shogan suggest, however, that Moe's efforts to provide a clearer and more realistic picture of the administrative dynamics that adhere to the modern presidency may have inadvertently erased any meaningful difference between modern and traditional practice. Had the progressive ideal of developing a neutral repository of information and managerial skill for policy makers taken hold, it might well have transformed the operations of American government categorically, but the fact that this ideal has proven difficult to realize in practice actually makes modern experience far less distinctive. Careful to avoid reference to nineteenth-century incumbents already well known for their strong assertions of executive power and control, Galvin and Shogan examine a range of presidential behaviors in the administrations of John Tyler, James Polk, and Rutherford B. Hayes to demonstrate that efforts by presidents to politicize executive branch operations or centralize power in the quest of administrative control are "neither distinctly modern or particularly extraordinary" (477).

This is a conclusion well worth pondering, for it suggests that more is at stake in debunking the modern difference than an empirical correction of the historical record. The findings of Galvin and Shogan imply that the politicization of central administration is an essential feature of the presidential office, an ingrained characteristic indifferent to development. This could, of course, open onto more nuanced arguments about the significance of context, but an unvarnished presentation cuts the other way. At the risk of putting too fine a point on it, peeling away the modern difference augurs a normalization of received understandings of contemporary maladies, a history stripped of its own standards of criticism, and a powerful justification for current practice. As we shall see in the next section, when it comes to presidential history today, there are no innocent corrections.

Of all the claims ventured on behalf of a paradigmatic divide in presidential history, Jeffrey Tulis's thesis—that the traditional presidency proscribed direct presidential appeals to the people for support on policy initiatives and that the modern presidency features distinctive rhetorical practices—has commanded the most sustained attention to date (Ellis 1998). In one especially instructive challenge, Mel Laracey (2002) questions the claim that nineteenth-century presidents did not "go public" with their commitments. He surveys the different mechanisms available for them to impress the people with their policy commitments, most especially the partisan press, and he documents their extensive use. Laracey presents the strongest arguments yet that contemporary presidential practice is not grounded in a historical reconceptualization of the office but is merely reflective of the technological means available for pursuing presidential interests.

With that argument, Laracey forces to the fore the key question on which debate about significance of development is likely to turn: the equivalence of forms. Tulis has responded to Laracey on precisely this ground. He insists that the nineteenth-century practice of presidents "going public" through intermediaries like parties and newspapers is not the same as "going public" today precisely because those earlier practices maintained an official distance from popular politics. He points to the fact that these early presidents could, but did not, make more direct appeals in their own name as confirmation of the potency of nineteenth-century norms foreign to contemporary practice. In the end, Tulis admits that the force of the distinction he has drawn now rests on further empirical research aimed at determining whether these indirect forms of popular communication actually did insulate the president from attributions of policy responsibility (Tulis 1998, 215–16). More generally, his response asks just how far arguments for functional equivalence can reach in discounting development.

Next to these efforts that challenge specific assertions about the distinctiveness of the modern presidency, work is proceeding apace that speaks more directly to variability within and across periods. These studies seek not only to test more directly the thesis that contemporary presidential politics is different, but also to specify that difference more accurately. Some of these findings comport well with received notions of the modern presidency; others less so. For example, recent work by Elvin Lim confirms the thesis that presidential rhetoric underwent a sea change in the twentieth century, and it breaks new empirical ground by tying changes in the form of communication more directly to changes in its content. As Lim documents, the professionalization and institutionalization of presidential speech writing has produced rhetoric that is by historical standards more simplistic, more hortatory, less substantive, and less informative (Lim 2008). Colleen Shogan's study of presidential moralizing presents more mixed results. She finds that there is nothing particularly modern about presidents employing moralizing rhetoric in their speech and that the decision to moralize or not turns on contextual variables that change from one administration to the next while recurring across periods. At the same time, she finds evidence supportive of Tulis and Lim that a rhetorical shift did occur around the Wilson era, at least to the extent that presidential moralizing began to detach itself from specific policy content (Shogan 2006).

Terri Bimes and Quinn Mulroy's (2004) study of populist rhetoric frames the issue a bit differently. They find that whatever else might be said about the rise of a plebiscitary presidency and the political implications of "going public," modern presidents have grown decidedly *less* combative in the modern period. Nineteenth-century presidential rhetoric, they observe, was far more varied than twentieth-century rhetoric, and a strong populist strand engaging the president directly in political and social conflict was substantially muted over the course of the twentieth century. Similarly, a study by David Lewis and James Strine (1996) shows a historic decrease in the rate of presidential vetoing as measured against congressional output, a finding that cuts against the notion that a state that once prized institutional deliberation and interbranch cooperation has been eclipsed by one organized around convulsive popular appeals. These studies suggest that, contrary to the common notion that leadership in the modern presidency is more highly politicized and divisive than it was in the traditional presidency, twentieth-century presidents may actually have become more fully integrated into and defensive of state power.

The picture of the modern presidency that is emerging from all this work is difficult to summarize. That is hardly a surprise. Candid testing for a modern difference has just begun, the number of possible variables is vast, and interest in rhetoric and communication has thus far consumed the lion's share of the energy. Clearly, however, development has emerged as a hotly contested category. Some of this research confirms development as we have come to understand it, some of it challenges the thesis of fundamental change and opens the door to more essentialist readings of the history, and some of it confirms a modern difference but does so in ways that run counter to what critics of the modern presidency have charged.

The promise of all this testing is that in pushing back against caricatures of the nineteenth-century presidency we will come to a clearer and more accurate understanding of the presidency today. Regardless of where the chips fall, that cannot but advance the field. There are, however, reasons to be cautious. First, it is clear that we are still far from the point at which we can discount or confirm the thesis that development has produced an office that is different in kind. Not only do we need to consider a much fuller range of political and institutional dimensions on which modern practice may be distinguished, but we also need to consider more deeply the issue of the comparability of the different forms through which actions that otherwise seem similar are displayed. Second, it is important to keep in mind that using the modern presidency thesis as a foil for empirical research can only take us so far. It is no substitute for providing an alternative history, and it will provide little insight of its own into problems and processes of institutional development. Issues that earlier scholarship identified in the layering of standards over one another or in the displacement of older forms in favor of new ones tend to be sidelined in this new literature, and to the extent they have been replaced, they appear to throw the discussion of political development back to a crude technological determinism. Finally, although this work seems to be motivated primarily by a methodological and empirical critique of the modern–traditional divide, it is not entirely innocent of normative implications. Whatever problems we may find in the progressives' assumptions about political transformation and governmental reinvention, there are weighty implications to the default alternative. Another line of scholarship is alerting us to exactly what these are.

DEVELOPMENT AS ORIGINAL INTENT

To date, the most formidable challenge to the paradigm of development in presidential history has not come from scholars disillusioned by the twentieth-century shift to "presidential government," nor has it come from those who now treat that shift as an untested assumption and return to the nineteenth century to determine its true scope and significance. The most formidable challenge has come from legal scholars and political theorists who anchor expansive powers for modern presidents in the original design of Constitution and reject in principle the notion that political developments since 1789 have changed, or can change, anything of significance. Elaborating what they call the "unitary theory" of the executive, these scholars are turning the progressive understanding of presidential history on its head (Calabresi and Rhodes 1992; Calabresi 1995). In place of a bifurcated frame featuring a reinvention of the presidency and an executive-centered reconstruction of American government, the unitary theorists present a seamless history in which seemingly sweeping claims of executive prerogative and presidential control follow directly from the intent of the Framers and of those who originally ratified their handiwork.

This is an ideologically charged and programmatic history, but in these respects it is no different from the history bequeathed to us by the reformers of the early twentieth century. Nor are the unitary theorists the first to look at the contemporary problem of presidential power from over the president's shoulder. Indeed, the coincidence of interest in this new line of scholarly advocacy for presidential power with the rise of a politically potent conservative insurgency in American politics at large marks it as the normative counterpart of the scholarly advocacy of presidential power which attended the progressive insurgency. Moreover, a moment's reflection on the case the progressives built for presidential power suggests why today's conservatives might have found it helpful to elaborate a different history. The progressives had emphasized institutional pragmatism, experimentation, and invention; they had placed their faith in the flexibility and adaptability of basic governing arrangements; above all, they had appealed to public opinion to allay concerns about constitutional form and the distribution of institutional prerogatives. These foundations are not well suited to a defense of presidential power when national opinion appears stubbornly divided over basic issues of governance and when much of the institutional experimentation looks toward reining in perceived presidential excesses.

On inspection, then, there is no simple way to characterize the unitary theory of the executive in relationship to scholarly positions previously staked out. Against the progressive position, the unitary theorists have abruptly returned to constitutional formalism in their analysis and justification of presidential power and sharply delimited the legitimate scope of institutional tinkering. But unlike the conservatives who wrote during the progressive period, they have not employed formalism to limit the reach of presidential power; the unitary theorists have used it instead as the vehicle for a more aggressive assertion of presidential independence and institutional dominance against innovations that threaten to restrict it. It is notable, in this regard, that as late as the 1950s and 1960s, American conservatives were still taking their cues from the hallowed Whig tradition of hostility to presidential power and executive pretension. Opposition to progressive political priorities and opposition to presidential dominance went hand in hand as conservative voices such as James Burnham, Willmoore Kendall, Alfred de Grazia, and James Buchanan looked to the Constitution to defend congressional and local prerogatives against the higher-order aggregations of presidency-centered government (Burnham 1959; Kendall 1960; De Grazia 1965; Lynch 2004). In place of this straightforward refutation of the progressives' case for presidentialism, today's conservatives have, in effect, bid trump. They have deployed the traditional conservative arguments for formalism, but they have repudiated the traditional conservative arguments against an expansive presidential power, and they have extended the progressive paradigm of presidency-centered government by jettisoning its historical and normative supports. The result is a wholly new formulation—an arresting marriage of formalism with presidentialism—which is blazing its own path through presidential history.

There are, to be sure, powerful developmental claims ventured by these theorists, but the significant shifts in authority that they bring into view all occur before 1789. In determining the scope and legitimate application of presidential power, they look, in the first instance, to the long history of thinking about the executive in England and the West prior to the constitutional convention in America. This history eyes the practical advantages of a prerogative power in government and situates the American Constitution as the culmination of efforts to tap that kind of power within a government of laws (Mansfield 1989; McDonald 1994; Kleinerman 2007). More immediately, the scope and legitimate application of presidential power are anchored in the ratification of a new system of American government in 1789, a system that not only displaced the Articles of Confederation but also allegedly repudiated and jettisoned governing norms associated with the failed constitutional experiments that had been ushered in by the Declaration of Independence.

Indeed, the key claim is that chief among the norms discarded during the post-independence interregnum was the revolutionaries' skepticism toward broad executive prerogatives. That is to say, in adopting a new Constitution organized around separate and equal branches, the people allegedly repaired to, and with minor modifications incorporated, common European understandings of what an independent executive power entailed. Evidence of this incorporation is gleaned from the ratification debates and from prominent clauses of Article II: the vesting of all "executive power" in a single officer, the oath charging the president to "preserve, protect and defend the nation," the designation of the president as commander in chief, and the stipulation of presidential responsibility for the faithful execution of the laws (Calabresi 1994, 1995; Calabresi and Prakash 1994; Yoo 2005, 2006).

These historical inferences are likely to frame debates over presidential history long into the future (Pfiffner 2008). In some respects, the issues engaged are familiar ones. In 1793, when Alexander Hamilton, writing as Pacificus, drew a broad construction of executive power in the American Constitution from European history and theory, James Madison, writing as Helvidius, countered by challenging the relevance of ideas hatched in monarchical regimes to a republic that had rejected monarchy and reconstituted governing authority by its lights. The question the unitary theorists press is whether opinions Madison expressed in 1793, in the heat of a new political debate and a realignment of party divisions *under* the Constitution, are a reliable guide to what the people actually ratified 1789 when the friends of the Constitution stood united against the overweening power of popular assemblies and argued for the reestablishment of a unified, independent, and energetic executive. To the extent that their conception of executive unity, independence, and energy was not wholly original but guided by the precepts and examples available to them at the time, they may well be seen to have sharply delimited the legitimate reach of the other branches, to have set aside a vast and exclusive domain for presidential action in foreign and domestic affairs, and to have established a closed hierarchy of administrative control commanded at the top by the president alone. In any case, it is that view of what the people originally ratified that the unitary theorists employ to adjudicate later constitutional interpretations and delimit the legitimate domain of later-day experimentation.

It will be observed that, in one way or another, each of the steps traced in this chapter away from the progressive's paradigm of development has nudged toward a new paradigm of essentialism. In the unitary theory, that movement assumes its starkest and most explicit form. Steven Calabresi and his collaborators have now sketched a comprehensive history of the presidency along these lines (Calabresi and Yoo 1997, 2003; Yoo, Calabresi, and Nee 2004; Yoo, Calabresi, and Colangelo 2005). It documents the stubbornly persistent affirmation of the unitary theory by incumbents themselves and, in the process, disavows any meaningful distinctions in understandings of this office that might be drawn between Federalist presidents and Republican presidents, populist presidents and Whig presidents, strong presidents and weak presidents, or nineteenth-century presidents and twentieth-century presidents. To the extent that those who have been most directly responsible for the executive power are the appropriate judges of what their job entails and requires, the storyline is uniform and unyielding.

Modern developments that have expanded the reach of American national power abroad and the role of the national government at home did not, by this reading, call for any categorical reconfiguration of the presidency and its relationship to the rest of the government. Innovations that have enhanced the presidents' resources for independent action at home and abroad merely acknowledge what is necessary for presidents to continue to fulfill their original constitutional obligations. Presidential power did not have to catch up to developments on the ground; rather, developments on the ground finally caught up to the Framers' capacious provisions and engaged the president's inherent powers more directly. Likewise, institutional innovations that have sought new ways to constrain presidential action in foreign and administrative affairs are exposed by this history as misguided experiments that threaten "a serious reduction in the constitutional standing of the presidency" (Arkes 1987, 642).

In this last respect, the unitary theorists agree with the post-progressive critics of the modern presidency: they too see that modern American political development has led to the derangement of American institutions. The source of that derangement, however, is not traced by the unitary theorists to overzealous and imperial presidents who usurped power and mocked constitutional constraints. On the contrary, it is traced to court rulings and congressional intrusions that have besieged the presidency over the course of the twentieth century and thwarted its incumbents in the fulfillment of their constitutional duties. The creation of independent regulatory commissions, of an independent Comptroller General to monitor accounts, of civil service protections for high-level employees, of a Congressional Budget Office, of war power restrictions, independent prosecutors, and legislative vetoes—all mark modern American political development as an alarming experiment in congressional overreach, a concerted assault on the unitary executive as it was enshrined in the Constitution and consistently defended over the course of the nineteenth century. So, too, the majority opinion of the Supreme Court in *Humphrey's Executor*, which secured the independence of the regulatory commissions, and Justice Jackson's concurring opinion in *Youngstown Co. v. Sawyer* (the *Steel Seizure Case*), which attempted to calibrate extraordinary claims of presidential power to measures of the breadth of political support. This analysis reverses the field of presidential history completely. As the unitary theorists see it, the developments of the twentieth century have left the presidency in a "diminished state;" their question is whether incumbents will be able to fulfill responsibilities that are "preeminently [their] own and whether [they are] in a position any longer to fulfill the design of the American Constitution" (Arkes 1987, 642).

Nowhere is this reversal of the historical perspective more instructive than in the repositioning of the administrative practices of the nineteenth century as a leading indicator of the president's essential constitutional role and institutional prerogative. Calabresi's history treats the spoils system—the political appointment and wholesale rotation of administrative officers—as an emblem of original ideals. The practice of displacing administrative officers *en masse* bespeaks a general acceptance of the president's singular responsibility to the electorate for the performance of the executive during his term and of the bureaucracy's strict subordination to presidential direction. Gone from this reading is the progressives' understanding of the spoils system as a source of executive weakness. Gone too is their contention that a more powerful and independent presidency might be rendered more responsible in action by building a system of managerial oversight on norms of neutral competence and shared information. Gone as well is the post-progressive understanding of the spoils system as an administrative arrangement designed to assure collective control of government through the mechanism of the political party.

The unitary theory denies constitutional standing to notions like administrative neutrality and collective responsibility and thereby rules them out of bounds. Indeed, it is striking just how far it goes toward converting the fully "politicized presidency" into a constitutional ideal. This history renders modern administration an extension of the president's personal political will, and, impeachment aside, it renders his priorities legitimate subjects for review only briefly in quadrennial elections. The plebiscitary standards of legitimacy so roundly renounced by post-progressives critics may, in this way, yet find accommodation as an expression of the Framers' original intent.

The Current Opening
for Historical Research

Histories of the presidency written through the lens of the unitary theory portend a paradigmatic shift in our understanding of this subject. Whether or not they succeed in securing their alternative, they have rendered it all but impossible for presidency scholars to continue to take their historical bearings for granted. The developmental perspective that has long provided our working history, that has directed our enquiries into contemporary operations and lent meaning to our findings, stands exposed and the alternative is up for grabs. It is no longer clear what changes, if any, have been fundamental, in which direction they point, or what the meaningful indicators of strength and weakness are. The stakes of historical research in this field have been correspondingly altered. The time when historical researchers could rest content to fill in the back story has passed; for the near future, they will be contesting the basic contours of the storyline itself.

At issue is our definition of what constitutes a problem. We know that presidents routinely seek support in the public at large for the implementation of their policy preferences, that they often choose to act unilaterally rather than work through Congress, that they struggle to gain control over the agencies of the executive branch, that it is hard for them to alter public opinion. But it is harder now to say why these are concerns or whether they are right on. Historical research on the presidency has always served to frame the significance of such facts; at present it is hosting a contest over their significance.

Two paths lie open to a resolution of this contest. One is political. As has grown increasingly apparent in recent decades, the state of scholarly opinion about the presidency tends to reflect the state of political opinion at large. It may be that a reliable working history cannot sort itself out until a broader political consensus emerges—a consensus the likes of which we have not seen since the middle decades of the twentieth century.

The second, more promising path is empirical. It entails capitalizing on the current weakening of assumptions and the proliferation of alternative readings of presidential history with more open-ended investigations of different dimensions of institutional change and more rigorous tests of their political significance. As we have seen, this empirical work is still in its infancy. Moreover, it has to date been directed almost exclusively at debunking the strong assumptions of development that under-lie the modern presidency construct, and in that guise, it, perhaps inadvertently, enhances the plausibility of essentialist readings of the history like those put forward by the unitary theorists. To tap its full potential, this empirical work will need to proceed with greater awareness of the larger implications of its own findings, to test assumptions on *all* sides, to indicate what changes have made a difference and how.

It is strange to think that an arena as well trodden by scholars as presidential history could suddenly emerge as an exciting frontier in research. That it has is testimony to the simplicity and power of the assumptions that have long informed our approach to the subject. By the same token, the one sure way to attenuate the great research opportunity afforded by the current opening would be to fall too quickly into line behind other, equally simple assumptions. Better to revel a bit in the present uncertainty and direct our sights close to the ground. The new history to be written in this way is likely to be more subtle than those currently contending. But no one ever said that a subtle history cannot be fresh and true.

References

ACKERMAN, B. A. 2005. *Failure of the Founding Fathers: Jefferson, Marshall, and the Rise of Presidential Democracy.* Cambridge, MA: Belknap Press of Harvard University Press.

ADLER, D. G. 1988. The Constitution and Presidential Warmaking: The Enduring Debate. *Political Science Quarterly,* 103: 1–36.

—— 2003. Presidential Greatness as an Attribute of Warmaking. *Presidential Studies Quarterly,* 33: 466–84.

—— 2006. George Bush as Commander-in-Chief: Toward the Nether World of Constitutionalism. *Presidential Studies Quarterly,* 36: 525–40.

ARKES, H. 1987. On the Moral Standing of the President as an Interpreter of the Constitution: Some Reflections on Our Current "Crises." *PS* 20: 637–42.

ARNOLD, P. E. 1986. *Making the Managerial Presidency: Comprehensive Reorganization Planning, 1905–1980.* Princeton, NJ: Princeton University Press.

—— 1996. Policy Leadership in the Progressive Presidency: The Case of Theodore Roosevelt's Naval Policy and his Search for Strategic Resources. *Studies in American Political Development,* 10: 333–59.

—— 2003. Effecting a Progressive Presidency: Roosevelt, Taft, and the Pursuit of Strategic Resources. *Studies in American Political Development,* 17: 61–81.

BAILEY, J. D. 2007. *Thomas Jefferson and Executive Power.* New York: Cambridge University Press.

BARILLEAUX, R. J. 1988. *The Post-Modern Presidency: The Office after Ronald Reagan.* New York: Praeger.

BIMES, T., and SKOWRONEK, S. 1998. Woodrow Wilson's Critique of Popular Leadership: Reassessing the Modern–Traditional Divide in Presidential History. In *Speaking to the People: The Rhetorical Presidency in Historical Perspective,* ed. R. J. Ellis. Amherst: University of Massachusetts Press.

—— and MULROY, Q. 2004. The Rise and Decline of Presidential Populism. *Studies in American Political Development,* 18: 136–59.

BURNHAM, J. 1959. *Congress and the American Tradition.* Chicago: H. Regnery.

BURNS, J. M. 1965. *Presidential Government: The Crucible of Leadership.* Boston: Houghton Mifflin.

CALABRESI, S. G. 1994. The Vesting Clauses as Power Grants. *Northwestern University Law Review,* 88: 1377–405.

—— 1995. Some Normative Arguments for the Unitary Executive. *Arkansas Law Review,* 48/1: 23–104.

—— and PRAKASH, S. B. 1994. The President's Power to Execute the Laws. *Yale Law Journal,* 104: 541–665.

CALABRESI, S. G., and RHODES, K. H. 1992. The Structural Constitution: Unitary Executive, Plural Judiciary. *Harvard Law Review*, 105: 1153–216.

——and YOO, C. S. 1997. The Unitary Executive during the First Half-Century. *Case Western Reserve Law Review*, 47: 1451–561.

——— 2003. The Unitary Executive during the Second Half-Century. *Harvard Journal of Law & Public Policy*, 26: 667–801.

CEASER, J. W., THUROW, G. E., TULIS, J., and BESSETTE, J. M. 1982. The Rise of the Rhetorical Presidency. In *Rethinking the Presidency*, ed. T. E. Cronin. Boston: Little, Brown.

DE GRAZIA, A. 1965. *Republic in Crisis: Congress against the Executive Force*. New York: Federal Legal Publications.

DICKINSON, M. 2003. Bargaining, Uncertainty, and the Growth of the White House Staff, 1940–2000. In *Uncertainty in American Politics*, ed. B. C. Burden. New York: Cambridge University Press.

——and LEBO, M. J. 2007. Reexamining the Growth of the Institutional Presidency, 1940–2000. *Journal of Politics*, 69: 206–19.

EDWARDS, G. C., III. 1989. *At the Margins: Presidential Leadership of Congress*. New Haven, CT: Yale University Press.

——2003. *On Deaf Ears: The Limits of the Bully Pulpit*. New Haven, CT: Yale University Press.

ELLIS, R. J. (ed.) 1998. *Speaking to the People: The Rhetorical Presidency in Historical Perspective*. Amherst: University of Massachusetts Press.

——and KIRK, S. 1998. Jefferson, Jackson, and the Origins of the Presidential Mandate. In *Speaking to the People: The Rhetorical Presidency in Historical Perspective*, ed. R. J. Ellis. Amherst: University of Massachusetts Press.

FARRAR-MYERS, V. 2007. *Scripted for Change: The Institutionalization of the American Presidency*. College Station: Texas A&M University Press.

FISHER, L. 1995. *Presidential War Power*. Lawrence: University Press of Kansas.

——and ADLER, D. G. 1998. The War Powers Resolution: Time to Say Goodbye. *Political Science Quarterly*, 113: 1–20.

FORD, H. J. 1898. *The Rise and Growth of American Politics: A Sketch of Constitutional Development*. New York: Macmillan Company.

GALVIN, D., and SHOGAN, C. J. 2004. Presidential Politicization and Centralization across the Modern–Traditional Divide. *Polity*, 36: 477–504.

GILLMAN, H. 1989. The Constitution Besieged: TR, Taft, and Wilson on the Virtue and Efficacy of a Faction-Free Republic. *Presidential Studies Quarterly*, 19: 179–201.

GREENSTEIN, F. I. 1978. Change and Continuity in the Modern Presidency. In *The New American Political System*, ed. A. King. Washington, DC: American Enterprise Institute.

——1983. The Need for an Early Appraisal of the Reagan Presidency. In *The Reagan Presidency: An Early Assessment*, ed. F. I. Greenstein. Baltimore: Johns Hopkins University Press.

——1988. Introduction: Toward a Modern Presidency. In *Leadership in the Modern Presidency*, ed. F. I. Greenstein. Cambridge, MA: Harvard University Press.

Humphrey's Executor v. *United States*, 295 US 602 (1935).

JAMES, S. C. 2005. The Evolution of the Presidency: Between the Promise and the Fear. In *The Executive Branch*, ed. J. D. Aberbach and M. A. Peterson. Oxford: Oxford University Press.

KENDALL, W. 1960. The Two Majorities. *Midwest Journal of Political Science*, 4: 317–45.

KERNELL, S. 1986. *Going Public: New Strategies of Presidential Leadership*. Washington, DC: CQ Press.

KLEINERMAN, B. A. 2007. Can the Prince Really Be Tamed? Executive Prerogative, Popular Apathy, and the Constitutional Frame in Locke's *Second Treatise*. *American Political Science Review*, 101: 209–22.

KRAUSE, G. A. 2002. Separated Powers and Institutional Growth in the Presidential and Congressional Branches: Distinguishing between Short-Run versus Long-Run Dynamics. *Political Research Quarterly,* 55: 27–57.

LARACEY, M. 2002. *Presidents and the People: The Partisan Story of Going Public.* College Station: Texas A&M University Press.

LEWIS, D. E., and STRINE, J. M. 1996. What Time Is It? The Use of Power in Four Different Types of Presidential Time. *Journal of Politics,* 58: 682–706.

LIM, E. 2008. *The Anti-Intellectual Presidency.* New York: Oxford University Press.

LOWI, T. J. 1985. *Personal President: Power Invested, Promise Unfulfilled.* Ithaca, NY: Cornell University Press.

LYNCH, G. P. 2004. Protecting Individual Rights through a Federal System: James Buchanan's View of Federalism. *Publius: The Journal of Federalism,* 34: 153–68.

McDONALD, F. 1994. *The American Presidency: An Intellectual History.* Lawrence: University Press of Kansas.

MANSFIELD, H. C., JR. 1989. *Taming the Prince: The Ambivalence of Modern Executive Power.* New York: Free Press.

MERRIAM, C. E. 1925. *New Aspects of Politics.* Chicago: University of Chicago Press.

MILKIS, S. M. 1993. *The President and the Parties: The Transformation of the American Party System since the New Deal.* New York: Oxford University Press.

—— and RHODES, J. H. 2007. George W. Bush, the Republican Party, and the "New" American Party System. *Perspectives on Politics,* 5: 461–88.

—— and TICHENOR, D. J. 1994. "Direct Democracy" and Social Justice: The Progressive Party Campaign of 1912. *Studies in American Political Development,* 8: 282–340.

MOE, T. M. 1985. The Politicized Presidency. In *The New Direction in American Politics,* ed. J. E Chubb and P. E. Peterson. Washington, DC: Brookings Institution.

NICHOLS, D. K. 1994. *The Myth of the Modern Presidency.* University Park: Pennsylvania State University Press.

PATTERSON, J. T. 1976. The Rise of Presidential Power before World War II. *Law and Contemporary Problems,* 40: 39–57.

PFIFFNER, J. P. 2008. *Power Play: The Bush Presidency and the Constitution.* Washington, DC: Brookings.

RAGSDALE, L., and THEIS, J. J., III. 1997. The Institutionalization of the American Presidency, 1924–92. *American Journal of Political Science,* 41: 1280–318.

ROSE, R. 1991. *The Postmodern President: The White House Meets the World.* Chatham, NJ: Chatham House.

SCHLESINGER, A. M., JR. 1973. *The Imperial Presidency.* Boston: Houghton Mifflin.

—— 2005. *War and the American Presidency.* New York: W. W. Norton.

—— 2007. *Journals, 1952–2000.* New York: Penguin Press.

SHOGAN, C. J. 2006. *The Moral Rhetoric of American Presidents.* College Station: Texas A&M University Press.

SKOWRONEK, S. 1982. *Building a New American State: The Expansion of National Administrative Capacities, 1877–1920.* New York: Cambridge University Press.

—— 1993. *The Politics Presidents Make: Leadership from John Adams to George Bush.* Cambridge, MA: Belknap Press.

—— 2008. *Presidential Leadership in Political Time: Reprise and Reappraisal.* Lawrence: University Press of Kansas.

TULIS, JEFFREY. 1987. *The Rhetorical Presidency.* Princeton, NJ: Princeton University Press.

TULIS, JEFFREY. 1998. Reflections on the Rhetorical Presidency in American Political Development. In *Speaking to the People: The Rhetorical Presidency in Historical Perspective*, ed. R. J. Ellis. Amherst: University of Massachusetts Press.

WHITE, M. G. 1947. The Revolt against Formalism in American Social Thought of the Twentieth Century. *Journal of the History of Ideas*, 8: 131–52.

WHITTINGTON, K. E., and CARPENTER, D. P. 2003. Executive Power in American Institutional Development, *Perspectives on Politics*, 1: 495–513.

WILSON, W. 1885. *Congressional Government*. Boston: Houghton, Mifflin & Company.

——1908. *Constitutional Government in the United States*. New York: Columbia University Press.

WOOLLEY, J. C. 2005. Drawing Lines or Defining Variables: Studying Big Changes in the Presidency. Available from <http://convention2.allacademic.com/one/apsa/apsa05/index.php?cmd=Down load +Document&key=unpublished_manuscript&file_index=2&pop_up=true&no_click_key=true&attachment_style=attachment&PHPSESSID=39492acd5628b9050fd522a14fd4ad2f >.

YOO, C. S., CALABRESI, S. G., and COLANGELO, A. 2005. The Unitary Executive in the Modern Era, 1945–2004. *Iowa Law Review*, 90/2: 601–731.

—— —— and NEE, L. 2004. The Unitary Executive during the Third Half-Century, 1889–1945. *Notre Dame Law Review*, 80: 1–110.

YOO, J. C. 2005. *The Powers of War and Peace: The Constitution and Foreign Affairs after 9/11.* Chicago: University of Chicago Press.

——2006. *War by Other Means: An Insider's Account of the War on Terror.* New York: Atlantic Monthly Press.

Youngstown Co. v. *Sawyer*, 343 US 579 (1952) (Jackson, J., concurring).

CHAPTER 33

WHOSE PRESIDENCY IS THIS ANYHOW?

HUGH HECLO

SINCE "reflection" stems from the Latin word for the act of bending back, I would like to begin by turning back some thoughts to an earlier time.

Not so long ago, there really was nothing that could be called "presidential studies." By that I mean it is only during the last half of the twentieth century that there came to be a distinctive group of scholars researching, publishing, and teaching within a specialized field called "the presidency." In the Eisenhower years, a person interested in the American presidency could have jammed all the scholarly books devoted to this particular subject into one of those large 1950s-style leather briefcases. Stuffed therein you might have found volumes by Edward Corwin, Louis Koenig, Clinton Rossiter, Pendleton Herring, Louis Brownlow, and probably not much more. As Richard Neustadt recalled those days, there was only one under-graduate course on the presidency at any major college campus—Clinton Rossiter's offering at Cornell.

Now, of course, things are different. A tractor-trailer might not suffice to carry around today's library of books that fall under the heading of presidential studies. I am making an obvious point, but it is a useful preliminary reminder for what follows. Looking back now, the growth of this specialized field seems not only understandable but inevitable, and the reasons for this are interesting to consider.

THE GROWTH OF PRESIDENTIAL STUDIES

The end of the Eisenhower years and movement into the 1960s marked an inflection point in the growth of presidential studies. As befits the subtlety of historical turning points, there was no single abrupt event to signpost this change. The inflection was carried out through the confusing currents of the time and scarcely recognized, as observers were carried along by those currents. In fact, among the tiny corps of scholars thinking about the presidency at the middle of the twentieth century, the question of a turning point had already been decided. This newly minted conventional view was roughly as follows. There had been such a thing as a pre-modern presidency. Its developmental tendencies had been fulfilled in the modern presidency that emerged with FDR. The public's personal identification with this modern presidency had been established through the radio, news media, and dramatic events of the Depression and the Second World War; the modern presidency's institutional turning point had been established in the 1939 creation of the Executive Office of the President.

However, the modern presidency that was said to be represented by FDR did not generate the growth of presidential studies we are considering here. For that, something more had to happen.

For one thing, after mid-century, Americans began rushing headlong into a new way of doing politics—through television. The advantage would now lie with presidents and would-be presidents as the visual focal point for Americans' attention to public affairs.

Things were also helped along by the personalities who now came under scrutiny by the new visual media. After Eisenhower retired to his Pennsylvania cattle farm, Americans experienced something resembling an ongoing psycho-drama in the Oval Office. It involved political celebrity, consuming ambition, and some remarkable personal quirkiness swirling around the White House. How could anyone *not* want to probe deeper into this fascinating world peopled by the likes of a Kennedy, Johnson, Nixon, and the rest of the cast of characters.

Of course there were also more substantive concerns driving the growth of presidential studies. Since the earliest days of the Republic, Americans had been struggling with the tension between what Alexander Hamilton called energy and safety in the presidency, or what modern scholars have aptly termed "the promise and the fear" of executive power (*Federalist*, Nos. 69–77; James 2005). Although this had been a long-standing tension, the realities of government after the 1950s demanded that more serious attention should be paid to the hopes and dangers attached to the presidency. After the complacency of the 1950s, the federal government was called on to enact an ever-expanding domestic policy agenda, an agenda of social reform vastly more ambitious than the New Deal's focus on economic security (Milkis and Mileur 2005). Kicking and screaming, America was being dragged into creating its own version of a modern welfare state. This entailed a vast expansion of executive branch responsibilities, though rarely was it accompanied by administrative capacities and knowledge commensurate to those responsibilities.

In addition, the progressive New Deal view of the subject—the modern presidency as the people's tribune leading an activist government—began taking on a darker tone after mid-century. The Cold War gave the name to an existential threat which continued to drag on, seemingly forever. The people's tribune, now also the "leader of the free world," not only had his finger on the nuclear trigger. From Cuba and Vietnam onwards, it also was becoming clear that presidents had their hands in all sorts of foreign intrigues—some public, some secret, and some possibly nefarious. One had to take notice.

Then too, internal dynamics in social science and the academy have no doubt also played their part in creating professional presidential studies. Mid-century ushered in the "behavioral" turn in the social sciences. Vast uncharted territory was opened up for new generations of scholars to explore, all in the name of systematically studying how the presidency *really* works. At the same time, a population boom in college students and academic jobs offered new opportunities for professional specialization in the social science marketplace. One could now make a career in academia out of being a "presidentialist."

For these and no doubt other reasons, the tractor-trailer load has kept growing. If one is in a reflective mood, this development can prompt two preliminary thoughts: puzzlements really.

The Decline of Practitioners' Accounts

First, compared with an earlier time, it is surprising how little is to be learned about the modern presidency from the people with White House and other executive branch experience over this eventful last half century. To be sure, there have been plenty of books produced by former officials and ex-presidents during these years. However, I think it is fair to say that, anecdotes aside, there is little significant knowledge about the presidency to be gained from reading these largely self-aggrandizing books. In fact, it appears that a general degeneration in thoughtfulness has occurred when these accounts by insiders are compared to the publications by former executive branch officials of the "pre-presidential studies" era. In the latter category one could think of the work of Herring and Brownlow, of course, but also of a Don Price, Dwight Waldo, Thurman Arnold, Marshall Dimock, James Landis, V. O. Key, Harold Seidman, and, not least of all, Richard Neustadt himself in the 1950s (Jones 2003).

Why is that? The possible answers are not pretty. The more recent crops of executive officials may not be as intellectually gifted as their predecessors. Or perhaps they are more influenced by our modern media culture to be pop-in-cocks rather than public servants. Or maybe the issues of modern government are not of the kind that would attract people who are seriously devoted to understanding government, compared with those people drawn to Washington to fight the Depression, the Second World War, and the early Cold War. Or it could be that talented people nowadays simply have more opportunities for cashing in on their high-level governmental experience and do not care to write books with much substance. As I said, the possible explanations are not very attractive. My own guess is that the earlier, more substantive work by executive branch veterans reflects the fact that by the 1960s an incipient higher civil service had developed in the environs of the Executive Office of the President. This produced people who wrote books with intellectual substance. In subsequent years that development was stopped in its tracks.

Knowing More and Doing Worse

A second and deeper puzzle about the ever-growing body of presidential scholarship is this. One might reasonably expect that this accumulating knowledge would be associated with some noticeable improvement in presidential performance. Granted, we live in a complex world. But a rough-hewn common sense would lead one to expect that the more that is known about an activity, the better people should become at carrying out that activity. Yet it would be very difficult to argue that the record of the last fifty years shows any such improved performance, either in the institutional presidency or the people occupying the office. In fact a stronger case could be made to the contrary. One sign is that serious discussions of impeachment have been directed against five of the nine presidents who held office from 1960 to 2008 (Johnson, Nixon, Reagan, Clinton, and George W. Bush). Again, there actually seems to have been a degeneration in performance compared to the era before the presidential studies enterprise began to accumulate its expert knowledge.

One might object that more knowledge may just as likely deepen the mystery of a thing, as in moving from Newtonian mechanics to quantum physics, or from dating the opposite sex to marrying one of them. The more we know, the more we realize how much we don't know.

But that problem should not apply in this case because so much of the scholarship in presidential studies is devoted to a kind of "practical" knowledge; in other words, knowledge that is meant to be is useful for understanding and guiding presidential actions. One of the striking things is how strongly presidential studies have continued to move in this direction originally signposted in 1960 by Richard Neustadt's book *Presidential Power*. In this broad mainstream of presidential studies, the emphasis is essentially on understanding the realpolitik of presidential leadership, its constraints and opportunities. The Big Question, if I may call it such, is this: how do and how can presidents try to get their way in governing? It is a good, important question, even if some people take it as evidence that the field of presidential studies suffers from a surfeit of political scientists who are White House aides-in-waiting.

THREE CURRENTS OF RESEARCH

It is in light of this Big Question that we can recognize three currents of mainstream presidential research that have developed since the 1950s. It may be helpful to sketch the way each perspective has addressed our presidents' governing problem.

Personal Influence

The first scholarly current focuses on a president's personal influence. Since governing power is widely shared under our Constitution, any president must operate largely by persuading rather than commanding other politically relevant actors. But these other power holders also need the president's help in doing their jobs. And so a president has the opportunity to negotiate mutually advantageous exchanges to align their self-interest with his purposes. To influence such a governing process and get more of what he (or someday she) wants, the president must always be looking ahead to leverage his resources into bargaining advantages. Thus, a wise president will make choices that protect and enhance his own chances for future effectiveness—his power stakes. This leads to considering how presidents organize their sources of information, protect their professional reputation with other bargainers, and use their prestige with the general public—all with an eye to maintaining and hopefully improving the president's prospects for getting his way.

It naturally follows that many researchers have gone on to study how, and to what effect, recent presidents have managed their staff (Haney 1997; Hess and Pfiffner 2002), public appeals (Kernell 1997), media relations (Kumar 2007), and especially their bargaining strategies with Congress (Edwards 1989; Peterson 1990; Jones 1994; Bond and Fleisher 2000).

Unfortunately for any neat model of presidential influence, complexity reigns. To paraphrase one summary of recent studies, presidents may have significant influence in setting Washington's policy agenda, but their sway in actually passing legislation depends mainly on the preexisting ideological and partisan make-up of Congress. When controlled by the opposition party, Congress has managed to constrain presidents' use of military force, mainly through public posturing rather than direct legislative action (Howell and Pevehouse 2007). Likewise, the public prestige of presidents is shaped by forces largely outside their control and generally has a small effect on legislative outcomes. As for a president's personal bargaining skills, research suggests they might be crucial in very exceptional circumstances, but mostly their impact is overwhelmed by other factors at work amid the complexities of governing (Dickinson 2005). These difficulties have been intensified for presidents because divided government between executive and legislative has become the modern norm. Indeed, if one considers "divided government" to include not only control of the two branches by different parties but also the sharper ideological divisions between the parties and within the Congress, then any period of unified government, in which a president might readily function as a party and opinion leader, is virtually unknown in our contemporary politics.

Closer analysis of presidents' efforts to get their way by "going public" reveals a similar complexity. Public appeals can heighten the salience of particular issues to Americans, and thus put pressure on Congress to act (Barrett 2004). However, despite what presidents themselves believe, such appeals appear to be ineffective in changing the public's substantive dispositions towards those issues (Edwards 2003). Presidents since Eisenhower have become more inclined to launch PR campaigns appealing to the general public, but they have tended to do so with regard to what are already popular domestic issues. Research indicates that presidential pandering to public opinion is conditional and mostly directed toward selling the president's cause, not deriving that cause from public opinion polls (Jacobs and Shapiro 2000). Typically it is marginally popular presidents facing reelection who trim their policy pronouncements to curry public favor, especially if the public will not learn of the consequences until after the election (Canes-Wrone 2005).

Moreover, going public appears to be a diminishing asset. Contemporary changes in the media environment (e.g., the proliferation of news sources, sites for contending political commentaries, and the ordinary citizen's information overload) appear to have weakened presidential capacities to rally public opinion by talking to their "fellow citizens" (Baum and Kernell 1999; Cohen 2008). Likewise, a generation of scholars has now documented the weakness of modern presidents as party leaders dealing with Congress and public leaders rallying American opinion (Pious 2002). This has not stopped recent presidents from trying to govern through a more or less "permanent campaign" aimed at selling their policies to the media, interest groups, and the public at large (Heclo 2000; Edwards 2008).

Reflecting on all this, one can appreciate why any administration might feel frustrated. However savvy a president might be in making decisions, however carefully he might protect his prospective resources for bargaining, the deck seems stacked against him. Barring a national crisis, the odds of getting his way in some clear, publicly persuasive manner are generally slim.

Unilateralism

There is, therefore, a profound disparity between public expectations for modern presidents to solve problems and the real world constraints on their bargaining strategies for doing so. Today's presidents have strong incentives to go it alone, in one way or another. Thus a second strand of mainstream presidential research has been growing in prominence during recent years. It emphasizes presidential unilateralism rather than bargaining, or as one important book in this field puts it, "power without persuasion" (Howell 2003).

In this approach to the Big Question, the view of "power" denominated in terms of personal influence (i.e. presidents relying on bargaining and opinion leadership to get their way) slips into the background. Attention now focuses on how presidents can use their "powers" to pursue their ends. The powers in question are not only those in the texts of the Constitution and congressional laws. They are also powers said to be inherent and implied by the president's position as a unitary chief executive, military commander-in-chief, and sole spokesman for the nation in international affairs.

It is important to distinguish traditional views on this subject from the more recent and far-reaching assertions. Every president since George Washington has embraced a theory of the unitary executive in the sense of claiming constitutional authority for the president to control and remove all policy-making officials in the executive branch (Calabresi and Yoo 2008). However, the Nixon administration inaugurated what was to become a far more ambitious series of moves to enhance presidential power.

This development first attracted attention during President Nixon's effort to gain control over the executive branch bureaucracy, especially its personnel and procedures for implementing policy (Heclo 1977; Nathan 1983). Theoretical justifications soon followed in the presidential literature. In a series of influential articles in the 1980s and 1990s, Terry Moe argued that the Neustadt school's focus on the personal bargaining calculus of presidents not only ignored the institutional side of presidential power developing across all recent administrations, but it also failed to recognize that in an increasingly volatile and hostile political environment, presidents had a legitimate need to surround themselves with executive branch personnel who are responsive, like-minded, and politically loyal (Moe 1985, 1993; Moe and Wilson 1994; Moe and Howell 1999).

Since then, this second strand of research has burgeoned with studies focusing on the theme of presidential unilateralism, that is to say, the use of strictly executive measures to make policy without going through Congress (Shull 2006). Such measures include impoundment of congressionally appropriated funds, "signing statements" putting on record the president's rationale for ignoring the law he is signing, and executive orders often creating a *de facto* system of policy making hidden in the executive branch (Mayer 2001; Cooper 2002; Warber 2006). The procedural manifestations of this trend include more centralized White House control over legislative proposals (Rudalevige 2005), judicial nominations (Goldman 1997; Abraham 1999), and promulgation of new government regulations and executive orders. In the course of this development, George W. Bush's presidency launched sweeping claims of inherent executive power related to the war on terror, claims that some saw as undermining the rule of law and long-standing constitutional principles (Fisher 2007, Pfiffner 2008).

For present purposes, the important point is this. Although coming at it from a different angle, those rebelling against the standard bargaining model have mainly reaffirmed the conventional approach in presidential studies. Whether by bargaining or unilateralism, the central issue remains a matter of investigating how presidents try to get their way in governing.

Contingent Influence

A third research current has emphasized the contingent relationship of presidential leadership to the array of political forces in different time periods (Skowronek 1993).

This attention to historical context has thrown into question the standard account of a flat landscape divided simply between a pre-modern and a modern presidency, with the great break occurring sometime between 1932 and 1945. Instead, scholars working from this perspective find similarities and differences cutting across presidential history. For example, the prospects for presidential leadership are different for leaders operating in an ideologically charged era of conviction politics and those who are not (Sykes 2000), just as they are different for presidents who win the White House as leaders of an opposition party versus presidents who move into office as part of an established political regime (Crockett 2002). What presidents are likely to be able to do in governing depends on where they find themselves in different configurations of political time.

Of course these three strands of presidential research are not mutually exclusive. It makes sense to think that when there is an underlying policy consensus and generally predictable political environment, presidential bargaining and negotiation can be prominent. By contrast, unilateralism and flexing of presidential powers might be favored when there is little political consensus and the surrounding political environment offers only uncertainty and no reliable bargaining partners. With this understanding, there is little reason to choose between Neustadt and Moe. Seen in the context of different historical periods, both can have their day.

In something called "reflections," I hope I will be excused for summarizing in such a crude way the substantial and varied merits of these three related and at times contending strands of presidential research. However, I think it is fair to say that in all three, the common thread lies in trying to understand the constraints and opportunities as presidents try to get their way in governing. That is the Big Question. And to repeat, it does seem a little strange that as we accumulate ever more knowledge on that subject, the record of presidential performance should be so widely regarded as disappointing.

We might flatter ourselves and say this is because presidents and their advisers do not read and learn from the literature produced by presidential scholars. But even if they did, do we really believe this would lead to greater presidential success and fewer failures? And what do we mean by "success" and "failure" anyway? Is a president who excels in getting his way in governing necessarily to be hailed as having a successful presidency? Before turning to this issue of evaluating success and failure in presidential performance, we might reflect on the gains and setbacks that have occurred in the conduct of presidential research itself.

THE RESEARCH ENTERPRISE

In reflecting on the presidential research enterprise itself, there have been marked gains since the early years. There have also been some growing difficulties.

The Positive Side

On the positive side of the ledger there are at least four features that deserve to be acknowledged.

First, in ways that could not have been imagined a few decades ago, advances in computer technology have facilitated the assembly of massive databases for creative analysis by presidential scholars. For example, impressive sets of data have been compiled with regard to the sources of presidential legislative programs (Rudalevige 2002), trends in political appointments (Lewis 2005), the use of executive orders (Kraus and Cohen 2000), and Senate confirmation of presidential nominations (McCarty and Razaghian 1999; Binder and Maltzman 2002).

This in turn has facilitated the use of quantitative techniques to test competing claims regarding subjects such as control of the president's program, presidential appeals to the public, and unilateral policy making. Rather than displaying technical virtuosity for its own sake, quantitative research on the presidency clearly has produced new knowledge and gained an increasingly respected standing in the field (Howell 2006). For example, thirty years ago I tried to write about the politicization of executive branch management associated with the presidential personnel process. Today, thanks to a combination of case studies and careful analysis of quantitative data, one can speak with much more confidence about the effects on agency performance produced by political appointees in the bureaucracy (Lewis 2008).

Third, use of presidential libraries has become more common, with Fred Greenstein leading the way to show some of the rich possibilities for researchers (Greenstein 1982). George W. Bush's presidency makes a total of twelve presidential libraries available to presidential scholars. As we shall see shortly, there are major problems in using these resources, but unlike fifty years ago, it is now a legal norm that records of every presidential administration belong to the American public and are potentially available for scholarly research. At least in terms of record keeping, it has been made clear that the presidency does not belong to presidents.

Finally, a whole new world of potentially useful information has opened up in databases outside the confines of the presidency. For example, the National Digital Newspaper Program is a joint project between the National Endowment for the Humanities and the Library of Congress (<www.loc.gov/chroniclingamerica/>). It contains 30 million pages of American newspapers from the nineteenth and early twentieth centuries, providing a rich body of material of potential relevance for studying public commentary on the presidency before the electronic media existed. And thanks again to recent modern technology, there are digitalized catalogues and finding aids to make constructive use of such resources. Obviously any researcher must bring intelligent, theoretically informed questions to these resources, but we have passed beyond a time when E. E. Schattschneider characterized political science as "a mountain of data surrounded by a vacuum" (1969, 8).

The Downside

There is also a downside to the research picture. Experience has shown that presidential studies face some very practical research problems, and indeed, certain obstacles seem to be growing for today's and tomorrow's presidential scholars. I will mention three.

We now have multi-million-dollar presidential libraries, monuments it would seem to people who are legends in their own minds. These imposing structures can be maddeningly cumbersome places for doing research. For example, the first presidential library to fall under the jurisdiction of the 1978 Presidential Records Act is the Ronald Reagan Presidential Library and Museum. Under this Act (44 USC chapter 22) the United States owns and controls all the records "created or received by the President, his immediate staff, or a unit or individual of the Executive Office of the President whose function is to advise and assist the President." This sounds promising for researchers but in practice the process of gaining any realistic access can be a nightmare.

For example, in a recent project trying to use these papers, researchers found that as of 2005 no more than 10 percent of the 50 million pages of presidential records were processed and available for study. Although a number of topics of general interest (e.g., Reagan's speeches) had been researched at the library, topics of specific interest were generally unavailable for study. Gaining access required filing Freedom of Information Act or (for national security documents removed from a file) mandatory review requests. Most of these requests produced no response. When they did, the waiting period before archivists would *begin* processing the requests ranged from three and a half to five years (Ebin 2005). In 2007, of the 78 million pages of documents and 20 million emails at the Clinton Library, approximately one-half of 1 percent was open to the public, with almost 300 Freedom of Information requests pending.

Second, and quite apart from a clogged process, obstacles to research in the libraries of our most recent presidents have been greatly magnified since 2001. In that year President Bush's Executive Order 13233 overturned much of the 1978 Act's intent. By this order, a sitting president is required to defer to the executive privilege claims of a former president or his designated representative to keep certain materials sealed. If a researcher objects, the onus is on him or her to mount a court challenge. For example, since November 2002, former President Clinton's request has been honored to withhold confidential communications involving foreign policy issues, "sensitive policy, personal or political" matters, "legal issues and advice," and all non-routine direct communications from the president, or between the president and vice president, first lady, or former presidents and vice president. That would seem to cover much, if not most, of what would be of interest to a presidential scholar.

Finally, we have entered a world where words that stay put on paper are often taking second place to words that disappear as electronic flickers on a screen. Obviously paper records are not being replaced, and the mountain of paper grows with each administration. But the value of such records may be decreasing. This is because the intervention of electronic communication means we cannot be sure the written records reflect a writer's intent. Moreover it seems that electronic records often go uncollected, and even if collected, mostly go uncatalogued.

For these reasons, it seems to me that however well we do with new databases and quantitative techniques, presidential research is going to have to rely heavily on the scholarly equivalent of investigative journalism. By that I mean ferreting out inside sources or former participants to interview, prompting sources to react to each other, and so on. It also means finding information sources among the "grunts" in the bureaucracy who keep the government running and becoming rather less enamored with the high-profile figures who make it into the news and talk shows.

In sum, presidential studies have experienced immense advances in research resources and methods over the last fifty years. The creation and quantitative analyses of new databases has gone far beyond anything imaginable in the pre-computer era. In the sense of embracing both quantitative and qualitative forms of analysis, the study of the presidency has become more technically sophisticated and well rounded. And while cumbersome to use, the network of presidential libraries has become an ever-burgeoning resource for researchers. What should one make of all this?

With the presidency now well established as a distinct research and teaching field, there is always a temptation to carry on by inertial force. Few of us would like to admit it, but things in academia can keep going just for the sake of extending publication lists, showcasing new analytic techniques, and building academic careers. So as this research field expands, I think we would do well to keep interrogating our own questions and answers about the presidency.

WHAT KIND OF KNOWLEDGE?

In 2002, the editor of *Presidential Studies Quarterly* invited several leading scholars in the field to reflect on the question, "What do we want to know about the Presidency—and why do we want to know it?" (Edwards 2002). This is a good question, but presidential studies have probably developed to a point where it is appropriate to probe deeper into our presuppositions. We should also ask ourselves a somewhat different and prior question. What kind of knowledge is it that we want? In other words, what is the nature of the learning we seek to acquire and disseminate to the rest of society concerning the presidency? That is asking us to consider what, at the end of the day, we actually mean to accomplish. Asking about performance in light of purpose—whether applied to presidents or presidential scholars—points us toward knowledge that is inherently normative in character.

Earlier I suggested that the kind of knowledge being sought throughout much, possibly most, of the field is oriented around matters of practice: descriptions, theories, and analyses of how presidents try to govern. In the competitive world of politics, this sort of inquiry makes perfectly good sense, and I am certainly not suggesting it should be sidelined, much less abandoned. Description and analysis of the actual exercise of power is an essential kind of knowledge.

However, the presidency does not belong to presidents and their aides. It also does not belong to presidential scholars, as if it were a lab specimen laid out for an ethically neutral examination. By its nature, the presidential office belongs to a larger constitutional order, and it therefore always makes sense to look beyond whether presidents are simply succeeding or failing to prevail in the political process. Seeing the presidency in terms of its constitutional purposes offers a standard in light of which performance is to be judged, and this applies to both presidents and presidential researchers. In other words, praxis needs to be understood in light of a broader constitutional-institutional perspective on performance and on the meaning of presidential "success." This is another kind of knowledge about the presidency that should be disseminated in the larger political society. Of course, many presidential scholars know this, but it has become very easy to lose sight of this larger picture.

If inattentive to that larger picture, presidential studies are prone to operate—usually implicitly—on a "great man" theory of history and politics. Success means prevailing over opponents and ostensibly shaping the course of public policy. This means that we gauge presidential success and failure by such things as high or low approval ratings, election and reelection margins, legislative batting averages, victories scored on particular policy issues, and the like. Success or failure is a matter of whether or not the president gets his way. In sliding down this slope, presidential scholarship can unconsciously transform itself into advocacy of presidential power. It is then left to the separate corps of congressional scholars and judicial scholars to offset any imbalance in the analysis. In effect, political science simply becomes a tripartite reflection of the Constitution's "invitation to struggle" among the three branches, instead of being an independent intellectual platform seeking an enlarged understanding of that struggle.

For example, we noted earlier that a generation of scholars has documented the weakness of modern presidents as party leaders dealing with Congress and as public leaders rallying American opinion. We also saw the temptation to read that situation as not merely explaining but also justifying presidential strategies of unilateralism and prerogative power. But a view of the larger institutional picture should make us wary of such claims. Given that researchers take "weakness" to mean the president has not prevailed in his legislative program and/or public appeals, what view of executive power would justify the subsequent strategy of going it alone? The only logical answer is to embrace a view that is the antithesis of "thinking constitutionally," namely, a view that the president is the one and only true representative and protector of the nation. Going down this dangerous path, presidents and presidential scholars alike can convince themselves that what is good for the president is good for the country—that what is to the president's political advantage defines what is in the public interest.

Put in such stark terms, few presidential observers would explicitly affirm such claims. But there is a subtle way we can drift into that way of thinking. Given the dominant public and scholarly focus on weakness and strength—success and failure—in presidents getting their way, it is a view that can tend to creep sideways into our thinking. The antidote is to give sustained attention to the presidency as an institutional office, seeing it as something that is both shaped by and reshaping a deeper constitutional order.

This is in fact a fourth current of presidential scholarship, and it contains a number of exemplary works. These range from textbooks used on many college campuses (Milkis and Nelson 2007) to constitutionally minded studies of presidential selection (Ceaser 1979), personal leadership (Lowi 1986; Landy and Milkis 2000), executive power (Mansfield 1993; Rudalevige 2005; Pfiffner 2008), and political demagoguery (Tulis 1987; Friedman 2008). I would argue that these are signposts pointing us toward a kind of knowledge that deserves much greater attention.

This knowledge is not a matter of simply treating the written Constitution as a base on which historical, organization, and operational studies are then layered. It means recognizing the constitutional dimension and spirit permeating our subject matter throughout all levels of analysis. In reflecting on what this country has experienced since the Eisenhower years, I believe this is an essential knowledge we need to cultivate and teach for the sake of the long-term political health of our nation.

Institutional Knowledge

At risk of belaboring the obvious, I should note that considering the presidency as an "office" involves two sorts of knowledge that are institutional in nature. One is narrowly focused and the other is a broader contextual understanding. The narrow-gauged view (which by no means do I intend to be a term of denigration) concerns itself with the staff work, bureaucratic units, and advisory processes located in both the White House Office and the Executive Office of the President (Burke 2003). The growing size and political weight of this institutional presidency has continued across many administrations, indicating that larger forces are at work than the particular management styles of individual presidents (Moe and Wilson 1994). Anyone seriously interested in the presidency has good reason to want to know more about such changes in the organization, procedures, and power of this institutional apparatus in the chief executive's office.

It is, however, a broader form of institutional knowledge that I want to emphasize at the end of these reflections. A few months before he left the White House, President Reagan observed, "You don't become president of the United States. You are given temporary custody of an institution called the Presidency, which belongs to our people."[1]

President Reagan's statement sounds good, and it resonates with many Americans' thinking today. But in terms of the institutional kind of knowledge I am trying to talk

---

[1] Address to the Republican National Convention, Aug. 15, 1988.

about, it is actually wrong and misguided. In our system of government, the office of the presidency does not belong to the people, not directly. It is an office that belongs to the Constitution—the fundamental set of rules for how to govern by the rule of law. It is the Constitution, not the presidential office, which is, in its turn, the creation and property of the people.

I do not think it is splitting hairs to recognize that the presidency belongs first to the Constitution and only indirectly to the people. Among other merits, this view invites us to understand presidential success or even greatness as an inherently constitutional idea. Institutionally understood, "success" means excelling in the context of a constitutional office, in this case an office holding the executive power. I realize that may sound unduly abstract. But the truth is that being careful about the meaning of words does matter for how we think about things. "Office" in its original and most meaningful sense entails obligations to act by virtue of being "positioned" in a certain place. The place being occupied is not a physical location but a moral space in a given order. Being "in office" is above all about being in a place of duty (Heclo 2008). Given our experience with presidents over the past fifty years, I think this seemingly old-fashioned notion of institutional "duty" is something presidential scholars have a scholarly obligation to reassert and disseminate as a form of knowledge about the presidency.

Constitutionalism

Ours is a constitutional democracy, not a plebiscitary form of government. It is easy enough to draw up a democratic Constitution. Someone simply writes laws stipulating that representatives of the people will be in charge of state structures of power; that those representatives are to be chosen through free, fair, and recurring elections; and so on. But it is quite another thing to draw out of the violent historical materials of any people something that can be called a constitutional democracy. The question now becomes not is a constitution democratic, but is a democracy constitutional?

To put it another way, the term "democratic constitution" is a concept that has no tension within itself. What are taken to be the defining characteristics of democracy are simply transcribed into provisions of a constitution that one can then call democratic. By contrast, constitutional democracy is an internally tensioned concept. "Democracy" says rule by the common people. "Constitutional" says not so fast, people; yours has to be a certain kind of rule, a rule observant of and subservient to fundamental law. We might even say that constitutional democracy is an anti-democratic concept, if by democratic we mean "an expression of human will that creates its own truths and values from day to day to suit its changing purposes." Lest a person agree too readily with that view of democracy, let me warn that it is actually a definition of fascism offered by Lawrence Dennis in 1936 (Dennis 1936, 105).

The principles and doctrines underlying this nation's political identity are not a day-to-day matter of the popular will. To the contrary, America's political identity—its self-understanding as a nation—is grounded and expressed in a historic achievement called constitutionalism. This is an achievement of immense human value anywhere in the world. It is the background understanding in which we Americans have placed our ultimate trust as a political society.

The Western idea of constitutionalism developed out of the thought and experiences of many centuries. The Founders who drafted the American Constitution understood that the revolutionary purpose for which they had fought was not to create a government based on the will of the majority. Willful government, whether based on the will of the one, the few, or the many, was simply a variation on the theme of perverted, arbitrary, self-interested rule. It was unfaithful to the purpose for which governments in all forms exist. Undergirding the whole subject of constitutional democracy is the idea that government exists to serve the interests of the governed, not the interests of the rulers. So they set out to design a formal constitution that would suppress the immediate "will" of the majority and instead elicit the judgment of majorities on matters conducive to general welfare of the whole people and the protection of their individual rights (cf. *Federalist* Nos. 10 and 51).

Since the first days of the Constitution's new national government, many Americans have regarded the Founders' design—the provisions for an indirect democracy aspiring to produce expressions of public judgment rather than majority will—as far too elitist. In the name of more direct popular government, parts of the Founders' design have been erased (indirect election of Senators), disregarded (state-level deliberations of the Electoral College), barely tolerated (federal judges' life terms of office), or supplanted (by communication technology, opinion polls, professional advocacy groups, transparency rules, and a series of other developments over the last fifty years) (Heclo 2009). And yet despite all of this, the idea of a government that is constitutional and not merely impulsively democratic remains central to our political identity. *Gore* v. *Bush* in 2000 was a recent trial of that claim, a trial that put faith in constitutionalism to an important test.

At the end of the day, the transfer of power occurred, the contending parties shook hands, and the streets remained free of rioters. But let us make no mistake about what happened. Citizens (many gnashing their teeth) simply went on about their daily business because of a priceless, if half-conscious, commitment to the constitutional rule of law, an inarticulate commitment that one might not be able to explain to a pollster, and all the more important because of that. Presidential scholars must never take this sort of background constitutionalism for granted or neglect the need to nourish it in their teachings. Ultimately it is because we care about constitutionalism that we should want to know more about the presidency.

Situational "Constitutionalism"

Certainly it is appropriate to continue studying how presidents try to get their way in governing. But today it seems more important than ever that research into the actions of presidents and their people be put in the larger context of our constitutional order as a going concern. Students of the presidency would be wise to consider their own work in light of what Steven Skowronek has called political time. I think doing so means facing up to some ugly truths about our political condition.

The political class as now constituted in America really does not seem to care very much about constitutional government, not in any deeply serious way. Perhaps largely as a result, neither do many (if not most) citizens. It is not difficult to fathom why this should be so. During the past fifty years politicians of both parties have been adept at teaching citizens a kind of "situational constitutionalism" (Pious 2002). Democrats and Republicans, liberals and conservatives, have supported and then pivoted 180 degrees to oppose expansive presidential powers, all depending on whether it was their man or the opposing party's man who was in the White House. Typically, the yearning for partisan advantage has overwhelmed any principled commitment to constitutional values. And likewise, thanks to this recent history, any twenty-first-century president can now expect to be engaged—from day one—in an ongoing struggle to establish the credibility of his words and the legitimacy of his actions. The result is presenting us today with a political theater of the absurd. Doing any job—much less being president—becomes strangely farcical if you must first convince people that the things you are saying are not lies and that what you are doing is not part of some sinister conspiracy. But in today's political culture, that is the state of affairs any president faces.

Ordinary Americans appear to have been learning well the lessons of situational constitutionalism that the political class has been teaching. President George W. Bush and officials in his administration repeatedly claimed broad, inherent executive powers, often connected with the war on terrorism. Most Americans seemed to respond simply based on whether or not they approved of the results obtained by such use of presidential power. Any constitutional understandings tended to be brushed aside as minor formalities or another part of the political spin process for gaming the system. President Bush's eventual plummet to a historic low in public approval ratings was a function of his failure to produce results, not of his unprecedented claims for executive power. The implication should be sobering. We may have reached a point in this country where a president who does deliver the popularly desired results, despite disregarding the constitutional rules of the game, can expect to be publicly applauded rather than condemned. This is a dangerous state of public understanding for a nation aspiring to be not only democratic but constitutional.

Rethinking Presidential Success

This brings us back to the issue of presidential success and failure. Researchers would do well to reexamine the narrow metrics they apply to this subject. By all the conventional measures of success-as-getting-your-way-in-governing—that is to say, high public approval ratings and reelection margins, a good legislative batting average, and evidence of transformative changes in domestic and foreign policy—the only president of the last fifty years who would rank as an approximate success is

Ronald Reagan. Not least of all, after the turmoil of the 1960s and 1970s Reagan restored a sense of the presidency as something manageable and dignified.

Yet for all his positive contributions to the image of the presidency, I would argue that Reagan was less successful in the context of the executive office known to the Constitution. Presidential legacies teach things, and Ronald Reagan did not teach us well about the executive power in our constitutional order. His zeal for rolling back Communist influence in Central America and his personal concern for the Americans held hostage in Lebanon led President Reagan and his aides into the non-constitutional and illegal activities of the Iran-Contra affair.

In the end most Americans seemed willing to forgive the Gipper as being merely uninformed or forgetful. But a constitutionally malignant trend had been reinforced. In asserting executive power Reagan and his officials violated congressional laws and the spirit of the Constitution. And equally clearly, they largely got away with it as a precedent for future years. The American presidency was left stronger, more manageable, and more dangerous.

I think we are in a time when presidential scholars owe it to their students and readers to give special emphasis to a broad-minded view of presidential performance, namely, success in the institutional terms of the office: How well has a president preserved any positive contributions to good government from preceding administrations? Has a president given the public reason to trust that the laws are being faithfully executed? How have a president's actions affected positively or negatively the leadership prospects of his successor, whatever the party? How well is a president teaching the American people about the realities of the challenges they face?

Obviously these and similar questions of this type cannot be answered by statistical measures. They require debatable judgments. But that should not stop us. I think scholars are charged by their duties of "office" to strive for judgments that are more rather than less well-informed, more even-handed rather than fashionably partisan. And if presidential scholars, who are also citizens, do not draw attention to and try to address these sorts of vital, institution-valuing questions, who will?

INTIMATIONS OF FORM

Whether or not one is a presidential scholar, the accumulated history should convince us of at least one thing about the presidency. It is a capacious office. It is capacious in the sense that both theoretically and practically, the presidency over time has been able to accommodate a wide variety of leadership styles and interpretations of executive power (Mansfield 1993). Informed by this history, presidential studies will always have to accept such ambivalence and resist the temptation to search out the one right model for presidential leadership.

As a constitutional office the presidency is capacious. But it is not formless. It derives its form from constitutionalism—the commitment to ordering power so that the rightful purpose of government, the interests of the governed, will be pursued through the rule of law. I have been arguing that constitutionalism is an important way of knowing about the presidency and that it should be more firmly inscribed in our studies of the subject.

Granted, we live in a modern culture deeply prejudiced against any talk of form and formality. So I should try to clarify what I mean by saying that the presidency is not formless and asserting there is a formal quality that should guide our understanding of performance.

Form, Formality, and Formalism

By "form" I mean the essential quality that is innate to something's nature. It is the controlling concept, the internal principle, which makes something what it is, rather than something else. For example, I think it is accurate to say that Abraham Lincoln understood the American Union in such "formal" terms. The Union was not something fundamentally united by its geography or institutions. It was united by a public dedication to justice centered on the equality of all men, the form having been articulated in the Declaration of Independence (Thurow 2000).

Likewise the presidency is a certain kind of executive power, the form of which is created by the Constitution. In this sense, the Constitution is the "formal cause" making the presidency the thing it is. I speak of "intimations" to suggest that form does not derive from simply the bare words in the Constitution. The grounding idea of constitutionalism itself imputes a form—a calling to appropriate behavior inherent within the structure of every president's situation in a constitutional democracy.

Respect for form does not decree stasis. Rather, it directs attention to the appropriateness of responses to changing circumstances. As new circumstances present themselves, appropriate responses are a developmental working out of what has heretofore lain hidden within the form of a constitutional chief executive. For example, as America emerged as a world power, it was wholly in keeping with the idea of a constitutional chief executive that the president should acquire new advisory and coordinating staffs such as the National Security Council. Without that, given changing circumstances, the form could not be realistically fulfilled.

By contrast, inappropriate responses—the breaking of form—consist in trying to build new things into the presidency, constructing as it were a new kind of office by adding materials from outside the form of a constitutional executive. Such additions "against form" make something less of what it is, not more. For example, the recent (but not unprecedented) tendency for retired high-ranking officers of the US military to not only advise but actively endorse presidential candidates is not illegal, but it does violate the form of the presidency as a constitutional executive. It does so because it both politicizes the public face of the military and militarizes what should be the wholly civilian identity of a constitutional commander-in-chief. Likewise the augmentation of presidential power through "signing statements" that nullify rather than either approve or veto legislation are a corruption rather than a fulfillment of constitutional form.

Without an appreciation for the transcendent value of constitutionalism, attention to form easily degenerates into formalism—in other words, meaningless gestures divorced from human realities. And this in turn provokes calls to "realism." But form *is* something real, not something concealing things as they really are.

Of course like everything else, formality can be distorted into something corrupt, an expression of hypocrisy. Yet that charge is itself revealing. As La Rochefoucauld's maxim puts it, "L'hypocrisie est un hommage que le vice rend à la vertu" ("Hypocrisy is the homage which vice pays to virtue"). Hypocrisy can work because there is something real to pretend about. Counterfeiting pays only if there is a currency of authentic value to be faked.

"Formality" that has not been corrupted into formalism is a mark of respect. Observing formalities is literally a bowing to and honoring of form. It means doing things with a conscious and careful appropriateness. Formality reveals and points to the intended purpose embodied in the form. For example, referring to the chief executive as "Mister President" is not an empty formality. It honors the formal idea of a person who is no more and no less than a citizen entrusted with executive power in our republican form of government. Or to take a less pleasant example, when Bill Clinton unleashed his libido in the president's Oval Office rather than the private residence upstairs, it was not just a case of personal high jinks or moral shortcoming. It was demonstrating a subversive disrespect for the constitutional form of the presidency.

I readily acknowledge that amid today's partisan warfare, what I am advocating can appear to be utterly naive. We live in a political culture of shouting and brute political force, not a place with regard for anything as delicate as "intimations." Moreover, as Tocqueville predicted, formality will be disdained in a democracy because it stands in the way of rushing directly to the object of desire. But as Tocqueville also pointed out, that is a tendency that should be resisted rather than accepted. He recognized that, more than other societies, democracies need formalities because they "serve as a barrier between the strong and the weak, the government and the governed, to hold back the one while the other has time to take his bearings" (1966, 673).

Far from being unrealistic and impractical, there are few things more practical than a serious regard for form. It cuts through the chaos of whatever understandings self-interested parties might arbitrarily seek to impose. It frees a person to think and work creatively with the nature of the situation rather than against the grain of things. To briefly conclude, let me suggest how a knowledge of form can help us take two particular bearings on the nature of the presidency, first as a collaborative office and second as a teaching office. Both are features embedded in the presidency as constitutionally given. Whether they are recognized and followed is another matter. Nonetheless, I would argue that they are two intimations of form that both presidents trying to succeed in the office and presidential scholars trying to understand the office ignore to their great disadvantage.

A Collaborative Office

There are only two promises in the presidential oath: to execute faithfully the office of president and to do one's utmost to safeguard the Constitution.[2] Those are not two separate duties but one duty facing in two directions. One aspect faces inward toward the work of the presidential office and the other outward toward the constitutional order containing that office. Logically it is the second aspect that puts the first in its place. Faithfully executing the work of the office must be consistent with and indeed subordinate to safeguarding the Constitution. If the Constitution-protecting clause is not preeminent, there is conceivably no constitutional office worth the name to execute.

As known to the Constitution, the executive power is singular but the executive branch is not unitary. The executive power is vested in a single person, not some plural head or collegial body. At the same time, the departments, agencies, and offices of the executive branch are created by acts of Congress. For their sustenance, they depend on the continuing flow of funds and authorizations from Congress. The substance of their work consists in laws and other types of guidance from Congress, often vague and inconsistent in nature.

This is, of course, the invitation to endless mutual dealing and struggle between divided institutions sharing powers. But it also imparts a form to appropriate behavior inherent within the structure of every president's situation under the Constitution. And that is not a calling to a "great man" theory of history or to executive unilateralism in governing. Rather the essential appropriateness inhering in the nature of this Constitution is a calling for presidential leadership to be heavily collaborative.

By this I do not mean to say that presidents should be expected to operate through committees or partnerships or collegially. Under our Constitution, the president has no equal colleague. By collaborative leadership, I mean laboring together with other parties responsible for governing, sometimes leading from the front but sometimes and under other circumstances leading from the middle or rear of the procession. The collaboration called for is an ever-churning mixture of struggle and cooperation. Rightly understood, presidential "weakness" is not an excuse for unilateralism but rather an invitation to more effective leadership in collaboration.

Given today's highly charged partisanship and the permanent campaign that has become a way of governing, I certainly do not intend to minimize the difficulty of collaborative leadership. However, this particular appreciation for form has very practical value. It is often said that only the most intractable problems make their

---

[2] "I do solemnly swear (or affirm) that I will faithfully execute the office of President of the United States, and will to the best of my ability, preserve, protect, and defend the Constitution of the United States."

way to the president's desk, the place where the truly tough decisions have to get made. But there is also a reverse dynamic at work. Problems can become intractable as participants anticipate unloading decisions onto a chief executive who always stands ready to provide the final word. Everything about our current system of endless campaigning helps suffocate the good sense that should make any leading politician very cautious about claiming to be America's answer-man.

A president who insists that other people bang their heads together to figure out some possible answers may be exercising a more subtle and productive form of leadership than the hyped-up kind of "follow me" drama beloved by our pop culture. Thus, it was basically in this collaborative form that the most "ideological" of our modern presidents, Ronald Reagan, achieved relative success in reforming social security and the federal tax code. Likewise it was the lack of such collaborative leadership that did much to produce Clinton's disastrous failure in health care reform and George W. Bush's even more disastrous invasion of Iraq. No modern president can go so far in a "hidden hand" direction as Lao-tzu recommended, but there is deep wisdom in his words: a leader is best when men barely know he is there, not so good when men obey and acclaim him.

In emphasizing the collaborative, subtle form of governing that is embedded in America's constitutional design, I am certainly not saying anything new. From the beginning, the Founders recognized that the constituent parts of the new federal government would be kept "in their proper places" by the constitutional necessity for their "mutual relations," which is to say, by their shared rather than cleanly partitioned powers (*Federalist* No. 51). In that sense I am merely urging further development of presidential research along a line already traced in several contemporary studies. Such research demonstrates the value of weighing presidential success and failure in terms of our larger governing system and not simply from the offices at 1600 Pennsylvania Avenue (Mayhew 1991; Jones 1994).

Even if it is not saying anything fundamentally new, to say the old things in the new context created by the experience of the last half century is to do new work. It is to help keep alive what could easily become a dead tradition. Political scientists obviously do not need to duplicate the massive literature on the presidency and Constitution that is available for them in law libraries. And as I noted earlier, presidential researchers are well aware of the Constitution's congressional and judicial checks on presidential power. The problem is that too often the big picture of constitutionalism, which I suggest is the ultimate reason for studying the presidency, gets overshadowed by the ostensibly Big Question of presidents getting their way in governing.

Political scientists are rightly concerned with the actual exercise of presidential power. But serious research and teaching on that subject has an obligation to understand governing as more than a horse race. Today that seems almost the only way we are able to see elections. If presidential studies cooperate in interpreting our whole constitutional system as an extension of horse-race thinking, then something has gone wrong in our approach. The effect is to turn the constitutional rules of the game into so much common material to be manipulated as partisans try to win at all costs. In that case we should at least be honest about what has happened. People might mouth nice feelings about the Constitution, but as a political society they will have given up on constitutionalism. And with that, the last chapter on this experiment in self-government will probably have begun to be written.

A Teaching Office

A second aspect of form that I would like to highlight concerns the didactic quality of the office. Despite everything that might be said about leadership-in-collaboration, the ground tone underlying the presidential office is singularity. There is nothing like it in our constitutional order. That is less because of the office's vast power and more because of its unique personal quality. A president can command the public's attention, emotions, and thoughts as no other person in the nation can, at least for as long as he retains credibility with the public.

This is another area where presidential studies have fallen prey to the strategic, Big Question, getting-his-way perspective and so have diminished the issue to matters of presidential "rhetoric" or "going public." The standard of success becomes electoral and legislative box scores, not education and enlightenment. But attention to constitutional form should tell us there is a didactic quality inherent within the structure of every president's situation. Teaching is not a "leadership style" to be picked up or put aside at will, and it is something much deeper than the smart use of public relations techniques to "sell" the president's agenda. In the constitutional structure of the situation there is no choice but to teach, in ways intended and unintended, with words and with deeds.

Great presidents have seemed to understand that—Washington in his deliberate setting of precedents and in his addresses concerning the new republic, Lincoln throughout his career but especially at Gettysburg and the Second Inaugural, and FDR in his carefully explained actions and fireside chats during depression and war. Whether it is done well or poorly, teaching is in the formal nature of the presidency given its personal quality in the constitutional order.

I believe it is here that one of Richard Neustadt's major insights has remained overlooked and undeveloped. The issue comes up in the context of asking why presidential prestige varies (Neustadt 1960, 94–105). In Neustadt's account popularity shifts are produced not by personality appraisals (which are fixed very early in a president's relationship with the public) but by perceptions of the office. What causes shifts in images of the office, and consequent shifts in presidential popularity, are the real life "happenings" that impinge on people's daily existence and what the president teaches people about those happenings.

Given the kind of knowledge I have been discussing, it is unfortunate that Neustadt took "the Big Question's" narrowly strategic view and simply asked how presidents in this situation can guard their popular "prestige." But his view of presidents' inherent teaching role is nevertheless instructive. As he rightly observes, presidents can make few choices that will control the large happenings that touch people's lives. To protect his prestige, the president is left with choices that teach people about the meaning of their encounter with happenings, meanings "that will foster tolerance for him." What Neustadt recognizes is that by the nature of his situation, a president is always teaching, to his benefit or harm. He is teaching people about himself by teaching them about events. The choice is not whether but when, how, and what to teach. A president teaches and people learn not so much by his words as by his actions or inactions.

Here, for our purposes, we come to the nub of the matter. What presidents must teach amounts to one word: realism. As Neustadt puts it, "the enemy of [presidential] prestige is unreality." The popular frustration that threatens prestige comes from people who lack a realistic understanding of the happenings that touch them. For the president's own sake, his must be "action that makes for enlightenment." Why? Because effective presidential teaching helps (a) disabuse the public of groundless hopes, "pleasures he cannot provide"; (b) reduce outrage and dismay when people "lack preparedness for pains he cannot stop"; and (c) promote forbearance to "make them think the hardship necessary... and make them want to bear it with grace."

CONCLUSION

At the outset I noted a puzzling fact about the last fifty years. As research on the presidency has grown exponentially, the performance of presidents has, if anything, deteriorated. During this time we have certainly had presidents who were extremely shrewd politicians—men (and people advising them) who were adept at calculating their power stakes and strategizing about how to get their way in governing. In fact it seems the more raw cleverness in the politician—say, a Nixon, Johnson, Clinton, or George W. Bush—the greater the ultimate failure. Might this have anything to do with a failure to abide by form, not least the form expressed in the collaborative and teaching nature of this constitutional office?

Now there is something worth a bit of reflection.

REFERENCES

ABRAHAM, H. J. 1999. *Justices, Presidents, and Senators: A History of the U.S. Supreme Court Appointments from Washington to Clinton*. Lanham, MD: Rowman & Littlefield.

BARRETT, A. W. 2004. Gone Public: The Impact of Going Public on Presidential Legislative Success. *American Politics Research*, 32: 338–70.

BAUM, M., and KERNELL, S. 1999. Has Cable Ended the Golden Age of Presidential Television? *American Political Science Review*, 93: 99–114.

BINDER, S., and MALTZMAN, F. 2002. Senatorial Delay in Confirming Federal Judges, 1947–1998. *American Journal of Political Science*, 46: 190–9.

BOND, J. R., and FLEISHER, R. (eds.) 2000. *Polarized Politics: Congress and the President in a Partisan Era*. Washington, DC: Congressional Quarterly Press.

BURKE, J. P. 2003. The Institutional Presidency. Pp. 399–424 in *The Presidency and the Political System*, ed. M. Nelson. Washington, DC: Congressional Quarterly Press.

CALABRESI, S. G., and YOO, C. S. 2008. *The Unitary Executive: Presidential Power from Washington to Bush*. New Haven, CT: Yale University Press.

CAMERON, C. 2000. *Veto Bargaining: The Politics of Negative Power*. New York: Cambridge University Press.

CANES-WRONE, B. 2005. *Who's Leading Whom?* Chicago: University of Chicago Press.

CEASER, J. W. 1979. *Presidential Selection: Theory and Development*. Princeton, NJ: Princeton University Press.

COHEN, J. E. 2008. *The Presidency in the Era of 24-Hour News*. Princeton, NJ: Princeton University Press.

COOPER, P. 2002. *By Order of the President: The Use and Abuse of Executive Direct Action*. Lawrence: University Press of Kansas.

CROCKETT, D. A. 2002. *The Opposition Presidency: Leadership and the Constraints of History*. College Station: Texas A&M University Press.

DENNIS, L. 1936. *The Coming American Fascism*. New York: Harper & Brothers.

DE TOCQUEVILLE, A. 1966. *Democracy in America*, ed. J. P. Mayer and M. Lerner, trans. G. Lawrence. New York: Harper & Row.

DICKINSON, M. J. 2005. Neustadt, New Institutionalism, and Presidential Decision Making: A Theory and Test. *Presidential Studies Quarterly*, 35: 259–89.

EBIN, J. 2005. Archives Essay. Pp. 543–5 in *President Reagan: The Triumph of Imagination*. ed. R. Reeves. New York: Simon & Schuster.

EDWARDS, G. C., III. 1989. *At the Margins: Presidential Leadership of Congress*. New Haven, CT: Yale University Press.

—— 2002. From the Editor. *Presidential Studies Quarterly*, 32: 641.

—— 2003. *On Deaf Ears: The Limits of the Bully Pulpit*. New Haven, CT: Yale University Press.

—— 2008. *Governing by Campaigning: The Politics of the Bush Presidency*, 2nd edn. New York: Longman.

FISHER, L. 2007. Invoking Inherent Powers: A Primer. *Presidential Studies Quarterly*, 37: 1–22.

FRIEDMAN, J. (ed.) 2008. *The Rhetorical Presidency* after Twenty Years. *Critical Review*, 19/2–3.

GOLDMAN, S. 1997. *Picking Federal Judges: Lower Court Selection from Roosevelt through Reagan*. New Haven, CT: Yale University Press.

GREENSTEIN, F. 1982. *The Hidden-Hand Presidency: Eisenhower as Leader*. New York: Basic Books.

HANEY, P. J. 1997. *Organizing for Foreign Policy Crises: Presidents, Advisers, and the Management of Decision-Making*. Ann Arbor: University of Michigan Press.

HECLO, H. 1977. *A Government of Strangers: Executive Politics in Washington*. Washington, DC: Brookings.

—— 2000. Campaigning and Governing: A Conspectus. In *The Permanent Campaign and its Future*, ed. N. J. Ornstein and T. E. Mann. Washington, DC: AEI Press.

—— 2008. *On Thinking Institutionally*. Boulder, CO: Paradigm Press.

—— 2009. The Corruption of Democratic Leadership. In *America at Risk: Dangers on the Horizon*, ed. R. Faulkner and S. Shell. Ann Arbor: University of Michigan Press.

HESS, S., with PFIFFNER, J. P. 2002. *Organizing the Presidency*, 3rd edn. Washington, DC: Brookings.

HOWELL, W. G. 2003. *Power without Persuasion: The Politics of Direct Presidential Action*. Princeton, NJ: Princeton University Press.

—— 2006. Executives: The American Presidency. In *The Oxford Handbook of Political Institutions*, ed. R. A. W. Rhodes, S. H. Binder, and B. A. Rockman. New York: Oxford University Press.

—— and PEVEHOUSE, J. C. 2007. *While Dangers Gather: Congressional Checks on Presidential War-Making Powers*. Princeton, NJ: Princeton University Press.

JACOBS, L., and SHAPIRO, R. Y. 2000. *Politicians Don't Pander: Political Manipulation and the Loss of Democratic Responsiveness*. Chicago: University of Chicago Press.

JAMES, S. C. 2005. The Evolution of the Presidency: Between the Promise and the Fear. In *Institutions of American Democracy: The Executive Branch*, ed. J. D. Aberbach and M. A. Peterson. New York: Oxford University Press.

JONES, C. O. 1994. *The Presidency in a Separated System*. Washington, DC: Brookings.

—— 2003. Richard Neustadt: Public Servant as Scholar. *Annual Review of Political Science*, 6: 1–22.

KERNELL, S. 1997. *Going Public: New Strategies of Presidential Leadership*. Washington, DC: Congressional Quarterly Press.

KRAUSE, G. A., and COHEN, J. E. 2000. Opportunity, Constraints, and the Development of the Institutional Presidency: The Case of Executive Order Issuance, 1939–1996. *Journal of Politics*, 62: 88–114.

KUMAR, M. J. 2007. *Managing the President's Message: The White House Communications Operation*. Baltimore: Johns Hopkins University Press.

LANDY, M., and MILKIS, S. M. 2000. *Presidential Greatness*. Lawrence: University Press of Kansas.

LEWIS, D. E. 2005. Staffing Alone: Unilateral Action and the Politicization of the Executive Office of the President, 1988–2004. *Presidential Studies Quarterly*, 35: 440–56.

—— 2008. *The Politics of Presidential Appointments: Political Control and Bureaucratic Performance*. Princeton, NJ: Princeton University Press.

LOWI, T. J. 1986. *The Personal President: Power Invested, Promise Unfulfilled*. Ithaca, NY: Cornell University Press.

McCARTY, N., and Razaghian, R. 1999. Advice and Consent: Senate Response to Executive Branch Nominations, 1885–1996. *American Journal of Political Science*, 43: 1122–43.

MANSFIELD, H. C., JR. 1993. *Taming the Prince: The Ambivalence of Modern Executive Power*. Baltimore: Johns Hopkins University Press.

MAYER, K. 2001. *With the Stroke of a Pen: Executive Orders and Presidential Power*. Princeton, NJ: Princeton University Press.

MAYHEW, D. R. 1991. *Divided We Govern: Party Control, Lawmaking, and Investigations, 1946–1990*. New Haven, CT: Yale University Press.

MILKIS, S. M., and MILEUR, J. M. (eds.) 2005. *The Great Society and the High Tide of Liberalism*. Amherst: University of Massachusetts Press.

—— and NELSON, M. 2007. *The American Presidency: Origins and Development, 1776–2007*, 5th edn. Washington, DC: CQ Press.

MOE, T. M. 1985. The Politicized Presidency. In *The New Direction in American Politics*, ed. J. E. Chubb and P. E. Peterson. Washington, DC: Brookings Institution.

—— 1993. Presidents, Institutions and Theory. *In Researching the Presidency: Vital Questions, New Approaches*, ed. G. C. Edwards III, J. H. Kessel, and B. A. Rockman. Pittsburgh: University of Pittsburgh Press.

MOE, T. M., and HOWELL, W. 1999. Unilateral Action and Presidential Power: A Theory. *Presidential Studies Quarterly,* 29: 850–72.

—— and WILSON, S. A. 1994. Presidents and the Politics of Structure. *Law and Contemporary Problems,* 7: 1–44.

NATHAN, R. P. 1983. *The Plot that Failed: Nixon and the Administrative Presidency.* New York: John Wiley & Sons.

NEUSTADT, R. 1960. *Presidential Power.* New York: John Wiley.

PETERSON, M. A. 1990. *Legislating Together: The White House and Capitol Hill from Eisenhower to Reagan.* Cambridge, MA: Harvard University Press.

PFIFFNER, J. P. 2008. *Power Play: The Bush Presidency and the Constitution.* Washington, DC: Brookings Institution.

PIOUS, R. M. 2002. Why Do Presidents Fail? *Presidential Studies Quarterly,* 32: 724–43.

RUDALEVIGE, A. 2002. *Managing the President's Program: Presidential Leadership and Legislative Policy Formation.* Princeton, NJ: Princeton University Press.

—— 2005. *The New Imperial Presidency: Renewing Presidential Power after Watergate.* Ann Arbor: University of Michigan Press.

SCHATTSCHNEIDER, E. E. 1969. *Two Hundred Million Americans in Search of a Government.* New York: Holt, Rinehart, Winston.

SHULL, S. A. 2006. *Policy by Other Means: Alternative Policymaking by Presidents.* College Station: Texas A&M University Press.

SKOWRONEK, S. 1993. *The Politics Presidents Make: Leadership from John Adams to George Bush.* Cambridge, MA: Harvard University Press.

SYKES, P. L. 2000. *Presidents and Prime Ministers: Conviction Politics in the Anglo-American Tradition.* Lawrence: University Press of Kansas.

THUROW, G. E. 2000. Abraham Lincoln and the Spirit of American Statesmanship. In *Educating the Prince: Essays in Honor of Harvey Mansfield,* ed. H. Claflin, M. Blitze, and W. Kristol. Lanham, MD: Rowman & Littlefield.

TULIS, J. K. 1987. *The Rhetorical Presidency.* Princeton, NJ: Princeton University Press.

WARBER, A. 2006. *Executive Orders and the Modern Presidency: Legislating from the Oval Office.* New York: Lynne Rienner.

YOO, J. 2005. *The Powers of War and Peace: The Constitution and Foreign Affairs after 9/11.* Chicago: Chicago University Press.

CHAPTER 34

POLITICAL SCIENTISTS AND THE PUBLIC LAW TRADITION

LOUIS FISHER

POLITICAL scientists, historians, and specialists in public administration have largely abandoned what was once an essential part of their discipline: public law. For some time now the study of the judiciary has been narrowly confined. Students take classes in constitutional law, perhaps reduced from two semesters to one. They are likely to be fed a steady diet of case law with little understanding of constitutional law in broader terms, including the contributions of Congress, presidents, executive agencies, the fifty states, and the general public. Professors teach courses on judicial politics and judicial process, but the substance of court rulings is subordinated to describing how judges go about their business. How are judges selected? What steps are involved in litigation? How does the judiciary fit into the larger political system? What are the limits of judicial power? How do judicial decisions impact society?

Professors are not expected to independently and authoritatively critique how well the judiciary interprets the Constitution. Courses in administrative law might focus on the content of judicial decisions, but this amounts primarily to the interpretation of statutes, not the Constitution. Those courses are devoted essentially to process. As to classes on the presidency, textbooks and course outlines cover the major court rulings on the president's removal power, delegation of legislative power, foreign affairs (*Curtiss-Wright*), the war power, and recent decisions on military tribunals,

Guantanamo, and enemy combatants. But the treatment is largely descriptive, not analytical. It is rare for a political scientist or historian to dissect a judicial opinion and find its legal reasoning deficient. Political scientists are unlikely to be called before a congressional committee to testify on constitutional and legal matters or even to be solicited for advice on those issues. It was not always so.

THE ORIGINAL PLAN

The first graduate school of political science, established at Columbia College in 1880, was devoted to the study of history, law, and philosophy. The college created a department called Public Law and Government. It kept that name for years until the late 1960s or early 1970s, when it morphed into the Department of Political Science. America's first journal of political science, *Political Science Quarterly*, invited manuscripts that explored the "Historical, Statistical and Comparative Study of Politics, Economics, and Public Law" (*Political Science Quarterly* 1886). The introductory essay regarded politics, economics, and law as "interdependent." Investigating one implied investigating the others. "Choose which you will, the others are necessary auxiliaries" (8).

When the American Political Science Association was founded in 1903, it adopted as its mission the scientific study of government, law, and administration. Of six distinct topics laid out, two focused on comparative legislation and political theory. The other four were on law: international law, including diplomacy; constitutional law, including law making and political parties; administrative law, including colonial, national, state, and local; and historical jurisprudence (Proceedings 1905, 11). The initial orientation of public administration was strongly toward law. Leonard D. White's 1939 edition of *Introduction to Public Administration* emphasized the pivotal importance of legal research (White 1939). The historian and presidential scholar Edward S. Corwin was regularly invited to Congress to testify on constitutional matters. So were other political scientists and historians.

Eventually, an artificial wedge was driven between the disciplines of political science and law. A 1963 study listed the fields of political science in which the most significant work was being done. At the top of the list: general politics and behavioralism. Next in importance came comparative government and international relations. Public administration, political theory, and American government and politics followed. Stranded at the bottom was public law (Somit and Tanenhaus 1963, 941).

The doctrine of mechanical jurisprudence and the supposed non-political character of the judiciary were convenient, if false, excuses for keeping political scientists from public law. Judicial rulings were seen as something remote instead of one more form of political activity. C. Herman Pritchett perceptively noted that political science and law drifted apart for semantic, philosophical, and practical reasons: "Law is a prestigious symbol, whereas politics tends to be a dirty word. Law is stability; politics is chaos. Law is impersonal; politics is personal. Law is given; politics is free choice. Law is reason; politics is prejudice and self-interest. Law is justice; politics is who gets there first with the most" (Pritchett 1969, 31).

Justices of the Supreme Court contribute to this misconception. The decision by courts not to rule on cases involving "political questions" encourages the belief that a gulf does indeed separate law and politics. Chief Justice John Marshall in *Marbury* v. *Madison* (1803) insisted that "Questions in their nature political ... can never be made in this court."[1] Yet in that very decision he established a political precedent of far-reaching importance: the right of the judiciary to review and overturn the actions of other branches. Justice Oliver Wendell Holmes, Jr., hearing a litigant claim that a dispute over a party primary was non-justiciable because of its political character, regarded objections of that nature as "little more than a play upon words."[2]

POLITICAL SCIENTISTS AS OUTSIDERS

The contemporary assumption that non-lawyers lack the capacity to interpret and analyze constitutional issues runs deep. On June 28, 1958, Justice Felix Frankfurter wrote to six of his colleagues, objecting to a request by Justice Hugo Black to delay the release of a decision until he could review some recent publications by political scientist J. A. C. Grant. Frankfurter found no reason for a delay: "Dr. Grant's articles, to which Brother Black makes reference, are valuable compilations of materials, but in good conscience, Grant does not add to the sum of ideas with which one is dealing with this problem has long been familiar. Dr. Grant is a political scientist and not a lawyer, and like almost all political scientists who write on constitutional law problems, even some of the best of them, like Dr. Corwin, they cavalierly disregard what to us lawyers is essential. The notion that Grant's articles should make us reverse the whole current of our constitutional law strikes me a bit odd" (D. J. Danelski, personal communication 2008). The phrase "our constitutional law" apparently reserved the founding document exclusively to attorneys.

Frankfurter's letter reminded me of an experience I had with the Congressional Research Service when I arrived in September 1970. I spent a lot of time in the library of the American Law Division (ALD). Attorneys there found it strange that a political scientist would want to read legal materials (much less understand them). After three or four of them had questioned my presence in their hallowed quarters, I asked one if he was familiar with the "Annotated Constitution," a massive tome of more than 2,000 pages. "Of course I am," he quickly replied. Did he know who wrote the initial

---

[1] 5 US (1 Cr.) 137, 170 (1803).   [2] *Nixon v. Herndon*, 273 US 536, 540 (1927).

edition? "Why yes I do. Edward Corwin." And do you think, I continued, he was a lawyer? Silence. I was left alone after that.

For a number of years, I was the only individual in the Library of Congress to testify before congressional committees on constitutional issues. ALD decided it would prepare memoranda and reports on constitutional and legal issues but would not have its attorneys testify. As a result, I had the field to myself for quite a stretch. After a while, ALD relaxed its policy and allowed a number of legal specialists to testify.

Almost fifty appearances before congressional committees have yielded many choice moments for me. Here are two. In 1985 I was asked to testify on the constitutionality of the Gramm–Rudman–Hollings deficit control bill. ALD had prepared a short memo concluding that the bill was free of constitutional defects. The Senate let the bill move forward without hearings. The House Government Operations Committee invited four people to testify: Office of Management and Budget Director Jim Miller, Comptroller General Charles Bowsher, Congressional Budget Office Director Rudy Penner, and me.

Miller, Bowsher, and Penner did not address constitutional issues. I came for that purpose and told the committee the bill was unconstitutional because it gave executive duties to the Comptroller General, an agent of the legislative branch. A committee member asked whether I was familiar with the ALD analysis that found no constitutional problems. I said I had read it. The member asked whether I was an attorney. I explained that my training was in political science but reiterated why Congress could not give executive duties to a legislative officer. The bill was enacted, litigated on an expedited basis, and reached the Supreme Court, which held that it was unconstitutional because Congress cannot vest in the Comptroller General duties of an executive nature.[3]

Here is a second example of a political scientist playing in the constitutional sandbox. In 1998 the Senate Intelligence Committee asked me to review a memo from the Office of Legal Counsel in the Justice Department. The memo concluded that a bill giving whistleblower rights to employees in the Central Intelligence Agency was unconstitutional because it interfered with the president's exclusive control over the executive branch. I prepared for the committee a memo highly critical of OLC's analysis. The committee asked me to testify on the bill. I appeared with a law professor, Peter Raven-Hansen, and both of us found the OLC analysis unpersuasive and misleading on many points. The committee asked me to return a week later to testify again, this time alongside an OLC attorney. We appeared and took questions. I recall that all of the Senators were there. After the hearing concluded a committee staffer called me at my office within a couple of hours and said the committee was reporting the bill nineteen to zero. OLC's constitutional interpretation encountered a bipartisan and unanimous rejection. I testified before the House Intelligence Committee, worked with both committees on bill language, and the bill became law.[4]

[3] *Bowsher* v. *Synar*, 478 US 714 (1986).
[4] Intelligence Community Whistleblower Protection Act of 1998, 112 Stat. 2413–17 (Oct. 20, 1998).

JETTISONING CONSTITUTIONAL LAW

The public law model developed by Corwin and others entered into a sharp decline after the Second World War. Prominent political scientists and historians decided to champion presidential power as the best hope for democracy, all at the cost of checks and balances. Separation of powers seemed to these scholars antiquated and irrelevant to contemporary needs. Constitutional liberties would be secured not by structure but by well-meaning and competent presidents. Part of the decision to trust in the presidency was the perceived need to vigorously combat international Communism. This new orientation was evident in the scholarly response to President Harry Truman going to war against North Korea in 1950. His initiative marked the first time in American history that a president took the country from a state of peace to a state of war without coming to Congress either for a declaration or an authorization (Fisher 2004, 81–100).

There were ample grounds for the academic community to challenge and reject the legality and constitutionality of Truman's action. He attempted to play down the constitutional significance of his military operation by resorting to semantics. Asked at a press conference whether the country was at war, he replied: "We are not at war" (Public Papers of the Presidents 1950, 504). A reporter enquired whether it would be more correct to call the conflict "a police action under the United Nations." Truman agreed with that assessment: "That is exactly what it amounts to" (ibid.). Other than supplying a veneer of legality, it was clear that the UN had no control over the war. The United States supplied the troops and the money and suffered the overwhelming number of casualties and deaths. The Security Council asked the United States to designate the commander of the forces and authorized the "unified command at its discretion to use the United Nations flag" (ibid. 52). Truman promptly selected General Douglas MacArthur to serve as commander of this so-called unified command (ibid.).

The question of whether the Korean conflict was a war or a UN police action eventually found its way into the courts. Judges had to interpret insurance policies that promised benefits when someone died in "time of war." Federal and state courts had no difficulty in concluding that the hostilities in Korea amounted to war.[5] During Senate hearings in June 1951, Secretary of State Dean Acheson stopped dancing around the issue and admitted the obvious: "In the usual sense of the word there is a war" (US Congress 1951, 2014).

To accept the UN Security Council as a substitute for Congress, in terms of "authorizing" military operations, one would have to argue that the president and the Senate, acting through the treaty process, could create an international body that dispensed with future congressional control. Through that process, the president and the Senate would obliterate the war power of the House of Representatives, the

---

[5] Weissman v. Metropolitan Life Ins. Co., 112 F. Supp. 420, 425 (SD Cal. 1953); Gagliomella v. Metropolitan Life Ins. Co., 122 F. Supp. 246 (D. Mass. 1954); Carius v. New York Life Insurance Co., 124 F. Supp. 388 (D. Ill. 1954); Western Reserve Life Ins. Co. v. Meadows, 261 SW 2d 554 (Tex. 1953).

political body closest to the people. Such an argument is too far fetched to be taken seriously. How did the academic community respond to Truman's action?

Truman's initiative in Korea was vigorously defended by a number of leading academics who saw in the presidency the qualities of energy, decisiveness, and centralized power needed to withstand Communism. Oddly, the public debate about the legality of the war centered around comments not from attorneys or political scientists but from three historians: Henry Steele Commager, Arthur M. Schlesinger, Jr., and Edward S. Corwin. The first two strongly supported Truman; the third did not.

HENRY STEELE COMMAGER

In an article for the *New York Times* on January 14, 1951, Commager set out to discredit Truman's critics. Senator Robert Taft said that the decision to send US troops to Korea without congressional authorization "usurped" power from Congress and "violated the laws and the Constitution of the United States." Those objections, Commager wrote, "have no support in law or in history." As to general constitutional principles, Commager found the historical pattern so clear and obvious and "so hackneyed a theme that even politicians might reasonably be expected to be familiar with it" (Commager 1951a, 11). Powerful claims, but Commager's own reading of law and history was shallow and uninformed.

Commager quoted John Quincy Adams for the proposition that however startled people may be at the idea that the president "has the power of involving the nation in war, even without consulting Congress, an experience of fifty years has proved that in numberless cases he has and must have exercised the power" (ibid.). Adams offered those remarks during a eulogy to James Madison, who died in 1836. What presidential wars could Adams (or Commager) have had in mind? For Commager, the Neutrality Proclamation of 1793 issued by President George Washington "might well have involved us in war with France" (ibid.). "Might well have"? That hardly counts as a presidential war. Washington's intent was to keep America out of war, not in it. Moreover, the proclamation was so lacking in legal authority that Washington had to appeal to Congress for statutory support, leading to the Neutrality Act a year later (Fisher 2004, 26–9).

When violations of the Neutrality Act ended up in court, federal judges repudiated the claim that a president could somehow start a war. The president did not possess the power of making war: "That power is exclusively vested in Congress."[6] Although the president has an implied power to resist invasions, there was a "manifest distinction" between defensive actions and offensive operations: "It is the exclusive province of Congress to change a state of peace into a state of war."[7]

---

[6] *United States* v. *Smith*, 27 Fed. Cas. 1192, 1230 (CCNY 1806) (No. 16,342).   [7] Ibid.

Commager next remarked: "On his own initiative John Adams overrode his cabinet and his party and sent commissioners to France to end the quasi-war with that country." Through this action, Adams obviously took steps to end a war, not start one. When he thought that war against France was necessary, he did not claim unilateral authority to order military operations. He came to Congress and sought statutory authority (Fisher 2004, 24). Commager's third example: "On his own initiative Jefferson, in theory a strict constructionist, inaugurated the war with the Barbary pirates" (Commager 1951a, 11). Military conflicts with the Barbary pirates had plagued presidents from the beginning of the Republic. Jefferson took certain *defensive* actions in the Mediterranean but came to Congress to seek authority for anything that went "beyond the line of defense." Congress enacted ten statutes to authorize military action by Presidents Jefferson and Madison in the Barbary wars (Fisher 2004, 32–7).

Commager claimed to find precedents in the Civil War. In *The Prize Cases* (1863), "involving the legality of Lincoln's blockade—and by implication of his powers to make war—the court held that it was for the President to determine when war comes, and that he is 'not only authorized but bound to resist force by force' " (Commager 1951a, 24). Commager confused defensive and offensive actions and failed to explain the difference between presidential actions at a time of domestic insurrection and military operations against another country. The Supreme Court saw clearly what Commager did not. Justice Robert C. Grier carefully limited the president's power to defensive actions within the country. The president, he said, "has no power to initiate or declare a war against either a foreign nation or a domestic State."[8] During oral argument, Richard Henry Dana, Jr., who was representing the White House, made precisely the same point. Lincoln's actions had nothing to do with "the right *to initiate a war, as a voluntary act of sovereignty.* That is vested only in Congress."[9]

Commager's final point explored the president's duty to implement treaties. In that process he found an independent source of presidential power to take the country to war: "[I]t is an elementary fact that must never be lost sight of that treaties are laws and carry with them the same obligation as laws. When the Congress passed the United Nations Participation Act it made the obligations of the Charter of the United Nations law, binding on the President" (ibid. 24). Commager ignored Truman's pledge to the Senate in 1945, the legislative history of the UN Charter, and the express language of the UN Participation Act.

During debate on the Charter, senators considered language calling for member states to enter into "special agreements" when sending military forces to the UN for collective action. President Truman wired this note to the Senate from Potsdam: "When any such agreements or agreements are negotiated it will be my purpose to ask the Congress for appropriate legislation to approve them" (US Congress 1945, 8185). He promised to seek advance statutory support from Congress. There was no claim of independent and inherent powers to act unilaterally. Article 41 of the UN Charter called on all member states to ratify the agreements "in accordance with their respective constitutional processes." Congress implemented that provision by passing the UN Participation Act

---

[8] *The Prize Cases*, 67 US 635, 668 (1863).   [9] Ibid. 660 (emphasis in original).

of 1945. Section 6 states with singular clarity that the special agreements "shall be subject to the approval of the Congress by appropriate Act of joint resolution."[10] The legislative history of the UN Charter and the UN Participate underscores congressional control over the initiation of war against other countries (Fisher 2004, 81–95).

Commager wrote a second piece for the *New York Times*, again defending Truman's action in Korea. He claimed that "the limitation on the Executive power—with a corresponding expansion of the legislative power—finds no justification in our history." While the generation of Thomas Jefferson and Thomas Paine looked back to the historical use of executive power as "always dangerous," Commager argued that the experience of democracy in America "teaches a different moral." Strong presidents who use their power boldly do not threaten democracy or the Constitution. "There is, in fact, no basis in our own history for the distrust of the Executive authority" (Commager 1951b, 15). Quite a selective reading of history! Commager saw no need for checks and balances or the system of separation of powers, all of which form the heart of popular and constitutional government. Some years later Commager would publicly retreat from his scholarship.

ARTHUR SCHLESINGER

Also defending Truman's war in Korea was Arthur Schlesinger. In a letter to the *New York Times*, he rejected Taft's statement that Truman "had no authority whatever to commit American troops to Korea without consulting Congress and without Congressional approval." Truman's action, Taft said, "simply usurped authority, in violation of the laws and the Constitution." Schlesinger dismissed Taft's position as "demonstrably irresponsible." Citing Jefferson's use of force against the Barbary pirates, Schlesinger argued that presidents "have repeatedly committed American armed forces abroad without prior Congressional consultation or approval." Schlesinger threw down this gauntlet: "Until Senator Taft and his friends succeed in rewriting American history according to their own specifications these facts must stand as obstacles to their efforts to foist off their current political prejudices as eternal American verities" (Schlesinger 1951, 28).

Years later, in the midst of the Vietnam War, Schlesinger would admit that his "facts" were illusory. It was he, not Taft, who attempted to rewrite American history. He, not Taft, relied on political prejudices. No similarity existed between Jefferson's defensive actions against the Barbary pirates and Truman's multi-year war in Korea. Jefferson came to Congress for authority; Truman did not. Jefferson understood congressional prerogatives and constitutional limits; Truman did not. As for all the "repeated" examples of presidents committing US forces abroad without seeking

[10] 59 Stat. 621, 6.

congressional approval, Schlesinger could not name a single precedent to justify Truman's actions in Korea.

Edward Corwin publicly rebuked Commager and Schlesinger, charging that they ascribed to the president "a truly royal prerogative in the field of foreign relations, and [did] so without indicating any correlative legal or constitutional control to which he is answerable." To Corwin, "our high-flying prerogative men appear to resent the very idea that the only possible source of such control, Congress to wit, has any effective power in the premises at all." He described Jefferson's actions in the Mediterranean as "only self-defensive" (Corwin 1951, 15). The vast majority of presidential military initiatives, Corwin pointed out, "involved fights with pirates, landings of small naval contingents in barbarous or semi-barbarous coasts, the dispatch of small bodies of troops to chase bandits or cattle rustlers across the Mexican border, and the like" (16).

Later, when the Vietnam War and Watergate once again highlighted the damage of unchecked presidential power, Schlesinger publicly expressed his regret for calling Taft's position "demonstrably irresponsible." He explained that he had responded with "a flourish of historical documentation and, alas, hyperbole" (Schlesinger 1973, 139). Even with an apology Schlesinger could not talk straight. The fault was not flourishes and hyperbole. It was a *lack* of historical documentation. Schlesinger knew what he was doing in 1950. It was to discredit Taft. For whatever reason, Schlesinger decided to abandon his professional duties and play a partisan, political card. Even before his 1973 expression of regret, he was counseling that "something must be done to assure the Congress a more authoritative and continuing voice in fundamental decisions in foreign policy" (Schlesinger and de Grazia 1967, 27–8). It should not take almost two decades for a renowned historian to understand that fundamental principle.

Commager told Congress in 1967 that there should be a reconsideration of executive–legislative relations in the conduct of foreign relations (US Congress 1967, 21). When he returned to Congress in 1971, he testified that "it is very dangerous to allow the president to, in effect, commit us to a war from which we cannot withdraw, because the warmaking power is lodged and was intended to be lodged in the Congress" (US Congress 1971, 62). If the Constitution lodged it there in 1971, it was lodged there in 1950. What had changed? The president in 1950 was a Democrat and in 1971 a Republican. With such interpretations there is no constitution. The time to respond to constitutional abuse is when it occurs, not two decades later.

THE IMPACT OF RICHARD NEUSTADT

Commager and Schlesinger did great damage to public law by defending a war that violated basic constitutional principles. In time, they admitted their errors. Legal standards suffered also from the writings of political scientist Richard Neustadt. Like

Commager and Schlesinger in 1950, he believed that whatever power flowed toward the president was all for the good. Like them, he could not conceive that any increase in presidential power would harm the country. Unlike Commager and Schlesinger, Neustadt's highly influential book *Presidential Power* gave no attention to the Constitution, even superficially.

Published in 1960, Neustadt's book was reissued as a paperback in 1964 and had an immense impact on the teaching of the presidency. Joseph Bessette and Jeffrey Tulis made this point in 1981: "what was truly distinctive about his approach was how little it had to say about specific constitutional provisions" (Bessette and Tulis 1981, 4). Andrew Rudalevige underscored Neustadt's advice to readers: "[W]hat is good for the country is good for the President, and vice versa" (Rudalevige 2005, 55). Neustadt's preoccupation with political techniques of influence and persuasion overshadowed the fundamental constraints of public law (Moe 1999, 266–7; 2004, 24–5). Political scientists like Clinton Rossiter and James McGregor Burns also saw in a strong presidency the best hope for democratic government (Rudalevige 2005, 54–5).

Neustadt began with a modest and beguiling theme. Presidential power "is the power to persuade" (Neustadt 1964, 23). Persuasive power "amounts to more than charm or reasoned argument . . . . For the men he would induce to do what he wants done on their own responsibility will need or fear some acts by him on his responsibility" (43). A little flavor of Machiavelli, but Neustadt's analysis promised no wholesale shift of power to the president. The formal powers of Congress and the president "are so intertwined that neither will accomplish very much, for very long, without the acquiescence of the other" (45). In language that seems consistent with the Framers' reliance on checks and balances, power at the national level "is a give-and-take" (47). Neustadt is famous for saying that the constitutional convention did not create a government of separated powers: "Rather, it created a government of separated institutions *sharing* powers" (42, emphasis in original). The implication: the president would not operate independently but would work jointly with Congress. Mutual accommodation seemed assured.

As the book progressed, a different theme emerged. Neustadt now began to urge presidents to take power, not share it. Power was something to be acquired and concentrated in the presidency, to be used for *personal* reasons. Neustadt's ideal president was Franklin D. Roosevelt, not Dwight D. Eisenhower: "The politics of self-aggrandizement as Roosevelt practiced it affronted Eisenhower's sense of personal propriety" (157). Does the explanation lie in Eisenhower's "personal propriety" or a deeper comprehension of the Constitution, including separation of powers and federalism? To Neustadt, it did not seem to matter. FDR had every right to seek power for his own use and enjoyment: "Roosevelt was a politician seeking personal power; Eisenhower was a hero seeking national unity" (ibid.). Because Eisenhower cared more for national unity than personal power, Neustadt dismissed him as an "amateur" (170, 171, 182). Surely a president, like Lincoln, can care about political power but also national unity and the Constitution.

How did Neustadt's analysis apply to Truman going to war single-handedly in Korea? Neustadt's book covers the Korean War, but only in part. He concluded that

Truman gave General Douglas MacArthur too much latitude and had to fire him. Neustadt also described Truman's effort to seize steel mills to prosecute the war in Korea and his defeat in the Supreme Court. But Neustadt says nothing about Truman's authority to initiate the war and nothing about Truman's inflated claims of emergency power that allowed the president to operate independently of Congress and the judiciary (Devins and Fisher 2004, 112–14). What happened to the "power to persuade"? Truman never came to Congress for authority to seize the plants. He claimed "inherent" power to do what he did. There was no talk or discussion about "shared power."

At least indirectly, Neustadt seemed to support Truman's intervention in Korea. It was Truman's job "to make decisions and to take initiatives." Among Truman's private values, "decisiveness was high upon his list." His image of the president was "man-in-charge" (Neustadt 1964, 166). With that orientation, there was no point in persuading others, entering into give-and-take, or seeking mutual accommodations. Making decisions and taking initiatives trumped competing values. Neustadt did not ask whether decisions and initiatives were constitutional and did not seem to care. Corwin's public law model had no appeal for him.

Neustadt's purpose was to write for "a man who seeks to maximize his power" (171). That political model could apply to an American president, Winston Churchill, Adolf Hitler, Benito Mussolini, or Joseph Stalin. In maximizing power the key ingredient for Neustadt was confidence: "Such confidence requires that his image of himself in office justifies an unremitting search for personal power" (172). This formula necessarily undermines a constitutional and legal system. Neustadt's advice: "The more determinedly a President seeks power, the more he will be likely to bring vigor to his clerkship. As he does so he contributes to the energy of government" (174). Neustadt measured success by action, vigor, decisiveness, initiative, energy, and personal power— attributes that easily describe the record of President George W. Bush after 9/11 (Fisher 2008a). As John Hart observed, Neustadt evaluated a president "on the basis of his influence on the outcome, but not on the outcome itself" (Hart 1977, 56). Throughout the book, Neustadt makes only two brief (and inconsequential) references to the Constitution, neither of which merits an entry in the index (Neustadt 1964, 51, 66).

Alexander Hamilton and other Framers valued "energy" in the executive, but it was energy within the law, not outside it; energy to carry out the laws, not make or break them. In the afterword to *Presidential Power*, added in 1964, Neustadt spoke about constitutional requirements in light of the Cuban missile crisis of 1962. He recognized "profound" consequences for the presidency (186–7). The Constitution originally contemplated that decisions of military force "should emanate from President *and* Congress" (187, emphasis in original). But the prospect of nuclear war had worked a fundamental change: "When it comes to action risking war, technology has modified the Constitution: the president perforce becomes the only such man in the system of exercising judgment under the extraordinary limits now imposed by secrecy, complexity, and time" (187–8).

Neustadt's argument on nuclear war had no application to Truman's conventional war in Korea. The afterword offered a remarkable framework: "The President remains our system's Great Initiator. When what we once called 'war' impends, he now becomes our system's Final Arbiter" (189).[11] Neustadt's book was reissued in 1990 under a different title: *Presidential Power and the Modern Presidents.* The preface contained a reformulation: "To share is to limit; that is the heart of the matter, and everything this book explores stems from it" (Neustadt 1990, x). However, the 1960 edition and the 1964 paperback had little to do with shared power and everything to do with presidents amassing personal power without regard to legal or constitutional limits. In one of his last publications, in 2004, Neustadt faulted the neoconservatives in the administration of George W. Bush for promoting the war in Iraq and other countries. He criticized "junior ministers" in the Bush administration who "appear to disregard the limits on the presidency embedded in the Constitution" (Neustadt 2004, 17). Neustadt spent decades systematically ignoring constitutional limits.

SOME REAWAKENING

With regular ups and downs, political scientists paid scattered attention to constitutional issues. The confrontations between President Richard Nixon and Congress in the late 1960s and early 1970s helped renew a focus on public law. In 1969, Joel Grossman and Joseph Tanenhaus pointed to a "renascence" of public law, a field that had "for a time drifted close to the outer margins of political science but is now fast returning to the fold" (Grossman and Tanenhaus 1969, 3). Similarly, Richard Pious in 1974 wrote about a "renaissance of public law" with regard to presidential studies (Pious 1974, 635–7). In 1975, Thomas Cronin wrote about the "cult of the presidency," the "halo" effect, and drew attention to the "textbook presidency" of the 1950s and 1960s that exalted both the office and the occupant (Cronin 1975).

In 1984, Richard Pious teamed up with Christopher Pyle to write a sophisticated volume called *The President, Congress, and the Constitution: Power and Legitimacy in American Politics.* They explained that the volume focused on "the *legitimacy* of power as well as the conditions of its exercise," helping to counterbalance a literature that "currently emphasizes amoral aspects of political behavior and the policy-making process" (Pious and Pyle 1984, xv, emphasis in original). In addition to providing introductory essays, Pious and Pyle included a collection of cases, materials, notes, questions, and original essays to encourage students to rethink and understand constitutional principles. By including selections from court cases, Pious and Pyle made it very clear that judicial opinions are merely one factor and hardly the final word. Over the enterprise of constitutional law "judges and lawyers can have no monopoly" (xvi).

Pious and Pyle continue their contributions to public law. In 2001, Pyle published a book on the practice of forcibly abducting suspected criminals and taking them

---

[11] Although Neustadt supposedly reprinted the 1960 version in subsequent editions unchanged, in 1990 the language of this passage is altered to: "The President remains our system's usual initiator. When what we once called 'war' impends, he now becomes our system's final arbiter" (Neustadt 1990, 182).

from one country to another for trial (Pyle 2001). Under the Bush II administration, this practice blossomed into "extraordinary rendition:" taking suspects from one country to another not for trial but for interrogation and torture (Fisher 2008b). In 2006, Pious published *The War on Terrorism and the Rule of Law*. He included many original documents and lead essays to take the reader through such topics as homeland security, domestic surveillance, material support and material witnesses, indefinite detention of suspects, interrogation techniques, and military tribunals (Pious 2006).

In 1981, Joseph Bessette and Jeffrey Tulis edited a thoughtful collection of essays on *The Presidency in the Constitutional Order*. They remarked that "[u]nlike most recent works of this type," their book "is authored by political scientists, not law professors" (Bessette and Tulis 1981, ix). In an introductory essay, Bessette and Tulis discussed a divorce between constitutional and political approaches to studying the presidency. The Corwin model had been effectively eclipsed by studies that abandoned public law. Political scientists could not see why constitutional interpretation was relevant to understanding contemporary political behavior, including the presidency. As a result, they "seem susceptible to the charge that it was the emancipation of presidential studies from a concern with legal and constitutional restraints that implicitly encouraged the abuses of executive power that we have recently witnessed" (7).

After nourishing the "imperial presidency," some liberals began to turn against it for a time because of the Vietnam War and Watergate. Yet there was a tendency among some scholars to regard those periods as tragic aberrations, attributable to the individuals serving as president rather than to the neglect of constitutional and institutional checks. Consequently, Neustadt's model of presidential power retained support (Hart 1977, 48–54). Textbooks in American government gave little attention to the source and limits of presidential authority. As shown by David Gray Adler and other scholars, students were left in doubt about how the Constitution allocates foreign relations and the war-making power. The general impression in class was that the president is the dominant and preeminent force in external affairs (Adler 2005). In other works by Adler and his co-editors, a more balanced understanding of the president's constitutional authority in foreign affairs and war emerged (Adler and Genovese 2002; Adler and George 1996).

The only consistent and principled critique of presidential power and support for constitutional checks came from a community of scholars who promoted conservative and Whiggish views. Some of those writings took their cue from *The Road to Serfdom* (1944) by Friedrich A. Hayek, who strongly opposed the shift of legislative power to "experts" in the executive branch. He warned that this trend posed a threat to democracy and would lead to arbitrary government and a weakened legislative branch (Hayek 1944, 61–71). Conservatives counted Hayek among their ranks, but in a thoughtful essay he declined full membership, preferring to classify himself as "an unrepentent Old Whig—with the stress on the 'old' " (Hayek 1964, 100). His caution is understandable and perceptive. Many contemporary conservatives, including neoconservatives, prefer to concentrate all power in the presidency and put their trust in one individual. More on that later.

A study by the conservative James Burnham in 1959 offered full support for congressional prerogatives: "The Founding Fathers believed that in a republican and representative governmental system the preponderating share of power was held and exercised by the legislature" (Burnham 1959, 92). Conservatives naturally favored "the relative power of Congress within the diffused power equilibrium," whereas liberals tended "to distrust Congress, and to favor the relative power of the executive" (119). He predicted that if Congress "ceases to be an actively functioning political institution, then political liberty in the United States will soon come to an end" (344).

Conservatives drew interesting contrasts between the legislative and executive branches. Willmoore Kendall, in an article called "The Two Majorities," looked to Congress as the primary institution for preserving a republic. He rejected the conventional belief that the president and the executive branch represent "high principle" while Congress stood for low principle, no principle at all, reaction, and unintelligence (Kendall 1960, 325, 345). Those stereotypes seemed to him not only hackneyed but profoundly wrong and destructive of the system of checks and balances. In 1960, Ronald Moe selected materials in an edited volume to underscore the fundamental importance of Congress in a constitutional order. He explained why he thought many professors leaned toward the presidency: "Historically, there has been a tendency for intellectuals to be wary of democratic legislatures," concluding that "they as a class would have more influence within the executive than in the legislative branch" (Moe 1970, 3).

During the Watergate period, some influential conservatives objected to critiques leveled at the presidency. Irving Kristol in 1974 wrote an article called "The Inexorable Rise of the Executive." He faulted liberals for opposing the "imperial presidency" when "until yesterday they were actively promoting the very tendency they now deplore." He parted company with conservatives who supported a strong legislative presence in foreign affairs. To give Congress "anything like an equal share" in the making of foreign policy was "absurd." Foreign policy, Kristol said, required secrecy, swiftness, and "an irreducible minimum of duplicitous scheming," all of which was beyond the public deliberations of a legislative body (Kristol 1974, 12). That line of reasoning reached full flower among neoconservatives with the war against Iraq in 2003.

Just as Ronald Moe predicted that liberals and intellectuals would favor the executive branch because of its power and leverage, many conservatives reached the same conclusion. Writing for the *National Review* in 1974, Jeffrey Hart focused on the "steady growth of the federal bureaucracy" and advised conservatives that if they wanted the executive branch to adopt their policies "they can do so only by supporting a powerful and activist Presidency" (Hart 1974, 1353). Concerned about what he considered to be the liberal media, Hart believed that of the three branches "only one has the capacity to contest the mass media where the focusing of opinion is concerned, and that, of course, is the Presidency" (1355).

Conservatives and neoconservatives were drawn increasingly to the presidency. To Norman Podhoretz, editor of *Commentary*, the attack on executive power in the

1970s did great damage to "the main institutional capability the United States possesses for conducting an overt fight against the spread of Communist power in the world" (Podhoretz 1976, 35). Charles Krauthammer saw things the same way. Writing in 1987, he reasoned that for the United States to remain a superpower and effectively oppose Communism, there had to be a "centralization and militarization of authority." An "imperial presidency" would be "a more coherent and decisive instrument than its legislative rival" (Krauthammer 1987, 23). Krauthammer and other conservatives criticized President Ronald Reagan for not defending what they regarded as presidential prerogatives during the Iran-Contra affair (Crovitz 1988).

In recent years, traditional conservatives have pushed back against the adulation of executive power. Mickey Edwards, former Republican member of Congress from Oklahoma, published *Reclaiming Conservatism* in 2008, attempting to steer some of his colleagues back toward constitutional government. He expressed concern that Congress in the post-9/11 period "had been nearly destroyed as a separate, independent, and equal institution." President George W. Bush "seemed to have little interest in maintaining even the slightest pretense of adherence to the Constitution's system of separated powers" (Edwards 2008, 9). Similarly, Gene Healy of the Cato Institute published a hard-hitting critique of the romance (both conservative and liberal) with presidential power (Healy 2008).

FUNCTIONING AS AN ENTREPRENEUR

Political scientists have many opportunities to influence the national debate over constitutional values and legal policy. One way is to appear before congressional committees and offer expert testimony. Law professors, even when they possess modest credentials on the issue before the committee, are routinely invited. Part of that pattern is the committee habit of reaching out to law professors. Also, law professors have better skills in marketing themselves. A number of political scientists have been invited to testify because of the strength of their scholarly work.

Robert Spitzer's book *The Presidential Veto* led to three appearances before House and Senate committees to discuss the pocket veto, the item veto, and the "inherent" item veto. His book on *The Politics of Gun Control* drew an invitation to testify before a Senate committee. Spitzer also studied the practice of law reviews in publishing articles without any peer review and how this shortcut method permits shoddy scholarship that would not be published anywhere else. His book, published in 2008, is called *Saving the Constitution from Lawyers: How Legal Training and Law Reviews Distort Constitutional Meaning*.

Katy Harriger's two books on *Independent Justice: The Federal Special Prosecutor in American Politics* and *The Special Prosecutor in American Politics* caught the attention of congressional committees studying revisions of the law. She has testified before

Congress and also submitted, separately, written testimony. Phillip Cooper's writings on executive orders, including his book *By Order of the President: The Use & Abuse of Executive Direct Action*, prompted an invitation from a House committee to testify on pending legislation. Another political scientist writing on executive orders is Kenneth R. Mayer, author of *With the Stroke of a Pen: Executive Orders and Presidential Power*. In 2001 he testified on executive orders before a House committee.

Mark Rozell's book *Executive Privilege: Presidential Power, Secrecy, and Accountability* drew the interest of committees seeking documents and testimony from the executive branch. He testified three times before congressional committees. In 2008 he co-authored a legal brief that challenged White House arguments regarding the firings of nine US attorneys and the immunity the Justice Department gave to current and past White House officials. His analyses of executive privilege disputes are frequently sought by reporters and appear in major newspapers.

In 2006, David T. Canon and Carol M. Swain testified before a Senate committee on the renewal of the Voting Rights Act. Thomas Mann and Norman Ornstein maintain close contacts with members of Congress and their committees, offering assistance both behind the scenes and during congressional testimony. Mann has testified on campaign finance, continuity of Congress, and biennial budgeting. Ornstein testified on those issues and also on the item veto, legislative veto, the balanced budget amendment, and proposals to lengthen the two-year term for House members. Mann and Ornstein co-authored the legal brief with Mark Rozell on US attorneys. Another political scientist, Mitchel Sollenberger, was the fourth co-author. He is the author of *The President Shall Nominate: How Congress Trumps Executive Power*. Allen Schick is invited to testify on a range of budget issues, including the item veto and the balanced budget amendment.

William Weaver, a political scientist with a law degree, has testified twice before congressional committees on the issue of federal whistleblowers. What rights and procedures are they entitled to? What legislation is needed? He has filed a number of briefs to challenge the Bush administration's policy on the state secrets privilege. Joining him on these briefs is Robert Pallitto, a political scientist who previously served as an attorney in New Jersey. They are the authors of *Presidential Secrecy and the Law*.

A number of political scientists have been active with the bipartisan Constitution Project, which issues position papers on a number of legal issues. I drafted the statement on "Reforming the State Secrets Privilege" and it was signed by former members of Congress, former federal judges, former executive officials, lawyers, law professors, and these political scientists: David Gray Adler, Phillip Cooper, Katy Harriger, Nancy Kassop, Christopher Kelley, Norman Ornstein, Robert Pallitto, James Pfiffner, Richard Pious, James Thurber, Michael Tolley, and William Weaver.

Political scientists would strengthen their visibility and influence by acting the part of the entrepreneur: publishing studies of direct interest to Congress and making sure that those materials are placed directly in the hands of key committee staffers, including the chief counsel and staff director. Regular contact will make your name known and promote your willingness to assist committee activities. Unfortunately, political science departments do not give much credit to professors who publish in law reviews, even when the analysis is solid and original. Some political scientists find their interests better served by working through executive agencies or by authoring or co-authoring legal briefs in court. After 9/11, I filed five amicus briefs under my own name on such issues as military tribunals, detaining US citizens without trial, and NSA surveillance. Lawyers have dominated the field of public law far too long. It is time not to encroach on their domain but to recapture territory unwisely vacated. We have much to contribute.

Those contributions will be modest unless political scientists reorient the way they study, teach, and write about the presidency. It is not enough to describe the behavior and conduct of someone in office. Presidential studies need a larger framework. Adding content without context is shallow. More important than how much presidents do something, or why they act as they do, is the source of their authority and limits to it. The president is part of a constitutional system and cannot, or should not, be isolated from it.

Studying the presidency without reference to legal boundaries and values is to treat the United States as any other country, including those that are authoritarian and fascist. Democracies decline when citizens become satisfied only with results and care little about procedures, legal sources, or their own participation. Political scientists have a duty to keep alive an appreciation for the values that made America unique. Those fundamental principles include the belief that citizens (not "subjects") have the capacity to develop their talents and participate in self-government; protecting the dignity and worth of the individual; relying on procedural safeguards to curb arbitrary power; and protecting rights and liberties through such structural arrangements as checks and balances and separation of powers. Elementary points, of course, but a review of presidential studies over the last half century underscores how much this public law heritage has lost ground to other pursuits.

REFERENCES

ADLER, D. G. 2005. Textbooks and the President's Constitutional Powers. *Presidential Studies Quarterly*, 35: 376.
—— and GENOVESE, M. A. (eds.) 2002. *The Presidency and the Law: The Clinton Legacy*. Lawrence: University Press of Kansas.
—— and GEORGE, L. N. (eds.) 1996. *The Constitution and the Conduct of American Foreign Policy*. Lawrence: University Press of Kansas.
BESSETTE, J. M., and TULIS, J. (eds.) 1981. *The Presidency in the Constitutional Order*. Baton Rouge: Louisiana State University Press.
BURNHAM, J. 1959. *Congress and the American Tradition*. Chicago: Henry Regnery.
COMMAGER, H. S. 1951a. Presidential Power: The Issue Analyzed. *New York Times Magazine*, Jan. 14.
—— 1951b. Does the President Have Too Much Power? *New York Times Magazine*, Apr. 1.
CORWIN, E. S. 1951. The President's Power. *New Republic*, Jan. 29.

CRONIN, T. E. 1975. *The State of the Presidency.* Boston: Little, Brown.

CROVITZ, L. G. 1988. How Ronald Reagan Weakened the Presidency. *Commentary,* Sept.

DEVINS, N., and FISHER, L. 2004. *The Democratic Constitution.* New York: Oxford University Press.

EDWARDS, M. 2008. *Reclaiming Conservatism: How a Great American Political Movement Got Lost—and How it Can Find its Way Back.* New York: Oxford University Press.

FISHER, L, 2004. *Presidential War Power,* 2nd edn. Lawrence: University Press of Kansas.

——— 2008a. *The Constitution and 9/11: Recurring Threats to America's Freedoms.* Lawrence: University Press of Kansas.

——— 2008b. Extraordinary Rendition: The Price of Secrecy. *American University Law Review,* 57: 1405.

GROSSMAN, J. B., and TANENHAUS, J. (eds.) 1969. *Frontiers of Judicial Research.* New York: John Wiley & Sons, Inc.

HART, J. 1974. The Presidency: Shifting Conservative Perspectives? *National Review,* Nov. 22.

——— 1977. Personal Power Revisited. *Political Studies,* 25: 48–61.

HAYEK, F. A. 1944. *The Road to Serfdom.* London: G. Routledge & Sons.

——— 1964. Why I Am Not a Conservative. In *What is Conservatism?,* ed. F. S. Meyers. New York: Holt, Rinehart & Winston.

HEALY, G. 2008. *The Cult of the Presidency.* Washington, DC: Cato Institute.

KENDALL, W. 1960. The Two Majorities. *Midwest Journal of Political Science,* 4: 317.

KRAUTHAMMER, C. 1987. The Price of Power. *New Republic,* Feb. 9.

KRISTOL, I. 1974. The Inexorable Rise of the Executive. *Wall Street Journal,* Sept. 20.

MOE, R. C. (ed.) 1970. *Congress and the President: Allies and Adversaries.* Pacific Palisades, CA: Goodyear Publishing.

——— 1999. At Risk: The President's Role as Chief Manager. In *The Managerial Presidency,* ed. J. P. Pfiffner. College Station: Texas A&M University Press.

——— 2004. Governance Principles: The Neglected Basis of Federal Management. In *Making Government Manageable,* ed. T. H. Stanton and B. Ginsberg. Baltimore: Johns Hopkins University Press.

NEUSTADT, R. E. 1964. *Presidential Power.* New York: Signet Books.

——— 1990. *Presidential Power and the Modern Presidents: The Politics of Leadership from Roosevelt to Reagan.* New York: The Free Press.

——— 2004. Challenges Created by Contemporary Presidents. In *New Challenges for the American Presidency,* ed. G. C. Edwards III and P. J. Davies. New York: Pearson/Longman.

PIOUS, R. M. 1974. Is Presidential Power "Poison?" *Political Science Quarterly,* 89: 627.

——— 2006. *The War on Terrorism and the Rule of Law.* Los Angeles: Roxbury Publishing Co.

——— and PYLE, C. H. 1984. *The President, Congress, and the Constitution: Power and Legitimacy in American Politics.* New York: Free Press.

PODHORETZ, N. 1976. Making the World Safe for Democracy. *Commentary,* Apr.

Political Science Quarterly. 1886. Front cover of Volume One.

PRITCHETT, C. H. 1969. The Development of Judicial Research, in *Frontiers of Judicial Research,* ed. J. B. Grossman and J. Tanenhaus. New York: John Wiley & Sons.

Proceedings of the American Political Science Association. 1905. Lancaster, PA: Wickersham Press.

Public Papers of the Presidents. 1950. Washington, DC: Government Printing Office.

PYLE, C. H. 2001. *Extradition, Politics, and Human Rights.* Philadelphia: Temple University Press.

RUDALEVIGE, A. 2005. *The New Imperial Presidency: Renewing Presidential Power after Watergate.* Ann Arbor: University of Michigan Press.

SCHLESINGER, A. M., JR. 1951. Presidential Powers: Taft Statement on Troops Opposed, Actions of Past Presidents Cited (letter). *New York Times*, Jan. 9.

——1973. *The Imperial Presidency*. Boston: Houghton Mifflin.

——and DE GRAZIA, A. 1967. *Congress and the Presidency*. Washington, DC: American Enterprise Institute.

SOMIT, A., and TANENHAUS, J. 1963 Trends in American Political Science: Some Analytical Notes. *American Political Science Review*, 57: 933.

US Congress. 1945. *Congressional Record*, 91: 8185.

——1951. Military Situation in the Far East (Part 3), Hearings before the Senate Committee on Armed Services and Foreign Relations, 82nd Cong., 1st Sess.

——1967. Changing American Attitudes towards Foreign Policy. Hearings before the Senate Committee on Foreign Relations, 90th Cong., 1st Sess.

——1971. War Powers Legislation. Hearings before the Senate Committee on Foreign Relations, 92nd Cong., 1st Sess.

WHITE, L. D. 1939. *Introduction to the Study of Public Administration*. New York: Macmillan.

CHAPTER 35

THE STUDY OF PRESIDENTIAL LEADERSHIP

GEORGE C. EDWARDS III

LEADERSHIP is perhaps the most commonly employed concept in politics. Politicians, pundits, journalists, and scholars critique and analyze public officials, attributing both success and failure to the quality of their leadership. When times are bad, the reflexive call is for new—and better—leadership.

The president is the most prominent focus of political leadership in the US, and the notion of the dominant president who moves the country and the government by means of strong, effective leadership has deep roots in American political culture. Those chief executives whom Americans revere—from Washington to Franklin D. Roosevelt—have taken on mythic proportions as leaders. Stories about the remarkable persuasive powers of presidents abound. Often these stories originate with presidential aides or admiring biographers, fed by the hagiography that envelops presidents and distorts both our memories and our critical facilities.

A century ago in the first article in the first issue of the *American Political Science Review*, A. Maurice Low criticized scholars who had complained of "executive usurpation" of power from Congress for "relying upon their rhetoric rather than their facts" (Low 1906). In fact, he argued, if there had been usurpation, it was on the part of the Senate, not the president. Thus, the critics had not gotten their facts straight and completely missed the real pattern of behavior.

A century later, political scientists are still exploring presidential leadership, yet for most of the decades since Low wrote, the study of the presidency was a backwater of the discipline. Nearly three decades ago, an impertinent young scholar minced few words in criticizing the presidency subfield for failing to adopt basic norms of social science. He argued that

Research on the presidency too often fails to meet the standards of contemporary political science, including the careful definition and measurement of concepts, the rigorous specification and testing of propositions, the employment of appropriate quantitative methods, and the use of empirical theory to develop hypotheses and explain findings.

(Edwards 1981, 146)

Scholars needed to think theoretically to develop falsifiable propositions about presidential leadership and test these systematically with relevant data and appropriate econometric techniques. They should seek to discover generalizations about behavior rather than produce discrete, ad hoc analyses, repeat colorful anecdotes from presidential press clippings, or reach facile conclusions about Lyndon Johnson's skill at swaying members of Congress or Ronald Reagan's ability to mobilize the public behind his proposals. Thus, the research on the presidency presented a striking irony: The single most important and powerful institution in American politics was the one that political scientists understood the least.

Research on the presidency has progressed significantly over the past three decades, but there is still much to learn. In this chapter, I argue that to advance our understanding of presidential leadership, we need to think more rigorously about it. More specifically, we need to reorient our focus from one that concentrates on presidential persuasion as the core of successful leadership to one that centers on facilitating change through the recognition and exploitation of opportunities in the president's environment.

LEADERSHIP AS PERSUASION

Despite all the attention to leadership, it remains an elusive concept, and there is little consensus even on what leadership is. According to James MacGregor Burns (1978, 2), "Leadership is one of the most observed and least understood phenomena on earth." Barbara Kellerman (1984, 70) lists ten different definitions of political leadership, as does Gary Yukl (2006).

Writers and commentators employ the term "leadership" to mean just about everything a person who occupies what we often refer to as a position of leadership does—or should do. When we define a term so broadly, however, it loses its utility. Making tough decisions, establishing an administration's priorities, and appointing good people to implement policy are core functions of the presidency. Yet these activities are quite different from, say, obtaining the support of the public, the Congress, or other nations for the president's policies.

There is no question that the Constitution and federal laws invest significant discretionary authority in the president. Making decisions and issuing commands are important and doing them well requires courage, wisdom, and skill. At times, the exercise of unilateral authority may lead to historic changes in the politics and policy of the country (see Howell 2003; Cooper 2002; Mayer 2001). In the extreme case, the president can choose to launch a nuclear attack at his discretion. The consequences would be vast. Most people, however, would not view such an act as one of leadership. In exercising discretionary authority, the president, in effect, acts alone. He does not have to *lead*. At its core, decision making represents a different dimension of the job of the chief executive than influencing others.

Persuasion refers to causing others to do something by reasoning, urging, or inducement. Influencing others is central to the conception of leadership of most political scientists. Scholars of the presidency want to know whether the chief executive can affect the output of government by influencing the actions and attitudes of others. In a democracy, we are particularly attuned to efforts to persuade, especially when most potentially significant policy changes require the assent of multiple power holders.

An important element of a chief executive's job may be creating the organizational and personal conditions that promote innovative thinking, the frank and open presentation and analysis of alternatives, and effective implementation of decisions by advisers and members of the bureaucracy. We may reasonably view such actions as leadership, and there is no doubt that the processes of decision making and policy implementation are critical to governing. For purposes of this essay, however, I focus on leadership of those who are not directly on the president's team and who are thus less likely to support his initiatives.

Richard Neustadt and the Power to Persuade

Perhaps the best-known dictum regarding the American presidency is that "presidential power is the power to persuade" (Neustadt 1990, 11). It is the wonderfully felicitous phrase that captures the essence Richard Neustadt's argument in *Presidential Power*. For half a century, scholars and students—and many presidents—have viewed the presidency through the lens of Neustadt's core premise.

Neustadt provided scholars with a new orientation to the study of the presidency. Published in 1960, his framework was strikingly different from those of Edward S. Corwin (1957) and Clinton Rossiter (1960) that had dominated presidential scholarship. These differences were to have important consequences for how many scholars would examine the presidency over the ensuing decades as the emphasis on persuasion encouraged moving beyond Corwin's focus on the formal powers of the presidency and Rossiter's stress on roles. In Neustadt's words, " 'powers' are no guarantee of power" (1990, 10) and "[t]he probabilities of power do not derive from the literary theory of the Constitution" (1990, 37). Power, then, is a function of personal politics rather than of formal authority or position. Neustadt placed people and politics in the center of research, and the core activity on which he focused was leadership. Indeed, the subtitle of *Presidential Power* is *The Politics of Leadership*. In essence, presidential leadership was the power to persuade.

Following Neustadt's lead, scholars began to focus on the people within institutions and their relationships with each other rather than to focus primarily on the institutions themselves and their formalities. It was not the roles of the president but the performance of those roles that mattered. It was not the boundaries of behavior but the actions within those boundaries that warranted the attention of scholars. In other words, scholars began to focus on presidents attempting to lead by persuading others to follow them. The president's need to exercise influence in several arenas led those who follow Neustadt's power perspective to adopt an expansive view of presidential politics that includes both governmental institutions and actors, such as the Congress, bureaucracy, and White House staff, and those outside of government, such as the public, the press, and interest groups. (Much of my own work has followed this path. See, for example, Edwards 1980a, 1980b, 1983, 1989, 2003, 2007.)

Two critical premises follow from Neustadt's argument that presidential power is the power to persuade. Both have had a powerful impact on studying the presidency. The first stems from the fact that power is a concept that involves relationships between people. By focusing on relationships and suggesting why people respond to the president as they do, Neustadt forced us into a more analytical mode. To understand relationships, we must explain behavior.

Equally important, Neustadt was concerned with the strategic level of power:

> There are two ways to study "presidential power." One way is to focus on the tactics ... of influencing certain men in given situations ... The other way is to step back from tactics on those "givens" and to deal with influence in more strategic terms: what is its nature and what are its sources? ... Strategically, [for example] the question is not how he masters Congress in a peculiar instance, but what he does to boost his chance for mastery in any instance.
>
> (1990, 4)

Neustadt, then, was less interested in what causes something to happen in one instance than in what affects the probabilities of something happening in every instance. To think strategically about power, we must search for generalizations and calculate probabilities. Although he employed neither the language nor the methods of modern social science, Neustadt was clearly a forerunner. His emphasis on reaching generalizations about presidential power discouraged ad hoc explanations and may have been his greatest contribution of all.

The emphasis on explaining relationships has had a positive impact on studying the presidency. Less benign has been the impact of a second implicit proposition. There is an important prescriptive element in *Presidential Power*. Neustadt's central motivation for writing the book was to offer advice to presidents to help them help themselves with their strategic problem of power, and he remained interested in the challenges of governing. Indeed, tying scholarship to governing is important, because—entertainment value aside—governing is the primary reason we study politics. Underlying his effort to aid presidents in leading was the premise that they *could succeed* in doing so if they were skilled enough at recognizing and protecting their interests and exploiting critical resources.

The view that presidents not only need to persuade but that they can do so has led scholars, commentators, and other observers of the presidency to focus on the question of *how* presidents persuade rather than the more fundamental question of *whether they can do so*. In addition, Neustadt's emphasis on the personal in politics—and the potential success of persuasion—has led some scholars to overlook the importance of the context in which the president operates as well as his institutional setting. Ironically, this focus has also discouraged reaching generalizations about the strategic level of power.

It would be unfair to argue that Neustadt had erected an impediment to understanding the broader patterns of presidential influence. His emphasis on the person in the office certainly discouraged it, however, especially among the less discerning of his readers. Similarly, many scholars and other commentators on the presidency have fallen prey to the personalization of politics and have uncritically accepted, for example, an exaggerated concept of the potential for using the "bully pulpit" to go public.

Presidential Power has remained the most influential, and most admired, book on the American presidency—and for good reason. Its focus on the influence relationships of presidents was a critical intellectual breakthrough that forced us to broaden and clarify our thinking and encouraged us to emphasize explanation and generalization in our research. Yet we must not *assume* the power to persuade. Instead, we need to explore the basic premises of presidential leadership.

"Transformational" Leaders

Although Neustadt encouraged the belief that presidential persuasion was possible, he began with the premise that presidents would have to struggle to get their way. As he put it (1990, 32), "The power to persuade is the power to bargain." Indeed, it was the inherent weakness of the presidency that made it necessary for presidents to understand how to use their resources most effectively. Not everyone has such restrained views of leaders, however.

A common premise underlying the widespread emphasis on political leadership as the wellspring of change is that some leaders have the capability to *transform* policy by reshaping the influences on it. Such "transformational" leadership is the holy grail of leadership studies. An internet search of the phrase "transformational leadership" will quickly produce more than a million hits. Websites, institutes, and research studies focus on understanding—and teaching—the principles of transformational leadership.

With so much attention to transformational leadership, there is no consensus definition of the concept. The most prominent advocate of transformational leadership is James MacGregor Burns (1978. Also see Burns 2003 and Burns and Dunn 2001). The essence of Burns's concept of transformation is elevating moral leadership, transforming both the leaders and the led. This change, in turn, leads to fundamental and comprehensive change in society, values, and political structures (Burns 1978, 4, 20, 455; 2003, ch. 2). In his work on leadership, Burns focuses more on the goals of leadership than on democratic political leaders actually leading.

Others have adopted the term "transformational" and infused it with broader meaning than Burns originally intended. Writing on the private sector views transformational leaders as visionaries and catalysts for change who sell their ideas and reshape their organizations. Common to most applications of the concept in the public sector is a belief in the potential of transformational leadership to change the opinions and behavior of followers in the public and actors in institutions and thus effect major change. (The address in one of the first hits in an internet search is aptly named ChangingMinds.org.) Burns himself asserts at various points that transformational leaders have an "extraordinary potential influence over followers" and "immense" potential for influence over them. They are event-making individuals who define the forks in history (see, for example, 1978, 13, 20, 33–4, 39–40, 43–4, 68–9, 454).

It would be easy to become enmeshed in debates about whether a particular president was "transformational." The issue is *not* whether major policy changes that presidents desire occur. They do. Neither is the issue one of determining when change is large enough that we may consider it to be transformational. That is a matter I leave to others. I, as I believe are most scholars, am interested in significant changes, whether or not they are "transformational." The fundamental question is whether presidents have the potential to persuade others to follow them. If significant changes in public policy occur, what is the explanation? Can presidents transform politics through persuasion? On the other hand, must presidents persuade in order to transform policy?

Explaining Change

Even though both the public and commentators are frequently disillusioned with the performance of individual presidents and recognize that stalemate is common in the political system, Americans eagerly accept what appears to be effective presidential leadership as evidence on which to renew their faith in the potential of presidential persuasion to engender change. After all, if presidential leadership works some of the time, why not all of the time?

The tenacity with which many commentators embrace the persuasive potential of political leadership is striking. They routinely explain historic shifts in public policy such as those in the 1930s, 1960s, and 1980s in terms of the extraordinary persuasiveness of Franklin D. Roosevelt, Lyndon Johnson, and Ronald Reagan.

Equally striking is the lack of evidence in support of the persuasive power of the presidency. Observers in both the press and the academy base their claims about the impact of such leadership on little or no systematic evidence and seemingly little reflection. *There is not a single systematic study that demonstrates that presidents can reliably move others to support them.*

Perhaps faith in the potential of persuasive leadership persists because such a view simplifies political analysis. Because broader forces that may influence changes in policy are complex, and perhaps even intractable, focusing primarily on the individual as leader eases the burden of explaining policy change. Faith in the persuasive presidency also simplifies the evaluation of the problems of governing. If it is reasonable to expect the White House to create opportunities for change, then failures of leadership must be personal deficiencies. If problems arise because the leader lacks the proper will, skills, or understanding, then the solution to our need for leadership is straightforward and simple: Elect presidents who are willing and able to lead. Because the system is responsive to appropriate leadership, it will function smoothly with the right leader in the Oval Office. The blame for unsuccessful leadership lies in the leader rather than the opportunities for change in the leader's environment.

LEADERSHIP AS FACILITATION

The American political system is not a fertile field for the exercise of presidential leadership. Most political actors are free to choose whether to follow the chief executive's lead; the president cannot force them to act. At the same time, the sharing of powers established by the Constitution prevents the president from acting unilaterally on most important matters and gives other power holders different perspectives on issues and policy proposals. Thus, the political system compels the president to attempt to lead while inhibiting his ability to do so.

These imperatives present the primary challenge to his political leadership. Harry Truman, writing to his sister, reflected on the job of president:

Aside from the impossible administrative burden, he has to take all sorts of abuse from liars and demagogues. . . . The people can never understand why the President does not use his supposedly great power to make 'em behave. Well, all the President is, is a glorified public relations man who spends his time flattering, kissing and kicking people to get them to do what they are supposed to do anyway.   (quoted in McCullough 1992, 584–5)

Despite Truman's frustration, presidents often succeed in achieving changes in public policy, some of which are of historic significance. Coupling this fact with the lack of systematic evidence that presidents succeed in persuasion and plenty of evidence that they frequently fail to achieve the policy changes they desire presents a conundrum. What explains their success when they have it? If persuasion is not the key, then what is?

If persuasion plays a minor part in presidential leadership, it does not follow that leadership is unimportant. Successful leadership may have another explanation. In some cases, presidents may not need to rely on persuasion because there is already sufficient support for their policy stances. In other instances, there may be latent support that requires activation by the president and his supporters. In all cases, presidents who are successful in obtaining support for their agendas have to evaluate the opportunities for change in their environments carefully and orchestrate existing and potential support skillfully. Although it is not common for students of politics to articulate leadership as recognizing and exploiting opportunities for change, these—rather than persuasion—may be the essential presidential leadership skills.

To sharpen our thinking about leadership, it is useful to contrast two broad perspectives on the presidency. In the first, the president is the *director* of change. Through his leadership, he creates opportunities to move in new directions, leading others where they otherwise would not go. The director establishes an agenda and persuades the public, organized interests, Congress, and others to support administration policies. Accordingly, the president is the moving force of the system. Some may term such leadership as "transformational," and all view it as based on successful persuasion.

A second perspective is less heroic. Here the president is primarily a *facilitator* of change. Facilitators understand the opportunities for change in their environments and fashion strategies and tactics to exploit them. Rather than create a constituency, they reflect and sometimes clarify, intensify, or channel their constituencies' aspirations, values, and policy views. Instead of persuading others to support them, they skillfully work at the margins of coalition building, perhaps influencing a few critical actors, to obtain support for their initiatives.

It is important not to underrate this role. The facilitator is *not* simply one who seizes opportunities as they present themselves and invites people to do what they already want to do. Change is not inevitable, and facilitators make things happen that otherwise would not. Effective facilitators are skilled leaders who must recognize the opportunities that exist in their environments, choose which opportunities to pursue, when and in what order, and exploit them with skill, energy, perseverance, and will.

The director reshapes the contours of the political landscape to pave the way for change, whereas the facilitator exploits opportunities presented by a favorable configuration of political forces. The director creates a constituency to follow his lead, whereas the facilitator endows his constituency's views with shape and purpose. The range and scope of the director's influence are broad, whereas those of the facilitator are narrower.

The question of the relative influence of context and personal skills has also occupied some scholars of leadership within Congress. In their innovative examination of leadership in the House of Representatives, Joseph Cooper and David Brady concluded that institutional context is more important than personal skills or traits in determining the influence of leaders. They found no relationship between leadership style and effectiveness and argue that the institutional context, especially party strength, in which leaders find themselves, determines their leadership style more than do their own personal traits (1981. See also Rohde and Shepsle 1987; Sinclair 1986).

The distinction between director and facilitator does not create exclusive categories: my goal is neither to classify presidents nor to resolve an academic dispute. Instead, I employ these types to aid our understanding of leadership by exploring its possibilities. Once we understand the possibilities of leadership, we are in a better position to assess both the performance of presidents and the opportunities for change. Equally important, we will be better positioned to *explain* the success or failure of presidential leadership.

The two categories of leader do not represent a straw man. Instead, they represent leadership types common in the literature on leadership. Sidney Hook (1943) contrasted the "eventful man," who influences developments noticeably, and the "event-making man," an eventful man whose actions are the consequences of outstanding capacities rather than accidents of position and who not only appears at but also helps define the forks in the road of history. (Hook expected few event-making leaders in democracies. His principal example of an event maker in the twentieth century was Lenin.)

Burns (1956, 399–402, 487), arguing that leaders can change contextual forces under certain conditions, criticized Franklin D. Roosevelt for being only an "eventful man." He goes on to argue that

There is an important difference between the politician who is simply an able tactician, and the politician who is a creative political leader. The former accepts political conditions as given and fashions a campaign and a set of policies best suited to the existing conditions. The latter tries consciously to change the matrix of political forces amid which he operates, in order that he may better lead the people in the direction he wants to go. The former operates within slender margins; the latter, through sheer will and conviction as well as political skill, tries to widen the margins with which he operates. He seeks not merely to win votes but consciously to alter basic political forces such as public opinion, party power, interest group pressure, the governmental system.   (1956, 401–2)

This description is a close match to my distinction between facilitators and directors of change.

There is of course a third possibility: a president who is disposed not to lead. Although some occupants of the Oval Office may have fit this description, it is not useful for our purposes. We may learn a great deal about leadership from those who do not succeed in their efforts, but we can learn little from those who do not make the effort.

Great Men vs. Historical Inevitability

It is useful to distinguish the leadership types I employ from the polar positions that characterize the debate over the "great man" interpretation of history. The two sides of this issue assumed their best-known forms in the nineteenth century. In *Heroes and Hero-Worship and the Heroic in History*, published in 1841, Thomas Carlyle argued that great men alone were responsible for the direction of history. The environment of the hero seems generally malleable and thus receptive to leadership.

George W. Bush shared this view of leadership. As conservative columnist David Brooks (2007) put it, "When Bush is asked about military strategy, he talks about the leadership qualities of his top generals. . . . When Bush talks about world affairs more generally, he talks about national leaders." Bush

is confident that in reading the individual character of leaders, he is reading the tablet that really matters. History is driven by the club of those in power. When far-sighted leaders change laws and institutions, they have the power to transform people.

Viewing history from quite a different perspective, various schools of social determinists, including the Spencerians, Hegelians, and Marxists, saw history as an inexorable march in one direction, with change occurring only when the culture was ripe for it. They concluded that great men could not have acted differently from the way they did. Tolstoy's portrayal of Napoleon in *War and Peace* is perhaps the most memorable depiction of this view.

Most will agree that these perspectives are inadequate, and we have no need to become mired in this ancient debate. My contrasting leadership types are much less extreme, and the issue is not whether leadership matters, but rather how much and in what ways. It is not sufficient to conclude, however, that sometimes the environment is receptive to change and at other times it is not. This view simply begs the question of whether leaders are able to influence the environment so as to create the opportunity for change. It also discourages enquiring about the role recognizing and exploiting opportunities plays in presidential success.

How Presidents Matter

It is common to argue that it makes a difference who the president is (see, for example, Greenstein 2004). For example, commentators often offer the example of the attempted assassination of President-elect Franklin D. Roosevelt on February 15, 1933, to make the point. If anarchist Giuseppe Zangara has succeeded in assassinating Roosevelt instead of Chicago mayor Anton Cermak, they argue, the history of the US would have been different. No doubt. It does not follow, however, that the difference Roosevelt made lay in his ability to build supportive coalitions through persuasive leadership.

Thus, I am *not* suggesting that presidents do not have transformative effects or that they are not independent agents in producing them. Stephen Skowronek (1993) maintains that the presidency's capacity to transform American government and politics results from its blunt and disruptive effects. Andrew Jackson forced the submission of the nullifiers and undermined the Bank of the US, Franklin Pierce deployed the resources of his office on behalf of the Kansas Nebraska Act, and Lincoln bludgeoned the South into submission. All were transformative acts that changed the landscape of American government and politics. I agree. And Skowronek agrees that persuasion was not central to any of these actions.

In addition, Skowronek (1993) argues that presidential failures can be as transformative as their successes, with retribution for failure driving political change, jarring loose governing coalitions, opening unforeseen alternatives, shifting the balance of power, and passing to successors an entirely new set of opportunities and constraints. Again, I agree. My focus, however, is on presidents attempting to obtain support for policies that *they* want.

The question, then, is not whether presidents matter. Of course they do. The question is *how* they matter—how do they bring about change? If we are going to understand the nature of presidential leadership and the potential of persuasion, we must not conflate persuasion with other dimensions of the presidency such as discretionary decision making. In addition, we must move beyond anecdotes and investigate presidential persuasion more rigorously. Finally, we need to investigate whether facilitative skills are another, and important, dimension of presidential leadership. Thus, it is reasonable to ask whether the most effective presidents reshape the political landscape to pave the way for change, or whether they recognize and skillfully exploit opportunities in their environments to achieve significant changes in public policy.

Until recently, scholars largely ignored the question of the impact of presidents on public opinion. Some innovative experimental studies found that supporters of the president were more likely to back policies when his name was attached to them (Sigelman 1980; Thomas and Sigelman 1985; Conover and Sigelman 1982), and one study concluded that presidents could exercise a small influence on public opinion on issues, but only when they themselves had high approval ratings (Page, Shapiro, and Dempsey 1987). The bulk of research, however, makes it clear that the White House is rarely able to move the public to support either the president or his policies (Sigelman and Sigelman 1981; Simon and Ostrom 1989; Mondak 1993; Cohen 1997; Baum and Kernell 2001; Edwards 2003, 2007, 2009; Canes-Wrone 2006). I discuss this research in an essay earlier in this volume.

Other essays in this volume focus on presidential leadership of Congress. The best evidence is that presidential persuasion is at the margins of congressional decision making. Even presidents who appeared to dominate Congress were actually facilitators rather than directors of change. They understood their own limitations and quite explicitly took advantage of opportunities in their environments. Working at the margins, they successfully guided legislation through Congress. When these resources diminished, they reverted to the more typical stalemate that usually characterizes presidential–congressional relations (Edwards 1989, 2009; Bond and Fleischer 1990, ch. 8; Fleischer, Bond, and Wood 2007).

In his important work on pivotal politics Keith Krehbiel (1998, chs. 7–8) examined votes to override presidential vetoes, focusing on those members of Congress who switched their votes from their original votes on the bill. He found that presidents attracted 10 percent of those who originally supported a bill but lost 11 percent of those who originally supported him and opposed it. Those closest in ideology to the president were most likely to switch to his side, which may indicate they voted their true views, rather than responding to other interests, when it really counted. Even among those most likely to agree with the White House, legislators within the cluster of pivotal or near-pivotal, the net swing was only 1 in 8. The majority of switchers were from the president's party, indicating that the desire to avoid a party embarrassment rather than presidential persuasiveness may have motivated their votes.

It is certainly possible that there is selection bias in votes on veto overrides. Presidents do not veto the same number of bills, and some veto no bills at all. Moreover, presidents may often choose to veto bills on which they are likely to prevail. In addition, most override votes are not close, allowing members of Congress more flexibility in their voting. Whatever the case, Krehbiel's data do not provide a basis for inferring successful presidential persuasion.

Thus, presidential legislative leadership is more useful in exploiting discrete opportunities than in creating broad possibilities for policy change. It operates in an environment largely beyond the president's control and must compete with other, more stable factors that affect voting in Congress in addition to party. These include ideology, personal views and commitments on specific policies, and the interests of constituencies. By the time a president tries to exercise influence on a vote, most members of Congress have made up their minds on the basis of these other factors. As a result, a president's legislative leadership is likely to be critical only for those members of Congress who remain open to conversion after other influences have had their impact. Although the size and composition of this group varies from issue to issue, it will almost always be a minority in each chamber. Whatever the circumstances, the impact of persuasion on the outcome will usually be relatively modest. Therefore, conversion is likely to be at the margins of coalition building in Congress rather than at the core of policy change.

In sum, the most effective presidents do not reshape the political landscape to pave the way for change. Instead, they exploit opportunities already present in their environments to achieve significant changes in public policy.

Some, especially those who desire significant changes in public policy, may find the role of facilitator unsatisfactory. Yet the nature of the American system is such that presidents will not bring about major changes in public policy through persuasion. Although it may be appealing to explain major changes in terms of personalities, the political system is too complicated, power too decentralized, and interests too diverse for one person, no matter how extraordinary, to dominate. American chief executives will not bring about major changes in public policy through transformational leadership. As Neustadt (1990, 265) observed, "if the President envisages substantial innovations, whether conservative or liberal, then almost everything in modern history cries caution to such hopes unless accompanied by crises with potential for consensus."

Moreover, we should not undervalue the facilitating skill required to recognize and exploit opportunities. Not everyone who occupies the Oval Office will be adept at building of coalitions for new policies. Facilitators are not unskilled leaders. Instead, they are leaders who depend on their environments for providing opportunities that they can exploit to accomplish their objectives. When the various streams of political resources converge to create opportunities for major change, facilitators are critical to engendering significant alterations in public policy.

Because presidents are not in strong positions to create opportunities for legislative success, recognizing those that already exist is especially significant. Indeed, it may be the most important skill of all. Analyzing the prospects for change with proper accuracy is difficult, however. As I discuss below, presidents often misestimate the opportunities in their environments. (In his memoirs, Bill Clinton (2004, 215) observes that he overestimated the pace and amount of change Americans could digest.)

Similarly, it takes considerable skill to fashion strategies and tactics to exploit opportunities. To repeat a point, facilitators are not merely conduits who grasp opportunities that appear and ask people to do what they already want to do. Change is not inevitable, and facilitators make things happen that otherwise would not. In essence, *facilitators can make crucial contributions to transforming policy without performing transformational leadership.*

THE IMPORTANCE OF
UNDERSTANDING LEADERSHIP

Debunking exaggerated claims of presidential persuasiveness is not an end in itself. Rejecting simplistic and inaccurate explanations for political phenomena is the first step to understanding how presidents actually engender change, however. And it is important that we do so.

Understanding the nature and possibilities of leadership puts us in a better position to evaluate both the performance of presidents and the opportunities for change. Equally important, we have a better sense of where to look for explanations of the success and consequences of presidential leadership.

If presidents cannot use persuasion to create opportunities for change, we should reassess the role of the chief executive within the American political system. To begin, we should adjust our expectations of presidential leadership and not expect persuasion to be at the core of engendering change.

To understand the presidency and the engines of change better, we should focus less exclusively on the president and devote more attention to the context in which the president seeks to lead. If there are significant limits on presidential persuasion, it follows that major changes in public policy require more than just the "right" person in the job, and may not turn on a president's leadership qualities.

It does not follow, of course, that we never should attribute failures of presidential leadership to the White House or that presidents have no control over the outcome of their relations with other political actors. The president may be a vital centralizing force, providing direction and energy for the nation's policy making. Properly understanding the potential of leadership does mean, however, that we should have a renewed appreciation for compromise and democratic constraints. More broadly, it means that we must continue to seek a better understanding of presidential leadership in order to think sensibly about the role of the chief executive in the nation's political system.

Similarly, presidential dependency on existing opportunities implies a critical interdependence between leaders and followers, which we miss when we focus only at the pinnacle of power. Moreover, there are many influences on followers and potential followers and many obstacles to influencing them. The president is an important agenda setter (Edwards and Barrett 2000), for example, but there are other key influences on the agenda as well (Edwards and Wood 1999). Thus, we need to devote more attention to thinking about politics from the bottom up as well as the top down and to the context in which the president seeks to lead.

I do not suggest, however, that we ignore presidents as individuals. Instead, we need to think more clearly about how presidents actually marshal resources to bring about change. Exploiting opportunities requires a different set of skills than creating them. It calls for presidents with the analytical insight necessary to evaluate their strategic positions correctly and the ability to take advantage of the possibilities in their environments.

In addition, a successful president requires the commitment, resolution, and strength to take full advantage of opportunities that arise. We would benefit from work that explores *systematically* the contribution of presidential energy, perseverance, and resiliency to presidential success.

If exploiting opportunities to steer true believers is more critical to engendering change than persuading the skeptical, much less converting the opposition, it follows that we should focus more on maintaining and managing coalitions and less on the verbal dexterity or interpersonal persuasiveness that is hypothetically necessary to expand coalitions and thus transform the political landscape.

Sustaining and channeling coalitions should encourage research on agenda setting, a topic that has played a modest role in scholarship on the presidency. Presidents come to office with an electoral platform. Yet they continually add to their agenda, often in response to unforeseen events. How skillful are chief executives at energizing their coalitions to support these new agenda items?

Likewise, if presidents cannot persuade, exercising discretionary authority may be a key to success. It is perhaps ironic that finding the potential of persuasiveness limited, some scholars are returning to a focus on the president's discretionary authority—the power to command (see Cameron 2000; Mayer 2001; Cooper 2002; Howell 2003; Warber 2006). In this regard, the revolution that Neustadt launched has come full circle.

At the same time, there are a number of possible means or venues of presidential leadership that require our attention. For example, Stephen Skowronek (1993) has called our attention to the role presidents may play in reconstituting the terms of discourse and thus structuring the choices of citizens and legislators, arguing that "to establish a common sense of the times ... is the primal act of leadership." His sweeping view of presidential history leads him to conclude, "All presidents change American politics, but rarely do they change it even roughly in the manner they intended."

For example, the typical political effect of such high-impact presidents as James Polk, Theodore Roosevelt, Lyndon Johnson, and George W. Bush has been "schismatic." Thus, he argues, "the political world seldom conforms to definitions and formulas; no matter how tight, skilled, or hands-on the controls exerted, events can be orchestrated to set terms only for so long." The president's opponents are unlikely to accept his terms of debate and "relentlessly and ruthlessly" provide an alternative view (2005, 818, 821, 826–7). Skowronek is correct about the importance of the terms of discourse, but we lack systematic understanding of the influence presidents may have on them and need to devote more attention to the topic.

Even if presidents are unlikely to *change* public opinion, it is possible for them to exploit *existing* public opinion as a resource for changing the direction of public policy. At the core of this strategy is choosing the issues they emphasize and the manner in which they present their policy initiatives. Although previous commitments, current crises, and unresolved problems left from their predecessors foist much of their agenda upon them, presidents still have substantial discretion to choose their own initiatives and the manner in which they present them to the public. From the perspective of the White House, "the key to successful advocacy is controlling the public agenda" (Kumar 2007, 9). As a result, the White House invests a substantial amount of staff, time, and energy into focusing the public's attention on the issues it wishes to promote and encouraging the public to see its proposals for dealing with those issues in a positive light.

Again, we know little about the impact of these endeavors, however. We need systematic studies of efforts to frame policy proposals and their consequences; the ability of the White House to increase the salience of its initiatives, clarify the public's wishes, and show how they are consistent with its policies; define themselves and their parties in ways that channel existing opinion on the issues into support for a party program over the longer term; and exploit the public's opinion fluidity or indifference regarding an issue.

Similarly, Jeffrey Tulis (1987) and David Zarefsky (1986), among others, have suggested that the impact of rhetoric may be in realms other than that of the general public. The real influence of rhetoric may be on elite debate, journalistic coverage, and congressional deliberation. Unfortunately, we know almost nothing about such impacts.

Seeing little potential for persuasion in a context of polarized politics, George W. Bush sought to transform policy on the basis of a 50 percent plus 1 majority (see, for example, Brownstein 2007). Rather than seeking compromise with his opponents by bringing them into an inclusive coalition and supporting legislation broadly acceptable to the electorate, the president sought to defeat the opposition, creating winners and losers in a zero-sum game. Similarly, in the 2004 presidential election Republican political strategist Matthew Dowd argued to Karl Rove that the presidential election was "about *motivation* rather than *persuasion*" (quoted in Draper 2007, 230). Thus, the campaign focused on mobilizing its base rather than undecided voters. In the process, the White House alienated large percentages of the country, reinforcing partisan polarization. A study in 2007 found that 77 percent of Americans felt there was a leadership crisis in the United States (Rosenthal et al. 2007, 2).[1]

It is appropriate to consider the broad implications of the limitations of presidential persuasion for basic strategies of governing. If presidents cannot persuade and if there is not a middle of the electorate that is persuadable, should presidents abandon attempts to govern from the center or to adopt an inclusive orientation to policy making? Do the limitations on presidential persuasion inevitably create incentives for polarizing politics in order to mobilize a president's base? Is one consequence of such a strategy that the president will rarely enjoy substantial public support and is likely to fall to very low ratings in tough times?

Answering such questions will be difficult. We do know, however, that there is a widespread desire to change basic features of our politics, including the tendency for civility to lose out to conflict, compromise to deadlock, deliberation to sound bites, legislative product to campaign issues, and public confidence to cynicism. A richer understanding of the true potential of leadership is a critical step in addressing these characteristics of contemporary politics.

---

[1] Interviews of the national sample were conducted on Sept. 4–17, 2007.

Lessons for the White House

The stakes of understanding the potential of persuasiveness are especially high for the White House. Although aiding presidents in governing has not been a primary motivation for the research on presidential leadership inspired by Neustadt, the results of those efforts contain important lessons for the chief executive.

If the conventional wisdom is wrong and presidents are not able to persuade, much less mobilize, the public or Congress, then presidents may be wasting their time and adopting governing styles that are prone to failure. Presidents—and the country—often endure self-inflicted wounds when they fail to appreciate the limits of their influence.

For example, in recent decades, presidents have tried to govern through a permanent campaign. Both politics and policy revolve around presidents' attempts to garner public support, both for themselves and for their policies. The ultimate goal, of course, is to influence Congress with a demonstration of public opinion favorable to the White House.

Three fundamental and widely shared premises about the relationship between public opinion and presidential leadership underlie this mode of governance. The first is that public support is a crucial political resource for the president, i.e., it is difficult for others who hold power to deny the legitimate demands of a president with popular support. The second premise supporting the White House's intense focus on public opinion is the view that the president must not only earn public support with his performance in office, but also must actively take his case to the people throughout his tenure. The final premise sustaining the public presidency is that through the permanent campaign the White House *can* successfully persuade or even mobilize the public if the president has the skill and will to exploit effectively the "bully pulpit." As a result, modern presidents choose to engage in a permanent campaign for the public's support as their core strategy for governing (Edwards 2003, 2007; Kernell 2007).

Given all the time and effort that the White House invests in attempting to persuade the public, it is especially interesting that presidential aides do not know how successful they have been. Martha Kumar found that communications staffers in both the Clinton and Bush White Houses agreed that their efforts to gauge the success of their salesmanship tended to be partial and impressionistic rather than comprehensive and scientific. Presidential Press Secretary Ari Fleischer attributed it to the fact that they had so little time to look back and take stock. "We move too fast to look back and have some type of empirical analysis or empirical accounting system like that. I think other than the use of your gut, you don't really do it" (Kumar 2007, 27–9, 57–60, 110–12, 147–8).

The White House need look no further than presidential scholarship for help with its dilemma. Research has challenged all three of the premises underlying the strategy of governing by campaigning. A sustained research agenda has found that the president's standing in the public has only marginal influence on his support in Congress (see, for example, Edwards 1989, 1997; Bond and Fleisher 1990; Bond, Fleisher, and Wood 2003).

We have already seen that presidents have shown little ability to move public opinion in their direction, undermining the third premise of the permanent campaign.

Presidents have not understood their limitations, however, and repeatedly adopted a core strategy of governing based on changing public opinion. Their mistaken belief that they can move the public has encouraged them to underestimate their opponents and eschew necessary compromises. Summing up Bill Clinton's health care reform debacle, Jacobs and Shapiro (2000, 115) concluded that the

fundamental political mistake committed by Bill Clinton and his aides was in grossly overestimating the capacity of a president to "win" public opinion and to use public support as leverage to overcome known political obstacles—from an ideologically divided Congress to hostile interest groups.

Similarly, George W. Bush began his second term by launching an intensive campaign to obtain the public's support for his proposal to reform Social Security. When he took his case to the people, however, they did not respond (Edwards 2007). At least they did not support his policies. Instead, the more the president advocated change, the less the public backed his proposals, and majorities opposed him. Congress was no more enthusiastic. One of the most explicit efforts to govern by campaigning in US history failed, apparently surprising the White House but not those who closely study the president's ability to move public opinion.

Overreaching may lead to even greater problems than the failure to achieve immediate policy goals. It may also result in political disasters. Not long after Bill Clinton failed to obtain even a vote in either house of Congress on his health care reform proposal, which was to have been his centerpiece legislation, the Democrats lost majorities in both the House and the Senate for the first time in four decades. The administration's health care proposal was the prime example of the Republicans' charge that the Democrats were ideological extremists who had lost touch with the wishes of Americans.

Similarly, George W. Bush's failed effort to reform Social Security reinforced the growing perception that he was not up to the job of president. When the Pew Research Center (2006) asked a national sample in March 2006 to describe the president in one word, the single word most frequently associated with Bush was "incompetent," followed closely by "idiot" and "liar." Such perceptions contributed to the Republicans losing both houses of Congress in the November midterm elections, giving back what they had won under Bill Clinton twelve years earlier.

Thus, the validity of the second premise, the necessity of the permanent campaign, is highly questionable. Presidents may not only fail to create new political capital by going public. Their efforts at persuading the public may also *decrease* their chances of success in bringing about changes in public policy. Governing by campaigning is antithetical to governing (Heclo 2000).

It is tempting to conclude that the relationship between the president and the public is a recent phenomenon and thus any inferences about the consequences of governing by campaigning are time bound. They are not. To illustrate this point, let us examine one of the most famous episodes of a president taking his case to the public: Franklin D. Roosevelt's effort to expand the Supreme Court. As we do so, we should remember that this was FDR at the height of his powers and occurred shortly after he won his greatest electoral victory as president.

FDR's Court Packing Plan

In February 1937, shortly after his landslide reelection and at the height of his powers, Franklin D. Roosevelt surprised the nation by proposing a plan to increase the size of the Supreme Court. His motivation was transparent: to add members who would support New Deal policies. It is telling that after the election, the president was so confident of his public support and his ability to channel it to support his initiatives that he did not consult with major groups of supporters such as leading liberals or leaders of labor unions and farm organizations on his proposal and ignored information on the public's fundamental support for the Court (Nelson 1988, 277–8).

According to historian William Leuchtenburg, "FDR's message generated an intensity of response unmatched by any legislative controversy of this century, save perhaps for the League of Nations episode," and the president's opponents, who seemed to include the vice president, enjoyed widespread support. Nevertheless, the president persisted, believing he had the country's support (1995, 134–47).

The story of the battle is a complicated one, and Roosevelt claimed success (a more responsive Court) even though his bill failed to pass. However we interpret the White House's success in achieving its immediate goal, there is little doubt that the entire episode was a costly one for the president. As Leuchtenburg put it, "Never again would FDR be as predominant, either on Capitol Hill or at the polling places, as he was when 1937 began" (1995, 156). The Court battle became a rallying point around which latent opposition to the New Deal could coalesce (Leuchtenburg 1963, 234; Maddox 1969, 10–11; Ekirch 1969, 97; Burns 1956, 307, 315),[2] and helped to weld together a bipartisan coalition of anti-New Deal senators. "For the first time Southern Congressmen in large numbers deserted the leader and the opposition found an issue on which it could openly take the field. Things were never quite the same again" (Tindall 1967, 623). Senators from both sides of the aisle soon organized a conservative bloc strong enough to deal Roosevelt his first serious setback in four years. The bloc was composed of the irreconcilable Democrats, Republicans, and, most important, previously loyal moderate Democrats—and the uncrowned leader of this group was Vice President Garner (Patterson 1967, 95; Leuchtenburg 1995, 157–8; Leuchtenburg 1963, 252).

The battle over the Court also deeply divided the Democratic Party, precipitating factional wars in states. These battles in turn led to a series of episodes, notably the purge campaign of 1938, that rubbed brine into the wounds. Some members of Congress who broke with FDR in 1937 never again would accord him the same degree of loyalty they had in his first term. Similarly, the dispute produced divisions among reformers of many types, undermining the bipartisan support for the New Deal and confirming for Republican progressives their suspicions that New Dealers were interested in self-aggrandizement and concentrating power in Washington. Finally, the attempt to pack the Court helped to diminish the middle-class backing Roosevelt had mobilized in the 1936 campaign (Leuchtenburg 1995, 158–60; 1963, 238–9).

---

[2] FDR's diminished authority resulted in part from other developments such as the harsh recession of 1937–8, anxiety over relief spending, and resentment at sit-down strikes (Leuchtenburg 1995, 156; 1963, 250).

As a result, the Court struggle helped to blunt the most important drive for social reform in American history and squandered the advantage of Roosevelt's triumph in 1936. The conservative coalition handed FDR a series of rebuffs at the special session of Congress in the autumn of 1937 and at the regular session the following year, and the prospects for reform diminished considerably. Years later Henry Wallace reflected: "The whole New Deal really went up in smoke as a result of the Supreme Court fight." At the end of the session, one reporter enquired, "How did the President slide so far—so fast?" (Leuchtenburg 1995, 157–8; 1963, 250–1, ch. 11).

By 1939, Congress was handling the president more roughly than it had previously and began moving aggressively to dismantle the New Deal. It slashed relief spending, killed appointments, eliminated what was left of the undistributed profits tax, and killed agencies with weak constituencies. Roosevelt was able to stave off other changes and occasionally win some battles, but his relations with Congress had changed from cooperation to stalemate (Leuchtenburg 1963, 272–4).

The Court fight also had implications for American foreign policy, for it distracted Roosevelt from the growing crisis in Europe, rekindled Americans' fear of executive power, and weakened the president's power at a time he needed it most (Leuchtenburg, 1995, 160–1). Robert Dallek (1979, 136–7, 140) argues that FDR accepted a mandatory law of neutrality in good part because he wished to avoid a congressional debate that could forestall action on judicial reform. He was in a weak position to ask for executive discretion in foreign affairs when critics were accusing him of seeking to destroy the Constitution and the courts.

Conclusion

Presidential power is *not* the power to persuade. Presidents cannot reshape the contours of the political landscape to pave the way for change by establishing an agenda and persuading the public, Congress, and others to support their policies. Instead, the essential presidential leadership skills are recognizing and exploiting opportunities rather than changing the minds of voters or legislators to create opportunities for change. If presidents exercise these skills effectively, they will increase the probability of achieving their goals. Moreover, if the opportunity structure in which they are governing is favorable to change, presidents may leave lasting marks on public policy and the political landscape. Facilitators are neither weak nor inconsequential. Instead, they are skilled leaders who have learned to govern in a system that is biased against change.

Leadership remains a core concept in the study of the presidency. Fortunately, this focus of scholarship has produced good news and even better news. The good news is that from the first book-length quantitative analysis of the presidency (Edwards 1980b) to the latest works employing rational choice theory (Howell 2003; Canes-Wrone 2006), recent decades have been bright ones for the study of presidential leadership.

The better news is that this advancement in our understanding of leadership has generated new issues for scholars to explore. Investigating these unresolved issues provides exciting prospects for the next generation of presidency research. Focusing on facilitating change rather than persuasion should open us to the study of the ways in which leaders actually do bring about change. From exercising unilateral power and maintaining coalitions to agenda setting and establishing the terms of debate over issues of public policy, there is much for us to learn.

REFERENCES

BAUM, M. A., and KERNELL, S. 2001. Economic Class and Popular Support for Franklin Roosevelt in War and Peace. *Public Opinion Quarterly*, 65: 198–229.

BOND, J. R., and FLEISHER, R. 1990. *The President in the Legislative Arena*. Chicago: University of Chicago Press.

—— and WOOD, B. D. 2003. The Marginal and Time Varying Effect of Public Approval on Presidential Success in Congress. *Journal of Politics*, 6: 92–110.

BROOKS, D. 2007. Heroes and History. *New York Times*, July 17.

BROWNSTEIN, R. 2007. *The Second Civil War: How Extreme Partisanship Has Paralyzed Washington and Polarized America*. New York: Penguin Press.

BURNS, J. M. 1956. *Roosevelt: The Lion and the Fox*. New York: Harcourt, Brace & World.

—— 1978. *Leadership*. New York: Harper & Row.

—— 2003. *Transforming Leadership*. New York: Grove Press.

—— and DUNN, S. 2001. *The Three Roosevelts: The Leaders Who Transformed America*. London: Atlantic Books.

CAMERON, C. M. 2000. *Veto Bargaining: Presidents and the Politics of Negative Power*. New York: Cambridge University Press.

CANES-WRONE, B. 2006. *Who Influences Whom?* Chicago: University of Chicago Press.

CLINTON, B. 2004. *My Life*. London: Hutchinson.

COHEN, J. E. 1997. *Presidential Responsiveness and Public Policy-Making*. Ann Arbor: University of Michigan Press.

CONOVER, P. J., and SIGELMAN, L. 1982. Presidential Influence and Public Opinion. *Social Science Quarterly*, 63: 249–64.

COOPER, J., and BRADY, D. W. 1981. Institutional Context and Leadership Style: The House from Cannon to Rayburn. *American Political Science Review*, 75: 411–25.

COOPER, P. J. 2002. *By Order of the President: The Use and Abuse of Executive Direct Action*. Lawrence: University Press of Kansas.

CORWIN, E. S. 1957. *The President, Office and Powers, 1787–1957*, 4th rev. edn. New York: New York University Press.

DALLEK, R. 1979. *Franklin D. Roosevelt and American Foreign Policy, 1932–1945*. New York: Oxford University Press.

DRAPER, R. 2007. *Dead Certain: The Presidency of George W. Bush*. New York: Free Press.

EDWARDS, G. C., III. 1980a. *Implementing Public Policy*. Washington, DC: Congressional Quarterly.

—— 1980b. *Presidential Influence in Congress*. San Francisco: W. H. Freeman.

—— 1981. The Quantitative Study of the Presidency. *Presidential Studies Quarterly*, 11: 146–50.

—— 1983. *The Public Presidency*. New York: St Martin's.

EDWARDS, G. C., III. 1989. *At the Margins: Presidential Leadership of Congress* New Haven, CT: Yale University Press.

——1997. Aligning Tests with Theory: Presidential Approval as a Source of Influence in Congress. *Congress and the Presidency*, 24: 113–30.

——2003. *On Deaf Ears: The Limits of the Bully Pulpit*. New Haven, CT: Yale University Press.

——2007. *Governing by Campaigning: The Politics of the Bush Presidency*, 2nd edn. New York: Longman.

——2009. *The Strategic President: Persuasion and Opportunity in Presidential Leadership*. Princeton, NJ: Princeton University Press.

——and BARRETT, A. 2000. Presidential Agenda Setting in Congress. In *Polarized Politics: Congress and the President in a Partisan Era*, ed. J. R. Bond and R. Fleisher. Washington, DC: Congressional Quarterly.

——and WOOD, B. D. 1999. Who Influences Whom? The President, Congress, and the Media. *American Political Science Review*, 93: 327–44.

EKIRCH, A. A., JR. 1969. *Ideologies and Utopias: The Impact of the New Deal on American Thought*. Chicago: Quadrangle Books.

FLEISHER, R., BOND, J. R., and WOOD, B. D. 2007. Which Presidents Are Uncommonly Successful in Congress? In *Presidential Leadership: The Vortex of Presidential Power*, ed. B. Rockman and R. W. Waterman. New York: Oxford University Press.

GREENSTEIN, F. I. 2004. The Presidential Difference: Leadership Style from FDR to George W. Bush. Princeton, NJ: Princeton University Press.

HECLO, H. 2000. Campaigning and Governing: A Conspectus. In *The Permanent Campaign and its Future*, ed. N. Ornstein and T. Mann. Washington, DC: American Enterprise Institute and Brookings Institution.

HOOK, S. 1943. *The Hero in History*. Boston: Beacon.

HOWELL, W. G. 2003. *Power without Persuasion*. Princeton, NJ: Princeton University Press.

JACOBS, L. R., and SHAPIRO, R. Y. 2000. *Politicians Don't Pander*. Chicago: University of Chicago Press.

KELLERMAN, B. 1984. Leadership as a Political Act. In *Leadership: Multidisciplinary Perspectives*, ed. B. Kellerman. Englewood Cliffs, NJ: Prentice-Hall.

KERNELL, S. 2007. *Going Public: New Strategies of Presidential Leadership*, 4th edn. Washington, DC: CQ Press.

KREHBIEL, K. 1998. *Pivotal Politics: A Theory of U.S. Lawmaking*. Chicago: University of Chicago Press.

KUMAR, M. J. 2007. *Managing the President's Message: The White House Communications Operation*. Baltimore: Johns Hopkins University Press.

LEUCHTENBURG, W. E. 1963. *Franklin D. Roosevelt and the New Deal, 1932–1940*. New York: Harper & Row.

——1995. *The Supreme Court Reborn: The Constitutional Revolution in the Age of Roosevelt*. New York: Oxford University Press.

LOW, A. M. 1906. The Usurped Powers of the Senate. *American Political Science Review*, 1: 1–16.

MCCULLOUGH, D. 1992. *Truman*. New York: Simon & Schuster.

MADDOX, R. 1969. Roosevelt vs. The Court. *American History Illustrated*, 4.

MAYER, K. R. 2001. *With the Stroke of a Pen: Executive Orders and Presidential Power*. Princeton, NJ: Princeton University Press.

MONDAK, J. J. 1993. Source Cues and Public Approval: The Cognitive Dynamics of Public Support for the Reagan Administration. *American Journal of Political Science*, 37: 186–212.

NELSON, M. 1988. The President and the Court: Reinterpreting the Court-Packing Episode of 1937. *Political Science Quarterly*, 103: 267–93.

NEUSTADT, R. E. 1990. *Presidential Power and the Modern Presidents*. New York: Free Press.

PAGE, B. I., SHAPIRO, R. Y., and DEMPSEY, G. R. 1987. What Moves Public Opinion? *American Political Science Review*, 81: 23–44.

PATTERSON, J. T. 1967. *Congressional Conservatism and the New Deal*. Lexington: University of Kentucky Press.

Pew Research Center for the People & the Press. 2006. Poll of March 8–12.

ROHDE, D. W., and SHEPSLE, K. A. 1987. Leaders and Followers in the House of Representatives: Reflections on Woodrow Wilson's Congressional Government. *Congress and the Presidency*, 14: 111–13.

ROSENTHAL, S. A., PITTINSKY, T. L., PURVIN, D. M., and MONTOYA, M. 2007. *National Leadership Index 2007: A National Study of Confidence in Leadership*. Cambridge, MA: Center for Public Leadership, John F. Kennedy School of Government, Harvard University.

ROSSITER, C. L. 1960. *The American Presidency*, 2nd edn. New York: Harcourt, Brace.

SIGELMAN, L. 1980. Gauging the Public Response to Presidential Leadership. *Presidential Studies Quarterly*, 10: 427–33.

—— and SIGELMAN, C. K. 1981. Presidential Leadership of Public Opinion: From "Benevolent Leader" to Kiss of Death? *Experimental Study of Politics*, 7/3: 1–22.

SIMON, D. M., and OSTROM, C. W., JR. 1989. The Impact of Televised Speeches and Foreign Travel on Presidential Approval. *Public Opinion Quarterly*, 53: 58–82.

SINCLAIR, B. 1986. Party Leadership and Policy Change. In *Congress and Policy Change*, ed. G. C. Wright, Jr., L. N. Rieselbach, and L. C. Dodd. New York: Agathon.

SKOWRONEK, S. 2005. Leadership by Definition: First Term Reflections on George W. Bush's Political Stance. *Perspectives on Politics*, 3: 817–31.

—— 1993. *The Politics Presidents Make*. Cambridge, MA: Harvard University Press.

THOMAS, D., and SIGELMAN, L. 1985. Presidential Identification and Policy Leadership: Experimental Evidence on the Reagan Case. Pp. 37–49 in *The Presidency and Public Policy Making*, ed. G. C. Edwards III, S. A. Shull, and N. C. Thomas. Pittsburgh: University of Pittsburgh Press.

TINDALL, G. 1967. *The Emergence of the New South, 1913–1945*. Baton Rouge: Louisiana State University Press.

TULIS, J. K. 1987. *The Rhetorical Presidency*. Princeton, NJ: Princeton University Press.

WARBER, A. L. 2006. *Executive Orders and the Modern Presidency: Legislating from the Oval Office*. Boulder, CO: Lynne Rienner.

YUKL, G. A. 2006. *Leadership in Organizations*, 6th edn. Upper Saddle River, NJ: Pearson Prentice Hall.

ZAREFSKY, D. 1986. *President Johnson's War of Poverty*. University: University of Alabama Press.

NAME INDEX

Abbott, K 699, 712
Abbott, P 60
Aberbach, J D 404, 589, 601, 602–3, 604, 673
Abraham, H J 627, 630, 637, 777
Abramoff, Jack 415
Abramowitz, A 292, 347
Abrams, E 153
Abrams, S 151, 233, 292, 294
Achen, C H 350
Acheson, Dean 801
Ackerman, B 62, 64–7, 758
Adams, John
   and image-based expectations of president 138
   and Supreme Court nominations 631
Adams, John Quincy 802
Adams, Sherman 516
Adler, D G 152, 444, 459, 650, 674, 726, 756, 809, 812
Agranoff, R 582, 596
Aldag, R J 505, 541
Aldrich, J H 290, 291, 292, 293, 294 n1, 301, 307, 390–1, 406, 414, 680
Alford, J R 346, 552
Alito, Samuel 411, 626, 638–9, 654
Allen, M 262–3
Allison, G T 329, 502, 507–11, 521, 522, 541, 668
Althaus, S L 167, 236, 244, 245, 246, 271, 276, 685
Ambrose, S E 340
Andersen, R 239
Anderson, J E 110, 119, 127
Andres, G 324, 325, 328, 408
Antczak, F J 208, 216, 221
Apple, R W 340
Arceneaux, K 236
Arkes, H 764, 765
Arnhart, L 459
Arnold, P E 75, 501, 519, 580, 602, 604, 614, 750, 758
Arnold, R D 343
Arnold, T 773
Arrow, K 561
Art, R J 509
Arterton, F C 150
Ashcroft, John 436–7
Atkeson, L R 347
Auerswald, D 671, 672, 681

Aufses, A 21, 439
Axelrod, R 520

Babington, C 345
Bacchus, W L 509
Bachrach, P 126
Bae, H-S 259
Bailey, J D 459, 463, 758
Bailey, M 121, 634, 635, 655
Baker, Howard 465
Baker, James A 100, 183, 516
Baker, N V 466
Baker, W 737
Baldwin, S E 460
Balutis, A P 255, 344
Baratz, M S 126
Barber, D 554
Barber, J 10 n1, 137, 140, 465
Barger, H M 152
Barilleaux, R J 757
Barker, D C 275
Barkow, R E 649
Barnes, J A 340
Barnes, R 437
Barnhurst, K G 256
Baron, D P 43, 44 n4, 364
Barratt, B 688
Barrett, A W 18, 21, 38–9, 125, 126, 267, 295, 305, 315, 318, 379, 389–90, 776, 828
Barron, D J 657
Barrow, D J 630
Bartels, L M 165, 166, 173, 174, 193, 238, 299
Bauer, R A 342
Baum, M 18, 115, 176, 187, 218, 234, 239, 240, 246, 247, 272, 273, 274, 674, 678, 679, 680, 681, 685, 776, 826
Baumgartner, F R 109, 110, 111, 116–17, 124, 194, 198, 199, 278, 420, 587, 683
Bazan, E B 436
Bazerman, M H 532
Beard, E 509
Beasley, V B 216
Beck, P A 272
Begala, Paul 439
Behn, R 615

SUBJECT INDEX